T0205755

# Lecture Notes of the Institute for Computer Sciences, Social Informatics and Telecommunications Engineering 462

More information about this series at https://link.springer.com/bookseries/8197

Fengjun Li · Kaitai Liang · Zhiqiang Lin ·
Sokratis K. Katsikas (Eds.)

# Security and Privacy in Communication Networks

18th EAI International Conference, SecureComm 2022
Virtual Event, October 2022
Proceedings

 Springer

*Editors*
Fengjun Li 🔟
University of Kansas
Lawrence, KS, USA

Kaitai Liang 🔟
Delft University of Technology
Delft, The Netherlands

Zhiqiang Lin 🔟
The Ohio State University
Columbus, OH, USA

Sokratis K. Katsikas 🔟
Norwegian University of Science and Tech
Gjøvik, Norway

ISSN 1867-8211                 ISSN 1867-822X (electronic)
Lecture Notes of the Institute for Computer Sciences, Social Informatics
and Telecommunications Engineering
ISBN 978-3-031-25537-3        ISBN 978-3-031-25538-0 (eBook)
https://doi.org/10.1007/978-3-031-25538-0

This Springer imprint is published by the registered company Springer Nature Switzerland AG
The registered company address is: Gewerbestrasse 11, 6330 Cham, Switzerland

# Preface

We are delighted to introduce the proceedings of the 18th EAI International Conference on Security and Privacy in Communication Networks (SecureComm 2022). This conference brought together researchers and practitioners working in academia, industry, government, to explore important research directions in the field.

These proceedings contain 40 papers, which were selected from 126 submissions (an acceptance rate of 31.7%) from universities, national laboratories, and the private sector from the Americas, Europe, Asia, Australasia, and Africa. All the submissions went through an extensive review process by internationally recognized experts in cybersecurity. The accepted papers are authored by researchers from 11 countries, with China and the USA being the top two countries with the most papers. These proceedings also contain three papers from the International Workshop on Security and Privacy-preserving Solutions in the Internet of Things (S/P-IoT).

Any successful conference requires the contributions of different stakeholder groups and individuals, who have unselfishly volunteered their time and energy in disseminating the call for papers, submitting their research findings, participating in the peer reviews and discussions, etc. First and foremost, we would like to offer our gratitude to the entire Organizing Committee for guiding the entire process of the conference. We are also deeply grateful to all the Technical Program Committee members for their time and efforts in reading, commenting, debating, and finally selecting the papers. We also thank all the external reviewers for assisting the Technical Program Committee in their particular areas of expertise as well as all the authors, participants, and session chairs for their valuable contributions. Support from the Steering Committee and EAI staff members was also crucial in ensuring the success of the conference. It was a great privilege to be working with such a large group of dedicated and talented individuals.

The 18th SecureComm Conference was originally planned to be held in Kansas City, KS, USA. It is unfortunate that we had to revert to an online conference in 2022. We hope that the discussions and interactions were enjoyable, and that the proceedings will stimulate further research.

October 2022

Fengjun Li
Kaitai Liang
Zhiqiang Lin
Sokratis K. Katsikas

# Conference Organization

## Steering Committee

Imrich Chlamtac — Bruno Kessler Professor, University of Trento, Italy
Guofei Gu — Texas A&M University, USA
Peng Liu — Pennsylvania State University, USA
Sencun Zhu — Pennsylvania State University, USA

## Organizing Committee

### General Co-chairs

Fengjun Li — University of Kansas, USA
Kaitai Liang — TU Delft, The Netherlands

### TPC Chair and Co-chair

Zhiqiang Lin — The Ohio State University, USA
Sokratis Katsikas — Norwegian University of Science and Technology, Norway

### Sponsorship and Exhibit Chair

Drew Davidson — The University of Kansas, USA

### Local Chairs

Bo Luo — The University of Kansas, USA
Alex Bardas — The University of Kansas, USA

### Workshops Chairs

Lannan Luo — George Mason University, USA
Fatih Turkmen — University of Groningen, The Netherlands

### Publicity and Social Media Chairs

Peng Liu — Pennsylvania State University, USA
Jingqiang Lin — University of Science and Technology of China, China

**Publications Chairs**

Jun Shao                        Zhejiang Gongshang University, China
Stjepan Picek                   Radboud University, The Netherlands

**Web Chair**

Apostolis Zarras                TU Delft, The Netherlands

## Technical Program Committee

Ali Abbasi                      Ruhr-University Bochum, Germany
Sharif Abuadbba                 CSIRO's Data61, Australia
Mohiuddin Ahmed                 Edith Cowan University, Australia
Nadeem Ahmed                    The University of New South Wales (UNSW),
                                  Australia
Magnus Almgren                  Chalmers University of Technology, Sweden
Ehab Al-Shaer                   Carnegie Mellon University, USA
Marios Anagnostopoulos          Aalborg University, Denmark
Giovanni Apruzzese              University of Liechtenstein, Liechtenstein
David Arroyo                    Spanish National Research Council, Spain
Elias Athanasopoulos            University of Cyprus, Cyprus
Razvan Beuran                   Japan Advanced Institute of Science and
                                  Technology, Japan
Silvia Bonomi                   Sapienza University of Rome, Italy
Sanchuan Chen                   Fordham University, USA
Bo Chen                         Michigan Technological University, USA
Guoxing Chen                    Shanghai Jiao Tong University, China
Franco Chiaraluce               Università Politecnica delle Marche, Italy
Fabio Di Franco                 ENISA, Greece
Shanqing Guo                    Shandong University, China
Guillaume Hiet                  CentraleSupélec, France
Darren Hurley-Smith             Royal Holloway University of London, UK
Taeho Jung                      University of Notre Dame, USA
Nesrine Kaaniche                Télécom SudParis, France
Georgios Kavallieratos          Norwegian University of Science and Technology,
                                  Norway
Igor Kotenko                    St. Petersburg Institute for Informatics and
                                  Automation, Russia
Platon Kotzias                  Norton LifeLock Research Labs, USA
Shaofeng Li                     PengCheng Laboratory, China
Juanru Li                       Shanghai Jiao Tong University, China
Ming Li                         UT Arlington, USA
George Loukas                   University of Greenwich, UK

| | |
|---|---|
| Bo Luo | University of Kansas, USA |
| Xiapu Luo | The Hong Kong Polytechnic University, Hong Kong, China |
| Leandros Maglaras | De Montfort University, UK |
| Kalikinkar Mandal | University of New Brunswick, Canada |
| Evangelos Markatos | ICS-FORTH, Greece |
| Fabio Martinelli | Italian National Research Council, Italy |
| Wojciech Mazurczyk | Warsaw University of Technology, Poland |
| Weizhi Meng | Technical University of Denmark, Denmark |
| Nour Moustafa | UNSW Canberra, Australia |
| Mehari Msgna | Norwegian University of Science and Technology, Norway |
| Toni Perkovic | University of Split, Croatia |
| Roberto Di Pietro | Hamad Bin Khalifa University, Qatar |
| Nikolaos Pitropakis | Edinburgh Napier University, UK |
| Gabriele Restuccia | University of Palermo, Italy |
| Roland Schmitz | Stuttgart Media University, Germany |
| Thomas Schreck | Munich University of Applied Sciences, Germany |
| Georgios Spathoulas | Norwegian University of Science and Technology, Norway |
| Yuzhe Tang | Syracuse University, USA |
| Jacques Traore | Orange Labs, France |
| Ding Wang | Nankai University, China |
| Christos Xenakis | University of Piraeus, Greece |
| Qiben Yan | Michigan State University, USA |
| Guomin Yang | University of Wollongong, Australia |
| Xu Yuan | University of Louisiana at Lafayette, USA |
| Apostolis Zarras | TU Delft, The Netherlands |
| Yingpei Zeng | Hangzhou Dianzi University, China |
| Ning Zhang | Washington University in St. Louis, USA |
| Tianwei Zhang | Nanyang Technological University, Singapore |
| Xiaokuan Zhang | George Mason University, USA |
| Yue Zhang | The Ohio State University, USA |
| Qingchuan Zhao | City University of Hong Kong, Hong Kong, China |
| Ziming Zhao | University at Buffalo, USA |
| Haojin Zhu | Shanghai Jiaotong University, China |
| Urko Zurutuza | Mondragon Unibertsitatea, Spain |

# Contents

## Binary Analysis

## Blockchain

## Cryptography

## Data Security

## Intrusion Detection

## Mobile Security

## Security and Privacy-Preserving Solutions in the Internet of Things (S/P-IoT) Workshop

# AI for Security

# Classification-Based Anomaly Prediction in XACML Policies

Maryam Davari[✉] and Mohammad Zulkernine

School of Computing, Queen's University, Kingston, Canada
{maryam.davari,mz}@queensu.ca

**Abstract.** XACML (eXtensible Access Control Markup Language) has gained significant interest as a standard to define Attribute-Based Access Control (ABAC) policies for different applications, especially web services. XACML policies have become more complex and difficult to administer in distributed systems, which increases the chance of anomalies (redundancy, inconsistency, irrelevancy, and incompleteness). Due to the lack of effective analysis mechanisms and tools, anomaly detection and resolution are challenging, particularly in large and complex policy sets. In this paper, we learn the characteristics of various types of anomalies to predict anomaly types of unseen policy rules with the help of data classification techniques. The effectiveness of our approach in predicting policy anomalies has been demonstrated through experimental evaluation. The discovered correlations between the anomaly types and the number of subject and resource attribute expressions can help system administrators improve the security and efficiency of XACML policies.

**Keywords:** Access control policies · XACML · ABAC · Policy anomalies · Classification-based anomaly prediction · Security

## 1 Introduction

Access control policies have been used to secure and control resource sharing in distinct applications such as web services (e.g., [26]), grid systems (e.g., [24]), and database federations (e.g., [4]). In recent years, Attribute-Based Access Control (ABAC) [7] policies have gained popularity in open distributed environments [21]. ABAC defines permissions based on attributes that can be any information describing subjects, resources, and environments, rather than their identities. ABAC access control policies are specified by XACML (eXtensible Access Control Markup Language) [22], which is a general-purpose access control policy language. XACML has been utilized in a variety of applications ranging from healthcare to transportation [1].

Due to the sophisticated expressiveness and increasing size of XACML policies, the consequences and effects of developed policies are not obvious to policy administrators. Some anomalies such as redundancy, inconsistency, irrelevancy, and incompleteness may arise in developing access control policies when there are

© ICST Institute for Computer Sciences, Social Informatics and Telecommunications Engineering 2023
Published by Springer Nature Switzerland AG 2023. All Rights Reserved
F. Li et al. (Eds.): SecureComm 2022, LNICST 462, pp. 3–19, 2023.
https://doi.org/10.1007/978-3-031-25538-0_1

not enough mechanisms to analyze a large number of policies. One of the issues with ABAC policies is redundancy detection and removal. When the number of policies to be parsed affects the response time of access requests, redundancy has to be addressed to avoid processing of unnecessary policies. In a policy set, multiple policies may conflict with each other which is referred to as inconsistency. Inconsistent policies overlap and yield different decisions. Inconsistency detection can mitigate conflict resolution activities. Irrelevancy occurs when access control policies are not suitable for any user's access requests. Irrelevancy detection can help policy administrators eliminate unused policies and make policy maintenance easier. Incompleteness refers to a situation when the current access control policies cannot cover an access request. By detecting this anomaly, some security issues (e.g., mistakenly allowing access to intruders) can be avoided. However, anomaly detection in XACML policies is complicated due to the fact that XACML policies may be aggregated by various parties and maintained by multiple administrators.

In this paper, we propose a data classification-based approach to predict anomaly types (redundancy, inconsistency, irrelevancy, and incompleteness) in XACML policies. To the authors' knowledge, there are no XACML policy rule sets that include these four types of anomalies. Therefore, the proposed approach begins by building XACML policy rules. The rules are then clustered based on their similarities and policy anomaly detection technique [3] is applied to each cluster. Various data classification techniques (e.g., Random Forest, Decision Tree) are then trained on these rules to discover the behavior of anomalies and predict anomaly types of unseen rules. The experimental results show that the classification-based approach is effective in predicting anomalies in large rule sets. Furthermore, some correlations among the number of subject and resource attribute expressions, rule sizes, and anomaly types are found. These insights can assist system administrators to make XACML policies more secure and efficient.

The major contributions of this paper can be summarized as follows:

- The design and implementation of XACML policy anomaly prediction using classification techniques.
- The anomaly (redundancy, inconsistency, irrelevancy, and incompleteness) formalization for XACML policies.
- The discovery of correlations among anomaly types, rule sizes, and rule attributes.

The rest of the paper is organized as follows: Sect. 2 presents background information on XACML. Section 3 describes the XACML policy anomaly prediction approach, which includes the XACML policy analysis and policy learning procedure for anomaly prediction. In Sect. 4, the experiments are discussed and the findings are analyzed. The related work, conclusion, and future work are presented in Sects. 5 and 6, respectively.

## 2   Overview of XACML

In this section, we provide background information about XACML policies [22]. Access control policy specification and formalization in the XACML language have four parts: attributes and functions, rules, policies, and policy sets. XACML policies are centered around attributes and functions that represent the characteristics of subjects, resources, actions, and environments. A policy rule is made up of three parts: effect (indicating whether access will be permitted or denied), Boolean condition (specifying when the rule applies to an access request), and target (grouping subjects, resources, and actions).

A policy consists of a target, a set of rules, and a rule combining algorithm. A combining algorithm computes a decision when a policy has rules with conflicting effects such as *Deny-Overrides* (i.e., if any rule evaluates to "Deny", the final decision is "Deny"), *Permit-Overrides* (i.e., if any rule evaluates to "Permit", the final decision is "Permit"), and *First-Applicable* (i.e., the effect of the first rule that applies is the decision of the policy). A policy set is defined by a target, a set of policies, and a policy combining algorithm (which is the same as the rule combining algorithm). We provide formal definitions of XACML policies [27] in the following paragraphs.

**Definition 1** Rule. A rule $Ru = (S, R, A, C, E)$ specifies a set of subjects $S$ (containing a set of subject attributes) can perform a set of actions $A$ ($a_1, a_2, \cdots, a_m$) over a set of resources $R$ (consisting of a set of resource attributes) by effect $E$ under condition $C$. A policy $P = \{Ru_1, Ru_2, ..., Ru_m\}$ contains a set of rules $Ru_1, Ru_2, ..., Ru_m$.

**Definition 2** Subject Attribute. Attributes describe the characteristics of a subject. Let $S$ be a finite set of subjects and $Att_s$ is a finite set of subject attributes. The value of attribute $a \in Att_s$ for subject $s \in S$ is represented by the function $d_s(a, s)$. Some subject attributes have just one value, while others have multiple values. Single value attributes ($Att_{s,1}$) have a unique value for each subject (e.g., subject id), and multiple value attributes ($Att_{s,m}$) are a set of single values (e.g., courses).

**Definition 3** Resource Attribute. Attributes that describe the characteristics of resources. Let $R$ and $Att_r$ be finite sets of resources and resource attributes, respectively. The value of attribute $a \in Att_r$ for resource $r \in R$ is represented by function $d_r(a, r)$.

**Definition 4** Attribute Expression. An attribute expression contains a set of attributes, operators, and value tuples ($att\ op\ val$) (e.g., $security\_level > 10$). The operators we consider in this paper are $\{\leq, <, =, >, \geq\}$. A subject attribute expression ($e_S$) is a function $e$ that for each subject attribute $a \in Att_s$, $e_S(a)$ is either special value $\perp$ (that indicates there is no constraint on the value of attribute $a$) or a set of possible values. Similarly, resource attribute expression ($e_R$) is a function for resource attributes.

**Definition 5** Access Request. An access request is represented as a tuple $(S, R, A, C)$, with $S$ containing a finite set of subject attribute-value pairs $(att_{s1} = val1), (att_{s2} = val2), \cdots, (att_{sn} = valn)$. Similarly, $R$ is a finite set of resource attribute-value pairings $(att_{r1} = val1), (att_{r2} = val2), \cdots, (att_{rm} = valm)$. $A$ is the request action, and $C$ is a set of conditions.

**Definition 6** Any Value. If subject attributes or resource attributes of a rule are not specified, it signifies that they do not impose any constraints on attribute values, which we indicate with $att = *$.

In this paper, analysis and prediction are performed at the rule level, and the influence of combining algorithms is ignored. When the number of rules increases, the consequence of using the conflicting algorithms to override access control decisions can be unpredictable [21]. These algorithms can handle conflicts in incoming requests, but they were not developed to detect conflicts in policies.

**Table 1.** Sample policy rules.

| Rule | Subject | Resource | Action | Condition | Effect |
|------|---------|----------|--------|-----------|--------|
| $Ru_1$ | adminRole= accountant | type=budget | update | s.project=r.project | Permit |
| $Ru_2$ | isEmployee=true | type=task; proprietary=false | request | s.expertise=r.expertise; s.project=r.project | Permit |
| $Ru_3$ | adminRole= accountant, planner | type=budget | read, update | s.project=r.project | Permit |
| $Ru_4$ | isEmployee=true | type=task, proprietary=false | request | s.project=r.project | Deny |
| $Ru_5$ | isEmployee=true | type=schedule | update | s.project=r.project | Deny |
| $Ru_6$ | adminRole=planner | type=budget | request | s.project=r.project | Permit |

## 3   XACML Policy Anomaly Prediction

The classification-based anomaly prediction aims to learn the characteristics of rules with anomalies based on historical results and predict whether new rules are normal or anomalous. We regard the mapping between policy rules and anomaly types as a function of $f : x \rightarrow y$ in machine learning contexts, where $x$ is a rule and $y$ is a type of rule. $y$ indicates whether the rule is normal (i.e., has no anomaly) or anomalous (i.e., has an anomaly) in the binary classification. In the multi-class classification, $y$ can be normal or an anomaly type (redundancy, static and dynamic inconsistency, irrelevancy, and incompleteness). The main goal is to learn function $f$ to predict the type of an unseen rule. We provide XACML policy anomaly definitions in Sect. 3.1. Then, XACML policy rules are clustered and analyzed to identify the types of rules in Sect. 3.2. In the following section, we present a policy learning procedure (including data pre-processing and data-classification) that is required for anomaly prediction.

## 3.1   XACML Policy Anomaly Definitions

We begin by defining different types of anomalies for XACML policy rules. For further demonstration, we use some rules focusing on project management from [27] that are listed in Table 1.

**Definition 7** Redundancy (RED). Redundancy indicates similarities among rules. Attributes of two rules with the same identifiers have intersecting values. Detecting and removing redundancies can improve policy evaluation performance. Rule $Ru_j$ is redundant if and only if

- $\exists\, Ru_i \in ACP$.
- $\forall a \in Ru_j.e_S,\ \exists a' \in Ru_i.e_S,\ Att_s(a) = Att_s(a') \to a \cap a' \neq \varnothing \wedge$
  $\forall b \in Ru_j.e_R,\ \exists b' \in Ru_i.e_R,\ Att_r(b) = Att_r(b') \to b \cap b' \neq \varnothing \wedge Ru_i.A \cap$
  $Ru_j.A \neq \varnothing \wedge Ru_i.E = Ru_j.E$.

For example, rule $Ru_3$ in Table 1 specifies that an accountant and a planner assigned to a project can read and update the budget. Rule $Ru_1$ indicates that an accountant assigned to a project can update the project budget. As a result, rule $Ru_1$ is redundant in comparison to rule $Ru_3$.

**Definition 8** Inconsistency (INCON). Inconsistency can be divided into two categories: static and dynamic.

**Definition 8-1** Static inconsistency (SINCON). Static inconsistency refers to a situation when there are at least two similar rules (i.e., two rules with the same attribute identifiers have intersecting values) in the policy set that conflict with each other. Consider rules $Ru_i$ and $Ru_j$. These two rules are statically inconsistent if and only if

- $\forall a \in Ru_i.e_S,\ \exists a' \subset Ru_j.e_S,\ Att_s(a) = Att_s(a') \to a \cap a' \neq \varnothing \wedge \forall b \in Ru_i.e_R,\ \exists b' \in Ru_j.e_R,\ Att_r(b) = Att_r(b') \to b \cap b' \neq \varnothing \wedge Ru_i.A \cap Ru_j.A \neq \varnothing \wedge Ru_i.E \neq Ru_j.E$.

For example, rule $Ru_2$ specifies that an employee working on a project can request to work on a non-proprietary task whose required areas of expertise are among the employee's areas of expertise, while rule $Ru_4$ specifies that an employee working on a project cannot request to work on the non-proprietary task. Rules $Ru_2$ and $Ru_4$ are statically inconsistent.

**Definition 8-2** Dynamic inconsistency (DINCON). Dynamic inconsistency refers to a situation when an incoming access request triggers at least two rules with conflicting decisions. The dynamic inconsistency relies on access requests and occurs at runtime. Consider rules $Ru_m$ and $Ru_n$. These two rules are dynamically inconsistent with respect to request $req$ if and only if

- $\exists\, req = (S', R', A')$.

- $\exists Ru_m \in ACP \wedge Ru_n \in ACP | (\exists a \in S', \exists a' \in Ru_m.e_S, Att_s(a) = Att_s(a') \rightarrow a \cap a' \neq \varnothing) \wedge (\exists a''' \in S' \wedge \exists a'' \in Ru_n.e_S, Att_s(a''') = Att_s(a'') \rightarrow a''' \cap a'' \neq \varnothing) \wedge (\exists b \in R', \exists b' \in Ru_m.e_R, Att_r(b) = Att_r(b') \rightarrow b \cap b' \neq \varnothing) \wedge (\exists b'' \in R', \exists b'' \in Ru_n.e_R, Att_r(b''') = Att_r(b'') \rightarrow b''' \cap b'' \neq \varnothing) \wedge A' \cap Ru_m.A \neq \varnothing \wedge A' \cap Ru_n.A \neq \varnothing \wedge Ru_m.E \neq Ru_n.E.$

For example, when an incoming request is

$$<s.adminRole{=}accountant,\ s.isEmployee{=}true;\ r.type{=}\{budget,\ schedule\};$$
$$s.project{=}r.project;\ action\ {=}update>$$

dynamic inconsistency occurs. Both rules $Ru_1$ and $Ru_5$ satisfy the conditions, while they have conflicting effects. Therefore, rules $Ru_1$ and $Ru_5$ are dynamically inconsistent.

**Definition 9** Irrelevancy (IRR). Irrelevancy refers to a scenario where a rule is never triggered for any kind of access request. A rule is irrelevant if and only if

- $\exists Ru \in ACP.$
- $\nexists req = (S', R', A') | \forall a \in Ru.e_S, \exists a' \in S', Att_s(a) = Att_s(a') \rightarrow a \cap a' = a \wedge \forall b \in Ru.e_R, \exists b' \in Ru', Att_r(b) = Att_r(b') \rightarrow b \cap b' = b \wedge A' \cap Ru.A \neq \varnothing.$

As an example, rule $Ru_6$ specifies that a planner assigned to a project can request to get information about the project budget. However, according to rule $Ru_3$, an accountant and a planner assigned to a project can read and update the budget without sending the request. As a result, rule $Ru_6$ is irrelevant with respect to rule $Ru_3$.

**Definition 10** Incompleteness (INCOM). Rules are incomplete when existing rules are unable to cover an access request. A rule is incomplete if and only if

- $\exists req = (S', R', A').$
- $\nexists Ru \in ACP | \forall a \in Ru.e_S, \exists a' \in S, Att_s(a) = Att_s(a') \rightarrow a \cap a' = a \wedge \forall b \in Ru.e_R, \exists b' \in Ru', Att_r(b) = Att_r(b') \rightarrow b \cap b' = b \wedge A' \cap Ru.A \neq \varnothing.$

A contractor working on a project, for example, requests information regarding the project schedule. However, there is no policy to handle the request.

## 3.2   Rule Clustering and Analysis

Rule clustering makes the policy analysis scalable. A number of clustering algorithms exist such as K-means [10] and hierarchical clustering [12]. However, they face various challenges (e.g., determining the number of clusters, cluster initialization) and are not effective for XACML rules. In this paper, we present a clustering algorithm that groups rules sharing similarities into a cluster as the likelihood of anomalies (especially redundancies and static inconsistencies) among similar rules is high. Similarities between rules in terms of subjects ($S_s$), resources ($S_r$), actions ($S_{act}$), and conditions ($S_{con}$) are calculated for rules $Ru_i$ and $Ru_j$ as follows:

- $S(Ru_i, Ru_j) = w_s\, S_s(Ru_i, Ru_j) + w_r\, S_r(Ru_i, Ru_j) + w_a\, S_{act}(Ru_i, Ru_j) + w_c\, S_{con}(Ru_i, Ru_j)$
- $S_s(Ru_i, Ru_j) = \sum_{att_k \in (Ru_i.Att_s \cap Ru_j.Att_s)}[\,(d_s(att_k, Ru_i.s) \cap d_s(att_k, Ru_j.s))\,/\,(d_s(att_k, Ru_i.s) \cup d_s(att_k, Ru_j.s))\,]$
- $S_r(Ru_i, Ru_j) = \sum_{att_k \in (Ru_i.Att_r \cap Ru_j.Att_r)}[\,(d_r(att_k, Ru_i.r) \cap d_r(att_k, Ru_j.r))\,/\,(d_r(att_k, Ru_i.r) \cup d_r(att_k, Ru_j.r))\,]$
- $S_{act}(Ru_i, Ru_j) = [\,Ru_i.act \cap Ru_j.act\,]\,/\,[\,Ru_i.act \cup Ru_j.act\,]$
- $S_{con}(Ru_i, Ru_j) = [\,Ru_i.con \cap Ru_j.con\,]\,/\,[\,Ru_i.con \cup Ru_j.con\,]$

where $w_s + w_r + w_a + w_c = 1$. The weight assignment may depend on application needs. We consider weights of subject ($w_s$), resource ($w_r$), action ($w_a$), and condition ($w_c$) equal (all weights are assigned to 1/4). When the similarity score of two rules exceeds a threshold, they are grouped into a cluster. This score may fluctuate depending on the rule set. In our work, we use the threshold of 0.8 which was suggested by Lin et al. [14], and it works fine. Furthermore, each cluster has at least one rule, and each rule is grouped into one or more clusters. We consider *AND* operator in the rule definition. A rule containing Boolean expressions (e.g., *OR, NOT*) is split into several rules.

When the rules are clustered, we apply the formal tree-based policy modeling technique [3] for each cluster to analyze policy rules. To keep the tree as slim as possible, we define the data structure of the tree as follows. The first level of the tree is made up of action nodes, which show the actions of systems. Each action node in the tree points to the resource nodes on the second level. Each resource node is connected to the third level of the tree which contains subject nodes. Each subject node points to the condition nodes at the fourth level of the tree. Each condition node can then have one or two leaf nodes that represent the effects of the rule. Leaf nodes of each rule store *Rule ID* and a *Counter_ref* variable. The *Counter_ref* indicates whether the rule was triggered by any access request or not. Anomalies within each cluster are detected by traversing the policy trees from root to leaf node. Redundancies and static inconsistencies are detected in each cluster[1]. Dynamic inconsistencies, irrelevancies, and incompleteness can be detected by evaluating incoming access requests. When an incoming access request is issued, a cluster with the highest similarity to the request is identified. Then, rules in the corresponding cluster are evaluated with respect to the incoming access request according to Definitions 7-10 mentioned in Sect. 3.1.

### 3.3 Policy Learning Procedure for Anomaly Prediction

To discover the characteristics of rules with anomalies, machine learning techniques are applied to the rules generated by the XACML policy analysis (pre-

---

[1] For more details, please refer to [3].

sented in Sect. 3.2). Before applying the techniques, the rules need to be pre-processed as follows:

1) *Rules are parsed to organize attribute orders.* The rule components are divided into non-category and category attributes. Subject attributes, resource attributes, actions, conditions, and effects are non-category attributes. The type of rules that can be normal or anomalous is a category attribute.

2) *Missing attribute values are handled.* Missing attribute values can arise in any application. An approach for dealing with missing values is included in some classification algorithms. For example, a missing value of a numerical attribute is substituted with an average value of its attributes. They do not, however, take into account the semantics of data. We address missing values for subject and resource attributes using Definition 6. If values of action and effect components are missing, the effect of the rule becomes "not applicable".

3) *Continuous attributes are treated as some non-overlapping ranges to be efficient in data mining.* For example, the age attribute that has continuous numerical values is converted into a range (e.g., *infant, child, young adult*).

4) *Conditions in rules are addressed.* For example, a subject can access a resource during a specific time slot (*8am-5pm*) in a particular location (e.g., *office*). Permission is granted only if all the conditions are satisfied. Conditions, subject attributes, and resource attributes can be expressed as Boolean expressions; for example, *subject.security_level > 10*. In policy sets, rules are not uniformly structured necessarily. Rules may have complex Boolean expressions with variable lengths. To apply data classification techniques, we normalize these Boolean expressions. Boolean expression is converted to Disjunctive Normal Form (DNF) ($C_1 \vee C_2 \vee ... \vee C_i$). Then, the rule is divided into $i$ rules with distinct conditions.

5) *Intervals between rule components are managed.* We find all potential unique intervals among rule components when they overlap. For example, Rule 1 allows accountants and planners to change the project budget between *8am* and *5pm*. Rule 2 denies accountants the right to change the project budget between *12pm* and *1pm*. To convert the rules into non-overlapping rules, our algorithm identifies all the boundaries: *8am, 12pm, 1pm*, and *5pm*. The algorithm rewrites the rules as follows: Rule 1 allows accountants and planners to change the project budget between *8am* and *12pm*, Rule 2 denies accountants the right to change the project budget between *12pm* and *1pm*, Rule 3 allows planners to change the project budget between *12pm* and *1pm*, and Rule 4 permits accountants and planners to change the project budget between *1pm* and *5pm*.

6) *Imbalanced categories of anomalies in rule sets are addressed.* Usually, the number of instances with anomalies is far less than the number of instances without anomalies. Applying the classification techniques to an imbalanced rule set has a high likelihood of over-fitting [16] (i.e., the category with the dominant instance biases the classifier toward itself). We over-sample the

minority classes by generating synthetic instances using SMOTE (Synthetic Minority Oversampling Technique) [2].

Each rule is a feature vector containing subject attributes, resource attributes, actions, conditions, effects, and anomaly types. A subset of rules with anomalies are then utilized to learn anomaly characteristics. The accuracy of classification algorithms may vary depending on applications. There is no single algorithm that can outperform other algorithms in all feasible applications. Therefore, we apply five classification techniques from diverse categories (e.g., tree-based classifiers, distance-based classifiers, probabilistic classifiers) to the rules: Random Forest (RF), Decision Tree (DT), Naive Bayes (NB), Support Vector Machine (SVM), and K-Nearest Neighbors (KNN). The classifiers may have inherent classification inaccuracies, and various classifiers may provide different outcomes. As a result, we integrate the findings of multiple classifiers using the majority voting (MV) [18]. The majority voting technique ensures that the decisions of the classifiers are in agreement. Its decision, in particular, is a class that the majority of classifiers predict. When the classifiers' decisions are not in agreement, it chooses a class at random.

## 4    Experimental Evaluation

The primary goal of this section is to evaluate the effectiveness and efficiency of the proposed policy anomaly prediction approach. To achieve this, we perform various experimental evaluations as described below.

### 4.1    Rule Sets and Settings

We are unable to get large real-world rule sets to evaluate the proposed approach. Therefore, we create 18 synthetic rule sets. The number of subject attribute expressions and resource attribute expressions are selected based on a normal distribution with distinct means and variances. In the experiments, three means of attribute expression for both subjects and resources are set to 3, 4, and 5, and variances are set to 1. Six rule sets with size of 100, 1000, 2000, 3000, 4000, and 5000 are built for each mean. Rule sets $\{RS_1, \cdots, RS_6\}$, $\{RS_7, \cdots, RS_{12}\}$, and $\{RS_{13}, \cdots, RS_{18}\}$ are constructed for the means of attribute expressions 3, 4, and 5, respectively. Attribute values can have different domains in practice. We define attribute values as an integer type with values ranging from 1 to 100. Subject attributes and resource attributes each have a lower and upper threshold. The total number of subject and resource attributes is 20. Each rule can have [1, 10] actions and [0, 10] conditions that are uniformly and randomly selected. The effect of each policy is randomly picked as either "Permit" or "Deny".

We build a set of access requests to evaluate the effectiveness of the proposed approach in predicting dynamic inconsistencies, irrelevancies, and incompleteness. The mean of attribute expressions for the requests is set to 10 and the variance is set to 2. The request set contains more than 10,000 requests. We consider that requests only have one action. Requests with more than one action are rewritten as multiple requests with one single action. The proposed approach is implemented in Java 11. The experiments are conducted using an Intel Core i7 1.99 GHz processor with 16 GB of RAM.

## 4.2   Policy Analysis

Rule sets $\{RS_1, \cdots, RS_{18}\}$ are analyzed based on the approach described in Sect. 3.2. The analyzed rule sets are considered training rule sets for Sect. 4.3.

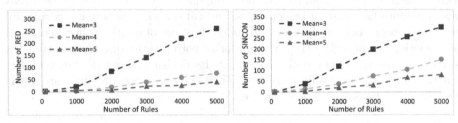

(a) Average Redundancy Rules.          (b) Average Static Inconsistency Rules.

**Fig. 1.** Average redundancy and static inconsistency rules for 18 rule sets.

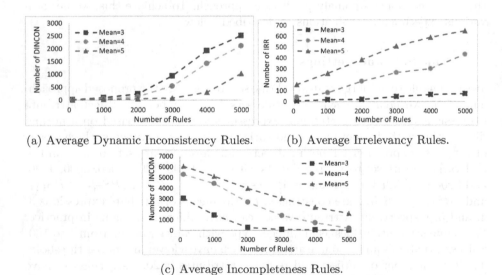

(a) Average Dynamic Inconsistency Rules.          (b) Average Irrelevancy Rules.

(c) Average Incompleteness Rules.

**Fig. 2.** Average dynamic inconsistency, irrelevancy, and incompleteness rules.

**Result Analysis.** Figures 1a and 1b show the average number of redundancies and static inconsistencies for 18 rule sets, respectively. On average, there is a significant number of redundancies and static inconsistencies. It is also observed that these two anomalies behave similarly with respect to the number of rules and means of attribute expressions. The average number of redundancies and static inconsistencies increases with the number of rules. However, as the means of attribute expressions increase, the growth rates of redundancies and static inconsistencies decrease.

Figure 2 shows the average number of dynamic inconsistencies, irrelevancies, and incompleteness for 18 rule sets. Figure 2a indicates that the behavior of dynamic inconsistencies is similar to the behavior of redundancies and static inconsistencies in terms of rule numbers and the means of attribute expressions. Similar behavior for static and dynamic inconsistencies was found by Liu et al. [15]. The average number of static inconsistencies is lower than the average number of dynamic inconsistencies. The reason is that policy administrators pay more attention to rules with similar attributes when creating policies. This can help decrease the number of static inconsistencies. It is difficult for administrators to determine whether rules with different attribute identifiers are inconsistent. Therefore, dynamic inconsistencies are ignored. As the majority of inconsistencies are dynamic inconsistencies, some of the static inconsistency detection approaches [11,13,21,25] may not successfully satisfy all actual system requirements.

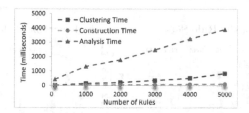

**Fig. 3.** Clustering, construction, and analysis time for 10,000 access requests for rule sets $RS_1, \cdots, RS_6$.

Despite the results shown in Figs. 1a, 1b, and 2a, the growth rates of irrelevancies increase when the means of attribute expressions increase (shown in Fig. 2b). Similar to redundancies, static inconsistencies, and dynamic inconsistencies, the average number of irrelevancies rises with the number of rules. On the other hand, the average number of incompleteness decreases with the number of rules. It can be observed from Fig. 2c that the average number of incompleteness increases as the number of attribute expressions grows. However, larger means of of attribute expressions have slower decreasing rates.

It can be observed from the above analysis that merely advising system administrators to employ a large number of attributes to generate inconsistency-free rule sets [15] is not effective. Although a high mean of attribute expressions can result in rule sets with fewer redundancies and (static and dynamic) inconsistencies, it can also raise irrelevancies and incompleteness. A low mean of attribute expressions, on the other hand, results in rule sets with fewer irrelevancies and incompleteness, while it can also result in more redundancies and (static and dynamic) inconsistencies. Redundancies and static inconsistencies rely on rules and are independent of access requests, while dynamic inconsistencies, irrelevancies, and incompleteness depend on access requests. As the number of access requests is far greater than the number of rules, rule sets with a low mean of attribute expressions can cause fewer anomalies.

As the anomaly detection technique needs to search all trees to find anomalies in the rule set, we collect time for building clusters, constructing policy trees, and analyzing access requests. These time-based metrics rely on the number of rules. In Fig. 3, we show the time for rule sets $RS_1, \cdots, RS_6$. As this figure indicates, rule clustering takes longer than tree construction. In addition, the policy analysis takes a longer time than clustering and tree construction, which is reasonable as we consider 10,000 access requests.

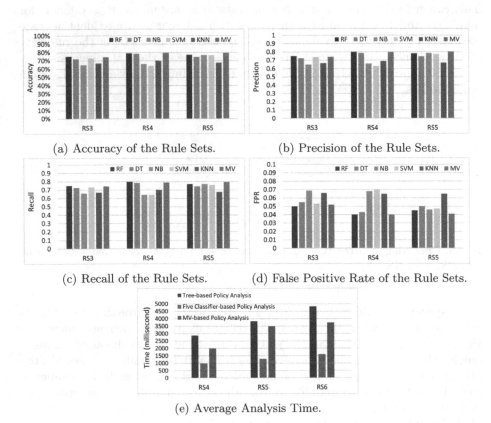

(a) Accuracy of the Rule Sets.

(b) Precision of the Rule Sets.

(c) Recall of the Rule Sets.

(d) False Positive Rate of the Rule Sets.

(e) Average Analysis Time.

**Fig. 4.** Efficiency of Anomaly Prediction for Rule Sets $RS_4$, $RS_5$, $RS_6$.

## 4.3   Anomaly Classification and Prediction

For the classification-based analysis, we use rule sets $RS_4$, $RS_5$, and $RS_6$. As the mean of the attribute expression is 3, the rule sets can balance the number of various anomalies (presented in the previous section). Various classifiers are constructed for the rule sets based on the approach presented in Sect. 3.3. We consider both binary and multi-class classifications. The classifiers are trained on 70% of the data and use 10-fold cross-validation and the Weka library [6], a set of machine learning algorithms for data mining tasks.

**Evaluation Metrics.**  To assess the efficiency of our classification-based anomaly detection approach, we report accuracy, precision, recall, and false positive rate (FPR) defined as follows:

$$Accuracy = \frac{TP + TN}{TP + TN + FP + FN} \tag{1}$$

$$Precision = \frac{TP}{TP + FP} \tag{2}$$

$$Recall = \frac{TP}{TP + FN} \tag{3}$$

$$FPR = \frac{FP}{FP + TN} \tag{4}$$

True Positive (TP) is the number of rules that are predicted as anomalies, and are truly anomalies. False Positive (FP) is the number of rules that are predicted as anomalies, while they are truly normal. False Negative (FN) is the number of rules that are predicted as normal, while they are truly anomalies. True Negative (TN) is the number of rules predicted as normal, and they are truly normal.

**Analysis Results.**  The effectiveness of multi-class classifiers is displayed in Fig. 4. The accuracy, precision, and recall of all five classifiers (excluding K-Nearest Neighbors) are above 70% using $RS_6$ as shown in Figs. 4a, 4b, and 4c, respectively. Figure 4d shows that the false positive rate ranges from 4% to 7%, which is critical for security. The low false positive rate shows that the classification-based detection methods are capable of detecting all anomalies. However, the effectiveness of a classification-based approach varies based on the employed classifiers. Some of the classifiers do not behave consistently. For example, K-Nearest Neighbors has about 70% accuracy, precision, and recall in $RS_4$. It improves slightly in $RS_5$, but it becomes worse in $RS_6$. The majority voting, on the other hand, achieves above 75% accuracy, precision, and recall for all rule sets. The binary class classifiers indicate that the average accuracy, precision, and recall for all six classification algorithms (including majority voting) are 99% and the average false positive rate is 0.8%.

Figure 4e depicts the average analysis time for discovering anomalies using the tree model, five classifiers, and majority voting technique. In general, classifiers outperform tree-based and majority voting policy analysis. The majority voting is slower than five classifiers as it integrates the results of all classifiers employed in classification-based policy analysis. However, it performs better than tree-based policy analysis. Therefore, it can be concluded that majority voting is effective in predicting policy anomalies.

## 5   Related Work

Policy anomaly assessment has attracted the attention of many researchers, and different approaches have been proposed in this area. There are some efforts to detect redundancies [11], inconsistencies [11,13,15,21,25], irrelevancies [17], and incompleteness [20] in XACML and ABAC policies. Jebbaoui et al. [11] proposed a semantic-based approach to detect redundancies and conflicts in XACML policies. The proposed approach was developed for a new set-based language named SBA-XACML. Shu et al. [21] focused on statically-conflicting rules and presented a method to detect conflicts in ABAC policies by using rule reduction and binary-search. They decomposed ABAC rules to identify redundancies and reduce the number of intersection operations. To enhance the efficiency of the proposed approach, they used binary search simultaneously. Liu et al. [15] presented a conflict detection method for ABAC policies based on the proposed definition of rule conflict. They transferred implicit conflicting rules to explicit conflicting rules and evaluated their approach by the proposed metrics.

The Satisfiability Modulo Theories (SMT) solver was another method for detecting conflict in XACML policies. The Boolean portion of satisfiability checking was separated from algorithms that employed property checking using SMT logic solvers [25]. Rami et al. [17] detected conflicts, unreachable policies (i.e., irrelevancies), and incompleteness by using Answer Set Programming (ASP). Expressing attributes that do not exist in AnsProlog [23] (e.g., strings) is difficult to be modeled. Also, there are no experimental results to show the applicability of their work. Fisler et al. [5] presented a tool called Margrave to analyze policies. It translates policies into Multi-Terminal Binary Decision Diagrams (MTBDDs) to answer user queries. Khoumsi et al. [13] proposed an automaton-based approach for modeling, developing, and analyzing policies. They divided firewall security policies into conflicting and non-conflicting anomalies.

There are a few works that use data mining-based and data classification techniques to detect anomalies in access control policies. Shaikh et al. [20] adopted data classification techniques to detect incompleteness in access control policies. This approach consisted of three steps. Attributes were ordered and Boolean expressions were normalized, a decision tree (which was a modification of C4.5) was generated, and the proposed anomaly detection algorithm was executed on the decision tree. In another study by Shaikh et al. [19], a modified C4.5 algorithm was proposed to detect inconsistencies and incompleteness in access control policies. When the number of XACML policies increases, the complexity and computation of some proposed algorithms grow, which makes the approach inapplicable. Abu Jabal et al. [9] proposed a framework based on the provenance technique for policy analysis. They proposed structure-based and classification-based approaches that focus on the RBAC domain.

Various approaches have been investigated to address the problem of anomalies in access control rules [8]. Most of the existing approaches were developed in the network management and RBAC domains. These studies are not effective for predicting all four types of anomalies in XACML policies. Our classification-based policy anomaly prediction approach is time efficient comparing tree-based anomaly detection. Furthermore, past policy analysis research has concentrated on only a few types of anomalies (the inconsistency being the most studied), whereas our approach attempts to discover all types of anomalies.

## 6  Conclusion and Future Work

A large number of XACML policies may raise the risk of anomalies (redundancy, inconsistency, irrelevancy, and incompleteness) in distributed systems. Anomaly detection, on the other hand, is a difficult and expensive operation. In this paper, we have presented an anomaly prediction approach for XACML policies based on the data classification techniques. The proposed approach extracts XACML policy rules and clusters them based on their similarities. Anomalies in each cluster are then detected using the policy anomaly detection technique. Various data classification techniques are trained on the rules to identify the behavior of anomalies and predict the anomaly types of new rules. The experimental results have shown that the majority voting technique can obtain accuracy, recall, and precision of 80% and a false positive rate of 4%. Therefore, the proposed approach has the capability to predict anomalies. Furthermore, the experiments have shown that anomaly types can be correlated to the number of rules and attribute expressions. It is notable that the limitation of the proposed approach is the lack of real-world policies. As part of the future work, we plan to find an appropriate number of attribute expressions to minimize the number of anomalies.

## References

1. https://www.oasis-open.org/ XACML references and products, version 1.85. https://www.oasis-open.org/committees/download.php/42588/xacmlRefs-V1-85. html#Products. (Accessed 28 Dec 2021)
2. Chawla, N.V., Bowyer, K.W., Hall, L.W., Kegelmeyer, W.P.: Synthetic minority over-sampling technique: SMOTE. J. Artifi. Intell. Res. **16**, 321–357 (2002)
3. Davari, M., Zulkernine, M.: Policy modeling and anomaly detection in ABAC policies. In: Luo, B., Mosbah, M., Cuppens, F., Ben Othmane, L., Cuppens, N., Kallel, S. (eds.) CRiSIS 2021. LNCS, vol. 13204, pp. 137–152. Springer, Cham (2022). https://doi.org/10.1007/978-3-031-02067-4_9
4. Dawson, S., Qian, S., Samarati, P.: Providing security and interoperation of heterogeneous systems. In: Security of Data and Transaction Processing, pp. 119–145. Springer (2000). https://doi.org/10.1007/978-1-4615-4461-6_5

5. Fisler, K., Krishnamurthi, S., Meyerovich, L.A., Tschantz, M.C.: Verification and change-impact analysis of access-control policies. In: Proceedings of the 27th International Conference on Software Engineering, pp. 196–205 (2005)
6. Hall, M., Frank, E., Holmes, G., Pfahringer, B., Reutemann, P., Witten. I.H.: The WEKA data mining software: an update. ACM SIGKDD Explorations Newsletter **11**(1), 10–18 (2009)
7. Hu, V.C., et al.: Guide to attribute based access control (ABAC) definition and considerations (draft). NIST Special Public. **800**(162), 1–54 (2013)
8. Jabal, A.A., et al.: Methods and tools for policy analysis. ACM Comput. Surv. (CSUR) **51**(6), 1–35 (2019)
9. Jabal, A.A., et al.: Profact: A provenance-based analytics framework for access control policies. IEEE Trans. Serv. Comput. (2019)
10. Jain, A.K., Dubes, R.C.: Algorithms for clustering data. Prentice-Hall Inc. (1988)
11. Jebbaoui, H., Mourad, A., Otrok, H., Haraty, R.: Semantics-based approach for detecting flaws, conflicts and redundancies in XACML policies. Comput. Elect. Eng. **44**, 91–103 (2015)
12. Johnson, S.C.: Hierarchical clustering schemes. Psychometrika **32**(3), 241–254 (1967)
13. Khoumsi, A., Erradi, M., Krombi, W.: A formal basis for the design and analysis of firewall security policies. J. King Saud Univ. Comput. Inf. Sci. **30**(1), 51–66 (2018)
14. Lin, D., Rao, P., Ferrini, R., Bertino, E., Lobo, J.: A similarity measure for comparing xacml policies. IEEE Trans. Knowl. Data Eng. **25**(9), 1946–1959 (2012)
15. Liu, G., Pei, W., Tian, Y., Liu, C., Li, S.: A novel conflict detection method for ABAC security policies. J. Ind. Inf. Integr. **22**, 100200 (2021)
16. Ostrand, T.J., Weyuker, E.J.: How to measure success of fault prediction models. In: 4th International Workshop on Software Quality Assurance
17. Ramli, C.D.P.K.: Detecting incompleteness, conflicting and unreachability XACML policies using answer set programming. arXiv preprint arXiv:1503.02732 (2015)
18. Ruta, D., Gabrys, B.: Classifier selection for majority voting. Inf. Fusion **6**(1), 63–81 (2005)
19. Shaikh, R.A., Adi, K., Logrippo, L.: A data classification method for inconsistency and incompleteness detection in access control policy sets. Int. J. Inf. Sec. **16**(1), 91–113 (2017)
20. Shaikh, R.A., Adi, K., Logrippo, L., Mankovski, S.: Detecting incompleteness in access control policies using data classification schemes. In: 5th International Conference on Digital Information Management (ICDIM), pp 417–422. IEEE (2010)
21. Shu, C.-c., Yang, E.Y., Arenas, A.E.: Detecting conflicts in ABAC policies with rule-reduction and binary-search techniques. In: International Symposium on Policies for Distributed Systems and Networks, pp. 182–185. IEEE (2009)
22. OASIS Standard. Extensible access control markup language (XACML) version 3.0. 2008. http://docs.oasis---open.or/xacmmL2.0/access_control-xacml-2.0core. spec---OS.pa1 (2013)
23. Sureshkumar, A., De Vos, M., Brain, M., Fitch, J.: Ape: An ansprolog* environment. See De Vos and Schaub **2007**, 101–115 (2007)
24. Thompson, M.R., Essiari, A., Mudumbai, S.: Certificate-based authorization policy in a PKI environment. ACM Trans. Inf. Syst. Sec. (TISSEC) **6**(4), 566–588 (2003)
25. Turkmen, F., den Hartog, J., Ranise, S., Zannone, N.: Analysis of XACML Policies with SMT. In: Focardi, R., Myers, A. (eds.) POST 2015. LNCS, vol. 9036, pp. 115–134. Springer, Heidelberg (2015). https://doi.org/10.1007/978-3-662-46666-7_7

26. Wimmer, M., Kemper, A., Rits, M., Lotz, V.: Consolidating the access control of composite applications and workflows. In: Damiani, E., Liu, P. (eds.) DBSec 2006. LNCS, vol. 4127, pp. 44–59. Springer, Heidelberg (2006). https://doi.org/10.1007/11805588_4
27. Xu, Z., Stoller, S.D.: Mining attribute-based access control policies. IEEE Trans. Depend. Sec. Comput. **12**(5), 533–545 (2014)

# An Evolutionary Learning Approach Towards the Open Challenge of IoT Device Identification

Jingfei Bian[1,2], Nan Yu[1,2], Hong Li[1,2], Hongsong Zhu[1,2(✉)], Qiang Wang[1,2], and Limin Sun[1,2]

[1] Beijing Key Laboratory of IOT Information Security Technology, Institute of Information Engineering, CAS, Beijing, China
{bianjingfei,yunan,lihong,zhuhongsong,wangqiang3113,sunlimin}@iie.ac.cn
[2] School of Cyber Security, University of Chinese Academy of Sciences, Beijing, China

**Abstract.** Internet of Things (IoT) device identification has become an indispensable prerequisite for secure network management and security policy implementation. However, existing passive device identification methods work under a "closed-world" assumption, failing to take into account the emergence of new and unfamiliar devices in open scenarios. To combat the open-world challenge, we propose a novel evolutionary model which can continuously learn with new device traffic. Our model employs a decoupled architecture suitable for evolutionary learning, which consists of device feature representation and device inference. For device feature representation, an auto-encoder based on metric learning is innovatively introduced to mine latent feature representation of device traffic and form independent compact clusters for each device. For device inference, the nearest class mean (NCM) classification strategy is adopted on the feature representation. In addition, to alleviate the forgetting of old devices during evolutionary learning with new devices, we develop a less-forgetting constraint based on spatial knowledge distillation and impose control on the distribution distance between clusters to reduce inter-class interference. We evaluate our method on the union of three public IoT traffic datasets, in which the accuracy is as high as 87.9% after multi-stage evolutionary learning, outperforming all state-of-the-art methods under diverse experimental settings.

**Keywords:** IoT device identification · Deep learning · Closed-world · Evolutionary model · NCM · Spatial knowledge distillation

## 1 Introduction

In recent years, deep learning has been employed to solve increasingly serious network security problems, especially passive IoT device identification [5,9,14,23–26,29], which has shown unlimited potential and achieved remarkable success. However, once the device identification model that performs well in the

F. Li et al. (Eds.): SecureComm 2022, LNICST 462, pp. 20–38, 2023.
https://doi.org/10.1007/978-3-031-25538-0_2

laboratory is deployed in a real open environment, it will fall into the dilemma of performance degradation [28]. One of the main reasons behind the dilemma is that the model is based on a biased assumption during the designing phase, that is, the IoT device types at training time and the IoT device types to be identified are from the same set of predefined types. However, the practical scenarios are complex and changeable, where new and unknown devices will continue to emerge. The knowledge acquired by the static model from the old device traffic will become outdated and unavailable in a short period. Hence, this assumption deviates from reality, which causes the notorious *open-world* [12] problem during the model deployment phase.

To address the problem of the open-world, most of the existing methods [9, 13] are based on the idea of Out-of-Distribution for detection. They not only allow the model to identify the known devices but also detects the unknown, which have made some progress. However, the methods merely mark unfamiliar devices as unknown without considering how to further recognize unknown devices. A realistic scenario for IoT device identification is, as time goes by when devices that have never been seen appear on the network, it is more imperative for the model to continuously learn, upgrade and evolve with the new data to adapt to the variations, rather than just to identify as the unknown. Therefore, we intend to solve the open-world problem in the field of IoT device identification from the perspective of model evolution. Our insight is that the fundamental solution for the open-world problem should be to accept new devices, not reject them, just as human beings always have the ability to continuously learn and internalize knowledge in new environments. To achieve the goal, we propose a novel evolutionary model which can continuously learn with new device traffic. And we borrow ideas from class incremental learning [15] and continuous learning [19] in the field of image recognition to overcome the inevitable catastrophic forgetting that arises in evolutionary learning. As far as we know, there is currently no evolutionary learning method in the field of passive network device identification, which is one of the motivations of this paper.

**Our Method.** We adopt a decoupled architecture for evolutionary learning, divided into representation and device inference. For representation, we design an automatic feature representation scheme for device traffic, which is data-centric. In specific, we propose an auto-encoder mapping algorithm based on metric learning to mine latent features suitable for evolutionary learning and automatically perform feature space layout with intra-class compactness and inter-class separation. Following, for device inference, we make use of the Nearest Class Mean (NCM) classification strategy on the latent representation. Additionally, to alleviate the catastrophic forgetting of old devices during evolutionary learning, we only leverage a tiny number of representative exemplars to ensure the continuity of knowledge in the evolutionary learning process based on the Spatial Knowledge Distillation.

**Contributions.** In summary, the paper has following main contributions:

- We innovatively propose an evolutionary learning method to overcome the open-world problem of passive IoT device identification. We introduce a decoupled architecture suitable for evolutionary learning, divided into device feature representation and device inference.

- To alleviate catastrophic forgetting during evolutionary learning, we develop a less-forgetting constraint based on Spatial Knowledge Distillation and introduce metric learning to control the inter-class distribution distance.
- We evaluate our method on the union of three public datasets [3,17,24], with traffic data from 66 different types of devices. The experimental results show that our method outperforms existing methods under diverse settings, with an accuracy of up to 87.9% after multi-stage evolutionary learning.

The remainder of the paper is organized as follows: Sect. 2 details our proposed method. The experiment and evaluation are presented in Sect. 3. Section 4 reviews related work and we discuss and conclude all the work in Sect. 5.

## 2  Proposed Method

### 2.1  Motivation and Problem Definition

Due to the rapid development of IoT applications, tens of thousands of new devices, which have never appeared before, emerge in the network every day [12]. Therefore, in practical scenarios, the network devices are usually in a process of dynamic change and continuous increase [28], which brings difficulties for passive IoT device identification. Actually, the main challenge in the open scenario is *the introduction of the new class.*

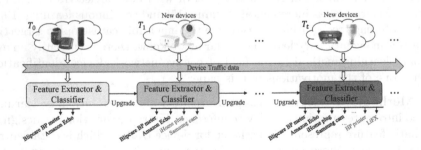

**Fig. 1.** General scenarios of model evolution.

We consider that the fundamental strategy to solve the open-world problem is to make the model continuously evolve during the life cycle to adapt to the transformation of the network. We regard the introduction of each batch of new devices as an evolution task. As shown in Fig. 1, in the open scenarios, the unknown number of tasks with previously unseen devices arrive at the model sequentially, denoted as $T_0, T_1, \cdots, T_t, \cdots$. The new traffic data contained in the task $T_t$ at time point $t$-th is $X_t = \{x_i^t, y_i^t\}_{i=0}^{N_t}$, where, $x_i^t$ and $y_i^t \in C_t$ is $i$-th device traffic sample and its label respectively. $N_t$ is the number of samples and $C_t$ represents the disjoint label set at time point $t$-th, where $C_t \wedge C_k =$

$\emptyset, \forall k \in \{0, 1, \cdots, t-1\}$. The model of the current stage can only be upgraded and evolved based on the currently visible new device data set and the model of the previous stage. And it would be evaluated on the test sets $Z_t$, whose label set is the union of all the encountered classes $\bigcup_{j=0}^{t} C_j$.

Our problem scope is how to effectively continuously evolve the model when traffic data for new devices is available or only a few traffic data is available. A naive idea is to use the latest traffic data to fine-tune the model of the previous task without much consideration when the new data arrives. However, the approach will lead to serious catastrophic forgetting [4]. Because the model will pay too much attention to the latest task, and the performance on the old tasks will drop significantly. The other simplest way is to store all the data that has appeared, and every time a new task comes, retrain a new model from scratch using all the data. However, this scheme greatly wastes storage and computing resources and even involves privacy protection issues, which is not feasible in practical applications. The above two ideas are extreme choices between consumption and performance, and also show the *main difficulty* of model evolution: how to avoid forgetting and achieve better performance while reducing the consumption of memory and computing resources.

## 2.2   Overall Framework

In this section, we present the overall framework of the method, as shown in Fig. 2. Following, we begin by describing our analysis and findings, which underlie our design.

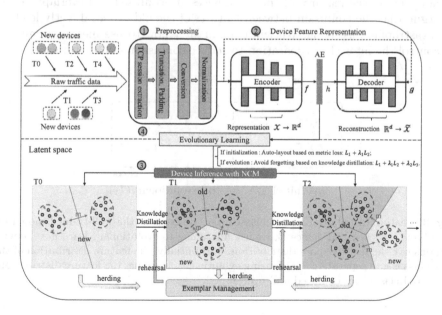

**Fig. 2.** The framework of our method.

1. *Feature representation of device traffic.* Most IoT device identification methods [23–26] rely on handcrafted features. But for evolutionary learning, it is impossible to expect current handcrafted features to be useful for modeling new device behaviors in the future. Therefore, it is necessary to design a traffic feature representation method suitable for evolutionary learning that directly relies on the data itself rather than hand-designed.

2. *Defects of traditional network architecture.* The usual classification neural network can be interpreted as a feature extractor followed by a classifier. For evolutionary learning, a universal feature extractor is crucial. If the extracted features only serve the current task, when a new device arrives, the parameters of the extractor will be drastically modified to regain new features favorable for the new task, which will exacerbate forgetting. In addition, the usual classifier is a linear fully-connected layer with as many softmax output nodes as classes observed so far. Rebuffi has shown in [20] that linear classification layers can become unstable and uncontrolled during evolutionary learning. Moreover, when learning to identify new devices, it is necessary to adjust and increase the output units of the network structure, which is cumbersome and inconvenient. In summary, traditional task-centric feature extraction methods and linear fully-connected classification are detrimental to evolutionary learning.

3. *Inter-class confusion and interference.* Figure 3 presents our findings from experiments on the IoT device dataset of UNSW [24]. The features of the well-trained devices form respective distribution regions, and there is no overlap between the features of base classes. However, with the introduction of the new device, the features of the old devices are confused and overlapped. We argue that the confusion between features of the old classes directly leads to catastrophic forgetting. We will explain later how to use metric learning to control the inter-class separation to reduce confusion and interference.

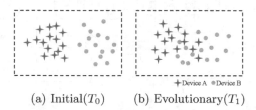

(a) Initial($T_0$)     (b) Evolutionary($T_1$)

**Fig. 3.** Feature distribution of old classes. On the basis of the well-trained model for classifying device A and device B, we use finetuning to evolutionary learn novel device and observe the feature space distribution. 3(a) Initially, the feature distribution of the base class is well separated. 3(b) During evolutionary learning, the feature distributions of the old classes are confused and overlapped.

## 2.3   Preprocessing

Generally, we can capture the traffic data by deploying sniffers on the gateway or the router. In the application scenarios, the devices will generate different traffic according to the special services. The service-related traffic behavior provides various device features, which facilitate IoT device identification [12]. However, most existing feature extraction methods rely on handcrafting. They are designed from closed scenarios where all training data is known. In the open world, it is impossible to anticipate which crafted features are useful to unknown devices. Therefore, hand-crafted methods are not suitable for evolutionary learning.

In contrast to methods that rely on hand-crafted features, we would like to make the model automatically mine latent features from traffic data. We find that when a device provides services, it always produces the natural sequences of TCP packets that are highly related to its services. In contrast, due to the connection-less nature of the UDP protocol, the network behavior based on UDP is less distinguishable than TCP, such as the largest number of UDP network services, NTP and DNS, the inadequacies of which have been discussed in [9]. Hence we consider using the TCP session as the basic unit to present traffic. In specific, we split a TCP session by the network five-tuple (source IP, source port, protocol, destination IP, destination port) and the session establishment or teardown flag. However, due to uncontrollable reasons such as network congestion, captured packets may be out of order, lost, or repeated, so we correct or ignore them according to the five-tuples, sequence numbers and timestamp intervals.

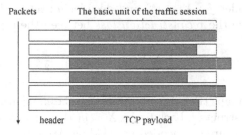

**Fig. 4.** The basic unit of TCP session.

Then, we extract the TCP payload of all sessions and drop the headers to avoid the model over-fitting with IP and MAC addresses [18]. A TCP session includes the whole process of network communication between a pair of device subjects, the dominant and responder. We arrange all communications of a session in a vertical request-response sequence, forming a 2D matrix. It is observed that most TCP sessions are short and compact, almost ending the session within the first 16 interactions. Therefore, we intercept the first 16 packets, keep the first 256 bytes of each payload, and pad any shortfalls with zeros so that we can express the TCP session with a smaller size. Additionally, for encrypted traffic of SSL/TLS, the first 16 packets always contain the entire process of key exchange and key negotiation, which is beneficial for the identification of encrypted traffic. Before the training data is fed into the neural network, the data will be converted from each byte to decimal and normalized. As shown in Fig. 5, we randomly sample 4 sessions of 6 devices from the public dataset UNSW [24] and visualize them using grayscale maps. It is found that behavioral patterns differed significantly between devices.

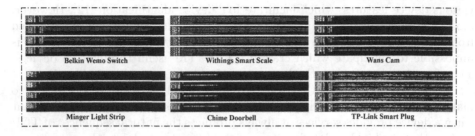

**Fig. 5.** Grayscale visualization of preprocessed data.

## 2.4   Device Feature Representation Learning

The analysis at the beginning of this section shows the limitations of traditional architectures. Thus we abandon the structural form of a task-centric extractor followed by the fully connected classifier, and creatively employ the stacked auto-encoder to learn latent representations for devices. Figure 2 shows the architecture of our method. We value the good representation ability of the auto-encoder. Given the inputs $X \in \mathcal{X}$ and features $h \in \mathbb{R}^d$, the auto-encoder can be divided into two parts: encoder $f : \mathcal{X} \rightarrow \mathbb{R}^d$ and decoder $g : \mathbb{R}^d \rightarrow \mathcal{X}$, which solves the mapping to minimize the *reconstruction loss* between the inputs and outputs:

$$L_1 = \frac{1}{N} \sum_{i=1}^{N} \| x_i - g[f(x_i)] \|_2^2 . \tag{1}$$

Here, encoder $f$ maps the original inputs $X$ to latent space features $h = f(X)$ and decoder $g$ reconstructs $h$ back to $X$, $\tilde{X} = g(h)$. The output $h$ of the encoder is named encoded feature or encoded embedding. We design the dimension $d$ of $h$ to be far smaller than the input, forcing the $f$ to capture the most prominent and representative features. Therefore, the captured features are good representations, as they do not serve a specific task, but work to characterize and express all latent information.

However, the auto-encoder is not well compatible with traditional fully connected classification layers, and auto-encoders cannot perform classification tasks independently. Hence, we introduce metric learning [21] into the representation of auto-encoder to automatically achieve independent compact spatial distributions. Specifically, we combine ideas from auto-encoding and metric learning to produce a compact, representative, and class-separable embedding space:

$$L_2 = \frac{1}{N} \sum_{i=1}^{N} \max \left( \| f(x_i^a) - f(x_i^p) \|_2^2 - \| f(x_i^a) - f(x_i^n) \|_2^2 + m, 0 \right) . \tag{2}$$

Equation (2) refers to the triplet loss [21], which takes a triple of samples $(x_i^a, x_i^p, x_i^n)$ and enforce the $x_i^a$ (*anchor sample*) of a certain device to be closer to all $x_i^p$ (*positive sample*) of the same device than to $x_i^n$ (*negative sample*) of any other device in the feature space. Here, $\|f(x_i^a) - f(x_i^p)\|_2^2$ represents the Euclidean distance metric between the anchor and the positive, and $\|f(x_i^a) - f(x_i^n)\|_2^2$ represents the Euclidean distance metric between the anchor and the negative. $m$ is the minimum interval between positive and negative samples relative to the anchor sample. As illustrated in the latent space in Fig. 2, The loss function intents to ensure that any traffic samples from different devices are sufficiently far apart.

As shown in Fig. 2, combining with Eq. (1) and Eq. (2), encoder $f$ can map the traffic to a latent space with tight clusters classes of different devices, which could be used for identification. The process is like we employ an encoder to assign the most appropriate and compact feature distribution for each device. Our representation learning method is not task-centric. The metric-based encoding algorithm can extract common latent features, which solves **the problem of traditional feature extractors**. In addition, we can intervene in the spatial layout by controlling the parameter $m$, which we will discuss in subsequent experiments to address **the problem of confusion and interference**. It is worth mentioning that, during evolutionary learning, we do not need to add neurons in the output layer of a deep network model to accommodate new devices, but can easily expand new devices in the latent representation space.

---

**Algorithm 1:** Device Inference

---

**Input:** Devices data set $X = \{x_0, \cdots, x_{N-1}\}$; devices class $Y = \{y_1, \cdots, y_K\}$; the number of samples in each class subset is $N^1, \cdots, N^K$; the test set $(\widehat{x}_j, \widehat{y}_j) \in Z$, where $j = 0, \cdots, \widehat{N} - 1$, $\widehat{N}$ is the total number of test samples; The encoder $f$.

**Output:** The inferred device class $y$.

1   **for** class $k = 1$ to $K$ **do**
2     $\mu_k = \frac{1}{N^k} \sum_{i=0}^{N^k - 1} f(x_i^k)$ ;        // The mean of the class k
3   **end**
    // Device Inference
4   **for** $j = 0$ to $\widehat{N}$ **do**
5     **for** $k = 1$ to $K$ **do**
6       $d_j^k = \|\widehat{x}_j - \mu_k\|_2^2$
7     **end**
8     $y_j^* = \underset{k=1,2,\cdots,K}{\arg\min} \; d_j^k$ ;        // NCM Classification Strategy
9   **end**

---

## 2.5   Device Inference

In the device feature representation, we propose an auto-encoder mapping method based on metric learning to automatically perform feature space layout with intra-class compactness and inter-class separation. Following, for device inference, we properly make use of the nearest class mean (NCM) classification strategy [20]. As described in Algorithm 1, we first use an auto-encoder to map the traffic data of all devices into the feature space and then obtain the mean feature vector for each device. Finally, we assign class labels based on the smallest distance from the mean vector in the feature space. Figure 6 visualizes the main idea of our device inference method. The entire feature space can be regarded as a multidimensional Voronoi Diagram. The embeddings of traffic samples for each class form corresponding regions, called Voronoi cells, consisting of all points that are closer to the mean vector of the class than any other classes. The inference of the device type is to determine in which cell it is mapped.

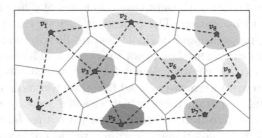

**Fig. 6.** Device inference with NCM. Combining metric learning and NCM strategy, the feature space is naturally formed similar to the Voronoi Diagram. Take the Voronoi diagram in 2-D space as an example, where $v_1, \cdots, v_9$ are the mean vectors of classes.

### 2.6   Evolutionary Learning

---

**Algorithm 2:** Exemplar Management

---

**Input:** Devices data set $X = \{x_0, \cdots, x_{N-1}\}$; devices class $Y = \{y_1, \cdots, y_K\}$; the number of samples in each class subset is $N^1, \cdots, N^K$; the encoder $f$; the size of exemplar set $S$.

**Output:** The exemplar set $P$.

1 **for** class $k = 1$ to $K$ **do**

2 $\quad \mu_k = \frac{1}{N^k} \sum_{i=0}^{N^k-1} f(x_i^k)$ ;                    // The mean of the class k

3 $\quad P^k = \{\}$ ;                                                    // Initialization

4 $\quad$ **for** $j = 0$ to $S - 1$ **do**

5 $\quad\quad p_j \leftarrow \underset{x \in X^k \setminus P^k}{\arg\min} \left\| \mu_k - \frac{1}{j} \left[ f(x) + \sum_{z=1}^{j-1} f(p_z) \right] \right\|$

6 $\quad\quad$ Add $p_j$ to $P^k$

7 $\quad$ **end**

8 $\quad P \leftarrow (P^1, P^2, \cdots, P^K)$ ;                           // Add to the set P

9 **end**

---

**Representative Exemplar Management.** We have designed a model archi-tecture suitable for evolutionary learning. However, during continuous learning with new devices, it is also necessary to overcome the inevitable forgetting of old devices. To help the model acquire knowledge from old classes, we use an exemplar manager to manage the most representative samples from old data for knowledge replay to avoid forgetting. When a set of new devices is added to the current model, we select a subset of the most representative samples from these classes and store them. In our work, we consider a manager with minimal storage compared to the original dataset, and select representative samples for each class to manage when new tasks arrive. For the selection of typical samples, we introduce the method of herding, which is detailed in Algorithm 2. When the device samples are added to the exemplar set, the algorithm guarantees that the average feature vector of the exemplar set most closely approximates the average feature vector of the overall sample set.

---

**Algorithm 3:** Evolutionary Learning

---

**Input:** A series of tasks arriving by time $T_0, \cdots, T_t$ and the training data of each task $X_0, \cdots, X_t$; the test tasks $\mathcal{Z}_0, \cdots, \mathcal{Z}_t$; the model $f$; the size of exemplar set $S$.

**Output:** Evolutionary model $f^*$; device identification results $Y$.

1 Preprocess raw traffic data from network devices;

   // Initial Stage

2 if the first task $T_0$ arrives then

3      $\mathcal{D}_0 \leftarrow \{(x, y) : x \in X_0\}$;

4      Run training with loss function:

$$f_0 \leftarrow \arg\min_f L_1 + \lambda_1 L_2, \qquad (3)$$

     that $L_1$ serves as Reconstruction Loss and $L_2$ serves as Metric Loss;

5      $P_0 \leftarrow ExemplarManage(\mathcal{D}_0, S)$;

6      $Y_0 \leftarrow DeviceInference(\mathcal{Z}_0, f_0)$;

7 end

   // Evolutionary Stage

8 while task $T_t \in \{T_1, T_2, T_3, \cdots\}$ arrive do

9      $\mathcal{D}_t \leftarrow \{(x, y) : x \in X_t\} \cup \bigcup_{j=0}^{t-1} \{(x, y) : x \in P_j\}$;

10      Knowledge replay with less consumption:

$$f_t \leftarrow \arg\min_f L_1 + \lambda_1 L_2 + \lambda_2 L_3, \qquad (4)$$

11      $P_t \leftarrow ExemplarManage(\mathcal{D}_t, S)$ ;        // get the exemplars set

12      $Y_t \leftarrow DeviceInference(\mathcal{Z}_t, f_t)$;

13 end

---

**Spatial Knowledge Distillation.** As described in Algorithm 3, evolutionary learning is divided into two stages: initialization and evolution. In general, the initial stage is the same as traditional learning, which learns to identify all IoT devices in $T_0$ by solving the constraint (3). The evolutionary stage is following the initial stage. As a sequence of tasks $T_0, T_1, \cdots, T_t$ arrive, the model needs to be re-learn based on the model obtained in the previous stage to continuously enhance the classification ability. During the training process for new tasks, we need to avoid using all the old training traffic data used in historical tasks, but not overly impair the ability to recognize old devices. So we introduce the method of *knowledge distillation* [7] into the stage of evolutionary training to alleviate the problem of catastrophic forgetting:

$$L_3 = \sum_{x_i \in \mathcal{D}_t} \delta_{x_i \in (P_0, P_2, \cdots, P_{t-1})} \|f_t(x_i) - f_{t-1}(x_i)\|_2^2, \tag{5}$$

where the term is named Spatial Knowledge Distillation, $\delta$ indicates true when $x_i \in (P_0, P_2, \cdots, P_{t-1})$. We regard the model of the previous stage as the teacher model and the model of the new stage as the student model. Then we transfer the knowledge from the model of the previous task stage $T_t$ to the next task stage $T_{t+1}$ with the constraint (5). In addition to learning the old knowledge, the student model needs to undertake more work. It not only needs to learn the knowledge of the teacher model in $T_t$ but also to learn new knowledge in the new task $T_{t+1}$. The process of dynamic evolution is visualized in Fig. 7.

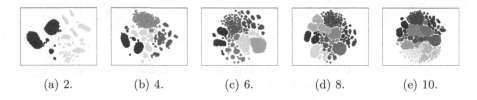

(a) 2.         (b) 4.         (c) 6.         (d) 8.         (e) 10.

**Fig. 7.** Visualization of dynamic evolution.

# 3    Experiments and Results

## 3.1    Experimental Setups and Datasets

Our experiments are based on three public datasets: IoT Traffic Traces of UNSW [24], Sentinel [17], and LSIF [3]. The detailed setup of the dataset and experiments will be described as follows.

**Traffic Traces of UNSW.** The dataset is open-source traffic data collected in 2018 by researchers at the UNSW in the process of studying IoT assets and tracking the behavior of IoT devices, recording daily traffic data for 3 month period. The dataset includes smart cameras, plugs, sensors, health monitors, etc., with a total of 30 network devices.

**IoT Sentinel.** The dataset is network device data generated by Miettinen [17] in the research on managing security and privacy risks posed by insecure IoT devices. The devices are mainly a representative set of consumer-oriented IoT devices, with 23 device data covering the most common types of devices such as smart lighting, home automation, and household appliances.

**LSIF.** Charyyev et al. [3] set up an experimental platform that automatically collects network traffic. The data set contains data on Internet devices produced by different manufacturers, which recorded network devices such as smart plugs, smart light bulbs, doorbells, and cameras. This dataset collects network traffic generated from experiments over approximately 20 d.

**Experimental Setups.** We choose the popular 18-layer ResNet as the underlying CNN network for all methods for comparative experiments. During the experiments, we use the Adam optimizer with which the learning rate starts at 0.001, the decay coefficient is set to 0.96, and the batch size is 256. In our method, the hyper-parameters $\lambda_1$ and $\lambda_2$ in the loss function are both set to 1 and the dimension of the encoding layer is set to 100. For the dataset, in order to perform multi-stage evolutionary learning, we merge all datasets together, remove the data of all duplicate devices, and then integrate the extracted TCP session data into a large dataset containing 66 different classes for experiments. We set the number of downsampling to 4000 and split the training and test sets with a ratio of 8:2. The number of exemplars per class is set to 50, which only accounts for a very small proportion of the original data, around 0.01. In addition, parameters such as task capacity $c$, number of exemplars per class $n$, and boundary distance $m$ will be discussed in detail in the later sections. In the experiments, we aim to answer the following research questions:

**Q1** - How about the accuracy of our proposed method after multi-stage evolutionary learning?

**Q2** - How well do various methods perform in evolutionary learning for the anti-forgetting of old devices?

**Q3** - How do key parameters affect evolutionary learning in experiments and how do we make trade-offs in performance, computational resources, and memory?

## 3.2 Accuracy Evaluation (Q1)

In this evaluation, our main purpose is to test the accuracy of our method after multi-stage evolutionary learning. We conduct comparative experiments with various state-of-the-art methods [15], including LwF-M [11], iCarl [20], LUCIR [8], EEIL [2] and il2m [1]. Note that the LwF-M here is an improvement of the original LwF method, adding the method of representative exemplars to improve the accuracy. In addition, we compare our method with the naive **finetune** method and **joint** learning method. Finetune is a naive idea and refers to fine-tuning models directly as new tasks arrive without any knowledge-preserving effort, which is considered as one of the baselines for models in evolutionary learning. The joint learning method represents storing all historical traffic data. Every time a new task is trained, a new model is reconstructed from scratch using all the data, which wastes huge computing resources and storage. Although the joint learning method is not available in practical scenarios, it can be regarded as the highest upper bound.

We set up a fair comparison experiment basis, all methods perform multiple comparisons at task capacities of 2, 5, and 10, respectively, where the task capacity refers to the number of new devices included in each task. The comparison results are shown in Fig. 8. We summarize the results as follows:

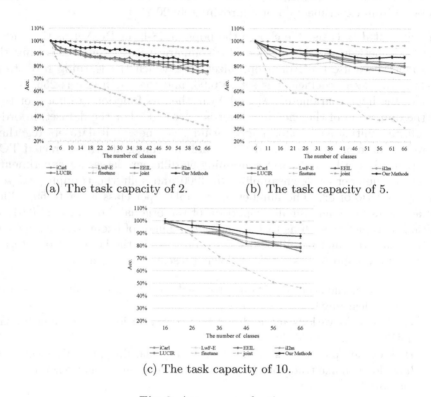

(a) The task capacity of 2.     (b) The task capacity of 5.

(c) The task capacity of 10.

**Fig. 8.** Accuracy evaluation.

- Our method significantly outperforms state-of-the-art methods under diverse experimental settings and is closest to the joint method. Furthermore, the memory consumption of our model is only 0.045, 0.09, and 0.165 of the joint method, respectively. Specifically, for the experiments with task capacities of 2, 5, and 10, we end up with an accuracy of $83.94 \pm 0.50\%$, $87.35 \pm 0.50\%$, and $87.96 \pm 0.50\%$, while the finetune is just 32.53%, 31.24%, and 46.61%. In addition to our method, il2m performs better in fewer task stages with an accuracy of 75.43%, 79.54%, and 82.21%. EEIL performs better in more task stages on tasks with an accuracy of 80.82%, 80.73%, and 78.51%.

– Since the total number of devices is 66, the smaller the task capacity, the more stages for evolutionary learning. Comparing the three experimental results, it can be found that as the number of task stages increases evolutionary learning becomes more difficult.

## 3.3   Anti-forgetting Evaluation (Q2)

As shown in Fig. 9, in the experiment with a task capacity of 10, we use the confusion matrix and F1 score to compare and analyze the forgetting that occurs in the evolutionary learning process of various methods. The vertical axis represents the correct device type, and the horizontal axis represents the predicted device type. LUCIR produces the worst forgetting problem. Its F1 score is only 75.65%. Additionally, other methods such as EEIL and LwF-E show an excessive preference for the latest learned devices. In contrast, our method performs well on both old and new devices, producing a better confusion matrice where the activations are mostly distributed at the diagonal. The F1 score of our method is 88.31%. In conclusion, our method effectively alleviates the forgetting of old devices during evolutionary learning.

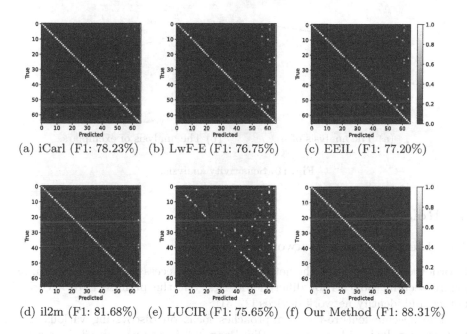

(a) iCarl (F1: 78.23%)   (b) LwF-E (F1: 76.75%)    (c) EEIL (F1: 77.20%)

(d) il2m (F1: 81.68%)   (e) LUCIR (F1: 75.65%)   (f) Our Method (F1: 88.31%)

**Fig. 9.** Confusion matrix and F1.

## 3.4   Sensitivity Analysis (Q3)

As mentioned earlier, the farther the boundaries of different classes in the feature space are, the less likely they are to interfere and confuse each other. Therefore, we discuss the contribution of the parameter $m$ to the accuracy of evolutionary learning. In this experiment, the task capacity is set to 10, and other hyperparameters are set to the default configuration. As shown in Fig. 10(a), it can be found that when the $m$ becomes larger and larger, the final accuracy rate also becomes higher. When $m$ is 1, the accuracy rate can reach about 84%, and when $m$ is 10, the accuracy rate can reach about 88%. This result proves our findings, and also shows that the greater the spatial distance, the better the effect of evolutionary learning in the process of evolutionary learning.

As shown in Fig. 10(b), the experiments investigate the effect of the number of exemplars in the exemplar manager for evolutionary learning. It is found that as the number of exemplars decreases, the accuracy also decreases, which is the same result as we expected. Because the larger the number of exemplars, the more knowledge of old IoT devices can be represented, and therefore more knowledge can be retained with the distillation loss. However, we have to take into account that as the number of samples increases, so does the memory footprint, so ultimately we have to strike the right balance between performance and memory.

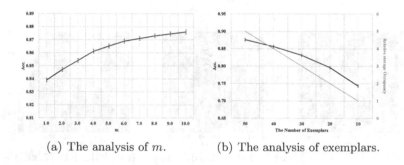

(a) The analysis of $m$.                (b) The analysis of exemplars.

**Fig. 10.** Sensitivity analysis.

## 4   Related Work

### 4.1   Identification of Network Devices

In order to better manage the network space, it is necessary to implement appropriate security policies for different devices, but the premise is to accurately detect and identify network devices [22,31].

The specific feature-based approaches focus on discovering various useful features for device identification. PingPong [26] introduces an efficient way to automatically extract packet-level signatures from traffic. Then, Wan et al. [27] propose an improved method for PingPong. Sivanathan proposes statistical properties of more than 20 IoT devices in his research work [25]. Then, in his recent research works [23,24], it is found that using the Naive Bayes classifier on the activity period, port number, domain name, and cipher suite can achieve better performance in classifying 28 commercial IoT devices. Feng [6] proposes a method to automatically generate rule features and annotate IoT devices. In addition, deep learning technology is also gradually applied in device identification. Meidan et al. [16] design a multi-stage meta classifier for IoT devices. [14,29] shows that the best IoT device classification results can be obtained by combining CNN and RNN. Fan [5] proposes a semi-supervised model based on CNN and multi-task learning.

Although the above methods have made some progress, when the processed device is not in the training set, the above methods will encounter the critical open-world problem. Yu [30] proposes an identification scheme with good scalability, but the limitation is that it depends on the traffic of the network connection stage. Recently, Hu [9] proposes out-of-distribution (OOD) with EVT to detect unknown devices to improve generalization.

### 4.2 Class Incremental Learning

Human learning mechanisms are different from machine learning models. Humans can continue to learn new knowledge without forgetting, but machine learning models usually only perform well on the latest learning tasks. Once they continue to learn new knowledge, they will forget the previous [19]. Therefore, it has drawn attention to class incremental learning [15].

The *regularization-based* method aims to constrain the optimization direction of the model in the new task and minimize the interference caused by the old task. Kirkpatrick [10] introduces an additional regularization term that consolidates important parameters from the previous task. Then, LwF [11] is the first to use the idea of knowledge distillation to preserve knowledge from past tasks. The idea based on *bias correction* aims to address the problem of task bias. Castro [2] proposes an efficient bias correction-based end-to-end incremental learning method. EEIL [8] develops a unified processing framework with three components to reduce the impact of imbalance. Belouadah et al. [1] propose an incremental learning approach that utilizes finetuning and a dual memory mechanism il2m to reduce the negative effects of catastrophic forgetting. The *rehearsal-based method* is considered to be the most promising method, aiming at replaying some key knowledge of old tasks when learning new tasks, just like reviewing old knowledge when learning new knowledge. iCaRL [20] combines playback and distillation loss to transfer knowledge, which inspires the method proposed in this paper.

## 5    Conclusion and Future Work

This work is devoted to solving the open-world problem of IoT device recognition from the perspective of model evolution. We propose a novel evolutionary model which can continuously learn with new device traffic. In specific, we represent the traffic rationally and introduce a metric learning-based auto-encoder to mine latent features of device traffic. Then we utilize the NCM classification strategy for device inference. We find that the less-forgetting constraint based on knowledge replay and the independent compact spatial distribution can cope with the catastrophic forgetting of old devices in evolutionary learning. During evolutionary learning, our method does not need to store all the device data and only requires very few representative samples to achieve high performance. The results of comparative experiments show that our method outperforms the state-of-the-art incremental learning methods. In future work, we will study how to use the few-shot learning method to reduce the workload of manual annotation, thereby improving the efficiency of model evolutionary learning.

**Acknowledgement.** This work was supported by the National Key Research and Development Program of China (Grant No.2018YFB0803402), the Young Scientists Fund of the National Natural Science Foundation of China (Grant No.61702504) and the Industrial Internet Innovation and Development Project (Grant No.KFZ0120200004).

# References

1. Belouadah, E., Popescu, A.: Il2m: Class incremental learning with dual memory. In: Proceedings of the IEEE/CVF International Conference on Computer Vision, pp. 583–592 (2019)
2. Castro, F.M., Marín-Jiménez, M.J., Guil, N., Schmid, C., Alahari, K.: End-to-end incremental learning. In: Ferrari, V., Hebert, M., Sminchisescu, C., Weiss, Y. (eds.) ECCV 2018. LNCS, vol. 11216, pp. 241–257. Springer, Cham (2018). https://doi.org/10.1007/978-3-030-01258-8_15
3. Charyyev, B., Gunes, M.H.: Iot traffic flow identification using locality sensitive hashes. In: ICC 2020–2020 IEEE International Conference on Communications (ICC), pp. 1–6. IEEE (2020)
4. Delange, M., et al.: A continual learning survey: Defying forgetting in classification tasks. IEEE Trans. Pattern Anal. Mach. Intell. (2021)
5. Fan, L., et al.: An iot device identification method based on semi-supervised learning. In: 2020 16th International Conference on Network and Service Management (CNSM), pp. 1–7. IEEE (2020)
6. Feng, X., Li, Q., Wang, H., Sun, L.: Acquisitional rule-based engine for discovering {Internet-of-Things} devices. In: 27th USENIX Security Symposium (USENIX Security 18), pp. 327–341 (2018)
7. Hinton, G., Vinyals, O., Dean, J., et al.: Distilling the knowledge in a neural network, vol. 2(7). arXiv preprint arXiv:1503.02531 (2015)
8. Hou, S., Pan, X., Loy, C.C., Wang, Z., Lin, D.: Learning a unified classifier incrementally via rebalancing. In: Proceedings of the IEEE/CVF Conference on Computer Vision and Pattern Recognition, pp. 831–839 (2019)
9. Hu, X., Li, H., Shi, Z., Yu, N., Zhu, H., Sun, L.: A robust IoT device identification method with unknown traffic detection. In: Liu, Z., Wu, F., Das, S.K. (eds.) WASA 2021. LNCS, vol. 12937, pp. 190–202. Springer, Cham (2021). https://doi.org/10.1007/978-3-030-85928-2_15
10. Kirkpatrick, J., et al.: Overcoming catastrophic forgetting in neural networks. Proc. Natl. Acad. Sci. **114**(13), 3521–3526 (2017)
11. Li, Z., Hoiem, D.: Learning without forgetting. IEEE Trans. Pattern Anal. Mach. Intell. **40**(12), 2935–2947 (2017)

12. Liu, Y., Wang, J., Li, J., Niu, S., Song, H.: Machine learning for the detection and identification of internet of things (iot) devices: A survey. arXiv preprint arXiv:2101.10181 (2021)
13. Liu, Z., Cai, L., Zhao, L., Yu, A., Meng, D.: Towards open world traffic classification. In: Gao, D., Li, Q., Guan, X., Liao, X. (eds.) ICICS 2021. LNCS, vol. 12918, pp. 331–347. Springer, Cham (2021). https://doi.org/10.1007/978-3-030-86890-1_19
14. Lopez-Martin, M., Carro, B., Sanchez-Esguevillas, A., Lloret, J.: Network traffic classifier with convolutional and recurrent neural networks for internet of things. IEEE Access **5**, 18042–18050 (2017)
15. Masana, M., Liu, X., Twardowski, B., Menta, M., Bagdanov, A.D., van de Weijer, J.: Class-incremental learning: survey and performance evaluation on image classification. arXiv preprint arXiv:2010.15277 (2020)
16. Meidan, Y., et al.: Profiliot: a machine learning approach for iot device identification based on network traffic analysis. In: Proceedings of the Symposium On Applied Computing, pp. 506–509 (2017)
17. Miettinen, M., Marchal, S., Hafeez, I., Asokan, N., Sadeghi, A.R., Tarkoma, S.: Iot sentinel: Automated device-type identification for security enforcement in iot. In: 2017 IEEE 37th International Conference on Distributed Computing Systems (ICDCS), pp. 2177–2184. IEEE (2017)
18. Ortiz, J., Crawford, C., Le, F.: Devicemien: network device behavior modeling for identifying unknown iot devices. In: Proceedings of the International Conference on Internet of Things Design and Implementation, pp. 106–117 (2019)
19. Parisi, G.I., Kemker, R., Part, J.L., Kanan, C., Wermter, S.: Continual lifelong learning with neural networks: A review. Neural Netw. **113**, 54–71 (2019)
20. Rebuffi, S.A., Kolesnikov, A., Sperl, G., Lampert, C.H.: icarl: Incremental classifier and representation learning. In: Proceedings of the IEEE Conference on Computer Vision and Pattern Recognition, pp. 2001–2010 (2017)
21. Schroff, F., Kalenichenko, D., Philbin, J.: Facenet: A unified embedding for face recognition and clustering. In: Proceedings of the IEEE Conference On Computer Vision And Pattern Recognition, pp. 815–823 (2015)
22. Shahid, M.R., Blanc, G., Zhang, Z., Debar, H.: Iot devices recognition through network traffic analysis. In: 2018 IEEE International Conference on Big Data (Big Data), pp. 5187–5192. IEEE (2018)
23. Sivanathan, A.: Iot behavioral monitoring via network traffic analysis. arXiv preprint arXiv:2001.10632 (2020)
24. Sivanathan, A., et al.: Classifying iot devices in smart environments using network traffic characteristics. IEEE Trans. Mob. Comput. **18**(8), 1745–1759 (2018)
25. Sivanathan, A., et al.: Characterizing and classifying iot traffic in smart cities and campuses. In: 2017 IEEE Conference on Computer Communications Workshops (INFOCOM WKSHPS), pp. 559–564. IEEE (2017)
26. Trimananda, R., Varmarken, J., Markopoulou, A., Demsky, B.: Pingpong: Packet-level signatures for smart home device events. arXiv preprint arXiv:1907.11797 (2019)
27. Wan, Y., Xu, K., Wang, F., Xue, G.: Iotathena: Unveiling iot device activities from network traffic. IEEE Trans. Wireless Commun. **21**(1), 651–664 (2021)
28. Yang, L., et al.: {CADE}: Detecting and explaining concept drift samples for security applications. In: 30th {USENIX} Security Symposium ({USENIX} Security 2021) (2021)

29. Yin, F., Yang, L., Wang, Y., Dai, J.: Iot etei: End-to-end iot device identification method. In: 2021 IEEE Conference on Dependable and Secure Computing (DSC), pp. 1–8. IEEE (2021)
30. Yu, L., Liu, T., Zhou, Z., Zhu, Y., Liu, Q., Tan, J.: Wdmti: wireless device manufacturer and type identification using hierarchical dirichlet process. In: 2018 IEEE 15th International Conference on Mobile Ad Hoc and Sensor Systems (MASS), pp. 19–27. IEEE (2018)
31. Yu, L., Luo, B., Ma, J., Zhou, Z., Liu, Q.: You are what you broadcast: Identification of mobile and {IoT} devices from (public){WiFi}. In: 29th USENIX security symposium (USENIX security 2020). pp. 55–72 (2020)

# SecureBERT: A Domain-Specific Language Model for Cybersecurity

Ehsan Aghaei[1(✉)], Xi Niu[1], Waseem Shadid[1], and Ehab Al-Shaer[2]

[1] University of North Carolina at Charlotte, Charlotte, USA
{eaghaei,xniu2,waseem}@uncc.edu
[2] Carnegie Mellon University, Pittsburgh, USA
ehab@cmu.edu

**Abstract.** Natural Language Processing (NLP) has recently gained wide attention in cybersecurity, particularly in Cyber Threat Intelligence (CTI) and cyber automation. Increased connection and automation have revolutionized the world's economic and cultural infrastructures, while they have introduced risks in terms of cyber attacks. CTI is information that helps cybersecurity analysts make intelligent security decisions, that is often delivered in the form of natural language text, which must be transformed to machine readable format through an automated procedure before it can be used for automated security measures.

This paper proposes SecureBERT, a cybersecurity language model capable of capturing text connotations in cybersecurity text (e.g., CTI) and therefore successful in automation for many critical cybersecurity tasks that would otherwise rely on human expertise and time-consuming manual efforts. SecureBERT has been trained using a large corpus of cybersecurity text. To make SecureBERT effective not just in retaining general English understanding, but also when applied to text with cybersecurity implications, we developed a customized tokenizer as well as a method to alter pre-trained weights. The SecureBERT is evaluated using the standard Masked Language Model (MLM) test as well as two additional standard NLP tasks. Our evaluation studies show that Secure-BERT outperforms existing similar models, confirming its capability for solving crucial NLP tasks in cybersecurity.

**Keywords:** Cyber automation · Cyber threat intelligence · Language model

## 1 Introduction

The adoption of security automation technologies has grown year after year. Cyber security industry is saturated with solutions that protect users from malicious sources, safeguard mission-critical servers, and protect personal information, healthcare data, intellectual property, and sensitive financial data. Enterprises invest in technology to handle such security solutions, typically aggregating a large amount of data into a single system to facilitate in organizing and

F. Li et al. (Eds.): SecureComm 2022, LNICST 462, pp. 39–56, 2023.
https://doi.org/10.1007/978-3-031-25538-0_3

retrieving key information in order to better identify where they face risk or where specific traffic originates or terminates. Recently, as social networks and ubiquitous computing have grown in popularity, the overall volume of digital text content has increased. This textual contents span a range of domains, from a simple tweet or news blog article to more sensitive information such as medical records or financial transactions. In cybersecurity context, security analysts analyze relevant data to detect cyber threat-related information, such as vulnerabilities, in order to monitor, prevent, and control potential risks. For example, cybersecurity agencies such as MITRE, NIST, CERT, and NVD invest millions of dollars in human expertise to analyze, categorize, prioritize, publish, and fix disclosed vulnerabilities annually. As the number of products grows, and therefore the number of vulnerabilities increases, it is critical to utilize an automated system capable of identifying vulnerabilities and quickly delivering an effective defense measure.

By enabling machines to swiftly build or synthesize human language, natural language processing (NLP) has been widely employed to automate text analytic operations in a variety of domains including cybersecurity. Language models, as the core component of modern text analytic technologies, play critical role in NLP applications by enabling computers to interpret qualitative input and transform it into quantitative representations. There are several well-known and well-performing language models, such as ELMO [20], GPT [21], and BERT [12], trained on general English corpora and used for a variety of NLP tasks such as machine translation, named entity recognition, text classification, and semantic analysis. There is continuous discussion in the research community over whether it is beneficial to employ these off-the-shelf models as a baseline, and then fine-tune them through domain-specific tasks. The assumption is that the fine-tuned models will retain the basic linguistic knowledge in general English and meanwhile develop "advanced" knowledge in the domain while fine tuning [7].

However, certain domains, such as cybersecurity, are indeed highly sensitive, dealing with processing of critical data and any error in this procedure may expose the entire infrastructure to the cyber threats, and therefore, automated processing of cybersecurity text requires a robust and reliable framework. Cybersecurity terms are either uncommon in general English (such as *ransomware, API, OAuth, exfilterate*, and *keylogger*) or have multiple meanings (homographs) in different domains (e.g., *honeypot, patch, handshake*, and *virus*). This existing gap in language structure and semantic contexts complicates text processing and demonstrates the standard English language model may be incapable of accommodating the vocabulary of cybersecurity texts, leading to a restricted or limited comprehension of cybersecurity implications.

In this study, we address this critical cybersecurity problem by introducing a new language model called SecureBERT by employing the state-of-the-art NLP architecture called BERT [12], which is capable of processing texts with cybersecurity implications effectively. SecureBERT is generic enough to be applied in a variety of cybersecurity tasks, such as phishing detection [10], code and malware analysis [24], intrusion detection [2], etc. SecureBERT is a pre-trained cybersecurity language model that have the fundamental understanding of both the word-level and sentence-level semantics, which is an essential building block for any cybersecurity report. In this context, we collected and processed a large corpus of 1.1 billion words (1.6 million in vocabulary size) from a variety of cybersecurity text resources, including news, reports and textbooks, articles, research papers, and videos. On top of the pre-trained tokenizer, we developed a customized tokenization method that preserves standard English vocabulary as much as possible while effectively accommodating new tokens with cybersecurity implication. Additionally, we utilized a practical way to optimize the retraining procedure by introducing random noise to the pre-trained weights. We rigorously evaluated the performance of our proposed model through three different tasks such as standard Masked Language Model (MLM), sentiment analysis, and Named Entity Recognition (NER), to demonstrate SecureBERT's performance in processing both cybersecurity and general English inputs.

## 2 Overview of BERT Language Model

BERT (Bidirectional Encoder Representations from Transformers) [12] is a transformer-based neural network technique for natural language processing pre-training. BERT can train language models based on the entire set of words in a sentence or query (bidirectional training) rather than the traditional way of training on the ordered sequence of words (left-to-right or combined left-to-right and right-to-left). BERT allows the language model to learn word context based on surrounding words rather than just the word that immediately precedes or follows it.

BERT leverages Transformers, an attention mechanism that can learn contextual relations between words and subwords in a sequence. The Transformer includes two separate mechanisms, an encoder that reads the text inputs and a decoder that generates a prediction for the given task. Since BERTs goal is to generate a language model, only the encoder mechanism is necessary [27]. This transformer encoder reads the entire data at the same time instead of reading the text in order.

Building a BERT model requires two steps: pre-training and fine tuning. In pre-training stage, the model is trained on unlabeled data against two different pre-training tasks, namely Masked LM (MLM) and Next Sentence Prediction (NSP). MLM typically masks some percentage of the input tokens (15%) at random and then predicts them through a learning procedure. In this case, the final hidden vectors corresponding to the mask tokens are fed into an output softmax over the vocabulary. NSP is mainly designed to understand the relationship between two sentences, which is not directly captured by language modeling. In order to train a model that understands sentence relationships, it trains for a binarized next sentence prediction task that can be trivially generated from any monolingual corpus, in which it takes a pair of sentences as input and in 50% of the times in replaces the second sentence with a random one from the corpus. To perform fine-tuning, the BERT model is launched with pre-trained parameters and then all parameters are fine-tuned using labeled data from downstream tasks. BERT model has a unified architecture across different tasks, and there is a minor difference between pre-trained and final downstream architecture. The pre-trained BERT model used Books Corpus (800M words) and English Wikipedia (2,500M words) and improved the state-of-the-art for eleven NLP tasks such as getting a GLUE [28] score of 80.4%, which is 7.6% of definite improvement from the previous best results, and achieving 93.2% accuracy on Stanford Question Answering Dataset (SQuAD) [23].

A derivative of BERT, which is claimed to be a robustly optimized version of BERT with certain modifications in the tokenizer and the network architecture, and ignored NSP task during training, is called RoBERTa [19]. RoBERTa extends BERT's MLM, where it intentionally learns to detect the hidden text part inside otherwise unannotated language samples. With considerably bigger mini-batches and learning rates, RoBERTa changes important hyperparameters in BERT training, enabling it to noticeably improve on the MLM and accordingly the overall performance in all standard fine-tuning tasks. As a result of the enhanced performance and demonstrated efficacy, we develop SecureBERT on top of RoBERTa.

## 3   Data Collection

We collected a large number (98,411) of online cybersecurity-related text data including books, blogs, news, security reports, videos (subtitles), journals and conferences, white papers, tutorials, and survey papers, using our web crawler tool[1]. We created a corpus of 1.1 billion words splitting it to 2.2 million documents each with average size of 512 words using the Spacy[2] text analytic tool. Table 1 shows the resources and the distribution of our collected dataset for pre-training the SecureBERT.

This corpora contains various forms of cybersecurity texts, from basic information, news, Wikipedia, and tutorials, to more advanced texts such as CTI, research articles, and threat reports. When aggregated, this collection offers a wealth of domain-specific connotations and implications that is quite useful for training a cybersecurity language model. Table 2 lists the web resources from which we obtained our corpus.

## 4   Methodology

We present two approaches in this section for refining and training our domain-specific language model. We begin by describing a strategy for developing a customized tokenizer on top of the pre-trained generic English tokenizer, followed by a practical approach for biasing the training weights in order to improve weight adjustment and therefore a more efficient learning process.

---

[1] Sample data: https://dropbox.com/sh/jg45zvfl7iek12i/AAB7bFghED9GmkO5YxpP
LIuma?dl=0.

[2] https://spacy.io/usage.

**Table 1.** The details of collected cybersecurity corpora for training the SecureBERT.

| Type | No. Documents |
|---|---|
| Articles | 8,955 |
| Books | 180 |
| Survey Papers | 515 |
| Blogs/News | 85,953 |
| Wikipedia (cybersecurity) | 2,156 |
| Security Reports | 518 |
| Videos | 134 |
| **Total** | **98,411** |

| | |
|---|---|
| Vocabulary size | 1,674,434 words |
| Corpus size | 1,072,798,637 words |
| Document size | 2,174,621 documents (paragraphs) |

**Table 2.** The resources collected for cybersecurity textual data.

**Websites**

Trendmicro, NakedSecurity, NIST, GovernmentCIO Media, CShub, Threatpost, Techopedia, Portswigger, Security Magazine, Sophos, Reddit, FireEye, SANS, Drizgroup, NETSCOUT, Imperva, DANIEL MIESSLER, Symantec, Kaspersky, PacketStorm, Microsoft, RedHat, Tripwire, Krebs on Security, SecurityFocus, CSO Online, InfoSec Institute, Enisa, MITRE

**Security Reports and Whitepapers**

APT Notes, VNote, CERT, Cisco Security Reports, Symantec Security Reports

**Books, Articles, and Surveys**

*Tags: cybersecurity, vulnerability, cyber attack, hack*

ACM CCS: 2014-2020 , IEEE NDSS (2016-2020), IEEE Oakland (1980-2020)

IEEE Security and Privacy (1980-2020), Arxiv, Cybersecurity and Hacking books

**Videos (YouTube)**

Cybersecurity courses, tutorial, and conference presentations

## 4.1 Customized Tokenizer

A word-based tokenizer primarily extracts each word as a unit of analysis, called a token. It assigns each token a unique index, then uses those indices to encode any given sequence of tokens. Pre-trained BERT models mainly return the weight of each word according to these indices. Therefore, in order to fully utilize a pre-trained model to train a specialized model, the common token indices must match, either using the indices of the original or the new customized tokenizer.

For building the tokenizer, we employ a byte pair encoding (BPE) [25] method to build a vocabulary of words and subwords from the cybersecurity corpora, as it is proven to have better performance versus word-based tokenizer. Character based encoding used in BPE allows for the learning of a small subword vocabulary that can encode any input text without introducing any "unknown" tokens [22]. Our objective is to create a vocabulary that retains the tokens already provided in RoBERTa's tokenizer while also incorporating additional unique cybersecurity-related tokens. In this context, we extract $50,265$ tokens from the cybersecurity corpora to generate the initial token vocabulary $\Psi_{Sec}$. We intentionally make the size of $\Psi_{Sec}$ the same with that of the RoBERTa's token vocabulary $\Psi_{RoBERTa}$ as we intended to imitate original RoBERTa's design.

If $\Psi_{Sec}$ represents the vocabulary set of SecureBERT, and $\Psi_{RoBERTa}$ denotes the vocabulary set of original RoBERTa, both with size of $50,265$, $\Psi_{Sec}$ shares $32,592$ mutual tokens with $\Psi_{RoBERTa}$ leaving $17,673$ tokens contribute uniquely to cybersecurity corpus, such as *firewall, breach, crack, ransomware, malware, phishing, mysql, kaspersky, obfuscated,* and *vulnerability*, where RoBERTa's tokenizer analyzes those using byte pairs:

$$V_{mutual} = \Psi_{Sec} \cap \Psi_{RoBERTa} \rightarrow 32,592 \text{ tokens}$$

$$V_{distinct} = \Psi_{Sec} - \Psi_{RoBERTa} \rightarrow 17,673 \text{ tokens}$$

Studies [29] shows utilizing complete words (not subwords) for those are common in specific domain, can enhance the performance during training since alignments may be more challenging to understand during model training, as target tokens often require attention from multiple source tokens. Hence, we choose all mutual terms and assign their original indices, while the remainder new tokens are assigned random indices with no conflict, where the original indices refers to the indices in RoBERTa's tokenizer, to build our tokenizer. Ultimately, we develop a customized tokenizer with a vocabulary size similar to that of the original model, which includes tokens commonly seen in cybersecurity corpora in addition to cross-domain tokens. Our tokenizer encodes mutual tokens $V_{mutual}$ as original model, ensuring that the model returns the appropriate pretrained weights, while for new terms $V_{distinct}$ the indices and accordingly the weights would be random.

## 4.2 Weight Adjustments

The RoBERTa model already stores the weights for all the existing tokens in its general English vocabulary. Many tokens such as *email, internet, computer,* and *phone* in general English convey similar meanings as in the cybersecurity domain. On the other hand, some other homographs such as *adversary, virus, worm, exploit,* and *crack* carry different meanings in different domains. Using the weights from RoBERTa as initial weights for all the tokens, and then retraining against the cybersecurity corpus to update those initial weights will in fact not updating much leading to overfitting condition in training on such tokens because the size of the training data for RoBERTa (16 GB) is 25 times larger than that for SecureBERT. When a neural network is trained on a small dataset, it may memorize all training samples, resulting in overfitting and poor performance in evaluation. Due to the unbalance or sparse sampling of points in the high-dimensional input space, small datasets may also pose a more difficult mapping task for neural networks to tackle.

One strategy for smoothing the input space and making it simpler to learn is to add noise to the model during training to increase the robustness of the training process and reduces generalization error. Referring to previous works on maintaining robust neural networks [18,31,33], incorporation of noise to an unstable neural network model with a limited training set can act as a regularizer and help reduce overfitting during the training. It is generally stated that introducing noise to the neural network during training can yield in substantial gains in generalization performance in some cases. Previous research has demonstrated that such noise-based training is analogous to a form of regularization in which an additional term is introduced to the error function [8]. This noise can be imposed to either input data or between hidden layers of the deep neural networks. When a model is being trained from scratch, typically noise can be added to the hidden layers at each iteration, whereas in continual learning, it can be introduced to input data to generalize the model and reduce error [4,16].

For training SecureBERT as continual learning process, rather than using the initial weights from RoBERTa directly, we introduce a small "noise" to the weights of the initial model for those mutual tokens, in order to bias these tokens to "be a little away" from the original tokens meanings in order to capture their new connotations in a cybersecurity context, but not "too far away" from standard language since any domain language is still written in English and still carries standard natural language implications. If a token conveys a similar meaning in general English and cybersecurity, the adjusted weight during training will conceptually tend to converge to the original vector space as the initial model. Otherwise, it will deviate more from the initial model to accommodate its new meaning in cybersecurity. For those new words introduced by the cybersecurity corpus, we use the Xavier weight initialization algorithm [14] to assign initial weights.

We instantiated the SecureBERT by utilizing the architecture of pre-trained RoBERTa-base model, which consists of twelve hidden transformer and attention layers, and one input layer. We adopted the base version (RoBERTa-base) given the efficiency and usefulness. Smaller models are less expensive to train, and the cybersecurity domain has far less diversity of corpora than general language, implying that a compact model would suffice. The model's size is not the only factor to consider; usability is another critical factor to consider when evaluating a model's quality. Since large models are difficult to use and expensive to maintain, it is more convenient and practical to use a smaller and portable architecture.

Each input token is represented by an embedding vector with a dimension of 768 in pre-trained RoBERTa. Our objective is to manipulate these embedding vector representations for each of the 50,265 tokens in the vocabulary by adding a small symmetric noise. Statistical symmetric noise with a probability density function equal to the normal distribution is known as Gaussian noise. We introduce this noise by applying a random Gaussian function to the weight vectors. Therefore, for any token $t$, let $\vec{W}_t$ be the embedding vector of token $t$ as follows:

$$\vec{W}_t = [w_1^t, w_2^t, ..., w_{768}^t] \tag{1}$$

where $w_k^t$ represents the $k$th element of the embedding vector for token $t$.

Let notation $\mathcal{N}(\mu, \sigma)$ be normal distribution where $\mu$ denotes the mean and $\sigma$ the standard deviation. For each weight vector $\vec{W}_t$, the noisy vector $\vec{W}_t'$ is defined as follows:

$$\vec{W}_t' \leftarrow \vec{W}_t \oplus (\vec{W}_t \odot \epsilon), \epsilon \sim \mathcal{N}(\mu, \sigma) \tag{2}$$

where $\epsilon$ represents the noise value, and $\oplus$ and $\odot$ means element-wise addition and multiplication, respectively.

The SecureBERT model is designed to emulate the RoBERTa's architecture, as shown in 1. To train SecureBERT for a cybersecurity language model, we use our collected corpora and customized tokenizer. SecureBERT model contains 12 hidden layers and 12 attention heads, where the size of each hidden state has the dimension of 768, and the input embedding dimension is 512, the same with RoBERTa. In RoBERTa ($768 \times 50265$ elements), the average and variance of the pretrained embedding weights are $-0.0125$ and $0.0173$, respectively. We picked $mu = 0$ and $sigma = 0.01$ to generate zero-mean noise value since we want the adjusted weights to be in the same space as the original weights. We replace the original weights in the initial model with the noisy weights calculated using Eq. 2.

## 5   Evaluation

We trained the model against MLM using dynamic masking using RoBERTa's hyperparameters running for $250,000$ training steps for $100\,\mathrm{h}$ on $8\,\mathrm{T}$ V100 GPUs with $Batch\_size = 18$, the largest possible mini-batch size for V100 GPUs. We evaluate the model on cybersecurity masked language modeling and other general purpose underlying tasks including sentiment analysis and named entity recognition (NER) to further show the performance and efficiency of Secure-BERT in processing the cybersecurity text as well as reasonable effectiveness in general language.

### 5.1   Masked Language Model (MLM)

In this section, we evaluate the performance of SecureBERT in predicting the masked word in an input sentence, known as the standard Masked Language Model (MLM) task.

Owing to the unavailability of a testing dataset for the MLM task in the cybersecurity domain, we create one. We extracted sentences manually from a high-quality source of cybersecurity reports - MITRE technique descriptions,

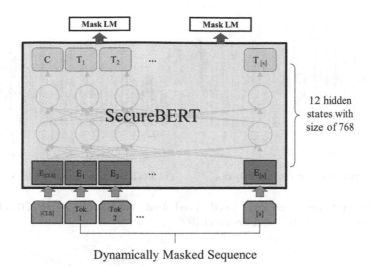

**Fig. 1.** SecureBERT architecture for pre-training against masked words.

which are not included in pre-training dataset. Rather than masking an arbitrary word in a sentence, as in RoBERTa, we masked only the verb or noun in the sentence because a verb denotes an action and a noun denotes an object, both of which are important for understanding the sentence's semantics in a cybersecurity context. Our testing dataset contains $17,341$ records, with $12,721$ records containing a masked noun ($2,213$ unique nouns) and $4,620$ records containing a masked verb ($888$ unique masked verbs in total). Figure 2a and 4b show the MLM performance for predicting the masked nouns and verbs respectively. Both figures present the prediction hit rate of the masked word in $topN$ model prediction. SecureBERT constantly outperforms RoBERTa-base, RoBERTa-large and SciBERT even though the RoBERTa-large is a considerably large model trained on a massive corpora with $355M$ parameters (Fig. 1).

Our investigations show that RoBERTa-large (much larger than RoBERTa-base which we used as initial model) is pretty powerful language model in general cybersecurity language. However, when it comes to advance cybersecurity context, it constantly fails to deliver desired output. For example, three cybersecurity sentences are depicted in Fig. 3, each with one word masked. Three terms including *reconnaissance, hijacking*, and *DdoS* are commonly used in cybersecurity corpora. SecureBERT is able to understand the context and properly predict these masked words, while RoBERTa's prediction is remarkably different When it comes to cybersecurity tasks including cyber threat intelligence, vulnerability analysis, and threat action extraction [1,3], such knowledge is crucial and utilizing a model with SecureBERT's properties would be highly beneficial. The models do marginally better in predicting verbs than nouns, according to the prediction results.

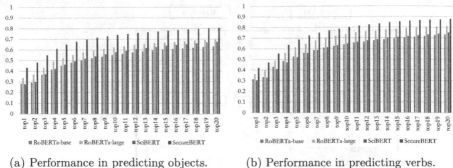

(a) Performance in predicting objects.   (b) Performance in predicting verbs.

**Fig. 2.** Cybersecurity masked word prediction evaluation on RoBERTa-base, RoBERTa-large, SciBERT, and SecureBERT.

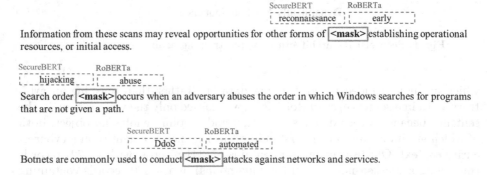

**Fig. 3.** A comparative example of predicting masked token. SecureBERT shows a good understanding of cybersecurity context while other models constantly failed in advanced texts.

## 5.2 Ablation Study

SecureBERT outperforms existing language models in predicting cybersecurity-related masked tokens in texts, demonstrating its ability to digest and interpret in-domain texts. To enhance its performance and maintain general language understanding, we used specific strategies such as the development of custom tokenizers and weight adjustment.

SecureBERT employs an effective weight modification by introducing a small noise to the initial weights of the pre-trained model when trained on a smaller corpus than off-the-shelf large models, enabling it to better and more efficiently fit the cybersecurity context, particularly in learning homographs and phrases carrying multiple meanings in different domains. As a result of the noise, this technique puts the token in a deviated space, allowing the algorithm to adjust embedding weights more effectively.

In Table 3, given a few simple sentences containing common homographs in cybersecurity context, we provide the masked word prediction of four different models, including SB (SecureBERT), SB* (SecureBERT trained without weight adjustment), RB (RoBERTa-base), and RL (RoBERTa-large). For example, word *Virus* in cybersecurity context refers to a malicious code that spreads between devices to damage, disrupt, or steal data. On the other hand, a *Virus* is also a nanoscopic infectious agent that replicates solely within an organism's live cells. In simple sentence such as " *Virus causes <mask>.*", four models deliver different prediction, each corresponding to associated context. RB and RL return *cancer, infection* and *diarrhea,* that are definitely correct in general (or medical) context, they are wrong in cybersecurity domain though. SB* returns a set of words including *problem, disaster* and *crashes,* which differ from the outcomes of generic models, yet far away from cybersecurity implication. Despite, SB predictions which are *DoS, crash,* and *reboot* clearly demonstrate how weight adjustment helps in improved inference of the cybersecurity context by returning the most relevant words for the masked token.

Customized tokenizer, on the other hand, also plays an important role in enhancing the performance of SecureBERT in MLM task, by indexing more cybersecurity related tokens (specially complete words as mentioned in Sect. 4.1). To further show the impact of SecureBERT tokenizer in returning correct mask word prediction, we train SecureBERT with original RoBERTa's tokenizer without any customization (but with weight adjustment). As depicted in Fig. 4a and Fig. 4b, when compared to the pre-trained tokenizer, SecureBERT's tokenizer clearly has a higher hit rate, which highlights the significance of creating a domain-specific tokenizer for any domain-specific language model.

## 5.3   Fine-Tuning Tasks

To further proof the performance of SecureBERT in handling the general NLP tasks, we conduct two training experiments including sentiment analysis as well as named entity recognition (NER).

### Task1: Sentiment Analysis

In the first task, we intend to evaluate the SecureBERT in comprehending general English language in form of sentiment analysis. Thus, we use publicly available Rotten Tomatoes dataset[3] that contains corpus of movie reviews used for sentiment analysis. Socher et al. [26] used Amazon's Mechanical Turk to create fine-grained labels for all parsed phrases in the corpus. The dataset is comprised of tab-separated files with phrases from the Rotten Tomatoes dataset. Each Sentence has been parsed into many phrases by the Stanford parser. Each phrase has a "Phrase Id" and each sentence contains a "Sentence Id" while there is no duplicated phrase included in the dataset. Phrases are labeled with five sentiment impressions including negative, somewhat negative, neutral, somewhat positive, and positive. We build a single layer MLP on top of the four models as classification layer to classify the phrases to the corresponding label. We

---

[3] https://www.kaggle.com/c/movie-review-sentiment-analysis-kernels-only.

**Table 3.** Shows the masked word prediction results returned by SecureBERT (SB), SecureBERT without weight adjustment (SB*), RoBERTa-base (RB) and RoBERTa-large (RL) in sentences containing homographs

| Masked sentence | Model predictions |
| --- | --- |
| Virus causes <mask> | **SB**: DoS \| crash \| reboot |
| | **SB***: problems \| disaster \| crashes |
| | **RB**: cancer \| autism \| paralysis |
| | **RL**: cancer \| infection \| diarrhea |
| Honeypot is used in <mask> | **SB**: Metasploit \| Windows \| Squid |
| | **SB***: images \| software \| cryptography |
| | **RB**: cooking \| recipes \| baking |
| | **RL**: cooking \| recipes \| baking |
| A worm can <mask> itself to spread | **SB**: copy \| propagate \| program |
| | **SB***: use \| alter \| modify |
| | **RB**: allow \| free \| help |
| | **RL**: clone \| use \| manipulate |
| Firewall is used to <mask> | **SB**: protect \| prevent \| detect |
| | **SB***: protect \| hide \| encrypt |
| | **RB**: protect \| communicate \| defend |
| | **RL**: protect \| block \| monitor |
| zombie is the other name for a <mask> | **SB**: bot \| process \| trojan |
| | **SB***: worm \| computer \| program |
| | **RB**: robot \| clone \| virus |
| | **RL**: vampire \| virus \| person |

trained two version of the SecureBERT called raw SecureBERT and modified SecureBERT. The former model is the version of our model in which we utilized customized tokenizer and the weight adjustment method, while the latter is the original RoBERTa model trained as is, using the collected cybersecurity corpora. We trained the model for 1,500 steps with $learning rate = 1e - 5$ and $Batch\_size = 32$, to minimize the error of $CrossEntropy$ loss function employing $Adam$ optimizer and $Softmax$ as the activation function in the classification layer. Figure 6 shows the SecureBERT's architecture for sentiment analysis Fig. 5.

In Table 4, we show the performance of both models and compared it with original RoBERTa-base and SciBERT, fine-tuned on Rotten Tomatoes dataset. As illustrated, despite the fact that SciBERT is trained on a broader range of domains (biomedical and computer science), both SecureBERT versions perform quite similarly to SciBERT. In addition, the 2.23% and 2.02% difference in accuracy and F1-score with RoBERTa-base demonstrates the effectiveness of SecureBERT in analysing the general English language as well. Furthermore, the

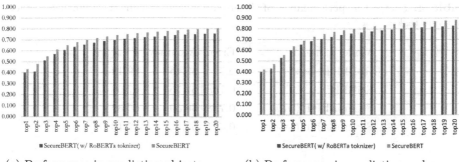

(a) Performance in predicting objects.    (b) Performance in predicting verbs.

**Fig. 4.** Demonstrating the impact of the customized tokenizer in masked word prediction performance.

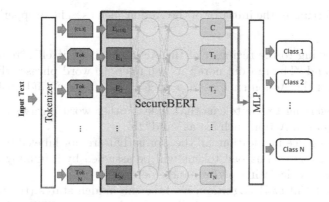

**Fig. 5.** SecureBERT architecture for sentiment analysis downstream task.

modified model perform slightly better than the raw version by 0.34% accuracy and 0.71% F1-score improvement. In the second task, we fine-tune the Secure-BERT to conduct cybersecurity-related name entity recognition (NER). NER is a special task in information extraction that focuses on identifying and classifying named entities referenced in unstructured text into predefined entities such as person names, organizations, places, time expressions, etc.

Since general purpose NER models may not always function well in cybersecurity, we must employ a domain-specific dataset to train an effective model for this particular field. Training a NER model in cybersecurity is a challenging task since there is no publicly available domain-specific data and, even if there is, it is unclear how to establish consensus on which classes should be retrieved from the data. Nevertheless, here we aim to fine-tune the SecureBERT on a relatively small sized dataset that is related to cybersecurity just to show the overall performance and compare it with the existing models. MalwareTextDB [17] is a dataset containing 39 annotated APT reports with a total of 6,819 sentences. In

**Table 4.** Shows the performance of different models on general English sentiment analysis task.

| Model name | Error | Accuracy | F1-score |
|---|---|---|---|
| RoBERTa-base | 0.733 | 69.46 | 69.12 |
| SciBERT | 0.768 | 67.76 | 67.08 |
| SecureBERT (raw) | 0.788 | 66.89 | 66.39 |
| SecureBERT (modified) | 0.771 | 67.23 | 67.10 |

the NER version of this dataset, the sentences are annotated with four different tags including:

**Action**: referring to an event, such as "registers", "provides" and "is written".

**Subject**: referring to the initiator of the Action such as "The dropper" and "This module"

**Object**: referring to the recipient of the Action such as "itself", "remote persistent access" and "The ransom note"; it also refers to word phrases that provide elaboration on the Action such as "a service", "the attacker" and "disk".

**Modifier**: referring to the tokens that link to other word phrases that provide elaboration on the Action such as "as" and "to".

In each sentence in addition, all the words that are not labeled by any of the mentioned tags as well as pad tokens will be assigned by a dummy label ("O") exclude them in calculating performance metrics.

For Named Entity Recognition, we take the hidden states (the transformer output) of every input token from the last layer from SecureBERT. These tokens are then fed to a fully connected dense layer with $N$ units where $N$ equals to the total number of defined entities. Since SecureBERT's tokenizer breaks some words into pieces (Bytes), in such cases we just predict the first piece of the word.

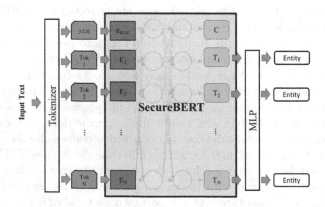

**Fig. 6.** SecureBERT architecture for named entity recognition (NER).

**Table 5.** Shows the performance of different models trained on MalwareTextDB dataset for NER task.

| Model name | Precision | Recall | F1-score |
|---|---|---|---|
| RoBERTa-base | 84.92 | 87.53 | 86.20 |
| SciBERT | 83.19 | 85.84 | 84.49 |
| SecureBERT (raw) | **86.08** | 86.81 | 86.44 |
| SecureBERT (modified) | 85.24 | **88.10** | **86.65** |

We trained the model in 3 epochs with $learning rate = 2e-5$ and $batch size = 8$, to minimize the error of $CrossEntropy$ loss function using $Adam$ optimizer and $Softmax$ as the activation function in the classification layer.

Similar to the previous task, Table 5 shows the performance of both Secure-BERT's version as well as two other models. As depicted, modified Secure-BERT outperforms all other models, despite the fact that MalwareTextDB dataset still contains many sentences with general English meaning and is not an cybersecurity-specific corpora.

## 6   Related Works

Beltagy *et al.* [7] unveiled SciBERT following the exact BERT's architecture, a model that improves performance on downstream scientific NLP tasks by exploiting unsupervised pretraining from scratch on a $1.14M$ multi-domain corpus of scientific literature, including 18% computer science and 82% biomedical domain.

In a similar work on biomedical domain, Gu *et al.* [15] introduced BioBERT focusing particularly on biomedical domain using BERT architecture and publicly available biomedical datasets. This work also creates a benchmark for biomedical NLP featuring a diverse set of tasks such as named entity recognition, relation extraction, document classification, and question answering. Clinical-BERT [5] is another domain adaptation model based on BERT which is trained on clinical text from the MIMIC-III database.

Thus far, utilizing language models such as BERT for cybersecurity applications is quite limited. CyBERT [6] presents a classifier for cybersecurity feature claims by fine-tuning a pre-trained BERT language model for the purpose of identifying cybersecurity claims from a large pool of sequences in ICS device documents. There are also some other studies working on fine-tuning of BERT in cybersecurity domain. Das *et al.* [11] fine-tunes BERT to hierarchically classify cybersecurity vulnerabilities to weaknesses. Additionally, there are several studies on fine-tuning BERT for NER tasks such as [9,32] and [13]. Yin *et al.* [30] fine-tuned pre-trained BERT against cybersecurity text and developed a classification layer on top of their model, ExBERT, to extract sentence-level semantic features and predict the exploitability of vulnerabilities. There is also another model called SecBERT[4] published in Github repository which trains

---

[4] https://github.com/jackaduma/SecBERT.

BERT on cybersecurity corpus from "APTnotes"[5], "Stucco-Data: Cyber security data sources"[6], "CASIE: Extracting Cybersecurity Event Information from Text"[7], and "SemEval-2018 Task 8: Semantic Extraction from CybersecUrity REports using Natural Language Processing (SecureNLP). However, at the time of submitting this paper, we could not find any article to learn more about the details and the proof-of-concept to discuss.

## 7    Conclusions and Future Works

This study introduces SecureBERT, a transformer-based language model for processing cybersecurity text language based on RoBERTa. We presented two practical ways for developing a successful model that can capture contextual relationships and semantic meanings in cybersecurity text by designing a customized tokenization tool on top of RoBERTa's tokenizer and altering the pre-trained weights. SecureBERT is trained to utilize a corpus of 1.1 billion words collected from a range of online cybersecurity resources. SecureBERT has been evaluated using the standard Masked Language Model (MLM) as well as the named entity recognition (NER) task. The evaluation outcomes demonstrated promising results in grasping cybersecurity language.

## References

1. Aghaei, E., Al-Shaer, E.: Threatzoom: neural network for automated vulnerability mitigation. In: Proceedings of the 6th Annual Symposium on Hot Topics in the Science of Security, pp. 1–3 (2019)
2. Aghaei, E., Serpen, G.: Host-based anomaly detection using eigentraces feature extraction and one-class classification on system call trace data. J. Inf. Assurance Sec. (JIAS) 14(4), 106–117 (2019)
3. Aghaei, E., Shadid, W., Al-Shaer, E.: ThreatZoom: hierarchical neural network for CVEs to CWEs classification. In: Park, N., Sun, K., Foresti, S., Butler, K., Saxena, N. (eds.) SecureComm 2020. LNICST, vol. 335, pp. 23–41. Springer, Cham (2020). https://doi.org/10.1007/978-3-030-63086-7_2
4. Ahn, H., Cha, S., Lee, D., Moon, T.: Uncertainty-based continual learning with adaptive regularization. In: Advances in Neural Information Processing Systems 32 (2019)
5. Alsentzer, E., et al.: Publicly available clinical bert embeddings. arXiv preprint arXiv:1904.03323 (2019)
6. Ameri, K., Hempel, M., Sharif, H., Lopez, J., Jr., Perumalla, K.: Cybert: Cybersecurity claim classification by fine-tuning the bert language model. J. Cybersec. Privacy 1(4), 615–637 (2021)
7. Beltagy, I., Lo, K., Cohan, A.: Scibert: A pretrained language model for scientific text. arXiv preprint arXiv:1903.10676 (2019)

---

[5] https://github.com/kbandla/APTnotes.
[6] https://stucco.github.io/data/.
[7] https://ebiquity.umbc.edu/_file_directory_/papers/943.pdf.

8. Bishop, C.M.: Training with noise is equivalent to tikhonov regularization. Neural Compu. **7**(1), 108–116 (1995). https://doi.org/10.1162/neco.1995.7.1.108

9. Chen, Y., Ding, J., Li, D., Chen, Z.: Joint bert model based cybersecurity named entity recognition. In: 2021 The 4th International Conference on Software Engineering and Information Management, pp. 236–242 (2021)

10. Dalton, A., et al.: Active defense against social engineering: The case for human language technology. In: Proceedings for the First International Workshop on Social Threats in Online Conversations: Understanding and Management, pp. 1–8 (2020)

11. Das, S.S., Serra, E., Halappanavar, M., Pothen, A., Al-Shaer, E.: V2w-bert: A framework for effective hierarchical multiclass classification of software vulnerabilities. In: 2021 IEEE 8th International Conference on Data Science and Advanced Analytics (DSAA), pp. 1–12. IEEE (2021)

12. Devlin, J., Chang, M.W., Lee, K., Toutanova, K.: Bert: Pre-training of deep bidirectional transformers for language understanding. arXiv preprint arXiv:1810.04805 (2018)

13. Gao, C., Zhang, X., Liu, H.: Data and knowledge-driven named entity recognition for cyber security. Cybersecurity **4**(1), 1–13 (2021). https://doi.org/10.1186/s42400-021-00072-y

14. Glorot, X., Bengio, Y.: Understanding the difficulty of training deep feedforward neural networks. In: Proceedings of the Thirteenth International Conference On Artificial Intelligence And Statistics, pp. 249–256. JMLR Workshop and Conference Proceedings (2010)

15. Lee, J., et al.: Biobert: a pre-trained biomedical language representation model for biomedical text mining. Bioinformatics **36**(4), 1234–1240 (2020)

16. Li, X., Yang, Z., Guo, P., Cheng, J.: An intelligent transient stability assessment framework with continual learning ability. IEEE Trans. Industr. Inf. **17**(12), 8131–8141 (2021)

17. Lim, S.K., Muis, A.O., Lu, W., Ong, C.H.: MalwareTextDB: A database for annotated malware articles. In: Proceedings of the 55th Annual Meeting of the Association for Computational Linguistics (Volume 1: Long Papers), pp. 1557–1567. Association for Computational Linguistics, Vancouver, Canada (July 2017). https://doi.org/10.18653/v1/P17-1143, https://aclanthology.org/P17-1143

18. Liu, X., Cheng, M., Zhang, H., Hsieh, C.-J.: Towards robust neural networks via random self-ensemble. In: Ferrari, V., Hebert, M., Sminchisescu, C., Weiss, Y. (eds.) ECCV 2018. LNCS, vol. 11211, pp. 381–397. Springer, Cham (2018). https://doi.org/10.1007/978-3-030-01234-2_23

19. Liu, Y., et al.: Roberta: A robustly optimized bert pretraining approach. arXiv preprint arXiv:1907.11692 (2019)

20. Peters, M.E., et al.: Deep contextualized word representations. arXiv preprint arXiv:1802.05365 (2018)

21. Radford, A., Narasimhan, K., Salimans, T., Sutskever, I.: Improving language understanding by generative pre-training (2018)

22. Radford, A., et al.: Language models are unsupervised multitask learners. OpenAI Blog **1**(8), 9 (2019)

23. Rajpurkar, P., Zhang, J., Lopyrev, K., Liang, P.: Squad: 100,000+ questions for machine comprehension of text. arXiv preprint arXiv:1606.05250 (2016)

24. Sajid, M.S.I., Wei, J., Alam, M.R., Aghaei, E., Al-Shaer, E.: Dodgetron: Towards autonomous cyber deception using dynamic hybrid analysis of malware. In: 2020 IEEE Conference on Communications and Network Security (CNS), pp. 1–9. IEEE (2020)

25. Shibata, Y., et al.: Byte Pair Encoding: A Text Compression Scheme That Accelerates Pattern Matching (1999)
26. Socher, R., et al.: Recursive deep models for semantic compositionality over a sentiment treebank. In: Proceedings of the 2013 Conference On Empirical Methods in Natural Language Processing, pp. 1631–1642 (2013)
27. Vaswani, A., et al.: Attention is all you need. In: Advances in Neural Information Processing Systems, pp. 5998–6008 (2017)
28. Wang, A., Singh, A., Michael, J., Hill, F., Levy, O., Bowman, S.R.: Glue: A multitask benchmark and analysis platform for natural language understanding. arXiv preprint arXiv:1804.07461 (2018)
29. Wang, C., Cho, K., Gu, J.: Neural machine translation with byte-level subwords. In: Proceedings of the AAAI Conference on Artificial Intelligence, vol. 34, pp. 9154–9160 (2020)
30. Yin, J., Tang, M., Cao, J., Wang, H.: Apply transfer learning to cybersecurity: Predicting exploitability of vulnerabilities by description. Knowl.-Based Syst. **210**, 106529 (2020)
31. You, Z., Ye, J., Li, K., Xu, Z., Wang, P.: Adversarial noise layer: Regularize neural network by adding noise. In: 2019 IEEE International Conference on Image Processing (ICIP), pp. 909–913. IEEE (2019)
32. Zhou, S., Liu, J., Zhong, X., Zhao, W.: Named entity recognition using bert with whole world masking in cybersecurity domain. In: 2021 IEEE 6th International Conference on Big Data Analytics (ICBDA), pp. 316–320. IEEE (2021)
33. Zur, R.M., Jiang, Y., Pesce, L.L., Drukker, K.: Noise injection for training artificial neural networks: A comparison with weight decay and early stopping. Med. Phys. **36**(10), 4810–4818 (2009)

# CapsITD: Malicious Insider Threat Detection Based on Capsule Neural Network

Haitao Xiao[1,2], Chen Zhang[1], Song Liu[1], Bo Jiang[1,2], Zhigang Lu[1,2],
Fei Wang[3], and Yuling Liu[1,2(✉)]

[1] Institute of Information Engineering, Chinese Academy of Sciences, Beijing, China
{xiaohaitao,zchen,liusong1106,jiangbo,luzhigang,liuyuling}@iie.ac.cn
[2] School of Cyber Security, University of Chinese Academy of Sciences,
Beijing, China
[3] Institute of Computing Technology, Chinese Academy of Sciences, Beijing, China
wangfei@ict.ac.cn

**Abstract.** Insider threat has emerged as the most destructive security
threat due to its secrecy and great destructiveness to the core assets. It
is very important to detect malicious insiders for protecting the security of enterprises and organizations. Existing detection methods seldom
consider correlative information between users and can not learn the
extracted features effectively. To address the aforementioned issues, we
present CapsITD, a novel user-level insider threat detection method.
CapsITD constructs a homogeneous graph that contains the correlative
information from users' authentication logs and then employs a graph
embedding technique to embed the graph into low-dimensional vectors
as structural features. We also design an anomaly detection model using
capsule neural network for CapsITD to learn extracted features and identify malicious insiders. Comprehensive experimental results on the CERT
dataset clearly demonstrate CapsITD's effectiveness.

**Keywords:** Insider threat detection · Capsule neural network · Graph
embedding

## 1 Introduction

Nowadays, insider threats are acknowledged as one of the most dangerous cyber
threats to an organization's network and data security. Insider threats are harder
to detect than external threats since insiders are generally permitted to access
internal information systems and are knowledgeable about the organization's
structure and security procedures. According to Securonix's insider threat report
2020 [1], 80% of employees who are about to terminate their employment with
their company tend to take some sensitive data with them. The insider threat
report 2021 issued by Gurucul shows that 98% of organizations feel vulnerable

F. Li et al. (Eds.): SecureComm 2022, LNICST 462, pp. 57–71, 2023.
https://doi.org/10.1007/978-3-031-25538-0_4

to insider attacks and 49% of organizations can not detect insider threats or can only detect them after data has left the organization [2]. Security problems caused by insiders are becoming more and more serious. It is vital to detect insider threats accurately and promptly.

In order to detect malicious insiders, many approaches have been proposed. These approaches can be divided into signature-based approaches and anomaly-based approaches. Signature-based approaches mainly depend on known-bad events' signatures and can not detect unknown threats. Current anomaly-based approaches are mainly focused on user behavior profiles and use machine learning algorithms [3], deep learning algorithms [4,5] to detect malicious insiders. There are two limitations in the previous approaches. Firstly, previous approaches [3,5] have not considered the correlative information between users. The correlative information can reflect the user's aggregation. Users with the same behavior tend to have similar attributes, and such correlative information can help detect malicious insiders. Secondly, previous approaches [4] fail to learn the extracted features effectively, and there is an urgent need to find a more suitable learning method that can adequately learn the extracted features.

To overcome these limitations, we propose CapsITD, a user-level malicious insider threat detection method based on capsule neural network, which leverages graph embedding technique and capsule neural network. First, we extract statistical features based on users' daily activities and communications. Then, we construct a homogeneous graph using the users' authentication logs to represent the correlative information. To efficiently learn correlative information, graph embedding is employed to embed the graph into low-dimensional vectors as structural features. Finally, we design an anomaly detection model using capsule neural network to learn statistical features and structural features adequately. According to the experimental results, CapsITD outperforms both traditional machine learning methods and state-of-the-art deep learning methods.

Our contributions can be summarized as follows:

- We construct a homogeneous graph that contains the correlative information from users' authentication logs and use a graph embedding technique to generate structural features which are helpful for user-level insider threat detection.
- We design a deep learning-based anomaly detection model, which can learn the extracted features effectively and achieve improved performance for detecting malicious insiders.
- We evaluate our method using a universal insider threat dataset (CERT version 4.2). The results show that our method is effective, competitive, and able to achieve state-of-the-art performance.

The remaining part of the paper proceeds as follows. Section 2 reviews the related studies. Section 3 presents the proposed methods and explains the learning algorithm. Section 4 covers the experiments and results analysis. Finally, Sect. 5 contains the conclusions.

# 2  Related Work

## 2.1  Insider Threat Detection

At present, existing insider threat detection methods can mainly be divided into two categories: signature-based methods and anomaly-based methods [6].

Signature-based method is to design a signature for each known insider threat, match incoming user behavior data with existing signatures, and identify users that match the signatures as insiders. Nguyen et al. [7] built a series of rules for exposing unusual system calls relating to the file system and detecting known abnormal actions effectively. However, the signature-based method heavily relies on domain expertise and can not cope with previously unknown insider threats.

Anomaly-based method is to calculate the deviation of current behavior from normal behavior and identify users that have a large deviation as insiders. Most existing anomaly-based methods are based on machine learning or deep learning and generally build an anomaly detection model based on historical user behavior data. Then use the fitted model to determine whether the user is an insider. Le et al. [3] adopted self-organizing map and C4.5 decision tree to detect malicious insiders using the numerical features extracted from user behavior data. Jiang et al. [4] proposed a graph convolutional network based model to identify users with abnormal behavior. Gayathri et al. [5] employed a pre-trained deep convolutional neural network for anomaly detection to identify malicious insiders. These methods either ignore the correlative information between users or can not learn the extracted features effectively.

## 2.2  Graph Embedding

Graph embedding aims at learning the representative embeddings as low dimensional vectors for each node in a graph. The embedding vectors represent the structure of nodes and can be used in downstream prediction tasks, such as node classification and link prediction.

Graph embedding technique is also used in the anomaly detection field. Wei et al. [8] used graph embedding to capture comprehensive relationships for detecting anomalous logon activities. Bowman et al. [9] built an authentication graph and used graph embedding to learn latent representations of the authenticating entities. Then, they identified low-probability authentication events to detect anomalous users. The above methods improve the learning performance by using the graph embedding technique.

## 2.3  Capsule Neural Network

Capsule neural network was first proposed by Hinton [10]. Unlike traditional neural network, capsule neural network uses vector instead of scalar as a neuron in traditional neural network and drops the pooling operation to retain feature spatial information. By this means, the capsule neural network has a momentous improvement compared to the traditional neural network. The capsule neural network is widely utilised in the field of anomaly detection. For example, Zhang et al. [11] presented a capsule neural network based intrusion detection method. Li et al. [12] employed a capsule neural network to detect anomalous images. They have proved the great power of the capsule neural network for feature learning.

## 3    Methodology

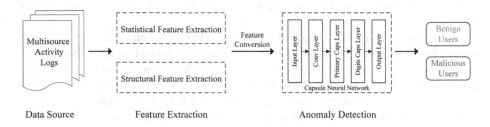

**Fig. 1.** The framework of CapsITD

Figure 1 illustrates the framework of CapsITD. CapsITD consists of two components: feature extraction module and anomaly detection module.

In the feature extraction module, we first count frequency-based and content-based information about user behavior from users' multisource activity logs as statistical features. Then we construct a homogeneous graph based on users' authentication logs and embed the graph into low-dimensional vectors as structural features. We concatenate and convert statistical features and structural features into the form of feature matrices, which are suitable as input to the neural network for the next module.

In the anomaly detection module, we train the anomaly detection model based on a capsule neural network to detect the users as benign or malicious using the feature matrices generated in the previous module.

### 3.1    Feature Extraction Module

The goal of the feature extraction module is to collect useful users' characteristics to identify malicious insiders. To obtain more comprehensive and effective features from users' multisource activity logs, as shown in Fig. 2, we extract the features from the statistical aspect and structural aspect respectively.

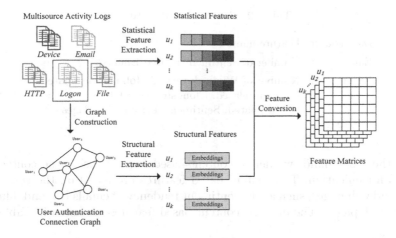

**Fig. 2.** The process of feature extraction

**Statistical Feature Extraction.** Statistical features can reflect the behavioral patterns of users and help us identify potential malicious users. In this work, we design 31 statistical features from users' multisource activity logs based on [13,14]. The statistical features can be categorised into frequency-based features and content-based features.

**Table 1.** Frequency-based features

| Data source | Feature name |
|---|---|
| Logon | Logon/Logoff times, Off work Logon/Logoff times, Number of PC for Logon/Logoff |
| Device | Number of Device Connection, Number of Off-work Device Connection, Number of PC for Device Connection |
| File | Number of Different Files, Number of Total Files, Number of Off-work Files, Number of .exe Files, Number of PC for Files |
| Email | Number of Sent Emails, Number of Out Organization Emails, Number of In Organization Emails, Average Email Size, Number of Email Attachments, Number of Receivers of Sent Emails, Number of Off-work Sent Emails, Number of PC for Emails |
| HTTP | Number of Web Pages Browsed, Number of Off-work Web Pages Browsed |

On the one hand, we derive frequency-based features from users' daily activities using the frequency information, which can reveal the typical behavioral patterns of users. The frequency-based features are the daily average counts of different types of actions the user performs, such as logon and logoff times, off-work hours logon and logoff times, and the number of PCs for emails. Based on the aggregation of logon and logoff activities, we define the work time as 8:00 to 19:00 [14]. Table 1 lists the detailed frequency-based features.

**Table 2.** Content-based features

| Data source | Feature name |
| --- | --- |
| Email | Number of Sentiment-related Emails |
| HTTP | Number of Wikileak-related, Jobhunting-related, Hacking-related, Cloudstorage-related, Social-related, Sentiment-related Web Pages |

On the other hand, we derive content-based features using the contents of users' communication. The content-based features are based on the content of emails and web pages, such as the sentiment tendency of emails [13] and different types of web pages. The detailed content-based features are listed in Table 2.

**Structural Feature Extraction.** Structural features can reflect the correlative information of users. The correlative information of users is represented by the edges of the graph, and users with similar behaviors tend to be closer together. This information can help us detect malicious insiders. Structural feature extraction can be separated into two steps: graph construction and graph embedding. The first step is to construct a user authentication connection graph based on the users' authentication logs. Then, we use graph embedding to derive latent node representations from the previously constructed graph and embed the nodes into low-dimensional vectors containing the correlative information of users. The low-dimensional vectors generated by graph embedding are used as structural features.

*Graph Construction.* The user authentication connection graph is defined as a homogeneous graph $G = (V, E)$. This graph has a node type mapping $\phi : V \to A$ and an edge type mapping $\psi : E \to R$ , where $V$ denotes the node set and $E$ denotes the edge set, $A = \{user\}$ and $R = \{connection\}$. We define two users have a connection only if they log on to the same computer. Specifically, if $user_i$ logs on to the $computer_k$ and $user_j$ logs on to the $computer_k$ too, there is a connection between $user_i$ and $user_j$.

*Graph Embedding.* Graph embedding is the process of transforming a graph into a low-dimensional space while preserving the graph's information. The goal is to convert each node in the graph $G$ into a low-dimensional vector while retaining relations between nodes.

The process of user authentication connection graph embedding is divided into two steps: First, we sample graph $G$ using fixed-length random walks. Specifically, we explore $r$ fixed-length random walks for any node in the graph $G = (V, E)$ and generate node sequences set $S = \{s_1, s_2, ..., s_m\}$, where the $i$th random walk sequence is denoted as $s_i$ and the total number of sequences is denoted as $m$. Then, we learn a $d$-dimensioal representation for each unique user $u$. In this step, the skip-gram model is utilised to acquire the embedding vector of each node over the sequence set $S$ by maximizing the objective function $f$ as Eq. 1.

$$f = \sum_{u \in W} logP(N(u) \mid u) \tag{1}$$

where $W$ is the vocabulary of unique nodes representing users. $N(u)$ is the set of neighborhoods of node $u \in V$. The probability of observing nodes $P(N(u)|u)$ is defined by a softmax unit:

$$P(N(u) \mid u) = \prod_{n_i \in N(u)} \frac{\exp \left( v_{n_i}'^T v_u \right)}{\sum_{w=1}^{|W|} \exp \left( v_w'^T v_u \right)} \tag{2}$$

where $v$ and $v'$ are two vectors which represent of the node $u$. And $v$ is the ultimately embedding vector of node $u$. If two nodes have similar authentication patterns, their embedding vectors will commonly occur together after the convergence of the skip-gram model.

**Feature Conversion.** Feature conversion is to transform the extracted features into a form that is suitable for the input of the capsule neural network based anomaly detection model. We directly concatenate the statistical feature vectors with structural feature vectors as concatenating features. Then the concatenating features will be normalized by min-max normalization, which limits the value range to $[0, 1]$. The normalization can eliminate the magnitude differences between features and avoid the impact on the detection model. Finally, we convert normalized concatenating features to $6 \times 6$ two-dimensional feature matrices as the input of the anomaly detection model.

## 3.2 Anomaly Detection Module

The goal of the anomaly detection module is to detect anomalous users and identify malicious insiders. A strong learning model is required for learning the extracted features in the previous module. Neural networks generally have excellent feature learning capabilities over other algorithms. The convolutional neural network is one of the most classic algorithms in neural networks. As described in Sect. 2, capsule neural network can make up for the shortage of convolutional neural network. So we choose the capsule neural network as our anomaly detection model. The model architecture is made up of convolutional layer, primary capsule layer, and digit capsule layer as shown in Fig. 3.

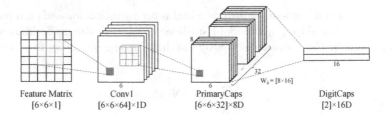

**Fig. 3.** Structure of capsule neural network

In the convolutional layer(Conv1), Conv1 has 64 channels each make up of $3 \times 3$ filters with a stride of 1, a padding of 1, and ReLu activation applied to a $6 \times 6 \times 1$ matrix which represents the concatenating features. Conv1 outputs 64 channel matrices of features with the size $6 \times 6$. This layer transforms pixel intensities into local feature detector activity, which is subsequently sent into the primary capsules.

The primary capsule layer is a convolutional capsule layer. This layer is made up of 32 channels of convolutional 8D capsules. Each primary capsule has eight convolutional units, each having a $3 \times 3$ kernel and a stride of 1. We execute primary capsule operation on 64 channel matrices of features and generate $6 \times 6 \times 32$ outputs. Each capsule in the $6 \times 6$ grid shares its weights with the others.

The third layer is digit capsule layer. This layer contains one 16D capsule for each digit class, and each of these capsules gets input from every capsule in the layer beneath it. As shown in Eq. 3, the overall input to capsule $s_j$ is a weighted sum over all prediction vector $\hat{\mathbf{u}}_{j|i}$ from the capsules in the layer beneath it and the coupling coefficients $c_{ij}$ determined by the iterative dynamic routing process. The $\hat{\mathbf{u}}_{j|i}$ is produced by the Eq. 4, where $\mathbf{W}_{ij}$ is a weight matrix.

$$s_j = \sum_i c_{ij} \hat{\mathbf{u}}_{j|i} \tag{3}$$

$$\hat{\mathbf{u}}_{j|i} = \mathbf{W}_{ij} \mathbf{u}_i \tag{4}$$

The coupling coefficients $c_{ij}$ is produced by the Eq. 5, where $b_{ij}$ is the log prior probabilities that capsule $i$ coupled to capsule $j$.

$$c_{ij} = \frac{\exp(b_{ij})}{\sum_k \exp(b_{ik})} \tag{5}$$

The probability of an entity is represented by the length of the output vector of a capsule. Thus, we utilise a non-linear squashing function to ensure that short vectors get shrunk to almost zero length and long vectors get shrunk to a length slightly below 1. Equation 6 shows the squashing function, where $\mathbf{v}_j$ is the capsule $j$ 's vector output and $s_j$ is its overall input.

$$\mathbf{v}_j = \frac{\|s_j\|^2}{1 + \|s_j\|^2} \frac{s_j}{\|s_j\|} \tag{6}$$

To update the parameters of the entire network, we use the margin loss function $L_k$ for each digit capsule, $k$:

$$L_k = T_k \max \left(0, m^+ - \|\mathbf{v}_k\|\right)^2 + \lambda \left(1 - T_k\right) \max \left(0, \|\mathbf{v}_k\| - m^-\right)^2 \tag{7}$$

where $T_k = 1$ if the class $k$ is present, otherwise $T_k = 0$. The two hyperparameters, $m^+$ and $m^-$ are set to 0.9 and 0.1. $\lambda$ is a regularization parameter and is set to 0.5. To achieve better accuracy, we add reconstruct loss into the final loss as well.

## 4    Experiments and Results

This section is devoted to evaluating the performance of CapsITD. First, we introduce the dataset utilised for evaluation. Then, we describe the evaluation metrics and experiment setup specifically. The experiment results are then discussed and compared to three classical machine learning algorithms (logistic regression, support vector machine, and random forest) as well as two deep learning algorithms (convolutional neural network and graph convolutional network [4]). We also set a comparative experiment between statistical features and concatenated features to evaluate the effort of correlative information and test the influence of different anomalous sample ratios to verify the robustness of CapsITD.

### 4.1    Dataset

We use a universal insider threat dataset (CERT version 4.2) from Carnegie Mellon University [15]. This dataset consists of multisource activity logs of 1000 users and 1003 computers over a period of 17 months from January 2010 to May 2011. The multisource activity logs contain user login, removable device usage, file access, email communication, and web browsing history. The dataset covers 70 malicious insiders and three insider threat scenarios, which are data exfiltration, intellectual property theft, and IT sabotage.

### 4.2    Evaluation Metrics

In the experiments, four well-known metrics are adopted for our evaluation: Accuracy, F-measure, AUC (Area Under the ROC Curve), and Recall. Accuracy is the ratio of correctly predicted observations to total observations. F-measure is the weighted average of precision and recall. AUC is a metric for evaluating the pros and cons of a binary classification model. Recall is the ratio of correctly predicted positive observations to all observations in the true class.

### 4.3   Experiment Setup

Our experiments are performed on a PC with Intel Core i5-10500 CPU @ 3.10GHz, 16GB RAM, and 64-bit Windows 10 Professional OS. We use Sklearn 0.24.1 to implement the machine learning algorithm and PyTorch 1.7.1 to implement the deep learning algorithm.

In the CERT dataset, we process the multisource activity logs of users and derive statistical features from these logs as demonstrated in Sect. 3. The dimension of statistical features is 31. Then we construct the user authentication connection graph using 1000 users' authentication logs and embed the nodes into low-dimensional vectors. The hyperparameters of graph embedding are as follows: We set the walk length $l = 30$ and the number of walks per node $r = 200$ in random walk. We set the vector's dimension $d = 5$ and the window size to 10 in skip-gram. After that, we concatenate and transform the extracted features into a $6 \times 6$ feature matrix as the input to the capsule neural network for each user. The hyperparameters of the capsule neural network are set as follows: The training epoch is set to 50, and the learning rate is set at 0.001.

### 4.4   Experimental Results

To evaluate the proposed method comprehensively, we first compare CapsITD with three classical machine learning methods and two deep learning methods. Then we expand the experiment to evaluate the effectiveness of correlative information and the robustness of CapsITD.

Table 3. Comparison results with other methods

| Method | Accuracy | F-measure | AUC | Recall |
|--------|----------|-----------|-----|--------|
| LR | 0.910 | 0.794 | 0.755 | 0.533 |
| SVM | 0.920 | 0.811 | 0.761 | 0.533 |
| RF | 0.920 | 0.803 | 0.747 | 0.500 |
| CNN | 0.965 | 0.926 | 0.897 | 0.800 |
| GCN | 0.945 | – | – | 0.833 |
| CapsITD | **0.980** | **0.958** | **0.933** | **0.867** |

**Comparison with Other Methods.** We compare the experimental results of the CapsITD with three classical machine learning algorithms such as Logistic Regression (LR), Support Vector Machine (SVM), Random Forest (RF), and two deep learning algorithms such as Convolutional Neural Network (CNN), and Graph Convolutional Network (GCN) [4]. However, since the GCN method does not describe its algorithm in detail, we only refer to the detection results of the CERT dataset as shown in [4] and set up the same dataset partition. The training set and test set are selected the same way as the [4]. The training set contains

160 normal users and 40 abnormal users, and the test set contains 170 normal users and 30 abnormal users. The comparison results between CapsITD and other methods on the CERT dataset are shown in Table 3. We can observe that CapsITD outperforms the other five competing algorithms. The deep learning algorithms outperform the other three machine learning algorithms. Compared with the GCN model proposed by [4], CapsITD is higher 3.5% accuracy and 3.4% recall than the GCN model. CapsITD is competent for insider threat detection since the performance of CapsITD outperforms other existing models.

**Table 4.** Comparison between statistical features and concatenated features

| Method | Accuracy | F-measure | AUC | Recall |
|--------|----------|-----------|-----|--------|
| $LR_{stat}$ | 0.895 | 0.764 | 0.732 | 0.500 |
| $LR_{conc}$ | **0.910** | **0.794** | **0.755** | **0.533** |
| $SVM_{stat}$ | 0.905 | 0.779 | 0.738 | 0.500 |
| $SVM_{conc}$ | **0.920** | **0.811** | **0.761** | **0.533** |
| $RF_{stat}$ | 0.895 | 0.715 | 0.664 | 0.333 |
| $RF_{conc}$ | **0.920** | **0.803** | **0.747** | **0.500** |
| $CNN_{stat}$ | 0.950 | 0.889 | 0.847 | 0.700 |
| $CNN_{conc}$ | **0.965** | **0.926** | **0.897** | **0.800** |
| $CapsITD_{stat}$ | 0.970 | 0.936 | 0.900 | 0.800 |
| $CapsITD_{conc}$ | **0.980** | **0.958** | **0.933** | **0.867** |

**The Effectiveness of Correlative Information.** To evaluate the effectiveness of correlative information, we compare the models with statistical features and concatenated features. The experimental results are shown in Table 4, where the subscripts are *stat* for only statistical features and *conc* for concatenated features. The concatenated features, which incorporate correlative information, are improved in all three machine learning methods and two deep learning methods compared to only statistical features. The most significant improvement is the random forest, where the random forest model using concatenated features improves accuracy by 2.5% compared to the random forest model using only statistical features. CapsITD with concatenated features outperforms CapsITD with only statistical features in terms of 1% accuracy, 2.2% F-measure, 3.3% AUC, and 6.7% recall. In general, correlative information can further improve the performance of detecting malicious insiders.

**Table 5.** Different anomalous sample ratios

| Anomalous sample ratio | Normal | Abnormal |
|---|---|---|
| 10% | 280 | 28 |
| 15% | 280 | 42 |
| 20% | 280 | 56 |
| 25% | 280 | 70 |

**Performance on Different Anomalous Sample Ratios.** To evaluate the robustness of CapsITD, we compare the models with different anomalous sample ratios. Table 5 shows the data with varying ratios of anomalous samples. Since the total number of anomalous samples in the dataset is 70, we set the number of normal samples at 280 to ensure that different anomalous sample ratios can be selected. In this experiment, we test the models on different ratios of anomalous samples. The proportion of training set to test set is 6:4.

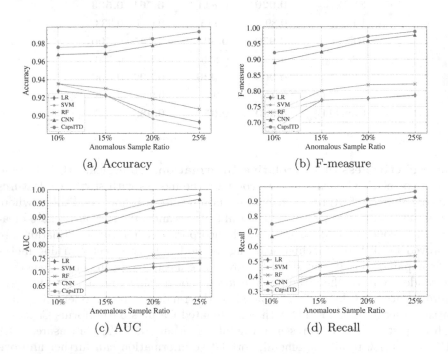

**Fig. 4.** Performance on different anomalous sample ratios

As shown in Fig. 4, they are the performance of three machine learning algorithms: Logistic Regression (LR), Support Vector Machine (SVM), Random Forest (RF), and two deep learning algorithms: Convolutional Neural Networks (CNN) and Our Proposed Method (CapsITD). We make the following observations: CapsITD is always higher than CNN of the four metrics. And deep learning-based approaches have significant improvements over machine learning-based approaches. According to Fig. 4(d), the ability of all models to detect malicious insiders increases as the ratio of anomalous samples rises. However, Fig. 4(a) shows the accuracy of machine learning-based approaches decreases as the ratio of anomalous samples rises. This is due to the poor ability to identify anomalous samples by machine learning-based approaches.

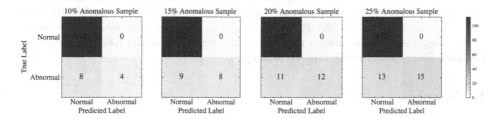

**Fig. 5.** The confusion matrix of RF on different anomolous sample ratios

As shown in Fig. 5, they are the confusion matrices of the random forest model under different anomalous sample ratios. It can be seen that the random forest can detect all normal samples under different anomalous sample ratios, but has a poor ability to identify anomalous samples. As the ratio of anomalous samples increases, the random forest model can gradually distinguish anomalous samples, but the accuracy tends to slightly decrease due to the large base of normal samples. The situation for the other machine learning-based approaches is the same as random forest. It demonstrates that machine learning-based approaches are unable to learn from the extracted features to classify normal and abnormal samples effectively. Meanwhile, deep learning-based approaches show an increasing trend in all metrics as the ratio of anomalous samples rises. It means that deep learning-based approaches can learn more from the extracted features to classify normal and abnormal samples precisely. In summary, CapsITD still outperforms other methods on different anomalous sample ratios. This experiment shows the robustness of CapsITD.

## 5  Conclusion

In this paper, we present CapsITD, a novel user-level approach for insider threat detection. This approach can effectively detect malicious insiders from users' multisource activity logs. Firstly, we extract statistical features based on users' daily activities and communications. Secondly, we construct a homogeneous graph based on users' authentication logs. The constructed graph can represent the correlative information between users. We then use a graph embedding technique to embed the graph into low-dimensional vectors as structural features. Thirdly, we design an anomaly detection model using capsule neural network to learn statistical features and structural features adequately. The results of the comparative experiments reveal that our proposed approach has superior performance compared with other existing approaches. In our expansive experiments, we verified the effectiveness of correlative information and the robustness of CapsITD.

**Acknowledgment.** This work is supported by National Key Research and Development Program of China (No.2021YFF0307203, No.2019QY1300), and NSFC (No. 61902376), Youth Innovation Promotion Association CAS (No.2021156), the Strategic Priority Research Program of Chinese Academy of Sciences (No. XDC02040100). This work is also supported by the Program of Key Laboratory of Network Assessment Technology, the Chinese Academy of Sciences, Program of Beijing Key Laboratory of Network Security and Protection Technology.

# References

1. 2020 Securonix Insider Threat Report. https://www.securonix.com/resources/2020-insider-threat-report/. (Accessed 29 Dec 2021)
2. 2021 Insider threat report. https://gurucul.com/2021-insider-threat-report. (Accessed 29 Dec 2021)
3. Le, D.C., Zincir-Heywood, A.N.: Evaluating insider threat detection workflow using supervised and unsupervised learning. In: 2018 IEEE Security and Privacy Workshops (SPW), pp. 270–275. IEEE (2018)
4. Jiang, J., et al.: Anomaly detection with graph convolutional networks for insider threat and fraud detection. In: MILCOM 2019–2019 IEEE Military Communications Conference (MILCOM), pp. 109–114. IEEE (2019)
5. Gayathri, R., Sajjanhar, A., Xiang, Y.: Image-based feature representation for insider threat classification. Appl. Sci. **10**(14), 4945 (2020)
6. Liu, L., De Vel, O., Han, Q.L., Zhang, J., Xiang, Y.: Detecting and preventing cyber insider threats: A survey. IEEE Commun. Surv. Tutorials **20**(2), 1397–1417 (2018)
7. Nguyen, N., Reiher, P., Kuenning, G.H.: Detecting insider threats by monitoring system call activity. In: IEEE Systems, Man and Cybernetics Society Information Assurance Workshop, vol. 2003, pp. 45–52. IEEE (2003)
8. Wei, R., Cai, L., Yu, A., Meng, D.: Age: authentication graph embedding for detecting anomalous login activities. In: Zhou, J., Luo, X., Shen, Q., Xu, Z. (eds.) ICICS 2019. LNCS, vol. 11999, pp. 341–356. Springer, Cham (2020). https://doi.org/10.1007/978-3-030-41579-2_20
9. Bowman, B., Laprade, C., Ji, Y., Huang, H.H.: Detecting lateral movement in enterprise computer networks with unsupervised graph ai. In: 23rd International Symposium on Research in Attacks, Intrusions and Defenses (RAID 2020), pp. 257–268 (2020)
10. Hinton, G.E., Krizhevsky, A., Wang, S.D.: Transforming auto-encoders. In: Honkela, T., Duch, W., Girolami, M., Kaski, S. (eds.) ICANN 2011. LNCS, vol. 6791, pp. 44–51. Springer, Heidelberg (2011). https://doi.org/10.1007/978-3-642-21735-7_6
11. Zhang, X., Yin, S.: Intrusion detection model of random attention capsule network based on variable fusion. J. Commun. **41**(11), 160 (2020)
12. Li, X.: Anomaly Detection Based on Disentangled Representation Learning. Ph.D. thesis, Université d'Ottawa/University of Ottawa (2020)

13. Jiang, J., et al.: Prediction and detection of malicious insiders' motivation based on sentiment profile on webpages and emails. In: MILCOM 2018–2018 IEEE Military Communications Conference (MILCOM), pp. 1–6. IEEE (2018)

14. Chattopadhyay, P., Wang, L., Tan, Y.P.: Scenario-based insider threat detection from cyber activities. IEEE Trans. Comput. Soc. Syst. **5**(3), 660–675 (2018)

15. Glasser, J., Lindauer, B.: Bridging the gap: A pragmatic approach to generating insider threat data. In: 2013 IEEE Security and Privacy Workshops, pp. 98–104. IEEE (2013)

# Towards High Transferability on Neural Network for Black-Box Adversarial Attacks

Haochen Zhai, Futai Zou[✉], Junhua Tang, and Yue Wu

School of Electronic Information and Electrical Engineering,
Shanghai Jiaotong University, Shanghai, China
{516021910264,zoufutai,junhuatang,wuyue}@sjtu.edu.cn

**Abstract.** Adversarial examples are one of the biggest potential risks faced by the modern neural networks, threatening the application with high sensitiveness. To improve the efficiency of black-box attacks, and eventually achieve the purpose of reducing the query number by a large margin when keeping a high attack success rate, we propose a NES-based gradient estimation method, which greatly reduces the queries via a heuristic way. We also use ADAM-based perturbation update rules to improve the strength of iterative attacks. Besides, to make the whole method more flexible, meta learning is introduced to generate gradients on multiple substitute models and train an initial meta model with stronger generalization ability for online attacks. Experiments on MNIST and CIFAR10 show that META-NES-ADAM attack greatly reduces query number while sacrificing a little attack success rate when attacking black-box models.

**Keywords:** Black-box attack · Meta learning · Adversarial examples · Query

## 1 Introduction

With the wide application of neural network, its lack of interpretability and formal description is one of the problems restricting its further development. Under normal conditions, neural network can calculate the final task-related prediction value through internal reasoning, while there is no explicit reasoning mode for human understanding in the intermediate process. The exploration of its reasoning basis is an independent research. Sometimes mapping the output value of the shallow neural network back to the original input space can obtain some useful clues related to the final task, but for the complex (nonlinear) deep network, its deep reasoning basis is still unclear. This will lead to two serious technical challenges in the application of neural network: firstly, malicious input will lead to the network to get far away from the actual output results, such as the adversarial examples in image and natural language; Secondly, due to its unclear internal reasoning mechanism, it is impossible to set up limited rules to

F. Li et al. (Eds.): SecureComm 2022, LNICST 462, pp. 72–88, 2023.
https://doi.org/10.1007/978-3-031-25538-0_5

make up for the reasoning logic of the network, and the reliability of reasoning depends entirely on the robustness of the network. The above challenges lead to the current application of neural network is still in the level of easy to attack and difficult to defend. In the face of applications with high-security requirements, such as face recognition and automatic driving, it often needs additional physical information to ensure security, or human intervention to prevent accidents, which makes the deployment and application process of neural network have large technology overlap and excessive resource allocation.

To understand and infer the internal operation mechanism of neural network, we try to control the input and output parts of neural network from the perspective of attackers, so as to provide a powerful analysis and verification means for the establishment of subsequent defense mechanisms. We will focus on how to attack efficiently under specific conditions (the attacker does not grasp the specific structure and parameter information of neural network) in the process of adversarial examples construction. Attacking efficiently here mainly includes two meanings: one is how to search for perturbation vector with high success rate at low query cost, and the other is how to attack as many unknown models as possible with one perturbation vector. However, in the process of research, we also notice the limitations of current algorithms: most of the research scenarios are limited to white-box conditions, and lack analysis methods and tools for unknown models, which greatly hinders our comprehensive understanding of neural networks. Our preliminary empirical analysis shows that the perturbations searched from a large number of neural networks with different structures are indeed closely related. For the black-box model, the perturbation calculated from the white-box model can be easily transferred to the black-box for effective attack. For the query times, although the query number needed for gradient estimation has been greatly optimized by ZOO [1] and AutoZOOM [2], and there have been many active researches in recent years, it is still in its infancy [1,3].

At present, many attack algorithms are directly related to gradient in white-box scenario, while gradient estimation method and iteration strategy need to be further considered in black-box scenario. Complex gradient estimation and inefficient iteration strategy are the two reasons for the unsatisfactory query efficiency and performance. At the same time, the requirement of black-box transferability is more and more strict. The success rate of attacking unknown model transferred from the perturbation of typical white-box attack is usually limited, and it needs to consume a certain number of queries to transfer effectively to improve the attack success rate. Typical schemes for transferring include autoencoder [2], natural evolution strategy [4] and so on. Based on the technical challenges and research status, this paper combines ADAM update rules and NES, and then introduces the meta learning frameworks, obtaining a high-transferability and efficient-estimation black-box attack method, which is called META-NES-ADAM attack.

This paper mainly makes the following contributions:

1. We combine ADAM update rules and NES for the first time, which makes full use of the historical information in the gradient estimation process ignored by the traditional algorithm. Without introducing additional query consump-

tion, the average attack success rate of black-box attack is improved as high as 8%.
2. We integrate the meta learning into the step of gradient estimation, and introduce the periodic gradient estimation strategy. Although a small amount of attack success rate is sacrificed, the query number is greatly reduced, so as to ensure the efficient operation of the whole method.
3. Our method has a high degree of adaptive learning ability and transforms the idea of black-box attack from "attack specific model" to "learn how to attack". It can carry out long-term offline learning in different types of datasets and models, and then obtain an initial meta model with stronger generalization ability, which can quickly adapt to any dataset and model online.

## 2   Related Work

**White-Box Attack**. Typical white-box attack methods include FGSM [5], PGD [6], DeepFool [7] and C&W attack [8] whose important assumption is that the attacker can grasp the specific structure and parameter information of neural network to obtain gradient and loss. Other white-box attack algorithms [9–11] mainly make great improvements to FGSM. For example, [9] introduces momentum into the iterative FGSM to accelerate and stabilize the whole iterative search process. Considering neural networks have the translation-invariant property, [10] optimizes an adversarial image by using a set of translated images to improve the generalization ability of white-box attack.

**Black-Box Attack**. In contrast, the black-box attack setting prohibits any access to internal configurations, which is more in line with the real scene. [12] trains a substitute model and deploys a white-box attack to it, so the attack transferability from the substitute model to the target model determines the effectiveness of black-box attacks. Because the black-box model can't get the gradient by back propagation, finite difference method [13] is a classical way of black-box attack to estimate gradient. [1] proposes a coordinate descent-based method employing only the zeroth order oracle without gradient information, and attains comparable performance to C&W attack. To reduce queries and increase efficiency in finite difference, RG (Random Grouping) and PCA (Principal Component Analysis) are introduced [14].

**NES**. Natural Evolution Strategies(NES) is introduced into deep learning by salimans et al. to solve derivative-free optimization problems [15]. NES maximizes the expected value of the loss function under the search perturbation instead of directly maximizing the objective function $F(x)$. [4] proposes the variant of NES to construct adversarial examples in the query-limited setting, using NES for the black-box gradient estimation and employing PGD with the estimated gradient. This method does not require the substitute network and allows gradient estimation in much fewer queries than the typical finite difference method. Besides, many researchers applies NES to the project successfully[15,16].

**Meta Learning.** The core idea of meta learning is to make machine learning model have the ability to learn new concepts and skills with only a small amount of data [17]. A good meta learning model should have strong adaptability and generalization ability. Different from the traditional method, meta learning can change the parameters of the model through the adaptive process which is called Few Shot Learning(FSL). The model completes the transformation from the original domain to the target domain, and then it can perform tasks in the target domain. OpenAI develops first-order meta learning algorithm: Reptile [18], which trains to minimize loss on the expectation over training tasks and optimizes for within-task generalization. In fact, there are many examples of applying meta learning to the field of adversarial Attacks[19–21]. [21] proposes a query-efficient meta attack method, which obtains prior information from the successful attack patterns and uses it for efficient optimization without sacrificing too much attack performance.

## 3  Method

### 3.1  NES-Based Gradient Estimation Algorithm

We introduce antithetic sampling [4] based on the original NES. More specifically, random Gaussian distribution is chosen as the search distribution; That is, we have $\theta = x + \sigma\delta$ around the image, where $\delta \sim N(0, I)$. We sample half of the Gaussian noise for $i \in \{1, ..., \frac{n}{2}\}$ rather than directly generate n values from the distribution and the other half is set to be negative: $\delta_j = -\delta_{n-j+1}$, where $j \in \{(\frac{n}{2} + 1), ..., n\}$. This optimization approach has been empirically proven to improve the performance of NES [4,15]. Therefore, the gradient estimation function we actually used is shown as follows:

$$\nabla\mathbb{E}[\mathcal{M}(\theta)] \approx \frac{1}{\sigma n} \sum_{i=1}^{n} \delta_i M(\theta + \sigma\delta_i) \qquad (1)$$

NES gradient estimation algorithm is shown in Algorithm 1. Here, loss function $\mathcal{L}(\cdot)$ is

$$f(x, t) = max\{max_{i \neq t} log[M(x)]_i - log[M(x)]_t, -\kappa\} \qquad (2)$$

where $\kappa \geq 0$, $log0$ is defined as $-\infty$ and $\kappa$ is a constant used to control the distance between target category $log[M(x)]_t$ and most similar category $max_{i \neq t}[F(x)]_i$.

### 3.2  ADAM-Based Perturbation Update Rules

For non-linear models, the direction of one-step iteration may not be completely accurate, while multi-step iteration can gradually adjust to find a better direction. There are different strategies for multi-step iteration. In white-box attack such as PGD [6], the most direct iterative method is adopted while in black-box attack, due to the uncertainty of gradient estimation, more complex strategies

---

**Algorithm 1.** NES Gradient Estimation Algorithm

---

**Input:** Model$\mathcal{M}$, image(x,y), loss function $\mathcal{L}(\cdot)$
**Output:** Gradient $\nabla M(y|x)$ with respect to input (x, y)
**Parameters:** Standard deviation of Gaussian distribution $\sigma$, number of samples $n$, input dimension N

1. Initialize gradient $g \leftarrow \mathbf{0}_n$
2. **for** i $\leftarrow$ 1 to n **do**
3.     Randomly sample from Gaussian distribution $u_i \leftarrow \mathcal{N}(0_N, I_{N \cdot N})$
4.     $g \leftarrow g + \mathcal{L}(\mathcal{M}(y|x + \sigma \cdot u_i)) \cdot u_i$
5.     $g \leftarrow g - \mathcal{L}(\mathcal{M}(y|x - \sigma \cdot u_i)) \cdot u_i$
6.     **end for**
7. return $\frac{1}{2n\sigma} g$

---

are usually used to reduce the impact of gradient estimation. For instance, ZOO [1] adopts stochastic coordinate descent, which makes it update coordinates by small batches for each iteration, instead of updating the coordinates of the whole space. The reason for this is that the query-efficiency of the finite difference method is quite low and if the conventional stochastic gradient descent method is used, one complete iterative attack will reach millions of queries, which is an extraordinary attack cost.

Our method uses NES based gradient estimation, so the query number for one-step attack of the whole space is not high. The low estimation accuracy of NES makes it need more iteration steps than other strategies (such as finite difference method) to reflect its advantages, and more iteration steps mean more optimization space. Zeroth order stochastic coordinate descent with Coordinate-wise ADAM [22] is proposed in ZOO and our optimization update strategy draws on their success, proposing a non coordinate descent version of ADAM-based iterative approximate update rules shown in Algorithm 2.

---

**Algorithm 2.** ADAM-based Iterative Approximate Update Rules

---

**Input:** Input image x, step size $\alpha$, timestep T, $M$, v
**Output:** Adversarial example $\hat{x}$
**Parameters:** ADAM hyper-parameters: $\beta_1 = 0.9, \beta_2 = 0.999, \epsilon = 10^{-8}$

1. $M \leftarrow 0, v \leftarrow 0, T \leftarrow 0$
2. **while not** converged **do**
3.     Estimate $\hat{g}$ using algorithm 1
4.     $T_i \leftarrow T_i + 1$
5.     $M \leftarrow \beta_1 M + (1 - \beta_1)\hat{g}, v \leftarrow \beta_2 + (1 - \beta_2)\hat{g}^2$
6.     $\hat{M} = M/(1 - \beta_1^T), \hat{v} = v/(1 - \beta_2^T)$
7.     $\delta^* = -\alpha \frac{\hat{M}}{\sqrt{\hat{v}} + \epsilon}$
8.     Update $x \leftarrow x + \delta^*$
9. **end while**

---

### 3.3   Meta Attack Algorithm

To further reduce the query consumption of black-box attack, we use meta learning framework to train the meta attacker. By learning a large number of prior gradient information of the model in advance, the meta attacker learns to infer the gradient of the target model only through a few queries. After getting such a meta attacker, we replace the original gradient estimator with a meta attacker to directly output the gradient. The following will describe the training process and implementation details of the meta attacker.

The acquisition of prior information needs to collect a series of classification models $\mathcal{M}_1, ..., \mathcal{M}_n$ to generate the corresponding input and output gradient information. After inputting image x into each pre-trained classification model, we calculate the loss $l_1, ..., l_n$ for each model. By performing a one-step back propagation to the image x, the gradient information about the input can be obtained. Finally, we collect n sets of data to train meta attacker $\mathcal{X} = \{x_i\}, \mathcal{G} = \{g_i\}, i = 1, ..., n$.

Due to the inherent different attributes of classification tasks, the training process of meta attacker samples each task $\mathcal{T}_i$. In each iteration, we extract K samples from the task $\mathcal{T}_i$, calculate the feedback loss $\mathcal{L}_i$, and then update the model parameters $\theta$ to $\theta'$ by using gradient descent method $\theta'_i = \theta - \alpha \nabla_\theta \mathcal{L}_i(\mathcal{A}_\theta)$. Eventually, we use the meta model update strategy of Reptile to summarize the parameters of all tasks and update them to the model parameters:

$$\theta = \theta + \epsilon \frac{1}{n} \sum_{i=1}^{n} (\theta'_i - \theta) \tag{3}$$

In addition, we use the average square error loss in the internal round update:

$$\mathcal{L}_i(\mathcal{A}_\theta) = ||\mathcal{A}_\theta(\mathcal{X}_f) - \mathcal{G}_i^s||_2^2. \tag{4}$$

Here, $(\mathcal{X}_f, \mathcal{G}_j^f)$ is the K samples used in the internal update. Usually K is very small, so the goal of the above update strategy is to find a good initial point of meta attacker, and then quickly adapt to the new data distribution through only a few steps of fine-tuning. Therefore, the feature can be naturally applied to black-box attacks to estimate the gradient information of the target model. Algorithm 3 shows more details of Reptile-based meta attacker training process.

To estimate the gradient information efficiently, we introduce a periodic interval update strategy to realize the gradient learning and mapping of the meta model, as shown in Algorithm 4. Specifically, we use the meta attacker above to generate gradient information after carrying out the adaptive process to match the target model. Suppose the input image is perturbed to $x_t$ in the t-th iteration, if (t+1) mod m =0, the finite difference estimation or NES estimation is performed ,and then we fine tune the gradient $g_t$ after getting it. In the remaining iterations, we directly use the fine-tuned meta attacker to output the gradient $y_t = \mathcal{A}_\theta(x)$.

Our method can greatly reduce the query number, because every M-time interval in the attack process will actually perform a gradient estimation operation that consumes queries, and the total number of queries will be reduced by

---

**Algorithm 3.** Reptile-based Meta Attacker Training Algorithm

---

**Input:** Input images $\mathcal{X}$, corresponding gradients $\mathcal{G}$ as task $\mathcal{T}_i$
**Output:** Meta model $\mathcal{A}_\theta$
**Parameters:** $\alpha, \epsilon, K$

1. Randomly initialize $\theta$
2. **while not** converged **do**
3.    **for all** $\mathcal{T}_i$ **do**
4.      Sample K sample pairs $(\mathcal{X}, \mathcal{G})$ from $\mathcal{T}$
5.      Calculate the loss $\mathcal{L}_i(\mathcal{A}_\theta) = ||\mathcal{A}_\theta(\mathcal{X}_f) - \mathcal{G}_i^s||_2^2$
6.      Update $\theta_i' = \theta - \alpha\nabla_\theta\mathcal{L}_i(\mathcal{A}_\theta)$
7.    **end for**
8.    Update $\theta \leftarrow \theta + \epsilon\frac{1}{n}\sum_{i=1}^n(\theta_i' - \theta)$
9. **end while**

---

m times. When we directly output the gradient in the meta attacker, there is no need for additional query consumption. Here, the larger the update interval m, it means fewer queries, but the effect of the attacker will also decline.

---

**Algorithm 4.** Reptile-based Meta Attacking Algorithm

---

**Input:** Test image $x_0$ and its label t, meta attacker $\mathcal{A}_\theta$, target model $\mathcal{M}_{tar}$
**Output:** Adversarial example $\hat{x}_0$
**Parameters:** Iteration interval $m$

1. **for** t=0,1,2,... **do**
2.    **if** (t+1) mod m = 0 **then**
3.      Perform NES gradient estimation to generate $g_t$
4.      Fine-tune the meta attacker with $L = ||\mathcal{A}_\theta(x_t) - g_t||_2^2$
5.    **else**
6.      Generate $g_t$ from meta attacker
7.    **end if**
8.    Update $x_t = x_t + \beta g_t$;
9.    **if** $\mathcal{M}_{tar}(x_t) \neq t$ **then**
10.     return $x_t$;
11.   **else**
12.     $x_{t+1} = x_t$
13.   **end if**
14. **end for**

---

## 3.4 META-NES-ADAM Attack

The final attack approach is called META-NES-ADAM attack, which is composed of the above algorithms and forms a high-transferability black-box attack system, as shown in the Fig. 1. The whole attack process is divided into two parts: offline and online. Offline part needs to train classification models to pre-process gradient extraction, and then carry out meta learning based on Reptile to form an offline model. When running online, for each sample, the offline model are called and updated intermittently to achieve the purpose of quickly adapting to the target model. For the target model, we also integrate a very efficient ADAM-NES gradient estimation strategy, so that the whole attack process can run online highly efficiently.

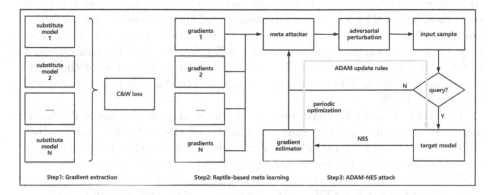

**Fig. 1.** The overall workflow is divided into three steps. The first step is gradient extraction. Based on the C&W loss from the logit layer, the input and corresponding gradients are extracted from the trained substitute models. The second step is Reptile-based meta learning. The third step is ADAM-NES attack. Here, NES is used as gradient estimator, ADAM is used to update and iterate, and the periodic optimization strategy is introduced to update meta attack model.

This paper uses a lot of advanced deep learning technologies, and they have been adopted by many researchers in their solutions, such as MetaAttack [21], which is similar to our attack process. The same point is that we all introduce meta learning strategy into the black-box attack, and achieve very good results. However, there are many differences between two attack methods, which are also our advantages:

1. **Gradient Estimation Strategy.** Instead of using the finite difference method as the final gradient estimation strategy, we introduce NES, which can improve the query efficiency. It is worth mentioning that in MetaAttack, in order to reduce the query number, the author sorts all the gradients and selects top-q coordinates for finite difference estimation. This step requires a certain amount of computing resources, and adopting the top-q method will reduce the accuracy of finite difference, while our method does not need these complex operations and the whole gradient estimation process can be completed highly efficiently.
2. **Perturbation Update Strategy.** Instead of using the simple superposition in FGSM, we employ ADAM-based iterative approximate update rules, which makes our perturbation iteration more accurate.

## 4    Experiments

### 4.1    Settings and Evaluation Metrics

In this paper, experiments are carried out on two datasets: MNIST and CIFAR10. On MNIST, models A and B are designed and well trained. The specific architectures of two models are shown in Table 1. In training, we set the batch size to 100, and each pixel is normalized to [0,1]. Model A has two convolutional layers and one fully connected layer, while model B has three convolutional layers. The accuracy of the test sets of the two models reaches 99.2%. On CIFAR10, we also set the batch size to 100, and each pixel is normalized to [0,1]. The two target models we used are ResNet-18[23] and WideResNet-28-10[24], and the accuracy is 93.1% and 93.7%. The performance of the model is shown in Table 2. The meta attack model architecture used in this paper is shown in Table 3.

For MNIST and CIFAR10, our search range of perturbation is limited to [0,0.4] and [0,0.03]. In the parameter selection of the finite difference method (FD), we set $\delta = 0.01$ by default. For all iterative attacks (including white-box attacks), we use the same step size $\alpha = 0.01$ on MNIST and $\alpha = 1.0$ on CIFAR10, and run 40 iterations on MNIST and 10 iterations on CIFAR10. For attack algorithms using NES, we set the number of iterations to 160 on MNIST and 20 on CIFAR10, and the number of samples n to 25 on MNIST and 200 on CIFAR10. All the standard deviations are 0.001. For attack algorithms optimized by meta learning, on MNIST, we set the attack interval to 8 and the number of iterations to 160 and the number of samples n to 200. On CIFAR10, we set the attack interval to 4 and the number of iterations to 80 and the number of samples n to 200 to keep the attack intensity close.

**Table 1.** Model architectures on MNIST. Conv is convolutional layer and FC is fully connected layer.

| A | B |
|---|---|
| Conv (64,5,5) + ReLU | Dropout (0.2) |
| Conv (64,5,5) + ReLU | Conv (64,8,8)+ReLU |
| Dropout (0.25) | Conv (128,6,6)+ReLU |
| FC (128) + ReLU | Conv (128,5,5)+ReLU |
| Dropout (0.5) | Dropout (0.5) |
| FC + Softmax | FC + Softmax |

We will use ASR, Avg. L2 and Avg. Queries as the evaluation metrics in the experiments.

1. **Attack Success Rate, ASR**. ASR is the main evaluation metric, which measures the success ratio of achieving the attack target: for untargeted

**Table 2.** Performance of target models

| Dataset | Classifier | Top-1 Acc. (%) |
|---------|-----------|----------------|
| MNIST | ModelA | 99.2 |
| MNIST | ModelB | 99.2 |
| CIFAR10 | ResNet18 | 93.1 |
| CIFAR10 | ResNet-28-10 | 93.7 |

**Table 3.** Meta attack model architectures, Conv is convolutional layer and DeConv is deconvolutional layer.

| MNIST | CIFAR10 |
|-------|---------|
| Conv (16,3,3,1) + ReLU + BN | Conv (32,3,3,1) + ReLU + BN |
| Conv (32,4,4,2) + ReLU + BN | Conv (64,4,4,2) + ReLU + BN |
| Conv (64,4,4,2) + ReLU + BN | Conv (128,4,4,2) + ReLU + BN |
| Conv (64,4,4,2) + ReLU + BN | Conv (256,4,4,2) + ReLU + BN |
| DeConv (64,4,4,2) + ReLU + BN | DeConv (256,4,4,2) + ReLU + BN |
| DeConv (32,3,3,2) + ReLU + BN | DeConv (128,4,4,2) + ReLU + BN |
| DeConv (16,4,4,2) + ReLU + BN | DeConv (64,4,4,2) + ReLU + BN |
| DeConv (8,4,4,2) + ReLU + BN | DeConv (32,3,3,1) + ReLU + BN |

attack, the model classification error is considered as success; For targeted attack, the model needs to be classified to the specified category before it can be considered as successful. It should be noted that the actual model is not completely correct, so we do not attack the samples without correct classification to evaluate the effectiveness of algorithms more accurately.

2. **Avg. L2**. To evaluate the perturbation, we use the average L2 distortion distance between the original image and the adversarial example as the evaluation metric: $|\hat{x} - x| = \frac{1}{N} \sum_{i=1} N||\hat{x}_i - x_i||_2$. When different attacks achieve similar attack success rate, the lower the Avg. L2 is, the better the attack effect is, because lower Avg. L2 means that it is harder to be perceived.

3. **Avg. Queries**. For the black-box attack, query number represents the average times the black-box attack needs to visit the model. The metric has strong practical significance, because in the real world system, visitors are usually not allowed to visit indefinitely. Under the premise of the same success rate, the attack algorithm with lower query consumption has stronger robustness and generalization ability.

## 4.2 Comparison

This section mainly compares the attack method proposed in this paper with the classic white-box attack and black-box attack methods. The results show that our attack has the similar attack success rate and L2 distance with other attacks, but it greatly reduces the query number.

**Comparison of Untargeted Attacks.** For untargeted attack, the attacker only needs to distort the classification result of target model to any other category to succeed. The results of various untargeted attacks on MNIST and CIFAR10 are shown in Table 4 and 5.

**Table 4.** Results of different types of untarget attacks on MNIST

| Attacks | Black | Model-A | | | Model-B | | |
|---|---|---|---|---|---|---|---|
| | | ASR | Avg. $L_2$ | Avg.#Q | ASR | Avg. $L_2$ | Avg. #Q |
| One-step attack | | | | | | | |
| FGSM | ✗ | 92.7% | 6.2 | N.A. | 91.4% | 6.9 | N.A |
| FD | ✓ | 94.1% | 5.9 | 1568 | 93.7% | 6.9 | 1568 |
| PCA-FD | ✓ | 90.5% | 6.0 | 200 | 93.2% | 6.5 | 200 |
| RG-FD | ✓ | 60.4% | 5.9 | 196 | 83.5% | 7.3 | 196 |
| Iterative attack | | | | | | | |
| $PGD_\infty$ | ✗ | 100.0% | 2.3 | N.A. | 100.0% | 1.3 | N.A |
| IFD | ✓ | 100.0% | 2.3 | 62720 | 100.0% | 1.3 | 62720 |
| PCA-IFD | ✓ | 100.0% | 2.8 | 8000 | 100.0% | 1.5 | 8000 |
| RG-IFD | ✓ | 90.3% | 2.6 | 7840 | 98.9% | 3.1 | 7840 |
| NES | ✓ | 99.8 % | 2.4 | 8000 | 100.0% | 1.5 | 8000 |
| ADAM-NES | ✓ | 100.0% | 2.6 | 8000 | 99.9% | 1.9 | 8000 |
| META-ADAM-NES | ✓ | 100.0% | 3.8 | 1450 | 100.0% | 2.9 | 946 |

We can observe that the performance of FD exceeds the white-box attack in most cases, which shows that it is an effective scheme to use the finite difference method to estimate the gradient and then carry out black-box attack. The first four rows and the middle four rows of data in the table represent one-step attack and iterative attack results of this algorithm. It shows that whether white-box or black-box attack is in iterative mode, the success rate of two different models on MNIST and CIFAR10 is greatly improved, which proves the effectiveness of iterative attack. In addition, we note that the L2 distance do not increase with iterations: On MNIST, the perturbation of iterative attack is half or more less than that of one-step attack. The same phenomenon can be observed in the results of CIFAR10. The results show that the structure of the deep neural network is most likely nonlinear, because when the attack mode changes from one-step to multi-step and the structure is a linear classifier, the gradient of the loss to the input is fixed and the direction of perturbation never changes; But for the nonlinear model, the direction of one step is not necessarily accurate, and the multi-step iteration can find a better direction through gradual adjustment. From the query number, the query efficiency of FD is extremely low, so we use RG (Random Grouping) and PCA to optimize it. For RG, the number of groups is set to 8. The results show that RG-FD can effectively reduce the query number of FD, and it is related to the number of groups: for one-step and iterative attacks, the query number is reduced to one eighth of the original on

**Table 5.** Results of different types of untarget attacks on CIFAR10

| Attacks | Black | ResNet18 | | | ResNet-28-10 | | |
|---|---|---|---|---|---|---|---|
| | | ASR | Avg. $L_2$ | Avg.#Q | ASR | Avg. $L_2$ | Avg. #Q |
| One-step attack | | | | | | | |
| FGSM | × | 89.1% | 1.6 | N.A. | 94.7% | 1.6 | N.A |
| FD | ✓ | 92.0% | 1.6 | 6144 | 93.5% | 1.6 | 6144 |
| PCA-FD | ✓ | 69.2% | 1.6 | 800 | 74.3% | 1.6 | 800 |
| RG-FD | ✓ | 63.8% | 1.6 | 800 | 69.4% | 1.6 | 800 |
| Iterative attack | | | | | | | |
| $PGD_\infty$ | × | 100.0% | 0.3 | N.A. | 100.0% | 0.3 | N.A |
| IFD | ✓ | 100.0% | 0.9 | 61440 | 100.0% | 1.0 | 61440 |
| PCA-IFD | ✓ | 99.0% | 0.6 | 8000 | 100.0% | 0.4 | 8000 |
| RG-IFD | ✓ | 99.8% | 0.4 | 7680 | 100.0% | 0.4 | 7680 |
| NES | ✓ | 99.7% | 0.7 | 8000 | 99.8% | 0.7 | 8000 |
| ADAM-NES | ✓ | 100.0% | 1.2 | 8000 | 100.0% | 1.2 | 8000 |
| META-ADAM-NES | ✓ | 100.0% | 1.2 | 960 | 99.8% | 1.2 | 960 |

both MNIST and CIFAR10. However, on MNIST, the success rate of one-step attack decreases by 33.7% when attacking model A and 10.2% when attacking model B. Similar results can be observed on CIFAR10. ASR is obviously the first factor to be considered in the attack, so we think that RG-FD does not have practical significance. In contrast, the effect of PCA-FD is better, and its success rate does not have much impact when the query number is similar to RG-FD.

Finally, according to the last three rows of data in the table, we can draw the following conclusions. The gradient estimation method using NES can achieve relatively high attack success rate with low query cost. The success rates of the two models on CIFAR10 are 99.7% and 99.8%, which are only 0.3% and 0.2% lower than those of FD, but the query number of NES are only one eighth of FD. The NES optimized by ADAM update rules can further improve ASR to 100%. Although negative effects are produced in some models, ADAM can actually improve NES as a whole. In particular, the meta attack model can greatly reduce the query number. META-NES-ADAM reduces the query number to 1450 and 946 on MNIST, which is 18.1% and 11.8% of the original. It performs better on CIFAR10, with only 12% of the original query number when attacking both two models. It can be seen that the introduction of meta learning strategy greatly improves the query efficiency of black-box attack, and does not sacrifice too much attack success rate.

**Comparison of Targeted Attacks.** In the scenario with high requirements, attackers are often required to specify the classification results of target model to a certain category, which is called targeted attack. The results of various targeted attacks on MNIST and CIFAR10 are shown in Tables 6 and 7.

We can clearly observe that the overall success rate of one-step targeted attack is low and less than 50%, so it is not suitable for black-box attack. Although iterative attack improves the success rate, it also greatly increases the query number. For example, the success rate of IFD on MNIST is 66.0% higher than that of FD, but at the same time, the query number becomes 40 times of the original. RG-IFD and PCA-IFD reduce the query number to some extent, but sacrifice too much success rate, so they can not be adopted in practice.

Similar to untargeted attack, we can also say that the gradient estimation method using NES can achieve relatively high attack success rate with low query cost in target attack and ADAM-NES can further improve ASR in most cases. Besides, on CIFAR10, The success rate of META-ADAM-NES is 97.4%, 15.6% higher than that of ADAM-NES and it reduces the query number by 72.0% on ResNet18. Although on ResNet28-10 the success rate is 92.8% and decreases by 2.3%, the query number is reduced by 63.6%. The same conclusion can be obtained on MNIST.

**Table 6.** Results of different types of target attacks on MNIST

| Attacks | Black | Model-A | | | Model-B | | |
|---|---|---|---|---|---|---|---|
| | | ASR | Avg. $L_2$ | Avg.#Q | ASR | Avg. $L_2$ | Avg. #Q |
| One-step attack | | | | | | | |
| FGSM | × | 30.5% | 6.2 | N.A. | 24.4% | 7.3 | N.A |
| FD | ✓ | 30.3% | 6.3 | 1568 | 24.0% | 7.2 | 1568 |
| PCA-FD | ✓ | 25.4% | 6.0 | 200 | 22.0% | 6.5 | 200 |
| RG-FD | ✓ | 13.5% | 6.0 | 196 | 11.9% | 7.5 | 196 |
| Iterative attack | | | | | | | |
| $PGD_\infty$ | × | 96.6% | 3.1 | N.A. | 99.0% | 1.9 | N.A |
| IFD | ✓ | 96.3% | 3.1 | 62720 | 99.5% | 1.9 | 62720 |
| PCA-IFD | ✓ | 88.1% | 3.8 | 8000 | 96.8% | 2.2 | 8000 |
| RG-IFD | ✓ | 55.3% | 2.5 | 7840 | 89.0% | 2.3 | 7840 |
| NES | ✓ | 82.0 % | 3.2 | 8000 | 97.6% | 2.2 | 8000 |
| ADAM-NES | ✓ | 86.2% | 3.1 | 8000 | 96.6% | 2.3 | 8000 |
| META-ADAM-NES | ✓ | 94.7% | 4.7 | 2960 | 99.1% | 4.0 | 1960 |

## 4.3   Effects of Attack Methods under Different Parameters

This section compares the attack effects of different attack methods under different intensity. The results are shown in Fig. 2 and 3 where X-axis represents the step size and Y-axis represents the attack success rate. The two figures show the attack success rate of different attack methods using different step sizes when

**Table 7.** Results of different types of target attacks on CIFAR10

| Attacks | Black | ResNet18 | | | ResNet-28-10 | | |
|---|---|---|---|---|---|---|---|
| | | ASR | Avg. $L_2$ | Avg.#Q | ASR | Avg. $L_2$ | Avg. #Q |
| One-step attack | | | | | | | |
| FGSM | × | 33.6% | 1.6 | N.A. | 41.2% | 1.6 | N.A |
| FD | ✓ | 34.5% | 1.6 | 6144 | 42.2% | 1.6 | 6144 |
| PCA-FD | ✓ | 21.3% | 1.6 | 800 | 23.1% | 1.6 | 800 |
| RG-FD | ✓ | 17.3% | 1.6 | 800 | 20.6% | 1.6 | 800 |
| Iterative attack | | | | | | | |
| $PGD_\infty$ | × | 99.5% | 0.5 | N.A. | 100.0% | 0.5 | N.A |
| IFD | ✓ | 100.0% | 0.6 | 61440 | 100.0% | 0.6 | 61440 |
| PCA-IFD | ✓ | 75.0% | 0.9 | 8000 | 74.3% | 1.0 | 8000 |
| RG-IFD | ✓ | 88.0% | 0.6 | 7680 | 89.0% | 0.6 | 7680 |
| NES | ✓ | 81.8 % | 1.1 | 8000 | 95.1% | 0.7 | 8000 |
| ADAM-NES | ✓ | 91.9% | 1.1 | 8000 | 93.3% | 1.1 | 8000 |
| META-ADAM-NES | ✓ | 97.4% | 1.3 | 2244 | 92.8% | 1.4 | 2914 |

attacking model A on MNIST and ResNet18 on CIFAR10. Here, we mainly use the following attacks to compare: white-box attack: iterative FGS; Black box: PCA-based FD, NES, ADAM-NES and META-ADAM-NES. Because of the weak one-step attack, we do not adopt any one-step mode for the sake of fairness of comparison; At the same time, due to the original finite difference method has high query number, it has no practical significance. This paper uses PCA-based FD with the close of query number to compare, which is because the PCA optimization method is more successful than RG in ASR and the query number is optimized to some extent; The remaining three methods are the comparison of the improvement schemes proposed by us. The practical effect of each module proposed in this paper can be proved from the experimental results.

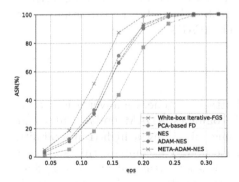

**Fig. 2.** Attack results on Model-A with $L_\infty$-norm

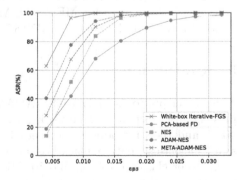

**Fig. 3.** Attack results on ResNet-18 with $L_\infty$-norm

From the experimental results, we can draw the following conclusions:

1. PCA-based FD relies on datasets, which can be observed from the results of MNIST and CIFAR10. It can achieve better effect on MNIST, but worse on CIFAR10.One of the possible reasons is that the distribution of MNIST is relatively simple while the pixel range of images on CIFAR10 is large. Therefore, PCA can not learn the overall data distribution as quickly as MNIST, leading to PCA can not provide an effective direction for black box attacks. However, a series of NES-based black-box attack methods proposed in this paper do not depend on the strength of datasets, and can better transfer between different datasets, which is one of the advantages of our methods.

2. ADAM-NES can effectively enhance the attack strength of NES. It can be observed from the two figures that the success rate of ADAM-NES can achieve stable improvement under various attack intensities, and this conclusion is applicable to different datasets and different models. This is because ADAM update rules make full use of the first-order historical information of the gradient. Compared with the original attack method which simply superimposes historical information, the gradient direction of ADAM is more accurate. At the same time, due to the introduction of the first-order momentum, the gradient direction in the iterative attack process is more stable. If there is fluctuation between iterations, the effective attack strength will be offset, and ADAM update rules can better alleviate the problem caused by this phenomenon.

3. The meta learning based attack method has little influence on ASR. According to the introduction of this paper, the role of meta learning is to greatly reduce the query number of black-box attack and improve the attack efficiency. The improvement design of ASR is limited, but we can still observe that when the perturbation intensity increases gradually, the success rate of META-ADAM-NES gradually approaches that of ADAM-NES. It should be noted that META-ADAM-NES on MNIST even exceeds the original algorithm under some perturbations, which shows the effectiveness of meta learning. The attack interval of meta model on MNIST is 8, and that on CIFAR10 is 4, which means that META-ADAM-NES reduces the perturbation by at least 8 times and 4 times on MNIST and CIFAR10.

## 5   Conclusion

This paper proposes META-NES-ADAM attack to generate adversarial examples against deep neural networks, which combines ADAM update rules and NES, and then introduces the meta learning, obtaining a high-transferability and efficient-estimation black-box attack method. We compare this approach with other classic one-step and iterative black-box attack algorithms, finding that it reduce query number by a wide margin while sacrificing a little attack success rate. Besides, We also discuss the benefits of NES, and the reasons for introducing ADAM and meta learning.

**Acknowledgments.** This work is supported by the National Key Research and Development Program of China (No.2020YFB1807500).

# References

1. Chen, P.Y., Zhang, H., Sharma, Y., et al.: Zoo: Zeroth order optimization based black-box attacks to deep neural networks without training substitute models. In: Proceedings of the 10th ACM Workshop on Artificial Intelligence and Security, pp. 15–26 (2017)
2. Tu, C.C., Ting, P., Chen, P.Y., et al.: AutoZOOM: autoencoder-based zeroth order optimization method for attacking black-box neural networks. AAAI **33**, 742–749 (2019)
3. Cheng, S., Dong, Y., Pang, T., et al.: Improving black-box adversarial attacks with a transfer-based prior. In: Advances in Neural Information Processing Systems, pp. 10934–10944 (2019)
4. Ilyas, A., Engstrom, L., Athalye, A., et al.: Black-box adversarial attacks with limited queries and information. ArXiv preprint arXiv:1804.08598 (2018)
5. Goodfellow, I.J., Shlens, J., Szegedy, C.: Explaining and harnessing adversarial examples. In: ICLR (2015)
6. Madry, A., Makelov, A,, Schmidt, L., et al.: Towards deep learning models resistant to adversarial attacks. In: ICLR (2018)
7. Moosavi-Dezfooli, S.M., Fawzi, A., Frossard, P.: Deepfool: a simple and accurate method to fool deep neural networks. In: Proceedings of the IEEE Conference On Computer Vision and Pattern Recognition, pp. 2574–2582 (2016)
8. Carlini, N., Wagner, D.: Towards evaluating the robustness of neural networks. In: 2017 IEEE Symposium On Security And Privacy (sp), pp. 39–57 (2017)
9. Dong, Y., Liao, F., Pang, T., et al.: Boosting adversarial attacks with momentum. In: Proceedings of the IEEE Conference on Computer Vision and Pattern Recognition, pp. 9185–9193 (2018)
10. Dong, Y., Pang, T., Su, H., et al.: Evading defenses to transferable adversarial examples by translation-invariant attacks. In: Proceedings of the IEEE Conference on Computer Vision and Pattern Recognition, pp. 4312–4321 (2019)
11. Lin, J., Song, C., He, K., et al.: Nesterov accelerated gradient and scale invariance for adversarial attacks. In: ICLR (2020)
12. Papernot, N., Mcdaniel, P., Goodfellow, I., et al.: Practical black-box attacks against machine learning. In: Computer And Communications Security, pp. 506–519 (2017)
13. Spall, J.C.: Introduction to stochastic search and optimization: estimation, simulation, and control. John Wiley & Sons (2005)
14. Bhagoji, A.N., He, W., Li, B., Song, D.: Practical black-box attacks on deep neural networks using efficient query mechanisms. In: Ferrari, V., Hebert, M., Sminchisescu, C., Weiss, Y. (eds.) ECCV 2018. LNCS, vol. 11216, pp. 158–174. Springer, Cham (2018). https://doi.org/10.1007/978-3-030-01258-8_10
15. Salimans, T., Ho, J., Chen, X., et al.: Evolution strategies as a scalable alternative to reinforcement learning. ArXiv preprint arXiv:1703.03864 (2017)
16. Huang, Z., Zhang, T.: Black-box adversarial attack with transferable model-based embedding. In: ICLR (2020)
17. Inn, C., Abbeel, P., Levine, S.: Model-Agnostic meta-learning for fast adaptation of deep networks. In: ICML (2017)

18. Nichol, A., Achiam, J., Schulman, J.: On first-order meta-learning algorithms. ArXiv preprint arXiv:1803.02999 (2018)
19. Zügner, D., Günnemann, S.: Adversarial attacks on graph neural networks via meta learning. ArXiv preprint arXiv:1902.08412(2019)
20. Edmunds, R., Golmant, N., Ramasesh, V., et al.: Transferability of adversarial attacks in model-agnostic meta-learning. In: Deep Learning and Security Workshop (DLSW) (2017)
21. Du, J., Zhang, H., Zhou, J.T., et al.: Query-efficient meta attack to deep neural networks. In: ICLR (2020)
22. Kingma, D.P., Ba, J.A.: A method for stochastic optimization. ArXiv preprint arXiv:1412.6980 (2014)
23. He, K., Zhang, X., Ren, S., et al.: Deep residual learning for image recognition. In: Proceedings of the IEEE Conference On Computer Vision and Pattern Recognition, pp. 770–778 (2016)
24. Zagoruyko, S., Komodakis, N.: Wide residual networks. ArXiv preprint arXiv:1605.07146 (2016)

# Coreference Resolution for Cybersecurity Entity: Towards Explicit, Comprehensive Cybersecurity Knowledge Graph with Low Redundancy

Zhengyu Liu[1], Haochen Su[1], Nannan Wang[1], and Cheng Huang[1,2](✉)

[1] School of Cyber Science and Engineering, Sichuan University, Chengdu, China
opcodesec@gmail.com
[2] Anhui Province Key Laboratory of Cyberspace Security Situation Awareness and Evaluation, Hefei, China

**Abstract.** Cybersecurity Knowledge Graph (CKG) has become an important structure to address the current cybersecurity crises and challenges, due to its powerful ability to model, mine, and leverage massive security intelligence data. To construct a comprehensive and explicit CKG with low redundancy, coreference resolution (CR) plays a crucial role as the core step in knowledge fusion. Although the research on coreference resolution techniques in Natural Language Processing (NLP) field has made notable achievements, there is still a great gap in the cybersecurity field. Therefore, the paper first investigates the effectiveness of the existing CR models on cybersecurity corpus and presents Cyber-Coref, an end-to-end coreference resolution model for cybersecurity entities. We propose an entity type prediction network that not only helps to improve mention representations and provide type consistency checks, but also enables the model to distinguish the coreference among different entity types and thus run the coreference resolution more granular. To overcome the problem of implicit contextual modeling adopted by the existing CR models, we innovative propose an explicit contextual modeling method for the coreference resolution task based on semantic text matching. Finally, we improve the span representation by introducing lexical and syntactic features. The experimental results demonstrate that CyberCoref improves the F1 values on the cybersecurity corpus by 6.9% compared to existing CR models.

**Keywords:** Coreference resolution · Security intelligence · Semantic text matching · Entity type

## 1 Introduction

With the development of artificial intelligence technology, its application in the cybersecurity domain is now striding forward from perception intelligence to cognition intelligence. Sufficient and well-formed data helps to realize the

© ICST Institute for Computer Sciences, Social Informatics and Telecommunications Engineering 2023
Published by Springer Nature Switzerland AG 2023. All Rights Reserved
F. Li et al. (Eds.): SecureComm 2022, LNICST 462, pp. 89–108, 2023.
https://doi.org/10.1007/978-3-031-25538-0_6

"perception" stage, however the key to achieving the leap to the next stage is to refine and fuse multi-source, multi-dimensional, and heterogeneous data into knowledge, making it easier for further reasoning.

The huge amount of cybersecurity intelligence data including threat intelligence, vulnerability intelligence, and asset intelligence, provide solid data foundation for the development of intelligent security. Among them, threat intelligence portrays key information such as threat source, attack purpose, attack techniques and tactics, etc. Vulnerability intelligence includes information related to existing disclosed vulnerabilities such as impact system and software, its version, patch information, associated attack events, etc. Asset intelligence includes information related to internal assets such as accounts, servers, system software, defense mechanisms, etc. How to model, integrate, and update the security intelligence knowledge base to support further reasoning determines the effectiveness of intelligence data in actual cybersecurity battlefields and becomes the core problem that related works are trying to solve.

Knowledge Graph, as its powerful ability to correlate and fuse multi-source heterogeneous data, as well as to support precise semantic retrieval and intelligent inference analysis, has become the optimal solution for current security intelligence carriers. Existing research on Cybersecurity Knowledge Graph (CKG) construction mainly focuses on information extraction, including steps such as entity recognition [1–7], relationship extraction [8,9], and event extraction [10]. However, there is still a gap in the study of knowledge fusion, including entity disambiguation and coreference resolution steps.

Coreference resolution is the process of linking different nouns, pronouns, noun phrases, and other expressions in a text that refer to the same entity. Those various expressions of entities are defined as mentions, which increase the flow and richness of the text, but also make it more obscure to understand. It is necessary to address the reference phenomena that commonly occur in unstructured security intelligence to extract complete and valuable knowledge. As shown in Fig. 1, coreference resolution will further improve and enrich the description of cybersecurity entities at different levels and perspectives, making the extracted entities and relationships more specific, clear, and comprehensive. In addition, it links the general and vague expression of entities to those more specific, reducing the data redundancy of the CKG and thus improving its overall quality.

Although there are extensive studies on coreference resolution in the NLP field, the challenges when running coreference resolution on articles involving cybersecurity domain specific entities shouldn't be overlooked. To be more specific, by comparing the cybersecurity corpus which we constructed in this work with the general corpus dataset Ontonotes 5.0 [11], we found that: (1) cybersecurity entities are longer in length and contain more noun phrases as well as verb-object structured phrases. (2) references in cybersecurity documents have a longer distance on average. (3) cybersecurity corpus has a smaller lexicon, which results in the phenomenon of the same or looked-like spans belonging to different coreference clusters is more frequent. (4) There are more domain-specific words, abbreviations, and aliases in the cybersecurity corpus. In terms of approach, the

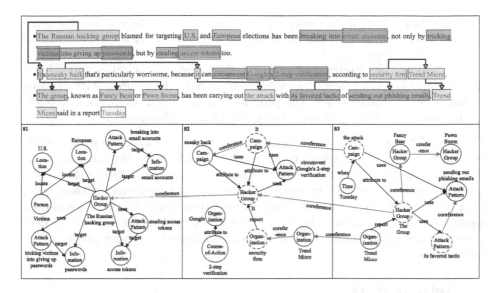

**Fig. 1.** Motivating example of coreference resolution on cybersecurity entities

existing state-of-the-art coreference resolution models heavily rely on BERT or its variants which are pre-trained on the large-scale general corpus and do not present expected performance when applied to domain-specific corpus [12–14]. Therefore, considering the above challenges, we need to review and evaluate the effectiveness of existing models on cybersecurity corpus and then further propose the best coreference resolution model for cybersecurity entities, targeting the characteristics of cybersecurity corpus.

Overall, our work's main contributions can be summarized as follows:

- We present CyberCoref, a document-level end-to-end coreference resolution model for cybersecurity entities, that can identify and cluster the referring cybersecurity entities within unstructured security intelligence reports in different kinds of grammatical forms including pronouns, noun phrases, verb object structures, security domain-specific structures, and etc.
- The paper proposes a type prediction network to introduce entity-type information which enables the model to improve mention representation and provide type consistency check between mention pairs. In addition, the entity-type information enables the model to distinguish the coreference relationship of different entity types and thus perform the coreference resolution task more granular.
- To overcome the problem of implicit contextual modeling adopted by the existing coreference models, we innovative propose an explicit contextual modeling method for coreference resolution task based on semantic text matching. It uses convolutional neural networks to extract the interaction information between utterances so as to emphasize the semantic relevance of the mentions' corresponding sentences. Besides, to resolve mentions with long expressions and complex syntactic structures, CyberCoref uses an additive

attention mechanism to incorporate lexical and syntactic features for head-word finding in span representations and help the model learn more general linguistic patterns.
- To validate the effectiveness of the CyberCoref, we collected and labeled a total of 536 documents including vulnerability disclosures, APT reports, and security-related news. The proposed dataset contains 43271 cybersecurity entities, 48745 coreference links, and 6657 coreference clusters.

The rest of this paper is organized as follows: Sect. 2 presents the related work. Section 3 presents the baseline model and the details of the three key improvements proposed in this paper. Section 4 shows the dataset construction, experimental setup, the comparison results of our approach and existing coreference models on cybersecurity corpus, and the ablation study. Section 5 provides a qualitative analysis of the proposed CyberCoref to demonstrate our model's strengths and limitations. The last section concludes this paper and proposes future work.

## 2 Related Work

In this section, we first review the recent landmark works on neural network-based coreference resolutions in the NLP field, and then analyze the research on coreference resolution in the cybersecurity domain.

**Coreference Resolution.** In recent years, adopting the idea of representation learning, the neural network-based coreference resolution models have replaced the traditional machine learning models on manual feature extraction, achieving better results in datasets such as GAP [15] and OntoNotes [11] used in the Conll-2012 shared task. Wiseman et al. 2015 [16] proposed the idea of using neural networks to learn a better feature representation for mention extraction and coreference resolution on the basis of the manually extracted features. Then, to bring in coreference cluster features, Wiseman et al. 2016 [17] used recurrent neural networks to learn the global representation of entity clusters. Similarly, Clark and Manning 2016 [13] used pooling operations to generate feature representations of referring cluster pairs based on mention pair features. The great milestone work of Lee et al. in 2017 [18] completely discarded hand-extracted features and instead used word embedding models as well as deep neural networks to generate feature representations based on the idea of representation learning. The proposed mention-ranking architecture, the objective function, and the representation of mentions and mention pairs in this work were all accepted, followed by numerous subsequent works on coreference resolution [19–22]. In 2018, Lee et al. [19] accomplished two important improvements to their previous model: the introduction of higher-order inference and the coarse-to-fine pruning algorithm. The former takes the idea of the entity-level coreference resolution framework and imports global information about the coreference cluster to the mention representation. The latter improves the accuracy of candidate antecedent filtering with bearable computational complexity and memory space occupation.

As the large-scale pre-trained model BERT swept various NLP tasks as the best model in 2018, Joshi et al. 2019 [20] used BERT instead of the original word embedding and BiLSTM-based context extraction methods to generate span representation with a substantial improvement in performance on the baseline dataset. Due to the importance of span representation in the coreference resolution task, Joshi [21] released SpanBERT in the same year which is more suitable for span boundary sensitive tasks, and achieves better results compared to the original BERT model. In addition, the corefBERT from Ye et al. 2020 [22], which uses coreference resolution as the self-training task of the BERT model, also has excellent performance.

The word-level coreference resolution model was proposed by Kirstain et al. in 2021 [23]. Dobrovolskii [24] inherited the idea from Kirstain et al. which is to accomplish the task from the word level rather than the span level, achieving similar results to the span-based coreference resolution model on the baseline datasets. The word-level model has the advantages of less search space in the coreference resolution step and avoidance of incorrect pruning in the mention detection step. However, using word embeddings directly instead of span representations will lead to missing certain information, especially when dealing with long and complex mentions. To evaluate the effectiveness of the word-level model in the cybersecurity domain, we compared their model in Sect. 4.

**Coreference Resolution in the Field of Security.** Although topics such as information extraction and knowledge graph construction [1–10,25,26] have been widely studied within the cybersecurity domain in recent years, research on coreference resolution in the cybersecurity domain is still relatively scarce. Hu et al. [27] modeled the coreference resolution task jointly with the relation extraction, treating the coreference relation as one of the inter-entity relation types. Zhang et al. [28] first extracts mentions from a given document by using a sequence labeling neural network, and then applies a random forest algorithm with custom rules to complete the resolution of extracted mentions. However, it should be noted that their works consider the coreference resolution as a cascading task of entity recognition that may suffer from error propagation. And also, their approaches regarding mention detection as a sequence labeling task are not able to cope with the nested entities natively, which would result in low recall rates.

## 3 Methodology

In this work, we used the model proposed in Joshi et al. 2019 [20] as our baseline model, which has achieved outstanding results on the OntoNotes 5.0 general corpus. The model adopts the higher-order inference as well as the coarse-to-fine pruning algorithm proposed by Lee et al. [18] and continues the classic task modeling, learning objectives, score architecture, and span representation proposed by Lee et al. 2017 [13]. Subsection 3.1 will focus on an overview of our baseline model.

As discussed in Sect. 1, running coreference references on the cybersecurity corpus is going to face more challenges than the general corpus. So, in order to better adapt to the characteristics of cybersecurity entities, we make the following improvements (Fig. 2) to the baseline model. First, to avoid the over-reliance on the similarity of words, lexical and syntactic features are introduced in the span representation to help the model learn more general language rules and improve its generalization ability, as detailed in Sect. 3.2. Secondly, inspired by the fact that human beings would significantly narrow down the search space by sifting out the mentions in the irrelevant sentences when finding the most appropriate antecedent, this work proposes an explicit contextual modeling network based on semantic text matching, as detailed in Subsect. 3.3. Finally, considering that different entity types do not share the same degree of reference matching, this work proposes an entity-type prediction network to keep the model aware of entity types in both mention detection and coreference resolution steps, as detailed in Subsect. 3.4.

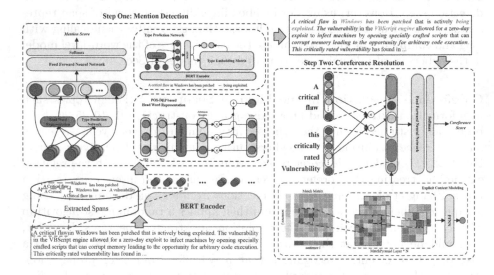

**Fig. 2.** Overview of CyberCoref architecture.

## 3.1   Baseline

The modeling for the coreference resolution task is shown below. Given a document $D$ containing $T$ words, it corresponds to $N = T(T + 1)/2$ spans. For all spans $i$ ($1 \leq i \leq N$), each of them could find an antecedent $y_i \in Y(i) = \{\epsilon, 1, 2, \ldots, i - 1\}$. If the span $i$ corresponds to a dummy antecedent $\epsilon$, it means that the span is not a mention, or the mention does not have a corresponding antecedent.

After encoding text segments by the BERT model, we can get the embedding of each token in the span $i$. Based on that, we can get the representation of the span $i$, i.e. $g_i$, including embeddings of its start and end positions, respectively, headword representation generated by an attention mechanism, and the span width feature. Through the mention score function $s_m(\cdot)$, we will get the score used to determine whether the span is a mention or not.

$$s_m(i) = FFNN_m(g_i) \tag{1}$$

For the spans $i$ and $j$ as the extracted mention and its candidate antecedent, respectively, we follow the coarse-to-fine pruning algorithm [18], using a simplified version of the coreference scoring function $s_c(\cdot)$ and a more precise coreference scoring function $s_a(\cdot)$ to determine whether there is a coreference relationship between them. For coreference scoring, the representation of the mention pairs contains $g_i$, $g_j$, $g_i \circ g_j$ and other features including representation of the distance between them.

$$s_c(i,j) = g_i^\top W_c g_j \tag{2}$$

$$s_a(i,j) = FFNN_a([g_i, g_j, g_i \circ g_j, \phi_a]) \tag{3}$$

where $W_c$ is a learned weight matrix, $\cdot$ denotes the dot product, $\circ$ denotes element-wise multiplication, and $FFNN$ denotes a feed-forward neural network that computes a nonlinear mapping from input to output vectors.

When it comes to specific inference, a three-step pruning will be performed to ensure computational efficiency. To start with, mentions will be filtered from all spans by using the unary function $s_m(\cdot)$. Then, for each extracted mention, we select top $K$ mentions as its candidate antecedents based on the score $s_m(i) + s_m(j) + s_c(i,j)$, and finally use the function $s_a(i,j)$ to achieve refined coreference scoring.

## 3.2   Combining Lexical and Syntactic Features

Suggested by the work [18] that generating the headword representation from word embedding vectors would still be error prone. Therefore, to more correctly represent those headwords in span representation, we use an additive attention mechanism based on lexical and syntactic dependency features instead of the original attention mechanism which only based on words themselves.

Given a span $i$ with a length $l$, the corresponding word embedding, part-of-speech embedding and syntactic dependencies embedding are $S_i \in \mathbb{R}^{l \times d_{word}}$, $P_i \in \mathbb{R}^{l \times d_{pos}}$ and $R_i \in \mathbb{R}^{l \times d_{deprel}}$, respectively. The additive attention scoring function $a$ and attention weights $\alpha$ based on lexical and syntactic dependency features are shown below. Where the lexical embedding matrix and word embedding matrix will be separately used as the key $K$ and the value $V$ of attention, and the syntactic role embedding matrix will be used as the query $Q$.

$$a_t = W_v^\top tanh(w_p p_t + w_r r_t) \tag{4}$$

$$\alpha_t^i = \frac{exp(a_t)}{\sum_{k=START(i)}^{END(i)} exp(a_k)} \tag{5}$$

where $w_p \in \mathbb{R}^{h \times d_{pos}}$ and $w_r \in \mathbb{R}^{h \times d_{deprel}}$ are the learnable weight matrices and $\alpha_{i,t}$ is the attention weight of the token corresponding to the position $t$ in span $i$. Therefore, obtained by the attention mechanism, the final headword representation of span $i$, i.e. $\widehat{s_i}$, which incorporates part-of-speech information and syntactic dependencies, is shown below.

$$\widehat{s_i} = \sum_{t=START(i)}^{END(i)} \alpha_t^i \cdot s_t^i \tag{6}$$

In addition, mean pooling of embedding of part-of-speech and syntactic features of the span are taken separately, and we concatenate them with the embedding of type information (detailed in Subsect. 3.4) and length of span to get the feature vector $\phi_m$. In summary, the representation of the span $i$ is shown below.

$$\phi_m(i) = [F_{type(i)}, F_{width(i)}, F_{pos(i)}, F_{deprel(i)}] \tag{7}$$

$$g_i = [s_{START(i)}^i, s_{END(i)}^i, \widehat{s_i}, \phi_{m(i)}] \tag{8}$$

## 3.3 Explicit Contextual Modeling

The baseline model uses only implicit contextual modeling, i.e., it relies on the contextual semantic word embeddings generated by the pre-trained model to reflect the relevance of encoded segments. However, we note that humans will first screen out candidate antecedents from completely irrelevant or conflicting statements and keep a small set of mentions that appear in closely related sentences based on context relevance. This intuitive idea is consistent with the fact that cybersecurity documents often repeatedly present descriptions of events, exploits, vulnerabilities, and attackers from different perspectives and degrees. Therefore, the relevance of context can become a very important factor in the task of coreference resolution. We aim to learn from semantic text matching models to explicitly model a closer context of mentions and their candidate antecedents, to determine whether their contexts have the same discussion objects or convey similar meanings.

Due to the powerful semantic modeling capability of the BERT model, the word embedding vector contains sufficient information for determining the semantic similarity of sentence pairs. Therefore, a simple and effective way is used in this paper to extract the local similarity features from the token-level matching matrix which can reflect the correlation between utterances. The main network structure refers to the MatchPyramid proposed by the work of Pang et al. [29], which uses a hierarchical CNN network to extract local information at a different level and introduces a dynamic pooling mechanism to handle pairs of sentences with different lengths.

For the extracted mention $i$ and the candidate antecedent $j$, we can get the corresponding sentence $S_i$ and $S_j$ with the length $n$ and $m$, respectively. The sentence representation $S_i = \{s_1^i, s_2^i, \ldots, s_n^i\}$ and $S_j = \{s_1^j, s_2^j, \ldots, s_m^j\}$, as well as the initial matching matrix $M$, can be obtained based on the embedding of each token. Calculation of each position of the initial matching matrix is shown as follows, where $Sim(\cdot)$ represents the word similarity score function, which can be dot product or cosine similarity. Finally, the MatchPyramid will be applied to extract features from the matching matrix and is followed by a feed forward network to get the fixed length $F_{sent-pair}$ feature which represents the contextual relevance.

$$M_{tk} = Sim(s_t^i, s_k^j) \tag{9}$$

$$F_{sent-pair} = FFNN_{context}(MatchPyramid(M)) \tag{10}$$

## 3.4   Entity Type Information

In the process of mention detection, for the span $i$ and the embedding $X_i$ of the sentence where $i$ is located encoded by the BERT model, we can get its corresponding embedding vector $\{x_{START(i)}^i, ..., x_{END(i)}^i\}$. Similarly, we use the idea of mention representation to predict the corresponding type of each span. The span representation $h_i$ used for type prediction consists of the embedding of the start and end token, the headword representation fused by the attention mechanism, and the feature to encode the span width. We use the embedding $X_i$ that represents a closer context (i.e., the sentence embedding) instead of the segment embedding $S_i$ to make the network more convenient for the pre-training on the type prediction subtask, which helps the network learn to classify the types of span.

$$a_t = FFNN_\alpha(X_i) \tag{11}$$

$$\alpha_t^i = \frac{exp(a_t)}{\sum_{k=START(i)}^{END(i)} exp(a_k)} \tag{12}$$

$$\widehat{x}_i = \sum_{t=START(i)}^{END(i)} \alpha_t^i \cdot x_t^i \tag{13}$$

$$h_i = [x_{START(i)}^i, x_{END(i)}^i, \widehat{x}_i, F_{width(i)}] \tag{14}$$

Next, we use a feed forward neural network to score the likelihoods of different types. For the type given the highest possibility, we also get its embedding $e_{type(i)} \in \mathbb{R}^{d_{type}}$ .

$$t_i = FFNN_{type}(h_i) \tag{15}$$

$$e_{type(i)} = Embedding_{type}(argmax(t_i)) \tag{16}$$

$$F_{type} = [t_i, e_{type(i)}] \tag{17}$$

During the coreference resolution, to provide an additional check of mention-pair type consistency, we add their type embeddings as well as the cosine similarity of their type likelihood scores to the mention-pair representation. Finally, $\phi_a$ is calculated as shown below:

$$\phi_a(i,j) = [F_{distance}, F_{sent-pair}, e_{type(i)}, e_{type(j)}, cos(t_i, t_j)] \tag{18}$$

To help the network generate the correct entity types based on the span and the given context, we pre-trained it with the entity type prediction subtask. The training samples are obtained from the mention detection steps of the baseline model, including the mentions and their corresponding sentences. The correct mentions are labeled with their corresponding entity types, while the wrongly extracted mentions are labeled as None. After sufficient training on this multi-classification subtask, the entity type prediction network can better distinguish between true and false mentions with similar boundaries and assign the correct entity type.

## 4    Evaluation

In this section, we will design a series of experiments to demonstrate the effectiveness and superiority of our proposed model CyberCoref especially towards the cybersecurity entity coreference resolution. Firstly, we will provide a comprehensive introduction to our dataset. Then, we clarify the experiment setup and show the results of CyberCoref and other representative coreference models in the NLP field on our dataset. Finally, we present a thorough ablation study on the proposed networks of CyberCoref.

### 4.1    Dataset

The experimental dataset is derived from publicly available security intelligence, including vulnerability disclosures[1], APT reports[2], and security-related news [10]. Our work refers to the ontology construction of UCO [30] and the threat intelligence sharing framework STIX2.1 [3] and redefines 29 cybersecurity entity types. And then we manually annotated 43,271 cybersecurity entities and 48,745 intra-document coreference links, which construct 6,657 coreference clusters, in 536 security-related articles. The specific entity definitions and annotation guidelines are detailed in our open source repository[4].

Regarding the data processing, we first extract plain text from rich text documents (e.g. pdf or html), and remove all embedded images, tables, and inserted code segments. Then we perform a simple data cleaning by replacing all non-ascii encoded characters with spaces and rewrite the protected forms from clicks by mistake of IP addresses, email addresses, and web addresses. Finally, we segment the long articles to ensure the best performance of the model.

The annotation of the dataset is conducted on the Brat platform [31]. The dataset annotation processes are as follows: firstly, we annotated the entities according to the defined entity types. Then, we annotate the coreference relations between the annotated entities, at the same time, proofread our previous annotation. The whole annotation work was done by two graduate students and one senior undergraduate student, which all major in cybersecurity.

---

[1]  https://github.com/pburkart/Vulnerability-Research-Blogs.
[2]  https://github.com/CyberMonitor/APT_CyberCriminal_Campaign_Collections.
[3]  https://oasis-open.github.io/cti-documentation/stix/intro.
[4]  https://github.com/jackfromeast/CyberCoref.

## 4.2 Evaluation Setup

The CyberCoref model is implemented with reference to the Bert-based c2f-coref model proposed by Joshi et al. 2019 [20], which is now open-sourced to the Github repository.

**Model Architecture.** We take the SpanBERT for word embedding, which is a pre-trained model from Hugging Face[5] at the based size with an embedding dimension of 768. We use the CoreNLP[6] for both part-of-speech and syntactic features extraction, and they all have an embedding dimension of 64. The embedding dimension of both entity type and context relevance features is 64 as well, and the distance and width features are binned into the following buckets [1, 2, 3, 4, 5–7, 8–15, 16–31, 32–63, 64–127, 128–255, 256–511, 512–1023, 1024+] and then embedded as 16-dimensional size vectors. The number of MatchPyramid layers is 2, the convolution kernel sizes are $5 \times 5$ and $3 \times 3$, the pooling layer sizes are $10 \times 10$ and $5 \times 5$, and the numbers of feature maps are 8 and 16, respectively. The hidden layer sizes of the feedforward neural networks $FFNN_m$ and $FFNN_a$ for mention and coreference scoring are both 1024, the hidden layer sizes of $FFNN_\alpha$ and $FFNN_{type}$ in the entity type prediction network are 512 and 1024, respectively, and in the context relevance representation network $FFNN_{context}$, the hidden layer size is 128. We adopt LeakyReLU [32]as the activation function, and the dropout rate is set to 0.3.

**Inference.** The pruning threshold $\lambda$ is set to 0.3, the maximum span length is 20. For each extracted mention or word, the number $K = 50$ of candidate antecedents are going to be selected. Referring to the experimental results in the work of Joshi et al. [20], the maximum segment length is set to 384 for word embedding. We use the higher-order inference algorithm based on antecedent distribution proposed by Lee et al. 2018 [19], and the number of iteration rounds is set to 2.

**Learning.** The optimizer for the models is AdamW, with a learning rate of 1e-5 for the pre-training weights of the BERT model and 3e-4 for the rest of the network structures. Such a learning rate setting allows the optimization of the models as a whole to be adjusted to the optimal position simultaneously. The training batch size for all models is 1, i.e., one article at a time. The models are all trained for up to 60 epochs. The training and validation sets are randomly divided in a 4:1 ratio. In addition, to avoid any degree of data leakage, training samples for the entity type prediction subtask are all from the training set.

---

[5] https://huggingface.co/.
[6] https://stanfordnlp.github.io/CoreNLP/.

**Compared Models.** For the replicated models used for comparison, the model architecture hyperparameters are set with reference to their original papers, and the inference parameters and training parameters are the same as above, except for the following notes. For the e2e-coref model proposed by Lee et al. 2017 [18], the optimizer is Adam with a learning rate of 3e-4. The word-level coreference resolution model wl-coref [24] also uses based size SpanBERT to complete word embedding, and the maximum segment length is set to 512. The remaining BERT-based span-level models [20–22] are all set to a maximum segment length of 384, and all use based size pre-trained models.

## 4.3   Coreference Results

Table 1 and Table 2 demonstrate the performance of CyberCoref and compared coreference resolution models on our cybersecurity corpus. The evaluation metrics are the MUC, B-Cubed, and $CEAF_{\phi_3}$ which were used in the conll-2012 coreference resolution shared task [11], and the LEA [33] evaluation metrics proposed by Moosavi et al. in 2016. Since these models heavily rely on span representation, they have high requirements for word embeddings. Models [20–24] using large-scale pre-trained dynamic word embeddings significantly perform better than using the embedding method combined GloVe, Turian, and Char-CNN [18]. The word-level model shows limited ability to distinguish long and complex spans, displaying lower scores compared to span-based models. In general, due to the vast differences between datasets, models that perform well on general corpora, like OntoNotes 5.0 and GAP, do not achieve the expected results on our dataset which is far more challenging. In contrast, the proposed CyberCoref achieves better results in the following four evaluation metrics and becomes the best coreference resolution model for cybersecurity entities.

**Table 1.** Results on the validation set of our cybersecurity corpus. The final column (Avg. F1) is the main evaluation metric, computed by averaging the F1 of MUC, B-cubed, and $CEAF_{\phi_3}$

| | $MUC$ | | | $B-cubed$ | | | $CEAF_{\phi_3}$ | | | |
|---|---|---|---|---|---|---|---|---|---|---|
| | Prec. | Rec. | **F1** | Prec. | Rec. | F1 | Prec. | Rec. | F1 | Avg. F1 |
| Lee et al. 2017 [18] | 9.8 | **58.8** | 16.7 | 2.0 | **81.6** | 4.9 | 4.0 | 18.2 | 6.7 | 9.4 |
| Joshi et al.2019a [20] | 62.2 | 27.6 | 36.2 | **80.7** | 63.7 | 69.4 | 65.5 | 29.2 | 38.6 | 48.1 |
| Joshi et al.2019b [21] | 56.4 | 38.9 | 43.6 | 74.2 | 72.0 | 71.7 | 59.8 | 39.0 | 45.0 | 53.4 |
| Ye et al. 2020 [22] | 59.2 | 35.9 | 42.4 | 80.3 | 68.1 | 72.3 | 61.5 | 37.7 | 44.7 | 53.1 |
| Kirstain et al. 2021 [24] | 24.5 | 23.3 | 22.8 | 61.3 | 62.4 | 61.0 | 31.2 | 28.6 | 28.8 | 37.5 |
| Proposed Model | **63.8** | 47.9 | 52.6 | 79.0 | 76.5 | **76.6** | **66.5** | **47.1** | **53.3** | **60.9** |

In terms of mention detection, the span-based model pursues a high recall rate so that as many mentions as possible are selected in a fixed number of extracted spans. While the selected non-mention spans and singletons will be screened in the following coreference resolution step later. As shown in Table 3, our proposed model achieves the best result for the mention detection by increasing in both recall and precision rates.

**Table 2.** Results on the validation set of our cybersecurity corpus with the LEA metric.

| | LEA | | |
|---|---|---|---|
| | Prec. | Rec. | F1 |
| Lee et al. 2017 [18] | 0.3 | **49.3** | 0.6 |
| Joshi et al. 2019a [20] | **56.0** | 19.6 | 26.2 |
| Joshi et al. 2019b [21] | 47.1 | 30.6 | 33.4 |
| Ye et al. 2020 [22] | 52.6 | 26.7 | 32.2 |
| Kirstain et al. 2021 [24] | 17.7 | 17.4 | 16.1 |
| Proposed model | 54.7 | 39.0 | **42.0** |

**Table 3.** Results of the mention detection step.

| | Prec. | Rec. | F1 |
|---|---|---|---|
| Lee et al. 2017 [18] | 15.6 | 65.9 | 25.2 |
| Joshi et al. 2019a [20] | 27.1 | 87.9 | 41.4 |
| Joshi et al. 2019b [21] | 26.8 | 87.8 | 41.1 |
| Ye et al. 2020 [22] | 27.1 | 88 | 41.4 |
| Kirstain et al. 2021 [24] | – | – | – |
| Proposed model | **28.3** | **92.1** | **43.3** |

## 4.4 Ablations

**Lexical and Syntactic Features.** The span representation plays a crucial role as the basis for the solution of both the mention detection and coreference resolution task. Four different ways of encoding part-of-speech and syntactic features are used as comparisons in this experiment. Due to the different token lengths of spans and each token corresponds to a separate part-of-speech and syntactic dependency label, this problem can be viewed as a variable-length category feature sequence encoding problem. The first and most straightforward idea is to embed the two features separately using the EmbeddingBags, and then average or sum the corresponding lexical and syntactic feature embeddings before concatenating them together. In the third approach, a Long short-term memory (LSTM) network is used for feature extraction of variable-length feature sequences, where the hidden state of the last non-padded time step is taken as the feature embedding. The last approach is our proposed additive attention mechanism, which is introduced in Sect. 3.

**Table 4.** Ablation study of the proposed architectures in CyberCore, where MD and CR stand for the mention detection and coreference resolution, respectively.

| | | MD | | CR | |
|---|---|---|---|---|---|
| | | Rec. | Prec. | Conll-2012 Avg. F1 | LEA F1 |
| | Baseline | 87.8 | 26.8 | 53.4 | 33.4 |
| Lexical & syntactic features | +EmbeddingBags-mean | 86.5 | 26.4 | 45.6 | 29.4 |
| | +EmbeddingBags-sum | 76.5 | 23.3 | 42.1 | 21.1 |
| | +LSTM | 85.6 | 26.5 | 41.6 | 29.8 |
| | +AttitiveAttention | **88.3** | **27.2** | **56.0** | **36.0** |
| Context modeling | +BiGRU | 87.4 | 27.0 | 53.1 | 33.4 |
| | +BiLSTM | 87.3 | 26.9 | 46.0 | 19.8 |
| | +Cos-MaxPooling | **87.8** | 26.4 | 46.3 | 20.3 |
| | +Cos-MatchPyramid [29] | 87.7 | 26.5 | 53.6 | 34.0 |
| | +Cos-Dot-MatchPyramid [29] | 87.7 | **26.8** | **55.6** | **36.8** |
| Entity type prediction | +Golden types | 95.5 | 29.4 | 70.9 | 59.2 |
| | +standalone-TPM | 90.5 | 27.4 | 56.2 | 36.2 |
| | +E2E-TPM with pre-trained weights | **92.0** | **28.4** | **59.9** | **40.2** |

The experimental result shows that the straightforward introduction of part-of-speech and syntactic features does not help the selection of mentions, while using the additive attention mechanism to introduce lexical and syntactic features for headword finding can better identify the most appropriate headword within a span and help its representation, thus improving the effectiveness of mention extraction and coreference resolution tasks in terms of precision rate.

**Context Relevance Modeling.** We come up with five explicit context modeling approaches to compare with the baseline model of Joshi et al. 2019b [21]. The first two approaches are based on recurrent neural networks, which encode the concatenated sentences where the mention and its candidate mentions are located in and take the hidden state at the last time step as the contextual feature of the two sentences. The last three approaches use matching matrices generated by cosine similarity or dot product function, which can better demonstrate the correlation between tokens than recurrent neural networks. The experimental results show that using MatchPyramid to extract features from the Cos and Dot matching matrices can demonstrate the relevance of sentences more precisely and provides valuable information for the coreference resolution of selected mentions.

**Entity Type Prediction.** The performance of different networks on the entity type prediction subtask is shown in Table 5. The previous works [34,35] demonstrated the noteworthy improvement of adding special tags (e.g., ⟨tag⟩ and ⟨/tag⟩) before and after the target span on span-related tasks such as entity typing and relationship extraction. Therefore, we investigate the effect of adding the boundary tags and compare the two proposed ways of span representation, i.e. concatenating the corresponding embedding of pre-and-post tags or performing average pooling for spans. The experimental result shows that tags can help the model better perceive the boundaries of span and grasp the semantics of content within the span tags, thus the concatenation of simple tag embedding can also lead to a good enough representation of spans. However, since the embedding of tags has not been pre-trained by BERT, its upper limit is inferior to the span representation proposed in this work, which consider the span boundary and overall content.

We then compare two ways of incorporating pre-trained entity type prediction network to CyberCoref: as a stand-alone model without participating in the parameter update of the overall model training to ensure the accuracy on the type prediction subtask; as part of the end-to-end model participating in the parameter update, sharing the weights of the BERT model which are pre-trained on the subtask of entity type prediction with the overall model. In addition, the performance of using exactly the right entity types (golden types) is also shown in Table 4. The result shows that the introduction of the entity type prediction network with pre-trained weights to initialize the end-to-end model works best.

Table 5. Performance of different networks on the entity type prediction subtask.

|  |  | Type Prediction |  |  |  |
| --- | --- | --- | --- | --- | --- |
|  |  | Prec. | Rec. | Micro-F1 | Weighted-F1 |
| Tagged [34] | +tag [34] | 81.9 | 76.8 | 76.8 | 77.9 |
|  | +mean [35] | 80.4 | 76.7 | 76.7 | 77.1 |
|  | +proposed network | 81.9 | 76.8 | 76.8 | 77.9 |
| Original | +mean | 79.8 | 75.8 | 75.9 | 76.3 |
|  | +proposed network | 83.4 | 78.3 | 78.3 | 79.4 |

## 5  Analysis

**Strengths.** After manually analyzing the errors on a set of validation samples, we found that for the more common and less error-prone coreferences, such as coreferences of pronouns or noun phrases in the same sentence or adjacent sentences, our model can determine them accurately based on the training with a large number of similar patterns and the guidance of entity types. The introduction of part-of-speech and syntactic features is helpful for the representation of longer mentions in the form of verb-object or other more complex structures. For example, in *(Subject)-Verb-Object sentence pattern* shown in Table 6, for Attack-Pattern, which are common in cybersecurity corpora and are usually used to describe the attack process or represent the attack features, CyberCoref can identify these mentions and complete the coreference resolution among them correctly. Furthermore, in APT or other cyber attack reports, we find that different parts of the article have obvious distinctions in discussion objects, as *Multi-discussion Objects in the same passage* shown in Table 6. The explicit sentence-based contextual modeling proposed in this work better reflects the relevance of sentences than the original segment-based implicit contextual semantic modeling. In this case, although the mention "new ransomware" appears twice, the key signals in the sentence such as "In other ransomware news" and the words interaction between their contexts help the model cluster them to different coreference groups rather than the same one.

**Weaknesses.** However, the coreference in the cybersecurity corpus is more complex than expected, and there are many challenging error-prone scenarios that make our model CyberCoref not always reliable. Many same or similar words that are commonly used in cybersecurity topics may refer to different entities, such as "vulnerability", "issue", "company", "attack", etc. This is similar to that of pronouns but the former is more difficult to handle, as these across coreference clusters high-frequency words are usually not constrained by distance but depend only on semantic expression. For example, as in the cases in *Same or Look-alike Strings*, CyberCoref is highly susceptible to the similarity of the words themselves, resulting in false positive resolutions, thus causing greater degradation in the evaluation metrics. In addition, the presence of many comparisons and citation descriptions in the cybersecurity corpus, some paragraphs will have the phenomenon of discussing multiple entities of the same type, making coreference resolution further difficult.

## 6   Conclusion and Future Work

In conclusion, we explore the effectiveness of existing coreference resolution models on cybersecurity corpus. To address the limitations of their performance, we propose CyberCoref, a document-level end-to-end coreference resolution model for cybersecurity entities. Based on the three improvements proposed in this work, including entity type prediction networks, explicit contextual modeling, and the introduction of lexical and syntactic features, CyberCoref improves the average F1 value of the four evaluation metrics by 6.9% on the dataset constructed in this work. However, when it comes to more complex coreference expressions, CyberCoref still has much room for improvement. In our future work, we will focus on solving the challenging coreference cases mentioned in Sect. 5.

**Acknowledgment.** This research is funded by the National Natural Science Foundation of China (No.61902265), National Key Research and Development Program of China (No.2021YFB3100500), Open Fund of Anhui Province Key Laboratory of Cyberspace Security Situation Awareness and Evaluation (No. CSSAE-2021-001).

# A  Challenging Coreference Cases

**Table 6.** Challenging coreference cases in our cybersecurity corpus. For better illustration, we only mark up the typical coreferences that reflects the displayed coreference types shown in the left side. Manual labels and results given by CyberCoref are shown in the right side.

| Challenging types | Examples | Results |
|---|---|---|
| Same or Look-alike Strings | This is only the latest exploit to hit Adobe Flash - earlier in June, a **zero-day Flash vulnerability(1)** was is being exploited in the wild in targeted attacks against Windows users in the Middle East, according to researchers. Adobe dealt with **another zero-day Flash vulnerability(2)** back in February, which was exploited by North Korean hackers | Golden: [(1)], [(2)] CyberCoref: [(1), (2)] |
| | Impacted is Adobe Flash Player Desktop Runtime, **Adobe Flash Player(1)** for Google Chrome; **Adobe Flash Player(2)** for Microsoft Edge and Internet Explorer 11; all for versions 31.0.0.153 and earlier | Golden:[(1)], [(2)] CyberCoref:[(1), (2)] |
| (Subject)-Verb-Object pattern | The only problem is that detecting either the hacked bank or the hacked ATM is almost impossible as most of the malicious behavior takes place via self-deleting malware and malicious PowerShell scripts executing in memory, **without leaving any artifacts on disk(1)**. Once the bank server/computer or the AMT is rebooted, most of **the clues are wiped from memory(2)** | Golden: [(1), (2)] CyberCoref: [(1), (2)] |
| | Microsoft Windows users beware of an unpatched memory corruption bug which could **be exploited to cause denial of service (DoS) attacks(1)** as well as other exploits If a user connects to a malicious SMB server, a vulnerable Windows client system may **crash and display a blue screen of death (BSOD) in mrxsmb20.sys(2)**, the advisory said | Golden: [(1), (2)] CyberCoref: [(1), (2)] |
| Multi-discussion Objects in the same paragraph | **Israeli mobile forensics firm(1) Cellebrite(2)** has announced that **it(3)** has suffered a data breach following an unauthorized access to an external web server. The confirmation comes a few hours after **Motherboard(4)** released general information about 900 GB of data that **they(5)** obtained and has supposedly been stolen from **the firm(6)**. The cache includes alleged usernames and passwords for logging into Cellebrite databases connected to **the company(7)**'s my.cellebrite domain, the publication noted | Golden: [(1), (2), (3), (6), (7)], [(4), (5)] CyberCoref: [(1), (2), (3), (7)], [(4), (5), (6)] |
| | **This vulnerability(1)** has been assigned **the CVE-2018-17456 ID(2)** and is similar to a previous **CVE-2017-1000117(3) option injection vulnerability(4)**. Like **the previous vulnerability(5)**, a malicious repository can create a .gitmodules file that contains an URL that starts with a dash | Golden: [(1), (2)], [(3), (4), (5)] CyberCoref: [(1), (2)], [(3), (4), (5)] |
| Multi-discussion Objects in the same passage | One tried-and-true technique continues to be hiding malware inside fake versions of popular files, then distributing those fake versions via app stores. To wit, last week researchers at the security firm ESET spotted **new ransomware(1) - Filecoder.E(2)** - circulating via BitTorrent, disguised as a"patcher" that purports to allow Mac users to crack such applications as Adobe Premiere Pro CC and Microsoft Office 2016 ... In other ransomware news, **new ransomware(3)** known as **Trump Locker(4)** - not to be confused with Trumpcryption - turns out to be a lightly repackaged version of VenusLocker ransomware, according to Lawrence Abrams of the security analysis site Bleeping Computer, as well as the researchers known as MalwareHunter Team | Golden: [(1), (2)], [(3), (4)] CyberCoref: [(1), (2)], [(3), (4)] |

# References

1. Jones, C.L., Bridges, R.A., Huffer, K.M., Goodall, J.R.: Towards a relation extraction framework for cyber-security concepts. In: Proceedings of the 10th Annual Cyber and Information Security Research Conference, pp. 1–4 (2015)
2. Mittal, S., Das, P.K., Mulwad, V., Joshi, A., Finin, T.: Cybertwitter: using twitter to generate alerts for cybersecurity threats and vulnerabilities. In: 2016 IEEE/ACM International Conference on Advances in Social Networks Analysis and Mining (ASONAM), pp. 860–867. IEEE (2016)
3. Liao, X., Yuan, K., Wang, X., Li, Z., Xing, L., Beyah, R.: Acing the ioc game: toward automatic discovery and analysis of open-source cyber threat intelligence. In: Proceedings of the 2016 ACM SIGSAC Conference on Computer and Communications Security, pp. 755–766 (2016)
4. Zhu, Z., Dumitras, T.: Chainsmith: automatically learning the semantics of malicious campaigns by mining threat intelligence reports. In: 2018 IEEE European Symposium on Security and Privacy (EuroS&P), pp. 458–472. IEEE (2018)
5. Ghazi, Y., Anwar, Z., Mumtaz, R., Saleem, S., Tahir, A.: A supervised machine learning based approach for automatically extracting high-level threat intelligence from unstructured sources. In: 2018 International Conference on Frontiers of Information Technology (FIT), pp. 129–134. IEEE (2018)
6. Zhao, J., Yan, Q., Li, J., Shao, M., He, Z., Li, B.: Timiner: automatically extracting and analyzing categorized cyber threat intelligence from social data. Comput. Secur. **95**, 101867 (2020)
7. Husari, G., Niu, X., Chu, B., Al-Shaer, E.: Using entropy and mutual information to extract threat actions from cyber threat intelligence. In: 2018 IEEE International Conference on Intelligence and Security Informatics (ISI), pp. 1–6. IEEE (2018)
8. Guo, Y., et al.: CyberRel: joint entity and relation extraction for cybersecurity concepts. In: Gao, D., Li, Q., Guan, X., Liao, X. (eds.) ICICS 2021. LNCS, vol. 12918, pp. 447–463. Springer, Cham (2021). https://doi.org/10.1007/978-3-030-86890-1_25
9. Pingle, A., Piplai, A., Mittal, S., Joshi, A., Holt, J., Zak, R.: Relext: relation extraction using deep learning approaches for cybersecurity knowledge graph improvement. In: Proceedings of the 2019 IEEE/ACM International Conference on Advances in Social Networks Analysis and Mining, pp. 879–886 (2019)
10. Satyapanich, T., Ferraro, F., Finin, T.: Casie: extracting cybersecurity event information from text. In: Proceedings of the AAAI Conference on Artificial Intelligence, vol. 34, pp. 8749–8757 (2020)
11. Pradhan, S., Moschitti, A., Xue, N., Uryupina, O., Zhang, Y.: Conll-2012 shared task: modeling multilingual unrestricted coreference in ontonotes. In: Joint Conference on EMNLP and CoNLL-Shared Task, pp. 1–40 (2012)
12. Brack, A., Müller, D.U., Hoppe, A., Ewerth, R.: Coreference resolution in research papers from multiple domains. In: Hiemstra, D., Moens, M.-F., Mothe, J., Perego, R., Potthast, M., Sebastiani, F. (eds.) ECIR 2021. LNCS, vol. 12656, pp. 79–97. Springer, Cham (2021). https://doi.org/10.1007/978-3-030-72113-8_6
13. Clark, K., Manning, C.D.: Improving coreference resolution by learning entity-level distributed representations. arXiv preprint arXiv:1606.01323 (2016)
14. Timmapathini, H., et al.: Probing the spanbert architecture to interpret scientific domain adaptation challenges for coreference resolution. In: SDU@ AAAI (2021)
15. Webster, K., Recasens, M., Axelrod, V., Baldridge, J.: Mind the gap: a balanced corpus of gendered ambiguous pronouns. Trans. Assoc. Comput. Linguist. **6**, 605–617 (2018)

16. Wiseman, S.J., Rush, A.M., Shieber, S.M., Weston, J.: Learning anaphoricity and antecedent ranking features for coreference resolution. In: Proceedings of the 53rd Annual Meeting of the Association for Computational Linguistics and the 7th International Joint Conference on Natural Language Processing, vol. 1: Long Papers. Association for Computational Linguistics (2015)
17. Wiseman, S., Rush, A.M., Shieber, S.M.: Learning global features for coreference resolution. arXiv preprint arXiv:1604.03035 (2016)
18. Lee, K., He, L., Lewis, M., Zettlemoyer, L.: End-to-end neural coreference resolution. arXiv preprint arXiv:1707.07045 (2017)
19. Lee, K., He, L., Zettlemoyer, L.: Higher-order coreference resolution with coarse-to-fine inference. arXiv preprint arXiv:1804.05392 (2018)
20. Joshi, M., Levy, O., Weld, D.S., Zettlemoyer, L.: Bert for coreference resolution: Baselines and analysis. arXiv preprint arXiv:1908.09091 (2019)
21. Joshi, M., Chen, D., Liu, Y., Weld, D.S., Zettlemoyer, L., Levy, O.: Spanbert: improving pre-training by representing and predicting spans. Trans. Assoc. Comput. Linguist. **8**, 64–77 (2020)
22. Ye, D., et al.: Coreferential reasoning learning for language representation. arXiv preprint arXiv:2004.06870 (2020)
23. Kirstain, Y., Ram, O., Levy, O.: Coreference resolution without span representations. arXiv preprint arXiv:2101.00434 (2021)
24. Dobrovolskii, V.: Word-level coreference resolution. arXiv preprint arXiv:2109.04127 (2021)
25. Liu, K., Wang, F., Ding, Z., Liang, S., Yu, Z., Zhou, Y.: A review of knowledge graph application scenarios in cyber security. arXiv preprint arXiv:2204.04769 (2022)
26. Fang, Y., Zhang, Y., Huang, C.: Cybereyes: cybersecurity entity recognition model based on graph convolutional network. Comput. J. **64**(8), 1215–1225 (2021)
27. Hu, Y., Guo, Y., Liu, J., Zhang, H.: A hybrid method of coreference resolution in information security. Comput. Mater. Continua **64**(2), 1297–1315 (2020)
28. Wang, X., Xiong, M., Luo, Y., Li, N., Jiang, Z., Xiong, Z.: Joint learning for document-level threat intelligence relation extraction and coreference resolution based on gcn. In: 2020 IEEE 19th International Conference on Trust, Security and Privacy in Computing and Communications (TrustCom), pp. 584–591. IEEE (2020)
29. Pang, L., Lan, Y., Guo, J., Xu, J., Wan, S., Cheng, X.: Text matching as image recognition. In: Proceedings of the AAAI Conference on Artificial Intelligence, vol. 30 (2016)
30. Syed, Z., Padia, A., Finin, T., Mathews, L., Joshi, A.: UCO: a unified cybersecurity ontology. In: Workshops at the Thirtieth AAAI Conference on Artificial Intelligence (2016)
31. Stenetorp, P., Pyysalo, S., Topić, G., Ohta, T., Ananiadou, S., Tsujii, J.: Brat: a web-based tool for nlp-assisted text annotation. In: Proceedings of the Demonstrations at the 13th Conference of the European Chapter of the Association for Computational Linguistics, pp. 102–107 (2012)
32. Xu, B., Wang, N., Chen, T., Li, M.: Empirical evaluation of rectified activations in convolutional network. arXiv preprint arXiv:1505.00853 (2015)

33. Moosavi, N.S., Strube, M.: Which coreference evaluation metric do you trust? a proposal for a link-based entity aware metric. In: Proceedings of the 54th Annual Meeting of the Association for Computational Linguistics, vol. 1: Long Papers), pp. 632–642 (2016)
34. Khosla, S., Rose, C.: Using type information to improve entity coreference resolution. arXiv preprint arXiv:2010.05738 (2020)
35. Soares, L.B., FitzGerald, N., Ling, J., Kwiatkowski, T.: Matching the blanks: distributional similarity for relation learning. arXiv preprint arXiv:1906.03158 (2019)

# Applied Cryptography

# Another Lattice Attack Against ECDSA with the wNAF to Recover More Bits per Signature

Ziqiang Ma[1], Shuaigang Li[2], Jingqiang Lin[3(✉)], Quanwei Cai[2], Shuqin Fan[4], Fan Zhang[5,6], and Bo Luo[7]

[1] School of Information Engineering, Ningxia University, Yinchuan, China
maziqiang@nxu.edu.cn
[2] State Key Laboratory of Information Security, Institute of Information Engineering, Chinese Academy of Sciences, Beijing, China
lishuaigang@iie.ac.cn
[3] School of Cyber Security, University of Science and Technology of China, Hefei, China
linjq@ustc.edu.cn
[4] State Key Laboratory of Cryptology, Beijing, China
fansq@sklc.org
[5] School of Cyber Science and Technology, College of Computer Science and Technology, Zhejiang University, Hangzhou 310027, China
fanzhang@zju.edu.cn
[6] Key Laboratory of Blockchain and Cyberspace Governance of Zhejiang Province, Hangzhou 310027, China
[7] Department of Electrical Engineering and Computer Science, University of Kansas, Lawrence, USA
bluo@ku.edu

**Abstract.** In the resource-constrained environment such as the Internet of Things, the windowed Non-Adjacent-Form (wNAF) representation is usually used to improve the calculation speed of the scalar multiplication of ECDSA. This paper presents a practical cache side channel attack on ECDSA implementations which use wNAF representation. Compared with existing works, our method exploits more information from the cache side channels, which is then efficiently used to construct

This work was supported in part by the Open Subject of the State Key Laboratory of Information Security, Institute of Information Engineering, Chinese Academy of Sciences under Grant 2020-MS-08; in part by the Ningxia Natural Science Foundation of China under Grant 2021AAC03078; in part by the Key RD plan of Ningxia Hui Autonomous Region, China under Grant 2021BEB04047; in part by the National Key RD Plan of China under Grant 2020YFB1005803; in part by National Natural Science Foundation of China under Grant 62072398, by National Key Laboratory of Science and Technology on Information System Security, by State Key Laboratory of Mathematical Engineering and Advanced Computing, and by Key Laboratory of Cyberspace Situation Awareness of Henan Province.

F. Li et al. (Eds.): SecureComm 2022, LNICST 462, pp. 111–129, 2023.
https://doi.org/10.1007/978-3-031-25538-0_7

lattice attacks in the ECDSA private key recovery. First, we additionally monitor the invert function which is related to the sign of the wNAF digits, and obtain a Double-Add-Invert chain through the Flush+Flush cache side channel. Then, we develop effective methods extracting 154.2 bits information of the ephemeral key per signature for 256-bit ECDSA from this chain, much more than the best known result which extracts 105.8 bits per signature. Finally, to efficiently use the extracted information, we convert the problem of recovering the private key to the Hidden Number Problem (HNP) and the Extended Hidden Number Problem (EHNP) respectively, which are solved by lattice reduction algorithms. We applied the attack on ECDSA with the secp256k1 curve in OpenSSL 1.1.0h. The experimental results show that only 3 signatures are enough to recover the private key. To the best of our knowledge, this work exploits the signs of the wNAF representation, along with the Double-Add chain against ECDSA, to recover the private key with *the least number of signatures*.

**Keywords:** ECDSA · windowed Non-Adjacent-Form · Lattice attack · Hidden number problem · Extended hidden number problem · Cache side channel

# 1 Introduction

The ECDSA [5] digital signature scheme based on the elliptic-curve cryptography (ECC), is widely used in lots of popular applications, such as OpenPGP [14], smartcard [27], TLS [30] and Bitcoin [21]. The scalar multiplication is the core operation of ECDSA and its speed determines the total efficiency of ECDSA. Exploiting the windowed Non-Adjacent Form (wNAF) [22,29] of the ephemeral key (the scalar) is a commonly used method to accelerate the scalar multiplication [1,2], especially in resource-constrained environments such as IoT. While this method needs a pre-computed table, which costs many memory resources. Several works [11,18,34] have been put forward to improve the efficiency of wNAF. One of the most effective ways is to exploit the invert function to convert the negative digits into positive digits during the calculation, which can save half of the pre-computed storage space [20].

However, side channel attacks can extract information on the ephemeral key with the wNAF representation. As long as some bits of the ephemeral key are leaked, the ECDSA private key can be fully recovered [24]. With the cache side channel attacks [10,17,33], practical attacks [4,6,9,26,32] are proposed to attack ECDSA. These works [6,9,26,32] observe the execution of ECDSA through cache side channels, and observe the ordered sequence of points addition and doubling during the ECDSA signing. Then, they extract and exploit the different information of the ephemeral key from this chain, and translate the problem of recovering the ECDSA private key to the Hidden Number Problem (HNP) or the Extended Hidden Number Problem (EHNP), which is then solved by lattice reduction algorithms. However, They infer the information of the ephemeral key's wNAF representation *only* from the Double-Add chain, so that for one signature the number of bits extracted hits the ceiling. The method proposed by Fan [9] is believed to infer almost all the available bits from the Double-Add chain, which performs remarkably better than other attacks [6,26,32]. Although another attack proposed by Allan [4] additionally monitored the invert function of the scalar multiplication implementation, they exploited the analytical method of Van de Pol [26] and obtained 71.4 bits per signature. Naturally, more bits are obtained from the side channels, and fewer signatures are required for recovering the ECDSA private key. For example, existing methods [4,6,9,26,32] require 6, 4, 200, 13, and 85 signatures, respectively, to recover the private key.

In this paper, we propose a more efficient attack against the wNAF implementation with the invert function of ECDSA, which obtains on average 154.2 bits per signature for 256-bit ECDSA and requires only 3 signatures to recover the ECDSA private key. First, we monitor the invert function of the implementation of the scalar multiplication, along with points addition and doubling functions using the cache side channel, and then construct a Double-Add-Invert chain instead of the Double-Add chain [6,9,26,32]. The invert function is invoked only when the sign of the current non-zero digit of the ephemeral key's wNAF representation is opposite to the previous one in the scalar multiplication. Through this information, we can extract the signs of the non-zero digits. Then, taking full advantage of information obtained through the Double-Add-Invert chain, we construct the HNP and EHNP instances respectively, to recover the ECDSA private key. We apply our attacks to the secp256k1 curve in OpenSSL 1.1.0h. The Flush+Flush [10] attack is used to monitor the functions of double, add and invert, and construct the Double-Add-Invert chain. From this chain, we successfully determine whether each digit of the ephemeral key's wNAF representation is zero or not, and also the signs of the non-zero digits. We extract on average 154.2 bits from one signature through the perfect Double-Add-Invert chain for 256-bit ECDSA. With the HNP problem, we need about 248 signatures to recover the private key with a success probability of 1.5% (in Sect. 4). While using the EHNP problem, 3 signatures are enough with a success probability no less than 69.9% (in Sect. 5).

Our contributions are summarized as follows:

- We present an efficient cache side channel attack to recover the private key of ECDSA with the invertible wNAF representation. First, we construct a Double-Add-Invert chain by additionally monitoring the invert function. Then, we propose two new lattice attacks to exploit the positions and signs of all non-zero digits in the ephemeral key's wNAF representation obtained through the Double-Add-Invert chain.
- We apply our methods to attack the secp256k1 curve in OpenSSL 1.1.0h. Through the cache side channel, 154.2 bits are obtained per signature on average. The experiments show that only 3 signatures are enough to recover the private key with a success probability no less than 69.9%.

The rest of this paper is organized as follows. Section 2 introduces the preliminaries. Section 3 shows how to improve the cache side channel to get more information. Sections 4 and 5 construct the lattice attacks with HNP and EHNP, respectively. Section 6 compares our attacks with existing works. And, Sect. 7 draws the conclusion.

## 2    Preliminaries

In this section, we first present the related concepts about the ECDSA and the wNAF. Then, we describe the attack method of the cache side channels. Also, the hidden number problem and the extended hidden number problem are introduced to utilize the data obtained from cache side channels.

### 2.1    The Elliptic Curve Digital Signature Algorithm

ECDSA [5,15] is based on the intractability of the elliptic curve discrete logarithm problem in finite field. We define a prime $p$, and set $E$ as the elliptic curve on the finite field $\mathbb{F}_p$. $G$ is the generator of the group with order $q$, which is a fixed point on the curve. We set an integer $\alpha$ as the private key of ECDSA that should satisfy $0 < \alpha < q$. The point $Q = \alpha G$ is the corresponding public key. Also the information about the elliptic curve is public. Given a message $m$, the ECDSA signature is generated as follows:

1. Generate a random number $k$, $0 < k < q$, as the ephemeral key.
2. Compute $(x, y) = kG$, and then set $r = x \bmod q$; return to 1 if $r$ equals 0.
3. calculate $s = k^{-1}(h(m) + r \cdot \alpha) \bmod q$, $h$ is a hash function; return to 1 if $s$ equals 0.

Thus, the computed ECDSA signature of $m$ is $(r, s)$.

### 2.2    The Scalar Multiplication Using wNAF Representation

Scalar multiplication $kG$ is caculated in the second step of ECDSA signature generation. Several algorithms (e.g. Montgomery Ladder) can be used to implement the scalar multiplication. Among them, the window Non-Adjacent Form (wNAF) algorithm [29] is most commonly used due to its speed. In wNAF, the ephemeral key $k$ is expressed as $k = \sum 2^i k_i$. That means $k$ is represented as a sequence of digits $k_i$. Each digit is either zero or an odd number satisfying $-2^w < k_i < 2^w$. $w$ is the window size. In this representation, any non-zero digit is required to follow at least $w$ zero digits.

For the scalar multiplication using the wNAF algorithm, during the initialization phase, it need to choose a window size $w$. Then the points $\{\pm G, \pm 3G, ..., \pm(2^w - 1)G\}$ are precomputed and stored. The multiplication $kG$ is calculated as described in Algorithm 1, after $k$ is under the wNAF representation.

In Algorithm 1, the if-then block (Line 4) uses $k_i$ to determine whether running into the branch. This is a vulnerability to cache attacks. An attacker can apply the cache attacks by using a spy process to monitor add and double function and get a Double-Add chain to determine whether $k_i$ is zero or not.

---

**Algorithm 1.** Implementation of $kG$ with wNAF

---

**Input:** Scalar $k$ in wNAF: $k_0$, $k_1$, ..., $k_{l-1}$, precomputed points $\{\pm G, \pm 3G, ..., \pm (2^w - 1)G\}$

**Output:** $kG$

  1: $Q \leftarrow G$
  2: **for** $i$ from $l - 1$ to $0$ **do**
  3:     $Q \leftarrow 2 \cdot Q$
  4:     **if** $k_i \neq 0$ **then**
  5:         $Q \leftarrow Q + k_i G$
  6:     **end if**
  7: **end for**
  8: **return** $Q$

---

### 2.3 The Scalar Multiplication with Invert Function

Here, we adopt OpenSSL 1.1.0h as the example to describe the implementation of the wNAF with the invert function (called the invertible wNAF representation). The core computation of the function is shown in Algorithm 2.

In this function, if the digit is non-zero, it runs into the if-then block in Line 6, and then determines whether an invert function is needed. The invert function is to compute the inverse of a point (the internal value of $kG$ here). If the sign of the non-zero digit $k_i$ is opposite to the previous non-zero digit, the invert operation (EC_POINT_invert()) is performed (Line 13), which makes it only need to precompute and store the points $\{G, 3G, ..., (2^w - 1)G\}$, and saves half of the storage space.

From Algorithm 2, it can be found that two conditional branches are vulnerable. First is the double-addtion branch which is already used to determine whether each digit of $k$ is zero or not in the attack. Second is the invert branch, which is related to the signs of the non-zero digits. Combining with the sequence of the double and addition operations, the information of the sign can be inferred.

### 2.4 Cache Side Channel Attacks

The cache side channel attack was firstly proposed in 2002 [25]. It exploited the fact that accessing data from caches is much faster than from memory. An attacker can use these time variations of cache hits or misses to infer the operations executed by the victim process and then extract the secret information. In this section, we introduce the Flush+Flush [10] attack as the example which is used in our work.

The spy and the victim processes have shared momeory, which is the basis of the Flush+Flush [10] attack. Then the attacker can apply a spy process to detect the state of the specific memory lines in the caches of the victim process. The execution time of the clflush instruction is measured in Flush+Flush attack to infer if the specific cache is padding or not. If the cache is padding, the execution time of clflush is longer, and if the cache is empty, the execution time is shorter. The Flush+Flush attack obtaining information involves three steps:

**Algorithm 2.** The Implementation of the Scalar Multiplication in OpenSSL

**Input:** Scalar $k$ in wNAF $\{k_0, k_1, ..., k_{l-1}\}$, precomputed points $\{G, 3G, ..., (2^w-1)G\}$
**Output:** $kG$

1: $r \leftarrow 0$, $is\_neg \leftarrow 0$, $r\_is\_inverted \leftarrow 0$
2: **for** $i$ from $l-1$ to $0$ **do**
3:    **if** $r \neq 0$ **then**
4:        $EC\_POINT\_dbl(r)$   // double
5:    **end if**
6:    **if** $k_i \neq 0$ **then**
7:        $is\_neg \leftarrow (k_i < 0)$
8:        **if** $is\_neg$ **then**
9:            $k_i \leftarrow -k_i$
10:       **end if**
11:       **if** $is\_neg \neq r\_is\_inverted$ **then**
12:           **if** $r \neq 0$ **then**
13:               $EC\_POINT\_invert(r)$   // invert
14:           **end if**
15:           $r\_is\_inverted \leftarrow !r\_is\_inverted$
16:       **end if**
17:       **if** $r = 0$ **then**
18:           $r \leftarrow EC\_POINT\_copy(k_iG)$
19:       **else**
20:           $r \leftarrow EC\_POINT\_add(r, k_iG)$   // add
21:       **end if**
22:    **end if**
23: **end for**
24: **return** r

- **Flush:** The attacker flushes out the specific target memory lines from the caches by the `clflush` instruction.
- **Idle:** In this step, the attacker waits the victim running for a little time slot.
- **Flush:** The attacker executes the `clflush` instruction again and measures the instruction execution time. The shorter time means that the victim does not access the target memory lines. Otherwise, it means that the victim accesses the target memory lines.

Therefore, the attacker infers the victim's memory activities by the execution time, and further inferences the secret information.

### 2.5    The (Extended) Hidden Number Problem and Lattice Attack

The attacker cannot obtain all the private key information from the cache side channel attack against the wNAF algorithm. So the lattice attack is always needed to infer the complete private key. The attacker can use the partial information obtained to construct the (Extended) Hidden Number Problem and solve it through the lattice reduction algorithm to recover the private key.

The Hidden Number Problem (HNP) is presented to recover the secret key of Diffie-Hellman key exchange [7], DSA [13] and ECDSA [24], when some consecutive bits of the ephemeral key are known. We have a positive $l$, a prime number $q$, and randomly chose $t_1, t_2, ..., t_d$ in $\mathbb{F}_q$. The number pairs $(t_i, u_i)$ are known, and satifsy

$$v_i = |\alpha t_i - u_i|_q \le q/2^{l+1}, \quad 1 \le i \le d.$$

The $\alpha \in \mathbb{F}_q$ is the unknown number which is called the hidden number. Thus the HNP is to recover the unknown $\alpha$. In this expression, $|\cdot|_q$ denotes the reduction modulo $q$ into the range $[-q/2, ..., q/2)$.

The Extended Hidden Number Problem (EHNP) introduced in [12] also can be used to recover the private key [9] of ECDSA. We have a prime number $N$ and $u$ congruences

$$\beta_i x + \sum_{j=1}^{l_i} a_{i,j} k_{i,j} \equiv c_i \mod N, \quad 1 \le i \le u .$$

In these congruences, $0 < x < N, \beta_i, a_{i,j}, c_i, l_i$ and $\varepsilon_{i,j}$ are all known. $k_{i,j}$ and $x$ are unknown and they satisfy $0 \le k_{i,j} \le 2^{\varepsilon_{i,j}}$. The EHNP is to recover the unknown $x$ satisfying the congruences above.

For the ECDSA algorithm, attackers take advantage of the signature equation $s = k^{-1}(h(m) + r \cdot \alpha) \mod q$. Based on the partial information related to the ephemeral key obtained by the attackers through the cache side channels, they transform this equation to satisfy the form of HNP or EHNP. Then the private key as the hidden number can be calculated and recovered by solving the SVP/CVP problem in lattice converted from HNP or EHNP using the lattice reduction algorithm such as LLL [16] or BKZ [28].

## 3    Improving Cache Side Channel Attack on Invertible wNAF Representation

This section proposes how to get more bits of the ephemeral key with the wNAF representation through the cache side channel. First, we analyze the invert function implemented in the wNAF representation in ECDSA and show how to use the Double-Add-Invert chain obtained from the cache side channel to extract the information about the ephemeral key. Then we implement the Flush+Flush attack against the secp256k1 curve in OpenSSL 1.1.0h to obtain the cache side channel information.

### 3.1    Attacking Invertible wNAF Through the Cache Side Channel

As shown in Algorithm 2, each digit of $k$ performs a double function. If the digit is not zero and the sign of the digit is opposite to the prior one, the invert function is called. Finally, the addition function is called to add the internal value of $kG$ with a precomputed point indexed by the absolute value of the digit.

We use the vulnerability that the invert function is called conditionally to improve the attack to obtain more valid data. We use a spy process to monitor the double, add and invert functions during computing the scalar multiplication. The time is divided into slots, and in each slot, the spy determines whether the three functions are performed or not by monitoring the cache hits/misses. Then we obtain a Double-Add-Invert chain. According to the Double and Add in this chain, we determine whether each digit of $k$ is zero or not, as done in previous works. Then, based on the Invert in this chain, we infer the sign of each non-zero digit.

When we use the Double-Add-Invert chain to extract the digits of $k$, the Double represents the double function is called, and the Add represents both double and add are called. The Invert represents the invert function is called. Therefore, the appearance of Double means that $k_i$ is zero and the Add means that $k_i$ is not zero. We use the Invert to determine the sign of $k_i$. The sign of $k_i$ is related to the previous non-zero digit. First, the Invert comes out together with Add. If the Invert appears, it represents that the sign of $k_i$ is opposite to the previous non-zero digit. While, if the Invert does not appear when Add comes out, it represents that the sign of this digit is the same as the previous non-zero one. In the wNAF representation, the most significant digit is always positive. Thus, we can determine the sign of all non-zero digits. In this way, we obtain both the positions and signs of all non-zero digits.

### 3.2    The Implementation of Flush+Flush Attack

We use the Flush+Flush technique instead of the Flush+Reload to monitor the functions. First, the cost of Flush is about 160 cycles [10] less than the cost of Reload. Second, the measurement stage and flush stage are merged into one stage, because in the measurement stage the execution of `clflush` also plays the role of flushing the cache. Thus, the precision is much higher than the Flush+Reload. Moreover, compared with Allan's method [4] , using Flush+Flush does not additionally degrade the performance of the system, nor does it increase the risk of being detected by the victim.

We launched the Flush+Flush attack on an Acer Veriton T830 running Ubuntu 16.04. The machine has an Intel Core i7-6700 processor with four execution cores and an 8 MB LLC. The attacking target is the ECDSA implemented in OpenSSL 1.1.0h, which uses wNAF representation in the scalar multiplication. We attack the 256-bit curve secp256k1 for the experiments.

**Threshold.** We monitor the time to execute the `clflush` instruction. For each address of the monitored functions, we record the time of flushing the cache 1000 times, and take the time larger than 99 percent of samples plus 6 cycles as the threshold for this address. The thresholds are recalculated every time before the attack is mounted.

**Time Slot.** For the attack, time slots are set approximately 2000 cycles. In each slot, the spy process flushes the memory lines of the add, double and invert functions (`EC_POINT_dbl()`, `EC_POINT_add()` and `EC_POINT_invert()`) out of the caches.

**Experimental Results.** Figure 1 shows a fragment of outputs by the spy process when performing the ECDSA with the secp256k1 curve. In this figure, $\square$, $\lozenge$ and $\triangle$ represent "double", "add" and "invert" respectively. From this fragment, three operations are clearly distinguished, so we can easily obtain the Double-Add-Invert chain.

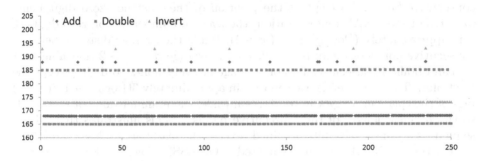

**Fig. 1.** A fragment of the output of the Flush+Flush attack.

# 4    Recover the ECDSA Private Key with HNP

After we obtain the information from the cache side channel, the most intuitive idea is that first recovering some consecutive bits of the ephemeral key $k$ from the Double-Add-Invert chain and then constructing the HNP or EHNP with these bits. So we first recover the consecutive bits at the position of every non-zero digits of $k$. Then we construct the HNP problem using these bits and solve it by the approximate CVP/SVP Problem with the lattice reduction algorithm to recover the ECDSA private key.

## 4.1    Recovering Consecutive Bits

First, we denote the wNAF representation of $k$ as $k = \sum k_i 2^i$, and the binary representation as $k = \sum b_i 2^i$. When we know the information about whether $k_i$ is zero and the sign of the non-zero $k_i$, we can simply determine some bits of $k$. For example, if we obtain the sign of the least non-zero $k_j$, we can infer that $b_j$ is one and $b_i$ is zero for $0 \leq i < j$. But for arbitrary non-zero digits, it can not directly determine whether the bit corresponding to the position of the digit is zero or one.

Set $m$ and $m + n$ as the positions of two consecutive non-zero digits of the wNAF representation, and $w$ be the window size. That is, $k_m, k_{m+n} \neq 0$ and

$k_{m+i} = 0$ for all $0 < i < n$. We analyse the transformation method between the binary and wNAF representation, getting the following result:

$$b_{m+n} = \begin{cases} 0, & k_m < 0 \\ 1, & k_m > 0 \end{cases}, \quad b_{m+i} = \begin{cases} 0, & k_m > 0 \\ 1, & k_m < 0 \end{cases}, \quad w \leq i \leq n-1 \quad (1)$$

And if $m$ is the position of the least non-zero digit of $k$,

$$b_i = \begin{cases} 1, & i = m \\ 0, & 0 \leq i < m \end{cases}. \quad (2)$$

In this way, at the position of every non-zero digit we can obtain $n - w + 1$ consecutive bits of $k$ except at the position of the least non-zero digit being $m + 1$. For the wNAF representation, the average number of non-zero digits of $k$ is approximately $(\lceil \log_2 q \rceil + 1)/(w + 2)$. While the average distance between consecutive non-zero digits is $w + 2$, i.e. on average $n = w + 2$, meaning that we can obtain 3 consecutive bits on average at every non-zero digit (except the least one). Thus, on average we can obtain approximately $3(\lceil \log_2 q \rceil + 1)/(w+2)$ bits of the ephemeral key $k$ in total. Meanwhile, the minimal value of $n$ is $w + 1$, so the minimal length of the consecutive bits is 2. This illustrates that all the sequences of consecutive bits obtained (except the least) are no less than 2 bits.

For the secp256k1 curve implemented in OpenSSL, $\lceil \log_2 q \rceil + 1 = 257$, $w = 3$. So the total number of bits per signature we obtain is $3(\lceil \log_2 q \rceil + 1)/(w + 2) = 154.2$. In theory, two signatures would be enough to recover the 256-bit private key as $2 \times 154.2 = 308.4 > 256$.

## 4.2   Constructing the Lattice Attack with HNP

In this section, we transform the problem of recovering the private key to the HNP instance, and further convert it to the CVP/SVP instance in a lattice. Our method is based on the analysis from [23]. And we make the following improvements to it. First, the length of the consecutive bits used to construct the lattice is variable while the prior work fixes the length, which may lose some information. Second, in our method the position of consecutive bits is arbitrary in the ephemeral key and does not need to be fixed, while the prior work needs all the consecutive bits at the same position. Finally, from one signature we obtain multiple sequences of consecutive bits, and all of them can be used for constructing the lattice as long as the length of the sequence is satisfied, while the prior work only generates one sequence of consecutive bits for one signature.

To construct an HNP instance using arbitrary consecutive bits, we use the standard analysis from [23]. Assuming that we have the $l$ consecutive bits of $k$ with the value of $a$, starting at some known position $j$. So $k$ is represented as $k = 2^j a + 2^{l+j} b + c$ for $0 \leq a \leq 2^l - 1$, $0 \leq b \leq q/2^{l+j}$ and $0 \leq c < 2^j$. We determine the following values

$$\begin{cases} t = \lfloor r\lambda s^{-1} \rfloor_q \\ u = \lfloor (2^j a - s^{-1} h(m))\lambda \rfloor_q \end{cases}, \quad (3)$$

where $\lfloor\cdot\rfloor_q$ denotes the reduction modulo $q$ into range $[0,...,q)$. where $(r,s)$ is the ECDSA signature, $\lambda$ satisfies that $|\lambda|_q < q2^{-j-l/2}$ and $|\lambda2^{j+l}|_q \leq q/2^{j+l/2}$, and $\lfloor\cdot\rfloor_q$ denotes the reduction modulo $q$ into range $[0,...,q)$.

It satisfies that

$$|\alpha t - u|_q < q/2^{(l/2-1)}. \tag{4}$$

This way, an HNP instance is constructed.

In practice, OpenSSL uses $k+q$ as the ephemeral key. So the Eq. 3 remains the same, but the Inequality 4 turns into

$$|\alpha t - u|_q < q/2^{(l/2-\log_2 3)}. \tag{5}$$

Note that, the Eq. 5 represents that the $l/2 - \log_2 3 - 1$ most significant bits of $\lfloor\alpha t\rfloor_q$ is $u$, based on the definition of the HNP. So it should satisfy that $l/2 - \log_2 3 - 1 \geq 1$, i.e. $l > 7$. That means the length of the consecutive bits used to construct the HNP instance should be larger than 7, although we could use all the sequences of the consecutive bits of the ephemeral key in theory.

Next we turn the HNP instance into the lattice problem. We use $d$ triples $(t_i, u_i, l_i)$ to construct a $d+1$ dimensional lattice $L(B)$ spanned by the rows of the following matrix:

$$B = \begin{pmatrix} 2^{l_1+1}q & 0 & \cdots & 0 & 0 \\ 0 & 2^{l_2+1}q & \ddots & \vdots & \vdots \\ \vdots & & \ddots & 0 & \vdots \\ 0 & \cdots & 0 & 2^{l_d+1}q & 0 \\ 2^{l_1+1}t_1 & \cdots & \cdots & 2^{l_d+1}t_d & 1 \end{pmatrix}.$$

Let the vector $\mathbf{x} = (2^{l_1+1}\alpha t_1 \bmod q, ..., 2^{l_d+1}\alpha t_d \bmod q, \alpha)$, and the vector $\mathbf{u} = (2^{l_1+1}u_1, ..., 2^{l_d+1}u_d, 0)$. It can be proved that the vector $\mathbf{x}$ is one of the closest vectors to $\mathbf{u}$. Inputing $B$ and $\mathbf{u}$, and solving the approximate CVP problem, the vector $\mathbf{x}$ is revealed. hence the private key $\alpha$ is recovered.

The approximate CVP problem can be transformed to an approximate SVP instance. $d$ triples $(t_i, u_i, l_i)$ can construct a lattice $L(B')$ with the dimension $d+2$ spanned by the rows of the following matrix

$$B' = \begin{pmatrix} B & 0 \\ \mathbf{u} & q \end{pmatrix}.$$

Similarly, the vector $\mathbf{x}' = (2^{l_1+1}(\alpha t_1 - u_1) \bmod q, ..., 2^{l_d+1}(\alpha t_d - u_d) \bmod q, \alpha, -q)$ belonging to the lattice $L(B')$ is a very short vector. But this lattice also contains another vector $(-t_1, ..., -t_d, q, 0) \cdot B = (0, ..., 0, q, 0)$, which also is a very short vector in the lattice. Therefore we expect the two shortest vectors in a reduced basis of the lattice contain $\mathbf{x}'$ with a suitably lattice reduction algorithm. Then we acquire the secret key $\alpha$.

**Table 1.** The success probability of solving SVP with different parameters.

| Dimension | Block size | | | | | |
|---|---|---|---|---|---|---|
| | $l \geq 9$ | | $l \geq 10$ | | $l \geq 11$ | |
| | 10 | 20 | 10 | 20 | 10 | 20 |
| 50 | 0 | 0 | 0 | 0 | 0 | 0 |
| 60 | 0 | 0 | 0 | 0 | 3.0 | 7.5 |
| 70 | 0 | 0 | 0.5 | 1.0 | 29.5 | 30.5 |
| 80 | 1.0 | 1.5 | 4.0 | 8.5 | 49.0 | 65.0 |
| 100 | 0.5 | 4.0 | 21.0 | 33.5 | 70.5 | 83.5 |
| 120 | 2.0 | 4.5 | 21.5 | 35.0 | 77.5 | 92.0 |
| 140 | 3.0 | 8.0 | 29.0 | 46.0 | 88.5 | 99.0 |
| 160 | 2.5 | 13.0 | 27.5 | 49.0 | 94.0 | 99.5 |
| 180 | 3.5 | 11.5 | 37.0 | 57.0 | 97.0 | 100.0 |
| 200 | 9.5 | 26.0 | 46.0 | 66.0 | 99.0 | 100.0 |
| 220 | 15.0 | 29.0 | 51.0 | 72.5 | 100.0 | 100.0 |

### 4.3    Lattice Attack on Secp256k1

We apply the lattice attack to the curve secp256k1 and assume the Flush+Flush attack is perfect, which means we correctly obtain the Double-Add-Invert chain and recover all the information about the digits of the ephemeral key it contains.

In the experiments, we use the BKZ algorithm implemented in `fplll` [31] to solve the SVP problem converted from the HNP problem. We denote the success probability as the amount of successfully recovering the private key divided by the total number of the lattice attacks. We want to find the optimal strategy for our attack in terms of the following parameters:

– the minimal value of $l$ (length of the consecutive bits of $k$)
– the block size of BKZ
– the lattice dimension

Table 1 shows the success probability for different dimensions and block sizes of solving the SVP instance. In each case, we run 200 experiments and compute the success probability. Although in Sect. 4.2 the HNP problem introduced requires that $l$ should be larger than 7. But in our experiments, when $l = 8$, the private key can not be successfully recovered. We can successfully recover the private key of a 256-bit ECDSA only need 60 sequences of consecutive bits with a success probability of 7.5%. These 60 sequences come from up to 60 signatures. That means we just need about 60 signatures satisfied the length requirement to successfully recover the ECDSA private key.

We analysed 10000 signatures. 32.33% signatures contain the sequence of consecutive bits that $l \geq 9$, 17.44% signatures contain the sequence that $l \geq 10$ and 9.08% signatures contain the sequence that $l \geq 11$. So, obtaining 60 satisfying signatures $(l \geq 11)$ needs 661 signatures totally. However, when using 80 signatures that satisfy $l \geq 9$, the total number of signatures needed is the least, just 248.

# 5  Recover the ECDSA Private Key with EHNP

We can see that the restriction on the length of the bits has a great influence on the number of signatures we need to observe. Although we have exploited the sign information of the wNAF representation, the result is not as expected, worse than Allan's attack [4], which only needs 6 signatures. So, in this section, we directly exploiting the wNAF representation to construct EHNP problem with the known information from the Double-Add-Invert chain to recover the ECDSA private key. The final result shows this method only needs 3 signatures, better than existing results.

## 5.1  Extracting More Information

Suppose in the obtained Double-Add-Invert Chain, the numbers of $A$ is $l$, whose positions are $\lambda_i (1 \leq i \leq l)$, separately. So we can easily have

$$k = \sum_{i=1}^{l} k_i' 2^{\lambda_i}, \qquad k_i' \in \{-7, -5, -3, -1, 1, 3, 5, 7\}. \tag{6}$$

On the other hand, from the Invert chain, we can easily know that the $k_i'$ is a positive integer or a negative integer. Suppose $k_i' = (-1)^{h_i} k_i^*$ , where $(-1)^{h_i}$ is the sign of $k_i'$ which is known, $k_i^* \in \{1, 3, 5, 7\}$. Write $k_i^* = 2k_i + 1$ , where $k_i \in \{0, 1, 2, 3\}$. Then we have

$$k = \sum_{i=1}^{l} (-1)^{h_i} k_i^* 2^{\lambda_i} = \sum_{i=1}^{l} (-1)^{h_i} (2k_i + 1) 2^{\lambda_i} = \bar{k} + \sum_{i=1}^{l} (-1)^{h_i} k_i 2^{\lambda_i + 1} \tag{7}$$

where $\bar{k} = \sum_{i=1}^{l} (-1)^{h_i} 2^{\lambda_i}$, $h_i$, $\lambda_i$ are known and the only unknowns are $k_i \in \{0, 1, 2, 3\}$.

For the secp256k1 curve implemented in OpenSSL, from Eq.(7), there are approximately 51.4*2= 102.8 bits being unknown, which means the number of the known bits is about $257 - 102.8 = 154.2$ on average. It is about 1.5 times of the number of bits in [9]. In theory, we just need two signatures to recover the 256-bit private key, because the least integer $m$ is 2 such that $m \cdot 154.2 > 256$.

## 5.2  Find the Target Vector with New Lattice

Similar to [9], we translate to the EHNP problem to recover ECDSA private key. Then we further construct a lattice and solve the approximate SVP using lattice reduction algorithm.

**Reduction to EHNP Problem.** Transforming the expression of the signature and we can have the equation

$$\alpha r - sk + H(m) = 0 \quad \mod q. \tag{8}$$

Substitue (8) with Eq. (7), we get Eq. (9)

$$\alpha r - \sum_{i=1}^{l}((-1)^{h_i}2^{\lambda_i+1}s)k_i - (s\bar{k} - H(m)) + hq = 0. \tag{9}$$

where $\alpha, k_i(1 \leq i \leq l)$ and $h \in \mathbb{Z}$ is unknown.

If we have $u$ signatures $(r_i, s_i)$ of different messages $m_i(1 \leq i \leq u)$ with the same private key $\alpha$. From (9) we can easily have

$$\begin{cases} \alpha r_1 - \sum\limits_{j=1}^{l_1}((-1)^{h_{1,j}}2^{\lambda_{1,j}+1}s_1)k_{1,j} - (s_1\bar{k}_1 - H(m_1)) + h'_1 q = 0 \\ \quad \vdots \\ \alpha r_i - \sum\limits_{j=1}^{l_i}((-1)^{h_{i,j}}2^{\lambda_{i,j}+1}s_i)k_{i,j} - (s_i\bar{k}_i - H(m_i)) + h'_i q = 0 \\ \quad \vdots \\ \alpha r_u - \sum\limits_{j=1}^{l_u}((-1)^{h_{u,j}}2^{\lambda_{u,j}+1}s_u)k_{u,j} - (s_u\bar{k}_u - H(m_u)) + h'_u q = 0 \end{cases} \tag{10}$$

the number of non-zero digits is $l_i$. $(-1)^{h_{i,j}}k_{i,j}$ is the $j$-th non-zero digit in the $i$-th signature, $\lambda_{i,j}$ is its position, $\bar{k}_i = \sum\limits_{j=1}^{l_i}(-1)^{h_{i,j}}2^{\lambda_{i,j}} \mod q$ and $\alpha, h'_i, k_{i,j}$ are unknown elements in the equations.

Given Eq. (10), find $0 < \alpha < q$ and $0 \leq k_{i,j} \leq 2^{w-1} - 1$. We denote this problem DSA-EHNP.

**Constructing the Target Vector.** Next we will translate the DSA-EHNP problem to the problem of finding the short vector of a related lattice, which uses the same way of [9].

Notice that we have $k_{i,j} \in \{0, 1, \cdots, 2^{w-1}-1\}$. For $1 \leq i \leq u$ and $1 \leq j \leq l_i$, denote $c_{i,j} = (-1)^{h_{i,j}+1}2^{\lambda_{i,j}+1}s_i \mod q$, $\beta_i = H(m_i) - s_i\bar{k}_i \mod q$. The lattice $L$ is spanned by the following matrix $B$ in Eq. (11).

It is easy to check there exists

$$\begin{aligned} \mathbf{w} &= (h'_1, \cdots, h'_\mu, \alpha, k_{1,1}, \cdots, k_{1,l_1}, \cdots, k_{u,1}, \cdots, k_{u,l_u}, -1)\mathbf{B} \\ &= (0, \cdots, 0, \tfrac{\alpha}{q}\delta - \tfrac{\delta}{2}, \tfrac{k_{1,1}}{4}\delta - \tfrac{\delta}{2}, \cdots, \tfrac{k_{1,l_1}}{4}\delta - \tfrac{\delta}{2}, \cdots, \\ &\quad \tfrac{k_{u,1}}{4}\delta - \tfrac{\delta}{2}, \cdots, \tfrac{k_{u,l_u}}{4}\delta - \tfrac{\delta}{2}, -\tfrac{\delta}{2}) \in L(\mathbf{B}), \end{aligned}$$

and the Euclid norm of the vector $\mathbf{w}$ satisfies $\|\mathbf{w}\| \leq \tfrac{\delta}{2}\sqrt{n-u}$, where $n$ is the dimension of the lattice, i.e., $n = \sum\limits_{i=1}^{u} l_i + u + 2$.

**Table 2.** The success probability for solving the EHNP problem. (merge: elimination and merging, MSD: recovering the MSDs, SMSD: enumeration of the MSD.)

| Number of signatures | Optimization methods | Success probability (%) | Time (s) |
|---|---|---|---|
| 3 | n_merge_n_MSD_n_SMSD | 69.9 | 341 |
| | n_merge_MSD_n_SMSD | 87.5 | 242 |
| | n_merge_MSD_SMSD | 89.1 | 273 |
| 4 | merge_n_MSD_n_SMSD | 99.8 | 497 |
| | merge_MSD_n_SMSD | 100 | 300 |
| | merge_MSD_SMSD | 100 | 320 |

$$\mathbf{B} = \begin{pmatrix} q & & & & & & & & & & \\ & \ddots & & & & & & & & & \\ & & q & & & & & & & & \\ r_1 & \cdots & r_u & \frac{\delta}{q} & & & & & & & \\ c_{1,1} & & & & \frac{\delta}{4} & & & & & & \\ \vdots & & & & & \ddots & & & & & \\ c_{1,l_1} & & & & & & \frac{\delta}{4} & & & & \\ & & & & & & & \ddots & & & \\ & c_{\mu,1} & & & & & & & \frac{\delta}{4} & & \\ & \vdots & & & & & & & & \ddots & \\ & c_{\mu,l_\mu} & & & & & & & & & \frac{\delta}{4} \\ \beta_1 & \cdots & \beta_u & \frac{\delta}{2} & \frac{\delta}{2} & \cdots & \frac{\delta}{2} & \cdots & \frac{\delta}{2} & \cdots & \frac{\delta}{2} & \frac{\delta}{2} \end{pmatrix} \tag{11}$$

The determinant of lattice $L(\mathbf{B})$ is $\|L\| = \frac{1}{2}q^{u-1} \cdot \delta^{n-u}(\frac{1}{4})^{n-u-2}$. The target vector $\mathbf{w}$ may not be the shortest vector, however, if we choose a appropriate value of $\delta$, the target vector $\mathbf{w}$ which will be a pretty short vector which can be found by lattice reduction algorithm ([3,8,16,28]), thus, the secret key $\alpha$ can be recovered.

### 5.3   Attacking the Secp256k1

We apply this lattice attack to the curve secp256k1 and also assume that the Flush+Flush attack is perfect. In the experiments, we use the BKZ with block size 30 to solve the SVP problem converted from the EHNP problem.

Fan [9] proposed three optimization methods: elimination and merging, recovering the MSDs, and enumeration of the MSD. In our experiments, we measure the success probability of the lattice attack with these optimization methods.

Table 2 shows the success probability for different number of signatures and optimization selections. We can successfully recover the private key of a 256-bit ECDSA only need 3 signatures for at least 69.9%. We also tried to use 2 signatures to recover the ECDSA private key, but it can not succeed. Although we already reach the best result, the same as in [19], theoretically we only need 2 signatures to recover the private key. That means we can still make improvements on it to reach the theoretical optimal number.

**Table 3.** Comparison with previous attack methods

| Methods | Exploited information | HNP or EHNP | # of bits | # of signatures |
|---|---|---|---|---|
| Benger et al. [6] | LSB | HNP | 2 | 200 |
| Van de Pol et al. [26] | Half positions of non-zero digits | HNP | 47.6 | 13 |
| Wang et al. [32] | Positions of two non-zero digits and the length of the wNAF representation of $k$ | HNP | $\geq 2.99$ | 85 |
| Allan et al. [4] | Half positions and signs of non-zero digits | HNP | 71.4 | 6 |
| Fan et al. [9] | All positions of non-zero digits | EHNP | 105.8 | 4 |
| Micheli et al. [19] | All positions of non-zero digits | EHNP | 105.8 | 3 |
| Ours | All positions and signs of non-zero digits | HNP | 154.2 | 248 |
| | | EHNP | 154.2 | 3 |

## 6   Comparison with Other Lattice Attacks

In this section, we compared our method with the previous attacks. Generally, through cache side channels attackers obtain the Double-Add or Double-Add-Invert chain and extract partial information about $k$. Then, the private key recovery from incomplete information of $k$ is transformed into a problem that can be solved by lattice reduction, such as the HNP or EHNP problem. Finally, through being converted to the CVP/SVP problem in the lattice, the ECDSA private key is recovered.

With the HNP problem, several works have been proposed. They all used the Flush+Reload attack to obtain the Double-Add chain. Then they used the different information extracted from the Double-Add chain, especially the least significant bits (LSBs) of the ephemeral key [6], half of the consecutive non-zero digit [26], and the positions of two non-zero digits and the length of the wNAF representation [32]. These methods extracted restricted bits from the Double-Add chain, so that they need many signatures to recover the private key.

Besides, Allan et al. [4] first used the Flush+Reload attack to monitor the invert function and used a performance degradation attack to increase the attack accuracy. Then they exploited Van de Pol's method to construct the HNP problem with the extra information to recover the ECDSA private key. This method can extract 71.4 bits per signature on average for the secp256k1 curve and recover the private with 6 signatures.

While with the EHNP problem, Fan et al. [9] extracted all positions of digits from the Flush+Reload attack and took advantage of them to construct an EHNP instance. They managed to obtain on average 105.8 bits per signature for the secp256k1 curve. With some optimization only 4 signatures are needed to recover the private key with the probability being 8%. Subsequently, Micheli et al. [19] improved Fan's work and optimized the lattice to recover the ECDSA private by only 3 signatures.

We compare these attacks with ours in detail in four aspects as shown in Table 3. Our method exploits both the signs and the positions of the non-zero digits of the ephemeral key $k$ achieved from the Flush+Flush attack. It extracts the largest amount of information, on average 156.2 bits per signature for the secp256k1 curve. We use both the HNP and EHNP problems to recover the ECDSA private key. Although the using HNP problem needs 248 signatures, using EHNP problem the number of signatures needed to recover the private key is only 3 with the success probability being not less than 69.9%.

## 7   Conclusion

In this paper, we demonstrate a practical attack on the ECDSA algorithm implemented with the scalar multiplication using the wNAF representation. We improve the cache side channel attack by using the Flush+Flush technique and adding an extra monitor to the invert function. Through them, we get the extra information, i.e., the signs of all non-zero digits of the ephemeral key. Then, we construct the HNP and EHNP instances respectively, to utilize the extracted information for the ECDSA private key recovery.

This work obtains the information about the signs of the non-zero digits of the ephemeral key without using performance degradation and uses the least number of signatures to recover the ECDSA private key. We applied the Flush+Flush attack to the secp256k1 curve in OpenSSL 1.1.0h to verify the availability of monitoring the invert function. from the Double-Add-Invert chain we extract on average 154.2 bits of information per signature. If the obtained Double-Add-Invert chain is perfect, 3 signatures are enough to recover the ECDSA private key by using the EHNP problem with a success probability no less than 69.9%. This result reaches the best one as ever known with higher success probability.

## References

1. Cryptlib Encryption Toolkit. https://www.cs.auckland.ac.nz/pgut001/cryptlib/ (2020)
2. The Legion of the Bouncy Castle (2020). http://www.bouncycastle.org/
3. Albrecht, M.R., Ducas, L., Herold, G., Kirshanova, E., Postlethwaite, E.W., Stevens, M.: The general sieve kernel and new records in lattice reduction. In: Ishai, Y., Rijmen, V. (eds.) EUROCRYPT 2019. LNCS, vol. 11477, pp. 717–746. Springer, Cham (2019). https://doi.org/10.1007/978-3-030-17656-3_25

4. Allan, T., Brumley, B.B., Falkner, K., van de Pol, J., Yarom, Y.: Amplifying side channels through performance degradation. In: Proceedings of the 32nd Annual Conference on Computer Security Applications (ACSAC), pp. 422–435 (2016)
5. American National Standards Institute: ANSI X9.62-2005, Public Key Cryptography for the Financial Services Industry: The Elliptic Curve Digital Signature Algorithm (ECDSA) (2005)
6. Benger, N., van de Pol, J., Smart, N.P., Yarom, Y.: "ooh aah... just a little bit" : a small amount of side channel can go a long way. In: 16th International Workshop on Cryptographic Hardware and Embedded Systems (CHES), pp. 75–92 (2014)
7. Boneh, D., Venkatesan, R.: Hardness of computing the most significant bits of secret keys in diffie-hellman and related schemes. In: Koblitz, N. (ed.) CRYPTO 1996. LNCS, vol. 1109, pp. 129–142. Springer, Heidelberg (1996). https://doi.org/10.1007/3-540-68697-5_11
8. Chen, Y., Nguyen, P.Q.: BKZ 2.0: better lattice security estimates. In: Lee, D.H., Wang, X. (eds.) ASIACRYPT 2011. LNCS, vol. 7073, pp. 1–20. Springer, Heidelberg (2011). https://doi.org/10.1007/978-3-642-25385-0_1
9. Fan, S., Wang, W., Cheng, Q.: Attacking OpenSSL implementation of ECDSA with a few signatures. In: Proceedings of the 2016 ACM SIGSAC Conference on Computer and Communications Security (CCS), pp. 1505–1515 (2016)
10. Gruss, D., Maurice, C., Wagner, K., Mangard, S.: Flush+ Flush: a fast and stealthy cache attack. In: 13th International Conference on Detection of Intrusions and Malware, and Vulnerability Assessment, pp. 279–299 (2016)
11. Hai, H., Ning, N., Lin, X., Zhiwei, L., Bin, Y., Shilei, Z.: An improved wnaf scalar-multiplication algorithm with low computational complexity by using prime precomputation. IEEE Access 9, 31546–31552 (2021)
12. Hlaváč, M., Rosa, T.: Extended hidden number problem and its cryptanalytic applications. In: Biham, E., Youssef, A.M. (eds.) SAC 2006. LNCS, vol. 4356, pp. 114–133. Springer, Heidelberg (2007). https://doi.org/10.1007/978-3-540-74462-7_9
13. Howgrave-Graham, N.A., Smart, N.P.: Lattice attacks on digital signature schemes. Des. Codes Cryptogr. 23(3), 283–290 (2001)
14. Callas, J., Donnerhacke, L., Finney, H., Shaw, D., Thayer, R.: OpenPGP Message Format (RFC 4880) (2007)
15. Johnson, D., Menezes, A., Vanstone, S.: The elliptic curve digital signature algorithm (ECDSA). Int. J. Inf. Secur. 1(1), 36–63 (2001)
16. Lenstra, A.K., Lenstra, H.W., Lovász, L.: Factoring polynomials with rational coefficients. Mathematische Annalen 261(4), 515–534 (1982)
17. Liu, F., Yarom, Y., Ge, Q., Heiser, G., Lee, R.B.: Last-level cache side-channel attacks are practical. In: IEEE Symposium on Security and Privacy, S&P 2015, pp. 605–622 (2015)
18. Liu, S., Qi, G., Wang, X.A.: Fast and secure elliptic curve scalar multiplication algorithm based on a kind of deformed fibonacci-type series. In: 2015 10th International Conference on P2P, Parallel, Grid, Cloud and Internet Computing (3PGCIC), pp. 398–402 (2015)
19. De Micheli, G., Piau, R., Pierrot, C.: A tale of three signatures: practical attack of ECDSA with wNAF. In: Nitaj, A., Youssef, A. (eds.) AFRICACRYPT 2020. LNCS, vol. 12174, pp. 361–381. Springer, Cham (2020). https://doi.org/10.1007/978-3-030-51938-4_18
20. Möller, B.: Algorithms for multi-exponentiation. In: International Workshop on Selected Areas in Cryptography, pp. 165–180 (2001)

21. Nakamoto, S.: Bitcoin: a peer-to-peer electronic cash system (2008). https://bitcoin.org/bitcoin.pdf
22. Nguyen, P.Q.: The dark side of the hidden number problem: lattice attacks on DSA. In: Cryptography and Computational Number Theory, pp. 321–330 (2001)
23. Nguyen, P.Q., Shparlinski, I.E.: The insecurity of the digital signature algorithm with partially known nonces. J. Cryptol. $15(3)$, 151–176 (2002)
24. Nguyen, P.Q., Shparlinski, I.E.: The insecurity of the elliptic curve digital signature algorithm with partially known nonces. Des. Codes Cryptogr. $30(2)$, 201–217 (2003)
25. Page, D.: Theoretical use of cache memory as a cryptanalytic side-channel. IACR Cryptol. ePrint Arch. $2002$, 169 (2002)
26. van de Pol, J., Smart, N.P., Yarom, Y.: Just a little bit more. In: The Cryptographers' Track at the RSA Conference (CT-RSA), pp. 3–21 (2015)
27. Rankl, W.: Smart card applications: design models for using and programming smart cards (2007)
28. Schnorr, C.P., Euchner, M.: Lattice basis reduction: improved practical algorithms and solving subset sum problems. Math. Program. $66(1)$, 181–199 (1994)
29. Solinas, J.A.: Efficient arithmetic on koblitz curves. Des. Codes Cryptogr. $19(2)$, 195–249 (2000)
30. Dierks, T., Rescorla, E.: The Transport Layer Security (TLS) Protocol Version 1.2 (RFC 5246) (2008)
31. The FPLLL development team: fplll, a lattice reduction library (2016). https://github.com/fplll/fplll
32. Wang, W., Fan, S.: Attacking OpenSSL ECDSA with a small amount of side-channel information. Sci. China Inf. Sci. $61(3)$, 032105:1–032105:14 (2017)
33. Yarom, Y., Falkner, K.: Flush+Reload: a high resolution, low noise, L3 cache side-channel attack. In: Proceedings of the 23rd USENIX Conference on Security Symposium, pp. 719–732 (2014)
34. Zhao, S.l., Yang, X.Q., Liu, Z.W., Yu, B., Huang, H.: An improved wnaf scalar-multiplication algorithm with low computational complexity. Acta Electonica Sinica, 1–7 (2022)

# MAG-PUF: Magnetic Physical Unclonable Functions for Device Authentication in the IoT

Omar Adel Ibrahim[1(✉)], Savio Sciancalepore[2,3], and Roberto Di Pietro[1]

[1] College of Science and Engineering (CSE), Information and Computing Technology (ICT) Division, Hamad Bin Khalifa University (HBKU), Doha, Qatar
{oaibrahim,rdipietro}@hbku.edu.qa
[2] Department of Mathematics and Computer Science, Eindhoven University of Technology (TU/e), Eindhoven, The Netherlands
s.sciancalepore@tue.nl
[3] Eindhoven Artificial Intelligence Systems Institute (EAISI), Eindhoven, The Netherlands

**Abstract.** Authenticating Internet of Things (IoT) devices is still a challenge, especially in deployments involving low-cost constrained nodes. The cited class of IoT devices hardly support dynamic re-keying solutions, hence being vulnerable to several attacks. To provide a viable general-purpose solution, in this paper we propose MAG-PUF, a novel lightweight authentication scheme based on the usage of unintentional magnetic emissions generated by IoT devices as Physical Unclonable Functions (PUFs). Specifically, through MAG-PUF, we collect unintentional magnetic emissions produced by the IoT devices at run-time while executing pre-defined reference functions, and we verify the match of such emissions with the profiles collected at enrolment time, providing device authentication. MAG-PUF enjoys unique flexibility, allowing the selection of an unlimited number and types of reference functions. We extensively assessed the performance of MAG-PUF through experiments on 25 Arduino devices and a set of exemplary reference functions. We obtained an authentication accuracy above 99%, hence proving the feasibility of using code-driven magnetic emissions as a lightweight, efficient, and robust PUF for IoT devices.

**Keywords:** Magnetic emissions · PUF · Authentication · IoT

## 1 Introduction

Internet of Things (IoT) devices are nowadays increasingly deployed in homes, offices, medical, electricity, and transportation domains, to name a few [41], with an installed base of a few billions, and counting [42]. Unfortunately, as acknowledged by several reports [39], security issues are still one of the most critical

F. Li et al. (Eds.): SecureComm 2022, LNICST 462, pp. 130–149, 2023.
https://doi.org/10.1007/978-3-031-25538-0_8

concerns, preventing the unleashing of the full potential behind the IoT. On the one hand, IoT devices often find applications in natively-insecure environments, being the ideal target of various attacks. On the other hand, such devices are usually so constrained in their processing, memory, and energy resources that they cannot support Public Key Infrastructure (PKI) at all, and sometimes even the usage of symmetric key cryptography techniques might significantly affect their lifetime and usability [34]. Moreover, when symmetric cryptography operations are supported, several devices use hard-coded cryptography materials. However, due to the simple design of the devices and the unattended nature of many IoT deployments, attackers can capture the devices and easily recover such keys, fully compromising them [7].

To address the above-described issues, Physical Unclonable Functions (PUFs) have been proposed as a viable and effective alternative [28] to authenticate devices. In a nutshell, PUFs leverage the finding that, despite Integrated Circuits (ICs) are assembled in a precise fabrication process, unintentional variations always occur at the sub-micrometer level, causing any two ICs to be never exactly identical. PUFs take into account such unique properties of any specific device, allowing to generate lightweight chip-dependent unique signatures, that are almost impossible to reproduce either synthetically or by using other devices [46]. Thus, when applied appropriately in the IoT domain, PUFs can efficiently and effectively bypass the need for both complex cryptography operations and hard-coded secrets, allowing system administrators to authenticate IoT devices at low-cost [40].

Despite the above introduced advantages, PUFs are still hardly usable in the IoT context. Indeed, many of the schemes proposed in the literature leverage unique properties of specific memory modules and low-layer circuits, difficult to generalize and to use in low-cost general-purpose IoT devices. Other solutions, such as the ones based on RF emissions, usually do not scale well for large deployments, providing limited security guarantees (see Sect. 5 for more details).

**Contribution.** In this paper, we design *MAG PUF*, a novel and lightweight scheme exploiting the unique randomness of unintentional magnetic emissions produced by IoT devices when computing a function to generate Physical Unclonable Functions. Specifically, deploying *MAG-PUF*, the IoT system owner can select a theoretically-unlimited number of reference functions to be used for authentication purposes. The profile of the unintentional magnetic emissions radiated by the devices when executing the reference functions is first acquired at enrolment time, and then checked for consistency at run-time. To this aim, as a novel building block in the PUF area, *MAG-PUF* features Machine Learning (ML)-based classification tools, used to model the magnetic emissions and check for the match of a specific acquisition with the expected profile. Our extensive experimental performance assessment, performed considering 25 Arduino IoT devices and a set of exemplary reference functions, reported a remarkable classification accuracy of above 99%, as well as PUF-related metrics very close to the optimal ones (Intra-PUF Distance of 0.02 and Inter-PUF Distance of 0.51).

Overall, thanks to the customized usage of near-field magnetic emissions and the integration of ML tools, *MAG-PUF* emerges as a novel, lightweight, and secure primitive for authenticating constrained IoT devices, natively offering scalability and robustness features for safety-critical IoT deployments.

**Roadmap.** This paper is organized as follows: Sect. 2 describes the scenario; Sect. 3 describes *MAG-PUF* in details; Sect. 4 reports an extensive performance assessment and highlights further research directions; Sect. 5 reviews related work; and, finally, Sect. 6 concludes the paper and outlines future work.

# 2    Scenario, Use-Cases, and Requirements

In this section, we introduce our considered scenarios, assumptions and the considered requirements.

## 2.1    Scenario and Assumptions

We consider a generic IoT network, i.e., a ubiquitous ecosystem where devices communicate and exchange information without the need for human intervention [3]. Our solution is also built on some realistic assumptions. First, we assume that the IoT devices are resource-constrained in terms of memory and energy. As a result, they cannot use a PKI, because of the overwhelming computational cost. Also, we consider a network where the IoT devices do not have specific tools or capabilities, such as ML-based functionalities or Software-defined radio (SDR) capabilities. Conversely, the devices rely on external equipment to collect and process their unintentional magnetic emissions (either the *PUF Manager* or the *verifier*, see below). The IoT devices in the network can be connected with each other or directly with a central network manager using either a wired or wireless interface, depending on the specific deployment, setup, and security requirements.

From the security perspective, we aim to provide physical-layer authentication of the IoT devices. Indeed, not featuring PKI-based solutions, the IoT devices should be able to prove their identity leveraging features (e.g., non-idealities) available at the physical-layer. In our work, we aim to reach the aforementioned objective by establishing a PUF-based challenge-response pairs (CRP) database (in a form of a trained ML model), utilizing random reference functions and their unintentional magnetic emissions to authenticate the devices.

## 2.2    Adversary Model

We consider a powerful adversary, namely, $\mathcal{A}$, characterized by both passive and active capabilities. We assume $\mathcal{A}$ has access to a much more powerful equipment than the deployed IoT devices, not characterized by any energy or processing limitations. Also, $\mathcal{A}$ could use advanced wireless reception tools, such as directional antennas, to boost its reception capabilities. We also consider an omnipresent adversary, present in the field before, during, and after the deployment of the IoT devices. Overall, $\mathcal{A}$ aims to authenticate itself as a legitimate node in the deployed IoT network, in place of a target IoT device. To this aim, we assume $\mathcal{A}$ can mimic other devices' messages, initiate a session, eavesdrop packets, and replay captured messages. In this context, the objective of ($MAG$-$PUF$) is to thwart such an adversary by providing physical-layer authentication of the IoT devices in the network.

## 2.3  Requirements

PUF-based solutions conceived to provide authentication of the IoT devices has to fulfill several requirements, outlined below [24].

- $Constructibility$: A PUF class $\mathbb{P}$ is said to be constructible if it is possible to produce a random $puf$ instance by invoking a specific $Create$ function: $puf \leftarrow \mathbb{P}.Create$.
- $Evaluability$: A PUF class $\mathbb{P}$ is said to be evaluable if it is constructible and it is possible to evaluate a response $y$ for any random PUF instance $puf \in \mathbb{P}$ and any random challenge $x \in \mathbb{X}$: $y \leftarrow puf(x).Eval$.
- $Reproducibility$: A PUF class $\mathbb{P}$ is said to be reproducible if it is evaluable, and the probability of the $Intra$-$PUF$ $Distance$ being small is high. The $Intra$-$PUF$ $Distance$ is defined as the difference between two separate evaluations (responses) of the same challenge produced by the same device, preferably averaging values close to 0.
- $Uniqueness$: A PUF class $\mathbb{P}$ is said to exhibit uniqueness if it is evaluable, and the probability of the $Inter$-$PUF$ $Distance$ being large is high. The $Inter$-$PUF$ $Distance$ is defined as the difference between two separate evaluations (responses) of the same challenge produced by different devices, preferably averaging values close to 0.5.
- $Identifiability$: A PUF class $\mathbb{P}$ is said to be identifiable if it is reproducible and unique, and the probability that $Inter$-$PUF$ $Distance$ being greater than the $Intra$-$PUF$ $Distance$ is high.

In Sect. 4.2, we will prove the conformity of $MAG$-$PUF$ with all the cited requirements.

# 3   Proposed Framework

In this section, we provide the details of $MAG$-$PUF$, our solution to provide authentication of energy-constrained IoT devices via magnetic-based PUFs.

## 3.1  $MAG$-$PUF$ in a Nutshell

Figure 1 provides an overview of our proposed solution. Overall, $MAG$-$PUF$ allows a verifier (e.g., the local system administrator or another system/device on

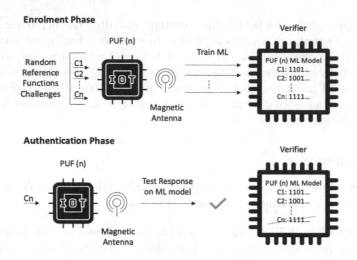

**Fig. 1.** Overview of *MAG-PUF*.

its behalf) to authenticate a prover (an IoT device), through the analysis of the profile of the unintentional magnetic emissions generated by the prover during the execution of a *reference function*, i.e., a sequence of operations appropriately selected by the verifier.

In brief, *MAG-PUF* consists of two phases, i.e., the *enrolment Phase* and the *Authentication Phase*. The former is executed upon manufacture, by: (i) supplying several *reference functions* to the prover; (ii) extracting the corresponding unintentional magnetic emissions generated by the device; and, (iii) creating the corresponding *reference models*, via ML algorithms. At run-time, when the system administrator or any other entity (namely, the verifier) requires authentication of the IoT device(s), it randomly chooses one or more of the available *reference functions*, it captures the corresponding unintentional magnetic emissions, and it checks if the corresponding real-time profile of the unintentional magnetic emissions matches the one available for the prover, via ML-based classification tools. If there is a match, the prover IoT device is authenticated successfully; otherwise, authentication fails.

## 3.2 Actors

Overall, *MAG-PUF* involves the following three entities.

- *Prover.* It is an IoT device, to be deployed in a specific scenario. We do not make any assumption for this device, besides the integration of communication capabilities to interact with other systems (PUF Manager) or devices (verifier).
- *PUF Manager.* It is a local entity, managed by a specific system administrator. Its role is manifold: (i) deciding on a set of *reference functions*; (ii) running them on the prover before the deployment; (iii) acquiring the corresponding

unintentional magnetic emissions; (iv) generating their profile, via ML-based tools; (v) storing such profiles on a dedicated server; and, finally, (vi) making them available to the verifier. Thus, we assume it is equipped with the tools necessary to acquire magnetic emissions, such as magnetic antennas, and signal analysis tools (e.g., SDR).

– *Verifier.* It is a remote system or device, interested in authenticating the prover. To this aim, it interacts both with the prover, to acquire its run-time unintentional magnetic emissions, and with the PUF Manager, to download the profile of the unintended magnetic emissions of the prover and the specific reference function submitted to the prover. Similar to the PUF Manager, the verifier also features tools to acquire magnetic emissions and run signal analysis.

## 3.3 Modules

*MAG-PUF* relies on four modules, described below.

– **Emissions Extraction Module.** This module, installed on the PUF manager and the verifier, is responsible for recording the unintentional magnetic emissions generated from specific IoT devices when executing particular reference functions. The collected raw data of magnetic emissions include: (i) timestamp, in msec; (ii) acquisition frequency, in Hz; and, (iii) value of the Received Signal Strength (RSS), in dBm. The collected data are provided as input to the *Features Extraction Module*.

– **Features Extraction Module.** This module, installed on the PUF Manager and on the verifier, is responsible for extracting the relevant features from the data collected by the Emissions Extraction Module. It operates in three stages, i.e., *Data Normalization, Regions Definitions*, and *Features Computation*.

 • **Data Normalization.** We first normalize the magnetic emissions power spectral density readings recorded in dBm to the range $[0\ldots1]$. Specifically, assuming that $x_i$ is a sample of the readings, and $X_{MIN}$ and $X_{MAX}$ are the minimum and the maximum value of the readings, the normalized sample $\hat{x}_i$ is calculated as: $\hat{x}_i = \frac{x_i - X_{MIN}}{(X_{MAX} - X_{MIN})}$. This step is important to allow for cross-comparison between different recordings, by eliminating small differences in the measured power levels due to minor misalignment of the measurement setup.

 • **Regions Definition.** In the collected data, each sample of magnetic emissions power level in dBm is associated with a specific timestamp and frequency. In this step, we divide each trace of magnetic emissions into a specific number of regions, with each region comprising the power level readings collected at a specific range of time and frequency. More details on the specific number and organization of regions are provided in Sect. 4.

 • **Features Computation.** In this step, we compute the following five statistical features on each region defined in the previous step: (i) mean; (ii) standard deviation; (iii) variance; (iv) skewness; and, (v) kurtosis.

The output of this phase is a matrix of features that is passed either to the Training Module (PUF Manager) or to the Classification Module (verifier).

- **Training Module.** This module, installed on the PUF Manager, is responsible for using the features matrix produced by the *Features Extraction Module* to train a ML model. The aim of the model is to discriminate uniquely the devices and the responses of the device to different reference functions. The trained ML model is made available online on request to the verifier, to be used in the authentication stage to authenticate different devices. In this work, we use a one-class Support Vector Machine (SVM) algorithm with cubic kernel to train the ML model, so as to uniquely identify each device and reference function. Indeed, for each class considered, the SVM algorithm creates a standalone profile mapping the acquired emissions [33].

- **Classification Module.** This module, installed on the verifier, is responsible for testing the profile of the recorded magnetic emissions from the IoT device against the trained ML model made available by the PUF Manager. For each test sample, the one-class SVM provides an evaluation score, indicating the likelihood that the particular sample belongs to a specific class in the trained ML model [33]. The closest the score is to the value 0, the more likely the sample is consistent with the tested model.

## 3.4   Phases of *MAG-PUF*

*MAG-PUF* includes two main phases, namely, the *Enrolment Phase* and the *Authentication Phase*, detailed below.

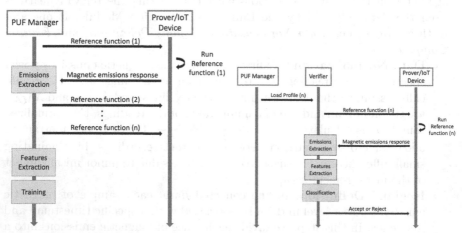

(a) Sequence diagram of the Enrolment phase of *MAG-PUF*.

(b) Sequence diagram of the different steps of the Authentication phase of *MAG-PUF*.

**Fig. 2.** Sequence diagrams of *MAG-PUF*.

**Enrolment Phase.** Figure 2a shows the sequence diagram of the Enrolment Phase. Upon manufacture and before deployment, the *PUF Manager* chooses at random several *reference functions*, and submits them to the prover, requesting their execution. Note that a *reference function* can be either a single specific operation or a combination of several operations. Moreover, due to the specific application, each system administrator can freely choose the reference functions most suitable for *MAG-PUF*. For instance, the system administrator can choose the primitives (or combinations thereof) providing the most unique profile of unintentional magnetic emissions for the IoT device.

At the same time, using the *Emissions Extraction Module*, the *PUF Manager* acquires the unintentional magnetic emissions generated by the prover while executing the specified reference function(s). For each tested reference function, using the *Features Extraction Module*, the *PUF Manager* extracts some features of the recorded signal, builds an SVM model using the *Training Module*, and uploads the model to an online database.

**Authentication Phase.** The Authentication phase steps are detailed in Fig. 2b. Upon any authentication exchange, the verifier extracts at random one (or more) of the reference functions whose profiles are available from the PUF Manager, and instructs the prover to execute such function(s). At execution time, the verifier records the unintentional magnetic emissions emitted from the prover thanks to the *Emission Extraction Module* and analyzes them, thanks to the *Features Extraction Module*, to extract the relevant features. Then, using the *Classification Module*, the verifier checks if the model of the features just extracted and computed match the available profile. If the profile acquired at run-time matches the one downloaded from the PUF Manager, the prover is authenticated. Otherwise, authentication fails.

## 4    Experimental Performance Assessment

In this section, we provide the results of our experimental assessment, carried out to evaluate the performance of *MAG-PUF*. Specifically, Sect. 4.1 introduces the experimental testbed, in Sect. 4.2 we report the results of our analysis, in Sect. 4.3 we report some performance metrics for PUF robustness, and finally, Sect. 4.4 summarizes our investigation.

### 4.1    Experimental Setup

In our experimental campaign, we used the following equipment.

- **Arduino Uno Boards.** We tested the performance of *MAG-PUF* with a set of 25 identical Arduino UNO IoT boards [45]. Each board is equipped with an 8-bit microcontroller ATmega328P, featuring a 16 MHz ceramic resonator, 2 KB of internal SRAM, and a 32KB of Flash memory.

– **Aaronia PBS2 EMC Probe set**. To collect the unintentional magnetic emissions response when running different reference functions, we used the Aaronia PBS2 EMC Probe Kit [1]. This equipment enables simple measurements in the frequency range from DC (1 Hz) to 9 GHz, as well as the monitoring of magnetic emissions. We used the PBS-H3 25 mm magnetic (H3) field antenna as a probe. The antenna is covered with an insulating layer that provides a safe measurement environment for the Arduino's oscillators and mains lines. The UBBV2 40dB EMC RF pre-amplifier is connected to the probe, providing for a clear distinction between the relevant signal and the background noise. The probe is connected via a low-impedance cable to a spectrum analyzer, used to collect and store the magnetic emissions.

– **Rohde & Schwarz FSW8 Spectrum Analyzer**. We used the Rohde & Schwarz FSW8 Spectrum Analyzer to record the unintentional magnetic emissions captured by the probe over a large frequency span, up to 80 MHz. This equipment converts raw I-Q samples into spectral power density measurements. Specifically, it performs a Fast Fourier Transform (FFT) on the collected data and, for each time frame, it generates a tuple containing the timestamp (in ms), the frequency (in Hz), and the power level (in dBm).

– **Matlab R2021a**. Matlab R2021a has been used to extract features from the collected magnetic emissions data of different reference functions run by the Arduino IoT devices. Matlab was also used to train and test the ML model for the classifications of samples, using the one-class SVM model with a cubic kernel as the classification algorithm.

All the experiments described below have been conducted in regular laboratory conditions, without any effort to reduce the environmental noise. Our measurement setup is shown in Fig. 3.

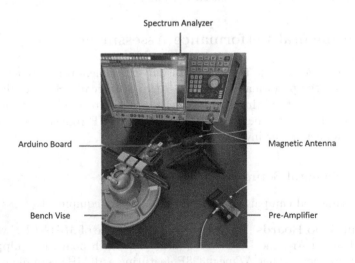

**Fig. 3.** Measurements setup

We placed the Arduino board on a Bench Vise, to hold it in a fixed position and allow for uniform recording conditions. We also placed the magnetic antenna directly above the IoT boards, to clearly capture the magnetic emission from the micro-controller and surrounding chips. The position of the magnetic antenna can be precisely controlled by a mechanical arm to ensure consistent positioning on the Arduino device in each sample collection. Alternatively, a special opening in the cover case of Arduino device can be made to exactly fit the magnetic antenna, ensuring precise placement with every measurement. Finally, we saved the collected emissions from each reference function run on the Arduino on the Spectrum analyzer.

## 4.2   Experimental Results

In the following, we provide several experimental results.

**Spectral Power Density of Sample Reference Functions.** We first evaluated the profile of unintended magnetic emissions generated by an Arduino IoT device when running different reference functions. To this aim, we defined the following operations: (A1) empty loop; (A2) first encrypt, later decrypt a 128 bit long message, using AES128, Block Cipher Mode (CBC); (A3) comparison of the similarity between two 11-bytes long strings; and, (A4) reading of input data from a DHT11 temperature and humidity sensor. We use the above-listed reference functions as examples to test our proposed *MAG-PUF* solution, as they are supported by almost any IoT device. Note that the usage of AES does not contradict our initial hypothesis on the constraints affecting IoT devices. Indeed, even if IoT devices could support symmetric encryption algorithms, they often cannot feature effective re-keying algorithms, being those often based on public-key cryptography. We also recall that each system administrator can choose the reference functions she finds most suitable for *MAG-PUF*, e.g., choosing the ones that provide the most unique profile of unintentional magnetic emissions for the device.

Figure 4 shows the spectral power density of the unintentional magnetic emissions of the full 80 MHz bandwidth acquired by the spectrum analyzer, with reference to the functions defined above, separated by dashed black lines. Each function lasts for around 120 ms. Because of the normalization phase executed during the *Features Extraction module*, all the RSS of samples of unintentional magnetic emissions recorded in dBm are normalized to a value between 0 and 1. Specifically, the blue color corresponds to values in the range [0–0.25], the cyan maps values in the range [0.25–0.5], the yellow indicates values in the range [0.5–0.75], while the red color is related to values in the range [0.75–1].

First, we can notice the clear color differences in the spectral power density between (A1) and (A3) compared with (A2) and (A4). Indeed, (A2) and (A4) are computationally-intensive operations, which require more processing power than (A1) and (A3). Furthermore, we can also see the similarity between the unintentional magnetic emissions of (A1) and (A3). Indeed, the string comparison operation (A3) is lightweight, it does not involve any complex mathematical

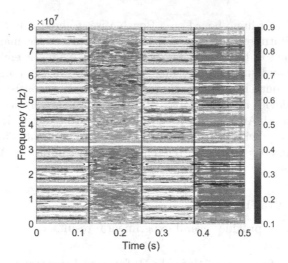

**Fig. 4.** Unintentional magnetic emissions recorded for around 120 ms of each of the four reference functions, using 80 MHz bandwidth, separated by black lines. (Color figure online)

operations, and it does not consume much more processing power than (A1), leading to similar spectral power profiles. We recall that the system administrator can select the best reference functions for its objective, i.e., the ones with distinct unintentional magnetic emissions, excluding others achieving worst performances in the field, so as to guaranteeing reliable IoT devices authentication. Overall, the results above demonstrate the fulfilment of the *Constructibility* requirement introduced in Sect. 2.3, as the PUF can be constructed by invoking the specific function, as well as the PUF *Evaluability*, being $x$ the function run by the prover and $y$ the unique profile of the emissions generated for each PUF.

**Classification Results.** For the verifier to authenticate the prover, we utilize the MATLAB provided one-class cubic SVM ML model. We consider the functions above described, each run separately inside a *For* loop on each of the 25 IoT boards. We collected the related magnetic emanations for around 6,000 slot-frames, each lasting 12 ms long. We divided each trace into 10 frames segments, getting 600 samples for each trace of the magnetic emanations recorded on a given IoT board when running a specific function. With the described procedure, the duration of a single instance of a function is 8 ms, i.e., each segment (120 ms) comprises the magnetic emanations of around 15 iterations of a given function. We collected each trace twice across four different days, to ensure robustness against temporary phenomena in the surrounding environment. This procedure resulted in $600 \cdot 2 = 1,200$ samples of each function running on each individual IoT board. We divided those 1,200 samples into 80% (960 samples) for training of the ML model, and the remaining 20% (240 samples) for testing the trained model. Overall, we have 25 IoT boards, with 960 samples for each

reference function, returning 24, 000 samples of each reference function for training, and 25 boards with 240 samples of each reference function, returning 6, 000
samples of each reference function running on the 25 IoT boards for testing.

As a result of many experiments and tests, we considered a 20 MHz acquisition bandwidth and a fixed observation window of 10 frames (120 ms) for each
of the collected traces of magnetic emissions, to allow a fair cross-comparison
between different traces. Each time window is further divided into a number
of time and frequency regions. Then, we computed the following five statistical
features over each of them: mean, standard deviation, variance, skewness, and
kurtosis. Overall, we considered 95 features, computed as follows. First, we computed the five (5) statistical features over the whole observation window of 10
frames (120 ms), generating 5 features. Then, we further divided the observation
window of 120 ms into two time regions, each 60 ms long, and we computed the
same 5 statistical features for each of them, resulting in 10 additional features.
Then, we further divided each of the time regions generated in the previous step
into eight (8) frequency regions, each with a bandwidth of 2.5 MHz. For each of
the $2 \cdot 8$ frequency regions, we computed the same aforementioned five statistical
features, resulting in $2 \cdot 8 \cdot 5 = 80$ features. By summing the three stages, we
have a total of $5 + 10 + 80 = 95$ features.

For each IoT board, we report the data coming from the authentic IoT
device as green squares (240 samples per class), while the black dots (5, 760
samples) represent the non-authentic ones. In the vast majority of experiments,
the authentic IoT devices reported values very close to 0, while the other IoT
devices executing even the same function reported lower scores. Given that the
model of each IoT device is trained and validated on its own, we selected a
threshold value for each one, and we decided to accept it as authentic if the
evaluation score is higher than the selected threshold.

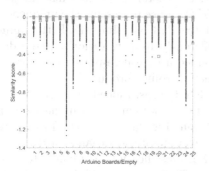 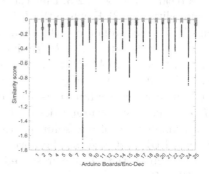

(a) Classification results of (A1) on 25 IoT   (b) Classification results of (A2) on 25 IoT
devices, using 20 MHz bandwidth.            devices, using 20 MHz bandwidth.

**Fig. 5.** Classification results for reference functions (A1) and (A2).

Figures 5a, 5b, 6a, and 6b show the similarity scores generated by the cubic
SVM model, produced by the considered IoT boards' classes, each considering

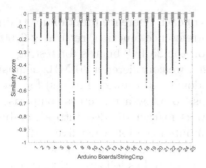 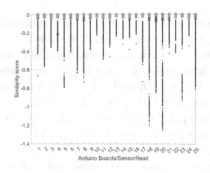

(a) Classification results of (A3) on 25 IoT   (b) Classification results of (A4) on 25 IoT
devices, using 20 MHz bandwidth.             devices, using 20 MHz bandwidth.

**Fig. 6.** Classification results for reference functions (A3) and (A4).

specific reference functions, using 20 MHz out of the total 80 MHz acquired bandwidth, over the 95 features previously-described. The average accuracy of each function across the IoT boards is 99.3%, 99.4%, 99.7%, and 99.6%, respectively. Such remarkable performances definitely prove also the *uniqueness* and *reproducibility* of *MAG-PUF* (see Sect. 2.3).

### 4.3   PUF Robustness Evaluation

In this section, we discuss the feasibility of using magnetic emissions as PUFs, through the *Intra-PUF Distance* (as a measure for the PUF *Reliability*) and *Inter-PUF Distance* (as a measure of the PUF *Uniqueness*).

We recall, from Sect. 2.3, that the *Intra-PUF Distance* provides insights into the reliability of a PUF, while the *Inter-PUF Distance* represents the uniqueness of the PUF. We cannot use the standard Intra-PUF and Inter-PUF Hamming distances to evaluate *MAG-PUF* since, differently from traditional PUFs discussed in Sect. 5, *MAG-PUF* does not produce a digital response. Conversely, *MAG-PUF* utilizes the differences of magnetic profiles produced as a response when similar reference functions are run on IoT boards. Indeed, from the *MAG-PUF* classification accuracy detailed in Sect. 4.2, we can confirm the reliability and uniqueness of our solution. In addition, Fig. 7a reports the Intra-PUF and Inter-PUF distances as the normalized average of the variance of the most prominent 20 statistical features used for ML classification. We computed the *Inter-PUF Distance* as the average variance of 600 groups, each group consisting of 25 magnetic samples taken from specific IoT device when executing a specific function, e.g., (A1) in Fig. 7a (other functions produced similar results, and are omitted for the sake of space). Each sample contains the top 20 features extracted at 20 MHz bandwidth. The *Intra-PUF Distance*, instead, is computed as the average variance of the features of 600 samples of each IoT device. Note that the most prominent normalized average variance for the Intra-PUF Distance (same device) is in the range [0–0.0005], while it is in the range [0.8–1] for

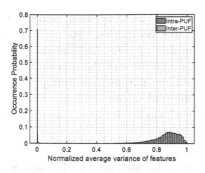
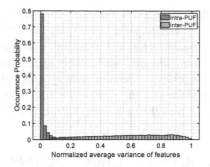

(a) Average variance of the most promi- (b) Average variance of the 95 features ex-
nent 20 features extracted at 20 MHz tracted at 20 MHz bandwidth from each
bandwidth from each IoT board.     IoT board.

**Fig. 7.** Average variance of the features extracted from the 25 IoT boards.

the Inter-PUF Distance (different devices). The ideal values of the *Inter-PUF Distance* and *Intra-PUF Distance* discussed in the literature are $\approx 0.5$ and 0, respectively [26]. In our case, the geometric mean of the normalized average variance of the 95 features used in *MAG-PUF*, reported in Fig. 7b, is approx. 0.51 for the *Inter-PUF Distance* and 0.02 for the *Intra-PUF Distance*, almost coincidental with the optimal values. Such results prove the reliability and uniqueness of *MAG-PUF*, and the suitability of the usage of magnetic emissions as PUFs.

### 4.4 Discussion and Limitations

**Impact of the Environmental Noise.** As mentioned in Sect. 4.1, we used a near field magnetic antenna to collect the emissions of the IoT devices. Such a setup allows for transparently mitigating the effect of surrounding environmental noises, as the antenna only captures a small near field around its location, i.e., on top of the electronic chips of the device. In addition, since any PUFs are susceptible to noise, the authentication can be done using a set threshold of multiple CRP to check against the CRP database. This threshold of CRP can be proportional to the amount of noise in the environment and to the total number of PUF devices that need to be distinguished [20].

**PUF Replay and Reuse Attacks.** The main attack applicable on PUFs is the replay and reuse attack, where the adversary has a temporary access to the PUF during the authentication exchange. This allows the opportunity for modeling the responses and launching a replay attack. Conversely to the RF-PUF proposed in [8], our solution enjoys the possible usage of a potentially unlimited number of reference functions. As such, *MAG-PUF* can abide to a one-time use protocol [30], so as to prevent PUF reuse and modeling attacks. In one-time use protocols, each nonce (in our case, reference function) is used only once, thus not being re-usable in case of replay and reuse.

**Scaling up CRPs Pairs.** Using *MAG-PUF*, several methods can be adopted to scale up CRPs pairs. One is to use different reference functions. As depicted in Fig. 4, each reference function has a unique profile of unintentional magnetic emissions, depending on the utilization of the micro-controller resources. To accommodate a large number of IoT devices, different reference functions can be used for specific sets of provers. Moreover, different reference function combinations and different acquisition bandwidths can also be used to scale up CRP pairs.

**ML Modeling Attacks.** *MAG-PUF* can also be the target of ML-based attacks, aiming at modeling the magnetic emission responses to reference functions through repeated eavesdropping of the exchanged authentication CRPs. On the one hand, *MAG-PUF* utilizes supervised ML to identify the magnetic emissions radiated when executing specific reference functions. On the other hand, as discussed in [8], the attacker would have to resort to unsupervised ML approaches to classify the eavesdropped CRPs streams. Thus, the modeling time is proportional to the number of CRPs possessed by attacker, and the accuracy of the model depends on the ratio of the CRPs possessed to the total length of the CRP database [11]. As discussed above, *MAG-PUF* can be scaled to use theoretically unlimited number of reference functions, and thus, CRPs pairs, making the task of such attacker harder.

**Table 1.** Qualitative comparison of *MAG-PUF* against competing solutions.

| Ref. | Type | Strong PUF | No RF interface | Near-field emissions | Hardware-agnostic |
|------|------|:----------:|:---------------:|:--------------------:|:-----------------:|
| [8] | RF | ✓ | ✗ | ✗ | ✓ |
| [15] | RF | ✓ | ✗ | ✓ | ✗ |
| [10] | RF | ✓ | ✗ | ✓ | ✗ |
| [31,44] | Delay | ✓ | ✓ | N/A | ✗ |
| [4,27,47] | Delay | ✗ | ✓ | N/A | ✗ |
| [2,6] | Memory | ✓ | ✓ | N/A | ✗ |
| [23] | Memory | ✗ | ✓ | N/A | ✗ |
| [9,13,14,17] | Memory | ✗ | ✓ | N/A | ✗ |
| [25] | Memory | ✗ | ✓ | N/A | ✗ |
| [43] | Memory | ✗ | ✓ | N/A | ✗ |
| ***MAG-PUF*** | Magnetic | ✓ | ✓ | ✓ | ✓ |

## 5   Related Work and Comparison

*MAG-PUF* enforces authentication using unintentional magnetic emissions radiated by IoT devices when executing specific functions, such as PUFs. A preliminary discussion of this idea appears in [18]. Thus, both EM-based *code fingerprinting* and PUF techniques are closely related to our work.

**EM-based Code Fingerprinting.** Code fingerprinting techniques leveraging Electro-Magnetic (EM) emissions have been used for several purposes. For instance, Sehatbakhsh et al. [38] introduced an EM physical side-channel vulnerability caused by the regular use of power management units in computers. Using such a side-channel, an attacker can create a covert channel to extract sensitive information. Similarly, Sangodoyin et al. [32] leveraged EM signals leaked from IoT devices to infer on programs activities and extract information. Sehatbakhsh et al. [36] presented EMMA, i.e., an attestation method based on EM emanations emitted from the prover when executing specific code. Both the above schemes are used to attest the functions execute by the device, but not to authenticate it. Another contribution is IDEA [21,22], i.e., a framework exploiting EM emanations to detect anomalous activities on embedded devices and Cyber-Physical Systems (CPS). Additional contributions for EM-based detection of Malware and deviations in program execution are presented in [5,16,29,35,37]. Moreover, Ibrahim et al. [19] used unintentional magnetic emissions to fingerprint USB flash drives. Their approach fingerprints the boot of the USB device, thus being not applicable for run-time authentication. Overall, the cited works prove the feasibility of using EM emanations to fingerprint specific devices' functions, but were never applied for run-time authentication.

**Physical Unclonable Functions.** From their introduction in [12], several PUFs have been proposed.

*Delay-based PUFs* use delays in the ICs of the devices for authentication. To name a few, Suh et al. [44] used them for authentication and secret key generation, while the authors in [31,48] designed multiplexer-based arbiter PUFs.

*Radio-frequency (RF)-based PUFs* exploit non-idealities in the transmitted RF signals for authentication. For instance, Deejan et al. [10] introduced RF-based Certificates of Authenticity (COA) to identify counterfeits, Chatterjee et al. [8] used deep neural networks to identify wireless transmitters, while Guajardo et al. [15] leveraged the peaks in the frequency response of IC to identify them.

*Memory-based PUFs* authenticate devices based on unique randomness of memory elements. To name a few, the authors in [2,6] used the randomness in the Resistive Random Access Memory (ReRAM), while the authors in [9,13,17], and [14] focused on the power-up of the static random access memory (SRAM). Other elements used are flip-flops [25] and latches [43].

Table 1 summarizes the PUF contributions above discussed, along relevant features. A novel element characterizing *MAG-PUF* is the independence from specific hardware. In addition, the magnetic emanations used by *MAG-PUF* can be captured mainly from the near-field of the prover, requiring the attacker to be in close proximity. Conversely, RF-based PUFs emissions can be eavesdropped from long distances, widening the attack scenario. *MAG-PUF* provides also a Strong PUF, easily allowing for the extraction of a large number of challenge-response pairs, and it does not require the presence of any RF interface in the device, as in the case of RF PUFs. Finally, *MAG-PUF* can utilize a theoretically unlimited number of reference functions; conversely, RF-PUFs use wireless messages, leveraging mostly identical digital data-streams.

## 6   Conclusions

In this paper, we proposed *MAG-PUF*, a novel and lightweight physical-layer authentication solution for resource-constrained IoT devices. *MAG-PUF* authenticates IoT devices using the uniqueness of the unintentional magnetic emissions radiated by the devices when executing specific functions. Our conceptual framework is supported by an extensive experimental campaign. Using 25 Arduino IoT boards and a set of exemplary reference functions, we revealed an outstanding classification accuracy (over 99%), high flexibility, robustness, and very limited overhead. At the same time, our investigation shows the robustness of using magnetic emissions for PUFs, with relevant metrics very close to the ideal values.

Overall, *MAG-PUF* emerges as an ideal solution to authenticate constrained IoT devices, especially where field devices cannot afford complex cryptography operations. Future work will consider the extraction of emissions on the IoT devices, with the integration of very-low bandwidth embedded magnetic sensors.

**Acknowledgements.** This publication was partially supported by award GSRA6-1-0528-19046, from the QNRF-Qatar National Research Fund, a member of Qatar Foundation. The information and views set out in this publication are those of the authors and do not necessarily reflect the official opinion of the QNRF. This publication was also partially supported by the INTERSECT project, Grant No. NWA.1162.18.301, funded by Netherlands Organization for Scientific Research (NWO) and the NATO Science for Peace and Security Programme - MYP G5828 project "SeaSec: DronNets for Maritime Border and Port Security".

## References

1. Aaronia: PBS2 EMC Probe (2021). https://tinyurl.com/2syhszbw, Accessed 31 July 2022
2. Afghah, F., Cambou, B., Abedini, M., Zeadally, S.: A reram physically unclonable function (reram puf)-based approach to enhance authentication security in software defined wireless networks. Int. J. Wirel. Inf. Netw. **25**(2), 117–129 (2018)
3. Al-Fuqaha, A., Guizani, M., Mohammadi, M., Aledhari, M., Ayyash, M.: Internet of things: a survey on enabling technologies, protocols, and applications. IEEE Commun. Surv. Tutor. **17**(4), 2347–2376 (2015)
4. Bossuet, L., Ngo, X.T., Cherif, Z., Fischer, V.: A puf based on a transient effect ring oscillator and insensitive to locking phenomenon. IEEE Trans. Emerg. Topics Comput. **2**(1), 30–36 (2013)
5. Callan, R., Behrang, F., Zajic, A., Prvulovic, M., Orso, A.: Zero-overhead profiling via em emanations. In: Proceedings of the 25th International Symposium on Software Testing and Analysis, pp. 401–412 (2016)
6. Cambou, B., Orlowski, M.: Puf designed with resistive ram and ternary states. In: Proceedings of the 11th Annual Cyber and Information Security Research Conference, pp. 1–8 (2016)

7. Camurati, G. et al.: Screaming channels: when electromagnetic side channels meet radio transceivers. In: ACM CCS, pp. 163–177 (2018)
8. Chatterjee, B., Das, D., Maity, S., Sen, S.: Rf-puf: enhancing IoT security through authentication of wireless nodes using in-situ machine learning. IEEE Internet Things J. 6(1), 388–398 (2018)
9. Claes, M., van der Leest, V., Braeken, A.: Comparison of SRAM and FF PUF in 65 nm technology. In: Laud, P. (ed.) NordSec 2011. LNCS, vol. 7161, pp. 47–64. Springer, Heidelberg (2012). https://doi.org/10.1007/978-3-642-29615-4_5
10. DeJean, G., Kirovski, D.: RF-DNA: radio-frequency certificates of authenticity. In: Paillier, P., Verbauwhede, I. (eds.) CHES 2007. LNCS, vol. 4727, pp. 346–363. Springer, Heidelberg (2007). https://doi.org/10.1007/978-3-540-74735-2_24
11. Delvaux, J., Verbauwhede, I.: Side channel modeling attacks on 65 nm arbiter PUFs exploiting CMOS device noise. In: 2013 IEEE International Symposium on Hardware-Oriented Security and Trust (HOST), pp. 137–142. IEEE (2013)
12. Gassend, B., Clarke, D., Van Dijk, M., Devadas, S.: Silicon physical random functions. In: Proceedings of the 9th ACM Conference on Computer and Communications Security, pp. 148–160 (2002)
13. Guajardo, J., Kumar, S.S., Schrijen, G.-J., Tuyls, P.: FPGA intrinsic PUFs and their use for IP protection. In: Paillier, P., Verbauwhede, I. (eds.) CHES 2007. LNCS, vol. 4727, pp. 63–80. Springer, Heidelberg (2007). https://doi.org/10.1007/978-3-540-74735-2_5
14. Guajardo, J., Kumar, S.S., Schrijen, G.J., Tuyls, P.: Physical unclonable functions and public-key crypto for fpga ip protection. In: 2007 International Conference on Field Programmable Logic and Applications, pp. 189–195. IEEE (2007)
15. Guajardo, J.: Anti-counterfeiting, key distribution, and key storage in an ambient world via physical unclonable functions. Inf. Syst. Front. 11(1), 19–41 (2009)
16. Han, Y., Etigowni, S., Liu, H., Zonouz, S., Petropulu, A.: Watch me, but don't touch me! contactless control flow monitoring via electromagnetic emanations. In: Proceedings of the 2017 ACM SIGSAC Conference on Computer and Communications Security, pp. 1095–1108 (2017)
17. Holcomb, D.E., Burleson, W.P., Fu, K.: Power-up sram state as an identifying fingerprint and source of true random numbers. IEEE Trans. Comput. 58(9), 1198–1210 (2008)
18. Ibrahim, O.A., Sciancalepore, S., Di Pietro, R.: Mag-puf - authenticating iot devices via magnetic physical unclonable functions. In: Proceedings of the 15th ACM Conference on Security and Privacy in Wireless and Mobile Networks, WiSec 2022, pp. 290–291. ACM, New York (2022)
19. Ibrahim, O.A., Sciancalepore, S., Oligeri, G., Pietro, R.D.: Magneto: fingerprinting usb flash drives via unintentional magnetic emissions. ACM Trans. Embedded Comput. Syst. (TECS) 20(1), 1–26 (2020)
20. Islam, M.N., Kundu, S.: Enabling ic traceability via blockchain pegged to embedded puf. ACM Trans. Des. Autom. Electron. Syst. (TODAES) 24(3), 1–23 (2019)
21. Khan, H.A., Sehatbakhsh, N., Nguyen, L.N., Prvulovic, M., Zajić, A.: Malware detection in embedded systems using neural network model for electromagnetic side-channel signals. J. Hardware Syst. Secur. 3(4), 305–318 (2019)
22. Khan, H.A., et al.: Idea: intrusion detection through electromagnetic-signal analysis for critical embedded and cyber-physical systems. IEEE Trans. Depend. Secure Comput. (2019)
23. Kumar, S.S., Guajardo, J., Maes, R., Schrijen, G.J., Tuyls, P.: The butterfly puf protecting ip on every fpga. In: 2008 IEEE International Workshop on Hardware-Oriented Security and Trust, pp. 67–70. IEEE (2008)

24. Maes, R.: Physically Unclonable Functions: Constructions, Properties and Applications. Springer, Heidelberg (2013). https://doi.org/10.1007/978-3-642-41395-7
25. Maes, R., Tuyls, P., Verbauwhede, I.: Intrinsic pufs from flip-flops on reconfigurable devices. In: 3rd Benelux Workshop on Information and System Security (WISSec 2008), vol. 17, p. 2008 (2008)
26. Maiti, A., Casarona, J., McHale, L., Schaumont, P.: A large scale characterization of ro-puf. In: 2010 IEEE International Symposium on Hardware-Oriented Security and Trust (HOST), pp. 94–99. IEEE (2010)
27. Maiti, A., Schaumont, P.: Improved ring oscillator puf: an fpga-friendly secure primitive. J. Cryptol. **24**(2), 375–397 (2011)
28. McGrath, T., et al.: A PUF taxonomy. Appl. Phys. Rev. **6**(1), 011303 (2019)
29. Nazari, A., Sehatbakhsh, N., Alam, M., Zajic, A., Prvulovic, M.: Eddie: em-based detection of deviations in program execution. In: Proceedings of the 44th Annual International Symposium on Computer Architecture, pp. 333–346 (2017)
30. Ostrovsky, R., Scafuro, A., Visconti, I., Wadia, A.: Universally composable secure computation with (malicious) physically uncloneable functions. In: Johansson, T., Nguyen, P.Q. (eds.) EUROCRYPT 2013. LNCS, vol. 7881, pp. 702–718. Springer, Heidelberg (2013). https://doi.org/10.1007/978-3-642-38348-9_41
31. Sahoo, D.P., Mukhopadhyay, D., Chakraborty, R.S., Nguyen, P.H.: A multiplexer-based arbiter puf composition with enhanced reliability and security. IEEE Trans. Comput. **67**(3), 403–417 (2017)
32. Sangodoyin, S., et al.: Remote monitoring and propagation modeling of em side-channel signals for iot device security. In: 2020 14th European Conference on Antennas and Propagation (EuCAP), pp. 1–5. IEEE (2020)
33. Schölkopf, B., Smola, A.J., Bach, F., et al.: Learning with Kernels: Support Vector Machines, Regularization, Optimization, and Beyond. MIT press, Cambridge (2002)
34. Sciancalepore, S., Oligeri, G., Piro, G., Boggia, G., Di Pietro, R.: EXCHANge: securing IoT via channel anonymity. Comput. Commun. **134**, 14–29 (2019)
35. Sehatbakhsh, N., Alam, M., Nazari, A., Zajic, A., Prvulovic, M.: Syndrome: spectral analysis for anomaly detection on medical iot and embedded devices. In: 2018 IEEE International Symposium on Hardware Oriented Security and Trust (HOST), pp. 1–8. IEEE (2018)
36. Sehatbakhsh, N., Nazari, A., Khan, H., Zajic, A., Prvulovic, M.: Emma: Hardware/software attestation framework for embedded systems using electromagnetic signals. In: Proceedings of the 52nd Annual IEEE/ACM International Symposium on Microarchitecture, pp. 983–995 (2019)
37. Sehatbakhsh, N., Nazari, A., Zajic, A., Prvulovic, M.: Spectral profiling: observer-effect-free profiling by monitoring em emanations. In: 2016 49th Annual IEEE/ACM International Symposium on Microarchitecture (MICRO), pp. 1–11. IEEE (2016)
38. Sehatbakhsh, N., Yilmaz, B.B., Zajic, A., Prvulovic, M.: A new side-channel vulnerability on modern computers by exploiting electromagnetic emanations from the power management unit. In: 2020 IEEE International Symposium on High Performance Computer Architecture (HPCA), pp. 123–138. IEEE (2020)
39. Semiconductor Eng.: IoT Device Security Makes Slow Progress (2019). https://semiengineering.com/iot-device-security-makes-slow-progress/, Accessed 31 July 2022
40. Shamsoshoara, A., Korenda, A., Afghah, F., Zeadally, S.: A survey on physical unclonable function (PUF)-based security solutions for Internet of Things. Comput. Netw. **183**, 107593 (2020)

41. Siow, E., et al.: Analytics for the Internet of Things: a survey. ACM Comput. Surv. (CSUR) **51**(4), 1–36 (2018)
42. Statista: Internet of Things (IoT) and non-IoT active device connections worldwide from 2010 to 2025 (2020). https://www.statista.com/statistics/1101442/iot-number-of-connected-devices-worldwide/, Accessed 31 July 2022
43. Su, Y., Holleman, J., Otis, B.P.: A digital 1.6 pj/bit chip identification circuit using process variations. IEEE J. Solid-State Circ. **43**(1), 69–77 (2008)
44. Suh, G.E., Devadas, S.: Physical unclonable functions for device authentication and secret key generation. In: 2007 44th ACM/IEEE Design Automation Conference, pp. 9–14. IEEE (2007)
45. Treedix: Arduino UNO (2021). https://tinyurl.com/TreedixArduinoUNO, Accessed 31 July 2022
46. Tuyls, P., Škoric, B., Kevenaar, T.: Security With Noisy Data: On Private Biometrics, Secure Key Storage and Anti-Counterfeiting. Springer, Heidelberg (2007). https://doi.org/10.1007/978-1-84628-984-2
47. Yin, C.E., Qu, G.: Temperature-aware cooperative ring oscillator puf. In: 2009 IEEE International Workshop on Hardware-Oriented Security and Trust, pp. 36–42. IEEE (2009)
48. Zalivaka, S.S., Ivaniuk, A.A., Chang, C.H.: Reliable and modeling attack resistant authentication of arbiter puf in fpga implementation with trinary quadruple response. IEEE Trans. Inf. Forensics Secur. **14**(4), 1109–1123 (2018)

# A Cross-layer Plausibly Deniable Encryption System for Mobile Devices

Niusen Chen[1], Bo Chen[1(✉)], and Weisong Shi[2]

[1] Department of Computer Science, Michigan Technological University, Michigan, USA
bchen@mtu.edu
[2] Department of Computer Science, Wayne State University, Michigan, USA

**Abstract.** Mobile computing devices have been used to store and process sensitive or even mission critical data. To protect sensitive data in mobile devices, encryption is usually incorporated into major mobile operating systems. However, traditional encryption can not defend against coercive attacks in which victims are forced to disclose the key used to decrypt the sensitive data. To combat the coercive attackers, plausibly deniable encryption (PDE) has been introduced which can allow the victims to deny the existence of the sensitive data. However, the existing PDE systems designed for mobile devices are either insecure (i.e., suffering from deniability compromises) or impractical (i.e., unable to be compatible with the storage architecture of mainstream mobile devices, not lightweight, or not user-oriented).

In this work, we design CrossPDE, the first cross-layer mobile PDE system which is secure, being compatible with the storage architecture of mainstream mobile devices, lightweight as well as user-oriented. Our key idea is to intercept major layers of a mobile storage system, including the file system layer (preventing loss of hidden sensitive data and enabling users to use the hidden mode), the block layer (taking care of expensive encryption and decryption), and the flash translation layer (eliminating traces caused by the hidden sensitive data). Experimental evaluation on our real-world prototype shows that CrossPDE can ensure deniability with a modest decrease in throughput.

**Keywords:** PDE · Mobile devices · Coercive attacks · Confidentiality · Cross-layer · Flash memory

## 1 Introduction

With the increased use of mobile computing devices, a large amount of sensitive data are collected, stored, and managed in them. To protect sensitive data, full disk encryption (FDE) has been integrated into major mobile operating systems including Android and iOS. FDE transparently encrypts/decrypts all the user data at the block layer and, without having access to the secret key, an adversary will not be able to learn the sensitive data even if the adversary can steal the

© ICST Institute for Computer Sciences, Social Informatics and Telecommunications Engineering 2023
Published by Springer Nature Switzerland AG 2023. All Rights Reserved
F. Li et al. (Eds.): SecureComm 2022, LNICST 462, pp. 150–169, 2023.
https://doi.org/10.1007/978-3-031-25538-0_9

entire disk. FDE however, cannot defend against a coercive attacker who can capture the device owner and coerce the owner for the secret key. For example, a human right worker may be forced to disclose the encrypted data stored in his/her smartphone when crossing the border of a country in conflict. To defend against the coercive attacker, plausibly deniable encryption (PDE) was proposed. Its main idea is, the sensitive data are encrypted in such a way that, only if the *true* secret key is used for decryption, the original sensitive data will be revealed, but if a *decoy* key is used, the decryption will result in some non-sensitive data; therefore, when a device owner is coerced, the owner can simply disclose the decoy key, protecting the true key as well as the hidden sensitive data.

To implement PDE in a mobile device, currently there are three options: 1) deploying the PDE at the block layer of a mobile device [8,9,17,22,31,37] (Category I), and 2) integrating the PDE with a flash-specific file system YAFFS [11,30] (Category II), and 3) integrating the PDE with the flash translation layer [10,12,23,25] (Category III). The mobile PDE systems in the Category I are **insecure** due to the potential deniability compromises when the adversary can have access to the internal flash memory and extract traces of hidden sensitive data which are invisible to the block layer [14,23]. The mobile PDE systems in the Category II are strongly coupling with YAFFS which is rarely used in today's mobile computing devices; instead, a vast majority of the existing mobile computing devices (including the ever-growing IoT devices) use flash memory cards via flash translation layer (FTL) and, the Category-II PDE systems are **incompatible** with this mainstream flash storage architecture. The mobile PDE systems in the Category III integrate the entire PDE (i.e., with expensive operations like disk encryption [10,23,25], WOM codes [12] or dummy writes [10,25]) into the FTL, turning it a **"heavyweight"** software component. However, the FTL was originally designed for handling unique nature of NAND flash, which is usually run by low-end internal hardware [18] of a flash-based block device (e.g., a microSD card), and the heavyweight FTL may significantly decrease the I/O throughput of the PDE system. In addition, the Category-III mobile PDE systems are located at the lower FTL layer which stays far away from users staying at the application layer, and hence may be difficult to be managed by users (i.e., **not user-oriented**).

The limitations observed from the existing mobile PDE systems motivate us to re-consider the PDE system design in a holistic manner. Our resulted design, **CrossPDE**, is the first mobile PDE system which simultaneously satisfies four properties: (P1) *resistance against the coercive attackers*, i.e., the design is secure even if the adversary can have access to the internal flash memory; and (P2) *being compatible* with the architecture of mainstream mobile computing devices; and (P3) *keeping the FTL lightweight*; and (P4) *being user-oriented*. Our key idea is to decouple the PDE functionality, and to separate them among different storage layers (i.e., the file system layer, the block device layer, and the FTL layer) of a mobile device. The outcome is the first cross-layer PDE system design for mobile devices. To be resistant against the coercive attackers (P1), we distill the minimal functionality necessary for eliminating deniability compromises on the flash memory, and place it to the FTL layer. In this way, the FTL remains thin and the extra overhead imposed on the less powerful [18] internal hardware of the flash-based block device will be minimized (P3). Note that the expensive PDE functionality including disk encryption/decryption as well volume management are conducted at the block layer which will be run by the more powerful hardware of the host computing device. In addition, the file system layer provides an immediate interface for the user to manage the PDE functionality at the lower layers (P4). Last, such a design is immediately compatible with mainstream mobile computing devices using flash memory cards via FTL (P2).

However, after decoupling the PDE functionality and moving them across multiple storage layers, we face a few new challenges:

1) To avoid deniability compromises, the FTL should be informed if the user is working in a hidden mode which manages hidden sensitive data. However, the user is typically located at the application layer, and how can he/she securely convey such information to the low-layer FTL? This issue becomes more challenging due to the deployment of disk encryption at the block layer, since everything going through the block layer will be encrypted transparently. To resolve this challenge, we have reserved a few logical block addresses which are accessible to the FTL, and used the file system as a bridge to issue I/Os on the reserved block addresses with secret patterns, so that the messages from the application layer can be conveyed stealthily to the FTL.

2) The loss of hidden sensitive data is a general issue for all PDE systems and, in our setting, this issue turns even more challenging, due to the separation of PDE functionality across multiple layers. Resolving this challenge requires coordinating the file system layer, the block layer and the FTL layer. By hiding an encrypted hidden volume at the end of an encrypted public volume, and deploying in the public volume a file system which has a low probability of writing the end of disk by nature, we can significantly mitigate loss of hidden sensitive data, without touching the lower FTL layer.

3) Eliminating all potential deniability compromises in the flash memory is challenging. We have identified two new deniability compromises in the flash memory and carefully mitigated all the known compromises discovered to date.

**Contributions.** We summarize our contributions as follows:

- We have discovered new PDE compromises in the underlying flash memory of mobile devices which have not been identified in the literature. We have also provided novel mitigation strategies.
- We have designed the first cross-layer PDE system that meets all following requirements: 1) being secure, and 2) being compatible with the mainstream storage architecture of mobile devices, and 3) imposing small burden on the underlying flash device and, 4) providing interface for users to manage the system.
- We have implemented CrossPDE by modifying and integrating a few open-source projects. In addition, we have ported our prototype to a real-world testbed for mobile devices to assess its performance.

# 2  Background and Related Work

## 2.1  Background Knowledge

**Flash Memory.** NAND flash has dominated storage media of today's mobile devices due to its high I/O speed and low noise. The NAND flash is usually divided into blocks (a few hundreds of KBs in size), and each block is divided into pages (a few KBs in size). Each flash page has a small out-of-band ($OOB$) area, which can store extra information like error correction code. Compared to regular hard disk drives (HDD), NAND flash exhibits some unique characteristics: 1) The unit of I/O is a page, but the unit of erasure is a block. 2) A flash block can not be re-programmed before it is erased. Therefore, flash memory typically performs out-of-place instead of in-place updates. 3) A flash block can only be programmed/erased for a limited number of times.

**Flash Translation Layer (FTL).** To use flash memory, the most popular approach today is to emulate it as a block device via flash translation layer (FTL). In this way, traditional block-based file systems (e.g. FAT32, EXT4) can be directly deployed. The FTL stays between the file system and the raw NAND flash, and implements four core functions: address translation, garbage collection, wear leveling, and bad block management.

Flash memory performs out-of-place updates, i.e., for an overwrite operation performed by the OS, the FTL will place the new data to a empty page, and invalidate the page storing the old data. From the OS's view, the logical block address ($LBA$) of the data remains the same. However, the physical block address ($PBA$) of the data has been changed. Therefore, the FTL needs to keep track of mappings between LBAs and PBAs for *address translation*. In addition, since the overwrite operations will invalidate flash pages storing the old data, *garbage collection* is needed to reclaim those blocks with a large number of invalid pages. Each flash block can be only programmed/erased for a limited number of times. Therefore, we need a mechanism which can distribute programmings/erasures (P/Es) evenly across the entire flash to prolong its service life. *Wear leveling* is such a mechanism which can even out P/Es among flash blocks by relocating frequently updated data to blocks with less P/Es. Flash memory is vulnerable to wear and, over time, a flash block may turn "bad" making it unable to reliably store data. *Bad block management* can manage those bad blocks.

**Full Disk Encryption (FDE).** FDE encrypts/decrypts the entire disk transparently to users. FDE includes both software-based and hardware-based disk encryption. The software-based FDE is usually deployed at the block layer, so that any data written to or read from the disk can be transparently encrypted or decrypted. Popular implementations include TrueCrypt [2], BitLocker [27], etc.

**Plausibly Deniable Encryption (PDE).** To implement PDE, we can use a steganographic file system, which hides sensitive data in either regular files or randomness arbitrarily filled. We can also use *the hidden volume technique*. The entire disk is filled with random data initially. Two volumes, a public and a hidden volume, are deployed on the disk. The public volume is used to store non-sensitive data, and the hidden volume is used to stored sensitive data. The public volume is encrypted via FDE using a *decoy key* and placed across the entire disk. The hidden volume is encrypted via FDE using a truly secret key (i.e., *true key*), and placed to the end of the disk starting from a secret offset. In view of the public volume, *the space filling with the randomness is just the empty space and can be used to store public data.* Therefore, the public data may overwrite the hidden data, causing data loss. Upon being coerced, the device owner can simply disclose the decoy key; the adversary uses the decoy key to decrypt the public volume, but is unaware of existence of the hidden volume.

## 2.2   Related Work

**Upper-Layer PDE Systems.** Steganographic file systems [4,5,21,26,29] hide sensitive data among either regular files or random data, and maintain additional redundancies of hidden data across the disk to avoid their loss. Image steganography has also been leveraged to construct PDE systems [13]. VeraCrypt [3]/TrueCrypt [2] introduces a hidden volume technique, which hides sensitive data in a dedicated volume that is stored hidden at a secret offset towards the end of the disk. Mobiflage [31,32] extends the hidden volume technique for Android OS. Other follow-up works enhance the mobile PDE systems supporting various features, e.g., multi-level deniability [22,37], file system friendliness [8], dynamic mounting of hidden volumes [17,22]. Major limitations of the aforementioned PDE systems are, they are purely deployed at upper layers, and do not consider deniability compromises in the underlying flash memory.

**Lower-Layer PDE Systems.** DEFY [30] and INFUSE [11] both integrated a PDE design into flash file system YAFFS, which unfortunately is rarely used nowadays. DEFTL [23] and PEARL [12] have moved the PDE to the FTL, but all of them suffer from some common drawbacks: 1) They impose a significant burden on the flash memory firmware (managed by low-end internal hardware of the flash device), rendering them impractical for broad deployment. Especially, DEFTL performs the expensive disk encryption and decryption purely in the FTL. PEARL achieves PDE by encoding (i.e., WOM codes) both the public and the hidden data together in the FTL and, since both public and hidden data are "entangled", I/Os on either one would be expensive. 2) They do not consider upper layers and the user is difficult to manage the PDE staying in the FTL. Liao et al. [25] proposed a TrustZone-enhanced mobile PDE system which isolates sensitive data in the memory to avoid memory leaks. However, they still heavily rely on the FTL to isolate the sensitive data in the external storage.

## 3   Model and Assumptions

**System Model.** We consider a mobile computing device (Fig. 1) which is equipped with a flash-based block device, e.g., an MMC/eMMC card, an SD/miniSD/microSD card, or a UFS card. We do not consider powerful flash

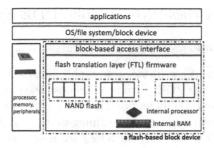

**Fig. 1.** The architecture of a mainstream mobile device.

devices like SSDs, which are typically used in the more powerful personal computers. Each flash device is equipped with its internal processor and RAM, and manages the raw NAND flash via the FTL. It usually exposes a block-based access interface, so that conventional block-based file systems like EXT4, FAT32, NTFS can be seamlessly deployed on top of it.

**Adversarial Model.** We consider a computationally-bounded adversary, which can capture a victim user and his/her mobile device. The adversary can access the external storage of the device, and coerce the user for keys to decrypt any encrypted sensitive data. The adversary does not trust the user and may try all means to identify the existence of PDE. For example, the adversary may enter the public mode and use it as a regular user to check any traces of hidden data; the adversary may check the file system in the public mode for anything abnormal in the file hash; moreover, the adversary may perform forensic analysis [24] on the disk. For analysis purposes, we assume the adversary can acquire a copy of the raw flash memory image via state-of-the-art laboratory techniques [6].

**Assumptions.** We rely on a few common assumptions which are also required in prior mobile PDE systems [8,23,31]: 1) The adversary is assumed to be rational and will stop coercing the victim once convinced that the decryption key is disclosed [31]. 2) The adversary cannot capture a victim user when he/she is right working in the hidden mode; otherwise, the hidden data are disclosed trivially. 3) We assume the bootloader and the OS are not infected by the malware controlled by the adversary; otherwise, the malware can monitor the system and trivially know the existence of PDE. In addition, the user will not use untrusted apps controlled by the adversary while working in the hidden mode, in case that sensitive information about the hidden mode will be leaked to those apps. 4) We assume the adversary will not perform reverse engineering over the code of the device after capturing it. To prevent the adversary from capturing the victim device multiple times and correlating the disk images captured each time to compromise PDE, we assume each time after the user is caught and released, he/she will take various actions including but not limited to: disconnecting the device from the network, scanning the device via antivirus tools, copying out the data, conducting a factory reset, etc.

# 4    CrossPDE: A Cross-layer Mobile PDE System

## 4.1    Design Rationale

Typically, we can rely on either the steganographic file system or the hidden volume technique to build a mobile PDE system. We choose the hidden volume technique (Sect. 2.1) which is more I/O efficient and fits the mobile devices better: First, the steganographic file system requires maintaining multiple redundant copies of hidden data across the disk to mitigate data loss, leading to significant storage overhead. On the contrary, the hidden volume technique does not require maintaining redundant sensitive data by smartly hiding them at the end of the disk. Second, the steganographic file system incurs significant overhead when writing the hidden data due to writing the redundant copies. On the contrary, the hidden volume technique can efficiently write the hidden data as no redundant writes are needed. Using the hidden volume technique, there are two modes. A *public mode* and a *hidden mode*, will be introduced which allow the user to manage the public and the hidden volume, respectively. Upon booting, if the user provides the decoy key, the OS will mount the public volume and the system will enter the public mode; otherwise if the user provides the true key, the OS will mount the hidden volume and the system will enter the hidden mode.

This simple adoption of the hidden volume technique is insufficient as the adversary can compromise PDE by having access to the underlying flash memory. Unlike prior works [12,23] which integrate the entire PDE with the flash translation layer to avoid the aforementioned compromise, we instead divide the PDE functionality and to separate them into multiple layers: the flash translation layer will manage flash blocks associating with the hidden mode to eliminate any deniability compromises; the block layer will manage both volumes and perform disk encryption/decryption; the file system layer will manage the file system deployed on each volume, and act as a bridge for the user to manage the hidden mode in lower layers of the storage system. An overview of our design is shown in Fig. 2, with three key ideas elaborated below:

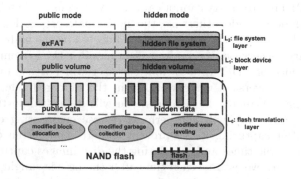

**Fig. 2.** An overview of our design.

**Idea 1: Mitigating Loss of Hidden Sensitive Data.** Loss of hidden data is a general problem for any PDE systems [4], as sensitive data are hidden among public data and, to ensure plausible deniability, the public mode should not be aware of the existence of the hidden data, and may overwrite them unintentionally. To avoid data loss at the block layer, we embed the hidden volume at the end of the disk, with three extra considerations: 1) The public volume and the hidden volume should be managed by a separate file system, i.e., a *public file system* for the public volume, and a *hidden file system* for the hidden volume. 2) To prevent the public file system from writing the end of the disk, we choose exFAT as the public file system, a mobile file system which writes data sequentially from the beginning of the disk, and has a low probability of overwriting the sensitive data stored hidden at the end of the disk. 3) The user is suggested to pay attention to the disk space used by the public data, because the public data are allowed to use the entire space of the disk (Sect. 2.1) and, if the disk is filled, the hidden data will be overwritten unavoidably.

A unique hardware feature of mobile devices is the use of flash memory, which is encapsulated inside the flash-based block device. Therefore, preventing data loss merely at the block layer may not be sufficient. We need to ensure that there is no data loss at the flash translation layer (FTL) as well. We argue that by embedding a hidden volume at the end of the disk and deploying exFAT as the public file system, we will not suffer from loss of hidden sensitive data at the FTL because: The entire disk (i.e., the block layer) is initially filled with random data, and from the view of the FTL, those random data are written by upper layers and hence are all valid. The sensitive data written to the hidden volume are stored stealthily among random data and, the flash blocks storing them will not turn invalid if they are not overwritten by the public file system deployed at the block layer. Our deployed public file system exFAT has a low probability of writing the end of the disk, and hence has a low probability of overwriting the hidden volume stored stealthily at the end of the disk. Therefore, the flash blocks storing hidden sensitive data will not be turned invalid and hence will not be reclaimed by garbage collection of the FTL.

**Idea 2: Thoroughly Eliminating Deniability Compromises in the Flash Translation Layer.** Merely deploying a hidden volume at the block layer will suffer from deniability compromises as the underlying flash translation layer (FTL) will not be aware of the existence of the hidden volume at the block layer and hence will not hide those traces created by the hidden data [23]. Prior works

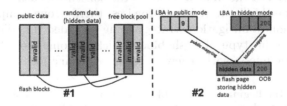

**Fig. 3.** Newly discovered deniability compromises in the flash memory.

have identified a few such compromises [14,23]. We have discovered two new compromises which have not been identified before (see Fig. 3):

*New Deniability compromise #1:* Initially, the hidden volume technique fills the entire disk with randomness which establishes an initial mapping[1] between the block layer and the flash memory blocks. At the block layer, the public file system writes at the beginning of the disk; therefore in the flash memory, the public data will occupy those blocks at the beginning of the flash memory. In addition, the hidden file system writes data at the end of the disk; therefore in the flash memory, the hidden data will occupy those blocks at the end of the flash memory. Without PDE, as the public file system writes data sequentially from the beginning of the disk, only the blocks at the beginning of the flash memory may be invalidated and moved to the free block pool. However, with PDE, the user may enter the hidden mode to delete/overwrite hidden data, and the blocks located at the end of the flash memory may be invalided and move to the free block pool. Such a difference may lead to compromise of PDE.

*New Deniability Compromise #2:* The hidden volume is part of the public volume. Therefore, a flash page used by the hidden volume data may be also used by the public volume data. The effect is, a flash page which stores hidden data may be mapped to two different LBAs, one for the public volume and the other for the hidden volume. Note that the FTL typically maintains a mapping table keeping track of mappings between LBAs and PBAs; to allow restoring this table upon sudden failures (e.g., power loss), the OOB area of each flash page will also keep its corresponding LBA. Therefore, when writing a flash page in the hidden mode, the OOB area of the page will keep track of its corresponding LBA of the hidden volume. This will be detected by the adversary, leading to compromise of PDE.

To mitigate the compromise #1, our strategy is: when working in the hidden mode, the FTL will not move flash blocks to the free block pool. Especially, the FTL in the hidden mode will work differently with the modified functions (i.e., the block allocation, garbage collection, wear leveling function specified for the hidden mode) and new data structures (i.e., the mapping table specified for the hidden mode). To mitigate the compromise #2, our strategy is: when writing a flash page in the hidden mode, the FTL will always commit the flash page's corresponding LBA of the public mode (rather than that of the hidden mode) to its OOB. The downside is that the OOB of the flash pages in the hidden mode cannot be used to restore the mapping table maintained in this mode upon sudden failures. This downside can be alleviated by embedding the corresponding LBA of the hidden mode to the content of each flash page.

Besides our newly discovered compromises, there is one compromise identified by [14], without a mitigation strategy being provided [14]. The compromise comes from a special type of flash block which is completely filled with undecryptable randomness, with a few pages in arbitrary locations of the block

---

[1] Data stored at the beginning of the block layer are mapped to those blocks at the beginning of the flash memory, as the system usually fills randomness sequentially from the beginning of the disk, and the FTL uses a log-structured writing strategy.

invalidated. This type of flash block is generated when the user modifies some of hidden sensitive data. To mitigate this compromise, we introduce an independent data structure to keep track of pages invalidated by the hidden data, and this data structure is only visible to the hidden mode. In other words, a page invalidated by the hidden data still appears as valid in the public mode. Finally, to ensure all the deniability compromises can be eliminated, we also handle those old compromises identified in [23] via strategies introduced in their work, including: 1) the hidden data will not share flash blocks with public data; 2) and if the hidden data cannot fill a flash block upon quitting the hidden mode, the remaining space of this block will be filled with randomness.

**Idea 3: Secure Cross-Layer Communication.** Our design is cross-layer and, therefore, components of the hidden mode will stay at different layers and need to communicate with each other securely. Especially, when entering the hidden mode, the user should securely inform the FTL that he/she is now in the hidden mode and the FTL should actively eliminate special traces in the flash memory caused by hidden data; when quitting the hidden mode, the user should inform the FTL as well. A strawman solution is that, the user crafts a special string and writes it to the disk via the regular "write" system call. The FTL will monitor any write requests issued by the block layer and, once it detects this special string, it will know that the user has conveyed a request. This solution is problematic because: The hidden volume is encrypted by FDE at the block layer and, all data written to the hidden volume will be encrypted before passing to the FTL; therefore, to search this special string, the FTL may need to decrypt all the data being received, which is expensive.

Our solution is, in the hidden mode, the user issues a request to the hidden file system and, upon receiving such a request, the hidden file system will pass it to the FTL. To allow the hidden mode to communicate with the hidden file system without affecting existing system calls, we create a unique file in the hidden file system, and the hidden mode can issue I/Os on this file via the regular system calls; the hidden file system can monitor I/Os on this special file to communicate with the hidden mode. To allow the hidden file system to send a request to the FTL without affecting the existing I/O interface of the block device, we reserve a few special LBAs, and the hidden file system will issue I/Os on the reserved LBAs via the regular block I/O interface; the FTL can monitor I/Os on the reserved LBAs to communicate with the hidden file system. To prevent this "hidden interface" of the FTL from being abused, authentication needs to be incorporated. Specifically, this "hidden interface" can only be activated if I/Os with a secret pattern are performed on the reserved LBAs and only the hidden file system knows this secret pattern.

## 4.2   Design Details

Following the rationale, we have designed CrossPDE, the first cross-layer mobile PDE system. CrossPDE separates PDE functionality into major layers of a mobile storage system: the flash translation layer $(L_0)$, the block layer $(L_1)$, and the file system layer $(L_2)$. Design details of each layer are elaborated below:

$L_0$ : Flash Translation Layer. CrossPDE modifies a few major functions in the FTL to support PDE. The bad block management function does not cause deniability compromises and therefore, we do not need to modify it.

**Block Allocation.** *In the public mode*, the FTL uses the log-structured writing, which typically writes public data to blocks from the beginning of the entire flash. *In the hidden mode*, the block allocation should be carefully performed to avoid deniability compromises. There are a few rules: 1) When writing hidden data, the FTL should not use empty pages from those blocks occupied by the public data. 2) When writing hidden data, the FTL should use those blocks located at the end of the flash (they are typically mapped to the areas located at the end of the block layer which are very unlikely overwritten by the public mode). Especially, the FTL in the hidden mode will allocate blocks in a reverse direction starting from the end of the flash, excluding the free blocks reserved initially. When allocating a block[2], the FTL will read all the LBAs from the OOBs of this block (also copy out the valid data if there are any, which need to be written back after block erasure), and immediately erase this block. The hidden data will be written sequentially to empty pages of this block. Note that when writing a page in the hidden mode, we will reuse the LBA of the public mode, and commit it to the corresponding OOB to avoid deniability compromises (Sect. 4.1). The empty pages of the block will be used until they are exhausted in the hidden mode. If the user quits the hidden mode and there are still unused empty pages in a block, the empty pages should be filled with randomness. A special case is an overwrite on the existing hidden data, in which the corresponding flash pages should be first invalidated. For deniability, the FTL should maintain an independent data structure (i.e., page validity table) keeping track of which pages are invalidated in the hidden mode. The page validity table is only used by the hidden mode and remains invisible to the public mode.

**Garbage Collection.** The garbage collection is performed periodically during the idle time. *In the public mode*, the garbage collection runs as follows: The FTL finds a dirty block which has the largest number of invalid pages, copies all valid data in this block to a free block, and places the dirty block to the free block pool. *In the hidden mode*, however, the garbage collection should be performed differently, since its dirty blocks should not be placed to the free block pool (Sect. 4.1). Especially, among those flash blocks storing hidden data, the FTL will find a dirty block which has the largest number of invalid pages; it will then handle the dirty block as follows: 1) It reads all the LBAs from the OOBs of the dirty block, and copies out all the valid data from this block; 2) It erases the dirty block; 3) It writes the valid data back to the block, sequentially from the first page; the remaining empty pages should be filled with randomness. When writing each page, the original LBA should be committed to its OOB.

---

[2] Those blocks which are 1) reserved for the hidden mode, and 2) entirely or partially filled with actual randomness, can be allocated.

**Wear Leveling.** *In the public mode*, the wear leveling runs as follows: Upon a certain wear leveling threshold is reached, the FTL: 1) selects a block (X) which is currently in use with the smallest erasure count; and 2) selects another block (Y) from free block pool with the largest erasure count; and 3) erases block Y and copies all data from block X to block Y; and 4) updates the mapping table. The rationale is that the data stored in block X is cold and should be relocated to block Y, which has the largest erasure count. *In the hidden mode*, wear leveling needs to be implemented differently as the blocks for the hidden mode cannot be placed to the free block pool (Sect. 4.1). When a certain threshold is reached, the FTL selects a block (X) with the largest erasure count and a block (Y) with the smallest erasure count among blocks for the hidden mode; it then exchanges the data between block X and block Y (under the help of RAM or a free block, but the free block should be cleaned after it). Note that: 1) The hidden mode should maintain its own table for keeping track of erasure counts for its reserved blocks, and this erasure count table is invisible to the public mode. 2) The wear leveling in the public mode usually will not use blocks reserved for the hidden mode, as it only swaps blocks storing public data with those in the free block pool, but the blocks storing hidden data will never enter the free block pool.

**Other Operations.** The FTL monitors I/Os issued by the upper layer on some reserved LBAs. If such I/Os have been detected, the FTL will determine the request type based on the I/O patterns. The most important requests are "start" and "quit" request. For the "start" request, the FTL knows that the hidden mode is activated, and starts to use the data structures (e.g., the mapping table, the page validity table, the erasure count table) and functions (block allocation, garbage collection, wear leveling) specifically for the hidden mode. For the "quit" request, the FTL knows that the hidden mode terminates. It will identify the block occupied by the hidden data but has not been completely filled, and fill the empty pages with randomness.

$L_1$ : Block Layer. The public/hidden volume is deployed on the block layer. Both volumes are encrypted by full disk encryption (run by the processor and memory of host computing device) via the decoy and the true key, respectively. The public volume will be managed by the public mode via the public file system and, any data written by the user in the public mode will be passed down by the public file system, and encrypted transparently with the decoy key at the block layer before being passed to the FTL. Similarly, the hidden volume will be managed by the hidden mode via the hidden file system and, any data written by the user in the hidden mode will be passed down by the hidden file system, and encrypted transparently with the true key at the block layer. Reading data from both volumes will be performed in a reverse manner.

$L_2$ : File System Layer. *In the public mode*, we deploy exFAT, a block-based mobile file system which writes data sequentially from the beginning of disk. *In the hidden mode*, we can deploy any block-based file system on the hidden volume. This hidden file system acts as a "bridge" between the user working in the hidden mode and the lower storage layers. To enable this bridge, we modify the hidden file system as follows: We maintain a "special file", which is created when the user enters the hidden mode for the first time. Note that the name for this special file should be unique and different from other files in the system, and a large enough random number can be used for this file name. The hidden file system will monitor I/Os on this special file and, once an I/O request is issued by the user on the file, it will determine the request type and issue I/Os (for different user requests, the hidden file system will use different secret I/O patterns) to the reserved LBAs. Note that we can easily convert the sector addresses on the block layer to the LBAs, e.g., if the sector size is 512 bytes, and the page size is 2KB, each sector address is translated to the LBA by dividing 4.

### 4.3   User Steps

To process non-sensitive data, the user should boot into the public mode via the decoy key. The user should use this mode regularly to ensure a better plausibility [31]. To process sensitive data, the user should boot into the hidden mode via the true key. Upon entering the hidden mode, the user can issue a "start" request to the "special file" maintained by the hidden file system, and the hidden file system will then issue a "start" request downwards; similarly, upon quitting the hidden mode, the user can issue a "quit" request to the "special file", and the hidden file system will then issue a "quit" request downwards. To prevent traces of hidden sensitive data from remaining in the memory, the user is suggested to power-off the device upon quitting the hidden mode.

## 5   Analysis and Discussion

**Security Analysis of** CrossPDE. We first show that by running the public mode, the adversary is not able to identify the existence of PDE. Using the decoy key coerced from the victim, the adversary can boot into the public mode, and can have access to all data files, configuration files, system logs, file system metadata, etc. However, all the aforementioned data belong to the public mode and, none of the data belonging to the hidden mode can be found as both modes are strictly isolated. In addition, the adversary may perform forensic analysis over the memory (e.g., extracting the memory content using memdump) in the public mode. This would not help, as CrossPDE requires the user to shut down the device when quitting the hidden mode and the traces should have been eliminated from the memory. The adversary may also analyze the raw data on the disk (the block layer), but will not be able to identify the existence of the hidden volume which is stored stealthily among the randomness.

We also show that by analyzing the raw data on the flash memory, the adversary is not able to identify the existence of PDE. By modifying the major functionality (e.g., block allocation, garbage collection, wear leveling) of the FTL, CrossPDE successfully eliminates all the traces caused by the hidden mode, so that a flash block storing hidden sensitive data cannot be differentiated from a flash block storing random data. Therefore, by analyzing the raw data on the flash memory, the adversary can only identify 3 types of flash blocks: 1) a flash block filled with public non-sensitive data; and 2) a flash block stores public data at the beginning and the remaining pages are empty; and 3) a flash block filled with (valid) random data. This is no different from a flash storage medium which is initially filled with randomness and has an FDE (via decoy key) deployed on the entire disk. In addition, the adversary is not able to identify the existence of PDE in the free block pool as well as the OOB areas of flash pages.

**Mitigating Multi-snapshot Adversaries.** CrossPDE can defend against a multi-snapshot adversary which can access the victim device multiple times, assuming that the victim is alert and will reset the device each time after being captured and released. To reset the device, the victim will 1) back up the data, and 2) conduct a full reset to clear both the memory and the external storage (via secure deletion [20]), and 3) re-fill new randomness and re-write the public and the hidden data back to the device, encrypted with a new decoy and true key, respectively. Such a reset operation allows the victim to plausibly deny the changes over the empty space of the disk.

**Denying the Existence of a Partition Filled with Random Data.** CrossPDE requires filling the entire disk with randomness initially. A plausible explanation can be, the user has securely erased the content in the partition using a tool which erases data by overwriting it with random data [28].

**Mitigating Timing Attacks.** Yu et al. [37] discovered a booting-time attack, which may happen when authenticating a given key (decoy or true key) for entering the corresponding mode. The reason is: given the decoy key, the public mode can be entered fast, as the bootloader will always try to boot the public volume first; however, given a wrong key, the bootloader will return slowly, as it first tries to boot the public volume and then the hidden volume, and finally returns with an error prompt which takes more time. To obfuscate this time difference, we can add extra time delay when booting with the decoy key [37].

**Protecting the PDE Code.** CrossPDE relies on an assumption that the adversary will not conduct reverse-engineering attacks over the code. To relax this assumption, a potential solution is to leverage the obfuscation technique [36] to obfuscate the code, concealing its purpose of PDE. This will be further investigated in our future work.

**Pre-boot Authentication.** To enter either the public or the hidden mode, the user needs to provide the corresponding key for authentication (i.e., the *pre-boot authentication*). We can derive the decoy/true key from the corresponding password [31], and choose strong passwords following certain security guidelines [33].

The password-based pre-boot authentication however, will essentially reduce the security provided by CrossPDE, as a memorable password implies that the adversary would be easier to guess it. Another option is to use NFC cards [7] to store keys so that the user does not need to memorize them.

# 6    Implementation and Evaluation

## 6.1    Implementation

We have implemented CrossPDE by integrating and modifying a few open-source software projects: OpenNFM [15] for the flash translation layer, VeraCrypt [3] for the block layer, and exFAT [16] for the file system layer. OpenNFM was used as the FTL. VeraCrypt was used to manage (e.g., create, encrypt, etc.) both the public and the hidden volume at the block layer. It also took care of initialization and pre-boot authentication. The exFAT was deployed as the file system for both the public and the hidden volume and, especially for the hidden volume, we deployed a modified exFAT, such that the hidden mode can communicate with the FTL using exFAT as a bridge (this implies that VeraCrypt and OpenNFM should be modified accordingly).

**Modifications to OpenNFM.** For the hidden mode, we implemented the new block allocation, garbage collection, and wear leveling, but reused the existing bad block management. We also modified the FTL_Read function, so that once the reserved LBAs are read, the FTL knows that there is a request from the user in the hidden mode. We implemented different read patterns to differentiate the starting and the quitting request.

**Modifications to VeraCrypt.** Each time when mounting a volume, we first check whether it is the public volume or the hidden volume. If it is the public volume, it will be mounted as usual. Otherwise, we will perform an I/O on a special file (we will create this special file when entering the hidden volume for the first time). In addition, when unmounting the hidden volume, we will perform another I/O on this special file.

**Modifications to exFAT.** We modified the function exfat_get_block() in super.c so that exFAT can monitor I/Os on the special file and, once it detects an I/O on this file, it will issue I/Os on some reserved disk sector addresses which will be translated deterministically to some reserved LBAs in the flash memory. In our case, the disk sector address can be translated to a corresponding LBA by dividing 4, considering a disk sector is 512 bytes in size and a flash page is 2KB in size. Note that exFAT is not in the kernel (V4.4.194) of Firefly AIO 3399J originally, but we made exFAT as a kernel module when re-compiling the kernel.

## 6.2 Evaluation

**Experimental Setup.** We ported our developed prototype to a self-built mobile device testbed [14], which consists of a flash-based block device and a host computing device. The flash-based block device was built using a USB header development prototype board LPC-H3131 [1] (ARM9 32-bit ARM926EJ-S, 180Mhz, 32MB RAM, and 512MB NAND flash) and our modified OpenNFM as the FTL [34,35]. The host computing device was an embedded development board, Firefly AIO-3399J (Six-Core ARM 64-bit processor, 4GB RAM, and Linux kernel 4.4.194). Our modified exFAT and modified VeraCrypt were deployed to the Firefly AIO-3399J. The LPC-H3131 connects to the USB 2.0 interface of Firefly AIO-3399J via a USB A to Mini Cable. Using the VeraCrypt, we created both the public and the hidden volume, and the original exFAT was deployed on the public volume, and the modified exFAT was deployed on the hidden volume. For comparison, we created a baseline by deploying the original VeraCrypt on top of the same testbed, in which the original exFAT was used in both the public and the hidden volume, and the original OpenNFM was used as the FTL. We believe that VeraCrypt is representative, as other block-based mobile PDE systems [8,17,22,31,37] all implement a similar technique. For simplicity, we call the baseline "VeraCrypt", which is vulnerable to deniability compromises in the flash memory. The I/O throughput of CrossPDE and VeraCrypt were both measured using benchmark tool fio [19]. We also compared CrossPDE with the represented FTL-based PDE systems DEFTL [23] and PEARL [12].

We compare the I/O throughput of CrossPDE with VeraCrypt in Table 1. We can observe that: 1) For the public mode, CrossPDE exhibits similar I/O throughput with VeraCrypt, because we do not change the read/write operations in the public mode. 2) For the hidden mode, the read throughput of CrossPDE is similar to that of VeraCrypt, but the write throughput is reduced 50%–60%. This is because: The read operations of the hidden mode are similar to those of the public mode; however, the write operations in the hidden mode require extra steps including reading the LBAs, erasing the block, etc.

To justify the benefits of moving the disk encryption/decryption from the FTL to the block layer, we also evaluated the I/O throughput without disk encryption, i.e., "no encryption" (as implemented by the original OpenNFM [15]), as well as the I/O throughput when deploying disk encryption/decryption in the FTL [23]. Both results are shown in Table 2. From Table 1 and 2, we can observe that: compared to "no encryption", the throughput of CrossPDE decreases 3%–12% in the public mode, and 4%–64% in the hidden mode; but "encryption in the FTL" decreases the throughput more than 10× in both modes. This confirms that CrossPDE makes the FTL much more lightweight compared to those which perform disk encryption/decryption in the FTL.

To assess the benefits of CrossPDE in keeping the FTL lightweight, we have compared the I/O throughput among CrossPDE, DEFTL [23] and PEARL [12]. The comparison is shown in Table 3, in which we estimated the throughput decrease of each aforementioned PDE system compared to a normal system without a PDE deployed, based on our own experimental results as well as the

**Table 1.** Throughput comparison between VeraCrypt and CrossPDE. SR - sequential read; RR - random read; SW - sequential write; RW - random write

| Patterns | VeraCrypt (KB/s) | | CrossPDE (KB/s) | |
|----------|------------------|-------------|-----------------|-------------|
|          | Public mode | Hidden mode | Public mode | Hidden mode |
| SR | 2508 | 2473 | 2460 | 2424 |
| RR | 2174 | 2030 | 2086 | 2000 |
| SW | 2599 | 2372 | 2535 | 948 |
| RW | 1897 | 1842 | 1910 | 839 |

**Table 2.** Throughput of "no encryption" and "encryption in FTL"

| Patterns | No encryption (OpenNFM)(KB/s) | Encryption in FTL (KB/s) |
|----------|-------------------------------|--------------------------|
| SR | 2538 | 172 |
| RR | 2206 | 170 |
| SW | 2639 | 168 |
| RW | 2176 | 165 |

**Table 3.** Estimation of throughput decrease in different FTL-based PDE schemes, compared to a regular system without a PDE deployed.

|              | PEARL [12] | DEFTL [23] | CrossPDE |
|--------------|------------|------------|----------|
| Public Read  | 41%   | 92%–93%     | 3.1%–5.4%  |
| Public Write | 48%   | 92.4%–93.6% | 3.9%–12.2% |
| Hidden Read  | 80%   | 92%–93%     | 4.5%–9.3%  |
| Hidden Write | 90.4% | 92.4%–93.6% | 61%–64%    |

experimental results from PEARL. We can observe that: 1) For the public read, the public write and the hidden read, CrossPDE decreases slightly in throughput, but PEARL (41%–80% decreases) and DEFTL (more than 90% decreases) significantly decrease in throughput. 2) For the hidden write, CrossPDE has a modest decrease in throughput (61%–64%), but PEARL and DEFTL both significantly decrease in throughput (more than 90%). The comparison can justify that CrossPDE performs much better in I/O throughput by decoupling the PDE functionality and separating them across multiple layers of the mobile system. This is because: unlike DEFTL and PEARL, the expensive operations of PDE in CrossPDE are separated from the FTL and moved to the block layer and hence processed by the more powerful host computing device.

# 7   Conclusion

In this work, we propose CrossPDE, a cross-layer PDE system for mobile computing devices which has integrated the PDE functionality into major layers of a mobile storage system. Experimental evaluation on our developed real-world prototype shows that CrossPDE can ensure deniability with a modest decrease in performance compared to the insecure block-layer PDE systems.

**Acknowledgments..** This work was supported by US National Science Foundation under grant number 1928349-CNS, 1928331-CNS, 1938130-CNS, and 2043022-DGE.

# References

1. Lpc-h3131. https://www.olimex.com/Products/ARM/NXP/LPC-H3131/
2. Truecrypt. http://truecrypt.sourceforge.net/
3. Veracrypt. https://www.veracrypt.fr/code/VeraCrypt/
4. Anderson, R., Needham, R., Shamir, A.: The steganographic file system. In: Aucsmith, D. (ed.) IH 1998. LNCS, vol. 1525, pp. 73–82. Springer, Heidelberg (1998). https://doi.org/10.1007/3-540-49380-8_6
5. Barker, A., Sample, S., Gupta, Y., McTaggart, A., Miller, E.L., Long, D.D.E.: Artifice: a deniable steganographic file system. In: 9th {USENIX} Workshop on Free and Open Communications on the Internet ({FOCI} 19) (2019)
6. Breeuwsma, M., De Jongh, M., Klaver, C., Van Der Knijff, R., Roeloffs, M.: Forensic data recovery from flash memory. Small Scale Dig. Dev. Forensics J. **1**(1), 1–17 (2007)
7. Chang, B., et al.: User-friendly deniable storage for mobile devices. Comput. Secur. **72**, 163–174 (2018)
8. Chang, B., Wang, Z., Chen, B., Zhang, F.: Mobipluto: file system friendly deniable storage for mobile devices. In: Proceedings of the 31st Annual Computer Security Applications Conference, pp. 381–390 (2015)
9. Chang, B., et al.: Mobiceal: towards secure and practical plausibly deniable encryption on mobile devices. In: 2018 48th Annual IEEE/IFIP International Conference on Dependable Systems and Networks (DSN), pp. 454–465. IEEE (2018)
10. Chen, B.: Towards designing a secure plausibly deniable system for mobile devices against multi-snapshot adversaries-a preliminary design. arXiv preprint arXiv:2002.02379 (2020)
11. Chen, C., Chakraborti, A., Sion, R.: Infuse: invisible plausibly-deniable file system for nand flash. Proc. Priv. Enhan. Technol. **4**, 239–254 (2020)
12. Chen, C., Chakraborti, A., Sion, R.: Pearl: plausibly deniable flash translation layer using wom coding. In: The 30th Usenix Security Symposium (2021)
13. Chen, N., Chen, B., Shi, W.: MobiWear: a plausibly deniable encryption system for wearable mobile devices. In: Chen, B., Huang, X. (eds.) AC3 2021. LNICST, vol. 386, pp. 138–154. Springer, Cham (2021). https://doi.org/10.1007/978-3-030-80851-8_10
14. Chen, N., Chen, B., Shi, W.: The block-based mobile pde systems are not secure - experimental attacks. In: EAI International Conference on Applied Cryptography in Computer and Communications. Springer, Heidelberg (2022). https://doi.org/10.1007/978-3-031-17081-2_9

15. Google Code. Opennfm (2011). https://code.google.com/p/opennfm/
16. exfat file system specification. https://docs.microsoft.com/en-us/windows/win32/fileio/exfat-specification
17. Feng, W., et al.: Mobigyges: a mobile hidden volume for preventing data loss, improving storage utilization, and avoiding device reboot. Fut. Gener. Comput. Syst. **109**, 158–171 (2020)
18. Typical hardware of flash storage devices. https://snp.cs.mtu.edu/techdoc/flash-devices.html
19. Freecode. fio (2014). http://freecode.com/projects/fio
20. Gutmann, P.: Secure deletion of data from magnetic and solid-state memory. In: Proceedings of the Sixth USENIX Security Symposium, San Jose, CA, vol. 14, pp. 77–89 (1996)
21. Han, J., Pan, M., Gao, D., Pang, H.: A multi-user steganographic file system on untrusted shared storage. In: Proceedings of the 26th Annual Computer Security Applications Conference, pp. 317–326 (2010)
22. Hong, S., Liu, C., Ren, B., Huang, Y., Chen, J.: Personal privacy protection framework based on hidden technology for smartphones. IEEE Access **5**, 6515–6526 (2017)
23. Jia, S., Xia, L., Chen, B., Liu, P.: Deftl: implementing plausibly deniable encryption in flash translation layer. In: Proceedings of the 24th ACM Conference on Computer and Communications Security. ACM (2017)
24. Johnson, N.F., Jajodia, S.: Steganalysis: the investigation of hidden information. In: 1998 IEEE Information Technology Conference, Information Environment for the Future (Cat. No. 98EX228), pp. 113–116. IEEE (1998)
25. Liao, J., Chen, B., Shi, W.: Trustzone enhanced plausibly deniable encryption system for mobile devices. In: 2021 IEEE/ACM Symposium on Edge Computing (SEC), pp. 441–447. IEEE (2021)
26. McDonald, A.D., Kuhn, M.G.: StegFS: a steganographic file system for linux. In: Pfitzmann, A. (ed.) IH 1999. LNCS, vol. 1768, pp. 463–477. Springer, Heidelberg (2000). https://doi.org/10.1007/10719724_32
27. Microsof. Bitlocker (2013). https://technet.microsoft.com/en-us/library/hh831713.aspx
28. Plausible deniability. https://www.veracrypt.fr/en/Plausible%20Deniability.html
29. Pang, H., Tan, K.-L., Zhou, X.: Stegfs: a steganographic file system. In: Proceedings 19th International Conference on Data Engineering (Cat. No. 03CH37405), pp. 657–667. IEEE (2003)
30. Peters, T.M., Gondree, M.A., Peterson, Z.N.J.: Defy: a deniable, encrypted file system for log-structured storage (2015)
31. Skillen, A., Mannan, M.: On implementing deniable storage encryption for mobile devices. In: 20th Annual Network and Distributed System Security Symposium, NDSS 2013, San Diego, California, USA, 24–27 February 2013 (2013)
32. Skillen, A., Mannan, M.: Mobiflage: deniable storage encryption for mobile devices. IEEE Trans. Depend. Secure Comput. **11**(3), 224–237 (2014)
33. How to create a strong password (and remember it). https://www.howtogeek.com/195430/how-to-create-a-strong-password-and-remember-it/
34. Tankasala, D., Chen, N., Chen, B.: A step-by-step guideline for creating a testbed for flash memory research via lpc-h3131 and opennfm. Technical report, Department of Computer Science, Michigan Tech (2020)
35. Tankasala, D., Chen, N., Chen, B.: Creating a testbed for flash memory research via lpc-h3131 and opennfm - linux version. Technical report, Department of Computer Science, Michigan Tech (2022)

36. Wroblewski, G.: General method of program code obfuscation (2002)
37. Yu, X., Chen, B., Wang, Z., Chang, B., Zhu, W.T., Jing, J.: MobiHydra: pragmatic and multi-level plausibly deniable encryption storage for mobile devices. In: Chow, S.S.M., Camenisch, J., Hui, L.C.K., Yiu, S.M. (eds.) ISC 2014. LNCS, vol. 8783, pp. 555–567. Springer, Cham (2014). https://doi.org/10.1007/978-3-319-13257-0_36

# Binary Analysis

# Language and Platform Independent Attribution of Heterogeneous Code

Farzaneh Abazari[1], Enrico Branca[1], Evgeniya Novikova[2],
and Natalia Stakhanova[1(✉)]

[1] University of Saskatchewan, Saskatoon, Canada
{faa851,enb733,natalia}@usask.ca
[2] Saint Petersburg Electrotechnical University, Saint Petersburg, Russia

**Abstract.** Code authorship attribution aims to identify the author of source or binary code according to the author's unique coding style characteristics. Recently, researchers have attempted to develop cross-platform and language-oblivious attribution approaches. Most of these attempts were limited to small sets of two-three languages or few platforms. However, rapid development of cross-platform malware and general language, platform and architecture diversity raises concerns about the suitability of these techniques. In this paper, we propose a unified approach that supports attribution of code irrespective of its format. Our approach leverages an image-based code abstraction that preserves the developer's coding style and lends itself to spatial analysis that reflects hidden patterns. We validate our approach on a set of Android applications achieving accuracy 82.8%–100% with source and byte code. We further explore the robustness of our approach in attributing developers' code written in 27 programming languages, compiled on 14 instruction set architectures types and 18 intermediate compiled versions. Our results on the GitHub dataset show that in the worst case scenario the proposed approach can discriminate authors of code in heterogeneous format with at least 68% accuracy.

**Keywords:** Source code and Binary attribution · Authorship attribution

## 1 Introduction

Code authorship attribution aims to identify a developer of a given code based on unique characteristics that reflect a developer's coding style. The underlying premise of the attribution techniques is the existence of inherent distinctive coding style, unique to an author and easily distinguishable from others. This style is reflected through variables, data structures, control flow logic, use of APIs, libraries, employed development tools, and other characteristics. A quantified representation of this coding style can be viewed as a developer's fingerprint. This coding style is unique to an author and invariant across all software programs written by this author.

© ICST Institute for Computer Sciences, Social Informatics and Telecommunications Engineering 2023
Published by Springer Nature Switzerland AG 2023. All Rights Reserved
F. Li et al. (Eds.): SecureComm 2022, LNICST 462, pp. 173–191, 2023.
https://doi.org/10.1007/978-3-031-25538-0_10

One of the main difficulties in code stylometry is compiling a fingerprint that provides efficient and accurate characterization of a coding style, remains consistent across programming languages, and survives compilation stages. This is particularly critical in security applications of code authorship attribution - software forensics [42], malware analysis [10,16,20,28], code plagiarism and theft detection [26,37] - where attribution analysis of any available code is often an essential task. Yet, the traditional attribution methods focus exclusively on the attribution of source code files expecting a homogeneous set of files written in traditional languages (typically, Java, C or Python), or attribution of binary files compiled in the same architecture. This is rarely possible in practice. Developers routinely use multiple languages for various tasks. For example, analyzing GitHub repositories Mayer and Bauer found that developers may use from 1 to 36 languages in their projects [32].

Beyond diversity of programming languages, there are other reasons that present significant challenges to attribution process in practice. Since source code is not always available, attribution is expected to be performed on a mixed set of binary files and code samples at various stages of compilation. Yet, the majority of the existing approaches almost exclusively focus on attribution of either source or binary code.

With rapidly evolving market of IoT devices, instruction set architectures (ISAs)-oblivious attribution becomes essential. Binary files might be generated on different ISAs which leads to significant differences in their instruction set even when the files are compiled from the same source code base.

Different compilers and variable compiler configurations (e.g., optimization levels) might also bring considerable changes to the resulting file structure. These reasons make it difficult or even infeasible for traditional attribution methods to attribute mixed code in a form of binary, source code, and code at different stages of compilation across architectures and compiling configurations.

To address these problems, we propose an attribution approach that supports attribution of code irrespective of its format. One of the main difficulties that the existing attribution techniques face in this context is the inherit dependence of feature engineering on the underlying nature of the code.

To address this challenge, we treat code as a binary stream, an abstraction independent of the actual code structure, and convert it to a format-oblivious gray-scale image. This approach preserves structural similarities of code segments and lends itself well to spatial analysis.

Spatial analysis is widely applied in many fields for exploratory analysis. It utilizes statistical techniques to reveal non-obvious patterns by analyzing spatial relationships of pixels. We thus analyze spatial properties of the images generated from author's code samples to derive patterns that describe a developer's style. In essence, our approach is based on the assumption that individual coding style is unique and preserved across programming languages and architectures.

We validate our approach on a set of 348 programs from 50 Android developers. Our approach can successfully attribute app's source code and byte code to its author with 82.8%–100% accuracy. We designed a set of experiments with source code in 27 languages, binaries in 14 ISAs and 18 compilers' versions. On GitHub data, our approach was able to accurately attribute source code with 71.5%, compiled binaries with 72.7% and intermediate stage of compiled files with 73.8% accuracy.

One of the practical applications of code attribution lies in malware analysis field where analysts are often challenged to attribute malware samples to its source. Since modern malware is typically obfuscated, any author attribution approach needs to be obfuscation-resistant. We show that our approach can achieve 72.5% attribution accuracy even in a presence of complex control-flow obfuscation transformations.

Finally, we compare the performance of our attribution approach to three techniques developed binary [21] and source [14, 44] code attribution. The code and datasets used in this study are publicly available:[1].

The following is a summary of our contributions:

- *Code format - oblivious attribution*: Unlike traditional attribution methods that focus exclusively on the attribution of homogeneous set of files written in traditional languages, we propose an accurate attribution approach for a mix of code in a form of binary and source code, code at different stages of compilation across architectures and compiling configurations. Our approach does not require a prior knowledge of programming language, ISA, or file format specifics.
- *Style-preserving abstraction*: We present an effective abstraction scheme optimized for detecting developer's coding characteristics in any code format.
- *Obfuscation-resilient attribution*: Our presented approach is resilient to the advanced data and control-flow obfuscation transformations applied by the off-the-shelf Tigress obfuscator.

## 2  Related Work

A comprehensive overview of the code attribution techniques is provided by Kalgutkar et al. [27]. The earliest studies in the field were primarily limited to an analysis of a single language, and as a result, experimented with programming language-dependent features [18]. More recently, researchers began analyzing features that represented the underlying semantics of the program behavior and moved to explore language-agnostic attribution [2, 3, 41]. Very few of the studies included experiments with more than one language (typically, Java, C and/or Python) [2, 3, 12, 44]. The majority of these studies leveraged Abstract Syntax Trees(ASTs) to capture language-independent syntactical features [12, 14, 41, 44]. AST can be helpful in representing source code. However, its construction and parsing is language-dependent and time-consuming, while the amount of generated features is unscalable for analysis. To resolve this, some employed control flow (CFG) and data flow analysis for source code attribution [42, 44]. Although these approaches are programming language-agnostic,

---

[1] https://cyberlab.usask.ca/anycodeattribution.html.

**Table 1.** Related work

| References | Code type | | Cross-lang. characteristics | | Cross-platform features | | Obf. | Malware |
|---|---|---|---|---|---|---|---|---|
| | Src. | Bin. | Languages | #of Lang per author | Compilers | ISA | | |
| Abuhamad et al. [2] | ✓ | | 4 (C, C++, Java, Python) | 2 | | | | ✓ |
| Abuhamad et al. [3] | ✓ | | 3 (C++, Java, Python) | 1 | | | | |
| Kurtukova et al. [31] | ✓ | | 13 | | | | | ✓ |
| Alsulami et al. [12] | ✓ | | 2 (C++, Python) | 1 | | | | |
| Ullah et al. [42] | ✓ | | 3 (C++, C#, Python) | | | | | |
| Ullah et al. [41] | ✓ | | 3 (C++, C#, Java) | | | | | |
| Zafar et al. [44] | ✓ | | 3 (C++, Python, Java) | 3 | | | | ✓ |
| Caliskan et al. [14] | ✓ | | 3 (C, C++, Python) | | | | | ✓ |
| Frantzeskou et al. [19] | ✓ | | 2 (C, C++) | 1 | | | | |
| Alrabaee et al. [7] | | ✓ | | | 5 with different optimization levels: gcc, g++, CLANG, ICC, MS VS 2010, 2012 | 3 (x86, ARM, MIPS) | ✓ | ✓ |
| Alrabaee et al. [6] | | ✓ | | | 5 with different optimization levels: gcc, g++, CLANG, ICC, MS VS 2010, 2012 | 1 (x86) | | ✓ |
| Alrabaee et al. [11] | | ✓ | | | 4 with different optimization levels: gcc, g++, CLANG, ICC, MS VS 2010 | | ✓ | |
| Hendrikse [24] | | ✓ | | | 3 with different optimization levels: gcc, ICC, MS VS | | ✓ | |
| Haddadpajuh et al. [21] | | ✓ | | | | | | ✓ |
| Our approach | ✓ | ✓ | 27 (listed in Table 4) | 1–8 (src code) | 3 with different optimization levels (gcc, ICC, MS VS) | 14 | ✓ | ✓ |

Empty table cell corresponds to the case when the data about given approach feature is not explicitly discussed or mentioned in the research paper, or not applicable to the approach.

their performance is dependent on the availability of parsers, and hence similarly support limited number of languages.

Strictly speaking, only a few studies in the field offer verifiable language agnostic approaches [2,44]. In these cases, authors with several programming languages are considered in both design and experimentation. The rest of the research studies either explicitly mention the use of homogeneous code per author or simply remain silent about this aspect.

As code authorship attribution evolved and found its application in security domain, it faced one of the main research challenges, i.e., unavailability of source code. So, several approaches have been presented in literature to attribute binaries [9,15,33,39]. Recently researchers become interested in the impact of different compilers, optimization levels and obfuscation techniques on the accuracy of authorship attribution. Most notable study was conducted by Alrabaee et al. [10]. Their study showed that attribution of a binary code is challenging, i.e., solely relying on instruction level features results in significant accuracy degradation, while utilizing only features extracted from CFG is sensitive to obfuscation. This result is consistent with the findings of other studies [9,15,39].

Several recent studies focused on adding an intermediate representation (IR), e.g., LLVM-IR, of disassembled binary code as an architecture-agnostic representation to unify files for feature extraction [6,7,11,23]. Alrabaee et al. [6,7] showed that relying on attributes extracted from lifted binaries to LLVM-IR in combination with deep learning supports multi-platform binary authorship identification and scales well to a significant number of authors. Several researchers [21,38] focused on problem of APT malware attribution and attribution of Android apks [20,25,28,29].

Table 1 presents an overview of attribution approaches that could be considered either language or platform independent. As opposed to the existing attribution approaches that focus on either source or binary code, we focus on language, platform, and architecture oblivious solution. We propose a simple yet effective method for attributing code, regardless of its format, without any prior knowledge of code specifics.

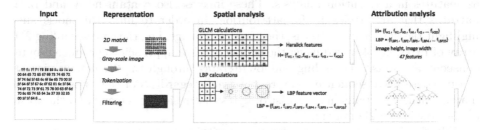

**Fig. 1.** The flow of the proposed approach

# 3    Approach

One of the main challenges that source or binary code attribution faces is engineering of features that are resistant to compilation process and persistent across programming languages and platforms.

In our work, we represent code regardless of its type as a set of consecutive bytes. This consequently allows us to generate a gray-scale image and leverage spatial analysis for deeper textural analysis of the image. Through this analysis, we can capture changes in adjacent bytes and derive characteristic byte patterns. As the last step, the characteristic patterns across all author's works are explored to derive a uniform representation of an author's coding style. Figure 1 summarizes the flow of our attribution approach.

## 3.1    Representation

Visualization of binary files have been used in many areas of security, e.g., for detection of obfuscation tools [25], malware detection and classification [13,34]. We leverage visualization of code as an intermediate representation to abstract the underlying format and platform specifics. The flow of the representation is shown in Fig. 2. Given that any code can be represented as a set of bytes, we read input in a raw binary format.

The input code either in human readable or machine readable format is converted into a gray-scale image following the approach introduced by Nataraj et al. [35]. The raw byte stream (or the corresponding ASCII values in case of source code) is transferred into a 2D matrix with a fixed width $d$, which is calculated based on the size of the original code file.

The resulting 2D matrix is treated as a 2D array of 1 byte vectors. Depending on the byte's value, each vector is then converted to a decimal value in range of $[0, 255]$ that further determines the gray-scale value of the pixel (0 for black and 255 for white). This approach preserves all patterns that exist in the original format of the input file.

The resulting images vary in size which allows us to use width and height as features in attribution analysis. These images also contain noisy and rare patterns that are irrelevant for attribution. In order to filter this noise and highlight the significant patterns, the generated image, i.e., the corresponding 2D array of bytes, is tokenized using the sliding window approach to produce n-byte consecutive grams. The sliding window iterates through the 2D matrix viewed as one consecutive sequence to extract n-grams regardless of their position in a matrix. Hence, n-grams may consist of bytes that reside at the end and the start of the row in the 2D matrix.

Filtering is based on n-gram frequency within the corresponding image and significance according to information gain (IG) value. For each file, we select the top most frequent n-grams, which results in a set of (sometime overlapping) n-grams across all samples per author. We further use Information Gain (IG) to measure each n-grams' importance for attributing samples to each author. Hence, in this process the distinctiveness of each n-gram for an author is assessed. For further analysis, we retained n-grams with IG $\geq 0.01$. All occurrences of these selected n-grams are retained in their original order. The remaining n-grams are 'squeezed out' of the image, hence preserving the original order of frequent n-grams which is important for the following spatial analysis.

## 3.2  Spatial Analysis

Since image is a numerical representation of byte values, image texture represents the spatial organization of the gray-levels of the pixels in a code sample. Although many numeric texture analysis approaches were introduced in the past decade, statistical method is seen as the one of the most powerful image analysis techniques [22].

The deeper insight into relationships between individual pixels can be derived through second-order statistics that look at correlations between pixels. We employ two well known approaches to statistical analysis of image texture, namely, analysis based on the gray-level co-occurrence matrix (GLCM) introduced by Haralick et al. [22] and Local Binary Patterns (LBP) [36].

**GLCM.** GLCM characterizes image by analyzing frequency of neighbouring pixels at selected distances and orientations over the entire image. Let $i$ and $j$

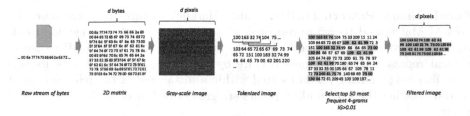

**Fig. 2.** The flow of the representation step.

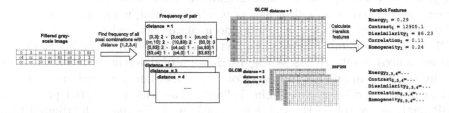

**Fig. 3.** An example of Haralick features' calculation.

be gray-scale values, the entry of GLCM is the probability that a pixel with value $i$ will be found adjacent to a pixel of value $j$ in the image separated by vector distance $d$ which can be further expressed in terms of absolute distant $d$ and the direction defined by the angle $\theta$ [22]. In this work, we set $d = 1, 2, 3, 4$; and $\theta = 0°$. In other words, the neighbouring pixels located at various distances are analyzed at an angle $0°$ to form four different GLCMs. Each of the GLCMs serves as a basis for calculation of Haralick features [22] that describe texture features of GLCM. We derive five features to reflect specific patterns of an image (Table 2). Since we employ four directions $d$, each image is represented by $4 \times 5 = 20$ Haralick features which we refer to as a *Haralick vector*. Figure 3 shows the process of GLCM calculation with the corresponding Haralick features. After the GLCM matrix is calculated for d=[1..4], we calculate $p_{i,j}$ for each GLCM cell by calculating probability of combination of pair (i,j) (e.g. dividing the cell's value to the summation of all elements in GLCM).

**Table 2.** The Haralick features derived from GLCM

| Name | Description | Formula |
|---|---|---|
| Energy | Shows randomness of the spatial distribution | $\sqrt{\sum_{i,j=0}^{255} P_{i,j}^2}$ |
| Contrast | Measures gray level variations between the reference pixel and its neighbour | $\sum_{i,j=0}^{255} P_{i,j}(i-j)^2$ |
| Dissimilarity | Shows average of differences in pixel values | $\sum_{i,j=0}^{255} P_{i,j}|i-j|$ |
| Correlation | Measures the linear dependency of gray level values | $\sum_{i,j=0}^{255} P_{i,j}\frac{(i-\mu_i)(j-\mu_j)}{\sigma_i \sigma_j}$ |
| Homogeneity | Indicates dominant values | $\sum_{i,j=0}^{255} \frac{P_{i,j}}{1+(i-j)^2}$ |

**Local Binary Pattern (LBP).** Unlike Haralick features that are based on GLCM Matrix and therefore represent global patterns, LBP conveys local patterns that are extracted directly from the image [43]. To do this, LBP measures a local representation of image texture by comparing each pixel with its surrounding neighbouring pixels located within a distance $d$ of the reference point to test whether the surrounding points are greater or less than the central pixel value.

Figure 4 shows the process of converting patterns represented by neighbouring pixels to a binary value. Those neighbours with value less than referenced pixels are denoted as *1* and others as *0*. The resulting values are stored in an 8-bit binary array (or a corresponding decimal number), which is referred to as *LBP value*. This number reflects the texture (i.e., pattern) of the image around the referenced point. To assess the distribution of different LBP values across the image, we compute the frequency of each LBP value (i.e., each pattern) and assign it to the corresponding bin. Following the widely accepted practice in LBP analysis, we divide the range (0 to 255) into 25 equally distributed bins, each representing a set of LBP patterns.

Finally, the resulting histogram tabulates the number of times each LBP pattern occurs. The frequency of the bins is treated as *LBP feature vector* (Fig. 4). These features have highly discriminative nature that help the classifier to predict the author with higher accuracy [4,5].

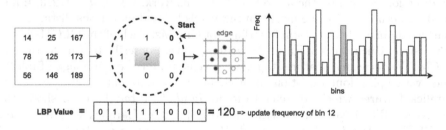

**Fig. 4.** An example of LBP value calculation for each pixel

### 3.3 Attribution

The attribution of code is based on the derived 47 features that include Haralick and LBP vectors, and image height and width.

Previous studies in source code authorship attribution employed various classification algorithms for attribution analysis [27]. Among them, Random Forest (RF) was one of the most common classifiers [1] that performs well in comparison with many standard methods.

We employ RF algorithm with 100 trees ("n_estimators" = 100) from a sample drawn with replacement from the training set with "entropy" criteria and maximum number of features is set to "sqrt". We set "min_samples_split" to 2 and "min_samples_leaf" to 1.

**Table 3.** The employed datasets' statistics

| Filtered dataset | # of lang. or formats per author | # of authors | # of files | Range of samples per author | Range LOC or size | Avg. LOC or size | Range char. per line | Avg char. per line |
|---|---|---|---|---|---|---|---|---|
| Android validation set (Java src code) | 1 | 50 | 7,594 | 5–856 | 3–4,253 | 172.1 | 1–1,464 | 36.1 |
| Android validation set (.dex binary code) | 1 | 50 | 413 | 5–25 | 12.4–11,640.7(KB) | 3158.9 | – | – |
| GCJ (src code) | 2–5 | 3,000 | 63,682 | 10–157 | 1–3,039 | 80.1 | 1–95,567 | 23.45 |
| GitHub (src code) | 2–8 | 475 | 114,461 | 11–5,005 | 2–164,684 | 327 | 1–4,723,481 | 46.5 |
| GitHub (binary code) | 1–3 | 378 | 13,577 | 5–641 | 0.1–89,309(KB) | 675(KB) | – | – |

# 4  Data Corpus

The critical aspect of this work is the analysis of our approach in the presence of heterogeneous code formats. We thus ventured to collect mixed code in a form of binary, source code, and code at different stages of compilation across different architectures and compiling configurations.

All datasets were prepared to ensure presence of at least 5 samples for each format of file per author[2]. Moreover, for GitHub and GoogleCodeJam sets, the authors were selected to contain more than one type of file's format in the dataset, i.e., each author has files of at least 2 format and thus has at least 10 unique samples. The details of our collected datasets are given in Table 3.

**Validation Dataset.** In recent years, there has been an increasing interest for attributing Android APKs based on analysis of dex files [20], strings [28] and even specific features of the app such as permissions [45]. For our validation, we attribute APKs to their authors based on bytecode contained in dex files and original Java source files. We collected a set of 348 Android projects written by 50 authors from the open source Android application market F-Droid[3]. To ensure that our set does not include authors that use different alias for different repositories, we verified the authors' identities through the official GitHub, Gitlab, SourceForge, BitBucket platforms. Our collected set has authors with varying number of APKs ranging from 5 to 22, dex code ranging from 5 to 25 and Java source code from 5 to 856.

**GitHub Repository.** GitHub, an open-source software development platform. The programs in GitHub are typically more complex, include variety of programming languages, third-party libraries, several encodings and binaries focus

---

[2] In the rest of this work, by file's format we mean source code in a programming language, file's compiled version on some platform or architecture, or a file at different stages of compilation with various compiling configurations.

[3] https://www.f-droid.org/.

on solving diverse tasks (e.g., from game development to middleware). Performing authorship attribution on data retrieved from GitHub is more challenging due to presence of library and shared code. Due to these facts most of the previous works evaluated their approach on GoogleCodeJam dataset [2,3,42] and confirmed that the result of their paper would be different in the real-world dataset such as GitHub [44].

We collected programs from January until October 2020 by using the GitHub action logs. We consider repositories with at least one commit log, those that contain at least two different languages. Although it is difficult to guarantee sole authorship of any code posted online, we took reasonable precautions by filtering repositories marked as forks, as these are typically copies of other authors' repositories and do not constitute original work. An additional check for multiple-author repositories was performed by examining the commit logs. Repositories with logs containing more than one unique name and email address combination (potentially indicating an involvement of several authors) were also excluded. We download the latest master file. After removing duplicated files and filtering authors with less than 5 samples, 475 authors are remained with at least two languages (source code data) and 378 authors with multiple binary file formats (Table 3). For this analysis, we collected source and binary code of programs written in 25 programming languages, compiled for 14 architectures and in 18 intermediate stages of compilation from 3602 master files in GitHub. The distribution of files between languages and binary types are given in Table 4 and Table 5, respectively.

**GoogleCodeJam dataset (GCJ).** Since the majority of the existing studies employ data extracted from GoogleCodeJam programming competition[4], an annual international coding competition hosted by Google, for our analysis we also assembled a dataset containing code from the 2008 to 2018 competitions with authors that have code written in more than one language. We randomly selected 3000 authors with source code files written in 15 programming languages (2–5 different languages per author). The distribution of files across languages is provided in Table 4.

## 5   Experiments

We perform several experiments to validate our approach and examine its attribution effectiveness for various types of code. To estimate accuracy of attribution analysis, we used stratified 4-fold cross-validation that ensures that all developers are present in all folds. Note that strategy randomly partitions all author's code samples regardless of language, platform, or format, hence, different folds are likely to represent different subsets of languages. To evaluate our results, we employ a commonly used metric in attribution studies indicating the attribution accuracy or the *accuracy* in short. We use weighted-average accuracy defined as

---

[4] https://code.google.com/codejam/.

**Table 4.** GitHub and GCJ source code datasets

| Language | # of samples GitHub | # of samples GCJ | Array | Scripting | Compiled | Concurrent | Curly-bracket | Extension | Imperative | Interactive mode | Functional | Impure |
|---|---|---|---|---|---|---|---|---|---|---|---|---|
| Python | 12072 | 14663 | ✓ | | | | | | ✓ | ✓ | ✓ | ✓ |
| C | 947 | 4668 | | | ✓ | | ✓ | | ✓ | | | |
| C++ | 2500 | 20584 | | | ✓ | | ✓ | | ✓ | | | ✓ |
| C# | 65497 | 4494 | ✓ | | ✓ | ✓ | ✓ | | ✓ | ✓ | ✓ | |
| Ruby | 1454 | 1617 | ✓ | | | | | | ✓ | ✓ | | ✓ |
| Golang | 285 | 757 | | | ✓ | ✓ | ✓ | | ✓ | | | |
| Java | 40880 | 14062 | | | ✓ | ✓ | ✓ | | ✓ | | ✓ | ✓ |
| Javascript | 30072 | 612 | ✓ | | | | ✓ | ✓ | ✓ | ✓ | ✓ | ✓ |
| LUA | 186 | 96 | ✓ | | | | | | ✓ | ✓ | ✓ | |
| Kotlin | 875 | 0 | | | ✓ | ✓ | ✓ | | | | | ✓ |
| PHP | 3943 | 769 | ✓ | | | | ✓ | | ✓ | ✓ | ✓ | |
| Perl | 533 | 724 | ✓ | | | | ✓ | ✓ | ✓ | ✓ | ✓ | ✓ |
| CSS | 8228 | 0 | ✓ | | | | | | | | | |
| S | 57 | 0 | ✓ | | | | | | | | | |
| Tcl | 17 | 0 | | ✓ | | | | | ✓ | ✓ | ✓ | ✓ |
| Cmake | 247 | 0 | | | | | | | | | | |
| Dart | 364 | 0 | | | | ✓ | | | | ✓ | ✓ | |
| Objective-c | 25 | 0 | | | | | ✓ | | | | | |
| Powershell | 52 | 0 | | ✓ | | | ✓ | | ✓ | ✓ | ✓ | |
| Verilog | 123 | 0 | | | | | | | | | | |
| Swift | 37 | 91 | | | ✓ | | ✓ | | ✓ | ✓ | ✓ | |
| Coffee | 44 | 59 | | | | | | | | | | |
| TypeScript | 848 | 0 | | | | | ✓ | | | | | |
| Groovy | 278 | 0 | | ✓ | | | ✓ | | ✓ | ✓ | ✓ | |
| Gradle | 340 | 0 | | | | | | | | | | |
| Pascal | 0 | 389 | | | | | | | ✓ | | | |
| Lisp | 0 | 97 | | | | | | | | | | ✓ |
| **Total** | 114,461 | 63,682 | | | | | | | | | | |

**Table 5.** GitHub dataset (binary and intermediate code)

*Compiled binary files:*

| File Type | Architecture | # of samples |
|---|---|---|
| ELF | ARM 32-bit | 468 |
| | 386 32-bit | 174 |
| | MIPS 32-bit | 4 |
| | AVR 32-bit | 14 |
| | 68HC12 32-bit | 4 |
| | PPC 32-bit | 1 |
| | ×86 64-bit | 503 |
| | AARCH64 64-bit | 64 |
| | MIPS 64-bit | 2 |
| PE32 | I386 32-bit | 1131 |
| | ARMNT 32-bit | 2 |
| | AMD64 32+ -bit | 630 |
| | ARM64 32+ -bit | 1 |
| | IA64 32+ -bit | 1 |

*Files at intermediate stages of compilation:*

| Compiler | Version | # of samples |
|---|---|---|
| Python | 3.6 | 1178 |
| | 3.5 | 311 |
| | 2.7 | 240 |
| | 3.4 | 168 |
| | 2.6 | 3 |
| Java | 1.2 | 12 |
| | 1.3 | 11 |
| | 1.5 | 640 |
| | 1.6 | 457 |
| | 1.7 | 439 |
| | 1.8 | 5281 |
| | 1.9 | 645 |
| | 1.10 | 59 |
| | 1.11 | 297 |
| | 1.12 | 71 |
| | 1.13 | 199 |
| | 1.14 | 102 |
| | 1.15 | 22 |

a percentage of code samples correctly attributed to the corresponding authors over the total number of samples, where accuracy of each class is weighted by the number of samples from that class. All experiments were performed on an Intel server equipped with 384 GB of RAM and 32 CPU cores.

***Selection of Parameters.*** Although n-grams are commonly applied in author attribution domain, their effect on the accuracy is often uncertain and depends on nature of the code. Since our approach leverages the top most frequent n-

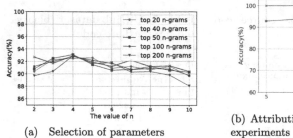
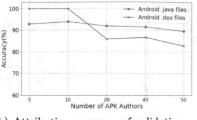

(a)   Selection of parameters

(b)  Attribution accuracy of validation
experiments (Android datasets)

**Fig. 5.** The experimental analysis.

grams for analysis, we investigate the optimal quantity of n-grams and the best values of $n$ on a subset of GCJ dataset with 50 authors and 841 source code samples. Previous studies (e.g., [30]) explored the values of $n$ ranging between 2 and 10 concluding that 4-grams generally produce the best results. We therefore also explore this range of n-grams. As Fig. 5a shows, the attribution accuracy for varying number of n-grams and the top $m$ most frequent n-grams is similar. This result is beneficial as voluminous feature vectors generated during the analysis may make analysis prohibitively expensive and sometimes infeasible. Hence, reducing the number of n-grams while retaining similar accuracy is beneficial in many resource-constraint environments. Although the results show low variability across different $n$ and $m$ values, the top 50 4-grams produce the best accuracy (93.1%). We choose these values to tokenize our input.

***Validation Results.*** For this experiment, we leverage our validation dataset that contains APKs related files at two granularity levels: original Java source code and byte code derived from dex files. Figure 5b shows that the accuracy for all levels varies between 100% and 82.8%. The most consistent attribution is achieved with source code (92.8% for 5 authors and 89.6% for 50 authors). This is consistent with our expectations (and the previous studies) that source code inherently preserves the developer's coding style and serves as a reliable characteristic. The best accuracy (100%) was obtained with dex files for 5–10 authors, which however dropped to 82.8% for 50 authors.

***Feature Set Analysis.*** In our analysis, we rely on a set of 47 features that include, in addition to Haralick and LBP features, image width and height. To understand their role in the final attribution, we explore the importance of each of these features on a subset of GCJ dataset with 50 authors. The majority of features (42 features) have information gain > 0.01, i.e., their contribution to the result is meaningful. The image width and height along with Haralick features appeared to be among the top performing features.

## 5.1   Authorship Attribution of Source Code

To examine the performance of our approach on multi-language source code dataset, we design a set of experiments to analyze the effect of the dataset size

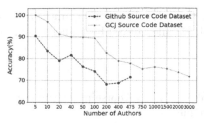

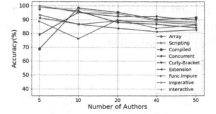

(a)    Attribution accuracy of source code

(b) Source code attribution of language paradigms

**Fig. 6.** Attribution accuracy of source code

and number of languages on the accuracy of attribution. We randomly select subsets of authors from GitHub and GCJ datasets to explore behaviour of our approach on smaller sets.

Figure 6a shows that our approach can obtain attribution accuracy of more than 70% in most cases. As been noted by several studies, experiments with GitHub data in almost all cases give lower accuracy than with GCJ programs [1, 12,17]. For authorship attribution, the use of GCJ data has been extensively criticized mostly owing to its artificial setup [15,17,33]. The researchers argued the existing competition setup gives little flexibility to participants resulting in somewhat artificial and constrained program code.

The variability of languages further impact the results. The GitHub dataset has more languages (25) than GCJ set (15). For example, with 5 authors that have 2 different languages each in GCJ and 5 languages in GitHub set, our approach obtains perfect accuracy (100%) with GCJ and only 90.4% with GitHub.

Yet, with the increase in number of authors and number of languages, the performance of our approach on GCJ deteriorates. The total set of GitHub authors (475 authors) with 25 languages is attributed with 71.5% accuracy, while GCJ set with 3000 authors and 15 languages shows 71.8%. It should be also noted that the difference in performance remains somewhat consistent between two sets (around 20%).

## 5.2    Authorship Attribution of Binary Files

Most of the previous works focused on analysis of files compiled for a single ISA [6,8], e.g., ×86, that makes their binary authorship attribution solution ineffective for analyzing modern malware which can be designed for various ISA. The performance of our approach in attributing binaries extracted from GitHub repository is shown in Fig. 7.

As the results show, the attribution is reasonably better on compiled binaries (ELF and PE) than binaries at intermediate stages of compilation (Java class and compiled Python). Table 5 shows the distribution of GitHub binaries in 14 compiled and 18 intermediate compiled binaries. The accuracy dips from 82.7% (5 authors) to 66.2% (200 authors) for Java class files. The results on Python compiled files are higher for smaller sets (96.5% for 10 authors) and lower for larger sets (72.9% for 50 authors). Overall, PE files have the highest accuracy (84.6%) on 50 authors.

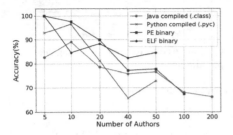

**Fig. 7.** Accuracy attribution of GitHub binary dataset

**Table 6.** Authorship attribution of GitHub dataset

| Group | Number of authors | Accuracy |
|---|---|---|
| Compiled | 142 | 72.7% |
| Inter.stage compiled | 248 | 73.8 % |
| All binaries | 378 | 68.3% |
| Binary and Source | 761 | 68% |

To investigate how the combination of datasets impacts the overall performance of authorship attribution, we combine GitHub files from two sets (source and binary) in 4 groups: 1) Intermediate stage compiled, 2) Compiled, 3) All binary code, and 4) Source and binary code.

The results of attribution on these four groups are shown in Table 6. The number of authors in the mixed set is less than the total number in individual sets due to overlap of authors in different groups. We are able to obtain the highest accuracy on a set of files at intermediate stages of compilation (73.8% accuracy). The least accuracy is achieved on the set of combined binary and source code (68% for 761 authors). Note that this set represents source code samples written in 25 different languages. This experiment clearly illustrates that the design of our approach allows to accurately attribute any file to a corresponding author in the worst case with at least 68% accuracy.

### 5.3   Authorship Attribution of Obfuscated Source Code

In this experiment, we investigate the impact of obfuscation techniques on attribution of source code. In our experiments, we use Tigress [40], an obfuscator tool designed for the C language. For this experiment, we randomly selected a subset of GCJ dataset, consisting of 50 authors with 7 samples per author on average (361 samples written in C), and obfuscate the whole set using several types of obfuscations (Table 7). The main reason behind using GCJ as opposed to GitHub is a lack of C samples within our GitHub set. Only GCJ set had enough C samples to perform experiments with 50 authors.

As expected, the accuracy of attributing obfuscated code is lower than original accuracy. However, for control obfuscation the performance drops only by 8.5% compared to the original source code (72.5% vs 81%). Note that including virtualization transformation (Advanced control obfuscation) only slightly

**Table 7.** Accuracy attribution of obfuscated source code (C language)

| Dataset | Obfuscation methods | Accuracy | |
|---|---|---|---|
| | | Zafar et al. [44] | Our approach |
| Original src code | – | 65.7 % | 81% |
| Data obf. | Literals encoding, Encode arithmetic | 58.9% | 70% |
| Control obf. | Opaque Predicates, Control flow Flattening, Insertion of random functions | 57.5 % | 72.5% |
| Advanced control obf. | Virtualization, Opaque Predicates, Control flow Flattening, Insertion of random functions | 57.5% | 70.5% |

decreases our approach's accuracy (by 1.5%). Virtualization generates arbitrarily complex virtual instruction sets (i.e., customized ISA), which are then interpreted on-the-fly during program execution. The results also show that our approach is more obfuscation resilient than the recent language and obfuscation oblivious method proposed by Zafar et al. [44]. While the authors reported higher accuracy in the presence of obfuscation (on average ranging from 83% to 95% for C++ samples), their analysis only included trivial layout transformations (e.g., symbol name replacement, removal of spaces, comments, etc.). While our evaluation with advanced control obfuscation showed superior resiliency of our approach.

## 5.4   Comparison with the Existing Approaches

To better assess the proposed approach, we compare the performance of our attribution approach with three techniques: MVFCC, binary code attribution approach developed by Haddadpajouh et al. [21] and the state-of-the-art source code, language oblivious attribution methods proposed by Zafar et al. [44] and Caliskan et al. [14][5]

For fair comparison, we obtained an original dataset employed in Haddadpajouh et al.'s [21] study that consists of 5 APT malware groups with a total of 1463 samples. To compare with Caliskan et al.'s and Zafar et al.'s approaches, we selected subsets of the GCJ dataset with Java and C++ source code to ensure at least 7 code samples per author.

The comparison results given in Table 8 show that *our proposed approach achieves higher accuracy in most cases, while providing more flexible and broader framework for attribution of code in various formats without prior knowledge.* In case of MVFCC, we were able to attribute samples of APT malware groups with accuracy of 96.3%, which is comparable with the results reported in the original study (95.2%). Our approach performs better in terms of accuracy and efficiency than the Caliskan et al.'s approach [14]. Relying on AST n-grams, Caliskan et al.'s approach results in more than 35,000 features for 100 authors present in

---

[5] The authors of the other cross-platform and languages-oblivious studies [7,8,12] could not provide us with their code for comparison.

**Table 8.** Comparison of the attribution approaches

| Java source code dataset | Accuracy | | |
|---|---|---|---|
| | Caliskan et al. [14] | Zafar et al. [44] | Our approach |
| GCJ (5 authors) | 89% | **100%** | 98.7% |
| GCJ (10 authors) | 83.3% | **100%** | 97.2% |
| GCJ (20 authors) | 85.7% | 86.3% | **95%** |
| GCJ (40 authors) | 81.4% | 81.3% | **93%** |
| GCJ (50 authors) | 80.3% | 80.8% | **92%** |
| GCJ (100 authors) | 75.2% | 77.5% | **90%** |
| **C++ source code dataset** | **Caliskan et al. [14]** | **Zafar et al. [44]** | **Our approach** |
| GCJ (5 authors) | 98.6% | 86.6% | **100%** |
| GCJ (10 authors) | **96.4%** | 93.9% | 94.2% |
| GCJ (20 authors) | 90.9% | 82.8% | **92.9%** |
| GCJ (40 authors) | **92.3%** | 73.4% | 90.3% |
| GCJ (50 authors) | 88.1% | 73.4% | **90.1%** |
| GCJ (100 authors) | 85.2% | 69.1% | **86.6%** |
| **Mixed source code dataset** (50 authors) | **Zafar et al. [44]** | | **Our approach** |
| Scripting languages | 76% | | **86.3%** |
| Compiled languages | 85.6% | | **91.3%** |
| Concurrent languages | **88.1%** | | 84.1% |
| Curly-Bracket languages | 77.9% | | **89.6%** |
| Extension languages | 55.6% | | **82.5%** |
| Functional Impure languages | 75.3% | | **86.1%** |
| Imperative languages | 77.1% | | **88.3%** |
| Interactive languages | 77.3% | | **87.6%** |
| **Binary dataset** | **MVFCC [21]** | | **Our approach** |
| APT malware set [21] | 95.2% | | **96.3%** |

our set, in comparison, our approach generates only 47 features which as a result leads to faster attribution.

Zafar et al. approach on the other hand showed a slightly higher accuracy for Java source code compared to our approach for a small number of authors (100% for attributing 5 and 10 authors vs 98.7% and 97% with our approach). Yet, its accuracy dropped significantly for larger sets of 20 and more authors (77.5% for 100 authors). With the C++ dataset and a set with mixed languages, our approach in most cases showed better performance. With the limited applicability of Zafar et al. approach (source code only), our framework is better equipped to provide a more versatile and accurate attribution in practice.

## 6   Conclusion

In the field of security, code attribution finds its application in many contexts, e.g., software forensics, malware analysis, code plagiarism and intellectual property theft detection. The uncertainty of field requires the presence of suitable techniques capable of attributing any given code. The existing authorship attribution approaches fail to provide necessary support. This work offers a unified approach for accurate code attribution. We adopt a coding style preserving abstraction scheme which enables us to accurately attribute code to its corresponding author without any knowledge of code format.

This paper's findings have important implications for developing a heterogeneous system that can relate any form of user output to the corresponding author.

# References

1. Abazari, F., Branca, E., Ridley, N., Stakhanova, N., Dallapreda, M.: Dataset characteristics for reliable code authorship attribution. IEEE Trans. Depend. Secure Comput. (2021)
2. Abuhamad, M., AbuHmed, T., Mohaisen, A., Nyang, D.: Large-scale and language-oblivious code authorship identification. In: Proceedings of the 2018 ACM SIGSAC Conference on Computer and Communications Security, pp. 101–114 (2018)
3. Abuhamad, M., Rhim, J.S., AbuHmed, T., Ullah, S., Kang, S., Nyang, D.: Code authorship identification using convolutional neural networks. Future Gener. Comput. Syst. **95**, 104–115 (2019)
4. Ahonen, T., Hadid, A., Pietikainen, M.: Face description with local binary patterns: application to face recognition. IEEE Trans. Pattern Anal. Mach. Intell. **28**(12), 2037–2041 (2006)
5. Ahonen, T., Matas, J., He, C., Pietikäinen, M.: Rotation invariant image description with local binary pattern histogram fourier features. In: Salberg, A.-B., Hardeberg, J.Y., Jenssen, R. (eds.) SCIA 2009. LNCS, vol. 5575, pp. 61–70. Springer, Heidelberg (2009). https://doi.org/10.1007/978-3-642-02230-2_7
6. Alrabaee, S., Debbabi, M., Wang, L.: On the feasibility of binary authorship characterization. Digital Invest. **28**, S3–S11 (2019)
7. Alrabaee, S., Debbabi, M., Wang, L.: Cpa: accurate cross-platform binary authorship characterization using lda. IEEE Trans. Inf. Forensics Secur. **15**, 3051–3066 (2020)
8. Alrabaee, S., Karbab, E.M.B., Wang, L., Debbabi, M.: BinEye: towards efficient binary authorship characterization using deep learning. In: Sako, K., Schneider, S., Ryan, P.Y.A. (eds.) ESORICS 2019. LNCS, vol. 11736, pp. 47–67. Springer, Cham (2019). https://doi.org/10.1007/978-3-030-29962-0_3
9. Alrabaee, S., Saleem, N., Preda, S., Wang, L., Debbabi, M.: Oba2: an onion approach to binary code authorship attribution. Digital Invest. **11**, S94–S103 (2014)
10. Alrabaee, S., Shirani, P., Debbabi, M., Wang, L.: On the feasibility of malware authorship attribution. In: Cuppens, F., Wang, L., Cuppens-Boulahia, N., Tawbi, N., Garcia-Alfaro, J. (eds.) FPS 2016. LNCS, vol. 10128, pp. 256–272. Springer, Cham (2017). https://doi.org/10.1007/978-3-319-51966-1_17
11. Alrabaee, S., Shirani, P., Wang, L., Debbabi, M., Hanna, A.: On leveraging coding habits for effective binary authorship attribution. In: Lopez, J., Zhou, J., Soriano, M. (eds.) ESORICS 2018. LNCS, vol. 11098, pp. 26–47. Springer, Cham (2018). https://doi.org/10.1007/978-3-319-99073-6_2
12. Alsulami, B., Dauber, E., Harang, R., Mancoridis, S., Greenstadt, R.: Source code authorship attribution using long short-term memory based networks. In: Foley, S.N., Gollmann, D., Snekkenes, E. (eds.) ESORICS 2017. LNCS, vol. 10492, pp. 65–82. Springer, Cham (2017). https://doi.org/10.1007/978-3-319-66402-6_6

13. Azab, A., Khasawneh, M.: Msic: malware spectrogram image classification. IEEE Access **8**, 102007–102021 (2020)
14. Caliskan-Islam, A., Harang, R., Liu, A., Narayanan, A., Voss, C., Yamaguchi, F., Greenstadt, R.: De-anonymizing programmers via code stylometry. In: 24th {USENIX} Security Symposium ({USENIX} Security 2015), pp. 255–270 (2015)
15. Caliskan-Islam, A., et al.: When coding style survives compilation: de-anonymizing programmers from executable binaries. In: The Network and Distributed System Security Symposium (NDSS 2018) (2018)
16. Chouchane, R., Stakhanova, N., Walenstein, A., Lakhotia, A.: Detecting machine-morphed malware variants via engine attribution. J. Comput. Virol. Hack. Tech. **9**(3), 137–157 (2013). https://doi.org/10.1007/s11416-013-0183-6
17. Dauber, E., Caliskan-Islam, A., Harang, R., Greenstadt, R.: Git blame who?: stylistic authorship attribution of small, incomplete source code fragments. arXiv preprint arXiv:1701.05681 (2017)
18. Ding, H., Samadzadeh, M.H.: Extraction of java program fingerprints for software authorship identification. J. Syst. Softw. **72**(1), 49–57 (2004)
19. Frantzeskou, G., Stamatatos, E., Gritzalis, S., Chaski, C., Howald, B.: Identifying authorship by byte-level n-grams: the source code author profile (scap) method. Int. J. Digit. Evid. **6** (2007)
20. Gonzalez, H., Stakhanova, N., Ghorbani, A.A.: Authorship attribution of android apps. In: Proceedings of the Eighth ACM Conference on Data and Application Security and Privacy, CODASPY 2018, pp. 277–286. Association for Computing Machinery, New York (2018)
21. Haddadpajouh, H., Azmoodeh, A., Dehghantanha, A., Parizi, R.M.: Mvfcc: a multi-view fuzzy consensus clustering model for malware threat attribution. IEEE Access **8**, 139188–139198 (2020)
22. Haralick, R.M., Shanmugam, K., Dinstein, I.: Textural features for image classification. IEEE Trans. Syst. Man Cybern. SMC **3**(6), 610–621 (1973)
23. Heitman, C., Arce, I.: Barf: a multiplatform open source binary analysis and reverse engineering framework. In: XX Congreso Argentino de Ciencias de la Computación (Buenos Aires 2014) (2014)
24. Hendrikse, S.: The Effect of Code Obfuscation on Authorship Attribution of Binary Computer Files. Ph.D. thesis, Nova Southeastern University (2017)
25. Jain, A., Gonzalez, H., Stakhanova, N.: Enriching reverse engineering through visual exploration of android binaries. In: Proceedings of the 5th Program Protection and Reverse Engineering Workshop, pp. 1–9 (2015)
26. Ji, J.H., Woo, G., Cho, H.G.: A plagiarism detection technique for java program using bytecode analysis. In: Third International Conference on Convergence and Hybrid Information Technology, 2008, ICCIT 2008, vol. 1, pp. 1092–1098. IEEE (2008)
27. Kalgutkar, V., Kaur, R., Gonzalez, H., Stakhanova, N., Matyukhina, A.: Code authorship attribution: methods and challenges. ACM Comput. Surv. **52**(1) (2019)
28. Kalgutkar, V., Stakhanova, N., Cook, P., Matyukhina, A.: Android authorship attribution through string analysis. In: Proceedings of the 13th International Conference on Availability, Reliability and Security. ARES 2018. Association for Computing Machinery, New York (2018)
29. Kaur, R., Ning, Y., Gonzalez, H., Stakhanova, N.: Unmasking Android obfuscation tools using spatial analysis. In: 2018 16th Annual Conference on Privacy, Security and Trust (PST), pp. 1–10. IEEE (2018)

30. Kothari, J., Shevertalov, M., Stehle, E., Mancoridis, S.: A probabilistic approach to source code authorship identification. In: Fourth International Conference on Information Technology, 2007, ITNG 2007, pp. 243–248. IEEE (2007)
31. Kurtukova, A., Romanov, A., Shelupanov, A.: Source code authorship identification using deep neural networks. Symmetry **12**(12), 2044 (2020)
32. Mayer, P., Bauer, A.: An empirical analysis of the utilization of multiple programming languages in open source projects. In: Proceedings of the 19th International Conference on Evaluation and Assessment in Software Engineering, EASE 2015. Association for Computing Machinery, New York (2015)
33. Meng, X., Miller, B.P.: Binary code multi-author identification in multi-toolchain scenarios (2018)
34. Nataraj, L.: A signal processing approach to malware analysis. University of California, Santa Barbara (2015)
35. Nataraj, L., Karthikeyan, S., Jacob, G., Manjunath, B.S.: Malware images: visualization and automatic classification. In: Proceedings of the 8th International Symposium on Visualization for Cyber Security, pp. 1–7 (2011)
36. Ojala, T., Pietikainen, M., Maenpaa, T.: Multiresolution gray-scale and rotation invariant texture classification with local binary patterns. IEEE Trans. Pattern Anal. Mach. Intell. **24**(7), 971–987 (2002)
37. Prechelt, L., Malpohl, G., Philippsen, M.: Finding plagiarisms among a set of programs with jplag. J. UCS **8**(11), 1016 (2002)
38. Rosenberg, I., Sicard, G., David, E.O.: DeepAPT: nation-state APT attribution using end-to-end deep neural networks. In: Lintas, A., Rovetta, S., Verschure, P.F.M.J., Villa, A.E.P. (eds.) ICANN 2017. LNCS, vol. 10614, pp. 91–99. Springer, Cham (2017). https://doi.org/10.1007/978-3-319-68612-7_11
39. Rosenblum, N., Zhu, X., Miller, B.P.: Who wrote this code? identifying the authors of program binaries. In: Atluri, V., Diaz, C. (eds.) ESORICS 2011. LNCS, vol. 6879, pp. 172–189. Springer, Heidelberg (2011). https://doi.org/10.1007/978-3-642-23822-2_10
40. Taylor, C., Colberg, C.: A tool for teaching reverse engineering. In: 2016 USENIX Workshop on Advances in Security Education (ASE 16). Austin, TX (2016)
41. Ullah, F., Jabbar, S., Al-Turjman, F.: Programmers' de-anonymization using a hybrid approach of abstract syntax tree and deep learning. Technol. Forecast. Social Change **159**, 120186 (2020)
42. Ullah, F., Wang, J., Jabbar, S., Al-Turjman, F., Alazab, M.: Source code authorship attribution using hybrid approach of program dependence graph and deep learning model. IEEE Access **7**, 141987–141999 (2019)
43. Wang, L., He, D.C.: Texture classification using texture spectrum. Pattern Recogn. **23**(8), 905–910 (1990)
44. Zafar, S., Sarwar, M.U., Salem, S., Malik, M.Z.: Language and obfuscation oblivious source code authorship attribution. IEEE Access **8**, 197581–797596 (2020)
45. Zhang, L., Thing, V.L., Cheng, Y.: A scalable and extensible framework for android malware detection and family attribution. Comput. Secur. **80**, 120–133 (2019)

# Multi-relational Instruction Association Graph for Cross-Architecture Binary Similarity Comparison

Qige Song[1,2], Yongzheng Zhang[3], and Shuhao Li[1(✉)]

[1] Institute of Information Engineering, Chinese Academy of Sciences,
Beijing, China
{songqige,lishuhao}@iie.ac.cn
[2] School of Cyber Security, University of Chinese Academy of Sciences,
Beijing, China
[3] China Assets Cybersecurity Technology CO., Ltd., Beijing, China
zhangyz@cacts.cn

**Abstract.** Cross-architecture binary similarity comparison is essential in many security applications. Recently, researchers have proposed learning-based approaches to improve comparison performance. They adopted a paradigm of instruction pre-training, individual binary encoding, and distance-based similarity comparison. However, instruction embeddings pre-trained on external code corpus are not universal in diverse real-world applications. And separately encoding cross-architecture binaries will accumulate the semantic gap of instruction sets, limiting the comparison accuracy. This paper proposes a novel cross-architecture binary similarity comparison approach with multi-relational instruction association graph. We associate mono-architecture instruction tokens with context relevance and cross-architecture tokens with potential semantic correlations from different perspectives. Then we exploit the relational graph convolutional network (R-GCN) to perform type-specific graph information propagation. Our approach can bridge the gap in the cross-architecture instruction representation spaces while avoiding the external pre-training workload. We conduct extensive experiments on basic block-level and function-level datasets to prove the superiority of our approach. Furthermore, evaluations on a large-scale real-world IoT malware reuse function collection show that our approach is valuable for identifying malware propagated on IoT devices of various architectures.

**Keywords:** Cross-architecture binary similarity comparison · IoT malware defense · instruction association graph · Relational graph convolutional network

## 1  Introduction

Cross-architecture binary similarity comparison task aims at measuring the functional semantic similarity of binary snippets compiled from different CPU architectures. It is of great significance in many systems security applications, such

F. Li et al. (Eds.): SecureComm 2022, LNICST 462, pp. 192–211, 2023.
https://doi.org/10.1007/978-3-031-25538-0_11

as vulnerability detection, patch analysis, and malware detection. In this paper, we explore its application in malware defense of the Internet of Things (IoT) environments. IoT devices have been widely used in various real-life scenarios in recent years. However, the security protection of many IoT devices is not yet perfect, leaving hidden dangers such as weak authentication services and security vulnerabilities, which have attracted the attention of malware developers. Many attackers use malware as a weapon to invade vulnerable devices to build large-scale IoT botnets and operate them to launch Distributed Denial of Service (DDoS) attacks, causing severe damage [1,5,16].

Due to the diversity of underlying hardware architectures of IoT devices, malware developers often reuse source code to generate malware binaries of multiple architectures, thereby infecting more devices and expanding the scale of attacks. Cozzi *et al.* [6] conducted empirical analysis on over 93k IoT malware emerged between 2015 and 2018, and results have shown that the samples involve more than a dozen kinds of architectures, with *ARM* and *MIPS* in the majority. They also found the prevalence of code reuse across malware samples of different families and architectures. Wang *et al.* [44] deployed IoT honeypots in real-world network environments and captured a large number of wild IoT malware samples. After code-level analysis, they confirmed that many samples with the same code origin are reused and propagated on IoT devices of different architectures. Therefore, an effective cross-architecture binary code similarity comparison approach can help discover reused IoT malware fragments under different architectures, providing solutions for defending against IoT attacks.

Traditional binary similarity comparison approaches are categorized into two main technical routes, static analysis-based approaches and dynamic analysis-based approaches. The former compares the syntactic or statistical features of disassembly instruction sequences [17,21,34], or design hash algorithms to calculate the similarity of binary fragments [11,37,47]. However, since different architectures have separate instruction sets, the mnemonics, registers, and memory access strategies are different, making it difficult to achieve decent performance. Dynamic-based approaches compare the runtime state information [20] or the input-output pairs of binary code fragments to measure their semantic similarity [7,32]. But it is challenging to perform scalable analysis on large-scale binary collections. Meanwhile, supporting diverse architectures and compilation settings will lead to extra workload for dynamic analysis environment configuration.

Considering the above disadvantages, researchers have recently shifted their focus to learning-based approaches. They generally adopted the following working paradigm: (i) Generate the initial representations of disassembly instructions by manually-designed features or external pre-training mechanism. (ii) Exploit deep neural encoders to individually extract vectorized representations of each binary snippet. (iii) Calculate the similarity score based on the distance metrics. Specifically, `Gemini` [46] extracted statistical vectors of basic blocks within the control-flow-graph of binary function pairs, then encoded the overall graph with the *structure2vec* network and measured their cosine similarity. INNEREYE [50] used *word2vec* to learn the assembly instructions embeddings (numerical vectors) on external code corpus, then deployed RNN encoders to separately generate sequential features of instruction sequences, and evaluated the similarity of cross-architecture binary snippets based on the *Manhattan* distance. SAFE [31] set up similar instruction representation and sequence encoding modules, with additional self-attention layers to automatically assign high weights to important instructions, improving the semantic similarity matching performance. Although showing promising results, these approaches have two main dilemmas:

- First, these approaches individually encode binaries of different architectures and then perform similarity comparisons on their vectorized representations. However, the semantic representation spaces of the cross-architecture instruction sets have a clear gap. The separate binary characteristics encoding mechanism will accumulate this gap, resulting in inaccurate comparison results. This phenomenon will be more pronounced for larger binary snippets.
- Second, although state-of-the-arts have proved that pre-trained instruction representations perform better than statistical features [40,48,50], it relies on high-quality, large-scale external code corpora. Considering real-world binaries are generated under diverse architectures and compilation settings, especially for IoT environments, collecting a comprehensive corpus for instruction pre-training generally takes considerable time and effort.

In this paper, we design a novel cross-architecture binary similarity comparison approach with *multi-relational instruction association graph*, which can effectively alleviate these two deficiencies. For a pair of binary snippets, we first associate mono-architecture opcode and operand token pairs with the operational relationship or co-occurrence-based relevance. Then we associate the cross-architecture token pairs with multi-perspective potential semantic correlations, including prefix-match, value-match, type-match and heuristic position alignment dependencies. The mono-architecture associations can effectively enhance the functional semantic representation of instructions without external instruction pre-training. The cross-architecture associations can effectively bridge the gap in the semantic feature spaces of instructions under different architectures, and significantly improve the cross-architecture binary similarity matching performance. We apply the relational graph convolutional network (R-GCN) to propagate information on the constructed multi-relational instruction association graph. R-GCN groups different types of relations and uses a separate neighbor message-passing mechanism, which can effectively aggregate multi-type associations and iteratively refine the semantic representations of instruction tokens.

Our major contributions can be summarized as follows:

- We creatively design a novel cross-architecture similarity binary comparison approach with multi-relational instruction association graph. It can associate the semantic dependencies of instructions from different perspectives, bridge the gap in the representation spaces of cross-architecture instructions, and significantly improve binary comparison performance.
- We implement our solution as an end-to-end cross-architecture binary similarity comparison system and conduct extensive evaluations at two granularities,

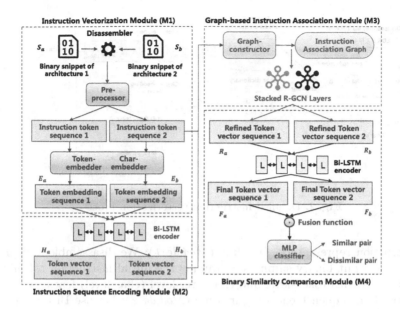

**Fig. 1.** The workflow of our proposed multi-relational instruction association graph-based cross-architecture binary similarity comparison approach. M1 is the abbreviation of *Module 1*.

basic block-level and function-level. Results show that our approach significantly outperforms the existing learning-based approaches (AUC = 0.9924 for basic block-level and Precision@1 = 0.9216 for function-level).
– We further evaluate our approach on a large-scale cross-architecture reuse function dataset (460,386 pairs) constructed from IoT malware in real-world environments. Promising results prove that our method is valuable for defending against malware spread on IoT devices of different architectures.

## 2 Overview

### 2.1 Problem Statement

In this section, we give a formal definition of the cross-architecture binary code similarity comparison problem. The input is a pair of binary code snippets compiled on two different CPU architectures, and the output is a semantic similarity score. We set the output value in the range of 0 to 1, where 1 represents that the input binary snippets are compiled from the exact same source code, and 0 means that their source code implements completely different functions.

### 2.2 System Workflow

Our approach is implemented as an end-to-end cross-architecture binary code similarity comparison system. Figure 1 shows the overall system workflow, including four major modules:

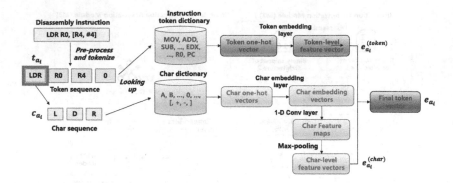

**Fig. 2.** Detailed instruction vectorization process.

- Instruction representation module (*Module 1*): We disassemble and preprocess the input binary snippets, obtaining the initial instruction token representations with token-level and character-level (char-level) features.
- Instruction sequence encoding module (*Module 2*): We use Bi-LSTM as the backbone encoder to extract the sequential representations of disassembly instruction token sequences.
- Graph-based instruction association module (*Module 3*): We construct the corresponding instruction association graph of the input pair of binary snippets, then generate the refined token representations by relational graph convolutional network.
- Binary similarity comparison module (*Module 4*): We fuse the final representation vectors of the binary snippets and generate the similarity comparison score by Multilayer Perceptron (MLP) network.

## 3   Instruction Vectorization Module

The input pair of binary snippets $S_a$ and $S_b$ are originally discrete byte streams, and we first extract their corresponding disassembly instruction sequences. Each instruction contains an opcode and a set of operands. The opcode specifies the operation performed by the instruction, and the operands represents the operation object, like registers and immediate literals. We tokenize raw disassembly instruction sequences and treat each independent opcode or operand as a token unit for vectorization. The input pair can be represented as token sequence $T_a = (t_{a_1}, t_{a_2}, ..., t_{l_a})$, and $T_b = (t_{b_1}, t_{b_2}, ..., t_{l_b})$. $l_a$ and $l_b$ are the length of the sequences. To improve generality, we preprocess the original token sequence, replacing the numerical constants with 0 while preserving the negative signs.

Figure 2 shows the working process of our instruction token vectorization module. We create a token lookup dictionary for the processed opcode and operand units. The initial representation of each token is a sparse one-hot vector based on its index within the dictionary, and then we set a trainable token embedding layer to learn the discrete dense vector $\mathbf{e}_{a_i}^{(token)}$ of token $t_{a_i}$.

We further extract the char-level features to enrich the instruction token representations with lexical information. We extract the corresponding character (char) sequences of the tokens and generate a char lookup dictionary. Then each token can be represented as a sequence of one-hot vectors of the chars. Similar to the token embedding process, we set up an embedding layer to obtain the dense vector of each char. After that, we deploy a one-dimensional-Convolutional (1D-Conv) layer to extract the local-spatial features of the char sequences. It will slide fixed-size 1D-Conv filters over the char vector sequence of the instruction token and generate corresponding feature maps. Then we process the feature maps by a max-pooling layer to generate the final char-level representations. In specific, for token $t_{a_i}$ with char one-hot sequence $(\mathbf{c}_{a_{i1}}, \mathbf{c}_{a_{i2}}, ..., \mathbf{c}_{a_{iM}})$ of length $M$, its char-level vectorized representation is generated as follows:

$$\mathbf{e}_{a_i}^{(char)} = \text{max-pooling}\,(\text{1D-Conv}\,(\mathbf{c}_{a_{i1}}, \mathbf{c}_{a_{i2}}, ..., \mathbf{c}_{a_{iM}})) \tag{1}$$

The final vectorization result $\mathbf{e}_{a_i}$ of the instruction token $t_{a_i}$ is the concatenation of token embedding features and character-level features. Note that our initial instruction vectorization process is implemented entirely through learnable parameters without relying on any external pre-trained instruction embeddings.

$$\mathbf{e}_{a_i} = \text{Concat}\left(\mathbf{e}_{a_i}^{(token)}; \mathbf{e}_{a_i}^{(char)}\right) \tag{2}$$

## 4    Instruction Sequence Encoding Module

From the instruction vectorization module, we obtain the instruction token vector sequences $\mathbf{E}_a = (\mathbf{e}_{a_1}, \mathbf{e}_{a_2}, ..., \mathbf{e}_{l_a})$ and $\mathbf{E}_b = (\mathbf{e}_{b_1}, \mathbf{e}_{b_2}, ..., \mathbf{e}_{l_b})$ of binary snippets $S_a$ and $S_b$. Our next goal is to encode the functional semantics of the overall binary sequences and generate their meaningful representations. The recurrent neural network (RNN) has a strong sequential context modeling ability and has been widely used in text sequence characterization. We apply it into our binary instruction sequence encoding process. To prevent the gradient vanishing and exploding problems that are prone to occur when encoding long sequences, we apply the LSTM variant instead of the vanilla RNN. We deploy the bidirectional LSTM (Bi-LSTM), with two LSTMs separately encoding forward and backward information. The hidden state $\mathbf{h}_{a_i}$ of token $t_{a_i}$ is generated as follows:

$$\overrightarrow{\mathbf{h}_{a_i}} = \overrightarrow{\text{LSTM}}\,(t_{a_1}, t_{a_2}, ..., t_{a_i}), \overleftarrow{\mathbf{h}_{a_i}} = \overleftarrow{\text{LSTM}}\,(t_{l_a}, t_{l_a-1}, ..., t_{a_i}) \tag{3}$$

$$\mathbf{h}_{a_i} = \text{Concat}\left(\overrightarrow{\mathbf{h}_{a_i}}; \overleftarrow{\mathbf{h}_{a_i}}\right) \tag{4}$$

After the encoding layers, the binary snippets are represented as the sequences of token hidden vectors, $\mathbf{H}_a = (\mathbf{h}_{a_1}, \mathbf{h}_{a_2}, ..., \mathbf{h}_{l_a})$, $\mathbf{H}_b = (\mathbf{h}_{b_1}, \mathbf{h}_{b_2}, ..., \mathbf{h}_{l_b})$. We keep all tokens' hidden states without any aggregation or pooling operation. They will be used for subsequent instruction association and instruction representation refinement process.

# 5    Graph-Based Instruction Association Module

## 5.1    Multi-relational Instruction Association Graph

In this section, we give a specific description of our designed instruction association graph schema. Our goal is to model dependencies of instructions from multiple perspectives and refine the quality of instruction token representations. For the instruction token sequence $T_a$ and $T_b$ processed from the input binary snippets, we regard each token as a node and establish the corresponding instruction association graph $\mathcal{G} = (\mathcal{T}, \mathcal{E}, \mathcal{R})$. $\mathcal{T}$ is the node set, $\mathcal{E}$ denotes the edge set, and $\mathcal{R}$ is the type set of the edges. Note that we construct an independent instruction association graph for each binary pair to be compared, so the graph structure will change dynamically for different input pairs.

We design the following six types of edges to represent the semantic relationships between instruction token nodes, including edges of mono-architecture token pairs and edges of cross-architecture token pairs.

### Mono-architecture Association Edges

- **Mono-architecture opcode-operate-operand edge** ($e_0$) : We associate the opcode with each operand within the same disassembly instruction, indicating the operational relationship.
- **Mono-architecture operands co-occurrence edge** ($e_1$) : We associate each operand pair within a disassembly instruction, displaying their co-occurrence-based relevance.

In specific, for the instruction "$MOV \sim R0, R4$", we associate token "$MOV$" with tokens "$R0$" and "$R4$" by edges of type $e_0$, indicating that opcode "$MOV$" operates on registers "$R0$" and "$R4$". Meanwhile, tokens "$R0$" and "$R4$" are associated with the $e_1$ edge, denoting that they co-occurred within the same disassembly instruction. These two types of edges will establish context-based dependencies of the mono-architecture token sequence, improving the semantic representations of opcodes and operands without resorting to external instruction pre-training.

### Cross-Architecture Association Edges

- **Cross-architecture opcodes prefix-match edge** ($e_2$) : We connect two cross-architecture opcodes with the same $n$ prefix characters. Although different architectures have separate instruction sets, some opcodes that perform similar operations have similar char-level lexical characteristics. Such as "$SUB$", "$SUBSD$", "$SUBPD$", "$SUBSS$" of the $x86$ architectures, and "$SUB$", "$SUBS$" of the $ARM$ architecture will perform similar operations, and they all contain the "$SUB$" prefix. This type of edge is meaningful for identifying instruction sequences implementing similar functions.

- **Cross-architecture operands value-match edge** ($e_3$) : We associate two cross-architecture operands with the same value after preprocessed. It will establish dependencies between numeric constants, identical symbols, and identical string literals of different architectures, assisting the semantic comparison process of disassembled code fragments.
- **Cross-architecture operands type-match edge** ($e_4$) : For a similar purpose to $e_3$, we associate cross-architecture operands with the same fine-grained category. We consider three fine-grained operand types: registers, immediate literals, and memory address pointers.
- **Cross-architecture heuristic position alignment edge** ($e_5$) : We define heuristic rules to establish positional associations between the token pairs of cross-architecture instruction sequences. Specifically, tokens $t_{a_i}$ and $t_{b_j}$ of sequences $T_a$ and $T_b$ will be associated if they meet the following conditions:

$$\left| \frac{a_i \times l_a}{l_b} - b_j \right| < \iota \tag{5}$$

$a_i$ and $b_j$ are the position indices of the tokens in the respective sequences. $l_a$ and $l_b$ are the lengths of the sequences. $\iota$ is a pre-defined threshold.

The $e_5$ edge is inspired by Redmon *et al.* [40]. We set the edge weights of the instruction association graph as their statistical frequencies, $e_0$ is unidirectional, and $e_1$ to $e_5$ are undirected edges. The same endpoint token nodes may be associated with multiple different types of edges, and our strategy of utilizing multi-type of dependencies will be illustrated in the next subsection.

## 5.2    Relational Graph Convolutional Network

After building the instruction association graph, we expect to refine the semantic representation of instruction tokens with the multi-relational graph schema. Graph neural network (GNN) [42] has strong graph structures representation abilities, and it has achieved promising performance in diverse tasks such as node classification and link prediction. The classic GNN is a message-passing framework with two core operations, neighbor node information aggregation and node representation update. It iteratively aggregates neighbor node information and updates the vectorized representations of nodes with local subgraph features.

Specifically, for a token node $t_v$ of set $\mathcal{T}$ with the corresponding neighbor set $\mathcal{N}(t_v)$, the neighbor node information aggregation and node representation update process of a GNN layer are performed as:

$$\mathbf{h}_{t_v} = \mathcal{F}\left(\mathbf{x}_{t_v}, AGG\left(\{\mathbf{h}_{t_u} : t_u \in \mathcal{N}(t_v)\}\right)\right) \tag{6}$$

$\mathbf{x}_{t_v}$ is the initial representation of $t_v$, and $\mathbf{h}_{t_v}$ denotes the updated representation calculated by the aggregated neighbor node features and the fusion function $\mathcal{F}$.

Our instruction association graph connects instruction token pairs with semantically distinct edges. To better exploit the multi-type dependencies, we choose the relational graph convolutional network (R-GCN) [43], a GNN variant that can efficiently handle multi-relational graph data. R-GCN extends the

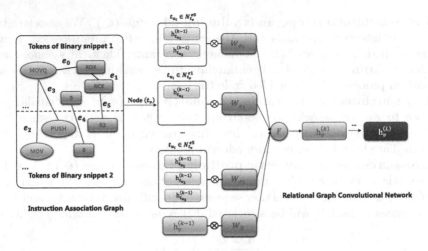

**Fig. 3.** Refine instruction representation with instruction association graph and R-GCN layers.

classic GNN framework with type-specific parameters to model the relations of different types separately. For token node $t_v$, the $l^{th}$ R-GCN layer maps its neighbor node-set $\mathcal{N}_{(t_v)}^{e_r}$ associated with edge type $e_r$ to a unified vector space through relation-specific transformation matrix $W_{e_r}^l$, and aggregates the transformed vectors in the normalized summation way. The node's characteristics of the previous layer $\mathbf{h}_{t_v}^l$ is preserved by a separate feature transformation matrix $W_0^l$. The overall $l^{th}$ layer node representation refinement process is as follows:

$$\mathbf{h}_{t_v}^{l+1} = \sigma \left( \sum_{e_r \in \mathcal{R}} \sum_{t_u \in \mathcal{N}_{t_v}^{e_r}} \frac{1}{|\mathcal{N}_{t_v}^{e_r}|} W_{e_r}^l \mathbf{h}_{t_u}^l + W_0^l \mathbf{h}_{t_v}^l \right) \tag{7}$$

A Single R-GCN layer can only aggregate first-order neighbor information. We stack multiple R-GCN layers to propagate multi-hop neighbor messages, learning the substructure of different scales within the instruction association graph. For token $t_{a_i}$, its corresponding input node attributes of the first R-GCN layer are the hidden states $\mathbf{h}_{a_i}$ generated by the previous token vectorization layers and the Bi-LSTM encoder, which contains the tokens' lexical semantics and the sequential information of the mono-architecture binary sequence. The final R-GCN layer will output its refined representation $\mathbf{r}_{a_i}$, and $B_a$ and $B_b$ will be represented as $\mathbf{R}_a = (\mathbf{r}_{a_1}, \mathbf{r}_{a_2}, ..., \mathbf{r}_{l_a})$ and $\mathbf{R}_b = (\mathbf{r}_{b_1}, \mathbf{r}_{b_2}, ..., \mathbf{r}_{l_b})$.

Figure 3 is the technical explanation of the overall graph-based instruction association module. The left side is an instruction association graph schema corresponding to an input pair of disassembly instruction sequences. We reserve one example edge for each type. On the right is the node representation refinement process performed by R-GCN layers.

# 6 Binary Similarity Comparison Module

The graph-based instruction association module will generate refined instruction token representation sequences $\mathbf{R}_a$ and $\mathbf{R}_b$. We send the sequences to another Bi-LSTM layer to strengthen the sequential context information, and then employ a max-pooling layer to generate the final binary snippet representations $\mathbf{F}_a$, $\mathbf{F}_b$. The process can be simplified as follows:

$$\mathbf{F}_a = \text{max-pooling}\,(\text{Bi-LSTM}\,(\mathbf{r}_{a_1}, \mathbf{r}_{a_2}, ..., \mathbf{r}_{l_a})) \tag{8}$$

We set up a fusion function to aggregate the final vector $\mathbf{F}_a$ and $\mathbf{F}_b$, and then feed the result into a one-layer MLP classifier with the *softmax* function to predict the similarity score of $S_a$ and $S_b$. The fusion function is based on [4], including the concatenation, element-wise difference, and element-wise product of $\mathbf{F}_a$ and $\mathbf{F}_b$, as follows:

$$\mathbf{F}_{(a,b)} = \text{Concat}\,(\mathbf{F}_a; \mathbf{F}_b; \mathbf{F}_a - \mathbf{F}_b; \mathbf{F}_a \odot \mathbf{F}_b) \tag{9}$$

This fusion way ensures that the MLP classifier can identify the boundary of the two representation vectors, and calculate the similarity between $F_a$ and $F_b$ more accurately. The overall neural model is optimized by minimizing the cross-entropy loss between the predicted scores and the ground truth pair labels.

# 7 Evaluation

## 7.1 Preliminary

**Dataset.** We evaluate our approach on three datasets with two granularities:

(i) **Dataset1** is a collection of basic block pairs provided by INNEREYE [49] with annotated ground truth, compiled from coreutils-8.29, findutils-4.6.0, diffutils-3.6, binutils-2.30, and OpenSSL-1.1.1-pre1 packages by the clang-6.0.0 compiler and O2 optimization, into *x86* and *ARM* architectures.

(ii) We build the function-level **Dataset2** from the same packages of Dataset1 by two compilers, clang-6.0.0 and GCC-5.4.0, also with O2 optimization.

(iii) We construct **Dataset3** with seven families of IoT malware samples captured by honeypots deployed in real-world network environments. We select samples spread on *ARM* and *MIPS* architectures, which are widely used in IoT devices, and build a large-scale cross-architecture malware reuse function matching dataset.

We annotate the ground truth of Dataset2 and Dataset3 with binary name and function name as the unique ID to identify functions compiled from the same source code. When building Dataset3, we filtered out functions of stripped binaries whose names could not be correctly identified by the disassembler. Table 1 shows the information of our datasets. The last two columns represent the average number of edges of the instruction-association graphs, and the average number of disassembly instructions contained in each binary snippet.

**Table 1.** Statistical information of evaluation datasets

| Dataset | Architectures | Granularity | # Pairs | Average # Edges | Average # Instructions |
|---------|---------------|-------------|---------|-----------------|------------------------|
| Dataset1 | x86-ARM | Basic-Block | 11,2019 | 239.50 | 7.09 |
| Dataset2 | x86-ARM | Function | 74,841 | 1142.31 | 28.38 |
| Dataset3 | ARM-MIPS | Function | 460,386 | 737.21 | 33.49 |

**Evaluation Metrics.** We consider two groups of metrics in evaluation:

(i) For basic block-level evaluation, we follow the prior art [40,50] and use AUC-ROC (Area under ROC curve) as the evaluation metric.
(ii) For function-level evaluation, we set up the function search task as the prior art [28,31,48]. It will compare a query binary function with multiple candidate functions and rank the corresponding similarity scores. In our experiments, we set one positive candidate similar to the query function, together with $N_{neg}$ dissimilar candidates. We adopt two commonly used evaluation metrics, precision@1 and MRR (Mean Reciprocal Rank). For each query function, the precision@1 value indicates whether the score of the positive candidate function is ranked first, and the MRR value is calculated as the reciprocal of the positive candidate's ranking position.

**Implementation Details.** We implement the proposed method with the *PyTorch* framework, *PyTorch Geometric* library [14], and *radare2* disassembler [38]. The parameters are optimized by Adam with a learning rate of 1e-3. The dimension of the instruction token embedding layer is set to 128, and the char embedding dimension is 32. The size of char 1-D convolutional filters is 2, and the number is 64. We set up one Bi-LSTM layer and two R-GCN layers with the hidden dimension of 256. The $n$ value of the *Cross-architecture opcode prefix-match edge* ($e_2$) is set to 3, and the $\iota$ threshold of the *Cross-architecture heuristic position alignment edge* ($e_5$) in the Eq. 5 is set to 2. Under this setting, our system can achieve the best results on the development sets. For Dataset2 and Dataset3, the number of negative candidates $N_{neg}$ for each query function is 20.

### 7.2  Basic Block-Level Experiments

**Comparisons with the Prior Art.** In this section, we evaluate our approach at the basic block-level dataset and compare it with two manually designed baselines and three state-of-the-art cross-architecture binary similarity comparison approaches. The implementations of the comparison methods are as follows:

– String edit distance: We use `python-Levenshtein` [25] to compute edit-distance-based similarity scores of the cross-architecture basic block pairs.
– Char n-gram: We extract the char n-gram sets of the assembly instruction sequences and calculate their Jaccard similarity score. 4-gram performs best in our evaluation.

- **Gemini** [46] features + SVM: Xu *et al.* extracted the statistical features to represent a basic block, such as the number of instructions, calls, and numeric constant. Following Zuo *et al.* [50], we concatenate the features of two blocks and use SVM with RBF kernel to predict their similarity.
- INNEREYE [50]: Zuo *et al.* used *word2vec* to pre-train assembly instruction embeddings on external code corpus. Then encode the cross-architecture instruction sequences by two individual LSTM networks and generate the similarity score based on the distance metric.
- Redmon *et al.* [40] proposed an instruction pre-training method based on joint objectives. They establish position-based alignments of cross-architecture instruction pairs, and set the mono-architecture and cross-architecture objectives to training instruction embeddings.

**Table 2.** Basic block-level cross-architecture binary similarity comparison results on Dataset1.

| Approaches | ROC-AUC |
|---|---|
| String edit distance | 0.8087 |
| Char n-gram | 0.7746 |
| Gemini features + SVM [46] | 0.8647 |
| INNEREYE [50] | 0.9764 |
| Redmond *et al.* [40] | 0.9069 |
| (- Mono-arch edges) | 0.9917 |
| (- Cross-archs edges) | 0.9885 |
| (- Type-specific aggregation) | 0.9825 |
| **Our approach** | **0.9924** |

We use the instruction embedding files of INNEREYE [49] and Redmond et al. [39] to make fair comparison. The AUC-ROC on Dataset1 are shown in the upper part of Table 2. From the results, we can mainly draw the following conclusions:

- The performance of edit distance, char n-gram, and **Gemini** + SVM is not ideal, which shows the syntax or statistical-features based comparison can not handle the significant differences of cross-architecture instruction sets.
- INNEREYE and our approach outperform other methods by large margins, which proves that exploiting deep neural networks to automatically extract the features of disassembly instruction sequences is a very effective solution.
- Our approach can achieve the best performance. The improvement is mainly because our graph-based instruction association module can effectively bridge the gap in the representation spaces of cross-architecture instructions. Furthermore, we do not rely on external pre-training to generate initial instruction embeddings, avoiding the additional workload and time consumption.

**Ablation Studies.** We design three ablation variants of our approach to evaluate the core components of our graph-based instruction association module: (i) Remove the mono-architecture association edges ($e_0$ and $e_1$). (ii) Remove the cross-architecture association edges ($e_2 \sim e_5$). (iii) Remove the type-specific neighbor message aggregation mechanism of R-GCN layers and use the classic graph convolutional network [22]. The lower part of Table 2 presents the results of the ablation experiments. It proves that the mono-architecture and cross-architecture associations all contribute to performance improvement. And separately aggregating neighbor messages from different types of dependencies can more effectively refine the instruction representation and improve the cross-architecture similarity comparison performance.

### 7.3   Function-Level Experiments

In this section, we evaluate our approach at the function-level Dataset2 and compare it with two existing approachs. We set up the binary function search task on Dataset2. The first work we make comparison with is INNEREYE, which performs best in the basic block-level experiments. The second is another function-level binary similarity comparison approach, SAFE [31]. It also used *word2vec* to implement instruction pre-training, and deployed the Bi-GRU network to encode disassembly instruction sequences. Then it added the self-attention mechanism to generate instruction representation weights. Instructions that are more important for binary semantic comparison results will be assigned higher weights.

Since the pre-trained instruction vocabulary provided by INNEREYE are pretrained on the code corpus compiled by clang, while Dataset2 also involves the GCC compiler, 42.12% of the instructions are out-of-vocabulary ($OOV$). Meanwhile, the instruction embeddings provided by SAFE are also generated by the external corpus inconsistent with the compilation environment of Dataset2. Therefore, we use the trainable instruction embedding and concatenate the char-level features similar to our approach for their instruction vectorization. This phenomenon also illustrates the limitations of the external instruction pre-training approach. Since it is difficult to accurately predict the binary compilation settings in practical applications, serious instruction $OOV$ issue is prone to occur.

**Table 3.** Function-level cross-architecture binary similarity comparison results on Dataset2.

| Approach | Precision@1 | MRR |
|---|---|---|
| INNEREYE (42.12% $OOV$) | 0.5014 | 0.6619 |
| INNEREYE + Char-features | 0.6386 | 0.7665 |
| SAFE + Char-features | 0.7097 | 0.7828 |
| **Our approach** | **0.9216** | **0.9550** |

Table 3 shows the comparison results on Dataset2. From the table, we can see that our approach has significant performance advantages, with at least 21.19 points improvement of the precision@1 value and 17.22 points improvement of the MRR value than the variants of INNEREYE and SAFE. Compared with the results of basic block-level experiments, our function-level improvement is more prominent. On the one hand, the reason is that the instruction sequences of function-level binary snippets are longer and implement more complex semantic functional modules, which increases the difficulty of cross-architecture binary semantic comparison. As shown in Table 1, our instruction association graph will establish more multi-type edges on Dataset2, and the effect of bridging the semantic representation space of binary snippets of different architectures is more significant. On the other hand, the function search task needs to compare the query function with multiple candidates and rank the similarity scores, which is more challenging than the pairwise comparison conducted at basic block-level.

### 7.4  Real-World IoT Malware Reuse Function Matching Experiments

In this section, we use Dataset3 to evaluate the scalability and practicability of our method in real-world applications. Dataset3 is constructed from malware captured in the public network by IoT honeypots. We use *radare2* to process unstripped malware samples of *ARM* and *MIPS* architectures and construct a large-scale dataset containing over 460k cross-architecture function pairs, characterizing malicious behaviors from a more refined perspective. We also make comparisons with INNEREYE and SAFE. Since their pre-trained instruction embeddings did not support *MIPS* architecture, we still compare with their variants using trainable embeddings and char-level features for instruction vectorization.

**Table 4.** Cross-architecture binary similarity comparison results on Dataset3.

| Approach | Precision@1 | MRR | Offline training-time (seconds/epoch) | Online prediction-time (milliseconds/pair) |
|---|---|---|---|---|
| INNEREYE + Char-features | 0.7780 | 0.8366 | 101 | 1.58 |
| SAFE + Char-features | 0.7840 | 0.8386 | 318 | 1.84 |
| **Our approach** | **0.9375** | **0.9597** | 823 | 3.72 |

Table 4 shows the performance of the three approaches on Dataset3, along with their offline training time (seconds per epoch) and online prediction time (milliseconds per function pair). The results show that our method significantly outperforms the variants of INNEREYE and SAFE, with precision@1 and MRR values improving at least 16.97 and 12.11 points, respectively. Due to the instruction association graph construction and the R-GCN-based multi-type dependencies aggregation on the graph, the training time and prediction time of our method are increased. However, the online prediction speed is still acceptable as inferencing the similarity score of a binary function pair can be completed in 3.72 ms. Meanwhile, we do not need additional time collecting external code corpus consistent with the specific application's compilation settings and pre-training disassembly instruction embeddings. In conclusion, our method can be effectively applied to large-scale real-world cross-architecture binary similarity comparison collection and provides a valuable solution for defending against malware reused and propagated on IoT devices of different architectures.

## 8   Related Work

### 8.1   Traditional Binary Similarity Comparison Approaches

Traditional binary similarity comparison approaches are mainly divided into two categories, static analysis techniques comparing syntax or structural features [2,19,21,24,29,36,37,41] and dynamic analysis techniques comparing behavioral semantics [20,27,32,33,45]. For static analysis-based methods, Rendezvous [21] extracted the instruction n-perms, control flow sub-graphs, and constants of binary code to construct a code search engine. Qiao et al. [37] used the *simhash* algorithm to generate basic block signatures, then exploited inverted index to achieve fast reuse function detection. CoP [29] first checked block-level semantic equivalence with theorem prover, and then performed the breadth-first search on the inter-procedural control-flow-graph (I-CFG) to compute path-level binary semantic similarity. These approaches are designed for mono-architecture binary comparison without handling the differences in instruction sets of different architectures. For dynamic analysis-based methods, Ulf et al. [20] recorded the execution traces and output values of a binary pair when given same input, and used matching features to identify programs with similar semantics but different syntax characteristics. BinSim [32] performed enhanced dynamic slicing and extracted the symbolic formulas of the code fragments to check the semantic equivalence. Dynamic analysis will meet challenges when analyzing large binary collections, and it requires additional efforts to configure execution environments supporting diverse architectures and compilation settings.

To support cross-architecture comparison, some existing work converted the instructions of different architectures into the intermediate representation (IR) [3,12,18,35]. Specifically, Multi-MH [35] first converted binary code into platform-independent VEX-IR, then used the input-output pairs of basic blocks to construct their semantic signatures. XMATCH [12] conducted static analysis on IR and extracted conditional formulas as semantic features, improving the binary vulnerability search accuracy. These methods may be limited by the adaptability and precision of IR extraction tools. Esh [7] decomposed binary procedures into small fragments, named strands, then checked the semantically equivalence of strand pairs and used statistical reasoning for procedure-level similarity comparison, but it also suffers the unscalable issue on the large-scale collections.

## 8.2   Learning-Based Binary Similarity Comparison Approaches

Recently, deep learning technology has achieved promising improvements in intelligent program analysis. To improve the effectiveness and efficiency of the binary similarity comparison task, researchers pay attention to learning-based approaches [8–10,13,15,23,26,28,30,31,46,48,50]. $\alpha$-diff exploited the siamese-CNN network to achieve cross-version binary code similarity detection. They adopted in-batch random negative sampling and contrastive loss to optimize the model. Asm2Vec [8] used the PV-DM model to implement binary function vectorization, achieving accurate binary clone detection against changes introduced by code obfuscation and optimization techniques.

For cross-architecture binary similarity comparison, Gemini [46] extracted the attribute control flow graph (ACFG) of the binary functions. Then it used the *structure2vec* network and cosine similarity to implement bug search for IoT firmware images. VulSeeker [15] extends ACFG into labelled semantic flow graph (LSFG) by adding additional data flow edges. INNEREYE [50] leveraged *wordvec* to pre-train instruction embeddings on external code corpus, then implemented binary comparison by LSTM encoders and Manhattan distance. SAFE [31] added the self-attention mechanism to calculate the importance weights of the instructions within the disassembled code sequence, improving the cross-architecture binary similarity matching accuracy. The common dilemma of existing learning-based approaches is that the cross-architecture binary snippets are encoded separately by neural layers and then compared based on the similarity metrics. The significant difference between cross-architecture instruction sets will lead to a considerable gap in their semantical representation spaces, which limits the comparison performance. Our method utilizes the multi-relational instruction association graph and R-GCN layers to close the gap in the semantic spaces of cross-architecture instructions, effectively alleviating the deficiency.

## 9   Conclusion

In this paper, we propose a novel cross-architecture binary similarity comparison approach. We design an instruction association graph schema to bridge the gap in the semantic spaces of instruction sets from different architectures. It consists of six types of dependencies, which respectively define the context relevance of mono-architecture instruction tokens and multi-perspective semantic associations of cross-architecture tokens. We leverage the R-GCN network to propagate the multi-type dependencies within the graph and improve the cross-architecture binary matching performance. We conduct extensive experiments on datasets of different granularities. Results show that it outperforms existing learning-based approaches on basic block-level and function-level comparisons. Furthermore, our approach can achieve effective cross-architecture reuse function detection on a large-scale IoT malware dataset collected from the real-world network environment, which is meaningful for identifying malware spread on IoT devices of various architectures and defending against IoT attacks.

# References

1. Antonakakis, M., et al.: Understanding the mirai botnet. In: 26th USENIX Security Symposium (USENIX Security 17), pp. 1093–1110 (2017)
2. Cesare, S., Xiang, Y., Zhou, W.: Control flow-based malware variantdetection. IEEE Trans. Dependable Secure Comput. **11**(4), 307–317 (2013)
3. Chandramohan, M., Xue, Y., Xu, Z., Liu, Y., Cho, C.Y., Tan, H.B.K.: BinGo: cross-architecture cross-OS binary search. In: Proceedings of the 2016 24th ACM SIGSOFT International Symposium on Foundations of Software Engineering, pp. 678–689 (2016)
4. Conneau, A., Kiela, D., Schwenk, H., Barrault, L., Bordes, A.: Supervised learning of universal sentence representations from natural language inference data. In: Proceedings of the 2017 Conference on Empirical Methods in Natural Language Processing, EMNLP 2017, Copenhagen, Denmark, 9–11 September 2017 (2017)
5. Costin, A., Zaddach, J.: IoT malware: comprehensive survey, analysis framework and case studies. BlackHat USA **1**(1), 1–9 (2018)
6. Cozzi, E., Vervier, P.A., Dell'Amico, M., Shen, Y., Bilge, L., Balzarotti, D.: The tangled genealogy of IoT malware. In: Annual Computer Security Applications Conference, pp. 1–16 (2020)
7. David, Y., Partush, N., Yahav, E.: Statistical similarity of binaries. ACM SIGPLAN Not. **51**(6), 266–280 (2016)
8. Ding, S.H., Fung, B.C., Charland, P.: Asm2Vec: boosting static representation robustness for binary clone search against code obfuscation and compiler optimization. In: 2019 IEEE Symposium on Security and Privacy (SP), pp. 472–489. IEEE (2019)
9. Duan, Y., Li, X., Wang, J., Yin, H.: DeepBinDiff: learning program-wide code representations for binary diffing. In: Proceedings of the 27th Annual Network and Distributed System Security Symposium (NDSS 2020) (2020)
10. Eschweiler, S., Yakdan, K., Gerhards-Padilla, E.: discovRE: efficient cross-architecture identification of bugs in binary code. In: NDSS (2016)
11. Farhadi, M.R., Fung, B.C., Charland, P., Debbabi, M.: BinClone: detecting code clones in malware. In: 2014 Eighth International Conference on Software Security and Reliability (SERE), pp. 78–87. IEEE (2014)
12. Feng, Q., Wang, M., Zhang, M., Zhou, R., Henderson, A., Yin, H.: Extracting conditional formulas for cross-platform bug search. In: Proceedings of the 2017 ACM on Asia Conference on Computer and Communications Security, pp. 346–359 (2017)
13. Feng, Q., Zhou, R., Xu, C., Cheng, Y., Testa, B., Yin, H.: Scalable graph-based bug search for firmware images. In: Proceedings of the 2016 ACM SIGSAC Conference on Computer and Communications Security, pp. 480–491 (2016)
14. Fey, M., Lenssen, J.E.: Fast graph representation learning with PyTorch Geometric. In: ICLR Workshop on Representation Learning on Graphs and Manifolds (2019)
15. Gao, J., Yang, X., Fu, Y., Jiang, Y., Sun, J.: VulSeeker: a semantic learning based vulnerability seeker for cross-platform binary. In: 2018 33rd IEEE/ACM International Conference on Automated Software Engineering (ASE), pp. 896–899. IEEE (2018)
16. Herwig, S., Harvey, K., Hughey, G., Roberts, R., Levin, D.: Measurement and analysis of Hajime, a peer-to-peer IoT botnet. In: Network and Distributed Systems Security (NDSS) Symposium (2019)

17. Hu, X., Shin, K.G., Bhatkar, S., Griffin, K.: MutantX-S: scalable malware clustering based on static features. In: 2013 USENIX Annual Technical Conference (USENIX ATC 2013), pp. 187–198 (2013)
18. Hu, Y., Zhang, Y., Li, J., Gu, D.: Cross-architecture binary semantics understanding via similar code comparison. In: 2016 IEEE 23rd International Conference on Software Analysis, Evolution, and Reengineering (SANER), vol. 1, pp. 57–67. IEEE (2016)
19. Huang, H., Youssef, A.M., Debbabi, M.: BinSequence: fast, accurate and scalable binary code reuse detection. In: Proceedings of the 2017 ACM on Asia Conference on Computer and Communications Security, pp. 155–166 (2017)
20. Kargén, U., Shahmehri, N.: Towards robust instruction-level trace alignment of binary code. In: 2017 32nd IEEE/ACM International Conference on Automated Software Engineering (ASE), pp. 342–352. IEEE (2017)
21. Khoo, W.M., Mycroft, A., Anderson, R.: Rendezvous: a search engine for binary code. In: 2013 10th Working Conference on Mining Software Repositories (MSR), pp. 329–338. IEEE (2013)
22. Kipf, T.N., Welling, M.: Semi-supervised classification with graph convolutional networks (2016)
23. Lageman, N., Kilmer, E.D., Walls, R.J., McDaniel, P.D.: BINDNN: resilient function matching using deep learning. In: Deng, R., Weng, J., Ren, K., Yegneswaran, V. (eds.) SecureComm 2016. LNICST, vol. 198, pp. 517–537. Springer, Cham (2017). https://doi.org/10.1007/978-3-319-59608-2_29
24. Lee, Y.R., Kang, B., Im, E.G.: Function matching-based binary-level software similarity calculation. In: Research in Adaptive and Convergent Systems, RACS 2013, Montreal, QC, Canada, 1–4 October 2013, pp. 322–327. ACM (2013)
25. python Levenshtein. https://pypi.org/project/python-Levenshtein/
26. Liang, H., Xie, Z., Chen, Y., Ning, H., Wang, J.: FIT: inspect vulnerabilities in cross-architecture firmware by deep learning and bipartite matching. Comput. Secur. **99**, 102032 (2020)
27. Lindorfer, M., Di Federico, A., Maggi, F., Comparetti, P.M., Zanero, S.: Lines of malicious code: Insights into the malicious software industry. In: Proceedings of the 28th Annual Computer Security Applications Conference, pp. 349–358 (2012)
28. Liu, B., et al.: αdiff: cross-version binary code similarity detection with DNN. In: Proceedings of the 33rd ACM/IEEE International Conference on Automated Software Engineering, pp. 667–678 (2018)
29. Luo, L., Ming, J., Wu, D., Liu, P., Zhu, S.: Semantics-based obfuscation-resilient binary code similarity comparison with applications to software plagiarism detection. In: Proceedings of the 22nd ACM SIGSOFT International Symposium on Foundations of Software Engineering, pp. 389–400 (2014)
30. Massarelli, L., Di Luna, G.A., Petroni, F., Querzoni, L., Baldoni, R.: Investigating graph embedding neural networks with unsupervised features extraction for binary analysis. In: Proceedings of the 2nd Workshop on Binary Analysis Research (BAR) (2019)
31. Massarelli, L., Di Luna, G.A., Petroni, F., Baldoni, R., Querzoni, L.: SAFE: self-attentive function embeddings for binary similarity. In: Perdisci, R., Maurice, C., Giacinto, G., Almgren, M. (eds.) DIMVA 2019. LNCS, vol. 11543, pp. 309–329. Springer, Cham (2019). https://doi.org/10.1007/978-3-030-22038-9_15
32. Ming, J., Xu, D., Jiang, Y., Wu, D.: BinSim: trace-based semantic binary diffing via system call sliced segment equivalence checking. In: 26th USENIX Security Symposium (USENIX Security 2017), pp. 253–270 (2017)

33. Ming, J., Xu, D., Wu, D.: Memoized semantics-based binary diffing with application to malware lineage inference. In: Federrath, H., Gollmann, D. (eds.) SEC 2015. IAICT, vol. 455, pp. 416–430. Springer, Cham (2015). https://doi.org/10.1007/978-3-319-18467-8_28

34. Ng, B.H., Prakash, A.: Expose: discovering potential binary code re-use. In: 2013 IEEE 37th Annual Computer Software and Applications Conference, pp. 492–501. IEEE (2013)

35. Pewny, J., Garmany, B., Gawlik, R., Rossow, C., Holz, T.: Cross-architecture bug search in binary executables. In: 2015 IEEE Symposium on Security and Privacy, pp. 709–724. IEEE (2015)

36. Pewny, J., Schuster, F., Bernhard, L., Holz, T., Rossow, C.: Leveraging semantic signatures for bug search in binary programs. In: Proceedings of the 30th Annual Computer Security Applications Conference, pp. 406–415 (2014)

37. Qiao, Y., Yun, X., Zhang, Y.: Fast reused function retrieval method based on simhash and inverted index. In: 2016 IEEE Trustcom/BigDataSE/ISPA, pp. 937–944. IEEE (2016)

38. radare2. https://www.radare.org/n/radare2.html

39. Redmond, K., Luo, L., Zeng, Q.: https://github.com/nlp-code-analysis/cross-arch-instr-model/

40. Redmond, K., Luo, L., Zeng, Q.: A cross-architecture instruction embedding model for natural language processing-inspired binary code analysis. arXiv preprint arXiv:1812.09652 (2018)

41. Ruttenberg, B., et al.: Identifying shared software components to support malware forensics. In: Dietrich, S. (ed.) DIMVA 2014. LNCS, vol. 8550, pp. 21–40. Springer, Cham (2014). https://doi.org/10.1007/978-3-319-08509-8_2

42. Scarselli, F., Gori, M., Tsoi, A.C., Hagenbuchner, M., Monfardini, G.: The graph neural network model. IEEE Trans. Neural Networks **20**(1), 61–80 (2008)

43. Schlichtkrull, M., Kipf, T.N., Bloem, P., van den Berg, R., Titov, I., Welling, M.: Modeling relational data with graph convolutional networks. In: Gangemi, A., et al. (eds.) ESWC 2018. LNCS, vol. 10843, pp. 593–607. Springer, Cham (2018). https://doi.org/10.1007/978-3-319-93417-4_38

44. Wang, B., Dou, Y., Sang, Y., Zhang, Y., Huang, J.: IoTCMal: towards a hybrid IoT honeypot for capturing and analyzing malware. In: ICC 2020–2020 IEEE International Conference on Communications (ICC), pp. 1–7. IEEE (2020)

45. Wang, S., Wu, D.: In-memory fuzzing for binary code similarity analysis. In: 2017 32nd IEEE/ACM International Conference on Automated Software Engineering (ASE), pp. 319–330. IEEE (2017)

46. Xu, X., Liu, C., Feng, Q., Yin, H., Song, L., Song, D.: Neural network-based graph embedding for cross-platform binary code similarity detection. In: Proceedings of the 2017 ACM SIGSAC Conference on Computer and Communications Security, pp. 363–376 (2017)

47. Xu, Z., Chen, B., Chandramohan, M., Liu, Y., Song, F.: Spain: security patch analysis for binaries towards understanding the pain and pills. In: 2017 IEEE/ACM 39th International Conference on Software Engineering (ICSE), pp. 462–472. IEEE (2017)

48. Yu, Z., Cao, R., Tang, Q., Nie, S., Huang, J., Wu, S.: Order matters: semantic-aware neural networks for binary code similarity detection. In: Proceedings of the AAAI Conference on Artificial Intelligence, vol. 34, pp. 1145–1152 (2020)
49. Zuo, F., Li, X., Young, P., Luo, L., Zeng, Q., Zhang, Z.: https://nmt4binaries.github.io/
50. Zuo, F., Li, X., Young, P., Luo, L., Zeng, Q., Zhang, Z.: Neural machine translation inspired binary code similarity comparison beyond function pairs. In: 26th Annual Network and Distributed System Security Symposium, NDSS 2019, San Diego, California, USA, 24–27 February 2019 (2018)

# Cost-Effective Malware Classification Based on Deep Active Learning

Qian Qiang[1,2,3](✉), Yige Chen[1,2], Yang Hu[4], Tianning Zang[1,2], Mian Cheng[3], Quanbo Pan[1,2], Yu Ding[1,2], and Zisen Qi[1,2]

[1] Institute of Information Engineering, Chinese Academy of Sciences, Beijing, China
{qiangqian,chenyige,zangtianning,panquanbo,dingyu,qizisen}@iie.ac.cn
[2] School of Cyber Security, University of Chinese Academy of Sciences, Beijing, China
[3] China National Computer Network Emergency Response Technical Team/Coordination Center, Beijing, China
chengmian@cert.org.cn
[4] Haier (Beijing) IC Design Co., Ltd., Beijing, China
huy@haier-ic.com

**Abstract.** Malware has now grown up to be one of the most important threats to internet security. As the number of malware families has increased rapidly, a malware classification model needs to classify the samples for further analysis. Recent success in deep learning-based malware classification, however heavily relies on the large number of labeled training samples, which may require considerable human effort. In this paper, we propose a novel malware classification framework for the cost issue, which is capable of building a competitive classifier via a limited amount of labeled training instances in an incremental learning manner. A cost-effective sample selection strategy is leveraged to focus expert efforts on labeling samples that are most informative for the classifier. We first convert the malware byte sequences into fixed-size gray-scale images through data visualization. Afterward, based on the strategy designed and oriented towards informative malware acquisition, we select samples through Convolutional Neural Network (ConvNet) to query experts for annotation according to the estimated gradients towards the last linear layer. The updated labeled dataset is then fed into the network for further fine-tuning progressively. To evaluate the capability of our method for acquiring informative malware from a pool of unknown samples, we conduct a series of experiments on a benchmark dataset named BIG 2015. Compared to random selection and other existing high-performance strategies, the proposed system can achieve a promising performance rise cost-effectively with less labeling effort wasted. The effectiveness of sample selection towards different families is also analyzed and further proves the efficiency of labeling cost. Moreover, the initialization methods and the pre-defined number of samples queried are studied for practical implementation.

Supported by National Key Research and Development Project (2020YFB1820102).

**Keywords:** Deep active learning · Malware classification ·
Cost-effective

# 1 Introduction

Currently, the volume of global threats against business endpoints has increased by more than 10% year-over-year. This emphasizes the importance of developing efficient approaches to analyze as well as classify malicious samples. Malware classification as a fundamental task has been a huge burden for analysts due to its fast-emerging speed, and deep learning (DL) methods have shown impressive performance on related tasks [1]. However, labeling samples, which is crucial for DL, is often a cost-sensitive task since it involves human experts. How to select the most informative samples that can improve the predictive capability of classifiers is an essential question that DL-based methods should focus on. A promising solution is active-learning, noted as AL, a learning protocol where samples can be selected for experts' annotation in a sequential, feedback-driven fashion. The selected samples sent to experts for labeling are defined as query samples by the algorithm. It has a great practical significance to develop a framework combining DL and AL, which can jointly learn features and classifiers from informative samples effectively.

In particular, we propose an AL-based malware classification framework using a ConvNet called cost-effective malware classification (CEMC). Different from the existing malware-related works that utilize machine learning methods, our CEMC leverages AL based on ConvNet. The contributions of our paper can be summarized below:

- We develop a cost-effective malware classification framework based on ConvNet with an AL strategy integrated, which is capable of informative sample selection according to the estimated gradients towards the last linear layer.
- The performance of CEMC is evaluated on a dataset named BIG 2015 in terms of accuracy, precision, recall, and F1-score. The experimental results demonstrate that CEMC outperforms random selection and other active learning strategies in terms of performance and stability.
- The effectiveness of CEMC is analyzed from the family perspective, which further proves that the proposed framework achieves the main goal to select the most informative samples while neglecting the less important ones for relatively higher performance. The impact of initialization and the number of query samples, termed query number is explored as well. Some interesting conclusions are drawn for future implementation.

The rest of this paper is organized as follows. Related works are illustrated in Sect. 2. In Sect. 3, the proposed framework is described. The experiments are elaborated in detail in Sect. 4. Finally, the conclusion of the whole paper and the future work are stated in Sect. 5.

## 2    Related Works

Traditionally, malware analysis methods can be divided into two main categories including static approaches and dynamic approaches. In static approaches, malware is checked by analyzing its executable binaries or codes without executing [2]. In contrast, dynamic approaches trace the malware process and record the behavior features, such as system calls, registry change, or traffic flows, in a controlled environment such as a virtual environment, simulator, and sandbox [3].

As the above hand-crafted malware analysis approaches need a lot of effort to extract features, researchers have introduced deep learning methods into malware classification tasks to improve efficiency. With the help of deep learning technology, features can be learned automatically and malware classification models can be built without expert knowledge.

Nataraj et al. were the first to start the research based upon digit gray-scale images converted from malware binaries [4]. Since then, classifiers trained on image-based malware data have shown to be very promising in massive research. Coull et al. [5] confirmed the effectiveness of ConvNet for malware classification and tried to find the parts which contribute most to the classification task. Yakura et al. [6] applied ConvNet with attention mechanism to images converted from binary data and generated attention maps for further analysis.

Although DL-based approaches can efficiently obtain ideal classification results, they need large amounts of labeled samples for training. Aiming at improving the existing models by incrementally selecting and annotating the most informative unlabeled samples, active learning (AL) has been well studied in the past few decades. In the AL methods, the model is first initialized with a relatively small set of labeled training samples. Then it is continuously boosted by selecting and pushing some of the most informative samples, which are called query samples, to experts for annotation. The informativeness of a sample is often measured by either the uncertainty of the model about this sample, the expected model change after training on this sample, or how representative the samples are about other unlabeled samples [7]. The key of AL is the design of query strategies and the most common strategies belong to the category called "uncertainty" which considers the most valuable sample is the one with the highest uncertainty.

Inspired by the success of AL, there are researches introduced AL to various kinds of malware tasks since then. The scholars from Microsoft Research Center designed a system called ALADIN which used active learning combined with rare class discovery and uncertainty identification to statistically train a network traffic classifier based on Logistic Regression (LR) [8]. Min Zhao et al. proposed a malware detection framework named RobotDroid using Support Vector Machine (SVM) and an active learning algorithm for smartphones [9]. Nir Nissim et al. designed "Exploitation" based on the SVM classification algorithm using the radial basis function kernel and acquired most probably malicious samples [10]. Bahman Rashidi et al. presented an malicious Android application detection framework based on SVM with 206 features and active learning technologies [11]. Chin-Wei Chen et al. proposed an approach that combines SVM and active learning by learning (ALBL) techniques for malware family classification [12] using statistical features.

As we can see, all the related works used AL strategies based on machine learning models, and most of them are SVM-based frameworks. The strategies designed for machine learning models can not be directly borrowed by DL with guaranteened performance improvement. What's more, compared to DL, machine learning methods are relatively "shallower" and can not handle features with high dimensions and feature engineering is a prerequisite for these methods.

To cope with this issue, it becomes a necessity to study the classification framework combining DL and AL.

# 3  Cost-Effective Malware Classification

## 3.1  Framework Overview

Suppose there is a training dataset of $m$ malware families initially with no labels denoted by $D$. The randomly selected malware set for network initialization is identified as $D_0^L$. The target of CEMC is to select the most informative query samples for expert labeling and expand the labeled training set $D_i^L$ progressively, where $i \in \{0, 1, ..., T\}$, while the unlabeled pool shrinks accordingly.

Motivated by the insights from a significant amount of previous ConvNet-based malware classification research as well as the recently proposed active learning techniques, i.e., CEAL [13], BADGE [14], we address the above-mentioned issues by AL-based ConvNet.

During the $i$-th round, our proposed CEMC scrutinizes the samples from the unlabeled data set $D_i^U$ and selects the top $q$ most informative samples, where $q$ represents the query number per round. These samples with newly acquired labels from malware experts are then merged into the labeled dataset $D_i^L$ as the training set for the next $(i + 1)$-th round.

Figure 1 illustrates the framework of CEMC, and the details of implementation will be discussed in the following.

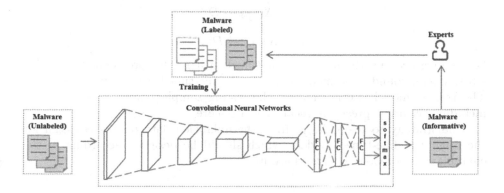

**Fig. 1.** The overview of the proposed cost-effective malware classification system

### 3.2   Malware Visualization

This part is considered as the data preprocessing module as well. Inspired by Nataraj et al. [4], gray-scale images of different malware samples appear visually similar from a given family and distinct from those belonging to different families. Based on the observation, the binaries of malware are processed line by line and the corresponding pixels are placed one after another in a row, with a width of 224. The size of the output images is fixed to 224 × 224 which is a routine size for image-related tasks. All the characters except bytes are ignored including newline characters and line labels. The redundant bytes are discarded and if the bytes cannot fill the entire image, black pixels are padded in the end. After this data preprocessing module, raw malware binaries can be converted into gray-scale images which are suitable for ConvNet to handle for feature extraction.

### 3.3   Model Initialization

The model can be initialized by $D_0^L$ directly, and this kind of initialization is termed INIT_DIRECT. Additionally, since the raw malware samples have been transformed into gray-scale images, some research has testified transfer learning methods for malware-related tasks that borrowed knowledge from models pre-trained with the dataset of the computer vision area, noted as CV [1,15,16]. Consequently, we can also take advantage of transfer learning ahead of direct initialization and this two-stage initialization method is denoted by INIT_TRANS in the discussion below. For INIT_TRANS, $D_0^L$ is also necessary obviously.

### 3.4   Model Training and Evaluation

After initialized, the model is fed with unlabeled samples remaining in $D$ referred to as $D_0^U$. Query sample set $X_{info}$ are selected for experts to annotation and the labeled traning set $D_0^L$ is updated as well as unlabeled pool $D_0^U$:

$$D_0^L \cup X_{info} \rightarrow D_1^L$$

$$D_0^U \backslash X_{info} \rightarrow D_1^U$$

For the next round, the model is fine-tuned with $D_1^L$ for pre-defined $e$ epochs. After several rounds, the model is gradually fine-tuned for classification tasks. The trained model is evaluated on the testing samples based on four merits, including accuracy, precision, recall, and F1-score.

The strategy to select $X_{info}$ from the unlabeled data pool is essential for the quality of fine-tuned models, which should be designed according to the characteristics of ConvNet and malware.

### 3.5   Informative Sample Selection

As mentioned before, the labeling cost to train a high-performance DL-based model is troublesome in practice. AL methods designed to select query samples based on DL-based models can help to deal with this cost issue. The selection should be carried out according to the appearance of the unlabeled samples out of the neural networks, which is the estimation of the real impact with the true labels attached afterward.

Batch Active learning by Diverse Gradient Embeddings (BADGE), which is designed as a practical, general-purpose, label-efficient AL method for deep neural networks has been proposed to offer a solution for the above demand [14]. BADGE creates diverse batches of informative examples. The uncertainty is measured by the gradient magnitude concerning parameters in the final linear layer. Meanwhile, to capture the diversity, a batch of samples is collected whose gradients span a diverse set of directions.

Consider a neural network $f(., W, V)$, where $W = (W_1, ..., W_m) \in \mathbb{R}^{K \times m}$ are the weights of the last linear layer, and $V$ consists of weights of all previous layers. For most of the classifiers, the last nonlinearity is a softmax layer, denoted by $\phi(.)$. Given a malware sample $x$ with label $y$, the corresponding outputs of the network is $P = f(x, W, V) = \phi(W \cdot Z(x, V))$, where $Z$ maps $x$ to the output of the network's penultimate layer.

Define $g_j$ as the gradient of the cross-entropy loss $l_{CE}$ of $x$ to $W_j$, according to the definition of cross-entropy loss, $g_j$ can be concluded as:

$$g_j = \frac{\partial l_{CE}}{W_j} = Z(x, V)_j (P_j - I(y = j)) \tag{1}$$

Note that each component of the gradient is a scaling of the corresponding one of $Z(x, V)$, which is the output of the penultimate layer of the network with $x$ as the input. Suppose $\hat{y} = argmax_{i \in m} P_i$, the norm and direction of $y^{\hat{y}}$ can be used to estimate the influence brought by sample $x$ on the current model.

To fulfill the demand for diversity at the same time, k-means++ algorithm is adopted. The algorithm for CEMC is described in Algorithm 1.

---

**Algorithm 1.** CEMC: Cost-effective Malware Classification

---

**Require:**

    Unlabeled pool of samples $D_0^U$, initialization training set $D_0^L$, initialized network $f$ with INIT_TRANS or INIT_DIRECT, number of rounds $T$, query number $q$ and number of epochs $e$ for each round

1: **for** $i = 0, 1, ..., T$ **do**
2:     Train $f$ for $e$ epochs on $D_i^L$
3:     **for** each sample $x$ from $D_i^U$ **do**
4:         Compute its hypothetical label $\hat{y} = f(x)$
5:         Compute the gradient $g_x$ based on Equa. 1
6:     **end for**
7:     Generate $X_{info}$ with $q$ samples using k-MEANS++ algorithm on $g_x : x \in D_i^U$
8:     Label samples in $X_{info}$ by experts
9:     $D_{i+1}^U = D_i^U \backslash X_{info}$
10:    $D_{i+1}^L = D_i^L \cup X_{info}$
11: **end for**

---

## 4  Experiments

### 4.1  Malware Dataset and Experimental Setup

In this section, we evaluate the performance of CEMC on the benchmark dataset provided by Microsoft Malware Classification Challenge in 2015 which is also referred to as BIG 2015. The dataset has 10868 malware samples in the training set and 10873 in the test set both from 9 families. This is a highly unbalanced dataset in which the largest family called Kelihos_ver3 has 2942 samples and the smallest Simba family has only 42 as shown in Table 1.

**Table 1.** Family description of BIG 2015 traning set

| Family name | Count | Family name | Count |
|---|---|---|---|
| Ramnit | 1541 | Tracur | 751 |
| Lollipop | 2478 | Kelihos_ver1 | 398 |
| Kelihos_ver3 | 2942 | Obfuscator.ACY | 1228 |
| Vundo | 475 | Gatak | 1013 |
| Simba | 42 | | |

For the effectiveness of CEMC does not rely on the ConvNet architectures, we use AlexNet [17] as the structure of CEMC.

Following the settings in most DL methods, we randomly select 90% samples of each family to form the unlabeled sample pool, and the rest 10% as the test set in our experiments. It should be noted that after the split, the number of samples from Simba for test is only 4, which will lead to severe fluctuations in performance. To smooth the performance toward this family, the test samples of Simba are increased to 14 on purpose, and the training samples are decreased accordingly. We randomly select 200 samples with labels from the unlabeled pool to initialize the network and the rest are for the incremental learning process.

After several trials, the learning rate of all layers is set to 0.005, and the model is fine-tuned for 50 epochs per round. The fine-tuning is carried out for 30 rounds with 50 query samples selected for each round at first and the performance with different query numbers is also checked to measure the impact induced by query numbers. If not specified, 5-fold strategy is applied and the execution results are averaged as the final result to get rid of the influence of randomness.

To provide persuasive results, we compare CEMC to several baseline strategies borrowed directly from ML-based AL methods which are embedded into ConvNet as well, including:

*Random Sampling (RS).* This is not an active learning method yet, it is actually the "lower bound" of the selection methods.

*LeastConfidence Sampling (LS).* An uncertainty-based active learning algorithm that selects top $q$ samples with the smallest predicted class probability, as $max_{i \in m} p_i$, just as Wang et al. [18].

*Entropy Sampling (ES).* An uncertainty-based strategy that selects the top $q$ samples according to the entropy of the predictive probability distribution, defined as $H(P) = \sum_{i=1}^{m} p_i \ln 1/p_i$ [13] .

*KMeans Sampling (KS).* This strategy clusters the output of the last linear layer $z = Z(x, V)$ for each unlabeled sample $x$ via K-Means into $q$ clusters and selects the samples nearest to the center of each cluster [7]. KS is a diversity-based strategy the same as the strategy used in this paper.

The above methods share the same ConvNet architecture with CEMC on identical training sets and test sets. The only difference lies in the sample selection criteria which is the target of evaluation.

### 4.2   Oevrall Performance Comparison

For this comparison, the averaged performance measures are recorded with 50 query samples after INIT_TRANS initialization. The measures of performance after 15/30 rounds of all strategies are listed in Table 2.

**Table 2.** Performance after 15- and 30-round fine-tuning of CEMC and baseline strategies

| Rounds | Strategy | Accuracy | Precision | Recall | F1-score |
|--------|----------|----------|-----------|--------|----------|
| 15 | RS | 90.10 ± 0.00% | 86.38 ± 0.04% | 83.39 ± 0.05% | 84.31 ± 0.04% |
| | KS | 88.71 ± 0.02% | 86.74 ± 0.10% | 80.44 ± 0.01% | 81.21 ± 0.02% |
| | ES | 92.70 ± 0.00% | 91.30 + 0.06% | 87.59 ± 0.03% | 88.86 ± 0.03% |
| | LS | 92.61 ± 0.07% | 90.11 ± 0.17% | 86.42 ± 0.16% | 87.73 ± 0.16% |
| | CEMC | **04.60 ± 0.00%** | **93.63 ± 0.08%** | **89.98 ± 0.01%** | **91.17 ± 0.02%** |
| 30 | RS | 92.08 ± 0.00% | 89.05 ± 0.04% | 85.53 ± 0.04% | 86.56 ± 0.05% |
| | KS | 90.67 ± 0.01% | 87.86 ± 0.16% | 83.43 ± 0.01% | 84.06 ± 0.03% |
| | ES | 95.99 ± 0.00% | 96.30 ± 0.00% | 91.25 ± 0.00% | 93.05 ± 0.00% |
| | LS | 96.30 ± 0.00% | 95.61 ± 0.03% | **92.94 ± 0.00%** | **93.98 ± 0.00%** |
| | CEMC | **96.34 ± 0.00%** | **96.36 ± 0.00%** | 92.36 ± 0.00% | 93.90 ± 0.00% |

It can be seen that the performance improvement of CEMC compared to the second-best strategy ES is about +2% for all measures after 15 rounds. But after 30 rounds, ES and LS show comparable performance to our CEMC.

For more detail, the performance of CEMC through 30 rounds compared to the other strategies is depicted as learning curves in Fig. 2.

The performance of these 5 methods can be separated into 2 groups in a clear margin. The first group consists of our CEMC, LS and ES, whose performance

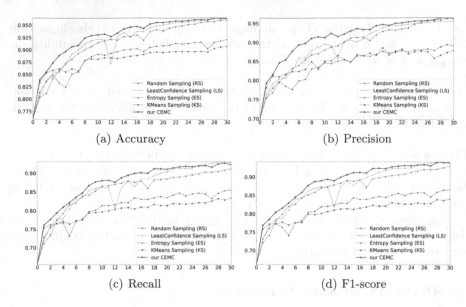

(a) Accuracy
(b) Precision

(c) Recall
(d) F1-score

**Fig. 2.** Performance comparison through 30 rounds with 50 query samples and INIT_TRANS initialization

outperforms KS and RS in the other group. Moreover, the gap between these two groups has no trend to narrow down along with the increase of labeled samples for more rounds. This gives an assumption that the sample selection strategy is deterministic that once fixed, the upper bound of classification performance is set.

It can also be observed that not until the first 1 or 2 rounds, does CEMC stand out in terms of performance and stability. The closest competitors seem to be LS and ES. LS performs even better in terms of recall and F1-score after about 22 rounds but the difference is so small that can be negligible.

At the end of fine-tuning, the performance of CEMC, LS and ES gradually approach together, which implies the advantage obtained through careful sample selection is compensated by the growing number of labeled samples.

From the above results and analysis, it is clear that our proposed framework CEMC performs consistently better than other methods through fair comparisons and that improvement is the main goal of this study. Additionally, this also indicates that CEMC can effectively select the informative query samples for outstanding performance.

### 4.3 Family Perspective Performance

In this section, we compare CEMC versus other strategies based on the performance and selection process concerning all families.

First, Fig. 3 presents the confusion matrix of CEMC after 15-round fine-tuning based on one of the 5-fold datasets.

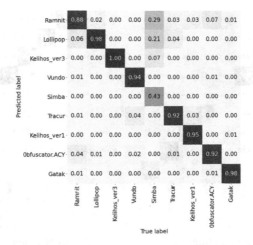

**Fig. 3.** Confusion matrix of CEMC after 15-round fine-tuning

Meanwhile, Fig. 4 illustrates the confusion matrix of baseline strategies with identical settings for comparison.

As can be seen, our method obtains the highest accuracy for 7 out of 9 families, while ES and KS both perform best for 3 out of 9. This stable and outstanding performance indicates the effectiveness of CEMC.

However, when it comes to the selection process, the situation is complex and varied for different families. They can be separated into 3 categories, denoted as SAME, MORE, and LESS, based on the number of query samples selected by CEMC compared to RS:

*SAME (Lollipop, Obfuscator.ACY, Gatak and Vundo).* CEMC selects almost the same number of samples from these 4 families as RS and other strategies as shown in Fig. 5. The performance of CEMC is better or at least almost the same compared to other strategies concerning these four families.

*LESS (Kelihos_ver3 and Kelihos_ver1).* CEMC selects much less samples from these 2 families than RS as shown in Fig. 6.

All the AL-based strategies perform perfectly with above 95% accuracy on these 2 families, while RS only recognizes 87% of the samples correctly from Kelihos_ver1 in the test set. This gives a signal that there are samples more informative than others in Kelihos_ver1. The model can yield better performance once trained with these samples selected and labeled. And this task is completed by CEMC with the least labeling cost. For Kelihos_ver3, the excellent accuracy obtained by all strategies implies high similarity among samples from this family. Acquiring samples in common is a waste of manual analysis resources and CEMC performs especially outstanding as well as its closest competitors (ES and LS) that they barely query experts for labeling samples from Kelihos_ver3.

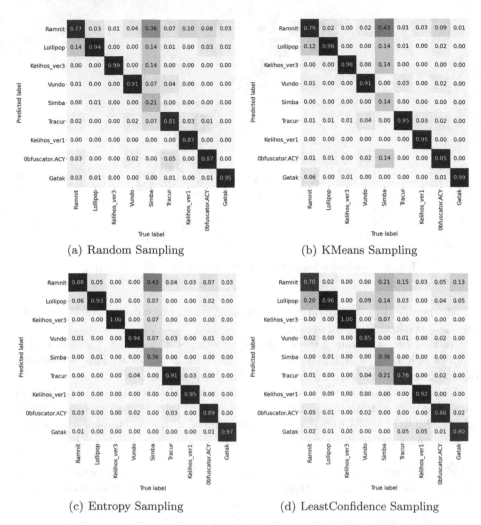

(a) Random Sampling

(b) KMeans Sampling

(c) Entropy Sampling

(d) LeastConfidence Sampling

**Fig. 4.** Confusion matrix of baseline strategies after 15-round fine-tuning

*MORE (Ramnit, Tracur and Simba).* CEMC selects more samples from these families than RS as in Fig. 7. The situation needs to be analyzed individually due to the complexity of situations in this category.

Ramnit has the third most samples among all the families in the unlabeled pool, but the best accuracy achieved by CEMC and ES is only 88% as shown in Fig. 3 and Fig. 4. This phenomenon implies that more informative samples are needed from Ramnit for a better recognition rate. Our CEMC, LS and ES are intended to fulfill this demand and continuously select almost the same amount

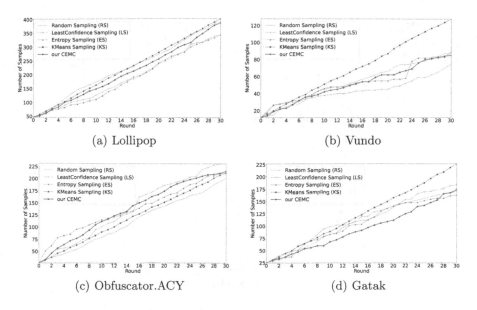

**Fig. 5.** Number of labeled samples per family in SAME category through 30 rounds

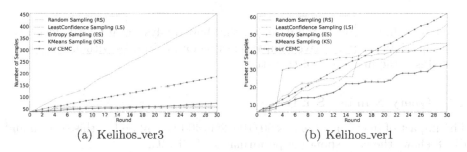

**Fig. 6.** Number of labeled samples per family in LESS category through 30 rounds

of samples through the training process. In contrast, KS selects less informative samples and RS performs the worst.

For Tracur, CEMC outperforms RS and LS, and shows comparable accuracy to KS and ES. LS does not perform well as expected and the accuracy for Tracur is only 76% which is worse than RS.

We leave Simba which has the least samples and worst performance to the last for the interesting result related to this family. There are only 25 samples from Simba in the unlabeled pool after initialization. CEMC succeeds to dig all of these 25 samples out of 9575 candidates, which is like looking for a needle in a haystack. ES and LS managed to select 22 samples, while RS and KS failed to find the informative samples belonging to Simba with crashed performance towards this specific family.

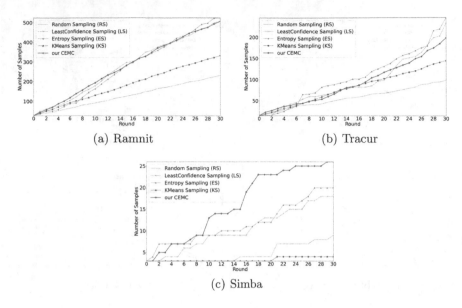

(a) Ramnit    (b) Tracur

(c) Simba

**Fig. 7.** Number of labeled samples per family in MORE category through 30 rounds

We can draw a conclusion based on the above analysis that CEMC yields the best capability of informative sample selection for all families without exception. And this is the main goal of this study.

### 4.4  Query Number Study

The impact of query numbers as 50/100/200/400 is explored in this section and Fig. 8 shows the corresponding performance of CEMC.

The y-axis represents the number of selected samples instead of rounds.

As can be seen, most of the time, a smaller query number shows an advantage over a larger one. It seems that identifying and acquiring more samples does not benefit the classifier consequently. This phenomenon may be due to the assumption that there exists an optimal set of informative samples and the advantage brought by this set can be disrupted by the samples out of it.

However, it cannot simply state that fewer query samples means better performance. Instead, in order to receive a maximal contribution from the suggested framework, the query number should be carefully tracked and defined. Additionally, it should be noticed that with more labeled training samples, the performance difference is tended to disappear.

### 4.5  Initialization Analysis

In this section, we want to discover the impact of initialization methods. As mentioned before, there are two kinds of initialization to induce the initial model, INIT_DIRECT and INIT_TRANS. Figure 9 presents the performance of INIT_DIRECT in CEMC versus baseline strategies.

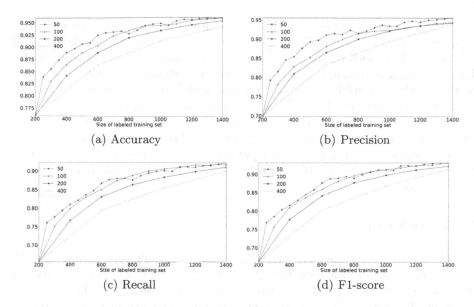

**Fig. 8.** Performance of CEMC with different query numbers with INIT_TRANS initialization

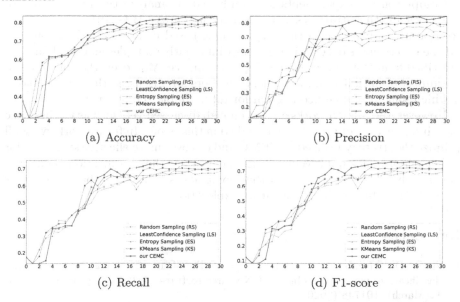

**Fig. 9.** Performance of INIT_DIRECT comparison through 30 rounds with 50 query samples

The performance of CEMC with INIT_DIRECT shows an advantage after almost 10 rounds, which means a longer start-up window and more query samples compared to INIT_TRANS. Additionally, the advantage of CEMC is no longer as obvious as INIT_TRANS, although still can be observed after start-up.

This phenomenon illustrates the importance of high-performance initialization, and this conclusion is reasonable due to the theoretical considerations of all AL-based methods below. AL algorithms select the most informative samples based on the assumption that the prediction can estimate the real contribution introduced by the specific sample with a true label. If the classifier is not accurate enough to provide knowledge consistent with that assumption, the estimation will fail to reflect the real impact from samples and we may miss the real informative ones. Without transfer learning, the model is just initialized using a few labeled samples (200 samples in our paper), and the performance turns out to be very poor (lower than 40%), which will fail to estimate the real impact of most samples.

## 5    Conclusion

In this paper, we propose a malware classification framework named CEMC, which employs a well-designed, ConvNet-oriented AL strategy. This strategy can progressively select the most informative samples according to the estimated gradients towards the last linear layer. These samples are sent to experts for labeling and integrated into the training set afterward for model fine-tuning.

Comprehensive experiments are conducted to analyze the performance of CEMC versus other strategies on the benchmark dataset BIG 2015. CEMC shows a competitive advantage in the deep learning-based malware classification task and the effectiveness of selecting the most informative samples across all families is justified from the family perspective performance. Moreover, the contribution and impact of initialization and query numbers are discussed thoroughly, based on which some useful advice is given for future implementation.

However, the related works are not enough discussed yet, such as the best size of the informative sample set is not studied in this paper. In future work, we shall optimize the strategy utilized in CEMC and discover more effective strategies for further performance improvement with ConvNet as the classification algorithm. Additionally, there is no research that combines AL and RNN-based networks so far. This is also a subject for future exploration.

## References

1. Vasan, D., Alazab, M., Wassan, S., Safaei, B., Zheng, Q.: Image-based malware classification using ensemble of CNN architectures (IMCEC). Comput. Secur. **92**(March), 101748 (2020)
2. Gibert, D., Mateu, C., Planes, J., Vicens, R.: Classification of malware by using structural entropy on convolutional neural networks. In: Proceedings of the 30th Innovative Applications of Artificial Intelligence Conference, IAAI 2018, pp. 7759–7764 (2018)
3. Huang, Y.-T., Chen, Y.-Y., Yang, C.-C., Sun, Y., Hsiao, S.-W., Chen, M.C.: Tagging malware intentions by using attention-based sequence-to-sequence neural network. In: Jang-Jaccard, J., Guo, F. (eds.) ACISP 2019. LNCS, vol. 11547, pp. 660–668. Springer, Cham (2019). https://doi.org/10.1007/978-3-030-21548-4_38

4. Nataraj, L., Karthikeyan, S., Jacob, G., Manjunath, B.S.: Malware images: visualization and automatic classification. In: ACM International Conference Proceeding Series (2011)

5. Coull, S.E., Gardner, C.: Activation analysis of a byte-based deep neural network for malware classification. In: Proceedings - 2019 IEEE Symposium on Security and Privacy Workshops, SPW 2019, pp. 21–27 (2019). https://doi.org/10.1109/SPW.2019.00017

6. Yakura, H., Shinozaki, S., Nishimura, R., Oyama, Y., Sakuma, J.: Malware analysis of imaged binary samples by convolutional neural network with attention mechanism. In: CODASPY 2018 - Proceedings of the 8th ACM Conference on Data and Application Security and Privacy 2018-January (3), pp. 127–134 (2018). https://doi.org/10.1145/3176258.3176335

7. Zhdanov, F.: Diverse mini-batch active learning (2019). http://arxiv.org/abs/1901.05954

8. Stokes, J.W., Platt, J.C., Kravis, J.: ALADIN: Active Learning of Anomalies to Detect Intrusion. Microsoft (2008)

9. Zhao, M., Zhang, T., Ge, F., Yuan, Z.: RobotDroid: a lightweight malware detection framework on smartphones. J. Networks 7(4), 715–722 (2012)

10. Nissim, N., Moskovitch, R., Rokach, L., Elovici, Y.: Novel active learning methods for enhanced PC malware detection in windows OS. Expert Syst. Appl. 41(13), 5843–5857 (2014)

11. Rashidi, B., Fung, C., Bertino, E.: Android malicious application detection using support vector machine and active learning. In: 2017 13th International Conference on Network and Service Management, CNSM 2017, 1–9 January 2018 (2017)

12. Chen, C.W., Su, C.H., Lee, K.W., Bair, P.H.: Malware family classification using active learning by learning. In: International Conference on Advanced Communication Technology, ICACT 2020, pp. 590–595 (2020)

13. Wang, K., Zhang, D., Li, Y., Zhang, R., Lin, L.: Colloids and surfaces a: physicochemical and engineering aspects 12(d), 1–13 (2016)

14. Ash, J.T., Zhang, C., Krishnamurthy, A., Langford, J., Agarwal, A.: Deep Batch Active Learning by Diverse, Uncertain Gradient Lower Bounds (2019)

15. Lo, W.W., Yang, X., Wang, Y.: An xception convolutional neural network for malware classification with transfer learning. In: 2019 10th IFIP International Conference on New Technologies, Mobility and Security, NTMS 2019 - Proceedings and Workshop, pp. 1–5 (2019). https://doi.org/10.1109/NTMS.2019.8763852

16. Bhodia, N., Prajapati, P., Di Troia, F., Stamp, M.: Transfer learning for image-based malware classification. In: ICISSP 2019 - Proceedings of the 5th International Conference on Information Systems Security and Privacy, pp. 719–726 (2019)

17. Krizhevsky, A., Sutskever, I., Hinton, G.: ImageNet classification with deep convolutional neural networks. In: Neural Information Processing Systems vol. 25 (2012). https://doi.org/10.1145/3065386

18. Wang, D., Shang, Y.: A new active labeling method for deep learning, pp. 112–119 (2014). https://doi.org/10.1109/IJCNN.2014.6889457

# Blockchain

# CTDRB: Controllable Timed Data Release Using Blockchains

Jingzhe Wang[✉] and Balaji Palanisamy

University of Pittsburgh, Pittsburgh, PA, USA
{jiw148,bpalan}@pitt.edu

**Abstract.** The notion of Timed Data Release (TDR) supports time-based sensitive data protection in such a way that sensitive data can be accessed only after a prescribed amount of time has passed. With recent advancements in blockchain techniques, practical solutions to support decentralized TDR using blockchains (BTDR) is gaining importance. Briefly, such designs entrust blockchain decentralized networks to serve as a decentralized time agent to protect the data and release the data at a prescribed release time. However, as a variant of outsourced data management service, BTDR inherently incurs the tension between data confidentiality protection as well as data control. Unfortunately, the off-the-shelf arts only strive to protect the data without rigorous support for the control of data.

In this paper, we design a controllable framework for BTDR called *CTDRB*. At a high level, *CTDRB* realizes data access control as well as data lifetime control while protecting data confidentiality. The novel technical contributions of *CTDRB* are three-fold: first, we adopt a temporal CP-ABE cryptographic scheme, serving as a basis, to enable the data access control; second, on top of such a design, we enable data lifetime control by carefully designing a time token control service on Ethereum. We then design two representative data lifetime control primitives, namely *Data Revocation* and *Data Release Time Modification*. The former refers to revoking the data before its prescribed release time while the latter modifies the release of data at a time ahead of its prescribed release time; third but not the least, we perform security analysis of *CTDRB* and implement it using the *Ethereum* blockchain. Our results show that *CTDRB* incurs only a moderate on-chain *gas consumption* and demonstrates high efficiency.

**Keywords:** Timed data release · Blockchain · Smart contract

## 1 Introduction

Timed data release (TDR) is a time-based data protection primitive that aims at protecting sensitive data by making it accessible only after a prescribed amount of time has passed. Several real-world applications require TDR. For example, in secure voting mechanisms, votes are not permitted to be accessed until the close of the polling process. With recent advancements in blockchain techniques, practical solutions to support decentralized TDR using blockchains (BTDR) is gaining importance [4,10,16–18,20–22,24,32,33]. Briefly, such designs entrust blockchain decentralized networks to serve as a decentralized time agent to protect the data and release the data at a

© ICST Institute for Computer Sciences, Social Informatics and Telecommunications Engineering 2023
Published by Springer Nature Switzerland AG 2023. All Rights Reserved
F. Li et al. (Eds.): SecureComm 2022, LNICST 462, pp. 231–249, 2023.
https://doi.org/10.1007/978-3-031-25538-0_13

prescribed release time. Given the open nature of blockchain decentralized networks, in which a large number of mutually distrusted nodes exist, protecting data confidentiality against adversarial actions in such environments before the release time is inherently challenging. Various off-the-shelf arts have developed effective designs for data protection. Specifically, both strong cryptographic constructions [20–22] as well as practical realizations in the Ethereum blockchain [10, 16–18, 24, 32, 33] have been designed.

As a variant of outsourced data management service, however, BTDR inherently meets the tension between data confidentiality protection as well as data control. One can imagine a scenario when a data sender wants to reduce the data access scope after the release time in such a way that the data is only accessible to a selected list of recipients who are eligible to access it instead of making the data public. As another scenario, after the data is released, the data sender may become aware of some incorrect information in the data. Under this scenario, the sender would like to revoke the data before the prescribed release time. Thus, supporting BTDR to serve a broad range of real-world applications to perform dynamic data control is of significant importance. Current techniques, however, invariably fail to meet such necessity and supporting dynamic data control in BTDR while protecting data confidentiality is still largely open.

In this paper, we take the first step towards designing a controllable framework for BTDR, coined as *CTDRB*. At a high level, *CTDRB* realizes data access control as well as data lifetime control while protecting data confidentiality. Specifically, in CTDRB, we investigate the controllable primitive from the two aspects namely data access control and data lifetime control. The former refers to limiting the access scope of the data. The latter is an attractive feature supported by our framework, in which a data sender can flexibly tweak the data publishing time. Our work starts with enabling data access control. Specifically, we adopt TAFC [14], a cryptographic construction that employs ciphertext-policy attribute-based encryption (CP-ABE) [12] with timed release encryption [27], to enable data access control in CTDRB. Briefly, TAFC encrypts the data with an access structure (access policy) that embeds a time trapdoor, corresponding to a prescribed release time. Later, at the release time, a trusted authority generates and publishes a time token. Anyone holding satisfying attributes as well as the time token is able to decrypt the data.

While adopting TAFC realizes the data access control, such a construction fails to meet our need for providing data lifetime control. It is attributed to the following challenges: *first*, TAFC only provides theoretical constructions of basic encryption and decryption operations. Directly adopting such constructions limits the data sender's ability to perform lifetime control over the data such as revoking the data before the release time; *second*, TAFC heavily relies on a trusted central time agent to publish a time token. In CTDRB, however, it is impractical that such a trusted time agent exists in a fully decentralized blockchain network. To address this challenge, we design a novel time token control service on the Ethereum blockchain to support data lifetime control. Concretely, our design adopts a hierarchical key management scheme. The time token is encrypted using a public key and stored at a decentralized storage platform. The protection of the corresponding private key is delegated to a group of Ethereum network nodes, namely trustees, who jointly protect such a private key and release it when the release time arrives. With the help of such a design, a sender can manually tweak the release time of the private key to impact the release time of the time token, which then realizes the data lifetime control. However, due to the inherent risk in BTDR design [17], trivially provisioning such a service inevitably exposes to the following two threats: drop attack and release-ahead attack. Drop attack may render the private key unavailable, which impacts the availability of the time token control service. Release-ahead poses a risk of pre-maturely releasing the data, in which adversaries may collude with the trustees as well as the recipients to illegally get access to the data at a time earlier than the prescribed one by getting the time token as well as a satisfying attribute set. Thus, to mitigate the aforementioned threats, we design the service with the following two countermeasures: (1) to lessen the impact of the drop attack, we adopt Shamir's $(t, n)$ threshold secret share scheme [28] to split the private key into multiple shares, in which at least $t$ shares of the private key can make it recoverable, (2) to set barriers for the adversaries seeking to prematurely release the data, we keep the identities of the trustees as well as the recipients private, which increases the efforts requires from the adversaries to launch such an attack. Grounded on the proposed time token delivery service, we then materialize two representative data lifetime control primitives, namely data revocation and data release time modification. Data revocation refers to revoking the data before its prescribed release time while data lifetime control modifies the release of data at a time ahead of its prescribed one. These primitives are practically supported by our carefully designed interactive protocol.

We provide rigorous security analysis by quantitatively measuring the attack resilience of our proposed framework. We also implement proof-of-concept smart contracts programmed in *Solidity* [7] and test it on the *Rinkeby* network to evaluate corresponding gas consumption. By performing case studies, we demonstrate that our proposed data revocation and data release time modification primitive only incur moderate gas cost under various service conditions.

**Contributions.** Concretely, we make the following key contributions in this paper:

- We propose a controllable framework for blockchain-based timed data release to realize both data access control as well as data lifetime control while protecting the confidentiality of the data.
- We first adopt TAFC, a variant of CP-ABE scheme, to provide data access control. Atop such a scheme, we propose a novel time token control service on the Ethereum blockchain to enable data lifetime control. Two representative data lifetime control primitives namely data revocation and data release time modification are developed.
- We rigorously analyze the security guarantee of our framework.
- We implement our prototype in *Ethereum* and perform extensive case studies.

**Organization.** The rest of the paper is organized as follows. In Sect. 2, we provide preliminaries adopted in this paper. A high-level description of *CTDRB* as well as corresponding security assumptions are given in Sect. 3. In Sect. 4, we construct *CTDRB* with technical details. We analyze our proposed *CTDRB* in Sect. 5. In Sect. 6, we discuss the *proof-of-concept* implementations in smart contracts. Related work is discussed in Sect. 7. We conclude this paper in Sect. 8.

## 2 Preliminaries

In this section, we first introduce some background about Ethereum blockchains in Sect. 2.1. Then, in Sect. 2.2, we introduce the major cryptographic primitives adopted in our work.

### 2.1 A Primer on the Ethereum Blockchain

*Ethereum* [2] is a pioneering platform that integrates the abstraction of smart contracts [29] with blockchains. Informally, an *Ethereum* smart contract is composed of a piece of computer code executed and stored on the *Ethereum* blockchain. Such code contractually enforces predefined policies among users (accounts) in *Ethereum*. The cryptocurrency associated with *Ethereum* is called *Ether*.

The two types of accounts, namely Externally Owned Account (*EOA*) and Contract Owned Account (*CA*), perform activities in the *Ethereum* account network. An *EOA*, controlled by some users on Internet, is associated with a unique public-private key pair as well as a balance of *Ether*. A *CA*, without a private key, is responsible for storing the smart contract code and maintaining a balance of ether. All interactions between *EOAs* and *CAs* rely on the concept of transaction. A transaction is initialized and signed with a private key of *EOA*.

The low-level *peer-to-peer* network maintained by *Ethereum* workers (miner nodes) provide a decentralized context for the submission and execution of transactions. The *Gas* mechanism in Ethereum drives the flow of transactions from an incentive perspective. The *Gas* is measured by *Ether*. For example, to submit a new transaction, a user needs to pay some gas for Ethereum workers to execute the transaction. The powerful consensus algorithm, *Proof-of-Work (PoW)*, guarantees the confirmation and correctness of transactions, which brings Ethereum with the attractive characteristics of *tamper-resistance* and *immutability*.

### 2.2 Cryptographic Primitives

In our work, we use the following cryptographic primitives.

**Cryptographic Hash Function**: We denote $hash(\cdot)$ to indicate a cryptographic hash function guaranteeing a collision resistant property. Specifically, in *CTDRB*, we adopt the *Keccak256* implementation supported by the *Ethereum* blockchain, where $hash(\cdot) := Keccak256(\cdot)$.

**Cryptographic Digital Signature**: Our work heavily relies on the cryptographic digital signature primitive to realize verifications. Specifically, we denote $Sig(\cdot)$ as the *ECDSA* signature scheme adopted in the Ethereum blockchain.

**TAFC-Time and Attribute Factors Combined Access Control:** *TAFC* [14] is a cryptographic scheme that integrates *timed-release encryption* (TRE) [27] with *cipertext-policy attribute-based encryption* (CP-ABE) [12] to realize timed-control primitives in CP-ABE. We next briefly introduce the adopted *TAFC*, which consists of the following algorithms:

$TAFC.Setup \rightarrow (pk, mk)$: The **Setup** algorithm takes an implicit security parameter. It outputs a public parameter $pk$ and a master key $mk$.

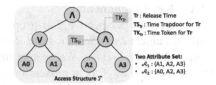

**Fig. 1.** TAFC sketch

$TAFC.KeyGen(mk, \mathcal{A}) \rightarrow sk_{\mathcal{A}}$: On input of a master key $mk$ and an attribute set $\mathcal{A}$, the **Key Generation** algorithm outputs a secret key $sk_{\mathcal{A}}$ corresponding to $\mathcal{A}$.

$TAFC.Encryption(pk, D, \mathcal{T}) \rightarrow CD$: The **Encryption** algorithm takes as input a public key $pk$, a data plaintext $D$, and a specified access structure $\mathcal{T}$. It generates a ciphertext $CD$.

$TAFC.TokenGen(mk, t) \rightarrow TK_t$: On input of a master key $mk$ and a time point $t$, the **Time Token Generation** algorithm generates a time token $TK_t$.

$TAFC.TrapdoorExp(TK, CD) \rightarrow CD'$: The **Trapdoor Exposure** algorithm takes as input a time token $TK$ and a ciphertext $CD$. It generates a modified ciphertext $CD'$.

$TAFC.Decryption(CD', sk_{\mathcal{A}}) \rightarrow D$: The **Decryption** algorithm takes as input a modified ciphertext $CD'$ and a secret key $sk_{\mathcal{A}}$ corresponding to an attribute set $\mathcal{A}$. It outputs a plaintext $D$.

As an example, in Fig. 1, assume that we expect that the data $D$ can be accessible at the release time $T_r$. We embed a time trapdoor $TS_{T_r}$ corresponding to $T_r$ into the access structure $\mathcal{T}$ and encrypt $D$ by adopting $TAFC.Encryption$ to get a ciphertext $CD$. A user, say user 1, holding the attribute set $\mathcal{A}_1 : \{A_1, A_2, A_3\}$ can adopt $TAFC.KeyGen$ to get his/her own secret key, namely $sk_{\mathcal{A}_1}$. At $T_r$, a time token $TK_{T_r}$, corresponding to $T_r$, is generated and released by $TAFC.TokenGen$. Then, user 1 can expose $TS_{T_r}$ in $\mathcal{T}$ by adopting $TAFC.TrapdoorExp$, which gives a modified ciphertext $CD'$. After the exposure of $TS_{T_r}$, user 1 can decrypt $CD'$ using his/her own secret key. Such a scheme guarantees that the user holding both $TK_r$ and $sk_{\mathcal{A}_1}$ can successfully decrypt the ciphertext.

**Shamir's $(t, n)$ Threshold Secret Share Scheme:** Shamir's secret share scheme [28] splits an original secret into $n$ different shares such that any $t$ shares are capable of reconstructing the original secret. We use $sss(t, n)$ to denote such a scheme.

## 3    *CTDRB:* In a Nutshell

In this section, we first introduce the overview of the CTDRB framework and discuss the security assumptions in *CTDRB*.

### 3.1    Framework Overview

We formally discuss the lifecycle of *CTDRB*. We begin by describing the role of each entity and we provide the formal definition of the data control primitives. We then present a high-level workflow formed among such components.

### 3.1.1 Key Components

At a high-level perspective, our proposed *CTDRB* consists of the following four key entities, namely *Data Sender, Data Recipient, Time Token Control Service*, and *Decentralized Storage Service*. We present the design as follows: (1) **Data Sender:** A data sender, denoted as $S$, is in possession of data $D$ and needs a timed-release service. In *CTDRB*, $S$ files a Ethereum smart contract, denoted as $\mathcal{SC}$, to support an incoming service. $S$ then takes charge of strategically provisioning an incoming timed data release service to enable data access control as well as data lifetime control. (2) **Time Token Control Service:** The time token control service (T2CS) aims at providing data lifetime control support by designing a hierarchical key management scheme with the help of the Ethereum blockchain. Such a design is contractually enforced by $\mathcal{SC}$. Specifically, the sender $S$ generates a time token $TK_{T_r}$ related to a release time $T_r$. $S$ then adopts a public key encryption approach to encrypt the $TK_{T_r}$ with the public key. $S$ then splits the corresponding private key into multiple secret shares by adopting Shamir's threshold secret share scheme. A group of trustees, denoted as $TE$ will be recruited from the $\mathcal{SC}$ to jointly protect the shares before $T_r$ and release the shares at $T_r$. At $T_r$, when getting the shares and reconstructing the private key, the encrypted time token can be decrypted. The data lifetime control is realized by temporally adjusting the secret share of the private key. (3) **Data Recipient:** Recipients receive the data at the release time from the timed data release service. Each recipient holds his/her own attributes as well as a published time token to decrypt the data. Without loss of generality, such recipients are formally captured by $\mathcal{R} = \{R_1, ..., R_m\}$. (4) **Decentralized Storage Service:** In our framework, we use IPFS [11] to provide a decentralized storage service. In particular, IPFS takes charge of storing the encrypted data and related information in T2CS.

### 3.1.2 Data Control Primitives

Keeping the key entities of *CTDRB* in mind, we formally introduce two types of controllable data primitives supported by our framework, namely *data access control* and *data lifetime control*. Formal descriptions are given as follows: (1) *data access control:* the data access control aims at limiting the access scope of the data in a timed release service. After getting the time token, only the recipients holding satisfying attribute set can decrypt the encrypted data. (2) *data lifetime control:* we design two representative data lifetime control primitives, namely *data revocation* and *data release time modification*. The data revocation primitive refers to revoking the data, by the data sender $S$, at a time, namely $T'$, before $T_r$. The completeness of such a primitive renders the data inaccessible to anyone except for $S$; the data release time modification primitive is also issued by the sender $S$, which allows the encrypted data to be accessible at a time before $T_r$.

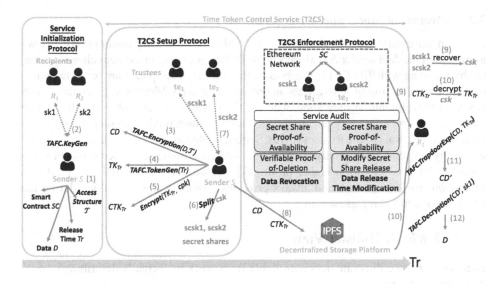

**Fig. 2.** CTDRB overview

### 3.1.3 Workflow Overview

To systematically support such primitives, the proposed approach tightly couples the four entities by carefully designing a suite of protocols, consisting of *Service Initialization Protocol*, *T2CS Setup Protocol*, and *T2CS Enforcement Protocol*. We first sketch the proposed protocols at a high-level here and we present detailed constructions in Sect. 4. As shown in Fig. 2, CTDRB starts with the service initialization protocol. In this protocol, the sender $S$ aims at initializing the basic service information (step 1) and enabling the data access control by distributing attribute secret key to the recipients (step 2). After the initialization protocol, CTDRB moves to the T2CS phase, which enables the data lifetime control. Specifically, T2CS consists of two protocols, T2CS setup protocol and T2CS enforcement protocol. In the T2CS setup protocol, $S$ encrypts the data $D$ with the specified access structure $\mathcal{T}$ to generate the ciphertext $CD$ (step 3) and generates a time token $TK_{T_r}$ related to the release time $T_r$ (step 4) and encrypts $TK_{T_r}$ to get the ciphertext $CTK_{T_r}$ with the public key $cpk$ (step 5). The corresponding private key $csk$ is then split to multiple shares by adopting $sss(t, n)$ (step 6). $S$ then distributes the shares to a set of trustees (step 7). At the end of this protocol, $S$ uploads $CD$ and $CTK_{T_r}$ to IPFS (step 8). After the setup, the T2CS enforcement protocol starts. It includes two suites of protocols to support the data revocation primitive and the data release time modification primitive, which are issued upon $S$'s request. If no data lifetime control is needed, after the release time $T_r$, any recipients, say $R_1$, first retrieves the secret shares from the Ethereum network and recovers the $csk$ (step 9). $R_i$ then decrypts the encrypted time token $CTK_{T_r}$ to get $TK_{T_r}$. Followed by exposing the time trapdoor (step 11), $R_i$ can adopt his/her attribute key, $sk_1$, to get the original data $D$ (step 12).

## 3.2   Adversarial Model and Assumptions

From an adversarial model standpoint, we make the following assumptions: (1) we assume that the data sender $S$ is always honest when engaging in a timed release service, (2) by agreeing with $TAFC$ [14], we assume that the set of recipients are prone to launch collusion attacks among $\mathcal{R}$ to access an unauthorized data. Moreover, given the $T2CS$ design, the recipients, if they know who are the trustees, are also able to collude with the trustees to pre-maturelly release the time token, which renders an illegal pre-mature release of the data, (3) the trustees in T2CS are modeled as rational adversaries who are driven by self-interest and only choose to violate timed-release service protocol when doing so let him/her earn a higher profit [17], (4) we assume that $IPFS$ may act in a *honest-but-curious* manner and always provides a reliable storage service during the lifecycle of a timed release service.

## 4   *CTDRB:* A Holistic View

In this section, we illustrate our controllable framework by formally describing its concrete constructions.

### 4.1   Service Initialization Protocol

*CTDRB* starts with the Service Initialization Protocol, namely $\Pi_{init}$. $\Pi_{init}$ aims at initializing the service parameters (Phase-1) and distributing the attribute secret key (Phase-2) to enable data access control. $\Pi_{init}$ includes the following assumptions: (1) we assume that $S$ and $\mathcal{R}$ know each other *apriori* and are in possession of the public key of each other; also, they adopt the symmetric key encryption approach in [17] to realize private communications. (3) only step-3 is an on-chain operation, and it is publicly known. We adopt the boxed convention to indicate on-chain operations in the rest of this paper. The details of $\Pi_{init}$ are shown below:

---

**Protocol: Service Initialization $\Pi_{init}$**

**Phase 1: Service Parameter Initialization**
**Sender $S$:**
1. $(pk, mk) \leftarrow TAFC.Setup$
2. prepares $D$, specifies an expected release time $T_r$, and prepares an universal set of attribute $\mathcal{U}$.
   $\boxed{3}$. deploys a smart contract $\mathcal{SC}$ on *Ethereum* and publish $T_r, \mathcal{U}$ in $\mathcal{SC}$.
**Phase 2: Attribute Secret Key Distribution:**
**Sender $S$:**
4. sends a request, $req_i$, to each recipient $R_i$ through a secure off-chain channel. $req_i :=$ $\{'\text{init}', \mathcal{U}, T_r, Addr(\mathcal{SC}), Sig_{privk_s}(hash('\text{init}', \mathcal{U}, T_r, Addr(\mathcal{SC})))\}$
**Recipient $R_i \in \mathcal{R}$:**
5. upon getting $req_i$, verifies the service information $T_r, \mathcal{U}$.
6. prepares an attribute set $\mathcal{A}_i$ further adopted to perform decryption in *TAFC*.
7. issues a response, $resp_i$, to $S$ for his/her secret key, $sk_{\mathcal{A}_i}$. Concretely, we have $resp_i :=$ $\{'\text{request secret key}', \mathcal{A}_i, Sig_{privk_{R_i}}(hash('\text{request secret key}', \mathcal{A}_i))\}$
**Sender $S$:**

---

8. upon receiving $resp_i$, generates the data decryption key $sk_{\mathcal{A}_i} \leftarrow TAFC.KeyGen(mk, \mathcal{A}_i)$

9. issues a new message, namely $dist_i$ to $R_i$ to distribute the generated $sk_{\mathcal{A}_i}$, where $dist_i := \{'\text{secret key}', sk_{\mathcal{A}_i}, Sig_{privk_S}(hash('\text{secret key}', sk_{\mathcal{A}_i}))$

## 4.2 T2CS Setup Protocol

After the provisioning in $\Pi_{init}$, *CTDRB* moves to the T2CS Setup protocol, namely $\Pi_{setup}$. The objectives of $\Pi_{setup}$ are two-fold: (1) in Phase-1, $S$ individually encrypts $D$ and generates a time token, (2) in Phase-2, $S$ interactively communicates with the trustees to provision T2CS to enable the data lifetime control. Several key designs are mentioned as follows: (1) In step-6, we assume that there are already $N$ trustees registered in $\mathcal{SC}$, where $N > n$. Specifically, we provide an interface in $\mathcal{SC}$ to let anyone who wants to participate in T2CS by submitting his/her EOA address, public key, and a security deposit $d$ to $\mathcal{SC}$ at any time point, (2) As mentioned in Sect. 3.2, *CTDRB* is under the risk of the collusion between the trustees as well as the recipients. As a countermeasure, we henceforth privately keep the recruitment evidence of the selected trustees, which keeps the recipients and the trustees double-blind. Moreover, to further help sender to retrieve the shares, in step-10, $S$ generates a cryptographic nonce for each selected trustee $te_j$, namely $rn_j$, to build a map to index the hash of each share without revealing the real identity of each selected trustee in $\mathcal{SC}$. The details of $\Pi_{setup}$ are illustrated below. After the execution of $\Pi_{setup}$, the time travel of $D$ normally starts.

---

**Protocol: T2CS Setup $\Pi_{setup}$**

**Phase 1: Data Encryption and Time Token Generation**
**Sender $S$:**
1. specifies an access structure $\mathcal{T}$ for $D$ and gets $CD \leftarrow TAFC.Encryption(pk, D, \mathcal{T})$
2. generates a time token $TK_{T_r}$ for $T_r$, where $TK_{T_r} \leftarrow TAFC.TokenGen(mk, T_r)$
**Phase 2: T2CS Provisioning**
**Sender $S$:**
3. generates a pair of keys to encrypt $TK_{T_r}$, namely *time token control key pair*, involving a control public key $cpk$, and a control private key $csk$.
4. $S$ encrypts $TK_{T_r}$ with $cpk$ to get $CTK_{T_r}$.
5. $S$ splits $csk$ into a list of shares by parameterizing $sss(t, n)$ with a pre-determined $t$ and $n$. We denote $SS = \{scsk_1, ..., scsk_n\}$ to represent list of shares of $csk$.
6. $S$ randomly selects $n$ trustees from $\mathcal{SC}$ to form a set of trustees, denoted as $TE = \{te_1, ..., te_n\}$, to further jointly take charge of protecting $SS$ until $T_r$.
7. $S$ issues a request $rec\_req_j$ to $te_j$ through an off-chain channel, specifically $rec\_req_j := \{'\text{recruit}', T_r, Addr(\mathcal{SC}), Sig_{privk_S}('\text{recruit}', hash(T_r, Addr(\mathcal{SC})))\}$.
**Each Selected Trustee: $te_j \in TE$:**
8. first performs verification when receiving $rec\_req_j$, then in case of agreeing with participation, $te_j$ sends $S$ a response as follows:
$rec\_res_j := \{'\text{agree}', Sig_{privk_{te_j}}(hash('\text{agree}', T_r, Addr(\mathcal{SC})))\}$.
**Sender $S$:**
9. Upon getting $rec\_res_j$ from $te_j$, $S$ first generates a cryptographic nonce for $te_j$, denoted as $rn_j$.
10. hashes $scsk_j$ to get $hash(scsk_j)$ and constructs a tuple $M_j$ to index $rn_j$ through the address of $te_j$, where $M_j := \{Addr(te_j), rn_j\}$; also, $S$ constructs another tuple, $MH_j := \{rn_j, hash(scsk_j)\}$ to index the share hash through $rn_j$.

11. distributes $scsk_j$ to $te_j$ by sending a share distribution message: $dist\_share_j :=$ $\{'share', scsk_j, Sig_{privks}(hash('share', scsk_j))\}$.
12. After receiving all responses from $TE$, $S$ ends the protocol as follows:
12.a uploads $CD$ as well as $CTK_{T_r}$ to IPFS, which gives $S$ two pointers, namely $pt(CD)$ and $pr(CTK_{T_r})$ respectively.
12.b builds two maps, one is $\mathcal{M}$, the other is $\mathcal{MH}$. Specifically, $\mathcal{M} := \bigcup_{j=1}^{n} M_j$, and $\mathcal{MH} := \bigcup_{j=1}^{n} MH_j$
| 12.c | keeps $\mathcal{M}$ private and publishes $\mathcal{MH}$, $pt(CD)$, as well as $pt(CTK_{T_r})$ on $\mathcal{SC}$.
| 12.d | updates the state in $\mathcal{SC}$

## 4.3 T2CS Enforcement Protocol

The T2CS Enforcement Protocol forms a key part of *CTDRB*. It aims at systematically supporting the data revocation as well as the data release time modification primitive. Concretely, the expected data control primitives will be realized in terms of controlling the publishing lifecycle of the time token $TK_{T_r}$. Naturally, it is equivalent to manually controlling the lifecycle of the $csk$ in terms of temporally adjusting the publishing of the secret shares of $csk$. Thus, in this protocol, we temporally control the shares held by the set of trustees. The T2CS enforcement protocol consists of four sub-protocols: (1) Secret Share Proof-of-Availability, (2) Data Revocation, (3) Data Release Time Modification and (4) Service Audit, which are detailed as follows:

**(1) Secret Share Proof-of-Availability** ($\Pi_{poa}$): $\Pi_{poa}$ aims at checking the availability of the secret shares $SS$ of $csk$ before performing the data lifetime control primitives, which is shown as follows:

---

**Protocol: Secret Share Proof-of-Availability** $\Pi_{poa}$

At a time point $T'$, where $T' < T_r$
**Phase 1 Challenging the Availability of the Secret Share**
**Sender $S$:**
1. locally indexes $\mathcal{M}$ to check the set of responsible trustees.
2. sends a challenge request, $avail\_challenge_j$ for each $te_j$ in $\mathcal{M}$ one by one, specifically $avail\_challenge_j := \{'check share', Sig_{privks}(hash('check share'))\}$
**Phase 2 Availability Proof Generation:**
**Challenged Trustee $te_j$:**
3. After verifying $avail\_challenge_j$, $te_j$ attaches $scsk_j$ to a response message to $S$, denoted as $avail\_resp_j := \{'share', scsk_j, Sig_{privkte_j}(hash('share', scsk_j))\}$.
**Phase 3 Sender Verification:**
**Sender $S$:**
4. After getting $scsk_j$, $S$ hashes $scsk_j$ in terms of adopting $h' \leftarrow hash(scsk_j)$ to get $h'$.
5. $S$ checks $h'$ with the original one in $\mathcal{MH}$ in $\mathcal{SC}$.
5.a If they match, $S$ continues to challenge next trustee;
| 5.b | otherwise, $S$ publishes the misbehavior on $\mathcal{SC}$
6. $S$ ends the availability check as follows:
| 6.a | Case 1: $S$ is confirmed that at least $t$ shares are available, which successfully ends $\Pi_{poa}$. $\Pi_{poa}$ outputs $TRUE$, and $S$ updates the state in $\mathcal{SC}$

| 6.b | Case 2: $S$ is confirmed that the available shares cannot recover $csk$. $\Pi_{poa}$ outputs $FALSE$. This aborts the current timed data release service.

With the help of $\Pi_{poa}$, next, we show the detailed design of the data revocation and the data release time modification primitive.

**(2) Data Revocation ($\Pi_{rvk}$):** $S$ performs the data revocation primitive by executing $\Pi_{rvk}$. Specifically, inspired by [13], $\Pi_{rvk}$ incorporates $\Pi_{poa}$ with our proposed *Verifiable Proof-of-Deletion* (VPoD) mechanism to realize the data revocation primitive. The proposed VPoD aims at deleting the shares of $csk$ held by the set of trustees. This operation then makes the decryption of $CTK_{T_r}$ impossible. In case $TK_{T_r}$ is not available by decrypting $CTK_{T_r}$ at $T_r$, even the recipients that hold satisfying attributes, cannot decrypt $CD$. The details of $\Pi_{rvk}$ are shown as follows:

---

**Protocol: Data Revocation $\Pi_{rvk}$**

At a time point $T'$, where $T' < T_r$, the following steps capture the data revocation primitive:

**Phase 1: Check Availability**

**Sender $S$:**

1. updates the state of $SC$ to $RVK\_P$ (revocation pending)
2. interacts with each $te_j$ in $TE$ to check availability in terms of adopting $\Pi_{poa}$. If $\Pi_{poa}$ gives $TRUE$, $S$ moves to step 3; otherwise, $S$ aborts the current service.

**Phase 2: Verifiable Proof-of-Deletion**

3. $S$ sends each $te_j$ a deletion request one by one, denoted as $del\_req_j$, where $del\_req_j :=$ $\{'share\ deletion', Sig_{privk_S}(hash('share\ deletion'))\}$

**Each Trustee $te_j$ who have passed $\Pi_{poa}$ :**

4. Upon receiving $del\_req_j$, $te_j$ deletes the share $scsk_j$.
5. After the deletion, $te_j$ generates a deletion response with an evidence, denoted as $del\_resp_j$, where $del\_resp_j := \{'deleted', Sig_{privk_{te_j}}(hash('deleted', scsk_j))\}$

**Sender $S$:**

| 6. | After getting the corresponding $del\_resp_j$, $S$ validates it and publishes it on-chain in $SC$. Specifically, $S$ only needs to guarantee that $(n - t + 1)$ shares are deleted.

| 7. | Once $S$ already gets $(n - t + 1)$ share deletion evidences, $S$ ensures that the $csk$ is unrecoverable. $S$ then transfers the state from $RVK\_P$ to $RVK\_E$ and ends the service.

---

In $\Pi_{rvk}$, the design of step-5 and step-6 enables verifiable capability. Specifically, since $S$ publishes the recruitment relationship as well as the evidence in step-6, anyone discovering the deleted share can perform verification. We will introduce the detailed verification design, namely *Cheating Misbehavior in VPoD*, in the service audit protocol.

**(3) Data Release Time Modification ($\Pi_{mod}$):** We next discuss the realization of the data release time modification primitive. Specifically, after checking the availability, we modify the release time by informing each $te_i$ to release the share of $csk$ at $T_r'$, a new release time before $T_r$. The detailed protocol $\Pi_{mod}$ is illustrated as follows:

---

**Protocol: Data Release Time Modification $\Pi_{mod}$**

At a time point $T'$, **Sender $S$** would like to modify the originally prescribed release time $T_r$ to $T_r'$, where $T' < T_r' < T_r$. $S$ performs the following steps:

1. $S$ updates the prescribed time $T_r$ in $\mathcal{SC}$ to $T'_r$ and the state of $\mathcal{SC}$ to a new state $MOD\_P$ (modification pending).
2. $S$ notifies the recipients $\mathcal{R}$ the modification.
3. $S$ interacts with each $te_j$ in $TE$ to check availability by adopting $\Pi_{poa}$. If $\Pi_{poa}$ gives $TRUE$, $S$ moves to step 4; otherwise, $S$ aborts the current service.
**Each Trustee $te_j$:**
4. $S$ sends a release time modification proposal, denoted as $mod\_req_j$ to each $te_j$, where $mod\_req_j := \{'\text{modification}', T'_r, Sig_{privk_S}(hash('\text{modification}', T'_r))\}$.
5. After validating $mod\_req_j$, $te_j$ constructs an agreement, denoted as $mod\_resp_j := \{'\text{agree}', Sig_{privk_{te_j}}(hash('\text{agree}', scsk_j, T'_r))$ and sends to $S$.
**Sender $S$:**
6. $S$ updates the state of $\mathcal{SC}$ to $MOD\_A$ (modification approved)
When the time hits $T'_r$, **Each Trustee $te_j$:**

7. $te_j$ publishes his/her share $scsk_j$ with a signature $Sig_{privk_{te_j}}(hash(scsk_j))$ on $\mathcal{SC}$.
After $T'_r$, **Each Recipient $R_i \in \mathcal{R}$:**
8. Retrieves all the submitted shares in terms of interacting with $\mathcal{SC}$.
9. Reconstructs $csk$ from the secret sharing scheme.
10. Verifies $csk$ with the original one in $\mathcal{SC}$ in terms of checking hash. In case verification successes, $R_i$ then gets $pt(CTK_{T_r})$ as well as $pt(CD)$ from $\mathcal{SC}$ to retrieve IPFS and decrypt $CTK_{T_r}$ with $csk$ to get $TK_{T_r}$.
11. By holding $TK_{T_r}$, $R_i$ adopts $TAFC.TrapdoorExp(TK_{T_r}, CD)$ to expose the time trapdoor, which gives $R_i$ a modified ciphertext of $CD$, namely $CD'$
12. $R_i$ adopts $TAFC.Decryption(CD', sk_{\mathcal{A}_i})$ to get $D$ at $T'_r$.

**(4) Service Audit ($\Pi_{aud}$):** Since our controllable primitives highly depend on the decentralized $T2CS$ design, guaranteeing the completeness of the execution of the primitives is quite important. In this part, we provide the Service Audit Protocol, which captures the corresponding misbehavior as well as makes the execution of the controllable primitives transparent. We outline the detailed design below.

---

**Protocol: Service Audit $\Pi_{aud}$**

**Cheating Misbehavior in *VPoD*:** Any trustee or recipient who discovers $scsk_j$ after $T'$ can adopt the following steps to submit a misbehavior report:
1. Anyone jointly holding the state of $\mathcal{SC}$ is $RVK\_E$, a discovered share $scsk_j$, the public key of the corresponding trustee $pubk_{te_j}$, as well as the evidence submitted by $te_j$, $Sig_{privk_{te_j}}(hash('\text{deleted}', scsk_j))$, can locally verify and report them with $\mathcal{SC}$, then the reporter can get rewards.
**Missing Share Report in $\Pi_{mod}$:** Any recipients failing to get the original secret recovered can adopt the following steps to submit a missing share report:
2. In case $R_i$ fails to verify the reconstructed $R_i$, $R_i$ submits a request to $S$.
3. $S$ then publishes the recruitment relationship.
4. $R_i$ verifies the shares one by one by checking the original hash of shares published by $S$.
5. $R_i$ reports the misbehavior trustees and aborts the current service ahead of time.

---

# 5 Security Analysis

In this section, we analyze the security of *CTDRB* from the following aspects:

**Collusion Attacks Among the Recipients:** As we mention in Sect. 3.2, after getting the published time token, the set of recipients may perform collusion misbehavior in such a way that the colluding recipients pool their secret keys together to forge a new secret key associated with a satisfying attribute set to decrypt the data. Due to the construction in $TAFC.KeyGen$, each user's $sk_{\mathcal{A}_i}$ corresponding to the attribute set $\mathcal{A}_i$ is associated with a secure random number. Such a number will be adopted in the $TAFC.Decryption$ phase. In case an adversary tries to combine different secret keys coming from different sets of attributes to forge a new secret key, the forged one will render a different random number. Even though the collusion behavior may acquire a satisfying attribute set, the wrong random number will lead to a failed decryption. Therefore, by seamless adopting $TAFC$, $CTDRB$ is resistant to the collusion attacks among the recipients.

**Data Confidentiality:** In *CTDRB*, we prevent the time token release-ahead attack by anonymizing the recruitment relationship of the selected trustees. Though such a countermeasure sets a barrier to the adversary, is it important to quantitatively measure the protection effectiveness of the scheme. We provide the details of our analysis, we highlight the key settings first. We assume that there are totally $N$ registered trustees in the smart contract $\mathcal{SC}$. The secret share scheme $sss(t, n)$, determined by the sender, has two fixed parameters, $t$ and $n$. We also have the ordered relationship $t \leq n < N$. With our rational adversarial setting of the trustees, we assume that the deposit of each trustee is denoted as $d$. By following the common attack strategy in [18], we consider the attack approach, namely bribery attack [18]. Such an attack is launched by the adversary by deploying a bribery contract to tempt each trustee to disclose his/her share.

**Resilience to Bribery Attack:** We analyze the resilience in terms of capturing the success probability of such an attack. Given a determined secret share scheme $sss(t, n)$, the notion of authorized sets refers to the set of parties that are able to reconstruct the original secret. In $sss(t, n)$, any set of trustees consisting of at least $t$ members is an authorized set. Without loss of generality, in $TE$, we capture the collection, namely $\mathcal{TE}_t$, of all the subsets of $TE$ consisting of at least $t$ trustees, as follows: $\mathcal{TE}_t = \{TE' \subseteq \{te_1, te_2, ..., te_n\} : |TE'| \geq t\}$. We also denote $n(TE')$ as the number of the subsets of $TE$ that consists of at least $t$ trustees. Hence, $n(\mathcal{TE}_t) = \sum_{i=t}^{n} \binom{n}{i} \leq 2^n$. In our scheme, $\mathcal{TE}_t$ is the target collection which the adversary aims for. Bribing any one set involved in $\mathcal{TE}_t$ can render the bribery attack successful. However, due to our anonymization design, from the list in $\mathcal{SC}$ consisting of all registered trustees, the adversary cannot distinguish which trustees are selected. We assume that there are totally $N$ registered trustees. Thus, the number of the subset of $N$ registered trustees is $2^N$. The attack success probability is then defined as a function in $N$, where $p(N) = \frac{n(\mathcal{TE}_t)}{2^N}$. Since $f(N) = 2^{-N}$ is negligible and $n(\mathcal{TE}_t)$ is a constant, $p(N)$ is also negligible. Therefore, our anonymization design renders the success probability of the bribery attack very small and negligible.

# 6  Evaluations

We discuss the details of our implementation and evaluation in this section. We start by describing the key implementations adopted in our framework in Sect. 6.1. We first provide detailed smart contract implementations with gas cost in Sect. 6.2.1. Then, in Sect. 6.2.2, we discuss the extensive case studies we performed.

## 6.1 Implementations and Environment

We implement the cryptographic constructions of *TAFC* in *Charm* [8], a cryptographic library implemented in *Python* [5]. For the secret sharing operation, we adopt the shamir's secret sharing implemented in *Charm*. We adopt the *Keccak256* hash implementation in *Web3.py* [6]. For the digital signature, we use the *ECDSA* implementation supported by *Web3.py*.

We use *Brownie* [1] to provide an interactive environment to work with *Ethereum*. Specifically, in *Brownie*, we implement the design of $\mathcal{SC}$ in *Solidity* [7], a smart contract oriented programming language supported by *Ethereum*. We create multiple accounts in *Brownie* acting as the sender $S$, the set of recipients $\mathcal{R}$, as well as the set of trustees $TE$. For IPFS, we employ Infura [3] to use the service.

## 6.2 Evaluations

### 6.2.1 Smart Contract Implementation

**Table 1.** Key functions & gas cost

| Protocol | Step | Function | Gas cost |
|---|---|---|---|
| Service Initialization | $\Pi_{init}.3$ | *deployment* | 665964 |
| | $\Pi_{init}.3$ | *newService* | 132024 |
| T2CS Setup | $\Pi_{setup}.12.c$ | *setOriHash* | 106864 |
| | $\Pi_{setup}.12.c$ | *submitCDPointer* | 42707 |
| | $\Pi_{setup}.12.c$ | *submitCTKPointer* | 42706 |
| T2CS Enforcement | $\Pi_{mod}.1$ | *modifyReleaseTime* | 28149 |
| | $\Pi_{rvk}.6$ | *submitDeletionEvidence* | 63117 |
| | $\Pi_{mod}.7$ | *submitShare* | 41757 |
| | $\Pi_{mod}.7$ | *submitShareSignature* | 24781 |
| | $\Pi_{poa}.5.b$ | *reportUnavailableShare* | 41021 |
| Service Audit | $\Pi_{aud}.1$ | *cheatingDeletionReport* | 43594 |
| | $\Pi_{aud}.3$ | *publishRelationship* | 63684 |
| | $\Pi_{aud}.5$ | *missingShareReport* | 42860 |
| Others | - | *trusteeRegistration* | 78121 |
| | - | *reward* | 41213 |
| | - | *stateTransition* | 21042 |

In Table 1, we show our implemented functions with corresponding gas cost in the smart contract. Gas cost is a key metric to economically measure the cost-effectiveness of a deployed smart contract. By analyzing the table, we observe that there are three functions, *deployment* (665964), *newService* (132024), as well as *setOriHash* (106864), incurring a relatively higher gas cost in comparison with the others. Since such functions will only be invoked once for each timed data release service, their gas cost is a one-time cost.

Next, we highlight the key functions associated with the data revocation primitive as well as the data modification primitive: **Data Revocation:** The function invocations of the data revocation primitive consist of the following scenarios: (1) If no unavailable share and no cheating proof-of-deletion behavior exists, the revocation primitive involves *submitDeletionEvidence* and *stateTransition*; (2) In case of the existence of unavailable shares as well as cheating proof-of-deletion behaviors, the revocation primitive totally involves *submitDeletionEvidence, stateTransition*, as well as *reportUnavailableShare*. **Data Release Time Modification:** The function invocations of the data release time modification primitive consist of the following scenarios: (1) If no unavailable share and no missing share, the modification primitive involves *modifyReleaseTime, submitShare*, as well as *submitShareSignature*; In case of the existence of unavailable shares as well as missing shares, the primitive totally involves *modifyReleaseTime, submitShare, submitShareSignature, publishRelationship*, as well as *missingShareReport*.

### 6.2.2  Case Study

We perform case studies to investigate gas consumption for our data revocation as well as data release time modification primitives.

**Case 1-No Misbehavior:** In this case study, we assume that all the trustees honestly follow the T2CS service. The objective of this study is to study the gas consumption of the two primitives when selecting different number of trustees. We set the threshold $t$ of $sss(t, n)$ as $t = 8$ in this case study. In Fig. 3a, we observe that the gas cost incurred by the two control primitives linearly increases with the growing number of selected trustees. Such an observation follows our design, since in the data revocation protocol $\Pi_{rvk}$- step 6, the sender $S$ must guarantee that $(n - t + 1)$ trustees have performed proof-of-deletion and publish them on-chain; also, for the data modification protocol $\Pi_{mod}$-step-7, we require all the selected trustees to submit his/her share.

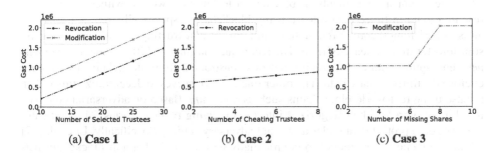

(a) **Case 1**          (b) **Case 2**          (c) **Case 3**

**Fig. 3.** Case study results

**Case 2-Cheating Proof-of-Deletion Existence:** In this case study, we study the impact of number of cheating trustees on the gas consumption of the data revocation primitive. We assume that all trustees have passed the proof-of-availability check. Also, we adopt $sss(8, 15)$ as the secret sharing scheme in this case. Figure 3b gives us the gas evaluation results. Specifically, we observe that the gas cost incurred by the data revocation primitive linearly grows with the increasing number of cheating trustees. Such an observation empirically validates our design in $\Pi_{aud}$ step-1, since the cheating behavior will trigger the auditing protocol when performing a data revocation primitive, in which anyone captures such a misbehavior prefers to report with $\mathcal{SC}$ to earn rewards. The rising number of cheating trustees renders an increasing number of invocations of *cheatingDeletionReport*, which inevitably incurs more gas cost.

**Case 3-Missing Share Existence:** In this case study, we study the impact of number of missing shares on the gas cost when performing a data release time primitive. We assume that all the selected trustees have passed the proof-of-availability check. Also, we adopt $sss$ $(8, 15)$ as the secret sharing scheme in this case. Figure 3c shows the evaluation results. The results show two interesting observations, which are described as follows: *first*, when the number of missing shares is less than the threshold $t$, say 2, 4, and 6, the gas cost of the data release time modification primitive does not grow with the increasing number of missing shares. Here also, this observation follows our design as the recipient can recover the $csk$ from the remaining shares, which will not trigger the auditing protocol; *second*, when we miss 8 shares, the gas cost dramatically increases. This empirical result validates our design in $\Pi_{aud}$ step-3 and step-5. Since the remaining shares cannot recover $csk$, $\Pi_{aud}$ will be triggered. The sender $S$ will publish the relationship on $\mathcal{SC}$ in terms of issuing transactions, which causes more gas cost. Moreover, when we miss 10 shares, the gas cost remains the same. This observation is attributed to the number of the invocations of $publishRelationship$ that only relies on the total number of selected trustees.

# 7    Related Work

## 7.1    Timed Data Release Using Blockchains

With the recent advancements in blockchain techniques, we are witnessing a rising research trend in timed data release using blockchains. Specifically, one line of work aims at enriching theoretic foundations in terms of constructing elegant cryptographic solutions for timed release of time. The techniques outlined in [20–22] incorporate witness encryption with cryptographic puzzles constructed from blockchains to securely enclose the timed-release data. The other line of work strives to decentralize timed data release using real-world blockchains such as *Ethereum*. Based on adversarial contexts, this line of work can be categorized into the following two categories. The first category seeks to protect data under a rational adversary setting. Specifically, Li et al. [17] adopted a game theory model to contractually enforce the Ethereum blockchain networks to behave honestly in a timed data release service. As a concurrent work, Ning et al. [24] proposed a provable cryptographic construction to guarantee the protection of the data with the help of Shamir's threshold secret share scheme and smart contracts.

By considering a potential attack launched by a data sender, the techniques developed by Bacis et al. [10] incorporated secure multiparty computation with the *Ethereum* smart contracts to jointly perform data protection. Recently, SilentDelivery [18] suggested a novel design to realize anonymity and scalability in blockchain-based timed data release. Recent work also has investigated a mixed adversarial environment, where both fully malicious adversaries as well as fully rational adversaries exist. Specifically, Wang et al. [32,33] proposed a reputation-aware timed data release protocol on top of Ethereum to achieve high attack resilience in a mixed adversarial environment. All the current techniques, however, only focus on the issue of data protection. In contrast, our proposed work in this paper augments the existing blockchain-based timed data release techniques with practically controllable primitives.

### 7.2 Temporal-Aware Data Control in Public Outsourced Environments

There have been several efforts on supporting temporal data controls in outsourced environments. The first line of work focuses on realizing data lifetime control in untrusted storage environment, namely *assured file deletion*. Such a notion starts from the design [26] proposed by Perlman, which theoretically constructs a system that manually specifies the expiry time of a file and permanently deletes it after the expiry time with the help of public key infrastructure [25]. FADE [30], proposed by Tang et al., further generalizes the primitive in [26] as *policy-based file assured deletion* in real-world storage platforms. Specifically, such a design specifies policy to regulate file lifetime and assured file deletion request. The work presented in [31] enrich this design with access control by using CP-ABE [12]. Our work differs from this line of work along the following two aspects: (i) unlike prior work that focused on the assured deletion primitive, the proposed work focuses on the timed data release scheme and (ii) while prior work on data lifetime control primitive assumed a centralized key management service, we note that it is impractical in a decentralized blockchain environment. Therefore, directly adopting such prior techniques to perform data lifetime control in our blockchain-based timed data release framework is infeasible. (2) The second line of work enhances cloud-based applications with temporal-aware access control primitives. Specifically, Zhu et al. [36] developed temporal access control by adopting cryptographic integer comparisons and proxy re-encryption encryption scheme. LoTAC [9] enables location and time-based access control on cloud-stored data with the help of ElGamal encryption and tag-based encryption, which specifically grants access to data by considering the location as well as time information of a user. Adopting CP-ABE [12] to realize temporal-aware access control is proposed in [14,15,19,23,34,35], where time is treated as an attribute in CP-ABE. This line of work, however, only focused on enabling data access control with temporal-related constraints. Such techniques fail to meet our joint objective of data lifetime control and data access control.

## 8   Conclusion

In this paper, we propose *CTDRB*, a controllable timed data release framework using blockchains, which offers both data access control as well as data lifetime control while protecting the confidentiality of the data. With the help of TAFC, a variant ciphertext-policy attribute-based encryption construction, we realize the data access control in *CTDRB*. We implement data lifetime control by designing a time token control service on Ethereum. On top of such a design, two representative data lifetime control primitives namely, data revocation and data release time modification are carefully designed. Our security analysis demonstrates the attack resilience of *CTDRB*. We prototype *CTDRB* by implementing smart contracts on Ethereum and perform gas cost evaluations. By performing case studies under various service conditions, we demonstrate that our data lifetime control primitives incur only a modest gas cost.

**Acknowledgement.** This material is based upon work supported by the National Science Foundation under Grant #2020071. Any opinions, findings, and conclusions or recommendations expressed in this material are those of the author(s) and do not necessarily reflect the views of the National Science Foundation.

# References

1. Brownie. https://eth-brownie.readthedocs.io/en/stable/
2. Ethereum. https://ethereum.org/en/
3. Infura. https://infura.io/
4. Kimono: trustless secret sharing using time-locks on ethereum. https://github.com/hillstreetlabs/kimono
5. Python. https://www.python.org/
6. A python interface for interacting with the ethereum blockchain and ecosystem. https://github.com/ethereum/web3.py
7. Solidity. https://docs.soliditylang.org/en/v0.8.10/
8. Akinyele, J.A., et al.: Charm: a framework for rapidly prototyping cryptosystems. J. Cryptographic Eng. **3**(2), 111–128 (2013)
9. Androulaki, E., Soriente, C., Malisa, L., Capkun, S.: Enforcing location and time-based access control on cloud-stored data. In: 2014 IEEE 34th International Conference on Distributed Computing Systems, pp. 637–648. IEEE (2014)
10. Bacis, E., Facchinetti, D., Guarnieri, M., Rosa, M., Rossi, M., Paraboschi, S.: I told you tomorrow: practical time-locked secrets using smart contracts. In: The 16th International Conference on Availability, Reliability and Security, ARES 2021, New York, NY, USA. Association for Computing Machinery (2021)
11. Benet, J.: IPFs-content addressed, versioned, p2p file system. arXiv preprint arXiv:1407.3561 (2014)
12. Bethencourt, J., Sahai, A., Waters, B.: Ciphertext-policy attribute-based encryption. In: 2007 IEEE Symposium on Security and Privacy (SP 2007), pp. 321–334. IEEE (2007)
13. Hao, F., Clarke, D., Zorzo, A.F.: Deleting secret data with public verifiability. IEEE Trans. Dependable Secure Comput. **13**(6), 617–629 (2016)
14. Hong, J., et al.: TAFC: time and attribute factors combined access control for time-sensitive data in public cloud. IEEE Trans. Serv. Comput. **13**(1), 158–171 (2017)
15. Huang, Q., Yang, Y., Fu, J.: Secure data group sharing and dissemination with attribute and time conditions in public cloud. IEEE Trans. Serv. Comput. **14**, 1013–1025 (2018)
16. Jiang, P., Qiu, B., Zhu, L.: Toward reliable and confidential release for smart contract via id-based TRE. IEEE Internet Things J. **9**(13), 11422–11433 (2022)

17. Li, C., Palanisamy, B.: Decentralized release of self-emerging data using smart contracts. In: 2018 IEEE 37th Symposium on Reliable Distributed Systems (SRDS), pp. 213–220. IEEE (2018)
18. Li, C., Palanisamy, B.: SilentDelivery: practical timed-delivery of private information using smart contracts. IEEE Trans. Serv. Comput. (to appear)
19. Li, Y., Dong, Z., Sha, K., Jiang, C., Wan, J., Wang, Y.: TMO: time domain outsourcing attribute-based encryption scheme for data acquisition in edge computing. IEEE Access **7**, 40240–40257 (2019)
20. Liu, J., Garcia, F., Ryan, M.: Time-release protocol from bitcoin and witness encryption for sat. Korean Circulation J. **40**(10), 530–535 (2015)
21. Liu, J., Jager, T., Kakvi, S.A., Warinschi, B.: How to build time-lock encryption. Des. Codes Crypt. **86**(11), 2549–2586 (2018)
22. Liu, J., Kakvi, S.A., Warinschi, B.: Extractable witness encryption and timed-release encryption from bitcoin. IACR Cryptology ePrint Archive, 2015:482 (2015)
23. Liu, Z., Jiang, Z.L., Wang, X., Yiu, S.-M., Zhang, R., Wu, Y.: A temporal and spatial constrained attribute-based access control scheme for cloud storage. In: 2018 17th IEEE International Conference on Trust, Security And Privacy In Computing and Communications/12th IEEE International Conference on Big Data Science and Engineering (TrustCom/BigDataSE), pp. 614–623. IEEE (2018)
24. Ning, J., Dang, H., Hou, R., Chang, E.-C.: Keeping time-release secrets through smart contracts. IACR Cryptology ePrint Archive, p. 1166 (2018)
25. Perlman, R.: The ephemerizer: Making data disappear (2005)
26. Perlman, R.: File system design with assured delete. In: Third IEEE International Security in Storage Workshop (SISW 2005), p. 6. IEEE (2005)
27. Rivest, R.L., Shamir, A., Wagner, D.A.: Time-lock puzzles and timed-release crypto (1996)
28. Shamir, A.: How to share a secret. Commun. ACM **22**(11), 612–613 (1979)
29. Szabo, N.: Formalizing and securing relationships on public networks. First Monday (1997)
30. Tang, Y., Lee, P.P.C., Lui, J.C.S., Perlman, R.: FADE: secure overlay cloud storage with file assured deletion. In: Jajodia, S., Zhou, J. (eds.) SecureComm 2010. LNICST, vol. 50, pp. 380–397. Springer, Heidelberg (2010). https://doi.org/10.1007/978-3-642-16161-2_22
31. Tang, Y., Lee, P.P.C., Lui, J.C.S., Perlman, R.: Secure overlay cloud storage with access control and assured deletion. IEEE Trans. Dependable Secure Comput. **9**(6), 903–916 (2012)
32. Wang, J., Palanisamy, B.: Attack-resilient blockchain-based decentralized timed data release. In: 36th Annual IFIP WG 11.3 Conference on Data and Applications Security and Privacy (DBSec2022) (2022, to appear)
33. Wang, J., Palanisamy, B.: Protecting blockchain-based decentralized timed release of data from malicious adversaries. In: 2022 IEEE International Conference on Blockchain and Cryptocurrency (2022)
34. Xia, Q., et al.: TSLS: time sensitive, lightweight and secure access control for information centric networking. In: 2019 IEEE Global Communications Conference (GLOBECOM), pp. 1–6. IEEE (2019)
35. Yang, K., Liu, Z., Jia, X., Shen, X.S.: Time-domain attribute-based access control for cloud-based video content sharing: a cryptographic approach. IEEE Trans. Multimedia **18**(5), 940–950 (2016)
36. Zhu, Y., Hu, H., Ahn, G.-J., Huang, D., Wang, S.: Towards temporal access control in cloud computing. In: 2012 Proceedings IEEE INFOCOM, pp. 2576–2580. IEEE (2012)

# FairBlock: Preventing Blockchain Front-Running with Minimal Overheads

Peyman Momeni[1]($\boxtimes$), Sergey Gorbunov[1,2], and Bohan Zhang[1]

[1] University of Waterloo, Waterloo, Canada
{pmomeni,sgorbunov,bohan.zhang}@uwaterloo.ca
[2] Axelar Network, Waterloo, Canada

**Abstract.** While blockchain systems are quickly gaining popularity, front-running remains a major obstacle to fair exchange. In this paper, we show how to apply identity-based encryption (IBE) to prevent front-running with minimal bandwidth overheads. In our approach, to decrypt a block of $N$ transactions, the number of messages sent across the network only grows linearly with the size of decrypting committees, $S$. That is, to decrypt a set of $N$ transactions sequenced at a specific block, a committee only needs to exchange $S$ decryption shares (independent of $N$). In comparison, previous solutions are based on threshold decryption schemes, where each transaction in a block must be decrypted separately by the committee, resulting in bandwidth overhead of $N \times S$. Along the way, we present a model for fair block processing and build a prototype implementation. We show that on a sample of 1000 messages with 1000 validators our system saves 42.53 MB of bandwidth which is 99.6% less compared with the standard threshold decryption paradigm.

**Keywords:** Blockchain · Front-running · DeFi · Identity-based encryption · Smart contract · Security

## 1 Introduction

Maximal (or Miner) Extractable Value (MEV) is one of the central problems that prevent fairness [39,70] and trust in decentralized exchanges and other decentralized applications (dApps) [5,24,29,52,71]. MEV allows a block proposer to influence the order of transactions to extract some "value" for themselves before they are executed by the application. By rearranging the order, the block proposer may inject extra transactions to extract profit. For example, if the block proposer sees a transaction $Tx_{org}$ that tries to buy an asset from a decentralized exchange, it may include another transaction $Tx_f$ (or a sequence of transactions) in the block that first buys the asset and then sells it to the sender in $Tx_{org}$ for a higher fee.

MEV is defined as the revenue other than transaction fees and block rewards which can be extracted by reordering, censoring, and adding transactions in blocks [5,24,29,52,71]. MEV is present on any blockchain infrastructure that includes a party that is responsible for transaction ordering such as miners in

© ICST Institute for Computer Sciences, Social Informatics and Telecommunications Engineering 2023
Published by Springer Nature Switzerland AG 2023. All Rights Reserved
F. Li et al. (Eds.): SecureComm 2022, LNICST 462, pp. 250–271, 2023.
https://doi.org/10.1007/978-3-031-25538-0_14

Ethereum [67], validators in Cosmos [22], or sequencers in Layer 2 solutions such as roll-ups [42,46]. Most of the extracted MEV happens in the form of a front-running attack whereby a party other than the block proposer itself closely observes the submitted transactions to the public mempool and exploits this information to detect profitable opportunities such as arbitrages, liquidations, and mispriced non-fungible tokens (NFT). After detecting them, the adversary makes sure that their profitable transaction will be executed in a high order by offering a high transaction fee to the block proposer or any party that is responsible for ordering. They do so by submitting it either in the public mempool or a private backchannel. Lower-bound estimates show that sophisticated bots and their affiliated miners are making up to 5M USD in 24 h with the total amount of over 607M USD million from 2020 to date just in the Ethereum network [42,50,67]. These attacks lead to serious problems such as high gas fees, network congestion, and even consensus instability [24].

Threshold decryption schemes are one of the most promising and well-known methods to prevent front-running [17,32]. The idea was proposed in 1994 [51], and recently explored by blockchain projects such as Sikka, F3, and Anoma [2, 32,58,69]. In this approach, every transaction sent to the blockchain is first encrypted by the user using a global public key. A committee of decryptors (e.g. validators or set of users) holds shares of the corresponding private key. After a block of encrypted transactions is finalized and sequenced by the consensus layer, they collectively decrypt each transaction in a block to see its cleartext values. Subsequently, the transactions must be executed in the order in which they were finalized prior to the decryption. It is easy to see that this mechanism solves many forms of front-running attacks: the validators must finalize a block of encrypted transactions and fix their order, they cannot see the information in them, and hence it is much harder for them to influence the outcome.

While this approach may be used to solve the problem, it introduces significant bandwidth overheads on the network. To be more specific, due to the high cost of distributed key generation process, decryption should happen without revealing private key shares. Consequently, for each encrypted transaction in a block, every committee member must propagate a separate decryption share, and a designated individual can aggregate decryption shares to reveal the transaction. For a $N$-transactions block and $S$-members committee, this results in decryption complexity of $N \times S$ broadcast messages. As an example, for $N = 1000$ transactions of size 64 bytes, $S = 1000$ of validators with a two-thirds honest majority, this adds an extra 42.7 MB of traffic on the network. This increases the bandwidth required to process transactions non-linearly resulting in significant scalability constraints. We refer the reader to Sect. 2 for limitations of other front-running prevention mechanisms.

## 1.1   Our Contributions

In this work, we construct a front-running protection protocol with minimal bandwidth overheads – linear in the number of users or validators called keepers. Our construction, called FairBlock, is based on well-studied cryptographic assumptions. In particular, the scheme is based on identity-based encryption where one can exploit the linearity and secret sharing of the IBE private keys [9,19,56]. In FairBlock, a committee composed of keepers that run a distributed key generation (DKG) [33,48] protocol to generate a shared master key $msk$ associated with a system-wide master public key $mpk$ for an IBE scheme. Next, we associate each block identifier $h$ with an IBE "identity". Consequently, clients can commit to their transactions by encrypting their information with $mpk$ and identity for a future block $h$ (or a range of blocks). Validators run the consensus and sequence all encrypted transactions in a block. Finally, to decrypt the block with minimal overheads, each keeper $k$ (a) computes a share $b_h^k$ of the private key $b_h$ (named block key) for the IBE identity corresponding to block $h$, and (b) broadcasts it over the blockchain. After sufficiently many keepers propagated their shares $b_h^k$, anyone can perform the key extraction process to obtain the private key $b_h$ that allows decryption of all transactions encrypted under identity $h$ with no further communication. In FairBlock, another set consists of users or validators named "relayers" (which can overlap with keepers) is responsible for key extraction and decryption. The original sender of the transaction can also reveal the plaintext transaction without block key extraction and decryption to avoid paying fees.

FairBlock is a general solution that can be applied to all smart contract blockchains. The scheme is practical and can be applied in real systems as IBE constructions that support the linearity properties that we leverage are efficient. FairBlock does not have basic commit-reveal challenges, which can facilitate denial of service attacks, whereby a client commits to a transaction and reveal it later only if subsequent transactions make it profitable [17,29].

Compared to the solutions [18,27,40,65] that leverage time-lock puzzles [7], we do not introduce significant delays or high computational complexity in decryption. Moreover, our work does not rely on secure enclaves [68] to realize a private pool [60]. Unlike the standard threshold decryption approach, FairBlock bandwidth overhead is minimal as the number of messages in this system grows linearly with the number of keepers.

## 1.2    Paper Organization

The remainder of the paper is organized as follows. In Sect. 2, we describe related works and their limitations. In Sect. 3, we review the cryptographic building blocks of FairBlock and define blockchain front-running. In Sect. 4, we present our security model, followed by describing FairBlock protocol and details of our architecture. Section 5 describes our prototype implementation and evaluation. We also indicate future research directions and challenges in Sect. 6, before concluding in Sect. 7.

## 2    Related Works

Several academic works and projects have attempted to either limit or prevent front-running. For instance, Flashbots [24] has mitigated front-running and bidding war consequences such as high gas fees and network congestion with a private channel for front-runners to make bids directly to miners through relayers. However, relayers and white-listed miners in this approach have full access to the transaction content in clear which makes it prone to front-running and censorship. LibSubmarine [12] conceals the transaction among other similar transactions by locking the amount of the transaction to a generated address that is indistinguishable from an address that has not been used on Ethereum previously. However, the security of this solution is not based on strong cryptographic assumptions, and also the contents of the transactions are still in plaintext and prone to front-running.

DEXes and AMMs [1,61], as the main target of front-running [5,42] have tried to limit front-running consequences such as transactions failure and gas waste using slippage. This approach has interestingly led to near-guaranteed sandwich attacks by taking a deal and selling it again to the buyer with a higher price to the maximum extent that slippage allows. CowSwap [23] protects DEX users from sandwich attacks by matching simultaneous users off-chain, whenever a user is buying an asset and another is selling the same asset. Currently, this approach is limited as it cannot prevent general front-running on transactions in the public mempool.

Recent projects including Secret Network [44] and Fairy [60] leverage secure enclaves namely Intel SGX [68] to build private mempools at the cost of potential latency, storage limits, and security risks due to several successful recent attacks on secure enclaves [53,64]. The basic commit-reveal approach relies on clients to reveal their transactions after the finalization of the commitment phase which leads to connectivity issues, and denial-of-service attacks (selective revealing based on the market output). As a way to address basic commit-reveal issues, time-lock encryption [18,27,40,49] relies on the secure implementation of verifiable delay functions (VDF) [7] and time-lock puzzles at the expense of long delays between transaction inclusion and execution e.g. 3 or 7 min delay in VeedDo implementation by Starkware [65].

Shutter Network [57] leverages threshold decryption and distributed key generation as their tools to prevent front-running by generating a private key for each epoch but additional research is needed to validate their cryptographic protocols. Projects such as Ferveo [32], Sikka [58], Helix [2], and F3 [69] employ threshold decryption with high communication overhead as decryption of every single message requires all members of the decryption committee to send their partial decryption shares.

# 3    Background

## 3.1    Cryptographic Preliminaries

**Identity-Based Encryption.** An identity-based encryption (IBE) [9,19,56] allows to establish a global master key in the system that can be used to derive identity-specific public keys (and associated private keys). For instance, it enables a sender, Alice, to encrypt a message for receiver Bob using his identifier information such as email address, phone number, and IP address. The receiver Bob, having obtained a private key associated with his identity information from Trusted Third Party (TTP), can decrypt the ciphertext. An IBE scheme consists of a tuple of algorithms: *Setup*, *Extract*, *Encrypt*, and *Decrypt* satisfying the following semantics:

- *Setup*($1^\lambda$): On input corresponding to the security parameter $\lambda$, the setup algorithm outputs a master key $msk$ and its associated master public key $mpk$ which is publicly known.

- *Encrypt*($mpk, ID, m$): On input of the master public key $mpk$, an identity $ID$ and a message $m$, the encryption algorithm outputs a ciphertext $C$.

- *Extract*($ID, msk$): On input of the master key $msk$ and identity $ID$, the extraction algorithm returns a private key $d_{ID}$ for user with identity $ID$.

- *Decrypt*($d_{ID}, C$): On input of the private key $d_{ID}$ and ciphertext $C$, the decryption algorithm recovers the plaintext message $m$.

We build FairBlock using an IBE that is semantically secure under the BDH assumption in a random-oracle model [9]. In particular, we use the Boneh-Franklin IBE [9]. Our construction will use an IBE in a non-black box way and exploit two common properties. Other IBE schemes [8,41] may also be used assuming they satisfy these two properties:

1. Support efficient distributed key generation (DKG) protocols.
2. Support linear homomorphic operations over the private keys for identities. That is, given a share of a master key, one should be able to compute a share of the corresponding private key for any identity $ID$, such that given a collection of shares, anyone can extract the private key for $ID$.

The central TTP in the described IBE algorithms is a single point of failure and contradictory to the distributed nature of blockchains. As suggested in [9], Shamir's secret sharing (SSS) [55] technique can replace the TTP by distributing the shares of $msk$ among a group of keepers with an honest majority. In this work, we show how to employ a distributed key generation [48] to eliminate the trusted dealer in SSS to achieve complete decentralization.

**Cryptographic Commitment.** In order to ensure that transactions cannot be modified, censored, or added after decryption by relayers, our protocol should verify that decrypted transactions are in fact the ones that have been encrypted. To realize this, we have leveraged a basic non-interactive hash-based commitment [11,37,43] with computational binding and hiding properties in the random oracle model based on a collision-resistant hash function $H_c$. The hiding property is vital for our commitment scheme, as an adversary should not acquire any information about the transaction. We also need binding, so a relayer cannot submit a different transaction with the correct commitment to censor the original transaction. The simple and efficient hash-based cryptographic commitment in this work can be replaced with more advanced commitment schemes [36,37,47] with stronger security guarantees.

## 3.2 Blockchain Front-Running

In this paper, we define blockchain front-running as follows:

**Definition 1.** *Blockchain front-running is a family of strategies in which a malicious party directly or indirectly manipulates the order of transactions in a blockchain architecture such that a transaction $tx_2$ which is broadcasted in time $t_2$ executes before the transaction of victim $tx_1$ which is broadcasted in time $t_1$ where $t_1 < t_2$.*

In practice, front-runners may be the parties who are responsible for sequencing transactions themselves including miners, validators, roll-up providers, or relayers. Alternatively, front-runners may indirectly influence the order of transaction by offering high tips (gas price) to block proposers, performing attacks in the network layer such as DDOS attacks, or utilizing high-speed networks similar to high-frequency traders in traditional financial markets. Typically, front-runners such as sophisticated bots actively listen to pending transactions in the public mempool or in the peer-to-peer network to exploit the revealed (but not executed) information of transactions to make profits by broadcasting a transaction and front-running the victim's transaction to capture the opportunity. This form of front-running attacks significantly increases the cost of transaction fees for normal users, unfairly steal many profitable opportunities, and makes the user experience much more complex and slow by failing the victim's transaction. Front-running and MEV-related transactions can also result in significant network congestion. For instance, Bank for International Settlements [3] has reported that up to one out of thirty transactions in Ethereum blocks from 2020 to 2022 were included for MEV extraction purposes. Moreover, several works in the literature [24,29,46] have also discussed the potential threat of front-running attacks to the consensus mechanism of blockchain networks due to the high profitability of these opportunities which incentivize some players such as miners to sabotage the whole network. We refer the reader to Appendix A for a summary on the nature of front-running attacks.

## 4    FairBlock

In this section, we formalize the security model in Sect. 4.1, present FairBlock's architecture in Sect. 4.2, and finally prove the correctness and security of the protocol in Sects. 4.3 and 4.4.

## 4.1   Model

**Players.** In this protocol, we define three types of players:

- **Users:** Parties who wish to communicate with a target smart contract without being front-runned. Users submit a transaction containing their encrypted message e.g. trading information to our system.
- **Keepers:** Parties that are responsible for generating a distributed secret key and submitting their shares for each block key. Keepers set can be composed of any parties in the network including users, consensus validators, decentralized oracle networks (DON) [17], or decentralized autonomous organizations (DAO) [25].
- **Relayers:** Parties that are responsible for aggregating block key shares, computing block keys, and decrypting committed transactions. Relayers set can be composed of users, keepers, consensus validators, decentralized oracle networks (DON) [17], or decentralized autonomous organizations (DAO) [25]. In practice, keepers can also play the relayers' role; however, we have defined an independent set to highlight the fact that they can be a very large group competing to decrypt transactions. Also, even just a single honest party e.g. the next block proposer would suffice.

**Setup.** In our protocol, a set of $n$ keepers $P = \{P_1, P_2, ..., P_n\}$ generate a shared master key $msk$ and a system-wide public key $mpk$. Users pick a desired block identifier $h$ as the $ID$ of the block (or range of blocks) in which their encrypted transaction should be executed without being front-runned.

Assume that the associated groups of a symmetric bilinear pairing, $\mathbb{G}_1$ and $\mathbb{G}_T$ have order $q$, that is, the pairing is $\hat{e} \colon \mathbb{G}_1 \times \mathbb{G}_1 \to \mathbb{G}_T$. Two cryptographic hash functions $H_1$ and $H_2$ are also used. $H_1$ maps block identifier $h \in \{0,1\}^*$ to $\mathbb{G}_1$, and $H_2$ maps $\mathbb{G}_T$ to transaction information $t_x$ of bitlength $l_1$. Additionally, a collision-resistant hash function $H_c$ is used for the cryptographic commitment. Also assume that a generator $g \in \mathbb{G}_1$ is available to all entities.

**Threat Model.** We assume that the adversary is computationally bounded and our cryptographic schemes including IBE, DKG, and Commitments are secure. In this work, we work with an honest majority assumption on the keepers. That is, an adversary controls at most $t$ keepers, whereas a collaboration of $t + 1$ keepers is required to extract the block key and also the presence of at least one honest relayer is necessary to perform decryption. Assuming that keepers are running Pedersen's DKG [48] protocol, the adversary must control at most $t \leq \frac{n-1}{2}$ keepers. In the case of consensus-level implementation, the underlying BFT-style [13] consensus algorithm may enforce a two-thirds honest majority assumption. In this case, the adversary must control at most $t \leq \frac{n-1}{3}$ keepers' shares as consensus validators also play keepers' roles. A party controlled by the adversary may deviate arbitrarily from the specified protocol. We consider an adaptive adversary, in the sense that it can decide which parties to corrupt at any point during the protocol execution.

**Correctness.** Our construction should also satisfy correctness. We define this property as follows: Given a sequence of encrypted transactions submitted by the users, every player should be able to learn the cleartext transactions and their correct execution order after the block key reconstruction phase.

**Security Model.** We now describe a security model that captures the notion of fairness. In essence, it states that no adversary that controls less than the corruption threshold of parties can influence the order or censor transactions in the system. We follow the formal notion of fairness in recent works [17,39,70] and aim to provide fairness by satisfying both order-fairness and secure causality preservation [15,28]. Order-fairness requires that if a large fraction of nodes $\gamma$ receive $T_1$ before $T_2$, then $T_1$ should not be executed after $T_2$. We refer the reader to [17,39,70] for further formal discussion and technical detail of order-fairness. Also, the security conditions of secure causality-preservation [15,28] require formally that no information about a transaction becomes known before the finalization of its order in the block. Until that time, the system must not reveal any information to an adversary in a cryptographically strong sense. In Sect. 4.4, we show how FairBlock satisfies both secure causality-preservation and order-fairness.

## 4.2 Protocol

In this section, we show how to apply FairBlock to any dApp by adding special-purpose smart contracts to the system. However, one can similarly apply Fair-Block at the consensus level, where keepers and relayers are replaced by the validators that maintain the shared master key and contribute to the decryption on chain [32,58]. We will further discuss consensus-level Implementation.

**Smart Contracts.** To implement FairBlock using smart contracts as the communication layer, we introduce five smart contracts:

1. Participate(dep, val): This contract keeps track of keeper and relayers sets. It may also lock security deposits $dep$ and the value of an encrypted transaction $val$ so it can be transferred to the target contract.
2. DKG($m_{DKG}$): During the distributed key generation protocol, keepers submit their broadcast messages $m_{DKG}$ and read others' from this contract. At the end of the protocol, it may also store the system-wide public key $mpk$ and other public system parameters, so users can read it and encrypt transactions.
3. Commit(enc($t_x$), $H_c(t_x)$): This contract stores received encrypted transactions $enc(t_x)$ and cryptographic commitments $H(t_x)$. The main purpose of this contract is to preserve the order of received transactions.
4. IBE($b_h^k$): This contract receives block key shares $b_h^k$ from each keeper $k$, so the relayer can aggregate them to construct the block key.

What follows is a brief description of FairBlock's architecture in six phases:

**Phase 0: Enrollment.** Keepers and relayers enroll in participating in the protocol by calling a function in Participate and sending an amount of deposit as an entry fee. Clients may also lock the value of their transaction in Participate, so the value could be automatically transferred to the target contract in the last phase.

**Phase 1: Distributed Key Generation.** Keepers generate a shared public key, and an associated shared master key split across all of them using a DKG protocol [48]. DKG protocols are generally slow as they typically require time quadratic in $n$ [38,48,62]; however, it only runs once in the setup phase and afterward very infrequently anytime the keepers set changes. Keepers set is expected to be stable as they are collecting rewards for their honest co-operation and being penalized for malicious behavior. The following is a brief description of Pedersen's DKG protocol [48]:

1. *Sharing:* Each keeper $P_i$ randomly picks a secret $s_i \in \mathbb{Z}_q^*$. Next, $P_i$ sets $a_{i0} = s_i$ and chooses a random polynomial $f_i(z)$ over $\mathbb{Z}_q^*$ of degree $t$ as follows:

$$f_i(z) = a_{i0} + a_{i1}z + \cdots + a_{it}z^t. \tag{1}$$

   $P_i$ broadcasts Feldman [31] commitments $A_{ik} = g^{a_{ik}}$ for $k \in [0, t]$ using DKG. $P_i$ computes the share $s_{ij} = f_i(j) \bmod q$ for $j$ in $[1, n]$ and sends $s_{ij}$ through secure private channels to $P_j$.
2. *Share Verification:* Each keeper $P_j$ verifies each received share $s_{ij}$ sent by $P_i$. To do so, $P_j$ checks Feldman's VSS [31] validity condition: $g^{s_{ij}} \stackrel{?}{=} \prod_{k=0}^{t} A_{ik}^{j^k}$.
3. *Dispute:* If $t$ or more keepers complain against a keeper $P_f$ by broadcasting the complaint on DKG, $P_f$ will be considered faulty and disqualified. Subsequently, $P_f$ can make a complaint and claim its honesty by revealing the share $s_{fv}$ for each complaining user $P_v$. If any of the revealed shares fails the check again, $P_f$ is disqualified.
4. *Public Key:* Assuming that $T$ is the set of qualified (not disqualified in the previous phase) keepers, the system-wide public key $mpk$ is computed as follows:

$$mpk = \prod_{i \in T} A_{i0} = \prod_{i \in T} g^{s_i}. \tag{2}$$

5. *Master Key Shares:* Each keeper $k \in T$ compute its master key share $w_k = \sum_{i \in T} s_{ik}$.

Although there is no need to reconstruct the $msk$ through our protocol, it is defined as sum of qualified keepers' secrets: $msk = \sum_{i \in T} s_i$. Note that secret $s_f$ for a disqualified keeper $P_f$ is set to zero.

**Phase 2: Encryption and Commitment.** Clients encrypt their message $m$ using public key $mpk$ for block identifier $h$. To encrypt transaction information $t_x \in \{0,1\}^{l_1}$, a client computes $Q_h = H_1(h)$ followed by selecting a random integer $r \in \mathbb{Z}_q^*$, and a random string $x \in \{0,1\}^{l_2}$. Afterward, it sets $m = t_x \| x$ and $R = g^r$ [9]. Having them, $U$ is calculated as follows:

$$U = m \oplus H_2(\hat{e}(Q_h, mpk)^r). \tag{3}$$

Finally, it submits a encrypted message $C = (R, U)$ alongside a commitment $H_c(m)$ to Commit.

**Phase 3: Broadcasting Block Key Shares.** At least $t + 1$ out of $n$ keepers compute their block key shares $b_h^k$ [9] and propagate it using IBE. Keeper $k$ computes its share for block $h$ as $b_h^k = H_1(h)^{w_k}$.

**Phase 4: Decryption.** Relayers compute the block key $b_h$ after receiving at least $t + 1$ valid shares from IBE. Next, they use $b_h$ to decrypt each of the encrypted messages for the block $h$. Relayers are incentivized to decrypt correctly as fast as possible by rewards for each correct decryption. Each Relayer can extract block key $b_h$ after the following steps:

1. *Share Verification:* Relayer verifies received shares $b_h^k$ from each keeper $k$ by checking the following condition [9]:

$$\hat{e}(\prod_{i=0}^{t} V_i^{k^i}, H_1(h)) \stackrel{?}{=} \hat{e}(g, b_h^k), \tag{4}$$

   where $V_i$s are public verification values for keepers $i \in [0, t]$ in the DKG protocol defined as $V_i = \prod_{k \in T} A_{ki}$.
2. *Block Key Extraction:* After verifying the shares, the block key for block $h$ is extracted as follows:

$$b_h = \prod_{k=1}^{t+1} (b_h^k)^{L_k}, \tag{5}$$

   where $L_k$s are proper Lagrange coefficients for point 0 defined as $L_k = \prod_{\substack{r=1 \\ r \neq k}}^{t+1} \frac{r}{r-k}$. The derived key $b_h$ is indeed the IBE key for identity $h$ that would have been extracted by the TTP. See Sect. 4.3 for correctness discussion.
3. *Decryption:* Let $C = (R, U)$ be the ciphertext for block identifier $h$. A Relayer decrypts $C$ using the private key $b_h$ as:

$$m = U \oplus H_2(\hat{e}(b_h, R)). \tag{6}$$

In the event that relayers are unable to include the decrypted transactions in the blockchain before or at the block specified in the commitments, an application-specific policy determines if the submitted encrypted transactions should fail or be decrypted in a later block. However, we expect that this case is very rare with a proper incentivization mechanism.

**Phase 5: Execution.** Given a list of decrypted messages $m_1, ..., m_n$, Process extracts $x$ and $t_x$ for each of the messages. Next, it checks the validity of each transaction $t_x$ e.g. user's balance in Participate which should be more than the transaction value. Finally, it verifies that a) none of the committed transactions is censored, b) all of them have been decrypted correctly, and c) their received order follows the specified ordering policy. This verification can be simply done by recomputing the cryptographic commitment for each of decrypted messages, and then reading previously submitted cryptographic commitments $H_c(m)$ from Commit for each of them. The verification can be done in a single step by computing the hash of all commitments as $H_c(m_1, \cdots, m_n)$ and comparing them. Finally, it executes the batch by calling the target contract for each of the decrypted transactions.

**Consensus-Level Implementation.** An alternative to using smart contracts as the communication layer is implementing FairBlock in the consensus layer [2, 58]. In this case, there will be no need to maintain sets of keepers and relayers, as the normal validators who are responsible for mining the blocks will also perform these tasks. To be more specific, validators receive private key shares in proportion to their stake and submit their block key shares as an extension to messages in the voting round in a BFT-style consensus algorithm [13]. Next, the next block proposer computes the block key by aggregating submitted shares, decrypting, and including the plaintext transaction in the next block.

Alternatively, validators can submit their block key shares as a message in the blockchain, and any other user can compute the block key and submit decrypted transactions as a message to collect rewards. Hash of submitted decryptions should be compared to the commitments which are previously sent alongside the encrypted transactions to verify the correctness of the block key extraction and decryption process. The original sender of the encrypted message is able to submit its plaintext transaction immediately without block key extraction and decryption in order to avoid system fees. In the event that the original sender is no longer online or refuses to reveal in time, other parties will compete to decrypt the transactions as soon as possible to collect rewards.

### 4.3 Correctness

Correctness follows by the linearity of secret sharing and IBE extraction algorithm. In particular, it is easy to see that shares of the private key can be reconstructed to obtain the IBE key. We refer the reader to Appendix B for correctness proof.

### 4.4 Security

**Secure Causality Preservation.** Assuming the honest majority of keepers described in Sect. 4.1, and at least one honest relayer, we show that our system satisfies causality-preservation based on the security of DKG and IBE schemes.

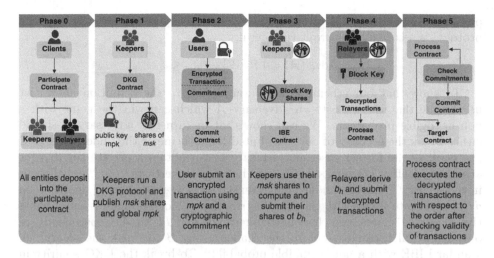

**Fig. 1.** Architecture of FairBlock

In particular, at the end of phase 1, the adversary cannot learn any information of the $msk$ given $t \leq \frac{n-1}{2}$ shares of the $msk$. Furthermore, given block keys $b_h$ for block identifiers $h \in S_h$, the adversary cannot learn about the block key of other block identifiers $h^* \notin S_h$ by the properties of IBE.

We prove security of FairBlock by defining a security game $G$ between a polynomially bounded adversary $\mathcal{A}$ controlling at most $t$ keepers and a challenger. The adversary's goal is to front-run a client, defined as being able to distinguish between two challenge encrypted messages containing transaction information. We define the security game as follows:

- The challenger runs DKG and IBE $Setup(1^\lambda)$ algorithm.
- The adversary receives shares of $msk$, $(w_1, ..., w_k)$ for $k \leq t$.
- The adversary computes $Encrypt(mpk, h, m)$ for arbitrary message $m$ and any block identifier $h \in S_h$.
- The adversary receives $q \leq n$ shares for the block key $b_h$.
- The adversary chooses two distinct message $m_0$, $m_1$, and a block identifier $h^* \notin S_h$ and sends them to the challenger.
- The challenger selects random bit $b$ and sends $C^* = Encrypt(mpk, h^*, m_b)$ to the adversary alongside up to $t - k$ shares of the block key $sk_{h^*}$. The number of received shares in this phase cannot be more than $t - k$, as the adversary can exploit its shares of $msk$ and extract additional $k$ shares for $sk_{h^*}$. In case of receiving more than $t - k$ shares of the challenge block key, the adversary can trivially extract the challenge block key by combining more than $t$ shares of $sk_{h^*}$ shares.
- The adversary can still query the oracle to get $q \leq n$ shares of the block key $b_h$ for any $h \neq h^*$, and finally outputs a guess for $b$.

Let $W$ be the event that an adversary succeeds in the game $G$ by correctly guessing $b$ in polynomial time, and $\varepsilon$ be a negligible function of the security parameter $\lambda$ which is fed to the scheme in the setup phase. We say that the protocol is secure against front-running if:

$$\mathsf{Adv}_G(\mathcal{A}) = \mid \Pr[W] - 0.5 \mid \leq \varepsilon \tag{7}$$

To show that our scheme is secure according to the definition above, let us assume that there exists an adversary $\mathcal{A}$ which can win the game with a non-negligible probability. We can show that in turn this adversary $\mathcal{A}$ should either break the security of our distributed IBE scheme or the underlying DKG protocol. In the former case, an adversary $\mathcal{B}$ can obtain a private key $d_{ID}$ for arbitrary identity $ID$ alongside the two challenge ciphertexts from the challenger in the security game of standard IBE. Next, it runs a secret sharing algorithm on $d_{ID}$ to generate shares with the same distribution of block key shares and submits the generated shares, two challenge ciphertexts, and $ID$ to $\mathcal{A}$. Consequently, $\mathcal{A}$ outputs $b$ which can be sent to the challenger by $\mathcal{B}$ to break the security of standard IBE with a non-negligible probability. To break the DKG security in latter, $\mathcal{A}$ should have the ability to distinguish between the distribution of master key shares and master public key tuple $(w_1, ..., w_k, mpk)$ as the output of a simulator $\mathsf{Sim}$ and $(w_1, ..., w_k, mpk')$ as the output of the real DKG protocol [33, 48]. Consequently, as we have not modified the DKG protocol in FairBlock, an adversary $\mathcal{C}$ can simply use $\mathcal{A}$ as an oracle to break the security of the original DKG protocol.

**Order-Fairness.** FairBlock achieves order-fairness by executing transactions in the order that their commitments have been received and written to Commit or alternatively distributed public ledger (in the case of consensus-level implementation) without duplication. No party including miners in the decryption and execution phase can influence the fixed order of executed transactions. Moreover, no party including miners can insert transactions before the decrypted batch or directly submit transactions to the target contract to frontrun or out-race Fair-Block transactions as the target contract only accepts messages received through FairBlock.

To achieve order-fairness, we follow the literature on "fairness" [17,39,70] which favors the transactions that are received earlier. This property has been a subject of debate in the blockchain community lately [17,24,58]. In some applications e.g. auctions or networks, it is vital to preserve the order of received transactions for the correctness of the auction or incentivize parties to act with the lowest possible latency e.g. arbitragers in AMMs. The other side of this trade-off is that this property may be exploited to perform blind front-running in some applications e.g. initial coin offerings (ICO) or attacks based on metadata. To the extent of our knowledge, blind front-running and attacks based on metadata are negligible in current applications. However, FairBlock can be easily modified to prevent this type of attack by shuffling the ordering of transactions. The source of shuffling can be the hash of the concatenation of random strings $x$ of all messages which cannot be pre-determined or influenced. Kelkar et al. [39] propose executing all the received transactions in parallel which is implemented in Chainlink fair sequencing service (FSS) [17] and also compatible with FairBlock's encryption mechanism. We have further discussed other solutions to combat metadata-based attacks by anonymizing the transaction's sender in Sect. 6.

# 5 Implementation

## 5.1 Implementation Details

We have built prototype implementations of FairBlock for both consensus-level and smart contracts approaches. Smart contracts are implemented in Solidity and consensus-level blockchain is built based on Cosmos SDK [22] in Go. For consensus-level implementation, validators can submit their block key shares as a message in the FairBlock blockchain, and other parties can compute the block key and submit decrypted transactions as a message to collect rewards. However, a more efficient implementation would be submitting block key shares as an extension to messages in the voting round in a BFT-style consensus algorithm [13]. This implementation can be realized in FairBlock blockchain after release of ABCI++ [21] which allows validators in a Cosmos-based blockchain to extend their votes in the consensus voting phase with their shares of block key [32,58].

Our implementation of the distributed IBE is built on top of Vuvuzela cryptography library [66] in Go and assembly. For simplicity, we have described FairBlock using symmetric pairings with the same source groups. However, we have implemented our protocol using type 3 pairings (BLS12-381) with different source groups for better efficiency as the Boneh-Franklin BasicIdent IBE [9] can also be described with type 3 pairings [10]. For the DKG part, we have used Pedersen's scheme [48], as it is efficient, fast, and can be explained simply in this paper. However, this DKG scheme can be replaced with implementations and schemes such as [33–35,38,54,62] to achieve better properties. Both implementations can be readily employed for auctions, gaming, and various other DeFi use cases. Moreover, other PoS blockchain networks including [4,20,30,59] can also prevent front-running in their network by including FairBlock in their consensus mechanism. Source code of FairBlock including distributed IBE and smart contracts is available on GitHub[1]. Source code of FairBlock implementation in the consensus layer is also available on GitHub[2].

## 5.2 Performance Evaluation

To measure performance of our Distributed IBE implementation, we use a 2nd Gen Intel Xeon 2.50 GHz server with 1 core and 2 GB of RAM. In order to determine an average performance, we ran the experiments 100 times for each keepers set size. We test the implementation for systems of up to 500 keepers and

---

[1] https://github.com/pememoni/FairBlock-SC.
[2] https://github.com/pememoni/FairBlock.

present average execution times in Table 1 along with 95% two-sided confidence intervals. Our results show the feasibility of our basic implementation using basic hardware resources for even the fastest proof-of-stake (PoS) and proof-of-work (PoW) public blockchains. For instance, average block key extraction time (composed of block key shares aggregation, verification, and block key computation) for 100 keepers is 147.39 ms which is significantly less than the block finalization time of PoW blockchains such as Ethereum (12–14 s), and current fastest PoS blockchain namely Avalanche [4] (1–3 s). We have also measured encryption and decryption execution time of random 256 byte messages for 1000 runs. On average, decryption takes 1.54 ms and encryption takes 5.27 ms which are neglectable compared to block key extraction time and can be easily parallelized with the same execution time. For larger message sizes, our work employs hybrid encryption [26]. Using hybrid encryption, identity-based encryption is used to encrypt a key and an efficient symmetric encryption scheme such as AES-GCM or ChaCha20 [16] is used to encrypt the actual transaction with the key.

**Table 1.** Mean values of encryption, block key extraction, and decryption execution time for various keepers set sizes.

| Keepers | Block key extraction (ms) | Decryption (ms) | Encryption (ms) |
|---------|---------------------------|-----------------|-----------------|
| 5 | 8.07 ± 0.05 | 1.57 ± 0.04 | 5.29 ± 0.03 |
| 10 | 16.97 ± 0.06 | 1.54 ± 0.04 | 5.24 ± 0.02 |
| 20 | 29.5 ± 0.10 | 1.50 ± 0.02 | 5.21 ± 0.01 |
| 50 | 72.91 ± 0.18 | 1.52 ± 0.04 | 5.22 ± 0.02 |
| 100 | 147.39 ± 0.29 | 1.60 ± 0.07 | 5.28 ± 0.04 |
| 200 | 294.90 ± 0.63 | 1.53 ± 0.04 | 5.30 ± 0.02 |
| 500 | 771.72 ± 1.38 | 1.59 ± 0.03 | 5.35 ± 0.03 |

We have compared the bandwidth overhead of FairBlock and the threshold decryption approach in two realistic scenarios. In scenario I, there are 1000 keepers and 1000 encrypted transactions that should be decrypted every 24 h. In scenario II, there are 100 keepers and 100 transactions to be decrypted in 10 s. Using IBE, we need at least two-thirds of keepers to send their shares (of size 256 byte in our implementation) for the block key extraction. In threshold decryption, at least two-thirds of keepers should compute partial decryptions (of size 64 byte in our implementation) for each of the committed transactions. Table 2 shows the result of our experiment. In scenario I, the total message size of IBE approach is only 0.4% of the threshold decryption approach. Similarly, the total message size of IBE approach is approximately 25 times less than the other approach in scenario II.

**Table 2.** Comparison of bandwidth overhead in identity-based encryption and threshold decryption (assuming two-thirds honest majority)

| System size | | Bandwidth overhead | |
|---|---|---|---|
| Transactions | Keepers | Identity-based encryption | Threshold decryption |
| 1000 | 1000 | 170.8 KB | 42.7 MB |
| 100 | 100 | 17.2 KB | 326.4 KB |

# 6   Challenges and Future Work

One of the main challenges that arises in all privacy-preserving implementations is to protect leakage of information through transaction metadata. In particular, although the data field will not leak any information about the encrypted transaction itself, signature of the transaction can leak the sender's identity. In theory, an adversary with just the knowledge of the transaction's sender can perform front-running. For example, traders can be front-runned just based on their regular trading times of specific assets. Preventing such attacks requires mitigations that avoid leakage of metadata as well. As an alternative to using complex ring signatures [45], a client can avoid this risk and hide the real sender of the transaction by asking another party to send its transaction; or alternatively, replace the sender's signature with a PoW puzzle. Other privacy-enhancing technologies such as [6,14,63] can also be applied to prevent front-running based on the sender's public key or other forms of metadata namely IP addresses.

# 7   Conclusions

This paper designs and implements FairBlock, the first front-running prevention mechanism based on distributed IBE. Our work does not have many limitations of previous front-running mechanisms. Specifically, FairBlock significantly outperforms the most well-known approach based on threshold decryption in bandwidth overhead. We have implemented and evaluated our prototype using both smart contracts and consensus-layer as the communications layer. The source code of our implementation is also open-sourced.

# A   Front-Running Strategies

In this appendix, we discuss two families of the most common front-running strategies with the goal of familiarizing the reader with the MEV space and nature of the front-running attacks.

**Sandwiching Attack.** Sandwich attacks are the most notorious form of front-running attacks. Predatory parties observe profitable pending transactions in the public mempool or exploit their privileged access to plaintext orders in centralized exchanges or relayer services. At its core, they manipulate the transaction ordering in a block and ensure that their front-running transaction $tx_1$ executes before the victim's transaction $tx_{org}$ and their back-running transaction $tx_2$ executes immediately after the victim's transaction. The profitability of this strategy is based on the assumption that demand for assets results in a higher price. In simple terms, when the attacker observes a pending buy order, it can buy the same asset before the original trade, and immediately sell after execution of the original trade to enjoy price increases thanks to a) its back-running transaction and b) the victim's transaction. For a concrete example, assume the scenario that Alice broadcasts $tx_{org}$ to trade 100 USDC for DAI with a standard 0.3% transaction fee and 1% slippage tolerance in a decentralized exchange (DEX) that has 1000 DAI and 1000 USDC reserve. Following the standard automatic market maker (AMM) model [1] in DEXes, Alice is expecting to receive 90.66 DAI in return. However, Bob observes this trade in the mempool and front-runs Alice by submitting $t_1$ to trade 5.23 USDC for 5.19 DAI which increases the price of DAI to the maximum limit that Alice can tolerate due to 1% slippage. Consequently, Alice's trade $t_{org}$ returns 1% less DAI (89.75 DAI) and even further increases DAI price. Finally, Bob pockets 1.05 USDC (ignoring gas fees) in profit by submitting $t_2$ and trading its 5.19 DAI for 6.28 USDC. To realize this strategy Bob should manipulate the ordering by offering gas prices (price for computing each unit of computation) to block proposers such that $t_1$ and $t_2$ sandwich $t_{org}$. Block proposers normally sort transactions with respect to gas price; and for a successful attack, Bob has the challenge to strategically offer a gas price that overbids competitors and still be profitable which makes this strategy complex for Bob. However, Flashbots [24] allows front-runners to sandwich users with much less risk as they can offer a bundle of transactions containing $t_1$, $t_2$, $t_{org}$, and a bid directly to the block proposer without submitting it to the mempool. Then the block proposer chooses the most profitable bundles and executes them in their profitable order. Consequently, Bob can almost guarantee his profit by only paying for the bid and fees only if the block proposer executes $t_1$, $t_2$, $t_{org}$ in the specified order.

**Generalized Front-Running.** Blockchain networks such as Ethereum [67] and Avalanche [4] are modelled as a distributed state machine and their global state changes from block to block with respect to a pre-defined set of rules. This means that any party can observe a pending transaction $tx_{org}$ and simulate its resulting state change. Consequently, generalized front-runners can simulate all pending transactions and determine the profitability of them by checking the balances of the transactions' senders. In case of a net increase in the original sender's balance, the generalized front-runner copies the same transaction fields and signs it with its private key. Next, it simulates the copied transaction locally to check that the transaction is indeed profitable e.g. not a trap smart contract. Finally, the generalized front-runner submits transaction $tx_1$ to front-run $tx_{org}$ and capture the profit. This strategy enables parties that have access to the mempool to extract profits by mimicking a pending transaction (even blindly) and outbidding competitors and the original sender. While the generalized front-runner may be able to simulate all pending transactions in order to find the most profitable ones, due to the high number of pending transactions and cost of simulating, the front-runner can also filter specific target addresses and markets which is expected to have more profitable opportunities including NFT markets, DEX and CEX liquidity pools, yield aggregators, or well-known traders.

# B    Correctness and Consistency

## B.1    Consistency of IBE Encryption and Decryption

Let $C = (R, U)$ be encryption of message $m$ for block identifier $h$ using the public key $mpk$. In encryption, $m$ is bitwise XORed with the hash of $\hat{e}(Q_h, mpk)^r$. Subsequently in decryption, $U$ is bitwise XORed with the hash of $\hat{e}(b_h, R)$. These two masks are equal since:

$$\hat{e}(Q_h, mpk)^r = \hat{e}(Q_h, g)^{r.msk} = \hat{e}((Q_h)^{msk}, g^r) = \hat{e}(b_h, R) \tag{8}$$

## B.2    Correctness Proof for Distributed Private Key Extraction

The following proof shows that $b_h$ is indeed the IBE key that a trusted third party extracts for the identity $h$ by raising the hash of the identity $H_1(h)$ to its private key $msk$:

$$b_h = \prod_{k=1}^{t} (b_h^k)^{L_k} = \prod_{k=1}^{t} (H_1(h)^{w_k})^{L_k} = \prod_{k=1}^{t} H_1(h)^{w_k L_k} = H_1(h)^{\sum_{k=1}^{t} w_k L_k} \tag{9}$$

And by Lagrange interpolation formula we have:

$$H_1(h)^{\sum_{k=1}^{t} w_k L_k} = H_1(h)^{msk} \tag{10}$$

# References

1. Adams, H., Zinsmeister, N., Salem, M., Keefer, R., Robinson, D.: Uniswap v3 core. Technical report, Uniswap (2021)
2. Asayag, A., et al.: A fair consensus protocol for transaction ordering. In: 2018 IEEE 26th International Conference on Network Protocols (ICNP), pp. 55–65 (2018). https://doi.org/10.1109/ICNP.2018.00016
3. Auer, R., Frost, J., Vidal Pastor, J.M.: Miners as intermediaries: extractable value and market manipulation in crypto and DeFi. https://www.bis.org/publ/bisbull58.htm. Accessed 07 July 2022
4. Avalanche whitepaper. https://www.avalabs.org/whitepapers. Accessed 12 Mar 2021

5. Bartoletti, M., Chiang, J.H.Y., Lluch-Lafuente, A.: Maximizing extractable value from automated market makers. arXiv preprint arXiv:2106.01870 (2021)
6. Bojja Venkatakrishnan, S., Fanti, G., Viswanath, P.: Dandelion: redesigning the bitcoin network for anonymity. Proc. ACM Meas. Anal. Comput. Syst. **1**(1) (2017). https://doi.org/10.1145/3084459
7. Boneh, D., Bonneau, J., Bünz, B., Fisch, B.: Verifiable delay functions. In: Shacham, H., Boldyreva, A. (eds.) CRYPTO 2018. LNCS, vol. 10991, pp. 757–788. Springer, Cham (2018). https://doi.org/10.1007/978-3-319-96884-1_25
8. Boneh, D., Boyen, X.: Efficient selective-ID secure identity-based encryption without random oracles. In: Cachin, C., Camenisch, J.L. (eds.) EUROCRYPT 2004. LNCS, vol. 3027, pp. 223–238. Springer, Heidelberg (2004). https://doi.org/10.1007/978-3-540-24676-3_14
9. Boneh, D., Franklin, M.: Identity-based encryption from the Weil pairing. In: Kilian, J. (ed.) CRYPTO 2001. LNCS, vol. 2139, pp. 213–229. Springer, Heidelberg (2001). https://doi.org/10.1007/3-540-44647-8_13
10. Boyen, X.: A tapestry of identity-based encryption: practical frameworks compared. Int. J. Appl. Crypt. **1**(1), 3–21 (2008)
11. Brassard, G., Chaum, D., Crépeau, C.: Minimum disclosure proofs of knowledge. J. Comput. Syst. Sci. **37**(2), 156–189 (1988)
12. Breidenbach, L., Daian, P., Tramèr, F., Juels, A.: Enter the hydra: towards principled bug bounties and exploit-resistant smart contracts. Cryptology ePrint Archive, Report 2017/1090 (2017)
13. Buchman, E., Kwon, J., Milosevic, Z.: The latest gossip on BFT consensus. arXiv preprint arXiv:1807.04938 (2018)
14. Bünz, B., Agrawal, S., Zamani, M., Boneh, D.: Zether: towards privacy in a smart contract world. In: Bonneau, J., Heninger, N. (eds.) FC 2020. LNCS, vol. 12059, pp. 423–443. Springer, Cham (2020). https://doi.org/10.1007/978-3-030-51280-4_23
15. Cachin, C., Kursawe, K., Petzold, F., Shoup, V.: Secure and efficient asynchronous broadcast protocols. In: Kilian, J. (ed.) CRYPTO 2001. LNCS, vol. 2139, pp. 524–541. Springer, Heidelberg (2001). https://doi.org/10.1007/3-540-44647-8_31
16. ChaCha20 and Poly1305 for IETF protocols. https://www.rfc-editor.org/rfc/rfc7539.txt. Accessed 04 Mar 2022
17. Chainlink 2.0 and the future of decentralized oracle networks — chainlink (2021). https://chain.link/whitepaper
18. Cline, D., Dryja, T., Narula, N.: Clockwork: an exchange protocol for proofs of non front-running (2020)
19. Cocks, C.: An identity based encryption scheme based on quadratic residues. In: Honary, B. (ed.) Cryptography and Coding 2001. LNCS, vol. 2260, pp. 360–363. Springer, Heidelberg (2001). https://doi.org/10.1007/3-540-45325-3_32
20. Cosmos: The internet of blockchains. https://cosmos.network/. Accessed 18 Mar 2022
21. Abci++. https://github.com/tendermint/spec/blob/master/rfc/004-abci++.md. Accessed 04 Mar 2022
22. Cosmos sdk - cosmos network. https://v1.cosmos.network/sdk. Accessed 26 Mar 2022
23. CoW Swap - meta DEX aggregator. https://cowswap.exchange/. 12 Mar 2021
24. Daian, P., et al.: Flash boys 2.0: frontrunning, transaction reordering, and consensus instability in decentralized exchanges. arXiv preprint arXiv:1904.05234 (2019)
25. Dao — aragon. https://aragon.org/dao. Accessed 04 Jan 2022

26. Dixit, P., Gupta, A.K., Trivedi, M.C., Yadav, V.K.: Traditional and hybrid encryption techniques: a survey. In: Perez, G.M., Mishra, K.K., Tiwari, S., Trivedi, M.C. (eds.) Networking Communication and Data Knowledge Engineering. LNDECT, vol. 4, pp. 239–248. Springer, Singapore (2018). https://doi.org/10.1007/978-981-10-4600-1_22

27. Doweck, Y., Eyal, I.: Multi-party timed commitments (2020)

28. Duan, S., Reiter, M.K., Zhang, H.: Secure causal atomic broadcast, revisited. In: 2017 47th Annual IEEE/IFIP International Conference on Dependable Systems and Networks (DSN), pp. 61–72 (2017). https://doi.org/10.1109/DSN.2017.64

29. Eskandari, S., Moosavi, S., Clark, J.: SoK: transparent dishonesty: front-running attacks on blockchain. In: Bracciali, A., Clark, J., Pintore, F., Rønne, P.B., Sala, M. (eds.) FC 2019. LNCS, vol. 11599, pp. 170–189. Springer, Cham (2020). https://doi.org/10.1007/978-3-030-43725-1_13

30. Ethereum upgrades. https://ethereum.org/en/upgrades/. Accessed 18 Mar 2022

31. Feldman, P.: A practical scheme for non-interactive verifiable secret sharing. In: 28th Annual Symposium on Foundations of Computer Science (SFCS 1987), pp. 427–438 (1987). https://doi.org/10.1109/SFCS.1987.4

32. Ferveo. https://anoma.network/blog/ferveo-a-distributed-key-generation-scheme-for-front-running-protection/. Accessed 12 Mar 2021

33. Gennaro, R., Jarecki, S., Krawczyk, H., Rabin, T.: Secure distributed key generation for discrete-log based cryptosystems. J. Cryptol. **20**(1), 51–83 (2007)

34. Groth, J.: Non-interactive distributed key generation and key resharing. Cryptology ePrint Archive, Report 2021/339 (2021)

35. Gurkan, K., Jovanovic, P., Maller, M., Meiklejohn, S., Stern, G., Tomescu, A.: Aggregatable distributed key generation. In: Canteaut, A., Standaert, F.-X. (eds.) EUROCRYPT 2021. LNCS, vol. 12696, pp. 147–176. Springer, Cham (2021). https://doi.org/10.1007/978-3-030-77870-5_6

36. Halevi, S.: Efficient commitment schemes with bounded sender and unbounded receiver. In: Coppersmith, D. (ed.) CRYPTO 1995. LNCS, vol. 963, pp. 84–96. Springer, Heidelberg (1995). https://doi.org/10.1007/3-540-44750-4_7

37. Halevi, S., Micali, S.: Practical and provably-secure commitment schemes from collision-free hashing. In: Koblitz, N. (ed.) CRYPTO 1996. LNCS, vol. 1109, pp. 201–215. Springer, Heidelberg (1996). https://doi.org/10.1007/3-540-68697-5_16

38. Kate, A., Goldberg, I.: Distributed private-key generators for identity-based cryptography. In: Garay, J.A., De Prisco, R. (eds.) SCN 2010. LNCS, vol. 6280, pp. 436–453. Springer, Heidelberg (2010). https://doi.org/10.1007/978-3-642-15317-4_27

39. Kelkar, M., Zhang, F., Goldfeder, S., Juels, A.: Order-fairness for byzantine consensus. In: Micciancio, D., Ristenpart, T. (eds.) CRYPTO 2020. LNCS, vol. 12172, pp. 451–480. Springer, Cham (2020). https://doi.org/10.1007/978-3-030-56877-1_16

40. Khalil, R., Gervais, A., Felley, G.: TEX - a securely scalable trustless exchange. IACR Cryptology ePrint Archive, p. 265 (2019)

41. Libert, B., Quisquater, J.-J.: Identity based encryption without redundancy. In: Ioannidis, J., Keromytis, A., Yung, M. (eds.) ACNS 2005. LNCS, vol. 3531, pp. 285–300. Springer, Heidelberg (2005). https://doi.org/10.1007/11496137_20

42. Mev-Explore. https://explore.flashbots.net/. Accessed 12 Mar 2021

43. Naor, M.: Bit commitment using pseudorandomness. J. Cryptol. **4**(2), 151–158 (1991). https://doi.org/10.1007/BF00196774

44. Secret Network: Secret markets: front running prevention for automated market makers. https://scrt.network/blog/secret-markets-front-running-prevention. Accessed 22 June 2022

45. Noether, S.: Ring signature confidential transactions for monero. IACR Cryptology ePrint Archive, p. 1098 (2015)
46. Obadia, A., Salles, A., Sankar, L., Chitra, T., Chellani, V., Daian, P.: Unity is strength: a formalization of cross-domain maximal extractable value (2021)
47. Pedersen, T.P.: Non-interactive and information-theoretic secure verifiable secret sharing. In: Feigenbaum, J. (ed.) CRYPTO 1991. LNCS, vol. 576, pp. 129–140. Springer, Heidelberg (1992). https://doi.org/10.1007/3-540-46766-1_9
48. Pedersen, T.P.: A threshold cryptosystem without a trusted party. In: Davies, D.W. (ed.) EUROCRYPT 1991. LNCS, vol. 547, pp. 522–526. Springer, Heidelberg (1991). https://doi.org/10.1007/3-540-46416-6_47
49. Protocol, V.: Blockchain derivatives. https://vega.xyz/. Accessed 22 June 2022
50. Qin, K., Zhou, L., Gervais, A.: Quantifying blockchain extractable value: how dark is the forest? (2021)
51. Reiter, M.K., Birman, K.P.: How to securely replicate services. ACM Trans. Programm. Lang. Syst. (TOPLAS) **16**(3), 986–1009 (1994)
52. Robinson, D., Konstantopoulos, G.: Ethereum is a dark forest - paradigm. https://www.paradigm.xyz/2020/08/ethereum-is-a-dark-forest/. Accessed 3 Dec 2021
53. van Schaik, S., Kwong, A., Genkin, D., Yarom, Y.: SGAxe: how SGX fails in practice (2020)
54. Schindler, P., Judmayer, A., Stifter, N., Weippl, E.: EthDKG: distributed key generation with ethereum smart contracts. Cryptology ePrint Archive, Report 2019/985 (2019)
55. Shamir, A.: How to share a secret. Commun. ACM **22**(11), 612–613 (1979). https://doi.org/10.1145/359168.359176
56. Shamir, A.: Identity-based cryptosystems and signature schemes. In: Blakley, G.R., Chaum, D. (eds.) CRYPTO 1984. LNCS, vol. 196, pp. 47–53. Springer, Heidelberg (1985). https://doi.org/10.1007/3-540-39568-7_5
57. Shutter Network. https://shutter.ghost.io/. Accessed 3 Dec 2021
58. Sikka. https://sikka.tech/projects/. Accessed 3 Dec 2021
59. Solana. https://solana.com/. Accessed 18 Mar 2022
60. Stathakopoulou, C., Rüsch, S., Brandenburger, M., Vukolic, M.: Adding fairness to order: Preventing front-running attacks in BFT protocols using tees (2021)
61. Sushiswap. https://sushi.com/. Accessed 3 Dec 2021
62. Tomescu, A., et al.: Towards scalable threshold cryptosystems. In: 2020 IEEE Symposium on Security and Privacy (SP), pp. 877–893. IEEE (2020)
63. Tornado Cash. https://tornado.cash/. Accessed 5 Dec 2021
64. Van Bulck, J., et al.: Foreshadow: extracting the keys to the Intel SGX kingdom with transient out-of-order execution. In: 27th USENIX Security Symposium (USENIX Security 18), pp. 991–1008 (2018)
65. Veedo. https://github.com/starkware-libs/veedo. Accessed 30 Mar 2022
66. vuvuzela cryptography libraries. https://github.com/vuvuzela/crypto. Accessed 3 Apr 2022
67. Wood, G.: Ethereum: a secure decentralized generalized transaction ledger (2014)
68. Xing, B.C., Shanahan, M., Leslie-Hurd, R.: Intel software guard extensions (Intel SGX) software support for dynamic memory allocation inside an enclave. In: Proceedings of the Hardware and Architectural Support for Security and Privacy 2016. Association for Computing Machinery, New York (2016). https://doi.org/10.1145/2948618.2954330
69. Zhang, H., Merino, L.H., Estrada-Galinanes, V., Ford, B.: F3B: a low-latency commit-and-reveal architecture to mitigate blockchain front-running. arXiv preprint arXiv:2205.08529 (2022)

70. Zhang, Y., Setty, S., Chen, Q., Zhou, L., Alvisi, L.: Byzantine ordered consensus without byzantine oligarchy. In: 14th USENIX Symposium on Operating Systems Design and Implementation (OSDI 20), pp. 633–649. USENIX Association, November 2020
71. Zhou, L., Qin, K., Torres, C.F., Le, D.V., Gervais, A.: High-frequency trading on decentralized on-chain exchanges. In: 2021 IEEE Symposium on Security and Privacy (SP), pp. 428–445 (2021)

# Blockchain-Based Ciphertext Policy-Hiding Access Control Scheme

Ruizhong Du[1,2] and Tianhe Zhang[1(✉)]

[1] School of Cyber Security and Computer, Hebei University, Baoding 071002, China
ztian73817@gmail.com
[2] Hebei Provincial Key Laboratory of High Credibility Information System,
Baoding 071000, China

**Abstract.** Ciphertext policy attribute encryption(CP-ABE) can realize one-to-many fine-grained access control, which can effectively solve the security problem of shared data. However, most existing CP-ABE protocols exhibit a single point of failure and access policy privacy disclosure problems. To resolve these issues, a blockchain-based ciphertext policy-hiding access control scheme is proposed. First, we propose a vector generation algorithm using vector compression techniques that can improve the efficiency of our scheme. Then, the privacy policy is protected by combining CP-ABE and inner product encryption. We then solve the user attribute revocation problem and single point of failure in the cloud-based access control models using ethereum. Finally, security analysis, the theoretical results, and experimental results show that the proposed solution is secure and efficient.

**Keywords:** Fine-grained access control · Blockchain · Policy-hiding · Inner product encryption

## 1 Introduction

As an emerging data interaction mode, cloud computing has dramatically transformed people's way of life, more individual and organizational users store their data online and share them remotely. People can access and obtain data as they wish. However, data stored in the cloud may contain private and confidential information. Thus, an attack or lack of monitoring may cause major accidents, such as data tampering or privacy leakage [4]. Data encryption is considered to be an effective method to achieve data security.

CP-ABE [5] can achieve fine-grained access control of user outsourced data and has higher flexibility and practicability, which has attracted extensive attention in industry. In CP-ABE, the ciphertext is related to the access policy, and the decryption key is related to the user's attributes. The trusted authority generates encryption-related parameters for the data owner to encrypt and sends the decryption key to the user. If the user attributes match the access policy, the user can decrypt the ciphertext to obtain the plaintext.

© ICST Institute for Computer Sciences, Social Informatics and Telecommunications Engineering 2023
Published by Springer Nature Switzerland AG 2023. All Rights Reserved
F. Li et al. (Eds.): SecureComm 2022, LNICST 462, pp. 272–289, 2023.
https://doi.org/10.1007/978-3-031-25538-0_15

In many current CP-ABE schemes, the data owner typically uploads encrypted data to a cloud server. The reliability of data access control thus depends to a large extent on the cloud server [6,25], and there may be a single point of failure. The blockchain can solve this problem well and improve the trustworthiness of the entire system. However, due to blockchain transparency, deploying access policies directly on the blockchain may reveal users' private data. For example, in a distributed access control system, Alice stores her electronic medical record access control policy in a blockchain. If the policy states that it can only be accessed by a cardiologist, Based on this access policy, an attacker can then infer that Alice may have a heart attack without obtaining her medical records. That is, an attacker could infer Alice's condition by knowing the contents of the access policy without accessing the contents of the medical records. Therefore, preventing malicious users from obtaining private information from access policies is a critical issue [21].

Currently, existing policy-hiding CP-ABE schemes have two forms: full policy-hiding [23] and partial policy-hiding [26]. In CP-ABE schemes with full policy-hiding, the entire attribute (name and value) is protected. Generally, full policy-hiding can be implemented by converting the access policy and user attributes into two vectors. Only when the result of multiplying the transformed two vectors is zero, the attribute set can satisfy the corresponding access policy. In this way, sensitive information is hidden by representing the access policy as a vector. Partial policy-hiding cannot protect all attributes, only attribute values, but not attribute names. Although full policy-hiding is not as efficient as partial policy-hiding, it can provide better privacy protection. For privacy-sensitive systems, any leakage of sensitive information can seriously threaten the data owner. Therefore, it is necessary to protect the personal information of data owners by implementing full policy hiding.

To resolve these issues, this study proposes a blockchain-based ciphertext policy-hiding scheme that achieves distributed fine-grained access control and protects the privacy of access policy. The main research contents of this study are as follows:

- We propose an efficient vector generation algorithm using vector compression techniques. Using ABE and inner product operation, we design a CP-ABE scheme with full policy hiding that can avoid leaking privacy-sensitive attribute information. Also, the proposed scheme performs constant bilinear pairing operations during decryption.
- We use the interplanetary file system to store encrypted information and store the ciphertext hash address using smart contracts. The storage overhead of the blockchain is reduced while achieving distributed and trustworthy access control. Revocation contract protects the private key from abuse.
- The security is demonstrated based on its application to difficult problems, and the performance is analyzed and explained via simulations, which verify the effectiveness of the scheme.

## 2    Related Works

### 2.1    Blockchain-Based Access Control Scheme

Saini et al. [20] built a distributed access system to achieve the goal of being patient-centric and accessible to medical records, which stored encrypted data on cloud servers, reducing the storage overhead of blockchain, but its scheme has scalability and performance problems. Zhang et al. [30] combine ethereum and traditional access control schemes and proposes a scheme to realize distributed access control through smart contract interaction. Their framework includes a policy management contract, two attribute management contracts, and an access contract for executing access control. Due to the openness and transparency of the blockchain, this scheme has the risk of attribute leakage. Ding et al. [9] proposed a scheme for the Internet of Things and used blockchain technology to simplify the access control process. The attributes of IoT devices are uploaded to the blockchain through transactions, and data access is allowed when the attributes meet the conditions of the access policy. Wang et al. [22] proposed a fine-grained access control framework based on blockchain. However, this scheme has the problems of access policy privacy leakage and poor scalability. Gao et al. [11] proposed an attribute hiding scheme based on blockchain and inner product encryption. The performance of this scheme degrades with increasing attributes in the system. Also, the scheme is constructed based on composite order bilinear groups (COBG), and the computational cost is relatively high.

Thus, these solutions primarily concentrates on enhancing the reliability and automation of the system, and there are some problems in terms of efficiency, scalability and user privacy.

### 2.2    Traditional Encryption Scheme

Phuong et al. [18] proposed an algorithm that uses Viete's formula and inner product encryption to achieve full policy hiding, but this scheme is less efficient. Subsequently, a series of policy hiding schemes [7,14] based on this algorithm appeared, despite some performance issues. Gan et al. [10] proposed a partial policy hiding scheme based on prime order bilinear groups, and added a decryption test algorithm in the system, which reduced the decryption overhead within a certain range, but the efficiency of the scheme was still low. Lai et al. [15] proposed a scheme to protect policy privacy, which only supports partial policy hiding. In addition, the decryption efficiency is low because the larger the access policy, the more the number of bilinear pairings. Based on [15], Zhang et al. [29] built a novel privacy protection scheme. Although this scheme can protect users' attribute privacy, its decryption overhead is still large. Liu et al. [17] built a multiauthorization outsourced scheme to solve the problem of complex decryption and key leakage, which achieves full policy hiding and has traceability. However, this scheme exhibits both attribute and user revocations. Hao et al. [12] proposed an efficient full policy-hiding scheme using Bloom filters, but their scheme cannot defend against attribute guessing attacks [31]. Zhang et al. [28] designed a scheme to resist attribute guessing attacks based on the linear secret sharing scheme, but its decryption algorithm is inefficient, and resource consumption on IoT devices is large. Hu et al. [13] constructed a highly efficient policy hiding scheme to protect privacy, but their study only supports partial policy hiding and cannot perform attribute revocation. Xiong et al. [24] achieved partial policy hiding using the linear secret sharing scheme. However, its scheme has many exponentiation operations and pairing processes during the execution of the system, which results in low efficiency. There are also some policy hiding schemes based on COBG [16,19,27], whose efficiency is low.

Thus, traditional encryption schemes have many disadvantages, such as inefficiency, privacy leakage and attribute revocation. So we propose a blockchain-based ciphertext policy-hiding access control scheme to avoid these problems. While protecting user privacy, this scheme overcomes the problems of attribute revocation and inefficiency.

## 3 Preliminaries

### 3.1 Bilinear Operation

We let $\mathbb{G}_1$, $\mathbb{G}_2$ and $\mathbb{G}_T$ be three cyclic groups of prime order $p$, where $\mathbb{G}_1 \neq \mathbb{G}_2$, and there are no efficiently computable homomorphisms between $\mathbb{G}_1$ and $\mathbb{G}_2$. $e$: $\mathbb{G}_1 \times \mathbb{G}_2 \to \mathbb{G}_T$ is considered to be an asymmetric bilinear operation if

- For all $g \in \mathbb{G}_1, h \in \mathbb{G}_2$, and $a, b \in \mathbb{Z}_p^*$, $e\left(g^a, h^b\right) = e(g, h)^{ab}$.
- $e(g, h) \neq 1$.
- $e(g, h)$ for all $g \in \mathbb{G}_1$ and $h \in \mathbb{G}_2$ can be calculated efficiently.

### 3.2 Complexity Assumption

**Asymmetric Decisional Bilinear Diffie-Hellman Problem (DBDH).** There are the following two distributions, where $g \in \mathbb{G}_1, h \in \mathbb{G}_2, a, b, c \in \mathbb{Z}_p^*$ and $T \in \mathbb{G}_T$ are all randomly generated.

$$-\mathcal{P}_A := \left(g, g^a, g^c, h, h^a, h^b, e(g, h)^{abc}\right) \in \mathbb{G}_1^3 \times \mathbb{G}_2^3 \times \mathbb{G}_T$$

$$-\mathcal{R}_A := \left(g, g^a, g^c, h, h^a, h^b, T\right) \in \mathbb{G}_1^3 \times \mathbb{G}_2^3 \times \mathbb{G}_T$$

$Adv_{\mathcal{A}}^{DBDH}$ is the advantage of algorithm $\mathcal{A}$ to distinguish the following two distributions. Specifically as follows:

$$Adv_{\mathcal{A}}^{DBDH} = |\Pr[\mathcal{A}(D) = 1] - \Pr[\mathcal{A}(R) = 1]|,$$

$D$ and $R$ are selected from $\mathcal{P}_A$ and $\mathcal{R}_A$, respectively.

An algorithm $\mathcal{B}$ has advantage $Adv_{\mathcal{A}}^{DBDH} = \epsilon$ in solving the $DBDH$ problem if:

$$| \Pr\left[\mathcal{B}\left(g, g^a, g^c, h, h^a, h^b, e(g, h)^{abc}\right) = 0\right]$$
$$- \Pr\left[\mathcal{B}\left(g, g^a, g^c, h, h^a, h^b, T\right) = 0\right] | \geq \epsilon$$

where the probability is above the random choice of generators $g \in \mathbb{G}_1$ and $h \in \mathbb{G}_2$, exponents $a, b, c \in \mathbb{Z}_p^*, T \in \mathbb{G}_T$ and the random bits used by $\mathcal{B}$.

**Definition 1.** If for any $PPT$ algorithms $\mathcal{A}$, the function $Adv_{\mathcal{A}}^{DBDH}(\lambda)$ is a negligible function of $\lambda$, we consider the $DBDH$ to hold for $\mathcal{G}$, where $\mathcal{G}$ is a bilinear group generator.

To justify the security of the access policy, another assumption needs to be introduced.

### $\mathcal{P}$-Asymmetric Decisional Bilinear Diffie-Hellman Problem ($\mathcal{P}$-DBDH)

The following two distributions are similar to those in the $DBDH$ assumption, with the difference that $T \in \mathbb{G}_1$ instead of $T \in \mathbb{G}_T$.

$$-\mathcal{D}_N := \left(g, g^a, g^{ab}, g^c, h, h^a, h^b, g^{abc}\right) \in \mathbb{G}_1^4 \times \mathbb{G}_2^3 \times \mathbb{G}_1$$

$$-\mathcal{D}_R := \left(g, g^a, g^{ab}, g^c, h, h^a, h^b, T\right) \in \mathbb{G}_1^4 \times \mathbb{G}_2^3 \times \mathbb{G}_1$$

$Adv_{\mathcal{A}}^{\mathcal{P}-DBDH}$ is the advantage of algorithm $\mathcal{A}$ to distinguish the following two distributions. Specifically as follows:

$$Adv_{\mathcal{A}}^{\mathcal{P}-DBDH} = |\Pr[\mathcal{A}(N) = 1] - \Pr[\mathcal{A}(P) = 1]|$$

$N$ and $P$ are selected from $\mathcal{D}_N$ and $\mathcal{D}_R$, respectively.

An algorithm $\mathcal{B}$ has advantage $Adv_{\mathcal{A}}^{\mathcal{P}-DBDH} = \epsilon_{\mathcal{P}}$ in solving the $\mathcal{P} - DBDH$ problem if:

$$|\Pr\left[\mathcal{B}\left(g, g^a, g^{ab}, g^c, h, h^a, h^b, g^{abc}\right) = 0\right]$$

$$-\Pr\left[\mathcal{B}\left(g, g^a, g^{ab}, g^c, h, h^a, h^b, T\right) = 0\right]| \geq \epsilon_{\mathcal{P}}$$

where the probability is above the random choice of generators $g \in \mathbb{G}_1$ and $h \in \mathbb{G}_2$, exponents $a, b, c \in \mathbb{Z}_p^*, T \in \mathbb{G}_1$ and the random bits used by $\mathcal{B}$.

**Definition 2.** If for any $PPT$ algorithms $\mathcal{A}$, the function $Adv_{\mathcal{A}}^{\mathcal{P}-DBDH}(\lambda)$ is a negligible function of $\lambda$, we consider the $\mathcal{P} - DBDH$ to hold for $\mathcal{G}$, where $\mathcal{G}$ is a bilinear group generator.

### 3.3   Access Structure

We let $U = \{U_1, U_2, \cdots, U_L\}$ be attributes, $U_k \in \{"+", "-"\}$; let $P = \{P_1, P_2, \cdots, P_L\}$ be an access policy, $P_k \in \{"+", "-", "*"\}$, where $k \in \{1, 2, \cdots, L\}$. The wildcard "$*$" means that both "$+$" and "$-$" are accepted. For example:

We assume that $U = \{U_1 = AI, U_2 = CE, U_3 = Faulty, U_4 = Student\}$, where "$AI$" and "$CE$" represent artificial intelligence and communications engineering, respectively. Anna is an AI faculty member, and Bell is a CE student. $P_1$ can be matched by all CE faculties without being in the AI, and $P_2$ can be matched by all AI faculty members and students, excluding those in the CE. User attributes and access policies are shown in Table 1.

**Table 1.** User attributes and access policies

| Attribute | $A_1$ | $A_2$ | $A_3$ | $A_4$ |
|---|---|---|---|---|
| Description | AI | CE | Faculty | Student |
| Anna | + | − | + | − |
| Bell | − | + | − | + |
| $P_1$ | − | + | + | − |
| $P_2$ | + | − | * | * |

### 3.4 Viete's Formulas

There are two vectors $p = (p_1, p_2, \cdots p_l)$ and $u = (u_1, u_2, \cdots u_l)$. Vector $p$ contains positive signs, negative signs and wildcards, and vector $u$ only contains positive signs and negative signs. The set of positions $I = \{i_1, \ldots, i_n\} \subseteq \{1, 2, \cdots l\}$ represents the positions of the wildcards in the vector $p$.

If there is a one-to-one correspondence between the attributes of the user and the attributes contained in the access policy, then $((p_i = u_i) \vee (p_i = *))$, $i \in [1, l]$, converted into mathematical form as shown in (1):

$$\sum_{i=1, i \in I}^{l} p_i \prod_{k_w \in I} (i - k_w) = \sum_{i=1}^{L} u_i \prod_{k_w \in I} (i - k_w) \tag{1}$$

We let $\prod_{k_w \in I} (i - k_w) = \sum_{j=1}^{n} a_j i^j$. So Eq. 2 can be obtained as follows:

$$\sum_{i=1, i \in I}^{l} p_i \prod_{k_w \in I} (i - k_w) = \sum_{j=0}^{n} a_j \sum_{i=1}^{L} u_i i^j \tag{2}$$

Then we choose a random number $B_i$ to hide the information in Eq. (2) and put $p_i, u_i$ as the exponents of $B_i$. Thus, we can obtain the following formula:

$$\prod_{i=1, i \notin I}^{L} B_i^{p_i \prod_{k=I}^{(i-k)}} - \prod_{j=0}^{n} \left( \prod_{i=1}^{l} B_i^{u_i i^j} \right)^{a_j} \tag{3}$$

According to Viete's formulas, the coefficients $a_j$ in Eq. (2) can be represented by $k_w$:

$$a_{n-j} = (-1)^j \sum_{1 \leq i_1 \leq i_2 \leq \ldots < i_j \leq n} k_i k_{i_2} \cdots k_{i_j}, 0 \leq j \leq n = |I| \tag{4}$$

For example, if we have $I = \{3, 4\}$, then we can get $(x - 3)(x - 4)$, and $a_2 = 1, a_1 = -(3 + 4) = -7, a_0 = 3 * 4 = 12$.

## 4 System Overview

### 4.1 System Model

The system model built in this study is illustrated in Fig. 1. The model includes five entities: the data owner (DO), data user (DU), consensus nodes (CN),

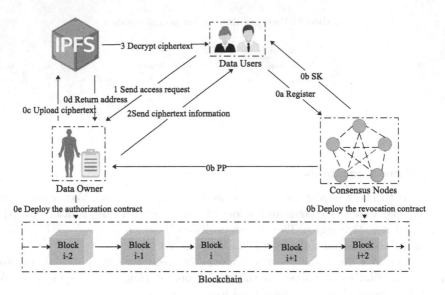

**Fig. 1.** System model

blockchain (BC) and interplanetary file system (IPFS). We suppose that communication between any two of the five entities is secure In this system, the access control workflow can be divided into a preparation phase (0a-0e) and an execution phase (1–3). The preparation phase primarily involves the distribution of keys, the deployment of contracts and the upload of ciphertext information. The execution phase mainly judges the access request.

**Preparation Phase**: First, the DU registers, and CN generate relevant parameters and deploy the revocation contract. DO encrypts the message M on the basis of the public key and access policy and stores the ciphertext on IPFS. After that, DO deploys the authorization contract and stores the ciphertext related information on the blockchain through transactions.

**Execution Phase**: First, the DU generates access information according to their own needs and send them to DO. After verifying the identity of the DU, the DO sends the ciphertext-related information to the DU. Du decrypts the ciphertext after performing the integrity check on the ciphertext.

**DO**: A DO specifies with which attributes users can access their own data and encrypt the data, after which the encrypted data are uploaded to the IPFS, and its hash address is kept on Ethereum through the authorization contract.

**DU**: A DU generates access information according to their own needs and send them to DO, obtains the ciphertext address after passing the verification of the authorization contract, and then decrypts the ciphertext.

**CN**: We displace the trusted authority in the traditional encryption system with a set of pre-defined trusted consensus nodes, which are responsible for generating system parameters and deploying revocation contracts.

**BC**: A BC includes the authorization contract and the revocation contract. The revocation contract is responsible for revoking retired or resigned users, and the authorization contract is responsible for the release of ciphertext information and the judgment of access requests.

**IPFS**: A IPFS is a distributed system that stores ciphertexts and returns hashed addresses.

## 4.2   Security Model

We now define selective IND-CPA security for CP-ABE with hidden access policy. The solution in this paper needs to implement IND-CPA security and access policy security. This paper proves IND-CPA security by using $DBDH$ assumption, and proves the security of access policy by $\mathcal{P} - DBDH$ assumption. We define the following security game $\Gamma_w$ for our scheme.

- **Initialization**. Adversary $\mathcal{A}$ outputs two challenge vectors $p_0$ and $p_1$ to challenger $\mathcal{B}$.
- **Setup**. $\mathcal{B}$ runs the Setup $(\lambda, n)$ algorithm and gives a public key $PK$ to $\mathcal{A}$.
- **Phase 1**: $\mathcal{A}$ may adaptively make a polynomial number of queries to create a secret key for the attribute $u$ subject to the restrictions that $\langle p_0, u \rangle \neq 0$ and $\langle p_1, u \rangle \neq 0.\mathcal{B}$ generates a secret key and inform $\mathcal{A}$ of it.
- **Challenge**: $\mathcal{A}$ outputs challenge messages $M_0$, and $M_1$. $\mathcal{B}$ chooses a random bit $w$. $\mathcal{A}$ given $C_T \leftarrow$ Encrypt $(PP, M_w, p_w)$.
- **Phase 2**: Same as Phase 1.
- **Guess**: $\mathcal{A}$ outputs a bit $w' \in \{0, 1\}$ for $\mathcal{B}$ and wins the game if $w' = w$. Thus, we define the advantage $\mathcal{A}$ as:

$$Adv_{\mathcal{A}}^{IND-sPH-CPA}(\lambda) = \left| \Pr\left[ w' = w \right] - \frac{1}{2} \right|$$

We say that the scheme is selective IND-CPA secure and policy-hiding if $Adv_{\mathcal{A}}^{IND-sPH-CPA}(\lambda)$ is negligible.

## 4.3   Attribute Vector and Policy Vector Generation Algorithms

A policy vector and attribute vector generation algorithm is proposed in [18], but the algorithm must generate three vectors: (one policy vector and two attribute vectors), markedly increasing the computational cost of this scheme. Based on [18], We propose an algorithm using vector fusion technology, which only needs to generate an attribute vector and a policy vector, and the algorithm is also applicable to other wildcard-based access structures. Since our vector generation algorithm generates fewer vectors, fewer policy matches are performed during the system execution phase, so it is more efficient. Specifically, this algorithm can be described as follows:

**Algorithm 1.** Vector Generation Algorithm

**Input:** An attribute set $U = \{U_1, U_2, \cdots, U_L\}$ and a policy set $P = \{P_1, P_2, \cdots, P_L\}$.

**Output:** A policy vector and an attribute vector.

(1): Positive, negative and wildcard symbols in an access structure are first separated into three position sets J, K and I;

(2): while $k_w \in I$ do

(3): Expand $\prod_{k_w \in I}(i - k_w) = \sum_{j=0}^{n} a_j i^j$ to derive coefficients $a_j$

(4): for $k_w \in I$ and $i \in J$ do

(5): Compute $\prod_J = + \sum_{i \in J} \prod_{k_w \in I}(i - k_w)$

(6): for $k_w \in I$ and $i \in K$ do

(7): Compute $\prod_K = + \sum_{i \in K} \prod_{k_w \in I}(i - k_w)$

(8): Compute $\Pi = \Pi_J + \Pi_K$

(9): end for

(10): Positive and negative symbols in a user attribute set are also separated into two position sets $J'$ and $K'$;

(11): for $i = 1$ to $l$ and $i \in J'$ do

(12): Compute $u_j = + \sum_{i \in J'} i^j$

(13): for $i = 1$ to $l$ and $i \in K'$ do

(14): Compute $u'_j = + \sum_{i \in K'} i^j$;

(15): Compute $u = u_j + u'_j$

(16): Return policy vector $\overrightarrow{p} = (a_0, a_1, \cdots, a_n, 0_{n+1}, \cdots, 0_l, \Pi)$, att-ribute vector $\overrightarrow{u} = (u_0, u_1, \cdots, u_l, -1)$

For instance, as shown in Table 1, $p_2 = (+, -, *, *)$ for the set of wildcard positions $I = \{3, 4\}$, the set of positive positions $J = \{1\}$ and the set of negative positions $K = \{2\}$. Based on Viete's formulas, we can obtain:

$$a_2 = 1; a_1 = -7, a_0 = 12$$

Therefore, the policy vector can be obtained as shown in Table 2.

**Table 2.** Policy vector

|     | 0 | 1 | 2 | 3 |
|-----|----|----|----|----|
| $p_2$ | 12 | -7 | 1 | $(1-3)(1-4) + (2-3)(2-4)$ |

Andy's attribute set $u_{Andy} = (+, -, +, -)$. The set of positive positions $J' = \{1, 3\}$ and the set of negative positions $K' = \{2, 4\}$. Therefore, the attribute vector can be obtained as shown in Table 3.

Then, we can calculate $p_2 \cdot u_{Andy} = 12 \times 4 - 7 \times 10 + 1 \times 30 - 8 = 0$. Therefore, Andy's attributes satisfy the access policy $p_2$.

## 4.4 Smart Contract Design

In our system, smart contracts mainly include authorization contracts and revocation contracts, as follows:

**Table 3.** Attribute vector

|           | 0           | 1           | 2           |
|-----------|-------------|-------------|-------------|
| +         | $1^0 + 3^0$ | $1^1 + 3^1$ | $1^2 + 3^2$ |
| −         | $2^0 + 4^0$ | $2^1 + 4^1$ | $2^2 + 4^2$ |
| $u_{Andy}$ | 4          | 10          | 30          |

(1) Revocation Contract: This contract is deployed by CN and is responsible for managing users who have left or retired in the system. It mainly includes the following functions:

updateAssert(): This function is responsible for updating the revocation list, and putting resigned or retired users into the revocation list.

getAssert(): This function returns true or false to determine whether the user has been revoked.

(2) Authorization Contract: This contract is deployed by DO and is responsible for storing ciphertext-related information. When DU sends an access request, it calls the revocation contract to check the identity of DU, so as to determine whether to send ciphertext-related information. It mainly includes the following functions:

initStorage(): This function is responsible for storing ciphertext related information.

judge(): In the access control phase, this function calls the getAssert() function in the revocation contract, and decides whether to send the ciphertext information according to the result.

### 4.5 Our Construction

Our solution consists of the following six procedures:

**Setup**$(\lambda, n)$: The algorithm generates relevant parameters for the system and is executed by the CN. Given a security parameter $\lambda$ and n attributes, CN pick random values $(z, a_0, a_1, \ldots, a_n) \in \left(\mathbb{Z}_p^*\right)^{n+2}$ and set them as follows:

$$g_1 = g^{a_1}, \ldots, g_n = g^{a_n}, g_0 = g^z, \quad h_1 = h^{a_1}, \ldots, h_n = h^{a_n}, h_0 = h^{a_0}$$

The MSK and the PP are given by:

$$\text{MSK} = (h, h_0, h_1, \cdots, h_n),$$
$$PP = (g, g_0, g_1, \cdots, g_n, e(g, h_0))$$

**KeyGen**(PP, MSK, $u$): The algorithm generates decryption key for DU and is done by CN, which randomly chooses $R \in \mathbb{Z}_p^*$, and based on public parameters, master key and attribute vector $u$. The CN then generate $sk_u = (sk_1, sk_2, u)$ as:

$$sk_1 = h_0 \prod_{i=1}^{n} h_i^{u_i R}, sk_2 = h^R$$

**Encrypt**(PP, $p$, M): The algorithm is performed by the DO. Relying on PP and access policy $p$, the DO selects a random $s \in \mathbb{Z}_p^*$ and generates the encrypted message $C_T = (c_0, c_1, c_{2,1}, \cdots, c_{2,n})$ as below:

$$c_0 = M \cdot e(g, h_0)^s, c_1 = g^s, c_{2,i} = g_0^{p_i s} g_i^s \ for \ 1 \leq i \leq n.$$

**On-blockchain**: This algorithm is also performed by the DO, which stores ciphertext-related information on the blockchain through the authorization contract:

$$Tx = (id_T, storeAddress, sign)$$

where $id_T$ is the identifier; and $storeAddress$ is the hash address of the ciphertext. Because IPFS is based on content addressing, it is also the ciphertext integrity check code. After obtaining the ciphertext, the user can use it to perform an integrity check first and then decrypt it. $sign$ is the digital signature. DU can judge whether the encrypted data is what they want based on the digital signature.

**Decrypt**($sk_u$, CT): This algorithm is implemented by the DU, which obtains ciphertext-related information after passing the verification of the authorization contract. The DU first verifies the digital signature of the DO; obtains the ciphertext and verifies its integrity; and finally recovers message $M$ if the user attributes meet the attributes specified by the data owner. We can obtain the plaintext information M by the following calculation:

$$M = e(c_1, sk_1)^{-1} \cdot e\left(\prod_{i=1}^{n} (c_{2,i})^{u_i}, sk_2\right) \cdot c_0 = M \cdot e(g, h)^{zsR\langle p,u\rangle}$$

If $\langle p, u \rangle = 0$, then we get $M$.

**Revocation**: We now assume that the $DU_1$ no longer has attribute $u_1$. Because $DU_1$ has asked for and obtained $sk_{u_1}$, it is able to obtain message $M$ encrypted under access policy $p_1$.

To solve this problem, CN map user addresses to true and false through the mapping type in Solidity. Specifically, as follows:

$$mapping(address => bool) \ public \ identify$$

if $DU_1$ has the attribute $u_1$.

$$identify[userAddress] => true$$

otherwise:

$$identify[userAddress] => false$$

When the $DU_1$ accesses the message, the authorization contract can determine whether to send ciphertext information through the key value corresponding to the user's address.

# 5    Security Proof

## 5.1    Security Analysis of Blockchain Operations

**Trustability**: Many current schemes introduce a central entity to generate relevant parameters in the system, but when this central entity fails, the entire system will be paralyzed. We ensure the trust of access control by storing ciphertext addresses on the blockchain. During the access authorization stage, each DU is verified by the authorization contract, achieving trusted authorization with less human intervention.

**Privacy**: Most of the existing methods directly store the access policy on the blockchain, from which attackers can easily obtain DO information. To protect privacy, it is quite important to protect the access structure. The proposed scheme can hide access policies through vector representations. Data are encrypted and stored on an IPFS, and its hash address is kept on Ethereum, which ensures that malicious users cannot obtain sensitive data and also decreases the cost of saving data in Ethereum.

**Integrity**: We store the ciphertext hash address on the blockchain through smart contracts, which improves system scalability. However, after the DO saves the ciphertext address on Ethereum, it is still possible to change the ciphertext content. In order to ensure that DU can obtain the latest information, we save the ciphertext hash value on the blockchain through a smart contract for users to check the integrity of the ciphertext content. Also, storing the ciphertext hash address on the blockchain avoids a situation where the DO refuses to provide their personal data, ensuring that any unrevoked user will have access to the.

**Traceability**: Because our scheme is based on blockchain, any authorization information will be recorded as an immutable access transaction, making the proposed scheme traceable.

## 5.2    Security Analysis of Scheme

**Theorem 1.** *If the DBDH assumption and the $\mathcal{P} - DBDH$ assumption hold, then any PPT attacker cannot selectively get plaintext information and access policy information.*

The detailed security proof of Theorem 1 is omitted to conserve space. Please contact the author to obtain it.

# 6    Comparisons and Performance Analysis

## 6.1    Implementation Details

In order to verify the practical feasibility of the proposed method, we finished the proposed scheme in JAVA using the JPBC Library 2.0.0 [8]. Experiments were implemented on a computer with 8 GB RAM and an Intel i5-9400 2.90 GHz CPU. We used Type-A pairing, which is constructed by elliptic curve $y^2 = x^3 + x$. We

utilised Remix-Solidity IDE [2] to edit and compile the authorization contract
and the revocation contract, and then used Ropsten [3] as the test network. After
we have written the smart contract on the Remix-Solidity IDE, we will deploy
the smart contract on the Ropsten test network through Metamask [1], Ropsten
and Ethereum have the same consensus mechanism.

## 6.2    Comparison of Functional Characteristics

In this part, we compare our scheme with the proposed existing methods, which
are shown in Table 4. We primarily compare the access revocation, type of hiding
and other performance features. Comparative results illustrate that our scheme
has certain advantages in different properties. As shown in Table 4, the scheme
in this paper and the method in reference [7,11,14] achieve full policy hiding,
whereas other schemes [10,13,15,24,28,29] only achieve partial policy hiding.
Also, in these schemes that achieve full policy hiding, only the proposed scheme
and the scheme [11] are based on blockchain. However, scheme [11] is constructed
based on COBG, and in the plaintext recovery stage, the more attributes of the
user, the lower the decryption efficiency. Additionally, only the scheme in this
paper and the method in reference [7,14] are wildcard constructions. Among
these wildcard-based schemes, only our method is implemented using asymmetric
pairing and supports access revocation.

**Table 4.** Properties comparison

| Scheme | Type of hiding | Asymmetric pairing | Wildcard | Blockchain | Access revocation |
|---|---|---|---|---|---|
| [15] | Partially hidden | ✓ | ✗ | ✗ | ✗ |
| [29] | Partially hidden | ✓ | ✗ | ✗ | ✗ |
| [24] | Partially hidden | ✗ | ✗ | ✗ | ✗ |
| [13] | Partially hidden | ✗ | ✗ | ✗ | ✓ |
| [11] | Fully hidden | ✗ | ✗ | ✓ | ✗ |
| [14] | Fully hidden | ✗ | ✓ | ✗ | ✗ |
| [7] | Fully hidden | ✗ | ✓ | ✗ | ✗ |
| [10] | Partially hidden | ✗ | ✗ | ✗ | ✗ |
| [28] | Partially hidden | ✗ | ✗ | ✗ | ✓ |
| Our scheme | Fully hidden | ✓ | ✓ | ✓ | ✓ |

## 6.3    Deployment Cost and Operating Cost

Some energy must be expended to deploy smart contracts on Ethereum and
run some functions in the smart contract. Ethereum uses a unit called "gas" to
describe how much energy it takes to perform an operation, such as deploying
a smart contract or run some functions. The more complex the task, the more
gas it consumes.

Table 5 shows the gas paid for some operations. We can see that deploying the contract costs relatively more, while executing some ABIs cost relatively little. Please note that since the Ropsten test network is used in the scheme, the gas values obtained are only experimental values and cannot represent the real situation. In a real system, we can reduce gas values by using a consensus mechanism with high consensus efficiency.

**Table 5.** Gas cost for some operations

| Blockchain operation | Gas |
|---|---|
| Deploy the authorization contract | 286352 |
| Deploy the revocation contract | 288549 |
| Access revocation | 29394 |
| Upload ciphertext information | 25984 |

**Table 6.** Notations for comparison

| Notation | Description |
|---|---|
| $|G_i|$ | Length of element in $G_1$, $G_2$ and $G_T$ |
| $|Z_p|$ | Length of element in $Z_p$ |
| $E_i$ | Exponentiation in $G_1$, $G_2$ and $G_T$ |
| $P$ | Pairing computation |
| $l$ | The number of rows of the LSSS |
| $s$ | The number of attributes of DU |
| $c$ | The number of the attribute categories |
| $\omega$ | The number of wildcards |
| $W$ | All minimal rowsets |
| $k$ | The size of W |

## 6.4   Theoretical Results

We now consider comparing the storage and computational costs of some of the studies in Table 4 that are more relevant to the content of this paper with the solution in this paper. Table 7 is the storage cost, and Table 8 is the computation cost. Related notations are described in Table 6. We compare the PK, CT and SK sizes of these schemes in Table 7. Table 7 shows that the PK length in [28] is the shortest; compared to [7], the proposed protocol achieves a shorter PK. The storage costs of [7] and the proposed method depend on the number of wildcards in the policy made by DO, which typically requires a shorter storage overhead than [10,13,28]. Obviously, the storage overhead of the three aspects of the scheme in this paper is smaller than [7]. Therefore, the storage cost required by the proposed scheme is minimal.

In Table 8, encryption time, secret key generation time and decryption time in schemes [10, 13, 28] are all related to the number of user attributes. The more attributes, the greater the computational overhead. The computational costs of [7] and the scheme of this paper are only related to the number of wildcards. In real systems, the number of wildcards will generally be significantly less than the number of user attributes, especially in attribute-sensitive systems. During decryption, pairing operations in these schemes increase with the number of attributes or wildcards, resulting in a long decryption time and a large computational cost for the decryption algorithms. The number of pairing calculations for the scheme in this paper is certain in the decryption phase and is thus more efficient. As a result, compared with other schemes in the table, the scheme in this paper has the highest efficiency.

**Table 7.** Storage cost

| Scheme | Size of PK | Size of CT | Size of SK |
|---|---|---|---|
| [13] | $7\lvert G_1\rvert + \lvert G_T\rvert$ | $(5l+2)\lvert G_1\rvert + 2\lvert G_T\rvert$ | $(4s+2)\lvert G_1\rvert$ |
| [10] | $5\lvert G_1\rvert + \lvert G_T\rvert$ | $(s+2)\lvert G_1\rvert$ | $(15l+10)\lvert G_1\rvert + 2\lvert G_T\rvert$ |
| [28] | $4\lvert G_1\rvert + \lvert G_T\rvert$ | $(c+3)\lvert G_1\rvert$ | $(4l+2)\lvert G_1\rvert + 2\lvert G_T\rvert$ |
| [7] | $(\omega+5)\lvert G_1\rvert + \lvert G_T\rvert$ | $(\omega+4)\lvert G_1\rvert + \lvert G_T\rvert$ | $(\omega+4)\lvert G_1\rvert$ |
| Ours | $(\omega+2)\lvert G_1\rvert + \lvert G_T\rvert$ | $(\omega+1)\lvert G_1\rvert + \lvert G_T\rvert$ | $2\lvert G_1\rvert + \omega\lvert Z_p\rvert$ |

**Table 8.** Computational cost

| Scheme | Computation cost of Enc | Computation cost of SK | Computation cost of Dec |
|---|---|---|---|
| [13] | $(8l+3)E_1 + 2E_T$ | $(7c+3)E_1$ | $2kE_T + (3k+1)P$ |
| [10] | $(30s+15)E_1 + 2E_T$ | $(2s+3)E_1$ | $10sE_1 + sE_T + (10s+15)P$ |
| [28] | $(6l+2)E_1 + 2E_T$ | $(c+3)E_1$ | $(k+l)E_T + 2(k+l+1)P$ |
| [7] | $(\omega+5)E_1 + E_T$ | $(\omega+4)E_1$ | $(\omega+4)P$ |
| Ours | $(2\omega+1)E_1 + E_T$ | $(\omega+1)E_1$ | $\omega E_1 + 2P$ |

## 6.5 Experimental Results

Because the proposed scheme uses blockchain, its efficiency is restricted by the blockchain. In the proposed scheme, we store the ciphertext address on Ethereum to reduce the cost of storing the entire ciphertext on the blockchain and to improve system scalability. The efficiency of computing on the blockchain depends on the consensus algorithm it uses. The blockchain with high consensus algorithm efficiency will execute faster. Thus, we primarily focus on the efficiency of encryption algorithms and decryption algorithms, only comparing the metrics of our scheme with those of the schemes proposed in [7, 10, 28]. To facilitate display on the coordinate graph, we use attributes to describe the abscissa and evaluate the worst-case efficiency of the proposed scheme. Comparative results are shown in Figs. 2 and 3. The experimental data is the average of 20 runs on the computer.

In the encryption stage, the comparison result of the calculation cost between our study and other schemes is shown in Fig. 2. Obviously, the encryption time of the proposed scheme and other schemes is related to the number of attributes. The more attributes, the longer the encryption time. In terms of encryption efficiency, the encryption efficiency of the proposed scheme is much higher than that of scheme [10,28] and slightly lower than that of scheme [7], but the encryption time cost of our study and scheme [7] is not much different, and the growth rate of encryption time is basically the same.

It can be seen from the Fig. 3 that although the decryption time of each scheme increases with the increase of the number of user attributes, compared with the schemes in [7,10,28], the proposed scheme has a lower growth rate and the efficiency of this scheme is also the highest. Especially when the number of attributes in the system is large, the user decryption experience in the proposed scheme is the best. Due to the large computational cost of pairing operation, and the pairing operation in this paper is fixed, the scheme in this paper has high efficiency in the decryption stage.

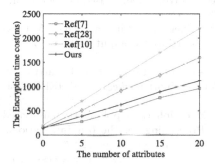

**Fig. 2.** Ciphertext generation stage

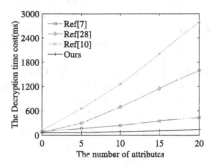

**Fig. 3.** Decryption phase

## 7   Conclusions

In this study, we built a blockchain-based ciphertext policy hiding access control scheme, which achieves distributed and reliable access control, and ensures user privacy and security. In addition, we use the revocation function by maintaining a revocation list through smart contracts, which protects users' private keys from abuse. Theoretical analysis and procedural data show that the our study is safe and effective. Because the efficiencies of operations using blockchain primarily depend on the consensus algorithm, we plan to consider using Ethereum 2.0 to implement the proposed scheme in future work to improve system throughput.

# References

1. Metamask (2022). https://metamask.io
2. Remix ide for Ethereum smart contract programming (2022). https://remix.ethereum.org
3. Ropsten Testnet Explorer (2022). https://ropsten.etherscan.io
4. Bertrand, Y., Boudaoud, K., Riveill, M.: What do you think about your company's leaks? A survey on end-users perception toward data leakage mechanisms. Front. Big Data, 38 (2020). https://doi.org/10.3389/fdata.2020.568257
5. Bethencourt, J., Sahai, A., Waters, B.: Ciphertext-policy attribute-based encryption. In: 2007 IEEE Symposium on Security and Privacy (SP 2007), pp. 321–334. IEEE (2007)
6. Butun, I., Österberg, P.: A review of distributed access control for blockchain systems towards securing the internet of things. IEEE Access **9**, 5428–5441 (2020)
7. Chen, Y., et al.: Efficient attribute-based data sharing scheme with hidden access structures. Comput. J. **62**(12), 1748–1760 (2019)
8. De Caro, A., Iovino, V.: jPBC: Java pairing based cryptography. In: 2011 IEEE Symposium on Computers and Communications (ISCC), pp. 850–855. IEEE (2011)
9. Ding, S., Cao, J., Li, C., Fan, K., Li, H.: A novel attribute-based access control scheme using blockchain for IoT. IEEE Access **7**, 38431–38441 (2019)
10. Gan, T., Liao, Y., Liang, Y., Zhou, Z., Zhang, G.: Partial policy hiding attribute-based encryption in vehicular fog computing (2021)
11. Gao, S., Piao, G., Zhu, J., Ma, X., Ma, J.: TrustAccess: a trustworthy secure ciphertext-policy and attribute hiding access control scheme based on blockchain. IEEE Trans. Veh. Technol. **69**(6), 5784–5798 (2020)
12. Hao, J., Huang, C., Ni, J., Rong, H., Xian, M., Shen, X.S.: Fine-grained data access control with attribute-hiding policy for cloud-based IoT. Comput. Netw. **153**, 1–10 (2019)
13. Hu, G., Zhang, L., Mu, Y., Gao, X.: An expressive "test-decrypt-verify" attribute-based encryption scheme with hidden policy for smart medical cloud. IEEE Syst. J. **15**(1), 365–376 (2020)
14. Jin, C., Feng, X., Shen, Q.: Fully secure hidden ciphertext policy attribute-based encryption with short ciphertext size. In: Proceedings of the 6th International Conference on Communication and Network Security, pp. 91–98 (2016)
15. Lai, J., Deng, R.H., Li, Y.: Expressive CP-ABE with partially hidden access structures. In: Proceedings of the 7th ACM Symposium on Information, Computer and Communications Security, pp. 18–19 (2012)
16. Li, Q., Zhang, Y., Zhang, T., Huang, H., He, Y., Xiong, J.: HTAC: fine-grained policy-hiding and traceable access control in mHealth. IEEE Access **8**, 123430–123439 (2020)
17. Liu, S., Yu, J., Hu, C., Li, M.: Traceable multiauthority attribute-based encryption with outsourced decryption and hidden policy for CIoT. Wirel. Commun. Mob. Comput. **2021**, 16 (2021)
18. Phuong, T.V.X., Yang, G., Susilo, W.: Hidden ciphertext policy attribute-based encryption under standard assumptions. IEEE Trans. Inf. Forensics Secur. **11**(1), 35–45 (2015)
19. Rana, S., Mishra, D.: Efficient and secure attribute based access control architecture for smart healthcare. J. Med. Syst. **44**(5), 1–11 (2020)
20. Saini, A., Zhu, Q., Singh, N., Xiang, Y., Gao, L., Zhang, Y.: A smart-contract-based access control framework for cloud smart healthcare system. IEEE Internet Things J. **8**(7), 5914–5925 (2020)

21. Shafeeq, S., Alam, M., Khan, A.: Privacy aware decentralized access control system. Futur. Gener. Comput. Syst. **101**, 420–433 (2019)
22. Wang, S., Zhang, Y., Zhang, Y.: A blockchain-based framework for data sharing with fine-grained access control in decentralized storage systems. IEEE Access **6**, 38437–38450 (2018)
23. Xiong, H., Yang, M., Yao, T., Chen, J., Kumari, S.: Efficient unbounded fully attribute hiding inner product encryption in cloud-aided WBANs. IEEE Syst. J. **16**, 5424–5432 (2021)
24. Xiong, H., Zhao, Y., Peng, L., Zhang, H., Yeh, K.H.: Partially policy-hidden attribute-based broadcast encryption with secure delegation in edge computing. Futur. Gener. Comput. Syst. **97**, 453–461 (2019)
25. Xu, G., Li, H., Dai, Y., Yang, K., Lin, X.: Enabling efficient and geometric range query with access control over encrypted spatial data. IEEE Trans. Inf. Forensics Secur. **14**(4), 870–885 (2018)
26. Yan, X., He, G., Yu, J., Tang, Y., Zhao, M.: Offline/online outsourced attribute-based encryption with partial policy hidden for the internet of things. J. Sens. **2020** (2020)
27. Zeng, P., Zhang, Z., Lu, R., Choo, K.K.R.: Efficient policy-hiding and large universe attribute-based encryption with public traceability for internet of medical things. IEEE Internet Things J. **8**(13), 10963–10972 (2021)
28. Zhang, W., Zhang, Z., Xiong, H., Qin, Z.: PHAS-HEKR-CP-ABE: partially policy-hidden CP-ABE with highly efficient key revocation in cloud data sharing system. J. Ambient Intell. Human. Comput. **13**, 1–15 (2021)
29. Zhang, Y., Zheng, D., Deng, R.H.: Security and privacy in smart health: efficient policy-hiding attribute-based access control. IEEE Internet Things J. **5**(3), 2130–2145 (2018)
30. Zhang, Y., Yutaka, M., Sasabe, M., Kasahara, S.: Attribute-based access control for smart cities: a smart-contract-driven framework. IEEE Internet Things J. **8**(8), 6372–6384 (2020)
31. Zhang, Z., Zhang, W., Qin, Z.: A partially hidden policy CP-ABE scheme against attribute values guessing attacks with online privacy-protective decryption testing in IoT assisted cloud computing. Futur. Gener. Comput. Syst. **123**, 181–195 (2021)

# Granting Access Privileges Using OpenID Connect in Permissioned Distributed Ledgers

Shohei Kakei[1]([envelope]) [iD], Yoshiaki Shiraishi[2] [iD], and Shoichi Saito[1] [iD]

[1] Nagoya Institute of Technology, Nagoya, Aichi, Japan
kakei.shohei@nitech.ac.jp
[2] Kobe University, Kobe, Hyogo, Japan

**Abstract.** Permissioned distributed ledger technology (DLT), in which only authenticated entities participate, assumes trust among the participants and implicit consent for data manipulation. In light of international regulations such as the GDPR, it is necessary to clarify the access privileges of user data, even for systems that assume the trust of the participants. In this paper, we propose an access privilege granting method for service providers that need to access user data in permissioned DLT systems. The proposed method separates the access privilege for user data in the distributed ledger from the execution privilege for smart contracts. By requesting a user to grant the access privilege, the participants can manipulate user data using smart contracts. The access privilege is represented by a token issued by OpenID Connect (OIDC). Smart contracts can directly verify the token without the participant's interference. In this way, all the participants in the DLT network can reach a consensus that data manipulation is based on the user's consent. We implemented the prototype system with Keycloak, an OIDC-compliant identity provider, and Hyperledger Fabric, a permissioned DLT, and then evaluated its performance. Finally, the overhead of access control is 0.21%, from which we conclude that the load on the system is very small.

**Keywords:** Distributed ledger technology · Smart contract · Access control · OpenID Connect · Hyperledger Fabric

## 1 Introduction

Distributed Ledger Technology (DLT) is known as a technology that can eliminate the cost of siloed business processes. In particular, a permissioned DLT system, which is built using multiple known nodes, fits the business use cases requiring the collaboration of multiple organizations because the permissioned DLT system can restrict the organizations that can join a DLT network [7]. In terms of the managed data handled by a DLT system, they can be classified into two main types: user data, such as healthcare [6,26], education [8] or energy [9], and non-user data, such as logistics [4] or the vehicular ad hoc networks [17].

© ICST Institute for Computer Sciences, Social Informatics and Telecommunications Engineering 2023
Published by Springer Nature Switzerland AG 2023. All Rights Reserved
F. Li et al. (Eds.): SecureComm 2022, LNICST 462, pp. 290–308, 2023.
https://doi.org/10.1007/978-3-031-25538-0_16

A smart contract (SC), which is used as an interface to manipulate data in a distributed ledger, enables secure and flexible data manipulation based on consensus among the organizations. In a permissioned DLT system, the execution of an SC is implicitly agreed upon because of the assumption of trust among participating organizations. In order to guarantee users the right to restrict access to user data and the right to data portability as required by regulations such as the General Data Protection Regulation (GDPR) [23], it is necessary to clarify access privileges to data in a distributed ledger.

Employing the classic method of sharing credentials such as passwords and passcodes for delegating access to resources often leads to unauthorized access and misuse of the provided credentials. Sudarsan et al. [21] classify the delegation-based authorization models into three types: (i) identity delegation at the authentication level, (ii) delegation by access control/authorization server, and (iii) power-of-attorney (PoA) based authorization, and discuss their strength and weakness. According to the authors, delegation by access control/authorization server and PoA-based authorization are similar in allowing authorization on the user's behalf. On the contrary, the difference is that delegation by access control/authorization server is performed via an authorization server, while PoA [20] is performed by the user's direct signature. In PoA-based authorization, since the user directly uses the private key, there is less dependence on third parties, but it is often hard to use private keys flexibly according to the environment. On the other hand, delegation by access control/authorization server requires trust in the authorization server but allows delegation from various devices through authentication via a web browser. Furthermore, security can be improved by multi-factor authentication [13].

In this paper, we propose an access privilege granting method for service providers to access user data in a permissioned DLT system. The proposed method separates the access privilege for user data in the distributed ledger from the execution privilege for SCs. A data owner gives consent for the service provider to access data, and the service provider manipulates the data under the consent. In other words, data owners need to eliminate unauthorized intervention by service providers and ensure that their consent is correctly transmitted to the DLT system. Our approach uses JSON Web Token (JWT) mechanism to transmit a claim as the user's consent. The JWT has a digital signature proving its claim and is often employed in distributed architectures such as microservices [5,10,19]. In our approach, the JWT provides the user's consent to the service provider, and the service provider uses the JWT to prove access privileges to the DLT system. By doing this, a data owner does not have to implicitly trust the service providers for data manipulation and can explicitly allow the service providers to manipulate data.

The main contributions of the paper are summarized as follows:

- We advocate separating data access privileges from SC execution privileges and propose an access control method based on user consent in permissioned DLTs.

- We designed the proposed method using JWT. In this method, JWT securely informs the SC about what a user is consenting to. For example, the user can consent to read or write data.
- We implement a prototype system for the proposed method with Hyperledger Fabric and evaluate the processing overhead of the proposed access control.
- We present limitations from the perspective of misuse of the privileges through security analysis and discuss the challenges in applying the proposed method to permissionless DLTs.

The rest of the paper is organized as follows. Section 2 presents background of the proposed method. Section 3 shows the access control model of the proposed method and provides the security requirements in access control using JWT. The proposed method is presented in Sect. 4, and is shown to satisfy the security requirements in Sect. 5. We present a prototype implementation and evaluate the performance in Sect. 6. Section 7 discusses the proposed method, and Sect. 8 concludes this paper.

## 2    Background and Related Works

### 2.1    OpenID Connect

OpenID Connect (OIDC) [18] is a mechanism that extends the OAuth 2.0 authorization protocol with the ability to issue ID tokens containing user information for user authentication. In OIDC, an ID Provider (IdP) issues an authorization code to an end-user (EU), and the EU passes the authorization code to a Relying Party (RP). The RP authenticates the EU by exchanging the authorization code for an ID token and verifying it. By porting RP's authentication function to the IdP, the EU does not need to authenticate individual RPs.

IdPs can issue an ID Token as a JSON Web Token (JWT) [14] consisting of a header part, a payload part, and a signature part. The header part typically consists of the type of the token and the signature algorithm being used. The payload part contains arbitrary attribute information called claims (e.g., issuer, subject, and expiration date). The signature part contains the signature of the IdP on the data in the header and payload parts.

In this way, a JWT can carry user information whose authenticity is guaranteed by an IdP. JWTs are suitable for carrying user authentication in distributed architectures because they can be verified locally and directly through the public key [19]. Karim et al. [15] raised a concern regarding rich user authentication in resource-constrained IoT environments. They proposed an authentication model based on OIDC for the IoT manufacturer platform, which will enable users to maintain IoT devices. Their model offloads the user authentication process to an IoT gateway. The gateway performs rule-based user authentication with JWTs. Xu et al. [24] raised a concern regarding account management in edge computing. They proposed a microservice security agent platform that enables edge computing clients to access the edge computing service with JWT.

## 2.2  Distributed Ledger Technology

Distributed ledger technology (DLT) is a technology that synchronizes tamper-resistant distributed ledgers using a consensus algorithm [1,2]. The distributed ledger is managed by multiple nodes that construct the DLT network and is divided into two components: a data store (DS), which stores data, such as an user, application, and system data, and a smart contract (SC), which is an interface for manipulating data in a DS. Only agreed-upon data are stored in the DS through the mutual confirmation of the execution results of the SC by multiple nodes.

DLT systems can be classified into "permissionless" and "permissioned" systems based on the participation of nodes [16]. Permissionless DLT systems, consisting of a DLT network with an unspecified number of nodes, are fault-tolerant because they do not require a central administrator as a single point of trust. However, even in the case of faults in SCs, a permissionless DLT system cannot be temporarily suspended. Thus, it is hard to patch vulnerable SCs [11,27]. This allows damage to spread easily. On the other hand, permissioned DLT systems comprise a consortium consisting of only specific organizations. Thus, a permissioned DLT system can be suspended for maintenance and to prevent further damage at the consortium's discretion, but trust in the consortium is vital. Ethereum and Bitcoin are known as permissionless DLT systems, and Hyperledger Fabric and Corda are known as permissioned DLT systems.

Researchers indicate that DLT is improving the GDPR compliance for user data sharing. Antwi et al. [6] identified key requirements of healthcare applications and created testing scenarios using Hyperledger Fabric to investigate the potential for the GDPR compliance with healthcare applications. Delgado-von-Eitzen et al. [8] proposed a GDPR-compliant academic certification system based on Hyperledger Fabric. Systems oriented toward GDPR compliance tend to employ permissioned DLT because it can restrict participants from manipulating data depending on user attributes. In addition to user data, there are also studies that share information about organizational data, such as cyber attacks [12]. Truong et al. [22] proposed a design concept with technical mechanisms for a blockchain-based GDPR-compliant personal data management platform. The platform manages the data with a database and ports the mechanisms (e.g., authentication and authorization, access control, and logging) to a blockchain network.

# 3   Access Control and Security Requirements for Distributed Ledgers

## 3.1  Access Control for Distributed Ledgers

Models of DLT-based services can be broadly classified into two types: one in which the DLT system operates at the front end, as shown in Fig. 1-(a), and the other in which the DLT system operates at the back end, as shown in Fig. 1-(b). The former model type is suitable for a permissionless DLT system that

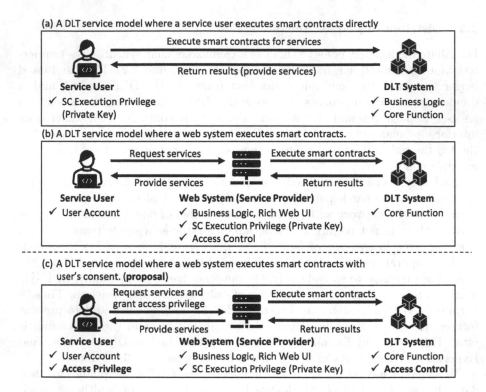

**Fig. 1.** Comparison of DLT service models and proposed DLT service model.

does not require a central administrator since the service user can execute SCs directly. There are two drawbacks of the permissionless DLT: one is the difficulty of implementing complex processing such as business logic or rich user interfaces due to its non-stoppable nature and the limitation of SCs. The other is that it forces all users to manage their private keys at their own risk. In contrast to the former model, in the latter model, core functions and complex processing can be separated into the DLT system and the web server, respectively. Thus, this model type is ideal for commercial services. The latter model is suitable for a permissioned DLT system that can restrict the entities executing SCs. The service user entrusts SC execution to the service provider (SP). The SP authenticates the service user, manipulates user data using SCs, and provides services using SC processing results. This model can achieve a rich DLT-based service and reduce the private key management cost for the service user, although the need for implicit trust in the SP arises.

When constructing a system using DLT, it is required to consider the characteristics of both. The systems oriented toward GDPR compliance described in Sect. 2.2 can be classified into the model shown in Fig. 1-(a). In this model, it is inevitable that usability will be sacrificed, although data manipulation is guaranteed to originate from the service user unless the private key is compromised.

For usability improvement, a new DLT service model is needed to resolve the problem with the model shown in Fig. 1-(b). In light of the above, this paper proposes the new DLT service model shown in Fig. 1-(c), which reduces the need for implicit trust in the SP.

Figure 1-(c) shows a new DLT service model that explicitly manages the access privilege for user data. In Fig. 1-(b), implicit trust arises because the SP controls data access as a single trust point. The proposed method moves the access control point from the SP to the DLT system, and the service user grants the access privilege to the SP. The SP has the SC execution privilege and executes SCs using the SC execution privilege and the access privilege.

In Fig. 1-(b), it is difficult to verify the legitimacy of manipulating data of users who are not in a service provision relationship because the SP is allowed to execute SCs that include the access privilege of user data. For example, when the service user provides user data with the DLT system, the service user expects that only the SP in use can access their data. However, it is difficult to guarantee such expectations in an environment where the access privilege is assigned to multiple organizations, including competitors. On the other hand, in the proposed model, the SP cannot access user data unless the service user grants the access privilege to the SP. When access to user data is required, the SP requests the service user to grant the access privilege. The access control point embedded in the SC determines whether data access is allowed or not based on the access privilege. The data manipulation is explicitly performed because multiple participants of the DLT network verify the access privilege.

### 3.2 Security Requirements for Access Control with JWT

In the model focusing on, the service user grants the SC the access privilege via the SP. For access privileges to be correctly conveyed from the user to the SC, the SC must be prevented from being interfered with and each node executing the SC must be able to correctly verify access privileges. In distributed architectures such as microservices, there are some mechanisms to directly authenticate user-related information asynchronously with the authentication server using the statelessness of JWT [5,10,19]. Therefore, the proposed model uses JWT, which can express a variety of claims, as access privileges.

The entity managing an access privilege can issue a JWT that includes the information necessary to verify access privileges as claims, and thereby the SC can know the access privilege of the service user simply by verifying the JWT. However, if the SP misuses the JWT, the access privileges will be violated. In order to mitigate the risk of misusing a JWT, the following requirements are required.

- **Req. 1:** The SC must only accept a JWT issued to legitimate a service user to use the legitimate service.
- **Req. 2:** The SC cannot use a JWT that has been used before.
- **Req. 3:** The SC cannot use a JWT that has been issued in the past.

Req. 1 is a requirement to prevent the use of access privileges of others or issued for other services. Req. 2 and Req. 3 are requirements to guarantee that the SP's use of access privileges originates from the SU's consent. If the SP could reuse a JWT, it would not be possible to guarantee that the execution of the SC originates from the SU. For the same reason, the act of retaining an unused JWT for later use by the SP must also be prevented.

## 4   Proposed Method

This paper proposes an access control method for user data in a distributed ledger. The proposed method guarantees that a service user accesses the user data based on user consent. An access token, which is a JWT in OIDC, represents a user's consent and is used as a temporary access privilege for the user data. A service user grants a service provider the access privilege by the access token. SC verifies the access token so that the user's consent is agreed upon among the participants of the DLT network.

### 4.1   Structure of the Proposed Method

The proposed method contains the following six components. The relationships with each component are shown in Fig. 2.

- **ID Provider (IdP):** The IdP is a component that issues ID tokens and access tokens in JWT format under the OIDC protocol. The IdP manages user accounts of SUs and issues authorization codes in response to SU requests. The authorization codes are exchanged by SPs to obtain ID tokens and access tokens. The IdP issues these tokens in the authorization code flow.
- **Service User (SU):** The SU is a service user of SPs and owns the rights to the SU's data in the DS. By granting the access privilege to the SP, the SU agrees to allow the SP to access the SU's data. In the proposed method, the access privilege is represented by the access token. The SU is the EU in OIDC.
- **Service Provider (SP):** The SP is a component that joins the DLT network according to the permission of the DLSP and provides services to the SU using SCs. Joining the DLT network gives the SP the privilege to execute the SCs. The SP trusts the IdP and authenticates the SU with the ID token issued from the IdP when providing services. If access to SU's data is required when providing services, the SP requests the access token from the SU and executes SCs with the access token.
- **Smart Contract (SC):** The SC is a part of a distributed ledger and is a set of code scripts that can process data in the DS. The SC can restrict the data manipulation by its code, and all SPs agree to the processing written in the SC. The processing of verifying access tokens is embedded in the SC, and the SC determines whether or not SU's data can be read or written according to access tokens.

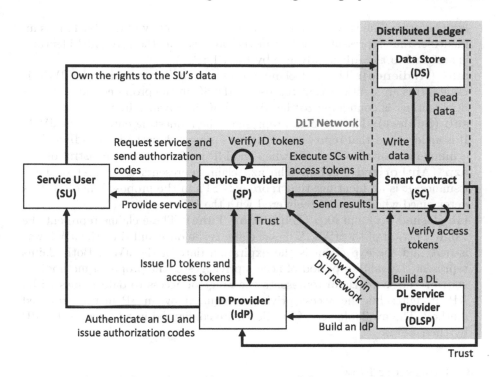

**Fig. 2.** Relationships with components of the proposed method.

- **Data Store (DS):** The DS is a part of a distributed ledger and can store any data. The DS is comprised of multiple instances of ledgers, which are maintained by each SP. In the proposed method, the DS stores application data (e.g., user data and configuration data) and system data (e.g., the identities of entities, the status of the access privileges, and public key certificates). The SU owns the rights to the SU's data, although the DS is managed under the DLT network.
- **Distributed Ledger Service Provider (DLSP):** The DLSP is a consortium of multiple organizations responsible for operating and managing a permissioned DLT network. Moreover, the DLSP is responsible for the DS's design, the SC's implementation, the management of participating SPs in the DLT network, and operates the IdP. The DLSP has to define access privileges according to a service design and implements the verification logic of a JWT in the SC.

## 4.2  Definition of Access Token and ID Token

The proposed method uses two types of JWTs signed by IdP: access tokens and ID tokens. The seven types of claims contained in a JWT that are used to construct the proposed method are listed below.

- **iss (Issuer):** The iss claim represents the issuing entity of the JWT. It is an identifier that represents the IdP in the proposed method. An IdP identifier is assigned to the IdP in advance by the DLSP.
- **aud (Audience):** The aud claim represents an RP to which the JWT is issued. It is an identifier that represents the SC in the proposed method. The SC identifier is configured to the IdP and SC in advance by the DLSP.
- **sub (Subject):** The sub claim represents the requesting entity of the JWT. It is an identifier that represents SUs in the proposed method. The IdP assigns a unique identifier to each SU when the IdP performs a user registration.
- **azp (Authorized Party):** The azp claim represents the target of JWT issuance. It is an identifier that represents SPs in the proposed method. It is determined when SPs are registered with the IdP.
- **iat (Issued At) and exp (Expiration Time):** These claims represent the validity period of the JWT. The iat claim is the date and time the JWT was issued, and the exp claim is the expiration date of the JWT. Both claims represent the validity period of access privileges in the proposed method.
- **scope:** The scope claim represents the range of access to data requested by RP. It represents the access privileges required by an SP in the proposed method. The available access privileges are configured in advance to the IdP by the DLSP.

### 4.3    Processing Flow

This section describes the four phases of the proposed method: setup phase, SP registration phase, SU registration phase, and service provision phase. In the setup phase, the DLSP launches the distributed ledger service by constructing the DS, the SC, and the IdP. In the SP Registration Phase, the DLSP qualifies an SP to participate in the DLT network and registers the SP as the RP with the IdP. In the SU registration phase, the DLSP registers an SU as a user of the distributed ledger service for the IdP. Finally, in the service provision phase, the SP provides services to the SU using SP's SC execution privilege and SU's DS access privilege. It is important to note that the DLSP has prepared the IdP, the SC, and the DS. The DLSP implements the SC to store these information types in the DS and stores the iss, aud claims, and IdP's public key $pk_{IdP}$ in the DS. Moreover, the DLSP has defined scopes and has set the scopes to the IdP.

**Setup Phase.** Figure 3 shows the processing flow of this phase. The DLSP generates the iss and aud claims and $pk_{IdP}$ and calls the SC to register these information types (Step 1-1). The SC writes these information types in the DS (Step 1-2). After this phase is performed for the first time, it is repeated each time the registration information is updated, such as following maintenance of the DLT network.

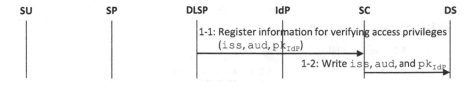

**Fig. 3.** Processing of the setup phase.

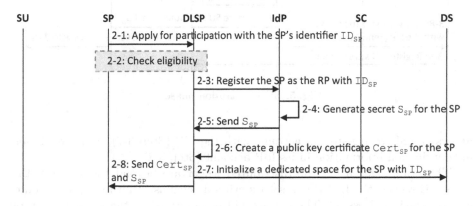

**Fig. 4.** SP registration phase.

**SP Registration Phase.** Figure 4 shows the processing flow of this phase. An SP applies to the DLSP for participation with its identifier $ID_{SP}$ (Step 2-1). When receiving the application, the DLSP checks whether the SP meets the criteria for participation in the DLT network (Step 2-2), and if it does, the DLSP registers the SP with the IdP as the RP with $ID_{SP}$ (Step 2-3). The IdP generates a secret $S_{SP}$ for the SP after confirming that $ID_{SP}$ is not already registered and issues $S_{SP}$ to the DLSP (Steps 2-4, 2-5). The DLSP creates a public key certificate $Cert_{SP}$, a qualification to participate in the DLT network, and initializes a dedicated space in the DS for the SP (Steps 2-6, 2-7). Finally, the DLSP issues $Cert_{SP}$ and $S_{SP}$ to the SP (Step 2-8).

The criteria for participating in the DLT network are beyond the scope of this paper. However, the DLSP can set its criteria, such as verifying the legal existence of the organization. The public key certificate and the secret generated in this phase are used to execute an SC and request access privileges in the service provision phase.

**SU Registration Phase.** Figure 5 shows the processing flow of this phase. When receiving a user registration from an SU, the DLSP determines whether or not the SU meets the criteria for using the distributed ledger (Steps 3-1, 3-2). If it does, the DLSP creates an account for the SU in the IdP (Step 3-3), and the IdP issues an SU's identifier $ID_{SU}$ (Steps 3-4, 3-5). Next, the DLSP creates the SU's account on the DS using the SC (Step 3-6), and the SC initializes settings, including the status of the access privilege (Step 3-7). Finally, the DLSP

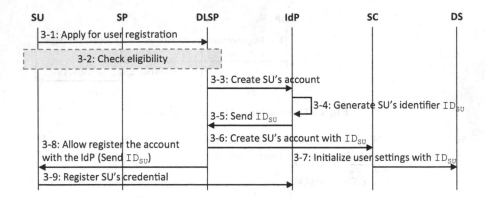

**Fig. 5.** SU registration phase.

allows the SU to register an account with the IdP (Step 3-7), and the SU sets authentication information in its IdP account (Step 3-8).

The criteria for using the distributed ledger are beyond the scope of this paper. However, the DLSP can set its criteria, such as confirming possession of a valid email address [3]. The details will be described at the service provision phase, but the date and time information of access tokens is stored to detect misuse. Then, in Step 3-7, the SC initializes that date and time information.

**Service Provision Phase.** Figure 6 shows the processing flow of this phase. When receiving a service request from an SU (Step 4-1), the SP decides on an SC to be executed (Step 4-2) and requests the necessary privileges to the SU using OIDC (Step 4-3). The SU, the SP, and the IdP execute the authorization code flow; the SU gives the SP an authorization code, and the SP obtains an ID token and an access token through the exchange of the authorization code. After the exchange of the tokens, the SP authenticates the SU using the sub claim of the ID token (Step 4-4) and executes the SC with arguments and the access token (Step 4-5).

The SC consists of the three processing: initiating the data manipulation (Step 4-6), executing the processing with DS read/write (Step 4-7), and finalizing the data manipulation (Step 4-8). In Step 4-6, the SC checks the validity of access privileges by checking the access token. The validation of the access privileges is performed as follows. Let $AT_t$ denote the access token at time $t$, and $iat_t$ denote the iat claim contained in $AT_t$. First, the integrity of $AT_t$ is verified to confirm that a legitimate IdP signs $AT_t$.

**Step V1:** The SC verifies the signature part of the $AT_t$ using the $pk_{IdP}$ registered in the DS.

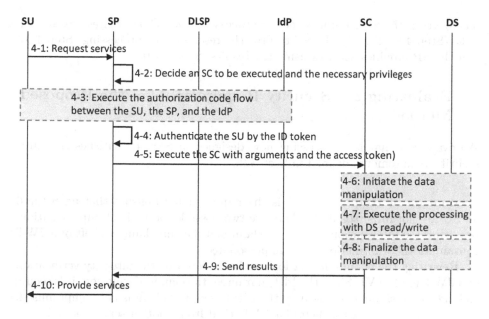

**Fig. 6.** Service provision phase.

Next, it is verified that the $AT_t$ is not reused.

**Step V2:** The SC compares $iat_t$ with $iat_{t-1}$ stored in the DS and verifies whether $iat_t$ is greater than $iat_{t-1}$, which means that $AT_t$ is the newer access token than the last used access token.

Next, it is verified that the legitimate IdP issues $AT_t$ to the legitimate SC, and the legitimate SP uses $AT_t$.

**Step V3:** The SC checks the executor of the SC with $Cert_{SP}$ and confirms that it is the same entity listed in the azp claim of $AT_t$.

**Step V4:** The SC compares the aud claim registered in the DS with the aud claim in $AT_t$ to confirm that the recipient of $AT_t$ is the SC itself.

**Step V5:** The SC compares the iss claim registered in the DS with the iss claim in $AT_t$ to confirm that the issuer of $AT_t$ is the legitimate IdP.

Finally, it is checked that $AT_t$ contains the necessary privileges for data manipulation.

**Step V6:** The SC verifies that the sub claim and the owner of the data to be manipulated match.

**Step V7:** Using the scope claims, the SC verifies that the access privileges meet the privileges required by the processing.

If any verification fails, the processing is aborted, and an error is returned to the SP. Next, in Step 4-7, the SC executes the processing for the DLT service and reads/writes the SU's data. After the processing, the SC overwrites $iat_{t-1}$ with $iat_t$ (Step 4-8). Finally, the SC returns the results of the processing (Step 4-9), and the SP provides services using the results (Step 4-10).

# 5  Evaluating the Security Requirements of the Proposed Method

We evaluated that the processing flow designed in Sect. 4.3 satisfies the three security requirements defined in Sect. 3.2.

**Evaluation of Req. 1.** Req. 1 is the requirement to ensure that an SP and an SU are not impersonated. There are two possible methods of impersonation: rewriting the information in the azp claim and the sub claim or theft of a JWT containing the information to be impersonated.

Rewriting the claim information can be detected by the integrity verification of a JWT in Step V1. Since the IdP guarantees the claim information, it is secure as long as the signing key used by the IdP to sign the claim is not compromised.

There are two cases of theft of a JWT: theft from another service domain and theft within the same service domain. The former can be detected by comparing the azp claim with an executor of the SC in Step V3 since the executor is identified by $Cert_{SP}$. Such attacks can be prevented if the signing key corresponding to the $Cert_{SP}$ is not compromised. In the latter case, the subject of $Cert_{SP}$ and the azp claim are equal; thus, there is a risk that an SP impersonates an SU. However, the risk can be reduced by Req. 2 and Req. 3, which restrict misuse of an access token.

**Evaluation of Req. 2.** Req. 2 is required to prevent an SP from reusing a previously used access token. During the service provision phase, the date and time information of the iat claim stored in a DS is updated at each time of SC execution. As a result, the reuse of an access token can be detected by Step V2.

One way to prevent the reuse of an access token can be using the jti claim that uniquely identifies a JWT. Since the IdP sets a different string in the jti claim for each JWT, an SP can detect the reuse of the access token if the SP saves the jti claim used once in the distributed ledger. However, the jti claims of the used tokens must be stored in the distributed ledger until the access tokens expire. Hence, the proposed method uses iat claims, which are ordered information.

**Evaluation of Req. 3.** Req. 3 is required to prevent an SP from retaining an unused access token for later use. In the proposed method, the date and time information of the iat claim saved in a DS is updated at each time of SC execution. As a result, even if the SP tries to use the unused access token later, it can be detected by Step V2 since the token retained will be invalid when an SU uses the new access token. To reduce the risk of unauthorized retention by SPs, the validity period of the access token should be kept to the minimum necessary that does not affect service provision. Specifically, the access token must be valid from Step 4-3 to Step 4-6.

# 6   Performance Evaluation

In the proposed method, the setup phase and the two registration phases are executed in advance, but the service provision phase is executed each time an SU requests a service. Therefore, latency for the service provision phase is a significant part of the overhead of the proposed method. In addition, the proposed method requires additional storage to manage the status of the access privilege. For this reason, we evaluate the processing time overhead and data size overhead during the service provision phase.

## 6.1   Experimental Setup

For this experiment, we implemented a data storage service with a permissioned DLT system as an experimental system and embedded the proposed access control mechanism into the experimental system. The experimental system has one scope **Change** and an SU can access its data with an access token that contains an SU's identity and the LIST scope. The scope regarding data registration is not defined because the SU's data are registered in the DS in advance for the experiment.

Our experiments were conducted on a machine running Linux kernel 4.15.0 on an Intel Core i9-9940X with 32 GB of main memory, Hyperledger Fabric v2.3.3 as a permissioned DLT system, and Keycloak v15.0.2 as an IdP system.

## 6.2   Experimental Result

All entities are deployed on a single experimental machine. The SU and the SP are implemented as the test script, while the two Docker containers in Hyperledger Fabric run the SC and the DS. We executed the test script for 1000 rounds with the processes from Step 4-1 to Step 4-10 as one round. The authorization code flow is a process that is generally executed in services that use OIDC; thus, we measured two kinds of processing times: Step 4-5 to Step 4-9 and Step 4-6 to Step 4-8, excluding Step 4-7. The former represents the service latency caused by Hyperledger Fabric, while the latter represents the pure overhead of the proposed method. In addition, because Hyperledger Fabric keeps records of DLT operations as a series of blocks, we measured the size of that block at the end of each round. We retrieved blocks using the "peer channel fetch" command.

Figure 7 shows trends in processing time in the experiment. The mean and variance of the processing times are $2282.7 \pm 6.9$ ms for requesting the chaincode and $4.8 \pm 0.7$ ms for the access control. The SC processing time is stable, with an overhead of only 0.21%. Figure 8 shows trends in data growth in the experiment. Both data sizes tend to increase monotonically. The mean and variance of data growth in each round are $7.884 \pm 0.002$ KB when the proposed method is applied,

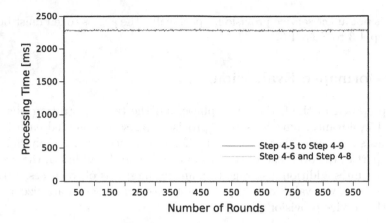

**Fig. 7.** Trends in processing time during the service provision phase. The blue line shows the small variation in the time that users are kept waiting by the smart contract. The red line indicates that the overhead is very small. (Color figure online)

and $6.118 \pm 0.002$ KB when the proposed method is not applied. The additional data size per processing in the proposed method is $1.766 \pm 0.002$ KB. Comparing the result without access control, the proposed method has an overhead 22.40%.

# 7    Discussion

## 7.1    Overhead of the Proposed Method

As shown in the experimental results, the overhead of the processing time is 0.21%, and the overhead of the data size is 22.40%. The result indicates that the proposed method has a negligible impact on the DLT service in terms of the overhead of the processing time. On the other hand, the result indicates that the proposed method requires a certain cost in data storage, but the cost can be estimated from the frequency of SC execution.

In contrast to the cost of the access control, the proposed method requires the cost to execute SCs in an invoke method. In Hyperledger Fabric, the invoke method executes a consensus algorithm, and it is known as a more time-consuming process than the query method that does not require executing the consensus algorithm. We found that the proposed method is well-suited for DLT services that change the state of user data as executed by the invoke method. In contrast, for DLT services that only read user data as executed by the query method, the proposed method bears the additional costs of executing the consensus algorithm.

## 7.2    Limitation of the Proposed Method

As shown in Step V2, the updated date and time of the iat claim causes all access tokens prior to that date and time to be determined as past. However,

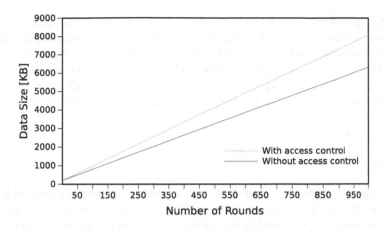

**Fig. 8.** Trends in data growth during the service provision phase. The graph shows that the data size increases monotonically with the number of SC executions with (red line) and without (blue line) the proposed method. (Color figure online)

the SP can obtain the latest unused access token by returning an error to the SU before the SP performs Step 4-5. Here, the SP can use the access token until it expires or the same SU requests the service. In order to detect such fraud, it is considered necessary to devise an auditing method that compares logs of IdPs, SCs, and SPs.

The work in [25] points out that processing with system clock should be done with caution because Hyperledger Fabric has non-deterministic risk. Our method uses system clock to verify the validity period of the access token. However, there is no problem except when executing a SC at the time of expiration since it is only used to compare access token expiration dates.

### 7.3 Access Privileges in Permissionless DLT and Importance of Separating Access Privileges in Permissioned DLT

When a permissionless DLT system is deployed as the front end, an SU operates the Web UI provided by an SP and executes an SC using its secret key. In other words, the SP does not execute the SC on behalf of the SU but supports the execution of the SC by the SU. Since the SC is executed mainly by the SU, access privileges are explicit, but the SU is responsible for managing its private key.

In Ethereum, a permissionless DLT system, private keys are associated with accounts, so a private key breach is equivalent to losing all assets associated with the account. On the other hand, in the proposed method, the SU does not need to manage private keys since it only needs to manage the credentials of IdP. In IdP authentication, not only password authentication but also FIDO authentication can be used, which is expected to improve user convenience. The IdP credentials are used to control granting access privileges to SPs, and credential breach is equivalent to losing that control. However, since the DLSP manages the access privileges itself, the DLSP can regain control by reconfiguring the authentication information of the SU. By separating the access privileges to the data in the distributed ledger from the execution privileges of SC, the proposed method can reduce the burden of managing confidential information required by permissionless DLT systems while achieving a clear operation of the access privilege.

# 8 Conclusion

In this paper, we propose a method that separates an access privilege for user data in a distributed ledger from a privilege to execute smart contracts and controls access to the data with the user's consent. In the proposed method, the access privilege is represented by an access token in the form of JWT in OpenID Connect, and security requirements for its secure operation are defined. We implemented the experimental system of the proposed method using Hyperledger Fabric and Keycloak and evaluated the performance of the proposed method.

Future works include designing and developing the proposed method to support any smart contract application and devising a method to audit the proposed method to reduce the risk of fraud in a service provider.

**Acknowledgement.** This work was supported by JSPS KAKENHI Grant Number JP22K17881. This research results were partly obtained from the commissioned research under a contract of "Research and development on IoT malware removal/make it non-functional technologies for effective use of the radio spectrum" among "Research and Development for Expansion of Radio Wave Resources (JPJ000254)", which was supported by the Ministry of Internal Affairs and Communications, Japan.

# References

1. Blockchain and distributed ledger technologies – Vocabulary. ISO 22739:2020 (2020)
2. Blockchain and distributed ledger technologies – Taxonomy and Ontology. ISO/TS 23258:2021 (2021)
3. How to prove and verify someone's identity (2022). https://www.gov.uk/government/publications/identity-proofing-and-verification-of-an-individual/how-to-prove-and-verify-someones-identity. Accessed 26 June 2022
4. IBM food trust: a new era in the world's food supply (2022). https://www.ibm.com/in-en/blockchain/solutions/food-trust. Accessed 26 June 2022
5. de Almeida, M.G., Canedo, E.D.: Authentication and authorization in microservices architecture: a systematic literature review. Appl. Sci. **12**(6) (2022). https://doi.org/10.3390/app12063023, https://www.mdpi.com/2076-3417/12/6/3023
6. Antwi, M., Adnane, A., Ahmad, F., Hussain, R., Habib UR Rehman, M., Kerrache, C.A.: The case of HyperLedger fabric as a blockchain solution for healthcare applications. Blockchain Res. Appl. **2**(1), 100012 (2021). https://doi.org/10.1016/j.bcra.2021.100012

7. Bedin, A.R.C., Capretz, M., Mir, S.: Blockchain for collaborative businesses. Mob. Netw. Appl. **26**(1), 277–284 (2020). https://doi.org/10.1007/s11036-020-01649-6
8. Delgado-von Eitzen, C., Anido-Rifón, L., Fernández-Iglesias, M.J.: Application of blockchain in education: GDPR-compliant and scalable certification and verification of academic information. Appl. Sci. **11**(10) (2021). https://doi.org/10.3390/app11104537
9. Guan, Z., Lu, X., Wang, N., Wu, J., Du, X., Guizani, M.: Towards secure and efficient energy trading in IIoT-enabled energy internet: a blockchain approach. Future Gener. Comput. Syst. **110**, 686–695 (2020). https://doi.org/10.1016/j.future.2019.09.027, https://www.sciencedirect.com/science/article/pii/S0167739X19315018
10. He, X., Yang, X.: Authentication and authorization of end user in microservice architecture. In: Journal of Physics: Conference Series, vol. 910, p. 012060. IOP Publishing (2017)
11. Huang, Y., Bian, Y., Li, R., Zhao, J.L., Shi, P.: Smart contract security: a software lifecycle perspective. IEEE Access **7**, 150184–150202 (2019). https://doi.org/10.1109/ACCESS.2019.2946988
12. Huff, P., Li, Q.: A distributed ledger for non-attributable cyber threat intelligence exchange. In: Garcia-Alfaro, J., Li, S., Poovendran, R., Debar, H., Yung, M. (eds.) SecureComm 2021. LNICST, vol. 398, pp. 164–184. Springer, Cham (2021). https://doi.org/10.1007/978-3-030-90019-9_9
13. Ibrokhimov, S., Hui, K.L., Abdulhakim Al-Absi, A., lee, H.J., Sain, M.: Multi-factor authentication in cyber physical system: a state of art survey. In: 2019 21st International Conference on Advanced Communication Technology (ICACT), pp. 279–284 (2019). https://doi.org/10.23919/ICACT.2019.8701960
14. Jones, M., Bradley, J., Sakimura, N.: JSON web token (JWT). RFC 7519 (2015). https://doi.org/10.17487/RFC7519
15. Karim, A., Adnan, M.A.: An OpenID based authentication service mechanisms for internet of things. In: 2019 IEEE 4th International Conference on Computer and Communication Systems (ICCCS), pp. 687–692 (2019). https://doi.org/10.1109/CCOMS.2019.8821761
16. Kuhn, R., Yaga, D., Voas, J.: Rethinking distributed ledger technology. Computer **52**(2), 68–72 (2019). https://doi.org/10.1109/MC.2019.2898162
17. Lu, Z., Liu, W., Wang, Q., Qu, G., Liu, Z.: A privacy-preserving trust model based on blockchain for VANETs. IEEE Access **6**, 45655–45664 (2018). https://doi.org/10.1109/ACCESS.2018.2864189
18. Sakimura, N., Bradley, J., Jones, M., de Medeiros, B., Mortimore, C.: OpenID Connect Core 1.0 (2014). https://openid.net/specs/openid-connect-core-1_0.html
19. ShuLin, Y., JiePing, H.: Research on unified authentication and authorization in microservice architecture. In: 2020 IEEE 20th International Conference on Communication Technology (ICCT), pp. 1169–1173 (2020). https://doi.org/10.1109/ICCT50939.2020.9295931
20. Sudarsan, S.V., Schelén, O., Bodin, U.: A model for signatories in cyber-physical systems. In: 2020 25th IEEE International Conference on Emerging Technologies and Factory Automation (ETFA), vol. 1, pp. 15–21 (2020). https://doi.org/10.1109/ETFA46521.2020.9212081
21. Sudarsan, S.V., Schelén, O., Bodin, U.: Survey on delegated and self-contained authorization techniques in CPS and IoT. IEEE Access **9**, 98169–98184 (2021). https://doi.org/10.1109/ACCESS.2021.3093327
22. Truong, N.B., Sun, K., Lee, G.M., Guo, Y.: GDPR-compliant personal data management: a blockchain-based solution. IEEE Trans. Inf. Forensics Secur. **15**, 1746–1761 (2020). https://doi.org/10.1109/TIFS.2019.2948287

23. Voigt, P., Von dem Bussche, A.: The EU general data protection regulation. GDPR), A Practical Guide (2017)
24. Xu, R., Jin, W., Kim, D.: Microservice security agent based on API gateway in edge computing. Sensors **19**(22) (2019). https://doi.org/10.3390/s19224905
25. Yamashita, K., Nomura, Y., Zhou, E., Pi, B., Jun, S.: Potential risks of hyperledger fabric smart contracts. In: 2019 IEEE International Workshop on Blockchain Oriented Software Engineering (IWBOSE), pp. 1–10 (2019). https://doi.org/10.1109/IWBOSE.2019.8666486
26. Zhang, A., Lin, X.: Towards secure and privacy-preserving data sharing in e-health systems via consortium blockchain. J. Med. Syst. **42**(8), 1–18 (2018). https://doi.org/10.1007/s10916-018-0995-5
27. Zhou, H., Milani Fard, A., Makanju, A.: The state of Ethereum smart contracts security: vulnerabilities, countermeasures, and tool support. J. Cybersecur. Privacy **2**(2), 358–378 (2022). https://doi.org/10.3390/jcp2020019

# Decentralized and Efficient Blockchain Rewriting with Bi-level Validity Verification

Kemin Zhang[1], Li Yang[1(✉)], Lu Zhou[1], and Jianfeng Ma[2]

[1] School of Computer Science and Technology, Xidian University, Xi'an, China
yangli@xidian.edu.cn
[2] School of Cyber Engineering, Xidian University, Xi'an, China

**Abstract.** Numerous studies have established that the immutability, a crucial property of blockchains, need to be delicately broken under certain circumstance as the content in blockchains could be compelled to redact for personal or legal reasons. Existing schemes ordinarily leverage policy-based chameleon hash (PCH) to perform fine-grained rewriting on blockchains, where modifiers with attributes satisfying the access policy can be authorized to modify the content in the blockchain. However, these schemes rely on a single trusted authority for managing rewriting permissions, which could be affected by a potential single point of failure. Meanwhile, heavy computations in such schemes might affect the performance in practical use.

To address these limitations, we propose a decentralized and efficient blockchain rewriting scheme with bi-level validity verification. With the integration of the multi-authorities attribute-based encryption, our scheme supports the modifier to obtain rewriting secret keys from various authorities for performing rewriting at transaction level. Moreover, computationally intensive operations in our scheme can be performed in stages and partially outsourced to the proxy server. As an assurance of security, our scheme provides bi-level validity verification for the rewriting secret key and the content on blockchain. Moreover, we present formal security analysis and conduct comparison experiments to illustrate the advantages in both functionality and performance.

**Keywords:** Blockchain rewriting · Attribute-based encryption · Chameleon hash · Outsource computing

## 1 Introduction

The concept of the blockchain was originally introduced by Satoshi Nakamoto to function as a distributed public ledger of the cryptocurrency Bitcoin [23]. It has raised a widespread concern in the community and has found wide applications in many fields such as supply chain [11], Internet-of-Things (IoT) [25] and healthcare services [8]. A blockchain is a continuously expanding list of records made

© ICST Institute for Computer Sciences, Social Informatics and Telecommunications Engineering 2023
Published by Springer Nature Switzerland AG 2023. All Rights Reserved
F. Li et al. (Eds.): SecureComm 2022, LNICST 462, pp. 309–328, 2023.
https://doi.org/10.1007/978-3-031-25538-0_17

up of cryptographically connected blocks, which is resistant to modifications since the transaction data in any fixed block cannot be modified retroactively without editing all subsequent blocks.

However, as a crucial property of the blockchain, the immutability could be a limiting factor for practical promoting in certain circumstance. From the perspective of privacy protection, the immutability is inherently incompatible with certain regulations that emphasize protecting user privacy and avoiding sensitive content, for instance, General Data Protection Regulation (GDPR) [30], since any data (e.g. transaction values) in such immutable blockchains cannot be erased. Moreover, the illicit content in blockchains such as pornography, violent narratives or viruses uploaded by malicious users could cause lasting and negative impact. Therefore, an urgent demand for schemes of redacting incorrect or even illicit contents in the blockchain is desirable in practical scenarios.

Earlier studies intended to perform block-level rewriting on blockchains, predominately by replacing the traditional hash function with a trapdoor-based chameleon hash [16]. Subsequently, for providing transaction-level redaction, several studies aimed to implement fine-grained and controlled blockchain rewriting by employing attribute-based encryption (ABE) [9, 14, 28, 33]. In these schemes, a predetermined access policy is embedded into a transaction and the modifier possessing a trapdoor could find hash collisions to modify the transaction if her attributes satisfy the embedded access policy.

Nevertheless, the aforementioned fine-grained blockchain rewriting schemes are still flawed to some extent. Specifically, these schemes either rely on a trusted authority for key distribution, which could be affected by a potential single point of failure, or necessitate heavy computation which might affect the performance in practical use. The requirement for a single trusted authority could be incompatible with the decentralized designing of the blockchain. Users with resource-constrained devices could not efficiently perform complex computations such as bilinear pairing operations in the hash or decryption phase. Moreover, the validity of the rewriting secret key received by the modifier and the transaction content cannot be verified.

To address these limitations, we propose a scheme of decentralized and efficient blockchain rewriting with bi-level validity verification. In our scheme, the transaction owner appends signatured transactions with the embedded access policy to the blockchain. Subsequently, the modifier obtains rewriting secret keys from multiple authorities and concurrently performs validity verification. As a consequence, the distribution of the rewriting secret key is decentralized which accordingly eliminates the risk of a potential single point of failure. Finally, the modifier requests partial decryption from the proxy server and further completes the decryption to rewrite and sign the transaction in the blockchain. Note that the computation of both hash and decryption are separated into two stages in our scheme. For this reason, the computational burden on the user side is significantly reduced, which is beneficial for practical implementation.

To the best of our knowledge, this scheme is the first to simultaneously address the aforementioned limitations, and the contributions of the work are summarized in the following four aspects:

- We introduce a framework of decentralized blockchain rewriting scheme that allows for transaction-level rewriting, based on multi-authority ABE. The modifier can perform transactions rewriting only if her attributes satisfy the access policy predetermined by the transaction owner, where the privilege to the modifier for rewriting is granted jointly by multiple authorities.
- We adopt offline/online hashing and outsourced computing in our scheme for reducing the computational burden on the user side. Specifically, the hash algorithm is separated into offline/online phases, and the decryption to be executed by the modifier is split into two phases for performing outsourced partial decryption.
- We provide a mechanism of bi-level validity verification, in order for the modifier to verify the validity of rewriting secret keys received from various attribute authorities, as well for any entity to verify the content in the blockchain.
- We build an instantiation of our scheme on firm theoretical grounds. All important properties of our scheme are formalized in Sect. 3, and the security of the proposed scheme is demonstrated via formal security analysis in Sect. 4.3. Besides, the experimental results of the comparison with previous schemes demonstrate that our scheme is advantageous in both functionality and performance.

### 1.1 Related Work

**Attribute-based Encryption.** Sahai and Waters [26] first introduced the concept of a public-key encryption scheme, namely attribute-based encryption (ABE), in which ciphertexts and secret keys are dependent upon attributes. Subsequently, Goyal et al. [12] developed a cryptosystem named *key-policy attribute-based encryption* (KP-ABE), in order to perform fine-grained sharing of encrypted data. In this scheme, ciphertexts are labeled with attributes and can be decrypted by private keys with respect to access structures. Bethencourt et al. [3] presented a system named *ciphertext-policy attribute-based encryption* (CP-ABE) to perform access control on the encrypted data. Guo et al. [13] introduced *identity-based offline/online encryption* (IBOOE), which separates identity-based encryption into online and offline phases for improving the computing efficiency. Afterwards, extensive research on KP-ABE or CP-ABE were proposed for better efficiency or security [7,15,17–19,21,31,32]. For instance, in [15], the vast majority of the work on encryption or secret key generation in ABE is performed offline to reduce the cost in practice. In [18], Lewko and Waters proposed a multi-authority ABE system which allows any party to become an authority, and thus avoids the performance bottleneck incurred by relying on a central authority.

**Blockchain Rewriting.** Blockchain rewriting has raised widespread concern in the community since the pioneering work [2]. In this work, chameleon hash (CH) function are deployed instead of the original SHA256 hash function for rewriting block contents in blockchains. Chameleon hash is collision resistant if the trapdoor is unknown, conversely, a modifier who is aware of the trapdoor can find collisions and perform rewriting operations while keeping the hash value.

Subsequently, Puddu et al. [24] proposed a mutable blockchain, named $\mu$chain, which provides mechanisms for removing record data from the blockchain and their modifications. Thyagarajan et al. [27] introduced a publicly verifiable layer *Reparo* to fix incorrect contracts and remove illicit contents from the blockchain. Deuber et al. [10] proposed an efficient redactable blockchain for permissionless setting based on consensus-based voting. It dispenses with sophisticated cryptographic techniques or trust assumptions. However, the block-level rewriting operation is coarse-grained, i.e. the whole block have to be replaced even only one transaction in a block is required to be modified.

To bridge this gap, a line of studies have been proposed to achieve the goal of fine-grained and controlled rewriting based on ABE scheme. For instance, Derler et al. [9] presented *policy-based chameleon hashes* (PCH) that integrate CP-ABE with *chameleon hash with ephemeral trapdoor* (CHET) [5] to perform fine-grained modifications on blockchains. Any modifier own the attributes which satisfy the access policy can find hash collisions and further rewrite the blockchain at transaction-level. In [28], the scheme of *policy-based chameleon hash with black-box accountability* (PCHBA) was proposed to identify responsible transaction modifiers in case of dispute while achieving the goal of fine-grained rewriting on blockchain. Subsequently, the authors further generalized their work to a permissionless setting [29], which leverages *dynamic proactive secret sharing* (DPSS) [22] to remove the trusted authority and utilize KP-ABE for fine-grained access control. In [33], a *multi-authority policy-based chameleon hash* (MAPCH) was proposed by combing CHET and multi-authority CP-ABE, for reducing the workload of a single authority. In [14], a new rewritable blockchain scheme, named OO-RB-AOC, was proposed to reduce computational overhead and improve the security by performing an auditable outsourced computation mechanism for some time-consuming operations.

## 2    Preliminaries

### 2.1    Bilinear Mapping

$\mathbb{G}_1$ and $\mathbb{G}_2$ are two cyclic groups of prime order $p$. Then a bilinear map $e : \mathbb{G}_1 \times \mathbb{G}_1 \to \mathbb{G}_2$ meets the following properties:

- Bilinearity: $\forall x, y \in \mathbb{Z}_p, \forall \alpha, \beta \in \mathbb{G}_1$, then $e(\alpha^x, \beta^y) = e(\alpha, \beta)^{xy}$.
- Non-degeneracy: $\exists \alpha \in \mathbb{G}_1$, such that $e(\alpha, \alpha) \neq 1_{\mathbb{G}_2}$, where $1_{\mathbb{G}_2}$ is the identity element of $\mathbb{G}_2$.
- Computability: $\forall \alpha, \beta \in \mathbb{G}_1$, the value of $e(\alpha, \beta)$ can be computed efficiently.

### 2.2    Multi-authority Ciphertext-Policy Attribute-Based Encryption (CP-ABE)

Multi-authority CP-ABE allows any entity to become an authority, and multiple authorities are responsible for managing the attribute sets of users. In this paper, we adopt the multi-authority CP-ABE scheme proposed in [20]. It executes hash function on users' global identifier *gid* [7] to integrate private keys of each user received form various authorities. This scheme simultaneously achieves the goals of autonomous key generation and collusion resistance. Specifically, multi-authority CP-ABE algorithm consists of the following five algorithms:

- *Global Setup*($\lambda$) $\rightarrow$ *GP*: Taking the security parameter $\lambda$ as the input, it outputs global parameter *GP* for the system.
- *Authority Setup*(*GP*) $\rightarrow$ $pk_{AA}, sk_{AA}$: Each authority runs the algorithm with *GP* to generate its own public and secret key pair ($pk_{AA}$, $sk_{AA}$).
- *KeyGen*($gid, GP, i, sk_{AA}$) $\rightarrow$ $SK_{i,gid}$: Taking an authority identity $gid$, global parameter *GP*, an attribute $i$, and the secret key $sk_{AA}$ as the input, the algorithm outputs $SK_{i,gid}$ for the attribute-identity pair.
- *Encrypt*($GP, \{pk_{AA}\}, \mathbb{A}, m$) $\rightarrow$ *CT*: The algorithm takes the global parameter *GP*, the set of public keys for related authorities $\{pk_{AA}\}$, access policy matrix $\mathbb{A} = (A, \rho)$, and a message $m$ as the input, and outputs a ciphertext *CT*.
- *Decrypt*($CT, GP, \{SK_{i,gid}\}$) $\rightarrow$ $m$: It takes the ciphertext *CT*, the global parameter *GP*, and a set of keys $\{SK_{i,gid}\}$ as the input. If the collection of attribute $i$ satisfies the access policy embedded in the ciphertext, the algorithm outputs the message $m$; otherwise the decryption cannot succeed.

### 2.3   Chameleon Hash (CH)

An arbitrary collision can be found in the domain of the function by using a trapdoor presented in chameleon hash functions [16]. On the message space $\mathcal{M}$, the chameleon hash employs the following four algorithms:

- *KeyGen*: The chameleon key pair ($pk, sk$) is computed by the security parameter $\lambda$ in this algorithm.
- *Hash*: This algorithm calculates a chameleon hash $h$ and a randomness $r$ using chameleon secret key $pk$ and a message $m$.
- *Verify*: The verify algorithm takes the chameleon public key $pk$, chameleon hash $h$, randomness $r$ and message $m$ as the input, and then outputs a bit $b \in \{0, 1\}$.
- *Adapt*: The chameleon private key $sk$, chameleon hash $h$, randomness $r$, original and new message ($m, m'$) are taken as the input, then a new randomness value $r'$ which could be used to recover the trapdoor is computed.

### 2.4   Bnoeh-Lynn-Shacham (BLS) Signature

We leverage BLS signature [4] to aggregate multiple signatures into a single signature without the interactions between each authority, in order for the modifier to verify the validity of the rewriting secret key. Specifically, the BLS signature algorithm consists of three algorithms listed below:

- *Ken*: This algorithm computes the public key $c$ and the secret key $a$.
- *Sign*: It takes $a$ and the message $m$ as the input, and outputs the signature $\sigma$.
- *Ver*: This algorithm takes $m$, $c$ and $\sigma$ as the input, and outputs a value $d \in \{0, 1\}$ which indicates the correctness of signatures.

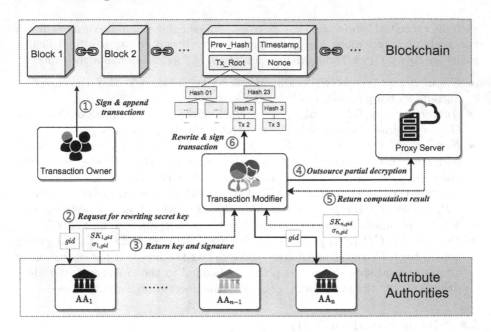

**Fig. 1.** System model

## 3    Models and Definitions

### 3.1    System Model

Our proposed system consists of four entities (shown in Fig. 1), namely Transaction Owner (TO), Attritube Authority (AA), Transaction Modifier (TM) and Proxy Server (PS). The interactions and functions of each entity are listed below:

**Transaction Owner (TO):** TO appends hashed transactions with signature to the blockchain. In our scheme, TO's devices are considered to be trusted and reliable yet could be resource-constrained (for instance, mobile phone).

**Attribute Authority (AA):** AAs are responsible for managing the attributes of users as well as generating and distributing the rewriting secret key associated with the TM's attribute set. There is no requirement for any global coordination amongst the authorities. Moreover, AA further signs the rewriting secret key in order for the TM to verify the validity.

**Transaction Modifier (TM):** The rewriting operation in blockchain is performed by the TM. Concretely, TM provides global identifier $gid$ to collect rewriting secret keys corresponding to her attribute set from AAs, and subsequently verifies the validity of keys by performing signature aggregation. Afterwards, TM requests partial decryption from PS and completes the rest of the computation. TM could find hash collision to perform transaction rewriting once its attributes satisfy the access policy predetermined by TO.

**Proxy Server (PS)**: PS performs partial decryption using transformation keys received from TM, and subsequently sends the result to the TM. As a consequence, the decryption load on TM's devices is reduced significantly.

## 3.2  Definition

Our proposed scheme is based on multi-authority ciphertext-policy attribute-based encryption (CP-ABE) and chameleon hash (CH) for decentralized rewriting on blockchain. It is comprised of the following five phases:

**Setup**: Arbitrary AA runs the *Global_Setup* algorithm to generate the global parameter. The *Auth_Setup* and *Modi_Setup* algorithms are used to generate the key pairs of all AAs and TM respectively;

**KeyGen**: Each AA runs *Rew_KeyGen* algorithm to generate and sign the rewriting secret keys associated with the attribute set of TM. Subsequently, TM runs *Trans_KeyGen* algorithm to generate and send the transformation keys to PS for outsourcing decryption;

**Hash**: TO firstly runs *Offline_Hash* algorithm to generate the intermediate ciphertext, which can be viewed as pre-computations for computing the final ciphertext. Afterwards, TO runs *Online_Hash* algorithm to generate chameleon hash, and subsequently signs the transaction for identification;

**Verify**: TM and any entity can respectively run *Aggre_Verify* and *Hash_Verify* algorithm, in order to verify the validity of the rewriting secret key and the transaction content;

**Adapt**: PS runs *Part_Decrypt* algorithm to execute partial decryption using transformation keys. TM subsequently runs *Full_Adapt* algorithm to find hash collision for rewriting, and signs the modified transaction for identification.

More precisely, the proposed scheme consists of the following algorithms:

- *Global_Setup*$(\lambda) \to GP$. Any AA could run the algorithm to compute global parameter $GP$ using security parameter $\lambda$.
- *Auth_Setup*$(GP) \to (pk_{AA}, sk_{AA}, pk_{sig}, sk_{sig})$. In accordance with $GP$, each AA computes public key $pk_{AA}$, the secret key $sk_{AA}$ and the key pair $(pk_{sig}, sk_{sig})$ for the signature.
- *Modi_Setup*$(GP) \to (spk, ssk)$. TM runs this algorithm to obtain a key pair $(spk, ssk)$ for signature using $GP$.
- *Rew_KeyGen*$(GP, gid, i, sk_{AA}, sk_{sig}) \to (SK_{i,gid}, \sigma_{i,gid})$. An authority owning the attribute $i$ inputs global parameter $GP$, global identity $gid$, attribute $i$ and secret keys $(sk_{AA}, sk_{sig})$, and computes rewriting secret key $SK_{i,gid}$ and signature $\sigma_{i,gid}$ for an attribute-identity pair $(i, gid)$.
- *Trans_KeyGen*$(GP, SK_{i,gid}) \to TK_{i,gid}$. Given the global parameter $GP$, TM transforms the $SK_{i,gid}$ into a transformation key $TK_{i,gid}$ which will be sent to a PS for partial decryption.

- *Offline_Hash*$(GP) \rightarrow (IC, IS)$. TO computes intermediate ciphertext $IC$ and intermediate state $IS$ using $GP$. The offline hash phase could accelerate the construction of the final ciphertext since it can be seen as the pre-computation of the online hash phase (detailed in Sect. 4.1). For reducing computational consumption, TO could execute the algorithm in the charging or idle time of the device.
- *Online_Hash*$(GP, \{pk_{AA}\}, IC, IS, \mathbb{A}, m) \rightarrow (h, r, \sigma_{user})$. Given $GP$, a set of public keys $\{pk_{AA}\}$ from multiple authorities, intermediate ciphertext $IC$, intermediate state $IS$, access policy $\mathbb{A} = (A, \rho)$ and message $m$, TO executes the algorithm to compute a hash $h$, a randomness $r$ and a signature $\sigma_{user}$.
- *Aggre_Verify*$(gid, \{\sigma_{i,gid}\}, pk_{sig}) \rightarrow 0$ or 1. TM could verify the validity of rewriting secret keys received from multiple authorities. Given $gid$ of TM, signatures set $\{\sigma_{i,gid}\}$ from all authorities owning TM's attribute set, and authorities' public key $pk_{sig}$ for signature verification, the $SK_{i,gid}$ is checked out to be valid if the algorithm returns 1, or else it returns 0.
- *Hash_Verify*$(m, h, r, \sigma_{user}) \rightarrow 0$ or 1. Any entity could take $m$, $(h, r)$ and signature $\sigma_{user}$ to verify whether the hash $h$ and signature $\sigma_{user}$ is valid. The output is a bit $b \in \{0, 1\}$.
- *Part_Decrypt*$(GP, CT, \{TK_{i,gid}\}) \rightarrow CT'$. PS could use $GP$, ciphertext $CT$ and transformation key $\{TK_{i,gid}\}$ to compute partial decryption result $CT'$.
- *Full_Adapt*$(h, r, m, m', \{TK_{i,gid}\}, \sigma_{user}) \rightarrow (r', \sigma'_{user})$. TM utilizes $(h, r)$, $m$, new message $m'$, $\{TK_{i,gid}\}$ and $\sigma_{user}$ to compute hash collision value $r'$ based on partial decryption result, and then generates signature $\sigma'_{user}$ of the modified transaction.

### 3.3   Security Model

We first briefly describe the relevant security assumptions. TO is honest and will correctly add transactions to the blockchain. TMs with trusted devices might collude to collect credentials required for decryption. Authorities might be corrupted. PS might attempt to gather extra information in the decryption stage, while the correctness of the partial decryption is not affected. In this paper, we consider the following security guarantees.

**Replayable Chosen Ciphertext Attack (RCCA) Security.** In this paper, we adopt RCCA security [6] which allows the ciphertext to be modified, provided that the fundamental message cannot be adjusted explicitly. To demonstrate the security, we define the following security games between adversary $\mathcal{A}$ and challenger $\mathcal{C}$.

- *Setup.* The challenger $\mathcal{C}$ executes *Global_Setup* algorithm and sends public parameters to $\mathcal{A}$.
- *Key Query Phase I.* $\mathcal{C}$ initializes an integer $j = 0$, an empty set $D$, and an empty table $T$. $\mathcal{A}$ could adaptively and repeatedly execute any following queries:

- *Create(S)*: $\mathcal{C}$ sets $j = j + 1$. For an attribute set $S$, $\mathcal{C}$ computes rewriting secret key and transformation key $(SK, TK)$ by *Rew_KeyGen* and *Trans_KeyGen* algorithms, where $SK = \{SK_{i,gid}\}_{i \in S}$, $TK = \{TK_{i,gid}\}_{i \in S}$. Then $\mathcal{C}$ stores entry $(j, S, SK, TK)$ into table $T$ and sends $TK$ to adversary $\mathcal{A}$.
- *Corrupt($\tau$)*: If the $\tau$th entry exists in $T$, $\mathcal{C}$ retrieves this entry $(\tau, S, SK, TK)$ and stores $S$ into $D$. Conversely, if the entry does not exist, it returns $\perp$.
- *Decrypt($\tau, CT$)*: If $T$ holds the $\tau$th entry, $\mathcal{C}$ queries entry $(\tau, S, SK, TK)$ and executes *Part_Decrypt* and *Full_Adapt* algorithms, and subsequently sends results to $\mathcal{A}$; otherwise, it returns $\perp$.
- *Challenge.* The adversary $\mathcal{A}$ sends to $\mathcal{C}$ two equal-length messages $m_0$, $m_1$. Meanwhile, $\mathcal{A}$ presents a challenge access policy $\mathbb{A}^* = (A^*, \rho^*)$ such that all attribute in $D$ does not satisfy $\mathbb{A}^*$. Then $\mathcal{C}$ randomly sets a bit $b \in \{0, 1\}$ and executes *Offline_Hash* and *Online_Hash* algorithms on message $m_b$ to compute a challenge ciphertext $CT^*_{m_b}$, and subsequently sends $CT^*_{m_b}$ to $\mathcal{A}$.
- *Key Query Phase II.* Repeating the phase I under following constraints:
  1) $\mathcal{A}$ cannot acquire the key that meets with $\mathbb{A}^*$.
  2) The message cannot be either $m_0$ or $m_1$ when $\mathcal{A}$ executes decryption query.
- *Guess.* The adversary $\mathcal{A}$ outputs a guess $b'$ for $b$.

**Definition 1.** *Our scheme satisfies RCCA security if a probabilistic polynomial-time (PPT) adversary win the security game with a negligible advantage $\varepsilon$:*

$$\mathsf{Adv}^{\mathrm{RCCA}}_{\mathcal{A}} = |\Pr[b' = b] - 1/2| \le \varepsilon. \tag{1}$$

**Existential Unforgeability Under Chosen-Message Attacks (EUF-CMA).** In this section, we introduce the existential unforgeability of BLS signature. We follow the definition of EUF-CMA in [4], and illustrate the security of the signature scheme against EUF-CMA by the following security game:

- *Setup.* $\mathcal{C}$ computes key pair $(c, a)$ by key generation algorithm *Ken*, and then sends the public key $c$ to $\mathcal{A}$.
- *Query Phase.* $\mathcal{A}$ queries for signature with respect to message $m$. $\mathcal{C}$ execute *Sign* algorithm to acquire signature $\sigma$ and sends it to $\mathcal{A}$.
- *Output.* $\mathcal{A}$ outputs $(m^*, \sigma^*)$. If $\mathsf{Ver}(c, m^*, \sigma^*) = 1$, $m^*$ is absent from the query phase, then $\mathcal{A}$ wins this security game.

Let $\mathcal{S}$ be the signing oracle which takes any public key $c$ and message $m$ as the input, and outputs a signature $\sigma$ satisfies $\mathsf{Ver}(c, m, \sigma)$. Given access to $\mathcal{S}$, the advantage of an adversary $\mathcal{A}$ is denoted as $\mathsf{Adv}^{\mathrm{EUF-CMA}}_{\mathcal{A}}$.

**Definition 2.** *$\mathcal{A}$ makes at most $q_H$ and $q_S$ queries to the hash function and signing oracle $\mathcal{S}$, respectively, up to $t$ time. If $\mathsf{Adv}^{\mathrm{EUF-CMA}}_{\mathcal{A}}$ is negligible, then the signature scheme is EUF-CMA secure.*

**Collision Resistance.** A collisions for a chameleon hash can be found by an adversary $\mathcal{A}$ if her secret key satisfies the policy embedded in that hash. The interactions between $\mathcal{A}$ and challenger $\mathcal{C}$ are listed below:

- *Setup.* $\mathcal{C}$ executes *Auth_Setup* to generate key pair and sends public key to $\mathcal{A}$, and subsequently initializes an empty table $Q$, an integer $j = 0$ and a message space $\mathcal{M}$.
- *Query.* $\mathcal{A}$ executes key generation and adaption queries, and then acquires transformation key $TK = \{TK_{i,gid}\}_{\forall i}$ and collision $(m^*, h^*, r^*, \sigma^*_{user}, m'^*, r'^*, \sigma'^*_{user})$, where $(\sigma^*_{user}, \sigma'^*_{user})$ is signature. The transformation key $TK$ and collision are recorded in $Q$.
- *Challenge.* $\mathcal{A}$ computes the hash collision. If the following equation holds: $Hash\_Verify(m^*, h^*, r^*, \sigma^*_{user}) = Hash\_Verify(m'^*, h^*, r'^*, \sigma'^*_{user})$, it returns 1; else returns 0.

The advantage of $\mathcal{A}$ is defined as follows:

$$\mathsf{Adv}^{\mathrm{CR}}_{\mathcal{A}} = \Pr[\mathcal{A} \to 1] \tag{2}$$

**Definition 3.** *If* $\mathsf{Adv}^{\mathrm{CR}}_{\mathcal{A}}$ *is negligible for any PPT adversaries $\mathcal{A}$, our scheme is collision resistance.*

**Indistinguishability.** Generally, indistinguishability implies that the adversary cannot distinguish whether the randomness of a chameleon hash is generated by the *Hash* algorithm or the *Adapt* algorithm. We define the following security game between an adversary $\mathcal{A}$ and a challenger $\mathcal{C}$:

- *Setup.* $\mathcal{C}$ executes the *Auth_Setup* algorithm and sends public key to $\mathcal{A}$.
- *Query Phase.* $\mathcal{C}$ selects a bit $b \in \{0, 1\}$ randomly. $\mathcal{A}$ executes HashOrAdapt queries $\mathcal{O}_{\mathtt{HashOrAdapt}}(., ., ., ., ., .)$, which takes global parameter $GP$, public key $pk_{\mathrm{AA}}$, messages $m, m'$, an access policy $\mathbb{A}$ and $TK = \{TK_{i,gid}\}_{\forall i}$ as the input. $\mathcal{C}$ runs *Offline_Hash* and *Online_Hash* algorithms and obtains $(h_b, r_b, \sigma_{userb})$, and subsequently returns them to $\mathcal{A}$.
- *Guess.* $\mathcal{A}$ outputs its guess $b'$.

The advantage of $\mathcal{A}$ in the security game is defined as:

$$\mathsf{Adv}^{\mathrm{IND}}_{\mathcal{A}} = |\Pr[b = b'] - 1/2| \tag{3}$$

**Definition 4.** *For all PPT adversaries $\mathcal{A}$, our scheme satisfies indistinguishability if* $\mathsf{Adv}^{\mathrm{IND}}_{\mathcal{A}}$ *is negligible.*

# 4    Instantiation

## 4.1    Construction of Our Scheme

The **Setup** phase consists of the following algorithms:

- *Global_Setup*$(\lambda) \rightarrow GP$. AA generates global parameters $GP = (\mathbb{G}_1, \mathbb{G}_2, p, e)$ by this algorithm, where $\mathbb{G}_1$ and $\mathbb{G}_2$ are bilinear groups of prime order $p$, $e$ is a bilinear map $\mathbb{G}_1 \times \mathbb{G}_1 \rightarrow \mathbb{G}_2$. The generator $g$ of $\mathbb{G}_1$ is chosen. In addition, a hash function $H_1 : \{0,1\}^* \rightarrow \mathbb{G}_1$ is determined, which projects global identities $gid$ to elements of $\mathbb{G}_1$. $H_1$ is regarded as a random oracle.
- *Auth_Setup*$(GP) \rightarrow (pk_{\text{AA}}, sk_{\text{AA}}, pk_{\text{sig}}, sk_{\text{sig}})$. Each authority is assumed to be responsible for one attribute in our scheme. Each AA owning attribute $i$ chooses three exponents $\alpha_i, y_i, x_i \in \mathbb{Z}_p$ and computes its public key $pk_{\text{AA}} = \{e(g,g)^{\alpha_i}, g^{y_i}\}_{\forall i}$ and secret key $sk_{\text{AA}} = \{\alpha_i, y_i\}_{\forall i}$. It keeps ($pk_{\text{sig}} = \{g^{x_i}\}_{\forall i}, sk_{\text{sig}} = \{x_i\}_{\forall i}$ as the key pair for signature.
- *Modi_Setup*$(GP) \rightarrow (spk, ssk)$. TM randomly selects $z_m \in \mathbb{Z}_p$ and computes $(spk = g^{z_m}, ssk = z_m)$ as its key pair.

The **KeyGen** phase is comprised of the following two algorithms:

- *Rew_KeyGen*$(GP, gid, i, sk_{\text{AA}}, sk_{\text{sig}}) \rightarrow (SK_{i,gid}, \sigma_{i,gid})$. For an authority owning attribute $i$, it executes operations listed below:
  1) Computing $SK_{i,gid} = g^{\alpha_i} H_1(gid)^{y_i}$ as the rewriting secret key for $gid$.
  2) Generating BLS signature $\sigma_{i,gid} = H_1(gid)^{x_i}$ for $gid$, and sending $SK_{i,gid}$ and $\sigma_{i,gid}$ to TM.
- *Trans_KeyGen*$(GP, SK_{i,gid}) \rightarrow TK_{i,gid}$. TM selects a randomness $z \in \mathbb{Z}_p$ and computes transformation key $TK_{i,gid} = (SK_{i,gid}^{1/z}, H_1(gid)^{1/z})$ for attribute $i$.

The **Hash** phase consists of the following two algorithms:

- *Offline_Hash*$(GP) \rightarrow (IC, IS)$. For attribute $j$, TO randomly selects exponents $\lambda_j', \alpha_j', y_j', \omega_j', r_j \in \mathbb{Z}_p$, then computes

$$C_{1j}' = e(g,g)^{\lambda_j'} \cdot e(g,g)^{\alpha_j' r_j}; \quad C_{2j}' = g^{r_j}; \quad C_{3j}' = g^{y_j' r_j} g^{\omega_j'};$$
$$CT_{1j} = e(g,g)^{\alpha_j r_j} \cdot e(g,g)^{-\alpha_j' r_j}; \quad CT_{2j} = g^{y_j r_j} g^{-y_j' r_j}.$$

Finally, $\{C_{1j}', C_{2j}', C_{3j}'\}_{\forall j}$ is reported as intermediate ciphertext $IC$, and $\{CT_{1j}, CT_{2j}\}_{\forall j}$ is regarded as intermediate state $IS$.
- *Online_Hash*$(GP, \{pk_{\text{AA}}\}, IC, IS, \mathbb{A}, m) \rightarrow (h, r, \sigma_{\text{user}})$. TO executes the following operations:
  1) TO defines a hash function $H_2 : \{0,1\}^* \rightarrow \mathbb{Z}_p$, then selects a randomness $r \in \mathbb{Z}_p^*$ and a trapdoor $T$, and finally computes $h' = g^m \cdot p_{CH}^r$, where $p_{CH} = g^{H_2(T)}$.
  2) TO publishes ciphertext $CT = (\mathbb{A}, C_0, C_0', IC, \{C_{4j}', C_{5j}'\}_{\forall j}, IS)$. $\mathbb{A}$ is an $n \times l$ access matrix $A$ with $\rho$ mapping its rows to attributes. Given a security hash function $H_3$, TO chooses a randomness $R \in \mathbb{G}_2$, and

computes $s = H_2(R, T)$, $u = H_3(R)$. Then TO selects randomly a vector $v \in \mathbb{Z}_p^l$ where $s$ is the first entry of $v$ and a vector $w \in \mathbb{Z}_p^l$ where 0 is the first entry of $w$. Let $\lambda_j$ denotes $A_j \cdot v$, $\omega_j$ denotes $A_j \cdot w$, and $A_j$ is the $j$th row of $A$. The ciphertext is computed as:

$$C_0 = R \cdot e(g, g)^s; \ C_0' = T \oplus u; \ C_{4j}' = \lambda_j - \lambda_j'; \ C_{5j}' = \omega_j - \omega_j'.$$

3) TO owns a signing key pair $(spk', ssk')$, where $spk' = g^{z_0} \in \mathbb{G}_1$ and $ssk' = z_0 \in \mathbb{Z}_p$. It computes signature $\sigma_{\text{user}} = H_1(h' \parallel \bar{r})^{ssk'}$, where $\bar{r} = g^{T+ssk'}$ denotes signed content.

Finally, TO outputs $(h, r, \sigma_{\text{user}}) = ((h', p_{CH}, CT), r, \sigma_{\text{user}})$, i.e. the hash, randomness and signature.

The **Verify** phase consists of the following two algorithms:

- *Aggre_Verify*$(gid, \{\sigma_{i,gid}\}, pk_{\text{sig}}) \to 0$ or 1. For reducing the cost of trial-and-error, The validity of rewriting secret key should be verified. TM aggregates the signatures $\{\sigma_{i,gid}\}$ from multiple authorities owning her attributes into one signature $\sigma_{gid} = \prod_i \sigma_{i,gid}$. Similarly, TM aggregates the signing public keys into $PK_{\text{sig}} = \prod_i (g^{x_i})$. The algorithm returns 1 if $e(\sigma_{gid}, g) = e(H_1(gid), PK_{\text{sig}})$, and returns 0 otherwise.
- *Hash_Verify*$(m, h, r, \sigma_{\text{user}}) \to 0$ or 1. Any entity could verify the transaction content on blockchain by checking whether all of the following satisfy: $h' = g^m \cdot p_{CH}^r$, $e(\sigma_{\text{user}}, g) = e(H_1(h' \parallel \bar{r}), spk')$. It returns 1 if all of them hold, and returns 0 otherwise.

The **Adapt** phase consists of the following two algorithms:

- *Part_Decrypt*$(GP, CT, \{TK_{i,gid}\}) \to CT'$. PS takes $GP$, ciphertext $CT$ encrypted under access matrix $\mathbb{A} = (A, \rho)$ and transformation key $\{TK_{i,gid}\}$ as the input. For $A_j$ ($j$th row of $A$), PS computes $C_{1j} = C_{1j}' \cdot CT_{1j} \cdot e(g, g)^{C_{4j}'}$, $C_{2j} = C_{2j}'$, $C_{3j} = C_{3j}' \cdot CT_{2j} \cdot g^{C_{5j}'}$, then chooses constant $c_j \in \mathbb{Z}_p$ such that $\sum_{j=1}^n c_j A_j = (1, 0, ..., 0)$, and computes $CT_1$, $CT_2$ as:

$$CT_1 = \prod_j \left( \frac{e(H_1(gid)^{\frac{1}{z}}, C_{3j})}{e(TK_{j,gid}^{\frac{1}{z}}, C_{2j})} \right)^{c_j} = \prod_j \left( \frac{e(H_1(gid), g)^{\frac{\omega_j}{z}}}{e(g, g)^{\frac{r_j \alpha_j}{z}}} \right)^{c_j},$$

$$CT_2 = \prod_j (C_{1j})^{c_j} = \prod_j \left( e(g, g)^{\lambda_j} e(g, g)^{\alpha_j r_j} \right)^{c_j}.$$

The partial decryption result $CT' = (C_0, C_0', CT_1, CT_2)$.

- *Full_Adapt*$(h, r, m, m', \{TK_{i,gid}\}, \sigma_{\text{user}}) \to (r', \sigma_{\text{user}}')$. The modifier holding transformation key $\{TK_{i,gid}\}$ executes the following operations to rewrite message $m$ to be $m'$:
  1) Verify the transaction content as described above (Sect. 4.1).

2) Decrypt trapdoor $T$. TM computes $R = C_0/(CT_1 \cdot CT_2^{\frac{1}{z}})^z$ and $u = H_3(R)$. Subsequently, TM computes $T = C_0' \oplus u$ and $s = H_2(R,T)$. If $C_0 = R \cdot e(g,g)^s$ and $CT_1 \cdot CT_2^{\frac{1}{z}} = e(g,g)^{\frac{s}{z}}$, the trapdoor $T$ is decrypted successfully; Otherwise, it outputs $\perp$.

3) Compute hash collision $r' = (m - m')/H_2(T)$.

4) Generate new signature $\sigma_{\text{user}}' = H_1(h' \parallel \bar{r}')^{ssk}$ for rewritten transaction, where $\bar{r}' = g^{T+ssk}$.

Finally, TM completes the rewriting operation and returns $(r', \sigma_{\text{user}}')$.

## 4.2   Correctness Analysis

In this section, we analyze whether the chameleon trapdoor $T$ can be correctly calculated when TM's rewriting secret key is valid and attributes satisfy the access policy. Firstly, in the $Part\_Decrypt$ algorithm, we have:

$$C_{1j} = C_{1j}' \cdot CT_{1j} \cdot e(g,g)^{C_{4j}'} = e(g,g)^{\lambda_j'} e(g,g)^{\alpha_j' r_j} e(g,g)^{\alpha_j r_j} e(g,g)^{-\alpha_j' r_j} e(g,g)^{\lambda_j - \lambda_j'}$$
$$= e(g,g)^{\alpha_j r_j} e(g,g)^{\lambda_j};$$

$$C_{2j} = C_{2j}' = g^{r_j}; C_{3j} = C_{3j}' \cdot CT_{2j} \cdot g^{C_{5j}'} = g^{y_j' r_j} g^{\omega_j'} g^{y_j r_j} g^{-y_j' r_j} g^{\omega_j - \omega_j'} = g^{y_j r_j} g^{\omega_j};$$

$$CT_1 = \prod_j \left( \frac{e(H_1(gid),g)^{\frac{\omega_j}{z}}}{e(g,g)^{\frac{r_j \alpha_j}{z}}} \right)^{c_j} = \frac{1}{e(g,g)^{\sum \frac{c_j r_j \alpha_j}{z}}};$$

$$CT_2 = \prod_j (C_{1j})^{c_j} = \prod_j \left( e(g,g)^{\alpha_j r_j} e(g,g)^{\lambda_j} \right)^{c_j} = e(g,g)^s e(g,g)^{\sum \alpha_j r_j c_j}.$$

Secondly, in the $Full\_Adapt$ algorithm, the correct $R$ can be calculated by substituting $C_0 = R \cdot e(g,g)^s$ into the following equation:

$$\frac{C_0}{\left( CT_1 \cdot CT_2^{\frac{1}{z}} \right)^z} = \frac{R \cdot e(g,g)^s}{\left( e(g,g)^{\sum \frac{c_j r_j \alpha_j}{z}} \left( e(g,g)^s e(g,g)^{\sum \alpha_j r_j c_j} \right)^{\frac{1}{z}} \right)^z} = \frac{R \cdot e(g,g)^s}{\left( e(g,g)^{\frac{s}{z}} \right)^z} = R.$$

Finally, the trapdoor $T$ could therefore be calculated as: $T = C_0' \oplus H_3(R)$.

## 4.3   Security Proof

In this section, we provide the security proof of the proposed scheme. The proofs of collision resistance and indistinguishability were established in [9], and the security proof of EUF-CMA was shown in [4]. Therefore, only the proof of the RCCA security is given here.

**Theorem 1.** *If the construction of Lewko-Waters (LW) scheme [18] is selectively CPA security, then in the random oracle model, our proposed scheme is RCCA security regarding Definition 1.*

*Proof.* Suppose there exist an adversary $\mathcal{A}$ that can attack our scheme with advantage $\varepsilon$ for any probabilistic polynomial-time (PPT). We subsequently build a simulator $\mathcal{B}$ that could successfully compromise the selective CPA security of LW scheme with advantage slightly less than $\varepsilon$.

- *Init.* $\mathcal{B}$ runs $\mathcal{A}$. $\mathcal{A}$ selects a challenge $\mathbb{A}^*$ and sends it to $\mathcal{B}$. $\mathcal{B}$ transmits this to the challenger of LW. We denote the LW challenger as $\mathcal{C}$.
- *Setup.* $\mathcal{B}$ computes the public parameters $PK = (e(g,g)^{\alpha_i}, g^{y_i})$ for all attributes $i$, and sends them to $\mathcal{A}$.
- *Phase I.* Then $\mathcal{B}$ initializes an empty set $D$, integer $j = 0$, and empty tables $T_1, T_2, T_3$. Subsequently, $\mathcal{B}$ answers the following queries from $\mathcal{A}$:
  - *Random Oracle Hash* $H_2(R,T)$: If there exists an entry $(R,T,s)$ in $T_1$, returns $s$; otherwise, select $s \in \mathbb{Z}_p$, store $(R,T,s)$ in $T_1$ and return $s$.
  - *Random Oracle Hash* $H_3(R)$: If there exists an entry $(R,u)$ in $T_2$, returns $u$. Otherwise, select $u \in \{0,1\}^k$, store $(R,u)$ in $T_2$ and return $u$.
  - *Create(S):* $\mathcal{B}$ sets $j = j + 1$. If $S$ does not satisfy $\mathbb{A}^*$, $\mathcal{B}$ executes the key generation algorithm to get $SK' = (PK, \{SK_{i,gid}\}_{i \in S})$. Then it selects $z \in \mathbb{Z}_p$ and sets $TK = (PK, \{SK_{i,gid}^{1/z}\}_{i \in S})$ and $SK = (z, TK)$. Else, if $S$ satisfies $\mathbb{A}^*$, $\mathcal{B}$ selects a randomness $d \in \mathbb{Z}_p$ and computes $SK'$ by executing *Rew_KeyGen* algorithm to construct a fake transformation key. Subsequently, $\mathcal{B}$ sets $TK = SK'$, $SK = (d, TK)$ where $TK$ is distributed appropriately for suitable selection of $d$. Finally, $\mathcal{B}$ stores $(j, S, SK, TK)$ in $T_3$ and returns $TK$ to $\mathcal{A}$.
  - *Corrupt(i).* If entry $(i, S, SK, TK)$ exists, $\mathcal{B}$ can obtain it, set $D = D \cup S$ and return $SK$ to $\mathcal{A}$.
  - *Decrypt(i, CT).* Suppose the ciphertext has been partially decrypted, both $\mathcal{A}$ and $\mathcal{B}$ could perform key transformation algorithm since they possesses transformation key $TK$. Let $CT = (C_0, C_0', CT_1, CT_2)$ related to $\mathbb{A}^*$. $(i, S, SK, TK)$ is acquired if it exists in $T_3$, and $\perp$ is returned if not or $S \notin \mathbb{A}^*$. In addition, if key $i$ does not satisfy $\mathbb{A}^*$, the following operations are performed:

1) Parse $SK = (z, TK)$, and calculate $R = C_0/(CT_1 \cdot CT_2^{1/z})^z$.
2) Obtain $(R, T_i, s_i)$ from $T_1$ if exists; otherwise return $\perp$.
3) If $\exists y \neq x$ that satisfies $(R, T_y, s_y)$ and $(R, T_x, s_x)$ are presented in $T_1$, $T_y = T_x$ and $s_y = s_x$, the simulation is terminated.
4) Otherwise, retrieve $(R, u)$ from $T_2$ if it exists. Else return $\perp$.
5) Verify if $C_0 = R \cdot e(g,g)^{s_i}$, $C_0' = T_i \oplus u$, $CT_1 \cdot CT_2^{1/z} = e(g,g)^{s_i/z}$ for each $i$.
6) If attribute $i$ exists and could pass the aforementioned checking, output $T_i$, else $\perp$.

If there exists $i$ that satisfies $\mathbb{A}^*$, then perform operations listed below:

1) Parse $SK = (d, TK)$, and calculate $\beta = (CT_1 \cdot CT_2^{1/d})^d$.
2) Check whether $\beta = e(g,g)^{s_i}$ for each entry $(R, T_i, s_i)$ in $T_1$.
3) If no such entry exists, $\mathcal{B}$ returns $\perp$.
4) If the entry that meets the condition is not unique, $\mathcal{B}$ terminates the operation.
5) Otherwise, let $(R, T, s)$ to be the only entry satisfied. Then obtain $(R, u)$ from $T_2$ if it exists, otherwise output $\perp$.

6) $\mathcal{B}$ verifies if $C_0 = R \cdot e(g,g)^s$, $C_0' = T \oplus u$, $(CT_1 \cdot CT_2^{1/d})^d = e(g,g)^s$.

7) Output $T$ if all conditions are met, else return $\perp$.

- *Challenge.* $\mathcal{A}$ sets two messages $(T_0^*, T_1^*)$. $\mathcal{B}$ randomly selects messages $(R_0, R_1) \in G_2^2$, then calls $\mathcal{C}$ to get ciphertext $CT = (C_0, \{C_{1j}, C_{2j}, C_{3j}\}_{\forall j})$ with $\mathbb{A}^*$. $\mathcal{B}$ randomly selects $C_0' \in \{0,1\}^k$ and sends $\mathcal{A}$ the challenge ciphertext $CT^* = (C_0, C_0', \{C_{1j}, C_{2j}, C_{3j}\}_{\forall j})$.

- *Phase II.* $\mathcal{B}$ performs the same answers operation as in Phase I except that the decryption query is either $T_0^*$ or $T_1^*$, then produces the test message.

- *Guess.* $\mathcal{A}$ should output a bit otherwise terminate the operation, while $\mathcal{B}$ would ignores it in any cases. $\mathcal{B}$ examines if any entry in $T_1$ and $T_2$ contains $R_0$ or $R_1$ as its first element. If neither randomness meets the condition, $\mathcal{B}$ returns its guess in $\{0,1\}$. If only $R_b$ exists, $\mathcal{B}$ outputs $b$. If a correct guess is proposed by $\mathcal{A}$, it implies that $\mathcal{A}$ is aware of $R_b$ with probability $\varepsilon$ and $R_b$ is retrieved through $H_1$ or $H_2$ oracle with $\varepsilon$. Then, $\mathcal{B}$ could produce a correct guess with the probability slightly larger than $\varepsilon$.

Therefore, if $\mathcal{A}$ could break our scheme with the given advantage $\varepsilon$, then with the same advantage, $\mathcal{B}$ could break the LW scheme [18]. Hence, the Theorem 1.

## 5 Performance Analysis

In this section, we evaluate the performance of our proposed scheme from the perspective of functionality comparison and computational burden.

**Functionality Comparison.** Table 1 provides the functionality comparison among our proposed scheme and several related rewritable blockchain schemes [9,10,14,28,33]. It is seen that our scheme is the only one that satisfies all of the properties, i.e. decentralized rewriting, fine-grained access control, offline/online hash, outsourced computation, and bi-level validity verification. Centralized attribute authority is not required in our scheme, instead, multiple attribute authorities share the responsibility for the distribution of the rewriting secret key. The schemes in [9,14,28] cannot support decentralized rewriting. The scheme in [14] makes use of multiple attribute authorities, nevertheless, it still requires

Table 1. Functionality comparison

| References | [10] | [9] | [28] | [33] | [14] | Ours |
|---|---|---|---|---|---|---|
| Decentralized rewriting | ✓ | × | × | ✓ | × | ✓ |
| Fine-grained access control | × | ✓ | ✓ | ✓ | ✓ | ✓ |
| Offline/Online hash | – | × | × | × | ✓ | ✓ |
| Outsourced computation | – | × | × | × | ✓ | ✓ |
| Bi-level validity verification | – | × | × | × | × | ✓ |

"✓":Well-done; "×":Not achieved; "–":Considered but needs further implements.

authorities to negotiate and share the same private key, implying that decentralization is not implemented in essence. The scheme in [10] cannot implement fine-grained access control. The scheme in [33] cannot perform offline/online hash and outsourced computation, as a result, users with resource-constrained devices may struggle to use in practice. Moreover, none of the above schemes have implemented the bi-level verification in blockchain rewriting.

**Computational Burden.** We implement our scheme in Python 3.8 and the Charm framework [1] on a workstation with Intel Xeon(R) E5-1620v4 CPU 3.50GHz and 128GB RAM. We adopt Type A curve from Pairing-Based Cryptography library for pairing, which has base field size of 512 bits. Specifically, we measure the running times of five major algorithms.

For comprehensive and fair comparison, we increase the attribute size from 10 to 100, and the corresponding access policy is set in the form of "$(S_1$ and $S_2)$ or $(S_3$ and $S_4)$ or...", where $S_i$ denotes an attribute. Each instance is run 100 times to estimate the average running time.

As illustrated in Fig. 2, the running times are basically invariant with the numbers of attributes in $Setup/Global\_Setup^1$ algorithms for each scheme, while our scheme achieves better performance. We conclude the reason is that our scheme dispenses with complex operations such as generating master keys during the setup phase, due to the decentralized design. Figure 3 shows that the running times of $KeyGen/Rew\_KeyGen$ algorithms grow approximately linear as attributes increasing in each scheme. The running time of our scheme is acceptable, which is less than most other schemes and only slightly higher than scheme in [9]. Figure 4 illustrates the running times of $Hash/Online\_Hash$ algorithms with the size of policies increasing. It is seen that the running time of our scheme is always kept to the lowest, while is present as increasing functions of policies for other schemes. It is due to the fact that the majority of computations (e.g. computation of $IC$ and $IS$) are executed offline, which reduces

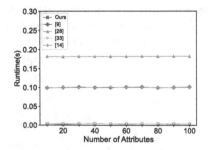

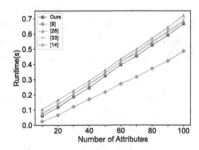

**Fig. 2.** Running time of $Setup/Global\_$ $Setup$

**Fig. 3.** Running time of $KeyGen/Rew\_$ $KeyGen$

---

[1] Algorithms separated by slashes represent functionally identical stages in various schemes, albeit with different names.

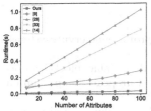
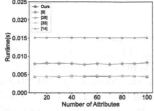
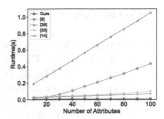

**Fig. 4.** Running time of *Hash/Online_Hash*

**Fig. 5.** Running time of *Verify/Hash_Verify*

**Fig. 6.** Running time of *Adapt/Full_Adapt*

the online computation cost. Likewise, as demonstrated in Fig. 5, our scheme and [33] achieve better performance in *Verify/Hash_Verify* algorithm. It takes 0.004 s to execute the algorithm with 100 attributes for our scheme, which is 0.011 s less than [28]. Moreover, our scheme achieves satisfactory running time in *Adapt/Full_Adapt* algorithm with increasing size of polices (shown in Fig 6). For reducing the computation burden of users, the majority of the computations in *Adapt* phase are separated out and executed by the proxy sever (partial decryption) in our scheme. As a result, with increasing size of policies, the running time of our scheme remains stably at the lowest, whereas of the schemes in [9, 28] grow appreciably.

# 6   Conclusion

In this paper, we proposed a scheme of decentralized and efficient blockchain rewriting with bi-level validity verification. The scheme overcomes the limitation of requiring a single trusted authority for the distribution of modification permissions compared to previous schemes, and supports multiple authorities to jointly manage and distribute the rewriting secret key. Meanwhile, the arrangement that separating the hash computation and the decryption into two stages can significantly reduce the computational burden on the user side, which is more conducive to the application in practice. Furthermore, the scheme supports validity verification for the modifier to check the validity of rewriting secret keys, as well for any entity to verify the content on blockchain. To the best of our knowledge, our scheme is the first to simultaneously support properties of decentralization, offline/online hash, outsourced computation and bi-level validity verification. Finally, extensive experimental results demonstrate that our scheme is advantageous in both functionality and performance.

**Acknowledgements.** We thank the anonymous reviewers for the valuable comments and suggestions. This work is supported by the National Natural Science Foundation of China (No. 62072359, No. 62072352, No. 61902292).

# References

1. Akinyele, J.A., et al.: Charm: a framework for rapidly prototyping cryptosystems. J. Cryptographic Eng. **3**(2), 111–128 (2013)
2. Ateniese, G., Magri, B., Venturi, D., Andrade, E.: Redactable blockchain-or-rewriting history in bitcoin and friends. In: 2017 IEEE European Symposium on Security and Privacy (EuroS&P), pp. 111–126. IEEE (2017)
3. Bethencourt, J., Sahai, A., Waters, B.: Ciphertext-policy attribute-based encryption. In: 2007 IEEE Symposium on Security and Privacy (S&P 2007), 20–23 May 2007, Oakland, California, USA, pp. 321–334. IEEE Computer Society (2007)
4. Boneh, D., Lynn, B., Shacham, H.: Short signatures from the weil pairing. J. Cryptology **17**(4), 297–319 (2004)
5. Camenisch, J., Derler, D., Krenn, S., Pöhls, H.C., Samelin, K., Slamanig, D.: Chameleon-hashes with ephemeral trapdoors. In: Fehr, S. (ed.) PKC 2017. LNCS, vol. 10175, pp. 152–182. Springer, Heidelberg (2017). https://doi.org/10.1007/978-3-662-54388-7_6
6. Canetti, R., Krawczyk, H., Nielsen, J.B.: Relaxing chosen-ciphertext security. In: Boneh, D. (ed.) CRYPTO 2003. LNCS, vol. 2729, pp. 565–582. Springer, Heidelberg (2003). https://doi.org/10.1007/978-3-540-45146-4_33
7. Chase, M.: Multi-authority attribute based encryption. In: Vadhan, S.P. (ed.) TCC 2007. LNCS, vol. 4392, pp. 515–534. Springer, Heidelberg (2007). https://doi.org/10.1007/978-3-540-70936-7_28
8. De Aguiar, E.J., Faiçal, B.S., Krishnamachari, B., Ueyama, J.: A survey of blockchain-based strategies for healthcare. ACM Comput. Surv. (CSUR) **53**(2), 1–27 (2020)
9. Derler, D., Samelin, K., Slamanig, D., Striecks, C.: Fine-grained and controlled rewriting in blockchains: chameleon-hashing gone attribute-based. In: 26th Annual Network and Distributed System Security Symposium, NDSS 2019, San Diego, California, USA, 24–27 February 2019. The Internet Society (2019)
10. Deuber, D., Magri, B., Thyagarajan, S.A.K.: Redactable blockchain in the permissionless setting. In: 2019 IEEE Symposium on Security and Privacy (SP), pp. 124–138. IEEE (2019)
11. Dutta, P., Choi, T.M., Somani, S., Butala, R.: Blockchain technology in supply chain operations: applications, challenges and research opportunities. Transp. Res. Part E: Logist. Transp. Rev. **142**, 102067 (2020)
12. Goyal, V., Pandey, O., Sahai, A., Waters, B.: Attribute-based encryption for fine-grained access control of encrypted data. In: Proceedings of the 13th ACM Conference on Computer and Communications Security, CCS 2006, Alexandria, VA, USA, October 30 - November 3, 2006, pp. 89–98. ACM (2006)
13. Guo, F., Mu, Y., Chen, Z.: Identity-based online/Offline encryption. In: Tsudik, G. (ed.) FC 2008. LNCS, vol. 5143, pp. 247–261. Springer, Heidelberg (2008). https://doi.org/10.1007/978-3-540-85230-8_22
14. Guo, L., Wang, Q., Yau, W.-C.: Online/offline rewritable blockchain with auditable outsourced computation. IEEE Trans. Cloud Comput., 1 (2021). https://doi.org/10.1109/TCC.2021.3102031
15. Hohenberger, S., Waters, B.: Online/Offline attribute-based encryption. In: Krawczyk, H. (ed.) PKC 2014. LNCS, vol. 8383, pp. 293–310. Springer, Heidelberg (2014). https://doi.org/10.1007/978-3-642-54631-0_17

16. Krawczyk, H., Rabin, T.: Chameleon signatures. In: Proceedings of the Network and Distributed System Security Symposium, NDSS 2000, San Diego, California, USA (2000)

17. Lewko, A., Okamoto, T., Sahai, A., Takashima, K., Waters, B.: Fully secure functional encryption: attribute-based encryption and (Hierarchical) inner product encryption. In: Gilbert, H. (ed.) EUROCRYPT 2010. LNCS, vol. 6110, pp. 62–91. Springer, Heidelberg (2010). https://doi.org/10.1007/978-3-642-13190-5_4

18. Lewko, A., Waters, B.: Decentralizing attribute-based encryption. In: Paterson, K.G. (ed.) EUROCRYPT 2011. LNCS, vol. 6632, pp. 568–588. Springer, Heidelberg (2011). https://doi.org/10.1007/978-3-642-20465-4_31

19. Lewko, A., Waters, B.: New proof methods for attribute-based encryption: achieving full security through selective techniques. In: Safavi-Naini, R., Canetti, R. (eds.) CRYPTO 2012. LNCS, vol. 7417, pp. 180–198. Springer, Heidelberg (2012). https://doi.org/10.1007/978-3-642-32009-5_12

20. Lewko, A.B., Waters, B.: Decentralizing attribute-based encryption. In: Proceedings of Advances in Cryptology - EUROCRYPT 2011–30th Annual International Conference on the Theory and Applications of Cryptographic Techniques, Tallinn, Estonia, 15–19 May 2011, vol. 6632, pp. 568–588 (2011)

21. Li, J., Zhang, Y., Ning, J., Huang, X., Poh, G.S., Wang, D.: Attribute based encryption with privacy protection and accountability for cloudiot. IEEE Trans. Cloud Comput. **10**, 762–773 (2020)

22. Maram, S.K.D., et al.: Churp: dynamic-committee proactive secret sharing. In: Proceedings of the 2019 ACM SIGSAC Conference on Computer and Communications Security, pp. 2369–2386 (2019)

23. Nakamoto, S.: Bitcoin: A peer-to-peer electronic cash system. Decentralized Bus. Rev. 21260 (2008)

24. Puddu, I., Dmitrienko, A., Capkun, S.. μchain: How to forget without hard forks. Cryptology ePrint Archive (2017)

25. Qi, S., Lu, Y., Zheng, Y., Li, Y., Chen, X.: Cpds: enabling compressed and private data sharing for industrial internet of things over blockchain. IEEE Trans. Ind. Inf. **17**(4), 2376–2387 (2020)

26. Sahai, A., Waters, B.: Fuzzy identity-based encryption. In: Cramer, R. (ed.) EUROCRYPT 2005. LNCS, vol. 3494, pp. 457–473. Springer, Heidelberg (2005). https://doi.org/10.1007/11426639_27

27. Thyagarajan, S.A.K., Bhat, A., Magri, B., Tschudi, D., Kate, A.: Reparo: publicly verifiable layer to repair blockchains. In: Borisov, N., Diaz, C. (eds.) FC 2021. LNCS, vol. 12675, pp. 37–56. Springer, Heidelberg (2021). https://doi.org/10.1007/978-3-662-64331-0_2

28. Tian, Y., Li, N., Li, Y., Szalachowski, P., Zhou, J.: Policy-based chameleon hash for blockchain rewriting with black-box accountability. In: Annual Computer Security Applications Conference, pp. 813–828 (2020)

29. Tian, Y., Liu, B., Li, Y., Szalachowski, P., Zhou, J.: Accountable fine-grained blockchain rewriting in the permissionless setting. arXiv preprint arXiv:2104.13543 (2021)

30. Voigt, P., von dem Bussche, A.: The EU General Data Protection Regulation (GDPR), vol. 1. Springer, Cham (2017). https://doi.org/10.1007/978-3-319-57959-7

31. Xie, M., Ruan, Y., Hong, H., Shao, J.: A CP-ABE scheme based on multi-authority in hybrid clouds for mobile devices. Future Gener. Comput. Syst. **121**, 114–122 (2021)

32. Yu, Y., Guo, L., Liu, S., Zheng, J., Wang, H.: Privacy protection scheme based on CP-ABE in crowdsourcing-IoT for smart ocean. IEEE Internet Things J. **7**(10), 10061–10071 (2020)
33. Zhang, Z., Li, T., Wang, Z., Liu, J.: Redactable transactions in consortium blockchain: controlled by multi-authority CP-ABE. In: Baek, J., Ruj, S. (eds.) ACISP 2021. LNCS, vol. 13083, pp. 408–429. Springer, Cham (2021). https://doi.org/10.1007/978-3-030-90567-5_21

# Cryptography

# TERSE: Tiny Encryptions and Really Speedy Execution for Post-Quantum Private Stream Aggregation

Jonathan Takeshita[1], Zachariah Carmichael[1], Ryan Karl[2], and Taeho Jung[1($\boxtimes$)]

[1] University of Notre Dame, Notre Dame, IN 46556, USA
{jtakeshi,zcarmich,tjung}@nd.edu
[2] Carnegie Mellon University, Pittsbufgh, PA 15213, USA

**Abstract.** The massive scale and performance demands of privacy-preserving data aggregation make integration of security and privacy difficult. Traditional tools in private computing are not well-suited to handle these challenges, especially for more limited client devices. Efficient primitives and protocols for secure and private data aggregation are a promising approach for private data analytics with resource-constrained devices. However, even such efficient primitives may be much slower than computation with plain data (i.e., without security/privacy guarantees).

In this paper, we present TERSE, a new Private Stream Aggregation (PSA) protocol for quantum-secure time-series additive data aggregation. Due to its simplicity, low latency, and low communication overhead, TERSE is uniquely well-suited for real-world deployment. In our implementation, TERSE shows very low latency for both clients and servers, achieving encryption latency on a smartphone of 0.0003 ms and aggregation latency of 0.0067 ms for 1000 users. TERSE also shows significant improvements in latency over other state-of-the-art quantum-secure PSA, achieving improvements of 1796× to 12406× for encryption at the client's end and 848× to 5433× for aggregation and decryption at the server's end.

**Keywords:** Public key cryptosystems · Lattice-based cryptography · Private Stream Aggregation

## 1 Introduction

**Motivation.** In modern computing and data analytics, aggregating a sum on data from many users is a frequently encountered problem. Ensuring security and privacy of user data in such aggregations while maintaining enough performance for practical deployment is a challenging issue, and is necessary to consider in order to comply with regulations for user protection such as GDPR. Secure and private data aggregation plays an important role in modern data analysis [31,37,57,66,67], with applications in statistical computation, smart metering, voting, advertising analytics, and federated learning. At the massive scale of

© ICST Institute for Computer Sciences, Social Informatics and Telecommunications Engineering 2023
Published by Springer Nature Switzerland AG 2023. All Rights Reserved
F. Li et al. (Eds.): SecureComm 2022, LNICST 462, pp. 331–352, 2023.
https://doi.org/10.1007/978-3-031-25538-0_18

the modern Internet, with billions of users and devices [1], there is a need for high-performance implementations to perform high-scale aggregations. The huge scale and unique characteristics of the modern era of computing world presents new challenges that require novel solutions.

There exist general cryptographic tools for secure and private computation. However, the generality and pitfalls of these tools make them unattractive or infeasible for real-world deployment. Homomorphic encryption [20,26,33] allows computation over encrypted data, but its computational intensity and ciphertext size are too high for use on resource-limited devices [64]. Secure multiparty computation [42] requires robust lines of communication for use in multiple rounds of communication, which may not be available in all locales, such as those in developing nations. Trusted Execution Environments such as Intel SGX [28] offer confidential computing, but face challenges at scale [53,72]. These challenges necessitate the development of efficient custom-built protocols for secure data aggregation.

To facilitate efficient secure and private aggregation, the study of Private Stream Aggregation (PSA) protocols has been undertaken and advanced in recent years [15,22,29,32,39–41,43,44,60,63,69]. Research in this area has focused on efficiency, though there is also work in fault tolerance and robustness. Many solutions for secure and private data analytics and outsourced computing focus on throughput on a large body of data [8,9,27,45,56,63]. In real-world deployments, the *latency* of a single computation, as opposed to the *throughput* across many epochs of time-series data, is of vital importance in real-time monitoring and reporting. Previous advances in secure aggregation have faced issues such as limited plaintext space, a lack of quantum security for future protection against quantum-capable attackers, high complexity and overhead due to the large ciphertext expansion, or focusing on throughput at the expense of latency due to the inherent computational intensity coming from the large ciphertext expansion.

**Our Work.** In this work, we present a more efficient PSA protocol with quantum security, minimal latency and communication overhead. Our new protocol TERSE: Tiny Encryptions and Really Speedy Execution for Post-Quantum PSA is truly practical for latency-critical applications, satisfying the requirements of high performance without sacrificing guarantees of security and privacy. As online (input-dependent) computations are most critical for latency, we consider this metric of latency of input-dependent operations as what users are most interested in. For this reason, we focus on reducing the online costs of computation and communication as much as possible. Our research goal is thus to construct efficient RLWE-based PSA overcoming these issues. TERSE' ciphertexts are quantum secure via RLWE, and its trusted setup can be implemented with quantum-secure TEE-based symmetric encryption [18,52] and quantum-secure signature schemes for TEE [17].

Our construction is enabled by three insights: 1) giving adversary RLWE samples one coefficient at a time does not improve their advantage, 2) no input-dependent ring polynomial multiplication is required for additive lattice-based PSA, and 3) lattice-based PSA inputs that are ring polynomials can have input encoded coefficientwise. Combining these, we construct a novel PSA protocol using single coefficients of ring polynomials, resulting in much smaller ciphertexts and extremely efficient input-dependent encryption and aggregation. Our protocol mitigates the practical disadvantages of RLWE-based cryptography by performing PSA with ring polynomials *one coefficient at a time*, and by precomputing intensive computations in advance of having inputs ready. This novel construction addresses the large ciphertext expansion that was inherent in previous lattice-based secure aggregation schemes, significantly reducing the latency of each aggregation. We show the real-world practicality of our novel construction with implementation results of both users and aggregators.

**Our Contributions**

1. We present TERSE, the first RLWE-based PSA scheme that can provide both low latency and high throughput, greatly reducing the size of a ciphertext for a single input. These novel traits allow TERSE to achieve operation latency measured in microseconds, making TERSE uniquely well-suited for performance-critical deployments.
2. We discuss the extension of TERSE with both well-known and cutting-edge extensions such as efficient ring polynomial arithmetic through RNS and NTT, SGX-based fault tolerance, and differential privacy. These extensions further support our goal of making private stream aggregation practically feasible for real-world use.
3. We implement TERSE and show experimental results demonstrating its performance and comparing it with plaintext aggregation. For $n = 1000$ users and a plaintext space of $|t| = 32$ bits, TERSE encryption achieves a latency of only 0.0003 ms, and aggregation and decryption run in 0.0067 ms. Our experiments with increasing numbers of users shows that TERSE is practically scalable for real-world deployments.

## 2  Related Work

### 2.1  Pre-Quantum PSA

The work of Shi et al. [60] established the field of PSA, creating the basic definitions and the first construction. The work of Shi et al. and Joye et al. rely respectively on the Decisional Diffie-Hellman (DDH) and the Decisional Composite Residuosity assumptions [38,60]. Other work based on the Discrete Logarithm problem has been proposed [39,41]. PSA has also been constructed for use in smart metering [58,62]. Chen et al. [24] presented a PSA scheme with dynamic joins/leaves and input tampering detection, based upon the DDH assumption. Wang et al. [70] created a scheme based on the Pallier cryptosystem [55] with fault tolerance and dynamic joins/leaves. These protocols are not secure against quantum-capable adversaries [61]; recent research has turned towards post-quantum PSA.

### 2.2  Post-Quantum PSA

The LaPS protocol [15] presented a PSA protocol integrating quantum security, improving upon previous bounds on the plaintext space, a generic and modular protocol with an instantiation, and the first implementation of a lattice-based PSA scheme. However, LaPS has several issues: it is extremely and needlessly complicated, and requires the black-box use of an FHE scheme (BGV [20] was used in their instantiation), reducing its practicality. Further, its security with the "encrypt-once" model is subject to a simple attack [69], though this can be mitigated by requiring fresh public matrices at each timestamp.

The SLAP protocol [63] presented many improvements over LaPS. Instead of using an FHE scheme as a black-box subprotocol, SLAP used custom-built RLWE-based cryptographic constructions for PSA. Due to this, SLAP is much simpler than LaPS and is much more lightweight, with computational improvements over LaPS of 20× for aggregation and 65× for user-side encryption, and ciphertexts that are up to 2730× smaller at larger parameters. SLAP showed large improvements over LaPS in throughput for communication and computation, as well as in complexity. However, SLAP, like LaPS, is still subject to the high degree of ciphertext expansion common to RLWE encryption, resulting in higher latency and communication overhead. Both LaPS and SLAP operate in the encrypt-once model, where an adversary only sees a single ciphertext for a user at a given time. While this model is sufficient for most practical purposes, stronger ones have been proposed [69].

Other quantum-secure schemes with even lower latency have also been presented that manage to have smaller ciphertexts by not using RLWE. The LaSS scheme of Waldner et al. [69] uses secret sharing, and the scheme of Ernst et al. [32] uses a "deterministic version of the LWE [Learning With Errors] problem" known as Learning With Rounding (LWR) and key-homomorphic pseudorandom functions. Both schemes achieve runtimes on the order of milliseconds and have smaller input-dependent communication overhead. These schemes do have some issues: LaSS's per-user keys are linear in the number of users, i.e., the total number of keys is quadratic in the total number of users, making practical deployment for memory-limited IoT devices infeasible for larger numbers of users. The security of LWR, upon which [32] is dependent, is still in contention due to the deterministic rounding used [30]. Multi-key fully homomorphic encryption can also be applied to PSA, but is too general and burdensome to be appealing for IoT deployments [6,54]. Bao et al. used AES with noninteractively generated keys for PSA with message integrity [13].

## 2.3   PSA for IoT and Limited Devices

Lu et al. [51] constructed a PSA scheme using modified Pallier encryption and message authentication codes to form IoT-friendly PSA with protection against input tampering. Zhuo et al. [71] created a cloud-assisted protocol to compute on users' aggregated data, relying on the Diffie-Hellman and discrete logarithm assumptions and the BGV homomorphic encryption scheme. He et al. [36] create a scheme with the discrete logarithm and Diffie-hellman assumptions aimed at smart grids, which is able to withstand many different types of internal attacks. Li et al. [48] construct private dual-function aggregation by relying on the BGV homomorphic encryption scheme [19]; their scheme's practical performance is difficult to infer, as they only give an asymptotic performance analysis.

# 3    Background

## 3.1    Private Stream Aggregation

We consider the scenario where $n$ users send inputs to a cloud server that is tasked with summing all user inputs. We assume that channels of communication are authenticated and nonmalleable; attackers impersonating users or modifying their messages in transit are outside the scope of this work. We use an honest-but-curious adversary model, where an adversary may view compromised parties' data, but will otherwise faithfully execute the protocol. This attacker model is commonly used for work in PSA [15,32,60,69]. PSA schemes are formally described with the following three algorithms:

1. $Setup(\lambda \in \mathbb{N}, \cdots)$: Takes a security parameter $\lambda \in \mathbb{N}$, along with other parameters such as the number of users and the plaintext space. Distribute secret keys $s_i$ to each user and an aggregation key $s'$ to the aggregator, and distribute publicly known parameters to all parties.
2. $Enc(s_i, ts, x_{i,ts}, r_{i,ts})$: Takes a user's input $x_{i,ts}$ at a particular timestamp $ts$, possibly along with differentially private noise $r_{i,ts}$. User $i$ will call this function with their secret key $s_i$. Returns a ciphertext $c_i$.
3. $Agg(s', ts, c_{0,ts}, \cdots, c_{n-1,ts})$: The aggregator will call this function at timestamp $ts$, using its aggregation key $s'$. It will aggregate the ciphertexts $c_{0,ts}, \cdots, c_{n-1,ts}$, and output $y_{ts} = \sum_{i=0}^{n-1} x_{i,ts} + r_{i,ts}$.

Intuitively, we want to require that any adversary against a PSA scheme learns nothing more than they would when executing an idealized, black-box protocol that allows the aggregator to learn the sum of users' data. Inherent in this definition is that an adversary compromising the aggregator and $n-1$ users can inevitably learn information about the last user's data. In general, collusions of users and the aggregator have the ability to learn about information from uncorrupted users. This is a common issue in privacy-preserving protocols; preserving user privacy in the face of such attacks is a problem left to differential privacy. The $Setup$ functionality is assumed to be performed by a trusted party, or collaboratively in a trusted format (e.g., using secure multiparty computation).

In the encrypt-once model, we assume that users will only produce a single input per timestamp. This model is used in prior work [15,63], and is a reasonable model of how real-world PSA deployments would function.

## 3.2    Definition of Security

**Definition 1.** *A PSA scheme is aggregator oblivious in the encrypt-once model if any probabilistic polynomial-time (PPT) adversary has no more than negligible advantage with respect to a security parameter $\lambda$ in the following security game:*
**Setup.** *The challenger runs the Setup algorithm, returning any public parameters to the adversary.*
**Queries.** *The adversary may make up to $poly(\lambda)$ of following types of queries adaptively:*

- *Encrypt: The adversary may specify $(i, ts, x_{i,ts}, r_{i,ts})$ and ask for the ciphertext. The challenger returns the ciphertext $c_{i,ts} = Enc(s_i, ts, x_{i,ts}, r_{i,ts})$ to the adversary.*
- *Compromise: The adversary specifies a party $i \in [0, n) \cup \{\Box\}$. If $i = \Box$, the challenger returns the aggregator's decryption key $s'$ to the adversary (i.e., the aggregator is compromised.). Otherwise, the challenger returns user $i$'s secret key $s_i$, to the adversary (i.e., user $i$ is compromised).*
- *Challenge: This query is only made once. The adversary specifies a set of participants $U$ and a time $ts$, such that neither $ts$ nor any $i \in U$ was previously argued to Compromise. For each user $i \in U$, the adversary chooses a pair of inputs (user input, along with noise if applicable) $(x_{i,ts}^0, r_{i,ts}^0)$ and $(x_{i,ts}^1, r_{i,ts}^1)$. The challenger then chooses a random bit $b$, and returns the ciphertexts $\{c_{i,ts} = Enc(s_i, ts, x_{i,ts}^b, r_{i,ts}^b)\}_{i \in U}$ to the adversary.*

***Guess.*** *The adversary attempts to guess $b$.*

*The adversary wins if they can guess the bit $b$, and if the aggregator was compromised, then $\sum x_{i,ts}^0 + r_{i,ts}^0 = \sum x_{i,ts}^1 + r_{i,ts}^1$.*

Aggregator obliviousness essentially states that nothing more leaks from the protocol's execution than what a collusion of parties can derive from their inputs and output [60].

## 3.3  Ring Learning with Errors

Many modern cryptographic constructions draw their hardness assumptions from the Ring Learning With Errors (RLWE) problem, due to its conjectured difficulty for quantum adversaries and convenient mathematical structure. We briefly summarize RLWE here; the reader is referred to other work for a more in-depth discussion of RLWE [33,52]. Consider the negacyclic ring $R_q = \mathbb{Z}_q[x]/(x^N + 1)$ for a large number $q$ and power-of-two $N$. We denote the modular reduction of $x$ modulo $q$ as $[x]_q$, which is applied coefficientwise to polynomials. For a desired security level $\lambda \in \mathbb{N}$, there exist standard choices for $q$ and $N$ to guarantee at least $\lambda$ bits of security in solving the RLWE problem for these parameters [4,5]. We say that a distribution is $B$-bounded if the values drawn from it have an infinity norm bounded above by $B$ with all but negligible probability.

The RLWE problem is as follows: let $\mathbf{s}$ be chosen randomly from $R_q$, and consider random distributions $\chi, \zeta$ on $R_q$. In practice, the distribution $\zeta$ is often chosen to be 1-bounded [33], while $\chi$ is uniformly random on $R_q$. Summarized succinctly, the RLWE problem states that terms of the form $[\mathbf{A}_i \cdot \mathbf{s} + \mathbf{e}_i]_q$ or $[\mathbf{A}_i \cdot \mathbf{s} + t \cdot \mathbf{e}_i]_q$ are computationally indistinguishable from random when $gcd(q, t) = 1$, $\mathbf{A}_i \leftarrow \chi$ is publicly known, and $\mathbf{e}_i \leftarrow \zeta$ [16,20,59].

In RLWE-based cryptosystems, elements of $R_q$ are large objects, using kilobytes or even megabytes of memory [65]. RLWE-based cryptosystems thus superficially seem impractical for secure aggregation with resource-limited devices. Our key innovation is a novel strategy to allow using only small portions of these terms, keeping the guarantee of quantum security, while achieving the functionality of additive aggregation.

### 3.4 The Random-Oracle Model

In cryptography, it is often convenient to assume the existence of a "random-oracle" hash function. A random-oracle hash function operates as a black-box functionality available to users, guaranteeing them random output for given inputs with the caveat that identical inputs will yield identical outputs. While the assumption of the existence of random-oracle hash functions was previously contentious [21], there is little practical evidence of any security risks from using random-oracle hashes [46].

## 4  Basic Construction

In this section, we review the previous state-of-the-art quantum-secure aggregation scheme, and show how to modify it for more efficient aggregation. We then show it satisfies the security definition of aggregator obliviousness. Guaranteeing user input privacy through the addition of differentially private noise is not our novel contribution, and is left to Sect. 5.1.

### 4.1 Prior State-of-the-Art RLWE-Based PSA

The LaPS protocol [15] brought several new developments in PSA, including post-quantum security, more generous plaintext spaces, and better efficiency. Their efficiency gains were demonstrated with their implementation and more thorough experimental results, as compared to previous work. However, LaPS left much room for improvement; it is overly complex, affecting both usability and practical performance. This was partially due to their use of FHE.

The SLAP scheme [63] improved upon these issues by eschewing the black-box approach to additive homomorphism used by LaPS. Instead, SLAP used purpose-built homomorphic lattice arithmetic in their scheme. This resulted in more efficient operations and much smaller ciphertexts. SLAP also found that noise-scaled message encoding is more efficient than message-scaled encoding; we follow their example by using noise-scaled encoding in TERSE. SLAP focused on practical throughput from message packing, but their latency was slightly greater than that of other state-of-the-art post-quantum PSA [32,69]. However, these schemes not using RLWE have disadvantages such as large key storage requirements or doubts on security [30], which leads us to focus on optimizing RLWE-based PSA.

SLAP and LaPS have some similarities. First, being related to RLWE or its A-LWE variant, public values **A** dependent on a timestamp were (or should have been) used. As is common to many PSA schemes [38,60], additively correlated secret keys are used. While SLAP represented a great leap forward in the state of the art, it still faced limitations in communication overhead. The ciphertexts of SLAP are ring polynomials in $R_q$, which may be as large as megabytes for common parameter settings. This makes it less practical for highly constrained users. SIMD batching still helps SLAP achieve high throughput, but the overall ciphertext size cannot be reduced. This necessitates either filling the remaining SIMD slots with junk data (greatly reducing throughput), or waiting for enough data to fill a ring polynomial, which may be undesirable in time-sensitive aggregations. These schemes consider security in the encrypt-once model, assuming each user will only produce a single encryption at a given timestamp – a reasonable security model for most applications.

Other work in quantum-secure PSA not using RLWE [32,69] is able to achieve much smaller ciphertexts. However, these schemes have some disadvantages. The security of the Learning With Rounding problem upon which [32] is based is of concern [30]. Using secret-sharing for aggregation [69] is not practical for large numbers of users, due to the quadratic growth in key storage needed. It is thus desirable to construct RLWE-based secure stream aggregation with smaller ciphertexts.

### 4.2   A More Performant Protocol: TERSE

We now show how to further break down lattice arithmetic for an even more efficient protocol, with smaller ciphertexts. Our path forward hinges on a few key ideas: first, with precomputation of user values, no expensive input-dependent polynomial multiplication is required, and the computation of these terms can be done ahead of time or prepared concurrently. (Phones and other limited devices can do this while plugged in and idling, or in a separate process, or they may outsource the precomputations to a synced computer.) This means that all input-dependent polynomial arithmetic is only addition, scalar multiplication, and base conversion, which can be done coefficient-wise. Second, transmitting elements of $R_q$ one coefficient at a time does not give adversaries any additional information about users' secret data. Third, SLAP can apply a simple coefficient-wise SIMD batching to improve the throughput of their scheme. Packing the coefficients in this manner means that coefficients can be packed into a polynomial or extracted at any point in the addition-only computation, without affecting correctness.

Combining these insights gives us the core idea: we can perform aggregation and decryption *one polynomial coefficient at a time*, which does not impact security or correctness, and reduces the ciphertext size needed to send a single element of $\mathbb{Z}_t$ by a factor of $N$, which usually ranges from $2^{10}$ to $2^{16}$. We can now describe TERSE, which applies the key ideas above. Essentially, we parse a timestamp into two parts, with one part used to index coefficients of polynomials in $R_q$. Then, we simply use coefficients at that index from the precomputed product of the user's secret key and the public hash.

Let $\lambda \in \mathbb{N}$ be the bits of guaranteed security, and let $\mathbf{A}_\theta = h(\theta)$ be a random-oracle hash function mapping the high bits $\theta$ of timestamps $ts = (\theta, \tau)$ to $R_q$. We consider a small error distribution $\zeta$ and a uniformly random distribution $\chi$, drawing either polynomials or singleton values from $R_q$ or $\mathbb{Z}_q$ as appropriate. Denote the $i$-th coefficient of a polynomial $\mathbf{x}$ as $\mathbf{x}[i]$. Differential privacy is an orthogonal extension, as discussed in Sect. 5.1, so we do not go into detail on the mechanisms of differentially private noise added through the terms $r_{i,ts}$. We describe TERSE as follows:

1. $TERSE.Setup(\lambda, t, n)$: For a plaintext space of $\mathbb{Z}_t$ and $n$ users, choose the ciphertext modulus $q$ such that $log_2(3) + log_2(n) + log_2(t) < log_2(q)$ and $q, t$ are coprime. Choose $N$ to ensure at least $\lambda$ bits of security for the RLWE problem on $R_q$ [4,5], and $H(\cdot)$ to be a random hash mapping timestamps to $R_q$. Choose users' secret keys $s_0 \cdots s_{n-1}$ randomly from $\chi$. Finally, choose the additively correlated aggregator's key $s' = -[\sum_{i=0}^{n-1} s_i]_q$. Users and the aggregators parse timestamps into most significant and least significant bits as $ts = (\theta, \tau)$, with $\tau \in \mathbb{Z}_N$, i.e., $\tau$ is represented using up to $|N|$ bits.
2. $TERSE.Enc(s_i \in R_q, ts = (\theta, \tau), x_{i,ts} \in \mathbb{Z}_t, r_{i,ts} \in \mathbb{Z}_t)$: Choose the user's RLWE error $e_{i,ts} \in \mathbb{Z}_t$ from $\zeta$. Set $p_{i,ts} = (\mathbf{A}_\theta \cdot s_i)[\tau]$. (Note that these steps can and should be precomputed before the user's time-series input $x_{i,ts}$ is available.) The user's ciphertext is $c_{i,ts} = \lfloor p_{i,ts} + t \cdot e_{i,ts} + [x_{i,ts} + r_{i,ts}]_t \rfloor_q$.
3. $TERSE.Agg(s' \in R_q, ts = (\theta, \tau), c_{0,ts} \cdots c_{n-1,ts})$: Precompute $p'_{ts} = (\mathbf{A}_\theta \cdot s'_{i,ts})[\tau]$. The sum of users' inputs $x_{i,ts}$ is $y_{ts} = [[p'_{ts} + \sum_{i=0}^{n-1} c_{i,ts}]_q]_t$.

Correctness is easy to see. Note that $p'_{ts} = -\sum p_{i,ts}$. Then $[p'_{ts} + \sum_{i=0}^{n-1} c_{i,ts}]_q = [\sum_{i=0}^{n-1} t \cdot e_{i,ts} + [x_{i,ts} + r_{i,ts}]_t]_q$. Reducing this modulo $t$ removes the noise terms, and we avoid noise overflow so long as the bounds in $TERSE.Setup$ are observed.

Note that the input-dependent portion of encryption in TERSE is extremely simple, requiring only base conversion from base $t$ to base $q$, followed by one modular addition in base $q$. Similarly, the online portion of aggregation of TERSE only needs the additive aggregation of all user ciphertexts and $p'_{ts}$, followed by a base conversion. This simplicity leads to highly efficient operations for both the user and aggregator, as shown in Sect. 6.

Improving upon other work in RLWE-based PSA, TERSE achieves a relatively small ciphertext expansion - for a single input in $\mathbb{Z}_t$, a ciphertext is an element of $\mathbb{Z}_q$, so that the expansion factor is only $q/t$, and only $|q|$ bits are needed for ciphertexts – in practice, this is usually only 64 or 128 bits!

### 4.3 Proof of Security

**Lemma 1.** *In attempting to solve the RLWE problem (in either of the Search or Decision versions in Sect. 3.3), an adversary does not gain any advantage from seeing elements of $R_q$ one coefficient at a time.*

**Theorem 1.** *TERSE is an aggregator oblivious PSA scheme.*

*Proof.* We follow previous work [3,15] and assume for simplicity that adversaries can choose the differentially private noise terms $r_{i,ts}$ during the Challenge phase. We will construct a reduction from RLWE to TERSE by showing that given an adversary $\mathcal{A}$ that can win the game of aggregator obliviousness (see

Definition 1) in polynomial time, we can construct an adversary $\mathcal{B}$ able to distinguish RLWE terms from random in polynomial time, thus solving the Decisional version of RLWE. For simplicity, we consider a real-or-random version of the game of aggregator obliviousness, again following previous work [15, 60, 63]. As noted in Sect. 3.1, aggregator obliviousness does not protect against the case where all but one party is compromised, so we suppose that $\mathcal{A}$ will not attempt to make Compromise queries for $n$ distinct parties.

First, consider a challenger $\mathcal{C}$ who tests the ability of $\mathcal{B}$ to attack RLWE. $\mathcal{B}$ will compute and return TERSE parameters including $R_q, t, n$ for a given security level $\lambda$ to $\mathcal{A}$ as a response to a Setup query from $\mathcal{A}$. $R_q$ is the ring for which $\mathcal{B}$ will attempt to attack RLWE. $\mathcal{B}$ will then choose two distinct parties $j, k \in [0, n) \cup \{\Box\}$, and draw secret keys $s_i \leftarrow \chi$ for $i \notin \{j, k\}$ (exactly as in $TERSE.Setup$). As noted in previous work [15, 63], $\mathcal{B}$'s choices $j, k$ must be in the set of at least two users $\mathcal{A}$ will not attempt to compromise, which occurs with probability $\frac{1}{n^2}$.

Next, $\mathcal{B}$ needs to prepare to match RLWE samples with the values it is able to send to $\mathcal{A}$. If $\mathcal{A}$ will make Encrypt queries for (up to) $\mathcal{P} = poly(\lambda)$ different timestamps, $\mathcal{B}$ will simply ask for $\mathcal{Q} = \lceil \frac{\mathcal{P}+1}{N} \rceil$ RLWE samples from $\mathcal{C}$. From this, $\mathcal{B}$ will receive a set of pairs $\mathcal{S} = \{(\mathbf{a}_\sigma, \mathbf{b}_\sigma)\}_{\sigma \in \mathbb{Z}_\mathcal{Q}}$. Note that $\theta$ and $\sigma$ are both in $\mathbb{Z}_\mathcal{Q}$. Then, $\mathcal{B}$ will select $H(\cdot)$ such that for each of the $\mathcal{P}$ values $ts = (\theta, \tau)$, $H(ts) = \mathbf{a}_\theta[\tau]$, and distribute this function as part of $TERSE.Setup$.

When $\mathcal{A}$ makes an Encrypt query $(i, x_{i,ts}, r_{i,ts}, ts)$ to $\mathcal{B}$, if party $i$ is not compromised and the pair $i, ts$ has not been used in a previous Encrypt query, $\mathcal{B}$ will compute and return the TERSE encryption $NoisyEnc(\mathbf{s}_i, ts, x_{i,ts}, r_{i,ts})$ if $i \notin \{j, k\}$. For the parties $j, k$, $\mathcal{B}$ will eventually set $j$'s secret key to be the secret RLWE value, and will (implicitly) let user $k$'s secret key be the sum of all other users' keys. If $i = j$, with $ts = (\theta, \tau)$, then $\mathcal{B}$ finds the tuple $(\mathbf{a}_\tau, \mathbf{b}_\tau)$, and returns $\mathbf{b}_\theta[\tau] + (x_{j,ts} + r_{j,ts})$ to $\mathcal{A}$. If $i = k$, $\mathcal{B}$ again finds the appropriate value $\mathbf{b}_\theta[\tau]$, and returns $-\mathbf{b}_\theta[\tau] - (\mathbf{a}_\theta \cdot \sum_{\ell \notin \{j,k\}} \mathbf{s}_\ell)[\tau] + (x_{k,ts} + r_{k,ts})$ to $\mathcal{A}$.

When $\mathcal{A}$ makes a Compromise query for a party $i \in ([0, n) \cup \{\Box\}) \setminus \{j, k\}$, $\mathcal{B}$ simply returns $\mathbf{s}_i$ to $\mathcal{A}$. We denote the set of never-compromised users as $K \subseteq [0, n) \cup \{\Box\}$. If $i \in \{j, k\}$, i.e., $\mathcal{A}$ tried to compromise a user that $\mathcal{B}$ assumed would remain uncompromised, then $\mathcal{B}$ will simply abort.

When $\mathcal{A}$ makes a Challenge query, it will choose a set of uncompromised users $U \in K$, and will send input-noise pairs $\{(x_{u,ts'}, r_{u,ts'})\}_{u \in U}$, where $ts' = (\theta', \tau')$ was not previously used in any Encrypt query. At this point, up to $\mathcal{Q} - 1$ timestamps have been used in Encrypt queries, leaving at least one unused value remaining. Then, $\mathcal{B}$ will compute the values $\mathbf{c}_{i,ts} = NoisyEnc(\mathbf{s}_i, ts', x_{i,ts}, r_{i,ts})$ for $i \in U \setminus \{j, k\}$, $c_{j,ts} = \mathbf{b}_{\theta'}[\tau'] + (x_{j,ts} + r_{j,ts})$, and $c_{k,ts} = -\mathbf{b}_{\theta'}[\tau'] - (\mathbf{a}_{\theta'} \cdot \sum_{\ell \notin \{j,k\}} \mathbf{s}_\ell)[\tau'] + (x_{k,ts} + r_{k,ts})$. Finally, $\mathcal{B}$ will return $\mathbf{c}_{i,ts}$ for $i \in [0, n) \cup \{\Box\}$ to $\mathcal{A}$.

To make a decision on whether it was given real RLWE terms or random values, $\mathcal{B}$ will use the decision of $\mathcal{A}$. If $\mathcal{A}$ decides that it was given ciphertexts that are simply messages padded with random values, then $\mathcal{B}$ will decide that it was given random values. On the other hand, if $\mathcal{A}$ decides that it is in a real version of TERSE and had received TERSE ciphertexts, then $\mathcal{B}$ will decide that it received RLWE values from $\mathcal{C}$. Thus if $\mathcal{A}$ can achieve a greater-than-negligible advantage (i.e., a success rate non-negligibly better than a random guess) against the aggregator obliviousness of TERSE, then $\mathcal{B}$ can use this to gain a greater-than-negligible advantage against RLWE. This completes the reduction from RLWE to TERSE.

## 5   Extensions and Improvements

### 5.1   Differential Privacy

Previously, we have introduced TERSE and discussed its security in the context of aggregator obliviousness, where the aim is to provide security against external attackers and leak no additional information to an honest-but-curious aggregator or user, or a collusion thereof. To construct a PSA protocol that is truly private, users should also have some notion of input privacy against the honest-but-curious aggregator. In particular, a user will want to avoid having the aggregator learn anything about its input. To this end, PSA schemes utilize differential privacy to obscure user inputs.

Differential privacy for PSA is well-known in the literature [15,32,60,63,69]. The exact mechanism of differential privacy (choosing values $r_{i,ts}$, based upon $n$, $t$, and the desired or acceptable accuracy and error) is an orthogonal issue to our work. We thus follow previous work in noting that differential privacy from adding noise to user inputs is preserved when executed in a PSA protocol [68,69]. Thus, TERSE is easily able to encapsulate both security and privacy, both of which are important concerns for users.

In practical use, it should be noted that implementing differential privacy into PSA (or any computation) can affect the accuracy of the computation. In RLWE-based PSA schemes with finite and possibly limited plaintext spaces, needing to account for noisy user input can significantly affect the practical parameter selection [15,63].

### 5.2   Network Faults or Disconnects

While previous work in quantum-secure PSA [15,32,63,69] has centered primarily upon efficient PSA construction, practical PSA should take fault tolerance into consideration. In several precursor works in PSA, user keys are correlated, such that the absence of a single user's input will result in failure of decryption [15,60,63,69]. As noted by Karl et al. [43], there are two prominent strategies of enhancing aggregation schemes with fault tolerance: recovering from faults by having a trusted party substitute missing inputs [2,12,13,49], or by having users provide redundant inputs as a precaution against future faults [14,24,25]. The Cryptonite protocol [43] uses trusted hardware, specifically Intel SGX, as a trusted third party for fault tolerance.

Intel SGX is a Trusted Execution Environment that provides confidentiality and integrity to a trusted portion of a program, which runs in an encrypted memory enclave that maintains integrity against even a malicious operating system [28]. While SGX provides strong guarantees of security to computations, it can be limited for computations at a very large scale, due to the practically limited size of its memory enclave and the overhead of encryption when paging memory in or out of the enclave [7,10,28,34,47].

Cryptonite used an aggregator-colocated SGX to read all user inputs and to generate encryptions of zero from missing users, using pre-received users' secret keys held securely in trusted memory. The more efficient variant of Cryptonite has the SGX only output encryptions of zero corresponding to missing users, so that the aggregation with ciphertexts from all users can be more efficiently performed in untrusted space. We note that for our model of honest-but-curious adversaries, it is reasonable for the SGX to trust that the aggregator will faithfully relay the set of faulted users. Then, the SGX does not need to take in $O(n)$ ciphertexts, but only a list of missing users, yielding a much smaller buffer that is passed to the enclave. Further, we can have the SGX return only a single aggregated ciphertext from all missing users, greatly reducing the amount of data that needs to be passed out of the enclave.

We include Cryptonite with these optimizations in our implementation (see Sect. 6.1). While other methods of fault tolerance exist, we chose to study the novel integration of SGX-based fault tolerance and post-quantum PSA due to their non-interactive fault recovery without additional client work or interaction. This is the first work investigating the implementation and use of SGX-based fault tolerance and PSA featuring aggregation on order of microseconds.

There exists other work in PSA dealing with dynamic join/leave of users [22, 40]. Dynamic user groups are outside the scope of this work, which is concerned with the basic primitive of efficient aggregation.

### 5.3  Optimizing Ring Arithmetic

In $R_q = \mathbb{Z}_q[x]/(x^N + 1)$, both $N$ and $q$ may be large - $N$ commonly ranges from $2^{10}$ to $2^{16}$, and $q$ may be hundreds of bits. These large operands are an obstacle to efficient computation. Residue Number System (RNS) arithmetic can decompose an element of $\mathbb{Z}_q$ into a tuple of numbers modulo smaller coprimes, allowing the use of multiple single-precision operations instead of expensive multiprecision arithmetic [11,35]. The Number-Theoretic Transform (NTT) reduces the asymptotic complexity of polynomial multiplication from $O(N^2)$ to $O(N \cdot log(N))$, greatly improving the runtime of algorithms whose dominant operation is polynomial multiplication [50]. We use these optimizations in implementing TERSE. Due to the design of TERSE in minimizing input-dependent computation, both users and the aggregator will perform all of their polynomial multiplication ahead of time, so the benefits of NTT are seen in the runtime of precomputation.

# 6   Experimental Evaluation

## 6.1   Implementation and Environment

We implemented client and server programs to test the performance of TERSE. Both implementations use RNS and NTT as described in Sect. 5.3. Runtime tests generally report averages of at least 50 iterations; for longer-running tests at least 5 iterations were used. Both implementations were in C++.

We tested the client version of TERSE on a Google Pixel 4a with 6 GB memory and a CPU running at up to 2.2 GHz. The client version assumes pre-computation of users' values $p_{i,ts}$, but does not do so for the noise terms $t \cdot e_{i,ts}$. As described earlier, this is a reasonable assumption to make - these larger polynomial products can be outsourced to users' synced laptops for smartphone clients, or computed "out-of-band" in a separate process, because one polynomial generates thousands of $p_{i,ts}$ terms, and the key retrieval and computation of $p_{i,ts}$ only needs to occur once per $N$ aggregations. Drawing error terms is a fast operation, and can done as input becomes available.

Our server tests were run on a computer with an Intel Xeon CPU running at 3.7 GHz, with 128 GB of RAM. Our server code integrates a modified version of the Cryptonite protocol for fault-tolerance, as described in Sect. 5.2. Our client and server implementations are available at https://gitlab.com/jtakeshi/slap-iot-cryptonite-client and https://gitlab.com/jtakeshi/slap-iot-cryptonomial-server, respectively. Our profiling of precomputations (see Sect. 6.3) is included in the client implementation repository.

**Table 1.** TERSE Parameter settings and precomputation times for 128-bit RLWE security and 1000000 aggregations

| Users | Plaintext space (bits) | Minimum ciphertext space (bits) | Ciphertext moduli | RLWE polynomial modulus degree | Secret keys generation (ms) | Derivation of $A_\theta$ (ms) | Multiplicative precomputation (ms) |
|---|---|---|---|---|---|---|---|
| 100 | 32 | 41 | 1 | 2048 | 6.75889 | 28.0973 | 451.451 |
| 1000 | 32 | 44 | 1 | 2048 | 66.5254 | 28.049 | 450.521 |
| 10000 | 32 | 48 | 1 | 2048 | 666.651 | 28.1002 | 451.375 |
| 100000 | 32 | 51 | 1 | 2048 | 6650.29 | 28.0568 | 450.602 |
| 1000000 | 32 | 54 | 1 | 2048 | 66587.6 | 28.0712 | 450.984 |
| 10000000 | 32 | 58 | 2 | 4096 | 1715910 | 100.646 | 1128.82 |
| 100000000 | 32 | 61 | 2 | 4096 | 17164700 | 99.7437 | 1132.2 |
| 1000 | 1 | 13 | 1 | 1024 | 33.7708 | 22.1876 | 221.474 |
| 1000 | 2 | 14 | 1 | 1024 | 33.842 | 22.2518 | 222.798 |
| 1000 | 4 | 16 | 1 | 1024 | 33.7107 | 22.1595 | 221.613 |
| 1000 | 8 | 20 | 1 | 1024 | 33.7945 | 22.1702 | 221.553 |
| 1000 | 16 | 28 | 1 | 2048 | 66.5783 | 28.1416 | 450.641 |
| 1000 | 32 | 44 | 1 | 2048 | 66.5213 | 28.0544 | 450.474 |
| 1000 | 48 | 60 | 2 | 4096 | 171.914 | 99.7837 | 1128.89 |

## 6.2　Parameters and Communication

A plaintext space of up to 48 bits is practical for a wide variety of practical uses, e.g., electronic voting for up to $2^{47}$ participants, or averaging patient ages for $2^{40}$ patients, or aggregating 65,536 users' 32-bit inputs for use in machine learning or data mining. Further, it allows us to keep TERSE ciphertexts small, and TERSE plaintexts within a single computer word. In our implementations of TERSE, we used standard RLWE parameters for 128-bit classical security [4,23]. For $|t| \leq 64$, only one or two RNS moduli represented in 64-bit words were required, making TERSE's communication overhead very lightweight. Parameter settings for our experiments are shown in Table 1.

## 6.3　Results

**Impact of Aggregation Scale.** We first tested the impact of high scale and increasing users on our protocol's runtime. The aggregator's server-side performance is shown in Fig. 1. The server achieves aggregation latency of 0.0067 ms for $n = 1000$ users, which is much more efficient than other state-of-the-art work in post-quantum PSA (see Sect. 6.4). The results from our Android user-side implementation are shown in Figure 2a. One of the strengths of TERSE as compared to aggregation schemes based upon secret sharing [69] is that users' computation (and memory to store keys) is not linearly dependent upon the number of other participants, making TERSE much more practical for deployment to users with limited devices such as smartphones or IoT devices. This is borne out by the minimal changes in users' encryption runtimes as the number of users increases. Most notably, user-side encryption on an Android smartphone can take place in *less than 0.3 microseconds for 1 billion users*!

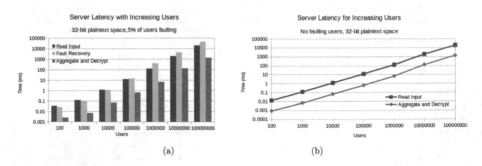

(a)　　　　　　　　　　　　　　　(b)

**Fig. 1.** Experimental results for server performance with increasing users. (a) Without faults (b) With faults

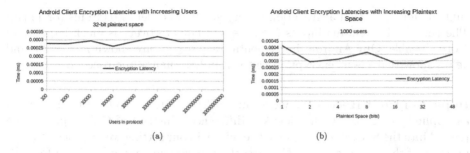

(a)                                    (b)

**Fig. 2.** Experimental results for client performance. (a) Increasing users (b) Increasing plaintext space

**Impact of Input Size.** We investigated the impact of an increasing plaintext space upon runtime. As described in Sect. 6.2, we expect very little asymptotic effect from larger plaintext spaces up to the 64 bits used in our implementation, as only one or two ciphertext moduli are required in all cases. The server-side results from increasing the plaintext space are shown in Fig. 3. In both cases, the

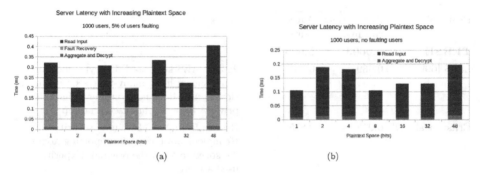

(a)                                    (b)

**Fig. 3.** Experimental results for server performance with increasing plaintext space. (a) With faults (b) Without faults space

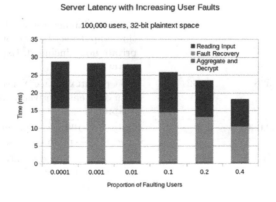

**Fig. 4.** Server performance for varying user faults

runtime for the actual aggregation is very small, on order of 0.001 ms (or 1 ms!). The runtime for reading inputs from file and fault recovery is much larger, and more variable. Our Android implementation's results are shown in Fig. 2b, and again show that client encryption can run in less than a microsecond.

**Impact of Fault Recovery.** We evaluate Cryptonite-based fault tolerance [43] as applied to TERSE with a few key differences. Instead of $O(n)$ inputs being passed into the SGX's secure memory enclave, in our setting we only need to pass in a list of the *faulting* users. This greatly reduces the paging overhead for calls into the enclave. We also only return a single ciphertext, reducing the paging overhead from returning to untrusted memory. Our experimental results for fault tolerance with TERSE are shown in Fig. 4. As the proportion of faulting users increases, the time to aggregate and read user input from file decreases slightly. This is logical: with fewer user inputs, there is less work for these portions of the computation (Table 2).

**Table 2.** Runtime in ms of TERSE vs. Reported results from other work (1000 users and at least 16 bits plaintext space, unless noted)

| Protocol | Encryption runtime | Aggregation runtime | Notes |
|---|---|---|---|
| **TERSE** | **0.0003** | **0.006** | |
| LaSS [69] | 0.539 | 0.509 | 256-bit AES keys used. Encrypt-once model times shown here, many-time security much slower. Also does not consider differential privacy. Experiments used a laptop |
| Ernst et al. [32] | 0.913 | 0.875 | Results from $\lambda = 114$ bits of security. Reimplements LaSS [69], reporting about a 2× speedup from the original. Experiments used a laptop |
| LaPS [15] | 3.722 | 1.964 | Results from $\lambda = 80$ bits of security. Runtimes at 128 bits of security are an order of magnitude greater. Experiments used a laptop. |
| SLAP [63] | 1.17 | 3.26 | Ordinary latency reported, practical throughput may be improved. Differentially private noise included. Experiments used a server |
| Lu et al. [51] | 0.328 | 0.062 | 8-bit plaintext space, runtime slightly higher with differential privacy. Experiments used a laptop. |
| Zhuo et al. [71] | ≈0.0001 | 6 | Only $N = 100$ users, plaintext space not specified. Experiments used a desktop |
| He et al. [36] | 6.66 | 3433.4 | Both figures only estimates, no implementation. Results estimated from a Pentium IV system |

**Precomputation.** While TERSE's precomputations do not directly affect online latency, it is informative to observe their performance. To concretely observe the burden of precomputation, we tested the latency of the generation of secret keys (done by trusted setup), public hash derivation (done by both client and server), and finding multiplicative terms $\mathbf{A}_\theta \cdot \mathbf{s}_i$. Table 1 shows the runtimes of these operations when precomputing values for 1000000 aggregations. As expected, runtime for secret key generation increases linearly with the number of users. Deriving the public values $\mathbf{A}_\theta$ takes only hundreds of milliseconds at the most, and the per-aggregation burden is low when considering amortization for a million aggregations. Similarly, computing the terms $\mathbf{A}_\theta \cdot \mathbf{s}_i$ for a million aggregations takes only seconds at most. We note that the precomputations of TERSE need occur only once every $N$ aggregations, while other post-quantum PSA need to calculate their public terms for every aggregation (while LaPS does not explicitly require this, it is needed for security [69]).

### 6.4 Comparison with Other Work

Differences in hardware platform, programming languages, and input types can make direct performance comparisons between different PSA protocols challenging. Still, we can make rough comparisons of protocol runtimes and communication overhead from reported experimental results. In Table 1, we report runtimes of TERSE and other schemes, using a plaintext space of at least 16 bits and at least 1000 users (unless otherwise noted). We note that these minimal bounds for scheme parameters are quite small, and TERSE is likely to perform even better relatively at scale; we chose smaller floors to show the best-possible runtime of other schemes. Against the 4 quantum-secure PSA schemes LaSS, Ernst et al., LaPS, and SLAP, TERSE shows improvements in latency of 1796× to 12406× for encryption and 848× to 5433× for aggregation.

## 7  Conclusion

In this paper, we presented TERSE, a quantum-secure PSA protocol uniquely well-suited for minimal latency. TERSE features highly efficient operations, minimally expansive ciphertexts, and a very simple and highly extensible design.

Our experimental results show that TERSE achieves encryption latency of 0.0003 ms and aggregation latency of 0.0067 ms for 1000 users and a 16-bit plaintext space, with improvements of two to three orders of magnitude as compared to prior post-quantum PSA. The performance improvements of TERSE for client-side operations are especially important, as the client-side implementation of TERSE was tested on a smartphone as opposed to prior implementations of PSA on laptops or desktops. These microsecond-latency operations for users and aggregators make RLWE-based PSA truly practical for real-world deployments.

**Acknowledgement.** This work was supported by Facebook as a winner of the Role of Applied Cryptography in a Privacy-Focused Advertising Ecosystem Facebook RFP. Any opinions, findings and conclusions or recommendations expressed in this material are those of the authors and do not necessarily reflect those of the sponsor.

# References

1. Internet of Things (IoT) connected devices installed base worldwide from 2015 to 2025. https://rb.gy/cbrasa. Accessed 15 Oct 2021
2. Han, S., Zhao, S., Li, Q., Ju, C.-H., Zhou, W.: PPM-HDA: privacy-preserving and multifunctional health data aggregation with fault tolerance. IEEE TIFS **11**(9), 1940–1955 (2015). IEEE
3. Ács, G., Castelluccia, C.: I Have a DREAM! (DiffeRentially privatE smArt Metering). In: Filler, T., Pevný, T., Craver, S., Ker, A. (eds.) IH 2011. LNCS, vol. 6958, pp. 118–132. Springer, Heidelberg (2011). https://doi.org/10.1007/978-3-642-24178-9_9
4. Albrecht, M., et al.: Homomorphic encryption security standard. HomomorphicEncryption.org, Toronto, Canada, Technical report (2018)
5. Albrecht, M.R., et al.: Estimate all the LWE, NTRU schemes! In: Catalano, D., De Prisco, R. (eds.) SCN 2018. LNCS, vol. 11035, pp. 351–367. Springer, Cham (2018). https://doi.org/10.1007/978-3-319-98113-0_19
6. Ananth, P., Jain, A., Jin, Z., Malavolta, G.: Multi-key fully-homomorphic encryption in the plain model. In: Pass, R., Pietrzak, K. (eds.) TCC 2020. LNCS, vol. 12550, pp. 28–57. Springer, Cham (2020). https://doi.org/10.1007/978-3-030-64375-1_2
7. Arnautov, S., et al.: {SCONE}: Secure linux containers with intel {SGX}. In: 12th USENIX OSDI, pp. 689–703 (2016)
8. Babuji, Y.N., Chard, K., Gerow, A., Duede, E.: Cloud kotta: enabling secure and scalable data analytics in the cloud. In: 2016 IEEE International Conference on Big Data (Big Data), pp. 302–310. IEEE (2016)
9. Bailey, S.F., et al.: Secure and robust cloud computing for high-throughput forensic microsatellite sequence analysis and databasing. Forensic Sci. Int. Genet. **31**, 40–47 (2017)
10. Bailleu, M., Thalheim, J., Bhatotia, P., Fetzer, C., Honda, M., Vaswani, K.: {SPEICHER}: Securing lsm-based key-value stores using shielded execution. In: 17th USENIX FAST, pp. 173–190 (2019)
11. Bajard, J.-C., Eynard, J., Hasan, M.A., Zucca, V.: A Full RNS variant of FV Like somewhat homomorphic encryption schemes. In: Avanzi, R., Heys, H. (eds.) SAC 2016. LNCS, vol. 10532, pp. 423–442. Springer, Cham (2017). https://doi.org/10.1007/978-3-319-69453-5_23
12. Bao, H., Lu, R.: DDPFT: secure data aggregation scheme with differential privacy and fault tolerance. In: 2015 IEEE ICC, pp. 7240–7245. IEEE (2015)
13. Bao, H., Lu, R.: A new differentially private data aggregation with fault tolerance for smart grid communications. IoT-J **2**(3), 248–258 (2015)
14. Bao, H., Lu, R.: A lightweight data aggregation scheme achieving privacy preservation and data integrity with differential privacy and fault tolerance. Peer-to-Peer Networking Appl. **10**(1), 106–121 (2017)

15. Becker, D., Guajardo, J., Zimmermann, K.-H.: Revisiting private stream aggregation: lattice-based PSA. In: NDSS (2018)
16. Blanco-Chacón, I.: On the RLWE/PLWE equivalence for cyclotomic number fields, pp. 1–19. Applicable Algebra in Engineering, Communication and Computing (2020)
17. Boneh, D., Eskandarian, S., Fisch, B.: Post-quantum EPID signatures from symmetric primitives. In: Matsui, M. (ed.) CT-RSA 2019. LNCS, vol. 11405, pp. 251–271. Springer, Cham (2019). https://doi.org/10.1007/978-3-030-12612-4_13
18. Bonnetain, X., Naya-Plasencia, M., Schrottenloher, A.: Quantum security analysis of AES. IACR Trans. Symmetric Cryptology **2019**(2), 55–93 (2019)
19. Brakerski, Z., Gentry, C., Vaikuntanathan, V.: (Leveled) fully homomorphic encryption without bootstrapping. ACM Trans. Comput. Theor. (TOCT) **6**(3), 1–36 (2014)
20. Brakerski, Z., Vaikuntanathan, V.: Fully homomorphic encryption from ring-lwe and security for key dependent messages. In: Rogaway, P. (ed.) CRYPTO 2011. LNCS, vol. 6841, pp. 505–524. Springer, Heidelberg (2011). https://doi.org/10.1007/978-3-642-22792-9_29
21. Canetti, R., Goldreich, O., Halevi, S.: The random oracle methodology, revisited. J. ACM (JACM) **51**(4), 557–594 (2004)
22. Chan, T.-H.H., Shi, E., Song, D.: Privacy-preserving stream aggregation with fault tolerance. In: Keromytis, A.D. (ed.) FC 2012. LNCS, vol. 7397, pp. 200–214. Springer, Heidelberg (2012). https://doi.org/10.1007/978-3-642-32946-3_15
23. Chen, H., Han, K., Huang, Z., Jalali, A., Laine, K.: Simple encrypted arithmetic library v2. 3.0. Microsoft Research, December 2017
24. Chen, J., Ma, H., Zhao, D.: Private data aggregation with integrity assurance and fault tolerance for mobile crowd-sensing. Wirel. Networks **23**(1), 131–144 (2017)
25. Chen, L., Lu, R., Cao, Z.: PDAFT: a privacy-preserving data aggregation scheme with fault tolerance for smart grid communications. Peer-to-Peer Networking Appl. **8**(6), 1122–1132 (2015)
26. Cheon, J.H., Kim, A., Kim, M., Song, Y.: Homomorphic encryption for arithmetic of approximate numbers. In: Takagi, T., Peyrin, T. (eds.) ASIACRYPT 2017. LNCS, vol. 10624, pp. 409–437. Springer, Cham (2017). https://doi.org/10.1007/978-3-319-70694-8_15
27. Conti, F., et al.: An IoT endpoint system on-chip for secure and energy-efficient near-sensor analytics. IEEE Trans. Circuits Syst. I: Regul. Papers **64**(9), 2481–2494 (2017)
28. Costan, V., Devadas, S.: Intel SGX explained. IACR Cryptol. ePrint Arch. **2016**(86), 1–118 (2016)
29. Danezis, G., Fournet, C., Kohlweiss, M., Zanella-Béguelin, S.: Smart meter aggregation via secret-sharing. In: ACM SEDAy, pp. 75–80 (2013)
30. Ding, J., Gao, X., Takagi, T., Wang, Y.: One sample ring-LWE with rounding and its application to key exchange. In: Deng, R.H., Gauthier-Umaña, V., Ochoa, M., Yung, M. (eds.) ACNS 2019. LNCS, vol. 11464, pp. 323–343. Springer, Cham (2019). https://doi.org/10.1007/978-3-030-21568-2_16
31. Du, J., Jiang, C., Gelenbe, E., Xu, L., Li, J., Ren, Y.: Distributed data privacy preservation in IoT applications. IEEE Wirel. Commun. **25**(6), 68–76 (2018)
32. Ernst, J., Koch, A.: Private stream aggregation with labels in the standard model. PETS **4**, 117–138 (2021)
33. Fan, J., Vercauteren, F.: Somewhat practical fully homomorphic encryption. IACR Cryptol. ePrint Arch. 2012, 144 (2012)

34. Gjerdrum, A.T., Pettersen, R., Johansen, H.D., Johansen, D.: Performance of trusted computing in cloud infrastructures with Intel SGX. In: CLOSER, pp. 668–675 (2017)
35. Halevi, S., Polyakov, Y., Shoup, V.: An improved RNS variant of the BFV homomorphic encryption scheme. In: Matsui, M. (ed.) CT-RSA 2019. LNCS, vol. 11405, pp. 83–105. Springer, Cham (2019). https://doi.org/10.1007/978-3-030-12612-4_5
36. He, D., Kumar, N., Lee, J.-H.: Privacy-preserving data aggregation scheme against internal attackers in smart grids. Wireless Netw. **22**(2), 491–502 (2016)
37. Jiang, M., Jung, T., Karl, R., Zhao, T.: Federated dynamic graph neural networks with secure aggregation for video-based distributed surveillance. ACM Trans. Intell. Syst. Technol. (TIST) **13**(4), 1–23 (2022)
38. Joye, M., Libert, B.: A scalable scheme for privacy-preserving aggregation of time-series data. In: Sadeghi, A.-R. (ed.) FC 2013. LNCS, vol. 7859, pp. 111–125. Springer, Heidelberg (2013). https://doi.org/10.1007/978-3-642-39884-1_10
39. Jung, T., et al.: Privacy-preserving data aggregation without secure channel: multivariate polynomial evaluation. In: 2013 Proceedings IEEE INFOCOM, pp. 2634–2642. IEEE (2013)
40. Jung, T., Han, J., Li, X.-Y.: PDA: semantically secure time-series data analytics with dynamic user groups. TDSC **15**(2), 260–274 (2016)
41. Jung, T., Li, X.-Y., Wan, M.: Collusion-tolerable privacy-preserving sum and product calculation without secure channel. TDSC **12**(1), 45–57 (2014)
42. Karl, R., Burchfield, T., Takeshita, J., Jung, T.: Non-interactive MPC with trusted hardware secure against residual function attacks. In: Chen, S., Choo, K.-K.R., Fu, X., Lou, W., Mohaisen, A. (eds.) SecureComm 2019. LNICST, vol. 305, pp. 425–439. Springer, Cham (2019). https://doi.org/10.1007/978-3-030-37231-6_25
43. Karl, R., et al.: Cryptonite: a framework for flexible time-series secure aggregation with online fault tolerance. Cryptology ePrint Archive, Report 2020/1561 (2020). https://rb.gy/tdcsfs
44. Karl, R., Takeshita, J., Mohammed, A., Striegel, A., Jung, T.: Cryptonomial: a framework for private time-series polynomial calculations. In: Garcia-Alfaro, J., Li, S., Poovendran, R., Debar, H., Yung, M. (eds.) SecureComm 2021. LNICST, vol. 398, pp. 332–351. Springer, Cham (2021). https://doi.org/10.1007/978-3-030-90019-9_17
45. Karl, R., Takeshita, J., Mohammed, A., Striegel, A., Jung, T.: Cryptogram: fast private calculations of histograms over multiple users' inputs. In: 2021 17th International Conference on Distributed Computing in Sensor Systems (DCOSS), pp. 25–34. IEEE (2021)
46. Koblitz, N., Menezes, A.J.: The random oracle model: a twenty-year retrospective. Des. Codes Crypt. **77**(2), 587–610 (2015)
47. Kunkel, R., Quoc, D.L., Gregor, F., Arnautov, S., Bhatotia, P., Fetzer, C.: Tensorscone: a secure tensorflow framework using Intel SGX. arXiv preprint arXiv:1902.04413 (2019)
48. Li, C., Lu, R., Li, H., Chen, L., Chen, J.: PDA: a privacy-preserving dual-functional aggregation scheme for smart grid communications. Secur. Commun. Netw. **8**(15), 2494–2506 (2015)
49. Li, Q., Cao, G.: Efficient privacy-preserving stream aggregation in mobile sensing with low aggregation error. In: De Cristofaro, E., Wright, M. (eds.) PETS 2013. LNCS, vol. 7981, pp. 60–81. Springer, Heidelberg (2013). https://doi.org/10.1007/978-3-642-39077-7_4

50. Longa, P., Naehrig, M.: Speeding up the number theoretic transform for faster ideal lattice-based cryptography. In: Foresti, S., Persiano, G. (eds.) CANS 2016. LNCS, vol. 10052, pp. 124–139. Springer, Cham (2016). https://doi.org/10.1007/978-3-319-48965-0_8

51. Lu, R., Heung, K., Lashkari, A.H., Ghorbani, A.A.: A lightweight privacy-preserving data aggregation scheme for fog computing-enhanced IoT. IEEE Access **5**, 3302–3312 (2017)

52. Lyubashevsky, V., Peikert, C., Regev, O.: On ideal lattices and learning with errors over rings. J. ACM (JACM) **60**(6), 1–35 (2013)

53. Mofrad, S., Zhang, F., Lu, S., Shi, W.: A comparison study of intel SGX and AMD memory encryption technology. In: HASP, pp. 1–8 (2018)

54. Mukherjee, P., Wichs, D.: Two round multiparty computation via multi-key FHE. In: Fischlin, M., Coron, J.-S. (eds.) EUROCRYPT 2016. LNCS, vol. 9666, pp. 735–763. Springer, Heidelberg (2016). https://doi.org/10.1007/978-3-662-49896-5_26

55. Paillier, P.: Public-key cryptosystems based on composite degree residuosity classes. In: Stern, J. (ed.) EUROCRYPT 1999. LNCS, vol. 1592, pp. 223–238. Springer, Heidelberg (1999). https://doi.org/10.1007/3-540-48910-X_16

56. Park, H., Zhai, S., Lu, L., Lin, F.X.: {StreamBox-TZ}: secure stream analytics at the edge with {TrustZone}. In: 2019 USENIX Annual Technical Conference (USENIX ATC 19), pp. 537–554 (2019)

57. Pu, Y., et al.: Two secure privacy-preserving data aggregation schemes for IoT. Wirel. Commun. Mobile Comput. **2019** (2019)

58. Rastogi, V., Nath, S.: Differentially private aggregation of distributed time-series with transformation and encryption. In: SIGMOD/PODS, pp. 735–746 (2010)

59. Rosca, M., Stehlé, D., Wallet, A.: On the ring-LWE and polynomial-LWE problems. In: Nielsen, J.B., Rijmen, V. (eds.) EUROCRYPT 2018. LNCS, vol. 10820, pp. 146–173. Springer, Cham (2018). https://doi.org/10.1007/978-3-319-78381-9_6

60. Shi, E., Chan, T.H., Rieffel, E., Chow, R., Song, D.: Privacy-preserving aggregation of time-series data. NDSS **2**, 1–17 (2011)

61. Shor, P.W.: Algorithms for quantum computation: discrete logarithms and factoring. In: FOCS, pp. 124–134. IEEE (1994)

62. Sui, Z., de Meer, H.: An efficient signcryption protocol for hop-by-hop data aggregations in smart grids. IEEE J. Sel. Areas Commun. **38**(1), 132–140 (2019)

63. Takeshita, J., et al.: SLAP: simple lattice-based private stream aggregation protocol. IACR Cryptol. ePrint Arch. **2020**, 1611 (2020)

64. Takeshita, J., Karl, R., Mohammed, A., Striegel, A., Jung, T.: Provably secure contact tracing with conditional private set intersection. In: Garcia-Alfaro, J., Li, S., Poovendran, R., Debar, H., Yung, M. (eds.) SecureComm 2021. LNICST, vol. 398, pp. 352–373. Springer, Cham (2021). https://doi.org/10.1007/978-3-030-90019-9_18

65. Takeshita, J., Reis, D., Gong, T., Niemier, M., Hu, X.S., Jung, T.: Algorithmic acceleration of B/FV-like somewhat homomorphic encryption for compute-enabled RAM. In: Dunkelman, O., Jacobson Jr., M.J., O'Flynn, C. (eds.) SAC 2020. LNCS, vol. 12804, pp. 66–89. Springer, Cham (2021). https://doi.org/10.1007/978-3-030-81652-0_3

66. Tang, W., Ren, J., Deng, K., Zhang, Y.: Secure data aggregation of lightweight e-healthcare IoT devices with fair incentives. IoT-J **6**(5), 8714–8726 (2019)

67. Tonyali, S., Akkaya, K., Saputro, N., Uluagac, A.S., Nojoumian, M.: Privacy-preserving protocols for secure and reliable data aggregation in IoT-enabled smart metering systems. FGCS **78**, 547–557 (2018)

68. Valovich, F., Aldà, F.: Computational differential privacy from lattice-based cryptography. In: Kaczorowski, J., Pieprzyk, J., Pomykała, J. (eds.) NuTMiC 2017. LNCS, vol. 10737, pp. 121–141. Springer, Cham (2018). https://doi.org/10.1007/978-3-319-76620-1_8
69. Waldner, H., Marc, T., Stopar, M., Abdalla, M.: Private stream aggregation from labeled secret sharing schemes. IACR Cryptol. ePrint Arch. **2021**, 81 (2021)
70. Wang, X., Liu, Y., Choo, K.-K.R.: Fault-tolerant multisubset aggregation scheme for smart grid. IEEE Trans. Ind. Inf. **17**(6), 4065–4072 (2020)
71. Zhuo, G., Jia, Q., Guo, L., Li, M., Li, P.: Privacy-preserving verifiable data aggregation and analysis for cloud-assisted mobile crowdsourcing. In: INFOCOM, pp. 1–9. IEEE (2016)
72. Takeshita, J., McKechney, C., Pajak, J., Papadimitriou, A., Karl, R., Jung, T.: GPS: integration of graphene, PALISADE, and SGX for large-scale aggregations of distributed data. Cryptol. ePrint Arch. (2021)

# Symmetrical Disguise: Realizing Homomorphic Encryption Services from Symmetric Primitives

Alexandros Bakas$^{(\boxtimes)}$, Eugene Frimpong, and Antonis Michalas

Tampere University, Tampere, Finland
{alexandros.bakas,eugene.frimpong,antonios.michalas}@tuni.fi

**Abstract.** Homomorphic Encryption (HE) is a modern cryptographic technique that allows direct computations on encrypted data. While relatively new to the mainstream debate, HE has been a solid topic in research for decades. However, and despite the technological advances of the past years, HE's inefficiencies render it impractical for deployment in realistic scenarios. Hence research in the field is still in its initial phase. To overcome certain challenges and bring HE closer to a realization phase, researchers recently introduced the promising concept of Hybrid Homomorphic Encryption (HHE) – a primitive that combines symmetric cryptography with HE. Using HHE, users perform local data encryptions using a symmetric encryption scheme and then outsource them to the cloud. Upon reception, the cloud can transform the symmetrically encrypted data to homomorphic ciphertexts without decrypting them. Such an approach can be seen as an opportunity to build new, privacy-respecting cloud services, as the most expensive operations of HE can be moved to the cloud.

In this work, we undertake the task of designing a secure cryptographic protocol based on HHE. In particular, we show how HHE can be used as the main building block of a protocol that allows an analyst to collect data from multiple sources and compute specific functions over them, in a privacy-preserving way. To the best of our knowledge, this is the first work that aims at demonstrating how HHE can be utilized in realistic scenarios, through the design of a secure protocol.

**Keywords:** Homomorphic Encryption · Hybrid Homomorphic Encryption · Multi-client · Storage protection

## 1 Introduction

Cloud computing has become an integral part of our lives. It has not only impacted our daily functions but also how businesses and organizations manage

This work was partially funded from the Technology Innovation Institute (TII), Abu Dhabi, United Arab Emirates, for the project ARROWSMITH: Living (Securely) on the edge.
This work was partially funded by the Harpocrates project, Horizon Europe.

F. Li et al. (Eds.): SecureComm 2022, LNICST 462, pp. 353–370, 2023.
https://doi.org/10.1007/978-3-031-25538-0_19

their data and customers. The wide use of cloud-services has, as expected, raised a plethora of challenging security and privacy problems. One of the main security concerns related to cloud computing has to do with so-called internal attacks. This is, a corrupted cloud service provider (CSP) exploiting customer data for its own benefit, e.g. sharing customer data with third parties. To alleviate these concerns CSPs have introduced support for data encryption. However, the problem of creating real privacy-respecting cloud services is not as easy as applying encryption on the stored data. For this reason, the research community has started looking into solutions that are not based on traditional encryption and can successfully protect user data from internal attacks without jeopardizing the main benefits of cloud computing. One of the most common solutions is Structured Encryption (SE) [30], where data is encrypted locally with a key that is unknown to the CSP. Hence, the CSP, which does not have access to the encryption key cannot learn anything about the content of user data. Furthermore, whenever a user wishes to access her files, she can search directly over the encrypted data for specific keywords. While this approach solves part of the problem, (i.e. users do not have to download and decrypt the whole database), ciphertexts remain "useless" in the sense that one can not operate on them as if as they were plaintexts. With a view to addressing this issue, a number of approaches to make ciphertexts "more useful" and operate on encrypted data have been developed. The most promising solutions is Homomorphic Encryption (HE) [37] and Functional Encryption [28] – two modern encryption techniques that allow authorized entities (i.e. users, the cloud or third parties) to perform computations on the encrypted data without accessing their contents.

*Homomorphic Encryption.* Often dubbed as *"the holy grail of cryptography"*. In an HE scheme a user first generates a public/private key pair (pk, sk) and an evaluation key evk[1]. Then, given two ciphertexts $c_1$, $c_2$ encrypting messages $x_1$ and $x_2$ respectively and the evaluation key evk, it is possible to compute $f(c_1, c_2)$, where $f$ is a function associated either with addition or multiplication. Moreover, what is fascinating about HE, is that in computing $f(c_1, c_2)$ there are no leaks about the underlying plaintexts $x_1$ and $x_2$ while decrypting the result in only feasible by possessing the secret key sk. Naturally, this opens up tremendous possibilities as, for the first time ever, it becomes possible to not only outsource data, applications and services but also *computations* to the cloud, in a privacy-preserving manner. However, despite its advantages, HE is unfortunately characterized by its inefficiency. Homomorphically encrypting big loads of data requires powerful machines and is time-consuming. As a result, to this day HE is a topic of interest mainly among members of the academic community. To address these inefficiencies however, researchers recently turned their attention to Hybrid Homomorphic Encryption (HHE) [22].

*Hybrid Homomorphic Encryption.* In an HHE scheme, a user encrypts data locally using a symmetric key K of a symmetric-key encryption scheme SKE. Subsequently, K is encrypted under HE's public key pk and is outsourced to the

---

[1] Sometimes, in literature, the evaluation key is part of the public key.

cloud along with the ciphertexts and the evaluation key evk. Upon reception, the CSP can transform the symmetrically encrypted data to homomorphic cipher-texts and hence operate on them. This promising approach significantly reduces computation costs on the client side by moving the most expensive computations on the cloud, where powerful machines are used traditionally for the processing and storage of the data. In this work, while we do not design a novel HHE scheme, we design a detailed protocol that aims at showing the applicability and functionality of HHE in real-world scenarios.

*Contributions*: While multiple different HHE schemes have been proposed over the past few years, to the best of our knowledge, none of these describe in detail how HHE can be used as the main building block of a secure protocol. We believe this is an important step forward that can bridge the gap between theoretical cryptographic concepts and security engineering and can pave the way for the implementation of a vast amount of privacy-respecting cloud services. The core contributions of this work can be summarized as follows:

**C1.** We design a protocol that utilizes the concept of HHE and allows multiple users to securely store and process their data in the cloud.
**C2.** We provide an efficient and novel way of using HE to securely store and analyze data stored in a remote location. More precisely, our scheme can run in any device that can run a typical symmetric encryption algorithm.
**C3.** We prove the security of our protocol in the presence of a malicious adversary modelled after the Dolev-Yao adversarial model [24].
**C4.** Our theoretical evaluation, is coupled with extensive experimental results that prove our protocol's efficiency and applicability.

## 2  Related Work

- *Homomorphic Encryption*: While HE has attracted a lot of attention in the recent years, it was first mentioned by Rivest et al. in 1978 [37]. How-ever, the first HE constructions allowed only for one specific operation on encrypted data. The operation could either be addition, using the Paillier cryptosystem [36], or multiplication, under RSA [38]. It was not until 2009 and the work of Gentry that the first fully homomorphic encryption (FHE) scheme was developed [26]. This was a major breakthrough in the field of cryp-tography as, in theory, by using a FHE scheme one can perform any operation directly on encrypted data. While fascinating, this work was unfortunately characterized by its inefficiency. However, it produced a series of publications in the field [14,15,18,19,25]. These works addressed the impracticalities of Gentry's work and lead to novel and more efficient schemes.

- *Hybrid Homomorphic Encryption*: HHE was first introduced as a con-cept in [35], but the first formal definition was presented very recently in [23]. The first approaches for the design of HHE schemes, relied on existing and well-established symmetric ciphers, like AES [17,21,27]. However, AES was not a good suitor for building HHE schemes, mainly due to its large multiplicative depth. Thus, research on the field of HHE took a new turn where the main focus has been shifted to the design of symmetric ciphers with different optimization criteria, depending on the use-case each work addresses [5,16,20,22,23,29,32]

- *Different Approaches*: Another emerging cryptographic primitive that can be used to outsource computations in a privacy-preserving is Functional Encryption (FE). In FE, each decryption key $sk_f$ is connected to a function $f$. Unlike traditional public-key cryptography, the use of $sk_f$ on a ciphertext $Enc(x)$ does *not* recover $x$ but a function $f(x)$. In this way, the actual value $x$ remains private. A more recent work [28] has introduced the general and promising notion of multi-input FE (MIFE). Here, when ciphertexts $Enc(x_1), \ldots, Enc(x_n)$ are provided, $sk_f$ can be used to recover $f(x_1, \ldots, x_n)$. To this day, most works in FE revolve around designing schemes for sums [8,11,13], inner products [1–3], as well as quadratic functions [40]. Unfortunately, except a handful works that rely on Multi-Party Computation (MPC) [11,12], most of FE schemes are highly centralized and require the existence of a fully trusted central authority.

- *Provable Secure Protocols for Cloud Security using HHE*: Designing provable secure protocols that utilize modern cryptography is not novel. Indeed, multiple solutions have been proposed [6,7,33,34], based on Attribute-Based Encryption (ABE) [4,39], as well as on Symmetric Searchable Encryption (SSE) [9,10]. However, to the best of our knowledge, this is the first work that aims at designing a provable secure protocol leveraging the functionality of HHE.

## 3   Preliminaries

*Notation.* If $\mathcal{Y}$ is a set, we use $y \xleftarrow{\$} \mathcal{Y}$ if $y$ is chosen uniformly at random from $\mathcal{Y}$. Concatenation of two strings $x, y$ is denoted by $x \| y$. A probabilistic polynomial time (PPT) adversary $\mathcal{ADV}$ is a randomized algorithm for which there exists a polynomial $p(z)$ such that for all input $z$, the running time of $\mathcal{ADV}(z)$ is bounded by $p(|z|)$. A function $negl(\cdot)$ is called negligible if $\forall c \in \mathbb{N}, \exists \epsilon_0 \in \mathbb{N}$ such that $\forall \epsilon \geq \epsilon_0 : negl(\epsilon) < \epsilon^{-c}$.

**Definition 1 (Homomorphic Encryption).** *A (public-key) homomorphic encryption scheme is a quadruple of PPT algorithms* HE = (HE.KeyGen, HE.Enc, HE.Dec, HE.Eval) *such that:*

- *Key Generation: The Key Generation algorithm* (pk, evk, sk) ← He.Keygen $(1^\lambda)$ *takes as input a unary representation of the security parameter $\lambda$, and outputs a public key* pk, *a public evaluation key* evk *and a secret decryption key* sk.
- *Encryption: This algorithm* $c \leftarrow$ HE.Enc(pk, m) *takes as input the public key* pk *and a message $m$ and outputs a ciphertext $c$.*

- **Decryption:** *This algorithm $m \leftarrow$ HE.Dec(sk, $c$), takes as input the secret key sk and a ciphertext $c$, and outputs a plaintext $m$.*
- **Homomorphic Evaluation:** *This algorithm $c_f \leftarrow$ He.Eval(evk, $f$, $c_1, \ldots, c_n$) takes as input the evaluation key evk, a function $f$, and a set of $n$ ciphertexts, and outputs a ciphertext $c_f$.*

**Correctness:** An HE scheme is said to be correct if and only if:

$$\Pr[\mathsf{HE.Dec_{sk}}\,(\mathsf{HE.Eval_{evk}}\,(f, c)) \tag{1}$$
$$\neq f(m)|\mathsf{HE.Enc_{pk}}\,(m) = c] \leq negl(\lambda)$$

Before we proceed with the formal definition of HHE, we discuss its functionality at a high-level. An HHE scheme is built on top of a traditional HE scheme as well as a symmetric cipher SKE. The *Key Generation* algorithm of HHE invokes the corresponding algorithms of both the HE and SKE and outputs (pk, sk, evk) for the HE scheme, and K for the SKE scheme. As a next step, the *Encryption* algorithm takes as input a message $m$, HE's public key pk, and K. The message $m$ will be encrypted symmetrically using K, resulting to a ciphertext $c$. Moreover, the symmetric key K will be homomorphically encrypted under pk, resulting to another ciphertext $c_K$. These two ciphertexts will then be given as input, along with the decryption function of SKE, to HHE's *Decompression* algorithm. This algorithm homomorphically performs the symmetric decryption circuit to transform the symmetric ciphertext $c$ into a homomorphic ciphertext $c'$, by invoking the evaluation algorithm of the HE scheme. Finally, the evaluation and decryption algorithms of HHE, are identical to those of the HE scheme.

**Definition 2 (Hybrid Homomorphic Encryption).** *Let* HE *be a Homomorphic Encryption scheme and* SKE = (Gen, Enc, Dec) *be a symmetric-key encryption scheme. Moreover, let* $\mathcal{M} = (m_1, \ldots, m_n)$ *be the message space and* $\lambda$ *the security parameter. An* HHE *scheme then consists of five PPT algorithms such that* HHE = (KeyGen, Enc, Decomp, Eval, Dec) *and it is constructed as follows (Fig. 1):*

---

HHE.KeyGen($1^\lambda$):

(pk, sk, evk) $\leftarrow$ HE.KeyGen($1^\lambda$)
**Return** (pk, sk, evk)

HHE.Enc:
K $\leftarrow$ SKE.Gen($1^\lambda$)
$c_K \leftarrow$ HE.Enc(pk, K)
$c \leftarrow$ SKE.Enc(K, $m$)
**Return** ($c_K$, $c$)

HHE.Decomp(evk, $c$, $c_K$):

$c' \leftarrow$ HE.Eval(evk, SKE.Dec, $c_K$, $c$)
**Return** $c'$

HHE.Eval(evk, $f$, $c'_1, \ldots, c'_n$):
**Return** HE.Eval(evk, $f$, $c'_1, \ldots, c'_n$)

HHE.Dec(sk, $c'$) :
**Return** HE.Dec(sk, $c'$)

---

**Fig. 1.** Hybrid Homomorphic Encryption Scheme

The correctness of an HHE scheme follows directly from the correctness of the underlying public-key HE scheme.

For the security of HHE we rely on the following theorem that was first proved for the KEM/DEM paradigm in [31], and then later modified for HHE in [23]:

**Theorem 1.** *Let* HE *be an IND-CPA secure public-key homomorphic encryption scheme. Moreover, let* SKE *be an IND-CPA secure symmetric-key encryption scheme. Then the* HHE *scheme instantiated by* HE *and* SKE *is IND-CPA secure.*

# 4  Architecture

For the needs of our construction, we assume the existence of the following three entities:

- **Cloud Service Provider (CSP):** An honest-but-curious cloud service provider that is primarily responsible for gathering symmetrically encrypted data from multiple sources. The CSP undertakes the task of transforming the symmetrically encrypted data to homomorphic ciphertexts and, upon request, operate on them in a blind way.
- **Analyst (A):** The analyst is an entity that wishes to perform computations on the data of various users. **A** is the only entity in our construction that can perform the homomorphic decryption and thus, gain insights from user data.
- **Users ($\mathcal{U}$):** Users encrypt their data locally using a symmetric-key encryption scheme and outsource them to the CSP.

# 5  Symmetrical Disguise

Before we proceed with the formal construction of the scheme, we provide a high-level overview.

## 5.1  High-Level Overview

An analyst **A** generates (pk, sk, evk) for the HHE scheme, outsources evk to the CSP and publishes pk. As a next step, each user $u_i$ ($u_i \in \mathcal{U}$), can generate a symmetric key locally, encrypt their data, and outsource them to the CSP along with a homomorphic encryption of the symmetric key under $A$'s public key. Upon reception, the CSP transforms the symmetric ciphertexts to homomorphic, and stores them online in its database. **A** can request the evaluation of a function $f$ on the collection of the ciphertexts from the CSP. The CSP uses evk and outputs an encrypted result which then sends back to **A**. Finally, **A** decrypts the result using their secret key sk.

## 5.2  Formal Construction

We are now ready to present SD that constitutes the core of this paper's contribution. For the realization of our construction we rely on the following building blocks:

- An IND-CPA secure symmetric cipher $\mathsf{SKE} = (\mathsf{Gen}, \mathsf{Enc}, \mathsf{Dec})$.
- An IND-CPA secure homomorphic encryption scheme $\mathsf{HE} = (\mathsf{KeyGen}, \mathsf{Enc}, \mathsf{Dec}, \mathsf{Eval})$.
- A CCA2 secure public-key encryption scheme $\mathsf{PKE} = (\mathsf{Gen}, \mathsf{Enc}, \mathsf{Dec})$
- An EUF-CMA secure signature scheme $\mathsf{S} = (\mathsf{sign}, \mathsf{ver})$.
- A first and second pre-image resistant hash function $H$.

SD is built around three main protocols: $\mathsf{Setup}, \mathsf{Add}, \mathsf{Query}$ such that:

$\boxed{\textbf{SD.Setup:}}$  Each entity from the described architecture generates a signing/ver-ification key pair for an EUF-CMA secure signature scheme S and publishes its verification key while keeping the signing key private. Apart from that, the CSP, generates a public/private key pair $(\mathsf{pk}, \mathsf{sk})$ for a CCA2-secure public-key encryption scheme PKE. Finally, the analyst A runs HHE.KeyGen to generate the public, secret and evaluation keys for an IND-CPA secure homomorphic encryption scheme HE, and each user $u_i$ runs SKE.KeyGen to generate a symmetric key $K_i$ for an IND-CPA secure symmetric cipher SKE. Below we provide a list of the generated keys:

- Signing/Verification keys for each entity.
- $(\mathsf{pk_{CSP}}, \mathsf{sk_{CSP}})$: Public/private key pair of the CSP.
- $(\mathsf{pk_A}, \mathsf{sk_A}, \mathsf{evk_A})$: Public/private/evaluation keys of A.
- $K_i$: Symmetric key for each user $u_i$.

Once the keys are generated, $\mathbf{A}$ outsources its evaluation key $\mathsf{evk}$ to the CSP via $m_1 = \langle t_1, \mathsf{Enc}(\mathsf{pk_{CSP}}, \mathsf{evk}), \sigma_A(H(t_1\|\mathsf{evk}))\rangle$, where $t_1$ is a timestamp, $\sigma_A$ is a signature encrypted with $\mathbf{A}$'s private key, and $H$ is a hash function. Upon reception, the CSP verifies the signature of $\mathbf{A}$, using $\mathbf{A}$'s verification key, and the freshness of the message through the timestamp. If a verification fails, the CSP aborts the protocol and outputs $\perp$. Otherwise, the CSP stores $\mathsf{evk_A}$.

$\boxed{\textbf{SD.Add:}}$  This protocol is initiated by any user $u_i \in \mathcal{U}$ that wishes to outsource some data $\mathbf{x} = (x_1, \ldots, x_n)$ to the CSP. To do so, $u_i$ first runs $c_i \leftarrow \mathsf{SKE.Enc}(K_i, x_i)$. As a next step, $u_i$, homomorphically encrypts is symmetric key $K_i$ under $\mathbf{A}$'s public key, by running $c_{K_i} \leftarrow \mathsf{HE.Enc}(\mathsf{pk_A}, K_i)$. Finally, the $(\mathbf{c}, c_{K_i})$ pair is outsourced to the CSP via the following message:

$$m_2 = \langle t_2, \mathbf{c} = (c_i, \ldots, c_n), c_{K_i} \sigma_{u_i}(H(t_2\|\mathbf{c}\|c_{K_i}))\rangle.$$

Upon receiving $m_2$, the CSP verifies the freshness and integrity of the message. If the verifacation fails, CSP outputs $\perp$. Otherwise, it transforms the symmetric ciphertext $c_i$ to a homomorphic one, by running $c_i' \leftarrow \mathsf{HHE.Decomp}(c_i, c_{K_i}, \mathsf{evk_A})$. Finally, the CSP stores $c_i'$ in its database.

SD.Query: The Query protocol is initiated by **A** whenever she wishes to issue a query to the encrypted data for a function $f$. To do so, A sends $m_3 = \langle t_3, \mathsf{Enc}(\mathsf{pk_{CSP}}, f), \sigma_A(H(t_3 \| f)) \rangle$ to the CSP. Upon reception, the CSP verifies both the integrity and the freshness of the message. If the verification fails, the CSP will abort the protocol and output the error symbol $\perp$. Otherwise, it runs $\mathsf{HHE.Eval}(f, \mathsf{evk_A}, c'_1, \ldots, c'_n) \to c_{\mathsf{res}}$ to get an encrypted result $c_{\mathsf{res}}$. Due to the homomorphic properties of the encryption scheme HE, the encrypted result $c_{\mathsf{res}}$ can be viewed as an encrypted version of $f(x'_1, \ldots, x'_n)$, where each $x'_i$ corresponds to a ciphertext $c'_i$, and that can only be dercypted using **A**'s secret key sk. Subsequently, the CSP forwards $c_{\mathsf{res}}$ to A via $m_4 = \langle t_4, c_{\mathsf{res}}, \sigma_{CSP}(H(t_4 \| c_{\mathsf{res}})) \rangle$. Upon reception, A verifies both the integrity and the freshness of the message. If a verification fails, A aborts the protocol and outputs $\perp$. Otherwise, they run $\mathsf{HHE.Dec}(\mathsf{sk}, c_{res}) \to \mathsf{res}$ to retrieve the result res. Having acquired the result in plaintext, **A** can use it to perform statistics or data analysis, in a privacy-preserving manner, since she never got access to the actual plaintexts. Our protocol is illustrated in Fig. 2.

## 6  Threat Model

In this section, we define the threat model under which we prove the security of SD. More specifically, we formalize the capabilities of the adversary $\mathcal{ADV}$ through the following set of possible attacks:

**Attack 1 (Analyst Substitution Attack).** *Let $\mathcal{ADV}$ be a malicious adversary. $\mathcal{ADV}$ successfully performs an Analyst Substitution Attack if she manages to convince the users that their data are processed for the needs of an analyst **A**, while in reality they are processed for an analyst $\mathbf{A}^{\mathcal{ADV}}$.*

**Attack 2 (Ciphertext Substitution Attack).** *Let $\mathcal{ADV}$ be a malicious adversary. $\mathcal{ADV}$ successfully launches a Ciphertext Substitution Attack if she manages to replace the ciphertexts sent by users to the CSP in an indistinguishable way.*

**Attack 3 (Query Substitution Attack).** *Let $\mathcal{ADV}$ be a malicious adversary. $\mathcal{ADV}$ successfully launches a Query Substitution Attack if she manages to replace the query sent by A to the CSP, with another one of her choice, in an indistinguishable way.*

**Attack 4 (Result Substitution Attack).** *Let $\mathcal{ADV}$ be a malicious adversary. $\mathcal{ADV}$ successfully launches a Result Substitution Attack if she manages to replace the result sent by the CSP to the analyst A, in an indistinguishable way.*

In our threat model, we assume that the CSP cannot collude with the Analyst **A**. This is a valid assumption as otherwise we would be required to prove security in a setting where the decryption keys are publicly-available.

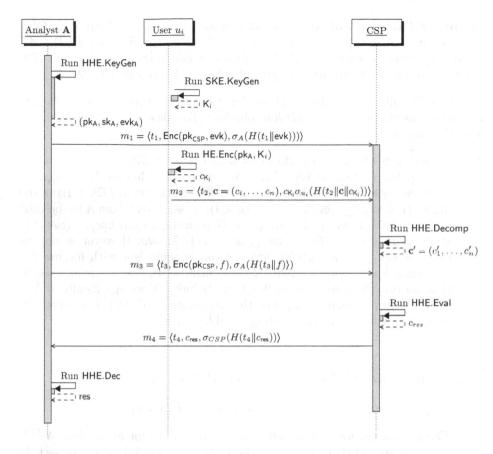

**Fig. 2.** Complete run of our protocol with one user $u_i$. More users would behave exactly like $u_i$.

## 7    Security Analysis

We are now ready to prove the security of our construction assuming the threat model defined in Sect. 6. In particular, we will prove the following theorem:

**Theorem 2 (SD Security in the presence of Malicious Adversaries).**
*Let* PKE *be an INC-CPA secure public-key encryption scheme and* S *an EUF-CMA secure signature scheme with security parameter* $\lambda$. *Moreover, let* SKE *be an IND-CPA secure symmetric-key encryption scheme with security parameter* $\kappa$. *Finally, let* $\mathcal{ADV}$ *be a malicious adversary. Then,* SD *is secure against the threat model defined in Sect. 6.*

*Proof.* To prove Theorem 2, we will start with a sequence of lemmas. Then, we will combine our results to derive a proof for the main theorem.

**Lemma 1 (Analyst Substitution Attack Soundness).** *Let* PKE *be an INC-CPA secure public-key encryption scheme. Moreover, let* S *be an EUF-CMA secure signature scheme and* $\mathcal{ADV}$ *a malicious adversary. In this case* $\mathcal{ADV}$ *cannot successfully launch an Analyst Substitution Attack against SD.*

*Proof.* $\mathcal{ADV}$ will successfully launch an Analyst Substitution Attack, by targeting either the SD.Setup or the SD.Add protocol. To this end, we distinguish the following cases:

**C1:** Attacking SD.Setup: To perform an attack against SD.Setup, $\mathcal{ADV}$ needs to swap the evaluation key of A, $evk_A$, with an evaluation key $evk_{\mathbf{A}^{\mathcal{ADV}}}$, for an analyst $\mathbf{A}^{\mathcal{ADV}}$ such that $A \neq \mathbf{A}^{\mathcal{ADV}}$. To this end, ADV targets the $m_1 = \langle t_1, \mathsf{Enc}(\mathsf{pk}_{\mathsf{CSP}}, evk), \sigma_A(H(t_1\|evk)))\rangle$ message sent from A to the CSP and tries to swap $evk_A$ with $evk_{\mathbf{A}^{\mathcal{ADV}}}$. Generating a valid $\mathsf{Enc}_{\mathsf{pk}_{\mathsf{CSP}}}(evk'_A)$ is straightforward for $\mathcal{ADV}$ as $\mathsf{pk}_{\mathsf{CSP}}$ is publicly known. However, swapping $evk_A$ for $evk'_A$ in the $\sigma_A(H(t_1\|evk))$ term, is equivalent with forging A's signature, and given the EUF-CMA security of the signature scheme S, this can only happen with negligible probability. More specifically, if $\lambda$ is the security parameter of S, then the advantage $\epsilon_1$ of $\mathcal{ADV}$ is successfully tampering with $m_1$ in an indistinguishable way is:

$$\epsilon_1 = negl(\lambda) \tag{2}$$

**C2:** Attacking SD.Add: Another option for $\mathcal{ADV}$ is to target

$$m_2 = \langle t_2, \mathbf{c} = (c_i, \ldots, c_n), c_{\mathsf{K}_i}\sigma_{u_i}(H(t_2\|\mathbf{c}\|c_{\mathsf{K}_i}))\rangle.$$

The motivation for this attack is to use user data for an analyst $\mathbf{A}^{\mathcal{ADV}}$ while the users believe that their data will be processed for an analyst A. Recall that $c_{\mathsf{K}_i}$ is generated as $c_{\mathsf{K}_i} \leftarrow \mathsf{HE.Enc}_{\mathsf{pk}_A}(\mathsf{K}_i)$. Hence, for $\mathcal{ADV}$ to successfully attack this protocol, they need to **simultaneously** satisfy the following three conditions:

(a) Guess the symmetric key $\mathsf{K}_i$;
(b) Encrypt it with the public key of another analyst $\mathbf{A}^{\mathcal{ADV}}$;
(c) Tamper with $m_2$ in an indistinguishable way.

However, assuming that the symmetric cipher SKE is IND-CPA secure, the probability of correctly guessing the key (e.g. brute force attack) is negligible in the security parameter $\kappa$ of SKE. Hence, if the advantage of $\mathcal{ADV}$ in guessing they key is $\epsilon_2$:

$$\epsilon_2 = negl(\kappa) \tag{3}$$

Since condition (1) can never be fulfilled, except with negligible probability, there is no need to separately examine conditions (2) and (3).

Hence, we conclude that in every case, $\mathcal{ADV}$ can successfully launch an Analyst Substitution Attack with only negligible probability.

**Lemma 2 (Ciphertext Substitution Attack Soundness).** *Let* PKE *be an INC-CPA secure public-key encryption scheme. Moreover, let* S *be an EUF-CMA secure signature scheme and* $\mathcal{ADV}$ *a malicious adversary. Then* $\mathcal{ADV}$ *cannot successfully launch a Ciphertext Substitution Attack against SD.*

In contrast with the previous attack that aimed at processing real user data, this attack aims at substituting the actual ciphertexts $(c_1, \ldots, c_n)$ with a sequence of data $(c'_1, \ldots, c'_n)$ generated by $\mathcal{ADV}$. By succeeding in this attack, $\mathcal{ADV}$ can control the outcome of a query to the CSP and hence, manipulate the analyst **A**.

*Proof.* Successfully performing a Ciphertext Substitution Attack, requires attacking the SD.Add protocol. More precisely, when a user $u_i$ outsources their data to the CSP via $m_2 = \langle t_2, \mathbf{c} = (c_i, \ldots, c_n), c_{K_i} \sigma_{u_i}(H(t_2 \| \mathbf{c} \| c_{K_i})) \rangle$, $\mathcal{ADV}$ needs to substitute $\mathbf{c} = (c_i, \ldots, c_n)$ with $\mathbf{c}' = (c'_1, \ldots, c'_n)$. Apart from that $\mathcal{ADV}$ needs to generate a $c_{K'}$ term where $K'$ is the key used to encrypt $\mathbf{c}'$. More precisely, $\mathcal{ADV}$ needs to successfully:

1. Generate a symmetric key $K_{\mathcal{ADV}}$;
2. Use $K'$ to generate a sequence of ciphertexts $\mathbf{c}' = (c'_1, \ldots, c'_n)$;
3. Encrypt $K_{\mathcal{ADV}}$ with $\mathsf{pk}_A$ to get $c_{K_{\mathcal{ADV}}}$;
4. Tamper with $m_2$ in an indistinguishable way.

Conditions (1), (2) and (3) are trivial to achieve. Moreover, substituting $\mathbf{c}$ with $\mathbf{c}'$ and $c_{K_i}$ with $c_K$ in the first part of $m_2$ is straightforward. However, these terms are also included in the signature and hence, successfully substituting the terms is equivalent to forging $u_i$'s signature. Given the EUF-CMA security of the signature scheme S, this can only happen with negligible probability in the security parameter $\lambda$ of S. As a result, the advantage $\epsilon_2$ in tampering with $m_2$ in an indistinguishable way is:

$$\epsilon_3 = negl(\lambda) \tag{4}$$

**Lemma 3 (Query Substitution Attack Soundness).** *Let* PKE *be an INC-CPA secure public-key encryption scheme. Moreover, let* S *be an EUF-CMA secure signature scheme and* $\mathcal{ADV}$ *a malicious adversary. Then* $\mathcal{ADV}$ *cannot successfully launch a Query Substitution Attack against SD.*

*Proof.* For $\mathcal{ADV}$ to successfully perform a Query Substitution Attack, they need to attack the SD.Query protocol. More precisely, when A sends $m_3 = \langle t_3, \mathsf{Enc}(\mathsf{pk}_{CSP}, f), \sigma_A(H(t_3 \| f)) \rangle$ tries to substitute the function $f$ with another function $f'$ of their choice. Since $f$ is encrypted with the public key of the CSP $\mathsf{pk}_{CSP}$, $\mathcal{ADV}$ simply needs to encrypt $f'$ under $\mathsf{pk}_{CSP}$ as well. However, $f$ is also included in the signature part of $m_3$ and hence, tampering with $m_3$ requires forging $\mathbf{A}^{\mathcal{ADV}}$s signature. Given the EUF-CMA security of the signature scheme S this can only happen with negligible probability in the security parameter $\lambda$ of S.

As a result, $\mathcal{ADV}$'s advantage $\epsilon_4$ is in tampering with $m_3$ in an indistinguishable way is:

$$\epsilon_4 = negl(\lambda) \tag{5}$$

**Lemma 4 (Result Substitution Attack Soundness).** *Let* PKE *be an INC-CPA secure public-key encryption scheme. Moreover, let* S *be an EUF-CMA secure signature scheme and* $\mathcal{ADV}$ *a malicious adversary. Then* $\mathcal{ADV}$ *cannot successfully launch a Result Substitution Attack against SD.*

*Proof.* The proof is identical to that of Lemma 3 with the main difference being that $\mathcal{ADV}$ targets $m_4$ instead of $m_3$. Hence, following the exact same reasoning as in the proof of Lemma 3, we conclude that the advantage $\epsilon_5$ of $\mathcal{ADV}$ is in tampering with $m_4$ in an indistinguishable way is:

$$\epsilon_4 = negl(\lambda) \tag{6}$$

Having examined each possible attack separately, what remains to be done is to prove that the overall advantage $\epsilon_{total}$ of $\mathcal{ADV}$ is negligible. Given the security parameter $\lambda$ and grouping up the results from Eqs. 2- 6 we get that:

$$\epsilon_{total} = \epsilon_1 + \epsilon_2 + \epsilon_3 + \epsilon_4 + \epsilon_5 \tag{7}$$
$$= 4 \cdot negl(\lambda) + negl(\kappa)$$

However, it is a standard result in real analysis that the finite sum of negligible functions is still negligible and hence:

$$\epsilon_{total} = negl'(\lambda, \kappa), \tag{8}$$

where $negl'(\lambda, \kappa)$ is negligible function produced as a linear combination of $negl(\lambda)$ and $negl(\kappa)$.     $\square$

## 8   Evaluation

In this section, we evaluate the performance of the core algorithms of our protocol. Our primary testbed for these experiments was an Intel Core i7 laptop with 16 GB RAM running an Ubuntu 20.04 operating system. For these experiments, we utilized the SEAL cryptographic library [41] for basic HE operations, PASTA library [23] to implement the secure symmetric cipher, and OpenSSL[2]. PASTA was chosen over more established Symmetric ciphers such as AES due to its low multiplicative index. All HE operations in this section were based on the BFV [14] scheme, with a polynomial modulus degree of 16384. We note that the choice of polynomial modulus degree impacted the efficiency of the implemented scheme and increased the size of the ciphertexts, however, this was necessary due to the complex operations involved. Finally, to provide a comprehensive overview of each algorithm's performance, each experiment was conducted 50 times with the average taken.

---

[2] https://github.com/openssl/openssl.

## 8.1   Performance of Core Protocols

In this phase of our evaluations, we focused on the performance of the SD.Setup, SD.Add, and SD.Query protocols.

SD.Setup : When evaluating the SD.Setup protocol, we first measured the time taken to generate an RSA public and private key pair (2048 bit long), which we used for both Signing/Verification and Encryption/Decryption, and the time taken to generate the HE keys for the Analyst (i.e., Public, Secret and Evaluation keys). On an average, it took 34.6 ms to generate the RSA public and private keypair, and 88.4 ms to generate the HE keys. Finally, we measured the time taken by a user to construct $m_1 = \langle t_1, \mathsf{Enc}(\mathsf{pk}_{\mathsf{CSP}}, \mathsf{evk}), \sigma_A(H(t_1 \| \mathsf{evk})) \rangle$, and the time taken by the CSP to verify $m_1$ and decrypt $\mathsf{Enc}(\mathsf{pk}_{\mathsf{CSP}}, \mathsf{evk})$. Constructing $m_1$ took 1.478 ms, while verifying and decrypting $m_1$ took 1.174 ms (Table 2).

SD.Add : For the SD.Add protocol, we evaluated the cost of homomorphically encrypting the symmetric key ($\mathsf{HE.Enc_{pk}}$), cost of symmetrically encrypting the user's data (SKE.Enc), and cost of transforming the symmetric ciphertext to a homomorphic ciphertext (HHE.Decomp). Additionally, we measured the time taken for a user to construct $m_2 = \langle t_2, \mathbf{c} = (c_i, \ldots, c_n), c_{\mathsf{K}_i} \sigma_{u_i}(H(t_2 \| \mathbf{c} \| c_{\mathsf{K}_i})) \rangle$, and time taken for the CSP to verify $m_2$. Each experiment was run with a varying number of user data from 1 to 200. It is worth re-iterating that one of the primary advantages of SD is that irrespective of the amount of data being outsourced, $\mathsf{HE.Enc_{pk}}$ is executed once. The cost of executing $\mathsf{HE.Enc_{pk}}$ once was 18 ms. When outsourcing one data value, it took 7 ms to execute the SKE.Enc algorithm and 17.7 s to run the HHE.Decomp algorithm on average. On the other hand, when outsourcing 200 data values, the SKE.Enc algorithm took 1.22 s to execute, while the HHE.Decomp algorithm took 3824 s to execute (Table 1). Constructing $m_2$ took 1.057 ms, while verifying $m_2$ took 0.101 ms (Table 2).

SD.Query : Meanwhile for the SD.Query protocol, we focused on the cost of executing the HHE.Eval and HHE.Dec algorithms. Once again, each experiment was run with a varying number of user data from 1 to 200. Additionally, for the HHE.Eval algorithm, we evaluated a simple squaring function. For a single data value, it took 91 ms to execute the HHE.Eval algorithm, and 5 ms to execute the HHE.Dec algorithm. While for 200 data values, the HHE.Eval algorithm took on average 16.9 s to execute, with the HHE.Dec algorithm taking 1.07 s to execute (Table 1). Furthermore, the analyst takes 1.098 ms to construct $m_3 = \langle t_3, \mathsf{Enc}(\mathsf{pk}_{\mathsf{CSP}}, f), \sigma_A(H(t_3 \| f)) \rangle$, while the CSP takes 1.56 ms to verify $m_3$ and decrypt $\mathsf{Enc}(\mathsf{pk}_{\mathsf{CSP}}, f)$. Finally, the CSP took 1.118 ms to construct $m_4 = \langle t_4, c_{\mathsf{res}}, \sigma_{CSP}(H(t_4 \| c_{\mathsf{res}})) \rangle$ (Table 2).

From our evaluations, it is quite obvious that the HHE.Decomp algorithm is the most computationally expensive function, which explains why it is executed by the CSP. We provide a complete overview of SD protocol measurements when outsourcing 200 data values in Table 2.

**Table 1.** Algorithm execution

| Data Values | SKE.Enc | HHE.Decomp | HHE.Eval | HHE.Dec |
|---|---|---|---|---|
| 1 | 7 ms | 17765 ms | 91 ms | 5 ms |
| 50 | 0.31 s | 990.2 s | 4.916 s | 0.275 s |
| 100 | 0.61 s | 1920.8 s | 8.418 s | 0.54 s |
| 150 | 0.93 s | 2832.1 s | 12.592 s | 0.81 s |
| 200 | 1.22 s | 3823.8 s | 16.902 s | 1.07 s |

## 8.2  Comparison with Plain BFV

To provide concrete evidence of the efficiency of SD, we compare the operations at its user side with that of a plain BFV scheme. To be more precise, we measured the performance of a plain BFV scheme where a user continuously encrypts each data value homomorphically before the data is outsourced to the CSP. We used the same encryption parameters as with SD. For these experiments, we compared the total cost of executing the $HE.Enc_{pk}$ and SKE.Enc algorithms of the SD.Add protocol, and the cost of continuously using HE encryption in the plain BFV.

As with the previous experiments, we vary the amount of data from 1 to 200. For a single data value, SD.Add takes 25 ms to execute, while the plain BFV scheme takes 21 ms to perform one HE encryption. It is worth mentioning that for a single data value, the plain BFV scheme is marginally faster than SD at the user side. However, this is easily attributed to the fact that SD requires two operations (a symmetric encryption operation plus an HE encryption operation) at the user side, while the plain BFV scheme involves just the one HE encryption operation. When the number of data values is increased to 200, the SD.Add algorithm executes in 1.22 s, while the plain BFV scheme executes in 3.1 s. Figure 3 provides an overview of all the results obtained from this phase of our experiments. From these results, it is evident that SD considerably reduces the computational costs of the user and transfers majority of the computational costs to the CSP.

**Table 2.** Protocol measurements in the case of 200 data values

| Sub-Protocol | Messages | Analyst Functions | User Functions | CSP Functions | Time (s) |
|---|---|---|---|---|---|
| SD.Setup | $m_1$ | PKE Keygen<br>HHE.KeyGen<br>$m_1$ construction | PKE Keygen | PKE Keygen<br>$m_1$ verification | 0.19 |
| SD.Add | $m_2$ | - | HHE.Enc<br>SKE.Enc<br>$m_2$ construction | $m_2$ verification<br>HHE.Decomp | 3825 |
| SD.Query | $m_3, m_4$ | $m_3$ construction | - | $m_3$ verification<br>HHE.Eval<br>$m_4$ construction | 16.91 |

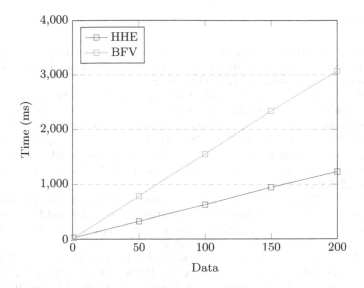

**Fig. 3.** Computation time on the user's side

*Science and Reproducible Research:* To support open science and repro-ducible research, and provide other researchers with the opportunity to use, test, and hopefully extend our scheme, the source code used for the evaluations is publicly available online[3].

## 9   Conclusion

In this paper we presented SD; a secure cryptographic protocol based on Hybrid Homomorphic Encryption. The security and applicability of our construction have been demonstrated through a detailed security analysis and an extensive experimental evaluation. It is our firm belief that in the years to come, cloud storage services will rely less on traditional cryptographic primitives and more on modern cryptographic techniques allowing flexible computations over the encrypted data – such as HE. To this end, we believe it is vital to start designing realistic architectures based on HE in an attempt to demonstrate the feasibility and applicability of modern cryptography. We hope that our work will incentivize other researchers to look into the same direction. Most importantly, though, we hope it will help companies to create modern privacy-respecting cloud services.

---

[3] https://github.com/iammrgenie/HHE-Protocol.

# References

1. Abdalla, M.D., Fiore, D., Gay, R., Ursu, B.: Multi-input functional encryption for inner products: function-hiding realizations and constructions without pairings. In: Advances in Cryptology - CRYPTO 2018 (2018)
2. Abdalla, M., Bourse, F., De Caro, A., Pointcheval, D.: Simple functional encryption schemes for inner products. In: Katz, J. (ed.) PKC 2015. LNCS, vol. 9020, pp. 733–751. Springer, Heidelberg (2015). https://doi.org/10.1007/978-3-662-46447-2_33
3. Abdalla, M., Gay, R., Raykova, M., Wee, H.: Multi-input inner-product functional encryption from pairings. In: Coron, J.-S., Nielsen, J.B. (eds.) EUROCRYPT 2017. LNCS, vol. 10210, pp. 601–626. Springer, Cham (2017). https://doi.org/10.1007/978-3-319-56620-7_21
4. Agrawal, S., Chase, M.: Fame: Fast attribute-based message encryption. In: Proceedings of the 2017 ACM SIGSAC Conference on Computer and Communications Security, CCS 2017, pp. 665–682. Association for Computing Machinery, New York (2017). https://doi.org/10.1145/3133956.3134014
5. Albrecht, M.R., Rechberger, C., Schneider, T., Tiessen, T., Zohner, M.: Ciphers for MPC and FHE. In: Oswald, E., Fischlin, M. (eds.) EUROCRYPT 2015. LNCS, vol. 9056, pp. 430–454. Springer, Heidelberg (2015). https://doi.org/10.1007/978-3-662-46800-5_17
6. Bakas, A., Dang, H.V., Michalas, A., Zalitko, A.: The cloud we share: access control on symmetrically encrypted data in untrusted clouds. IEEE Access 8, 210462–210477 (2020). https://doi.org/10.1109/ACCESS.2020.3038838
7. Bakas, A., Michalas, A.: Modern family: a revocable hybrid encryption scheme based on attribute-based encryption, symmetric searchable encryption and SGX. In: Chen, S., Choo, K.-K.R., Fu, X., Lou, W., Mohaisen, A. (eds.) SecureComm 2019. LNICST, vol. 305, pp. 472–486. Springer, Cham (2019). https://doi.org/10.1007/978-3-030-37231-6_28
8. Bakas, A., Michalas, A.: Multi-input functional encryption: efficient applications from symmetric primitives. In: 2020 IEEE 19th International Conference on Trust, Security and Privacy in Computing and Communications (TrustCom), pp. 1105–1112. IEEE (2020)
9. Bakas, A., Michalas, A.: Power range: Forward private multi-client symmetric searchable encryption with range queries support. In: 2020 IEEE Symposium on Computers and Communications (ISCC), pp. 1–7 (2020). https://doi.org/10.1109/ISCC50000.2020.9219739
10. Bakas, A., Michalas, A.: Nowhere to leak: a multi-client forward and backward private symmetric searchable encryption scheme. In: Barker, K., Ghazinour, K. (eds.) DBSec 2021. LNCS, vol. 12840, pp. 84–95. Springer, Cham (2021). https://doi.org/10.1007/978-3-030-81242-3_5
11. Bakas, A., Michalas, A., Dimitriou, T.: Private lives matter: a differential private functional encryption scheme. In: Proceedings of the Twelfth ACM Conference on Data and Application Security and Privacy, CODASPY 2022, pp. 300–311. Association for Computing Machinery, New York (2022). https://doi.org/10.1145/3508398.3511514
12. Bakas, A., Michalas, A., Frimpong, E., Rabbaninejad, R.: Feel the quantum functioning: instantiating generic multi-input functional encryption from learning with errors (extended version)? Cryptology ePrint Archive, Paper 2022/629 (2022). https://eprint.iacr.org/2022/629

13. Bakas, A., Michalas, A., Ullah, A.: (F)unctional sifting: a privacy-preserving reputation system through multi-input functional encryption. In: Asplund, M., Nadjm-Tehrani, S. (eds.) NordSec 2020. LNCS, vol. 12556, pp. 111–126. Springer, Cham (2021). https://doi.org/10.1007/978-3-030-70852-8_7

14. Brakerski, Z.: Fully homomorphic encryption without modulus switching from classical GapSVP. In: Safavi-Naini, R., Canetti, R. (eds.) CRYPTO 2012. LNCS, vol. 7417, pp. 868–886. Springer, Heidelberg (2012). https://doi.org/10.1007/978-3-642-32009-5_50

15. Brakerski, Z., Gentry, C., Vaikuntanathan, V.: (leveled) fully homomorphic encryption without bootstrapping. ACM Trans. Comput. Theor. (TOCT) **6**(3), 1–36 (2014)

16. Canteaut, A., et al.: Stream ciphers: a practical solution for efficient homomorphic-ciphertext compression. J. Cryptology **31**(3), 885–916 (2018)

17. Cheon, J.H., et al.: Batch fully homomorphic encryption over the integers. In: Johansson, T., Nguyen, P.Q. (eds.) EUROCRYPT 2013. LNCS, vol. 7881, pp. 315–335. Springer, Heidelberg (2013). https://doi.org/10.1007/978-3-642-38348-9_20

18. Cheon, J.H., Kim, A., Kim, M., Song, Y.: Homomorphic encryption for arithmetic of approximate numbers. In: Takagi, T., Peyrin, T. (eds.) ASIACRYPT 2017. LNCS, vol. 10624, pp. 409–437. Springer, Cham (2017). https://doi.org/10.1007/978-3-319-70694-8_15

19. Chillotti, I., Gama, N., Georgieva, M., Izabachène, M.: TFHE: fast fully homomorphic encryption over the torus. J. Cryptology **33**(1), 34–91 (2020)

20. Cid, C., Indrøy, J.P., Raddum, H.: Fasta - a stream cipher for fast fhe evaluation. Cryptology ePrint Archive, Report 2021/1205 (2021). https://ia.cr/2021/1205

21. Coron, J.-S., Lepoint, T., Tibouchi, M.: Scale-invariant fully homomorphic encryption over the integers. In: Krawczyk, H. (ed.) PKC 2014. LNCS, vol. 8383, pp. 311–328. Springer, Heidelberg (2014). https://doi.org/10.1007/978-3-642-54631-0_18

22. Dobraunig, C., et al.: Rasta: a cipher with low ANDdepth and few ANDs per bit. In: Shacham, H., Boldyreva, A. (eds.) CRYPTO 2018. LNCS, vol. 10991, pp. 662–692. Springer, Cham (2018). https://doi.org/10.1007/978-3-319-96884-1_22

23. Dobraunig, C., Grassi, L., Helminger, L., Rechberger, C., Schofnegger, M., Walch, R.: Pasta: A case for hybrid homomorphic encryption. IACR Cryptol. ePrint Arch. **2021**, 731 (2021)

24. Dolev, D., Yao, A.: On the security of public key protocols. IEEE Trans. Inf. Theor. **29**(2), 198–208 (1983). https://doi.org/10.1109/TIT.1983.1056650

25. Fan, J., Vercauteren, F.: Somewhat practical fully homomorphic encryption. IACR Cryptol. ePrint Arch. **2012**, 144 (2012)

26. Gentry, C.: Fully homomorphic encryption using ideal lattices. In: Proceedings of the Forty-First Annual ACM Symposium on Theory of Computing, pp. 169–178 (2009)

27. Gentry, C., Halevi, S., Smart, N.P.: Homomorphic evaluation of the AES circuit. In: Safavi-Naini, R., Canetti, R. (eds.) CRYPTO 2012. LNCS, vol. 7417, pp. 850–867. Springer, Heidelberg (2012). https://doi.org/10.1007/978-3-642-32009-5_49

28. Goldwasser, S., et al.: Multi-input functional encryption. In: Nguyen, P.Q., Oswald, E. (eds.) EUROCRYPT 2014. LNCS, vol. 8441, pp. 578–602. Springer, Heidelberg (2014). https://doi.org/10.1007/978-3-642-55220-5_32

29. Hebborn, P., Leander, G.: Dasta-alternative linear layer for rasta. In: IACR Transactions on Symmetric Cryptology, pp. 46–86 (2020)

30. Kamara, S., Moataz, T., Ohrimenko, O.: Structured encryption and leakage suppression. In: Shacham, H., Boldyreva, A. (eds.) CRYPTO 2018. LNCS, vol. 10991, pp. 339–370. Springer, Cham (2018). https://doi.org/10.1007/978-3-319-96884-1_12

31. Katz, J., Lindell, Y.: Introduction to Modern Cryptography. CRC Press, Boca Raton (2020)

32. Méaux, P., Carlet, C., Journault, A., Standaert, F.-X.: Improved filter permutators for efficient FHE: better instances and implementations. In: Hao, F., Ruj, S., Sen Gupta, S. (eds.) INDOCRYPT 2019. LNCS, vol. 11898, pp. 68–91. Springer, Cham (2019). https://doi.org/10.1007/978-3-030-35423-7_4

33. Michalas, A., Bakas, A., Dang, H.V., Zalitko, A.: Abstract: access control in searchable encryption with the use of attribute-based encryption and sgx. In: Proceedings of the 2019 ACM SIGSAC Conference on Cloud Computing Security Workshop, CCSW 2019, p. 183. Association for Computing Machinery, New York (2019). https://doi.org/10.1145/3338466.3358929

34. Michalas, A., Bakas, A., Dang, H.-V., Zaltiko, A.: MicroSCOPE: enabling access control in searchable encryption with the use of attribute-based encryption and SGX. In: Askarov, A., Hansen, R.R., Rafnsson, W. (eds.) NordSec 2019. LNCS, vol. 11875, pp. 254–270. Springer, Cham (2019). https://doi.org/10.1007/978-3-030-35055-0_16

35. Naehrig, M., Lauter, K., Vaikuntanathan, V.: Can homomorphic encryption be practical? In: Proceedings of the 3rd ACM Workshop on Cloud Computing Security Workshop, pp. 113–124 (2011)

36. Paillier, P.: Public-key cryptosystems based on composite degree residuosity classes. In: Stern, J. (ed.) EUROCRYPT 1999. LNCS, vol. 1592, pp. 223–238. Springer, Heidelberg (1999). https://doi.org/10.1007/3-540-48910-X_16

37. Rivest, R.L., Adleman, L., Dertouzos, M.L., et al.: On data banks and privacy homomorphisms. Found. Secure Comput. 4(11), 169–180 (1978)

38. Rivest, R.L., Shamir, A., Adleman, L.: A method for obtaining digital signatures and public-key cryptosystems. Commun. ACM 21(2), 120–126 (1978)

39. Sahai, A., Waters, B.: Fuzzy identity-based encryption. In: Cramer, R. (ed.) EUROCRYPT 2005. LNCS, vol. 3494, pp. 457–473. Springer, Heidelberg (2005). https://doi.org/10.1007/11426639_27

40. Sans, E.D., Gay, R., Pointcheval, D.: Reading in the dark: classifying encrypted digits with functional encryption. IACR Cryptology ePrint Archive 2018, 206 (2018)

41. Microsoft SEAL (release 4.0). https://github.com/Microsoft/SEAL, March 2022. Microsoft Research, Redmond, WA

# Replicated Additive Secret Sharing with the Optimized Number of Shares

Juanjuan Guo[1,2], Mengjie Shuai[1,2], Qiongxiao Wang[1,2], Wenyuan Li[1,2],
and Jingqiang Lin[3(✉)]

[1] State Key Laboratory of Information Security, Institute of Information
Engineering, Chinese Academy of Sciences, Beijing 100089, China
[2] School of Cyber Security, University of Chinese Academy of Sciences,
Beijing 100089, China
[3] School of Cyber Security, University of Science and Technology of China,
Hefei 230027, Anhui, China
linjq@ustc.edu.cn

**Abstract.** Replicated additive secret sharing (RSS) schemes introduce the threshold for additive secret sharing, and are known for computational efficiency and flexibility. While the traditional RSS schemes usually have a huge storage overhead with each server holding multiple shares, recent variations have tried reducing storage overhead but at the expense of computational performance. In this work, we focus on optimizing the number of shares to reduce storage overhead without introducing excessive computational cost. First, we construct a 2-of-$n$ RSS (i.e., any two among $n$ servers could reconstruct the secret value), which generates secret shares incrementally so that the storage increases almost linearly with $n$, and achieves the optimal number of shares as we proved. Then, we extend 2-of-$n$ RSS to a general $t$-of-$n$ RSS. Moreover, the incrementally-generate mechanism makes our scheme support a server to join dynamically that refrain existing shares from being modified. Our empirical study across 60 servers supports that our scheme largely reduces the storage overhead while obtaining an efficient runtime. Storage efficiency shows an improvement of up to two orders of magnitude and online runtime is within microsecond scale in our experimental settings.

**Keywords:** Secret sharing · Replicated additive secret sharing · Secure multiparty computation · Data privacy

## 1 Introduction

Secret sharing (SS) [4,31] has been extensively studied since it is important not only for sensitive data storage but also as a fundamental building block for

This work was partially supported by National Key R&D Program of China under Grant No. 2020YFB1005800.

F. Li et al. (Eds.): SecureComm 2022, LNICST 462, pp. 371–389, 2023.
https://doi.org/10.1007/978-3-031-25538-0_20

multiparty computation (MPC) [34]. The basic idea of SS is to (1) split the secret value into shares, and (2) ensure that the value can be reconstructed only with the predefined threshold number of shares. In sensitive data storage, the shares are stored among a set of non-colluded servers, preventing the adversary from reconstructing the secret value. Further, in secure multiparty computation, these servers cooperatively process these shares to complete the computation over the secret values without reconstructing them.

Two split mechanisms have been proposed for secret sharing. One is Shamir's secret sharing scheme [31], which splits the secret value by setting it as the constant coefficient of a random polynomial. The other is additive secret sharing scheme [18], which splits the secret value with a number of random values, ensuring the summation of the shares equal to the secret value. Shamir's secret sharing scheme [31] requires heavy modular exponentiation (and multiplication) in data split and complicated process of degree reduction for computing multiplication of secret values, which results in rare adoption in the secure multiparty computation [5]. In contrast, the additive secret sharing scheme is more efficient, as it only needs modular addition for data split, and a lightweight algorithm (i.e., Beaver triples [2,3]) has been proposed to multiply the secret values.

Therefore, additive secret sharing is widely adopted in secure multiparty computation, e.g., privacy-preserving machine learning (PPML) [10,11,22,23,23–26,29,30,32] and threshold signature [9]. In PPML, the secret values (e.g., medical data, finance data) are split into shares, and processed (e.g., addition, multiplication, comparison) by integrating additive secret sharing with garbled circuit [27], oblivious transfer [33], and/or homomorphic encryption [7,12], to complete the training and/or inference in machine learning. In threshold signature [9,14–16,21], the private key is split with additive secret sharing scheme among a number of servers, and a threshold number of servers cooperatively process the shares with the to-be-signed message, to generate a valid signature of the message.

Replicated additive secret sharing (RSS) [18] is proposed to introduce the threshold in additive secret sharing, by replicating shares in multiple servers, i.e., one server maintains multiple shares of the secret value. For example, $t$-of-$n$ RSS only needs the shares from $t$ servers among the whole $n$ ones. ISN [18], the first RSS, designs an access structure to ensure any $t$ servers can obtain all the shares. However, ISN needs a large storage (i.e., $C_n^t$, the number of $t-sized$ subset of $n-sized$ set). CDI [13] and KCI [19] reduce the storage overhead, by converting Shamir's secret share into additive secret share. However, a large computational overhead is introduced during the conversions of shares.

Various PPML schemes attempt to integrate RSS for improving the flexibility. However, the effect is still limited due to the heavy computation or storage overhead of $t$-of-$n$ RSS when $t$ and $n$ is large. For example, AFL [1,17] adopts ISN and only supports 2-of-3 RSS, PPML schemes [10,24,26,29] only support 2-of-3 or 2-of-4 RSS.

In this paper, we propose a new RSS scheme for additive secret sharing scheme, which reduces the storage significantly, without introducing excessive computational overhead. We first construct an optimal 2-of-$n$ RSS to split the value incrementally, i.e., first split the secret value in 2-of-2 setting, then 2-of-3 RSS until 2-of-$n$ RSS, which makes the storage increase almost linear with $n$, reduce the storage remarkably compared to ISN. Then, we extend 2-of-$n$ RSS to $t$-of-$n$ RSS, with a 3-of-$n$ RSS. Moreover, the proposed incrementally-generate mechanism supports a new server to join dynamically that refrain existing shares from being modified. We have implemented the propose RSS scheme, the evaluation demonstrates the significant decrease of storage and modest computation performance.

The main contributions are as follows.

- We design a new 2-of-$n$ RSS scheme and prove the optimal storage overhead theoretically.
- We extend the optimal 2-of-$n$ RSS to a general $t$-of-$n$ RSS, to support an arbitrary threshold. The analysis demonstrate that our scheme needs much less storage compared to ISN.
- Our scheme support the dynamical join of a new server in secret sharing, which generates the share while the shares remain unchanged.

## 2  Preliminaries

**Additive Secret Sharing.** Additive secret sharing(ASS) is a technique that splits the secret into shares that add up to the original secret. The additive secret sharing algorithm chooses $n$ strings $(s_1, ..., s_n)$ uniformly at random subject to the requirement that $\sum_{i=1}^{n} s_i = s$ (this can be done by choosing $s_1,...,s_{n-1} \in \mathbb{Z}_{2^l}$ uniformly at random, and then setting $s_n = s - \sum_{i=1}^{n-1} s_i$. The reconstruction algorithm simply adds all the shares to reconstruct the secret. ASS guarantees that each share does not reveal any information about the secret. Traditional additive secret sharing is a full-threshold secret sharing that requires all parties (servers) cooperate to reconstruct the secret, and no single point of failure is allowed.

**Replicated Additive Secret Sharing.** Replicated additive secret sharing (RSS) [13,18,19] has an access structure $\Gamma$. An access structure is defined by qualified sets $Q \in \Gamma$, which are the sets of parties who are granted access, and the remaining sets of the parties are called unqualified sets. In the context of this work we only consider threshold structures in which any set of $t-1$ or fewer parties is not authorized to learn information about private values (i.e., they form unqualified sets), while any $t$ or more parties are able to jointly reconstruct the secret (and thus form qualified sets). RSS can be defined for any $n > t \geq 2$. To secret-share private $s$ using RSS, we treat $s$ as an element of a finite ring $\mathbb{Z}_{2^l}$ and additively split it into shares $s_T$ such that $s = \sum_{T \in \tau} s_T$ (in $\mathbb{Z}_{2^l}$), where $\tau$ consists of all maximal unqualified set of $\Gamma$ (i.e., all sets of $t-1$ parties in our case). Then each party $i \in [1, n]$ stores shares $s_T$ for all $T \in \tau$ subject to $i \notin T$.

In $t$-of-$n$ replicated additive secret sharing, the secret is shared among $n$ parties and the secret can be reconstructed when $t$ parties cooperate.

## 3   2-of-$n$ Replicated Additive Secret Sharing

Replicated additive secret sharing (RSS) with a small threshold has become popular over the last few years [15,24,26]. We design a 2-of-$n$ RSS scheme, which is proved to achieve the minimum number of shares in 2-of-$n$ RSS.

**The System Model.** In our secret sharing scheme there is one dealer and $n$ parties (servers). The dealer generates shares of the secret and distributes them to $n$ parties, only when $t$ parties cooperate will the secret be reconstructed. In our 2-of-$n$ RSS, $t$ is 2. We denote $n$ parties who receive shares after share generation as (share holder) parties, and $t$ parties who reconstruct the secret corporately as reconstruct parties.

**The Adversary Model.** We assume that an adversary in our scheme can be divided into two kinds. An eavesdropping adversary learns all the information stored at the corrupted parties. A halting adversary may also disturb corrupted parties to stop sending messages during the execution of the protocol. Our scheme can tolerate up to $t-1$ eavesdropping parties and up to $n-t$ halting parties. We assume that the dealer is a trusted party.

### 3.1   2-of-$n$ Replicated Share Generation

Our 2-of-$n$ replicated additive secret sharing generates shares incrementally by adding parties one by one in turn. In our 2-of-$n$ RSS, multiple share sets will be generated, and each share set contains two shares whose sum is equal to the secret $s$. We denote share as $s_a^b$, the subscript $a$ indicates the order of share set that this share belongs to, and the superscript $b$ indicates the order of a share in its share set. The value of $b$ is 1 or 2, and the value of $a$ is related to the number of parties $n$. The party whose id is $i$ is denoted as $P_i$.

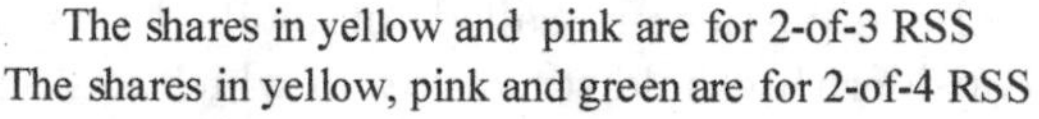

The shares in yellow are for 2-of-2 ASS
The shares in yellow and pink are for 2-of-3 RSS
The shares in yellow, pink and green are for 2-of-4 RSS

**Fig. 1.** 2-of-4 replicated share generation.

In our 2-of-$n$ replicated share generation, the dealer generates shares beginning with 2-of-2 additive secret sharing, then extends it to arbitrary 2-of-$n$ replicated share generation. We take 2-of-4 replicated share generation as an example, which shows in Fig. 1.

1) In 2-of-2 additive secret sharing, the dealer samples two additive shares $s_1^1$, $s_1^2$ in $\mathbb{Z}_{2^l}$ satisfying $s_1^1 + s_1^2 = s$, and sends $s_1^1$ to $P_1$, $s_1^2$ to $P_2$.

2) The 2-of-3 replicated share generation is based on 2-of-2 additive secret sharing, the dealer sends $P_1$'s share $s_1^1$ to $P_3$. Now $P_2$ can reconstruct the secret $s$ with either $P_1$ or $P_3$, but $P_1$ and $P_3$ cannot reconstruct the secret $s$ because they hold the same share. Thus we consider $P_1$ as the conflict party of $P_3$, or $P_1$ and $P_3$ are conflict parties. It is necessary for the dealer to generate the second share set $s_2^1$, $s_2^2$, and send $s_2^1$ to $P_1$, $s_2^2$ to $P_3$. So $P_1$ and $P_3$ can reconstruct the secret $s$ using $s_2^1$ and $s_2^2$.

3) The 2-of-4 replicated share generation is based on 2-of-3 replicated share generation. The dealer sends $P_2$'s share $s_1^2$ to $P_4$, now $P_4$ can reconstruct $s$ with either $P_1$ or $P_3$, but cannot reconstruct $s$ with $P_2$ because they hold the same share of the first share set. It is necessary for the dealer to send $s_2^1$ to $P_2$, $s_2^2$ to $P_4$ to enable $P_2$, $P_4$ reconstruct the secret.

In summary, $P_1$, $P_2$ hold $\{s_1^1\}$, $\{s_1^2\}$ respectively in 2-of-2 additive secret sharing; $P_1$, $P_2$, $P_3$ hold $\{s_1^1, s_2^1\}$, $\{s_1^2\}$, $\{s_1^1, s_2^2\}$ respectively in 2-of-3 RSS; $P_1$, $P_2$, $P_3$, $P_4$ hold $\{s_1^1, s_2^1\}$, $\{s_1^2, s_2^1\}$, $\{s_1^1, s_2^2\}$, $\{s_1^2, s_2^2\}$ respectively in 2-of-4 RSS.

Similar to 2-of-4 RSS, We design a 2-of-$n$ RSS incrementally through adding parties one by one. Since our goal is to make parties possess the minimum number of shares, and the dealer always distributes a new set of shares, each to the new party and its conflict party, we choose one of the parties holding the minimum number of shares as $P_{conflict}$, whose shares will be copied to the new party by the dealer. According to our rules, we find the conflict id of $P_i$ ($i \geq 3$) is $conflict = (i - 2^{(\lceil log_2 i \rceil - 1)})$ in 2-of-$n$ RSS. It can be seen that $P_{conflict}$ holds the minimum number of shares at present. For example, the conflict parties of $P_3$, $P_4$ are $P_1$, $P_2$ respectively, and the conflict parties of $P_5$, $P_6$, $P_7$, $P_8$ are $P_1$, $P_2$, $P_3$, $P_4$ respectively. The dealer will totally generate three share sets if $n$ ranges from 5 to 8, four share sets if $n$ ranges from 9 to 16, ..., according to the rules, we find that the dealer will generate $\lceil log_2 n \rceil$ share sets when the number of parties is $n$ where $\lceil \bullet \rceil$ represents ceiling function in math.

---

**Algorithm 1. Shr_2ofn: 2-of-$n$ replicated share generation**

**Input:** The number of parties $n$.
**Output:** Shares for all parties.

1: Generate $\lceil log_2 n \rceil$ share sets $(s_1^1, s_1^2), (s_2^1, s_2^2), ..., (s_{\lceil log_2 n \rceil}^1, s_{\lceil log_2 n \rceil}^2)$.
2: Set an array $rawshare_1$ to store the first share of share sets $s_1^1, s_2^1, ..., s_{\lceil log_2 n \rceil}^1$, and set an array $rawshare_2$ to store the second share of share sets $s_1^2, s_2^2, ..., s_{\lceil log_2 n \rceil}^2$.
3: Set an array $vshare$ containing $n$ sub-arrays, and each corresponds to a party.
4: Add $rawshare_1[1]$ to $vshare[1]$, add $rawshare_2[1]$ to $vshare[2]$.
5: **for** $3 \leq i \leq n$ **do**
6:     Compute the conflict id of $P_i$ as $conflict = i - 2^{\lceil log_2 i \rceil - 1}$.
7:     Copy $vshare[conflict]$ to $vshare[i]$.
8:     Add $rawshare_1[\lceil log_2 i \rceil]$ into $vshare[conflict]$ and add $rawshare_2[\lceil log_2 i \rceil]$ into $vshare[i]$.
9: **end for**
10: Output $vshare[i]$ to share holder $P_i$, where $1 \leq i \leq n$.

---

We describe 2-of-$n$ replicated share generation Shr_2ofn executed by the dealer in Algorithm 1. In order to reduce communication rounds, the dealer sends shares in one round after generating all shares for $n$ parties. Each party receives shares that have been arranged in ascending order of share sets. Specifically, $P_i$ holds at most $\lceil log_2 n \rceil$ shares in $vshare[i]$. These shares, in turn, belong to the first share set, the second share set, ..., the $\lceil log_2 n \rceil$th share set, so the index of a share in $vshare[i]$ represents the share sets to which it belongs.

**Proposition 1.** *In 2-of-$n$ RSS that splits the secret into multiple sets with each set containing 2 shares, the number of shares of the party holding the most shares in our scheme reaches the minimum.*

*Proof.* Let $Min(n)$ denotes the minimum number of shares of the party holding the most shares, we prove by mathematical induction and contradiction that $Min(n)$ is $\lceil log_2 n \rceil$ in 2-of-$n$ RSS.

Base case: Show that the statement holds for the smallest $n$ in 2-of-$n$ secret sharing: $n = 2$, $Min(2) = \lceil log_2 2 \rceil = 1$ is clearly true because the dealer has to generate one share set in this case.

Inductive step: Show that for any $k > 2$, if $Min(k) = \lceil log_2 k \rceil$ holds, then $Min(k+1) = \lceil log_2 (k+1) \rceil$ also holds. We consider two cases:

1) $k$ satisfies $\lceil log_2 (k+1) \rceil = \lceil log_2 k \rceil$. According to our share generation algorithm, $P_{k+1}$ will get all shares of $P_{conflict}$, then the dealer distributes one share of the $\lceil log_2 (k+1) \rceil$th share sets to $P_{conflict}$, and distributes the other share to $P_{k+1}$, now these two conflict parties hold $\lceil log_2 (k+1) \rceil$ shares. $Min(k)$ is $\lceil log_2 k \rceil$, it means that the rest parties except two conflict parties still hold $\lceil log_2 k \rceil$ shares. Because $\lceil log_2 (k+1) \rceil = \lceil log_2 k \rceil$, all parties hold $\lceil log_2 k \rceil$ shares at most. As $\lceil log_2 k \rceil$ is the minimum for $k$ parties, it is obviously for $(k+1)$ parties. Thus, $Min(k+1) = \lceil log_2 (k+1) \rceil$ holds.

2) $k$ satisfies $\lceil log_2 (k+1) \rceil = \lceil log_2 k \rceil + 1$. We prove this by contradiction. We first suppose that $\lceil log_2 k \rceil$ shares are enough for $k+1$ parties. In this case, $\lceil log_2 k \rceil = log_2 k$. The secret can be reconstructed only if the shares held by any two parties are not all the same. Each party holds $log_2 k$ shares and $log_2 k$ share sets each contains 2 shares in our method, so at most $2^{log_2 k} = k$ share combinations can be generated according to combination theorem. When the dealer distributes $k$ combinations of shares to $k + 1$ parties, there will definitely be two parties holding the same combination of shares, making it impossible for them to reconstruct the secret, which violates our suppose. Therefore, a new set of shares needs to be generated, $Min(k+1) = \lceil log_2 k \rceil + 1 = \lceil log_2 (k+1) \rceil$ holds.

### 3.2   2-of-$n$ Replicated Secret Reconstruction

In our 2-of-$n$ replicated additive secret sharing, each party holds at most $\lceil log_2 n \rceil$ secret shares. Before reconstructing the secret, two reconstruct parties exchange their id $id_1, id_2$ that $id_2 > id_1$. Each reconstruct party determines which share will be used to reconstruct the secret according to the id of the other party. Finally, the secret can be reconstructed by adding the two selected shares.

Since our 2-of-$n$ share generation is an incremental scheme, we design the secret reconstruction algorithm following the inverse idea of share generation described in Subsect. 3.1. The conflict id of the larger party $P_{id_2}$ can be computed as $conflict = id_2 - 2^{(\lceil log_2(id_2) \rceil - 1)}$.

1) If $conflict = id_1$, it means that shares of $P_{id_1}$ were copied to $P_{id_2}$ during share generation phase, so $P_{id_1}$ and $P_{id_2}$ can reconstruct the secret using their first different share, which is $\lceil log_2(id_2) \rceil$th share they hold.
2) If $conflict \neq id_1$, according to our share generation algorithm, the dealer copies the shares of $P_{conflict}$ to $P_{id_2}$, so $P_{id_2}$ can use these copied shares to reconstruct the secret with any other party except $P_{conflict}$. Now that $id_1 \neq conflict$, $P_{id_2}$ will only use the shares copied from $P_{conflict}$ to reconstruct the secret. Therefore, $P_{id_2}$ can be regarded as $P_{conflict}$ in this case. Now the secret reconstruction between $P_{id_1}$ and $P_{id_2}$ has transformed into the secret reconstruction between $P_{id_1}$ and $P_{conflict}$, so $P_{id_2}$ rolls its id $id_2$ back to $conflict$. Then each reconstruct party finds the larger id between $id_1$ and $conflict$, and computes the conflict id of it.

Executing the above operations for two reconstruct ids in a loop which stops until two ids are in conflict or the larger id is 2. If the larger id is 2, the smaller id must be 1 so that two reconstruct parties choose the first share to reconstruct the secret.

The algorithm Rec_2ofn executed by each reconstruct party to select the correct share is described in Algorithm 2, where $recparty$ is an array containing reconstruct id in ascending order, each reconstruct party $P_i(i \in \{id_1, id_2\})$ executes the algorithm, and obtain the correct share that will be used to reconstruct the secret.

---

**Algorithm 2.** Rec_2ofn: 2-of-$n$ replicated secret reconstruction

---

**Input:** $recparty$.
**Output:** The share that used to reconstruct the secret.

1: **while** True **do**
2:   **if** $recparty[2] == 2$ **then**
3:     output $vshare[i][1]$.
4:   **else**
5:     $conflict = recparty[2] - 2^{(\lceil log_2(recparty[2]) \rceil - 1)}$
6:     **if** $conflict == recparty[1]$ **then**
7:       output $vshare[i][\lceil log_2(recparty[2]) \rceil]$
8:     **else**
9:       Replace $recparty[2]$ with $conflict$ in $recparty$, and sort ids in $recparty$.
10:     **end if**
11:   **end if**
12: **end while**

---

# 4   $t$-of-$n$ Replicated Additive Secret Sharing

The threshold of RSS introduced in Sect. 3 is limited to 2, however, there are also some scenarios that requires larger threshold [16,28]. We extend the threshold to an arbitrary number, achieving $t$-of-$n$ RSS.

## 4.1   $t$-of-$n$ Replicated Share Generation

In $t$-of-$n$ replicated share generation, the dealer generates secret shares in an incremental way, similar to 2-of-$n$ RSS. It starts from $t$-of-$t$ additive secret sharing, then to $t$-of-$(t + 1)$ RSS, ... , $t$-of-$n$ RSS.

**$t$-of-$t$ Additive Secret Sharing.** The dealer begins with $t$-of-$t$ additive secret sharing, it generates shares $s_1^1, s_1^2, ..., s_1^t$ in $\mathbb{Z}_{2^l}$, satisfying $s_1^1 + s_1^2 + ... + s_1^t = s$. Then allocates $s_1^1$ to $P_1$, $s_1^2$ to $P_2$, ... , $s_1^t$ to $P_t$ so that the $t$ parties can reconstruct the secret $s$.

**$t$-of-$(t+1)$ Replicated Share Generation.** The dealer generates $t$-of-$(t + 1)$ RSS based on $t$-of-$t$ additive secret sharing above.

  The dealer allocates the share $s_1^1$ of $P_1$ to $P_{t+1}$, we consider $P_1$ as the conflict party of $P_{t+1}$, or $P_1$, $P_{t+1}$ are conflict parties. Now $t$ parties $\{P_1, P_2, ..., P_t\}$ or $\{P_2, P_3, ..., P_{t+1}\}$ can reconstruct the secret $s$ using $s_1^1, s_1^2, ..., s_1^t$. However, any $t$ parties including both $P_1$ and $P_{t+1}$ cannot reconstruct the secret $s$ because they hold the same share $s_1^1$ at present.

  To solve this, the dealer will generate and allocate shares to enable any $t$ parties including both $P_1$ and $P_{t+1}$ to reconstruct the secret $s$. The dealer samples two shares $s_2^1$, $s_2^2$ in $\mathbb{Z}_{2^l}$, then allocates $s_2^1$ to $P_1$ and allocates $s_2^2$ to $P_{t+1}$. Next, the dealer computes $\delta_1 = s - s_2^1 - s_2^2$. The new secret $\delta_1$ needs to be shared among the rest $t - 1$ parties, achieving any $t - 2$ parties from the rest parties can reconstruct the new secret $\delta_1$, and further any $t$ parties among $\{P_1, P_2, ..., P_{t+1}\}$ can reconstruct the secret $s$. In other words, when reconstructing the secret $s$, $P_1$, $P_{t+1}$ uses $s_2^1$, $s_2^2$ respectively, and the rest parties use their share which can reconstruct $\delta_1$.

  When we generate shares for $(t - 2)$-of-$(t - 1)$ RSS of the new secret $\delta_1$, it is a sub-problem of generating shares for $t$-of-$(t + 1)$ RSS of the original secret $s$. Thus, we design a recursive algorithm to solve sub-problem $(t - 2)$-of-$(t - 1)$ RSS, in which sub-problem $(t - 4)$-of-$(t - 3)$ RSS will be called, ..., until the recursion reaches its bound 2-of-3 or 3-of-4 determined by whether $t$ is even or odd respectively since $t$ reduces by 2 in each recursion. The 2-of-$n$ replicated share generation algorithm has been given in Sect. 3. The 3-of-$n$ replicated share generation algorithm is similar to 2-of-$n$ replicated share generation, which we will give at the end of this section.

**$t$-of-$n$ Replicated Share Generation.** Our scheme adds $P_{t+2}$ based on $t$-of-$(t + 1)$ share generation described above, then adds $P_{t+3}$, ..., $P_n$ similarly to achieve $t$-of-$n$ RSS. When $P_i$ ($i \geq t + 1$) is added, the dealer copies the shares of its conflict party $P_{i-t}$ to $P_i$, then samples two shares $s_*^1$ and $s_*^2$ and sends each of them to $P_{i-t}$, $P_i$ respectively. Next, the dealer computes $\delta = s - s_*^1 - s_*^2$, and generates shares for $(t-2)$-of-$(i-2)$ RSS of the new secret $\delta$, it is a sub-problem of generating shares for $t$-of-$i$ RSS of the original secret $s$. Thus, we design a recursive algorithm to solve sub-problem $(t-2)$-of-$(i-2)$ RSS, in which sub-problem $(t-4)$-of-$(i-4)$ RSS will be called, ..., until the recursion reaches its bound that the threshold of secret sharing to be called is 2 or 3.

---

**Algorithm 3.** $\mathcal{F}_{maxlevel}(t, n)$

1: **if** t==2 **then**
2:     return $maxlevel = \lceil log_2 n \rceil$
3: **else if** t==3 **then**
4:     return $maxlevel = n - 2$
5: **else if** t==n **then**
6:     return $maxlevel = 1$
7: **else then**
8:     return $maxlevel = \mathcal{F}_{maxlevel}(t, n-1) + \mathcal{F}_{maxlevel}(t-2, n-2)$
9: **endif**

---

In our $t$-of-$n$ replicated additive secret sharing, the number of share sets generated by the dealer can be calculated using $t$ and $n$ as described in Algorithm 3. The cases that $t$ is 2 and $t$ is 3 have proved before. When considering the $n$th party $P_n$, the dealer allocates shares of $P_{n-t}$ to $P_n$ on the basis of $t$-of-$(n-1)$ share generation, and executes $(t-2)$-of-$(n-2)$ RSS for the other $n-2$ parties excluding $P_{n-t}$ and $P_n$. Therefore, the total number of share sets of $t$-of-$n$ secret sharing is $\mathcal{F}_{maxlevel}(t, n-1) + \mathcal{F}_{maxlevel}(t-2, n-2)$.

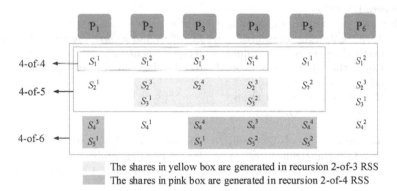

The shares in yellow box are generated in recursion 2-of-3 RSS
The shares in pink box are generated in recursion 2-of-4 RSS

**Fig. 2.** 4-of-6 replicated share generation.

Figure 2 shows an example of 4-of-6 replicated share generation. We describe our $t$-of-$n$ share generation Shr_tofn in Algorithm 4 and define the following parameters:

- 2-tuple($sharelevel$, $sharevalue$): It describes a share, $sharelevel$ is the order of the share set to which it belongs, and $sharevalue$ is its value.
- $vparty$: an array containing ids of all parties (share holders).

– *vshare*: a two-dimensional array that records the 2-tuples of $n$ parties. After the share generation algorithm ends, *vshare*[$i$] contains all 2-tuples of $P_i$. *vshare* is initialized as an empty two-dimensional array, and because it will be modified in every recursion, it is set as a global variable.

– *maxlevel*: an integer indicating maximum order of share sets that have been generated so far, *maxlevel* is initialized to 1. It will be modified in every recursion, so we set it as a global variable.

– *genlevel*: an integer indicating the *sharelevel* of share that is generated during the present recursion, it is initialized to 1. As our share generation is incremental, the *sharelevel* of new shares must not be the same as the shares that have already been generated, thus *genlevel* is always set to *maxlevel*+1.

The algorithm Shr_tofn takes threshold $t$, secret $s$, *genlevel* and *vparty* as input. It has no output, because all shares that are generated will be added into array *vshare*.

---

**Algorithm 4.** Shr_tofn($t$, $s$, *genlevel*, *vparty*)

---

**Input:** threshold $t$, secret $s$, *genlevel*, *vparty*.

1: **if** $t==2$ **then**
2:     Shr_2ofn($s$, *genlevel*, *recurparty*)
3: **else if** $t=3$ **then**
4:     Shr_3ofn($s$, *genlevel*, *recurparty*)
5: **else**
6:     Sample shares $s_1, s_2, ..., s_t \xleftarrow{\$} \mathbb{Z}_{2^l}$ such that $\sum_{i=1}^{t} s_i = s$.
7:     Set *sharelevel* = *genlevel*, add 2-tuple(*sharelevel*, $s_i$) to *vshare*[*vparty*[$i$]] where $1 \le i \le t$.
8:     **for** $i = t + 1; i \le$ sizeof(*vparty*); $i++$ **do**
9:         Traverse 2-tuples in *vshare*[*vparty*[$i-t$]] to find *vshare*[*vparty*[$i-t$]][*ord*] such that *vshare*[*vparty*[$i - t$]][*ord*].*sharelevel*=*genlevel*.
10:        Copy the shares from *ord*th to the last in *vshare*[*vparty*[$i - t$]] to *vshare*[*vparty*[$i$]].
11:        **if** *genlevel*>*maxlevel* **then**
12:            *maxlevel* = *genlevel*.
13:        **end if**
14:        Sample $s_1'$, $s_2'$ in $\xleftarrow{\$} \mathbb{Z}_{2^l}$, add 2-tuple(*maxlevel*+1, $s_1'$) into *vshare*[*vparty*[$i - t$]], add 2-tuple(*maxlevel* + 1, $s_2'$) into *vshare*[*vparty*[$i$]].
15:        Add *vparty*[$m$] into an empty array *recurparty* where $1 \le m<i$ and $m! = i-t$.

16:        Shr_tofn($t - 2$, $s - s_1' - s_2'$, *maxlevel*+1, *recurparty*)
17:    **end for**
18: **end if**

---

The 3-of-$n$ replicated share generation Shr_3ofn called in Shr_tofn is also incrementally generated, similar to 2-of-$n$ share generation. The dealer begins with 3-of-3 additive secret sharing, sends $s_1^1$, $s_1^2$, $s_1^3$ to $P_1$, $P_2$, $P_3$ respectively. When adding $P_i$ ($i \ge 4$), the dealer generates a new set of shares $s_2^1, s_2^2, s_2^3$, and sends $s_2^1$ to $P_{i-3}$, $s_2^2$ to $P_i$, $s_2^3$ to $P_j$ where $1 \le j<i$ and $j \ne i-3$. The dealer needs

to generate $n-2$ sets of shares in total in our 3-of-$n$ replicated share generation. Considering the parameter compatibility when Shr_3ofn and Shr_2ofn are called in Shr_tofn, it is necessary to introduce parameters *sharelevel, genlevel, vparty,* etc. based on 3-of-$n$ and 2-of-$n$ replicated share generation we described before.

## 4.2 $t$-of-$n$ Replicated Secret Reconstruction

In $t$-of-$n$ replicated additive secret sharing, each party holds multiple shares. The $t$ reconstruct parties exchange their ids, and each party selects a correct share according to $t$ reconstruct ids, then the secret can be reconstructed by computing the sum of $t$ shares that have been selected.

Our $t$-of-$n$ secret reconstruction follows the reverse strategy of share generation. Now that share generation is in an incremental way, reconstruction will start from maximum reconstruct id to minimum. After exchanging id with other reconstruct parties, each party holds the ids of all reconstruct parties as $\{id_1, id_2, ..., id_t\}$ in ascending order. The correct share selection starts from maximum id $id_t$, and computes the conflict id of $id_t$ as $conflict = id_t - t$.

1) If $P_{conflict}$ is also a reconstruct party, it means that the dealer copied shares of $P_{conflict}$ to $P_{id_t}$ during share generation. Therefore, $P_{conflict}$ and $P_{id_t}$ shall choose the first different share of them to reconstruct the secret. As their first different share is generated on the basis of $t$-of-$(id_t - 1)$ RSS, the *sharelevel* of which is $\mathcal{F}_{maxlevel}(t, id_t - 1) + 1$. The rest parties execute the secret reconstruction algorithm in a recursion, and with a threshold $t - 2$ after two conflict parties are removed.

2) If $P_{conflict}$ is not a reconstruct party, shares of $P_{id_t}$ that are generated after the conflict with $P_{conflict}$ will not be used. Instead, $P_{id_t}$ will choose one from shares that are copied from $P_{conflict}$. Therefore, $P_{id_t}$ can be regarded as $P_{conflict}$ in this case, similar to 2-of-$n$ secret reconstruction. Thus, $P_{id_t}$ rolls its id back to *conflict*. Then reconstruct parties sort ids of refreshed reconstruct parties in ascending order.

If no parties are in conflict, each reconstruct party chooses the first share in the present recursion to reconstruct the secret.

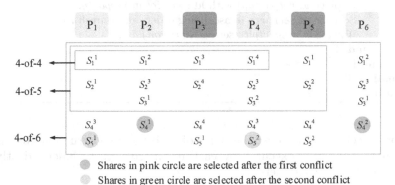

   Shares in pink circle are selected after the first conflict
   Shares in green circle are selected after the second conflict

**Fig. 3.** 4-of-6 replicated secret reconstruction.

Figure 3 shows an example of 4-of-6 replicated secret reconstruction that the reconstruct parties are $\{P_1, P_2, P_4, P_6\}$, The conflict party of maximum party $P_6$ is $P_2$, so they choose their first different share $s_4^1$ and $s_4^2$. The rest reconstruct parties $\{P_1, P_4\}$ call 2-of-4 secret reconstruction, where share holders are $\{P_1, P_3, P_4, P_5\}$, as $P_2$ and $P_4$ are excluded. In recursion 2-of-4 called by 4-of-6 secret reconstruction, the conflict party of maximum party $P_4$ is $P_1$, so they choose their first different share $s_5^1$ and $s_5^2$. Because $s_5^1 + s_5^2 = s - s_4^1 - s_4^2$ holds during share generation, it is obviously that four shares selected can reconstruct the secret $s$.

---

**Algorithm 5.** Rec_tofn($vparty$, $recparty$, $reclevel$, $recid$, $vshare[recid]$)

---

**Input:** $vparty$, $recparty$, $reclevel$, $recid$, $vshare[recid]$.
**Output:** The share that used to reconstruct the secret .
1: Set threshold $t$=sizeof($recparty$)
2: **if** $t==2$ **then**
3:    Rec_2ofn($vparty$, $recparty$, $reclevel$, $recid$, $vshare[recid]$)
4: **else if** $t==3$ **then**
5:    Rec_3ofn($vparty$, $recparty$, $reclevel$, $recid$, $vshare[recid]$)
6: **else**
7:    **while** True **do**
8:       **if** $recparty[t] == party[t]$ **then**
9:          Output 2-tuple.$sharevalue$ if 2-tuple.$sharelevel = reclevel$.
10:       **else**
11:          Generate an array $ind$ containing $t$ parameters indicating the indexes of $t$ reconstruct parties in $vparty$, compute $conflict = vparty[ind[t] - t]$.
12:          **if** $conflict$ **in** $recparty$ **then**
13:             Set $reclevel=\mathcal{F}_{maxlevel}(t, recparty[t] - 1)+1$.
14:             **if** $recid == conflict$ or $recid == recparty[t]$ **then**
15:                Output 2-tuple.$sharevalue$ if 2-tuple.$sharelevel = reclevel$.
16:             **else**
17:                Remove id $recparty[t]$ and $conflict$ from $vparty$ and $recparty$.
18:                Rec_tofn($vparty$, $recparty$, $reclevel$, $recid$, $vshare[recid]$)
19:             **end if**
20:          **else**
21:             Replace id $recparty[t]$ with id $conflict$ in $recparty$.
22:             Sort ids of $recparty$ in ascending order, and refresh $ind$.
23:             If $recid = recparty[t]$, set $rectid = conflict$.
24:          **end if**
25:       **end if**
26:    **end while**
27: **end if**

---

More specifically, we describe our $t$-of-$n$ secret reconstruction Rec_tofn in Algorithm 5, which is executed by each reconstruct party independently. We define the following parameters:

- $vparty$: an array containing ids of all parties (share holders) in ascending order.

- *recparty*: an array containing reconstruct party ids in ascending order.
- *ind*: an array containing indexes of $t$ reconstruct parties in *vparty*. Conflict id of maximum reconstruct party $recparty[t]$ is $vparty[ind[t] - t]$.
- *reclevel*: an integer, when two reconstruct parties are in conflict, they will choose shares whose *sharelevel* is equal to *reclevel* to reconstruct the secret. Furthermore, suppose $id_1$ is conflict with $id_2$, they will choose their first different share which is generated after $t$-of-$(id_2 - 1)$ RSS. Since maximum *sharelevel* of $t$-of-$(id_2 - 1)$ RSS is $\mathcal{F}_{maxlevel}(t, id_2 - 1)$, *reclevel* is set to $\mathcal{F}_{maxlevel}(t, id_2 - 1) + 1$. *reclevel* is initialized to 1.
- *recid*: an id of reconstruct party who executes secret reconstruction algorithm. $P_{recid}$ holds $vshare[recid]$ as its own shares, which is the input of secret reconstruction algorithm.

The 3-of-$n$ replicated secret reconstruction Rec_3ofn called in Rec_tofn follows inverse intuition of Shr_3ofn, which is similar to 2-of-$n$ RSS. Three reconstruct ids are $id_1$, $id_2$, $id_3$ where $id_1 < id_2 < id_3$. Firstly reconstruct parties computing conflict id of maximum party $P_{id_3}$ as $conflict = id_3 - 3$. If $conflict$ is equal to $id_1$ or $id_2$, reconstruct parties use the $(id_3 - 2)$th share to reconstruct the secret. If $conflict$ is not equal to $id_1$ or $id_2$, replace $id_3$ with id $conflict$ and rearrange three reconstruct ids in ascending order, and find new maximum id of them. Then execute the above operations for three reconstruct ids in a loop and stop until any two of three reconstruct parties are in conflict or maximum id is 3, then reconstruct parties choose the first share if maximum id is 3. Considering the parameter compatibility when Rec_3ofn and Rec_2ofn are called in Rec_tofn, it is necessary to introduce parameters *sharelevel*, *reclevel*, *vparty*, etc. based on 3-of-$n$ and 2-of-$n$ secret reconstruction we described before.

**Security Analysis.** Our $t$-of-$n$ RSS is a semi-honest scheme, privacy will be violated if less than $t$ parties can reconstruct the secret. During share generation, dealer generates multiple independent sets of shares, and each set contains $t$ shares whose sum is the secret $s$. Since each party only holds at most one share in the same set in our scheme, less than $t$ parties cannot reconstruct the secret, thus privacy is guaranteed.

## 5  Related Work

Existing solutions have some inherent flaws, such as huge storage overhead, poor computational overhead and fixed little threshold.

**Storage Inefficient RSS.** ISN [18] realizes $t$-of-$n$ replicated additive secret sharing with each party holding $C_{n-1}^{t-1}$ shares, which causes huge storage overhead. CT12 [8] presents a scheme for the evolving 2-threshold access structure in which the share size of party $t$ is linear in $t$. KNY16 [20] designs a secret sharing for the evolving 2-threshold access structure and an $l$-bit secret in which the share size of party $t$ is $logt + (l + 1)loglogt + 4l + 1$ bits. The storage overheads of CT12 and KNY16 are unbalanced, and the share size held by the party with a larger id is much larger than that of the party with a smaller id.

**Computational Inefficient RSS.** CDI [13] and KCI [19] achieve threshold additive secret sharing by converting Shamir secret share into additive secret share. The share conversion process needs to calculate Lagrange interpolation, which brings huge computational overhead. DKLs18 [15] and DKLs19 [16] are two threshold schemes that convert Shamir secret shares of private key into additive secret shares, and then combine additive secret sharing and oblivious transfer to accomplish threshold signature.

**RSS with a Fixed Threshold.** AFL [1,17] follows the share generating method of ISN to design a 2-of-3 MPC protocol, then TYAO [17] adapts AFL to a fully malicious case. Besides, ABY3 [26] and Sharemind [6] are 2-of-3 MPC schemes based on 2-of-3 replicated secret sharing. In these 2-of-3 MPC schemes based on replicated additive secret sharing, each party holds 2 shares. There are also some schemes [10,24,26,29] applied in PPML that only realize RSS with a fixed small threshold $t$ and a fixed number of parties $n$, such as 2-of-3 or 2-of-4 RSS.

From the perspective of extendibility, some existing replicated additive secret sharing schemes [10,11,18,26,29] split the secret into one share set, and each party holds multiple shares of the set. PrivPy [24] is sightly different from the previous schemes, which splits the secret into multiple sets of shares, and each party holds one share of each share set.

# 6   Evaluation

We evaluate the storage and computational overhead of our scheme. Our storage efficiency is up to two orders of magnitude faster than the best prior work, and the online runtime of the protocol is in the microsecond level. We test replicated share generation (offline) executed by the dealer, and replicated secret reconstruction (online) executed by reconstruct party. In order to measure performance, we implement a prototype in C++. We run single-threaded simulations on Ubuntu 18.04 with an Intel Xeon(R) Silver 4216 CPU 2.10 GHz, with 32 GB of RAM.

## 6.1   Storage Cost

**Table 1.** Comparision of threshold and storage.

| Algorithm | Threshold | Storage(bits) |
|-----------|-----------|---------------|
| ABY3 [26],etc | 2-of-3 | $2l$ |
| PrivPy [24] | 2-of-4 | $2l$ |
| ISN [18] | $t$-of-$n$ | $C_{n-1}^{t-1} \cdot l$ |
| Our Shr_2ofn | 2-of-$n$ | $\lceil log_2 n \rceil \cdot l$ |
| Our Shr_3ofn | 3-of-$n$ | $(n-2) \cdot l$ |
| Our Shr_tofn | $t$-of-$n$ | $\leq \mathcal{F}_{maxlevel}(t,n) \cdot (l+\sigma)$ |

We compare the storage overhead of our Shr_2ofn, Shr_3ofn, Shr_tofn with existing schemes in Table 1, where the length of *sharevalue*, *sharelevel* is $l$, $\sigma$ bits respectively. The existing schemes [1,6,10,17,24,26,29] realize 2-of-3, 2-of-4 RSS by having each party hold 2 shares. Our Shr_2ofn (Shr_3ofn) replicated share generation expands the number of parties to an arbitrary $n$ by having each party hold $\lceil log_2 n \rceil$ shares ($(n-2)$ shares). Our scheme obtains the same storage cost as existing schemes when $n$ is 3 or 4.

In our replicated share generation Shr_tofn, the number of shares held by distinct parties is different. The maximum number of shares held by a party is $\mathcal{F}_{maxlevel}(t, n)$, which is described in Algorithm 3. Each party not only stores the shares, but also stores their corresponding *sharelevel*. Therefore, the party who holds the most shares needs to store $\mathcal{F}_{maxlevel}(t, n) \cdot (l + \sigma)$ bits. In order to compare the storage overhead with ISN intuitively, we set $l$ as 64 like most schemes (i.e., ABY3, PrivPy), and set $\sigma$ as 32, which is much larger than the size of the maximum *sharelevel* in most cases (i.e., the length of *sharelevel* of 4-of-60 or 5-of-60 is only 10 or 12 respectively). We test the cases when $t$ is 4 and $n$ ranges from 10 to 50, and depict storage comparison in Fig. 4. The result shows our storage efficiency is up to two orders of magnitude faster than ISN. When we increase $t$, the storage gap between ISN and our Shr_tofn will be larger.

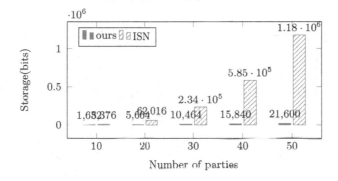

**Fig. 4.** Storage comparison between our Shr_tofn and ISN.

## 6.2   Computational Cost

**Table 2.** Runtime of share generation executed by the dealer(ms).

|         | $n = 10$ | $n = 20$ | $n = 30$ | $n = 40$ | $n = 50$ | $n = 60$ |
|---------|----------|----------|----------|----------|----------|----------|
| $t = 2$ | 0.03 | 0.04 | 0.06 | 0.07 | 0.08 | 0.09 |
| $t = 3$ | 0.03 | 0.08 | 0.12 | 0.21 | 0.28 | 0.36 |
| $t = 4$ | 0.06 | 0.21 | 0.46 | 0.82 | 1.17 | 1.63 |
| $t = 5$ | 0.06 | 0.42 | 1.24 | 2.60 | 4.50 | 7.60 |
| ... |  |  |  |  |  |  |
| $t = 9$ | 0.02 | 4.31 | 77.19 | 694.21 | $3 \times 10^3$ | $16 \times 10^3$ |
| $t = 10$ | 0.01 | 8.04 | 535.02 | $11 \times 10^3$ | $103 \times 10^3$ | $103 \times 10^3$ |

Runtime of replicated share generation is shown in Table 2. Only millisecond generation time is required when $t$ is 2 or 3, while runtime explodes when both $t$ and $n$ are large, for example, runtime of 10-of-60 share generation is 10 min. In fact, other schemes [13,18] also incur huge overhead when $t$ and $n$ are large.

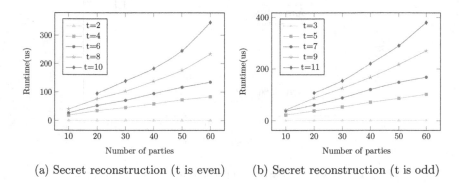

(a) Secret reconstruction (t is even)      (b) Secret reconstruction (t is odd)

**Fig. 5.** Runtime of secret reconstruction executed by reconstruct party.

Runtime of replicated secret reconstruction is plotted in Fig. 5. We test runtime of selecting the correct share, excluding exchanging ids among reconstruct parties and adding shares to reconstruct the secret. Runtime of exchanging ids depends on network performance and adding shares is fast so it can be ignored. We test the runtime in two cases: Rec_tofn will call Rec_2ofn if $t$ is even, and call Rec_3ofn if $t$ is odd. Runtime of distinct reconstruct subsets are different, so we test a large number of distinct subsets and finally take the average. It only takes 1 or 2 microsecond (us) for each party to select the correct share when $t$ is 2 or 3, and only 400 us selection time is required in 10-of-60 secret reconstruction.

# 7   Conclusion

In this paper, we first propose a 2-of-$n$ RSS scheme including a share generation algorithm, which generates shares incrementally and a secret reconstruction algorithm, which follows inverse intuition of share generation. Our 2-of-$n$ scheme is theoretically proved to achieve the optimal number of shares in 2-of-$n$ RSS. Then we design a more general $t$-of-$n$ RSS based on our 2-of-$n$ RSS, which supports an arbitrary threshold. It achieves a far better storage performance than existing schemes by making each share capable of reconstructing the secret in more subsets of parties. Since our RSS scheme generates shares in an incremental way, it realizes a extendibility that existing shares should not be changed when a new party joins in RSS. However, our RSS scheme can only compute addition operations in MPC, not multiplication operations in MPC. In the future, we will combine our RSS scheme with oblivious transfer to realize threshold multiplication operation in MPC, which can be directly applied in practical scenarios such as privacy-preserving machine learning and threshold signature.

# References

1. Araki, T., Furukawa, J., Lindell, Y., Nof, A., Ohara, K.: High-throughput semi-honest secure three-party computation with an honest majority. In: Proceedings of the 2016 ACM SIGSAC Conference on Computer and Communications Security, pp. 805–817 (2016)
2. Bar-Ilan, J., Beaver, D.: Non-cryptographic fault-tolerant computing in constant number of rounds of interaction. In: Proceedings of the eighth annual ACM Symposium on Principles of Distributed Computing, pp. 201–209 (1989)
3. Beaver, D.: Efficient multiparty protocols using circuit randomization. In: Feigenbaum, J. (ed.) CRYPTO 1991. LNCS, vol. 576, pp. 420–432. Springer, Heidelberg (1992). https://doi.org/10.1007/3-540-46766-1_34
4. Blakley, G.R.: Safeguarding cryptographic keys. In: Managing Requirements Knowledge, International Workshop on, pp. 313–313. IEEE Computer Society (1979)
5. Blakley, G.R., Meadows, C.: Security of ramp schemes. In: Blakley, G.R., Chaum, D. (eds.) CRYPTO 1984. LNCS, vol. 196, pp. 242–268. Springer, Heidelberg (1985). https://doi.org/10.1007/3-540-39568-7_20
6. Bogdanov, D., Laur, S., Willemson, J.: Sharemind: a framework for fast privacy-preserving computations. In: Jajodia, S., Lopez, J. (eds.) ESORICS 2008. LNCS, vol. 5283, pp. 192–206. Springer, Heidelberg (2008). https://doi.org/10.1007/978-3-540-88313-5_13
7. Brakerski, Z., Gentry, C., Vaikuntanathan, V.: (leveled) fully homomorphic encryption without bootstrapping. ACM Trans. Comput. Theor. (TOCT) 6(3), 1–36 (2014)
8. Cachin, C.: On-line secret sharing. In: Boyd, C. (ed.) Cryptography and Coding 1995. LNCS, vol. 1025, pp. 190–198. Springer, Heidelberg (1995). https://doi.org/10.1007/3-540-60693-9_22
9. Castagnos, G., Catalano, D., Laguillaumie, F., Savasta, F., Tucker, I.: Bandwidth-efficient threshold EC-DSA. In: Kiayias, A., Kohlweiss, M., Wallden, P., Zikas, V. (eds.) PKC 2020. LNCS, vol. 12111, pp. 266–296. Springer, Cham (2020). https://doi.org/10.1007/978-3-030-45388-6_10

10. Chaudhari, H., Choudhury, A., Patra, A., Suresh, A.: Astra: high throughput 3pc over rings with application to secure prediction. In: Proceedings of the 2019 ACM SIGSAC Conference on Cloud Computing Security Workshop, pp. 81–92 (2019)

11. Chaudhari, H., Rachuri, R., Suresh, A.: Trident: efficient 4pc framework for privacy preserving machine learning. arXiv preprint arXiv:1912.02631 (2019)

12. Cheon, J.H., Kim, A., Kim, M., Song, Y.: Homomorphic encryption for arithmetic of approximate numbers. In: Takagi, T., Peyrin, T. (eds.) ASIACRYPT 2017. LNCS, vol. 10624, pp. 409–437. Springer, Cham (2017). https://doi.org/10.1007/978-3-319-70694-8_15

13. Cramer, R., Damgård, I., Ishai, Y.: Share conversion, pseudorandom secret-sharing and applications to secure computation. In: Kilian, J. (ed.) TCC 2005. LNCS, vol. 3378, pp. 342–362. Springer, Heidelberg (2005). https://doi.org/10.1007/978-3-540-30576-7_19

14. Dalskov, A., Orlandi, C., Keller, M., Shrishak, K., Shulman, H.: Securing DNSSEC keys via threshold ECDSA from generic MPC. In: Chen, L., Li, N., Liang, K., Schneider, S. (eds.) ESORICS 2020. LNCS, vol. 12309, pp. 654–673. Springer, Cham (2020). https://doi.org/10.1007/978-3-030-59013-0_32

15. Doerner, J., Kondi, Y., Lee, E., Shelat, A.: Secure two-party threshold ECDSA from ECDSA assumptions. In: 2018 IEEE Symposium on Security and Privacy (SP), pp. 980–997. IEEE (2018)

16. Doerner, J., Kondi, Y., Lee, E., Shelat, A.: Threshold ECDSA from ECDSA assumptions: the multiparty case. In: 2019 IEEE Symposium on Security and Privacy (SP), pp. 1051–1066. IEEE (2019)

17. Furukawa, J., Lindell, Y., Nof, A., Weinstein, O.: High-throughput secure three-party computation for malicious adversaries and an honest majority. In: Coron, J.-S., Nielsen, J.B. (eds.) EUROCRYPT 2017. LNCS, vol. 10211, pp. 225–255. Springer, Cham (2017). https://doi.org/10.1007/978-3-319-56614-6_8

18. Ito, M., Saito, A., Nishizeki, T.: Secret sharing scheme realizing general access structure. Electr. Commun. Japan (Part III: Fundamental Electronic Science) 72(9), 56–64 (1989)

19. Kikuchi, R., Chida, K., Ikarashi, D., Ogata, W., Hamada, K., Takahashi, K.: Secret sharing with share-conversion: Achieving small share-size and extendibility to multiparty computation. IEICE Trans. Fundam. Electron. Commun. Comput. Sci. 98(1), 213–222 (2015)

20. Komargodski, I., Naor, M., Yogev, E.: How to share a secret, infinitely. In: Hirt, M., Smith, A. (eds.) TCC 2016. LNCS, vol. 9986, pp. 485–514. Springer, Heidelberg (2016). https://doi.org/10.1007/978-3-662-53644-5_19

21. Kondi, Y., Magri, B., Orlandi, C., Shlomovits, O.: Refresh when you wake up: proactive threshold wallets with offline devices. In: 2021 IEEE Symposium on Security and Privacy (SP), pp. 608–625. IEEE (2021)

22. Koti, N., Pancholi, M., Patra, A., Suresh, A.: {SWIFT}: Super-fast and robust {Privacy-Preserving} machine learning. In: 30th USENIX Security Symposium (USENIX Security 21), pp. 2651–2668 (2021)

23. Kumar, N., Rathee, M., Chandran, N., Gupta, D., Rastogi, A., Sharma, R.: Cryptflow: secure tensorflow inference. In: 2020 IEEE Symposium on Security and Privacy (SP), pp. 336–353. IEEE (2020)

24. Li, Y., Xu, W.: Privpy: general and scalable privacy-preserving data mining. In: Proceedings of the 25th ACM SIGKDD International Conference on Knowledge Discovery & Data Mining, pp. 1299–1307 (2019)

25. Mishra, P., Lehmkuhl, R., Srinivasan, A., Zheng, W., Popa, R.A.: Delphi: A cryptographic inference service for neural networks. In: 29th USENIX Security Symposium (USENIX Security 20), pp. 2505–2522 (2020)
26. Mohassel, P., Rindal, P.: Aby3: A mixed protocol framework for machine learning. In: Proceedings of the 2018 ACM SIGSAC Conference on Computer and Communications Security, pp. 35–52 (2018)
27. Mohassel, P., Rosulek, M., Zhang, Y.: Fast and secure three-party computation: the garbled circuit approach. In: Proceedings of the 22nd ACM SIGSAC Conference on Computer and Communications Security, pp. 591–602 (2015)
28. Ohara, K., Watanabe, Y., Iwamoto, M., Ohta, K.: Multi-party computation for modular exponentiation based on replicated secret sharing. IEICE Trans. Fund. Electron. Commun. Comput. Sci. **102**(9), 1079–1090 (2019)
29. Patra, A., Suresh, A.: Blaze: blazing fast privacy-preserving machine learning. arXiv preprint arXiv:2005.09042 (2020)
30. Poddar, R., Kalra, S., Yanai, A., Deng, R., Popa, R.A., Hellerstein, J.M.: Senate: a {Maliciously-Secure}{MPC} platform for collaborative analytics. In: 30th USENIX Security Symposium (USENIX Security 21), pp. 2129–2146 (2021)
31. Shamir, A.: How to share a secret. Commun. ACM **22**(11), 612–613 (1979)
32. Wagh, S., Gupta, D., Chandran, N.: Securenn: efficient and private neural network training. Cryptology ePrint Archive (2018)
33. Yang, K., Weng, C., Lan, X., Zhang, J., Wang, X.: Ferret: fast extension for correlated OT with small communication. In: Proceedings of the 2020 ACM SIGSAC Conference on Computer and Communications Security. pp. 1607–1626 (2020)
34. Yao, A.C.C.: How to generate and exchange secrets. In: 27th Annual Symposium on Foundations of Computer Science (sfcs 1986), pp. 162–167. IEEE (1986)

# Generic 2-Party PFE with Constant Rounds and Linear Active Security, and Efficient Instantiation

Hanyu Jia[1,2], Xiangxue Li[1,3(✉)], Qiang Li[4], Yue Bao[5], and Xintian Hou[5]

[1] School of Software Engineering, East China Normal University,
Shanghai 200062, China
xxli@cs.ecnu.edu.cn

[2] Shanghai Key Laboratory of Privacy-Preserving Computation,
MatrixElements Technologies, Shanghai 201204, China

[3] Shanghai Key Laboratory of Trustworthy Computing, Shanghai 200062, China

[4] Institute of Cyber Science and Technology, Shanghai Jiaotong University,
Shanghai 200240, China
qiangl@sjtu.edu.cn

[5] CATARC Software Testing (Tianjin) Co., Ltd., Tianjin 300300, China
{baoyue,houxintian}@catarc.ac.cn

**Abstract.** The paper considers generic construction of 2-party private function evaluation (PFE) in the malicious adversary model. There is hitherto only one concrete design of actively secure 2-party PFE protocol (Liu et al. at PKC 2022, and LWY hereafter) with constant rounds and linear complexity. One interesting feature of LWY is its function reusability (i.e., the same function is involved in multiple executions of LWY) which makes its execution more efficiently from the second execution. Nevertheless, in its first execution (in particular for those settings where only one invocation of the function is required), LWY is quite involved and too inefficient to be of practical use. For these settings (of non-reusable private functions), we initiate a generic construction of 2-party PFE protocol with constant rounds and linear complexity in the malicious adversary model based on Yao's garbled circuit and singly homomorphic encryption. When instantiated with ElGamal encryption and Groth secret shuffle (J. Cryptology 2010), the generic construction effectuates a novel concrete design of 2-party PFE, which has better performance and reduces 51.2% communication bits and 52.4% computation costs, compared to LWY (in its first execution) at the same security level. It even outperforms several 2-party PFE protocols (Katz and Malka at AISACRYPT 2011, and Mohassel and Sadeghian at EUROCRYPT 2013) that are secure in the semi-honest adversary model from the communication perspective. The proposed PFE and LWY thus make optimal solutions available for non-reusable and reusable private functions, respectively.

**Keywords:** Private function evaluation · Active security · Two-party computation · Extended permutation

© ICST Institute for Computer Sciences, Social Informatics and Telecommunications Engineering 2023
Published by Springer Nature Switzerland AG 2023. All Rights Reserved
F. Li et al. (Eds.): SecureComm 2022, LNICST 462, pp. 390–410, 2023.
https://doi.org/10.1007/978-3-031-25538-0_21

# 1   Introduction

Secure multi-party computation (MPC) protocols allow a group of participants to perform a computation together without revealing the private input of any party [13,57]. Since its introduction by Yao in the 1980 s,s, MPC has evolved from a theoretical curiosity to an important tool for building large-scale privacy-preserving applications [3,10,12,15,16,25,43,51].

SFE AND PFE. There are two cases of MPC protocols, secure function evaluation (SFE) and private function evaluation (PFE), depending on whether the functions involved in the computation are public/private. In SFE, the function $f(\cdots)$ (multi-variable) is not private knowledge of any participant, but an open function that all the parties agree to compute. Suppose there are $n$ parties $P_1, \cdots, P_n$ and $P_i$ has private data $x_i$. At the end of SFE, $n$ parties are given $f(x_1, \cdots, x_n)$, but any $P_i$'s private data $x_i$ is not disclosed to any other parties. Many SFE protocols rely on translating $f$ into a Boolean or arithmetic circuit $\mathcal{C}_f$. For example, Yao's garbled circuit (GC) [37,58] and GESS [32] are applicable to 2-party computation. Multi-party computation protocols include GMW [20], BGW [7], and BMR [5], and computation rounds of GMW and BGW are linear with the circuit depth, and BMR is constant-round. In PFE, the function $f(\cdots)$ is private knowledge of one of the parties, who cooperates with data owners $P_1, \cdots, P_n$ (holding private $x_i$, respectively) to jointly compute $f(x_1, \cdots, x_n)$. At the end of PFE, the final result would be obtained while the private knowledge of each party is not disclosed. Existing PFE protocols are mainly based on translating private function $f$ into circuit $\mathcal{C}_f$ with $u$ input wires, $g$ gates, and $o$ output wires. Before executing PFE, function owner should open some parameters to data owners [9,27,29,30,42,46,48], such as the values of $u$, $g$, $o$ and some auxiliary parameters, as long as these public parameters would not help the adversaries learn the function $f$.

MPC SECURITY PROFILE. MPC security is generally divided into a semi-honest adversary model (for low security requirements, a.k.a. passive security model) and a malicious adversary model (for high security requirements, a.k.a. active security model) [13]. In the semi-honest adversary model, each corrupt party follows the prescribed protocol steps, except that he is curious (honest but curious) and tries to infer as much as possible other parties' private data from the transcripts. Therein, corrupt parties might collude with each other in an attempt to learn more knowledge. In the malicious adversary model, corrupt parties can deviate from the protocol arbitrarily. Besides the ability in the semi-honest adversary model, these corrupt parties can also take any action during the protocol execution. An actively secure PFE can detect the behavior of corrupt parties and eventually abort the protocol or kick out them to continue the protocol. The paper concentrates on actively secure PFE. Actively secure SFE [14,28,35,36,39,54] has been well studied, and relatively less attention is paid to actively secure PFE [29,42,48] besides UC-based designs.

GENERIC PFE: UC-BASED. Valiant proposes universal circuit (UC) to achieve PFE. UC can be programmed (letting $p_c$ be control bits) to encode any circuit

$C_f$ that needs to be protected [55]. Then UC could be public and $p_c$ is private to function owner. Now the problem of computing $C_f(x)$ from private circuit $C_f$ (of function owner) and private data $x$ (of data owner) is transformed into computing $UC(x, p_c)$ via SFE protocols. That is, we gain a technical routine of reducing PFE to SFE by securely computing publicly available universal circuits [1,26,31,34,40,41,55,60]. One may thereby attempt to optimize UC as the smaller the size of the constructed UC, the smaller the consumption required in SFE. The best asymptotic size of Valiant's UC is $12g \cdot \log g$ ($g$ is the number of gates in $C_f$) by Liu et al. [41] and seems to reach theoretical optimum. UC-based PFE designs (either passively or actively secure) would thereby comply with the logarithmic factor in the complexity of $\mathcal{O}(g \cdot \log g)$.

GENERIC PFE: BEYOND UC-BASED. Katz and Malka [30] present a specific 2-party PFE protocol (KM hereafter) with linear complexity $\mathcal{O}(g)$ from Yao's GC and singly homomorphic encryption (HE) in the semi-honest adversary model. Later, Mohassel and Sadeghian show a general framework (MS hereafter) of PFE in the semi-honest adversary model [46]. MS is divided into two subprotocols, oblivious extended permutation (OEP) and private gate evaluation (PGE). OEP hides the topology of the circuit and protects the relationship between individual gates. PGE is a private computation of individual gates, and the computation of the circuit $C_f$ is completed after computing $g$ gates one by one. OEP based on oblivious switched network design [47] can build PFE protocols with complexity $\mathcal{O}(g \cdot \log g)$, while OEP based on HE can build PFE protocols with complexity $\mathcal{O}(g)$. Mohassel et al. [48] further describe a generic framework of PFE with linear complexity in the malicious adversary model based on the framework MS [46]. Technical tools used therein include one-time MAC for checking data consistency and actively secure SFE for data distribution and reconstruction. In addition, the zero-knowledge proof protocol $\mathcal{ZK}_{EP}$ with $\mathcal{O}(g)$ complexity proves to data owner that function owner performs correct extended permutation (EP, see Definition 1). $\mathcal{ZK}_{EP}$ is the first zero-knowledge protocol with linear complexity proving correct EP operation, and it is a general framework but constructed with redundant computations. Jia and Li [29] propose a more succinct double shuffle protocol ($\mathcal{ZK}_{DS}$) to prove the correctness of EP operations, which is constructed more light-weight and retains the generic feature of $\mathcal{ZK}_{EP}$. In addition, they also construct [29] a general-purpose PFE framework with $\mathcal{O}(g)$ complexity based on $\mathcal{ZK}_{DS}$ for better efficiency in the malicious adversary model.

DDH-BASED CONCRETE PFE WITH FUNCTION REUSABILITY. Bicer et al. [9] propose a 2-party PFE protocol based on decisional Diffie-Hellman (DDH) assumption with linear complexity and function reusability in the semi-honest adversary model. Liu et al. [42] propose a specific zero-knowledge protocol for proving correct EP operation and transforming the 2-party PFE [9] with passive security to that with active security (LWY hereafter). Function reusability says that the same function could be invoked multiple times (for different data each time) so that protocol executions become more efficient from the second execution[1]. The more times of protocol being executed, the smaller of the aver-

---

[1] The overhead required due to the EP operation on the function is no longer needed from the second execution, which accounts for the major part of the total overhead.

age overhead will be. For detailed protocol design, we refer the readers to the original paper [9, 42].

**Table 1.** *PFE protocols with linear complexity $O(g)$.*

| PFE | Security | Parties | Round | Reusable |
|-----|----------|---------|-------|----------|
| [30] | Semi-honest | Two | Constant | No |
| [46] | Semi-honest | Multi & Two | Constant | No |
| [9] | Semi-honest | Two | Constant | Yes |
| [48] | Malicious | Multi | #Gates | No |
| [42] | Malicious | Two | Constant | Yes |
| [29] | Malicious | Multi | #Gates | No |

For ease of understanding, we list in Table 1 main PFE protocols with linear complexity.

### 1.1  Motivations

Consider 2-party PFE with constant rounds, linear complexity, and active security. Constructing actively secure PFE can be viewed as two divisions, one is to construct a passively secure PFE and another is to construct an efficient primitive proving to data owners that function owner correctly performs EP operation. The latter could be solved using the approach of zero-knowledge protocols [29, 42, 48]. There is hitherto only one concrete design (i.e., LWY) of actively secure 2-party PFE with constant rounds and linear complexity. One interesting feature of LWY is its function reusability. Nevertheless, in its first execution (in particular for those settings where only one invocation of the function is required), LWY is quite involved and too inefficient to be of practical use.

We note that privacy-preserving machine learning is a good solution to protecting both private models and sensitive data [8, 19, 44, 45, 56]. In this regard, the concrete PFE construction [42] with function reusability property could find its position in privacy-preserving inference. For privacy-preserving training however, the model parameters are updated continuously during the training process and now we confront intrinsically a series of non-reusable private functions. It naturally raises the following question:

*Can we pursue a generic 2-party PFE with constant rounds and linear active security for non-reusable private functions, whose instantiations might achieve less computation and communication consumption (compared to the first execution of LWY)?*

In this paper, we present a positive answer to the question. Next we start with some preparatory knowledge which inspire our constructions.

TWO-PARTY PFE PROTOCOL KM [30]. We briefly describe how KM works in the semi-honest adversary model. KM is based on Yao's GC and singly homomorphic encryption and we assume that the readers are familiar with GC. First, function owner ($P_1$) translates his private function $f$ into a circuit $C_f$ which has $u$ input wires, $g$ NAND gates and $o$ output wires (see Fig. 1). Each of these NAND gates is two fan-in and any fan-out. Let the $u$ input wires of $C_f$ and the output wires of the $g - o$ non-output gates be called outgoing wires, and the input wires of the $g$ gates be called incoming wires. Data owner ($P_2$) holds private data $x \in \{0, 1\}^u$. $P_2$ generates public-private key pair $(pk, sk)$ for singly homomorphic encryption (e.g., ElGamal encryption) and sends $pk$ to $P_1$. In addition, $P_2$ generates $u + g$ pairs of random wire keys, $(s_i^0, s_i^1)$ representing bits 0 and 1, respectively. $P_2$ encrypts the first $u + g - o$ pairs wire keys with $pk$

$$[Enc_{pk}(s_1^0), Enc_{pk}(s_1^1)], \cdots, [Enc_{pk}(s_{u+g-o}^0), Enc_{pk}(s_{u+g-o}^1)] \qquad (1)$$

and sends the ciphertexts to $P_1$. In Eq. (1), the first $u$ ciphertext pairs correspond to the wire keys of $u$ input wires of $C_f$ and the last $g - o$ ciphertext pairs correspond to the wire keys of output wires of non-output gates. $P_1$ knows the topology of $C_f$ and can extend $u + g - o$ ciphertext pairs to $2g$ ciphertext pairs by EP. These $2g$ pairs represent the wire keys of input wires of all gates. $P_1$ chooses $a_i, b_i, a_i'$, and $b_i'$, $i \in \{1, \cdots, g\}$, uniformly at random from appropriate domain, and encrypts them under $pk$. Then the $2g$ ciphertext pairs could be re-randomized due to the homomorphic property. For each gate $i \in \{1, \cdots, g\}$ of $C_f$, suppose that its left incoming wire is connected with some outgoing wire $l$ (of some preceding gate) and right incoming wire is connected with some outgoing wire $r$ (of some preceding gate). $P_1$ computes

$$\begin{aligned} &[Enc_{pk}(a_i \cdot s_l^0 + b_i), Enc_{pk}(a_i \cdot s_l^1 + b_i)] \\ &[Enc_{pk}(a_i' \cdot s_r^0 + b_i'), Enc_{pk}(a_i' \cdot s_r^1 + b_i')] \end{aligned} \qquad (2)$$

Finally, the re-randomized ciphertexts are returned to $P_2$, who can decrypt them to recover new wire keys representing input wires of each gate. The wire keys for output wires of each gate are generated by himself, so $P_2$ can create garbled tables. At this point, $P_2$ has the ability to perform GC protocol with $P_1$. $P_1$ knows the topology of $C_f$ and the random values in the re-randomization, so he has the ability to act as an evaluator and eventually gets the $o$ wire keys representing the output wires of $C_f$. $P_2$ receives these $o$ wire keys and obtains the result of $f(x)$.

THE DESIGN OF $\mathcal{ZK}_{EP}$ [48]. $\mathcal{ZK}_{EP}$ is a generic zero-knowledge protocol to prove that EP is correctly executed. It consists of three components, Dummy Placement Phase, Replication Phase, and Permutation Phase. The number of inputs (input size) in all three phases is $2g$. The first component is the shuffle operation, which takes as input $2g$ ElGamal ciphertexts, including $u + g - o$ wire keys on outgoing wires generated by $P_2$ and $g - u + o$ dummy values known to both. $P_1$ then performs shuffle and re-randomization, proving the correctness of his operation by using $\mathcal{ZK}_{shuffle}$ [17]. The second component is a copy operation whose inputs are the outputs of the first component. $P_1$ performs replication and re-randomization and uses $\mathcal{ZK}_{rep}$ [46] to prove the correctness of his operation. The third component takes as inputs the outputs of the second component, performs shuffle and re-randomization (not the same as the first one), and outputs

$2g$ ElGamal ciphertexts of the wire keys of the incoming wires. $P_1$ again proves to $P_2$ the correctness of his operation by $\mathcal{ZK}_{shuffle}$ [17]. $P_2$ believes that $P_1$ performs the correct EP if all three components are verified correctly.

THE DESIGN OF $\mathcal{ZK}_{DS}$ [29]. $\mathcal{ZK}_{DS}$ optimizes the $\mathcal{ZK}_{EP}$ protocol and consists of two succinct components, randomness-generating & outgoing-wires-determining (RG&OWD) and randomness-reusing & incoming-wires-determining (RR&IWD). In $\mathcal{ZK}_{DS}$, the inputs of RG&OWD are $u+g-o$ ElGamal ciphertexts of random wire keys provided by $P_2$. $P_1$ executes RG&OWD to generate $u + g - o$ new ElGamal ciphertexts of wire keys of outgoing wires, and proves that his execution is correct by $\mathcal{ZK}_{shuffle}$. $P_2$ receives a set $C$ of auxiliary parameters ($C$ does not disclose $C_f$) from $P_1$ before the protocol. Each element in $C$ tells how many times each random wire key[2] will be copied, and [29] proves that this does not decrease security. Then $P_1$ executes RR&IWD with the inputs being the ciphertexts of $2g$ random wire keys (generated by copying the inputs of RG&OWD according to $C$). Its outputs are $2g$ new ElGamal ciphertexts of the wire keys of incoming wires. $P_1$ uses $\mathcal{ZK}_{shuffle}$ to prove the correctness of his execution. Once these two components have been executed, $P_2$ gets the inputs and outputs of EP. Two $\mathcal{ZK}_{shuffle}$ executions suffice for $P_1$ to prove the correctness of EP.

## 1.2  Contributions

LWY is well suited for scenarios where private functions might be reused multiple times (for different private data). In its first execution (in particular for those settings where only one invocation of the function is required) however, LWY is quite involved and too inefficient to be of practical use. For these settings (non-reusable private functions), we initiate the first generic construction of 2-party PFE with constant rounds and linear complexity in the malicious adversary model.

By learning the above, one might perceive that $\mathcal{ZK}_{EP}$ (yet cumbersome) could be *directly* plugged into passively secure KM to produce an actively secure 2-party PFE. This will not work for $\mathcal{ZK}_{DS}$ due to its particular structure, however. We thus design a novel generic construction of 2-party PFE protocol that can exactly support the succinct structure of $\mathcal{ZK}_{DS}$ protocol. The resulting actively secure 2-party PFE is with constant rounds and linear complexity, and its instantiation has much less consumption of communication and computation. Any optimization of $\mathcal{ZK}_{shuffle}$ [4,11,17,21–24,50] would lead to performance improvement of $\mathcal{ZK}_{DS}$ (and surely of our PFE protocol). As an instantiation, we take the scheme in [22] as candidate $\mathcal{ZK}_{shuffle}$ in our 2-party PFE and $\mathcal{ZK}_{DS}$ would thereby require approximately $9g \cdot ||\mathbb{Z}_q||$[3] proof bits and $36g$ exponentiations to prove the EP of $C_f$. Together with ElGamal encryption, our instantiation of the proposed generic PFE construction has better performance and reduces 51.2% communication costs and 52.4% computation costs, respectively, compared to LWY (in its first execution) at the same security level. It

---

[2] Note that these random wire keys do not represent outgoing wires, but rather a shuffle and re-randomization with the outgoing wires.

[3] Usually $||\mathbb{Z}_q|| = 160$.

even outperforms passively secure KM [30] and MS [46] from the communication perspective.The proposed PFE and LWY thus make optimal solutions available for non-reusable and reusable private functions, respectively.

We provide in Sect. 3 detailed description of our 2-party PFE and in Sect. 4 detailed performance comparison.

## 2    Preliminaries

We denote the security parameter by $k$. $r \leftarrow_R \{0,1\}^k$ means that $r$ is a random number chosen uniformly at random from $\{0,1\}^k$. We use both bold and italic (lower-case or capital) letters to denote sets (e.g., $D$), and italic for values or elements in a set (e.g., $D_i$). For a set $S$, we denote the size of the set by $|S|$, and we write $S = \{S_i\}_{i=1}^{|S|}$. We use $\|\mathbb{G}\|$ to denote the bit length of a group element in the group $\mathbb{G}$. We use $s := s+r$ to denote reassigning a new value to element $s$. We denote a mapping function by $\pi$, e.g., $j = \pi(i)$ where $i$ is the preimage and $j$ is the corresponding image. We use $\pi_1$ and $\pi_2$ to denote bijective functions and $\pi_3$ a surjective function.

We use a singly homomorphic encryption scheme (Gen,Enc,Dec), whose plaintext space is $\mathbb{G}$ of prime order $q$. We then use $n$ to denote the security parameter of the homomorphic encryption scheme, i.e., $(pk, sk) \leftarrow \text{Gen}(1^n)$ denotes that a pair of public and private keys is generated. We want to encrypt the plaintext $m \in \{0,1\}^k$ and we can map $m$ to a group element in $\mathbb{G}$. For the convenience of representation, we directly use $c = \text{Enc}_{pk}(m)$ to denote encryption of plaintext $m$ into ciphertext $c$ with the public key pk. We use $m = \text{Dec}_{sk}(c)$ to denote decryption of ciphertext $c$ into plaintext $m$ with private key $sk$. Singly homomorphic encryption suitable for our protocol includes Elliptic curve (EC) ElGamal [18] and Paillier [52], etc. It is believed [27] that EC ElGamal encryption is more efficient to implement some known 2-party PFE protocols from GC [30]. We use EC ElGamal encryption as well, and for a detailed homomorphic addition step we suggest to read [[27] Sect. 4.3].

We also need a symmetric encryption scheme (sEnc, sDec) whose plaintext space and key space are both $k$-bits random numbers. Given a ciphertext $c = \text{sEnc}_{sk}(m)$ ($sk$ is the secret key in the symmetric cipher), we have $m = \text{sDec}_{sk}(c)$. The symmetric cipher would be used in our protocols to create standard Yao's GC for each garbled table (GT) and decrypt each GT. It is required [38] for (sEnc,sDec) that it has elusive and efficiently verifiable range. Additionally, we require that (sEnc,sDec) satisfies a weak form of related-key security, and the work of Applebaum et al. [2] can be used to construct a scheme that satisfies the security based on the decisional Diffie-Hellman assumption. Holz, Nissim et al. [27, Sect. 5.1] used an AES-128 encryption scheme [6] to construct the GC in the linear PFE protocol.

**Definition 1 (EP [46]).** *The inverse of $\pi_3$ is defined as an extended permutation function, i.e., $\pi_3^{-1}$. In the following, $|ow|$ elements would be copied and permuted to $|iw|$ elements, i.e., $ow_i = iw_{\pi_3^{-1}(i)}$.*

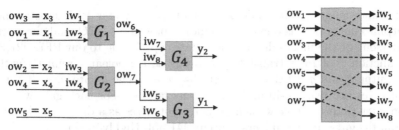

(a) A simple example circuit $C_f$ where $u = 5$, $g = 4$ and $o = 2$.

(b) EP relationship between $ow$ and $iw$ in $C_f$.

**Fig. 1.** A simple example of circuit $C_f$, and its corresponding EP relationship.

There are two players in our 2-party PFE protocol, function owner $P_1$ holding $f$ and data owner $P_2$ holding $x$. $P_1$ will privately translate the function $f$ into a Boolean circuit $C_f$ (see Fig. 1) with $u$ input wires, $g$ gates and $o$ output wires (in general, $u \approx o, u \ll g$). Let $N = u + g$ and $M = 2g$. Note that all the $g$ gates of $C_f$ in our protocol are NAND gates with two fan-in and more than one fan-out, so there is no need to hide the gate function. We declare that this is different from the standard Yao's GC protocol. The $C_f$ is like a directed acyclic graph, i.e., all the gates have topological order. We use $G = \{G_i\}_{i=1}^{g}$ to denote the $g$ gates that have been topologically sorted. We divide the $g$ gates into output and non-output gates according to the destination of each gate output wire, i.e., $\{G_i\}_{i=1}^{g-o}$ are non-output gates and $\{G_i\}_{i=g-o+1}^{g}$ are output gates. We refer to both the input wires of $C_f$ and the output wires of the non-output gates collectively as outgoing-wire (abbreviated as $ow$), and in addition refer to the input wires of all gates collectively as incoming-wire (abbreviated as $iw$). It is obvious that we can observe that $|ow| = N - o$, $|iw| = M$ and $|ow| \leq |iw|$. Since each gate of $C_f$ is the NAND gate, the problem of protecting the private function $f$ is transformed into the problem of protecting the EP relation from $ow$ to $iw$ ($iw_i = ow_{\pi_3(i)}$), i.e., $P_1$ hides the topological order of circuit $C_f$ from $P_2$. We decompose the EP problem ($\pi_3^{-1}$) into two permutation problems ($\pi_1$ and $\pi_2$).

## 3   Two-Party PFE with Linear Active Security

### 3.1   High-Level Description

Next, we describe our generic construction of actively secure 2-party PFE. We suppose the readers are familiar with Yao's GC. Our PFE has two parties, $P_1$ the function owner and $P_2$ the data owner. $P_1$ has private function $f(\cdot)$ (one-variable), and $P_2$ has private data $x$. In the original Yao's GC, function owner acts as the garbler of the circuit and data owner acts as the evaluator of the circuit. In our PFE however, they are assumed opposite roles, i.e., $P_2$ acts as the garbler of the circuit and $P_1$ acts as the evaluator of the circuit. The goal is that $P_1$ and $P_2$ cooperate to compute $y = f(x)$ (only disclosed to $P_2$), while $P_2$ cannot learn valid knowledge about $f$ and $P_1$ cannot learn $x$. Our PFE uses a singly homomorphic encryption as one of the building blocks. EC ElGamal encryption is currently one of the most effective candidates applicable to our PFE [27,30].

The function $f$ of $P_1$ is translated privately as a Boolean circuit $C_f$ with $u$ inputs, $o$ outputs and $g$ gates, and we let $N = u + g$. The $g$ gates are all NAND gates. All gates are two fan-in and can be any fan-out. For each gate with the fan-out greater than 1, we view each of its output wires as a different wire. This differs from the gates in the universal circuit [41,55]. Highly optimized hardware synthesis tools already exist for translating the function to Boolean circuits with a small number of (or optimized) NAND gates [27]. Since the output of each non-output NAND gate and the input of the circuit ($ow$) are used at least once in the circuit $C_f$, $P_1$ can compute a set $C$. $P_2$ has private data $x \in \{0,1\}^u$.

We view $u$, $o$, $g$ and $C$ as system parameters, which are not secret knowledge of $f$ and $x$, i.e., others can know these parameters but cannot recover $f$ and $x$ effectively. The topology of $C_f$ and $x$ should be only known to $P_1$ and $P_2$, respectively. In our protocol, $P_2$ does not know the topology of the circuit, so he cannot construct the garbled gates directly. Instead, we can take advantage of the property that the ciphertexts can be directly summed up in a homomorphic encryption: let $P_2$ provide $N$ - $o$ wire keys, encrypt these wire keys, and send the ciphertexts to $P_1$. According to the topology of the circuit, $P_1$ can perform permutation ($\pi_1$) and re-randomization on $N$ - $o$ ciphertexts to obtain new $N$ - $o$ ciphertexts about the $ow$, and then apply permutation ($\pi_2$) and re-randomization to the replication results of $N$ - $o$ ciphertexts to obtain new $2g$ ciphertexts about the $iw$. Note that the protocol here is different from KM protocol, where $P_2$ generates the wire keys about $ow$ directly. We say that $P_1$ constructs the encrypted garbled gate (abbreviated as $encGG_i$) for the $i$-th NAND gate in the circuit. By decrypting $encGG_i$, $P_2$ can obtain $3g$-$o$ new wire keys which can be used to create garbled tables. After $P_2$ gets $g$ $encGG$s, he can act as the garbler. As each wire key is re-randomized by $P_1$, $P_2$ cannot learn the topology of the circuit. We describe the protocol in detail below.

### 3.2   Specification

We decouple the PFE into three phases: the *offline* phase, the *initiation* phase, and the *evaluation* phase. Figure 2 shows the details.

**1) Offline Phase.** In this phase, $P_1$ translates the private function $f$ into a circuit $C_f$ and discloses the parameters $u$, $g$, $o$, and $C$. $P_2$ generates a public/private key pair ($pk,sk$) for a singly homomorphic encryption and discloses the public key $pk$. In addition, $P_2$ chooses uniformly $r_i \leftarrow_R \{0,1\}^k$, $i \in \{1,2\}$, where $k$ is the security parameter (say 128 [27]). These two random values would be used in creating the garbled tables.

Then, $P_2$ randomly generates a set of wire keys, $\boldsymbol{H} = \{h_i\}_{i=1}^N$. We assume that all the $N$ wire keys represent the bit value 0, which are written as $\boldsymbol{H}^0 = \{h_i^0\}_{i=1}^N$. Similarly, we use $\boldsymbol{H}^1 = \{h_i^1\}_{i=1}^N$ to represent the $N$ wire keys

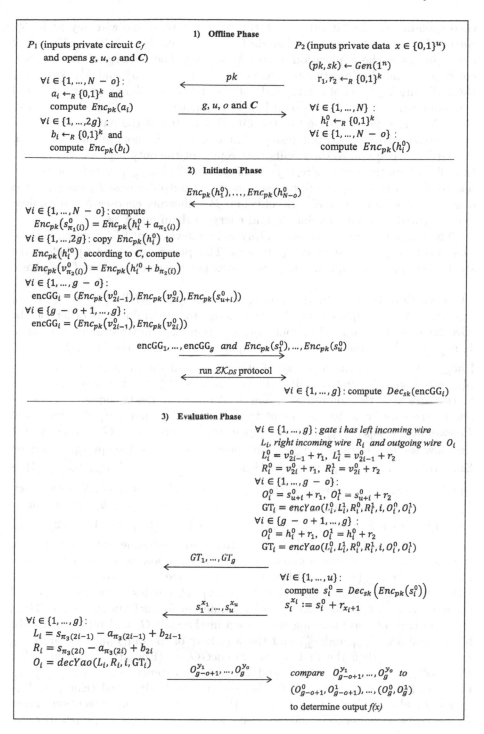

**Fig. 2.** Our 2-party PFE protocol. $\pi_3$ maps $2g$ incoming wires to $N-o$ outgoing wires.

corresponding to the bit value 1. Rather than sampling the wire key $h_i^1$ as $h_i^0$, we produce it by adding a global shift $r$ to $h_i^0$, i.e., $h_i^1 = h_i^0 + r$. This trick also appears in the application of *free-XOR* [33]. The security of Yao's protocol depends on the indistinguishability of the wire keys $h_i^0$ and $h_i^1$. Note that these $N$ wire keys do not correspond one-to-one[4] to the $N$-$o$ outgoing wires and $o$ output wires of $\mathcal{C}_f$. In the semi-honest adversary model [30], the first $u$ of these $N$ wire keys correspond to the bits that represent the data $x$, the next $g$ - $o$ correspond to the output results that represent the non-output gates, and the last $o$ correspond to the results that represent the output gates. We assume that $P_2$ selects the last $o$ wire keys in $\boldsymbol{H}^0$, i.e., $\{h_i^0\}_{i=N-o+1}^N$, which correspond one-to-one to the output results used for the $o$ output gates. $P_2$ encrypts the other $N$ - $o$ wire keys in $\boldsymbol{H}^0$. In addition, $P_1$ uniformly chooses $N$ - $o$ random values $a_i$ and $2g$ random values $b_i$ and encrypts them under $pk$.

The complexity of this phase is $\mathcal{O}(g)$ and we have about $\|\mathbb{G}\|$ communication bits and $8g$ exponentiation computations. This phase can be set up before the start of the protocol and thus one may freeze out the consumption of the phase.

**2) Initiation Phase.** In this phase, $P_2$ sends $\{\text{Enc}_{pk}(h_i^0)\}_{i=1}^{N-o}$ to $P_1$. Upon receiving $N - o$ ciphertexts, $P_1$ first needs to determine the order of the wire keys used for $\boldsymbol{ow}$. He applies permutation $(\pi_1)$ and re-randomization to $\{\text{Enc}_{pk}(h_i^0)\}_{i=1}^{N-o}$ to obtain $N$ - $o$ new ciphertexts $\text{Enc}_{pk}(s_i^0) = \text{Enc}_{pk}(h_{\pi_1^{-1}(i)}^0) + \text{Enc}_{pk}(a_i)$ based on the topology of the circuit and the property of homomorphic addition. The first $u$ plaintexts in $\{\text{Enc}_{pk}(s_i^0)\}_{i=1}^{N-o}$ correspond one-to-one to the wire keys that represent $x$. The next $g$ - $o$ plaintexts correspond one-to-one to the wire keys that represent the outputs of the non-output gates. Then $P_1$ extends $\{\text{Enc}_{pk}(h_i^0)\}_{i=1}^{N-o}$ to $2g$ ciphertexts according to $\boldsymbol{C}$ and we denote the new set as $\{\text{Enc}_{pk}(h_i'^0)\}_{i=1}^{2g}$. This process is a $(c_i$ - $1)$-copy operation on $\text{Enc}_{pk}(h_i^0)$, i.e., each ciphertext in $\{\text{Enc}_{pk}(h_{\sum_{j=1}^{i-1} c_j+1}'^0), \cdots, \text{Enc}_{pk}(h_{\sum_{j=1}^{i} c_j}'^0)\}$ is equal to $\text{Enc}_{pk}(h_i^0)$, where $c_i$ is the $i$-th value in $\boldsymbol{C}$, $i \in \{1, \cdots, N - o\}$. Next, $P_1$ applies permutation $(\pi_2)$ and re-randomization to $\text{Enc}_{pk}(h_j')$ to obtain $2g$ new ciphertexts $\text{Enc}_{pk}(v_j^0) = \text{Enc}_{pk}(h_{\pi_2^{-1}(j)}'^0) + \text{Enc}_{pk}(b_j)$, $j \in \{1, \cdots, 2g\}$. The plaintexts of these $2g$ new ciphertexts correspond one-to-one to the wire keys of the incoming wires of the $g$ gates that have been topologically sorted, i.e., the plaintexts of $\text{Enc}_{pk}(v_{2i-1})$ and $\text{Enc}_{pk}(v_{2i})$ correspond to the two wire keys of the $i$-th gate's two incoming wires, $i \in \{1, \cdots, g\}$. $P_1$ creates $g$ encrypted garbled gates $encGG_i$, where the first $g$ - $o$ have different forms from the last $o$. Thus, the wire keys of two incoming wires used in the gate $G_i$ and representing the bit value 0 are $v_{2i-1}^0$ and $v_{2i}^0$, and the wire keys of the outgoing wire are $s_{u+i}^0$, $i \in \{1, \cdots, g\}$, then the first $g$ - $o$ are $encGG_i = (\text{Enc}_{pk}(v_{2i-1}^0), \text{Enc}_{pk}(v_{2i}^0), \text{Enc}_{pk}(s_{u+i}^0))$ $(1 \le i \le g - o)$ and the last $o$ are $encGG_i = (\text{Enc}_{pk}(v_{2i-1}^0), \text{Enc}_{pk}(v_{2i}^0))$ $(g - o + 1 \le i \le g)$. $P_1$ then sends $\{encGG_i\}_{i=1}^g$ and $\{\text{Enc}_{pk}(s_i^0)\}_{i=1}^u$ to $P_2$. $P_1$ also applies $\mathcal{ZK}_{DS}$ to prove the correctness of his execution. Then, $P_2$ decrypts each $encGG_i$ and recovers the new wire keys in preparation for

---

[4] The *one-to-one* here means that the $i$-th element of the former set ($\boldsymbol{A}$) corresponds to the $i$-th element of the latter set ($\boldsymbol{B}$), i.e., $A_i$ corresponds to $B_i$.

constructing the GTs. From each of the first $g$ - $o$ $encGG_i$, $P_2$ obtains two input wire keys representing the bit value 0 of gate $G_i$, $v_{2i-1}^0$ and $v_{2i}^0$, and also the output wire keys representing the bit value 0, $s_{u+i}^0$, $i \in \{1, \cdots, g - o\}$. From each of the last $o$ $encGG_i$, $P_2$ gets only two input wire keys representing the bit value 0 of gates $G_i$, $v_{2i-1}^0$ and $v_{2i}^0$, $i \in \{g - o + 1, \cdots, g\}$. $P_2$ also decrypts $\{\text{Enc}_{pk}(s_i^0)\}_{i=1}^u$ and obtains $\{s_i^0\}_{i=1}^u$. Even with $\{s_i^0\}_{i=1}^{N-o}$ and $\{v_j^0\}_{j=1}^{2g}$, $P_2$ cannot learn about the topology of the circuit due to $P_1$'s re-randomization on these values.

The complexity of this phase is $\mathcal{O}(g)$ and we have approximately $(4u + 8g - 4o) \cdot ||\mathbb{G}|| + 9g \cdot ||\mathbb{Z}_q||$ communication bits and $39g$ exponentiation computations.

**3) Evaluation Phase.** By decrypting each $encGG_i$, $P_2$ can act as the circuit garbler in Yao's protocol. As shown in Fig. 3, we let $L_i$, $R_i$ and $O_i$ denote the left incoming wire, right incoming wire and outgoing wire of the gate $G_i$. Next, we use the global random values $r_1$ and $r_2$ generated in the offline phase to define the corresponding wire keys: $L_i^0 = v_{2i-1}^0 + r_1$, $L_i^1 = v_{2i-1}^0 + r_2$, and similarly, $R_i^0 = v_{2i}^0 + r_1$ and $R_i^1 = v_{2i}^0 + r_2$. There will be a bit different for outgoing wires. The wire keys about the $g$ - $o$ non-output gates are $O_i^0 = s_{u+i}^0 + r_1$ and $O_i^1 = s_{u+i}^0 + r_2$, $i \in \{1, \cdots, g - o\}$; the wire keys of the $o$ output gates are $O_i^0 = h_i^0 + r_1$ and $O_i^1 = h_i^0 + r_2$, $i \in \{g - o + 1, \cdots, g\}$. Garbled tables $\text{GT}_i$ can then be generated according to Yao's protocol, and the detailed implementation is shown in Fig. 4 where we use symmetric encipher sEnc. The secret keys of the symmetric encipher are the input keys $(L_i^0, L_i^1)$ and $(R_i^0, R_i^1)$ of $G_i$, and the plaintext is the output key $(O_i^0, O_i^1)$, $i \in \{1, \cdots, g\}$. This yields a truth table which needs to be randomly permuted to become a garbled table. In [27], sEnc is instantiated with AES-128. We emphasize that the input and output wire keys of each gate in the circuit are preprocessed and additive homomorphic operations are applied. More discussions on optimization techniques (e.g., point-and-permute [5], garbled row reduction [49,53], or half-gates [59]) might be found in [27]. After that, $P_2$ sends $\{\text{GT}_i\}_{i=1}^g$ to $P_1$.

Now $P_2$ needs to compute the wire keys representing the private data $x$. It may be noted that we have not used the $u$ wire keys about $\{s_i^0\}_{i=1}^u$. $P_2$ does not directly use these wire keys to represent the 0-bit in data $x$, but to perform the following computations. $P_2$ calculates $s_i^{x_i} := s_i^0 + r_1$ to denote $x_i = 0$ and $s_i^{x_i} := s_i^0 + r_2$ to denote $x_i = 1$, $i \in \{1, \cdots, u\}$, i.e., $s_i^{x_i} := s_i^0 + r_{x_i+1}$. We use the wire keys $\{s_i^{x_i}\}_{i=1}^u$ of the circuit input wires to denote $P_2$'s input bits $\{x_i\}_{i=1}^u$. $P_2$ sends these new wire keys to $P_1$.

**Fig. 3.** $L_i$ is the left incoming wire of $G_i$, $R_i$ the right incoming wire and $O_i$ the outgoing wire.

truth table      randomly permuted truth table

| $L_i$ | $R_i$ | $\overline{L_i \wedge R_i}$ |
|---|---|---|
| 0 | 0 | 1 |
| 0 | 1 | 1 |
| 1 | 0 | 1 |
| 1 | 1 | 0 |

$\rightarrow$

| $L_i$ | $R_i$ | $\overline{L_i \wedge R_i}$ |
|---|---|---|
| 1 | 0 | 1 |
| 0 | 0 | 1 |
| 1 | 1 | 0 |
| 0 | 1 | 1 |

$\rightarrow$

garbled table $GT_i$

$sEnc_{L_i^1 \| R_i^0 \| i \| 00}(O_i^1)$

$sEnc_{L_i^0 \| R_i^0 \| i \| 01}(O_i^1)$

$sEnc_{L_i^1 \| R_i^1 \| i \| 10}(O_i^0)$

$sEnc_{L_i^0 \| R_i^1 \| i \| 11}(O_i^1)$

**Fig. 4.** Create a garbled table.

$P_1$ has the ability to act as the circuit evaluator after receiving the input bit keys sent to him by $P_2$, and he has enough information to decrypt the garbled tables and then recover the wire keys for the output wires in this circuit. This decryption process is similar to Yao's GC method, but not exactly the same. Next $P_1$ decrypts the garbled table corresponding to the $g$ NAND gates one by one according to the topological order of the circuit. In order to decrypt the garbled table $GT_i$, $P_1$ recovers the keys used to encrypt the $GT_i$. Starting from $GT_1$, the two incoming wires of $G_1$ are the keys of the input bits about $x$, i.e., $s_1^{x_1}$ and $s_2^{x_2}$. $P_1$ knows the random values $a_1$ and $a_2$ used to re-randomize the two keys and also knows $b_1$ and $b_2$, so he can calculate $L_1^{x_1} = s_1^{x_1} - a_1 + b_1 = v_1^0 + r_{x_1+1}$ and $R_1^{x_2} = s_2^{x_2} - a_2 + b_2 = v_2^0 + r_{x_2+1}$. $P_2$ gets $L_1^{x_1}$ and $R_1^{x_2}$ to decrypt $GT_1$ and recovers the outgoing wire key $O_1^{NAND(x_1,x_2)}$, which is used to decrypt the garbled table(s) later. Thus $P_1$ decrypts the garbled tables one by one in topological order, and once all the garbled tables are computed, he obtains the output wire keys of the $o$ output gates $\{O_{g-o+1}, \cdots, O_g\}$, and sends these wire keys to $P_2$. $P_2$ receives $\{O_{g-o+1}, \cdots, O_g\}$ to recover the value of $f(x)$.

The complexity of this phase is $\mathcal{O}(g)$ and we have $(u + 4g + o) \cdot k$ communication bits and $u$ exponentiation computations. The costs of symmetric cipher are negligible.

To sum up, the computation complexity of the proposed protocol is $\mathcal{O}(g)$. We have the total communication overhead of $(4u + 8g - 4o + 1) \cdot ||\mathbb{G}|| + 9g \cdot ||\mathbb{Z}_q|| + (u+4g+o) \cdot k$ bits and approximately $39g$ exponentiation computations[5].

## 3.3 Heuristic Analysis

We next check whether it can resist against malicious adversaries. To achieve actively secure PFE protocol, malicious $P_1$ should be prevented from learning the valid knowledge of $P_2$'s private $x$, and malicious $P_2$ should be prevented from learning the valid knowledge of $P_1$'s private $f$. If one party cheats in the protocol, it should be checkable by another party or this cheating is useless. In addition, the function $f$ of $P_1$ should be irreversible, i.e., it should not be like $f(x) = x$.

---

[5] Exponentiation is the dominant computation in the protocol. We omit lightweight operations (e.g., symmetric cipher, addition, etc.).

We analyze above three phases (the values, the computation, and the interaction) one by one. Note that there is a takeaway in the protocol: we need to prove that $P_1$ uses the correct permutation maps $\pi_1$ and $\pi_2$. Fortunately, this can be resolved exactly by $\mathcal{ZK}_{DS}$ protocol. For the public key $pk$ sent by $P_2$ to $P_1$ in the *offline phase*, one can simply and efficiently verify that it is generated by ElGamal encryption. $P_2$ generates random values $r_1$ and $r_2$ as part of the keys used to represent the wires, and for his own security he does not fudge, and even if he does he cannot learn the valid knowledge of $f$. In the *initiation phase*, the $N$ - $o$ wire keys sent by $P_2$ to $P_1$ can also be verified simply and efficiently that these ciphertexts are well-formed corresponding to the public key $pk$. Then $P_1$ does a permutation ($\pi_1$) and re-randomization operation on the $N$ - $o$ wire keys generated by $P_2$, and a permutation ($\pi_2$) and re-randomization operation on the $2g$ extended wire keys. At the end of this phase, $P_2$ knows the ciphertexts of $v^0$ and $s^0$. Along with the knowledge of $C$, he knows the inputs and outputs of the two shuffles (permutation and re-randomization). $P_1$ can convince $P_2$ that he performs the correctly local work through the $\mathcal{ZK}_{DS}$ protocol. In the *evaluation phase* $P_2$ creates the garbled tables. If $P_2$ does not create these garbled tables correctly, it could be using fake wire keys or using the gates other than NAND. The former will be checked when $P_1$ decrypts the garbled table, and the latter is $P_2$ not getting the correct result. As long as $P_1$ does not tell $P_2$ in the process that he made an error in decrypting that one garbled table, $P_2$ cannot learn valid knowledge of $f$. The next $P_2$ sends $P_1$ the $u$ bit keys representing the data $x$. These ciphertexts are well-formed corresponding to the public key $pk$ and can be verified simply and efficiently, and $P_2$ cannot learn valid knowledge about $f$ by falsifying these ciphertexts. At the end, $P_1$ decrypts the $g$ garbled tables one by one, which are constructed using a symmetric encryption scheme. $P_1$ can only recover one row of the corresponding garbled table using the keys obtained in decrypting encrypted $GT_1$, and then calculates the keys to decrypt the subsequent garbled tables, and finally obtains $o$ wire keys $O_{g-o+i}^{y_i}$ (where $y_i$ is the $i$-th bit of $f(x)$), $i \in \{1, \cdots, o\}$. Since $P_1$ does not know the random values $r_1$ and $r_2$, the possibility of replacing $O_{y-o+i}^{y_i}$ with $O_{g-o+i}^{1-y_i}$ is negligible. If $P_1$ modifies $O_{g-o+i}^{y_i}$ privately, this can be checked by $P_2$ quite simply and effectively.

### 3.4   Security

**Theorem 1.** *The proposed 2-party PFE protocol has active security.*

*Proof sketch.* We can demonstrate the security of the proposed 2-party PFE protocol in the malicious adversary model by the real-ideal simulation paradigm. Intuitively, a protocol $\mathcal{P}$ is secure if anything a party sees can only be computed from that party's inputs and outputs.

We construct a simulator $\mathcal{S}_{2-party}$ that makes a poly-time environment $\mathcal{Z}$ unable to distinguish between the real protocol system and the ideal protocol system. We assume here that the corrupted adversary is malicious (active) and static. This simulator $\mathcal{S}_{2-party}$ runs a copy of the protocol given in Fig. 2, which relays messages between the parties and $\mathcal{Z}$ so that $\mathcal{Z}$ will see the same interface as when the actual protocol is interacted with. The next detailed description of $\mathcal{S}_{2-party}$ is presented in Table 2.

**Table 2.** Simulator $\mathcal{S}_{2-party}$

---

Simulator $\mathcal{S}_{2-party}$

---

**1) Offline Phase**

$P_2$ generates $(pk, sk)$.

– If $P_2$ is a corrupter. Simulator $\mathcal{S}_{2-party}$ verifies whether $pk$ is a well-formed public key, and if not, simulator aborts.

– If $P_2$ is not a corrupter. Simulator $\mathcal{S}_{2-party}$ honestly follows the protocol.

**2) Initiation Phase**

$P_2$ sends $N - o$ ciphertexts, $\{Enc_{pk}(h_i)\}_{i=1}^{N-o}$.

– If $P_2$ is the corrupter. Simulator $\mathcal{S}_{2-party}$ verifies whether $\{Enc_{pk}(h_i)\}_{i=1}^{N-o}$ are well-formed ciphertexts, and if not, simulator aborts.

– If $P_2$ is not a corrupter. Simulator $\mathcal{S}_{2-party}$ honestly follows the protocol.

$P_1$ performs two different shuffling operations on $\{Enc_{pk}(h_i)\}_{i=1}^{N-o}$, as described in Sect. 3.

– If $P_1$ is the corrupter. Simulator $\mathcal{S}_{2-party}$ randomly generates two mapping functions ($\pi_1$ and $\pi_2$) and sends them to $\mathcal{ZK}_{DS}$. Then, simulator aborts.

– If $P_1$ is not the corrupter. Simulator $\mathcal{S}_{2-party}$ waits for two mapping functions ($\pi_1$ and $\pi_2$) sent by $P_1$ and sends them to $\mathcal{ZK}_{DS}$.

In both cases, if $P_2$ aborts, simulator aborts.

**3) Evaluation Phase**

After $P_2$ decrypts the encrypted garbled gates, he creates $g$ garbled tables and calculates $u$ wire keys representing his data $x$.

– If $P_2$ is the corrupter. Simulator $\mathcal{S}_{2-party}$ randomly generates $g$ garbled tables and $u$ wire keys and proceeds to decrypt the garbled tables.

– If $P_2$ is not the corrupter. Simulator $\mathcal{S}_{2-party}$ follows the protocol honestly.

In both cases, if $P_1$ aborts, simulator aborts.

$P_1$ decrypts the garbled tables and recovers the $o$ wire keys

– If $P_1$ is the corrupter. Simulator $\mathcal{S}_{2-party}$ randomly generates $o$ wire keys and proceeds with the protocol.

– If $P_1$ is not the corrupter. Simulator $\mathcal{S}_{2-party}$ follows the protocol honestly

In both cases, if $P_2$ aborts, simulator aborts.

---

In order to see that the simulated process is indistinguishable from the real process, we will show that the view of the environment in the ideal process is computationally indistinguishable from the view in the real process. This view includes the honest player's inputs and outputs as well as the corrupted player's view of the protocol execution.

The views of the adversaries $P_1$ include: the public key $pk$, random values $\{a_i\}_{i=1}^{N-o}$ and $\{b_i\}_{i=1}^{2g}$, $\{Enc_{pk}(h_i^0)\}_{i=1}^{N-o}$, $\{Enc_{pk}(s_i^0)\}_{i=1}^{N-o}$, $\{Enc_{pk}(v_i^0)\}_{i=1}^{2g}$,

$\{GT_i\}_{i=1}^g$, $\{s_i^{x_i}\}_{i=1}^u$, $\{L_i\}_{i=1}^g$, $\{R_i\}_{i=1}^g$ and $\{O_i\}_{i=1}^g$. $\{s_i^{x_i}\}_{i=1}^u$, $\{L_i\}_{i=1}^g$, $\{R_i\}_{i=1}^g$ and $\{O_i\}_{i=1}^g$ are the results computed from the random values, which all look random and are therefore indistinguishable in real and ideal execution. Due to the randomness of $r_1$ and $r_2$, the probability that $P_1$ accurately computes $\{O_{g-o+i}^{1-y_i}\}_{i=1}^o$ based on $\{O_{g-o+i}^{y_i}\}_{i=1}^o$ is negligible, so in the evaluation phase, he must send the obtained $o$ wire keys to $P_2$ correctly, and malicious falsification of wire keys is easily detected by $P_2$. The ElGamal scheme is based on the DDH difficulty assumption, and the probability of recovering $sk$ according to $pk$ is negligible. $\{Enc_{pk}(h_i^0)\}_{i=1}^{N-o}$ are the ciphertexts encrypted by the ElGamal scheme, $sk$ is private to $P_2$ and therefore indistinguishable in the real and ideal execution. If the protocol is not aborted, $\{Enc_{pk}(s_i^0)\}_{i=1}^{N-o}$ and $\{Enc_{pk}(v_i^0)\}_{i=1}^{2g}$ are valid permuted and re-randomized ElGamal ciphertexts due to the verification of $\mathcal{ZK}_{DS}$. $\{GT_i\}_{i=1}^g$ are obtained based on the symmetric encryption scheme and random garbled, and is therefore indistinguishable in real and ideal execution.

The views of the adversaries $P_2$ include: the $pk$ and $sk$, random values $r_1$ and $r_2$, $\{Enc_{pk}(h_i^0)\}_{i=1}^{N-o}$, $\{Enc_{pk}(s_i^0)\}_{i=1}^{N-o}$, $\{Enc_{pk}(v_i^0)\}_{i=1}^{2g}$, $\{h_i^0\}_{i=1}^N$, $\{s_i^0\}_{i=1}^{N-o}$, $\{v_i^0\}_{i=1}^{2g}$, $\{L_i\}_{i=1}^g$, $\{R_i\}_{i=1}^g$, $\{O_i\}_{i=1}^g$, $\{GT_i\}_{i=1}^g$ and $\{s_i^{x_i}\}_{i=1}^u$. $\{s_i^{x_i}\}_{i=1}^u$, $\{s_i^0\}_{i=1}^{N-o}$, $\{v_i^0\}_{i=1}^{2g}$, $\{L_i\}_{i=1}^g$, $\{R_i\}_{i=1}^g$ and $\{O_i\}_{i=1}^g$ are the results computed from the random values, which all look random and are therefore indistinguishable in real and ideal execution. ElGamal ciphertexts all are indistinguishable in real and ideal execution. $P_2$ must ensure that the $\{GT_i\}_{i=1}^g$ created is correct, otherwise they will be checked by $P_1$ when decrypting the garbled, or $P_2$ doesn't get the correct result. If $P_2$ wants to successfully cheat $P_1$ and learn valid knowledge of $C_f$, he must guess exactly every mapping relation of the function $\pi_3$, which is obviously a negligible probability. The random values and wire keys all have uniform distribution in ideal and real execution.

As a result, it is indistinguishable between ideal and real execution for environment $\mathcal{Z}$.

## 4   Performance

In this paper, we initiate the first generic construction of 2-party PFE protocol with constant rounds and linear complexity in the malicious adversary model. In the case where the function is invoked once, we compare it (after instantiated by ElGamal encryption and Groth's secret shuffle [22]) with the only 2-party PFE protocol LWY [42] in the malicious adversary model. See Table 3. We consider the total communication costs and the exponentiation of the protocol. We let $||\mathbb{G}|| = 1024$ and $||\mathbb{Z}_q|| = 160$. The communication bits and exponentiation computations of our protocol are about $10144g$ and $39g$, respectively. For the same parameters, LWY requires about $20800g$ communication bits and $82g$ exponentiation (including $8g$ exponentiation in constructing and decrypting GTs). Our protocol reduces approximately 51.2% communication costs and 52.4% computation costs, compared to the first execution of LWY. We mention that from the second execution, LWY requires at least a total of $4096g$ communication bits and $8g$ exponentiation computations in each execution.

We also analyze the communication costs of all passively secure 2-party PFE protocols. The communication costs in the original KM protocol Sect.3.1 [30], optimal KM protocol Sect.3.2 [30], MS [46], and Bicer et al.'s protocol [9] are approximately $16896g$ bits, $8704g$ bits, $10752g$ bits, and $7168g$ bits, respectively. Thus our protocol even outperforms the original KM and MS that are passively secure from the communication perspective.

**Table 3.** Communication costs and exponentiation consumption in LWY and ours. $||\mathbb{G}|| = 1024$, $||\mathbb{Z}_q|| = 160$ and $k = 128$.

| PFE | Communication (bits) | | | Exponentiation | | |
|---|---|---|---|---|---|---|
| | $P_1$ | $P_2$ | *Total* | $P_1$ | $P_2$ | *Total* |
| LWY [42] | ~$15520g$ | ~$5280g$ | ~$20800g$ | ~$51g$ | ~$31g$ | ~$82g$ |
| Ours | ~$7584g$ | ~$2560g$ | ~$10144g$ | ~$18g$ | ~$21g$ | ~$39g$ |

## 5    Conclusion

Both our generic PFE and the concrete LWY are with constant rounds, linear complexity, and full security. They make optimal solutions available for non-reusable and reusable private functions, respectively. We believe that our constructions have practical relevance. In particular, we do expect our PFE could be both easier to implement and more efficient (for large circuits) than existing proposals (e.g., UC-based). We are also interested in constructing 2-party PFE with constant rounds and linear active security from other cryptographic primitives (to pursue better performance, e.g., without the usage of homomorphic encryption or reducing the number of exponentiations). We leave all above as future work.

**Acknowledgement.** Xiangxue Li is supported by National Natural Science Foundation of China (61971192), Shanghai Municipal Education Commission (2021-01-07-00-08-E00101), and Shanghai Trusted Industry Internet Software Collaborative Innovation Center.

## References

1. Alhassan, M.Y., Günther, D., Kiss, Á., Schneider, T.: Efficient and scalable universal circuits. J. Cryptol. **33**(3), 1216–1271 (2020)
2. Applebaum, B., Harnik, D., Ishai, Y.: Semantic security under related-key attacks and applications. In: Innovations in Computer Science - ICS 2011, pp. 45–60 (2011)
3. Barni, M., Failla, P., Kolesnikov, V., Lazzeretti, R., Sadeghi, A., Schneider, T.: Secure evaluation of private linear branching programs with medical applications. In: ESORICS 2009

4. Bayer, S., Groth, J.: Efficient zero-knowledge argument for correctness of a shuffle. In: Pointcheval, D., Johansson, T. (eds.) EUROCRYPT 2012. LNCS, vol. 7237, pp. 263–280. Springer, Heidelberg (2012). https://doi.org/10.1007/978-3-642-29011-4_17

5. Beaver, D., Micali, S., Rogaway, P.: The round complexity of secure protocols (extended abstract). In: STOC (1990)

6. Bellare, M., Hoang, V.T., Keelveedhi, S., Rogaway, P.: Efficient garbling from a fixed-key blockcipher. In: 2013 IEEE Symposium on Security and Privacy, SP 2013, pp. 478–492 (2013)

7. Ben-Or, M., Goldwasser, S., Wigderson, A.: Completeness theorems for non-cryptographic fault-tolerant distributed computation (extended abstract). In: STOC (1988)

8. Ben-Or, M., Goldwasser, S., Wigderson, A.: Completeness theorems for non-cryptographic fault-tolerant distributed computation (extended abstract). In: Simon, J. (ed.) Proceedings of the 20th Annual ACM Symposium on Theory of Computing, May 2–4, 1988, Chicago, Illinois, USA. pp. 1–10. ACM (1988). https://doi.org/10.1145/62212.62213

9. Bicer, O., Bingol, M.A., Kiraz, M.S., Levi, A.: Highly efficient and re-executable private function evaluation with linear complexity. IEEE Trans. Dependable Secure Comput. **19**(2), 835–847 (2020)

10. Brickell, J., Porter, D.E., Shmatikov, V., Witchel, E.: Privacy-preserving remote diagnostics. In: ACM CCS (2007)

11. Bünz, B., Bootle, J., Boneh, D., Poelstra, A., Wuille, P., Maxwell, G.: Bulletproofs: Short proofs for confidential transactions and more. In: 2018 IEEE Symposium on Security and Privacy, pp. 315–334 (2018)

12. Demmler, D., Schneider, T., Zohner, M.: ABY - A framework for efficient mixed-protocol secure two-party computation. In: NDSS (2015)

13. Evans, D., Kolesnikov, V., Rosulek, M.: A pragmatic introduction to secure multi-party computation. Found. Trends Priv. Secur. **2**(2–3), 70–246 (2018)

14. Frederiksen, T.K., Jakobsen, T.P., Nielsen, J.B., Nordholt, P.S., Orlandi, C.: Mini-LEGO: Efficient Secure Two-Party Computation from General Assumptions. In: Johansson, T., Nguyen, P.Q. (eds.) EUROCRYPT 2013. LNCS, vol. 7881, pp. 537–556. Springer, Heidelberg (2013). https://doi.org/10.1007/978-3-642-38348-9_32

15. Frikken, K.B., Atallah, M.J., Li, J.: Attribute-based access control with hidden policies and hidden credentials. IEEE Trans. Comput. **55**(10), 1259–1270 (2006)

16. Frikken, K.B., Atallah, M.J., Zhang, C.: Privacy-preserving credit checking. In: EC (2005)

17. Furukawa, J., Sako, K.: An efficient scheme for proving a shuffle. In: Kilian, J. (ed.) CRYPTO 2001. LNCS, vol. 2139, pp. 368–387. Springer, Heidelberg (2001). https://doi.org/10.1007/3-540-44647-8_22

18. Gamal, T.E.: A public key cryptosystem and a signature scheme based on discrete logarithms. IEEE Trans. Inf. Theor. **31**(4), 469–472 (1985)

19. Gilad-Bachrach, R., Dowlin, N., Laine, K., Lauter, K.E., Naehrig, M., Wernsing, J.: Cryptonets: Applying neural networks to encrypted data with high throughput and accuracy. In: Balcan, M., Weinberger, K.Q. (eds.) Proceedings of the 33nd International Conference on Machine Learning, ICML 2016, New York City, NY, USA, June 19–24, 2016. JMLR Workshop and Conference Proceedings, vol. 48, pp. 201–210. JMLR.org (2016)

20. Goldreich, O., Micali, S., Wigderson, A.: How to play any mental game. In: STOC, pp. 218–229 (1987)

21. Groth, J.: Linear algebra with sub-linear zero-knowledge arguments. In: Halevi, S. (ed.) CRYPTO 2009. LNCS, vol. 5677, pp. 192–208. Springer, Heidelberg (2009). https://doi.org/10.1007/978-3-642-03356-8_12

22. Groth, J.: A verifiable secret shuffle of homomorphic encryptions. J. Cryptol. **23**(4), 546–579 (2010)

23. Groth, J., Ishai, Y.: Sub-linear zero-knowledge argument for correctness of a shuffle. In: Smart, N. (ed.) EUROCRYPT 2008. LNCS, vol. 4965, pp. 379–396. Springer, Heidelberg (2008). https://doi.org/10.1007/978-3-540-78967-3_22

24. Groth, J., Lu, S.: Verifiable shuffle of large size ciphertexts. In: Okamoto, T., Wang, X. (eds.) PKC 2007. LNCS, vol. 4450, pp. 377–392. Springer, Heidelberg (2007). https://doi.org/10.1007/978-3-540-71677-8_25

25. Günther, D., Kiss, Á., Scheidel, L., Schneider, T.: Poster: Framework for semi-private function evaluation with application to secure insurance rate calculation. In: ACM CCS, pp. 2541–2543 (2019)

26. Günther, D., Kiss, Á., Schneider, T.: More efficient universal circuit constructions. In: Takagi, T., Peyrin, T. (eds.) ASIACRYPT 2017. LNCS, vol. 10625, pp. 443–470. Springer, Cham (2017). https://doi.org/10.1007/978-3-319-70697-9_16

27. Holz, M., Kiss, Á., Rathee, D., Schneider, T.: Linear-complexity private function evaluation is practical. In: Chen, L., Li, N., Liang, K., Schneider, S. (eds.) ESORICS 2020. LNCS, vol. 12309, pp. 401–420. Springer, Cham (2020). https://doi.org/10.1007/978-3-030-59013-0_20

28. Jawurek, M., Kerschbaum, F., Orlandi, C.: Zero-knowledge using garbled circuits: how to prove non-algebraic statements efficiently. In: ACM CCS, pp.955–966 (2013)

29. Jia, H., Li, X.: Pfe: Linear active security, double-shuffle proofs, and low-complexity communication. Cryptology ePrint Archive, Report 2022/219 (2022)

30. Katz, J., Malka, L.: Constant-round private function evaluation with linear complexity. In: Lee, D.H., Wang, X. (eds.) ASIACRYPT 2011. LNCS, vol. 7073, pp. 556–571. Springer, Heidelberg (2011). https://doi.org/10.1007/978-3-642-25385-0_30

31. Kiss, Á., Schneider, T.: Valiant's universal circuit is practical. In: Fischlin, M., Coron, J.-S. (eds.) EUROCRYPT 2016. LNCS, vol. 9665, pp. 699–728. Springer, Heidelberg (2016). https://doi.org/10.1007/978-3-662-49890-3_27

32. Kolesnikov, V.: Gate evaluation secret sharing and secure one-round two-party computation. In: Roy, B. (ed.) ASIACRYPT 2005. LNCS, vol. 3788, pp. 136–155. Springer, Heidelberg (2005). https://doi.org/10.1007/11593447_8

33. Kolesnikov, V., Schneider, T.: Improved garbled circuit: free XOR gates and applications. In: Aceto, L., Damgård, I., Goldberg, L.A., Halldórsson, M.M., Ingólfsdóttir, A., Walukiewicz, I. (eds.) ICALP 2008. LNCS, vol. 5126, pp. 486–498. Springer, Heidelberg (2008). https://doi.org/10.1007/978-3-540-70583-3_40

34. Kolesnikov, V., Schneider, T.: A practical universal circuit construction and secure evaluation of private functions. In: Tsudik, G. (ed.) FC 2008. LNCS, vol. 5143, pp. 83–97. Springer, Heidelberg (2008). https://doi.org/10.1007/978-3-540-85230-8_7

35. Lindell, Y.: Fast cut-and-choose-based protocols for malicious and covert adversaries. J. Cryptol. **29**(2), 456–490 (2015). https://doi.org/10.1007/s00145-015-9198-0

36. Lindell, Y., Pinkas, B.: An efficient protocol for secure two-party computation in the presence of malicious adversaries. In: Naor, M. (ed.) EUROCRYPT 2007. LNCS, vol. 4515, pp. 52–78. Springer, Heidelberg (2007). https://doi.org/10.1007/978-3-540-72540-4_4

37. Lindell, Y., Pinkas, B.: A proof of security of Yao's protocol for two-party computation. J. Cryptol. **22**(2), 161–188 (2008). https://doi.org/10.1007/s00145-008-9036-8

38. Lindell, Y., Pinkas, B.: A proof of security of yao's protocol for two-party computation. J. Cryptol. **22**(2), 161–188 (2009)

39. Lindell, Y., Riva, B.: Blazing fast 2pc in the offline/online setting with security for malicious adversaries. In: ACM CCS (2015)

40. Lipmaa, H., Mohassel, P., Sadeghian, S.: Valiant's universal circuit: Improvements, implementation, and applications, iACR Eprint 2016/017

41. Liu, H., Yu, Yu., Zhao, S., Zhang, J., Liu, W., Hu, Z.: Pushing the limits of valiant's universal circuits: simpler, tighter and more compact. In: Malkin, T., Peikert, C. (eds.) CRYPTO 2021. LNCS, vol. 12826, pp. 365–394. Springer, Cham (2021). https://doi.org/10.1007/978-3-030-84245-1_13

42. Liu, Y., Wang, Q., Yiu, S.: Making private function evaluation safer, faster, and simpler. IACR Cryptol. ePrint Arch. p. 1682 (2021)

43. Malkhi, D., Nisan, N., Pinkas, B., Sella, Y.: Fairplay - secure two-party computation system. In: USENIX Security (2004)

44. Mohassel, P., Zhang, Y.: Secureml: A system for scalable privacy-preserving machine learning. In: 2017 IEEE Symposium on Security and Privacy (SP). pp. 19–38 (2017). https://doi.org/10.1109/SP.2017.12

45. Mohassel, P., Rindal, P.: Aby$^3$: A mixed protocol framework for machine learning. In: Lie, D., Mannan, M., Backes, M., Wang, X. (eds.) Proceedings of the 2018 ACM SIGSAC Conference on Computer and Communications Security, CCS 2018, Toronto, ON, Canada, October 15–19, 2018, pp. 35–52. ACM (2018). https://doi.org/10.1145/3243734.3243760

46. Mohassel, P., Sadeghian, S.: How to hide circuits in MPC an efficient framework for private function evaluation. In: Johansson, T., Nguyen, P.Q. (eds.) EUROCRYPT 2013. LNCS, vol. 7881, pp. 557–574. Springer, Heidelberg (2013). https://doi.org/10.1007/978-3-642-38348-9_33

47. Mohassel, P., Sadeghian, S.: How to hide circuits in MPC an efficient framework for private function evaluation. In: Johansson, T., Nguyen, P.Q. (eds.) EUROCRYPT 2013. LNCS, vol. 7881, pp. 557–574. Springer, Heidelberg (2013). https://doi.org/10.1007/978-3-642-38348-9_33

48. Mohassel, P., Sadeghian, S., Smart, N.P.: Actively secure private function evaluation. In: Sarkar, P., Iwata, T. (eds.) ASIACRYPT 2014. LNCS, vol. 8874, pp. 486–505. Springer, Heidelberg (2014). https://doi.org/10.1007/978-3-662-45608-8_26

49. Naor, M., Pinkas, B., Sumner, R.: Privacy preserving auctions and mechanism design. In: EC (1999)

50. Neff, C.A.: A verifiable secret shuffle and its application to e-voting. In: CCS 2001, pp. 116–125 (2001)

51. Niksefat, S., Sadeghiyan, B., Mohassel, P., Sadeghian, S.S.: ZIDS: a privacy-preserving intrusion detection system using secure two-party computation protocols. Comput. J. **57**(4), 494–509 (2014)

52. Paillier, P.: Public-key cryptosystems based on composite degree residuosity classes. In: Stern, J. (ed.) EUROCRYPT 1999. LNCS, vol. 1592, pp. 223–238. Springer, Heidelberg (1999). https://doi.org/10.1007/3-540-48910-X_16

53. Pinkas, B., Schneider, T., Smart, N.P., Williams, S.C.: Secure two-party computation is practical. In: Matsui, M. (ed.) ASIACRYPT 2009. LNCS, vol. 5912, pp. 250–267. Springer, Heidelberg (2009). https://doi.org/10.1007/978-3-642-10366-7_15

54. Shelat, A., Shen, C.: Two-output secure computation with malicious adversaries. In: Paterson, K.G. (ed.) EUROCRYPT 2011. LNCS, vol. 6632, pp. 386–405. Springer, Heidelberg (2011). https://doi.org/10.1007/978-3-642-20465-4_22
55. Valiant, L.G.: Universal circuits (preliminary report). In: STOC (1976)
56. Wagh, S., Gupta, D., Chandran, N.: Securenn: 3-party secure computation for neural network training. Proc. Priv. Enhancing Technol. **2019**(3), 26–49 (2019)
57. Yao, A.C.: Protocols for secure computations. In: FOCS (1982)
58. Yao, A.C.C.: How to generate and exchange secrets. In: FOCS (1986)
59. Zahur, S., Rosulek, M., Evans, D.: Two halves make a whole. In: Oswald, E., Fischlin, M. (eds.) EUROCRYPT 2015. LNCS, vol. 9057, pp. 220–250. Springer, Heidelberg (2015). https://doi.org/10.1007/978-3-662-46803-6_8
60. Zhao, S., Yu, Yu., Zhang, J., Liu, H.: Valiant's universal circuits revisited: an overall improvement and a lower bound. In: Galbraith, S.D., Moriai, S. (eds.) ASIACRYPT 2019. LNCS, vol. 11921, pp. 401–425. Springer, Cham (2019). https://doi.org/10.1007/978-3-030-34578-5_15

# Data Security

# A Random Reversible Watermarking Scheme for Relational Data

Qiang Liu[1,2], Hequ Xian[1,2(✉)], Jiancheng Zhang[3,4], and Kunpeng Liu[4]

[1] College of Computer Science and Technology, Qingdao University, Qingdao, China
xianhq@126.com
[2] State Key Laboratory of Information Security, Institute of Information
Engineering, Chinese Academy of Sciences, Beijing, China
[3] Shandong Computer Science Center, Jinan, China
zhangjc@sdas.org
[4] Shandong Zhengzhong Information Technology Co., Ltd., Jinan, China
liukp@sdas.org

**Abstract.** In the era of Big Data, relational data is at risk of piracy
and misuse when distributed, shared and used. The use of digital watermarking technology is a reliable way to protect the copyright of relational
data. In order to protect the copyright of relational data and recover the
original data, many reversible watermarking schemes have been proposed
in recent years. But most of them cannot extract the watermark information completely under severe attacks. To address this problem, a random reversible watermarking scheme is proposed. Watermark embedding
algorithm, watermark integrity checking algorithm, watermark detection algorithm and data recovery algorithm are designed. The watermark capacity is increased by embedding multiple watermarks in selected
tuples, and the randomness of the watermark information distribution is
increased by embedding unequal proportions of watermarks in different
tuples. In extracting the watermark, the attacked bits are discarded to
improve the accuracy of watermark detection. In addition, only a partition with complete watermark information is selected for watermark
extraction. This not only improves the speed of watermark extraction,
but also avoids the risk of key leakage from other partitions. The experimental results show that the complete watermark information can be
extracted even when more than 90% of the tuples are under attack.

**Keywords:** Relational data · Reversible watermark · Copyright ·
Multiple verification

## 1 Introduction

There is currently an increasing amount of data on the internet due to the
widespread use of big data and cloud computing [1]. This data is stored on the
internet in various forms such as audio, video, images, text, and relational data.
As it circulates and used, this data constantly creates new value. These data can

F. Li et al. (Eds.): SecureComm 2022, LNICST 462, pp. 413–430, 2023.
https://doi.org/10.1007/978-3-031-25538-0_22

be easily copied, modified and distributed through public channels, which makes them more vulnerable to misuse. Information misuse has become a more frequent data security issue than information corruption or leakage [2]. How to protect data security and prove data ownership in an open and shared environment has become an urgent issue.

Digital watermarking is a technology used for copyright protection of multimedia data, such as images, audio, video, natural languages, and relational databases [3–7]. Database watermarking is a recently proposed technique for database copyright protection. Before distributing the data, Data owners embed their unique copyright mark into the data via a watermark embedding algorithm and then distributed the data through public channels. After obtaining the data, the malicious attacker will use various attacks to destroy the watermark in the data to interfere with the proof of copyright. Common attacks include tuple addition, tuple alteration, and tuple deletion attacks. The data owner extracts a unique copyright mark from the stolen data for copyright proofing.

In this paper, we propose a dynamic random distributed watermarking scheme for relational data, which improves the robustness of watermarking while reducing data distortion. Experimental results show that our scheme is better than the previous schemes in terms of robustness and data availability.

The subsequent sections of the paper are structured as follows: In Sect. 2, some related researches are provided. In Sect. 3, the proposed scheme is described in detail. In Sect. 4, experiments and results are discussed concisely. At last, the paper is concluded in Sect. 5.

## 2    Related Work

In 2002, Agrawal and Kiernan proposed the first watermarking scheme for relational data [7]. The author uses a key to select special bits for specific attributes and embeds some particular values forming the watermark. After that, Sion et al. proposed a different watermarking scheme [8]. This scheme uses a key to rearrange and repartition the tuples. The authors achieve the embedding of watermark information by changing the distribution characteristics of the data. However, this scheme has poor resistance to tuple deletion attacks. In 2003, Prof. Niu et al. proposed a scheme to embed meaningful strings into data [9]. This scheme embeds a matching relation in the selected attribute value of the tuple chosen, and the value of the watermarked bits is confirmed by verifying the existence of the matching relation when detecting the watermark. In 2008, Shehab et al. reduced digital watermarking to an optimization problem with constraints and proposed a digital watermarking scheme using genetic algorithms to reduce data distortion [10].

These intentionally introduced particular values will inevitably cause a certain degree of distortion to the data and, in some cases, will not meet the usability requirements. In 2006, Zhang et al. proposed the first reversible relational database watermarking scheme(HSW), which constructs histograms by exploiting the differences between attribute values and extends the histogram technique to achieve reversibility of database watermarking [11]. In the same year, Zhang et al. designed a reversible watermarking scheme for relational data by exploiting the reversible nature of exclusive or operations [12]. However, this technique cannot be used against attacks that target large numbers of tuples. In 2008, Gupta and Pieprzyk used the differential extended watermarking technique DEW to achieve reversible watermarking of relational data [13], but the robustness of this scheme is poor. In 2010, Farfoura and Horng proposed a prediction error extended watermarking technique (PEEW) [14], where the authors used a predictor to select the watermarked bits and features in the embedded data. In 2013, K. Jawad et al. first used genetic algorithms in database watermarking and designed a reversible watermarking scheme based on genetic algorithms and differential extended watermarking techniques (GADEW) [15]. The scheme uses a genetic algorithm to select the optimal attributes to reduce data distortion and increase the watermarking capacity, which improves the scheme's robustness. In 2015, Iftikhar et al. used genetic algorithms and data analysis methods from information theory to deal with the watermarking problem (RRW) [16]. They used genetic algorithms to generate optimal watermarks to reduce data distortion. However, developing the optimal watermark requires a large amount of computation time. Therefore the efficiency of the algorithm is too low when dealing with large amounts of data. In the same year, Franco-Contreras J et al. proposed a robust watermarking algorithm based on circular histograms by using circular histograms to modify data in plain text domains [17]. In 2017, Imamoglu M B et al. proposed a new reversible watermarking scheme for relational data (FFADEW) by combining differential extension techniques and the Firefly algorithm (FFA) [18]. The Firefly algorithm is another evolutionary algorithm that the authors use to select the optimal attribute-value pairs to achieve minimal distortion. In 2018, Hu et al. proposed a genetic algorithm-based histogram shift watermarking scheme (GAHSW) [19]. The authors used a genetic algorithm to partition the tuples and then used a histogram shift method to embed the watermark. This method improves the robustness of watermarking while reducing data distortion. In 2019, Li et al. proposed a low-distortion reversible database watermarking method based on histogram gaps (HGW) [20]. The method reduces data distortion without weakening the robustness of watermarking. Compared to GAHSW, this method reduces data distortion without cutting watermarking robustness. In 2020, Li et al. improved the histogram shifting scheme by proposing a non-redundancy shifting-based method. It changed the histogram shifting method to reduce the distortion caused by watermarking and slightly enhance the usability of the data [21]. In 2022, Xiang et al. proposed a robust watermarking algorithm based on order-preserving encryption scheme(OPES) and circular histograms [22].

The above schemes for relational data show that researchers are trying to improve the robustness and capacity of watermarking while reducing the impact of watermarking on the data. It seems that the robustness of watermarking and data availability cannot be achieved at the same time. To solve this problem, we propose a random reversible watermarking scheme in this work.

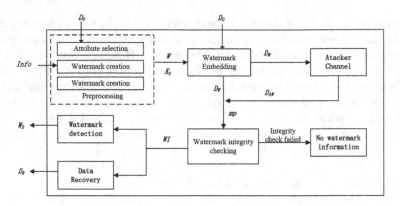

**Fig. 1.** System architecture.

## 3 Scheme

The main structure of the scheme is shown in Fig. 1. The scheme mainly includes the following five main phases: (1) preprocessing; (2) watermark embedding; (3) watermark integrity detection; (4) watermark extraction; (5) data recovery.

The watermark preprocessing is mainly to do some preparatory work before embedding watermark. The first step is encoding the data owner's copyright information into a watermark sequence that can be embedded in the database. The second step is filtering out the attribute columns suitable for embedding the watermark. The final step is to generate a random function to determine the proportion of each tuple in which the watermark will be embedded. The main task of the watermark embedding phase is to embed the watermark information into the data according to the key, and finally obtain the database with the watermark and return the auxiliary data. The watermark integrity check phase checks each partition's watermark integrity. The watermark extraction phase extracts the watermark information from the stolen watermarked data and implements the issue of proof of copyright. The data recovery phase removes the watermark from the data and restores the original data. Notation used in the scheme is given in Table 1.

**Definition 1.** Watermark Integrity, $WI$(Watermark Integrity), indicates the watermark's degree of integrity for each partition and. In some ways, it reflects the extent to which data has been corrupted. $WI = [f_1, f_2, f_3, ..., f_N](f_i \in 0, 1)$. Where $f_i$ is the identifier of the complete watermark of partition i.

We will select only one of the partitions with a full watermark for detection during watermark extraction. The use of watermark completeness improves the efficiency of watermark detection. It ensures that in case of severe attacks in the database, the data owner can still extract the complete watermark from the data.

**Table 1.** The meaning of the symbols in the scheme.

| Symbol | Description | Symbol | Description |
|---|---|---|---|
| $D_O$ | Original database | $D_W$ | Databases with embedded watermarks |
| $D_R$ | Restored database | $D_{AW}$ | Databases under attack |
| $1/\omega$ | Proportion of attribute embedding | $\lambda$ | Number of data partitions |
| $\sigma$ | Random number greater than the length of the watermark | $1/\eta$ | Proportion of tuples with watermarks embedded |
| $\xi$ | Length of watermarked information | $\nu$ | Number of bits in the least significant bit |
| $K_P$ | Data partition key | $K_S[i]$ | Watermark embedding key for partition $i$ |
| $r$ | Example tuple of data | $A_j$ | The jth attribute of the data |
| $bit[k]$ | The $k$th bit of the $LSB$ | $W[l]$ | kth bit of watermark information |
| $bit_W[k]$ | The $k$th watermarked bit of the LSB | $W_D[l]$ | The $l$th bit of the detected watermark |
| $Max$ | Proportional limit for embedding watermark attributes | $LSB$ | The least significant bit of the data |
| $mp$ | Auxiliary data | $MSB$ | The most significant bit of the data |
| $mp[i]$ | Auxiliary data for partition $i$ | $mpw$ | Auxiliary data for the data to be tested |
| $r.key$ | Primary key for tuple $r$ | $count[l]$ | Array of majority vote marks |
| $WI$ | Marker array | $bits$ | Bits to be embedded |
| $f_i$ | Markers for partition $i$ | $bitsl$ | Information about the watermarked bits stored |
| $bit_o$ | The original bits that be recovered | $bitwsl$ | The value of the $bitsl$ in the checked data |
| Mean | Mean value of the attribute | Std | Standard deviation of attributes |

## 3.1 Preprocessing

Before embedding the watermark, the data needs to be preprocessed. The main tasks in the preprocessing phase are: (1) selecting the appropriate attributes for watermark embedding; (2) creating watermark information for embedding; (3) determining a random function.

**Attribute Selection.** Not all attributes are suitable for embedding attributes, and for some attributes, small changes can significantly impact data quality. We select multiple attribute columns from the database as candidate attributes that can be used as identifiable features, and embedding a watermark in an attribute fewer impacts data quality. The candidate attributes are then reordered and numbered in ascending order, and the reordering enhances robustness against attribute attacks.

**Watermark Creation.** The watermark information is not only a carrier of the data owner's copyright information but also evidence of the owner's copyright claim. The unique identification information is converted into a binary sequence. Then the binary sequence is encoded with the data as watermark information. We embed the full watermark into the different partitions. We simply select the partition with the most complete watermark for the copyright claim. The watermark creation equation is shown in Eq. (1):

$$W = Info \text{ xor Rand} \tag{1}$$

$Info$ is the copyright information of the data owner, and $Rand$ is random number. By encode $Info$ with an $Rand$, the data owner's information can be effectively prevented from being leaked.

**Determine Random Function.** We embed an unequal number of watermarks in each tuple. The F function chooses the number of watermarks embedded in each tuple. The input to the F function is the tuple's primary key and key, and the output is a random integer of $[0, Max]$ to ensure that the number of watermarks embedded is random. The data owner can choose any generation function. In this case, the following function is selected by Eq.(2):

$$F(x, y, z) = H(x|H(x|y))\%z \tag{2}$$

### 3.2   Watermark Embedding

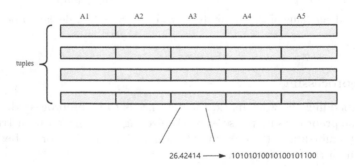

**Fig. 2.** Least significant bits

The main task of the watermark embedding phase is to embed the watermark into the database in an invisible way. After embedding the watermark, the data owner stores the auxiliary data $bitsl$ and uses them during the watermark integrity check, watermark extraction, and data recovery phases. The information stored in the auxiliary array $mp$ consists of the original data bit value $bit[k]$ and the subscript position $l$ of the watermark. $bit[k]$ is selected as shown in Fig. 2, and bits are generated by selecting one of the $LSB$ and dissociating $bit[k]$ with $W[l]$. $bitls$ are generated by processing the bits, and the final stored value $bitls$ is calculated according to Eq. (3).

$$bitsl = l + \sigma * bits \qquad (3)$$

$l$ is the subscript position of the embedded watermark $W$. $sigma$ is any random number bigger than the watermark length $\xi$. When extracting the stored information, if the value of $bitsl$ is bigger than $\xi$ or not, the value of bits is 1 or 0. When the value of $bitsl$ is less than $\xi$, the value of $l$ is $bitsl$. Otherwise, $l$ is calculated by Eq. (4). The specific watermarking process is shown in Algorithm 1.

$$l = bits - \sigma * bits \qquad (4)$$

---

**Algorithm 1.** Watermark embedding algorithm

---

**Input:** $D_O, K_P, K_S, W$
**Output:** $D_W, mp$
1: **for** each tuple $r \in D$ **do**
2:     $i = H(r.key, K_P, MSB) \bmod \lambda$
3:     **if** $H(r.key, K_S[i]) \bmod \eta = 0$ **then**
4:         **for** each $A_j$ in $r$ **do**
5:             $\omega = F(r.key, K_S[i], Max)$
6:             **if** $H(r.key, K_S[i], MSB) \bmod \lceil \omega \rceil = 0$ **then**
7:                 $W_{index} \ l = H(r.key, K_S[i]) \bmod \xi$
8:                 $bit_{index} \ k = H(r.key, K_S[i]) \bmod \upsilon$
9:                 $bits = bit[k]$ xor $W[l]$
10:                $bitsl = l + \sigma * bits$
11:                $Stroe(mp[i], bitsl)$
12:                $Update(bit[k], bits)$
13:            **end if**
14:        **end for**
15:    **end if**
16: **end for**
17: **return** $D_W, mp$

---

Here we take an arbitrary tuple $r$ as an example. Line 2 determines the partition of $r$. The primary key of the tuple and the key $K_P$ are hashed. Line 3 determines whether the tuple is watermarked or not, and $1/\eta$ is the parameter that controls the tuple embedding ratio. Line 4 determines for each attribute whether the attribute is embedded into a watermark bit or not. Lines 5 and 6 generate a random number and attributes in the tuple with a ratio of $1/\omega$ will be watermarked. The value of $\omega$ is determined by the key, the primary key of the tuple, and $Max$. This approach increases the watermarking capacity and the randomness of the watermark embedding. We can adjust the watermark capacity and control the data distortion by adjusting $Max$. Line 7 selects one bit from the watermark string as the embedded bit, $\nu$ being the length of the watermark. Line 8 selects the bit position for embedding, $\xi$ is the number of least significant bits. Line 9 combines the watermarked bits with the original information using an exception or operation to generate a new bit. Line 10 connects the embedded watermark bits with the subscript of the watermark where it is located to create the auxiliary data $bitsl$ with the embedded watermark and watermark position information via Eq. (3). Then, $store(mp[i], bitsl)$ means to store the $bitsl$ into the auxiliary array element $mp[i]$, $mp[i]$ represents the auxiliary data for partition $i$. $Update(bit[k], bits)$ in line 12 updates the $k$th bit of the least significant bit to bits. Finally, the algorithm returns the embedded watermarked data $D_W$ and the auxiliary data $mp$.

### 3.3   Watermark Integrity Detection

To ensure that the data owner can detect its watermark, we check the watermark integrity of all partitions. The watermark completeness check uses the $Check(mp_W[i], mp[i])$ function to check the watermark completeness of partition $i$. This function checks $\xi$ watermark positions in the $i$th partition. If the function detects at least one occurrence of watermark information in $\xi$ watermark positions, the partition's watermark information is considered complete and returns 1; otherwise, it returns 0. We have discarded the attacked watermark bits in the watermark extraction stage, so when each watermark bit is detected at least once in partition $i$, the correct result can be obtained by the majority voting mechanism. When extracting the watermark, the watermark is extracted for the partition with complete watermark information. The watermark integrity checking algorithm is shown in Algorithm 2.

**Algorithm 2.** Watermark integrity checking algorithm

---

**Input:** $D_W, K_P, K_S, mp$
**Output:** $WI$
1: **for** each tuple $r \in D_W$ **do**
2:      $i = H(r.key, K_P) \bmod \lambda$
3:      **if** $H(r.key, K_S[i]) \bmod \eta = 0$ **then**
4:          **for** each $A_j$ in $r$ **do**
5:              $\omega = F(r.key, K_S[i], Max)$
6:              **if** $H(r.key, K_S[i], MSB) \bmod \lceil \omega \rceil = 0$ **then**
7:                  $W_{index}\ l = H(r.key, K_S[i]) \bmod \xi$
8:                  $bit_{index}\ k = H(r.key, K_S[i]) \bmod v$
9:                  $bitwsl = l + \sigma * bit[k]$
10:                 **if** $bitwsl$ in $mp[i]$ **then**
11:                     $Store(mpw[i], bitwsl)$
12:                 **end if**
13:                 **if** $mpw[i].length\%\xi = 0$ **then**
14:                     $WI[i] = Check(mpw[i], mp[i])$
15:                 **end if**
16:             **end if**
17:         **end for**
18:     **end if**
19: **end for**
20: **return** $WI$

---

Lines 1 to 8 of Algorithm 2 are similar to the watermark embedding algorithm. Only line 3 has an additional line to determine the partition $i$ to which tuple $r$ belongs. If the watermark integrity token $WI[i]$ of partition i is already 1, the partition is no longer checked. Line 9 calculates the value of $bitwsl$ using Eq. 3. Lines 10–12 determine if $bitwsl$ is stored in $mp[i]$, and if so, store it in $mpw[i]$. Lines 13–15 determine the length of $mpw[i]$, and if the length is an integer multiple of $\xi$, perform a $Check(mpw[i], mp[i])$. This can greatly improve the detection efficiency by periodically checking whether the watermark is complete. When the marker array $WI[i]$ of partition $i$ is set to 1, no subsequent tuples of that partition are checked. The algorithm only detects all tuples when the data does not contain watermark information. When all partitions have a marker array of 0, the data does not contain copyright information.

### 3.4    Watermark Extraction

The data owner extracts the watermarked information from the data for copyright claim. This requires the watermark to be robust. Even in the case of a severe attack on the data, the data owner can still extract the complete watermark information from the data. We use majority voting in the watermark extraction process to reduce the attack's impact and improve the accuracy of watermark detection. The watermark extraction algorithm is shown in Algorithm 3.

---

**Algorithm 3.** Watermark extraction algorithm

---

**Input:** $D_W, K_P, K_S, mp, WI$
**Output:** $W_D$

1:   $get\ f_i = 1, f_i \in WI$
2:   $Initialize\ count = 0$
3: **for** each tuple $r \in D$ **do**
4:     $i = H(r.key, K_P) \bmod \lambda$
5:     **if** i $==$ $f_i$ **then**
6:       **if** $H(r.key, K_S[i]) \bmod \eta = 0$ **then**
7:         **for** each $A_j$ in $r$ **do**
8:           $\omega = F(r.key, K_S[i], Max)$
9:           **if** $H(r.key, K_S[i], MSB) \bmod \omega = 0$ **then**
10:            $W_{index}\ l = H(r.key, K_S[i]) \bmod \xi$
11:            $bit_{index}\ k = H(r.key, K_S[i]) \bmod \upsilon$
12:            $Get(mp[i], bitsl)$
13:            $bits = (bitsl - l)/\sigma$
14:            $bitws = bits$ xor $W[l]$
15:            $W_D[l] = bit_W[k]$ xor $bitws$
16:            **if** $W_D[l] = 1$ **then**
17:              $count[l] ++$
18:            **else**
19:              $count[l] --$
20:            **end if**
21:           **end if**
22:         **end for**
23:       **end if**
24:     **end if**
25: **end for**
26: **for** n=0 to $\xi - 1$ **do**
27:     **if** $count[n] > 0$ **then**
28:       $W_D[n] = 1$
29:     **else**
30:       $W_D[n] = 0$
31:     **end if**
32: **end for**
33: **return** $W_D$

---

In line 1, a partition with complete watermark information is selected, and only the tuples of this partition are watermark extracted next. Line 2 initializes the count variable. Lines 3 and 4 determine the partition to which the tuple belongs. Line 6 determines whether the tuple is a tuple with a watermark. Lines 7 to 11 search for the location of the watermark embedding. Line 12 $Get(bits, mp[i])$ extracts the $bitls$ from the auxiliary data of partition $i, mp[i]$. Line 13 calculates the value of the bits stored in the $bitsl$. Line 14 calculates the embedded watermark information. If $WD[l]$ is 1, the count value is added to 1, if $W_D[l]$ is 0, the count value is subtracted from 1. Lines 25 to 31 calculate the final vote result and finally return the detected watermark information $W_D$. $W_D$ is encrypted and is decrypted using a key to get $Info$. Info is the copyright information of the owner of the decrypted data.

### 3.5   Data Recovery

When the quality of the data is not sufficient to meet the demand, the data will be useless. The data owner licenses the key and supporting files to the data user, who then uses the key and data recovery algorithm to recover the original data. The data recovery algorithm is shown in Algorithm 4.

---

**Algorithm 4.** Data recovery algorithms

---

**Input:** $D_W$ $D_{AW}, K_P, K_S, mp, W$
**Output:** $D_R$
1: **for** each tuple $r \in D$ **do**
2:    $i = H(r.key, K_P)$ mod $\lambda$
3:    **if** $H(r.key, K_S[i])$ mod $\eta = 0$ **then**
4:       **for** each $A_j$ in $r$ **do**
5:          $\omega = F(r.key, K_S[i], Max)$
6:          **if** $H(r.key, K_S[i], MSB)$ mod $\lceil \omega \rceil = 0$ **then**
7:             $W_{index}$ $l = H(r.key, K_S[i])$ mod $\xi$
8:             $bit_{index}$ $k = H(r.key, K_S[i])$ mod $\upsilon$
9:             $Get(bitsl, mp[i])$
10:           $bits = (bitsl - l)/\sigma$
11:           **if** $bits$ in $mp[i]$ **then**
12:             $bit_o = bits$ Xor $W[l]$
13:             $Update(bit_w[k], bit_o)$
14:           **end if**
15:         **end if**
16:       **end for**
17:    **end if**
18: **end for**
19: **return** $D_R$

---

Lines 1 to 8 are same as the watermark embedding algorithm. Line 9 gets the value of the stored $bitsl$ from the auxiliary array. Lines 10 compute the values of $bits$. If the $bits$ is in the auxiliary data $mp[i]$, line 12 is an alias to the $bits$ to get the original $bit_o$. Line 13 uses $Update(bit_W[s], bit_o)$ to update the value of $bit_W[k]$ to $bit_o$, removing the watermark information. Finally, the recovered data is returned to $D_R$.

## 4   Experimental Analysis

This section evaluates various aspects of the scheme. The experiments aim to verify the accuracy and robustness of the scheme. The experiments include

(1) Statistical distortion experiments, (2) watermark capacity experiments, (3) robustness experiments. The experimental environment is: a 2.0 GHz Intel Core CPU, 16 GB RAM, Ubuntu 20.04LTS operating system, IDEA2021.1.3 development environment, and MariaDB 10.3.29 database. The experimental data were obtained using the Forest Cover dataset provided by the University of California(kdd.ics.uci.edu/databases/covertype/covertype.html). The dataset contains a total of 581012 tuples and 54 attributes. We selected 100000 tuples and 10 attributes from this data set and transformed them to be the experimental data.

Experimental parameters: number of data tuples n = 100000, number of data partitions $\mu = 10$, watermark tuple embedding ratio $1/\eta = 1/5$, F-function parameter $Max = 5$.

## 4.1   Statistical Distortion Experiments

Watermarking inevitably causes distortion of the data, and the longer the watermark, the more severe the distortion. Therefore, we compared some statistical metrics of the original and watermarked databases. The results of the comparison were compared with other schemes, such as DEW, GADEW, PEEW and GAHSW.

To visualize the effect of watermarking on data distortion, we calculate the mean, standard deviation and mean absolute error($MAE$) before and after watermark embedding data. And the value of $MAE$ is calculated from Eq. (5).

$$MAE = \frac{\sum_{i=1}^{n} |A_i - A_i^w|}{n} \tag{5}$$

where $A_i$ is the original attribute, $A_i^w$ is its watermarked version, and $n$ is the total number of attributes for all tuples in the database.

To make the experimental results more precise, the results were averaged from 10 experiments. Table 2 shows the experimental results for each attribute of the database, and the results are compared with other schemes in the table. To visualize the changes in mean and variance, the difference in mean (DM) and difference in standard deviation (DS) for each attribute are given in Table 3. DM and DS are calculated by Eq. (6) and Eq. (7):

$$DM = |Mean_D - Mean_{DW}| \tag{6}$$

$$DS = |Std_D - Std_{DW}| \tag{7}$$

where $Mean_D$ and $Std_D$ represent the original database's mean and standard deviation values, $Mean_{DW}$ and $Std_{DW}$ represent the mean and standard deviation of the watermarked database. In addition, the $MAE$ values for the different scenarios are shown in the last row of Table.

As shown in Table 3, the variation in our scheme's mean and standard deviation between the original and watermarked databases is minimal. The maximum

**Table 2.** Results of statistical distortion of the database.

| Attributename | Original database Mean | Std | DEW Mean | Std | GADEW Mean | Std | PEEW Mean | Std |
|---|---|---|---|---|---|---|---|---|
| Elevation | 2862.037 | 231.375 | 2862.037 | 231.375 | 2862.018 | 231.442 | 2862.037 | 231.375 |
| Aspec | 138.163 | 103.779 | 138.403 | 103.946 | 137.712 | 103.635 | 138.829 | 105.149 |
| Slope | 11.803 | 6.534 | 11.819 | 7.074 | 11.788 | 6.542 | 11.818 | 6.546 |
| H_D_To_Hydrology | 260.580 | 202.774 | 260.580 | 202.774 | 260.292 | 202.366 | 261.844 | 203.507 |
| V_D_To_Hydrology | 35.242 | 42.627 | 48.462 | 66.603 | 25.593 | 57.792 | 41.540 | 48.110 |
| H_D_To_Roadways | 3344.252 | 1776.873 | 3346.659 | 1781.056 | 3342.698 | 1779.658 | 3352.709 | 1780.346 |
| Hillshade_9am | 218.234 | 20.933 | 218.321 | 21.071 | 217.984 | 21.145 | 218.552 | 21.242 |
| Hillshade_Noon | 225.451 | 16.653 | 225.522 | 16.966 | 225.359 | 17.070 | 225.669 | 17.869 |
| Hillshade_3pm | 139.301 | 31.184 | 139.387 | 31.228 | 139.255 | 31.440 | 139.425 | 31.985 |
| H_D_To_Fire_Points | 3589.618 | 1781.439 | 3591.923 | 1786.310 | 3588.353 | 1781.782 | 3700.371 | 2071.255 |

| Attributename | GAHSW Mean | Std | OUR Mean | Std |
|---|---|---|---|---|
| Elevation | 2862.040 | 231.462 | 2862.071 | 231.375 |
| Aspec | 138.206 | 103.847 | 138.167 | 103.779 |
| Slope | 11.835 | 6.571 | 11.834 | 6.498 |
| H_D_To_Hydrology | 260.659 | 202.739 | 260.588 | 202.777 |
| V_D_To_Hydrology | 35.242 | 42.627 | 35.277 | 42.623 |
| H_D_To_Roadways | 3344.255 | 1776.972 | 3344.256 | 1776.875 |
| Hillshade_9am | 218.243 | 20.984 | 218.270 | 20.922 |
| Hillshade_Noon | 225.528 | 16.625 | 225.454 | 16.652 |
| Hillshade_3pm | 139.360 | 31.219 | 139.333 | 31.175 |
| H_D_To_Fire_Points | 3589.660 | 1781.533 | 3589.622 | 1781.438 |

variation caused is 0.035, which is negligible compared to DEW, GADEW, and PEEW. Although the variation in mean and standard deviation for the GAHSW scenario is also tiny, it is still worse than the results in our scheme. It is important to note that DEW and PEEW change 0 for some attributes, such as the first attribute shown in Table 3. This is because the watermark is not embedded in these attribute columns. In general, the smaller the variation in the mean and standard deviation, the smaller the impact of the watermarking scheme on the data quality. The same is also applicable to the $MAE$ for quantifying attribute distortion. The $MAE$ values for DEW, GADEW, and PEEW are not ideal, with their values being 28.395, 7.867, and 133.125, respectively. This means that these schemes introduce relatively large distortions into the data, which severely affect its usability of the data. The $MAE$ value of GAHSW is the lowest, at 0.775. Although this value is much lower than the other schemes, it is still higher than the value in our proposed scheme. Although the improvement is minor, it is still an improvement. Thus, the experiments show that our proposed scheme is highly effective and significantly outperforms the other schemes in terms of statistical distortion performance.

**Table 3.** Results of difference in Mean, difference in Std and $MAE$

| Attributename | DEW DM | DS | GADEW DM | DS | PEEW DM | DS | GAHSW DM | DS | OUR DM | DS |
|---|---|---|---|---|---|---|---|---|---|---|
| Elevation | 0 | 0 | 0.019 | 0.067 | 0 | 0 | 0.003 | 0.087 | 0.035 | 0 |
| Aspec | 0.240 | 0.167 | 0.451 | 0.144 | 0.666 | 1.37 | 0.043 | 0.068 | 0.004 | 0 |
| Slope | 0.016 | 0.540 | 0.015 | 0.008 | 0.015 | 0.012 | 0.032 | 0.037 | 0.031 | 0.036 |
| H_D_To_Hydrology | 0 | 0 | 0.288 | 0.408 | 1.264 | 0.733 | 0.079 | 0.035 | 0.008 | 0.003 |
| V_D_To_Hydrology | 13.220 | 23.976 | 9.649 | 15.165 | 6.298 | 5.483 | 0.872 | 0.503 | 0.035 | 0.004 |
| H_D_To_Roadways | 2.407 | 4.183 | 1.554 | 2.785 | 8.457 | 3.473 | 0.003 | 0.099 | 0.004 | 0.002 |
| Hillshade_9am | 0.071 | 0.313 | 0.092 | 0.417 | 0.218 | 1.216 | 0.077 | 0.028 | 0.036 | 0.011 |
| Hillshade_Noon | 0.086 | 0.044 | 0.046 | 0.256 | 0.124 | 0.801 | 0.059 | 0.035 | 0.004 | 0.001 |
| Hillshade_3pm | 0.087 | 0.138 | 0.250 | 0.212 | 0.318 | 0.309 | 0.009 | 0.051 | 0.032 | 0.009 |
| H_D_To_Fire_Points | 2.305 | 4.871 | 1.265 | 0.343 | 110.753 | 289.816 | 0.042 | 0.094 | 0.003 | 0.001 |
| $MAE$ | 28.395 | | 7.867 | | 133.125 | | 0.775 | | 0.624 | |

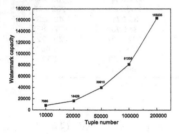

**Fig. 3.** Watermark capacity under different tuples

**Fig. 4.** Watermark capacity in different proportions

## 4.2    Watermark Capacity Experiment

Watermark capacity is a measure of the ability of a watermark to resist attacks. The more bits of information a watermark has in a certain amount of data, the more resistant the watermark will be against malicious attacks. However, the larger the watermark capacity, the greater the distortion of the data.

Figure 3 shows the change in watermark capacity under different number of tuples at $1/\eta = 1/5$. Figure 4 shows the difference in the number of embedded watermark bits by varying the value of $1/\eta$ when the number of tuples is 100000. Since our scheme embeds watermarks in the attributes of the selected tuple $1/\eta$ ratio, the value is randomly generated by the F function. Mathematical reasoning shows that there are about $N * (\ln\nu + C)/(\eta * Max)$ number of bits of information embedded in the data (C is the Euler constant). The experimental results are consistent with the inference results within the error tolerance.

## 4.3    Robustness Experiments

In this section, different attacks are performed on the watermarked data. These attacks include (1) tuple addition attack, (2) tuple alteration attack, and

(3) tuple deletion attack. We also compare our scheme with recent reversible database watermarking schemes, such as DEW, GADEW, PEEW, and RRW. Since the watermark detection rate criteria of GAHSW schemes are not the same as the previous ones, this scheme can't be compared.

**Tuple Addition Attack.** In this type of attack, the attacker adds some new tuples to the watermarked data set in an attempt to interfere with the watermark detection. The attacker may insert several randomly generated tuples into the watermarked data.

Watermark detection: As shown in Fig. 5, when the same amount increases the number of tuples as the original data, the detection accuracy of our scheme remains 100%. At this point, the detection accuracy of DEW is already less than 88%, and the accuracy of PEEW is only 98%.

Data recovery: As shown in Fig. 6, after inserting 100% of the tuples, 100% of the watermarked data can be recovered accurately. This is because the tuple addition attack does not destroy any original data or watermark, and the hash function and auxiliary data can pinpoint the location of the added watermark.

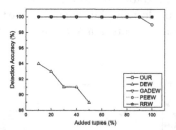

**Fig. 5.** Watermark detection accuracy after tuples addition attack

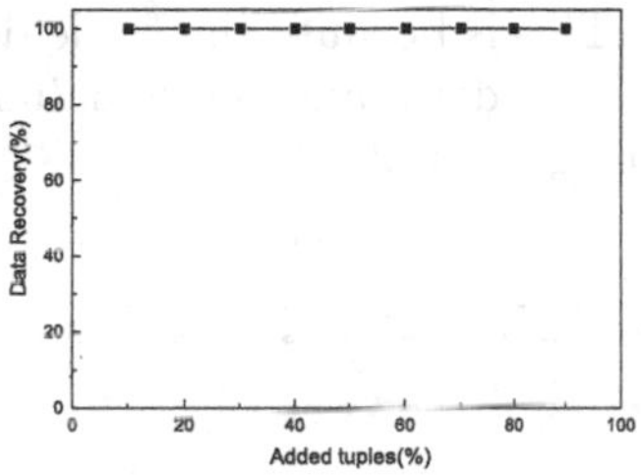

**Fig. 6.** Data recovery accuracy after tuples addition attack

**Tuple Alteration Attack.** In this type of attack, the attacker changes some tuples at random. Here we perform a bit-inversion attack on all attributes of a randomly selected tuple to interfere with the watermark detection.

Watermark detection: As shown in Fig. 7, when 90% of the tuples are alternated, our scheme still maintains 100% accuracy in watermark detection, while only RRW maintains 100% accuracy in the other schemes.

Data recovery: As shown in Fig. 8, it is almost impossible to perform complete data recovery on data knowing that it has been subjected to a tuple alteration attack. The experimental results are generally consistent with the results of the tuple deletion attack, and the scheme is still able to recover data that has not been attacked fully.

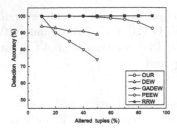

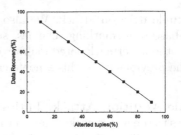

**Fig. 7.** Watermark detection accuracy after tuples alteration attack

**Fig. 8.** Data recovery accuracy after tuples alteration attack

**Tuple Deletion Attack.** In this attack, the attacker removes a certain number of tuples at random, trying to interfere with watermark detection by removing tuples containing watermark information.

Watermark detection: As shown in Fig. 9, when 90% of the tuples are deleted, our scheme can still maintain 100% watermark detection accuracy. When many tuples are deleted, the detection accuracy of GADEW, PEEW, GAHSW, and other methods, except RRW, decreases significantly.

Data recovery: As seen in Fig. 10, the original data can be recovered accurately. This is because the tuple deletion does not destroy the remaining part of the original data, and the remaining data can still be watermarked and restored to its original state.

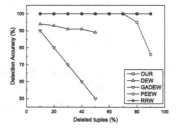

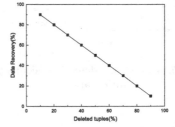

**Fig. 9.** Watermark detection accuracy after tuples deletion attack

**Fig. 10.** Data recovery accuracy after tuples deletion attack

## 5   Conclusion

Aiming at the problem that the watermark information extracted under severe attack is incomplete, a random reversible watermarking scheme based on LSB modification is proposed. Watermark embedding algorithm, watermark integrity checking algorithm, watermark detection algorithm, and data recovery algorithm are designed. The watermark capacity is improved by embedding multiple watermarks in the selected tuples. The randomness of watermark information distribution is increased by controlling different tuples to embed an unequal proportion of watermarks. When extracting the watermark, the accuracy of watermark detection is improved by discarding the attacked bits. Finally, the scheme's statistical distortion, watermark capacity, and robustness experiments are analyzed. We can draw some conclusions. Firstly, our scheme can resist severe tuple attacks. Secondly, the impact of embedded watermarks on data availability is small. Compared with DEW, GADEW, RRW, PEEW, and GAHSW, our scheme has better attack resistance and causes less data distortion, which can meet the requirements of most application scenarios.

# References

1. Liu, Y.-C., Ma, Y.-T., Zhang, H.-S., Li, D.-Y., Chen, G.-S.: A method for trust management in cloud computing: Data coloring by cloud watermarking. Int. J. Autom. Comput. 8(3), 280–285 (2011)
2. Cheng, L., Liu, F., Yao, D.: Enterprise data breach: causes, challenges, prevention, and future directions. Wiley Interdisc. Rev. Data Mining Knowl. Discov. 7(5), 1211 (2017)
3. Wong, P.W., Memon, N.: Secret and public key image watermarking schemes for image authentication and ownership verification. IEEE Trans. Image Process. 10(10), 1593–1601 (2001)
4. Saadi, S., Merrad, A., Benziane, A.: Novel secured scheme for blind audio/speech norm-space watermarking by arnold algorithm. Signal Process. 154, 74–86 (2019)
5. Venugopala, P., Sarojadevi, H., Chiplunkar, N.N.: An approach to embed image in video as watermark using a mobile device. Sustain. Comput.: Inform. Syst. 15, 82–87 (2017)
6. Brassil, J.T., Low, S., Maxemchuk, N.F.: Copyright protection for the electronic distribution of text documents. Proc. IEEE 87(7), 1181–1196 (1999)
7. Agrawal, R., Kiernan, J.: Watermarking relational databases. In: VLDB'02: Proceedings of the 28th International Conference on Very Large Databases, pp. 155–166. Elsevier (2002)
8. Sion, R., Atallah, M., Prabhakar, S.: Rights protection for categorical data. IEEE Trans. Knowl. Data Eng. 17(7), 912–926 (2005)
9. Niu, X., Zhao, L., Huang, W., Zhang, H.: Watermarking relational databases for ownership protection. Acta Electron. Sin. 31(S1), 2050 (2003)
10. Shehab, M., Bertino, E., Ghafoor, A.: Watermarking relational databases using optimization-based techniques. IEEE Trans. Knowl. Data Eng. 20(1), 116–129 (2008)
11. Zhang, Y., Yang, B., Niu, X.-M.: Reversible watermarking for relational database authentication. J. Comput. 17(2), 59–66 (2006)
12. Zhang, Y., Niu, X.-M.: Reversible watermark technique for relational databases. Acta Electron. Sin. 34(S1), 2425 (2006)
13. Gupta, G., Pieprzyk, J.: Reversible and blind database watermarking using difference expansion. Int. J. Digital Crime Forensics (IJDCF) 1(2), 42–54 (2009)
14. Farfoura, M.E., Horng, S.-J., Wang, X.: A novel blind reversible method for watermarking relational databases. J. Chin. Inst. Eng. 36(1), 87–97 (2013)
15. Jawad, K., Khan, A.: Genetic algorithm and difference expansion based reversible watermarking for relational databases. J. Syst. Softw. 86(11), 2742–2753 (2013)

16. Iftikhar, S., Kamran, M., Anwar, Z.: Rrw-a robust and reversible watermarking technique for relational data. IEEE Trans. Knowl. Data Eng. **27**(4), 1132–1145 (2014)
17. Franco-Contreras, J., Coatrieux, G.: Robust watermarking of relational databases with ontology-guided distortion control. IEEE Trans. Inf. Forensics Secur. **10**(9), 1939–1952 (2015)
18. Imamoglu, M.B., Ulutas, M., Ulutas, G.: A new reversible database watermarking approach with firefly optimization algorithm. Math. Problems in Eng. **2017**(2), 1–14 (2017)
19. Hu, D., Zhao, D., Zheng, S.: A new robust approach for reversible database watermarking with distortion control. IEEE Trans. Knowl. Data Eng. **31**(6), 1024–1037 (2018)
20. Li, Y., Wang, J., Ge, S., Luo, X., Wang, B.: A reversible database watermarking method with low distortion. Math. Biosci. Eng. **16**(5), 4053–4068 (2019)
21. Li, Y., Wang, J., Luo, X.: A reversible database watermarking method non-redundancy shifting-based histogram gaps. Int. J. Distrib. Sens. Netw. **16**(5), 1550147720921769 (2020)
22. Xiang, S., Ruan, G., Li, H., He, J.: Robust watermarking of databases in order-preserving encrypted domain. Front. Comp. Sci. **16**(2), 1–9 (2022). https://doi.org/10.1007/s11704-020-0112-z

# Enabling Accurate Data Recovery for Mobile Devices Against Malware Attacks

Wen Xie, Niusen Chen, and Bo Chen[✉]

Department of Computer Science, Michigan Technological University, Michigan, USA
bchen@mtu.edu

**Abstract.** Mobile computing devices today suffer from various malware attacks. After the malware attack, it is challenging to restore the device's data back to the exact state right before the attack happens. This challenge would be exacerbated if the malware can compromise the OS of the victim device, obtaining the root privilege. In this work, we aim to design a novel data recovery framework for mobile computing devices, which can ensure recoverability of user data at the corruption point against the strong OS-level malware. By leveraging the version control capability of the cloud server and the hardware features of the local mobile device, we have successfully built MobiDR, the first system which can ensure restoration of data at the corruption point against the malware attacks. Our security analysis and experimental evaluation on the real-world implementation have justified the security and the practicality of MobiDR.

**Keywords:** Mobile device · Data recovery · OS-level malware · Corruption point · FTL · TrustZone · Version control

## 1 Introduction

Mainstream mobile computing devices (e.g., smart phones, tablets, etc.) have been suffering from various malware attacks [8]. For example, ransomware encrypts the data of a victim device and asks for ransom; trojans first steal data from a victim device, send the data to the remote controller, and corrupt the data locally. Especially, there is one type of strong malware [15] which can compromise the OS, obtaining the root privilege. This type of OS-level malware is difficult to combat due to its high system privilege [15]. Data are extremely valuable for both organizations and individuals. Therefore, after a mobile device is attacked by the OS-level malware and the stored data are corrupted, it is of significant importance to ensure that the valuable data can be restored to the exact state right before the malware corruption (**data recovery guarantee**). We define the point of time right before the malware starts to corrupt the data as the "corruption point", and the data recovery guarantee requires restoring the data at the corruption point after malware attacks.

© ICST Institute for Computer Sciences, Social Informatics and Telecommunications Engineering 2023
Published by Springer Nature Switzerland AG 2023. All Rights Reserved
F. Li et al. (Eds.): SecureComm 2022, LNICST 462, pp. 431–449, 2023.
https://doi.org/10.1007/978-3-031-25538-0_23

To enable data recovery, existing works either 1) purely rely on a remote version control server [12,19,20], or 2) purely rely on the local device [9,10,22, 24,29,30]. Simply relying on the remote version control server cannot achieve the data recovery guarantee, as the OS-level malware may compromise the most recent data changes (i.e., *delta*) in the device which have not[1] been committed remotely and, the remote server can only allow restoring the historical state of the data rather than the exact state at the corruption point. Simply relying on the local storage cannot achieve the data recovery guarantee against the OS-level malware either, because: First, FlashGuard [22] and TIMESSD [30] retain historical data in the storage hardware for data recovery. This is essentially equal to maintaining a local version control system but, due to the limited local storage capacity, the historical data can only be retained for a short term (e.g., 20 d in FlashGuard). This implies that the data which are not retained any more may become irrecoverable if compromised by the malware. Second, MimosaFTL [29], SSD-Insider [9], and Amoeba [24] incorporate malware detection to avoid retaining too much unnecessary historical data, but the malware detection may suffer from false negatives and the data corrupted by the undetected malware may be lost. SSD-Insider++ [10] tries to compensate the false negatives, but their strategy is specific for the ransomware and, their lazy detection algorithm still suffers from potential false negatives.

In this work, we aim to achieve the data recovery guarantee against the OS-level malware. Our key idea is to build a secure version control system *virtually* across the mobile device and the version control server in an adversarial setting (Fig. 1), such that the most recent delta data are correctly maintained in the mobile device and the historical delta data are correctly stored in the cloud server. In this manner, any version of data is recoverable in the mobile device hence the version of data at the corruption point is always recoverable. A salient advantage of our design is that it does not rely on any malware detection mechanisms and hence does not suffer from false negatives and, meanwhile, it does not suffer from the storage capacity as the cloud storage can be easily scaled up. Towards the aforementioned goal, the first step of our design is to ensure that the OS-level malware cannot corrupt any newly generated delta data. Mobile devices today usually use flash memory as external storage and, a flash storage medium typically exhibits two salient hardware features: 1) performing out-of-place update internally, and 2) introducing a flash translation layer (FTL) to transparently handle the flash memory hardware. Therefore, we can simply hide the delta data in the flash memory [21,22]: due to the physical isolation, the malware cannot physically "damage" the delta data stored in the flash memory even if it can compromise the OS; additionally, as the flash storage performs out-of-place update, overwriting operations performed by the malware at the OS level can only invalidate rather than delete the delta data stored in the flash memory. Besides, our design needs to address extra challenges:

---

[1] Typically, delta data are committed to the remote server periodically rather than continuously, to reduce bandwidth/energy consumption imposed on the low-power mobile computing devices.

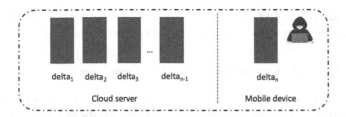

**Fig. 1.** A virtual version control system across the cloud server and the mobile device. We focus on defending against attackers in the mobile device side. Handling attackers in the cloud server side has been explored extensively before [12, 13, 18–20, 27, 32].

First, the malware may first overwrite the user data at the OS level, invalidating them in the flash memory, and then fill the entire disk (on top of the block device) to force the garbage collection in the flash memory to reclaim those flash blocks storing invalid data. To address this challenge, we periodically invoke a backup process which commits the new delta data to the cloud server and, before any new delta data are committed remotely, we will temporarily "freeze" the garbage collection over them. In other words, once the new delta data are committed remotely, the garbage collection on them can run normally.

Second, the OS-level malware may disturb the backup process, so that the delta data may not be securely extracted from the flash memory and correctly committed to the cloud server. To facilitate the backup process, we need a backup app which runs in the application layer, securely extracting delta data and committing them to the cloud server. Two issues need to be tackled:

1) How can we prevent the backup app from being compromised by the OS-level malware? Mobile devices today are broadly equipped with Arm processors, which provide a hardware-level security feature TrustZone. TrustZone can allow creating a trusted execution environment (i.e., a secure world) and, any code running in this environment cannot be compromised by the adversary which can compromise the OS. We therefore move critical components of the backup app into the secure world to avoid being compromised by the malware.

2) How can the backup app securely extract delta data from the flash memory? The backup app runs at the application layer and does not have access to the raw data in the flash memory. We therefore modify the FTL, so that upon the backup process, it can work with the backup app, extracting the raw flash memory data and sending them to the backup app. To prevent the malware from disturbing the extraction process, we incorporate a backup mode into the FTL and, if the mode is activated, the FTL will be exclusively working for the backup process. To activate the backup mode securely, authentication is performed based on the secret known by the backup app and the FTL. To prevent the malware from corrupting delta data sent from the FTL to the backup app, the FTL will compute cryptographic tags for the delta data using a secret key, and the backup app will verify the delta data before committing them remotely. To prevent the malware from replaying old delta data, the version number should be embedded

into each tag. Note that the FTL stays isolated from the OS, therefore the malware cannot compromise the tag computing process as well as the secret key.

**Contributions.** We summarize our contributions below:

- We have designed MobiDR, the first data recovery system for mobile computing devices, that can ensure recoverability of data at the corruption point against malware attacks. We consider the strong malware which is allowed to compromise the OS of the victim device.
- We have built two user-level apps, DRBack and DRecover, which make the proposed design usable by regular mobile users in the user space. The apps work together with our modified FTL (DRFTL) to enable secure data backup (periodically) and data recovery (upon failures).
- We have analyzed the security of MobiDR. In addition, we have implemented a real-world prototype of MobiDR using a few embedded boards and a remote version control server, and assessed the performance of MobiDR.

## 2    Background

**Flash Memory.** Flash memory especially NAND flash is widely used as the mass storage for mobile devices today. For instance, main-stream smartphones and tablets use eMMC and UFS cards; smart IoT devices use microSD cards. Flash memory is typically organized into blocks, each of which is further divided into pages. The number of pages in a flash block varies from 32 to 128, and the page size varies from 512, 2048, to 4096 bits. Each page usually contains a small spare out-of-band (OOB) area, used for storing metadata like error correcting code. Flash memory typically supports three operations: read, program, and erase. The read/program operation is performed on the basis of pages, while the erase operation is performed on the basis of blocks. Different from conventional mechanical drives, flash memory exhibits some unique characteristics. First, it follows an erase-then-write design. This means, re-programming a flash page usually requires first erasing it. However, since the erase operation can only be performed on blocks, re-programming a few pages would be expensive. Therefore, flash memory uses an *out-of-place update* strategy for small writes. Second, each block can be programmed/erased for a limited number of times, and a block would be worn out if it is programmed/erased too often. Therefore, wear leveling is usually integrated to distribute writes/erasures across the flash evenly.

**Flash Translation Layer (FTL).** Flash memory exhibits completely different nature compared to HDDs (hard disk drive). To be compatible with traditional block file systems (e.g., EXT4, FAT32) built for HDDs, a flash-based storage device is usually used as a block device. This is achieved by introducing an extra firmware layer, namely, the flash translation layer (FTL) to transparently handle unique characteristics of flash memory, exposing a block access interface. The FTL stays isolated from the OS, implementing a few unique functions

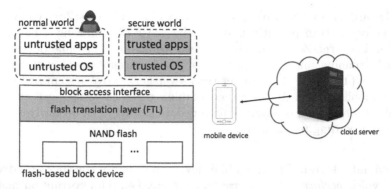

**Fig. 2.** Our system model. The part on the left is the architecture of the mobile device, in which the components in yellow color are isolated from the untrusted OS. (Color figure online)

including address translation, garbage collection, wear leveling, and bad block management. Address translation maintains the address mappings between the addresses (i.e., the Logical Block Addresses or *LBAs*) accessible to upper layers and the flash memory addresses (i.e., the Physical Block Addresses or *PBAs*). Garbage collection periodically reclaims the flash memory space occupied by obsolete data which have been invalidated by the FTL after the out-of-place update is performed. Wear leveling periodically swaps blocks so that the programmings/erasures performed over the entire flash blocks can be even out. Bad block management handles those blocks which have been worn out.

**TrustZone.** ARM TrustZone is a main-stream trusted execution environment (TEE) implementation for mobile devices. It is a hardware-based technology which provides security extension to ARM processors[2]. TrustZone separates two worlds, a secure world and a normal world. The two worlds have isolated memory space and different privilege level to peripherals. Applications running in the normal world cannot access memory space of the secure world, while applications running in the secure world can access memory space of the normal world in certain conditions. The processor can only run in one world at a certain time. A special *Non-secure* (NS) bit determines in which world the processor is currently running. A privileged instruction *Secure Monitor Call (SMC)* switches the processor between the normal and the secure world.

## 3    System and Adversarial Model

**System Model.** Our system mainly consists of two entities (Fig. 2): 1) a mobile computing device; and 2) a remote cloud server. The mobile device is equipped with a flash-based block device as external storage (e.g., an eMMC card, a

---

[2] TrustZone has been broadly supported since ARMv7.

microSD card, or a UFS card) and Arm processors with TrustZone enabled. The flash memory is transparently managed by the *FTL*, exposing a block access interface. The TrustZone can separate two worlds in the mobile device, a normal world running untrusted applications, and a *secure world* running *trusted applications* (TA). The cloud server runs a version control system and interacts with the mobile device. As the server is running as a cloud instance, its computational resources (i.e., computing power, data storage) can be easily scaling up and down according to the need.

**Adversarial Model.** In the mobile device, we mainly consider an adversary (Fig. 2) which *performs data corruption attacks*, i.e., data corruption malware. This can be ransomware which encrypts a victim device's data and asks for ransom. This can also be a piece of trojan or backdoor malware that first steals user data and then damages them locally in the victim device. We consider the strong OS-level malware [15] which can compromise the regular OS running in the TrustZone normal world and corrupt any data visible to the OS. Here "data" especially refers to the information having been committed to the external storage rather than those staying in the memory and not yet been committed.

The cloud server is assumed to correctly store and maintain the versioning data, and how to ensure integrity of the versioning data outsourced to an untrusted remote server has been explored extensively in prior works [12,18,20]. Other assumptions include: 1) TrustZone is secure, and the malware cannot compromise the secure world, including the trusted applications and data in it. This is a reasonable assumption in the domain of TrustZone technologies [21]. Although a few security leaks [25,31] have been found in TrustZone, hardening TrustZone has been explored extensively in the literature [28] and is not our focus. 2) The malware is not able to hack into the FTL. This is also reasonable as the FTL is isolated from the OS (Fig. 2) and there are no known attacks which can bypass the isolation utilizing the limited block access interface exposed by the flash device. 3) The communication channel between the mobile device and the cloud server is assumed to be protected by TLS/SSL. 4) The malware will not perform arbitrary behaviors like blocking user I/Os or conducting DoS attacks which would be easily noticed by the device's owner.

## 4    MobiDR

### 4.1    Design Rationale

To achieve the data recovery guarantee against the OS-level malware, MobiDR relies on the versioning data in the cloud server as well as the most recent delta stored in the local device. Periodically, MobiDR securely commits changes of data (i.e. delta) in the local device to the cloud server (*the backup phase*). After a malware attack, MobiDR will retrieve the versioning data from the server, applying the most recent delta (stored locally) to restore the data at the corruption point (*the recovery phase*).

**The Backup Phase.** The backup phase happens *periodically*. After each successful backup, the FTL will monitor write requests from the OS and, if a new flash page is written, it will push the corresponding PBA into a stack and the garbage collection on those new flash pages should be frozen[3] temporarily even if they are invalidated. Meanwhile, the FTL will monitor write requests on some reserved LBAs. Note that the LBAs are accessible to the OS, e.g., if a disk sector is 512-byte, and a flash page is 2 KB, every 4 sector addresses can be converted to one LBA. If a secret write sequence on the reserved LBAs is observed by the FTL, a new backup phase has been invoked by the backup app and the FTL will enter the backup mode. In the backup mode, the backup app will work with the FTL to extract the most recent delta data securely from the flash memory and to correctly commit them to the cloud server. The backup app will issue read requests (i.e., by writing the reserved LBAs) and, upon receiving a read request, the FTL will: 1) pop a PBA from the stack, read the data stored in the corresponding flash page, and identify the corresponding LBA; and 2) compute a cryptographic tag over a concatenation of the data, the LBA, the current version number as well as the sequence number (during each backup process, the sequence number starts from 0, and is increased by 1 after each read request), using a secret key; and 3) return the data, the LBA, and the tag for each read request. Upon receiving a response from the FTL, the backup app will verify the integrity of the data using the tag and the secret key. Once the stack is exhausted by the FTL, the backup app will verify and commit all the delta data together with their tags to the cloud server, and quit the backup mode. Note that critical components of the backup app should be run in the TrustZone secure world to avoid being compromised by the OS-level malware.

**The Recovery Phase.** Once a mobile device suffers from a malware attack and the stored data are corrupted, a data recovery phase will be activated to restore the data back to the *corruption point*. The malware is assumed to have been detected [15] at some point of time (i.e., the *detection point*) and eliminated[4] from the victim device and, therefore, the recovery app can be run in the normal world. As the backup phase is activated periodically, the device should have conducted a successful backup process (i.e., the *most recent backup point*) before the malware is detected. The corruption point should be located either between the most recent backup point and the detection point (if the malware detection is effective and can detect the malware immediately) or before the most recent backup point (if the malware detection suffers from false negatives). The recovery app will restore the data at the corruption point by: 1) retrieving versioning data from the remote server (correctness of the data is verified via the cryptographic

---

[3] An extreme case is that the device is almost filled and there are no unused blocks. In this case, if there is a flash block which stores invalid data that have not been backed up yet, MobiDR will back up those data immediately and garbage collection can be immediately performed on this block.

[4] If the malware is impossible to be eliminated, we can unplug the flash storage medium from the victim device and plug it into a clean device for the recovery phase.

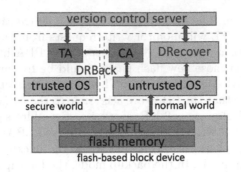

**Fig. 3.** The design overview of MobiDR.

tags), and 2) extracting the most recent delta preserved locally in the flash memory, and 3) approaching the corruption point by interacting with the user following a binary searching manner (details elaborated in DRecover of Sect. 4.2).

### 4.2 Design Details

**Overview.** The overview of MobiDR is shown in Fig. 3. The version control server runs a version control system which allows storing and retrieving versioning data. The DRFTL is a special flash translation layer tuned for MobiDR design, which can transparently manage the raw NAND flash and work with the user-level apps for data backup and recovery. The DRBack app consists of a client application (i.e. *CA*) which runs in the normal world (based on a rich untrusted OS) and a trusted application (i.e. *TA*) which runs in the secure world of TrustZone. The *backup phase* is conducted periodically by the DRBack app, which communicates with both the DRFTL via the OS (for extracting delta data from the flash memory) and the remote version control server (for storing the delta data remotely). The *recovery phase* is conducted by the DRecover app. The DRecover app communicates with the remote version control server (for retrieving necessary versioning data) and the DRFTL (for extracting the most recent delta preserved in the flash memory, reconstructing the data at the corruption point as well as placing the data back to the flash memory). In the following, we elaborate the design detail of each major component in MobiDR.

**The Version Control Server.** The cloud server runs a version control system [12,20] which allows the client to commit a new version of the data (e.g., via commit), or to retrieve an arbitrary historical version (e.g., via checkout). In MobiDR, the data committed during each backup phase are the most recent delta currently and the corresponding cryptographic tags. The data retrieved during the recovery phase are the collection of deltas (and their corresponding tags) from the initial version up to an arbitrary version. Each delta is a collection of raw data newly stored to the flash memory pages.

**DRFTL.** The DRFTL will keep track of delta data (not yet committed remotely), protecting them from being deleted by the malware. It will also collaborate with the DRBack to correctly extract and commit the delta data, and collaborate with the DRecover to restore the data to the corruption point.

To protect the delta data in the flash memory, we need to understand the delta a bit. Here the delta means the changes of data in the flash memory. In the user space, there are typically three operations: read, write, and delete. The read operation usually does not generate delta. The delete operation is typically handled by the OS as follows: the OS will mark the corresponding disk space as invalid by updating its metadata which may cause an overwrite operation in the flash memory. The write operation in the user space may either cause a new write or an overwrite in the flash memory. For a new write, the new content will be placed to a new PBA (corresponding to a physical flash page) in the flash memory; for an overwrite, the obsolete content in the old PBA will be invalidated, and the new content will be placed to a new PBA due to the out-of-place update. Therefore, our observation is that, the new content generated since the last backup process is always stored in the new PBAs and, therefore, we can simply keep track of all the new PBAs in the flash memory, following the order they are written. In addition, each flash page has an OOB area which typically records its corresponding LBA. Therefore, the content in a PBA contains all the information[5] needed for the recovery. Note that the malware cannot compromise the delta as the flash memory performs the out-of-place update, and only the garbage collection in the FTL can remove data.

To keep track of new PBAs, the DRFTL maintains a stack in the internal RAM of the flash device. To avoid data loss due to unexpected instances like power loss, we should periodically commit the data in the stack to the flash and, once the backup phase is finished, the data associated with the stack can be cleared from both the RAM and the flash. Once a backup phase is invoked, the DRFTL will pop a PBA from the stack, read the content from the corresponding flash page, and return it to the DRBack. The aforementioned step will be terminated when all the delta data are extracted (i.c., the stack is empty).

In order to differentiate the backup/recovery phase with the normal use, we define a backup and a recovery mode for the FTL, respectively. In the backup mode, the FTL will exclusively work with the DRBack for extracting and committing the delta and, in the recovery mode, the FTL will exclusively work with the DRecover to restore the data to the corruption point. Since only the DRBack knows when to enter the backup mode, it should inform the DRFTL once it launches the backup phase. This can be achieved by reserving some LBAs, and the DRBack will perform writes on those LBAs with some secret sequence known to the DRFTL. To avoid replay attacks, we can concatenate the sequence with an index (increased by one upon a new backup phase) and encrypt it using the secret key shared between the DRBack and the DRFTL. Similarly, the DRecover

---

[5] During recovery, we can simply place the content back to the LBA in the flash memory, since where the content will be physically located is not important.

will inform the DRFTL once it launches the recovery phase with another secret write sequence on the reserved LBAs.

To prevent reclaiming flash blocks which store the delta data that have not been committed remotely, the garbage collection on the delta data will be disabled temporarily, but will be resumed as soon as a following backup is finished (in which the delta data are committed to the remote server).

**DRBack.** The DRBack will work with the DRFTL to extract the most recent delta data from the flash memory, and send them to the cloud server after having verified their correctness. Note that the DRBack contains both a trusted application (TA) running in the TrustZone secure world (mainly responsible for verifying and committing the delta), and an untrusted client application (CA) running the normal world (used as a proxy for the TA to communicate with the DRFTL to extract the delta data).

Periodically, the TA of the DRBack will issue a secret write sequence (using CA as a proxy) to the reserved LBAs, changing the DRFTL to a backup mode. In the backup mode, the TA continuously reads a special LBA until having extracting all the new delta data since the last backup process. When the DRFTL receives a read request from the TA, it will read a flash page (the PBAs are kept in the stack), and compute a cryptographic tag for the data of the page. To defend against the replay attack, the current version number, the page sequence number, the LBA and the data of the page are combined together when computing the tag. The DRFTL will return the data of the page in the first read; the LBA, the current version number, the page sequence number in the current version, as well as the tag will be combined and returned in the second read. Therefore, to extract the delta data stored at a single page, the TA needs to perform two read operations. After all the new delta data are read, the DRFTL will inform the TA (this can be achieved by responding with some special content to the read request issued by the TA). The TA will verify the delta data and, if they are correct, the TA will commit them to the cloud server. It will then send a confirmation (together with a cryptographic tag, computed over the confirmation and the version number via the secret key shared between the TA and the DRFTL) to the DRFTL and, after the DRFTL has successfully verified the confirmation, it will quit the backup mode and return to a normal state.

**DRecover.** The DRecover will collaborate with the DRFTL to restore the data to the corruption point. The DRecover will first issue a different secret write sequence to the reserved LBAs to change the DRFTL to the recovery mode; it will then retrieve the most recent delta data from the flash memory. The most recent delta data can be stored in another computing device or committed remotely. Next, it will retrieve the most recent version of the data from the cloud server, verify its integrity, and place them back to the flash memory. The user needs to check whether this restored data version has any corruptions or not. If it has no corruptions, the corruption point is located somewhere between the most recent backup point and the detection point (*case #1*); otherwise, the corruption point is located somewhere between the initial point and the most recent backup point (*case #2*). After the recovery phase is finished, the DRecover will change the DRFTL back to the normal state.

Handling case #1: The DRecover will first restore the data to the most recent backup point, and then sort the most recent delta data based on the timestamps of each page in the increasing order (for simplicity, we call them the sorted delta data). The DRecover places the first half[6] of the sorted delta data back to the flash memory, and the user will check whether this restored version contains corrupted data or not. If it contains, the corruption point should be moved backwards; otherwise, the corruption point should be moved forwards. A binary searching will be continued in either half, recursively. The number of user involvement will be $O(log\ l)$, where $l$ is the total number of pages in the sorted delta. Note that the user involvement seems to be unavoidable, as only the user knows whether his/her data were corrupted or not.

Handling case #2: The DRecover will retrieve a historical version from the remote server which is at the middle of the initial point and the most recent backup point, and work with the DRFTL to place this version back to the flash memory. The user will check whether this restored version contains corrupted data or not. If it does, the corruption point is located at a point even earlier; otherwise, the corruption point is located at a point later. A binary searching will be continued in either half, recursively. After a target version is located, the corruption point can be further located similar to case #1. The number of user involvement will be $O(log\ n + log\ l)$, when $n$ is the total number of historical versions stored in the remote server and $l$ is the maximal number of pages in a delta.

## 5  Security Analysis and Discussion

<u>Security Analysis</u>. In the following, we show that MobiDR can ensure recovery of data at the corruption point against the OS-level malware.

**Any Newly Created Delta can be Correctly Committed to the Remote Server During the Backup Phase.** The newly created data which have been written to the flash memory will not be deleted by the garbage collection of the DRFTL before they are committed to the remote server. Therefore, regardless how the malware behaves at the OS level, e.g., over-writing the user data at the block layer to invalidate them in the flash memory, writing arbitrary data to the disk sectors, the new data will stay intact in the flash memory. Note that the DRFTL is transparent to the OS, and will not be affected malware. The DRBack runs in the user space, which is separated into two parts: one (CA) is running in the normal world and acts as a proxy to communicate with the DRFTL, and the other (TA) is running in the secure world and is responsible to verify the extracted data and to commit them remotely after the verification. The malware

---

[6] The description here is not very exact. In practice, a few pages together may belong to the same atomic operation and cannot be separated.

may affect the CA, e.g., when the CA is used as a proxy to extract data from the DRFTL, the malware may corrupt the data passing through the untrusted OS. This corruption attack can be mitigated as the DRFTL will compute cryptographic tags for the extracted data and, the corruption will be detected by the TA which will not be affected by the malware. If the corruption is detected, the TA will require the CA to extract the data again (note that if the corruption persists, the TA should notify the user, as there is a potential DoS attack); others, the TA will send the extracted data, together with the associated tags, to the server.

**The Most Recent Delta Data will not be Corrupted by the Malware.** After the latest backup process, any new data created by the user since then, cannot be compromised by the OS-level malware once they have been written to the flash memory. This is because, the data stored at the flash memory are not accessible to the OS, and can only be removed by the garbage collection of the FTL; however, DRFTL has modified the garbage collection strategy so that any newly created data, valid or not, will not be deleted from the flash memory before they are correctly committed to the remote server.

**MobiDR Can Always Recover Data at the Corruption Point During the Recovery Phase.** During the recovery phase, the device is always in a healthy state, either because the malware has been eliminated from the victim device or because a clean device has been used for recovery. Therefore, the DRecover can run correctly in the OS. An arbitrary historical version of the data can be retrieved correctly by the DRecover from the version control server (crytographic tags are used to verify the correctness of a historical version upon retrieval). In addition, the new data changes since the most recent committed version are preserved in the flash memory, and are extractable by the DRecover. Being able to have access to any version of the historical data, as well as the most recent delta data, the DRecover is able to restore data at any point over the history, surely including the corruption point.

**Discussion**. In the following, we discuss a few minor issues in MobiDR.

**Sharing Secret Keys Between the DRFTL and the TA**. During initialization, the device owner can generate the secret keys, and send them to the TA in the secure world; in addition, the secret keys can be passed to the FTL as follows: the FTL reserves an LBA and monitors the writes on this page; once the device owner writes the secret keys to this LBA, the FTL will read it, copy the keys to other area invisible to the OS, and clear the data in this LBA.

**Handling Device Failures.** If the device fails (e.g., suffering from power loss [23]) upon backup and the most recent delta has not been committed yet, the user could try mobile device forensics [11] to extract the most recent delta from the device, though there is no guarantee whether the delta can be extracted or not. If the device is lost/stolen, there is still a possibility that the latest delta would be backed up to the remote server if the "pickpocket" turns on the device and network connection is available for the device. In the worst case, the user can at least restore the data to the latest backup stored in the remote server. It seems no approach can completely address the aforementioned limitation, unless the device backs up every single operation to the remote server which is impractical.

**The Impact of "Freezing" Garbage Collection.** Freezing the garbage collection will not affect the system much because: 1) The garbage collection is only frozen for those data not yet been committed remotely. 2) The garbage collection on the not-yet-committed data is only frozen for a short period, e.g., if the device is backed up daily, the period is one day. 3) If the malware fills the entire storage on purpose (i.e., no unused flash blocks), the backup operation will be performed immediately, and the garbage collection will run normally after it.

**Moving the Entire** DRBack **into the TrustZone Secure World.** One alternative is to move the entire DRBack to the secure world to prevent DoS attacks conducted by the malware. However, accessing the external storage in the secure world is non-trivial. This may require incorporating extra software components into the secure world, including disk driver and other components along the storage path [15]. We will investigate this alternative in our future work.

# 6  Experimental Evaluation

We have implemented a prototype of MobiDR, which includes DRFTL, a DRBack app, a DRecover app, and a server program. DRFTL was implemented by modifying OpenNFM [16], an open-sourced flash controller framework written in C. The cryptographic tag was instantiated using HMAC-SHA1. The DRBack app, the DRecover app, and the server program were all written in C. The DRBack app consists of two major software components (both were implemented in C): one software component (CA) runs in the normal world, and the other software component (TA) runs in the secure world of ARM TrustZone. Our TA relies on the support of OP-TEE [4], an open source trusted execution environment implementing Arm TrustZone technology, which has been ported to many Arm devices and platforms. The code of the prototype is publicly available in [1].

**Experimental setup.** We ported the DRFTL to LPC-H3131 [3], a USB header development prototype board with ARM9 32-bit ARM926EJ-S (180 Mhz), 32 MB SDRAM, and 512 MB NAND flash. After the DRFTL is ported, LPC-H3131 can be used as a flash-based block device via USB 2.0. Both the DRBack (CA) and the DRecover were run as an application in another electronic development board Firefly AIO-3399J [2], equipped with Six-Core ARM 64-bit processor (up to 1.8 GHz) and 4 GB Dual-Channel DDR3. AIO-3399J acts as the host computing device of the mobile device to perform I/Os on the flash storage provided by LPC-H3131. Note that although the processor of Firefly AIO-3399J can support TrustZone, the manufacturer of this electronic board does not offer a free support for TrustZone development. We instead measured the TA of DRBack in TrustZone secure world provided by a cheap Raspberry Pi (version 3 Model B, with Quad Core 1.2 GHz Broadcom BCM2837 64bit CPU, 1 GB RAM) [5], by porting OP-TEE[7] to it. The remote version control server was run by a desktop (8 core Intel Core i7-9700K CPU, 3.60 GHz, 32GB RAM), which was connected to a local area network in our lab, and the electronic boards (Firefly AIO-3399J and Raspberry Pi) were both connected to the same local area network. Note that none of the prior works (Sect. 7) can ensure recoverability of the data at the corruption point over time under an adversarial setting; therefore, we did not experimentally compare MobiDR with them, considering that the goal of MobiDR is different from all of them and the comparison would not be fair.

**Evaluating The Backup Phase.** The backup process is conducted by DRBack, together with DRFTL and the remote version control server. The DRBack needs to first extract data from the raw flash memory to the user space, by working with the DRFTL. This sub-process is taken care by the CA of DRBack, which runs in the normal world (rather than TrustZone secure world). The DRFTL computes tags for the data being extracted. As shown in Fig. 4(a), the throughput for data extraction is approximately 1 MB/s, which is regular for a USB 2.0 interface. The throughput for computing the tags in LPC-H3131 is around 100 KB/s. This is reasonable for a low-power electronic board equipped with a 180 MHz processor. In practice, we can replace the cryptographic hash function SHA1 with a more efficient non-cryptographic hash function like XXH128, which was shown 30 times faster than SHA1 [7].

After having extracting the data, the DRBack will verify integrity of the data based on the associated tags, and send them (together with tags) to the remote server if the verification is successful. This sub-process is taken care by the TA of DRBack, which runs in the TrustZone secure world. As shown in Fig. 4(a), the throughput for these TA operations is approximately 250KB/s. The major computation in the TA (running in the TrustZone of Raspberry Pi) is to verify the correctness of the tag (HMAC-SHA1), which requires a similar computing workload compared to the tag generation (running in the LPC-H3131). The performance of the tag verification in Raspberry Pi is 2×-3× better than the tag generation in LPC-H3131, which makes sense since Raspberry Pi is more powerful than LPC-H3131.

**Evaluating The Recovery Phase.** The recovery phase is conducted by DRecover, together with DRFTL and the remote version control server. If the corruption happens after the most recent backup process, MobiDR will restore the device by retrieving the most recent data version from the remote server, and applying the local delta up to the corruption point. If the corruption happens before the most recent backup process, it implies that the malware detection

---

[7] Currently OP-TEE has not supported TLS yet, which can be implemented as "a glue layer between mbedTLS and the GP API provided [6]".

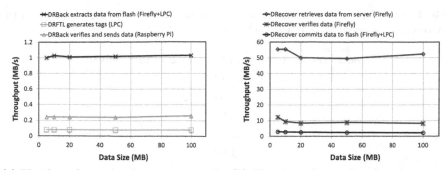

(a) The throughput of each component in the backup phase. (b) The throughput of each component in the recovery phase

**Fig. 4.** Performance in the backup and the recovery phase.

cannot detect the malware timely, or suffer from false negatives in the past. Therefore, the corruption point should be located anywhere from the initial data version to the most recent data version. For this case, we can retrieve the most recent data version, and localize the data version which is before but closest to the corruption point. The data at the corruption point can be restored by starting from the closest version, and applying the corresponding delta up to the corruption point. In the following, we assess the performance of two key steps: 1) retrieving the most recent data version from the remote server; and 2) localizing the closest data version from the most recent data version locally. As MobiDR performs data recovery by centering around the raw data in the flash memory (rather than the traditional file data), we also access whether it can recover a given file accurately or not.

**Retrieving the most recent data version from the server.** To retrieve the most recent data version, DRecover will retrieve all the deltas from the server, verifying them, and committing them back to the flash memory (by working with the DRFTL). The experimental results are shown in Fig. 4(b). The throughput for data retrieval is around 50 MB/s, which is reasonable since the communication happens in a local area network. The throughput for data verification is around 9 MB/s. This is because, Firefly AIO-3399J is a high-end electronic board with performance comparable to the desktop. The throughput for data commit is around 2.5 MB/s. This is reasonable for a USB 2.0 interface. Compared to the data extraction in Fig. 4(a), the throughput for data commit is 2× faster. This is because, the data extraction requires extra read operations for obtaining the tags, but the data commit does not need to write the tags.

**Localizing the Closest Data Version.** We have conducted an experiment in which there are 64 data versions in total, and the delta size is 2 MB (i.e., each version will generate 2 MB additional data compared to its immediate previous version). After the DRFTL has retrieved the most recent data version, it will

**Table 1.** The overhead for localizing a closest data version in DRecover, in which the most recent data version is 64, and each delta size is 2 MB.

| Closest version number | Time (s) | #User involvement |
|---|---|---|
| 8 | 39.10 | 3 |
| 16 | 33.84 | 2 |
| 32 | 22.96 | 1 |
| 48 | 35.17 | 2 |
| 56 | 41.63 | 3 |

localize a closest data version following a binary search manner, i.e., a new data version will be restored in the device and the user will get involved to determine how the "search" will be moved next. The results are shown in Table 1. We can observe that, if the targeted data version is 32, it will be localized with the minimal time, since the first version to be examined is version 32 based on the rule of binary search, and the total number of user involvements is 1; similarly, if the targeted data version is 16 or 48, it will take more time compared to version 32, since DRFTL needs to first examine version 32, and then examine version 16 or 48 (depending on the user feedback), and the total number of user involvement is 2. Without knowing where is the close data version, binary search would require at most log(n) user involvements, and the total number of versions needed to be examined is also bounded by log(n).

**Recovery Rate.** To evaluate whether MobiDR can recover a given file accurately by placing the raw data back to the flash memory, we tested 100 sample files, covering 5 categories and 30 file types (see Table 2), with file size varying between 1 MB to 100 MB. The results show that MobiDR can accurately recover all of them, which indicates a recovery rate of 100%.

**Table 2.** Summary of sample files used for testing the recovery rate.

| category | file type |
|---|---|
| text files | txt,pdf,rtf,ppt,odp,doc |
| image files | jpg,webp,tiff,gif,psd |
| video files | flv,mkv,3gp,mp4,wmv,webm,avi,f4v |
| audio files | mp3,ogg,wav,flac |
| others | zip,bin,db,tar,img,exe,msi |

## 7 Related Work

Continella et al. designed ShieldFS [17], a self-healing, ransomware-aware file system. ShieldFS can automatically shadow a copy whenever a file is modified and, the shadow copy can be used to recover the file corrupted by the ransomware. Subedi et al. proposed RDS3 [26], which hides backup data to an isolated storage space for data recovery. Both ShieldFS and RDS3 cannot combat the malware which can compromise the OS, as they are both deployed at the OS level.

Huang et al. proposed FlashGuard [22] to enable data recovery from ransomware attacks. FlashGuard needs to preserve all the historical versions of "possibly" attacked data locally in the flash memory to maximize probability of successful recovery. Wang et al. proposed TIMESSD [30] to enable data recovery by retaining past storage states in the local SSD. FlashGuard and TIMESSD try to support data recovery via the local version control, and both unavoidably suffer from the limited storage space in the local device. SSD-insider (Baek et al. [9]), and MimosaFTL (Wang et al. [29]) and Amoeba (Min et al. [24]) improved FlashGuard by incorporating a ransomware detection into the FTL, so that the local device does not need to preserve invalid data in the flash memory if the ransomware is not detected. This can save local storage space, but the malware detection unavoidably suffers from false negatives and, if a false negative happens, the data corrupted by the ransomware will become irrecoverable as they are no longer preserved locally. SSD-Insider++ [10] further employed instant backup/recovery and lazy detection algorithms to mitigate the data loss due to false negatives. However, the "lazy detection algorithm" still suffers from false negatives and, additionally, their design is only applicable to ransomware.

Guan et al. [21] proposed Bolt to enable system restoration after bare-metal malware analysis. However, Bolt is specifically designed to enable system restoration during the malware analysis, in which the malware analyst has a full control over the malware. It cannot be applied to our scenarios, in which the malware is out of the control of the victim, e.g., the malware may come anytime, and may behave arbitrarily. Chen et al. designed mobiDOM [14,15] which aims to combat malware which comes any time. However, mobiDOM can only restore data to a historical state, rather than the exact state at the corruption point. In addition, mobiDOM relies on the malware detection which suffers from both false positives and false negatives.

# 8   Conclusion

In this work, we have designed MobiDR, the first secure data recovery system which can allow a victim mobile device to restore its data at the corruption point when suffering from malware attacks. Security analysis and experimental evaluation confirm that MobiDR can ensure recoverability of data at the corruption point, at the cost of a modest extra overhead.

**Acknowledgment.** This work was supported by US National Science Foundation under grant number 1938130-CNS, 1928349-CNS, and 2043022-DGE.

# References

1. DRFlash - A Prototype of MobiDR. https://snp.cs.mtu.edu/drflash.html
2. Firefly AIO-3399J. https://en.t-firefly.com/product/industry/aio_3399
3. Lpc-h3131. https://www.olimex.com/Products/ARM/NXP/LPC-H3131/
4. Open Portable Trusted Execution Environment. https://www.op-tee.org/
5. Raspberry Pi 3 Model B. https://www.raspberrypi.org/products/raspberry-pi-3-model-b/
6. TLS support in OPTEE #4075. https://github.com/OP-TEE/optee_os/issues/4075
7. xxHash. https://cyan4973.github.io/xxHash/
8. Mobile Malware. https://usa.kaspersky.com/resource-center/threats/mobile-malware, 1998
9. Baek, S.H., Jung, Y., Mohaisen, A., Lee, S., Nyang, D.H.: Ssd-insider: Internal defense of solid-state drive against ransomware with perfect data recovery. In: Proceedings of ICDCS, pp. 875–884 (2018)
10. Baek, S., Jung, Y., Mohaisen, A., Lee, S., Nyang, D.: Ssd-assisted ransomware detection and data recovery techniques. IEEE Trans. Comput. **70**(10), 1762–1776 (2020)
11. Breeuwsma, M., De Jongh, M., Klaver, C., Van Der Knijff, R., Roeloffs, M.: Forensic data recovery from flash memory. Small Scale Digital Device Forensics J. **1**(1), 1–17 (2007)
12. Chen, B., Curtmola, R.: Auditable version control systems. In: Proceedings of NDSS (2014)
13. Chen, B., Curtmola, R., Dai, J.: Auditable version control systems in untrusted public clouds. In: Software Architecture for Big Data and the Cloud, pp. 353–366. Elsevier (2017)
14. Chen, N., Chen, B.: Defending against os-level malware in mobile devices via real-time malware detection and storage restoration. J. Cybersecur. Privacy **2**(2), 311–328 (2022)
15. Chen, N., Xie, W., Chen, B.: Combating the OS-level malware in mobile devices by leveraging isolation and steganography. In: Zhou, J., et al. (eds.) ACNS 2021. LNCS, vol. 12809, pp. 397–413. Springer, Cham (2021). https://doi.org/10.1007/978-3-030-81645-2_23
16. Google Code. Opennfm. https://code.google.com/p/opennfm/
17. Continella, A.: Shieldfs: a self-healing, ransomware-aware filesystem. In: Proceedings of ACSAC, pp. 336–347. ACM (2016)
18. Erway, C.C., Küpçü, A., Papamanthou, C., Tamassia, R.: Dynamic provable data possession. ACM Trans. Inform. Syst. Secur. (TISSEC), **17**(4), 1–29 (2015)
19. Esiner, E., Datta, A.: Auditable versioned data storage outsourcing. Futur. Gener. Comput. Syst. **55**, 17–28 (2016)
20. Etemad, M., Küpçü, A.: Transparent, distributed, and replicated dynamic provable data possession. In: Jacobson, M., Locasto, M., Mohassel, P., Safavi-Naini, R. (eds.) ACNS 2013. LNCS, vol. 7954, pp. 1–18. Springer, Heidelberg (2013). https://doi.org/10.1007/978-3-642-38980-1_1
21. Guan, L., et al.: Supporting transparent snapshot for bare-metal malware analysis on mobile devices. In: Proceedings of ACSAC, pp. 339–349 (2017)
22. Huang, J., Xu, J., Xing, X., Liu, P., Qureshi, M.K.: Flashguard: Leveraging intrinsic flash properties to defend against encryption ransomware. In: Proceedings of ACM CCS, pp. 2231–2244. ACM (2017)

23. Krishnan, A.S., Suslowicz, C., Dinu, D., Schaumont, P.: Secure intermittent computing protocol: Protecting state across power loss. In: 2019 Design, Automation & Test in Europe Conference & Exhibition (DATE), pp. 734–739. IEEE (2019)
24. Min, D., et al.: Amoeba: an autonomous backup and recovery ssd for ransomware attack defense. IEEE Comput. Archit. Lett. **17**(2), 245–248 (2018)
25. Qiu, P., Wang, D., Lyu, Y., Qu, G.: Voltjockey: Breaching trustzone by software-controlled voltage manipulation over multi-core frequencies. In: Proceedings of ACM CCS, pp. 195–209 (2019)
26. Subedi, K.P., Budhathoki, D.R., Chen, B., Dasgupta, D.: Rds3: Ransomware defense strategy by using stealthily spare space. In: Computational Intelligence (SSCI), 2017 IEEE Symposium Series on, pp. 1–8. IEEE (2017)
27. Vaidya, S., Torres-Arias, S., Curtmola, R., Cappos, J.: Commit Signatures for Centralized Version Control Systems. In: Dhillon, G., Karlsson, F., Hedström, K., Zúquete, A. (eds.) SEC 2019. IAICT, vol. 562, pp. 359–373. Springer, Cham (2019). https://doi.org/10.1007/978-3-030-22312-0_25
28. Wan, S., Sun, M., Sun, K., Zhang, N., He, X. Rustee: Developing memory-safe arm trustzone applications. In: Annual Computer Security Applications Conference, pp. 442–453 (2020)
29. Wang, P., Jia, S., Chen, B., Xia, L., Liu, P.: Mimosaftl: Adding secure and practical ransomware defense strategy to flash translation layer. In: Proceedings of the Ninth ACM Conference on Data and Application Security and Privacy, pp. 327–338 (2019)
30. Wang, X., Yuan, Y., Zhou, Y., Coats, C.C., Huang, J.: Project almanac: A time-traveling solid-state drive. In: Proceedings of the Fourteenth EuroSys Conference 2019, pp. 1–16 (2019)
31. Zhang, N., Sun, K., Shands, D., Lou, W., Hou, Y.T.: Trusense: Information leakage from trustzone. In: Proceedings of IEEE INFOCOM, pp. 1097–1105. IEEE (2018)
32. Zhang, Y., Blanton, M.: Efficient dynamic provable possession of remote data via update trees. ACM Trans. Storage (TOS) **12**(2), 1–45 (2016)

# Bootstrapping Trust in Community Repository Projects

Sangat Vaidya[1]($\boxtimes$), Santiago Torres-Arias[2], Justin Cappos[3], and Reza Curtmola[1]

[1] New Jersey Institute of Technology, Newark, NJ, USA
{ssv33,crix}@njit.edu
[2] Purdue University, West Lafayette, IN, USA
santiagotorres@purdue.edu
[3] New York University, New York, NY, USA
jcappos@nyu.edu

**Abstract.** Community repositories such as PyPI and NPM are immensely popular and collectively serve more than a billion packages per day. However, existing software certification mechanisms such as code signing, which seeks to provide to end users authenticity and integrity for a piece of software, are not suitable for community repositories and are not used in this context. This is very concerning, given the recent increase in the frequency and variety of attacks against community repositories. In this work, we propose a different approach for certifying the validity of software projects hosted on community repositories. We design and implement a *Software Certification Service (SCS)* that receives certification requests from a project owner for a specific project and then issues a project certificate once the project owner successfully completes a protocol for proving ownership of the project. The proposed certification protocol is inspired from the highly-successful ACME protocol used by Let's Encrypt and can be fully automated on the SCS side. It is, however, fundamentally different in its attack mitigation capabilities and in how ownership is proven. It is also compatible with existing community repositories such as PyPI, RubyGems, or NPM, without requiring changes to these repositories. To support this claim, we instantiate the proposed certification service with several practical deployments.

**Keywords:** Software certification · Trust establishment

## 1 Introduction

Community repositories such as PyPI [34], RubyGems [36], and NPM [32] are among the most popular and accessible ways of publishing and distributing open source software. Their immense popularity is illustrated by the large number of downloads: PyPI, the Python package manager, sees more than 600 million downloads per day [35]; npm, the Javascript package manager, more than 700 K downloads a day [33]; RubyGems, the public repository of Ruby packages, has seen more than 107 billion downloads since its creation (as of August 2022).

F. Li et al. (Eds.): SecureComm 2022, LNICST 462, pp. 450–469, 2023.
https://doi.org/10.1007/978-3-031-25538-0_24

Due to their popularity, attacks against community repositories have been on the rise in the recent past [1,3,4,7,10,13,15,16,37]. For instance, in July 2021, a PyPI package containing a backdoor was downloaded almost 30,000 times before the breach was detected [10]. In April 2020, a supply chain attack on RubyGems used packages with names similar to popular packages to infect the end user's system [37]. Similar types of supply chain attacks have become a rising concern for users of NPM as well [1,3,7,13].

This increase in frequency and variety of attacks against community repositories makes it necessary to improve the overall security stance of these popular custodians of open-source software. In this work, we focus on a fundamental question: *How can end users retrieve an authentic version of a community repository project, as intended by the project owner?* Trust in a software project can be bootstrapped by ensuring that what is retrieved is what the project owner intended. When a software project is digitally signed, this question becomes: *How can end users obtain an authentic version of the project owner's public key?*

Looking at existing mechanisms to certify software, we realized that they may not be appropriate in the context of community repositories. While code signing certificates [24–26] ostensibly provide a means to validate the identity of the software publisher, apart from a few large companies, they are rarely used in practice. This sort of certification often requires out-of-band verification and cannot be easily automated. As a result, unfortunately, the effort required to obtain a certificate is prohibitive, making these unsuitable for all types of software projects. We elaborate more in Sect. 3 on the limitations of existing certification mechanisms, including code signing.

In this work, we propose a different approach for certifying the validity of software projects hosted on community repositories. To leverage the existing PKI model of trust, our goal is to provide a way to bootstrap trust using this mechanism. In the PKI model, a certification authority binds a domain owner and a domain name to a public key. The domain owner provides proof of ownership in order to get the X.509 domain certificate. Similarly, we propose a solution where the software project owner proves the ownership of the project and gets a digital certificate that binds the project owner and the project name to a public key. We design and implement a *Software Certification Service (SCS)* that receives certification requests from a project owner for a specific project and then issues a project certificate once the owner successfully completes a procedure for proving project ownership. This project certificate validates a public key for the project.

Unlike in the code signing model, which seeks to establish trust in the identity of the software publisher using a cumbersome procedure, the proposed Software Certification Service relies on a certification protocol with the project publisher to establish ownership of the software. The proposed certification protocol is inspired from the highly-successful ACME protocol [2] used by Let's Encrypt [30] and can be fully automated on the SCS side. It is, however, fundamentally different in its attack mitigation capabilities (*i.e.*, compromise resiliency) and in how ownership is proven (*e.g.*, how to account for the specifics of software naming as opposed to domain names). It is also compatible with community repositories such as PyPI, RubyGems, NPM, without requiring changes to them.

In the ACME protocol, the owner of a domain proves ownership of that domain by provisioning a specific HTTP resource (*e.g.*, random token chosen by the Let's Encrypt CA) at a specific URL at that domain. In our approach, the project publisher proves ownership over a project by executing a certification protocol with the SCS, which requires the publisher to answer SCS challenges by provisioning certain HTTP resources (e.g., random tokens chosen by the SCS) at a specific location on the project's webpage. The ability to answer SCS challenges proves control over the project's repository. After successfully completing the certification protocol, the project owner gets a project certificate which binds a public key to a (project ID, project owner) tuple. The project owner signs the software project with the corresponding private key for distribution to end users.

The SCS certification protocol includes safeguards to provide resiliency against an adversary who is able to gain control of a project repository (*e.g.* by compromising the project repository credentials). First, the certification protocol is designed to last over an extended period of time. We raise the bar to adversaries who must maintain control over a project for a prolonged period of time, which is arguably more difficult to achieve while going undetected. Second, the SCS protocol requires that the response to a challenge must be placed on the project's repository in a publicly visible way (*i.e.*, the project's webpage). This will prevent an adversary to execute the certification protocol in a stealthy manner.

Finally, we instantiate the proposed service with several practical deployments. First, we use the service to automate the certification of community repositories projects. Our deployments include several popular community repositories: PyPI, RubyGems, and NPM. Second, we use the service to automate the delegation process in community repositories that rely on systems like TUF [12,18] to provide compromise resilience. We are actively working with Google and PyPI on integrating our service into existing cloud security frameworks.

## 2    Background on the ACME Protocol

The software certification protocol proposed in this paper is modeled after the Automatic Certificate Management Environment (ACME) protocol [2], which can be used by a certificate authority (CA) and an applicant to automate the process of verification and HTTPS certificate issuance. Certificate issuance using ACME resembles a traditional CA's issuance process, in that a user creates an account, requests a certificate for a domain, and proves control of the domain in that certificate in order for the CA to issue the requested certificate.

The entities interacting in the ACME protocol are the ACME client (*i.e.*, the applicant for the HTTPS certificate) and the ACME server (*i.e.*, the CA who issues HTTPS certificates). To begin the process of certificate issuance, the ACME client generates a key pair whose public key will be included in the HTTPS certificate to be generated by the CA. The client proves knowledge of the corresponding private key by signing a CSR (certificate signing request).

The client then engages in a protocol with the ACME server to prove control over the requested domain. For this, the client needs to complete a challenge issued by the ACME server. Once the validation is successful, the client sends a certificate signing request (CSR) just like in the traditional certificate issuance process. On receiving the request, the CA issues the certificate.

The ACME protocol is similar to a traditional certificate issuance protocol. However, the major difference lies in the step where the client proves control over the domain. For a traditional CA, this step requires human intervention. Instead, ACME automates these processes. Let's Encrypt [30] is a free, automated, and open CA which relies on ACME to issue domain certificates. Since its debut in September 2015, it has grown rapidly to become the largest CA on the web.

## 3   Existing Software Certification Mechanisms

### 3.1   Code Signing

The code signing model mirrors the PKI model used to issue domain validation TLS X.509 certificates. A software publisher applies for a publisher certificate with a Certificate Authority (CA) and proves its identity in the process. Having verified the publisher's identity, the CA issues a *code signing certificate* which binds the identity of the software publisher to a public key. The publisher then signs the software using the private key corresponding to the public key in the certificate. Finally, the user downloads the signed software, verifies the signature, and validates the publisher's certificate.

Code signing provides the following two guarantees: (1) Validation of the software publisher, *i.e.*, the software comes from a known publisher, and (2) Software integrity (*i.e.*, it has not been modified since it was signed and released by the publisher). The code signing certificate that accompanies the software provides a guarantee that certain checks were done by the CA about the identity of the publisher. As such, it fits best scenarios in which end users need to establish the trustworthiness of the publisher.

Unfortunately, to have its identity verified by the CA, the software publisher needs to go through a very cumbersome process. In addition to verifying that the publisher controls the domain name(s) listed on certificate, the CA need to verify the legal, physical and operational existence of the publisher's business before issuing the certificate. This requires the publisher to provide relevant documents and answer phone calls to complete validation. The CA must also verify the name, title, authority and signature of the person(s) requesting the certificate.

Given this manual and lengthy validation process, code signing certification cannot be automated and imposes large operational costs for the CA. The current code signing model is not suitable for all types of software, as it might be difficult for small businesses, start-ups, independent developers and freelancers to afford a code signing certificate (which few users will validate) that incurs significant costs. Another direct consequence of the cumbersome and intrusive certification process is the low adoption rate for code signing certificates. Besides limited use cases inside closed ecosystems such as Microsoft (for the Windows ecosystem and MS Office objects), Apple (for software developed using Xcode), and Adobe (for Adobe Air applications), code signing remains largely unused for the large majority of software, including open source software.

## 3.2 Package Signatures

Some community repositories allow their packages to be cryptographically signed with a private key so that end users can verify the packages with a public key. There are generally two types of package signing:

**Signed-By-Repository:** In community repositories such as NPM [32], the repository signs uploaded packages with a repository private key. The corresponding public key is publicized on Keybase [29] and is used by end users to verify downloaded packages. The repository private key is kept online to ensure that new packages can be signed as soon as possible. This results in a coarse-grained security guarantee. A compromise of the repository invalidates the security of all its packages. If, on the other hand, the repository private key remains secure, a package signature guarantees that the package uploaded to the repository is the package that an end user downloads. This in itself does not account for the possibility that an individual project's credentials were compromised (even for a brief amount of time) and a malicious version of a package was uploaded to the repository.

**Signed-By-Author:** In community repositories such as RubyGems [36], a package is signed by its author before being uploaded. The private key used for signing is kept offline. In turn, end users verify the end-to-end authenticity of the downloaded packages based on the corresponding public key. The problem with this model is that end users must discover the correct key by using out-of-band channels, a manual process that is vulnerable to fake key distribution attacks. Alternatively, the authenticity of a public key can be established using a PGP decentralized "web of trust", in which authors vouch for each other's GPG keys.

Some repositories, such as RubyGems, allow the project owner to upload a public key in a dedicated location of the repository – this is a mechanism that can be used to distribute the owner's public key. However, this solution is vulnerable to an attacker that gains control over a project's repository and replaces the owner's authentic public key. The solution we propose provides better resiliency against attackers that gain control over a project's repository.

## 4    System and Threat Model

### 4.1    System Model

Figure 1 describes the general architecture of the proposed software certification service. At a high level, our approach is similar to the model employed by code

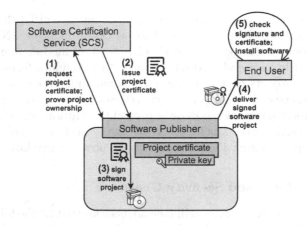

**Fig. 1.** The software certification architecture.

signing. A *software publisher* contacts the *Software Certification Service (SCS)* requesting a *project certificate* for a software project that it owns (*e.g.*, a Python package hosted on the PyPI community repository). The software publisher then proves ownership of the software project by executing a *software project certification* protocol with the SCS (Step 1). Once the certification protocol is completed successfully, the SCS issues a *project certificate* that binds together a *certificate public key* to a (project ID, project owner) tuple (Step 2). The software publisher then uses the corresponding private key to sign the software project (Step 3) for distribution to end users (Step 4). Finally, end users can verify the integrity of the retrieved software by checking the signature on the software and can get assurance that the software is authentic and originates with the project owner by checking the project certificate (Step 5).

The main difference from the code signing model is in Step 1. Whereas code signing seeks to establish trust in the identity of the software publisher based on a manual procedure that requires human intervention, our approach relies on a certification protocol that requires the software publisher to establish ownership of the software – a protocol designed to be fully automated on the SCS side.

Software publishers that wish to apply for a project certificate need to establish an account with the SCS. This account will be used by the SCS to track interactions with the software publisher. During the software certification protocol, messages sent by a software publisher to the SCS server are authenticated using the publisher's *SCS account key*. Software publishers use a different set of credentials to manage projects hosted on a community repository, referred to as a *repository key* (*e.g.*, a password used to log into the community repository).

**Community Repository.** We describe the salient features of a *community repository*, which hosts and distributes third party software that represents the main target for the proposed certification service. A community repository is a collection of individual projects which, usually, are open source and are developed using the same programming language. For example, PyPI [34] (the Python package index), RubyGems [36] (the Ruby package manager), NPM [32] (the JavaScript package manager), or CPAN [27] (the Perl module manager).

Each project has a web-based homepage with a standard format that is uniform across all projects hosted on the same community repository. Typically, a project's homepage contains several sections that can be edited by project owner, such as the project name, owner details, project description, and download links. The proposed certification service leverages the *project description* section of a project's homepage during the protocol used to prove ownership over a project.

### 4.2    Threat Model and Security Goals

We assume that the SCS service will face adversaries that fit the following threat model. The SCS service (*i.e.*, the SCS server) is trustworthy and the private key used by the SCS service for signing project certificates is out of the attacker's reach. We assume that a software publisher is able to protect her certificate signing key (this is the private key corresponding to the certificate public key). For example, this key can be stored offline, and only be used to sign new project releases. The communication between the SCS server and software publishers (acting as clients) happens over a secure channel (for example using SSL/TLS). We also assume that standard cryptographic primitives can be deployed, such as digital signatures that guarantee integrity and authenticity.

We consider the following types of adversaries:

A1: An attacker who gains access to the client's SCS account. This means that the attacker controls the SCS account key that is used to authenticate a publisher's messages to the SCS server. In this case, the attacker is able to impersonate a software publisher to the SCS service.

A2: An attacker who gains access to the project's repository account. This type of attacker controls the credential used by the project owner to manage the project on the community repository (*e.g.*, a password). This allows the attacker to arbitrarily change content in the project repository, including modifying the project description, adding/deleting project versions, or modifying the project files.

A3: An attacker who executes a network MITM attack between the SCS client and the SCS server. This type of attacker may be a nation state that has the ability to tamper with messages exchanged between the publisher and the SCS service as part of the software certification protocol.

Although an A2-type adversary may gain access to a project's repository account, we assume that the attacker does not control the entire infrastructure of the community repository. As such, the attacker cannot cause the community repository to provide different views of the project repository to different sets of clients. In addition, as our goal is to ensure the security of the certification protocol, we assume that the following attacks are outside the scope of this work:

– An attacker modifies the software package directly in the community repository, or its source code in the corresponding version control system (e.g., a

GitHub repository), and this goes unnoticed by the project owner/maintainer. We assume that proper checks are in place before a community repository project is signed for release.

- Name typosquatting attacks, in which the attacker registers a package with a similar name as a target package.

**Attacker Goals:** The attacker seeks to obtain a valid signed project certificate that binds a tuple (project ID, project owner) to a public key PK, such that the attacker is not the owner of this project and it possesses the private key corresponding to PK. This will allow the attacker to sign arbitrary versions of the project (*e.g.*, a malicious version that has a backdoor embedded).

**Security Goals.** Only the legitimate owner of a project should be able to complete a certification protocol for that project. Still, we need to account for occasional events when an attacker gains control over a project's repository, *i.e.*, we need to provide compromise resilience.

Of particular interest are adversaries that can gain control over a project for a short amount of time, during which they may try to obtain a project certificate by executing the certification protocol stealthily. If, on the other hand, adversaries must maintain control over a project for a prolonged period of time in order to successfully complete the certification protocol, this is arguably more difficult to achieve while going undetected. This is especially true if the certification protocol produces artifacts that are publicly visible on the project's webpage.

Concretely, we aim to achieve the following security goals:

SG1: Only an entity that controls an identifier should be able to successfully complete the certification for that identifier (by completing the given challenge). In particular, only the owner of a software project should be able to complete the certification protocol for that project.

SG2: Messages generated during one execution of the certification protocol for one account (i.e., between the SCS server and one client) cannot be used towards obtaining authorizations for other accounts.

SG3: Attackers that gain control over a project's repository for a short period of time should not be able to successfully complete the certification protocol. This prevents such attackers from obtaining a project certificate unbeknownst to the project owner.

SG4: Anyone who can access a project's webpage should be able to know whether an instance of the certification protocol is currently running for that project. In particular, the project owner should be able to tell if someone other than the project owner is trying to obtain a certificate for the project.

## 5   Software Certification Service

### 5.1   Preliminaries

**General Terms.** During the course of execution of the proposed protocol for software certification, we make use of the following terms:

- SCS server: The server software run by the Software Certification Service (SCS) acting as a Certification Authority (CA) that issues project certificates upon request by software publishers.
- SCS client: The client software run by a software publisher that interacts with the SCS server in order to obtain a project certificate for a project owned by that publisher.
- Project Repository: The repository used for hosting the project. This refers to an individual project repository hosted on a community repository.
- Project: The project/package for which the certificate is requested.
- Project Owner: The software publisher who owns the project for which certification is requested. The project owner controls the SCS client and the project hosted on the repository.
- End Users: The users that download the project distribution from the project repository for installation and use.

**Keys.** The SCS server has a *CA key pair*, and uses the CA private key to sign project certificates. The CA private key has high value and its compromise can have serious consequence for the security of the SCS service. As such, it must be kept offline, or protected using dedicated hardware (e.g., HSMs).

The following types of keys are used by the project owner:

- *SCS account keys* (public/private key pair): Used to authenticate an SCS account holder (acting as a client) to the SCS server. Specifically, the client uses the SCS account private key to sign the messages sent to the SCS server while executing the SCS certification protocol. There is only one SCS account key pair per client, generated by the client. Once registered with the SCS server, an SCS account key can be used to obtain multiple project certificates for multiple projects owned by the client.
- *certificate keys* (public/private key pair): This key pair is generated by the client (acting as a project owner) and its public key is included in the project certificate generated by the SCS. The corresponding private key will be used by the project owner to sign a software project.
- *repository key*: This is the credential used by a project owner to manage the project on the community repository. For example, it can be the password used by the project owner to log into her account with community repositories such as PyPI, RubyGems or NPM.

**High-Level Details.** As our proposed protocol is inspired from the ACME protocol, we reuse several of ACME's protocol design choices. We mention these details here, so as not to overload unnecessarily the actual protocol description.

*JSON Objects and Signatures.* Information exchanged between the SCS server and clients is encapsulated in objects encoded as JSON messages [14] carried over HTTPS. Typically, the client sends to the SCS server a stub object, and the server returns the object where various fields have been filled.

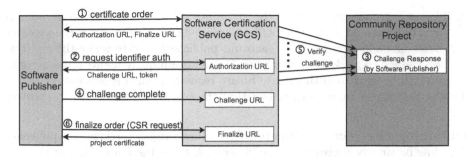

**Fig. 2.** SCS protocol overview (Phase 2: Obtaining a project certificate).

Messages sent by the client to the server are signed using the private key of the client's SCS account key pair. The server uses the corresponding public key to verify the authenticity and integrity of messages from the client.

*Nonces Against Replay Attacks.* To ensure protection against replay attacks, the protocol uses an anti-replay mechanism based on *nonces*: The server maintains a list of nonces issued to clients, and any signed request from the client must include a nonce. The server verifies that the nonces it receives from clients are among those that it has issued to clients, and ensures that nonces can be used at most once by clients.

### 5.2   Certification Protocol Description

We now describe the protocol used by the SCS to issue a software project certificate. The protocol has two major phases: 1) Register an account with the SCS server; 2) Request a project certificate. Phase 1 is carried out only once, when the publisher is communicating with the server for the first time. Each publisher creates an account with the SCS server, so that the SCS server can keep track of its interactions with different publishers. The same account can then be used to get certificates for multiple projects owned by the publisher. Phase 2, illustrated in Fig. 2, is carried out every time the publisher needs a certificate for a project. Appendix A provides a security analysis of the proposed certification protocol.

**SCS Account Registration.** The protocol execution is initiated by the publisher (*i.e.* project owner) using the SCS client. To register an account with the SCS server, a publisher emgages in the following protocol with the SCS server:

1. The client generates a fresh pair of SCS account keys (public/private keys).
2. The client sends to the SCS server a registration request that contains the following information: the contact details of the client (email address), the SCS account public key, and a signature over the entire registration request using the SCS account private key.

3. The SCS server verifies that the signature is valid and that no account is already registered under this SCS account public key. The server then creates an account and stores the SCS account public key used to verify the registration request. This SCS account key is used to uniquely identify the account and will be used to authenticate future requests from this account.
4. The SCS server informs the client that the account was successfully created.

**Obtaining a Project Certificate.** To obtain a project certificate, a publisher who has previously registered an SCS account, takes the following four steps:

*(1) Submit a project certificate order.* The client sends to the SCS server a project certificate order request that contains the software project identifier for which the certificate is requested (*e.g.*, project URL), and the certificate expiration date. Upon receipt of the order request, the SCS server performs some basic checks regarding the project identifier, such as checking the validity of the project URL. The server may also check if the project URL matches one of the participating community repositories.

The SCS server then informs the client that the order is created, together with an "**expires**" time by when the client needs to complete authorization of the requested project identifier. The server's response also contains an Authorization URL (a location on the server where the server makes available an identifier authorization resource associated with this new order request) and a Finalize URL (a location on the server where the client will inform the server that it has completed the project ownership proof requirement).

*(2) Obtain authorization over the project identifier.* The project identifier authorization process establishes that an SCS account holder is authorized to manage project certificates for a given project identifier. For this, the client must prove ownership over the project by completing multiple validation challenges chosen by the SCS server. To complete a validation challenge, the client provisions the challenge response on the project's repository (more details in Sect. 5.3). The following steps are executed in order to complete a validation challenge:

1. The client sends a request to the Authorization URL and the SCS server responds with an Authorization object that contains the project identifier (*i.e.*, the project URL), the Challenge URL, and a validation token for this challenge. The validation token is a string randomly generated by the SCS server for this challenge. The Challenge URL is a location on the SCS server where the client will notify the server that the challenge has been completed.
2. The client completes the challenge by provisioning the challenge response on the project's repository.
3. The client notifies the SCS server that the challenge was completed by sending a request to the Challenge URL.
4. The SCS server verifies that the challenge was completed.

To address the threat model described in Sect. 4.2, the SCS certification protocol requires a client to respond to multiple challenges spread over time, and the SCS server to check that the client's response to the challenges remains persistently visible on the project's repository. In Sect. 5.3, we provide details on how challenges are completed by the client and verified by the SCS server.

*(3) Finalize the order by submitting a CSR.* Once the client completes the server's requirements for this project certificate order, it generates a certificate key pair (public/private keys). It also creates a Certificate Signing Request (CSR) and requests to finalize the order by sending the CSR to the Finalize URL. The CSR contains the software project identifier for which the certificate is requested (e.g., project URL), the certificate public key, the project owner details (name, email address), temporal information (valid from date, expiration date), and a signature over the entire CSR using the certificate private key.

If the request to finalize the order is successful, the SCS server issues the project certificate, which is signed with the server's CA private key. The SCS server then responds to the client with a Certificate URL.

*(4) Download the project certificate.* The client downloads the project certificate by sending a request to the Certificate URL, located on the SCS server.

## 5.3  Identifier Authorization

An attacker who gains control over the project's repository for a brief period of time may be able to provision the challenge response on the project's repository, notify the server to validate the challenge, and then quickly remove the challenge response from the project's repository. In order to achieve security goal SG3 and mitigate attackers that can take control of the project repository for a brief period of time, we design the identifier authorization step to last over an extended period of time. In this way, a successful attacker needs to maintain control over the project repository for a longer period of time, which is arguably more difficult to achieve while going undetected.

Specifically, to obtain authorization over a project identifier, a project owner acting as a client in the certification protocol must complete not just one challenge, but multiple validation challenges spread over an *identifier validation window* of time. Additionally, for each challenge, the client must not only provision the challenge response on the project's repository, but must also maintain persistently this challenge response on the project's repository over a *challenge validation window* of time. For example, we may consider a 7-day identifier validation window[1] during which the server will send a new challenge every 24 h for 7 d in a row. For each challenge, the server will check the persistence of the challenge answer on the project's repository multiple times randomly during the 24-hour challenge validation window.

The project identifier authorization process establishes that an SCS account holder is authorized to manage project certificates for a given project identifier.

---

[1] We picked 7 d based on previous repository breaches, which were detected as early as a few hours in some cases or it took 5–7 d in other cases [21–23].

*Validation of individual challenges.* For each validation challenge, the client must provision a challenge response on the project's repository. In order to achieve security goal SG4 and deal with long-term adversarial presence, the validation requires that the response to a challenge must be placed on the project's repository in a publicly visible way. This will prevent an adversary to execute the certification protocol stealthily, as the legitimate project owner and/or other project maintainers will notice that a certification protocol is ongoing.

Specifically, to complete a challenge, the client must provision the challenge response in the *project description* section of the project's homepage. To preserve the functionality of the project description section and reduce confusion for the casual user who browses that project's homepage, the challenge response is placed at the end of the project description, using delimiters that make it clear they are not part of the actual project description. Placing the challenge response in the project description meets our requirement that the certification protocol must generate artifacts that are publicly visible.

The client generates the challenge response as a Base64-encoded string of characters generated by concatenating the validation token for the challenge with a key fingerprint, separated by a"." character:

Response = token || "." || base64(fingerprint(SCS account key)),

where "||" denotes concatenation of strings, and the fingerprint is computed as a SHA-256 digest of the SCS account key. The response is placed at the end of the project's description, using clear delimiters.

After notifying the server about completion of the challenge, the client needs to maintain the challenge response on the project homepage during the challenge validation window. The server checks the existence of the challenge response multiple times at random times within this window. If all the server checks during the challenge validation window are successful, the server deems the challenge as successfully completed, and generates the next challenge for the client.

## 6   Deployments

### 6.1   SCS Implementation Details

The SCS service has two components, the server and the client. We implemented the SCS server on top of Boulder [39], which is an open-source ACME-based CA built for Let's Encrypt and written in Go. We have adapted the code to process the Project ID (the project repository URL) instead of the domain names. For example, when the client requests a project certificate, the server verifies that the project URL comprises of a valid set of characters and that the URL belongs to one of the community repositories that the SCS service has been deployed to. We also implement the challenge-response protocol used for proving project ownership. The SCS server is engages by keeping track of the challenge-response process and how far the client is in the proof of ownership process. The process on the server side is automated and does not require manual intervention.

We implemented the SCS client on top of Lego [31], which is an ACME client implementation for Let's Encrypt, written in Go. The SCS client is responsible for initiating the certificate issuance process, by placing a request to the server. The client is also responsible for participating in the challenge-response protocol and for fulfilling the challenge issued by the server. The project owner gets the challenge response from the SCS client and provisions it on the project homepage. This is the only step that requires manual intervention during the challenge-response SCS protocol execution.

## 6.2 Deployment to Community Repositories

We deployed the SCS service to several community repositories to automate the issuance of certificates for the projects hosted on these repositories. By design, the SCS service does not require any changes to these community repositories, which makes it deployable right away and serves as an incentive for adoption.

The SCS service can be deployed to community repositories where each individual project has a dedicated webpage containing a project description section. Most community repositories fit this scenario, with the project description being normally used to provide basic information about the project. Although every community repository may have a different web layout for the project description, all the projects that are hosted on the same community repository have the same layout for the project description.

During the SCS protocol execution, the project owner provisions on the project description webpage the responses to challenges issued by the SCS server. To preserve the functionality of the project description field and reduce confusion for the casual user who browses the project's webpage, the challenge responses are placed at the end of the project description, using delimiters that make it clear they are not part of the actual project description (see Sect. 5.3). As shown in Fig. 3, the challenge response will be publicly visible on the project's webpage.

**SCS for PyPI.** PyPI [34] is used for hosting and distributing Python packages. We use the "Project description" page to display the SCS challenge response. For this, the project owner includes the challenge response in the project description section of the *setup.py* file, which generally contains the metadata for the Python package, and then builds the package and uploads it to PyPI.

**SCS for RubyGems.** RubyGems [36] is used for hosting and distributing Ruby projects, known as "gems". To display the SCS challenge response, we use a section on a project's webpage where the owner can provide a short description of the project, which can range from a single sentence to a few paragraphs. Also, the project page does not allow HTML or Markdown formatting and so, unlike in PyPI, project owners do not have any choice in the way a challenge response gets displayed in the section. The project owner includes the challenge response in the description field of the *gemspec* file, which generally contains the metadata for the gem, and then builds the package and uploads it to RubyGems.

Project description

Example Package

This is a sample project to test the SCS service.

Software certification service:

||SCS Response||+=+ qa0MBO_3AnSJv611SDJF_wrIiZAyCUB-P-Fgy8QM604.mkHMATCJqC2w-Ru93qIttSJqfGUqtHU03AU5WARUeeo +=+

📄 Readme          📄 Explore  (BETA)          📦 0 Dependencies

This is a sample project to test the SCS service.

Software certification service:

||SCS Response|| =+= rkzCCtSNDwIfFFRyHuURQZEjiGoObsgRFaUQoSvdojc.PVQWIwdDiKSmB-X7P11JfDtTmrcM_j0zPcJDmemMm8l =+=

(a) PyPI                        (b) NPM

**Fig. 3.** Challenge response on the project webpage for various community repos.

**SCS for NPM.** NPM [32] is the Node package manager used for hosting and distributing JavaScript packages. We use the "Readme" page to display the SCS challenge response. For this, the project owner includes the challenge response in the *package.json* file and then builds the package and uploads it to NPM.

### 6.3   Automating Delegations in Community Repositories

We consider a setting in which a system such as TUF [18] or Diplomat [12] is used to provide compromise resilience for a community repository such as PyPI. This type of protection is achieved through several mechanisms, such as the use of *roles* (which allow to separate responsibility in a system) and *delegations* (which allow to distribute responsibilities in a system).

For PyPI, there is a `root` role, which indicates which keys are authorized for other roles, such as the `projects`, `release`, and `timestamp` roles. The `projects` role is trusted to validate all the packages on PyPI. This role delegates trust for individual packages to the developers responsible for those packages. For example, the `projects` role may delegate the `BeautifulSoup` project to the public key belonging to the developer Alice, who is responsible for `BeautifulSoup`.

This delegation step can occur whenever a new project is created on PyPI, or an existing project wants to change an existing delegation. Currently, such a delegation involves manual operations on the part of the PyPI maintainers, which is not scalable since PyPI has over 345,000 projects (as of December 2021).

We automate this delegation step using the SCS service. To have her public key certified as trusted for the `BeautifulSoup` project, the developer responsible for `BeautifulSoup` engages in the SCS ownership-proving protocol with the entity responsible for the `projects` role (i.e., the PyPI server). If the developer successfully completes the SCS protocol, this serves as proof that the developer owns the `BeautifulSoup` project. As a result, the `projects` role will delegate trust for the `BeautifulSoup` project to the public key of this developer.

Specifically, once the ownership protocol is completed successfully, the server updates the top-level `projects` role to include a new "delegations" entry to a new role `BeautifulSoupOwner` that is in charge of `BeautifulSoup`. This entry will include the public key of the developer responsible for `BeautifulSoup`. Then, the developer creates the `projects` file for the `BeautifulSoupOwner` role.

# 7  Related Work

Previous works in the area of securing community repositories studied the design and implementation of community repositories and proposed attacks [5, 6] and defenses [11, 12, 17]. These works focus on designing more secure software ecosystems with properties such as compromise-resilience and supply chain integrity. [19] discusses the security issues with the programming language specific community repositories like PyPI, RubyGems or NPM. In addition, due to the rising number of vulnerabilities and malware in the NPM ecosystem, various works [8, 9, 40] have been proposed to find new vulnerabilities, isolate untrusted packages, evaluate risks and remediate issues. [20] discusses the typosquatting and combosquatting attacks on the Python software ecosystems like PyPI. Other frameworks, such as in-toto [17, 28] and Sigstore [38], focus on the security of the entire software supply chain. As opposed to previous work, our focus is on bootstrapping trust in a community repository project by ensuring that end users can retrieve an authentic version of a community repository project, as intended by the project owner. Specifically, we propose a new mechanism to certify software hosted in community repositories.

# 8  Conclusion

In this work, we have presented a new approach for certifying the validity of software projects hosted on community repositories. Towards this goal, we have introduced a Software Certification Service (SCS) which gives software publishers the ability to prove the ownership of their projects and then get a project certificate that binds the project owner and the project name to a public key. Although inspired from the ACME protocol in that it can be fully automated on the SCS side, the proposed certification protocol is fundamentally different in its attack mitigation capabilities and in how ownership is proven.

We deployed the SCS service to several community repositories, including PyPI, RubyGems, and NPM, to automate the issuance of certificates for projects hosted on these repositories. By design, the SCS service does not require any changes to these community repositories, which makes it deployable right away and serves as an incentive for adoption. We are currently working with Google and PyPI on integrating our service into existing cloud security frameworks. As future work, we plan to extend the SCS service to more community repositories (currently, we require that each individual project has a dedicated webpage containing a project description section) and to explore other use cases that can benefit from automated verification. We also plan to evaluate the usability aspects of the proposed SCS certification protocol; in particular, we need to better understand what are appropriate values for the validation windows, which should be chosen as a tradeoff between usability and security.

**Acknowledgments.** This research was supported by the US National Science Foundation under Grants No. CNS 1801430, DGE 1565478, and DGE 2043104.

# A    Security Analysis

We now turn to analyzing the security of the proposed SCS protocol. We first show that the protocol meets the security goals stated in Sect. 4.2, and then analyze the protocol's compromise resiliency.

**SG1:** *Only a project's owner should be able to complete the certification for that project.* To prove ownership over a project, which is required for completing the certification protocol, an entity must successfully complete the challenges generated by the SCS server. As such, for each challenge, the entity must both:

- Hold the private key of the SCS account key pair used to respond to the challenge. This is because the responses from the client to the SCS server must be signed with that key.
- Control the project in question. This is because successfully provisioning the challenge response on the project's homepage requires write-access to the project's repository.

Since only the project owner has write-access to the project's repository, a successful execution of the SCS protocol ensures that a specific SCS account holder is also the entity that controls a project (*i.e.*, the project owner).

**SG2:** *Messages generated during one execution of the certification protocol for one account (i.e., between the SCS server and one client) cannot be used towards obtaining authorizations for other accounts.* This is achieved because all messages sent by an SCS client to the SCS server are signed using that client's SCS account private key. Thus, such messages cannot be reused between instances of the certification protocol executed by different SCS account holders.

**SG3:** Attackers that gain control over a project's repository for a short period of time are not be able to successfully complete the SCS certification protocol. The certification protocol is designed so that the identifier authorization step lasts over an extended period of time. An entity attempting to complete the certification protocol for a project must complete multiple challenges. For each challenge, the challenge response must be maintained persistently on the project's homepage, because the SCS server will check multiple times randomly during the challenge validation window. If an attacker is able to briefly gain control over the project's repository, she maybe able to provision a valid challenge response for that challenge. However, such an attacker will not be able to successfully provision valid information for subsequent challenges.

**SG4:** We need to show that an attacker cannot complete an SCS certification for a project in a stealthy manner. The SCS protocol achieves this by requiring that all challenge responses must be placed on the project's repository in a publicly visible way (*i.e.*, on the project's homepage). This ensures that the legitimate project owner and/or other project maintainers will notice that a certification protocol is ongoing.

**Compromise Resiliency.** If an attacker is able to get hold of the *repository key* for a project, this allows the attacker unfettered access to the project repository, including making changes to the project's homepage. The attacker can register an account with the SCS server and then request a project certificate under this SCS account. Having access to the repository key, the attacker will be able to provision challenge responses on the project homepage.

The SCS protocol has two safeguards in place to deal with a repository key compromise. First, the certification protocol is designed to to last over an extended period of time. Thus, if the repository key compromise is detected early enough, the project owner can change the repository key, preventing the attacker from successfully completing the certification protocol. In this way, a successful attacker would have to maintain control over the project repository for a longer period of time, which is arguably more difficult to achieve while going undetected. Second, the SCS protocol requires that the response to a challenge must be placed on the project's repository in a publicly visible way (*i.e.*, the project's homepage). This will prevent an adversary to execute the certification protocol stealthily, as the legitimate project owner and/or other project maintainers will notice that a certification protocol is ongoing and will take steps to terminate such an active threat.

# References

1. Aguirre, J.: Fake npm Roblox API Package Installs Ransomware and has a Spooky Surprise. https://blog.sonatype.com/fake-npm-roblox-api-package-installs-ransomware-spooky-surprise (2021)
2. Barnes, R., Hoffman-Andrews, J., McCarney, D., Kasten, J.: Automatic Certificate Management Environment (ACME). RFC 8555 (Mar 2019). https://datatracker.ietf.org/doc/html/rfc8555
3. Barsan, A.: Dependency Confusion: How I Hacked Into Apple, Microsoft and Dozens of Other Companies. https://medium.com/@alex.birsan/dependency-confusion-4a5d60fec610/ (February 2021)
4. Burt, J.: Supply Chain Flaws Found in Python Package Repository. https://www.esecurityplanet.com/threats/supply-chain-flaws-found-in-python-package-repository/ (August 2021)
5. Cappos, J., Samuel, J., Baker, S., Hartman, J.H.: A look in the mirror: Attacks on package managers. In: Proceedings of the 15th ACM Conference on Computer and Communications Security, pp. 565–574. CCS '08, ACM, New York, NY, USA (2008)
6. Cappos, J., Samuel, J., Baker, S., Hartman, J.H.: Package Management Security. Tech. rep., University of Arizona (2008)
7. Cimpanu, C.: Malware found in npm package with millions of weekly downloads. https://therecord.media/malware-found-in-npm-package-with-millions-of-weekly-downloads/ (October 2021)
8. Decan, A., Mens, T., Constantinou, E.: On the impact of security vulnerabilities in the npm package dependency network. In: Proceedings of the 15th International Conference on Mining Software Repositories, pp. 181–191. MSR '18, ACM (2018)

9. Garrett, K., Ferreira, G., Jia, L., Sunshine, J., Kästner, C.: Detecting suspicious package updates. In: Proceedings of the 41st International Conference on Software Engineering: New Ideas and Emerging Results, pp. 13–16. ICSE-NIER '19, IEEE Press (2019). https://doi.org/10.1109/ICSE-NIER.2019.00012

10. Goodin, D.: Software downloaded 30,000 times from PyPI ransacked developers' machines. https://arstechnica.com/gadgets/2021/07/malicious-pypi-packages-caught-stealing-developer-data-and-injecting-code/ (July 2021)

11. Kuppusamy, T.K., Diaz, V., Cappos, J.: Mercury: Bandwidth-effective prevention of rollback attacks against community repositories. In: Proceedings of the 2017 USENIX Conference on Usenix Annual Technical Conference, pp. 673–688. USENIX ATC '17 (2017)

12. Kuppusamy, T.K., Torres-Arias, S., Diaz, V., Cappos, J.: Diplomat: Using delegations to protect community repositories. In: 13th USENIX Symposium on Networked Systems Design and Implementation (NSDI 16), pp. 567–581 (2016)

13. Lakshmanan, R.: Two NPM Packages With 22 Million Weekly Downloads Found Backdoored. https://thehackernews.com/2021/11/two-npm-packages-with-22-million-weekly.html (November 2021)

14. Rfc 8259. https://datatracker.ietf.org/doc/html/rfc8259

15. Ruohonen, J., Hjerppe, K., Rindell, K.: A Large-Scale Security-Oriented Static Analysis of Python Packages in PyPI. In: Proceedings of the 18th International Conference on Privacy, Security and Trust (PST). IEEE (2021)

16. Sharma, A.: Sonatype Catches New PyPI Cryptomining Malware. https://blog.sonatype.com/sonatype-catches-new-pypi-cryptomining-malware-via-automated-detection/ (June 2021)

17. Torres-Arias, S., Afzali, H., Kuppusamy, T.K., Curtmola, R., Cappos, J.: In-toto: Providing farm-to-table guarantees for bits and bytes. In: Proceedings of the 28th USENIX Conference on Security Symposium, pp. 1393–1410. SEC'19 (2019)

18. TUF: The Update Framework. https://www.updateframework.com/

19. Vaidya, R.K., Carli, L.D., Davidson, D., Rastogi, V.: Security issues in language-based sofware ecosystems. CoRR abs/1903.02613 (2019)

20. Vu, D.L., Pashchenko, I., Massacci, F., Plate, H., Sabetta, A.: Typosquatting and combosquatting attacks on the python ecosystem. In: 2020 IEEE European Symposium on Security and Privacy Workshops (EuroS PW). pp. 509–514 (2020). https://doi.org/10.1109/EuroSPW51379.2020.00074

21. Bitcoin gold issues critical alert. https://www.enterprisetimes.co.uk/2017/11/27/bitcoin-gold-issues-critical-alert

22. Npm packages disguised as roblox api code caught carrying ransomware. https://www.theregister.com/2021/10/27/npm_roblox_ransomware/

23. Typosquatting attacks on rubygems. https://thehackernews.com/2020/04/rubygem-typosquatting-malware.html

24. Introduction to Code Signing. https://docs.microsoft.com/en-us/previous-versions/windows/internet-explorer/ie-developer/platform-apis/ms537361(v=vs.85)

25. Minimum Requirements for the Issuance and Mgmt. of Publicly-Trusted Code Signing Certificates. https://casecurity.org/wp-content/uploads/2016/09/Minimum-requirements-for-the-Issuance-and-Management-of-code-signing.pdf

26. Leading Certificate Authorities and Microsoft Introduce New Standards to Protect Consumers Online. https://casecurity.org/2016/12/08/leading-certificate-authorities-and-microsoft-introduce-new-standards-to-protect-consumers-online/

27. Comprehensive Perl Archive Network. https://www.cpan.org/

28. in-toto. https://in-toto.io/
29. Keybase. https://keybase.io/
30. Let's Encrypt. https://letsencrypt.org/
31. ACME client implementation. https://letsencrypt.org/docs/client-options/
32. Javascript Node package manager. https://npmjs.com
33. NPM download stats. https://npmcharts.com/
34. Python Packaging Index. https://pypi.org
35. PyPI download stats. https://pypistats.org/packages/__all__
36. RubyGems statistics. https://rubygems.org/stats
37. Supply-chain attack hits RubyGems repository with 725 malicious packages. https://arstechnica.com/information-technology/2020/04/725-bitcoin-stealing-apps-snuck-into-ruby-repository/ (2020)
38. Sigstore. https://www.sigstore.dev/
39. ACME server Boulder. https://github.com/letsencrypt/boulder
40. Zimmermann, M., Staicu, C.A., Tenny, C., Pradel, M.: Small world with high risks: A study of security threats in the npm ecosystem. In: 28th USENIX Security Symposium (USENIX Security 19). pp. 995–1010 (2019)

# Intrusion Detection

# Assessing the Quality of Differentially Private Synthetic Data for Intrusion Detection

Md Ali Reza Al Amin[1(✉)], Sachin Shetty[1], Valerio Formicola[2],
and Martin Otto[3]

[1] Old Dominion University, Norfolk, VA 23508, USA
{malam002,sshetty}@odu.edu
[2] California Polytechnic State University, Pomona, California, USA
vformicola@cpp.edu
[3] Siemens Technology US, Princeton, NJ 08540, USA
m.otto@siemens.com

**Abstract.** Supervised learning is effectively adopted in Network Intrusion Detection Systems (IDS) to detect malicious activities in Information Technology (IT) and Operation Technology (OT). Sharing high-quality network data among cyber-security practitioners increases the chance of detecting new threat campaigns by analyzing updated traffic features. As data sharing brings privacy concerns, Differential-Privacy (DP) has emerged as a promising approach to performing privacy-preserving analytics. This paper presents an approach to generating high-quality synthetic network features using a differentially private Generative Adversarial Network (DP-GAN) based on the DoppleGANger https://github.com/fjxmlzn/DoppelGANger toolset. We assess the classification performance of several machine learning (ML) models on a privacy-preserved synthetic dataset derived from the NSL-KDD intrusion dataset. Experiments show ML algorithms achieve high classification accuracy on the synthetic data (95.95%) with a low privacy budget ($\varepsilon = 6.73$), i.e., low success rates for membership inference attacks. Hence, DP-GAN models offer a promising tool for sharing traffic features with bounded loss of privacy.

**Keywords:** Intrusion detection system · Differential privacy · Generative adversarial networks · Data sharing

## 1 Motivation

With the increasing adoption of Information Technology (IT) and Operation Technology (OT), Intrusion Detection System (IDS) is one of the most critical defensive mechanisms against cyber-attacks with potential impact on the cyber-physical system. Network IDS detects malicious or anomalous activities

V. Formicola—This work has been performed while at Siemens Technology US.

F. Li et al. (Eds.): SecureComm 2022, LNICST 462, pp. 473–490, 2023.
https://doi.org/10.1007/978-3-031-25538-0_25

within a network domain by analyzing network traffic characteristics (features). Detecting if network traffic is malicious or benign, or determining the attack category, is a classification problem. Several supervised machine learning models have been widely used to train IDS and improve detection accuracy with good success on known attack methods. However, as attackers develop new techniques, for example, developing and using variants of known attack tools, models have to be re-trained against new features. Updating a data-driven network IDS is more effective if information and data are shared among cyber-security practitioners in a timely manner. As a matter of fact, data sharing is very controlled and limited, despite the benefit, due to privacy concerns in the exposure of sensitive information.

Most anonymization techniques require a subset of real data to be shared among security practitioners. However, for some domains sharing real data with remote entities imposes a security threat. For example, intrusion detection datasets contain real attack signatures and sensitive information (i.e., source and destination IP addresses, port numbers, etc.). During data sharing, attackers can use the attack signature information to learn how to bypass the detection if the real data gets compromised. At the same time, large network-level intrusion data under attack scenarios can help to build good machine learning-based intrusion detection systems. However, the lack of such attack datasets has significantly hampered data-driven research. Sometimes, it is not feasible to share data among different teams, even within the organization. To guarantee no part of the attack datasets is being shared outside the organization's private network, we need an alternative method to sharing real data that can be used to build a robust machine learning model.

In this work, we leverage a tool, DoppleGANger (DG) [13] to build the synthetic data generation framework and investigate the synthetic data utility -i.e., classification of malicious traffic - while protecting the privacy of information contained in a dataset. DG is developed to generate synthetic networked time-series data using generative adversarial networks (GANs) while improving the data fidelity, i.e., long-term dependencies, complex multidimensional relationships, mode collapse. DG claims to achieve 43% better fidelity than other baseline models. DG also tackles the mode collapse issue of GANs by developing a custom auto-normalization heuristic method. Previous studies [5] have proposed synthetic data generation using Decision Trees, Random Forest, etc., by keeping the statistical properties like mean or median close to the original dataset. However, it is also important to test the machine learning model's performance (i.e., classification accuracy) on the original dataset when the model is trained on the synthetic dataset. One promising way to generate synthetic data that resembles original data for analytical tasks is to use GANs. GANs are neural networks that use random noise as input and generate realistic data samples. GANs have been widely used to generate synthetic data and translation in image and text data [2,9]. However, GAN-based models are prone to Membership Inference Attacks (MIA). In MIA, the attacker aims to identify whether a specific record was used to train the model. Moreover, GAN-based generation does not allow the user to quantify and assess the level of privacy achieved. To alleviate that issue, we apply the differential privacy on GAN, DP-GAN, generated synthetic data to make the privacy guarantee and make the machine learning model robust against MIA. The DP-GAN model consists of two networks, a generator and a discriminator, which can be modeled based on the application domain. Long Short Term Memories (LSTM) is used inside the generator to model continuous data, and Multilayer Perceptron (MLP) is used to model discrete data. To achieve the differential privacy guarantee, we used the Differentially Private Stochastic Gradient Descent (DP-SGD), proposed by [1], to train the discriminator and the Adam optimizer to train the generator.

We use a well-known Intrusion Detection Dataset, NSL-KDD, to conduct the experiments. To date, NSL-KDD has still been considered an intrusion detection benchmark because of its diverse attacks groups [18]. In summary, we provide the following contributions:

– Generate differentially private synthetic intrusion detection dataset from NSL-KDD while maintaining high accuracy for classification. Further, we assess the differential privacy achieved in the synthetic intrusion detection dataset. Even if GAN-based approaches are well studied, no quantification has been done so far regarding differential privacy and against membership inference attacks. Therefore, our investigation on differentially private intrusion detection, where we retain 95% classification accuracy, supports the research on synthetic data in the cyber-security community.
– We perform an assessment of detection accuracy by following a use case scenario where data is trained on a differentially private synthetic dataset and tested on the original dataset for validation. As a result, we achieve 90% accuracy in detecting malicious traffic from benign traffic.
– We find the parameters of DP-GAN to generate synthetic data that achieve a trade-off between privacy and accuracy for intrusion detection.

The rest of the paper is as follows: in Sect. 2, we describe the related work, Sect. 3 describes the Privacy-Preserving framework, Sect. 4 explains how we prepare the dataset and privacy we are protecting, and lastly, in Sect. 5, experimental results are presented.

## 2   Related Work

Privacy-preserving data sharing has been widely discussed in the past. However, organizations are still skeptical about sharing their own data for use in research. To improve the intrusion detection accuracy, a large volume of network data is needed. Previous technique for IDS like Snort [3] works with detection rule for known attack. The main drawback for the rule based method is that it does not perform well for novel attacks. This is why ML based methods are currently being used for the automated rule generation by the machine. Previous efforts [14,21] in intrusion detection heavily rely on large volumes of network data. Sharing these data with the research community is not practical as the dataset contains sensitive information that impose privacy guarantee.

There has been some work done on improving the detection accuracy using GAN using the dataset we have used in this paper. Authors in [12] propose a framework based on GANs to generate adversarial samples to improve intrusion detection. NSL-KDD dataset is used to test the feasibility of the model. The authors in [17] proposed a generative adversarial network (GAN) based intrusion detection system (G-IDS), where GAN generates synthetic samples, and IDS gets trained on them along with the original ones. GAN based IDS work focused on generating adversarial samples but does not guarantee the privacy. Several other approaches as in [8,16,22] use GANs to generate synthetic datasets for ad-hoc and Industrial Internet of Things (IIoT) networks. These models are focused on solving the imbalance problems in the intrusion detection dataset. Compared to these works, our work focuses on generating the synthetic intrusion detection dataset and assessing privacy while maintaining high-level classification accuracy.

The authors in [11], propose a framework to generate privacy-preserving synthetic data suitable for release for analytical purposes. To ensure the privacy, the principal of $t$-closeness is applied GAN model. PATE-GAN [10] is the Private Aggregation of Teacher Ensembles (PATE) framework which applies to the GANs. Another differentially private generative adversarial network approach described in [19] achieved differential privacy in GANs by adding carefully designed noise to gradients during learning procedure. The authors used MNIST and MIMIC-III dataset to do evaluation. However, to the best of our knowledge so far DP-GAN is not directly applied to the Network Intrusion Detection System dataset NSL-KDD. We also show that, DP-GAN is robust than the GAN to defend against membership inference attacks.

## 3   Privacy Preserving Framework

In this section, we elaborate on the design of privacy-preserving framework, a differentially private generative adversarial network, to mitigate privacy exposure and maintain desirable utility in the generated intrusion detection data. In our proposed approach, we first train a DG model using real data. After the training, the generator in the DG model can generate a sample dataset which can be used instead of real dataset. Then, differential privacy is applied on the GAN generated synthetic dataset to meet the privacy guarantee and defend against MIA. We elaborate the detail of data generation and preserving privacy in our approach further in this section.

### 3.1   Generation Using DG

GANs are a data-driven generative modeling technique that takes training data samples as an input (original data) and outputs a model that generates new samples from the same distribution of the input. A GAN consists of a generator $G$ and a discriminator $D$. First, the generator maps the noise vector to samples and generates plausible data. Then, the discriminator is trained by taking samples as input and classifying those samples as fake or real. More precisely, GANs assume to have a dataset of $n$ samples $O_1, ..., O_n$, where $O_i \in \mathbb{R}^p$, and each sample is drawn i.i.d. from some distribution $O_i \sim P_O$. The goal of GANs is to use these samples to learn a model that can draw samples from the distribution $P_O$, usually a Gaussian or a uniform. At the same time, the discriminator takes samples as input and classify as either real or fake. Backpropagation is used to minimize the errors in the classification task to train the parameters of both the generator and discriminator. As soon as the training begins, the generator generates fake data, and the discriminator learns that the data is fake. After some training rounds, the generator learns how to fool the discriminator, resulting in the identification of fake data as real data. The loss function for GANs is: $min_G max_D \mathbb{E}_{x \sim p_x}[log D(x)] + \mathbb{E}_{z \sim p_z}[log(1 - D(G(z)))]$. In contrast to the prior generative modeling approach, e.g., likelihood maximization of parametric models, GANs make very few assumptions about the original data structure. The original GAN process [6] is presented in Fig. 1

GAN has been widely used in fake image generation and vanilla GAN have proven the success. The real-valued or continuous variables in the image data can be modeled using Gaussian distribution. Generating images of specific categories rather than high quality is still a challenging task as high variance is present in the specific image category. The authors in [20] states that when min-max normalizer is used on pixel values data to normalize, it is followed the Gaussian-like distribution. However, it is not always true for continuous variables in domains like computer vision that the distribution come from Gaussian. Moreover, min-max normalization can lead to vanishing gradient descent problem. This raises the concerns to handle non-image continuous data and other discrete types data.

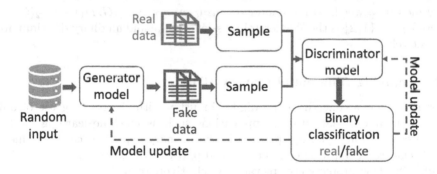

**Fig. 1.** GAN process

One of the well-known issue with the GAN is mode-collapse [6]. In mode-collapse, GAN generates a single type of output or small set of outputs despite being trained on diverse dataset. This issue happens when the generator finds a sample type that can fool the discriminator and it keeps generating that type as there is no incentive for the generator to change things up. Mode-collapse can cause serious issue when dealing with intrusion detection dataset as the dataset contains diverse types of data. Authors in the paper [13] claim to have dealt with the mode-collapse problem. Measurements of physical properties (metadata) can also influence the characteristics of the measurements. For example, a denial-of-service (DoS) attack can create a larger traffic than a probing attack. So that GAN needs to learn the joint distribution between metadata and their corresponding measurements. The following steps were used in the DG paper to generate synthetic data:

- Mode-collapse
- Capturing attribute relationship

To tackle the mode collapse, DG develops a custom *auto-normalization* heuristics. For example, we have a dataset which has two time series with different offsets (min max values). A standard normalization approach would first normalize the data by the global min and max and store them as global constants. Then, GAN model train on the normalized data where normalization is just scaling and shifting by a constant. So the mode collapse still occurs. Instead DG, normalize each time series signal individually and store the min/max as fake metadata. Thus GAN learns to generate fake metadata by identifying the min.max for each time series individually, which are then used to rescale measurements to a realistic range. In our case, intrusion detection dataset, we consider each network flow as an individual time series signal. As in the intrusion detection dataset, each traffic flow at each time-step defined as malicious or benign traffic.

DG achieves in capturing the attribute relationship by introducing an auxiliary discriminator. Because, generating metadata and measurements using a single discriminator is too difficult. The auxiliary discriminator only discriminates on metadata. The losses from discriminator and auxiliary discriminator are then combined by a weighted parameter $\alpha : min_G max_{D_1,D_2} \mathbb{L}_1(G, D_1) + \alpha \mathbb{L}_2(G, D_2)$ where $\mathbb{L}_i, i \in \{1, 2\}$ is the Wasserstein loss of original and auxiliary discriminator respectively.

### 3.2 Applying Differential Privacy (DP)

User privacy is a concern in the digital industry with the growing use of data for a multitude of data-driven applications such as machine learning models. In the case of data sharing, privacy is the primary aspect to consider due to the disclosure of sensitive content to third parties. An existing method such as de-identification protects user privacy by selectively removing information fields connected to user identities. However, de-identification is prone to reconstruction attacks, i.e., queries forged on a database to reconstruct individual records. Further, de-identified databases are prone to linkage attacks where malicious actors can re-identify users by correlating the remaining fields with background information, i.e., using auxiliary data sources and forming a big picture of user profiles.

Differential privacy ensures users' privacy from reconstruction attacks by manipulating the output of an analytical query on a database. A differentially private algorithm guarantees that its outcome changes under controlled conditions (privacy budget), regardless of the data's single records (elements).

In the case of machine learning, DP states that a model $\mathcal{M}$ is differentially private if for any pairs of training datasets $\mathcal{D}$ and $\mathcal{D}'$ that differ for a single user record, and for any input $z$, it holds that [13]

$$\mathcal{M}(z; \mathcal{D}) \leq e^{\epsilon} \mathcal{M}(z; \mathcal{D}') + \delta$$

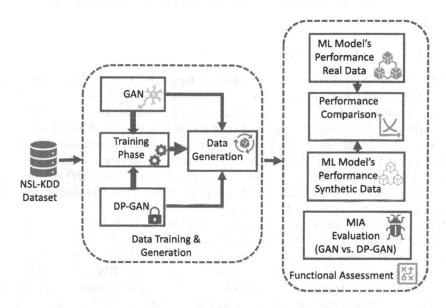

**Fig. 2.** Experimental flow diagram

where $\mathcal{M}(z; \mathcal{D})$ denotes a model trained on $\mathcal{D}$ and evaluated on $z$. Smaller values of $\epsilon$ and $\delta$ give more privacy. DoppleGANger's differential privacy framework is developed on top of the Google Tensorflow Privacy library [7]. The basic idea of Tensorflow Privacy is to modify the gradients used in stochastic gradient descent (SGD), which is the modified version of vanilla SGD. The first modification is done on the sensitivity of each gradient which is bounded by clipping the gradient computed for each training. The second modification is done with random noise sampled and added to the clipped gradients, hence making it impossible to identify which data point was used during training. The privacy optimizers share some privacy-specific parameters that need to be tuned before training the model, specifically [7]:

- *l2_norm_clip* : The maximum Euclidean (L2) norm of each individual gradient that is computed on an individual training example from minibatch.
- *noise_multiplier*: The amount of noise sampled and added to gradients during training the model.

Our experimental flow diagram is presented in Fig. 2. Initially, to understand the insights of the DG's GAN model where it captures the correlations between measurements and their metadata, we conducted the same experiment described in the paper [13]. Then, in the data training & generation phase, we first train the GAN framework by feeding the NSL-KDD dataset and then train the DP-GAN framework. Finally, both (GAN and DP-GAN) synthetic data is generated.

## 4 Use Case Scenario: Data Sharing for Algorithm Training

### 4.1 Dataset Description

KDDCUP'99 is the most widely used dataset for intrusion detection. Despite the fame, the dataset suffers from two critical issues that highly affect the performance of intrusion detection systems trained on it, resulting in a limited validity. The first issue is the significant number of redundant records, causing biases on the learning algorithm towards those frequent records. Another issue is the level of complexity, as authors in [18] show that various evaluations as accuracy, detection rate, and false-positive rate are not a proper use of the KDD dataset. To solve these problems, authors in [18] proposed the NSL-KDD dataset, which consists of selected records of the complete KDD dataset.

The NSL-KDD dataset contains network traffic extracted from the real network environment consisting of normal (benign) traffic and malicious traffic. There are four main categories of attacks, namely Probing (Probe), Denial of Service (DoS), user to Root (U2R), and Root to Local (R2L). Extracted features from the raw traffic data are labeled as benign or malicious traffic. The 41 features consist of 9 discrete and 32 continuous values. Features are also categorized based on 4 semantic categories, including *intrinsic*, *content*, *time-based traffic*, and *host-based traffic*, as presented in Fig. 3. The dataset has 125 k records for a total size of 20 MB.

We use the Pearson Correlation Coefficient (PCC) for feature extraction in our experiment. PCC measures the strength and direction of a linear relationship between two variables. For our case, correlation coefficients whose magnitude is 0.5 indicate variables that can be considered moderately correlated. There are 9 features have been selected form NSL-KDD dataset which are, *count*, *srv_serror_rate*, *serror_rate*, *dst_host_serror_rate*, *dst_host_srv_serror_rate*, *logged_in*, *dst_host_same_srv_rate*, *dst_host_srv_count*, *same_srv_rate*.

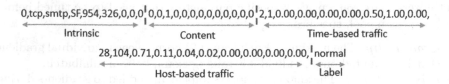

**Fig. 3.** Features description

**Table 1.** Non-identifier features examples

| Feature type | Features examples |
|---|---|
| Categorical | protocol_type, service, flag, label |
| Continuous | src_bytes, dst_bytes, num_failed_login |
| Discrete | logged_in, root_shell, su_attempted |

## 4.2  Privacy Concerns for the Dataset

IDS is one of the most effective defense mechanisms to protect from cyber-attacks if equipped adequately with updated rules and signatures. In particular, for machine learning-based IDS, the availability of high-quality and updated data is essential to deal with new versions of hacker tools. Data sharing offers a way to increase the knowledge base of security teams in a relatively short time and proactively. Privacy is, however, a key stumbling block for the research community because of contents not suitable to be shared. Privacy-sensitive data in IDSs can be found from three cases: IDS input data, IDS built-in data, and IDS generated data [15]. Privacy-sensitive fields in these cases can be present in two fields: privacy-preserving identifiers (i.e., user-names, IP address) and privacy-preserving non-identifiers (i.e., time-stamps, attack signature). In this paper, we focus on privacy-preserving non-identifiers, i.e., attack signatures.

IDS built-in data includes attack signatures to be used in misuse-based IDSs. Security vendors usually consider attack signatures as a piece of proprietary information to not be revealed to competitors. Furthermore, attackers can analyze signatures to learn potential vulnerabilities in target systems and design their exploits. Therefore, devices running an IDS can become an accessible source of information for attackers who want to learn and design new attacks. As we mentioned in the earlier section, there are four categories of attacks in the NSL-KDD dataset. All the fields in the dataset are non-identifiers, meaning there are no user names or IP addresses. Therefore, this paper aims to protect non-identifier information and generate a synthetic version of NSL-KDD while preserving the attack signature information. In Table 1, we show samples of non-identifier information from the dataset.

## 4.3  Data Preprocessing

Dataset needs to be processed before feeding into the training model. In our experiments we assess the performance with two synthetic data generation approaches as provided by DoppleGANger, a) intrusion detection accuracy without differential privacy, b) intrusion detection accuracy with differential privacy. Both approaches require us to pre-process the dataset.

**Pre-Processing for ML:** NSL-KDD dataset contains 41 features of multiple types and ranges. To apply the DG tools, we perform numeric conversion and normalization. Among the 41 features, 9 are discrete and 32 are continuous. In the case of 9 discrete features, 3 features are non-numeric and 6 features binary (0,1). We use one-hot encoding to convert the non-numeric values to numeric values, such as "protocol_type" (TCP, UDP, ICMP).

Further, we use standard scalar to eliminate the dimensional impact between features values. For all discrete and continuous features, the min-max normalization method is used to convert the numeric values into the interval of [0,1]:

$$y' = \frac{y - y_{min}}{y_{max} - y_{min}}$$

where, $y$ represents the value before normalization for a specific feature in the dataset and $y'$ is the value after the normalization.

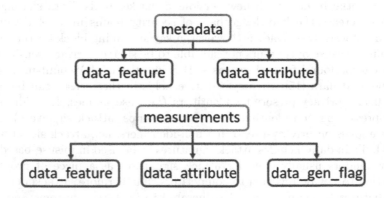

**Fig. 4.** Dataset formatting for DP-GAN

**Pre-Processing for DP-GAN:** To train the DP-GAN model, dataset needs to be formatted into the *metadata* and *measurements* categories [13] as show in Fig. 4. In the schema for *metadata*, *data_feature* and *data_attribute* represent a list of objects, indicating dimension, type, and normalization of each feature and attributes in the *Python Pickle format* (e.g., data_feature_output.pkl). The *data_attribute* in the *metadata* are *protocol_type*, *service*, *flag*. The remaining 38 features for dimension, type, and normalization are present in the *data_feature*.

In the schema for *measurements*, *data_feature* represents the value of different features in NumPy 3D array format. *data_attribute* represents the one-hot encoding of 3 categorical features (*protocol_type*, *service*, *flag*) and label of each record i.e. benign and malicious. *data_gen_flag* represents the time-series activation. All values are stored in an NPZ format with three arrays [13]:

– data_feature: Training features are stored in numpy float32 array format. The size is [(number of training samples) x (maximum length) x (total dimension of features)]. Categorical features are stored by one-hot encoding; for example,

**Table 2.** Accuracy in detection of normal and malicious traffic in original dataset

| Classification algorithm | Training accuracy | Testing accuracy |
|---|---|---|
| Random Forest | 99.42 | 98.69 |
| Linear Support Vector Machine | 97.84 | 97.8 |
| Logistic Regression | 96.99 | 96.99 |
| Gaussian Naive Bayes | 84.45 | 84.33 |
| Gradient Boosting | 98.24 | 98.21 |
| Multi-Layer Perceptron | 98.61 | 98.51 |

if a categorical feature has 3 possibilities, then it can take values between [1., 0., 0.], [0., 1., 0.], and [0., 0., 1.]

- data_attribute: Training attributes are stored in numpy float32 array format. The size is [(number of training samples) x (total dimension of attributes)]. Categorical attributes are stored by one-hot encoding; for example, if a categorical attribute has 3 possibilities, then it can take values between [1., 0., 0.], [0., 1., 0.], and [0., 0., 1.].
- data_gen_flag: Flags indicating the activation of features, in numpy float32 array format. The size is [(number of training samples) x (maximum length)]. 1 means the time series is activated at this time step, 0 means the time series is inactivated at this time step. In our case, data_gen_flag remains activated (1) all the time as the dataset does not have missing values.

## 5   Experimental Evaluation

We use Python (v3.7.10) and Tensorflow (v1.14.0) for the experiments. Tensorflow can be run on CPU or GPU; however, for our experiment, we use GPU_Task_Scheduler library, which is computationally faster than CPU. To record the intrusion detection accuracy, we tested 6 supervised machine learning models, specifically Random Forest (RF), Linear Support Vector Machine (LSVM), Logistic Regression (LR), Gaussian Naive Bayes (GNB), Gradient Boosting (GB), and Multi-Layer Perceptron (MLP).

To start with the normal and malicious traffic classification on the original NSL-KDD dataset, we process it as mentioned in Sect. 4. We adopt correlation-based feature selection to reduce dimensionality, thus obtaining a reduced set of 9 features. We divide the dataset in two, with 0.75 for training and 0.25 for testing. The accuracy in detecting normal and malicious traffic on the original dataset is presented in Table 2.

In the next phase of our experiment, we feed the processed dataset as described in Sect. 4. C to generate a pure GAN-based synthetic dataset. In Table 3, some of the core parameters of the GAN-based framework [13] are reported.

**Table 3.** GAN model parameter

| Parameter | Value | Meaning |
|-----------|-------|---------|
| batch_size | 100 | Training batch size |
| d_rounds | 1 | Number of discriminator steps per batch |
| g_rounds | 1 | Number of generator steps per batch |
| g_lr | 0.001 | Learning rate in Adam for training the generator (1/s) |
| d_lr | 0.001 | Learning rate in Adam for training the discriminator (1/s) |
| attr_disc_num_layers | 5 | Number of layers in the auxiliary discriminator |
| attr_disc_num_units | 200 | Number of units in each layer of the auxiliary discriminator |
| disc_num_layers | 5 | Number of units in each layer of the auxiliary discriminator |
| initial_state | random | "random" means setting the initial state to random numbers |
| l2_norm_clip | 1.0 | Bound the optimizer's sensitivity to individual training points |
| noise_multiplier | [1.0, 2.0, 4.0] | Amount of noise sampled and added to gradients during training |

**Table 4.** Accuracy in detection of normal and malicious traffic in synthetic dataset

| Classification algorithm | Training accuracy | Testing accuracy |
|--------------------------|-------------------|------------------|
| Random Forest | 99.99 | 99.6 |
| Linear Support Vector Machine | 98.25 | 97.93 |
| Logistic Regression | 96.85 | 96.44 |
| Gaussian Naive Bayes | 90.71 | 90.61 |
| Gradient Boosting | 99.28 | 99.15 |
| Multi-layer Perceptron | 99.15 | 98.92 |

After the training, the GAN framework generates samples with a mix of normal and malicious traffic. The pure GAN generates 125K samples for training and 50K samples for testing. The accuracy detection on the synthetic dataset

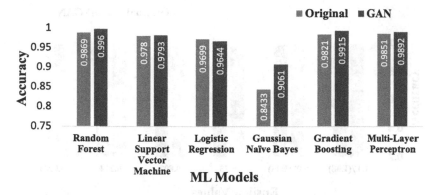

**Fig. 5.** Classification accuracy comparison (original vs GAN)

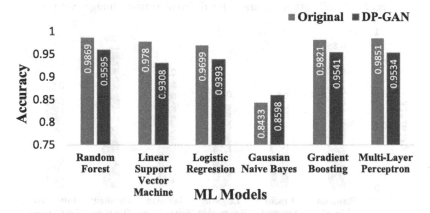

**Fig. 6.** Classification accuracy comparison (original vs DP-GAN)

is presented in Table 4. In Fig. 5, we present a comparison of testing accuracy between the original dataset and GAN-based synthetic data. It is notable from Fig. 5 that all the machine learning models perform well in classifying malicious traffic on the synthetic dataset than the original dataset. In the original NSL-KDD dataset, the distribution between malicious and normal traffic is imbalanced. On the other hand, the malicious and normal traffic distribution is balanced in the synthetic dataset. We observe that the GAN-based synthetic dataset gives high accuracy in classifying malicious traffic from normal traffic.

In the next phase of the experiments, we assess the accuracy of the differential privacy GAN (DP-GAN). We train the model using DoppleGANger's [13] differential privacy framework, which is based on the Google Tensorflow Privacy library [7]. The trained model generates synthetic samples for malicious and normal traffic. Machine learning models of the previous assessment are also applied to the differentially private synthetic dataset. Classification accuracy is presented in Fig. 6 for $\varepsilon = 6.73$. Here, we note that the detection accuracy for malicious traffic is close to the detection of malicious traffic on the original dataset. Since

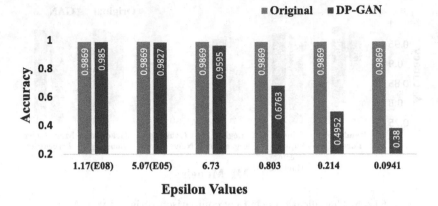

**Fig. 7.** Classification accuracy for different privacy budget values

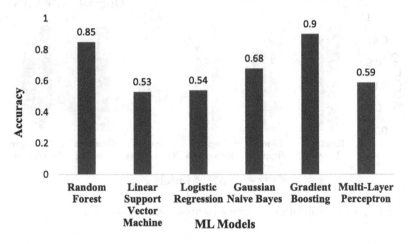

**Fig. 8.** Classification accuracy when ML models are trained on DP-GAN dataset and test on original dataset.

DP-GAN provides a model with a differential privacy budget, we can now assess the detection accuracy against several values of privacy parameters. In order to proceed in the assessment with DP, we record the accuracy for different $\varepsilon$ values as depicted in Fig. 7 for Random Forest algorithm. The value on the x-axis represents different epsilon values (the letter E represents power of 10 as exponent). We observe that lowering the budget value deteriorates the accuracy to an unacceptable level. We also observe that when the privacy budget parameter is $\varepsilon = 6.73$, the accuracy is 95%, which is close to the original accuracy. For $\varepsilon = 6.73$, we obtain a good trade-off between differential privacy and accuracy. Finally, we assess the DP-GAN model in a realistic scenario, where it is trained on the syntehtic dataset and it is tested on the original dataset, while keeping the same privacy budget parameter found above. The generated dataset has 126k samples

**Table 5.** Confusion Matrix when models are trained on synthetic dataset and tested on original dataset

| ML models | Accuracy | Precision | Recall | F1-score |
|---|---|---|---|---|
| RF | 0.8456 | 0.9127 | 0.7863 | 0.8448 |
| LSVM | 0.5292 | 0.6969 | 0.2112 | 0.3242 |
| LR | 0.5440 | 0.7711 | 0.2091 | 0.3290 |
| GNB | 0.6831 | 0.6348 | 0.9586 | 0.7638 |
| GB | 0.9038 | 0.9060 | 0.9149 | 0.9104 |
| MLP | 0.5893 | 0.7835 | 0.3203 | 0.4547 |

for training the ML models. We observe Random Forest and Gradient Boosting models perform well on the original dataset where the accuracy is 85% and 90% respectively, as shown in Fig. 8. However, the other models seem to suffer from generative effects, thus showing worse performance than training with original data.

To further understand ML models' performance, we use three well-known metrics: Precision, Recall, and F1-Score. These metrics depend on four basic attributes, as follows:

- True Positive (TP) - Attack data which is correctly classified as an attack.
- True Negative (TN) - Benign data which is correctly classified as benign.
- False Positive (FP) - Benign data which is incorrectly classified as an attack.
- False Negative (FN) - Attack data which is incorrectly classified as benign.

The accuracy is the percentage of total correct classifications, where precision - i.e., TP/(TP+FP) - measures the number of positive classifications that belong to the positive class. Recall - i.e., TP/(TP+FN) - quantifies the number of correct class predictions made out of all positive examples in the dataset. F1 score - i.e., (2*Precision*Recall)/(Precision+Recall) - provides the harmonic mean of precision and recall in one number. From Table 5, it is evident that Random Forest and Gradient Boosting both models F1-score is close to the value of accuracy. Hence, we can conclude that both models (RF and GB) performed well.

**Membership Inference Attacks Evaluation:** GAN models are susceptible to Membership Inference Attacks (MIA). In the membership inference attacks, the attacker aims at inferring whether trained data samples have been used to train a machine learning model, hence revealing content in the original dataset. A simple MIA model is presented in Fig. 9. Authors in [4] argue that a smaller training dataset leads to a higher risk of revealing information used in training. This raises the concern when dealing with a real-world privacy-sensitive dataset (e.g., intrusion detection samples), and differential privacy is an effective defense mechanism against MIA on GAN training models [4].

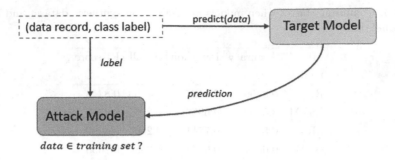

**Fig. 9.** Membership inference attack model

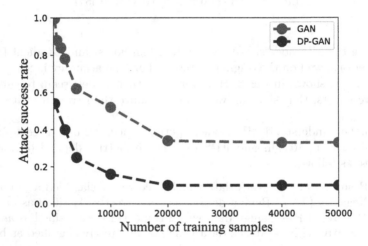

**Fig. 10.** Membership inference attacks against DP-GAN based dataset

To measure GAN model robustness against MIA, we use attack success rate [13] as a metric. We find that the attack success rate is high when the training sample size is small. For instance, with 200 training samples, the attack success rate is 0.998. However, increasing the sample size, the attack success rate decreases, as shown in Fig. 10. For the DP-GAN model, we note that, with 200 training samples, the attack success rate is 0.54, which is lower than GAN. Our results suggest that the differential privacy-based GAN model can effectively defend against MIA using more training data as compared to pure GAN models.

## 6    Conclusion

In this paper, we investigated methods to protect privacy in the case of data sharing and for training machine learning algorithms for intrusion detection. First, we assessed the quality of synthetic datasets generated with Generative Adversarial Networks (GANs) and Differential Privacy, particularly with the

DoppleGANger toolset. We assessed the quality of synthetic data in terms of detection accuracy, i.e., ability to classify malicious vs. benign network traffic. We use the well-known intrusion detection dataset NSL-KDD. The experimental results showed that the synthetic dataset with differential privacy (DP-GAN) could achieve high classification accuracy (95.95%) while maintaining a low privacy budget parameter ($\varepsilon = 6.73$), i.e., the low success rate for member inference attacks. We also observed a 90% accuracy when the model was trained on the DP-GAN dataset and tested on the original dataset. Our results suggested a practical guideline: dataset owners can generate differentially private synthetic datasets and share the dataset among researchers and cyber-security practitioners without privacy concerns. Then, the researcher can develop ML models to achieve high binary (malicious or benign) and multiclass (attack categories, i.e., probe, DoD, R2L, U2R) classification accuracy.

# References

1. Abadi, M., et al.: Deep learning with differential privacy. In: Proceedings of the 2016 ACM SIGSAC conference on computer and communications security, pp. 308–318 (2016)
2. Brock, A., Donahue, J., Simonyan, K.: Large scale gan training for high fidelity natural image synthesis. arXiv preprint arXiv:1809.11096 (2018)
3. Chakrabarti, S., Chakraborty, M., Mukhopadhyay, I.: Study of snort-based ids. In: Proceedings of the International Conference and Workshop on Emerging Trends in Technology, pp. 43–47 (2010)
4. Chen, D., Yu, N., Zhang, Y., Fritz, M.: Gan-leaks: A taxonomy of membership inference attacks against generative models. In: Proceedings of the 2020 ACM SIGSAC conference on computer and communications security, pp. 343–362 (2020)
5. Dandekar, A., Zen, R.A.M., Bressan, S.: A Comparative Study of Synthetic Dataset Generation Techniques. In: Hartmann, S., Ma, H., Hameurlain, A., Pernul, G., Wagner, R.R. (eds.) DEXA 2018. LNCS, vol. 11030, pp. 387–395. Springer, Cham (2018). https://doi.org/10.1007/978-3-319-98812-2_35
6. Goodfellow, I., et al.: Generative adversarial nets. In: Advances in Neural Information Processing Systems, vol. 27 (2014)
7. Google: Tensorflow privacy. https://github.com/tensorflow/privacy
8. Huang, S., Lei, K.: Igan-ids: an imbalanced generative adversarial network towards intrusion detection system in ad-hoc networks. Ad Hoc Netw. **105**, 102177 (2020)
9. Isola, P., Zhu, J.Y., Zhou, T., Efros, A.A.: Image-to-image translation with conditional adversarial networks. In: Proceedings of the IEEE Conference on Computer Vision and Pattern Recognition, pp. 1125–1134 (2017)
10. Jordon, J., Yoon, J., Van Der Schaar, M.: Pate-gan: Generating synthetic data with differential privacy guarantees. In: International conference on learning representations (2018)
11. Kotal, A., Piplai, A., Chukkapalli, S.S.L., Joshi, A., et al.: Privetab: Secure and privacy-preserving sharing of tabular data. In: ACM International Workshop on Security and Privacy Analytics (2022)
12. Lin, Z., Shi, Y., Xue, Z.: Idsgan: Generative adversarial networks for attack generation against intrusion detection. arXiv preprint arXiv:1809.02077 (2018)

13. Lin, Z., Jain, A., Wang, C., Fanti, G., Sekar, V.: Using gans for sharing networked time series data: Challenges, initial promise, and open questions. In: Proceedings of the ACM Internet Measurement Conference, pp. 464–483 (2020)
14. Mukherjee, S., Sharma, N.: Intrusion detection using naive bayes classifier with feature reduction. Procedia Technol. **4**, 119–128 (2012)
15. Niksefat, S., Kaghazgaran, P., Sadeghiyan, B.: Privacy issues in intrusion detection systems: a taxonomy, survey and future directions. Comput. Sci. Rev. **25**, 69–78 (2017)
16. Salem, M., Taheri, S., Yuan, J.S.: Anomaly generation using generative adversarial networks in host-based intrusion detection. In: 2018 9th IEEE Annual Ubiquitous Computing, Electronics & Mobile Communication Conference (UEMCON), pp. 683–687. IEEE (2018)
17. Shahriar, M.H., Haque, N.I., Rahman, M.A., Alonso, M.: G-ids: Generative adversarial networks assisted intrusion detection system. In: 2020 IEEE 44th Annual Computers, Software, and Applications Conference (COMPSAC), pp. 376–385. IEEE (2020)
18. Tavallaee, M., Bagheri, E., Lu, W., Ghorbani, A.A.: A detailed analysis of the kdd cup 99 data set. In: 2009 IEEE symposium on computational intelligence for security and defense applications, pp. 1–6. IEEE (2009)
19. Xie, L., Lin, K., Wang, S., Wang, F., Zhou, J.: Differentially private generative adversarial network. arXiv preprint arXiv:1802.06739 (2018)
20. Xu, L., Skoularidou, M., Cuesta-Infante, A., Veeramachaneni, K.: Modeling tabular data using conditional gan. In: Advances in Neural Information Processing Systems 32 (2019)
21. Yu, Z., Tsai, J.J.: A framework of machine learning based intrusion detection for wireless sensor networks. In: 2008 IEEE International Conference on Sensor Networks, Ubiquitous, and Trustworthy Computing (sutc 2008), pp. 272–279. IEEE (2008)
22. Zhang, L., Jiang, S., Shen, X., Gupta, B.B., Tian, Z.: Pwg-ids: An intrusion detection model for solving class imbalance in iiot networks using generative adversarial networks. arXiv preprint arXiv:2110.03445 (2021)

# Forensic Analysis and Detection of Spoofing Based Email Attack Using Memory Forensics and Machine Learning

Sanjeev Shukla[1]($\boxtimes$), Manoj Misra[1], and Gaurav Varshney[2]

[1] Department of Computer Science and Engineering, Indian Institute of Technology, Roorkee, India
{sanjufcc,manojfec}@iitr.ac.in
[2] Department of Computer Science and Engineering, Indian Institute of Technology, Jammu, India
gaurav.varshney@iitjammu.ac.in

**Abstract.** Emails encounter many types of cyber-attacks and email spoofing is one of the most common and challenging investigation problems. This paper identifies spoofing-based email attacks in an organization by analyzing received and replied emails. The detection works by capturing the email traces via memory forensics. Unlike the traditional approaches of capturing the entire physical memory, we only capture the memory of relevant processes for email header extraction. It significantly reduces the size of the memory dump and makes detection faster. We suggest a novel mechanism called URL extractor, which uses seven novel features from URL to identify the live running email message process by applying ML that traces received emails and captures their header fields for analysis. The authentication header fields of *SPF*, *DKIM*, *DMARC*, and *ARC* are examined closely to develop a detection algorithm for received emails. Similarly, novel header fields of *Reference* along with *MX record* are applied for the detection of replied emails. The MX record is fetched to verify the domain name by sending a forward ns-lookup query to DNS. It also includes an email attack alert mechanism for intimating IT admins of an organization regarding suspected attacks. The results thus obtained show that email detection takes 35 secs (apprx.) to complete with high accuracy and low false positives.

**Keywords:** Email forensics · Email spoofing · Memory forensics · Cyber security · Email attacks

## 1 Introduction

In the modern era of an IT-enabled society, consumers increasingly use digital communication as a preferred mode of interaction for their business and personal needs. Email is still a reliable, safe, and most widely used mode of data communication on the Internet. As email services have gained popularity, attackers are

© ICST Institute for Computer Sciences, Social Informatics and Telecommunications Engineering 2023
Published by Springer Nature Switzerland AG 2023. All Rights Reserved
F. Li et al. (Eds.): SecureComm 2022, LNICST 462, pp. 491–509, 2023.
https://doi.org/10.1007/978-3-031-25538-0_26

using email as a platform to launch cyber attacks [1]. *Email spoofing* is one of the prevalent attacks on the email platform. Most Business Email Compromises (BEC) and phishing attacks use email spoofing as the first step. In email spoofing, the attacker finds a way to deceive the receiver into trusting a false identity of the sender, eventually gaining a higher level of trust. Email spoofing is generally performed by finding out an open relay or open *simple mail transfer protocol (SMTP)* server which can relay the emails without any sender authentication.

## 1.1  Motivation

CSO Online article "Top cybersecurity facts, figures and statistics" and a survey by International Data Group (IDG) in 2020 report that email application is still mostly preferred for malicious propagation as found in 94% of cases. It also states that phishing accounts for 80% of reported security incidents [2]. It brings a unique challenge for organizations as it caters to both external and internal attack threats. The inbound emails (received emails) attacks pose a challenge of early detection so that necessary mitigation steps can be applied. Also, a malicious insider can use the organization's precious resources to launch an email spoofing attack. This outbound emails (sent emails) attack is more difficult to detect and needs urgent attention as it blacklists the IP addresses of the organization and brings a bad reputation. Therefore, the motivation of this work is to provide a mechanism for detection and early warning for admins and security experts to address email spoofing attacks precisely and timely.

## 1.2  Email Forensics

Email forensics is a sub-branch of network forensics that performs forensic investigation to extract digital evidence regarding an email for further analysis. Emails are subjected to threats and are vulnerable to spoofing, spamming [3], and phishing attacks [4]. Email spoofing [5] is a critical step to a successful phishing attack as the hacker impersonates someone whom the victim trusts [6]. This is due to the SMTP's inherent weakness, lacking source authentication or verification mechanisms. The email header analysis is crucial to email forensics investigation because the critical information related to the email sender along the path from sending *mail transfer agent (MTA)* to receiving MTA can be obtained through the email header metadata [7].

## 1.3  Memory Forensics

Memory forensics is a crucial element and upcoming sub-branch of digital forensics, where the current state of physical memory (RAM) of a compromised device or application is captured and dumped on the hard disk as a snapshot file for forensic investigation [8,9]. This snapshot file is referred to as a memory dump. The most significant advantage of using memory forensics is that it guarantees non-repudiation and can retrieve data even when end-to-end encryption is applied at the application or transport layer. Though memory forensics is quite effective in some instances, its practical application has some critical challenges. The biggest challenge is the size of memory dump file. Every snapshot of the entire physical memory is enormous in size and is proportional to the size of the RAM installed on a computing device. Periodically storing or processing memory for any analysis is expensive and time-consuming, and hence only near real-time solutions can be built using such analysis.

### 1.4  Contribution

This paper proposes a detection scheme that identifies spoofed emails in received and replied emails via live memory forensics. The traditional approach in memory forensics is to capture live memory dump of complete RAM resulting in a large file to be stored, which further requires a significant amount of time for processing and extracting the email header [10]. This approach was improved by capturing all the live processes associated with the browser having multiple tabs [11]. The above method can further be enhanced by addressing the research gap by identifying only the process (amongst all live browser running processes having multiple tabs and web pages opened for browsing) associated with email inbox messages and only capturing it. Therefore if user is running a chrome browser and is browsing ten websites (10 processes), then the objective is to find the one process out of 10 which is associated with the email inbox message. The significant contributions of this paper are, thus, as follows:

- We propose a resource-effective email header extraction process from live memory by identifying 7 novel features from URL to identify the live running email message process by using ML.
- We develop an email spoofing detection algorithm using novel header fields of *ARC* and *References* for received and replied emails.

## 2  Literature Survey

A literature survey for email spoofing detection techniques and approaches is carried out where research articles after 2013 are considered, as shown in Table 1.

P. Mishra et al. [12] proposed email date and time as measures to detect email spoofing. The algorithm checks the semantics of the date and time fields and matches the sending date and the last date of the received email. Finally, it calculates the threshold or margin of standard time taken by receiving email, which indicates it is a spoofed or legitimate email. S. Gupta et al. [13] proposed spoofed email detection of received emails by examining the header fields of email authentication standards like SPF, DKIM, DKIM-Signature, and DMARC. The proposed algorithm checks the header field values and decides the authenticity of an email. Small dataset and not finding accuracy are its limitation. R. P Iyer et al. [10] proposed spoofed email detection that uses the volatile memory of a system. They captured a host machine's complete volatile memory (RAM)

**Table 1.** Comparison of similar email spoofing detection schemes

| Author(s) | Novelty | Spoofed email detection uses | | | Email header used for | | Database | Dataset |
| | | Memory Forensic | Received Email | Replied Email | Received Email | Replied Email | | Size (Emails) |
|---|---|---|---|---|---|---|---|---|
| P. Mishra et al. [12] | To detect email spoofing using date and time fields | No | Yes | No | Date, Time | - | Self Generated | Total =3 (All S) |
| S. Gupta et al. [13] | Developed algorithm based on Authentication header field values | No | Yes | No | SPF, DKIM, D-Sig, DMARC | - | Self Generated | Total =10 (Mix) |
| R.P Iyer et al. [10] | Applied the concept of memory Forensic for the first time. | Yes | Yes | Yes | Message-ID | InReplyTo | Self Generated | Total =70 (All S) |
| S. Shukla et al. [11] | Reduced computational complexity By using process forensics | Yes | Yes | No | Message-ID MX record | – | Self Generated | G=50, S=50, Mix =100 |
| O. Oduni bosi [14] | Classification of email header Using ML to detect spoofing | No | Yes | No | From, Message-ID | - | Self Generated | 1000 |
| K. Konno et al. [15] | Detect false positive email deliveries In sender domain authentication | No | Yes | No | DMARC | - / – | Dmarc Report | 1 week D-marc Report |
| S. Maroof et al. [16] | Large-scale analysis of the adoption of email anti-spoofing schemes | No | Yes | No | SPF, DMARC | – | Open Source | 236 mil+ 32k (approx) |

G-Genuine, S-Spoofed, FP - False Positive, Mix - both Spoofed and Genuine emails

and extracted email header features from it. The detection algorithm used only one email header called message-ID to check whether the email was legitimate or spoofed. The limitation of this approach was the generation of a large size memory snapshot file resulting in significant time required for the detection algorithm. S. Shukla et al. [11] proposed an improved method where instead of capturing the entire RAM, only live running processes related to the browser were captured. It reduced the size of the captured file significantly and improved the capturing speed. The detection algorithm used message-ID and DNS lookup in real-time to verify the domain IP address. The limitation of this technique was that it captured all the live running processes since it could not identify the exact browser process of all. O. Odunibosi [14], in his work, proposed machine learning to perform email spoofing detection. He extracted the emails from the user inbox using python script, saved the headers in CSV format, and classified the user inbox message as spoofed or legitimate using the RF algorithm. The limitations of such an approach is its dependence on an email server for open-port or protocol for fetching emails, the necessity to write a new script for each email server, and the usage of only one header field (message-ID) to determine spoofed emails. K. Konno et al. [15] suggested an approach to identify legitimate IP addresses by using DMARC report. K-means clustering is applied to find false positives in sender domain authentication. The limitation is that it only works where DMARC is implemented, and it does not check false negatives. S. Maroofi et al. [16] studied and evaluated the adoption rate of SPF and DMARC across a vast set of domains. He proposed an algorithm to detect defensively registered domains and enumerated misconfigured SPF, deployment in sub-domains, and the possibility of sending spoofed emails in a non-existent subdomain by an end-to-end subdomain. The limitation of its approach is that it does not provide any detection algorithm and results in sharing recommendations.

# 3    Proposed Approach

The proposed scheme of *spoofed email attack detection* is designed to identify spoofed email attacks by analyzing the email header of both received and replied emails. This is achieved by capturing the memory of the live running process associated with an email inbox opened over the browser on the host. The email header information is then extracted from the live memory dump and passed to the detection algorithm to flag spoofed emails.

## 3.1    System Architecture

The architecture of the proposed system consists of two modules - *The email header capturing module* and *The detection module* - as shown in Fig. 1.

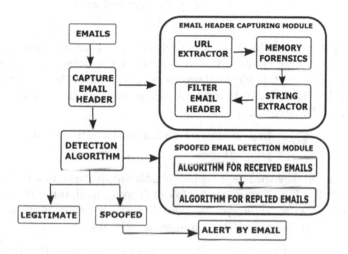

**Fig. 1.** Architecture diagram of the proposed work

Email header capturing module consists of four sub-modules:

**URL Extractor:** The task of this sub-module is to extract the URL of a process with an open email inbox and extract features from the URL representing an email transaction. In order to extract features, we have studied 35 most popular email servers currently used to provide email services [17]. Our experiment included extracting the open email URL. For this, we had to create email accounts on these servers. That gave us access to the email inbox. We even sent a few test emails and extracted open email URLs. After obtaining all the URLs from these email servers, we closely examined the structure of the complete URL to extract common features that can be attributed as distinguishable (i.e., features which can reliably be used to identify a URL as an email transaction URL).

**Feature Extraction:** Any webpage opened is referred to by its Uniform Resource Locator (URL). We have selected eight features (F1-F8) to identify an email based URL. While F1-F6 are Text-based Features that are searched to find the occurrence's of the keyword in URL, F7-F8 are other features. Out of eight features, F1-F7 are novel features and F8 is taken from literature. These features in the structure of opened email URL are discussed below:

- Mail: The 'mail' keyword is very commonly used in URLs, prefixing the domain name of an email server. This is a strong feature that is found in most email servers. E.g., ; is an email message opened URL. Here 'mail' prefixes the google.com domain. In some cases, if the mail keyword is not present as a prefix of a domain, then it is found in the structure of the email URL. Therefore we check the keyword 'mail' in the URL structure and its presence is considered as relevant URL.

$$F1 = \begin{cases} 1, & \text{if 'mail' keyword exists} \\ 0, & \text{otherwise} \end{cases} \quad (1)$$

- Message-ID: This is a long alphanumeric string of random characters that are very common in all email URLs. It represents the unique reference given to each message. E.g., https://mail.protonmail.com/inbox/bdb1RXwqXwqR8J-gUhUfMxVb; is an email-based URL where message-ID is mentioned at the end of the URL structure.

$$F2 = \begin{cases} 1, & \text{if the last alphanumeric string exists} \\ 0, & \text{otherwise} \end{cases} \quad (2)$$

- Inbox: 'Inbox' keyword is another significant feature found in an email opened URLs. E.g., https://www.fastmail.com/-mail/Inbox/ff47cec8a17710 ad.M6eb-41729aIn; some places, the 'inbox' keyword is represented by 'folder/1'. Its presence in URL is marked as relevant.

$$F3 = \begin{cases} 1, & \text{if 'inbox' keyword exists or 'folder/1' exist} \\ 0, & \text{otherwise} \end{cases} \quad (3)$$

- Messages: Some email servers use 'message' as a keyword to represent the email message in the URL. Its presence in URLs by some service providers is observed. E.g., https://in.mail.yahoo.com/d/folders/1/message/277?greferrer-a0cHM6-Ly9sb2dpanclBJ55Acd0YZH8t.

$$F4 = \begin{cases} 1, & \text{if 'message' keyword exists} \\ 0, & \text{otherwise} \end{cases} \quad (4)$$

- Home directory: This is represented by '/0'in the URL to mark the home directory. E.g., https://outlook.live.com/mail/0/inbox/id/ADAwATMwMtM2NmOC.

$$F5 = \begin{cases} 1, & \text{if '/0' exists} \\ 0, & \text{otherwise} \end{cases} \quad (5)$$

– User ID: The 'uid' or 'id' keyword is present in most URLs representing user ID. This feature is commonly cited in most email URLs. E.g., https://mail.yan-dex.com/?uid=1426701416#message/175921860444160001.

$$F6 = \begin{cases} 1, & \text{if 'uid' or 'id' keyword exists} \\ 0, & \text{otherwise} \end{cases} \tag{6}$$

– Special Character: The presence of a special character in a URL like '?' is acceptable. This is commonly found in email URLs. E.g., https://mail.tutanota.com/mail/id=?-MaDCBSW-7-2MaDCBXBUZ-2; Any other special symbol found like '@' can be malicious, phished, or irrelevant.

$$F7 = \begin{cases} 1, & \text{if '?' or no special character} \\ 0, & \text{otherwise} \end{cases} \tag{7}$$

– HTTPS/HTTP count: We count the number of occurrences of this feature (protocol) in the URL. More than one count is malicious while a single count of HTTPS/HTTP is genuine.

$$F8 = \begin{cases} 1, & \text{if https/http count is } > 1 \\ 0, & \text{otherwise} \end{cases} \tag{8}$$

In order to further experiment and find the significance of features, we use ML-based algorithms. Before applying ML, we need to prepare our dataset.

**Dataset** - Our dataset thus used comprises a total of 33080 URLs, of which 14350 URLs are downloaded from the 35 popular email servers having email features [17] and the rest are non-email URLs that are used from Alexa top websites [18]. We then prepare a CSV file have eight columns representing the eight features (discussed above) and the tuples represent the URL. We take the first tuple, check the keywords and mark them as 1 or 0 based on their presence in the URL. E.g., If a feature (named "mail") is present in the URL, it is marked as 1 (in the "mail" column) and if it is not, then it is represented as 0. In this way, each URL is searched to find the presence of the corresponding feature and they are marked as 1 or 0 in the csv file. The class is characterized as 1, if features are present and 0, if features are not present.

**Feature Selection** - Feature selection is the most critical part of any data model. Here, our aim is to select the most optimal features that should be independent of any bias in order to generate a highly efficient data model. To achieve this, we used Filtering Method, where we tried Chi-Square(CS) and Information gain (IG) techniques and we found that CS results were not appropriate for our problem due to their dependence on the significance level. Therefore, we chose IG. Further, a brief comparison was also made to understand the discrepancies between Gini Index (GI) and IG based on the Entropy quantifier. In contrast, GI facilitates the bigger distributions and is easy to implement, whereas the IG favors lesser distributions having small counts with multiple specific values. GI is predominantly used in CART algorithms, while IG is used in ID3, C4.5, and J48 algorithms. Also, GI operates on the categorical target variables, whereas IG computes the difference between entropy before and after the split and indicates the impurity in classes of elements. IG is thus applied to calculate the normalized average impurity using Eq. 9.

$$Gain(S, A) = Ent(S) - \sum_{v \in Values(A)} \frac{|Sv|}{S} Ent|Sv| \tag{9}$$

where, Values(A) is the all possible values of attribute A, and Sv is the subset of S for which attribute A has value v. Ent(Entropy) is calculated using Eq. 10.

$$Entropy(S) = -(P \oplus log_2 P \oplus + P \ominus log_2 P \ominus) \tag{10}$$

Where, $P\oplus$ is the portion of positive examples and $P\ominus$ is the portion of negative examples in S.

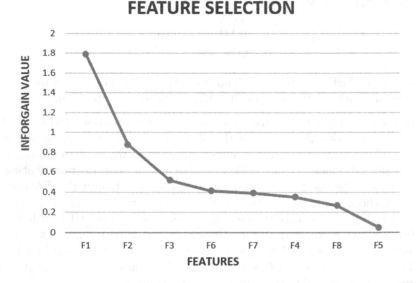

**Fig. 2.** Feature extraction

Figure 2 shows the ranking of all the features based on their information gain values, where the x-axis shows the features and the y-axis shows the Info Gain value. As we can observe from Fig 2, the gain value stagnates at F6, F7 and F4 and then takes a dip after F8. Thus we select the top 7 features which have the highest significance value and impact on the model.

**Classifier Selection:** The next step is to select an appropriate classifier based on its performance to predict the model correctly. We use binary classifiers to test our proposed method based on the features described above and classify the

URLs as relevant (for opened emails) or irrelevant (for non-email URLs). Next, 6 binary ML classifiers, Naive Bayes (NB), Support Vector Machine (SVM), Logical Regression (LR), Decision Tree (DT), Random Forest (RF) and K Nearest Neighbour (KNN), are compared with 7 features set (as obtained from feature extraction) where k-fold cross validation (k = 10) is applied.

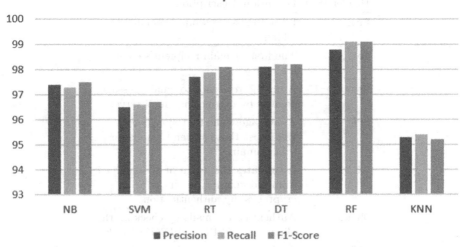

**Fig. 3.** Comparison of different ML classifier

All the chosen classifier performance is evaluated with precision, recall, and F1-score values, as shown in Fig. 3, respectively. We chose the RF classifier based on its performance (which is highest amongst all), avoids overfitting while model buildup time is marginally higher (1–2%). After the selection of the classifier, the dataset is used to train and test the model. The dataset is divided with various random data splits using 10-fold cross-validation.

Our program works as follows. Each instance of browser execution triggers the event listener of the URL extraction module to obtain the URL and Process ID(PID) of the browser tab and verify whether the URL is of relevance (email is opened in the browser). The relevance of URL is found by applying ML, which uses the 7 email URL features as explained above. If the URL is not relevant, it is immediately rejected, and the program (developed in python) stops.

**Memory Forensics:** The live active processes from memory associated with email are captured using PID (PID obtained from URL extraction module) by using Magnet Process Capturing Tool [19].

**Extract Strings:** From captured memory dump, we extract ASCII and UNICODE strings using Microsoft's Sysinternal Strings64 [20].

**Filter Email Header:** Finally, the email header fields that the Detection Algorithm will use are extracted from the Strings file.

## 3.2   Detection Algorithm for Received Emails

Email header analysis is essential to identify spoofing attacks in emails. Some of the header fields used in the detection algorithm are explained in Table 2:

**Table 2.** Header Field Description

| Header field | Definition/Description |
|---|---|
| From | E-mail message sender's email address |
| To | The first or main recipient's email address |
| Message-ID | A unique reference to email message created by originating email server |
| SPF | A message value that specifies a valid host that can send emails for that domain |
| DKIM | It validates the origin of an email from a domain through cryptography authentication |
| DMARC | Authenticates emails by checking the alignment of SPF and DKIM checks |
| ARC | Authenticates original email when it is modified between senders and receivers |
| References | It indicates threaded mail reading and message-ID added with each reply |
| MX Record | A DNS record that specifies a domain's valid mail server |

To detect spoofed emails received, we extract SPF, DMARC, DKIM, and ARC headers, analyze the values of each field as per Algorithm 1, and determine whether an email is spoofed or legitimate. In the case of legacy email servers or service providers that do not use authentication methods, we may not get header field values. In such cases, we rely on message-ID-based spoofing detection.

**Algorithm 1:** Spoofed Email Detection for Received Emails

```
Input: Received Email Headers
       Result: Genuine Email, Spoofed Email
while read header do
    if Header value != none then
        if DMARC = PASS then
        |   Genuine Email;
        else
            Check DKIM;
            if DKIM = PASS AND DKIM Signature domain value = domain value of message-ID field then
            |   Genuine Email;
            else
                Check SPF;
                if SPF = PASS AND ARC = PASS then
                |   Genuine Email;
                else
                |   Spoofed Email;
                end
            end
        end
    else
        compare (message-ID Domain = From email ID Domain);
        if matched then
        |   Genuine Email;
        else
        |   Spoofed Email;
        end
    end
    ReceivedLog = write (From, To, DMARC, DKIM, SPF, ARC)
end
```

## 3.3  Detection Algorithm for Replied Emails

Algorithm 2 detects spoofed emails replied by an employee by matching the header values of **Reference** and **To** fields. If they match, we declare it as a legitimate email else, we again check it by querying the DNS through forward ns-lookup to fetch **MX records**. The domain name thus obtained is matched with **Reference** field. In case of a match, we consider it as a genuine email else, we declare it as a spoofed email.

**Algorithm 2:** Spoofed Email Detection for Replied Emails

```
Input: Replied Email Headers
       Result: Genuine Email, Spoofed Email
while read header do
    From = From Field of Header;
    To = To Field of Header;
    References = References Field of Header;
    ToDName = GetDomainName (To);
    RefDName = GetDomainName (Reference);
    comp = Compare (ToDName, RefDName)
    if comp = TRUE then
    |   Genuine Email;
    else
        Check MX Record;
        nslkupMX = nslookup (ToDName);
        comp1 = Compare (nslkupMX, RefDName);
        if comp1 = TRUE then
        |   Genuine Email;
        else
        |   Spoofed Email;
        end
    end
    RepliedLog = write (From, To, References)
end
```

A local database of **MX records** is maintained to increase algorithm speed and reduce the bottleneck and dependency on internet connectivity. The algorithm first queries the local database and then queries the DNS and also saves this value to keep the database updated. The MX record matching is applied when a genuine email fails to match Reference with To field, as shown in Fig. 4.

```
References: <CADWDuKfwTDbv6icWv79zD2o474hD738xjFWDVgk85KpTrachXg@mail.gmail.com>
From: Sanjeev Shukla <sanjeevs.shukla@gmail.com>
To: ICDE <icde@iimraipur.ac.in>
```

Fig. 4. Genuine email fails in To and reference matching

It has been experimentally tested and identified that Reference matching fails when enterprises purchase email-related services from email vendors. For instance, if an enterprise (here, *iimraipur*) uses G-suite from Google, the emails will retain the original domain (*iimraipur.ac.in*), but the Reference generated by MTA of originating email-server (here, *Gmail*) has the Google domain. Comparing this with the To field domain will always show a legitimate email as spoofed. This shortcoming is resolved with MX record matching, as shown by our program in Fig. 5.

```
References: <CADWDuKfwTDbv6icWv79zD2o474hD738xjFWDVgk85KpTrachXg@mail.gmail.com>
Domain : iimraipur.ac.in
Reference matching with To Field fails - Starting DNS Lookup query (nslookup)

Domain iimraipur.ac.in:
iimraipur.ac.in MX preference = 1, mail exchanger = aspmx.l.google.com
iimraipur.ac.in MX preference = 5, mail exchanger = alt1.aspmx.l.google.com
iimraipur.ac.in MX preference = 5, mail exchanger = alt2.aspmx.l.google.com
iimraipur.ac.in MX preference = 10, mail exchanger = alt3.aspmx.l.google.com
iimraipur.ac.in MX preference = 10, mail exchanger = alt4.aspmx.l.google.com
iimraipur.ac.in MX preference = 20, mail exchanger = mx1.iimraipur.ac.in
iimraipur.ac.in MX preference = 20, mail exchanger = mx2.iimraipur.ac.in
iimraipur.ac.in MX preference = 20, mail exchanger = mx3.iimraipur.ac.in
================================================================
MX Record and Reference Field : MATCHED

Genuine Email
```

Fig. 5. MX record matching

## 4    Experimental Setup and Testing

### 4.1    Assumption

The laptop used for testing is free from any infection from malicious programs. Hence, it is assumed that the memory dump used for analysis contains an unmodified/authentic version of the live memory.

## 4.2  Experimental Setup

The proposed method is tested on a laptop having Intel(R) Core(TM) i5-7200U CPU @ 2.7 GHz as processor, x64-based processor with 64-bit Operating System (Windows 10), 16 GB and 1 TB HDD. To test legitimate and spoofed emails, both types of emails are sent. Fake emails were sent from anonymous or fake email services like anonymailer.net, sendanonymousemail.net, emkei.cz, and spoofbox.com, whereas genuine emails are sent from Gmail and Yahoo. The proposed method is deployed as a client-side solution with alert messages sent to the admin over HTTP. Every PC or laptop provided to the working employees in any organization has pre-loaded software installed, and this tool is expected to be one of them in commercial deployment whose primary task is to detect and report spoofed emails being received or replied by an employee in an organization to administrators.

Our program is developed in python, which runs as a listener event to check the browser instance to call back and activate the URL extractor function. The output of the URL extractor passes the PID to the process capturing tool, which generates memory snapshot file of the process associated with PID. This file is searched using String64 to finally extract the email headers. Further, the header field values are then extracted and saved to create a CSV file. This CSV file is used in our python code by using pandas (an open-source data analysis package) to implement a spoofing detection algorithm.

# 5  Results and Discussion

## 5.1  Results of URL Extractor

The performance of the URL extractor module to find relevant URLs is evaluated using accuracy-98.8, precision-98.9, recall-97.3, and F1 score-99.1. The results thus obtained show the model has performed better with an average metric score of 98%.

## 5.2  Detection Algorithm

In order to test the detection algorithm accuracy, a real case scenario consisting of both genuine and spoofed emails is taken. The dataset is collected via an automated browser extension program that can open the full path of email header metadata of emails in inboxes over the browser and dump them as a file to be used for header extraction. The browser extension uses a content script to read the contents of the *document object module (DOM)* and hence the raw text required for header extraction. The extension, however, needs to follow the email inbox DOM that has the necessary information to construct URLs that can lead us to the individual emails' original or raw headers information. The active tab permission is enough in the manifest file to allow browser extension to access the DOM of a page. The dataset thus obtained consists of 17200 emails (a mix of both spoofed and genuine emails where spoofed email = 2967 and genuine email = 14233). Emails from the 3 most popular public email servers of Gmail, Yahoo and Rediffmail are used for testing the detection algorithm. The dataset is further anonymized, and no privacy issues have been violated in preparing the dataset. A comparison of our proposed approach results with other standard state-of-art email spoofing detection methods is shown below in Table 3.

**Table 3.** Comparison of the proposed approach with other standard methods

| Approach | Accuracy | Precision | Recall | F1 score |
|---|---|---|---|---|
| P. Mishra [12] | Not given | | | |
| S. Gupta [13] | Not given | | | |
| R. P Iyer [10] | 96 | – | – | – |
| S. Shukla [11] | 98 | – | – | 99 |
| O.Odunibosi [14] | 1 | 99 | 1 | 1 |
| K. Konno [15] | SPF+DKIM FP=7%, DMARC FP=50% | | | |
| S. Maroof [16] | Recommendations | | | |
| Proposed | Received=96.15 | 96.9 | 97.89 | 97.39 |
| Method | Replied=95.09 | 95.68 | 97.51 | 96.59 |

## 5.3  Resource Utilization

Performance analysis is carried out by executing the proposed scheme on the user machine while considering various system parameters. Average values of *CPU* utilization, *disk* usage, *memory* consumption, and *time* required for the execution of the detection algorithm were observed as shown in Fig. 6.

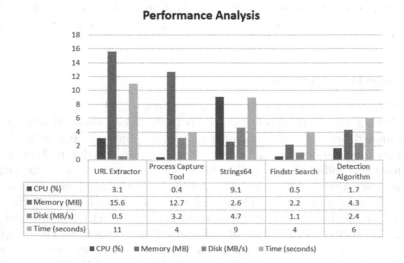

**Fig. 6.** Performance analysis

Figure 7 shows the detection time required for varying sizes of captured data files. These are the memory dump (dmp file) captured from live memory. The average detection time is 34.57 s for an average data file of size 161.7 MB.

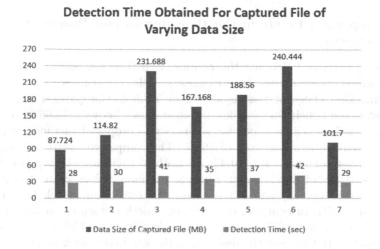

**Fig. 7.** Detection time with varying sizes of captured data file

Figure 8 contains *PM* as the proposed method and [10] and [11] as similar state-of-the-art references that are used for comparison.

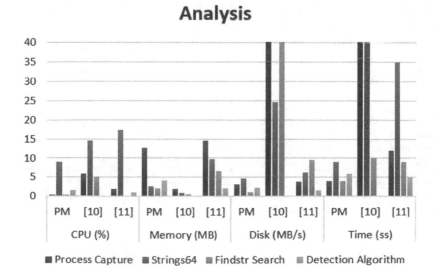

**Fig. 8.** Comparison of resource utilization

The total time, thus, required by the proposed method from capturing live process dump to detecting spoofed email is 35 sec approx. This is better than the 12 min time taken for performance analysis by a similar method [10] or the 1 min time taken by the process-based approach [11], as shown in Fig. 8.

## 5.4    Comparison Points in the Benchmarks and Proposed Framework

After recognizing and defining the comparative checklist issues, our proposed method was compared with those from other relevant studies with the help of a benchmarking checklist that is shown in Table 4. Comparison results show that most of the benchmark studies obtained scores between 16.66% to 83.33%, covering 1 to 5 benchmark points, whereas our proposed method covered all the points and obtained a score of 100%. The comparison score also validates our comparison analysis with [10,11], as both of them are the top two highest scores. The study of previous benchmarks was mainly focused on the inbound attack (received emails) and did not consider outbound attack by an inside user (relied email). In contrast, our proposed method focuses on both types of attacks. Though some studies saved detection results in log files, any kind of alert mechanism was not used in the past. Also, the key benchmark points missed by previous research studies were related to the number of header fields used for detection, dataset size, detection accuracy and detection time.

**Table 4.** Benchmarking checklist

| Comparison points | P. Mishra et al. [12] | S. Gupta et al. [13] | R.P. Iyer et al. [10] | S. Shukla et al. [11] | O. Oduni et al. [14] | K. Konno et al. [15] | S. Maroof et al. [16] | Proposed work |
|---|---|---|---|---|---|---|---|---|
| Handling received and replied emails | x | x | ✓ | ✓ | x | x | x | ✓ |
| Email alert mechanism | x | x | x | x | x | x | x | ✓ |
| Save the results as log files | x | x | ✓ | ✓ | x | x | x | ✓ |
| No of email headers used (more than 1) | ✓ | ✓ | ✓ | ✓ | ✓ | x | ✓ | ✓ |
| Large dataset greater then 1000 | x | x | x | x | ✓ | ✓ | ✓ | ✓ |
| Detection time (less than 1 min) | x | x | x | ✓ | x | x | x | ✓ |
| Accuracy greater than 95% | x | x | ✓ | ✓ | ✓ | x | x | ✓ |
| Score | 16.66% | 16.66% | 66.66% | 83.33% | 50% | 16.66% | 33.33% | 100% |
| Difference | 83.33% | 83.33% | 33.33% | 16.66% | 50% | 83.33% | 66.66% | − |

## 5.5    Commercial Applications and Limitations

The proposed tool can be deployed as a client-side tool that can detect email spoofing. The novelty of memory forensics is that the organization can even prevent email spoofing in scenarios where it does not own the email server used by the employee in the organization. The tool can detect email spoofing even when the email is received on a personal email service used by the employee on the host provided by the organization. The limitation of the proposed scheme is that it is currently tested on webmail-based email services.

# 6    Conclusion and Future Work

The advantage of using memory forensics in spoofed email detection is that it guarantees non-repudiation of a digital trace of the host in physical memory [8]. Further, by identifying the exact processes and only capturing them addresses the disadvantage of capturing the entire physical memory. In our work, we examine the current URLs to identify the ones related to opened emails and then capture this live process to perform header extraction and further apply detection algorithm to identify and store the results in respective log files. The alert mechanism of emailing the log file, thus, gives a threat profile and early warning to the IT admins and security team of the organization to initiate further forensic investigation [21] and adopt a suitable mitigation strategy for such threat scenarios [16]. Our performance analysis shows that the proposed work takes approximately 35 s to complete the email detection process with minimum false positives. This is achieved with minimal consumption of system resources, least overheads, and without interference with the normal functioning of the user's system. Also, the earlier practice of periodic program scheduling with a fixed time interval had challenges in determining the time interval and storage of irrelevant memory dumps. By replacing scheduling with the callback function to auto-trigger, any instance of browser execution saved system resources and overhead significantly. It is also better than the browser extension method of spoofed email detection due to the ease with which users can switch off the extension [22]. Also, the browser extension method is not browser independent and one has to write different extension codes for different browsers used. Future work can be extended to include other email client-side applications such as Outlook, Postbox, Apple Mail, Mozilla Thunderbird, etc. Similarly, the proposed scheme can be extended to mobile phones to test its performance and efficacy on android and apple OS used in mobiles.

**Compliance with Ethical Standards**

**Conflict of Interest.** The authors declare that they have no conflict of interest.

**Ethical Approval.** This article does not contain any studies with human participants or animals performed by any of the authors.

# References

1. Lutui, R.: A multidisciplinary digital forensic investigation process model. Bus. Horiz. **59**(6), 593–604 (2016)
2. Fruhlinger, J.: Top cybersecurity facts, figures and statistics. CSO Online, IDG (2020)
3. Sheikhalishahi, M., Saracino, A., Martinelli, F., Marra, A., Mejri, M., Mejri, N.: Digital waste disposal: an automated framework for analysis of spam emails. Int. J. Inf. Secur. **19**, 499–522 (2020)
4. Gupta, B.B., Arachchilage, N.A.G., Psannis, K.: Defending against phishing attacks: taxonomy of methods, current issues and future directions. Telecommun. Syst. J. **67**, 247–267 (2018)
5. Mooloo, D., Fowdu, T.P.: An ssl-based client-oriented anti-spoofing email application. Africon, pp. 1–5 (2013)
6. Hu, H., Peng, P., Wang, G.: Towards understanding the adoption of anti-spoofing protocols in email systems. In: IEEE Cybersecurity Development (SecDev 2018) (2018)
7. Hunt, R., Zeadally, R.: Network forensics: an analysis of techniques, tools, and trends. IEEE Comput. **45**(12), 36–43 (2012)
8. Pagani, F., Fedorov, S., Balzarotti, D.: Introducing the temporal dimension to memory forensics. ACM Trans. Priv. Sec. **22**(9), 1–21 (2019)
9. Parida, T., Das, S.: Pagedumper: a mechanism to collect page table manipulation information at run-time. Int. J. Inf. Secur. **20**, 603–619 (2021)
10. Iyer, R., Atrey, P.K., Varshney, G., Misra, M.: Email spoofing detection using volatile memory forensics. In: IEEE Conference on Communications and Network Security (CNS), Las Vegas, NV, pp. 619–625 (2017)
11. Shukla, S., Misra, M., Varshney, G.: Identification of spoofed emails by applying email forensics and memory forensics. In: Published in Proceeding of ACM Digital Online, 10th International Conference (ICCNS 2020), pp. 109–114 (2020)
12. Mishra, P., Pilli, E., Joshi, R.: Forensic analysis of e-mail date and time spoofing. In: Third International Conference on Computer and Communication Technology (2013)
13. Gupta, S., Pilli, E.S., Mishra, P., Pilli, S., Joshi, R.C.: Forensic analysis of e-mail address spoofing. In: 5th IEEE International Conference on the Next Generation Information Technology Summit, pp. 898–904 (2014)
14. Odunibosi, O.: The classification of email headers using random forest algorithm to detect email spoofing. School of Computing, National College, Ireland (2019)
15. Konno, K., Kitagawa, N., Yamai, N.: False positive detection in sender domain authentication by dmarc by dmarc report analysis. In: 3rd International Conference on Information Science and System ICISS, pp. 38–41 (2020)
16. Maroofi, S., Korczynski, M., Hölzel, A., Duda, A.: Adoption of email anti-spoofing schemes: A large scale analysis. IEEE Trans. Netw. Service Manage. 1–1 (2021)
17. Hu, H., Wang, G.: End-to-end measurements of email spoofing attacks. In: Proceedings of 27th USENIX Security Symposium (2018)
18. Alexa: Alexa most popular website. http://www.alexa.com/topsites
19. Magnet: Magnet process capture tool. https://www.magnetforensics.com/resources/magnet-process-capture/
20. Microsoft: Windows sysinternals strings v2.53. https://docs.microsoft.com/en-us/sysinternals/downloads/strings

21. Banday, M.T.: Analysing e-mail headers for forensic investigation. J. Digital Foren. Sec. Law **6**, 49–64 (2011)
22. Sanchez, P., Tapiador, J., Schneider, G.: After you, please: browser extensions order attacks and countermeasures. Int. J. Inf. Secur. **19**, 623–638 (2020)

# AttackMiner: A Graph Neural Network Based Approach for Attack Detection from Audit Logs

Yuedong Pan[1,2], Lijun Cai[1(✉)], Tao Leng[1,2], Lixin Zhao[1], Jiangang Ma[1], Aimin Yu[1], and Dan Meng[1]

[1] Institute of Information Engineering, Chinese Academy of Sciences, Beijing, China
{panyuedong,cailijun,lengtao,zhaolixin,majiangang,yuaimin,
mengdan}@iie.ac.cn
[2] School of Cyber Security, University of Chinese Academy of Sciences,
Beijing, China

**Abstract.** In an enterprise environment, intrusion detection systems generate many threat alerts on anomalous events every day, and these alerts may involve certain steps of a long-dormant advanced persistent threat (APT). In this paper, we present AttackMiner, an attack detection framework that combines contextual information from audit logs. Our main observation is that the same attack behavior may occur in various possible contexts, and combining various possible contextual information can provide more effective information for detecting such attacks. We utilize a combination of provenance graph causal analysis and deep learning techniques to build a graph-structure-based model that builds key patterns of attack graphs and benign graphs from audit logs. During detection, the detection system creates provenance graphs using the input audit logs. After being optimized by our customized graph optimization mechanism, it identifies whether an attack has occurred. Our evaluations on the DARPA TC dataset show that AttackMiner can successfully detect attack behaviors with high accuracy and efficiency. Through this effort, we provide security investigators with a new approach of identifying attack activity from audit logs.

**Keywords:** Host-based intrusion detection · Graph neural network · Attack migration

## 1 Introduction

Advanced Persistent Threats (APTs), as opposed to regular attacks, are a type of sophisticated attack performed by experienced adversaries employing a variety of offensive strategies and tools [23]. APTs typically involve multiple attack steps over an extended period of time. When a security analyst wants to determine whether an APT has occurred inside the system, he usually needs to conduct a lengthy and complex search and analysis of massive logs, and identify whether there are typical attack behaviors in these logs. This makes these

© ICST Institute for Computer Sciences, Social Informatics and Telecommunications Engineering 2023
Published by Springer Nature Switzerland AG 2023. All Rights Reserved
F. Li et al. (Eds.): SecureComm 2022, LNICST 462, pp. 510–528, 2023.
https://doi.org/10.1007/978-3-031-25538-0_27

attacks difficult to detect. Traditional detectors [7,25] can detect anomalous actions that do not fit into previously learned benign patterns. However, attackers can easily get around them because they treat system calls or network events as temporal sequences [6,7,29] and only consider the sequential relationship between log entries. Existing attack detection and response technologies (e.g., endpoint detection and response tools) rely on low-level indicators of compromise (IOCs) or adversarial tactics, techniques, and procedures (TTPs) criteria [1] being matched. However, simple rule-matching approaches are prone to a huge number of false positives, resulting in "alert fatigue".

Recent research [12,13,25–27,38] suggests that host-based intrusion detection might benefit from abundant contextual knowledge regarding data provenance. Compared to raw system audit data, data provenance offers more contextual information, which helps identify malicious behaviors from benign behaviors [12, 14]. Some anomaly-based graph kernel algorithms [12,25] dynamically model the entire graph and detect anomalous graphs through clustering methods. However, the provenance graph produced by covert intrusion activities carried out in a system may be similar to a benign system. Therefore, it is difficult for the graph kernel algorithm to detect the attack behavior with a few abnormal nodes in the feature graph. To a certain extent, malicious behavior can be detected by detecting anomalous paths in the provenance graph [38]. However, the activity of some complex threats (e.g., APTs) is frequently divided into several parts rather than appearing in a complete path, making path-level detection difficult.

In this paper, we aim to identify the key steps of attack activities from audit logs, helping security analysts identify whether a given audit log contains specific malicious behavior. We propose AttackMiner, a graph neural network-based attack detector capable of detecting attack patterns in various contextual scenarios. AttackMiner takes system audit logs as inputs and uses a graph neural network framework to learn rich contextual information from data sources. AttackMiner mainly includes three stages: (a) processing audit logs and creating provenance graphs based on the log sliding window; (b) constructing attack graphs containing specific attack patterns using attack migration and mutation techniques; and (c) learning to represent attack semantics using a graph neural network model, which aids in accurately determining whether a given audit log contains a specific attack pattern at detection time. Additionally, security analysts can conduct fast attack investigations from detected logs that contain attack behavior, saving significant time compared to investigation activity on massive logs.

Our approach is based on the insight that some complex malicious activities (e.g., APTs) are usually divided into several parts rather than appearing in a complete path. A 14-stage APT knowledge base is provided by the MITRE ATT&CK framework [1] to characterize adversary plans and methodologies for APTs. The Lockheed Martin Cyber Kill Chain [17] is a 7-stage methodology for characterizing APTs. However, the multiple stages of APTs span a long time and generate a large number of logs. This results in significant processing and storage overhead for over-redundant multi-stage models. Therefore, we focus on identifying key actions in the attack activity.

In summary, this paper makes the following contributions:

1. We propose AttackMiner, a GNN-based attack detection framework. Attack-Miner combines model learning techniques for natural language and provenance graph processing to help security analysts quickly detect attacks from audit logs.
2. We focus on attack migration, migrating various behaviors representing attacks into various possible log contexts. Through attack migration, attack behaviors with rich backgrounds can be constructed, providing rich data for model learning.
3. We implemented a set of provenance graph optimization methods that greatly reduce the number of redundant edges and nodes. The optimized provenance graph allows AttackMiner to build efficient GNN-based models to accurately detect attack activity.
4. We present a concrete implementation and evaluation of AttackMiner. The experimental results show that AttackMiner can accurately identify various attack behaviors, and the detection effect is better than other advanced attack behavior detectors.

The paper is organized as follows. Related work is introduced in Sect. 2. Motivation and assumptions about our work are introduced in Sect. 3. We introduce the overview of AttackMiner in Sect. 4. In Sect. 5, we provide the formal details of AttackMiner. The evaluation and conclusion are presented in Sect. 6 and Sect. 7, respectively.

## 2   Related Work

### 2.1   Log-Based Attack Analysis

Many works [9,10,24,32] use system audit logs to perform attack detection and forensic analysis. Disclosure [5] extracts statistical features from NetFlow logs to detect botnet C&C channels. Opera et al. [28] utilize DNS or web proxy logs to detect early infections in the enterprise. LogLens [6] is a real-time anomaly detection system that deploys an unsupervised learning approach to analyze log sequences. DeepLog [7] converts system logs into natural language sequences using the Long Short-term Memory (LSTM) network that can automatically learn benign patterns and alert anomalies from system behavior. Tiresias [34] utilizes Recurrent Neural Networks (RNNs) in logs to predict specific attack steps. Most of these log analysis methods treat the log as temporal sequences, which only preserves sequential relationships between log entries. AttackMiner takes into account the spatial and interactive relationships between system entities through the message-passing mechanism of graph neural networks.

### 2.2   Provenance Graph-Based Attack Detection

Provenance graph analysis is widely used in APT attack detection [35], forensic analysis [16], and attack scenario reconstruction [15,28]. Holmes [27] and

RapSheet [13] focus on alert generation, correlation, and scenario reconstruction for host-based threats, but they rely on the knowledge base of adversarial TTPs. Log2vec [23] uses logs to construct compositions, extracts log vectors based on graph embedding, and detects malicious logs based on clustering. It differs from the provenance-based approach because the nodes in the provenance graph are entities of the system rather than logs. StreamSpot [25] is a memory-efficient anomaly detection system that handles provenance graph heterogeneity and streaming challenges, but suffers from shortcomings in handling locally constrained graph features and dynamic cluster maintenance. With only a certain amount of benign data and a small amount of attack data, our method can learn key attack steps via the provenance graph. Models trained with optimized provenance graphs have better detection capabilities.

## 3   Motivation and Assumptions

**Motivation.** We define the attack detection problem as a subgraph detection problem. Specifically, we detect whether the provenance graph contains a subgraph representing an attack. If it does, it means that attack events have occurred. Otherwise, no attacks have occurred. The key insight behind our method is that the attack behavior expressed by the attack subgraph may occur at various moments when the system is running. In the context of different audit logs of the system, similar attacks have similar attack patterns, and the attack pattern is learned through deep learning. The representation of this context helps to detect attacks. Specifically, Fig. 1 shows a portion of the provenance graph where the attack occurs, with the shaded area representing a key attack behavior. This attack mainly starts by exploiting the vulnerability of Nginx. The attacker downloads and executes the malicious file */tmp/vUgefal*, triggering an alert for file execution. The attacker then writes to another file */var/log/devc*, communicates with the malicious server, and even attempts to inject into the *sshd* process. Likewise, this kind of aggressive behavior can occur in other situations as well. As long as attackers exploit the vulnerability of the software to invade the system, even if the system is running a background task different from that in Fig. 1, the attack behavior in Fig. 1 can be achieved.

That is to say, if the attacker performs some malicious behaviors after invading the system by exploiting a certain software vulnerability this time, the next time he intrudes the system may be through other vulnerabilities and perform similar malicious behaviors.

**Assumptions.** We assume that the underlying operating system and audit application are part of a trusted computing base (TCB), similar to previous research on provenance tracking [4, 30]. The audit logs used to build the provenance graph are hard to tamper with. The source of the attack is outside the enterprise. The attacker uses remote network access to infiltrate the system. The host audit system can normally capture a series of attack behaviors by attackers.

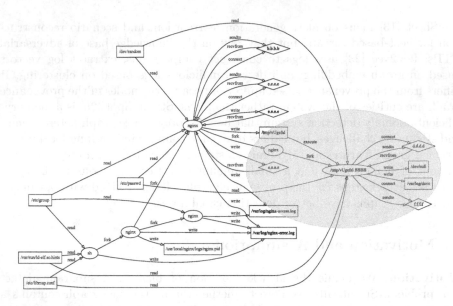

**Fig. 1.** A portion of the provenance graph where the attack occurs, with the shaded area representing a key attack behavior.

## 4   Approach Overview

### 4.1   Overview

AttackMiner is an attack detection tool that models attack and non-attack behaviors. Figure 2 gives an overview of the AttackMiner architecture. It mainly consists of four parts: dynamic log sliding window selection (a), provenance graph construction and optimization (b), deep learning model based on graph neural network (c), and attack detection (d). In the dynamic log window selection stage, we randomly and dynamically adjust the start time of two adjacent windows according to the time span of the current log window, which can improve the representativeness of the data to a certain extent. In the provenance graph construction stage, AttackMiner first constructs benign provenance graphs and then constructs malicious provenance graphs through attack migration technology. We adopt a series of graph optimization methods to reduce the size of the provenance graph while preserving the original semantics as much as possible. In the model training stage, AttackMiner uses a learning model based on a graph neural network to effectively embed the input data. During the attack detection stage, AttackMiner accurately determines whether an attack has taken place on given log files using a novel classifier we developed.

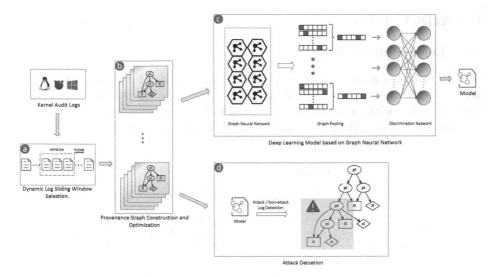

**Fig. 2.** Overview of AttackMiner architecture.

## 4.2   Challenges and Solutions

In this work, we first need to consider as much as possible the context in which the attack steps occur, and more importantly, we need to effectively aggregate the information contained in each provenance graph. Below, we present the challenges of designing AttackMiner and our corresponding solutions.

**Challenge 1.** How to construct provenance graphs to cover both benign and malicious behaviors as much as possible? Previous graph pattern matching models [2,21,39] analyzed small subgraphs but did not involve log window processing. In order to include as many benign and malicious behaviors as possible, we run a dynamic sliding window on the original logs (Sect. 5.1) and combine attack migration and attack mutation techniques (Sect. 5.3) to provide the model with realistic learning materials.

**Challenge 2.** How to optimize provenance graphs while keeping the original semantics as much as possible? With only a few behaviors in the massive audit log indicating a real attack, searching for traces of an attack is like "finding a needle in a haystack". In order to solve this problem, we adopt log compression methods based on semantic preservation (Sect. 5.2), which simplifies the provenance graph structure and improves the detection efficiency.

**Challenge 3.** How to effectively represent graph information? Previous work searches for provenance graph information by meta-path [25]. However, representing provenance graph information via meta-paths requires expert knowledge of the target system. Graph neural networks have been shown to learn complex graph patterns for downstream tasks such as memory forensic analysis [35] and binary code similarity detection [40]. In this work, we try to extract graph patterns with graph neural networks (Sect. 5.4).

## 5   AttackMiner

### 5.1   Log Window Sliding

Our main goal is not to detect a complete attack activity with a long time span but to focus on a typical steps of an attack, such as when the invaded process communicates with some malicious IP addresses after reading and writing a private file. These actions are usually completed within a certain time window.

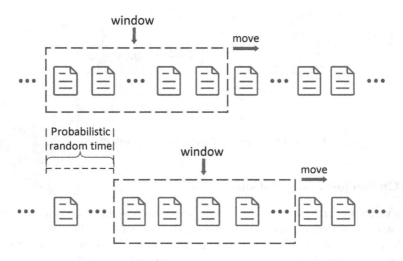

**Fig. 3.** Illustration of log sliding window in AttackMiner.

The log sliding window is used to select audit logs within a suitable time span for constructing provenance graphs. The two adjacent log windows are not completely separated. This is to cover various situations in the audit log as much as possible. Figure 3 is an illustration of a log sliding window. A window with a certain time span moves on the log in chronological order of events. After each move is completed, AttackMiner constructs the provenance graph with the log events in the current window. In order to cover as many events as possible, the distance that the window moves each time is a random time that varies according to the probability. Additionally, in order to gather useful information, we suggest choosing log windows with an appropriate length $L$ based on the target behavior. According to the findings of Sect. 6.5, AttackMiner still has high accuracy when $L$ is above 60 min.

### 5.2   Provenance Graph Construction and Optimization

AttackMiner first performs log window sliding on logs generated by benign environments and then converts the selected audit logs into a provenance graph. The provenance graph constructed with logs produced in benign environments

**Table 1.** A summarization of nodes and edges in provenance graphs

| Subject type | Object type | Attributes | Relations |
|---|---|---|---|
| Process | Process | Type, Name | Fork/Clone |
| | File | Type, File Name | Read, Write, Execute |
| | Socket | Type, Src/Dest IP | Recv, Send, Connect |

is called the benign provenance graph. The entities and events we use when building the provenance graph are shown in Table 1, where subjects and objects correspond to nodes in the graph and relations correspond to edges in the graph.

AttackMiner mainly uses three techniques for graph structure optimization.

First, AttackMiner eliminates isolated nodes in the provenance graph since these nodes do not have enough graph structure information. At the same time, we merge socket nodes with the same IP address connected to the same process. We do not differentiate whether a port is malicious or not in order to obtain a compact provenance graph.

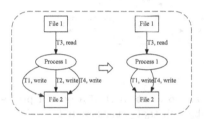

**Fig. 4.** Event reduction

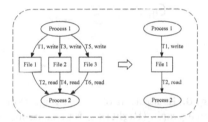

**Fig. 5.** Node reduction

Second, AttackMiner constructs provenance graphs from audit logs with distinct edges, removing redundant edges while preserving semantics [41]. When a node has an incoming edge, the incoming edge may affect the semantics of the node's outgoing edge. Specifically, as shown in Fig. 4, before the *read* at time $T3$ occurs, the *write* event at $T2$ is repeated with the *write* event at $T1$, so the *write* event at $T2$ can be removed. The *write* at $T4$ occurs after the *read* at $T3$, which affects *Process*1, so it should be retained.

Third, inspired by research [3], AttackMiner merges nodes and their edges whose incoming and outgoing edges are events of the same type. As shown in Fig. 5, file nodes *File*1, *File*2, and *File*3 are merged into one node *File*1 because they share same types of incoming edges (*read*) and outgoing edges (*write*).

## 5.3   Attack Provenance Graph Construction

We obtain attack information from threat intelligence or audit logs recording malicious behaviors, and use the extracted attack information to construct an attack subgraph $G_a$. Then we migrate $G_a$ to the benign provenance graph $G_b$ through the attack migration technique, and finally get a malicious provenance graph $G_m$ containing the attack subgraph. Figure 6 depicts an example of attack migration.

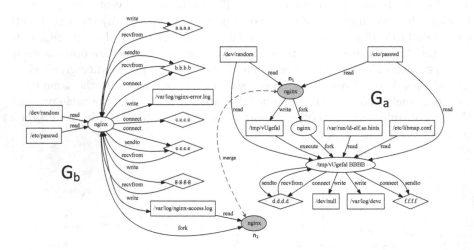

**Fig. 6.** Illustration of attack migration. (Left) $G_b$ represents part of a benign provenance graph. (Right) $G_a$ represents an attack subgraph that was extracted.

**Attack Migration.** The purpose of attack migration is to use various log contexts where malicious behaviors may occur as the background and construct attack samples with rich background information. So the trained model has the ability to shield the interference of background noise and pay attention to malicious behavior itself.

As shown in Fig. 6, $G_b$ represents a benign provenance graph. For the sake of illustration, we have selected a portion of the benign provenance graph. The right half of the figure, $G_a$, is an attack subgraph extracted from attack campaigns. The attack in $G_a$ invades the system through the vulnerability of *nginx*, and the shaded *nginx* node $n_1$ is the intrusion point for malicious behavior. In the benign provenance graph $G_b$, we find the target process node with the same type and name as the intrusion point (*nginx* node $n_2$ marked with shadow in $G_b$), and then we migrate the events associated with node $n_1$ to node $n_2$, so that node $n_1$ merges with $n_2$. Algorthim 1 explains our node merging algorithm in detail.

In addition, we randomly mutate the intruding process in the attack subgraph into another process in the benign provenance graph. And we mutate the name of the process with the same name as the intrusion process in the attack subgraph

---

**Algorithm 1:** Attack migration algorithm

---

**Input:** Benign provenance graph collection $List_{G_b}$; Attack subgraph collection $List_{G_a}$

**Output:** Malicious provenance graph $List_{G_m}$

1  $List_{Gm} \leftarrow Null$ ;
2  **for** $G_b$ *in* $List_{G_b}$ **do**
3     $\hat{V} \leftarrow$ random subject node in $G_b$ ;
4     $attr_{\hat{V}} \leftarrow$ attribute of $\hat{V}$ ;
5     **for** $Ga$ *in* $List_{Ga}$ **do**
6        $V \leftarrow$ intrusion subject node in $Ga$ ;
         // change the attribute of $V$, merge $\hat{V}$ and $V$
7        $attr_V \leftarrow attr_{\hat{V}}$;
         // migrate $G_a$ to $G_b$
8        $Gm \leftarrow migrateGraph(Ga, G_b)$;
9        $List_{Gm}$.append($G_m$)
10     **end**
11  **end**
12  return $List_{Gm}$

---

to the name after the mutation of the invading process. This process does not fundamentally change the attack pattern and, at the same time, increases the number of attack subgraphs that are not currently triggered but may appear in the future.

### 5.4  Deep Learning Model

**Input Embedding.** AttackMiner uses word2vec [20] for word embedding. We first convert complete events in the provenance graph into sentences, such as this sentence converted from an event: Process *nginx* write file *access.log*. Then we feed the sentence into the word2vec model and learn the embedding representation of each word in the sentence. Since each node in the provenance graph contains two attributes, type and name, the input feature $h_u$ of node $u$ can be computed as follows:

$$h_u = \text{Concat}(w_{type}^u, w_{name}^u) \tag{1}$$

where $w_{type}^u$ is the vector representation of the type word of the node $u$, and $w_{name}^u$ is the vector representation of the name word of the node $u$.

**Learning Model Based on Graph Neural Network.** Overly complex models bring certain difficulties to training. We tend to implement our models with simple network structures. We chose the graph attention network (GAT) [37] as the basic component of AttackMiner. The GAT is implemented by stacking simple graph attention layers, which introduce a self-attention mechanism in the propagation process, and the hidden state of each node is calculated by paying attention to its neighbor nodes. In our experiments, we use a multi-head attention mechanism with three heads. More details on GAT can be found in [37].

**A Classifier Combining Multiple Receptive Fields.** The general approach to graph classification is to add a multilayer perceptron (MLP) layer to the end of the graph network. However, we seek to strengthen the model's robustness while retaining the various traits of vectors. In contrast to the general approach, we try to perform 1D-convolution of node vectors with different receptive fields to obtain high-level features of embedding vectors. Then, we perform graph max-pooling and average-pooling operations on the convolution results, respectively, to obtain two graph embedding vectors. Finally, we concatenate the learned graph embedding vectors and feed them into MLP for multi-classification. The relevant expressions are as follows:

$$y_1 = \text{GraphPooling}(\text{ReLu}(\text{Conv}_1(H_G))) \tag{2}$$

$$y_2 = \text{GraphPooling}(\text{ReLu}(\text{Conv}_2(H_G))) \tag{3}$$

$$\tilde{y} = \text{softmax}(\sum \text{MLP}(\text{Concat}(y_1, y_2))) \tag{4}$$

where $H_G$ denotes the node vectors of graph $G$ following GNN embedding.

## 6    Evaluation

### 6.1    Implementation

AttackMiner is implemented in Python 3.8 with around 3100 lines of code (LoC). We use the Gensim [33] library to generate node embeddings for training graphs. The length of the initial node embedding vector is limited to 200 to reduce the size of the model. AttackMiner uses a two-layer GAT model to aggregate graph information. The input and output dimensions of node vectors in the model are 200 and 64, respectively. We optimize the model parameters through the Adam optimizer. We train the model for 20 epochs with the training batch size set to 64. The learning rate changes exponentially. The rate of change is 0.98 and the initial value is 0.01. We use Pytorch [31] as the backend and run our experiments on a server with two Intel Xeon E5-2630 v3 CPUs and 128 GB of memory. The server has two NVIDIA Tesla P4 GPUs and a 64-bit CentOS 7 operating system installed.

### 6.2    Dataset

We chose to evaluate our system using the DARPA TC [18] dataset, which was generated when the red team played against the blue team in April 2018. In total, we evaluated AttackMiner using four of these attack scenarios. We describe the scenarios and properties in Table 2.

For each attack scenario, we construct the corresponding attack subgraph. We leverage attack migration (detailed in Sect. 5.3) to generate datasets containing benign and malicious provenance graphs. The number of samples for each category of provenance graphs (including benign provenance graphs) is 6000, of which 80% are used as the training set. Before feeding the samples into the learned model, we use the graph optimization method described in Sect. 5.2 to optimize the structure of provenance graphs.

**Table 2.** Attack scenarios description

| Scenario | Short description | $|V(G)|$ | $|E(G)|$ |
|----------|-------------------|----------|----------|
| ATK-1 | Nginx vulnerability was exploited to attack CADETS FreeBSD. The attacker downloaded a file, elevated it to a new process running as root, and attempted to inject into the sshd process but fails | 22 | 36 |
| ATK-2 | Attackers exploited Nginx with malformed HTTP requests to attack CADETS, and downloaded the libdrakon implant file *.so to inject into the sshd process, but it crashed CADETS | 15 | 21 |
| ATK-3 | The shell connection connected to the operator console via HTTP. The attacker performed the micro apt implant without root privileges. The micro apt implant was connected to the C2's micro apt listener | 36 | 65 |
| ATK-4 | The Nginx vulnerability was exploited by attackers to cause the drakon implant executable to run from disk, resulting in a new drakon process with root privileges and operation with a new connection to the administrator console | 28 | 47 |

## 6.3 Effectiveness of Graph Optimization Algorithms

The effectiveness of AttackMiner lies in a set of optimization techniques integrated into its components. As described in Sect. 5.2, to reduce graph complexity, we construct provenance graphs using a set of custom graph optimization techniques. Here, we detail how these techniques contribute to its effectiveness. Figure 7 shows the number of entities and events before and after graph optimization when the log window length $L$ is set to 60 min. Compared to the original graph size, AttackMiner reduces the number of entities in provenance graphs by an average of 80.20% and the number of events by an average of 83.39%. AttackMiner removes redundant or irrelevant events and entities from massive logs that do not provide any semantics to detect different attack patterns. Therefore, the further extracted provenance graph is more representative as the input for model training.

**Table 3.** Results before and after provenance graph optimization.

| Category | Before optimization | | | | After optimization | | | |
|----------|----------|-------------|-----------|------------|----------|-------------|-----------|------------|
| | Recall % | Precision % | F1-score % | Accuracy % | Recall % | Precision % | F1-score % | Accuracy % |
| Benign | 92.52 | 68.70 | 78.85 | 85.15 | 98.46 | 91.89 | 95.06 | 97.72 |
| ATK-1 | 70.02 | 82.77 | 75.87 | | 99.14 | 99.06 | 99.01 | |
| ATK-2 | 92.79 | 100.00 | 96.26 | | 98.11 | 100.00 | 99.05 | |
| ATK-3 | 87.38 | 100.00 | 93.26 | | 99.12 | 100.00 | 99.56 | |
| ATK-4 | 81.49 | 82.61 | 82.05 | | 93.63 | 98.31 | 95.91 | |

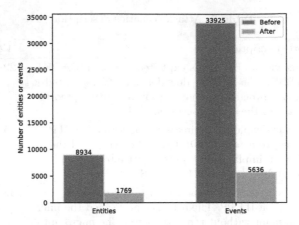

**Fig. 7.** Changes in average number of entities and average number of events before and after provenance graph optimization.

We present the detection results before and after graph optimization in Table 3 (log window length $L$ is 60 min). As shown in Table 3, the provenance graph optimization improves the overall accuracy by 14.76%, and the F1 scores of the five categories are increased by 20.56%, 30.49%, 2.90%, 6.76%, and 16.89%, respectively. This is because graph optimization removes redundant events from massive logs, making attack patterns more apparent. Overall, the optimized provenance graph serves as a highly representative training set and is used for model training, which significantly improves the generalization ability of the model.

### 6.4   Comparison Analysis

We implemented a set of cutting-edge approaches that can be used to replace the AttackMiner component and compared their attack detection performance to that of AttackMiner. We chose the time span of the log window to be 60 min. Table 4 and Fig. 8 summarize our results.

Support vector machines (SVM) [36]. To evaluate the effectiveness of graph neural network aggregation, we compare it with SVM. We obtain the embedding vector of each node on the graph through the input embedding method introduced in 5.4, and then perform the graph pooling operation to obtain the embedded representation of the provenance graph. In order to improve the accuracy of the classifier, we implement a multi-classifier by combining multiple binary classifiers and repeatedly adjusting the parameters C, gamma, and the number of iterations of the SVM. In the evaluation experiments, we use a linear kernel function with C=1.0, gamma="auto" and an iteration number of 1000. Although the average accuracy of SVM can reach 86.55%, it cannot detect some attack behaviors well, and its recall on ATK-1 is only 66.90%. The main limitation of SVM is its inability to model the connection relationships between different entities in the provenance graph, which is one of the key features reflecting attack patterns.

**Table 4.** The results of the comparison analysis.

| Category | SVM | | | | Random forest | | | |
|---|---|---|---|---|---|---|---|---|
| | Recall % | Precision % | F1-score % | Accuracy % | Recall % | Precision % | F1-score % | Accuracy % |
| Benign | 96.67 | 75.17 | 84.58 | 86.55 | 74.17 | 78.77 | 76.40 | 78.45 |
| ATK-1 | 66.90 | 98.98 | 79.84 | | 60.72 | 67.69 | 64.01 | |
| ATK-2 | 97.17 | 99.21 | 98.18 | | 98.71 | 98.80 | 98.75 | |
| ATK-3 | 97.78 | 81.97 | 89.18 | | 98.41 | 98.10 | 98.26 | |
| ATK-4 | 72.92 | 87.21 | 79.43 | | 59.08 | 50.91 | 54.70 | |
| Category | k-nearest neighbor | | | | GCN | | | |
| | Recall % | Precision % | F1-score % | Accuracy % | Recall % | Precision % | F1-score % | Accuracy % |
| Benign | 62.23 | 49.45 | 55.11 | 65.25 | 91.15 | 95.08 | 93.07 | 90.83 |
| ATK-1 | 48.89 | 48.06 | 48.47 | | 80.19 | 94.54 | 86.77 | |
| ATK-2 | 92.45 | 92.92 | 92.69 | | 99.91 | 74.47 | 85.34 | |
| ATK-3 | 85.87 | 90.62 | 88.18 | | 83.57 | 96.43 | 89.54 | |
| ATK-4 | 35.65 | 46.05 | 40.19 | | 99.83 | 100.0 | 99.92 | |
| Category | GraphSAGE | | | | AttackMiner | | | |
| | Recall % | Precision % | F1-score % | Accuracy % | Recall % | Precision % | F1-score % | Accuracy % |
| Benign | 98.46 | 85.23 | 91.37 | 95.88 | 98.46 | 91.89 | 95.06 | 97.72 |
| ATK-1 | 99.14 | 100.0 | 99.57 | | 99.14 | 99.06 | 99.01 | |
| ATK-2 | 97.85 | 98.45 | 98.15 | | 98.11 | 100.0 | 99.05 | |
| ATK-3 | 98.57 | 100.0 | 99.28 | | 90.12 | 100.0 | 99.56 | |
| ATK-4 | 85.14 | 98.14 | 91.18 | | 93.63 | 98.31 | 95.91 | |

Random Forest (RF) [22]. We chose the Gini coefficient as a function to measure segmentation quality. As can be seen from the Table 4, the accuracy of the RF classifier is much lower than that of the SVM. In addition, we also experimented with k-Nearest Neighbor (KNN) [8], which gives less classification performance than RF and SVM, and the classification accuracy is only 65.25%. Figure 8 visually shows the detection distribution of SVM, RF, and KNN. As shown in Fig. 8(a-c), the detection effects of SVM, RF, and KNN are inferior to those of GNN based methods. This is mainly because GNNs can effectively learn by fusing the attribute information of graphs.

In addition, we compare AttackMiner with GCN [19] and GraphSAGE [11] to evaluate the effectiveness of AttackMiner in detecting migration attacks based on various graph neural networks. GCN is a convolution operation defined on the graph structure. By defining the convolution operation on the graph, the structural information and node information in the graph are captured. GraphSAGE aggregates information by sampling neighbor nodes. As can be seen from Table 4, the accuracies of GCN and GraphSAGE are 90.83% and 95.88%, respectively, which are only 7.05% and 1.88% lower than the AttackMiner prototype, respectively. In total, the attack behavior in the original audit log is typically made more obvious by graph structure optimization and attack migration operations.

### 6.5   Influence of Log Window Size on Detection Effect

In the process of building the provenance graph, we adopt the log window sliding mechanism. Since log windows of different sizes contain different numbers of

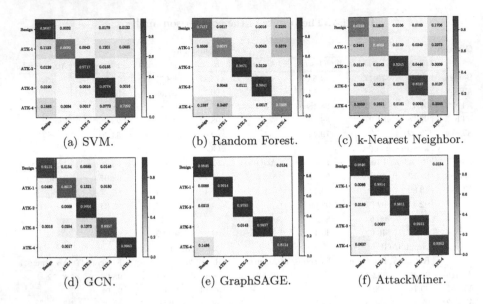

(a) SVM.        (b) Random Forest.        (c) k-Nearest Neighbor.

(d) GCN.        (e) GraphSAGE.        (f) AttackMiner.

**Fig. 8.** Confusion matrices result from comparison analysis.

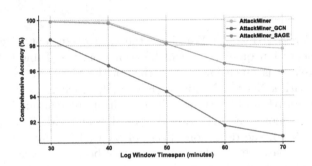

**Fig. 9.** Accuracy with different log window timespans.

**Table 5.** Results of different classifiers.

| Category | AttackMiner_Tra | | | | AttackMiner | | | |
|---|---|---|---|---|---|---|---|---|
| | Recall % | Precision % | F1-score % | Accuracy % | Recall % | Precision % | F1-score % | Accuracy % |
| Benign | 92.77 | 93.61 | 93.19 | 92.97 | 98.46 | 91.89 | 95.06 | 97.72 |
| ATK-1 | 80.36 | 94.65 | 86.92 | | 99.14 | 99.06 | 99.01 | |
| ATK-2 | 99.91 | 82.61 | 90.44 | | 98.11 | 100.00 | 99.05 | |
| ATK-3 | 93.57 | 96.24 | 94.89 | | 99.12 | 100.00 | 99.56 | |
| ATK-4 | 98.13 | 100.00 | 99.06 | | 93.63 | 98.31 | 95.91 | |

entities and events, the size of the log window will affect the detection effect to a certain extent. We evaluate the impact on detection results when the log window size is varied from 30 min to 70 min, where the results are evaluated every 10 min. Figure 9 shows the change in detection accuracy for different log window sizes. In Fig. 9, as the log window becomes larger, the detection accuracy decreases slightly, but still maintains a high accuracy (when the log window size becomes 70 min, the AttackMiner detection accuracy is still above 96%). This is because while normal entities and events occupy a larger proportion of log windows with large time spans, AttackMiner learns the characteristics of attack patterns in different contexts through attack migration. At the same time, our graph structure optimization methods make the attack pattern more prominent in the provenance graph, which is also beneficial to the detector detection.

### 6.6 The Effect of Changes in the Classifier on the Experiment

Traditional classifiers directly input node features into MLP for aggregation classification. Instead of using the traditional method, we designed a new classifier. Our classifier is based on convolutional layers and combines multiple receptive fields. The new classifier can aggregate features from different aspects of the feature vector by combining multiple receptive fields simultaneously. To understand the contribution of our classifier module, we created a variant of AttackMiner called AttackMiner_Tra using the traditional classifier. Table 5 shows the performance metrics for the above settings. Overall, AttackMiner's average precision, recall, and F1-score are all over 4.80% higher than AttackMiner_Tra. We believe that richer attack features can be learned due to the addition of convolutional layers after the graph neural network. The results show that our classifier improves the performance of attack detection.

## 7    Conclusion

We present AttackMiner, a GNN-based attack detection framework for detecting attack activity from system audit logs. AttackMiner combines provenance graph analysis, natural language processing, and graph neural network techniques. Through optimization and attack migration based on provenance graph structure, AttackMiner can identify high-level patterns of different attacks. We extensively evaluate AttackMiner on real public datasets. AttackMiner successfully detects all the attacks with high accuracy and efficiency. Our research demonstrates the successful application of graph neural networks in attack detection.

**Acknowledgment.** This work is supported by the Strategic Priority Research Program of Chinese Academy of Sciences, Grant No. XDC02040200.

## References

1. Adversarial tactics, techniques and common knowledge. https://attack.mitre.org/wiki/Main Page

2. Trace: Preventing advanced persistent threat cyberattacks(2018). https://archive.sri.com/work/projects/trace-preventing-advanced-persisten-threat-cyberattacks. (Accessed 1 April 2022)

3. Alsaheel, A., et al.: {ATLAS}: A sequence-based learning approach for attack investigation. In: 30th USENIX Security Symposium (USENIX Security 21), pp. 3005–3022 (2021)

4. Bates, A., Tian, D.J., Butler, K.R., Moyer, T.: Trustworthy whole-system provenance for the linux kernel. In: 24th USENIX Security Symposium (USENIX Security 15), pp. 319–334 (2015)

5. Bilge, L., Balzarotti, D., Robertson, W., Kirda, E., Kruegel, C.: Disclosure: detecting botnet command and control servers through large-scale netflow analysis. In: Proceedings of the 28th Annual Computer Security Applications Conference, pp. 129–138 (2012)

6. Debnath, B., et al.: Loglens: A real-time log analysis system. In: 2018 IEEE 38th International Conference On Distributed Computing Systems (ICDCS), pp. 1052–1062. IEEE (2018)

7. Du, M., Li, F., Zheng, G., Srikumar, V.: Deeplog: Anomaly detection and diagnosis from system logs through deep learning. In: Proceedings of the 2017 ACM SIGSAC Conference On Computer And Communications Security, pp. 1285–1298 (2017)

8. Fix, E., Hodges, J.L.: Discriminatory analysis. nonparametric discrimination: Consistency properties. International Statistical Review/Revue Internationale de Statistique $57(3)$, 238–247 (1989)

9. Goel, A., Feng, W.C., Maier, D., Walpole, J.: Forensix: A robust, high-performance reconstruction system. In: 25th IEEE International Conference on Distributed Computing Systems Workshops, pp. 155–162. IEEE (2005)

10. Goel, A., Po, K., Farhadi, K., Li, Z., De Lara, E.: The taser intrusion recovery system. In: Proceedings of the Twentieth ACM Symposium On Operating Systems Principles, pp. 163–176 (2005)

11. Hamilton, W., Ying, Z., Leskovec, J.: Inductive representation learning on large graphs. In: Advances in Neural Information Processing Systems 30 (2017)

12. Han, X., Pasquier, T., Bates, A., Mickens, J., Seltzer, M.: Unicorn: Runtime provenance-based detector for advanced persistent threats. arXiv preprint arXiv:2001.01525 (2020)

13. Hassan, W.U., Bates, A., Marino, D.: Tactical provenance analysis for endpoint detection and response systems. In: 2020 IEEE Symposium on Security and Privacy (SP), pp. 1172–1189. IEEE (2020)

14. Hassan, W.U., et al.: Nodoze: Combatting threat alert fatigue with automated provenance triage. In: Network and Distributed Systems Security Symposium (2019)

15. Hassan, W.U., Noureddine, M.A., Datta, P., Bates, A.: Omegalog: High-fidelity attack investigation via transparent multi-layer log analysis. In: Network and Distributed System Security Symposium (2020)

16. Homayoun, S., Dehghantanha, A., Ahmadzadeh, M., Hashemi, S., Khayami, R.: Know abnormal, find evil: frequent pattern mining for ransomware threat hunting and intelligence. IEEE Trans. Emerg. Top. Comput. $8(2)$, 341–351 (2017)

17. Hutchins, E.M., Cloppert, M.J., Amin, R.M., et al.: Intelligence-driven computer network defense informed by analysis of adversary campaigns and intrusion kill chains. Lead. Issues Inf. Warfare Sec. Res. $1(1)$, 80 (2011)

18. Keromytis, A.D.: Transparent computing engagement 3 data release (2018). https://github.com/darpa-i2o/Transparent-Computing

19. Kipf, T.N., Welling, M.: Semi-supervised classification with graph convolutional networks. arXiv preprint arXiv:1609.02907 (2016)
20. Le, Q., Mikolov, T.: Distributed representations of sentences and documents. In: International Conference On Machine Learning, pp. 1188–1196 (2014)
21. Li, Y., Gu, C., Dullien, T., Vinyals, O., Kohli, P.: Graph matching networks for learning the similarity of graph structured objects. In: International Conference on Machine Learning, pp. 3835–3845. PMLR (2019)
22. Liaw, A., Wiener, M., et al.: Classification and regression by randomforest. R news **2**(3), 18–22 (2002)
23. Liu, F., Wen, Y., Zhang, D., Jiang, X., Xing, X., Meng, D.: Log2vec: A heterogeneous graph embedding based approach for detecting cyber threats within enterprise. In: Proceedings of the 2019 ACM SIGSAC Conference on Computer and Communications Security, pp. 1777–1794 (2019)
24. Liu, Y., et al.: Towards a timely causality analysis for enterprise security. In: NDSS (2018)
25. Manzoor, E., Milajerdi, S.M., Akoglu, L.: Fast memory-efficient anomaly detection in streaming heterogeneous graphs. In: Proceedings of the 22nd ACM SIGKDD International Conference on Knowledge Discovery and Data Mining, pp. 1035–1044 (2016)
26. Milajerdi, S.M., Eshete, B., Gjomemo, R., Venkatakrishnan, V.: Poirot: Aligning attack behavior with kernel audit records for cyber threat hunting. In: Proceedings of the 2019 ACM SIGSAC Conference on Computer and Communications Security, pp. 1795–1812 (2019)
27. Milajerdi, S.M., Gjomemo, R., Eshete, B., Sekar, R., Venkatakrishnan, V.: Holmes: real-time apt detection through correlation of suspicious information flows. In: 2019 IEEE Symposium on Security and Privacy (SP), pp. 1137–1152. IEEE (2019)
28. Oprea, A., Li, Z., Yen, T.F., Chin, S.H., Alrwais, S.: Detection of early-stage enterprise infection by mining large-scale log data. In: 2015 45th Annual IEEE/IFIP International Conference on Dependable Systems and Networks, pp. 45–56. IEEE (2015)
29. Parveen, P., McDaniel, N., Hariharan, V.S., Thuraisingham, B., Khan, L.: Unsupervised ensemble based learning for insider threat detection. In: 2012 International Conference on Privacy, Security, Risk and Trust and 2012 International Confernece on Social Computing, pp. 718–727. IEEE (2012)
30. Pasquier, T., et al.: Practical whole-system provenance capture. In: Proceedings of the 2017 Symposium on Cloud Computing, pp. 405–418 (2017)
31. Paszke, A., et al.: Pytorch: An imperative style, high-performance deep learning library. In: Wallach, H., Larochelle, H., Beygelzimer, A., d'Alché-Buc, F., Fox, E., Garnett, R. (eds.) Advances in Neural Information Processing Systems, vol. 32, pp. 8024–8035. Curran Associates, Inc. (2019). http://papers.neurips.cc/paper/9015-pytorch-an-imperative-style-high-performance-deep-learning-library.pdf
32. Pohly, D.J., McLaughlin, S., McDaniel, P., Butler, K.: Hi-fi: collecting high-fidelity whole-system provenance. In: Proceedings of the 28th Annual Computer Security Applications Conference, pp. 259–268 (2012)
33. Rehurek, R., Sojka, P.: Software framework for topic modelling with large corpora. In: Proceedings of the LREC 2010 Workshop on New Challenges for NLP Frameworks. Citeseer (2010)
34. Shen, Y., Mariconti, E., Vervier, P.A., Stringhini, G.: Tiresias: Predicting security events through deep learning. In: Proceedings of the 2018 ACM SIGSAC Conference on Computer and Communications Security, pp. 592–605 (2018)

35. Song, W., Yin, H., Liu, C., Song, D.: Deepmem: Learning graph neural network models for fast and robust memory forensic analysis. In: Proceedings of the 2018 ACM SIGSAC Conference on Computer and Communications Security, pp. 606–618 (2018)
36. Suykens, J.A., Vandewalle, J.: Least squares support vector machine classifiers. Neural Process. Lett. **9**(3), 293–300 (1999)
37. Veličković, P., Cucurull, G., Casanova, A., Romero, A., Lio, P., Bengio, Y.: Graph attention networks. arXiv preprint arXiv:1710.10903 (2017)
38. Wang, Q., et al.: You are what you do: Hunting stealthy malware via data provenance analysis. In: NDSS (2020)
39. Wang, S., et al.: Heterogeneous graph matching networks for unknown malware detection. In: Proceedings of the 28th International Joint Conference on Artificial Intelligence, pp. 3762–3770. AAAI Press (2019)
40. Xu, X., Liu, C., Feng, Q., Yin, H., Song, L., Song, D.: Neural network-based graph embedding for cross-platform binary code similarity detection. In: Proceedings of the 2017 ACM SIGSAC Conference on Computer and Communications Security, pp. 363–376 (2017)
41. Zhu, T., et al.: General, efficient, and real-time data compaction strategy for apt forensic analysis. IEEE Trans. Inf. Forensics Secur. **16**, 3312–3325 (2021)

# Hiatus: Unsupervised Generative Approach for Detection of DoS and DDoS Attacks

Sivaanandh Muneeswaran[✉], Vinay Sachidananda, Rajendra Patil, Hongyi Peng, Mingchang Liu, and Mohan Gurusamy

National University of Singapore, Singapore, Singapore
e0503509@u.nus.edu, {comvs,rspatil,dcslium,gmohan}@nus.edu.sg, dcshongp@nus.edu

**Abstract.** Denial of Service (DoS) and Distributed Denial of Service (DDoS) attacks pose a serious threat to the internet community by disrupting the availability of services. The current methods for detecting DoS and DDoS attacks have several drawbacks including a high false-positive rate and are mostly supervised techniques. The datasets used lack recent attack types. To overcome these limitations, we propose Hiatus: two independent generative models as anomaly detectors: (1) Variational Auto Encoder (VAE), and (2) Generative Adversarial Network (GAN) to classify the traffic flow as either benign or DoS or DDoS. We make the following contributions: (1) two learning algorithms (VAE and GAN) are trained in an unsupervised fashion to detect DoS and DDoS traffic without the involvement of labeled data, (2) avoid external feature engineering, (3) both the learning algorithms are trained and tested on CICDDoS2019 dataset which consists of latest exploitation and reflection based attacks, and the models are benchmarked by testing them with CICIDS2017 and UNSW-NB15 dataset. With the evaluated results, the proposed approaches outperform existing state-of-the-art techniques and could be used for effective DoS and DDoS detection.

**Keywords:** Denial of Service · Distributed Denial of Service · Unsupervised learning · VAE · GAN · UNSW-NB15 · CICDDoS2019

## 1 Introduction

Network attacks pose a serious threat to the growing internet traffic. With high-speed internet access and the rapid expansion of computer networks, we see an increase in the number of cyberattacks. One of the most common network attacks is the Denial of Service or Distributed Denial of Service attacks. Such attacks tend to disrupt the availability of the resources in the network by overwhelming traffic from various sources. These DoS and DDoS attacks are focused on obtaining financial or economical benefits, besides being used as a tool for revenge and also for political and military advantages. According to the quarterly reports on

© ICST Institute for Computer Sciences, Social Informatics and Telecommunications Engineering 2023
Published by Springer Nature Switzerland AG 2023. All Rights Reserved
F. Li et al. (Eds.): SecureComm 2022, LNICST 462, pp. 529–546, 2023.
https://doi.org/10.1007/978-3-031-25538-0_28

DDoS attacks by Kaspersky[1], for the second quarter of 2021, the top three most attacked countries are the United States (36.00%), China (10.28%), and Poland (6.34%). Almost 60% of the attacks were UDP flood attacks, and the next being SYN flood attacks accounting for 23.67%.

Network Intrusion Detection Systems (NIDS) are employed to detect such DoS and DDoS attacks. NIDS can be classified into signature-based and anomaly-based. Signature-based NIDS attempts to match with the known attack signatures to detect intrusions. The main drawback of such systems is that they cannot detect unknown attacks. On the other hand, anomaly-based NIDS tries to capture the normal behavior of the network, and any deviation from such behavior is flagged as an intrusion. The main advantage of anomaly-based NIDS over signature-based NIDS is that it could even detect unknown attacks and hence the former is preferred over the latter.

Such anomaly-based detection systems are built through statistical methods besides using machine learning techniques. Deep learning has shown to be effective in various tasks due to the availability of data. Many such learning techniques have been proposed to detect the normal and DoS and DDoS records from the network flow. There are some drawbacks to the existing techniques. One such drawback is the limitation in the availability of labeled data which is required for the supervised learning techniques. To overcome this, unsupervised detection of DoS and DDoS traffic is required.

## 1.1   Motivation and Problem Statement

Most of the state-of-the-art approaches are based on supervised learning techniques. The major challenge with supervised learning techniques is the collection of large-scale labeled data which is quite tedious. Moreover, supervised learning techniques do not generalize well to unknown attacks. Even though some unsupervised learning techniques exist for detecting DDoS attacks, they suffer from a high false-positive rate. Moreover, the datasets used in existing works do not address the detection of up-to-date DDoS attacks.

The existing works rely on using the network traffic to detect the attacks. But all these network traffic features do not contribute to the detection of DoS or DDoS attacks. Therefore, the important features from the network traffic have to be extracted. Existing works apply different feature engineering techniques to extract the necessary data from network traffic. But these feature engineering techniques require expertise and vary with different data and algorithms. In addition, as the attacks are evolving on a daily basis, it is necessary for the system to be able to detect recent attacks.

In summary, existing DDoS detection systems suffer from heavy dependence on labeled data for training, unsatisfactory performance, complex feature engineering techniques. To solve the limitations of existing approaches, there is a need for a DoS and DDoS detection system which is capable of detecting up-to-date DoS and DDoS attacks from network traffic without relying much on labeled

---

[1] https://securelist.com/ddos-attacks-in-q2-2021/103424/.

data (i.e. in an unsupervised fashion). The proposed model should be capable of generating abstract features from high dimensional data without involving domain expertise and without deteriorating performance.

**Shortcomings.** Most of the above-mentioned techniques implement feature extraction through various techniques in order to develop the model which impedes the development of a model suitable across data from different origins and has to adapt to different algorithms. Moreover, highly accurate models require labeled data for development. Thus, we need a methodology to detect DoS, DDoS attacks without heavy dependence on labeled data and complex feature engineering techniques.

**Research Gaps.** Even though numerous solutions exist for the detection of DDoS attacks, the setbacks in the existing works lead to the following research questions:

- RQ-1: how to develop systems capable of detecting DoS, DDoS attacks without much reliance on labeled data?
- RQ-2: how to generate or extract abstract features from high dimensional data without any domain expertise?
- RQ-3: how to develop a detection system with a low false-positive rate along with less inference time capable of detecting recent attacks?

## 1.2 Approach Overview

To build a model for detecting DoS, DDoS attacks, we train two generative models in an unsupervised fashion. This will eliminate the reliance on labeled data to a larger extent. Therefore we train Variational Autoencoder (VAE) and Generative Adversarial Network (GAN) on a single category of data (either benign or malicious). Through this, we limit the usage of labeled data. We are aware that collecting one particular category of data without contamination is not feasible. Therefore, one of our models i.e. VAE is trained with a particular category of data along with a few records of another category as outliers. Through this, our model is robust to outliers in the training data.

Although many works exist for detecting such attacks through shallow and deep ML models, we propose the use of generative models to design the detection system. The main advantage of these generative models is the modeling and learning of the distribution of the training data. Since the model learns the distribution of the data, additional feature selection techniques are not required. Hence generative models are best suited to avoid domain expertise and complex feature engineering procedures.

## 1.3 Results Overview

We have conducted multiple sets of performance evaluation and benchmarking experiments. We evaluated Hiatus(VAE and GAN models) on multiple datasets like CICDDoS2019, CICIDS2017, and UNSW-NB15 datasets containing recent DoS, and DDoS attacks. The proposed GAN model achieves around 99% recall with a false positive rate of 4.16% on the CICDDoS2019 dataset. The proposed VAE model achieves 96.27% recall with a false positive rate of 0.08% on the CICIDS2017 dataset. Moreover, both the proposed models i.e. GAN and VAE achieve 99.93% and 98.87% accuracy along with the false-positive rates of 0.35% and 2.7% respectively.

**Our Contributions.** We make the following contributions to address the existing research gaps.

– We propose `Hiatus` - a DoS, DDoS detection system with two independent generative models VAE, and GAN trained in an unsupervised fashion to detect DoS and DDoS attacks.
– We train the generative models without any external feature engineering process. These generative models are robust to noise in training data.
– We train the models on CICDDoS2019, consisting of modern reflection-based attacks and exploitation-based attacks. Also, the models are trained and tested on datasets like CICIDS2017, UNSW-NB15 and benchmarked.

The remainder of this paper is organized as follows: Section 2 investigates the existing works, Sect. 3 provides a detailed discussion on the proposed models. In Sect. 4 and Sect. 5, the performance of the model along with its results in addition to comparison with existing state-of-the-art is provided. The evaluation results are discussed in Sect. 6, conclusion is provided in Sect. 7 with references at the end.

## 2    Related Work

Various methods for detecting DDoS attacks have been proposed in the literature. Some techniques use statistical methods to detect such attacks which resulted in increased computational complexity. Other techniques include data mining and machine learning methods to detect DDoS attacks. This section summarizes various machine learning techniques to detect DoS and DDoS attacks along with their missing gaps.

**Supervised Learning Techniques:** In [15], an ensemble of deep learning techniques (CNN, LSTM, RNN) is trained on the CICIDS2017 dataset to detect DDoS attacks. Two binary classifiers are trained individually and ensembled. In [29], DeepDefense - several variations of recurrent deep neural networks like LSTM, GRU, CNN-LSTM are trained on the ISCX2012 dataset to differentiate normal traffic from DDoS attacks. Generally, deep learning models involve a higher number of parameters than shallow machine learning models and hence involve higher inference time. However, there is only a 0.1% difference in F1 score between a Random Forest model and the proposed LSTM model. [14] proposed a deep Autoencoder for feature extraction followed by classification of normal and DDoS traffic through the k-Nearest Neighbour algorithm. The proposed work includes both binary and multi-class classification with the hyperparameters of k-NN and Autoencoder optimized through Bayesian optimization. General ML techniques like Random Forest, outperform the proposed AE + k-NN technique. [16] analyzes statistical features of four different DDoS attacks (SSH Brute-force, DNS Reflection, ICMP flood, TCP SYN) obtained from a simulated dataset. The technique aims to detect DDoS attacks from the source side. The pre-trained model in addition to several machine learning models like Decision Tree, Naive Bayes, K-means acts as an online learning mechanism i.e. using these predictions the pre-trained model can be updated. A combination of different algorithms could have affected the performance, especially in the case of unsupervised learning algorithms. [9] uses a RNN-autoencoder (autoencoder with RNN layers) as a feature extractor in the pre-training stage and a softmax classifier is used in fine-tuning stage to classify the normal and malicious traffic in CICDDoS2019 dataset. Though the dataset consists of around 11 types of DDoS attacks, the model is trained as a binary classifier. RNN has its benefits for sequence data. But the advantage of using it over feed-forward neural networks is not illustrated. One of the major issues of the supervised learning approach is the lack of labeled data. Obtaining labeled data on a large scale is costly in terms of computation. Moreover, these approaches employ additional feature engineering techniques which would vary over data and algorithms.

**Unsupervised Learning Techniques:** In the case of unsupervised learning, labeled data is not required for building the classifier. In [10], multivariate correlation analysis is performed on network features to show the degree of dependency. Clustering through DBSCAN algorithm is used to cluster normal and DDoS traffic with experiments on CAIDA DDoS dataset. Accuracy of 99.99% with only 3000 testing records could not account for the validity of the model. But DBSCAN falls behind with datasets where the density of normal and DDoS records are similar. In [4], K-means clustering is used for determining the cluster with experiments on CAIDA DDoS dataset. But K-means clustering does not work well with non-spherical cluster shapes. [22] proposed an autoencoder trained on CICIDS2017 dataset to obtain low-dimensional data. The low-dimensional normal traffic is used to train the One Class-SVM model to classify the DDoS traffic. Although the model has good accuracy of 99.35% accuracy, the false positive rate is quite high and also it requires noiseless normal traffic for training which is difficult to obtain in the real world setup. [19] proposed two Self-Organizing Maps (SOM) to label the unlabeled data. One SOM is used to mark the record as normal or suspicious and the other to mark the suspicious record as normal or DDoS attack. The labeled data is used to train an ensemble of Random Forest, Decision Tree, and Gradient Boosted Tree through max voting. If the input data has several hot spots, SOM might generate several smaller groups instead of one larger group. If there are discrepancies with the initial SOM model, it would adversely affect the classifier. The main drawback of unsupervised learning algorithms is the high false-positive rate.

**Semi-Supervised Learning Techniques:** To tackle the problem of high false rate, and the need for a large amount of labeled data, semi-supervised learning approaches have been proposed that work on labeled and unlabeled datasets. In [1], agglomerative clustering and K-means cluster the unlabeled data into two clusters, and initial labelling is done based on entropy. Labeling is done based on the voting of the two clustering techniques followed by supervised training and testing through SVM, Random Forest, k-Nearest Neighbours. A simulated dataset is used for training, and the model is evaluated using CICIDS2017 dataset. Even very slight differences in entropy values may mislead the initial labeling process and lead to bad clusters. In [17], Co-clustering is employed for dimensionality reduction, and the dataset (NSL-KDD and ISCX2012) is split into three clusters: 1. the cluster with DDoS traffic, 2. the cluster with normal traffic, 3. the cluster with DDoS-normal traffic. Cluster 2 is considered to be noisy normal traffic and thus it is eliminated and the remaining clusters are combined and trained with Extra-tree classifier.

In [21], the centroid of 14 clusters (13 attack types and normal) obtained through Fuzzy C-means clustering is predefined based on the available labeled data. The cluster for unlabeled data is determined using the membership value. Botnet 2014 dataset containing 13 DDoS attack types was used for experimentation. Noise in the available labeled data used for determining the initial clusters may lead to instability. [13] proposed constrained K-means clustering for distinguishing normal traffic from DDoS traffic. The centroid for the clusters is initialized through the labeled seed set with Lincoln Laboratory Scenarios(DDoS) 1.0 dataset. Though the time to converge is less than K-means, it works on the assumption that the initial labeling of the seed set is noise-free. In [12], the candidate feature set is obtained based on entropy difference and ranked through K-means based on the ratio of average sum of squares error to cluster distance (RSD) followed by Sequential Forward Selection. After feature selection, K-means clustering is performed with an allocation of initial cluster centers based on labeled data density. Experiments were performed on DARPA, CAIDA, CICIDS2017, and a real-world dataset independently. Feature selection leads to a very less number of features used for training and testing. With such less number of features and noise in the data points used for allocating initial cluster centers, this technique becomes unstable. [3] surveyed the machine learning approaches used to detect DDoS attacks.

## 3  Our Proposed Approach

We propose Hiatus - an unsupervised DoS and DDoS detection method based on generative models like Variational AutoEncoder (VAE) and Generative Adversarial Network(GAN) trained on datasets with recent DDoS attacks. VAE is preferred over AutoEncoder because the classification of normal and DDoS traffic is based on the reconstruction score which considers the variability of the distribution of variables rather than the reconstruction error of AutoEncoder which is deterministic. GAN is trained to fit the distribution of normal samples and based on its ability to reconstruct a sample from certain latent representations, the classification between normal and DDoS traffic is done. Both VAE and GAN can handle complex high dimensional data, thus eliminating the curse of dimensionality. Moreover, both techniques are trained in an unsupervised fashion.

## 3.1 Variational Autoencoder

Variational Autoencoder (VAE) [18] is an unsupervised directed probabilistic model whose structure is similar to that of an Autoencoder. It consists of an encoder, a latent distribution, and a decoder. The difference between Autoencoder and VAE is that Autoencoder is a deterministic model and could not produce new samples. But VAE is a probabilistic model and can produce new samples. The probabilistic encoder $e_\theta$ and the probabilistic decoder $d_\phi$ together form the Variational Autoencoder. The objective of VAE is the variational lower bound of the marginal likelihood of the data. The marginal likelihood of individual data points can be written as

$$logp_\theta(x^{(i)}) = -D_{KL}(q_\phi(z|x^{(i)})||p_\theta(z)) + E_{q_\phi(z|x^{(i)})}[logp_\theta(x|z)] \qquad (1)$$

where $q_\phi(z|x)$ is the approximate posterior to be modeled. This posterior can be denoted as $\mathcal{N}(\mu_\phi(x), \sigma_\phi(x))$ where $\mu_\phi(x)$ and $\sigma_\phi(x)$ are the mean and standard deviation of the posterior distribution derived through the VAE, $p_\theta(z)$ is the prior distribution of the latent variable $z$. $p_\theta(x|z)$ is the likelihood of $x$ given the latent variable $z$. The first term of equation(1) is the KL divergence between the approximate posterior and the prior. The second term of equation(1) is the reconstruction of $x$. VAE models the parameters (mean and standard deviation) of the distribution. VAE applies reparameterization by using a random variable from a standard normal distribution. The latent variable $z$ is reparameterized through a transformation $h_\phi(\epsilon, x)$ where $\epsilon$ is the random variable from a standard normal distribution.

$$z = h_\phi(\epsilon, x), \epsilon \sim \mathcal{N}(0, 1) \qquad (2)$$

This will ensure that the latent variable $z$ follows the distribution of the approximate posterior.

VAE is trained with one class of data (e.g. normal or with DDoS records) and with little noise from the other class. During testing, a number of samples are drawn from the encoder. For every sample, the decoder outputs the mean and standard deviation. Based on this, the probability of generating the input data from this distribution is calculated as the reconstruction score. The average reconstruction score is used as the score for detecting DDoS records.

The main advantage of VAE over Autoencoder is that VAE takes variability of the data into account which is not in the case of Autoencoder. It is possible that both normal and DDoS records share the same mean value but their variance can differ. Most of the techniques for anomaly detection including GAN require only one particular category of data without noise. Noise in such data will deteriorate the performance of the model. Since VAE takes variability into account, it could even work well with noise in the input data. The working of the proposed VAE is depicted in algorithm 1.

---

**Algorithm 1:** VAE for DoS and DDoS detection

---

**INPUT:** Training dataset $X$, Validation dataset $X_{val}$, Testing dataset $X_{test}^{(i)}$
$\quad\quad i = 1, ..., M$
**OUTPUT:** benign or anomalous
$\phi, \theta \leftarrow$ train a VAE using $X$ ;
$\alpha \leftarrow$ obtain through Validation dataset $X_{val}$;
**for** $i \leftarrow 0$ **to** $M$ **do**
$\quad \mu_{z^{(i)}}, \sigma_{z^{(i)}} = e_\theta(z|x^{(i)})$;
$\quad$ draw N samples from $z \sim \mathcal{N}(\mu_z(i), \sigma_z(i))$;
$\quad$ **for** $j \leftarrow 0$ **to** $N$ **do**
$\quad\quad \mu_{\hat{x}(i,j)}, \sigma_{\hat{x}(i,j)} = d_\phi(x|z^{(i,j)})$;
$\quad$ **end**
$\quad$ reconstruction score$(i) = \frac{1}{N}\sum_{n=1}^{N} p_\theta(x^{(i)}|\mu_{\hat{x}(i,n)}, \sigma_{\hat{x}(i,n)})$;
$\quad$ **if** *reconstruction score* $(i) < \alpha$ **then**
$\quad\quad x^{(i)}$ is not an anomaly
$\quad$ **end**
$\quad$ **else**
$\quad\quad x^{(i)}$ is an anomaly
$\quad$ **end**
**end**

---

## 3.2 Generative Adversarial Network

Our model is based on [11]. A generative module and discriminative module are trained for the detection of DoS and DDoS attacks. Both the generator network $G$ and the discriminator network $D$ are trained in an adversarial fashion. The generator is involved in mapping uniformly distributed noise sampled from the latent variable $z$ to the input space $\mathcal{X}$ through the mapping $G(z)$. The objective of the generator is to improve the generation of realistic data. Since the proposed work is based on traffic flows, instead of CNN, ANN is used in both generator and discriminator. The discriminator is aimed at mapping the input data to the probability that the given input to D is real or generated by the generator. The objective of the discriminator is to improve the identification of real and generator data. During training, both the generator and discriminator are optimized through a two-player min-max game.

$$min_G max_D V(D, G) = E_{x \sim p_{data}(x)}[log D(x)]$$
$$+ E_{z \sim p_z(z)}[log(1 - D(G(z)))] \quad (3)$$

After training, the generator is capable of mapping the latent variable $z$ to realistic data. To detect the anomaly, two components are used: the *residualloss* and *discriminatorloss*. The residual loss deals with the similarity between the generated data from the generator $G$ and the query data and it can be defined as

$$\mathcal{L}_R(z) = \sum |x - G(z)| \quad (4)$$

If the generator is perfectly trained, the residual loss will be zero and the discrimination loss is defined as:

$$\mathcal{L}_D(z) = \sum |f(x) - f(G(z))| \tag{5}$$

where f(.) represents the output of an intermediate layer of the discriminator. The idea is to obtain a better feature representation through the intermediate layer rather than relying on the scalar output of the discriminator. The GAN model is trained only with one particular category of data (either benign or anomalous data). In this way, the GAN model learns the representation of the input data. As the model is being trained only with one particular category of data, the GAN model could reconstruct that particular category of data. This ability could be used to find the anomalous data since both the loss components remain high for any other category of data. Therefore, the overall anomaly score can be defined as the sum of both residual loss and discriminator loss. The overall algorithm of the proposed GAN technique is given in Algorithm 2.

$$\mathcal{L}(z) = \mathcal{L}_R(z) + \mathcal{L}_D(z) \tag{6}$$

This anomaly score is used to detect DDoS attacks based on a threshold $\gamma$.

---

**Algorithm 2:** GAN for DoS and DDoS detection

---

**INPUT:** Training dataset $X$, Validation dataset $X_{val}$, Testing dataset $X_{test}^{(i)}$
$\quad\quad i = 1, ..., M$
**OUTPUT:** benign or anomalous
$G, D \leftarrow$ train a GAN using $X$ ;
$\alpha \leftarrow$ obtain through Validation dataset $X_{val}$;
**for** $i \leftarrow 0$ **to** $M$ **do**
$\quad$ draw $z \sim \mathcal{N}(0, 1)$;
$\quad \mathcal{L}_R(z) = |x^{(i)} - G(z)|$;
$\quad \mathcal{L}_D(z) = |f(x) - f(G(z))|$;
$\quad$ anomaly score($i$) $= \mathcal{L}_R(z) + \mathcal{L}_D(z)$;
$\quad$ **if** *anomaly score($i$) $< \alpha$* **then**
$\quad\quad |\quad x^{(i)}$ is not an anomaly
$\quad$ **end**
$\quad$ **else**
$\quad\quad |\quad x^{(i)}$ is an anomaly
$\quad$ **end**
**end**

---

## 4 Performance Evaluation

### 4.1 Datasets

In this section, we list the publicly available datasets consisting of DDoS attacks.

The CAIDA "DDoS Attack 2007" dataset [5] contains one hour of anonymous traffic traces from a DDoS attack. DARPA dataset [20] consists of LLDOS 1.0, which includes a DDoS attack by a novice attacker against a naive defender, LLDOS 2.0.2 which includes a DDoS attack by a stealthy attacker yet novice against a naive defender, and Windows NT Attack Dataset. NSL-KDD [27] contains four categories of attacks: Probe, DoS, R2L, and U2R. It contains 10 types of DoS attacks like Neptune, back, Teardrop, Pod, etc.

The main drawback of the above-mentioned datasets is that almost all of them are outdated. They do not contain recent types of DDoS attacks. In order to solve this issue, we use the CICDDoS2019 dataset [26] which remains as one of the largest public dataset and addresses the gaps in the existing datasets. It contains the most up-to-date DDoS attacks like SSDP, NTP, NETBIOS, etc. It consists of both reflection-based and exploitation-based attacks. 12 DDoS attacks were included during the training day and 7 DDoS attacks were included during the testing day.

Also, to validate the performance of our proposed approach and to compare it with existing literature, we use two more datasets. UNSW-NB15 dataset [23] is labeled and contains nine categories of attacks including DoS. It consists of 49 features with around 16,353 DoS attack records. CICIDS2017 dataset [25] is a labeled dataset and contains seven categories of attacks. It consists of both DoS and DDoS attack types like Hulk, GoldenEye, Slowloris, Slowhttptest, Heartleech, and Low Orbit Ion Canon attacks. We train our proposed model with these datasets and benchmark them. Table 1 contains the distribution of the above-mentioned datasets for both the proposed VAE and GAN models in case of training, validation, and testing sets.

**Table 1.** Distribution of datasets for VAE and GAN models.

| Dataset | Approach | Type of record | Training | Validation | Testing |
|---------|----------|----------------|----------|------------|---------|
| CICDDoS2019 | VAE | DDoS | 207880 | 36685 | 61142 |
| | | Benign | 1000 | 4327 | 38948 |
| | GAN | DDoS | 181894 | 32100 | 91713 |
| | | Benign | – | 4427 | 39848 |
| CICIDS2017 | VAE | DDoS | 22326 | 3941 | 11258 |
| | | Benign | 100 | 5990 | 539108 |
| | GAN | DDoS | 57127 | 10082 | 16803 |
| | | Benign | – | 6000 | 54000 |
| UNSW-NB15 | VAE | DDoS | 100 | 2819 | 11276 |
| | | Benign | 89250 | 15750 | 45000 |
| | GAN | DDoS | – | 2839 | 11356 |
| | | Benign | 76500 | 13500 | 60000 |

**Pre-Processing.** The first step in pre-processing is to obtain the DDoS records from various datasets. Benign and DDoS records are extracted from datasets like UNSW-NB15 and CICIDS2017 since these datasets contain other types of attacks also. Since CICDDoS2019 contains only DDoS records, the records are equally sampled from all the different DDoS attacks.

The features containing flow details like timestamp, source IP, destination IP, source port, destination port, etc. are removed. Also, the categorical features are one-hot encoded. Outliers in the dataset are removed using z-score. Normalization is important to convert all the features into a common scale. Hence the data is normalized using min-max normalization.

### 4.2  Experiments

In our experiments, VAE and GAN are trained and tested for different distributions of datasets. For both, VAE and GAN methods, a threshold $\gamma$ is required to classify the data as benign or malicious. This threshold $\gamma$ is calculated through the validation set.

**Model Setup for VAE.** The encoder consists of two hidden layers with 16 and 8 dimensions. The decoder consists of two hidden layers with 8 and 16 dimensions. The latent space consists of 2 dimensions. In addition to this, batch size, the number of epochs for every dataset is determined through hyper-parameter tuning. VAE is trained with only one class of data (either benign or DDoS data) with little noise from the other. During training, the data is preprocessed and passed into the probabilistic encoder where the latent vector learns the distribution of the training data. The average reconstruction loss of the testing data is calculated and the threshold is determined using the validation data.

**Model Setup for GAN.** The generator of GAN consists of two fully connected layers with 64 and 128 units respectively. The units in the output layer of the generator are the number of features. Therefore during training, the generator tunes the latent space accordingly to generate data similar to training data. The discriminator of GAN consists of three fully connected layers with 256, 128, 128 units respectively. The input to the discriminator is either the data generated by the generator or the original data and the discriminator classifies the input as original or fake. All these fully connected layers are activated with LeakyRelu and 20% dropout is applied. By calculating the sum of residual loss and discriminator loss from the generator and discriminator respectively, and comparing it against a threshold calculated through the validation set, the testing data is classified.

## 5  Results and Comparison

This section comprises the results of VAE and GAN implemented for the three datasets: CICDDoS2019, CICIDS2017, and UNSW-NB15. To evaluate the performance of the model, the metrics like Recall, Precision, F1-score, False Positive

Rate are calculated. Since the testing data is imbalanced, robust scoring metrics like F1-score, Area under ROC curve, and Area under PRC curve are calculated in order to avoid bias from the imbalanced data. Moreover to benchmark against the existing works, other metrics like Accuracy, Precision and Recall are also calculated. Results are also obtained by varying the size of datasets. The training size of datasets is varied from 50% to 90% and Receiver operating characteristic curve, Precision-Recall curve are plotted.

## 5.1   CICDDoS2019 Dataset

Table 2 shows the performance of our proposed GAN and VAE models for CICD-DoS2019 dataset in comparison with the existing models. It can be seen that GAN performs a little better than VAE because the training data for VAE contains noise (both categories of data) but GAN simply contains one category of data. It is a trade-off between the inclusion of noise in training data and the performance of the models. Although [6,9] are supervised approaches, our approach being unsupervised performs on par and better respectively in terms of higher accuracy and low false positive rate. Figure 1 shows the ROC curve along with Area Under the ROC value and Precision-Recall Curve (PRC) along with Area Under PRC value respectively for different sizes of the dataset for GAN and VAE models. Figure 1e and Fig. 1f show the comparison between the proposed VAE and GAN models in terms of ROC curve and Precision-Recall Curve.

**Table 2.** Performance of `Hiatus` on CICDDoS2019 dataset.

| Method | Precision(%) | Recall(%) | FPR(%) | F1(%) |
|---|---|---|---|---|
| DDoSNet [9] | 99% | 99% | – | 99% |
| Automatic Feature Selection [6] | 91.16% | 79.41% | – | 79.39% |
| Hiatus-GAN (Our approach) | 97.33 | 99.05 | 4.16 | 98.18 |
| Hiatus-VAE (Our approach) | 95.76 | 97.52 | 10.15 | 96.63 |

## 5.2   CICIDS2017 Dataset

Table 3 shows the performance of GAN and VAE for CICIDS2017 dataset. [28] generalizes higher-order features from attributed network flow graph and detects the network attack. [8] utilized convolutional neural networks to detect benign or malicious traffic flows. [24] performs unsupervised feature selection and computes initial cluster centers using a set of semi-identical instances and performs clustering. [7] classifies DDoS records from normal records through the Kernel Online Anomaly Detection algorithm which is unsupervised. [8] and [28] are supervised techniques. Although our proposed work is unsupervised, and it is not a head-to-head comparison, our proposed VAE model could perform equivalent to the state of the art and in fact could achieve a better false-positive rate than the state of the art. Our proposed GAN model could perform better than the other two existing works. Figure 2 shows the ROC curve along with Area Under ROC value and Precision-Recall Curve (PRC) along with Area Under PRC value respectively for different sizes of the dataset for GAN and VAE models.

## 5.3    UNSW-NB15 Dataset

Table 4 shows the performance of GAN and VAE for UNSW-NB15 dataset. In [2], Feature Correlation Map is extracted to detect malicious traffic from normal traffic. [17] utilizes network entropy estimation, co-clustering, and extra-tree

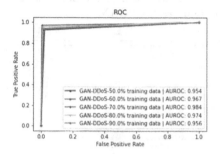

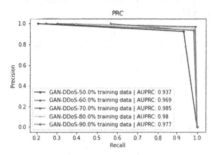

(a) ROC curve for different sizes of dataset for GAN.

(b) Precision-Recall curve for different sizes of dataset for GAN.

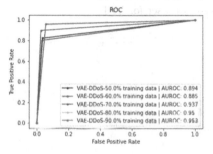

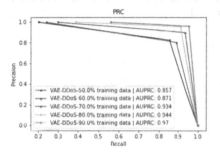

(c) ROC curve for different sizes of dataset for VAE.

(d) Precision-Recall curve for different sizes of dataset for VAE.

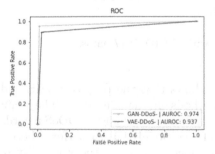

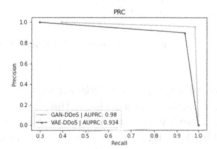

(e) Receiver Operating Characteristic curve for VAE and GAN.

(f) Precision-Recall curve for VAE and GAN.

**Fig. 1.** Results of VAE and GAN with CICDDoS2019 dataset.

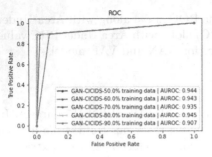

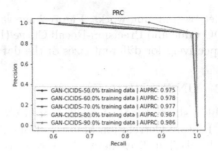

(a) ROC curve for different sizes of dataset for GAN.

(b) Precision-Recall curve for different sizes of dataset for GAN.

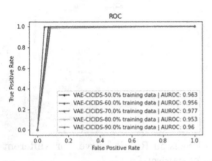

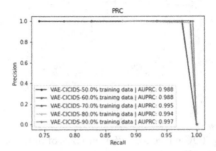

(c) ROC curve for different sizes of dataset for VAE.

(d) Precision-Recall curve for different sizes of dataset for VAE.

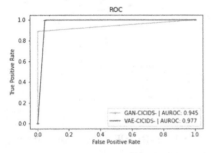

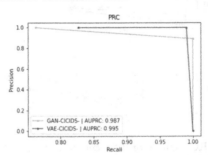

(e) Receiver Operating Characteristic curve for VAE and GAN.

(f) Precision-Recall curve for VAE and GAN.

**Fig. 2.** Results of VAE and GAN with CICIDS2017 dataset.

algorithm to detect DDoS attacks. Table 4 shows that the proposed VAE and GAN methods outperform the existing methods in the literature. The main reason for low performance in existing works is that the normal and DDoS records in UNSW-NB15 are similar. Hence most of the models fail to perform better or result in increased False Positive Rates. Since VAE takes the variability of the data into account, it could differentiate between normal and DDoS records effectively.

Table 3. Performance of Hiatus on CICIDS2017 dataset.

| Method | Accuracy(%) | FPR(%) | Precision(%) | Recall(%) | F1(%) |
|---|---|---|---|---|---|
| LUCID [8] | 98.88 | 1.79 | 98.27 | 99.52 | **98.89** |
| DeepGFL [28] | – | – | 75.67 | 30.24 | 43.21 |
| Cluster center initialization [24] | 81.98 | 59.68 | 79.16 | 81.98 | 80.54 |
| E-KOAD [7] | **99.55** | 0.23 | 95.24 | 95.24 | 95.24 |
| Hiatus-GAN (Our approach) | 91.59 | 11.01 | 73.85 | **100** | 84.96 |
| Hiatus-VAE (Our approach) | 99.28 | **0.08** | **99.55** | 96.27 | 97.86 |

Figure 3 shows the ROC curve along with Area Under ROC value and Precision-Recall Curve (PRC) along with Area Under PRC value respectively for different sizes of the dataset for GAN and VAE models. Figure 3e and 3f show the comparison between the proposed VAE and GAN models in terms of ROC curve and Precision-Recall Curve.

Table 4. Performance of Hiatus on UNSW-NB15 dataset.

| Method | Accuracy(%) | TPR(%) | FPR(%) | F1(%) |
|---|---|---|---|---|
| Feature Correlation Map [2] | 91.82 | 60.92 | 0.46 | 72.65 |
| Semi supervised machine learning [17] | 93.71 | – | 1.41 | – |
| **Hiatus-GAN (Our approach)** | **99.93** | **99.99** | 0.35 | **99.95** |
| **Hiatus-VAE (Our approach)** | 98.87 | 99.29 | 2.7 | 99.29 |

## 6   Discussion

The proposed generative models (VAE and GAN) have the advantage of less reliance on labeled data during training which makes the feasibility of collection of large-scale data easier. Considering the noise within a single category of data in the real-world environment, the proposed VAE model proves to be robust to noise and has on-par performance with the GAN model.

For different datasets and attacks, the existing works have relied on multiple rounds of feature selection in order to achieve good performance. However, the proposed approaches have eliminated the need for such expensive feature engineering techniques. The proposed approaches can handle all the features of the data and model it completely without any loss in potential information. Therefore, *Hiatus* can ingest network traffic data in real time and could detect the DoS and DDoS attacks without much latency as the system does not involve complex feature engineering practices and also considers all the information for detection.

In order to prove the robustness of our approaches, we have conducted multiple experiments with varying proportion of training and testing data in addition to using robust scoring metrics like Receiver Operating Characteristic (ROC)

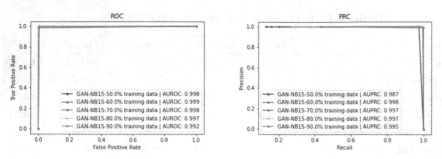

(a) ROC curve for different sizes of dataset for GAN.

(b) Precision-Recall curve for different sizes of dataset for GAN.

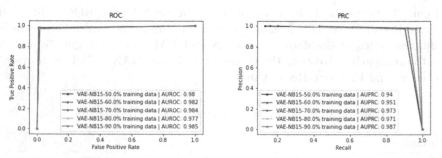

(c) ROC curve for different sizes of dataset for VAE.

(d) Precision-Recall curve for different sizes of dataset for VAE.

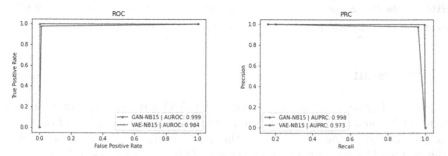

(e) Receiver Operating Characteristic curve for VAE and GAN.

(f) Precision-Recall curve for VAE and GAN.

**Fig. 3.** Results of VAE and GAN with UNSW-NB15 dataset.

curve, and Precision Recall Curve (PRC) and plotted their graphs for each of the dataset to show that our models achieve good performance while handling the data imbalance problem. Moreover, datasets containing recent attack types are used and the model is capable of classifying new attack patterns due to its unsupervised training nature.

# 7    Conclusion

In this work, we have presented two generative models for the detection of DDoS attacks which are capable of outperforming the performance of state-of-the-art models. The benefit of both models is that they do not require additional domain expertise for the feature selection and are unsupervised without any dependency on labels. Despite being an unsupervised technique, our models could achieve a low false-positive rate. To show the reliability of our approach, we have tested the models on benchmark datasets and produced the results.

# References

1. Aamir, M., Zaidi, S.M.A.: Clustering based semi-supervised machine learning for ddos attack classification. Journal of King Saud University - Computer and Information Sciences (2019). https://doi.org/10.1016/j.jksuci.2019.02.003, http://www.sciencedirect.com/science/article/pii/S131915781831067X
2. Amma, N.G.B., Subramanian, S.: Feature correlation map based statistical approach for denial of service attacks detection. In: 2019 5th International Conference on Computing Engineering and Design (ICCED), pp. 1–6 (2019)
3. Bhardwaj, A., Mangat, V., Vig, R., Halder, S., Conti, M.: Distributed denial of service attacks in cloud: State-of-the-art of scientific and commercial solutions. Comput. Sci. Rev. **39** 100332 (2021). https://doi.org/10.1016/j.cosrev.2020.100332, https://www.sciencedirect.com/science/article/pii/S1574013720304329
4. Bhaya, W., Manna, M.: A proactive ddos attack detection approach using data mining cluster analysis. J. Next Gener. Inform. Technol. **5** 36– 47 (D2014)
5. CAIDA: The caida ucsd "ddos attack 2007" dataset (2007)
6. Can, D.-C., Le, H.-Q., Ha, Q.-T.: Detection of distributed denial of service attacks using automatic feature selection with enhancement for imbalance dataset. In: Nguyen, N.T., Chittayasothorn, S., Niyato, D., Trawiński, B. (eds.) ACIIDS 2021. LNCS (LNAI), vol. 12672, pp. 386–398. Springer, Cham (2021). https://doi.org/10.1007/978-3-030-73280-6_31
7. Daneshgadeh Çakmakçı, S., Kemmerich, T., Ahmed, T., Baykal, N.: Online ddos attack detection using mahalanobis distance and kernel-based learning algorithm. J. Netw. Comput. Appl. **168** 102756 (2020). https://doi.org/10.1016/j.jnca.2020.102756, http://www.sciencedirect.com/science/article/pii/S1084804520302307
8. Doriguzzi-Corin, R., Millar, S., Scott-Hayward, S., Martinez-del Rincon, J., Siracusa, D.: Lucid: A practical, lightweight deep learning solution for ddos attack detection. IEEE Trans. Netw. Serv. Manage. **17**(2), 876–889 (2020). https://doi.org/10.1109/tnsm.2020.2971776, http://dx.doi.org/10.1109/TNSM.2020.2971776
9. Elsayed, M.S., Le-Khac, N.A., Dev, S., Jurcut, A.D.: Ddosnet: A deep-learning model for detecting network attacks. In: 2020 IEEE 21st International Symposium on "A World of Wireless, Mobile and Multimedia Networks" (WoWMoM), pp. 391–396 (2020). https://doi.org/10.1109/WoWMoM49955.2020.00072
10. Girma, A., Wang, P.: An efficient hybrid model for detecting distributed denial of service (ddos) attacks in cloud computing using multivariate correlation and data mining clustering techniques. Issues Inform. Syst. **19**(2), 12 (2018)
11. Goodfellow, I., et al.: Generative adversarial nets. In: Ghahramani, Z., Welling, M., Cortes, C., Lawrence, N., Weinberger, K. (eds.) Advances in Neural Information Processing Systems. vol. 27. Curran Associates, Inc. (2014). https://proceedings.neurips.cc/paper/2014/file/5ca3e9b122f61f8f06494c97b1afccf3-Paper.pdf

12. Gu, Y., Li, K., Guo, Z., Wang, Y.: Semi-supervised k-means ddos detection method using hybrid feature selection algorithm. IEEE Access **7**, 64351–64365 (2019)
13. Gu, Y., Wang, Y., Yang, Z., Xiong, F., Gao, Y.: Multiple-features-based semisupervised clustering ddos detection method. Math. Prob. Eng. **2017** (2017)
14. Görmez, Y., Aydin, Z., Karademir, R., Gungor, V.: A deep learning approach with bayesian optimization and ensemble classifiers for detecting denial of service attacks. Int. J. Commun. Syst. **33**(6), e4401 (2020). https://doi.org/10.1002/dac.4401
15. Haider, S., et al.: A deep cnn ensemble framework for efficient ddos attack detection in software defined networks. IEEE Access **8**, 53972–53983 (2020)
16. He, Z., Zhang, T., Lee, R.B.: Machine learning based ddos attack detection from source side in cloud. In: 2017 IEEE CSCloud, pp. 114–120 (2017)
17. Idhammad, M., Afdel, K., Belouch, M.: Semi-supervised machine learning approach for ddos detection. Appl. Intell. **48**(10), 3193–3208 (2018)
18. Kingma, D.P., Welling, M.: Auto-encoding variational bayes. CoRR abs/1312.6114 (2014)
19. Ko, I., Chambers, D., Barrett, E.: Self-supervised network traffic management for ddos mitigation within the isp domain. Future Gener. Comput. Syst. **112**, 524–533 (2020). http://www.sciencedirect.com/science/article/pii/S0167739X20302193
20. Laboratory, M.L.: 2000 darpa intrusion detection scenario specific datasets (2000)
21. Lysenko, S., Savenko, O., Bobrovnikova, K.: Ddos botnet detection technique based on the use of the semi-supervised fuzzy c-means clustering. In: ICTERI Workshops, pp. 688–695 (2018)
22. Mhamdi, L., McLernon, D., El-moussa, F., Raza Zaidi, S.A., Ghogho, M., Tang, T.: A deep learning approach combining autoencoder with one-class svm for ddos attack detection in sdns. In: 2020 IEEE Eighth International Conference on Communications and Networking (ComNet), pp. 1–6 (2020). https://doi.org/10.1109/ComNet47917.2020.9306073
23. Moustafa, N., Slay, J.: Unsw-nb15: a comprehensive data set for network intrusion detection systems (unsw-nb15 network data set). In: 2015 military communications and information systems conference (MilCIS), pp. 1–6. IEEE (2015)
24. Prasad, M., Tripathi, S., Dahal, K.: Unsupervised feature selection and cluster center initialization based arbitrary shaped clusters for intrusion detection. Comput. Secur. **99**, 102062 (2020). https://doi.org/10.1016/j.cose.2020.102062, http://www.sciencedirect.com/science/article/pii/S0167404820303357
25. Sharafaldin, I., Lashkari, A.H., Ghorbani, A.A.: Toward generating a new intrusion detection dataset and intrusion traffic characterization. In: ICISSP, pp. 108–116 (2018)
26. Sharafaldin, I., Lashkari, A.H., Hakak, S., Ghorbani, A.A.: Developing realistic distributed denial of service (ddos) attack dataset and taxonomy. In: 2019 International Carnahan Conference on Security Technology (2019)
27. Tavallaee, M., Bagheri, E., Lu, W., Ghorbani, A.A.: A detailed analysis of the kdd cup 99 data set. In: 2009 IEEE Symposium on Computational Intelligence for Security and Defense Applications, pp. 1–6. IEEE (2009)
28. Yao, Y., Su, L., Lu, Z.: Deepgfl: Deep feature learning via graph for attack detection on flow-based network traffic. In: MILCOM 2018–2018 IEEE Military Communications Conference (MILCOM), pp. 579–584 (2018)
29. Yuan, X., Li, C., Li, X.: Deepdefense: Identifying ddos attack via deep learning. In: 2017 IEEE International Conference on Smart Computing, pp. 1–8 (2017)

# Mobile Security

# What Data Do the Google Dialer and Messages Apps on Android Send to Google?

Douglas J. Leith[✉]

Trinity College Dublin, Dublin, Ireland
doug.leith@tcd.ie

**Abstract.** We report on measurements of the data sent to Google by the Google Messages and Google Dialer apps on an Android handset. We find that these apps tell Google when message/phone calls are made/received. The data sent by Google Messages includes a hash of the message text, allowing linking of sender and receiver in a message exchange. The data sent by Google Dialer includes the call time and duration, again allowing linking of the two handsets engaged in a phone call. Phone numbers are also sent to Google. In addition, the timing and duration of other user interactions with the apps are sent to Google. There is no opt out from this data collection. The data is sent via two channels, (i) the Google Play Services Clearcut logger and (ii) Google/Firebase Analytics. This study is therefore one of the first to cast light on the actual telemetry data sent by Google Play Services, which to date has largely been opaque. We informed Google of our findings and delayed publication for several months to engage with them. On foot of this work Google say that they plan to make multiple changes to their Messages and Dialer apps.

## 1 Introduction

We analyse the data sent to Google by Android handsets using the Google Messages and Google Dialer apps. Both are core apps for a mobile handset, the Messages app being used to send and receive SMS text messages and the Dialer app to make/receive phone calls. According to the Google Play store the Google Messages app is installed on > 1 Billion handsets. In the US, AT&T and T-Mobile recently announced all Android phones on their networks will use the Google Messages app[1] and the app also comes pre-loaded on recent Samsung handsets[2] and on Xiaomi and Huawei handsets. According to the Google Play store the Google Dialer app is also installed on > 1 Billion handsets.

---

[1] https://www.theverge.com/2021/6/30/22556686/att-android-phones-rcs-google-messages.

[2] https://support.google.com/messages/answer/10324785?hl=en.

---

This work was supported by Science Foundation Ireland grant 16/IA/4610.

F. Li et al. (Eds.): SecureComm 2022, LNICST 462, pp. 549–568, 2023.
https://doi.org/10.1007/978-3-031-25538-0_29

In summary, we find that:

1. When an SMS message is sent/received the Google Messages app sends a message to Google servers recording this event, the time when the message was sent/received and a truncated SHA256 hash of the message text. The latter hash acts to uniquely identify the text message. The message sender's phone number is also sent to Google, so by combining data from handsets exchanging messages the phone numbers of both are revealed.
2. When a phone call is made/received the Google Dialer app similarly logs this event to Google servers together with the time and the call duration.

This data is sufficient to allow discovery of whether a pair of handsets are communicating.

The data sent to Google is tagged with the handset Android ID, which is linked to the handset's Google user account and so often to the real identity of the person involved in a phone call or SMS message. For example, a working phone number is required to create a Google account, and if the person has paid for an app on the Google Play store or uses Google Pay then their Google account is also linked to their credit card/bank details. In this way real-world identities of the pair of people communicating may be revealed to Google.

In addition to logging the sending/receiving of SMS messages and phone calls, the Google Messages and Dialer apps send messages to Google recording user interactions with the app. For example, when the user views an app screen, an SMS conversation or searches their contacts the nature and timing of this interaction is sent to Google allowing a detailed picture of app usage over time to be reconstructed.

There is no opt out from this data collection.

The Google Messages and Dialer apps send data to Google via two channels: (i) the Google Play Services Clearcut logger service and (ii) Google/Firebase Analytics. Recent Android measurement studies have noted the large volume of data sent by Google Play Services to Google servers on most Android handsets [7, 9]. A substantial component of this data is sent by the Clearcut logger service within Google Play Services. However, the data transmission is largely opaque, being binary encoded with little public documentation [7,9].

The work reported here is the first close look at the actual data sent by the Clearcut logger component of Google Play Services. It is limited in nature – we focus only on the data that the Messages and Dialer apps send via Google Play Services. Nevertheless, our measurements are already enough to establish that the data sent goes beyond what is suggested by the Google Play Services support page and Google's public statements. The data sent is not simply system health data (battery and CPU statistics and the like), device configuration data needed to check for updates, syncing of contacts and account details etc., but rather extends to details of the phone calls and SMS messages sent/received by users, and of user interactions with the Messages and Dialer apps (which SMS conversations viewed and when, dialing of phone numbers and so on).

While we report here on Android 11 measurements, we observed the same behaviour on a Pixel 4a handset running Android 12.

## 1.1  GDPR

We report on a technical study here, not a legal one. Nevertheless, the data collection that we observe by Google raises obvious questions regarding GDPR data protection regulations in Europe (the measurements were all carried out within Europe using handsets purchased in Europe and so it is European data regulations that apply). Roughly speaking, there are three main basis under GDPR for data collection[3]: (i) the data is anonymised, i.e. cannot reasonably be linked to an individual person, and so is not personal data, (ii) with consent for a defined purpose and (iii) for the legitimate interests of Google.

**Lack of Anonymity.** Regarding anonymity, all of the events recorded via the Google Play Services Clearcut logger are tagged with the handset's Android ID. Via other data collected by Google Play Services this ID is linked to (i) the handset hardware serial number, (ii) the SIM IMEI (which uniquely identifies the SIM slot) and (iii) the user's Google account. When a SIM is inserted the Google Messages app also links the Android ID to the SIM serial number/ICCID, which uniquely identifies the SIM card.

By making a request using https://takeout.google.com/ for the data associated with the Google user account used in our tests we further confirmed that the data reported under the heading "Android Device Configuration Service" includes the Android ID for each handset used (as well as the handset serial number, SIM IMEI, last IP address used and mobile operator details).

When creating a Google account it is necessary to supply a phone number on which a verification text can be received. For many people this will be their own phone number. Use of Google services such as buying a paid app on the Google Play store or using Google Pay further links a person's Google account to their credit card/bank details. A user's Google account, and so the Android ID, can therefore commonly be expected to be linked to the person's real identity.

Additionally, when a message is received by the Google Messages app the sender's phone number is sent to Google via the Google Play Services Clearcut logger, see Sect. 5.2. By combining data from the pair of handsets involved in an exchange of messages (which seems perfectly feasible based on the hashes of the message text that we observe to be sent to Google) both phone numbers may be revealed and linked to the Android IDs. Similarly when the spam protection option is enabled in the Google Dialer (as it is by default), see Sect. 6.1.

All of the events recorded via Google Analytics are tagged with the user's Google Advertising ID and the sender app's Firebase ID. The app Firebase ID is directly linked to the handset Android ID when the app registers to use the Google Analytics service.

The linkage between the various identifiers is illustrated schematically on Fig. 1.

---

[3] E.g. see https://gdpr.eu/what-is-gdpr/.

**No Consent.** Specific consent has neither been sought nor given for the data collection by the Google Messages and Dialer apps that we observe, and there is no opt out.

**Legitimate Interest.** Invoking legitimate interest requires the data to be collected for a specific purpose, that the data is necessary for the purpose, that the data collection is balanced against the interests and freedoms of the individual, and so on[4]. The legitimate interest basis for data collection is the least clear, and probably best left to the lawyers. We note, however, that we could not find an app-specific privacy policy stating the specific purpose for which the data that we observe is collected and the basis used for data collection. We discuss this further next.

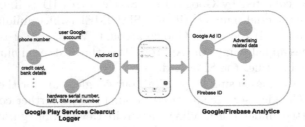

**Fig. 1.** Illustrating how handset data can be linked to a person's real identity. Handset data sent to Google via the Google Play Services Clearcut logger is tagged with the Android ID, which in turn is linked to the user's Google account and to device/SIM identifiers. The user's Google account in turn may be connected to the person's phone number, credit card/bank details etc. and so their real identity. Handset data sent to Google via Google/Firebase Analytics is tagged with the Google Advertising ID and the Firebase ID of the app carrying out the data collection. The Google Advertising ID links this data with other data collected for advertising-related purposes. The Firebase ID is linked to the Android ID, and so to the user Google account etc.

## 1.2 Lack of App-Specific Privacy Policy

**Google Messages.** Viewing the privacy policy of the Google Messages app is not straightforward. It is necessary to: (i) click on the three dots in search bar to open the Settings menu, (ii) scroll down to see an "About, terms and privacy" link, (iii) click on this to open a new menu that shows a "Privacy Policy" link, (iv) click on this link which opens a Google Chrome window to view the privacy policy web page at http://www.google.com/intl/en_IE/policies/privacy/ (note

---

[4] E.g.    see    https://ico.org.uk/for-organisations/guide-to-data-protection/guide-to-the-general-data-protection-regulation-gdpr/lawful-basis-for-processing/legitimate-interests/.

the use of http rather than https, although this redirects to https://policies. google.com/privacy?hl=en&gl=IE). Unfortunately, this is not an app-specific privacy policy but the rather general Google privacy policy. This is silent on the specific data collected by the Messages app, the associated app-specific purposes and the basis under which this app-specific data is collected. We note that during the loading of this privacy policy web page around 20 connections are made that appear to send telemetry to Google servers, see Sect. 5.4.

**Google Dialer.** The Google Dialer does not appear to have an app privacy policy link, only a privacy policy associated with the Support pages.

## 1.3   Response from Google

The apps studied here are in active use by many millions of people. We informed Google of our findings, delayed publication to allow them to respond and in fairness to Google they have engaged positively with us. In summary,

1. Google say they plan to change the app onboarding flow so that users are notified this is a Google app with a link to Google's consumer privacy policy. This will likely include opportunities to provide more "Privacy Tours" that walk the user through an overview of the app's data use and data collection. This will include a new on/off toggle to cover data collection that Google do not consider to be essential for the app to function.
2. Will halt the collection of the sender phone number via the CARRIER_ SERVICES log source, collection of the SIM ICCID and of a hash of sent/received message text by Google Messages (the latter change will be rolled out with version 10.9.160 of Google Messages, the other changes in the next release).
3. Will remove logging of call related events in Firebase Analytics from both Google Dialer and Messages.
4. Re the recommendation to use short-lived session identifiers for telemetry data, Google say they would like to see more logging moved to using the least long-lived identifier available whenever possible and that this an ongoing project.
5. Re the spam detection/protection service, Google note that this only occurs for phone numbers not in the handset contacts list and plan to (i) create a product tour explaining to new users and reminding current users that caller ID and spam protection is turned on for user protection, and letting them know how to disable it, (ii) add a visual indicator within the Messages app that indicates when spam protection is enabled, (iii) investigate whether an approach similar to the Safe Browsing hash prefix solution can be used. Google also state that the timestamp logged in the SCOOBY_EVENTS log message (see Section VI.A.4) is fuzzed to the nearest hour server-side, and will also be fuzzed client-side from version v75 onwards of the Dialer app.

6. Google state that there are back-end server controls to regulate joins between the Android ID and user account data, but the policy used to manage joins is not publicly available. Google also note that when a handset has multiple Google user accounts then its Android ID would be associated with all of those user accounts.

## 2   Related Work

While the Android ecosystem continues to evolve, most smartphone users remain largely unaware of the personal information disclosed by their devices and the apps they run [13]. This has motivated extensive privacy and security over recent years, e.g. see [4–6,10–12,14] and references therein, and triggered data protection legislation with nearly 100 articles laying out privacy requirements [3]. Its worth noting that much of this previous work uses static analysis i.e. inspection of the app binary to infer permissions used etc. While this scales well, allowing inspection of many apps, it essentially highlights potential rather than actual app behaviour i.e. can lead to "false positives" re privacy leakage. In the present work we employ dynamic analysis i.e. inspect the output of the running app. This has the great advantage that since actual app behaviour is recorded there are privacy false positives and stronger conclusions can therefore be drawn.

Probably closest to the present work are recent analyses of the data shared by Google Play Services [7–9]. The measurement study in [8] was motivated by the emergence of Covid contact tracing apps based on the Google-Apple Exposure Notification (GAEN) system, which on Android requires that Google Play Services to be enabled. This highlighted the extensive data collection Google Play Services. The follow-up work in [7] extended consideration to the data sent to Apple by an iPhone/IOS. Recently, in [9] the data sent by six variants of the Android OS, namely those developed by Samsung, Xiaomi, Huawei, Realme, LineageOS and e/OS, is measured (in [7,8] only Google-brand Android handsets were studied). While the focus was on data sent to non-Google servers, e.g. on the data sent to Samsung by a Samsung-brand handset, this study again highlighted the large volume of data uploaded to Google by Google Play Services on all handsets apart from the e/OS handset. The volume of data uploaded to Google was observed to be at least $10\times$ that uploaded by the mobile OS developer, rising to around $30\times$ for the Xiaomi, Huawei and Realme handsets. This occurs despite the 'usage & diagnostics" option being disabled for Google Play Services in these studies. These previous studies also note the opaque nature of this data collection by Google, with there being no public documentation, use of binary encoded payloads and obfuscated code.

The microG project[5] is an open source re-implementation of parts of the Google Play Services API used by popular apps (in particular the Fused Location, Maps, Firebase Cloud Messaging/push notifications, authentication and

---

[5] https://microg.org/.

SafetyNet components). However, the microG project has specifically avoided re-implementation of the analytics components of Google Play Services, including Google/Firebase Analytics and the Clearcut logger service, and it is these that we study here.

## 3  The Challenge of Seeing What Data Is Sent

It is generally straightforward to observe packets sent from a mobile handset. Specifically, we configure the handsets studied to use a WiFi connection to a controlled access point, on which we use `tcpdump` to capture outgoing traffic. However, this is of little use for privacy analysis because: *(i)* packet payloads are almost always encrypted due to the widespread use of HTTPS to transfer data; *(ii)* prior to message encryption, data is often encoded in a binary format for which there is little or no public documentation

### 3.1  Decrypting HTTPS Connections

Almost all of the data we observe is sent over HTTPS connections and so encrypted using TLS/SSL (in addition to any other encryption used by the app). However, decrypting SSL connections is relatively straightforward. We route handset traffic via a WiFi access point (AP) that we control, configure this AP to use `mitmdump` as a proxy [2] and adjust the firewall settings to redirect all WiFi HTTP/HTTPS traffic to mitmdump so that the proxying is transparent to the handset. When a process running on the handset starts a new network connection, the mitmdump proxy pretends to be the destination server and presents a fake certificate for the target server. This allows mitmdump to decrypt the traffic. It then creates an onward connection to the actual target server and acts as an intermediary, relaying requests and their replies between the app and the target server while logging the traffic.

System processes typically carry out checks on the authenticity of server certificates received when starting a new connection and abort the connection when these checks fail. For Google apps and services, installing the mitmproxy CA cert as a trusted certificate causes these checks to pass. Installing a trusted cert is slightly complicated in Android 10 and later, since the system disk partition, on which trusted certs are stored, is read-only and security measures prevent it being mounted as read-write. Fortunately, folders within the system disk partition can be overriden by creating a new mount point corresponding to the folder, and in this way the mitmdump CA cert can be added to the `/system/etc/security/cacerts` folder.

## 3.2   Google Play Services Telemetry

The Google Message and Dialer apps do not send data directly to Google, but rather send data to event logging services within Google Play Services. Specifically, to the Clearcut logger service and the Google/Firebase Analytics service. These Google Play Service components expose APIs that the app uses to communicate with them. The Clearcut logger and Google/Firebase Analytics services then batch up data received and forward it to Google servers. The Clearcut logger sends data to https://play.googleapis.com/log/batch while Google/Firebase Analytics sends data to https://app-measurement.com/. This process is illustrated schematically in Fig. 2.

The Clearcut logger and Google/Firebase Analytics services encode the data in different formats for sending to Google. We discuss these formats in more detail next.

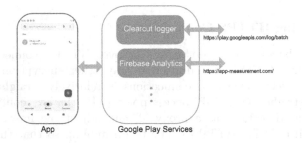

**Fig. 2.** Schematic illustrating app data flow. The app sends event data to Google Play Services via the Clearcut logger and Firebase Analytics APIs. These Google Play Services components then batch up the data and send it to Google servers. Note that Google Play Services provides many other APIs and services in addition to the Clearcut logger and Firebase Analytics.

## 3.3   Decoding Google Clearcut Logger Data

The Clearcut logger service within Google Play Services sends data to https://play.googleapis.com/log/batch. Each message sent includes an NID cookie and an x-server-token authentication token (which act as device identifiers), followed by the message body. The message body is encoded in a binary protobuf format[6]. Figure 3 shows the structure of the decoded message, including an example header message. Note that the sequence of log entries sent by each log source is encoded as a protobuf array. That is, as a sequence of <length/varint><protbuf> entries from which the individual log entry protobufs need to be extracted and decoded. Standard tools cannot decode a protobuf array but we have made software tools that we have developed for this publicly available, see below.

---

[6] https://developers.google.com/protocol-buffers/.

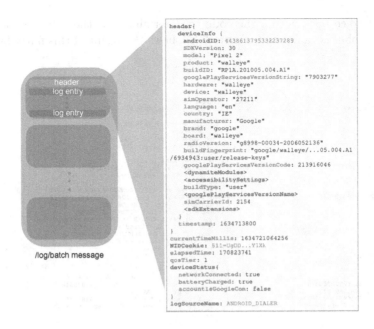

**Fig. 3.** Structure of messages sent to play.googleapis.com/log/batch by the Google Play Services Clearcut logger. Each message consists of one or more bundles of log entries, indicated in brown. Each bundle has a header containing device details and persistent identifiers (Google androidID, NID cookie) and specifying the log source. This header is followed by one or more log entries, the format of the log entries being determined by the log source.

Protobufs can be decoded without knowledge of the message content using the Google Protobuf compiler with the --decode_raw option. However, this means that the interpretation of values is missing and there is also sometimes ambiguity as to interpretation of the value types. Figure 4(a) shows an example of a log entry generated by the Google Messages app ANDROID_MESSAGING log source and decoded in this way. While the contents of the log entry can be viewed, it remains largely opaque since the interpretation of the various numerical and string values is not known.

Since there is no public documentation, to determine the meaning of these values we (i) decompile the Google Messages app, (ii) identify the protobuf used to encode the log entry within the decompiled code (this step is non-trivial since the Google Messages app contains more than 2000 distinct protobufs[7].) and

---

[7] The protobufs themselves are encoded within the app in compact protobuf format, which is undocumented although there are useful comments embedded in the Android source code, see https://cs.android.com/android/platform/superproject/+/master:external/protobuf/java/core/src/main/java/com/google/protobuf/RawMessageInfo.java.

then (iii) trace back within the code to determine how the value of each entry in the protobuf is calculated. Figure 4(b) shows the result of this fairly laborious process.

```
logEntry:{
1: 1635013045967
6 {
  1: 2
  3 {
    1: 1
    2: 1
    <...>
    5 {
      1: 1635013045028
      2: 898
    }
    8: 2
    9: 1282237833693804524
    12: 1
    14: 2
    16: 2
    17: 4
    18: 10
    19: 4
    20 {
      1: 30524580
      3: ""
    }
    21: 778
    27: 8480061162880308485
    31: "NOT_AVAILABLE"
    33: "-8443536869600326524"
    34: "5478611868067030819"
    <...>
```

```
logEntry:{
timestamp: 1635013045967
event {
  eventType: BUGLE_MESSAGE
  bugleMessage {
    messageProtocol: ONE_ON_ONE
    bugleMessageStatus: SENT
    <...>
    messageTiming {
      currentTime_ms: 1635013045028
      elapsedTimeSinceMsgSendRecv_ms: 898
    }
    bugleMessageSource: CONVERSATION_ACTIVITY
    usageStatsLoggingId: 12822378336938045248
    conversationType: ONE_ON_ONE
    sendAttempt: FIRST_ATTEMPT_TO_SEND
    wasRCS: HAS_ALWAYS_BEEN_XMS_CONVERSATION
    rcsStatus: RCS_AVAILABILITIES_ISSUES
    configStatus: CARRIER_SETUP_PENDING
    phoneNumberFormat2: PHONENUMBER
    carrierServicesData {
      versionCode: 30524580
      3: ""
    }
    messageSendClickToSentLatency: 778
    conversationIdSHA1: 8480061162880308485
    RcsConfig: "NOT_AVAILABLE"
    sha256HashMsg: "-8443536869600326524"
    sha256HashPrevMsg: "5478611868067030819"
    <...>
```

(a)                                    (b)

**Fig. 4.** Example of Google Messages ANDROID_MESSAGING Clearcut logger log entry: (a) protobuf decoded using Google Protobuf compiler with the --decode_raw option, (b) after reverse engineering the schema.

```
logEntry:{
  timestamp: 1635013503410
  event {
    impressionEvent {
      timestamp: 1635013503410
      deviceDetails {
        buildDevice: "walleye"
        buildModel: "Pixel 2"
        buildVersionRelease: "11"
        buildID: "RP1A.201005.004.A1"
        releaseStatus: RELEASE
        systemApp: true
        updatedSystemApp: true
        deviceClass: DEFAULT_GOOGLE_DEVICE
        simOperator: "Tesco Mobile"
        country: "ie"
        elapsedDaysSinceDialerInstall: 4678
        mobileOperator: "27205"
        installedBy: "com.android.vending"
        14: "0AFFFFFFFFFFFFFFFFFFFFFFFFFFFFFFFFFFFFFFFFFFFF"
      }
      AOSPEventType: MAIN_CLICK_FAB_TO_OPEN_DIALPAD
    }
  }
  subEvent: 1340
  tz_offset: 3600
  <...>
}
```

**Fig. 5.** Example of Google Dialer ANDROID_DIALER Impression event log entry recording event that dialpad has been opened.

```
logEntry:{
  timestamp: 1635013208570
  event {
    searchQuery {
      queryLength: 3
      searchTimeMillis: 47
      5: 1
    }
  }
  tz_offset: 3600
  <...>
}
```

```
callDetails {
  isIncoming: False
  callInitiationType: Dialpad
  lookupResultType: NOT_FOUND
  disconnectCause: REMOTE
  callDuration: 48605 // ms
  callSetupTiming {<...>}
  deviceDetails {<...>}
  callID: "d97ae1a6-...7d7ecb7"
  <...>
}
```

(a)

(b)

**Fig. 6.** More examples of Google Dialer ANDROID_DIALER log entries: (a) logging each key press when dialing a phone number, (b) call details sent upon completion of a call, including the call duration (in milliseconds).

Each log source sending data to the Clearcut logger service uses its own protobuf format for log entries, necessitating seperate reverse engineering of each in order to decode the message content.

Figure 5 shows an example of a decoded Google Dialer log entry generated in response to manually dialing a phone number. The AOSPEventType value MAIN_CLICK_FAB_TO_OPEN_DIALPAD records the fact that the dialpad was opened, and the timestamp records the time when this occurred. As the phone number is typed a searchQuery event is logged for each digit typed, see Fig. 5(a) for an example log entry sent in response to a keypress. When a phone call finishes this event is also logged, using a message similar to that in Fig. 5 but with AOSPEventType value USER_PARTICIPATED_IN_A_CALL and including additional data recording call details, including the call duration (in milliseconds), see Fig. 5(b).

### 3.4 Decoding Google/Checkin Message

Google Play Services sends periodic messages to https://android.googleapis.com/checkin that act to link together a number of persistent device and user identifiers, see [1,7–9]. The message contains the (i) Android ID (a long-lived device identifier that can only be changed by carrying out a factory reset), (ii) the IMEI (which uniquely identifies the handset SIM slot), (ii) the hardware serial number (which uniquely identifies the handset), (iv) the NID cookie (which acts as a persistent device identifier), (v) the Google account username/email (which identifies the handset user) and (vi) a user account authorisation token (which again identifies the handset user). As already noted, logging messages sent by the Clearcut logger to https://play.googleapis.com/log/batch are tagged with the AndroidID, and so via this /checkin message can be linked to long-lived device and user identifiers.

## 4  Experimental Setup

### 4.1  Hardware and Software Used

Google Pixel 2 running Android 11 (build RP1A.201005.004.A1) with Google Play Services ver. 21.39.16 (150400–402663742) rooted using Magisk v23.0.

Google Dialer ver. 70.05.401408800, Google Messages ver. 10.0.014. Although we only present measurements for Android 11 we also collected measurements from a Google Pixel 4a running Android 12 (build SP1A.210812.015), Google Play Services ver. 21.39.17 (190400–405802548), Google Dialer ver. 68.0.392726590, Google Messages ver 8.4.041. The behaviour observed is almost identical to that of Android 11.

## 4.2  Device Settings

At the start of each test we removed any SIM card and reflashed the handset with a fresh factory image. Following this, the handset reboots to a welcome screen and the user is then presented with a number of option screens. To mimic a privacy conscious user, we unchecked any of the options that asked to share data and only agreed to mandatory terms and conditions. Specifically, we deselected the (i) "Free up space" option, (ii) "Use location" option, (iii) "Allow scanning" option and (iv) the "Send usage and diagnostic data" option. Note that there is no option to deselect automatic updates. We did not log in to Google user account during the onboarding process. After onboarding we inserted a SIM.

## 4.3  Test Design

Following previous mobile handset privacy studies [7,9] we assume a privacy-conscious but busy/non-technical user, who when asked, does not select options that share data but otherwise leaves handset settings at their default values. This provides a baseline for privacy analysis, and we expect that the level of data sharing may well be larger for a less privacy-conscious user.

Both the Google Dialer and Messages app include spam detection/protection services. By default these are enabled for both apps, but can be disabled by a user via the settings menu in each app. To explore the impact of these services on data sharing we take measurements both with spam detection/protection enabled (the default) and with it disabled. Google documentation[8] also suggests that these spam detection/protection services may treat calls/messages from phone numbers that are already in the handset contacts database differently from numbers that not in handset contacts database.

With these considerations in mind we carry out the following experiments:

*Phone number in contacts:*

1. Start a pair of handsets following a factory reset (mimicking a user receiving a new phone), insert a SIM in each handset and disable mobile data.
2. Login in to a Google account. This downloads a list of contacts, including the calling number used in our tests.
3. Make/receive phone calls and send/receive SMS messages between the pair of handsets. Record the network activity.

---

[8] "Your chats stay private with spam detection", Google Support page https:// support.google.com/messages/answer/9327903.

4. Disable the "Caller ID and spam detection" option in Google Dialer and the "Spam protection" option on Google Messages (both default to "on").
5. Make/receive calls and send/receive SMS messages. Record the network activity.

*Phone number not in contacts:* As above, but do not login to Google account (the handset contacts database will be empty).

*Interacting With Apps:* During the above tests we interact with the apps to send/receive SMS messages and make/receive phone calls. Since our measurements in these tests established that user interactions (screens viewed, buttons clicked) are logged and sent to Google by the apps we then also additionally carried out tests where we (i) viewed the call history, (ii) viewed recent calls/favourites, (iii) viewed/edited contact details, (iv) opened the in-app settings menu and viewed the settings screens, (v) entered both text and phone numbers in the app search bar and

*App Privacy Policy:* We also tried to view the app privacy policy.

## 5  Results: Google Messages

### 5.1  Inserting SIM

When a SIM is inserted into the handset Google Messages records this event via the Google Play Services ANDROID_MESSAGING log source:

```
event {
  eventType: BUGLE_TELEPHONY_EVENT
  bugleTelephonyEvent {
    carrierInfo {
      simStatus: LOADED
      simInfoNotUpdated: true
      simOperator: "27211"
      <...>
      simSerialNumber: "09353111802...65506"
      simCarrierId: -1
}}}
```

and similarly via the Google Play Services CARRIER_SERVICES log source. The simOperator value specifies the SIM operator (in this case 48 Mobile Ireland). The simSerialNumber value is the SIM card serial number or ICCID, which uniquely identifies the SIM card. Since these event records are also tagged with the handset AndroidID (see Fig. 3) they act to link the handset and the SIM. Additionally, Google Play Services also separately sends SIM details and the AndroidID to https://android.clients.google.com/fdfe/uploadDynamicConfig, see [7,9].

### 5.2  Sending/Receiving an SMS Message

We present measurements when sending an SMS message between two handsets using Google Messages with the spam protection service disabled and the handset phone numbers not in their contacts list. However, we note that in our tests similar behaviour was also observed when spam protection is enabled and/or the handset phone numbers are in the contacts list.

**ANDROID_MESSAGING Log Source.** On the handset sending a text we observe, for example, the following sequence of event messages sent by Google Messages via the Google Play Services ANDROID_MESSAGING log source[9]:

```
1635968886592 BUGLE_MESSAGE bugleMessageStatus: CREATED
1635968886593 BUGLE_APP_CONFIGURATION
1635968886600 BUGLE_COMPOSE
1635968886623 BUGLE_P2P_SUGGESTION suggestionEventType: SENT_MESSAGE
1635968886735 BUGLE_MESSAGE bugleMessageStatus: MESSAGE_ID_CREATED
1635968887029 BUGLE_P2P_SUGGESTION suggestionEventType: REQUEST
1635968887562 BUGLE_MESSAGE bugleMessageStatus:
SENT sha256HashMsg: "247836537599431109" sha256HashPrevMsg: "200428458475182371"
```

The first BUGLE_MESSAGE event records the fact that a new message is created, the last BUGLE_MESSAGE event records the fact that the message was successfully sent. The BUGLE_APP_CONFIGURATION event records the orientation of the screen and whether the handset is in multi-window mode. The other events log internal app processing steps as a new message is sent for transmission.

At the receiving handset we observe the following corresponding sequence of event messages:

```
1635968888138 BUGLE_P2P_SUGGESTION suggestionEventType: REQUEST
1635968888460 BUGLE_MESSAGE bugleMessageStatus:
RECEIVED sha256HashMsg: "247836537599431109" sha256HashPrevMsg: "200428458475182371"
1635968888685 BUGLE_P2P_SUGGESTION suggestionEventType: RECEIVED_MESSAGE
1635968890295 BUGLE_NOTIFICATION
1635968890295 BUGLE_APP appLaunch: VIA_NOTIFICATION
1635968890426 BUGLE_CONTACT_BANNER
1635968890712 BUGLE_MESSAGE bugleMessageStatus: READ
```

The first BUGLE_MESSAGE records the receipt of the message. The BUGLE_P2P_SUGGESTION events record processing of the message by the Google suggestions service (which can suggest links for more information related to a message, quick replies etc.[10]). The BUGLE_APP event records launch of the app by the user clicking on the message arrival notification, and the final BUGLE_MESSAGE event records the fact that the received message has been displayed.

**CARRIER_SERVICES Log Source.** On the receiving handset the phone number of the SMS sender is transmitted to Google via the Google Play Services CARRIER_SERVICES log source, e.g.

```
timestamp: 1635968888300
event {
<...>
packageVersionName: "10.0.014 (Isengard_RC01.phone_dynamic)"
<...>
      incomingPhoneNumber: "+353872...351"
<...>
}
```

When a pair of handsets engage in a back-and-forth exchange of SMS messages, each handset sends the phone number of the other to Google via the CARRIER_SERVICES log source.

---

[9] Each event message is similar to that in Fig. 4 but for clarity and to save space we just show selected values from each message.

[10] https://support.google.com/messages/answer/9265111?hl=en.

**Google Analytics Event Logging.** On the handset sending a text an event message is sent to Google Analytics to record this, e.g.[11]:

```
1635968887562 data_str: "ConversationActivity" event_code: "ACTIVE_EVENT"
package_name: "com.google.android.apps.messaging"
google_ad_id: "916c714a-e838-479d-a7a6-3325d838da5f"
firebase_instance_id: "eVpvvohEDCqhfIGC7pXLnv"
```

On the receiving handset a corresponding event message is also sent to Google Analytics, e.g.

```
1635968894940 data_str: "ConversationActivity" event_code: "ACTIVE_EVENT"
package_name: "com.google.android.apps.messaging"
google_ad_id: "0fcb9970-3c60-426d-8186-452793942752"
firebase_instance_id: "fkT8O_dZhqxcNAfYucplGA"
```

These Google Analytics event messages act to link the SMS message exchange to the Google Advertising IDs of the handsets.

**Using Hashes to Identify Communicating Phones.** Google Messages also sends to Google a signature of each message sent/received that uniquely identifies the message. Observe that the sha256HashMsg and sha256HashPrevMsg values logged by the sender and receiver in the above measurements are the same.

The sha256HashMsg value is derived from the SHA256 hash of the time, in hours since 1st Jan 1970, when the message was sent/received concatenated with the message content i.e. the message text. This SHA256 hash is 32 bytes long, the lower 8 bytes are converted to a long int and then to a decimal string, which gives the sha256HashMsg value. The sha256HashPrevMsg value is the hash for the previous message sent/received in the conversation.

These sha256HashMsg and sha256HashPrevMsg values can therefore act to identify the SMS messages sent. Identifying whether a pair of handsets using Google Messages are communicating therefore simply involves comparing the pair of sha256Hash values sent by both handsets to Google. Even if there occasional pairs of hash collisions (the same pair of short text messages is sent around the same time by two handsets), it only needs one hash miss to reveal that a pair of handsets are communicating.

### 5.3   Interacting with Messages App

When a user interacts with the Google Message app, their actions are recorded and sent to Google both via the Google Play Services ANDROID_MESSAGING log source and via Google Analytics. The events logged include opening of the app, composing and reading a message, viewing a conversation (message exchanges between the same pair of handsets), entering text in the app search bar (where phone numbers, contact names etc. are entered), navigating to the app home screen.

---

[11] To save space we just show selected values from each message.

## 5.4   Viewing App Privacy Policy

As already noted, viewing the privacy policy of the Google Messages app is not straightforward. It is necessary to: (i) click on the three dots in search bar to open the Settings menu, (ii) scroll down to see an "About, terms and privacy" link, (iii) click on this to open a new menu that shows a "Privacy Policy" link, (iv) click on this link which opens a Google Chrome window. At this point the Messages app silently sends messages to Google Analytics https://app-measurement.com/ a logging the fact that the page with the privacy policy link has been viewed, e.g.

```
event_info {
  setting_code: "_pc" // firebase_previous_class
  data_str: "AboutPrivacyTermsActivity"
}
event_code: "_vs" // screen_view
event_timestamp: 1636311111608
}
package_name: "com.google.android.apps.messaging"
google_ad_id: "916c714a-e838-479d-a7a6-3325d838da5f"
firebase_instance_id: "eVpvvohEDCqhfIGC7pXLnv"
```

Agreeing to the Google Chrome terms and conditions loads the page at http://www.google.com/intl/en_IE/policies/privacy/ which redirects to https:// policies.google.com/privacy?hl=en&gl=IE. During the loading of this page (i) 20 connections are made to www.youtube-nocookie.com/youtubei/v1/log_event sending what appears to be telemetry, (ii) a connection is made to download https://www.google-analytics.com/analytics.js, (iii) and then connections are made to www.google-analytics.com/j/collect, https://stats.g.doubleclick.net/j/ collect and https://play.google.com/log.

# 6   Results: Google Dialer

## 6.1   Making/Receiving a Phone Call

We now present measurements when making a phone calls between two handsets using Google Dialer with the Caller and Spam ID option disabled. When this option is enabled additional event messages are sent to Google, but we will describe these later.

**ANDROID_MESSAGING Log Source.** On the handset initiating the phone call we observe, for example, the following sequence of event messages sent by the Google Dialer via the Google Play Services ANDROID_DIALER log source[12]:

---

[12] Each event message is similar to that in Figs. 5 and 6 but to save space we just show selected values from each message.

```
1635969033382  MAIN_CLICK_FAB_TO_OPEN_DIALPAD
1635969034630  searchQuery
1635969039257  queryLength: 1
1635969039478  queryLength: 2
1635969039881  queryLength: 3
1635969041305  queryLength: 4
1635969041680  queryLength: 5
1635969042060  queryLength: 6
1635969044085  queryLength: 7
1635969044556  queryLength: 8
1635969044906  queryLength: 9
1635969045359  queryLength: 10
1635969064139  PRECALL_INITIATED
1635969065267  TIDEPODS_STATUS_BAR_NOTIFICATION_SHOWED
1635969065297  TIDEPODS_BUBBLE_SHOWED
1635969085622  SCOOBY_CALL_LOG_SPAM_DISABLED
1635969085622  USER_PARTICIPATED_IN_A_CALL callDuration: 12344
1635969085720  ANNOTATED_CALL_LOG_FORCE_REFRESH_CHANGES_NEEDED
1635969085868  ANNOTATED_CALL_LOG_FORCE_REFRESH_NO_CHANGES_NEEDED
1635969085918  ANNOTATED_CALL_LOG_NOT_DIRTY
```

To make the call the dialpad in the app is opened and the phone number typed. The MAIN_CLICK_FAB_TO_OPEN_DIALPAD event records opening of the dialpad, the next sequence of SearchQuery event messages record each individual keypess as the phone number is typed, and also the timing of these keypresses. The PRECALL_INITIATED event through to the TIDEPODS_BUBBLE_SHOWED record the internal process of initating the call over the phone network and displaying the in-call user interface. The USER_PARTICIPATED_IN_A_CALL event records the termination of the call and, amongst other things, sends the call duration to Google (the value is in milliseconds so a value of 12344 corresponds to a call of 12.344 s duration). The last three CALL_LOG events record internal actions associated with updating the handset call log.

At the receiving handset we observe the following corresponding sequence of event messages:

```
1635969070066  CALL_SCREENING_SERVICE_MUSIC_IS_NOT_ACTIVE
1635969070096  INCOMING_CALL_SCREENED
1635969070639  TIDEPODS_BUBBLE_SHOWED
1635969070644  TIDEPODS_STATUS_BAR_NOTIFICATION_SHOWED
1635969072326  TIDEPODS_STATUS_BAR_NOTIFICATION_ANSWER
1635969085350  SCOOBY_CALL_LOG_SPAM_DISABLED
1635969085350  USER_PARTICIPATED_IN_A_CALL callDuration: 13065
1635969085483  ANNOTATED_CALL_LOG_FORCE_REFRESH_CHANGES_NEEDED
```

The first events record call screening, displaying a notification to the user that here is an incoming call and the user pressing the answer button. The USER_PARTICIPATED_IN_A_CALL event records the termination of the call and sends the call duration to Google. Note the close match in the call durations recorded by the sender and receiver i.e. 12.344 s and 12.865 s respectively. Presumably the small difference of 0.52 s is due to the telephone network delay between one phone hanging up and the other phone being informed of this.

**Google Analytics Event Logging.** On the handset initiating the phone call an event message is sent to Google Analytics to record this, e.g.

```
data_str: "LegacyInCallActivity" event_code: "OUTGOING_CALL_PLACED"
package_name: "com.google.android.dialer"
google_ad_id: "916c714a-e838-479d-a7a6-3325d838da5f"
firebase_instance_id: "f86VDMHLSSGcArM16Up973"
```

At the receiving handset the incoming call is also logged to Google Analytics:

```
data_str: "LegacyInCallActivity" event_code: "INCOMING_CALL_RECEIVED"
package_name: "com.google.android.dialer"
google_ad_id: "0fcb9970-3c60-426d-8186-452793942752"
firebase_instance_id: "cyoEhnfBQtChaUDIrYRfYB"
```

These Google Analytics event messages act to link the phone call to the Google Advertising ID of the sender handsets.

**Identifying Pairs of Communicating Handsets.** When the caller and receiver in a phone conversation are both using the Google Dialer, then the time when the time the call ended and the call duration are both sent to Google via the above event logging messages. This information can potentially be used to identify pairs of handsets engaged in phone conversations. For example, Fig. 7 shows the call times and durations sent to Google by a pair of handsets as they engage in a sequence of phone calls (at roughly 5 min, or 300 s, intervals). Clearly, by comparing the pattern of call times and call durations on a pair of handsets it may be possible to infer whether two handsets are communicating.

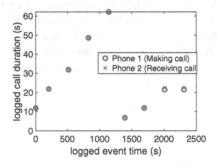

**Fig. 7.** Example of Google Dialer log entries on a pair of communicating handsets. The x-axis is the logged event timestamp (rescaled from milliseconds to seconds and offset so the first entry has timestamp 0), the y-axis is the logged callDuration value (again rescaled from milliseconds to seconds).

**Caller and Spam ID Enabled.** When the Caller and Spam ID option is enabled we observe additional events sent to Google via the Google Play Services SCOOBY_EVENTS log source (Scooby in the internal name for the spam scanning service). For example:

```
timestamp: 1635013551317
event {
  1 {
    packageName: "Dialer"
    packageVersionName: "70.05.401408800"
    incomingPhoneNumber: "+353872...351"
    <...>
  }
}
```

The `packageVersionName` value is the version name of Google Dialer app. Note that this SCOOBY_EVENTS message is sent every time a call is received and even if the phone number is in the handset contacts database. When a pair of handsets engage in a back-and-forth phone calls and both have the Caller and Spam ID option enabled, then each handset sends the phone number of the other to Google via the SCOOBY_EVENTS log source.

## 6.2 Interacting with Dialer App

Similarly to Google Messages, when a user interacts with the Google Dialer app, their actions are recorded and sent to Google both via the Google Play Services ANDROID_DIALER log source and via Google Analytics.

## 7 Summary

We report on measurements of the data sent to Google by the Google Messages and Google Dialer apps. We find that these apps tell Google when message/phone calls are made/received. The data sent by Google Messages includes a hash of the message text, allowing linking of sender and receiver in a message exchange, and by Google Dialer the call time and duration, again allowing linking of the two handsets engaged in a phone call. Phone numbers are also sent to Google. In addition, the timing and duration of user interactions with the apps are sent to Google. There is no opt out from this data collection. The data is sent via two channels, the Google Play Services (i) Clearcut logger and (ii) Google/Firebase Analytics. This study is one of the first to cast light on the actual telemetry data sent by Google Play Services, which to date has largely been opaque.

## References

1. Learn about the Android Device Configuration Service, Google Help Pages (Accessed 5 Aug 2020). https://support.google.com/android/answer/9021432?hl=en
2. Cortesi, A., Hils, M., Kriechbaumer, T., contributors: mitmproxy: A free and open source interactive HTTPS proxy (v5.01) (2020). https://mitmproxy.org/
3. European Parliament and Council of the European Union: Regulation on the protection of natural persons with regard to the processing of personal data and on the free movement of such data, and repealing directive 95/46/ec (data protection directive) (2016)
4. Gamba, J., Rashed, M., Razaghpanah, A., Tapiador, J., Vallina-Rodriguez, N.: An analysis of pre-installed android software. In: IEEE Symposium on Security and Privacy (S&P), pp. 1039–1055 (2020)
5. Jia, Q., Zhou, L., Li, H., Yang, R., Du, S., Zhu, H.: Who leaks my privacy: Towards automatic and association detection with gdpr compliance. In: Biagioni, E.S., Zheng, Y., Cheng, S. (eds.) Wireless Algorithms, Systems, and Applications, pp. 137–148 (2019)

6. Jin, H., et al.: Why are they collecting my data? inferring the purposes of network traffic in mobile apps. Proc. ACM Interact. Mob. Wearable Ubiquitous Technol. **2**(4), 1–27 (2018)

7. Leith, D.J.: Mobile handset privacy: measuring the data ios and android send to apple and google. In: Garcia-Alfaro, J., Li, S., Poovendran, R., Debar, H., Yung, M. (eds.) SecureComm 2021. LNICST, vol. 399, pp. 231–251. Springer, Cham (2021). https://doi.org/10.1007/978-3-030-90022-9_12

8. Leith, D.J., Farrell, S.: Contact Tracing App Privacy: What Data Is Shared By Europe's GAEN Contact Tracing Apps. In: Proc IEEE INFOCOM (2021)

9. Liu, H., Patras, P., Leith, D.J.: Android Mobile OS Snooping By Samsung,Xiaomi, Huawei and Realme Handsets. SCSS Tech Report, Oct 2021 (2021). https://www.scss.tcd.ie/doug.leith/Android_privacy_report.pdf

10. Razaghpanah, A., Nithyanand, R., Vallina-Rodriguez, N., Sundaresan, S.: Apps, Trackers, Privacy, and Regulators: A Global Study of the Mobile Tracking Ecosystem. In: Network and Distributed System Security Symposium (NDSS) (2018)

11. Reardon, J., Feal, Á., Wijesekera, P., On, A.E.B., Vallina-Rodriguez, N., Egelman, S.: 50 ways to leak your data: An exploration of apps' circumvention of the android permissions system. In: 28th USENIX Security Symposium (USENIX Security 19), pp. 603–620. USENIX Association, Santa Clara, CA (Aug 2019). https://www.usenix.org/conference/usenixsecurity19/presentation/reardon

12. Ren, J., Lindorfer, M., Dubois, D.J., Rao, A., Choffnes, D., Vallina-Rodriguez, N.: Bug fixes, improvements,... and privacy leaks. In: Network and Distributed System Security Symposium (NDSS) (2018)

13. Van Kleek, M., Liccardi, I., Binns, R., Zhao, J., Weitzner, D.J., Shadbolt, N.: Better the devil you know: Exposing the data sharing practices of smartphone apps. In: CHI Conference on Human Factors in Computing Systems, pp. 5208–5220 (2017)

14. Zhang, D., Guo, Y., Guo, D., Wang, R., Yu, G.: Contextual approach for identifying malicious inter-component privacy leaks in android apps. In: IEEE Symposium on Computers and Communications (ISCC), pp. 228–235 (2017)

# Detection and Privacy Leakage Analysis of Third-Party Libraries in Android Apps

Xiantong Hao, Dandan Ma, and Hongliang Liang$^{(\boxtimes)}$

TSIS Lab., Beijing University of Posts and Telecommunications, Beijing, China
{xiantonghao,ma21,hliang}@bupt.edu.cn

**Abstract.** Third-party libraries (TPL) make Apps' functionality diversified but introduce severe security risks. Precisely detecting and analyzing TPLs is challenging because their code usually is not publicly available or obfuscated. Prior studies do not perform well in detecting closed-source or obfuscated TPLs and analyzing their privacy risks.

In this paper, we propose a novel approach to detect TPLs in Android Apps and analyze privacy leakage caused by TPLs. The key idea of our approach is that it leverages the call frequencies of different types of APIs as features and conducts a clustering algorithm on these features, our approach works well on obfuscated TPLs, especially those with dead code removal and control flow randomization. We also analyze whether there is privacy leakage in a TPL by dynamically instrumenting privacy-related APIs and inspecting its call stack. We implement our approach in a tool named Libmonitor and evaluate it on 162 obfuscated Apps and 217 real-world Apps. Experimental results show that Libmonitor outperforms two state-of-the-art tools on two datasets. With obfuscated TPLs, Libmonitor improves 394.08% over Libradar and 26.32% over LibD on F1 metric, respectively. With closed-source TPLs, Libmonitor increases 18.66% over Libradar and 150.15% over LibD on F1 metric, respectively. Besides, Libmonitor found 5809 pieces of privacy leakage risks caused by 152 TPLs in 64 real-world Apps.

**Keywords:** Android · Third-party library detection · Clustering · Privacy leakage analysis

## 1 Introduction

Now Android is the most popular mobile operating system [1] while developing a practical Android application is getting more intricate. Today's Apps require many additional functions to assist, such as user portraits, personalized recommendations, socialization, etc. To cope with the ever-increasing demand for App development, existing developers on the Android platform integrate third-party libraries (TPL) into their Apps. These TPLs have complex sources, diverse types, and different functions, including advertising, location access, mobile payment, etc. Related research work [2] shows that each App contains an average of 1.59 TPLs. In extreme circumstances, some Apps use over 30 different TPLs. On

F. Li et al. (Eds.): SecureComm 2022, LNICST 462, pp. 569–587, 2023.
https://doi.org/10.1007/978-3-031-25538-0_30

average, over 60% of sub-packages in an App are from third-party libraries [3]. The TPL can reuse code, reduce development time, improve App quality, and let developers focus on the architecture of the App. However, improper use of TPL will introduce the following problems:

The first problem is the introduction of vulnerable code. If a developer uses a TPL with a vulnerability and does not update it in time, the TPL will introduce the vulnerable code into the App. For example, the SlowMist Security Team published a report in 2018 [4], there is an XSS 0-day vulnerability in a JavaScript library named *TradingView*, which can bypass the Cloudflare defense mechanism. Wu et al. [5] found 13 popular TPLs have open ports and 61.8% open-port actions in their App dataset are caused by TPL. Almanee et al. [6] conducted a study on 200 free Apps on Google Play, and tracked the version iterations of Apps using third-party native libraries between May 2013 and September 2020. The study found that 53 Apps use malicious versions of third-party libraries with known CVEs, of which 14 Apps have not updated the vulnerable versions in 2020. Since multiple Apps may use a same TPL, vulnerabilities in the third-party library will have an enormous impact, like viruses.

The second problem is the leakage of private information. TPLs may collect user information to achieve their functions, but sometimes, they may collect unauthorized or unnecessary data. For example, TPLs provided by Taomike and Baidu have been exposed to security vulnerabilities. They secretly monitor users' behaviors and upload sensitive information to remote servers [7]. According to a survey in 2019 [8], over 40% Apps collect users' personal information beyond their own function requirements.

Unfortunately, developers rarely list third-party libraries in their Apps. Some open-source TPLs can be accessed from Maven [9], GitHub [10], and other websites, however, commercial Apps may use closed-source TPLs. To detect TPLs in mobile Apps, several prior efforts [2,11,12] use the whitelist approach. However, closed-source TPLs and the growing of new TPLs make it difficult for researchers to maintain a complete whitelist. In addition, code obfuscation also makes the whitelist approach ineffective. Some studies [14,16,33] apply similarity comparison techniques. LibID [13] has two library detection schemes, using the textual representation in the basic block and class dependency as features, but it cannot resist dead code removal and control flow randomization. Libpecker [32] uses signature matching to get a similarity score between a library and an App. By internal class dependencies in the library, Libpecker generates strict signatures for each class. To resist the customization and removal of library code as much as possible, it uses fuzzy match when calculating library similarity. However, Libpecker requires pre-collection of TPLs to establish a feature database, so it can't detect closed-source TPL and is time-consuming.

Other studies leverage feature clustering technique. Libradar [15] uses feature clustering, but it requires an exact match of hash values in features, so it cannot deal with TPLs obfuscated with dead code removal. LibD [17] needs to traverse the decompiled code to build the directory tree and homogeny graphs, which is time-consuming and cannot detect TPLs obfuscated with control flow randomization.

As for privacy leakage analysis in Apps, some research efforts use taint analysis technique. For example, Taintdroid [18] and Taintman [19] work on Dalvik and ART, respectively. They use dynamic taint analysis to track data flow, but they need to modify system code and hence are hard to migration. Besides, their analysis target is a whole App instead of a TPL. Some studies analyze network traffic to find privacy leakage. For instance, He et al. [20] capture network packets to match private information and trace back to find the APIs that leak privacy. VULPIX [21] also collects network traffic to match private information, but it only considers network interfaces and ignores other interfaces such as logcat and short-message-service. These methods are either heavy weighted or incomplete for analyzing privacy leakage in TPLs.

In this paper, we propose a new clustering-based approach to detect TPLs in Android Apps and perform privacy leakage analysis on TPLs. We classify Android APIs into 15 categories and extract API call frequencies for every category as features. These features can resist control flow randomization because each API name is persistent in any call place and call time. Considering that different Apps may import a same TPL, we use fuzzy match to cluster feature vectors into different clusters and use cluster prediction to detect TPLs, which means the feature vectors in a cluster don't have to be exactly the same during cluster partitioning. In this way, the fuzzy match is not sensitive to dead code removal. We use dynamic instrumentation to monitor sensitive APIs and perform privacy leakage analysis. Dynamic instrumentation is light-weighted and hence easily applied on most sensitive interfaces like logcat, network, message and clipboard.

In summary, our contributions are as follows:

- We propose a feature matching approach for detecting TPLs. We divide Android APIs into 15 categories and extract API call frequency for each category as features, then perform fuzzy match to cluster feature vectors and detect TPLs by cluster prediction. Our approach can resist code obfuscation, especially dead code removal and control flow randomization.
- We develop a TPL privacy leakage analysis approach, which uses dynamic instrumentation to monitor source and sink APIs, then performs information match and call stack analysis.
- We implement the proposed approaches in a tool Libmonitor and evaluate it on 162 obfuscated Apps and 217 real-world Apps respectively. Experimental results show that Libmonitor outperforms two state-of-the art tools, Libradar and Libd. Moreover, Libmonitor found 5809 pieces of privacy leakage risks caused by 152 TPLs in 64 Apps.

## 2 Background

### 2.1 Code Obfuscation

Code obfuscation is the act of creating source or machine code that is difficult for humans to understand without destroying behaviors of a program. The purpose of code obfuscation is to prevent code from being tampered with or reverse-engineered. Code obfuscation is common in Android Apps, for example, Dong et al. [22] found that 43% of Google Play Apps and 73% of third-party market Apps have obfuscated code. Currently common obfuscation strategies in Android apps are: package flattening, identifier renaming, string encryption, control flow randomization, and dead code removal, the later two of which are difficult to deal with when detecting TPLs [28]. Existing well-known tools are Dasho and Proguard. Dasho provides all strategies above while Proguard supports the former two strategies.

## 2.2  Cluster Algorithm

Cluster analysis is the task to group a set of objects so that objects in the same cluster are more similar or more closely related to each other. Clustering is a common statistical data analysis technique. According to the cluster criteria, clustering algorithms can be divided into the following categories:

- *Hierarchical cluster*: samples are more related to objects at closer distances.
- *Centroid-based cluster*: each cluster is marked by a center point and the number of clustering centers needs to be determined in advance.
- *Density-based cluster*: clusters are defined as regions with a higher density than the other objects.

The advantage of cluster analysis over other machine learning algorithms is that cluster analysis is an unsupervised algorithm and is simple to operate. Cluster analysis is more cost-effective and time-efficient than other probability sampling methods, especially for widely distributed samples.

## 3  Design

### 3.1  Overview

In this section, we present Libmonitor, a third-party library detection and privacy leakage analysis system. Libmonitor consists of two modules: TPL detection and privacy leakage analysis.

We observe that a third-party library may be used in several Apps, so we can detect closed-source or obfuscated TPLs by clustering features of numerous Apps. The workflow of TPL detection is shown in Fig. 1. First, a large dataset of real-world Apps is collected from Android App markets, and API call frequencies of different types are extracted as features for each App. Then clustering of fuzzy match is performed, which means that the features are not exactly equal in a cluster, so our system can resist dead code removal.

The workflow of privacy leakage analysis is shown in Fig. 2. We get private information, e.g., AdvertiserID, AndroidID, IMEI, MacAddress, DeviceType, TimeZone, KernelVersion, through android debug bridge (adb) and dynamic instrumentation. They are encoded or encrypted into a processed information list (PIL). Then we adopt a dynamic instrumentation technique to separately monitor and record the invocations of private information related APIs, i.e., source and sink APIs. Finally, we match PIL with API invocation record and perform call stack analysis to generate privacy leakage analysis report for those TPLs in the TPL list, which is generated in TPL detection module.

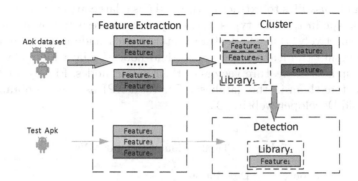

**Fig. 1.** Workflow of Third-party library detection

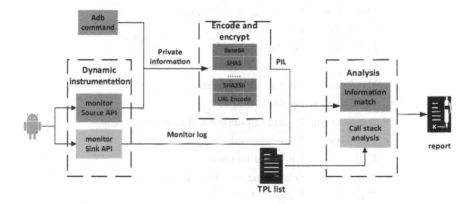

**Fig. 2.** Workflow of privacy leakage analysis

## 3.2   TPL Detection

**Collecting and Unpacking Apps.** We collect 10000 Apps from Androzoo [23], which contains millions of Apps from various App markets. Since Apps on Google play are more secure and popular, we mainly downloaded Google play Apps. After unpacking these Apps with apktool [24], we can analyze them from multiple aspects. Without source code, we need to analyze *smali* code or *dex* file. Generally, the *smali* code is more friendly for people to read. However, conversion to *smali* files is time-consuming, and the analysis of *smali* files is text analysis, which loses some structured information in binary, therefore we unpack Apps to get dex file.

**Feature Extraction.** In this section, we firstly categorize Android APIs into 15 categories according to the functions of the Android APIs, as shown in Table 1, then we parse *dex* files in an App and count the call frequency of each type of API in the App according to Algorithm 1. The call frequencies of these APIs rarely change in the process of obfuscation, and thus can represent the behaviors (or features) of TPLs in the App. As shown in Algorithm 1, we go through all *dex* files and *class* files to extract features. *AT* is a large array that maps an API to its API type in total 15 types, these types are represented by numbers from 0 to 14 respectively, thus the feature vector of each node is an array of length 15. We compute the feature vectors of child nodes in Java hierarchy tree and gradually update the feature vectors of their parent nodes. Finally, we integrate them and store them in the database. The total API list can be obtained from the Android Developer website [25].

**Table 1.** Classification of android APIs

| Type | Description |
| --- | --- |
| io | Write to and read file |
| Security | Security verification |
| Deviceinfo | Get IMEI, deviceId, etc. |
| Network | Related to network |
| Location | Get location |
| UI | UI and resource file |
| Hardware | Control of hardware |
| Multimedia | Radio, vedio, etc. |
| Application | Package manager and four components |
| Database | Manage database |
| Util | Universal method |
| System | Scheduling and Parallelization, etc. |
| Xml | Parse xml file |
| Time | Timezone, date, etc. |
| Datatype | Object of Int, String, json, etc. |

**Feature Clustering.** Common clustering algorithms include hierarchical clustering, center-based clustering, spectral clustering, etc. The center-based algorithm needs to determine the number of cluster centers in advance, which is unknown to us. Spectral clustering is used to deal with the division of nodes that are related to each other, but we regard each package as an individual node in our system, therefore this algorithm is not appropriate. Considering these facts, we adopt the hierarchical clustering method.

---

**Algorithm 1.** Extracting features from Dex files

---

**Require:**    $DF$: dex files; $AT$: The array that maps an API to its API type in total
    15 types.
**Ensure:**    $Dict$: features dictionary;
 1: dictionary initialize
 2: **for** each file in $DF$ **do**
 3:    Parse and construct dexfile object $O$
 4:    **for** each class $C$ in $O$ **do**
 5:        $C_f=[0]*15$
 6:        **for** each method in $C.methods$ **do**
 7:            $C_f[AT[method]]+=1$
 8:        **end for**
 9:        add $C_{name}$ and $C_f$ to $Dict$
10:        **while** $C$ is not root directory **do**
11:            $tmp = C$
12:            $C = C.parent$
13:            **if** $C$ in $Dict$ **then**
14:                $Dict[C]+ = Dict[tmp]$
15:            **else**
16:                $Dict[C] =Dict[tmp]$
17:            **end if**
18:        **end while**
19:    **end for**
20: **end for**

---

Android App code has a certain package structure, the obfuscation of identifier name will not affect the package structure, and the feature of one third-party library in different Apps are the same, for example, when *com.google.gson* is obfuscated into *com.a.b*, its feature value will not change. Even with dead code removal, the feature of TPL is similar within limits. Based on the above observations, we cluster the features at the same package structure level when implementing the feature cluster.

First, we read the feature vector from the feature database built in Sect. 3.2. There may be some features that are too small or simple, which can't represent a TPL. Considering the existence of these noise points, we filter the feature vector data to remove these invalid feature vectors. Then we normalize the feature vector data and use the Birch algorithm [26] to cluster these data. We only keep the clusters each of which has more sample points than a certain threshold. Finally, we build the map between a cluster label and a TPL according to package name that is not obfuscated in the cluster and persist the cluster model.

**TPL Detection.** After feature clustering, we get lots of potential third-party libraries in our cluster model. To detect TPLs in an App, we first extract its features and normalize the feature vector in the same way as Sect. 3.2. Then we conduct cluster prediction based on the models established in the clustering process. Our clustering model uses the hierarchical clustering strategy with a threshold, which means that the cluster prediction process performs fuzzy matching and is resistant to dead code removal. According to the map between labels and TPLs, we get a list of TPLs used in an App.

### 3.3 Privacy Leakage Analysis

**PIL Collection.** Compared with the user's personal information, the device information is fixed. We can use adb and instrumentation of the source APIs to obtain device-related information. Considering that an App may encrypt or encode the device information when transmitting it, we process acquired device information using common encoding and encryption algorithms, and finally, the processed information list (PIL) is obtained.

**Dynamic Instrumentation.** Sensitive APIs can be divided into source APIs and sink APIs as shown in Table 2. We record the return values of the source APIs called by an App and the parameters of the sink APIs as logs, and then collect the call stack information for subsequent analysis. We leverage dynamic instrumentation technique to monitor sensitive APIs as shown in Fig. 3. Specifically, dynamic instrumentation is composed of an Android device and a PC-side controller. The device is installed with frida server, a typical instrumentor for Android, and the PC-side controller is implemented as some scripts in JavaScript which are injected into the Android device. We use Monkey [27] to simulate a user's operations on the App. During the App's execution, the scripts record the running log for later analysis.

**Table 2.** Example source APIs and sink APIs

| Example | Type |
| --- | --- |
| android.location.LocationManager.getLastKnownLocation | Source |
| android.content.ClipboardManager.getPrimaryClip | Source |
| android.content.ContentResolver.query | Source |
| android.telephony.TelephonyManager.getDeviceId | Source |
| android.util.Log.i | Sink |
| okhttp3.OkHttpClient.newCall | Sink |
| android.telephony.SmsManager.sendDataMessage | Sink |
| android.util.LogPrinter.println | Sink |
| android.content.ClipboardManager.setPrimaryClip | Sink |

**Private Information Matching.** Private information can be divided into two categories: device information and user-specific personal information. The former includes deviceID, WifiInfo, etc., while the latter mainly includes user name, age, home address, etc. Part of the device information is fixed and can be obtained in advance, and another part of the information such as location information can

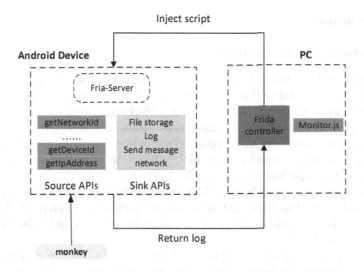

**Fig. 3.** Dynamic instrumentation

be obtained by instrumentation of the source APIs, this information is processed in Sect. 3.3 and we can get PIL. For logs of sink APIs, we match logs with PIL to determine whether there is private information flowing out of the sink APIs. For logs of source APIs, as long as source APIs are called, we define that the private information is matched but with low risk. Device information is generally a specific string, so it can be matched directly in the monitor log. For user-specific personal information, it is not fixed information but has a certain format, we can use regular expressions to match user-specific personal information.

**Call Stack Analysis.** Since our research object is third-party libraries in the Android App, we need to analyze the acquisition and transmission of private information by the third-party library. In the third-party library detection module, we can get a list of third-party libraries used in the application. The analysis of the call stack can help us know about the privacy leakage through the third-party library. As long as the privacy information is successfully matched, we will evaluate the privacy leakage risk of the third-party library by parsing the call stacks in logs of source APIs and sink APIs. In this paper, we divide the privacy leakage risk of third-party libraries into four levels according to the following rules:

- Level 0: No private information is matched;
- Level 1: Any TPL calls a source API directly or indirectly;
- Level 2: Any TPL indirectly calls a sink API, and any private information is matched in the API monitor log;
- Level 3: Any TPL directly calls a sink API, and any private information is matched in the API monitor log.

# 4    Evaluation

## 4.1    Dataset and Environment

To compare with state-of-the-art TPL detection tools, we get an App dataset from [28], which contains the ground truth of TPLs in Apps. The dataset consists of two parts: $Dataset_{ob}$ for evaluating obfuscation resistance capability and $Dataset_{per}$ for evaluating performance on precision and time cost. $Dataset_{ob}$ consists of Apps processed by Proguard and Dasho. However, the ground truth in the dataset only considers open-source TPL, we extend it to include closed-source TPLs and get a complete ground truth.

For privacy leakage analysis of TPL, there are no open-source tools for comparison and no widely used datasets, so we randomly selected 64 Apps from $Dataset_{per}$, these applications include categories of reading, video, shopping, image processing, etc.

The program runs on the ubuntu 18.04 operating system and the feature clustering algorithm is implemented with the scikit-learn toolkit. We use frida of version 15.1.14 for dynamic instrumentation. We wrote Libmonitor in python version 3.6.9.

## 4.2    TPL Detection

We compare our tool with two state-of-the-art clustering-based tools, i.e., Libradar and Libd. We do not consider those tools based on similarity comparison [13,14,16,32,33] because they can not detect closed-source TPLs. Both Libradar and LibD use the cluster-based approach to detect TPL, and we can get the profile database or source code of these two tools online. We design experiments to answer these questions:

**RQ1** How is Libmonitor's capability to resist obfuscation?
**RQ1** How does Libmonitor perform on detecting TPLs?
**RQ1** Is Libmonitor efficient compared to other tools?

**RQ1: How Is Libmonitor's Capability to Resist Obfuscation?** To evaluate the capability of resisting code obfuscation, we perform TPL detection on $Dataset_{ob}$ with 162 Apps, which are obfuscated respectively by Proguard and Dasho. We compare our tool with Libradar and Libd, and the statistical results are shown in Table 3. The results show that Libmonitor has best performance on F1 metrics for Apps obfuscated both by Dasho and Proguard, Libradar performs well for Proguard Apps, and Libd performs well for Dasho Apps.

We analyze the experimental results. On the one hand, different obfuscation tools have different effects on the results. Proguard generally employs identifier renaming while Dasho performs dead code removal and control flow randomization for Apps. Libradar requires an accurate comparison of hashes of API call frequencies and is sensitive to dead code removal. Libd needs to construct the control flow graph (CFG) to generate features, and thus is sensitive to control flow randomization caused by Dasho. Compared to exact matching detection methods or methods based on CFG, our clustering method uses fuzzy matching and thus performs better. On the other hand, since our method is based on clustering, dataset selection is important. Our clustering dataset contains a more updated version of Apps, so it has better detection results (Table 3).

**Table 3.** Experiment Result on $dataset_{ob}$

| Tool | Proguard | | | Dasho | | |
|------|----------|--------|--------|----------|--------|--------|
| | Precise | Recall | F1 | Precise | Recall | F1 |
| Libmonitor | 71.31% | 74.91% | 0.7307 | 91.50% | 63.76% | 0.7515 |
| Libradar | 94.08% | 58.19% | 0.7191 | 84.21% | 8.36% | 0.1521 |
| Libd | 54.06% | 61.50% | 0.5754 | 60.29% | 58.71% | 0.5949 |

**RQ2: How Does Libmonitor Perform on Detecting TPLs?** To measure the precision of third-party library detection for real-world applications, we use another dataset $dataset_{per}$ for evaluation, and the results can be seen in Table 4. Moreover, we extend the ground truth of the original dataset with 245 closed-source TPLs and count the experimental results of three tools respectively. The results show that Libmonitor outperforms other tools on F1 metrics when detecting closed-source TPLs. The F1 values of three tools are low according to original ground truth, because the clustering-based approach can detect many closed-source TPL, and the original ground truth doesn't consider about it. Libd hashes basic blocks and concatenates features, it can resist code obfuscation but doesn't perform well in restoring package names, so it causes many false positives. Compared with Libradar, our feature cluster process is based on the fuzzy match, hence feature vectors are easier to cluster and more clusters can be generated, so Libmonitor can detect more third-party libraries (Table 4).

**Table 4.** Experimental results on $Dataset_{per}$ and extended Dataset

| Tool | $Dataset_{per}$ | | | Extended Dataset | | |
|------|-----------------|--------|--------|------------------|--------|--------|
| | Precise | Recall | F1 | Precise | Recall | F1 |
| Libmonitor | 30.43% | 71.80% | 0.4275 | 79.07% | 83.98% | 0.8145 |
| Libradar | 37.77% | 50.74% | 0.4330 | 95.78% | 53.48% | 0.6864 |
| Libd | 9.52% | 8.70% | 0.0909 | 24.35% | 49.12% | 0.3256 |

**RQ3: Is Libmonitor Efficient Compared to Other Tools?** To evaluate the efficiency of Libmonitor, we run it and two baseline tools on $Dataset_{per}$ to compare their runtime cost. The experimental results are listed in Table 5. The performance of Libmonitor is significantly better than Libd, and slightly

weaker than Libradar. In order to represent the performance of these tools more intuitively, we plot their run time on top 40 Apps in Fig. 4. Obviously, Libmonitor and Libradar perform comparably while Libd is the most time-consuming.

**Table 5.** Run time on Dataset$_{per}$

| Tool | All | Average |
|------|-----|---------|
| Libmonitor | 6280.1 s | 28.9 s |
| Libradar | 5375.8 s | 24.8 s |
| Libd | 27477.0 s | 126.6 s |

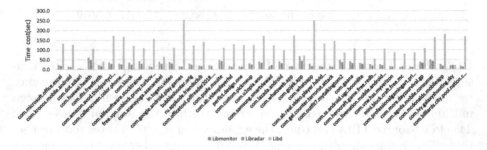

**Fig. 4.** Run time on top 40 apps in Dataset$_{per}$.

We explain the reasons behind the results as follows. First, Libd needs to build CFG and concatenates features of basic blocks, which is relatively time-consuming. Both Libradar and Libmonitor use the frequency of API calls as feature by parsing the dex files, and hence run quickly. Second, Libmonitor divides Android's APIs into more fine-grained types than ones in Libradar, causing slightly more run time.

### 4.3   Privacy Leakage Analysis

We use dynamic instrumentation technique to monitor sensitive APIs, then we perform information match and call stack analysis. Finally, we generate privacy leakage analysis reports for third-party libraries. We perform privacy leakage analysis on 64 Apps and obtain the following experimental results.

**Case Studies.** Some Apps may leak private information through interfaces other than the network interface. For instance, as shown in Fig. 5, *Cartola* App prints Advertiser_ID information through logcat interface. Besides, we found a serious security threat: *DoorDash* App transmits the passwords and email of users in plain text, which means that one can see users' password and email through logcat, as indicated in Fig. 6, where we hide some user data such as mobile phone and email. The App developers should take care of these behaviors when using TPLs.

{'method': "android.util.Log.v.overload('java.lang.String', 'java.lang.String')", 'srctype': 'Advertiser_ID', 'srcval': 'b5db678b-ab72-4a9f-973c-a6e7202679c5', 'formatch': 'Sending hit to service PATH: https: PARAMS: cd=Parciais_dos_times, a=2094971135, ht=1647671318431, an=Cartola FC, tid=UA-20936277-33, cd2=, cd1=, uid=, adid=b5db678b-ab72-4a9f-973c-a6e7202679c5, ate=1, t=appview, av=4.5.0, v=1, _u=.4nL, ul=zh-cn, aid=br.com.mobits.cartolafc, sr=1440x2392, cid=decef45a-96e6-4824-97f7-0827ed785d36, '}

**Fig. 5.** Case study: privacy leakage analysis on Cartola App.

{'method': "android.util.Log.d.overload('java.lang.String', 'java.lang.String')", 'srctype': 'email_pt', 'srcval': 'xxxxxxxxxxxxxxxxxxxxxx', 'formatch': '{"last_name":"nickname","phone_number":"xxxxxxxxxxx", "password":"0123456789","first_name":"test"," email":"xxxxxxxxxxxxxxxxxxxxxx"}'}

**Fig. 6.** Case study: privacy leakage analysis on DoorDash App.

**Experimental Results.** We define a piece of privacy leakage data that one TPL participates in as a privacy leak risk. For example, if a privacy leakage behavior involves two different TPLs, we will judge it as two privacy leakage risks. Libmonitor found 5809 pieces of privacy leakage risks caused by 152 TPLs in 64 applications, and the risks in level 1 to level 3 are 3118, 797 and 1894 respectively. Generally, private information is not necessarily leaked after obtained through source APIs, and may be used as user profile, so source APIs are called more frequently, i.e., risks in level 1 are the most. Risks of level 2 and level 3 represent privacy leakage through sink APIs called indirectly and directly by TPLs, respectively. Therefore, 46.3% of found risks involves privacy leakage caused by TPLs.

We count third-party libraries with more leakage risks, and record the types of private information that are leaked more frequently, as shown in Table 6 and Table 7. TPL will participate in the leakage of private information. It can be seen from the experimental results that *com.google.android.gms* has the most risks of privacy leakage, and AdvertiserID is the most easily leaked type of private information. Most of the applications in the dataset integrate Google's advertising service, so AdvertiserID is easy to be leaked. Most Apps on Google play rely on google mobile service(gms), so *com.google.android.gms* is used frequently.

**Table 6.** Top 10 privacy leaked by 152 TPLs

| Info. type | Freq. |
|---|---|
| AdvertiserID | 1163 |
| BuildNumber | 342 |
| DeviceType | 323 |
| Country | 280 |
| Date of birth | 99 |
| Timezone | 81 |
| AndroidID | 44 |
| Email | 34 |
| Uid | 14 |
| Kernel version | 12 |

**Table 7.** Top 10 TPLs leaking privacy

| PkgName | L1 | L2 | L3 | Total |
|---|---|---|---|---|
| com.google.android.gms | 1064 | 26 | 365 | 1455 |
| com.mopub | 93 | 269 | 341 | 703 |
| com.ironsource | 7 | 0 | 599 | 606 |
| com.google.firebase | 71 | 310 | 179 | 560 |
| io.fabric.sdk.android | 246 | 11 | 22 | 279 |
| com.facebook | 102 | 11 | 150 | 263 |
| com.crashlytics.android | 252 | 0 | 0 | 252 |
| com.applovin | 144 | 2 | 6 | 152 |
| com.unity3d | 23 | 61 | 58 | 142 |
| com.free.ads | 108 | 0 | 0 | 108 |

We counted the frequency of source APIs and sink APIs called in these privacy leakage risks, as shown in Table 9 and Table 8. As for sink APIs, APIs in *android.util.Log* are the interface of logcat whose call frequency is 328. Others are the interface of network whose call frequency is 3490. The proportion of logcat interface is 8.6%, which is ignored in [20,21], because they just collect network traffic information. In addition, there are SMS and clipboard interfaces. We did not find calls of these two types of interfaces in this experiment. As to source APIs, *android.provider.Settings$Secure.getString* is accessed by most TPLs, because androidID is a unique identifier which can be accessed easily without permission. Besides, *android.content.ContentResolver.query* is accessed frequently to query GSFID, image and vedio. Apps that integrate the Google framework are likely to access GSFID, while images and videos usually are accessed by multimedia related Apps.

**Table 8.** Top 10 sink APIs

| API | type | frequency |
|---|---|---|
| java.net.URL.$init.overload[2] | Network | 1336 |
| java.net.URL.$init.overload[0] | Network | 1315 |
| com.android.okhttp.internal.huc.HttpsURLConnection-Impl.setRequestProperty | Network | 742 |
| android.util.Log.i.overload[0] | Logcat | 219 |
| android.util.Log.d.overload[0] | Logcat | 89 |
| okhttp3.RequestBody.create.overload[2] | Network | 71 |
| android.util.Log.v.overload[0] | Logcat | 20 |
| okhttp3.RequestBody.create.overload[1] | Network | 12 |
| java.net.URL.$init.overload[5] | Network | 10 |
| org.apache.http.client.methods.HttpGet.$init.overload[0] | Network | 4 |

**Table 9.** Top 10 source APIs

| API | Frequency |
|---|---|
| android.provider.Settings$Secure.getString | 2589 |
| android.content.ContentResolver.query%GSFID | 572 |
| android.hardware.SensorManager.getDefaultSensor | 417 |
| android.content.ClipboardManager.getPrimaryClip | 97 |
| android.net.wifi.WifiInfo.getMacAddress | 86 |
| android.os.BatteryManager.getIntProperty | 84 |
| android.location.LocationManager.getLastKnownLocation | 49 |
| android.net.wifi.WifiInfo.getIpAddress | 27 |
| android.content.ContentResolver.query%image | 16 |
| android.content.ContentResolver.query%video | 16 |

# 5   Discussion

Libmonitor has limitations. First, Libmonitor can also detect open-source TPLs but it cannot accurately identify the specific version of each TPL. As a future work, we will combine clustering method and similarity comparison method to address this issue. Second, our approach to analyze privacy leakage cannot obtain complete data flow from source to sink, which needs to be improved in future work.

# 6   Related Work

## 6.1   Third-Party Library Detection

On third-party library detection, some prior studies use the simplest whitelist method. For example, Liu et al. [12] collected a whitelist of 400 SDKs to analyze the privacy leakage of third-party libraries and classified them according to the functions of the third-party libraries. The whitelist-based method generally requires manual collection and needs to be continuously updated as new third-party libraries appear. In addition, the code obfuscation in Android applications makes this method invalid.

Other research efforts perform feature extraction on Android applications and detect third-party libraries through similarity comparison. LibScout [16] uses class hierarchy analysis to construct a Merkle tree with a fixed depth of 3 as the configuration file of each library and proposes a matching algorithm to calculate the similarity with collected libraries. They collected 800 libraries (9623 versions in total) and constituted a tangible database to ensure accurate detection results. OSSPolice [29] uses normalized signatures and function centroids [30] as features, then uses a hierarchical indexing scheme to compare the similarity between the feature files and the tens of thousands of source files in the benchmark database. When analyzing the library version, OSSPolice uses the software birthmark [31]to accurately detect OSS versions. According to the identified third-party SDK version, OSSPolice reports the third-party SDK version that contains security vulnerabilities or violates the open-source agreement. OSSPolice has also built a third-party SDK whitelist, which contains 110 Java libraries authorized under GPL and AGPL terms.

ATVHUNTER [33] conducts candidate TPL decoupling by class dependency and uses features of two granularities for TPL matching, the coarse-grain feature is serial numbers assigned in the control flow graph, and the fine-grained feature is the hash of opcode in the basic block. ATVHUNTER builds a TPL database and can detect the version of the TPL. LibID [13] has two library identification schemes, designed for scalability and accuracy, respectively named LibID-S, LIbID-A. LibID-S uses textual representation in basic blocks as the feature, LidID-A makes use of class dependency to get accurate matching of the TPL version, besides, LibID uses LSH and minihash to speed up class matching. These similarity-based tools require building TPL profile in advance and can't detect closed-source TPLs.

## 6.2 Privacy Leakage Analysis

FlowDroid [34] is a static taint tracking system based on Soot, which simulates the complete Android application life cycle, and expresses the control flow call relationship between the Activity life cycle and all callback functions as a control flow graph(CFG). FlowDroid uses CFG to track the sensitive data flow from the source point to the sink point, but FlowDroid cannot analyze data flow of inter-component communication and uses static analysis which is prone to false positives. Enck et al. modified the source code of the Android system and designed the dynamic taint tracking system TaintDroid [18]. By modifying the Dalvik VM interpreter, the corresponding taint label was added to the private data, and four levels of taint were defined. TaintDroid provides logs to record private information behaviors and sends messages in the notification bar to warn users of privacy leakage. However, TaintDroid only implements data flow tracking but does not analyze control flow and native methods. Taintman [19] performs static instrumentation on target Apps and system libraries, and uses taint analysis technique to track data flow and control flow. In addition, Taintman uses an execution environment reconstruction technology called reference hijacking, which allows the target application to reference and modify the system library, so it can run on Android devices without root privilege. However, Taintdroid and Taintman need to modify system code, which is inconvenient for migration and adaptation.

## 7    Conclusion

In this paper, we present a novel approach to detect third-party libraries (TPLs) in Android Apps and analyze potential privacy leakage in TPLs. We implement a tool named Libmonitor. It leverages the call frequencies of different types of APIs as features and uses fuzzy match strategy when performing the clustering algorithm, and thus works well on obfuscated TPLs.

Experimental results of TPL detection show that Libmonitor outperforms two state-of-the-art TPL detection tools (i.e., Libradar and LibD) on two datasets. Besides, Libmonitor found 5809 pieces of privacy leakage risks caused by 152 TPLs in 64 real-world Apps.

# References

1. IDC. Smartphone Market Share. https://www.idc.com/promo/smartphone-market-share/os
2. Lin, J., Liu, B., Sadeh, N., et al.: Modeling users mobile app privacy preferences: restoring usability in a sea of permission settings. In: Proceeding SOUPS 2014 Proceedings of the Tenth USENIX Conference on Usable Privacy and Security, vol. 199 (2014)
3. Wang, H., Guo, Y., Ma, Z., Chen, X.: WuKong: a scalable and accurate two-phase approach to Android app clone detection. In: Proceedings of the 2015 International Symposium on Software Testing and Analysis, pp. 71–82. ACM, Baltimore (2015).https://doi.org/10.1145/2771783.2771795
4. Slowmist Knowledge-Base. https://github.com/slowmist/Knowledge-Base/blob/master/tradingview-xss-vul.md
5. Wu, D., Gao, D., Chang, R.K.C., He, E., Cheng, E.K.T., Deng, R.H.: Understanding open ports in android applications: discovery, diagnosis, and security assessment. In: Proceedings 2019 Network and Distributed System Security Symposium. Internet Society, San Diego (2019). https://doi.org/10.14722/ndss.2019.23171
6. Almanee, S., Unal, A., Payer, M., Garcia, J.: Too quiet in the library: an empirical study of security updates in android apps' native code. In: 2021 IEEE/ACM 43rd International Conference on Software Engineering (ICSE), pp. 1347–1359. IEEE, Madrid (2021). https://doi.org/10.1109/ICSE43902.2021.00122
7. Reardon, J., Feal, Á., Wijesekera, P.: 50 ways to leak your data: an exploration of apps' circumvention of the android permissions system, vol. 19 (2019)
8. Mobile application (App) data security and personal information protection white paper. http://www.caict.ac.cn/kxyj/qwfb/bps/201912/P020191230332039577332.pdf
9. Maven Repository. https://mvnrepository.com/
10. GitHub: Where the world builds software. https://github.com/
11. Lin, J., Sadeh, N., Amini, S., Lindqvist, J., Hong, J.I., Zhang, J.: Expectation and purpose: understanding users' mental models of mobile app privacy through crowdsourcing. In: Proceedings of the 2012 ACM Conference on Ubiquitous Computing - UbiComp 2012, p. 501. ACM Press, Pittsburgh (2012). https://doi.org/10.1145/2370216.2370290
12. Liu, B., Liu, B., Jin, H., Govindan, R.: Efficient privilege de-escalation for ad libraries in mobile apps. In: Proceedings of the 13th Annual International Conference on Mobile Systems, Applications, and Services, pp. 89–103. ACM, Florence (2015). https://doi.org/10.1145/2742647.2742668
13. Zhang, J., Beresford, A.R., Kollmann, S.A.: LibID: reliable identification of obfuscated third-party Android libraries. In: Proceedings of the 28th ACM SIGSOFT International Symposium on Software Testing and Analysis, pp. 55–65. ACM, Beijing (2019). https://doi.org/10.1145/3293882.3330563

14. Wang, Y., Wu, H., Zhang, H., Rountev, A.: ORLIS: obfuscation-resilient library detection for Android. In: Proceedings of the 5th International Conference on Mobile Software Engineering and Systems - MOBILESoft 2018, pp. 13–23. ACM Press, Gothenburg (2018). https://doi.org/10.1145/3197231.3197248

15. Ma, Z., Wang, H., Guo, Y., Chen, X.: LibRadar: of third-party libraries in Android apps. In: Proceedings of the 38th International Conference on Software Engineering Companion - ICSE 2016, pp. 653–656. ACM Press, Austin (2016). https://doi.org/10.1145/2889160.2889178

16. Backes, M., Bugiel, S., Derr, E.: Reliable third-party library detection in android and its security applications. In: Proceedings of the 2016 ACM SIGSAC Conference on Computer and Communications Security - CCS 2016, pp. 356–367. ACM Press, Vienna (2016). https://doi.org/10.1145/2976749.2978333

17. Li, M., et al.: LibD: scalable and precise third-party library detection in android markets. In: 2017 IEEE/ACM 39th International Conference on Software Engineering (ICSE), pp. 335–346 (2017). https://doi.org/10.1109/ICSE.2017.38

18. Enck, W., et al.: TaintDroid: an information flow tracking system for real-time privacy monitoring on smartphones. Commun. ACM. **57**, 99–106 . https://doi.org/10.1145/2494522

19. You, W., Liang, B., Shi, W., Wang, P., Zhang, X.: TaintMan: an ART-compatible dynamic taint analysis framework on unmodified and non-rooted android devices. IEEE Trans. Depend. Secure Comput. **17**, 209–222 (2020). https://doi.org/10.1109/TDSC.2017.2740169

20. He, Y., Yang, X., Hu, B., Wang, W.: Dynamic privacy leakage analysis of Android third-party libraries. J. Inf. Secur. Appl. **46**, 259–270 (2019). https://doi.org/10.1016/j.jisa.2019.03.014

21. Wongwiwatchai, N., Pongkham, P., Sripanidkulchai, K.: Comprehensive detection of vulnerable personal information leaks in android applications. In: IEEE INFOCOM 2020 - IEEE Conference on Computer Communications Workshops (INFOCOM WKSHPS), pp. 121–126. IEEE, Toronto (2020). https://doi.org/10.1109/INFOCOMWKSHPS50562.2020.9163043

22. Dong, S., et al.: Understanding android obfuscation techniques: a large-scale investigation in the wild. In: Beyah, R., Chang, B., Li, Y., Zhu, S. (eds.) SecureComm 2018. LNICST, vol. 254, pp. 172–192. Springer, Cham (2018). https://doi.org/10.1007/978-3-030-01701-9_10

23. Allix, K., Bissyandé, T.F., Klein, J., Le Traon, Y.: AndroZoo: collecting millions of Android apps for the research community. In: Proceedings of the 13th International Conference on Mining Software Repositories, pp. 468–471. ACM, Austin (2016). https://doi.org/10.1145/2901739.2903508

24. A tool for reverse engineering Android apk files. https://ibotpeaches.github.io/Apktool/

25. Android Developer. https://developer.android.com/reference/packages

26. Zhang, T., Ramakrishnan, R., Livny, M.: BIRCH: an efficient data clustering method for very large databases. SIGMOD Rec. **25**, 103–114 (1996). https://doi.org/10.1145/235968.233324

27. Monkey. https://developer.android.com/studio/test/monkey

28. Zhan, X., et al.: Automated third-party library detection for Android applications: are we there yet? In: Proceedings of the 35th IEEE/ACM International Conference on Automated Software Engineering, pp. 919–930. ACM, Virtual Event Australia (2020). https://doi.org/10.1145/3324884.3416582

29. Duan, R., Bijlani, A., Xu, M., Kim, T., Lee, W.: Identifying open-source license violation and 1-day security risk at large scale. In: Proceedings of the 2017 ACM SIGSAC Conference on Computer and Communications Security, pp. 2169–2185. ACM, Dallas (2017). https://doi.org/10.1145/3133956.3134048

30. Chen, K., Liu, P., Zhang, Y.: Achieving accuracy and scalability simultaneously in detecting application clones on Android markets. In: Proceedings of the 36th International Conference on Software Engineering - ICSE 2014, pp. 175–186. ACM Press, Hyderabad (2014). https://doi.org/10.1145/2568225.2568286

31. The protection of computer software - Its technology and applications: edited by Derrick Grover, 2nd Edition, 1992 (British Computer Society Monographs in Informatics - Cambridge University Press, Softcover), 307pp, £17.95 (US $32.95), ISBN 0-521-42462-3. Computer Law & Security Review. 8, 204 (1992). https://doi.org/10.1016/0267-3649(92)90069-L

32. Zhang, Y., et al.: Detecting third-party libraries in Android applications with high precision and recall. In: 2018 IEEE 25th International Conference on Software Analysis, Evolution and Reengineering (SANER), pp. 141–152. IEEE, Campobasso (2018). https://doi.org/10.1109/SANER.2018.8330204

33. Zhan, X., et al.: ATVHunter: reliable version detection of third-party libraries for vulnerability identification in android applications. In: ICSE (2021)

34. Arzt, S., et al.: FlowDroid: precise context, flow, field, object-sensitive and lifecycle-aware taint analysis for Android apps. In: Proceedings of the 35th ACM SIGPLAN Conference on Programming Language Design and Implementation - PLDI 2014, pp. 259–269. ACM Press, Edinburgh (2013). https://doi.org/10.1145/2594291.2594299

# Secure CV2X Using COTS Smartphones over LTE Infrastructure

Spandan Mahadevegowda[1]([✉]), Ryan Gerdes[1], Thidapat Chantem[1],
and Rose Qingyang Hu[2]

[1] Virginia Tech, Arlington, VA, USA
{spandan,rgerdes,tchantem}@vt.edu
[2] Utah State University, Logan, UT, USA
rose.hu@usu.edu

**Abstract.** With the proliferation of vehicle technologies to support sophisticated features like assisted and autonomous driving, advanced communication protocols like cellular-vehicle-to-everything (CV2X) have been proposed. However, practical large-scale deployments have been hindered due to caveats such as hardware, security, and cellular infrastructure demands. This work presents and evaluates a practical approach to utilizing ARM TrustZone to turn commercial off-the-shelf smartphones into secure CV2X radios that communicate over the LTE network. These smartphone-based CV2x radios communicate with each other via an intermediary server placed outside/within the LTE infrastructure without affecting normal operations of the phone, like using navigation, calls, and music. Vehicle owners would only have to install the CV2X application to use their smartphones as CV2X radios. The approach would boost the adoption of CV2X by reducing the requirement for dedicated hardware and reusing existing infrastructure. In this work, we empirically evaluate the on-device overhead coupled with various network topologies concerning the location of an intermediary server and the LTE infrastructure. We show that our proposed approach can meet the required real-time constraints for safe CV2X operation while ensuring the integrity of the on-device communication from manipulation by remote attackers.

**Keywords:** CV2X · COTS devices · LTE · Secure communication · TEE · Trustzone

## 1 Introduction

With the advancements in communication and processing technologies, modern vehicles and traffic infrastructure have become smarter, providing improved safety, security, and overall commuting experience. Today, we have automated

This work was supported by the National Science Foundation (NSF) under grant numbers 2038726 and 1941524.

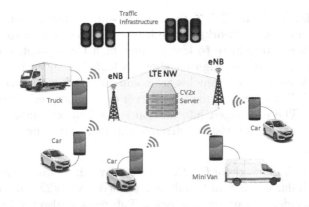

**Fig. 1.** Secure COTS based CV2X overview

driver assistance, cruise control, pedestrian detection, etc., that can save lives and increase commuter comfort while decreasing commute time. However, establishing connectivity among vehicles and the infrastructure is essential to enable the large-scale integration of such data-driven technologies. Features such as over-the-air updates and diagnostics of vehicle software have only been made possible from such connectivity [1]. One widely explored and investigated solution is the cellular vehicle to everything (CV2X) framework, which uses a high-speed cellular network to interconnect vehicles and traffic infrastructure. However, this has caveats. Enabling CV2X would mean significant investment in developing dedicated software and hardware. Moreover, it would require tedious integration of cellular modules into deployed vehicles or even mean waiting to replace older vehicles with new models. Additionally, enabling such complex communication means the exposure of vehicles to malicious entities. Research has already shown possible attacks and issues on vehicles made by Tesla with wireless/cellular connectivity that can threaten passenger safety and security [2,3].

Also, installing dedicated CV2X radios by vehicle manufacturers will likely require government mandates. Opportunely, modern-day smartphones that possess advanced processing power are ubiquitous. Moreover, these smartphones also come equipped with software and hardware techniques to provide secure data processing and privacy. For example, watching licensed media on Netflix, or securely storing/using fingerprints to perform financial transactions, utilizes said underlying software or hardware security mechanisms, such as TrustZone, a trusted execution environment on ARM-based processors [4]. Given how ubiquitous smartphones are, we could leverage smartphones instead of dedicated cellular modules to securely tether vehicles to the CV2X framework. The smartphone's universal serial bus (USB) port can be connected to the vehicle's on board diagnostics (OBD/OBD-II)port [5] with a dongle.

Vehicle owners would only need to install a secure application on their smartphones to use them as a CV2X radio while not significantly impacting the performance of other applications like navigation or music. However, since these cellular devices do not inherently support CV2X protocols and frameworks, we need to provide external servers that will behave as intermediaries to connect these smartphones to the CV2X framework. Furthermore, connecting cellular devices on commercial networks through intermediary servers to enable CV2X protocol still needs to adhere to low latency, high throughput, etc., for safety-critical CV2X applications. Figure 1 shows a high level overview of the framework. Smartphone tethered vehicles are communicating with each other for the purpose of CV2X via the intermediary server on the long term evolution (LTE) infrastructure. The exchanged information is used to communicate commands or data to the vehicles for assisted driving, warnings, etc. Therefore, our contributions are:

- We provide a framework for CV2X connectivity using commercial-off-the-shelf (COTS) cellular devices and analyze intermediary CV2X server on LTE/4G network considering various topologies. This work is also the first attempt to establish secure CV2X connectivity using COTS cellular devices to the best of our knowledge.
- We provide a secure framework using ARM TrustZone to mitigate security vulnerabilities such as replay and denial of service (DoS) attacks on the COTS devices running the CV2X application.
- We study and evaluate various network topologies by placing the CV2X server in various locations within the cellular infrastructure to ensure the real-time deployability of our approach.
- We evaluate and provide quantitative measurements for the overheads and latency incurred in the framework. Consequently, we analyze and discuss the feasibility of using COTS devices for CV2X.

## 2   Related Work

The objective of our work is provide a secure framework for CV2X using ARM TrustZone, a trusted execution environment (TEE) while analyzing the feasibility of using LTE as the underlying cellular network. Considerable work on using trusted execution can be found in literature. Similarly work on analysis and evaluating LTE for CV2X has been pursued for sometime. However, since our work looks at an intersection of both these research objectives, we discuss some relevant literature with overlap of such technologies. The use of trusted execution environment for real-time network use cases in internet of things has been studied in [6]. The authors discuss and evaluate how TrustZone can be used to meet IOT real-time requirements while ensuring security, specifically in the case of connected industrial systems. [7] discusses enhancing mobile application security using TEE with user services identity module (USIM) to provide secure billing and payment services. Ali Raza discusses the use of TEE on COTS devices used by public safety officers to secure mission critical services for public safety over private and commercial LTE networks in the work [8]. To enhance privacy and enable private conversations on mobile devices, Amit Ahlawat and Wenliang Du propose and evaluate a TrustZone based secure voice over internet protocol (VoIP) application in [9].

Given, the real-time demands of the CV2X applications, it is essential to study latency, packet drop and throughput of the network extensively. Sheng

Liu et al. provide an empirical study of LTE-4G based CV2X performance in [10]. The authors also study the performance of dedicated short range communication (DSRC), another vehicle-to-vehicle communication protocol and compare the two frameworks. [11] evaluates and studies the use of 4G LTE network for IoT applications with real-time latency demands less than 100ms. The paper discusses the feasibility of using LTE for such applications with fixed packet sized transmission. [12] discusses the latency radio access network bottle neck issue in the LTE network for V2X applications and evaluate the performance for latency critical use cases. [13] describes a study to measure the possibility of automated driving using V2X connectivity with 4G-LTE. The authors use certain assumption to restrict the physical proximity of the LTE subsytems and evaluate a real-world vehicle setup suggesting that V2X applications are possible with LTE under certain conditions.

While these prior works consider dedicated and trusted hardware, our approach tries to utilize smartphones connected to vehicles in lieu of such hardware, aiding in the acceleration of adopting and using CV2X. Additionally, our work tries to analyze and compare various network topologies with our COTS based CV2X device deployed on the same.

## 3    Preliminaries

This section provides an overview of the underlying technologies, ARM Trustzone, LTE Architectural Overview, and Open Portable Trusted Execution Environment (OP-TEE). We also include details on external constraints. For brevity, we only highlight the components relevant to this work, readers can refer to the cited work for more details.

**ARM Trustzone:** ARM Trustzone [14] is a hardware extension on ARM Cortex devices that provides a platform for creating and executing trusted execution environments via software. The extension divides the processor execution into secure and non-secure domains. The secure domain has access to the information and peripherals of both domains. In contrast, the non-secure domain can only access its data, code, and peripherals. Software or hardware modules within the secure extension like secure memory controller (SMC) and secure peripheral controller (SPC) control the access permissions. In the case of Cortex-A devices, ARM provides a default secure monitor called the ARM Trusted-Firmware (ARM TF) that acts as an intermediary to securely switch between the domains, preventing information leaks and unauthorized access. Whenever the non-secure domain wants to process critical data or a secure interrupt gets raised, the ARM TF discerns the call and routes it to the secure domain after handling the relevant context switches. Similarly, the ARM TF also handles the switching back to the non-secure domain.

**Open Portable Trusted Execution Environment (OP-TEE):** OP-TEE [15] is an open-source implementation of TEE that follows the GlobalPlatform Trusted Execution Environment specifications [16]. It consists of a secure kernel with a range of cryptographic libraries that accepts requests from the non-secure domain via a secure monitor to perform cryptographic operations and process critical data.

**Long-Term Evolution (LTE):** LTE [17] is the 4th generation of the universal terrestrial radio access network (UTRAN). The main components of the LTE infrastructure are the cellular devices or user devices(UE) like smartphones, radio access network (RAN), Evolved UTRAN Node (eNB), and the Evolved Packet Core (EPC). The UEs connect to the eNB at a given locality over RAN. The eNB schedules and controls the access of the UE connections and resources. Multiple eNBs connect to the EPC via dedicated interfaces specified by 3rd Generation Partnership Project (3GPP). The EPC is primarily composed of four components, (i) the Mobility Management Entity (MME), (ii) Home Subscriber Server (HSS), (iii)Serving Gateway (SGW), and (iv) Packet Gateway (PGW). MME and HSS are responsible for the user control signaling that authorizes and collects billing data, handles authorization and identification of users. The latter two components, SGW and PGW are the packets switching components that connect the UEs across networks or the internet for calls/data.

**Latency Requirements:** Many CV2X applications such as driver assistance, auotmated braking, etc. are safety critical in nature. Therefore, we have explicit latency requirements for exchanging information. European Telecommunications Standards Institute (ETSI) and U.S Department of Transportation (DOT) have analyzed various traffic and vehicle scenarios and laid out latency demands corresponding for the same [18]. These latency requirements are based on the scenario for vehicular applications. For example, a 100 ms latency is required for periodic vehicle-2-vehicle/pedestrian/infrastructure applications such as emergency electronic brake, stop sign assistance, lane change assistance, etc. Similarly, 1000 ms latency is mandated for vehicle-2-infrastructure warnings, while pre-crash sensing applications have a requirement of 20 ms. In order to cover majority of the scenarios and establish a basic CV2X framework, we set our latency constraint for 100 ms.

**Basic Safety Messages (BSMs):** BSM is a standardized messaging specification developed for V2X applications. Originally standardized as an ASN.1 encoded message in the SAE J2735 [19] specification, it carries information related to vehicle position, speed, direction and other safety extension data. In our work, we restrict the payload to carry only the position, speed and some vehicle information primarily obtained using a GPS [20,21] module. However we refer to this payload as BSM in the rest of the paper and it has an average size of 67 bytes.

## 4    System and Threat Models

The smartphones/user equipment (UE) capabilities and architecture considered for our CV2X framework, as well as attacker capabilities are discussed.

### 4.1    System Model

**UE and Vehicles.** The UE is an ARM Cortex-A device with TrustZone hardware extension and secure timers. It houses an LTE modem and a GPS module with typical cell phone peripherals. The TrustZone extension divides the processing/OS (Fig. 2) into secure (red) and non-secure domains (green). The device also has secure hardware extensions to control and configure access rights to peripherals and memory like the Secure Peripheral and Secure Memory Controllers.

Here, we perform the required cryptographic and secure processing using trusted applications and return relevant data to the non-secure world.

Finally, we expect that the drivers and/or the passengers connect their smartphones with the vehicle via the OBD-II port. Please note that from here on, we refer to smartphones and cellular devices as UEs. Vehicles tethered to the CV2X network via the UEs are referred to as UE enabled vehicles.

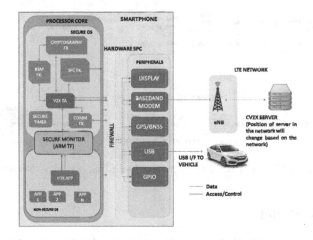

**Fig. 2.** Architectural overview of the UE with secure CV2X application

**LTE Network and Server.** There has been considerable research on using Device to Device (D2D) and dedicated side channel PC5 [22,23] for V2X communication on the LTE network. However, D2D and PC5 solutions require additional hardware provisions, which are not guaranteed to be available on LTE modules of smartphones. Therefore, to support majority of smartphones, we instead deploy a CV2X server facilitating the connection of various UE-enabled vehicles. The server after receiving BSMs from UEs, filters relevant BSMs based on GPS proximity and positional data within the BSM. These filtered BSMs are sent as response to relevant UEs. Given the latency constraint of the CV2X safety-critical applications, we assume that the server is equipped with sufficient processing capabilities and can communicate at the required bandwidths with negligible overheads in data transmission.

For the LTE network, we consider the most common setup of the commercially available 3GPP standardized architecture [17]. We do not delve into the specifics of the LTE network itself, given its vast expanse of intricacies and technicality. Instead, we look at the LTE at the network level, which suffices for the most part of our work. UEs attach to the eNB over RAN, and multiple eNBs connect to the EPC. Though the eNBs are interconnected over the X2 interface for handovers of moving UEs, we currently ignore this to simplify analysis. Data packets for general applications or calls on the UE take the traditional user data plane to connect to the internet or other UEs over the SPGW. Data/BSMs to and from the secure CV2X application can either follow the traditional path or modified paths depending on the position of the CV2X server within the LTE network. The four potential locations for the CV2X server would be (i) on the internet, (ii) at the end of the EPC, (iii) as a part of the EPC, and (iv) at the end of eNB as an edge computing server. We analyze the above network topologies in detail in Sects. 6 and 7, for ease of deployability and latency.

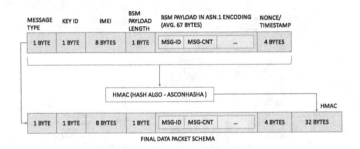

**Fig. 3.** Modified BSM data packet including security overhead

## 4.2 Threat Model

We consider an attacker that can access the smartphone remotely on the non-secure domain to gain complete access and control of the UE connected to the external world via internet or wireless interfaces. Since the attacker has complete control of the non-secure kernel, they have complete access to the LTE modem and the GPS module. Therefore, the attacker can read, modify and delete their respective data. Thus, the attacker can either corrupt/replay data or launch denial of service (DoS) attacks on the modem and GPS modules.

It is assumed that the attacker does not have physical access to the system. Any attack that requires physical access is considered out-of-scope for this work. Also, we assume that the integrity of the ARM Trustzone and OPTEE cannot be compromised. We consider that the CV2X application is installed in a secure environment and not manipulated before the installation, ensuring the integrity of the secure domain application. In this work, we also assume that the attacker is not capable of modifying user input by taking control of user interfaces such as physical buttons/touchscreen. However, this is a minor limitation and can be addressed as discussed in Sect. 5.4

## 5   Secure CV2X Framework

We now discuss the architecture, functionality and application flow of our Secure CV2X framework on COTS UE. Our approach considers both regular and attacker controlled (see threat model in Sect. 4.2) scenarios.

### 5.1   Secure CV2X Architecture

Our approach deploys a CV2X framework using UEs tethered to the vehicle over the OBD-II port. Commands or data for the vehicle are transmitted based on the exchanged location, speed, and direction information with nearby vehicles and infrastructure.

Recall from Sect. 3 that such information exchange requires very low latency. Inability to meet these demands, for example, not exchanging BSMs in a timely manner with nearby vehicles when performing maneuvers such as lane changes, may threaten passenger safety. Additionally, attackers may manipulate data and inject delays to enforce hazardous operating conditions. Therefore, to

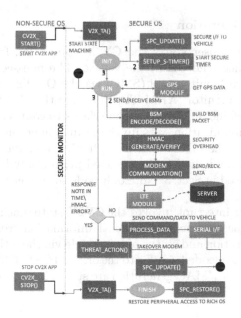

**Fig. 4.** Secure CV2X framework application flow

enable secure and low overhead BSM exchange, our CV2X application (Fig. 2) is deployed within the secure domain of the vehicle owner's TrustZone equipped UE. Our framework consists of a trusted application (CV2X TA) that sets up the CV2X state machine for periodically exchanging BSMs with other vehicles. The secure OS, OP-TEE, is modified to support the CV2X TA. The changes include the ability to encode and decode the ASN.1 BSM specification, support cryptography operations for encryption and hashing, modifying the SPC to control access to peripherals, drivers to utilize the LTE and GPS modems, and secure timer interrupt configuration to periodically trigger BSM exchanges.

Before we delve into how the CV2X TA operates, we first discuss the modifications required to the BSM data packet.

## 5.2    Modified BSM Data Packet

Figure 3 shows a modified BSM data packet with security overhead. Important additions include the following fields: a) "Message Type" to identify type based on the SAE J2735 specification [19], b) "Key ID" to allow us to identify rotated keys (to prevent brute-force key extraction) for HMAC [24] computation, c) "IMEI" that allows the CV2X server to identify individual UEs communicating with it without needing to perform an expensive lookup via the Home Subscriber System (HSS), d) "Payload Length" to support BSM packet compression by dropping unused bytes, and e) nonce that consists of a truncated timestamp and ascon-hash-a [25] based HMAC generated from the payload to validate integrity of data.

## 5.3    CV2X TA Operation

As seen in Fig. 4, the user starts the CV2X application from the non-secure OS, after they connect the UE to the vehicle. The non-secure CV2X application invokes a Secure Monitor Call (SMC) via the OP-TEE kernel driver which instructs the secure monitor, ARM TF, to invoke the CV2X TA. This sets up the CV2X state machine, initializes the interfaces to connect with the vehicle to perform secure communication, sets up the secure timer, and changes the internal state machine to the "RUN" state. No further user interaction is required. The secure timer is configured to be triggered periodically based on the latency requirements discussed in Sect. 3. Note only code in the secure domain can modify the secure timer.

The secure timer interrupt invokes the CV2X state machine which performs the following actions. It fetches positional information from the GPS/GNSS module, and the direction and status of the vehicle via the tethered interface. The information is ASN.1 encoded similar to the original SAE J2375 [19] specification for BSMs. The keys for HMAC generation are stored in the secure domain during the installation of the CV2X application. The CV2X TA utilizes the current timestamp as a nonce, rotates through the store to select a key to generate an HMAC based on BSM payload, which are then combined to create our final packet (Sect. 5.2). This packet is sent to the CV2X server. The server responds with data containing BSM packets of nearby vehicles. The response HMAC is verified before the payload is utilized for making vehicle maneuvering decisions. The state machine can be shut down by the user from the non-secure OS at the end of the commute.

## 5.4  Security Analysis Under Attack Conditions

Based on our threat model in Sect. 4.2, since the attacker may control the non-secure domain, the attacker could gain control over two components of our framework: LTE (and GPS) modem, and user input. We shall now look at how the system may operate when each of these components is compromised.

**Compromised LTE+GPS Modem.** The attacker may assume complete control over the shared LTE modem. The attacker then could modify, store and replay or deny the use of the LTE modem to the secure domain. Considering Fig. 4 and the elements of the data packet, we can detect an attack or discrepancy in the CV2X operation as follows:

- If the attacker manipulates the received data, the HMAC verification of the received data would fail. Here, we consider that the server is not compromised and use HMAC to validate any manipulations by an attacker at the device or the LTE network.
- If the attacker reads and saves a server response on the modem, then replays this message to the device to thwart the CV2X operation. The nonce in the data can be checked to validate the BSM payload freshness.
- If the attacker performs a denial of service attack on the modem by bombarding the modem with requests, or deletes data before it is read by the secure side. An internal alive counter is implemented to check for timeliness.

In all the cases, the secure application assumes that the smartphone is compromised and invokes the secure peripheral controller (SPC) function to modify the SPC to explicitly assign access rights of the modem and GPS to the secure domain. Once the access permissions are changed, the non-secure domain or the attacker in the non-secure domain cannot access the modem or data lines connected to the modem or GPS. The CV2X application would now continue in the secure safety mode and follows the flow as described in Sect. 5.3. Though the mitigation action is strict, it is necessary to ensure passenger safety. Similarly, attacker intent to disrupt any power to the UE or modem can be thwarted by taking over the power module of the device on the secure domain during the execution of the CV2X application.

**Compromised User Input.** The capability to start and stop the application is provided to the user. All other functionality of the CV2X application, such as generating BSM, computing HMAC and transmission are done automatically in the secure domain and are outside attacker control based on our threat model. By controlling user input, the attacker may have the capability to stop the CV2X application by overriding the user interface on the non-secure side. This can be countered by reassigning a General-Purpose I/O physical button (such as the volume rocker button), which becomes the sole mechanism to signal the CV2X application to stop. This ensures that if every other user input mechanism is compromised, the attacker cannot remotely shut-off the CV2X application while the vehicle is in motion.

# 6   Network Configuration and Topologies

As mentioned in the system model, we consider four network topologies based on the possible placement of the CV2X server within the LTE network as shown in the Fig. 8. In this section, we discuss each configuration in detail.

**CV2X Server on the Internet.** As shown in Fig. 5a, the CV2X server can be placed on the internet. However to support the real-time latency demands of the vehicular applications, the CV2X server (i) must be located at a geographical location closer to the UE to minimize round-trip latency, and (ii) must be on a high bandwidth network where its traffic is prioritized for real-time applications. Deploying the CV2X server on the internet does not require any additional modifications or constraints from the LTE infrastructure in terms of additional hardware or standards, other than the automatic selection and broadcast of the IP address of the nearest CV2X server.

Further, placing the CV2X server on the internet provides straightforward inter-connectivity between different network providers where various operators can use existing packet data networks (PDNs) to reach the same CV2X server in a given locality. This mechanism makes the CV2X server agnostic to the origin and destination of the data, but needs to still maintain the latency requirements of the applications even with tight bounds on geographical distance and high bandwidth networks. The round trip latency in this case, is the sum of the latency from (i) the EPC to the server over the internet, (ii) radio access network, and (iii) the S1 interface connecting eNB and EPC.

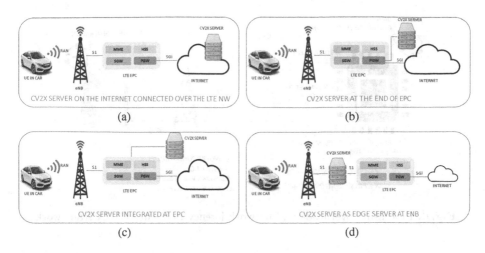

**Fig. 5.** Network topologies based on the position of the CV2X server in the LTE infrastructure

**CV2X Server at the End of the EPC.** As in Fig. 5b, the CV2X server is closer to the core LTE infrastructure when placed at the end of the EPC. This approach uses a dedicated subsystem at the end of the EPC core connected to the SPGW for CV2X, similar to IP multimedia systems (IMS) [26], which provide voice over internet protocol(VoIP), conference calls, etc. This placement strategy effectively eliminates the delays and network demands of public internet PDNs. The network round-trip delay is now reduced to latency in (i) radio access network, and (ii) the S1 interface connecting eNB and the EPC. Further, similar to IMS infrastructure, multiple network providers can exchange information across dedicated CV2X servers at the end of individual EPC centers.

**CV2X Server as Part of EPC.** As shown in Fig. 5c, the CV2X server can also be placed as a subsystem within the EPC core network connected to the mobility management entity (MME). However, such integration would require modifications to the standard interfaces within the LTE infrastructure. Moreover, exchanging BSMs and data across different network providers in this scenario would either require the development of novel standards for EPC subsystems or require implementing wrapper interfaces and modules to synchronize CV2X servers within EPCs across networks which could add computation and latency overheads. Due to the impracticality of placing the CV2X server as a part of the EPC, such a strategy is not included for further analysis.

**CV2X Server at End of the eNB.** By placing the CV2X server at the end of the eNB, we envision a mobile edge computing (MEC) platform [27,28] for the LTE infrastructure, as shown in Fig. 5d. A middlebox implementation [27] of an MEC server was recently proposed to reduce data processing latency without significant changes to the standard LTE network. This MEC server also acts

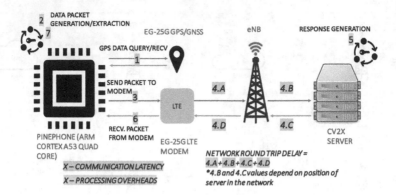

**Fig. 6.** Processing overheads and network latency in Secure CV2X framework

as a filter for processing local packets at the edge while forwarding other data packets to the SPGW. We modify this MEC server approach to integrate our CV2X server application, which could require having a CV2X server at every eNB. Alternatively, a server with increased computation capabilities at one eNB could be shared with other eNBs via the X2 interface.

## 7 Evaluation and Analysis

We discuss the proof of concept CV2X application built on open source UE and evaluate the considered network topologies. We describe the hardware, latency measurements, and simulations to understand the real-world scalability. Source code and relevant documentation can be found at https://github.com/spandan-m/secure_cv2x.

### 7.1 Hardware Setup

We use the ARM Cortex-A based Pinephone [29] as the UE to set up our proof of concept. The device houses a 64-bit quad-core Cortex A53 chipset at 1.152 GHz with 3 GB of LPDDR3 RAM. The device runs Arch ARM linux with kernel v5.8 as the rich OS (Non-secure domain) and OP-TEE OS v3.14.0-rc1 as the secure OS (Secure domain). The user application runs on the rich OS and allows the user to request the ARM Trusted Firmware to load the CV2X TA on OP-TEE.

**CV2X TA:** We implement most of the features of the CV2X TA as described in Sect. 5.1. However, since our aim is to measure latency, we omit some features such as:

- Since previous work [30,31] have already shown the effectiveness of the countermeasures, our goal here is to ensure that latency constraints are still met when the countermeasures are used. We assume that there is no attacker during our testing, so threat mitigation mechanisms, such as controlling modem access using SPC, are skipped. However, all packet processing code are considered in order to report overheads accurately.

- For testing latencies with respect to different number of BSM response packets, our CV2X server implementation sends the required number of responses containing random data. We do not implement a realistic CV2X server for simulating network overhead. Our tests incur negligible server overheads in generating random but valid HMAC verifiable data.
- We gather the latency for GPS separately as it is unfeasible to establish assisted GPS within our lab setup.

**Table 1.** UE processing and communication overhead measurements

|  | Action | No. BSMs sent as response from server | Mean [ms] | 95% CI [ms] |
|---|---|---|---|---|
| UE SEND | GPS Module data request and fetch | – | 1.2652 | 1.25874–1.27172 |
|  | Building data packet + HMAC | – | 0.0100 | 0.01002–0.01005 |
|  | Sending data packet to modem + ACK from Modem | – | 1.8080 | 1.80800–1.80801 |
| UE RECV | Receive data from Modem | 1 BSM | 4.8460 | 4.84371–4.84845 |
|  |  | 5 BSM | 6.3721 | 6.36952–6.37471 |
|  |  | 10 BSM | 8.3028 | 8.30093–8.30472 |
|  | Extract BSMs and Verify HMAC | 1 BSM | 0.0098 | 0.00984–0.00992 |
|  |  | 5 BSM | 0.0080 | 0.00800–0.00801 |
|  |  | 10 BSM | 0.0080 | 0.0080–0.0080 |
| *TOTAL OVERHEAD ON UE (SEND+RECV)* | | 1 BSM | **7.9388 ms** | |
|  | | 5 BSM | **9.4459 ms** | |
|  | | 10 BSM | **11.3938 ms** | |

**Network Setup for Server on the Internet:** As detailed in Sect. 6. We require a geographically close server with high processing and bandwidth capabilities. So, we use a server on amazon web services located about 27 miles from the test zone. We test the latency across an urban, suburban and highway terrain with vehicle speeds varying between 20–60 miles/hr.

**Network Setup for Server at the End of EPC:** In this topology, we established a private LTE network with the Open Air Interface (OAI) LTE eNB and EPC stacks on two computers. The eNB and EPC were hosted on Ubuntu 18.04 LTS on an Intel Core i5-6500 quad-core CPU running at 3.2 GHz with 8 GiB and 16 GiB of RAM, respectively. For the radio interface, we use USRP B210 and test the setup for 100 resource blocks of bandwidth.

**Network Setup for the Server at the End of eNB:** The network setup is similar to the network setup used in the case of the server at the end of EPC. Additionally, we use another computer for the MEC in between the eNB and EPC running the OAI stacks. The MEC setup runs Ubuntu 20.04 LTS on an Intel i7-10750H quad-core CPU at 2.6 GHz with 32 GiB of RAM.

## 7.2    Latency Evaluation and Analysis - Hardware POC

To understand the overheads and network latency of the proposed approach, it is better to split the same as shown in Fig. 6. We can split the overhead into two components: One from the processing of data on the UE and communication to/from the modem, and the second is the network round trip delay of the LTE infrastructure. Expanding further, during the sending phase, we have overhead to request the GPS/GNSS modem for GPS data. Then we have the processing delay in building a BSM packet, computing, and appending HMAC. Finally, we send the combined packet to the modem via UART at 3Mbit/s baud and wait for the modem to provide an acknowledgment. The overheads during the receive phase are the same, except that they occur in the inverse order of operation and do not include GPS query. The network round trip delay varies depending on the network topology discussed in earlier sections.

**Table 2.** Roundtrip latency for considered network topologies. We provide the mean and 95% CI for values collected for 5000 Send-Receive Cycles * Ideal Case: eNB-EPC negligible channel delay

| No. BSMs sent as response | Latency for server on Internet [ms] | Latency for server at the end of EPC* [ms] | Latency for server at eNB [ms] |
|---|---|---|---|
| 1 | 61.410 [60.391–62.429] | 29.139 [29.039–29.238] | 28.576 [28.369–28.783] |
| 5 | 77.039 [75.514–78.564] | 26.974 [26.773–27.175] | 27.900 [27.783–28.018] |
| 10 | 84.415 [81.922–86.908] | 40.085 [40.577–41.132] | 37.015 [37.015–37.576] |

We present the results in Tables 1 and 2 It is clearly evident that the COTS UE incurs minimal overhead for processing and exchanging data with the modem. We have a total overhead of 7.9388 ms when a single BSM/UE is sent as response from the server for every BSM. The average increases to 11.3938 ms for 10 BSM/UE as response from the server to every BSM. Therefore, even for 10 BSMs, the overall overhead is about 10% of a single core utilization on a low end open-source UE processor running at 1.152 GHz. We can expect even lesser overhead for processing on devices with proprietary hardware running at higher clock speeds. Additionally, the latency of communicating with the LTE modem can be further reduced by increasing the baud rate or choosing a parallel communication protocol if the hardware permits.

The network round-trip times (RTT) vary depending on the network topology. In the first scenario with the server on the internet, we see an average round trip delay of 61–84 ms depending on the number of BSMs that are sent in response to the UEs. These latency values could enable CV2X applications with latency constraints of 100ms but not guarantee the same. In the case of server at end of EPC and end of eNB, we obtain even lower RTT since the server is much closer to the UEs. However, note that for the topologies of the server at the end of EPC and end of eNB, the network RTT represents a lower bound (as both the cases use a private LTE setup). Also, in the real world, the EPC would not be as close to the eNB, and a single EPC services numerous eNBs. Thus, latency values would be higher than the values obtained above; however, placing servers with consideration for geographical proximity could provide satisfactory latency [13]. Additionally, the setup for the server at eNB with USRP antenna inconsistencies has very few UEs to measure any effects of Radio access resource contention and collisions. The measurements above hold if enough bandwidth is provided to the CV2X UEs. Therefore, in the worst-case scenario, when there are 100s of UEs trying to compete for resources from a single eNB, the latency exponentially increases, though mitigation may be possible [32]. Therefore, in the next Section, we try to evaluate and empirically determine the number of UEs that can meet CV2X latency constraints for a single eNB considering available bandwidth.

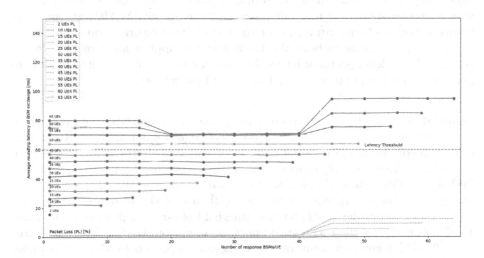

**Fig. 7.** Average latency and packet loss for 100 RBs (in increasing number of UEs starting from 2 and then in multiples of 5)

## 7.3   Simulation Evaluation

As discussed earlier, the primary bottleneck occurs in the radio access network of the LTE. Considering the most feasible topology for our use case(CV2X server as MEC at eNB), we modify the ns3 simulator(v3.26) [33] with MEC support [34] for our CV2X application. We wish to determine the possible number of UEs that a single eNB can service to measure the feasibility of our approach. For simplicity, we currently do not consider external traffic other than the CV2X application. We consider such robust realistic situations for the future.

**Simulation Model and Configuration.** For a given value of resource blocks, we consider an increasing number of UEs($n$) from 2 to 65. Starting from an ideal 1 response BSM per UE to the worst(each UE sending a BSM to each other), we have response BSMs/UE($r_n$) varying from 1 to $n-1$ for each $n$. Using the standard LTE configurations, we use the resource block values 25, 50, 100 for 5, 10 and 20 MHz(bandwidths of individual LTE bands) respectively. The smaller resource block values could be looked at as dedicated resource allocations within the larger 100RB scenario to understand the behavior if some bandwidth is explicitly reserved for CV2X. We modify the native UDP echo server of ns3 to mimic our CV2X application for measuring latency with varying BSMs/UE. The UDP echo client on UEs send a BSM every 100 ms, to which the UDP echo server responds with varying number of BSMs/UE. Additionally, to add a mobility scenario, we move the UE's randomly around a central eNB at 20 m/s using the ns3's 2D random direction mobility model. The eNB is configured to use an isometric $2 \times 2$ multiple-input multiple-output (MIMO) antenna. We utilize default ns3 configurations for the rest of the network parameters. Since, we are more concerned about the latency at the application level, we do not consider lower level protocol layers, but use the ns3's Flow monitor module to get the higher level network layer latency and packet loss.

**Simulation Analysis.** Even though the periodicity requirement of the application is 100 ms, we set a safe cutoff threshold of 60 ms for our analysis. Recall that our UE proof-of-concept does not consider any latency/overhead for actions from the vehicle. Also, we only measure the hardware overhead for response upto 10 BSMs/UE. The communication overhead of data between the UE processor and the modem would considerably increase with size of the response from server. Therefore, we consider a safe latency threshold of 60ms to determine the feasible number of UEs the eNB can support. As seen from the Fig. 7, for 100 RBs, a $2 \times 2$ MIMO antenna setup on the eNB can service up to 45–50 UEs under our latency threshold. We also only see packet loss when the number of UEs are above 50. In the case of 25 RBs and 50 RBs, we do see a local maxima for reduction in latency, but the latency overshoots our latency threshold bar for other arbitrary values of BSMs per UE. Therefore, from Fig. 8a and Fig. 8b, a safe value of number of UE that can be supported are 35 and 45 for 25 RBs and 50 RBs respectively.

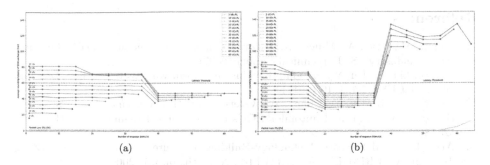

|     |     |
| --- | --- |
| (a) | (b) |

**Fig. 8.** Average latency and packet loss for (a) 25 RBs (b) 50 RBs (in increasing number of UEs starting from 2 and then in multiples of 5)

Given, that the commercial networks utilize more robust software and hardware like $4 \times 4$ MIMO antennas, proprietary scheduling algorithms and dedicated resources, the number of feasible UEs that could be supported would be slightly higher than the presented values.

## 8   Future Work

As mentioned, though we try to analyze the various topologies and COTS smartphone capabilities, there is still scope of further investigation. Considering the network, we assume no external traffic or influences for the simulation. Additionally, the hardware evaluation with a single UE does not provide a holistic discussion of the approach. So, we intend to further investigate the possibility of using LTE via enhanced simulations and a larger scale hardware test bed. Subsequently, our secure CV2X application on the UE is abstracted from the underlying cellular modem. So, we would like to explore the possibility of analysing our approach on the 5G or device-to-device (D2D) frameworks. A more interesting tangent we wish to also explore is to setup the above approach to connect with an actual vehicle over the OBD-II port, enabling us to analyze and investigate our approach for vehicle compatibility and driving applications. This would enable the end-to-end discussion of our whole idea.

## 9   Conclusion

In this paper we investigated a secure framework to enable CV2X using commercial of-the-shelf smartphones by leveraging device hardware security extensions. In particular, we look at using the smartphones as CV2X radios without degrading their performance for regular operation. Further, we explored possible threats to using such a framework on smartphones and provide mitigation approaches to thwart the same. Additionally, we also consider the whole LTE network in our framework and investigate the possible solutions of using a dedicated server to act as an intermediary between the UEs. Simulation results, backed by hardware measurements indicate that CV2X can be securely implemented using COTS smartphones.

# References

1. Shavit, M., Gryc, A., Miucic, R.: Firmware update over the air (FOTA) for automotive industry. (SAE Technical Paper) (2007)
2. Nie, S., Liu, L., Du, Y.: Free-fall: hacking tesla from wireless to can bus. Briefing, Black Hat USA **25**, 1–16 (2017)
3. Nie, S., Liu, L., Du, Y., Zhang, W.: Over-the-air: How we remotely compromised the gateway, BCM, and autopilot ECUs of Tesla cars. Briefing, Black Hat USA (2018)
4. Arm, L.: ARM Security Technology-Building a Secure System using TrustZone Technology. (PRD-GENC-C. ARM Ltd., Apr. (cit. on p.) (2009)
5. McCord, K.: Automotive Diagnostic Systems: Understanding OBD I and OBD II. (CarTech Inc.) (2011)
6. Pinto, S., Gomes, T., Pereira, J., Cabral, J., Tavares, A.: IIoTEED: an enhanced, trusted execution environment for industrial IoT edge devices. IEEE Internet Comput. **21**, 40–47 (2017)
7. Ahmad, Z., Francis, L., Ahmed, T., Lobodzinski, C., Audsin, D., Jiang, P.: Enhancing the security of mobile applications by using TEE and (U) SIM. In: 2013 IEEE 10th International Conference on Ubiquitous Intelligence and Computing and 2013 IEEE 10th International Conference on Autonomic And Trusted Computing, pp. 575–582 (2013)
8. Wang, Y., Gao, W., Hei, X., Mungwarama, I., Ren, J.: Independent credible: secure communication architecture of android devices based on TrustZone. In: 2020 International Conferences on Internet of Things (iThings) and IEEE Green Computing and Communications (GreenCom) and IEEE Cyber, Physical and Social Computing (CPSCom) and IEEE Smart Data (SmartData) and IEEE Congress on Cybermatics (Cybermatics), pp. 85–92 (2020)
9. Ahlawat, A., Du, W.: TruzCall: secure VoIP calling on android using ARM TrustZone. In: 2020 Sixth International Conference on Mobile and Secure Services (MobiSecServ), pp. 1–12 (2020)
10. Liu, S., Xiang, W., Punithan, M.: An empirical study on performance of DSRC and LTE-4G for vehicular communications. In: 2018 IEEE 88th Vehicular Technology Conference (VTC-Fall), pp. 1–5 (2018)
11. Hassebo, A., Obaidat, M., Ali, M.: Commercial 4G LTE cellular networks for supporting emerging IoT applications. In: 2018 Advances in Science and Engineering Technology International Conferences (ASET), pp. 1–6 (2018)
12. Amjad, Z., Sikora, A., Hilt, B., Lauffenburger, J.: Low latency V2X applications and network requirements: performance evaluation. In: 2018 IEEE Intelligent Vehicles Symposium (IV), pp. 220–225 (2018)
13. Pyykönen, P., Lumiaho, A., Kutila, M., Scholliers, J., Kakes, G.: V2X-supported automated driving in modern 4G networks. In: 2020 IEEE 16th International Conference on Intelligent Computer Communication and Processing (ICCP), pp. 271–275 (2020)
14. ARM Arm Security Technology Building a Secure System using TrustZone Technology. ARMDeveloper. https://developer.arm.com/documentation/PRD29-GENC-009492/c?lang=en
15. Linaro Open Portable Trusted Execution Environment. OPTEE Documentation. https://optee.readthedocs.io/en/latest/index.html
16. GlobalPlatorm Introduction to trusted execution environments (2018). https://globalplatform.org/resource-publication/introduction-to-trusted-execution-environments/. Accessed 30 Mar 2022

17. Paradisi, A., Yacoub, M.D., Figueiredo, F.L., Tronco, T.R. (eds.): Long Term Evolution. TIT, Springer, Cham (2016). https://doi.org/10.1007/978-3-319-23823-4
18. European Telecommunications Standards Institute. Service requirements for V2X services ETSI TS 122 185 V14.3.0. (2017)
19. Society of Automotive Engineers. V2X Communications Message Set Dictionary J2735_202007 (2020)
20. Bajaj, R., Ranaweera, S., Agrawal, D.: GPS: location-tracking technology. Computer **35**, 92–94 (2002)
21. Van Diggelen, F.: A-gps: Assisted gps, gnss, and sbas. Artech house (2009)
22. Nardini, G., Virdis, A., Campolo, C., Molinaro, A., Stea, G.: Cellular-V2X communications for platooning: design and evaluation. Sensors **18**, 1527 (2018)
23. Miao, L., Virtusio, J., Hua, K.: Pc5-based cellular-v2x evolution and deployment. Sensors **21**, 843 (2021)
24. Krawczyk, H., Bellare, M., Canetti, R.: HMAC: keyed-hashing for message authentication. (RFc 2104) (1997)
25. Dobraunig, C., Eichlseder, M., Mendel, F., Schläffer, M.: Ascon v1.2: lightweight authenticated encryption and hashing. J. Cryptol. **34**, 1–42 (2021)
26. Camarillo, G., Garcia-Martin, M.: The 3G IP Multimedia Subsystem (IMS): Merging the Internet and the Cellular Worlds. John Wiley & Sons, Hoboken (2007)
27. Li, C., et al.: Mobile edge computing platform deployment in 4G LTE networks: a middlebox approach. In: USENIX Workshop on Hot Topics in Edge Computing (HotEdge 2018) (2018)
28. Giust, F., et al.: MEC deployments in 4G and evolution towards 5G. ETSI White Paper **24**, 1–24 (2018)
29. Pine64 Pinephone. https://www.pine64.org/pinephone/
30. Oehler, M., Glenn, R.: HMAC-MD5 IP authentication with replay prevention (1997)
31. Lentz, M., Sen, R., Druschel, P., Bhattacharjee, B.: Secloak: arm trustzone-based mobile peripheral control. In: Proceedings of the 16th Annual International Conference on Mobile Systems, Applications, and Services, pp. 1–13 (2018)
32. Amjad, Z., Sikora, A., Lauffenburger, J., Hilt, B.: Latency reduction in narrowband 4G lte networks. In: 2018 15th International Symposium on Wireless Communication Systems (ISWCS), pp. 1–5 (2018)
33. Riley, G., Henderson, T.: The ns 3 network simulator. In: Modeling and Tools for Network Simulation, pp. 15–34 (2010)
34. Nin, J.: NS3-MEC: MEC model for NS-3. GitHub. https://github.com/mmajanen/ns3-MEC

# Network Security

# DQR: A Double Q Learning Multi Agent Routing Protocol for Wireless Medical Sensor Network

Muhammad Shadi Hajar[1]([✉]) [iD], Harsha Kalutarage[1] [iD],
and M. Omar Al-Kadri[2] [iD]

[1] Robert Gordon University, Aberdeen AB10 7GJ, UK
{m.hajar,h.kalutarage}@rgu.ac.uk
[2] Birmingham City University, Birmingham B4 7XG, UK
omar.alkadri@bcu.ac.uk

**Abstract.** Wireless Medical Sensor Network (WMSN) offers innovative solutions in the healthcare domain. It alleviates the patients' everyday life difficulties and supports the already overloaded medical staff with continuous monitoring tools. However, widespread adoption of these advancements is still restrained by security concerns and limitations of existing routing protocols. Routing is challenging in WMSN owing to the fact that some critical requirements, such as reliable delivery, have been neglected. To address these challenges, this paper proposes DQR, a double Q-learning routing protocol to meet WMSN requirements and overcome the positive bias estimation problem of the Q-learning based routing protocols. DQR uses a novel Reinforcement Learning (RL) model to reduce computational and communication overheads. It is combined with an effective trust management system to ensure a reliable data transfer and defeat packet dropping attacks. The experimental results demonstrate robust performance under various attacks with minimal resource footprint and efficient energy consumption.

**Keywords:** Double Q-learning · Routing · Reinforcement Learning · Trust management · Blackhole attack · Selective forwarding attack · Sinkhole attack

## 1 Introduction

Wireless Medical Sensor Network (WMSN) has become a critical element in the healthcare systems to monitor the physiological signs of the human body. This revolutionized technology provides medical staff with continuous real-time monitoring data without disturbing the patients. However, the widespread uptake of WMSN applications is still suppressed by security concerns. Ensuring a secure and reliable data transfer between the sensing units and the sink is still challenging despite the abundant routing protocols proposed for Wireless Sensor Network (WSN) [1,2]. Although WMSN is regarded as a branch of WSN, routing

© ICST Institute for Computer Sciences, Social Informatics and Telecommunications Engineering 2023
Published by Springer Nature Switzerland AG 2023. All Rights Reserved
F. Li et al. (Eds.): SecureComm 2022, LNICST 462, pp. 611–629, 2023.
https://doi.org/10.1007/978-3-031-25538-0_32

protocols and security countermeasures proposed for WSN do not necessarily fit WMSN due to its resource limitations, critical applications, and operating conditions.

Reinforcement Learning (RL) has been used recently to solve distributed optimization problems, such as routing [3]. RL-based routing protocols rely on an existence of a learning agent that acts with the environment and receives rewards based on its actions. By interacting with the network environment, the learning agents will be able to maximize their reward by making optimal forwarding decisions. Q-learning, which is a model-free RL algorithm, is the most used algorithm for both centralized and decentralized routing protocols [4]. Although this approach is able to produce an efficient routing protocol that can outperform other algorithms, it still has drawbacks. First, as it works without prior knowledge about the environment, it requires a series of randomly chosen actions to explore the environment before converging on the optimal solution. WMSN cannot tolerate a long learning period because of its sensitive applications. Second, Q-learning has an inborn overestimation problem which has been overlooked for a long time [5]. It uses the maximum value as an estimation for the maximum expected value. The routing performance may be impacted negatively due to this positive bias. Third, although different parameters have been considered in protocol design, ensuring reliable data transfer is still challenging as senders cannot predict the behaviour of other nodes in the path to the destination. Moreover, taking into consideration more parameters may optimize the routing decisions, but it involves a significant overhead increase, especially when information must be exchanged between learning agents. Therefore, a suitable solution is needed to overcome these aforementioned shortcomings.

The main contribution of this paper is threefold. First, the unique requirements for an efficient, lightweight and reliable routing protocol for WMSN are specified. Second, a double Q-learning trust-aware routing protocol for WMSN has been proposed. Third, extensive analysis has been carried out to ensure the robustness of our proposed protocol under different scenarios.

The rest of this article is organized into six sections as follows. Related work is given in Sect. 2. Section 3 overviews WMSN. DQR routing protocol is described in Sect. 4, followed by evaluation and performance results in Sect. 5. Finally, Sect. 6 concludes this article.

## 2    Related Work

Developing a secure, reliable and efficient routing protocol for WSN is still an open area of research, and it is more challenging in WMSN due to its resource scarcity and critical applications. Abundant research has been carried out to propose an efficient routing protocol using different metrics and methods. Recently, reinforcement learning has been widely used to find the optimal routing path with minimal overhead. Q-learning, which uses temporal difference (TD) to estimate the value of an action in a given state, is extensively used to build an efficient routing policy. However, Q-leaning suffers from an overestimation problem, which overlooks the optimal action in some cases [5]. Therefore, double

Q-learning, which is an off-policy RL algorithm, is introduced to solve the over-estimation problem by using double estimators to approximate the maximum expected value. To the best of our knowledge, only a few works used double Q-learning to develop a routing protocol. Authors in [6] proposed DQLR, a double Q-learning routing protocol for Delay Tolerant Networks (DTN). However, DQLR only used the number of hops between the source and the destination as a metric. It achieved an acceptable delivery ratio under normal operation. However, considering the hop count as the only metric is insufficient to deal with complicated scenarios.

On the other hand, researchers use various metrics to build the Q-learning reward function in order to achieve an efficient routing protocol, such as delivery delay, the number of hops, remaining energy and location information [3,7–9]. Although this kind of metrics could produce an efficient forwarding method, it cannot deal with malicious activities launched by insiders. Therefore, the routing protocol needs a different source of information to make an informed routing decision, such as Trust Management System (TMS). According to our literature review, only two routing protocols proposed integrating a TMS with Q-learning. Authors in [10] proposed a resource and security efficient routing protocol combined with a trust mechanism for WSN. However, this protocol is not reproducible due to missing some details. In [11], the authors integrate the beta distribution based trust scheme with the Q-learning algorithm to achieve a reliable routing protocol for WMSN. However, positioning information is to be periodically provided in order to choose the optimal path, which could not be practical for WMSN. Moreover, it needs further investigation under different packet dropping attacks.

## 3 Wireless Medical Sensor Network

With the rapid advancement of the low power and intelligent biomedical SNs, WMSN emerged as a special kind of WSN for healthcare applications. It consists of a set of tiny SNs that are distributed inside or offside the body to monitor the body's biosignals. This revolutionized technology empowers physicians to timely monitor their patients and intervene when necessary.

### 3.1 Network Model

This study assumes a WMSN of a ward in a field hospital as shown in Fig. 1. Due to the ongoing COVID-19 pandemic, field hospitals have become prevalent, especially in developing countries. The ward dimensions are 10 m × 50 m, where a number of hospital beds are distributed efficiently to provide the necessary care and save physical space. A network of 64 SNs was used to simulate the WMSN conforming to IEEE 802.15.6 [12]. The SNs have been distributed randomly across the hospital ward. The topology is star, with one SN acting as a sink. All sensed data is transmitted to the sink, which in turn forwards it to the medical server. The communication range is 5m. Thus, nodes need to cooperate and relay packets for other adjacent nodes.

## 3.2  Threat Model

The critical applications of WMSN necessitate a reliable routing protocol as dropped packets may carry sensitive information. Dropping attacks, such as blackhole and selective forwarding attacks, may not just disrupt the network operation but endanger the patient's life. This kind of attack is difficult to deal with as malicious nodes are usually legitimate nodes that pass cryptographic security countermeasures, such as authentication. Dropping attacks have various patterns and may happen for different reasons. An SN could get compromised and stop relaying packets for other nodes intentionally. Even benign nodes could act selfishly to save resources or could get overloaded by an inefficient routing protocol. Therefore, a reliable, efficient, lightweight routing protocol for WMSN that ensures secure data delivery between the sensing units and the sink is required. DQR assumes that all SNs nodes are mutually authenticated and have a copy of the security keys to ensure a high level of secure communication.

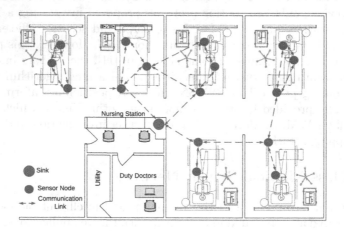

**Fig. 1.** Network model

# 4  Protocol Design

In this section, the proposed routing protocol is presented. The design requirements are justified and the proposed algorithms are comprehensively discussed.

## 4.1  Reinforcement Learning and Double Q-Learning

Multi-Agent Reinforcement Learning (MARL) is a subfield in RL that focuses on studying the behaviour of multiple agents co-existing in a shared environment. The agents are motivated by reward functions and interact with the environment and each other to compete or achieve a common goal. MARL is modeled using the Markov Decision Process (MDP), where the environment has a set of states

$s_t \in \mathbb{S}$ and each agent takes action $a_t \in \mathbb{A}$. In the network environment, each learning agent solves a multi objectives routing problem to make optimal routing decisions.

Q-Learning is an off-policy, model-free temporal difference (TD) algorithm to learn the value of an action in a particular state. However, due to its inborn overestimation problem, Q-Learning could perform poorly in some stochastic environments because the most optimal action could be obscured by overestimation [5]. Therefore, double Q-learning is introduced as an alternative method to approximate the maximum expected action-value by using double estimators.

### 4.2 Design Requirements

The unique characteristics of WMSN dictate rigorous requirements, which must be kept in mind when designing any potential routing protocol. Therefore, the proposed protocol must be efficient, lightweight, and attack-resistant.

The routing protocol must always choose the optimal path in order to achieve a high delivery ratio and low energy consumption. However, Q-learning-based routing protocols could suffer from poor performance due to the action-value overestimation problem. This biased estimation leads to bad routing decisions that negatively affect the packet delivery ratio. Moreover, increasing the number of transmissions aggravates the energy consumption as transmission activities account for around 80% of the total consumed energy [13]. Therefore, a new approach to achieve an efficient routing protocol is required.

WMSN has stringent resource constraints that make the inherited WSN routing methods not necessarily fit. The traditional RL model necessitates updating the Q table after each sent or forwarded packet, which is a resource depletion process [6,11]. Therefore, the routing engine of any proposed routing protocol must have a minimal resource footprint in terms of processing and memory.

Dropping attacks, such as blackhole and selective forwarding attacks, degrade the overall performance, and most importantly, it may endanger the patient's life. Moreover, the routing process itself could be prone to a specific kind of attack based on the used method, such as poisoning attacks. Therefore, WMSN requires a reliable and robust routing design. The delivery reliability allows the protocol to predict the malicious paths and avoid them, while the design robustness ensures high resiliency to routing attacks.

### 4.3 DQR Protocol

DQR is designed to fulfill all the above requirements. The reward function is defined as punishment to ensure that the learning agent always chooses the lowest-cost path. Moreover, in order to reduce the computational overhead of the traditional RL model, DQR reformulated the RL model, assuming that the network will be static for a short period, which is an acceptable assumption as nodes could be regarded as stationary for a short interval. This assumption allows the learning agent to perform the same action multiple times before receiving the corresponding reward, as illustrated in Fig. 2. Adopting this method reduces the computational overhead significantly by updating the Q tables periodically, which will be discussed comprehensively in Sect. 4.4. Furthermore, DQR incorporates an effective TMS to ensure reliable data transfer and avoid malicious paths.

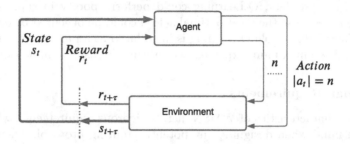

**Fig. 2.** Graphical representation of the proposed RL model

WMSN network represents the environment $\mathbb{E}$, which contains a set of SNs, one of which acts as a sink $S$. The learning agent in DQR is defined as the tuple $(\mathbb{S}, \mathbb{A}, \mathbb{R})$ where $\mathbb{S}$ represents a set of states, $\mathbb{A}$ is the set of actions the agent can take, and $\mathbb{R}$ is the reward function. At time step $t$, an agent at state $s \in \mathbb{S}$ could get a packet to send to destination $d$, and hence the agent takes action $a_t \in \mathbb{A}$ to forward the packet to one of its neighbors. The learning agent keeps taking the same action during the time window $[t, t + \tau]$. At the end of the time window, the learning agent receives $r_{t+1} \in \mathbb{R}$ from the environment and moves from state $s_t$ to $s_{t+1}$. DQR defines two Q functions $Q_{t+1}^{A(i)}(s_t^{(i)}, a_t^{(i)})$ and $Q_{t+1}^{B(i)}(s_t^{(i)}, a_t^{(i)})$ as the estimated future reward of agent $i$ at state $s_t$ taking the action $a_t$ as shown in Eq. 2 and Eq. 4. Each one of these estimators is updated using a value from the other estimator for the next state as shown in Eq. 1 and Eq. 2. Therefore, the actions $a_t^*$ and $b_t^*$ are the maximum valued actions for $Q_{t+1}^{A(i)}(s_t^{(i)}, a_t^{(i)})$ and $Q_{t+1}^{B(i)}(s_t^{(i)}, a_t^{(i)})$, respectively.

$$a_t^{*(i)} = \underset{a_t^{(i)} \in A}{argmax} Q_t^{A(i)}(s_{t+1}^{(i)}, a_t^{(i)}) \tag{1}$$

$$Q_{t+1}^{A(i)}(s_t^{(i)}, a_t^{(i)}) \leftarrow (1-\eta)Q_t^{A(i)}(s_t^{(i)}, a_t^{(i)}) + \eta[r_{t+1}^{(i)}(s_{t+1}^{(i)}) + \gamma Q_{t+1}^{B(i)}(s_{t+1}^{(i)}, a_t^{*(i)})] \tag{2}$$

$$b_t^{*(i)} = \underset{a_t^{(i)} \in A}{argmax} Q_t^{B(i)}(s_{t+1}^{(i)}, a_t^{(i)}) \tag{3}$$

$$Q_{t+1}^{B(i)}(s_t^{(i)}, a_t^{(i)}) \leftarrow (1-\eta)Q_t^{B(i)}(s_t^{(i)}, a_t^{(i)}) + \eta[r_{t+1}^{(i)}(s_{t+1}^{(i)}) + \gamma Q_{t+1}^{A(i)}(s_{t+1}^{(i)}, b_t^{*(i)})] \tag{4}$$

where $\eta \in [0, 1]$ is the learning parameter where small values decelerate the learning and large ones may prevent algorithm convergence, $\gamma \in [0, 1]$ is the future reward discount parameter where small values make the learning agent nearsighted by considering the only immediate reward.

DQR is designed to always choose the most reliable shortest path by defining the reward function as punishment, as shown in Eq. 5. The delivery reliability is achieved by incorporating trust information, which is discussed in Sect. 4.6, while the punishment design reduces the number of transmissions along the path to the destination to ensure an energy-efficient protocol. Moreover, energy information from the agent itself is also considered to optimize the network lifetime, which will be discussed further in Sect. 4.5

$$
r_{t+1}^{(i)}(s_{t+1}^{(i)}, j) = \begin{cases} -(1 - T_t^{(ij)}).F_t^{(i)} & if \quad O_t^{(ij)} \neq \{\phi\} \\ -(1 - T_{t-\delta}^{(ij)}).F_t^{(i)} & if \quad O_t^{(ij)} = \{\phi\} \wedge |O^{(ij)}| > \epsilon \\ 0 & Otherwise \end{cases} \tag{5}
$$

where $r_{t+1}^{(i)}(s_{t+1}^{(i)}, j)$ is the received reward by node $i$ for taking the action $a_t^{(i)} = j$ forwarding the traffic to the neighbor $j$ at time window $[t, t+\tau]$, $T_t^{(ij)}$ is the trust value of SN $j$ that maintained by SN $i$ at time window $t$ and is evaluated using Algorithm 4, $O_t^{(ij)}$ is the direct observations maintained by node $i$ for node $j$ at time window $t$, $\delta$ is a time lag used to obtain the last trust value, $\epsilon$ is a threshold to identify the minimum required evidence where higher values means more historical data is required to use the evaluated trust value.

The learning process must be continual due to network dynamicity and distributed as no agent has a full view of the network. DQR is a decentralized protocol where the learning agents exchange their best estimations with their neighbors, as illustrated in Algorithm 1. The received estimations are then used to update the $Q^A$ and $Q^B$ tables and specify the most optimal next hop. As the goal of the learning agent is to maximize the received reward in the long run, greedy action should not always be taken as routing task is a continual online task and exploiting the greedy action all the time prevents the convergence to the global optimum. Therefore, DQR uses $\varepsilon$-greedy method to balance between exploration and exploitation. The learning agent explores the environment with a probability of $\theta$ and exploits it with a probability of $(1 - \theta)$. Initially, the learning agents have no evidence from the network; hence their Q values are initialized to zeros, which is more practical to motivate the agents to explore the environment and does not require any hardware or positioning information like in [11, 14].

### 4.4  Synchronous and Asynchronous Updating

DQR adopted a synchronous Q tables updating method with a view to producing a lightweight routing protocol. Each action-value function is updated with the outcome of the other action-value function as shown in Algorithm 2. The actions $a^{*(i)}$ and $b^{*(i)}$ are the maximum value action in state $s_{t+1}$ for $Q^{A(i)}$ and $Q^{B(i)}$, respectively. Therefore, both Q tables are updated for the same problem but with a different set of evidence to produce an unbiased estimate for all action-value(s). Although the obtained experience is divided between two action-value functions, the algorithm is still data-efficient as selecting the optimal action is computed

---

**Algorithm 1:** Routing Protocol

---

**Input:**
The reward: $r_{t+1}^{(i)}(s_{t+1}^{(i)}, j)$
The Q tables: $Q_t^A$ & $Q_t^B$
The trust table: $T_t$
**Output:** Optimal next hop $a_t^{(i)}$
**Initialization:**

$$Q_0^{A(i)}(n^{(i)} \in N_t^{(i)}) = Q_0^{B(i)} = \begin{cases} 0 & if \quad n^{(i)} \neq S \\ 1 & if \quad n^{(i)} = S \end{cases} \qquad // \ N_t^{(i)} \text{ is the adjacent nodes of } i$$

$$T_0^{(i)}(n^{(i)} \in N_t^{(i)}) = E[uni(0,1)] = 0.5$$

$$a_1^{(i)} = \begin{cases} S & if \quad S \in N_1^{(i)} \\ n^{(i)} & | \quad n^{(i)} \in N_1^{(i)} \end{cases} \tag{6}$$

**while** *TRUE* **do**
  Wait $\tau$
  Broadcast $max(Q_t^{A(i)})$ & $max(Q_t^{B(i)})$
  **if** $\varepsilon - greedy > \theta$ **then**
    $a_t^{(i)} = \underset{a \in A}{argmax}(\frac{Q_t^{A(i)}(s,.)+Q_t^{B(i)}(s,.)}{2})$
    Calculate $r_{t+1}^{(i)}(s_{t+1}^{(i)}, a_t^{(i)})$ as in Eq. 5
    $Q_{t+1}^{A(i)}(s_t^{(i)}, a_t^{(i)})$ & $Q_{t+1}^{B(i)}(s_t^{(i)}, a_t^{(i)})$ Synchronous update as in algorithm 2
  **else**
    $a_t^{(i)} \leftarrow n_t^{(i)} | n_t^{(i)} \in N_t^{(i)}$
    Calculate $r_{t+1}^{(i)}(s_{t+1}^{(i)}, a_t^{(i)})$ as in Eq. 5
    $Q_{t+1}^{A(i)}(s_t^{(i)}, a_t^{(i)})$ & $Q_{t+1}^{B(i)}(s_t^{(i)}, a_t^{(i)})$ Synchronous update as in algorithm 2
  **end**
  $s_t^{(i)} \leftarrow s_{t+1}^{(i)}$
**end**

---

based on the average Q tables as illustrated in Algorithm 1. As the learning agents collaborate with each other by broadcasting their best estimation to a destination, this information is then used to keep the Q tables updated. However, the learning agent forwards the traffic to only one adjacent node during the time window $t$, and thus it can only calculate the reward for this action. For instance, node $i$ take the action $a_t^{(i)} = j$ during the time window $t$ and receives two updates from nodes $j$ and $k$. Consequently, DQR updates the action-value of $j$ with the calculated reward using double Q-learning, while it checks if there is enough evidence about node $k$ to update each action-value separately using Q-learning or keep it unchanged in case of not enough evidence. This method allows DQR to react quickly to any environment change, and at the same time, it immunizes DQR against utilizing false updates from malicious nodes.

On the other hand, although the synchronous updating method is computationally efficient, it may decelerate the convergence as the learning agent, especially in the exploration phase, may make wrong decisions, and thus keep forwarding the traffic to the wrong next hop. In traditional RL mode, the learning agent risks losing one packet each time to update the Q tables. However, by using only synchronous updating, more packets may be lost before updating the Q tables. This usually happens when loops occur. Therefore, DQR uses an

---

**Algorithm 2:** Synchronous Updating

---

**Input:**
The Q Table: $Q_t^{A(i)}$ and $Q_t^{B(i)}$
The reward: $r_{t+1}^{(i)}(s_{t+1}^{(i)}, j)$
The trust table: $T_t$
**Output:** $Q_{t+1}^{A(i)}$ and $Q_{t+1}^{B(i)}$
**while** *TRUE* **do**
    *Wait* $\tau$
    **foreach** $j \in N_t^i$ **do**
        **if** $j == a_t^i$ **then**
            $\rho \leftarrow rand(0,1)$
            **if** $\rho > 0.5$ **then**
                Define $a^{*(i)} = \underset{a \in A}{argmax} Q_t^{A(i)}(s_{t+1}^{(i)}, a_t^{(i)})$

$$Q_{t+1}^{A(i)}(s_t^{(i)}, a_t^{(i)}) \leftarrow (1 - \eta)Q_t^{A(i)}(s_t^{(i)}, a_t^{(i)}) + \eta[r_{t+1}^{(i)}(s_{t+1}^{(i)}) + \gamma Q_{t+1}^{B(i)}(s_{t+1}^{(i)}, a_t^{*(i)})]$$

            **else**
                Define $b^{*(i)} = \underset{a \in A}{argmax} Q_t^{B(i)}(s_{t+1}^{(i)}, a_t^{(i)})$

$$Q_{t+1}^{B(i)}(s_t^{(i)}, a_t^{(i)}) \leftarrow (1 - \eta)Q_t^{B(i)}(s_t^{(i)}, a_t^{(i)}) + \eta[r_{t+1}^{(i)}(s_{t+1}^{(i)}) + \gamma Q_{t+1}^{A(i)}(s_{t+1}^{(i)}, b_t^{*(i)})]$$

            **end**
        **else**
            **if** $|O^{ij}| > \epsilon$ **then**

$$Q_{t+1}^{A(i)}(s_t^{(i)}, j) \leftarrow (1 - \eta)Q_t^{A(i)}(s_t^{(i)}, j) + \eta[r_{t-\delta}^{(i)}(s_{t-\delta}^{(i)}, j) + \gamma \max_{j \in N_t^{(i)}} Q_t^{A(i)}(s_{t+1}^{(i)}, j)]$$

$$Q_{t+1}^{B(i)}(s_t^{(i)}, j) \leftarrow (1 - \eta)Q_t^{B(i)}(s_t^{(i)}, j) + \eta[r_{t-\delta}^{(i)}(s_{t-\delta}^{(i)}, j) + \gamma \max_{j \in N_t^{(i)}} Q_t^{B(i)}(s_{t+1}^{(i)}, j)]$$

            **else**
                $Q_{t+1}^{A(ij)} \leftarrow Q_t^{A(ij)}$
                $Q_{t+1}^{B(bij)} \leftarrow Q_t^{B(ij)}$
            **end**
        **end**
    **end**
**end**

---

asynchronous updating method to step up the learning process and makes the algorithm converge swiftly. Once a loop is detected or expected, such as when forwarding the packet to its source again, the asynchronous updating method is triggered to penalize both corresponding action-value(s) and allow the learning agent to take the appropriate action accordingly, as detailed in Algorithm 3.

## 4.5 Energy Model

Optimizing the network lifetime is still a challenging concern in WSN and WMSN in particular. Due to the critical applications of WMSN, dead nodes may have catastrophic consequences. Moreover, in some cases, replacing the battery may need surgical intervention. Considering the residual energy of the adjacent nodes is widely used to maximize the overall network lifetime [15,16]. However, exchanging energy information between adjacent nodes is neither energy nor

---

**Algorithm 3:** Asynchronous Updating

---

**Input:** A packet to forward: $P_t^{(sd)}$
**Output:** Updated Routing
**while** *TRUE* **do**

    **if** $\forall\, i \in \mathbb{N}$ *receives* $P_{t+\delta}^{(id)}$ **then**        // $P_{t+\delta}^{(id)}$ is a packet from $i$ to $d$ after time lag $\delta$

        **if** $\eta == 1$ **then**

           $\left|\quad r_{t+1}^{(i)}(s_{t+1}^{(i)}, j) = -e^{\eta}(1 - T_t^{(ij)}).F_t^{(i)}\right.$

        **else**

           $\left|\quad r_{t+1}^{(i)}(s_{t+1}^{(i)}, j) = -(1 - T_t^{(ij)}).F_t^{(i)}\right.$

        **end**

        **if** $RQ_{t-1}^{A(i)}(s_{t-1}^{(i)}, j) \wedge RQ_{t-1}^{B(i)}(s_{t-1}^{(i)}, j)$ **then**      // $RQ_{t-1}^{A(i)}(s_{t-1}^{(i)}, j)$ is the last expected future reward received from $j$

           update $Q_t^{A(ij)}$ and $Q_t^{B(ij)}$ using $r_{t+1}^{(i)}$, $RQ_{t-1}^{A(i)}$ and $RQ_{t-1}^{B(i)}$

        **else**                              // $\zeta$ is the loop penalising parameter

           $\left|\quad Q_{t+1}^{(i)}(s_t^{(i)}, a_t^{(i)} = n_j) \leftarrow Q_t^{(ij)} - \zeta\right.$

        **end**

         $a_t^{(i)} = \underset{n_t^{(i)} \in N_t^{(i)}}{argmax} \left(\dfrac{Q_t^{A(i)}(s,.) + Q_t^{B(i)}(s,.)}{2}\right)$

        Update $P_t^{(id)}$

        Send $P_t^{(id)}$

    **end**

    **if** $\forall\, i \in \mathbb{N}$ *receives* $P_t^{(jd)} \wedge a_t^{(i)} = j$ **then**

        **if** $\eta == 1$ **then**

           $\left|\quad r_{t+1}^{(i)}(s_{t+1}^{(i)}, j) = -e^{\eta}(1 - T_t^{(ij)}).F_t^{(i)}\right.$

        **else**

           $\left|\quad r_{t+1}^{(i)}(s_{t+1}^{(i)}, j) = -(1 - T_t^{(ij)}).F_t^{(i)}\right.$

        **end**

        **if** $RQ_{t-1}^{A(i)}(s_{t-1}^{(i)}, j) \wedge RQ_{t-1}^{B(i)}(s_{t-1}^{(i)}, j)$ **then**

           update $Q_t^{A(ij)}$ and $Q_t^{B(ij)}$ using $r_{t+1}^{(i)}$, $RQ_{t-1}^{A(i)}$ and $RQ_{t-1}^{B(i)}$

        **else**

           $\left|\quad Q_{t+1}^{(i)}(s_t^{(i)}, a_t^{(i)} = n_j) \leftarrow Q_t^{(ij)} - \zeta\right.$

        **end**

         $a_t^{(i)} = \underset{n_t^{(i)} \in N_t^{(i)}}{argmax} \left(\dfrac{Q_t^{A(i)}(s,.) + Q_t^{B(i)}(s,.)}{2}\right)$

        Forward $P_t^{(jd)}$

    **end**

**end**

---

computational efficient. In contrast, DQR only used local energy information with a view to reducing the computational overhead and avoiding filtering out false second-hand information. Moreover, it uses two sources of energy information with a view to load balancing energy consumption across the network. When the residual energy percentage is greater than a threshold $\vartheta$, this parameter does not contribute in evaluating the consumed energy ratio $E_t^{(i)} \in [0, 1]$ as shown in Eq. 7. In that case, SNs choose the most reliable shortest path, which in turn makes some nodes overloaded due to their trustworthiness and positions. Therefore, DQR defines the energy consumption ratio $C_t^{(i)}$ to evaluate the extra burden incurred by the node due to relaying activities, as shown in Eq. 8. The weighted average of $E_t^{(i)}$ and $C_t^{(i)}$ is calculated in Eq. 9. As integrating the energy into the reward function may influence the nodes routing decision to choose a malicious path, the energy factor is bounded by $\lambda \in [0,1]$ as shown in Eq. 10.

$$E_t^{(i)} = \begin{cases} 0 & if \quad \frac{e_{res}(t)}{e_{init}} > \vartheta \\ 1 - \frac{e_{res}(t)}{e_{init}} & Otherwise \end{cases} \tag{7}$$

$$C_t^{(i)} = 1 - \frac{c_n(t)}{c_a(t)} \tag{8}$$

$$\psi_t^{(i)} = \omega E_t^{(i)} + (1 - \omega) C_t^{(i)} \tag{9}$$

$$F_t^{(i)} = e^{\lambda \psi_t^{(i)}} \tag{10}$$

where $e_{res}(t)$ is the remaining energy at time $t$, $e_{init}$ is the initial energy, $\vartheta$ is the residual energy threshold, $c_n(t)$ is the node normal energy consumption rate, $c_a(t)$ is the overall energy consumption rate, $\omega$ is the average weight, $\lambda$ is the bound parameter where $\lambda = 0$ is used to disable the energy module.

## 4.6   Trust Model

DQR evaluates the trust relationship between the SNs using the Lightweight Trust Management System (LTMS) [17]. LTMS has been chosen for several reasons. It is a lightweight distributed trust scheme designed to fit WMSN requirements. The trust value is evaluated using a novel updating mechanism that can detect packet dropping attacks with different dropping patterns thanks to integrating the slopes $b_t$ and $d_t$ into the beta distribution shape parameters $\alpha_t$ and $\beta_t$, which gives more weight to bad activities and makes it difficult to eliminate. As TMSs can be manipulated by intelligent adversaries who launch on-off attacks, LTMS is provided by a protection module that can detect complicated on-off attacks by considering short and long-term trust values to detect repeated dropping patterns as illustrated in Algorithm 4.

# 5   Evaluation and Performance Results

In this section, our proposed DQR is analyzed under different conditions. Various simulation scenarios have been run to prove the merit of DQR.

## 5.1   Experimental Setup

A WMSN for a ward in a field hospital has been adopted, as shown in Fig. 1. The SNs have been distributed randomly over an area of 50 m × 10 m. A total number of 64 SNs has been used where one of them acts as a sink, which represents the maximum number of SNs according to IEEE 802.15.6 [12]. The traffic is randomly generated using an exponential distribution density function.

---

**Algorithm 4:** Secure Trust Evaluation

---

**Input:** Observations & beta shape parameters
**Output:** Trust value
initialization;
**while** *TRUE* **do**

    **if** $b_{t-1} \leq 0$ *&&* $d_{t-1} > 0$ **then**

        $\alpha_t = \lambda(\alpha_{t-1} + b_{t-1}) + s_t$;

        $\beta_t = \lambda(\beta_{t-1} + d_{t-1}) + u_t$;

        $b_t = \alpha_t - \alpha_{t-1}$;

        $d_t = \beta_t - \beta_{t-1}$;

    **else**

        $\alpha_t = \lambda . \alpha_{t-1} + s_t$;

        $\beta_t = \lambda . \beta_{t-1} + u_t$;

        $b_t = \alpha_t - \alpha_{t-1}$;

        $d_t = \beta_t - \beta_{t-1}$;

    **end**

    **if** $\alpha_t \leq 0$ **then**

        $Rep_t^{ij} = 0$;

    **else**

        $Rep_t^{ij} = \frac{\alpha_t}{\alpha_t + \beta_t}$;

    **end**

    **if** $T_{t-1}^{ij} \geq thr_1$ *&&* $Rep_t^{ij} < thr_1$ **then**

        **if** *malicious* $> 0$ **then**

            $cycle = t - malicious$;

            $malicious = 0$;

        **else**

            $malicious = t$;

        **end**

    **end**

    **if** $cycle > 0$ *&&* $Trust(t-1) < thr_2$ **then**

        $ShRep_t^{ij} = mean(T_{t-cycle:t}^{ij})$;

        $T_t^{ij} = min(ShRep_t^{ij}, Rep_t^{ij})$;

    **else**

        $T_t^{ij} = Rep_t^{ij}$;

        $cycle = 0$;

    **end**

**end**

---

DQR is benchmarked with QRT [11] routing protocol, which has been designed to handle non-cooperative and misbehaving SNs in WMSN. It has been proposed as a trust-based extension to RL_QRP [14], an RL-based routing protocol proposed to fit WMSN. QRT has been chosen as a benchmark because it is the only routing protocol proposed to deal with dropping attacks in WMSN. To ensure fair comparisons, we adopted the reported parameters setting of QRT as shown in Table 1. The experiments have been run using a discrete event simulator based on Simpy [18]. The simulation time is set to $200s$ where the first $50s$ represents the learning time. The exploration-exploitation rate is controlled by $\varepsilon$-greedy strategy and set to 10% as in QRT. Each experiment has been run 30 times to ensure the Gaussian distribution. The results are then averaged out and reported with one standard deviation.

## 5.2    Delivery Reliability Analysis

In these experiments, the delivery performance is evaluated under different network conditions ranging from normal operation to under complicated attacks.

The packet delivery ratio and hop counts are considered to compare the optimality of the routing decisions made by both protocols.

**Table 1.** Simulation parameters

| Parameter | Value |
| --- | --- |
| Application | Poisson random traffic |
| Traffic rate $\mu$ | 1, 2, 4, 8 |
| Radio range | 5 m |
| Propagation loss model | Range propagation loss |
| Number of SNs | 64 |
| Time unit | 1 s |
| Simulation time | 200 s |
| Learning period | 50 s |
| Learning rate $\eta$ | 0.5 |
| Discount factor $\gamma$ | 0.5 |
| $\varepsilon$−greedy | 0.1 |
| The average weight $\omega$ | 0.5 |
| Residual energy threshold $\vartheta$ | 0.7 |

The first experiment studies the performance under normal operation with variable traffic rates. Some SNs generate a low traffic rate of around $1p/s$, such as heart rate SNs [19]. Thus, four traffic rates have been chosen for simulation, starting at $1p/s$ and doubling it each time. No malicious SNs are considered in this experiment. Benign nodes may drop randomly 1% of the traffic. Figure 3a and 3d show the delivery ratio, and the hop counts for both protocols under normal operation, respectively. DQR show superior data delivery performance with optimum routing decision. QRT shows high variability in terms of delivery ratio and hop count, which indicates that QRT does not converge to the optimum action-value(s) all the time. Moreover, it finds difficulty working under low traffic rates.

In the second experiment, blackhole and selective forwarding attacks are launched during the simulation to study the robustness of both protocols. The blackhole attack is a dropping attack where malicious nodes drop all received traffic instead of relaying it. In the selective forwarding attack, the malicious nodes selectively choose some sources to drop their traffic. Both attacks may disrupt the network operation. Therefore, nodes should always choose the most reliable path to destinations. The performance has been evaluated for a variable number of malicious nodes, starting from 1 malicious nodes and up to 50% of the total number of SNs. Figure 3b, 3c, 3e and 3g shows the delivery ratio and the hop counts under blackhole and selective forwarding attacks, respectively. Across all scenarios, DQR chooses the most optimal reliable paths, as illustrated in the hop counts results. When the number of malicious nodes increases, DQR avoids malicious paths and tends to choose longer but reliable paths. On the other hand, QRT is not able to detect malicious paths, as shown in the decreasing hop counts when introducing more malicious nodes. This means that packets end up in malicious nodes, which explains the low delivery ratio.

In the third scenario, sinkhole, which is a route poisoning attack, is launched to study the impact of receiving dishonest updates from other agents on routing decisions. Different levels of poisoning are evaluated starting by increasing the updates by 25% and doubling it up to 100%, where the agents send the value zero, which is the highest Q value in DQR. The delivery and hop counts ratios are illustrated in Fig. 4a–Fig. 4f. The results show that DQR is robust under different poisoning levels and can achieve a high delivery ratio. It is worth noting that in the worst-case scenario when malicious SNs advertise zeros, DQR takes slightly longer paths as the received false updates influence not only the SN itself but also its neighbors. However, this behaviour does not affect the delivery ratio.

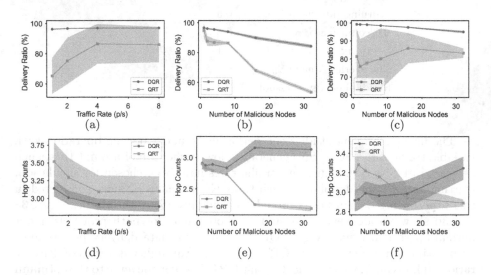

**Fig. 3.** Delivery and hop counts ratios under different conditions

## 5.3   Convergence

Q-learning is proved to converge to the optimum action-value(s) [20], as is double Q-learning [5]. However, convergence time is a crucial factor. A longer time to converge implies risking more packets to lose and consuming extra resources. In this experiment, the convergence time is evaluated in two scenarios, at the beginning of the simulation and when patients change their locations. Figure 5a demonstrates the convergence time at the beginning of the simulation, where SNs have no information about the environment and need to explore in order to converge. DQR converges faster than QRT thanks to its asynchronous updating algorithm. It took less than 50% time to converge compared to QRT. It is worth

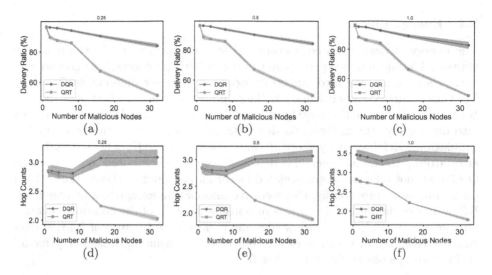

**Fig. 4.** Delivery and hop counts ratios under sinkhole attack

noting that QRT performs well at the early start because it is provided by positional information, while DQR works without any prior knowledge. In the second scenario, patient mobility is considered within the hospital ward. The patient could have up to three SNs. Thus the simulation is run for 1, 2 or 3 randomly chosen SNs at a time. Two movements have been considered at times $100s$ and $150s$. The simulation has been run for a hostile environment where 50% of the nodes are launching blackhole attacks. Figure 5b shows mobility results for only three SNs due to space constraints. The results show a fast convergence without any noticeable performance degradation for DQR protocol, which proves the robustness of our methods. On the other hand, QRT suffers from difficulty in re-converging, especially after the second movement.

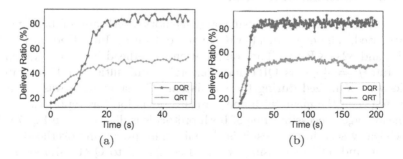

**Fig. 5.** The average convergence time

## 5.4    Energy Efficiency

The energy efficiency has been evaluated in two experiments. In the first, the network lifetime has been compared between both protocols. The second scenario shows the average consumed energy by a node for different traffic rates. Network lifetime could be defined as the running time until the first node dies [7]. Both simulation scenarios have been carried out under normal operation without introducing any attack. Figure 6a shows the percentage of alive nodes during the simulation. QRT has a very short lifetime compared to DQR. The first node dies after around $16s$ on average. This deficiency could be attributed to two reasons. QRT does not take any energy-related factor into account to choose the optimal path, and most importantly, the excessive information exchanging increases the RF activities significantly, which is responsible for 80% of the consumed energy. On the other hand, DQR shows superior performance because of its resource-conservative design, which is clearly reflected in consuming less energy for all traffic rates, as obviously seen in Fig. 6b.

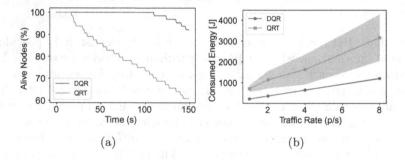

(a)                              (b)

**Fig. 6.** Energy efficiency results

## 5.5    Computational Overhead

In this experiment, the processing and memory overheads of both protocols are evaluated. The experiment was carried out on an Intel Core i9-10885H at 2.4 GHz and 32 GB RAM. The computational overhead has been evaluated for traffic rate $\mu = 4p/s$ as QRT has converging difficulties for lower rates. No attacks were launched during the simulation. The simulation was repeated 30 times, and then the mean with one standard deviation was reported.

The average processing time of both protocols is illustrated in Fig. 7a. What can be clearly seen in this result is the minimum processing overhead of DQR. It saves around 50% processing overhead compared to QRT. Moreover, unlike QRT, DQR has minimum variability. This proves that our novel RL model is resource-efficient. Moreover, the low variability of DQR indicates that DQR is always able to converge swiftly without any difficulties, proving its robustness.

Memory consumption is another crucial factor for constrained devices, such as SNs. Figure 7b depicts the average consumed memory of both protocols. During the simulation, the memory allocations were traced using a memory allocation module called tracemalloc [21]. The results show that DQR is able to save up to 80% of QRT consumed memory. Moreover, unlike QRT, DQR shows almost no variability, which indicates its robustness.

The results of this experiment show that DQR has a minimum footprint in terms of processing time and consumed memory. This lightweight computational overhead could be attributed to its resource-efficient design represented in synchronous and asynchronous Q tables updating algorithms. Furthermore, this novel design is able to converge swiftly with minimum variability allowing the packets to reach their destinations efficiently.

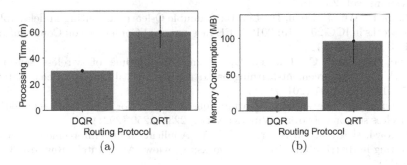

**Fig. 7.** The average processing time and memory consumption

## 6 Conclusion and Future Work

The resource scarcity and the sensitive applications have brought enormous challenges to WMSN routing protocols. The existing routing protocols for WSN cannot be directly adopted for WMSN due to overlooking some imperative requirements. In this paper, a lightweight, reliable and energy-efficient routing protocol for WMSN has been proposed. DQR is a double Q-learning routing protocol that uses a novel RL model. It uses two updating methods combined with trust management and energy models to ensure lightweight, reliable and resource-efficient data delivery. The experimental results show superior performance with minimal resource footprint. The performance of DQR will be further optimized by tuning the used hyper-parameters. Additionally, more experiments will be carried out to ensure robustness under further complicated dropping attacks.

# References

1. Barker, A., Swany, M.: Distributed cooperative reinforcement learning for wireless sensor network routing. In: 2022 IEEE Wireless Communications and Networking Conference (WCNC), pp. 2565–2570 (2022)
2. Keerthika, A., Berlin Hency, V.: Reinforcement-learning based energy efficient optimized routing protocol for WSN. Peer-to-Peer Network. Appl. **15**, 1685–1704 (2022)
3. Mammeri, Z.: Reinforcement learning based routing in networks: review and classification of approaches. IEEE Access **7**, 55916–55950 (2019)
4. Künzel, G., Indrusiak, L.S., Pereira, C.E.: Latency and lifetime enhancements in industrial wireless sensor networks: a Q-learning approach for graph routing. IEEE Trans. Ind. Inform. **16**, 5617–5625 (2020)
5. Hasselt, H.: Double Q-learning. In: Advances in Neural Information Processing Systems, vol. 23 (2010)
6. Yuan, F., Wu, J., Zhou, H., Liu, L.: A double Q-learning routing in delay tolerant networks in ICC 2019. In: 2019 IEEE International Conference on Communications (ICC), 1–6 (2019)
7. Guo, W., Yan, C., Lu, T.: Optimizing the lifetime of wireless sensor networks via reinforcement-learning-based routing. Int. J. Distrib. Sens. Netw. **15**, 1550147719833541 (2019)
8. Maivizhi, R., Yogesh, P.: Q-learning based routing for in-network aggregation in wireless sensor networks. Wireless Netw., 2231–2250 (2021)
9. Al-Rawi, H.A., Ng, M.A., Yau, K.-L.A.: Application of reinforcement learning to routing in distributed wireless networks: a review. Artif. Intell. Rev. **43**, 381–416 (2015)
10. Liu, G., Wang, X., Li, X., Hao, J., Feng, Z.: ESRQ: an efficient secure routing method in wireless sensor networks based on Q-learning. In: 2018 17th IEEE International Conference on Trust, Security And Privacy in Computing and Communications/12th IEEE International Conference On Big Data Science And Engineering (TrustCom/BigDataSE), pp. 149–155 (2018)
11. Naputta, Y., Usaha, W.: RL-based routing in biomedical mobile wireless sensor networks using trust and reputation. In: 2012 International Symposium on Wireless Communication Systems (ISWCS), 521–525 (2012)
12. IEEE. IEEE Standard for Local and metropolitan area networks - Part 15.6: Wireless Body Area Networks. IEEE Std 802.15.6-2012, 1–271, February 2012
13. Azdad, N., Elboukhari, M.: Wireless body area networks for healthcare: application trends and MAC technologies. Int. J. Bus. Data Commun. Network. (IJBDCN) **17**, 1–20 (2021)
14. Liang, X., Balasingham, I., Byun, S.-S.: A reinforcement learning based routing protocol with QoS support for biomedical sensor networks. In: 2008 First International Symposium on Applied Sciences on Biomedical and Communication Technologies, pp. 1–5 (2008)
15. Jiang, J., Zhu, X., Han, G., Guizani, M., Shu, L.: A dynamic trust evaluation and update mechanism based on C4. 5 decision tree in underwater wireless sensor networks. IEEE Trans. Veh. Technol. **69**, 9031–9040 (2020)
16. Krishnaswamy, V., Manvi, S.S.: Trusted node selection in clusters for underwater wireless acoustic sensor networks using fuzzy logic. Phys. Commun. **47**, 101388 (2021)

17. Hajar, M.S., Al-Kadri, M.O., Kalutarage, H.: LTMS: a lightweight trust management system for wireless medical sensor networks. In: 2020 IEEE 19th International Conference on Trust, Security and Privacy in Computing and Communications (TrustCom), pp. 1783–1790 (2020)
18. Matloff, N.: Introduction to discrete-event simulation and the SimPy language. In: Davis, C.A. (ed.) Department of Computer Science. University of California at Davis (2008). Accessed 2 Aug
19. Islam, M.N., Yuce, M.R.: Review of medical implant communication system (MICS) band and network. Ict Express **2**, 188–194 (2016)
20. Melo, F.S.: Convergence of Q-learning: a simple proof. Institute of Systems and Robotics, Technical Report, 1–4 (2001)
21. TRACEMALLOC - Trace memory allocations - Python 3.10.2 documentation. https://docs.python.org/3/library/tracemalloc.html. Accessed 8 Feb 2022

# Message Recovery Attack of Kyber Based on Information Leakage in Decoding Operation

Mengyao Shi[1,2], Zhu Wang[1,2(✉)], Tingting Peng[1,2], and Fenghua Li[1,2]

[1] Institute of Information Engineering, Chinese Academy of Sciences,
Beijing 100093, China
wangzhu@iie.ac.cn
[2] University of Chinese Academy of Sciences, Beijing 100049, China

**Abstract.** In this work, we propose practical side-channel attacks for message recovery in post-quantum key encapsulation mechanisms (KEM). As a target scheme, Kyber is a standardized algorithm in the ongoing NIST standardization process. Notably, this work is the first one that implements message recovery by exploiting the information leaked on computational operations during Kyber decoding. The main findings include 1. analyzing computational operations during decoding by power consumption information to effectively recover message; 2. recovering message by analyzing the time differences existing in decoding single bits; 3. by way of simple power analysis, using incremental storage leakage to recover the message.

**Keywords:** Lattice-based cryptography · Side-channel attacks · Message decoding · Kyber

## 1 Introduction

The rapid development of quantum computing technology has posed a severe challenge to the security of traditional modern cryptographic schemes. The unique physical properties of quantum systems, such as superposition and coherence, make quantum Turing machines more computationally efficient than classical Turing machines. In 1994, Peter w. Shor of Bell Labs [1] proposed quantum computing based on the discrete logarithm problem and the significant integer prime factorization problem, which makes it possible to solve a large number of decomposition problems in polynomial time; In 1996, Grover [2] proposed to speed up the key search by continuously doing the Mississippi transformation to increase the likelihood of the desired solution value. These contributions make public-key cryptosystems built on the assumption of computational hardness (e.g., RSA, ECC, and other algorithms) no longer secure, and also raise the issue of the security of protocols based on such algorithms and the security of products based on such protocols. Accordingly, research on post-quantum cryptosystems has become a frontier focus issue in the cryptographic field.

F. Li et al. (Eds.): SecureComm 2022, LNICST 462, pp. 630–647, 2023.
https://doi.org/10.1007/978-3-031-25538-0_33

Based on the new cryptosystem, post-quantum algorithms mainly include code-based cryptography, hash-based cryptography, lattice-based cryptography, multivariate cryptography and supersingular isogeny cryptography. At the end of 2016, the National Institute of Standards and Technology (NIST) launched the standard solicitation of post-quantum cryptography algorithm [3]. On July 5, 2022, NIST announced it has completed the third round of the post-quantum Cryptography standardization process. As a result, a total of four candidate algorithms have been selected for standardization. As one of four, Kyber [4] was successfully selected as a standardized algorithm for it strong security and excellent performance [5], and NIST expected it to work well in most applications.

The cryptographic algorithm ensures the algorithm's security through theory, but the mathematical security of algorithm design can not fully guarantee the security of the implementation. Side-channel attack is an effective technology that seriously threatens the safety of cryptographic implementation (cryptographic chip and cryptographic system). Side-channel attacks (refer to Fig. 1) mainly exploits the leakage of side information (such as time, power consumption, etc.) during the operation of the cryptographic algorithm. It achieves the attack by analyzing the dependency between the side-channel information and the secret information. Since timing attack [6] was proposed in 1996, after more than 20 years of development, the international standard algorithms 3DES, AES, Sha-3, RSA, ECC, etc. have been successfully analyzed using side-channel attacks. The mighty power of side-channel attack in analyzing classical cryptographic algorithms seriously threatens the security of cryptographic systems, which poses a severe challenge to the protection of cryptographic algorithms and has attracted extensive attention. Therefore, algorithm security is no longer limited to design safety, and the implementation of security has become an important indicator. Therefore, in the third round of evaluation, NIST pointed out that an important indicator to measure whether the post-quantum cryptography candidate algorithm can become a standard is to resist side-channel attack.

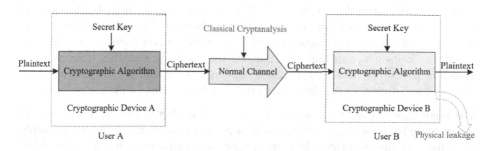

**Fig. 1.** Pictorial representation of the side-channel attack.

From classical cryptography to post-quantum cryptography, side-channel attack is not a simple transplant. Although assumptions are both based on mathematical difficulties, the post-quantum public key cryptosystem adopts an entirely different mathematical structure from the traditional public key cryptosystem. The side-channel information leaked in the implementation process and the subsequent side-channel attack methods are further from the conventional one, so the side-channel security can not be obtained by simply transplanting the attack methods. For post-quantum cryptography, the adversary must invest extra effort to find the key-dependent data required for side-channel attack. Therefore, to meet the urgent needs of formulating post-quantum cryptography algorithm standards, it is critical to carry out accurate and efficient side-channel security analysis on post-quantum cryptography.

## 1.1 Related Work

In the process of encryption and decryption, the cryptographic equipment will inevitably leak signals (power consumption, electromagnetic emanation, time, etc.). Unlike other forms of cryptographic analysis, side-channel attacks use the information leaked from the target device to find information related to the key, including the time or power consumption of the internal operation of the device or the error output generated by the device. Currently, the side-channel attack methods of post-quantum cryptography mainly focus on power consumption/ electromagnetic emanation, time and fault injection. In recent years, side-channel attacks related to Kyber algorithm mainly include: in 2019, Pessl and Primas [7] proposed a single power trace attack scheme for NTT in Kyber; In 2020, Ravi et al. [8] launched a chosen-ciphertext attack against a variety of lattice-based cryptographic algorithms such as Round5, LAC, Kyber, FrodoKEM, NewHope, etc., and its main attack targets are error correcting codes and FO-transformation [9]. In 2019, Ravi and Roy et al. [10] proposed a fault attack scheme against nonce random seeds of Gaussian distribution in NewHope, Kyber, FrodoKEM and other different cryptographic algorithms; In 2018, Albrecht and Deo et al. [11] launched cold boot attacks against NTT in Kyber and NewHope. The above attacks on Kyber and other algorithms mainly focus on core operators such as NTT, error correcting code and FO-transformation. In fact, there are more effective attack points than those mentioned above. Information leakage in the encoding and decoding process can also effectively recover message information.

In the key encapsulation mechanism, the message encoding and message decoding processes involve arithmetic operations on the message. The study of side-channel attacks on these two processes is described below separately.

**Message Encoding Process.** Amiet *et al.* [12] in PQCrypto 2020 used a single power trace to attack the message encoding operation in the C reference implementation of the NewHope key encapsulation mechanism submitted to NIST for the second round and found that it had a severe side-channel vulnerability. Under the Hamming weight leakage model, the power consumption of the processed sensitive intermediate value under two different values was very different, which leaked information about single bits of the message. When the compiler optimization level was -O0, the bit-by-bit recovery of the message could be realized only by using simple power attack. When the compiler optimization level reached -O3, 256 templates should be pre-processed. By combining the template attack and the brute-force search, the success rate of message recovery could reach 99%. Based on [12], Sim *et al.* [13] further explored the side-channel security of the message encoding operation in other lattice-based key encapsulation schemes that entered the third round of NIST evaluation. The author used a single power trace to analyze the message encoding phase of the key encapsulation scheme implemented by the C reference. It was found that the side-channel vulnerabilities in [12] commonly exist in Kyber, Saber, and FrodoKEM. In particular, when analyzing Saber and FrodoKEM, the author used a machine learning method to build templates to help recover the encoded message. Xu *et al.* [14] successfully attacked the memory-efficient and high-speed Kyber encoding operation in *pqm4* [15]. By taking specific preprocessing measures to filter POIs and calculate the threshold in the profiling stage, the author could use the two-stage recovery attack on the -O0 and -O3 compiler levels to recover the message with a 100% success rate.

**Message Decoding Process.** Ngo *et al.* [16] conducted a comprehensive study on the Saber scheme with masking implementation for IND-CCA security. In the reference implementation, the author found the side-channel leakage point of the "incremental storage" vulnerability in the message decoding process mentioned in [17] and the newly found poly_A2A() primitive also contains an exploitable point of "incremental storage" vulnerability. Based on this work, Ngo *et al.* [18] subsequently used the ciphertext malleability proposed by [17] to attack the decoding process of the Saber scheme with shuffling protection at the same time. As a result, the message recovery attack was realized. Ravi *et al.* [19] analyzed the decoding process of multiple lattice-based KEMs and successfully implemented horizontal message recovery attacks.

These attacks show some vulnerabilities in the lattice-based post-quantum cryptography schemes and strongly indicate that more potential vulnerabilities have not been discovered. Therefore, we believe that further research in this field is necessary to give the implementation scheme a complete security check and provide security recommendations for deploying these schemes in the real world.

## 1.2 Our Contribution

We perform side-channel attacks on the implementation of Kyber obtained from the *pqm4* public library, a testing and benchmarking framework for post-quantum cryptographic schemes on the ARM Cortex-M4 microcontroller. Refer to Fig. 2 for the pictorial description of our attacks (Attack_Decoding) targeting the message recovery. In this work, by focusing on the message decoding operation in the decapsulation phase, we comprehensively analyze the side-channel leakage about time and power consumption that can be used for message recovery in this process. The main contributions of this paper can be summarized as follows.

(1) **Novelty of attack target:** Existing attacks focus more on recovery attacks against the long-term key, while message recovery attacks leading to shared

session key recovery have received little attention. Compared with traditional PKE/KEM based on RSA and ECC, message in LWE/LWR-based PKE/KEM operates uniquely on each bit of message.

(2) **Universality of the attack:** In essence, our work exploits the algorithmic properties inherent in the LWE/LWR-based scheme since the decoding operation is unique to the LWE/LWR scheme. In this paper, we achieve full recovery of the message from the assembly level by analyzing the power leakage and the time leakage generated during the bitwise computation and storage of the message.

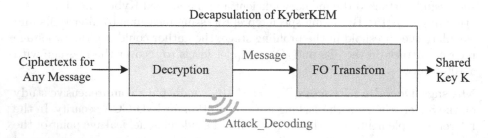

**Fig. 2.** Pictorial representation of our proposed attacks on the Kyber decapsulation procedure.

### 1.3   Outline

The rest of the paper is organized as follows. In the next section, we recall the Kyber algorithm and message recovery attacks. Section 3 consists of the detailed experimental environment. Section 4 shows some findings of our side-channel attacks on Kyber's message decoding process. Section 5 makes a complete and profound analysis of our experimental findings in Sect. 4. Finally, the conclusion is discussed in Sect. 6.

## 2   Background

### 2.1   Parameter Settings

The basic elements in Kyber are the polynomials in the ring $\mathbb{Z}_q[x]/(x^n + 1)$, denoted by $\mathcal{R}_q$, with $n = 256$ and $q = 3329$ in all variants of Kyber. The parameter $k$ represents the dimension of the matrix of polynomials in $\mathcal{R}_q$. Kyber has three variants aimed at different security levels. In order of increasing security they are Kyber512, Kyber768, and Kyber1024, and their parameters can be found in Table 1. The attack methods proposed in this paper are applicable to the above three security levels.

**Table 1.** Parameter sets for Kyber.

| Algorithm | NIST-level | $n$ | $q$ | $k$ |
|-----------|------------|-----|------|-----|
| Kyber512 | 1(AES-128) | 256 | 3329 | 2 |
| Kyber768 | 3(AES-192) | 256 | 3329 | 3 |
| Kyber1024 | 5(AES-256) | 256 | 3329 | 4 |

## 2.2 Module Learning with Errors Problem

The learning with errors (LWE) problem proposed by Regev [20] is one of the most well-known hard problems in the average case. It is considered computationally infeasible for both classical and quantum computers. There are two versions of the LWE problem - Search LWE and Decisional LWE. The search variant of the LWE problem requires the attacker to compute the secret value given several LWE samples. The decisional variant of the LWE problem requires the attacker to distinguish uniformly random samples from similar LWE samples.

As we know, several lattice-based NIST candidates are constructed based on LWE or algebraically structured variants of the standard LWE problem known as Ring/Module-LWE (RLWE/MLWE). The security of Kyber is based on the Module-LWE hardness assumption. MLWE differs from LWE in using the polynomial ring instead of the integer ring. The decision and search LWE problem over standard lattices can be extended to the decision and search MLWE problem over module lattices.

## 2.3 Kyber

Lattice-based IND-CPA schemes can be made secure against CCA by being transformed into IND-CCA schemes with the help of a post-quantum variant of the Fujisaki-Okamoto (FO) transformation [8]. The transformation is also used by Kyber to achieve IND-CCA security. Kyber KEM contains three algorithms: Key Generation, Encapsulation, and Decapsulation. Simplified versions of the three algorithms are described in the corresponding Algorithm 1, Algorithm 2, and Algorithm 3.

---

**Algorithm 1.** KYBER.CCAKEM.KEYGEN()

---

**Output:** Public key $pk \in \mathcal{B}^{12 \cdot k \cdot n/8+32}$
**Output:** Secret key $sk \in \mathcal{B}^{24 \cdot k \cdot n/8+96}$
1: $Z \leftarrow \mathcal{B}^{32}$
2: $(pk, sk') := $ KYBER.CPAPKE.KEYGEN()
3: $sk := (sk'||pk||\text{H(pk)}||z)$
4: **return** $(pk, sk)$

---

**Algorithm 2.** KYBER.CCAKEM.ENC($pk$)

---

**Input:** Public key $pk \in \mathcal{B}^{12 \cdot k \cdot n/8 + 32}$
**Output:** Ciphertext $c \in \mathcal{B}^{d_u \cdot k \cdot n/8 + d_v \cdot n/8}$
**Output:** Shared key $K \in \mathcal{B}^*$
1: $m \leftarrow \mathcal{B}^{32}$
2: $m \leftarrow \mathrm{H}(m)$
3: $(\overline{K}, r) := \mathrm{G}(m \| \mathrm{H}(pk))$
4: $c := $ KYBER.CPAPKE.ENC($pk, m, r$)
5: $K := \mathrm{KDF}(\overline{K} \| \mathrm{H}(c))$
6: **return** $(c, K)$

---

**Algorithm 3.** KYBER.CCAKEM.DEC($c, sk$)

---

**Input:** Ciphertext $c \in \mathcal{B}^{d_u \cdot k \cdot n/8 + d_v \cdot n/8}$
**Input:** Secret key $sk \in \mathcal{B}^{24 \cdot k \cdot n/8 + 96}$
**Output:** Shared key $K \in \mathcal{B}^*$
1: $pk := sk + 12 \cdot k \cdot n/8$
2: $h := sk + 24 \cdot k \cdot n/8 + 32 \in \mathcal{B}^{32}$
3: $z := sk + 24 \cdot k \cdot n/8 + 64$
4: $m' := $ KYBER.CPAPKE.DEC $(s, (\mathbf{u}, \mathbf{v}))$
5: $(\overline{K}', r') := \mathrm{G}(m' \| h)$
6: $c' := $ KYBER.CPAPKE.ENC $(pk, m', r')$
7: **if** $c = c'$ **then**
8:     **return** $K := \mathrm{KDF}(\overline{K}' \| \mathrm{H}(c))$
9: **else**
10:     **return** $K := \mathrm{KDF}(z \| \mathrm{H}(c))$
11: **end if**
12: **return** $K$

---

### 2.4 Message Recovery Attack

By analyzing the implementation of Kyber's encapsulation and decapsulation algorithm in the last part, it can be found that if an attacker can try to obtain the message $m$, he can easily calculate the shared session key through $m$ and known public values, which will seriously threaten the session security of both communication parties. In other words, the leakage of message values will seriously damage the confidentiality of the cryptosystem.

In the part of related work, we summarize the previous message recovery attacks completed in message encoding and decoding process through side-channel attacks. Theoretically, any operation related to the message can be used as a potential attack path to recover useful information about the message. Regarding the implementation process of Kyber, there are attack paths other than message encoding and decoding. In Kyber's encapsulation procedure Algorithm 2, step 1 involves the generation of random message $m$; step 2 is the hash operation H involving message $m$; In step 3, as part of the input, $m$ participates in the hash operation G; The message encoding process in step 4 is an effective and commonly used attack path. In Kyber's decapsulation procedure Algorithm 3, the first desirable attack path is the message encoding process included in step 4; step 5 here corresponds to step 3 of Algorithm 2, which is also desirable; Since the Kyber KEM to which the FO transformation is applied includes the re-encryption operation, there is step 6 similar to step 3 of Algorithm 2.

Considering the realizability of message recovery under above attack paths, this paper mainly focuses on the message decoding operation in the decapsulation procedure. In the following, we will prove that several side-channel vulnerabilities in the message decoding process can be used to recover the complete message.

```
1  void poly_tomsg(unsigned char msg[32],poly *a){
2      unsigned int k;
3      unsigned short t;
4      int i,j;
5      for(i=0;i<32;i++) {
6          msg[i] = 0;
7          for(j=0;j<8;j++) {
8              k = 8*i+j;
9              t = ((a)->coeffs[k] << 1 ) + 1664;
10             /*calculate message bit*/
11             t = ( t / 3329 ) & 1;
12             /*bit update in memory*/
13             msg[i] |= t << j;
14         }
15     }
16 }
```

**Listing 1.** C code snippet of message decoding operation in Kyber KEM.

## 3   Experimental Setup

The device under attack we use is an OSR407 development board with a 32bit ARM Cortex-M4 processor. The target message decoding implementation is from the public *pqm4* library, which provides NIST recommended optimized target for embedded software implementations. We use the original implementation it provides (refer to Listing 1 plus a trigger signal to simplify the recording of power traces. The device used to record power traces is the Lecroy 3000z oscilloscope with a sampling rate of 1.0 GSam/sec. Refer to Fig. 3 for our power-based SCA setup used for our experiments.

(a)                                    (b)

**Fig. 3.** Experimental setup for SCA.(a) SCA setup. (b) Zoomed-in view of the DUT.

# 4 SPA of ARM-Specific Implementation

In this section, we attacked the "ARM-Specific" reference implementation specifically optimized for ARM Cortex-M4 processor of Kyber from a side-channel perspective. Accordingly, we found three obvious side-channel leakages on message decoding operation during the decapsulation procedure of Kyber.

## 4.1 Power Consumption Leakage in Computation

Collecting power traces during Kyber decapsulation, it is found that there are significant differences in the power trace when decoding different message bits. Figure 4 interprets the power trace with the first message byte value of 2. In

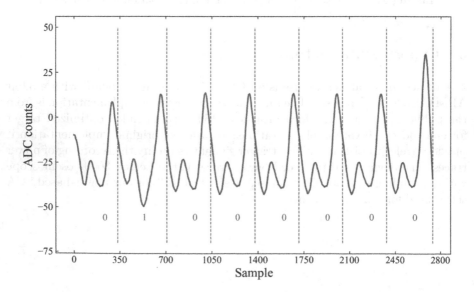

**Fig. 4.** A single trace measurement of $msg[0] = 2$ (binary 0000 0010).

the process of decoding this byte, the recovered bits are 0,1,0,0,0,0,0,0 orderly; that is, for the calculation results, only the second bit is different. The difference can be clearly seen in Fig. 4, because the power consumption fluctuation is more apparent when the recovered message bit value is 1. Therefore, each bit of a message byte can be directly recovered through simple power attack.

## 4.2  Timing Leakage

In order to better analyze the time difference in the process of decoding the message bits taking different values, we selected 0 and 255 as experimental objects. When the decoding process of message byte values 255 and 0 is repeated 32 times, we found that the former takes longer than the latter. Additionally, Fig. 5 shows the power traces of the first message byte value of 0 and 255, respectively. It can be clearly seen that when the start position of the two is the same, the sampling end time after decoding is different. Therefore, it can be inferred that processing bit 1 takes much longer than processing bit 0.

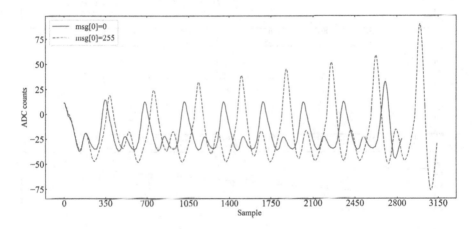

**Fig. 5.** Traces of $msg[0] = 0$ and $msg[0] = 255$.

## 4.3  Incremental Leakage

By comparing the power traces of message bytes with values of 0,1,2... 255 during message decoding, it is found that there is a fixed peak interval in the interval processing of adjacent bits, and the maximum power consumption in this interval is always greater than or approximately equal to the power consumption of the corresponding interval of the last bit. Figure 6 indicates the comparison details in the power traces where $msg[0]$ takes 0,1,2,34, and 255, respectively.

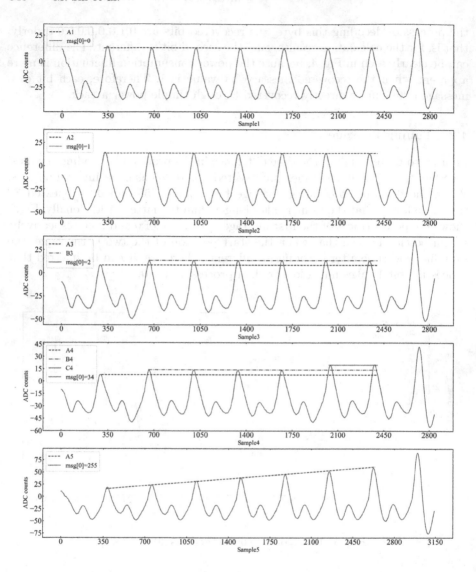

**Fig. 6.** Traces of $msg[0] = 0, 1, 2, 34, 255$ (top to bottom).

## 5   Analysis of Experimental Results

To better understand the execution details of the message decoding process on the actual embedded device, we use the arm-none-eabi-gcc compiler toolchain to further obtain the assembly code under -Os (refer to Listing 2) and -O0 compiler options. The analysis of these instructions can help us to complete effective message recovery attacks under the message decoding path.

```
1    .L3:
2        strb r6, [r0, #1]!
3        add r5, r1, r2, lsl #1
4        movs r4, #0
5    .L2:
6    /* t = ( (a)->coeffs[k] << 1 ) + 1664; */
7        ldrsh r3, [r5], #2
8        ldrsh ip, [r0]
9        lsls r3, r3, #1
10       add r3, r3, #1664
11       uxth r3, r3
12   /* t = ( t / 3329 ) & 1; */
13       udiv r3, r3, 3329
14       and r3, r3, #1
15   /* msg[i] |= t << j; */
16       lsls r3, r3, r4
17       adds r4, r4, #1
18       orr r3, r3, ip
19       cmp r4, #8
20   /* store msg[i] in memory*/
21       strb r3, [r0]
22       bne .L2
23       adds r2, r2, #8
24       cmp r2, #256
25       bne .L3
```

**Listing 2.** Assembly code snippet (at -Os) of a single iteration of the message decoding function in Kyber.

## 5.1   Power Consumption Analysis

**Power Consumption Analysis at -Os Level.** By comparing the power consumption during decoding, two significant differences in power trace segments were found when the resultant bits were 0 and 1, respectively. They are now labeled separately in Fig. 7. According to the execution of instructions, the two apparent differences are caused by the *udiv* instruction (integer division instruction) in one-bit processing and the *strb* instruction (storage instruction from register to memory) at the end of one-bit processing. The following analyzes the two differences, respectively.

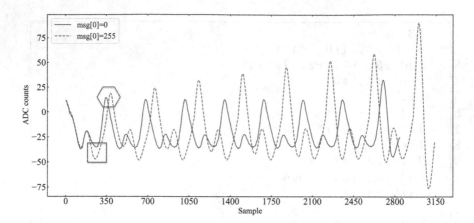

**Fig. 7.** Traces at -Os of $msg[0] = 0$ and $msg[0] = 255$ (two labels showing differences between message bit 0 and 1)

*udiv Instruction.* By analyzing the sampling interval of **udiv** instruction execution on power traces, it is found that the power fluctuation amplitude when the calculation result is 0 is much smaller than that when the calculation result is 1. This significant difference is marked in Fig. 7 with a blue rectangular box. Further observation shows that this difference exists in the eight times of decoding with $msg[0] = 0$ and 255, which is consistent with the above analysis. To prove the universality of the above analysis, we repeat the above experiment for 256 possible values of one byte, which is verified to be true. Since the difference is so significant that the calculation results can be read directly from the oscilloscope, the value of the message can be recovered from a single power trace through SPA. Figure 8 shows a single power trace. According to the above

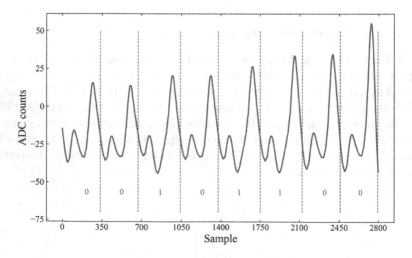

**Fig. 8.** A single trace measurement where $msg[0] = 52$.

analysis, the decoded message byte can be directly recovered bit by bit horizontally: 52 (binary representation: 00110100).

*strb Instruction.* It is well known that the storage operation divulges the Hamming weight of the stored value. Therefore, if an attacker can identify the Hamming weight of the median value of each message byte during the decoding operation, he can recover each bit value of the message byte under the leakage feature of incremental storage. According to the analysis of Fig. 6, for $msg[0] = 0$, at the peak position of 1-bit processing, the values of the first seven processes are approximately the same because the Hamming weight of the stored operand is 0 every time, so the power consumption of the corresponding instruction execution is roughly the same; For $msg[0] = 255$, at the peak position of 1-bit processing, the value of the first seven processing times is higher than that of the previous time. This is because each decoded message bit is 1. When it is connected to the median value of the message byte, the Hamming weight of the value increases by 1. Therefore, the power consumption of *strb* instruction execution rises with the increase of the Hamming weight of the operand. For the last bit, the decoding result of $msg[0] = 0$ is 0, and the decoding result of $msg[0] = 255$ is 1. At this time, the value of the spike position of 1-bit processing is always greater than the previous one. It can be seen from the assembly code snippet of Listing 2 that the power consumption sampling in this interval will include the subsequent *add* and *cmp* instructions, and thus the power fluctuation is more significant.

In general, the incremental storage leakage during the decoding operation can be used to recover the message byte except the first bit and the last bit. To prove the universality of the above analysis, we repeat the above experiment for 256 possible values of one byte, which is verified to be true. Since the leakage is so significant that the decoding result can be read directly from the oscilloscope, six bits of one message byte can be recovered from a single power trace through simple power analysis.

*The Horizontal Message Recovery Scheme.* Using the leakage on the *udiv* division instruction, we can recover the value of each message byte bit by bit on a single power trace. In order to make full use of the leaked information, a fault-tolerance scheme can be built with the leaked information on the *strb* instruction to assist in verifying that the message bits recovered through the *udiv* instruction leakage are correct, except the first bit and the last bit of one byte. For 256 possible values of one message byte, we demonstrate that the above horizontal message recovery scheme can recover the value of message bytes with a 100% success rate.

**Power Consumption Analysis at -O0 Level.** At the -O0 level, the division operation in the decoding process does not use the *udiv* instruction but the *umull* series of instructions. Through experimental analysis, it is found that the difference in power consumption is not apparent when the operand takes different values. Therefore, the message value cannot be recovered using the scheme proposed in the last part. The power consumption leakage found on the **udiv** instruction no longer applies to the analysis at -O0 compiler level.

To explore the applicability of the horizontal message recovery attack proposed in the last part at this compiler level, the compiler parameter is modified to -O0, and the experiment under -Os is repeated. To reduce the negative effect of noise, the decoding experimental data is sampled 1000 times and then averaged. Figure 9 shows two power traces during the message decoding process where $msg[0]$ is 0 and 255, respectively.

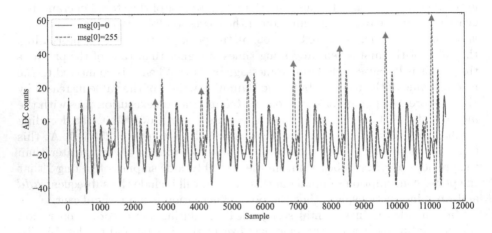

**Fig. 9.** Traces of $msg[0] = 0$ and $msg[0] = 255$.

For the decoding process with $msg[0] = 0$, the operand of **strb** instruction stored each time is 0, and the corresponding Hamming weight is also 0. Therefore, with the Hamming weight model, the power consumption of **strb** instruction execution is approximately equal in the eight intervals. For the decoding process with $msg[0] = 255$, the operands of **strb** instruction stored each time are 1,3,7,15,31,63,127,255, and the corresponding Hamming weight increases by one from 1 to 8. Therefore, under the Hamming weight model, the power consumption during the execution of **strb** instruction is gradually augmented during 8 intervals. Consequently, the average difference in **strb** instruction power consumption per bit of decoding processing should be increased. As the result, the interval in which the difference between the two values shown in Fig. 9 increases significantly in turn in 8 processes can represent the sampling interval of **strb** instruction execution. We express this interval as $w[i]$, where $i \in [0, 7]$. When a simple power analysis is made for the $w[i]$ interval of a single group of data, the power consumption values of w[i] in the eight processing processes are approximately the same in terms of $msg[0] = 0$; As far as $msg[0] = 255$ is concerned, the power consumption of $w[i]$ in the eight processes is significantly higher than that in the last process. This is consistent with the power consumption characteristics of Hamming weight model.

*The Horizontal Message Recovery Scheme.* For the attacked message decoding process, when recovering the message of one byte on the obtained power trace, first locate the $w[i]$ interval corresponding to the byte, where $i \in [0, 7]$. According to the analysis in the last section, for $i \in [1, 7]$, compare the power consumption value of $w[i]$ with the power consumption value of $w[i-1]$ corresponding to the previous process, and then recover the message value of the $i$th bit by bit; For the recovery of the message value of the 0th bit, firstly, build two templates with the corresponding bit value of $w[0]$ being 0 and 1 respectively, then calculate the similarity between $w[0]$ and the two templates respectively. Finally, take the value corresponding to the template with high similarity as the message bit recovery value of $w[0]$. As a result of the attack, the value of the message byte can be completely recovered.

## 5.2  Timing Leakage Analysis

Usually, the main reason for the leakage of time information is the use of branch statements. Kyber adopts nested for-loop in the decoding process, and its code implementation effectively avoids the timing attack based on branch statements. However, by analyzing the assembly code in the decoding process, we find that the number of clock cycles spent by **udiv** instructions depends on the value of the operand, while **strb**, **add**, **movs**, **ldrsh**, **lsls**, **uxth**, **orr**, **cmp** instructions are completed in fixed number of clock cycles. It can be seen that the time difference of different message intermediate byte values calculated depends on the time difference of **udiv** instruction execution.

For 256 different values of one message byte, we build 256 groups of ciphertext. Except that the values of the first byte are belonging to [0,255], the message values of other bytes after decoding are random. To obtain a clear and noise-weakened power trace, we repeat the decoding process 100 times and average the obtained power traces.

It is known that the number of sampling points = sampling rate $\times$ sampling time. From the power traces in Fig. 5, we can see that for a 1-byte message decoding process, the sampling interval of $msg[0] = 0$ is narrower than that of $msg[0] = 255$. Therefore, when the sampling rates are fixed, the execution time of decoding $msg[0] = 255$ is longer than that of $msg[0] = 0$. According to the clock cycle required for instruction execution, this difference is caused by the difference of the operand when the **udiv** instruction is executed. In the process of decoding $msg[0] = 0$, the result of 8 times of **udiv** instruction execution is 0; In the process of decoding $msg[0] = 255$, the result of 8 times of **udiv** instruction execution is 1. According to the statistics of the sampling points in the eight effective intervals of Fig. 5, there are significant differences in the sampling points processed in these eight segments: for $msg[0] = 0$, there are about 335 sampling points in an effective interval; For $msg[0] = 1$, the number of sampling points in an effective interval is about 373; As explained above, there is a significant difference in clock cycles spent by the **udiv** instruction in implementing the above two calculations.

Unlike -Os, which uses the *udiv* instruction to implement the division operation $t/Q$, the other four compiler levels -O0, -O1, -O2, and -O3 use a combination of multiplication *umull*, subtraction *subs*, and addition *add* instructions to implement the division operation. In particular, in the Kyber's specification, the author mentioned that on the ARM Cortex-M3 processor, the *umull* instruction is implemented within a variable number of clock cycles, and its execution time depends on the value of the operands involved in the operation, which is a possible source of timing leakage. However, as far as the ARM Cortex-M4 processor is concerned, this leakage does not exist because the *umull* instruction is guaranteed to complete within a single clock cycle. According to the number of clock cycles of instructions execution, the analysis of the remaining assembly instructions shows that when these four compiler optimizations are adopted, the message decoding process does not have side-channel leakage in the time dimension on the Cortex-M4 processor.

## 6   Conclusion

In this paper, we prove that Kyber's decoding process is vulnerable to side-channel attacks in terms of power consumption and time. Subsequently, We show a new type of horizontal message recovery attack. The proposed attack method can use a single power trace to recover the message value with a 100% success rate. Because of the severe threat to the security system, adding well-designed shuffling and masking schemes to the message decoding process may be an effective protection strategy.

## References

1. Shor, P.W.: Algorithms for quantum computation: discrete logarithms and factoring. In: Proceedings 35th Annual Symposium on Foundations of Computer Science, pp. 124–134. IEEE (1994)
2. Grover, L.K.: A fast quantum mechanical algorithm for database search. In: Proceedings of the Twenty-Eighth Annual ACM Symposium on Theory of Computing, pp. 212–219 (1996)
3. Chen, L., et al.: Report on post-quantum cryptography, vol. 12. US Department of Commerce, National Institute of Standards and Technology (2016)
4. Bos, J., et al.: CRYSTALS-Kyber: a CCA-secure module-lattice-based KEM. In: 2018 IEEE European Symposium on Security and Privacy (EuroS&P), pp. 353–367. IEEE (2018)
5. PQC Standardization Process: Announcing Four Candidates to be Standardized, Plus Fourth Round Candidates. https://csrc.nist.gov/News/2022/pqc-candidates-to-be-standardized-and-round-4
6. Kocher, P.C.: Timing attacks on implementations of Diffie-Hellman, RSA, DSS, and other systems. In: Koblitz, N. (ed.) CRYPTO 1996. LNCS, vol. 1109, pp. 104–113. Springer, Heidelberg (1996). https://doi.org/10.1007/3-540-68697-5_9
7. Pessl, P., Primas, R.: More practical single-trace attacks on the number theoretic transform. In: Schwabe, P., Thériault, N. (eds.) LATINCRYPT 2019. LNCS, vol. 11774, pp. 130–149. Springer, Cham (2019). https://doi.org/10.1007/978-3-030-30530-7_7

8. Ravi, P., Roy, S.S., Chattopadhyay, A., Bhasin, S.: Generic side-channel attacks on CCA-secure lattice-based PKE and KEMS. IACR Trans. Cryptogr. Hardw. Embed. Syst. **2020**(3), 307–335 (2020)
9. Fujisaki, E., Okamoto, T.: Secure integration of asymmetric and symmetric encryption schemes. In: Wiener, M. (ed.) CRYPTO 1999. LNCS, vol. 1666, pp. 537–554. Springer, Heidelberg (1999). https://doi.org/10.1007/3-540-48405-1_34
10. Ravi, P., Roy, D.B., Bhasin, S., Chattopadhyay, A., Mukhopadhyay, D.: Number "Not Used" once - practical fault attack on *pqm4* implementations of NIST candidates. In: Polian, I., Stöttinger, M. (eds.) COSADE 2019. LNCS, vol. 11421, pp. 232–250. Springer, Cham (2019). https://doi.org/10.1007/978-3-030-16350-1_13
11. Albrecht, M.R., Deo, A., Paterson, K.G.: Cold boot attacks on ring and module LWE keys under the NTT. Cryptology ePrint Archive (2018)
12. Amiet, D., Curiger, A., Leuenberger, L., Zbinden, P.: Defeating NEWHOPE with a single trace. In: Ding, J., Tillich, J.-P. (eds.) PQCrypto 2020. LNCS, vol. 12100, pp. 189–205. Springer, Cham (2020). https://doi.org/10.1007/978-3-030-44223-1_11
13. Sim, B.Y., et al.: Single-trace attacks on message encoding in lattice-based KEMs. IEEE Access **8**, 183175–183191 (2020)
14. Xu, Z., Pemberton, O.M., Roy, S.S., Oswald, D., Yao, W., Zheng, Z.: Magnifying side-channel leakage of lattice-based cryptosystems with chosen ciphertexts: the case study of Kyber. IEEE Trans. Comput. **71**, 2163–2176 (2021)
15. Kannwischer, M.J., Rijneveld, J., Schwabe, P., Stoffelen, K.: PQM4: post-quantum crypto library for the ARM Cortex-M4. https://github.com/mupq/pqm4
16. Ngo, K., Dubrova, E., Guo, Q., Johansson, T.: A side-channel attack on a masked IND-CCA secure saber KEM implementation. IACR Trans. Cryptographic Hardware Embedded Syst., 676–707 (2021)
17. Ravi, P., Bhasin, S., Roy, S.S., Chattopadhyay, A.: On exploiting message leakage in (few) NIST PQC candidates for practical message recovery and key recovery attacks. Cryptology ePrint Archive (2020)
18. Ngo, K., Dubrova, E., Johansson, T.: Breaking masked and shuffled CCA secure saber KEM by power analysis. In: Proceedings of the 5th Workshop on Attacks and Solutions in Hardware Security, pp. 51–61 (2021)
19. Ravi, P., Bhasin, S., Roy, S.S., Chattopadhyay, A.: On exploiting message leakage in (few) NIST PQC candidates for practical message recovery attacks. IEEE Trans. Inf. Forensics Secur. **17**, 684699 (2021)
20. Regev, O.: On lattices, learning with errors, random linear codes, and cryptography. J. ACM (JACM) **56**(6), 34 (2009)

# PII-PSM: A New Targeted Password Strength Meter Using Personally Identifiable Information

Qiying Dong[1], Ding Wang[1(✉)], Yaosheng Shen[2], and Chunfu Jia[1]

[1] College of Cyber Science, Nankai University, Tianjin 300071, China
wangding@nankai.edu.cn
[2] School of ECE, Peking University Shenzhen Graduate School, Shenzhen 518055, China

**Abstract.** In recent years, unending breaches of users' personally identifiable information (PII) have become increasingly severe, making targeted password guessing using PII a practical threat. However, to our knowledge, most password strength meters (PSMs) only consider the traditional trawling password guessing threat, and no PSM has taken into account the more severe targeted guessing threat using PII (e.g., name, birthday, and phone number). To fill this gap, in this paper, we mainly focus on targeted password strength evaluation in the scenario where users' PII is available to the attacker. First, to capture more fine-grained password structures, we introduce the high-frequency substring as a new grammar tag into leading targeted password probabilistic models TarGuess-I and TarMarkov, and propose TarGuess-I-H and TarMarkov-H. Then, we weight and combine our two improved models to devise PII-PSM, *the first practical* targeted PSM resistant to common PII-accessible attackers. By using the weighted Spearman (WSpearman) metric recommended at CCS'18, we evaluate the accuracy of our PII-PSM and its counterparts (i.e., our TarGuess-I-H and TarMarkov-H, as well as two benchmarks of Optimal and Min_auto). We conduct evaluation experiments on password datasets leaked from eight high-profile English and Chinese services. Results show that our PII-PSM is more accurate than TarGuess-I-H and TarMarkov-H, and is closer to Optimal and Min_auto, with WSpearman differences of only 0.014~0.023 and 0.012~0.031, respectively. This establishes the accuracy of PII-PSM, facilitating to nudge users to select stronger passwords.

**Keywords:** Password authentication · Targeted guessing · Password strength meter · Personally identifiable information · Password probabilistic model

## 1 Introduction

Identity authentication is the first line of defense to ensure information system security, and text passwords are the most widely used method [2]. The most

F. Li et al. (Eds.): SecureComm 2022, LNICST 462, pp. 648–669, 2023.
https://doi.org/10.1007/978-3-031-25538-0_34

common threat to password-based authentication is password guessing attacks, which can be divided into trawling attacks and targeted attacks based on the attacker's knowledge. By exploiting users' vulnerable behaviors (e.g., adopting popular passwords [1,18] and keyboard patterns [23]), a trawling attacker performs indiscriminate password guessing on all user accounts to crack as many accounts as possible. In contrast, to guess a specific user's password, a targeted attacker takes advantage of the user's personal information to facilitate guessing. This is realistic because users tend to employ a variety of personal information (e.g., name, birthday, and old/sister passwords) when generating passwords [4,9,15,22,24].

In recent years, there have been numerous data breaches containing users' personal information. For example, the LinkedIn breach [14] leaks 700 million users' full names, phone numbers, physical addresses, email addresses, geolocation records, LinkedIn usernames and profile URLs, personal and professional experiences and backgrounds, genders, and other social media accounts and usernames; the Facebook breach [5] leaks 533 million users' full names, Facebook IDs, phone numbers, locations, birthdays, biographies, and email addresses; the Nitro PDF breach [7] leaks 77 million users' email addresses, full names, bcrypt hashed passwords, titles, company names, IP addresses, and other system-related information. This provides sufficient material for targeted guessing, making it a more severe and realistic threat than traditional trawling guessing [24].

To nudge users to select strong passwords, nearly every respectable web service provider has deployed password strength meters (PSMs). However, as far as we know, apart from personalized password strength meter (PPSM) [15], leading PSMs (e.g., [3,6,13,21,26]) only consider trawling guessing scenarios. These trawling PSMs do not include the user's personal information in password strength evaluation, and are thus unable to accurately measure password strength when facing real-world attacks. Besides, the targeted PPSM [15] relies on sister passwords from different sites in evaluating password strength, which is highly impractical due to two reasons: 1) The server generally does not hold the user's old (sister) passwords; 2) Sister passwords are not easily accessible [4,24]. For example, Das et al. [4] analyzed 7.96 million accounts from different sites and found that only 152 (0.00191%) were successfully matched by email more than once; Wang et al. [24] analyzed 547.56 million accounts and found that less than 1.02% and 1.73% were successfully matched by email and username more than once. Comparatively, users often submit personally identifiable information (PII, such as name and phone number) when registering. Even if they do not submit, PII is easy to obtain (e.g., through social networks) by attackers. Thus, designing a PII-based PSM is urgent and necessary.

## Contributions

(1) **Two Improved Targeted Password Probabilistic Models.** We analyze passwords from eight high-profile English and Chinese services, and find that high-frequency substrings (HFSs) can capture more fine-grained password structures than popular passwords. Thus, we introduce the HFS as a new grammar tag into leading targeted probabilistic models TarGuess-I [24]

and TarMarkov [22], and propose the improved models TarGuess-I-H and TarMarkov-H.

(2) **A New Targeted Password Strength Meter (PSM).** We weight and combine our proposed TarGuess-I-H and TarMarkov-H to devise PII-PSM. It is *the first practical* targeted PSM resistant to common targeted attackers with personally identifiable information (PII), using the stochastic gradient descent approach to optimize the weights. In this way, the impact of randomly/manually setting the weights on PSM accuracy can be eliminated.

(3) **An Extensive Evaluation.** By using the weighted Spearman correlation coefficient (WSpearman) metric recommended by Golla et al. [8], we evaluate the accuracy of our PII-PSM and its counterparts (including our TarGuess-I-H and TarMarkov-H, as well as two benchmarks of Optimal and Min_auto). We perform experiments on eight large-scale password datasets with different user languages and service types. Results show that our PII-PSM is more accurate than TarGuess-I-H and TarMarkov-H, and is closer to Optimal and Min_auto, with WSpearman differences of only 0.014~0.023 and 0.012~0.031, respectively. This indicates the accuracy of PII-PSM, facilitating to help users set stronger passwords.

## 2   Preliminaries and Related Work

In this section, we introduce leading targeted password probabilistic models using personally identifiable information (PII), and elaborate on the preliminaries of targeted password strength meters (PSMs).

### 2.1   Targeted Password Probabilistic Models

A password probabilistic model (e.g., [6,9,13,21,22,24]) can assign password construction probabilities in the password space. It can be used to construct probability-based PSMs and password guessing models. A targeted guessing attacker usually utilizes the target user's personal information to improve guessing efficiency. There are various types of personal information, such as PII (e.g., name, user name, and email address), and user identification information (e.g., users' old passwords and sister passwords from different sites) [24]. Targeted password probabilistic models can be categorized according to the personal information incorporated, e.g., Personal-PCFG [9], TarGuess-I [24], and TarMarkov [22] that employ users PII; TarGuess-II [24], pass2path and PPSM [15], and Das et al.'s [4] that employ users sister passwords; TarGuess-III [24] including both PII and sister passwords. In this paper, we mainly focus on the most basic yet realistic targeted guessing scenario that exploits users' PII.

**Personal-PCFG.** Based on the probabilistic context-free grammar (PCFG) password model [25], Li et al. [9] proposed a targeted model Personal-PCFG. It divides personal information into six categories (i.e., **U**ser name, **E**mail, **N**ame, **B**irthday, **P**hone number, and **ID** number) and combines PCFG grammar tags (i.e., **L**etter string, **D**igit string, and **S**ymbol string). Besides, it determines the password structure according to the type and length of strings and personal information. For example, the password Li123! for a user named Hua Li is converted to $N_2 D_3 S_1$. The rest of the training and password generation approaches for Personal-PCFG [9] are the same as PCFG [25].

However, Wang et al. [24] have shown that the above length-based PII matching method of Personal-PCFG [9] is inaccurate to capture users' PII usage behaviors. For example, Personal-PCFG [9] transforms the passwords Hua123 and Liu456 of the users named Hua Li and Kai Liu into the same base structure $N_3 D_3$ during the training phase, and the password wang789 of the user named Lei Wang into $N_4 D_3$. However, the user Hua Li uses her given name to build passwords, while users Kai Liu and Lei Wang use their family names to build passwords. Such inherently different user behaviors are misleadingly characterized in Personal-PCFG [9].

**TarGuess-I.** Almost at the same time, Wang et al. [24] proposed TarGuess-I, which is based on PCFG but uses a novel type-based PII matching method. For instance, TarGuess-I [24] transforms the password Hua123 of the user named Hua Li into $N_4 D_3$, and passwords Liu456 and wang789 (of users named Kai Liu and Lei Wang) into the same base structure $N_3 D_3$. That is, TarGuess-I [24] uses the subscript $n$ to represent the *sub-type* of a specific PII type (e.g., Name $N$ and Birthday $B$), *not* the length of a specific PII type as in Personal-PCFG [9]. This well eliminates the misleading characterization of user behaviors in Personal-PCFG [9]. Taking $N_n$ as an example, for a user named Lei Wang, $N_1$ stands for leiwang, $N_2$ for lw, and $N_3$ for wang. The grammar $\mathcal{G}_{TarGuess-I} = (\mathcal{S}, \mathcal{V}, \mathcal{\Sigma}, \mathcal{R})$ is described as:

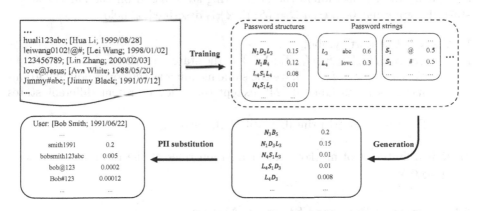

**Fig. 1.** An illustration of TarGuess-I [24].

1) $\mathcal{S} \in \mathcal{V}$ is the start symbol;
2) $\mathcal{V} = \{\mathcal{S}; L_n, D_n, S_n; N_n, B_n, U_n, E_n, I_n, T_n; \varepsilon\}$ is the set of grammar tags, where
   a) $L_n, D_n, S_n$ are the grammar tags of basic PCFG [25], representing the letter, digit, and symbol strings of length $n$, respectively;

b) $N_n, B_n, U_n, E_n, I_n, T_n$ are the grammar tags of TarGuess-I [24], representing the different forms of Name, Birthday, User name, Email, ID number, and Phone number distinguished by the number $n$;

c) $\varepsilon$ is the terminator;

3) $\Sigma$ is the set of 94 printable ASCII characters;

4) $\mathcal{R}$ is a finite set of rules of the form $A \to \beta$, with $A \in \mathcal{V}$ and $\beta \in \mathcal{V} \cup \Sigma$.

Different from PCFG [25], when guessing the target user $user_A$'s password, TarGuess-I [24] does not directly generate the final passwords for guessing, but first generates PII-tags and then replaces them with $user_A$'s PII, as shown in Fig. 1. The experimental results of Wang et al. [24] showed that within 1,000 guesses, the guessing success rate of TarGuess-I is 37.11% higher than Personal-PCFG [9].

In 2020, Xie et al. [27,28] modified TarGuess-I by introducing grammar tags of popular passwords, keyboard patterns, and special strings. However, their experiments showed that these modifications only marginally improved the guessing success rate of the model (increased by less than 2.62% within 100 guesses). Moreover, the guessing success rate decreased on password datasets of certain service types (e.g., the train ticketing service 12306). Besides, they only used passwords leaked from Chinese services in experiments, without considering the impact of different user languages (e.g., English and Chinese) on model performance. Therefore, we adopt the original TarGuess-I [24] for evaluation and comparison in this paper.

**TarMarkov.** Unlike Personal-PCFG [9] and TarGuess-I [24], TarMarkov [22] is a sequence model that infers the next string state based on the current string state. Its grammar $\mathcal{G}_{TarMarkov} = (\mathcal{S}, \mathcal{V}, \mathcal{R})$ is described as below:

1) $\mathcal{S} \in \mathcal{V}$ is the start symbol;

2) $\mathcal{V} = \{\mathcal{S}; N_n, B_n, U_n, E_n, I_n, T_n; \Sigma; \varepsilon\}$ is the state set, where

a) $N_n, B_n, U_n, E_n, I_n, T_n$ have the same meaning as the corresponding grammar tags in TarGuess-I [24], except that they represent different states here;

b) $\Sigma$ is the set of 94 printable ASCII characters;

c) $\varepsilon$ is the terminator;

3) $\mathcal{R}$ is a finite set of markov state transition rules of the form $s_1 \to s_2$, with $s_1, s_2 \in \mathcal{V}^*$.

## 2.2   Targeted Password Strength Meters

The above targeted password probabilistic models enable us to design targeted PSMs. Though academia has proposed a series of well-performed PSMs (e.g., [3,6,13,21,26]), the main focus is still trawling guessing scenarios, while paying little attention to the more threatening targeted guessing scenarios (especially when users' PII is available). Thus, we mainly focus on targeted PSMs using common PII.

**Users' Vulnerable Behaviors.** Users' password security/strength is intrinsically impacted by their vulnerable behaviors, mainly including [24]: (1) using popular passwords [1,10], (2) password reuse [11,12], and (3) using personal information [23]. Existing PSMs can prevent issue-1 and issue-2 well. For example, fuzzyPSM [21] can accurately capture users' password reuse behaviors and has a built-in base dictionary containing popular passwords. However, to the best of our knowledge, issue-3 has not been well addressed. This is because current practice using third-party corpora (e.g., common names and places) during training will result in PSM accuracy largely dependent on the corpus selection [23]. Besides, in a targeted guessing scenario where the attacker can obtain users' PII, the same password containing PII constructed by different users should be rated with different strengths. For instance, `Hua Li` and `Lei Wang` both select the password `Li123#`. The string `Li` is likely to be constructed by `Hua Li` using her family name, while for `Lei Wang` it may just be a random letter string. Thus, it is essential to propose a PSM that can accurately evaluate the strength of different users' passwords in targeted guessing.

**Ideal Targeted Password Strength Meter.** For the ideal PSM under trawling guessing scenarios, the formal definition given by Wang et al. [21] is as follows. For the function $M(\cdot)$ and password distribution $\mathcal{D}$, if

$$P_{\mathcal{D}}(pw_i) \geq P_{\mathcal{D}}(pw_j),\tag{1}$$

there is

$$\forall pw_i, pw_j \in \mathcal{D};\ M(pw_i) \geq M(pw_j).\tag{2}$$

Then, $M(\cdot)$ is called an ideal trawling PSM.

Analogously, targeted PSMs are adopted to evaluate the strength of the password $pw$ in the password space under the given users' PII, so we give the formal definition of the ideal targeted PSM as follows. Suppose $user_A$ uses her own PII to construct passwords; for the function $M(\cdot)$ and password distribution $\mathcal{D}_{user_A}$, if

$$P_{\mathcal{D}_{user_A}}(pw_i) \geq P_{\mathcal{D}_{user_A}}(pw_j),\tag{3}$$

there is

$$\forall pw_i, pw_j \in \mathcal{D}_{user_A};\ M(pw_i) \geq M(pw_j).\tag{4}$$

Then, $M(\cdot)$ is called an ideal targeted PSM.

**Table 1.** Basic info about our eight password datasets (PII = personally identifiable information).

| Dataset | Web service | Language | When leaked | Total passwords | With PII |
|---------|-------------|----------|-------------|-----------------|----------|
| Rootkit | Hacker forum | English | Feb. 2011 | 69,418 | ✓ |
| 12306 | Train ticketing | Chinese | Dec. 2014 | 129,303 | ✓ |
| Yahoo | Web portal | English | July 2012 | 453,491 | |
| 000webhost | Web hosting | English | Oct. 2015 | 15,299,907 | |
| CSDN | Programmer | Chinese | Dec. 2011 | 6,428,632 | |
| Dodonew | E-commerce | Chinese | Dec. 2011 | 16,283,140 | |
| Rockyou | Forum | English | Dec. 2009 | 32,603,387 | —† |
| Tianya | Forum | Chinese | Dec. 2011 | 29,513,716 | —† |

† We choose Rockyou and Tianya as base dictionaries of high-frequency substrings, so the users' PII contained in them is not considered.

**Table 2.** Basic info about our PII datasets (PII=personally identifiable information).

| Dataset | Items num | Types of PII |
|---------|-----------|--------------|
| PII-Rootkit | 69,330 | Email, User name, Name, Birthday |
| PII-12306 | 129,303 | Email, User name, Name, Birthday, Phone number |
| PII-Yahoo | 214 | Email, User name, Name, Birthday |
| PII-000webhost | 79,580 | Email, User name, Name, Birthday |
| PII-CSDN | 77,216 | Email, User name, Name, Birthday, Phone number |
| PII-Dodonew | 161,517 | Email, User name, Name, Birthday, Phone number |

# 3    Analysis of Real Password Data

In this section, we analyze the characteristics of real-world leaked password data, and provide the basis for our improved targeted probabilistic models TarGuess-I-H and TarMarkov-H and our proposed targeted PII-PSM.

## 3.1    Our Datasets and Ethical Considerations

**Datasets.** We analyze eight large-scale leaked password datasets and show basic information in Table 1. These datasets have different password strengths, languages, and service types, and have been widely used in password research (e.g., [8,13,16,21,23–26]). Referring to Wang et al.'s password data cleaning method [23], we first remove the junk information in the dataset, such as unnecessary headers, descriptions, footnotes, hash values, and strings containing symbols other than 94 printable ASCII characters and the space character. Besides, we remove those passwords longer than 30 for they are unlikely to be chosen by users but by password managers, while our concerned PSMs are designed to evaluate user-constructed passwords.

Two of our datasets, 12306 and Rootkit, contain certain types of users' PII (e.g., Email, User name, Name, Birthday, and Phone number). To make our targeted probabilistic models more extensible, we match the above two datasets containing users' PII with the remaining four datasets (i.e., Yahoo, 000webhost, CSDN, and Dodonew) through email, resulting in four datasets associated with PII (e.g., PII-Yahoo). The types of PII in each dataset and the number of passwords associated with PII are shown in Table 2.

**Ethical Considerations.** Despite the fact that these password datasets are ever publicly available and widely used, passwords are highly private and sensitive. Thus, we still process them with caution. We only show aggregated statistics (like total passwords, top-10 HFSs%, and given name%) and treat each account as confidential, so that our use will not make attackers gain extra advantages in password guessing. Besides, we process all our password-related data on computers not connected to the Internet, and delete sensitive info after finishing experiments. Furthermore, our use of these datasets is not only beneficial for research on targeted guessing and password strength evaluation, but also for security admins to protect user account security.

**Table 3.** Top-10 popular passwords (left) and high-frequency substrings (right).[†]

| Rank | English | | | | | | | |
| --- | --- | --- | --- | --- | --- | --- | --- | --- |
| | Rootkit | | Yahoo | | 000webhost | | Rockyou | |
| 1 | 123456 | 123456 | 123456 | 123456 | abc123 | abc123 | 123456 | 123456 |
| 2 | password | Password | Password | 101 | 123456a | 123456a | 12345 | 12345 |
| 3 | Rootkit | Rootkit | Welcome | ana | 12qw23we | 12qw23we | 123456789 | 123456789 |
| 4 | 111111 | 111111 | Ninja | 100 | 123abc | 123abc | Password | Password |
| 5 | 12345678 | 12345678 | abc123 | cat | a123456 | a123456 | iloveyou | iloveyou |
| 6 | qwerty | qwerty | 123456789 | red | 123qwe | 123qwe | Princess | Princess |
| 7 | 123456789 | 123456789 | 12345678 | star | secret666 | secret | 1234567 | 1234567 |
| 8 | 123123 | 123123 | Sunshine | dog | YfDbUfNjH10305070 | YfDbUfNjH10305070 | rockyou | rockyou |
| 9 | qwertyui | 12345 | Princess | 102 | asd123 | qwerty | 12345678 | 12345678 |
| 10 | 12345 | 1234 | qwerty | ard | qwerty123 | YfDbUfNjH10305070[‡] | abc123 | abc123 |
| % | 3.94 | 5.38 | 1.01 | 1.93 | 0.79 | 1.35 | 2.05 | 2.05 |
| Rank | Chinese | | | | | | | |
| | 12306 | | CSDN | | Dodonew | | Tianya | |
| 1 | 123456 | 123456 | 123456789 | 123456789 | 123456 | 123456 | 123456 | 123456 |
| 2 | a120456 | a120456 | 12345678 | 123456 | a123456 | a123456 | 111111 | 123 |
| 3 | 5201314 | 5201314 | 11111111 | 11111111 | 123456789 | 123456789 | 000000 | 111 |
| 4 | 123456a | 123456a | dearbook | dearbook | 111111 | 111111 | 123456789 | 12345678 |
| 5 | 111111 | 111111 | 00000000 | 00000000 | 5201314 | 520 | 123123 | 520 |
| 6 | woaini1314 | 123123 | 123123123 | 123123123 | 123123 | 123 | 123321 | 321 |
| 7 | 123123 | 000000 | 1234567890 | 1234567890 | a321654 | a321654 | 5201314 | 123123 |
| 8 | 000000 | woaini | 88888888 | 88888888 | 12345 | 123123 | 12345678 | 666666 |
| 9 | qq123456 | qq123456 | 111111111 | 111111111 | 000000 | 000000 | 666666 | 111 |
| 10 | 1qaz2wsx | 1qaz | 147258369 | 147258369 | 123456a | 1234 | 111222tianya | tianya |
| % | 3.28 | 3.78 | 10.44 | 10.44 | 0.79 | 1.75 | 7.43 | 16.33 |

† A high-frequency substring in blue indicates that it is different from the popular password of the same rank in the same password dataset. In Chinese, the homophonic meaning of 5201314 is "I love you (520) forever (1314)". The Chinese pinyin woaini means "I love you".

‡ The letter segment YfDbUfNjH can be mapped to a Russian word that means "navigator", and why it is so popular is beyond our comprehension.

## 3.2  High-Frequency Substrings (HFSs) and Popular Passwords

When constructing passwords, users may adopt more common and fine-grained HFSs as password components than popular passwords [20]. To investigate this issue, we count top-10 HFSs (see Sects. 4.1 and 5.1 for detailed identification approaches and parameter settings) and popular passwords in our eight password datasets, and calculate the proportion of passwords containing them in the dataset. The results are shown in Table 3. It can be seen that 1.35%~16.33% of the passwords contain top-10 HFSs, while only 0.79%~7.43% contain top-10 popular passwords. That is, *HFSs are more common in users' passwords than popular passwords, indicating that users may prefer to utilize HFSs to construct passwords*. In addition, when constructing passwords, Chinese users prefer to use simple digit strings (e.g., 123456, 00000000, and 123123) and some strings with semantics (e.g., 5201314 and woaini related to "love"). In contrast, English users tend to use a combination of letter and digit strings (e.g., abc123 and qwerty123) and common English words/phrases (e.g., password, iloveyou, and cat).

**Table 4.** Percentages (%) of users constructing passwords with (left) and only with (right) their heterogeneous personal information, popular passwords, and high-frequency substrings (HFSs).[†]

| Typical usages of PII (examples) | English | | | Chinese | | |
|---|---|---|---|---|---|---|
| | PII-Rootkit | PII-Yahoo | PII-000webhost | PII-12306 | PII-CSDN | PII-Dodonew |
| | (69,330) | (214) | (2,950) | (129,303) | (77,439) | (161,510) |
| Top-10 popular passwords (123456) | 2.45  2.14 | 0.06  0.02 | 0.79  0.47 | 1.56  1.01 | 9.32  8.42 | 4.61  2.18 |
| Top-100 popular passwords | 2.76  2.31 | 0.09  0.04 | 0.87  0.53 | 1.78  1.14 | 26.31  24.54 | 4.91  2.43 |
| Top-10 HFSs (123, abc) | 2.98  2.02 | 0.19  0.00 | 3.01  0.45 | 1.78  1.08 | 12.59  8.42 | 5.33  2.18 |
| Top-100 HFSs | 6.32  2.25 | 0.59  0.04 | 6.38  0.49 | 3.45  1.12 | 29.32  27.73 | 7.57  2.39 |
| Full name (hua li) | 1.38  0.75 | 2.34  1.87 | 2.44  1.32 | 5.02  1.13 | 4.85  1.81 | 4.68  0.82 |
| Family name (li) | 2.28  0.78 | 4.67  1.87 | 3.73  1.46 | 11.23  0.00 | 9.75  0.00 | 11.15  0.01 |
| Given name (hua) | 0.49  0.07 | 0.93  0.00 | 0.75  0.20 | 6.61  0.07 | 6.26  0.08 | 6.49  0.07 |
| Abbr. full name (lh, hl, hli) | 0.15  0.01 | 0.00  0.00 | 0.20  0.00 | 13.13  0.00 | 9.42  0.00 | 13.64  0.02 |
| Full Birthday (19980102, 01021998) | 0.08  0.06 | 0.47  0.00 | 0.10  0.07 | 4.33  1.77 | 6.29  5.16 | 3.12  1.00 |
| Year of birthday (1982) | 0.75  0.01 | 1.40  0.00 | 1.12  0.00 | 10.78  0.00 | 11.37  0.00 | 8.92  0.00 |
| Date of birthday (0102, 0201) | 0.44  0.01 | 0.47  0.00 | 0.58  0.00 | 10.03  0.00 | 11.84  0.00 | 8.32  0.00 |
| Abbr. birthday (199812, 980102) | 0.10  0.05 | 0.00  0.00 | 0.20  0.14 | 3.31  1.12 | 2.89  1.45 | 2.37  0.59 |
| User name strings (neko_10, neko) | 2.91  0.86 | 4.01  1.40 | 2.20  1.32 | 3.57  1.22 | 0.91  0.67 | 2.61  1.71 |
| Email strings (loveu@exa, loveu) | 0.77  0.49 | 4.38  1.87 | 1.32  0.78 | 3.23  1.95 | 4.65  2.48 | 5.37  3.08 |
| Phone strings (123-4567-8900) | —  — | —  — | —  — | 0.07  0.01 | 0.50  0.45 | 0.11  0.11 |

† All decimals in the table are in "%". For instance, 2.45 in the upper left corner means that 2.45% of the 69,330 PII-Rootkit users employ top-10 popular passwords to build passwords; 2.14 means that 2.14% of these 69,330 PII-Rootkit users' passwords are just top-10 popular passwords.

Further, we extract top-10 and top-100 HFSs and popular passwords, respectively, and use them together with some PII-tags (e.g., name and email) to mark and analyze passwords. The results are shown in Table 4. The left column corresponding to each dataset in Table 4 is the proportion of passwords containing the tag, and the right column is the proportion of passwords that are exactly the tag. For example, if the tag content is 123456, the counted passwords in the left column include 1234567 and a123456, and that in the right column only include 123456. It can be seen that passwords with a specific PII-tag account for a considerable portion, the highest being 13.64%, showing that users' vulnerable behaviors of using PII to construct passwords are common.

Here we focus on HFS and popular password tags, and find that: 1) For the same dataset, the proportion of passwords containing top-10/top-100 HFSs (on the left column) is greater than that of top-10/top-100 popular passwords (in two columns), indicating that *HFSs can capture more fine-grained password characteristics than popular passwords*; 2) The proportion of passwords that are exactly the top-10/top-100 HFS-tags (on the right column) is close to the proportion of top-10/top-100 popular passwords (in two columns), indicating that some HFSs are directly used by users as passwords and play the role of popular passwords; 3) A larger scale of HFS-tags (e.g., from top-10 to top-100) can significantly cover more passwords and capture more password characteristics.

### 3.3  Password Structures

To investigate how HFS-tags and popular password-tags characterize password structure, we convert the two types of tags into grammar tags of $\mathcal{G}_{TarGuess-I}$ and $\mathcal{G}_{TarMarkov}$. More specifically, we count the top-100 popular passwords and HFSs, labeled "$P_n$" which represents a popular password of length $n$ and "$H_n^i$" meaning an HFS ranked $i$ in those substrings of length $n$. Following the longest-prefix matching rule, we first match PII segments in a password, then use the remaining segments to match $P_n$ and $H_n^i$, and obtain password structures. We show the top-10 password structures and the proportions containing $P_n$ and $H_n^i$ in Table 5. We find that the top-10 password structures of these password

**Table 5.** Top-10 password structures marked with popular password tags ($P_n$; on the left) and high-frequency substring tags ($H_n^i$; on the right) of each dataset, and proportions of password structures containing the two tags ($P_n\%$ and $H_n^i\%$) in each dataset. ($P_n$=a popular password of length $n$, and $H_n^i$=a high-frequency substring ranked $i$ in those substrings of length $n$)

| Rank | English | | | | | | Chinese | | | | | |
|---|---|---|---|---|---|---|---|---|---|---|---|---|
| | Rootkit | | Yahoo | | 000webhost | | 12306 | | CSDN | | Dodonew | |
| 1 | $P_6$ | $H_6^1$ | $P_6$ | $H_6^1$ | $P_6$ | $H_6^1$ | $P_6$ | $H_6^1$ | $P_8$ | $D_8$ | $E_1$ | $E_1$ |
| 2 | $P_8$ | $H_8^1$ | $P_8$ | $H_8^1$ | $P_8$ | $H_8^1$ | $D_6$ | $H_6^2$ | $D_8$ | $H_8^1$ | $D_7$ | $H_7^3$ |
| 3 | $D_8$ | $H_6^2$ | $D_6$ | $H_6^2$ | $P_7$ | $H_6^2$ | $D_7$ | $D_6$ | $E_1$ | $E_1$ | $P_6$ | $H_6^1$ |
| 4 | $L_8$ | $H_8^2$ | $L_6$ | $H_8^2$ | $D_6$ | $H_7^1$ | $N_2D_6$ | $D_7$ | $B_1$ | $B_1$ | $D_6$ | $H_6^2$ |
| 5 | $P_7$ | $H_7^1$ | $L_8$ | $L_8$ | $D_8$ | $H_8^2$ | $U_1$ | $H_7^1$ | $D_9$ | $D_9$ | $D_8$ | $D_6$ |
| 6 | $N_2D_6$ | $H_6^3$ | $D_9$ | $D_9$ | $L_6$ | $N_1D_6$ | $D_8$ | $U_1$ | $N_2D_6$ | $N_2D_6$ | $N_2D_6$ | $N_2D_6$ |
| 7 | $D_5$ | $N_2H_6^1$ | $P_9$ | $P_9$ | $N_3D_1$ | $U_1D_1$ | $E_1$ | $D_8$ | $U_1$ | $U_1$ | $U_1D_7$ | $U_1D_7$ |
| 8 | $U_1D_1$ | $N_2D_6$ | $N_1D_1$ | $H_9^1$ | $N_4D_1$ | $N_1D_1$ | $N_2D_7$ | $E_1$ | $D_{11}$ | $D_{11}$ | $N_2D_7$ | $N_2D_7$ |
| 9 | $N_3D_1$ | $U_1D_1$ | $U_1D_1$ | $N_1D_1$ | $E_1D_3$ | $N_3D_1$ | $U_3$ | $N_2D_7$ | $N_2D_7$ | $N_2D_7$ | $U_1$ | $U_1$ |
| 10 | $N_4D_1$ | $D_5$ | $N_3D_1$ | $H_8^3$ | $D_{10}$ | $N_1$ | $U_2D_6$ | $N_2H_7^1$ | $D_{10}$ | $H_{10}^1$ | $U_2D_6$ | $U_2H_6^1$ |
| $P_n\%$ | 14.12 | | 16.78 | | 10.14 | | 6.31 | | 10.11 | | 4.25 | |
| $H_n^i\%$ | 30.13 | | 34.28 | | 26.13 | | 17.22 | | 16.12 | | 6.39 | |

datasets include a number of simple structures independent of PII-tags, such as single $P_n$, $H_n^i$, $L_n$, and $D_n$. Therefore, adding $P_n$ and $H_n^i$ tags to $\mathcal{G}_{TarGuess-I}$ and $\mathcal{G}_{TarMarkov}$ are likely to facilitate password probabilistic models to identify simple yet common strings in passwords more effectively, thereby helping to build more accurate PSMs.

What's more, $H_n^i$ can characterize more fine-grained password structures than $P_n$. For example, after introducing $H_n^i$ tags, the top-2 password structures of Rootkit are further refined into $P_6 \rightarrow H_6^1, H_6^2$ and $P_8 \rightarrow H_8^1, H_8^2$. Similarly, there are $P_9 \rightarrow H_9^1$; $L_8 \rightarrow H_8^1, H_8^2$; and $U_2 D_6 \rightarrow U_2 H_6^1$. This can help TarGuess-I [24] construct more HFSs rather than redundant segments when generating passwords. For TarMarkov [22], more refined and diverse password structures are helpful to well solve the long-standing issue of data sparsity. To sum up, we take $H_n^i$ as a new grammar tag to improve the leading targeted password probabilistic models TarGuess-I [24] and TarMarkov [22].

## 4   Methodology

In this section, we first propose two new targeted password probabilistic models, TarGuess-I-H and TarMarkov-H, which can identify HFSs in users' passwords. Based on these two models, we devise a new targeted PSM called PII-PSM.

### 4.1   Improved Password Probabilistic Models

To help construct accurate and practical targeted PSMs, we first need to devise well-performed password probabilistic models. Thus, we propose the improved TarGuess-I-H and TarMarkov-H as follows.

**Our TarGuess-I-H.** We introduce HFS as a new grammar tag into TarGuess-I [24], and propose a novel targeted password probabilistic model TarGuess-I-H. Its grammar $\mathcal{G}_{TarGuess-I-H} = (\mathcal{S}, \mathcal{V}, \Sigma, \mathcal{R})$ is described as below:

1) $\mathcal{S} \in \mathcal{V}$ is the start symbol;
2) $\mathcal{V} = \{\mathcal{S}; L_n, D_n, S_n; N_n, B_n, U_n, E_n, I_n, T_n; H_n^i; \varepsilon\}$ is the set of grammar tags, where
   a) $L_n, D_n, S_n$ are the grammar tags of basic PCFG [25], representing the letter, digit, and symbol strings of length $n$, respectively;
   b) $N_n, B_n, U_n, E_n, I_n, T_n$ are the grammar tags of TarGuess-I [24], representing the different forms of Name, Birthday, User name, Email, ID number, and Phone number distinguished by the number $n$;
   c) $H_n^i$ is proposed in this paper *for the first time*, representing the set of strings ranked $i$ among those substrings of length $n$ in descending order of frequency;
   d) $\varepsilon$ is the terminator;

3) $\Sigma$ is the set of 94 printable ASCII characters;
4) $\mathcal{R}$ is a finite set of rules of the form $A \rightarrow \beta$, with $A \in \mathcal{V}$ and $\beta \in \mathcal{V} \cup \Sigma$.

**Our TarMarkov-H.** TarMarkov [22] is a sequence model that infers the next string state based on the current string state. We introduce HFS as a new state into TarMarkov [22], and propose a novel targeted password probabilistic model TarMarkov-H. Its grammar $\mathcal{G}_{TarMarkov-H} = (\mathcal{S}, \mathcal{V}, \mathcal{R})$ is described as below:

1) $\mathcal{S} \in \mathcal{V}$ is the start symbol;
2) $\mathcal{V} = \{\mathcal{S}; N_n, B_n, U_n, E_n, I_n, T_n; H_n^i; \Sigma; \varepsilon\}$ is the state set, where
   a) $N_n, B_n, U_n, E_n, I_n, T_n$ and $H_n^i$ have the same meaning as the corresponding grammar tags in TarGuess-I-H, except that they represent different states in TarMarkov-H;
   b) $\Sigma$ is the set of 94 printable ASCII characters;
   c) $\varepsilon$ is the terminator;
3) $\mathcal{R}$ is a finite set of markov state transition rules of the form $s_1 \rightarrow s_2$, with $s_1, s_2 \in \mathcal{V}^*$.

**High-Frequency Substrings (HFSs).** In a password dataset, HFSs are password substrings with the frequency exceeding a certain threshold, and they can be identified by taking the following steps:

1) Record the count $C(p_s)$ of each password substring $p_s$ with the length $n \geq 3$;
2) Set the threshold $T_1$ and delete the substrings with a count less than $T_1$;
3) Modify the substring count record as

$$C(p_s)^{new} = C(p_s)^{old} - \sum_{c \in \Sigma} [C(c \mid p_s)^{old} + C(p_s + c)^{old}], \qquad (5)$$

   where $C(p_s)^{old}$ is the original count record of $p_s$, and $c + p_s$ and $p_s + c$ respectively mean that the character $c$ is concatenated to the beginning and end of $p_s$;
4) Set the threshold $T_2$ and identify $p_s$ as a HFS if $C(p_s)^{new} \geq T_2$;
5) Store HFSs with the same length $n$ into the set $H_n$ ($n \geq 3$), arrange them in descending order of count, and denote the set of substrings ranked $i$ in $H_n$ as $H_n^i$. The parsing process is shown in Fig. 2. Parameter setups of $T_1$, $T_2$, and $n$ are detailed in Sec. 5.1.

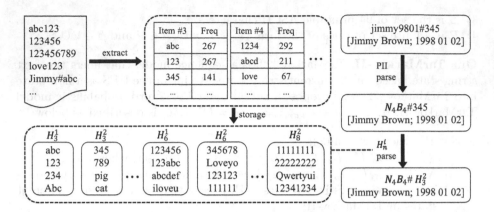

**Fig. 2.** An illustration of $H_n^i$-tag processing. $H_n^i$ denotes the high-frequency substring ranked $i$ in those substrings of length $n$.

## 4.2   Our Targeted PII-PSM

Our proposed password probabilistic models TarGuess-I-H and TarMarkov-H introduced above can be individually transformed into two targeted PSMs. Still, we combine these two models to construct a new targeted PSM called PII-PSM, because Dong et al. [6] found that: In online guessing scenarios (often guess number<$10^4$), PCFG-based password models usually outperform markov-based ones; on the contrary, in offline guessing scenarios (often guess number>$10^4$), markov-based password models usually outperform PCFG-based ones. Thus, taking into account PSM performance under both online and offline guessing, we construct our PII-PSM by weighing the strength scores of the PCFG-based TarGuess-I-H and markov-based TarMarkov-H. For a password $pw$, we denote the probabilities calculated by TarGuess-I-H and TarMarkov-H as $p_1$ and $p_2$, and the corresponding weights are $\alpha$ ($\alpha \in [0,1]$) and 1-$\alpha$ (detailed $\alpha$ setups are in Sect. 5.2). Then the strength score of $pw$ evaluated by PII-PSM under targeted guessing scenarios can be calculated as

$$Final\ score_{pw} = \alpha \times (-\log_2 p_1) + (1 - \alpha) \times (-\log_2 p_2). \qquad (6)$$

**Justification for PII-PSM.** Under targeted guessing scenarios, to evaluate the strength of the password $pw$ in the password space, it is ideal to obtain all of $user_A$'s personal data (e.g., all PII and all existing passwords), and compute $user_A$'s password distribution space as $P(pw|all\ user_A's\ personal\ data,\ public\ data)$. However, this is intrinsically/virtually impossible to obtain all of $user_A$'s personal data. Fortunately, $user_A$'s password distribution space can be approximated more accurately when $user_A$'s more personal data (e.g., common PII) is available. Accordingly, the password strength evaluation models under targeted guessing using PII hold that

$$\forall pw, user_A, user_B;$$

$$\forall P(pw|PII_{user_A}, \ public\ data) \neq P(pw|PII_{user_B}, \ public\ data). \qquad (7)$$

That is, the probabilities of $pw$ in $user_A$'s password space and $user_B$'s are different.

**Table 6.** Training and test settings for targeted password guessing and strength evaluation.

| Exp# | Language | Training set | Test set | Auxiliary dataset |
|---|---|---|---|---|
| 1 | English | 1/2 PII-Rootkit | 1/2 PII-Rootkit | Rockyou |
| 2 |  | 1/2 PII-Yahoo | 1/2 PII-Yahoo (1/2 Yahoo†) |  |
| 3 |  | 1/2 PII-000webhost | 1/2 PII-000webhost |  |
| 4 | Chinese | 1/2 PII-12306 | 1/2 PII-12306 | Tianya |
| 5 |  | 1/2 PII-CSDN | 1/2 PII-CSDN |  |
| 6 |  | 1/2 PII-Dodonew | 1/2 PII-Dodonew |  |

† Since PII-Yahoo size is small (only 214) and thus unable to evaluate targeted PSMs accurately, in targeted password strength evaluation, we randomly sample half of the passwords from Yahoo (226,731) as the test set. When an account in the test set lacks PII, PCFG-based and markov-based models degenerate into basic PCFG [25] and Markov [11].

It is worth noting that, when evaluating password strength, our PII-PSM first replaces the PII-related segments in $pw$ with corresponding PII-tags, and obtains a new password form $pw_{PII-tag}$. For example, if a user's name, birthday, and password are Li Wang, 1998/08/18, and wang980818abc, respectively, the converted $pw_{PII-tag}$ is $N_3B_8abc$. Since PII-PSM uses the same grammar rules for all users when calculating $pw_{PII-tag}$, there is

$$\forall pw_{PII-tag}, user_A, user_B;$$

$$P(pw_{PII-tag}|PII_{user_A}, \ public\ data) = P(pw_{PII-tag}|PII_{user_B}, \ public\ data).$$
$$(8)$$

when given users' PII, $pw$ is determined by $pw_{PII-tag}$, satisfying Eq. 7 under targeted guessing scenarios.

## 5   Experiments

In this section, we first experimentally quantify the improvement of our proposed TarGuess-I-H and TarMarkov-H over the basic TarGuess-I [24] and

TarMarkov [22]. Then, we evaluate the accuracy of our PII-PSM and its counterparts (including our TarGuess-I-H and TarMarkov-H, as well as two benchmarks of Optimal and Min_auto) using the weighted Spearman metric recommended in CCS'18 [8].

## 5.1   Validation of the Improvements

Many studies (e.g., [3,6,13,15]) have shown that password probabilistic models with good guessing ability can be used to construct accurate and practical PSMs. Therefore, we first perform password guessing experiments to demonstrate that our TarGuess-I-H and TarMarkov-H are indeed significantly improved over the original TarGuess-I [24] and TarMarkov [22], and thus are likely to be used to build more accurate targeted PSMs.

**Experimental Setups.** The user language, service type, and password policy are the three most influential factors on password security and strength in turn [23]. The closer the training set is to the passwords of the target site, the better [23]. Therefore, we sample the training and test sets from the same dataset, and show the experiment settings in Table 6. Taking Exp #1 as an example, we randomly divide PII-Rootkit into two equal-sized parts used for training and testing, respectively.

Since our TarGuess-I-H and TarMarkov-H have considered the impact of HFSs and introduced $H_n^i$ tags, we need to select third-party auxiliary datasets to build the HFS dictionary. We use Rockyou and Tianya as auxiliary datasets for English and Chinese training sets, respectively, because the two low-strength datasets contain a large number of weak passwords [6,16], and have been widely used in leading password research (e.g., [6,11,13,15,16,24,25]) in recent years. Besides, to make our TarGuess-I-H and TarMarkov-H perform well, we have implemented multiple experiments with different HFS parameter configurations, and finally set the HFS thresholds $T_1=500$ and $T_2=50$, the HFS length $3 \leq n \leq 8$, and the HFS dictionary composed of top-100 HFSs. The settings of targeted password probabilistic models are shown in Table 7.

**Table 7.** Settings of targeted password probabilistic models.

| Model | L/D/S-tags | PII-tags | $H_n^i$-tag | Model order | Probability threshold |
|---|---|---|---|---|---|
| TarGuess-I [24] | ✓ | ✓ | | — | $10^{-6}$ |
| TarMarkov [22] | | ✓ | | 3 | $10^{-6}$ |
| Our TarGuess-I-H | ✓ | ✓ | ✓ | — | $10^{-6}$ |
| Our TarMarkov-H | | ✓ | ✓ | 3 | $10^{-6}$ |

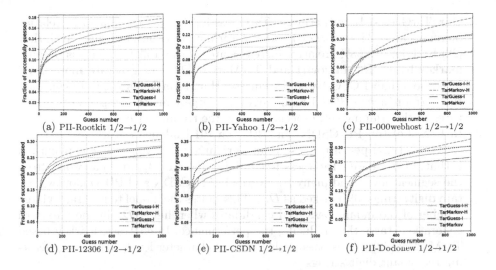

**Fig. 3.** Experimental results of targeted guessing scenarios on six different datasets. Sub-figures (a) to (c) are on datasets from English sites, and (d) to (f) are on datasets from Chinese sites.

**Experimental Results.** We show the experimental results in Fig. 3 and find that:

1) In Figs. 3(a)~3(d), the performances are ordered as our TarMarkov-H, our TarGuess-I-H, TarMarkov [22], and TarGuess-I [24]. In Figs. 3(e) and 3(f), it is our TarMarkov-H, TarMarkov [22], our TarGuess-I-H, and TarGuess-I [24]. On average, our added $H_n^i$-tags make the performances of our TarMarkov-H and TarGuess-I-H higher than the basic TarMarkov [22] and TarGuess-I [24] by 1.72% and 3.11%, respectively. The reasons are as follows: (a) According to Sec. 3.2, users tend to use HFSs when constructing passwords. Thus, password models with $H_n^i$-tags can well identify HFSs in passwords during training, and can better learn users' password construction habits when generating passwords, thereby improving model performance. (b) According to Sec. 3.3, password models with $H_n^i$-tags can more accurately capture password structures, such as $L_8 \rightarrow H_8^1, H_8^2$, and thus reduce redundant segments when generating passwords. (c) Introducing $H_n^i$-tags can increase the variety of password structures. For example, in Exp #1 of Table 6, the extracted password structures increase from 53,168 to 76,133 (a 43.19% increase). In this way, our TarMarkov-H can mitigate the inherent data sparseness issue of markov-based password models.

2) Our TarGuess-I-H outperforms TarGuess-I [24] by 2.02%~3.43% (relative
increases are 8.33%~15.22%) and our TarMarkov-H outperforms TarMarkov
[22] by 1.45%~2.63% (relative increases are 9.73%~15.22%). This is because
markov-based TarMarkov-H and TarMarkov [22] can generate more novel
passwords than PCFG-based TarGuess-I-H and TarGuess-I [24]. In contrast,
the performance of PCFG-based models is largely limited by password structures in the training set, especially when the training size is small.

3) In Figs. 3(e) (on PII-CSDN) and 3(f) (on PII-Dodonew), TarGuess-I-H and
TarGuess-I [24] perform worse than TarMarkov [22]. A possible explanation
is that, PCFG-based TarGuess-I-H and TarGuess-I [24] parse passwords from
the segment level, and many passwords in PII-CSDN and PII-Dodonew contain digit strings [6] (marked as $D_n$). This causes the model to generate a large
number of redundant password candidates when filling $D_n$ in the password
generation stage, thus reducing the performance. In contrast, markov-based
TarMarkov [22] parses passwords from the character level, reducing generating redundant digit strings.

**Summary.** By adding HFS tags, our TarGuess-I-H and TarMarkov-H significantly outperform the basic TarGuess-I [24] and TarMarkov [22] in most cases,
suggesting that our two models can be employed to build accurate targeted
PSMs.

## 5.2  PSM Accuracy Evaluation

**PSM Accuracy Evaluation Metric.** Accuracy is the most essential property
of a PSM. Only PSMs with accurate strength feedback can indeed nudge users to
choose stronger passwords [17,18]. In recent years, researchers have used various
metrics (e.g., Spearman and Kendall correlation coefficients) to measure PSM
accuracy [13,21,26]. At CCS'18, Golla et al. [8] tested 19 candidate metrics
for evaluating PSM accuracy and selected the weighted Spearman correlation
coefficient (WSpearman), because it is robust to monotonic transformations,
disturbances, and quantization. Thus, inspired by Golla et al.'s work [8], we use
WSpearman to evaluate PSM accuracy, calculated as

$$WSpearman(\mathbf{X}, \mathbf{Y}) = \frac{\sum_{i=1}^{n} [w_i(x_i - \bar{x})(y_i - \bar{y})]}{\sqrt{\sum_{i=1}^{n} [w_i(x_i - \bar{x})^2] \sum_{i=1}^{n} [w_i(y_i - \bar{y})^2]}}, \quad (9)$$

where $\mathbf{X}$ and $\mathbf{Y}$ are the weighted rank vectors of the ideal PSM and the tested
PSM, $x_i$ and $y_i$ are the members of $\mathbf{X}$ and $\mathbf{Y}$ ranked $i$ ($1 \leq i \leq n$) in descending
order of frequency, $\bar{x}$ and $\bar{y}$ are the weighted means of $\mathbf{X}$ and $\mathbf{Y}$, and $w_i$ is the
password frequency ranked $i$ in the test set. The higher the WSpearman value
(in [-1,1]), the more accurate the PSM.

**Experimental Setups.** TarGuess-I-H and TarMarkov-H in this section refer to targeted PSMs based on these two models. We show the experimental setups of targeted password strength evaluation in Table 6, and config the targeted PSMs and benchmarks for comparison and evaluation as follows:

- **Our TarGuess-I-H and TarMarkov-H.** The parameter settings of these two PSMs are shown in Table 7. The strength of the password $pw$ is evaluated as $-\log_2 p$, where $p$ is the construction probability of $pw$ under the corresponding model.
- **Our PII-PSM.** The password strength evaluated by our PII-PSM is obtained by weighting the strengths output by TarGuess-I-H and TarMarkov-H with $\alpha$ and 1-$\alpha$; see Eq. 6. $\alpha$ is initialized to a random value in [0,1], optimized by the stochastic gradient descent (SGD) approach with batchsize=$n$ (i.e., every $n$ passwords in the training/testing set are split into a batch). In this way, the impact of randomly/manually setting the $\alpha$ value on PSM accuracy can be eliminated. We calculate WSpearman for each batch in the test set and the corresponding batch in the training set, and use it as a loss to penalize $\alpha$ until $\alpha$ reaches convergence. The convergent $\alpha$ and SGD parameter setups are shown in Table 8. What's more, since the training set is known to our PII-PSM, the optimization for $\alpha$ is feasible, which contributes to the practicality of PII-PSM.

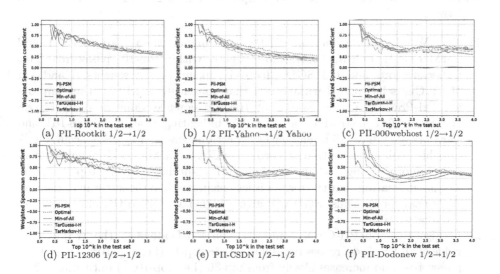

**Fig. 4.** Weighted Spearman correlation coefficient of our targeted PSMs. Sub-figures (a) to (c) are on datasets from English sites, and (d) to (f) are on datasets from Chinese sites.

- **Min_auto.** Min_auto is a PSM strength benchmark indicating a conservative approximation of password strength. It is proposed by Ur et al. [19] and is widely used in leading PSM research (e.g., [13,26]). Regarding a password, Min_auto takes the minimum value of the results of all evaluated PSMs as the password strength. In this paper, we also adopt Min_auto as a PSM strength benchmark, which is calculated as the minimum evaluation results of our TarGuess-I-H, TarMarkov-H, and PII-PSM.

**Table 8.** Convergent $\alpha$ and SGD setups.

| Exp# | $\alpha$ | SGD | | |
|------|----------|-----------|-------------|------------|
| | | Batchsize | Step length | $\Delta^\dagger$ |
| 1 | 0.623 | 50 | [0.2,0.8] | $10^{-5}$ |
| 2 | 0.629 | 100 | [0.5,1.0] | |
| 3 | 0.642 | 50 | [0.2,0.8] | |
| 4 | 0.612 | 50 | [0.2,0.8] | |
| 5 | 0.601 | 50 | [0.2,0.8] | |
| 6 | 0.617 | 50 | [0.2,0.8] | |

† When $|\alpha_{new} - \alpha_{old}| \leq \Delta$, SGD stops optimizing and chooses $\alpha$ as the optimal value.

- **Our Optimal.** To show the optimal evaluation capability that practical PSMs can achieve, we propose a new PSM strength benchmark, Optimal. Given a password, Optimal takes the one closest to the real frequency rank among the results of all evaluated PSMs (e.g., our TarGuess-I-H, TarMarkov-H, and PII-PSM in this paper) as the password strength. Note that an Optimal PSM is unlikely to be deployed in real-world scenarios, because one can hardly know the real password rank. Nevertheless, since the password rank is known in our experiments, Optimal is effective as a PSM strength benchmark.

**Experimental Results.** We show WSpearman of targeted PSMs in Fig. 4 and find that:

1) The Wspearman value of PII-PSM is higher than TarGuess-I-H and TarMarkov-H, and fluctuates more slightly within top-$10^2$ passwords. This is because our adopted SGD effectively optimizes the weights $\alpha$ and 1-$\alpha$ of TarGuess-I-H and TarMarkov-H that constitute PII-PSM, thus improving PII-PSM accuracy. Note that the convergence value of $\alpha$ in Table 8 is 0.601~0.642 instead of around 0.5, indicating that TarGuess-I-H and TarMarkov-H have different effects/contributions to PII-PSM accuracy. A possible explanation is that, according to Fig. 4, TarMarkov-H generally fluctuates more strongly than TarGuess-I-H (especially within top-$10^2$ passwords), indicating that the former is less accurate than the latter in evaluating weak passwords. Thus, SGD will give a higher weight to the more accurate TarGuess-I-H.

2) In Figs. 4(e) (on PII-CSDN) and 4(f) (on PII-Dodonew), the WSpearman value of all PSMs decreases rapidly in top-3~top-10 (i.e., top-$10^{0.5}$~top-$10^{1.0}$) passwords, and increases slowly from top-30 (i.e., top-$10^{1.5}$) until stable. The possible reason is that, in PII-CSDN and PII-Dodonew, the top-10 passwords account for a large proportion (8.33% and 7.91%), resulting in a more concentrated password probability distribution that can be accurately evaluated by PSMs. Thus, the WSpearman value is stable at 1 in top-10. While the followed passwords have a more uniform probability distribution and thus PSMs cannot accurately evaluate some of the passwords. As a result, the

WSpearman value decreases significantly. With more passwords being evaluated, PSMs can more accurately capture password distribution characteristics, so the WSpearman value gradually stabilizes.

3) Compared to individual TarGuess-I-H and TarMarkov-H, PII-PSM is closer to the Optimal benchmark, and the WSpearman differences are only 0.014~0.023. This suggests that PII-PSM has almost the optimal evaluation ability that the compared practical PSMs can achieve, and thus is more accurate. In addition, PII-PSM is also closer to the Min_auto benchmark, and the WSpearman differences are only 0.012~0.031. This indicates that PII-PSM evaluates password strength more strictly and conservatively, which may help nudge users to select stronger passwords.

**Summary.** Our PII-PSM obtained by combining and weighting TarGuess-I-H and TarMarkov-H is more accurate than both individual PSMs, and is closer to the PSM accuracy benchmarks Min_auto and our Optimal. This suggests that a rational combination of multiple PSMs that perform well in different guessing scenarios (e.g., online and offline guessing) is helpful for designing accurate targeted PSMs.

# 6   Conclusion

We have introduced the high-frequency substring (HFS) as a new grammar tag into leading targeted password probabilistic models TarGuess-I [24] and Tar-Markov [22], and proposed our improved models TarGuess-I-H and TarMarkov-H. Then, we weighted and combined our two models and, *for the first time*, devised a practical targeted password strength meter (PSM) called PII-PSM that exploits common personally identifiable information PII(e.g., name and birthday). Extensive evaluation experiments show that our PII-PSM is more accurate than individual TarGuess-I-H and TarMarkov-H, and is closer to two benchmarks of Optimal and Min_auto. What's more, eight large-scale password datasets across different user languages and service types indicate the practicality of our PII-PSM. We believe that our targeted probabilistic models and PII-PSM can shed light on both existing password practice and future password research.

**Acknowledgment.** The authors are grateful to the anonymous reviewers for their invaluable comments. Ding Wang is the corresponding author. This research was in part supported by the National Natural Science Foundation of China (Grant No.62172240), and by the Natural Science Foundation of Tianjin, China (Grant No.21JCZDJC00190).

# References

1. Bonneau, J.: The science of guessing: analyzing an anonymized corpus of 70 million passwords. In: Proceedings of IEEE S&P 2012, pp. 538–552 (2012)
2. Bonneau, J., Herley, C., van Oorschot, P., Stajano, F.: Passwords and the evolution of imperfect authentication. Commun. ACM **58**(7), 78–87 (2015)

3. Castelluccia, C., Dürmuth, M., Perito, D.: Adaptive password-strength meters from markov models. In: Proceedings of NDSS 2012, pp. 1–14 (2012)
4. Das, A., Bonneau, J., Caesar, M., Borisov, N., Wang, X.: The tangled web of password reuse. In: Proceedings of NDSS 2014, pp. 1–15 (2014)
5. Dellinger, A.: Personal data of 533 million Facebook users leaks online, April 2021. https://shorturl.at/dlHUV
6. Dong, Q., Jia, C., Duan, F., Wang, D.: RLS-PSM: a robust and accurate password strength meter based on reuse, Leet and separation. IEEE Trans. Inf. Forensics Secur. **16**, 4988–5002 (2021)
7. Gatlan, S.: Hacker leaks full database of 77 million nitro pdf user records, January 2021. https://shorturl.at/fjwI5
8. Golla, M., Dürmuth, M.: On the accuracy of password strength meters. In: Proceedings of ACM CCS 2018, pp. 1567–1582 (2018)
9. Li, Y., Wang, H., Sun, K.: A study of personal information in human-chosen passwords and its security implications. In: Proceedings of INFOCOM 2016, pp. 1–9 (2016)
10. Li, Z., Han, W., Xu, W.: A large-scale empirical analysis of Chinese web passwords. In: Proceedings of USENIX SEC 2014, pp. 559–574 (2014)
11. Ma, J., Yang, W., Luo, M., Li, N.: A study of probabilistic password models. In: Proceedings of IEEE S&P 2014, pp. 689–704 (2014)
12. Mazurek, M.L., et al.: Measuring password guessability for an entire university. In: Proceedings of ACM CCS 2013, pp. 173–186 (2013)
13. Melicher, W., et al.: Fast, lean, and accurate: modeling password guessability using neural networks. In: Proceedings of USENIX SEC 2016, pp. 1–17 (2016)
14. Morris, C.: Massive data leak exposes 700 million linkedin users' information, June 2021. https://shorturl.at/mDGQ1
15. Pal, B., Daniel, T., Chatterjee, R., Ristenpart, T.: Beyond credential stuffing: password similarity models using neural networks. In: Proceedings of IEEE S&P 2019, pp. 417–434 (2019)
16. Pasquini, D., Gangwal, A., Ateniese, G., Bernaschi, M., Conti, M.: Improving password guessing via representation learning. In: Proceedings of IEEE S&P 2021, pp. 1382–1399 (2021)
17. Tan, J., Bauer, L., Christin, N., Cranor, L.F.: Practical recommendations for stronger, more usable passwords combining minimum-strength, minimum-length, and blocklist requirements. In: Proceedings of ACM CCS 2020, pp. 1407–1426 (2020)
18. Ur, B., et al.: How does your password measure up? The effect of strength meters on password creation. In: Proceedings of USENIX SEC 2012, pp. 65–80 (2012)
19. Ur, B., et al.: Measuring real-world accuracies and biases in modeling password guessability. In: Proceedings of USENIX SEC 2015, pp. 463–481 (2015)
20. Veras, R., Collins, C., Thorpe, J.: On the semantic patterns of passwords and their security impact. In: Proceedings of NDSS 2014, pp. 1–16 (2014)
21. Wang, D., He, D., Cheng, H., Wang, P.: fuzzyPSM: a new password strength meter using fuzzy probabilistic context-free grammars. In: Proceedings of IEEE/IFIP DSN 2016, pp. 595–606 (2016)
22. Wang, D., Wang, P.: The emperor's new password creation policies. In: Proceedings of ESORICS 2015, pp. 456–477 (2015)
23. Wang, D., Wang, P., He, D., Tian, Y.: Birthday, name and bifacial-security: understanding passwords of Chinese web users. In: Proceedings of USENIX SEC 2019, pp. 1537–1555 (2019)

24. Wang, D., Zhang, Z., Wang, P., Yan, J., Huang, X.: Targeted online password guessing: an underestimated threat. In: Proceedings of ACM CCS 2016, pp. 1242–1254 (2016)
25. Weir, M., Aggarwal, S., De Medeiros, B., Glodek, B.: Password cracking using probabilistic context-free grammars. In: Proceedings of IEEE S&P 2009, pp. 391–405 (2009)
26. Wheeler, D.L.: zxcvbn: low-budget password strength estimation. In: Proceedings of USENIX SEC 2016, pp. 157–173 (2016)
27. Xie, Z., Zhang, M., Guo, Y., Li, Z., Wang, H.: Modified password guessing methods based on Targuess-I. Wirel. Commun. Mob. Comput. **2020**, 8837210:1–8837210:22 (2020)
28. Xie, Z., Zhang, M., Yin, A., Li, Z.: A new targeted password guessing model. In: Liu, J.K., Cui, H. (eds.) ACISP 2020. LNCS, vol. 12248, pp. 350–368. Springer, Cham (2020). https://doi.org/10.1007/978-3-030-55304-3_18

# Privacy

# Silver Surfers on the Tech Wave: Privacy Analysis of Android Apps for the Elderly

Pranay Kapoor[✉], Rohan Pagey, Mohammad Mannan, and Amr Youssef

Concordia University, Montreal, QC, Canada
{p_apoo,r_pagey}@live.concordia.ca, m.mannan@concordia.ca,
youssef@ciise.concordia.ca

**Abstract.** Like other segments of the population, elderly people are also rapidly adopting the use of various mobile apps, and numerous apps are also being developed exclusively focusing on their specific needs. Mobile apps help the elderly to improve their daily lives and connectivity, and their caregivers or family members to monitor the loved ones' well-being and health-related activities. While very useful, these apps also deal with a lot of sensitive private data such as healthcare reports, live location, and Personally Identifiable Information (PII) of the elderly and caregivers. While the privacy and security issues in mobile applications for the general population have been widely analyzed, there is limited work that focuses on elderly apps. We shed light on the privacy and security issues in mobile apps intended for elderly users, using a combination of dynamic and static analysis on 146 popular Android apps from Google Play Store. To better understand some of these apps, we also test their corresponding IoT devices. Our analysis uncovers numerous security and privacy issues, leading to the leakage of private information and allowing adversaries to access user data. We find that 95/146 apps fail to adequately preserve the security and privacy of their users in one or more ways; specifically, 15 apps allow full account takeover, and 9 apps have an improper input validation check, where some of them allow an attacker to dump the database containing elderly and caregivers' sensitive information. We hope our study will raise awareness about the security and privacy risks introduced by these apps, and direct the attention of developers to strengthen their defensive measures.

**Keywords:** Elderly privacy · Android apps privacy and security

## 1 Introduction

The adoption of mobile devices is forcing the elderly to navigate the treacherous waters of a complex digital world [5], wherein online threats can even translate into offline harm. While over 53% of all elderly own a smartphone [2], and are keenly adopting mobile technology [7,15], several studies have shown that older adults are more vulnerable to security and privacy threats than the general population [16]. According to US FBI and FTC, cybercrimes against older adults

F. Li et al. (Eds.): SecureComm 2022, LNICST 462, pp. 673–691, 2023.
https://doi.org/10.1007/978-3-031-25538-0_35

in the US have increased five times since 2014, costing over \$650 million in yearly losses [4]. A combination of low self-efficacy, mistrust and lack of awareness and understanding of security hazards [18] makes the elderly reluctant to adopt cyber-secure habits, hence vulnerable.[1]

Applications for the elderly offer various services such as care-giving, e-learning, and improving physical and mental health (e.g., apps for exercise and fitness). While these apps might be used daily by the elderly, their inherent privacy and security implications are not fully known. Weaknesses in elderly apps may expose sensitive private data, sometimes on a large scale, and endanger users' safety (online and in the real world). Recent studies [10] have revealed several security and privacy issues in Android apps, but most large-scale research has been done on apps used by the general population (also see Sect. 6). A few studies have exposed privacy issues in only one particularly vulnerable group (e.g., elderly or children) on a small scale. The work on elderly groups is limited to the study of elderly behavior concerning their privacy and security.

In this paper, we perform an in-depth analysis of 146 prominent elderly Android apps. We define a list of pertinent security and privacy related issues for these apps, and analyze them for such issues (e.g., security vulnerabilities, backend issues, presence of third-party trackers, and insecure data transmission). We also analyze three IoT devices to better understand the corresponding apps and their security implications. We combine the use of several existing tools that enable dynamic and static analysis to perform a wide range of security and privacy tests.

**Contributions and Notable Findings**

1. We design a hybrid approach of dynamic and static analysis for evaluating security and privacy issues in elderly apps (and their corresponding IoT devices). We inspect the apps' web traffic for personally identifiable information (PII) leakage, access control issues, improper authentication management, improper input validation, dangerous third-party library permissions, and the presence of third-party trackers.
2. We apply our analysis framework to 146 Android apps (and the IoT devices corresponding to three apps). Overall, 95/146 apps fail to adequately protect the security and privacy of users due to one or more vulnerabilities.
3. 4/146 Android apps (*GoldenApp, POC EVV, Senior Discounts, Damava*) do not properly authenticate their server API endpoints, allowing illegitimate access to view and obtain sensitive data such as elderly users' physical address, email, health reports, and private messages on the platform.
4. 15/146 Android apps (e.g., *40 Plus Senior Dating, All Well Senior Care, Seniority*) allow an attacker to easily compromise the account of elderly users and caregivers.
5. 9/146 (*Senior Dating, Empowerji, GoldenApp, Caring Village, EZ Care, Generations Homecare System, EllieGrid, Seniority, Tricella Health*) Android

---

[1] The term "vulnerable user" means a person "at-risk" due to his/her particular circumstances, and not to be confused with an app having a security "vulnerability".

apps have improper input validation with injection attack vulnerabilities such as SQL injection, allowing an adversary to dump and modify the application's database. We are assigned CVE-2022-30083 [6] for the code injection issue we found in *EllieGrid*.

6. 16/146 Android apps transmit PII via HTTP to their client-side servers (e.g., *Empowerji*, *GoldenApp*), while 8/146 apps transmit PII (6/146 via HTTP and 2/146 via HTTPS) to various third-party domains.

## 2    Potential Privacy and Security Issues and Threat Model

**Potential Security and Privacy Issues.** We primarily consider two types of data that can be leaked over the network: (1) personally identifiable information (PII) and (2) smartphone device information and usage. A PII leak is any data leak which can be used to identify an individual (e.g., email ID, location/address, password, date of birth, health data, unique device serial number). Device information and usage is the combination of the device data (e.g., manufacturer, model, OS, API level, IP address, screen, battery, cellular carrier, free memory/disk, language, time zone, orientation), and user interaction (e.g., session time, button clicks, visited web pages). Device information and usage leaks can be used to identify an individual or a group of individuals. We tested the most prominent vulnerability types from the OWASP top 10 for Android, based on their CVSS scores. From that base knowledge, we define the following list of potential security and privacy issues to evaluate elderly apps.

1. Improper authentication management: The ability of an attacker to gain access to a user's account (unauthorized login).
2. Improper access control: To be able to gain or observe other users' data on a given platform without their authorization.
3. Improper input validation: Possible injection attacks (e.g., SQL injection and code injection) resulting from missing/inadequate input validation, which may compromise sensitive user data.
4. Vulnerable backend: The use of remotely exploitable outdated server software, and misconfigured or unauthenticated backend service (e.g., Firebase).
5. Plaintext transmission of authentication secrets (e.g., passwords and session IDs), which can be easily captured by a network attacker to gain unauthorized access to user accounts.
6. Insecure PII, device information and usage transmission: PII and device information and usage from the client-end is sent without encryption (i.e., plain HTTP).
7. Data transmission to third-party: Any PII and device/usage information and usage data transmitted from the client side to third-party domains/ trackers, or library providers.
8. Inadequate security configurations: Android apps with misconfigured backend HTTP web servers (e.g., lack of Cross-Origin Resource Sharing or improper flash cross-domain policy), which may lead to large-scale attacks.

9. Dangerous permissions (e.g., Write External Storage, Access Fine Location) automatically acquired by a third-party library when requested by the elderly app, or by a malicious app using the same signed certificate third-party library as the elderly app developer.

**Threat Model.** We consider three attacker types with varying capabilities: (1) On-device attacker: a malicious app with limited permissions on the user's device. (2) On-path attacker: an attacker who is placed between the user's smartphone and its server. This attacker can eavesdrop, modify, and behave like a man-in-the-middle attacker between the user's device and the app's backend server. (3) Remote attacker: any attacker who can connect to an app's backend server. Our threat model does not consider attacks requiring physical access to the device.

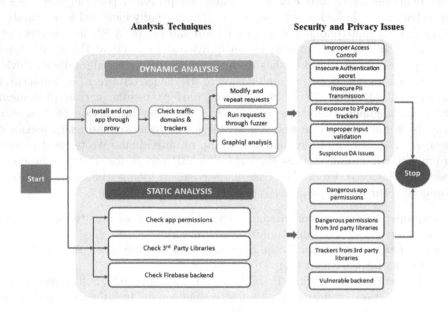

**Fig. 1.** Overview of our methodology

**Ethical Considerations and Responsible Disclosure.** We test vulnerabilities only against accounts that we own and we do not interact with the data of any legitimate user. We do not use an existing vulnerability to exfiltrate data or pivot to other systems, i.e., we stop our analysis when we have enough evidence of a vulnerability and its impact. We also refrain from running any automated scanners that might bombard the servers to cause denial of service. As part of the responsible disclosure, we contacted the developers of our vulnerable apps to share our detailed proof-of-concept and explain to them the related security consequences. 7/35 developers contacted us back, where 2/7 were automated replies to acknowledge our email, and 5/7 developers acknowledged the issues and forwarded them to their respective security teams.

# 3    Analysis Methodology

In this section, we explain how we perform our static and dynamic app analysis, and also how we select our Android test apps.

## 3.1    App Selection

We search Google Play Store for elderly apps (and also screen the best apps for older adults [12]), with relevant keywords.[2] The search was conducted on May 20, 2021, which provided us with 500 apps for further consideration. We shortlist the apps based on the criteria that the apps are specifically designed for elderly users, their caregivers and relatives. We exclude apps that required financial account details or verified identities (e.g., bank accounts, credit card numbers, social security numbers). We manually screen each app to check if it satisfies our key requirements. Our final dataset contains 146 apps. We found that 24/146 apps have a companion IoT device, where 5/24 apps are pill managing apps and 19/24 are elderly tracking apps. We purchased 3/24 IoT devices (available without any subscription and deliverable to our location) to better understand their functionality. Altogether, these apps have been downloaded 20.8M+ times, with a range between 10M+ (*NeuroNation*) to 1000+ downloads (*CareGo* IoT companion app). Note that each caregiver/EVV app may indirectly serve (and have access to) hundreds or thousands of elderly people.

## 3.2    Dynamic Analysis of Traffic Flow

We perform dynamic testing of the apps to simulate the real world usage for the apps so that we can observe the apps as they were intended. We set up test environments for each app (creating user accounts, setting up the IoT device, etc.), emulate user actions for 20 to 60 min depending on the feature-set of the app, collect traffic from the elderly apps and the IoT devices (up to 24 h), and then perform our analysis (explained further in this section). Figure 1 illustrates our methodology. We use Burp Suite[3] for manual dynamic analysis. Burp Suite is an integrated platform for security testing of web and mobile applications, using its various extensions. We also notice that some our apps use GraphQL [14]; note that the use of graph analytics is driving many important business applications from social network analysis to machine learning. To analyze GraphQL APIs, we use the official GraphQL IDE called GraphiQL [11] to test the network traffic on the apps using GraphQL. In-depth dynamic analysis with Burp Suite and GraphiQL[4] helps us find relevant security and privacy issues in our test apps.

The four main components for our dynamic analysis include the following: (1) *Proxy*, an intercepting proxy that lets us see and modify the contents of requests

---

[2] The keywords include: "elderly", "old", "senior", "dementia", "Alzheimer's", "retirement", "senior dating", "pension", "seniority", "caregiver", "memory", "maturity", "retiree", "Electronic Visit Verification", "EVV", "senior health", "memory games".

[3] https://portswigger.net/burp/releases/professional-community-2021-12-1.

[4] https://github.com/graphql/graphiql.

and responses while they are in transit. We use this component to analyze the complete network traffic of the app to check for insecure session management, insecure PII transmission to the app as well as to any third-parties, and look out for any suspicious activity from the app. (2) *Intruder*, a fuzzer used to run a set of values through an input point and perform brute-force attacks and testing rate limiting on apps. We use this component to enumerate user IDs (integer values), list of passwords and API endpoint parameters. (3) *Repeater* lets us send requests repeatedly with manual modifications to check for injection attacks and servers' response to unexpected values or requests. (4) *Decoder* lists the common encoding methods like URL, HTML, Base64, Hex, etc., when looking for chunks of data in values of parameters or headers.

We install each test app from Google Play Store and run it through Burp proxy. We analyze every request and response of the app's APIs (or any included third-party libraries) to the app server and to any third-party domain and tracker. We identify the known third-party trackers using EasyList and EasyPrivacy [8] filtering rules. We differentiate the requests with weak authentication, like the ones which are missing authentication headers or cookies, as they are more likely to be exploitable. This differentiation is done by inspecting the HTTP request headers and searching for the presence of session headers. We also identify the requests responsible for user login/logout or any transmission of user data. We pass these requests through Burp components to check for security and privacy issues. The requests transmitted via GraphQL are analyzed using GraphiQL. In particular, we first use an introspection query to read the GraphQL documentation. Then we inspect the whole documentation to read the available API calls (queries and mutations). Vulnerabilities in GraphQL are found by probing and tampering with the queries and mutations.

We assess the collected traffic to check for PII and transmitted authentication secrets, or leakage of PII to third-party domains that can be leaked via the request URL, Referer, HTTP Cookie, and requests' payload. If encoded data is observed, we use the decoder component in Burp to check for any suspicious data that is being transmitted to the domain. We also analyze the traffic to check for API endpoints with improper access control. APIs with weak authentication are checked first. We conclude that an app has improper access control if we can retrieve any other user's data (on the given app, tested using our own accounts) by changing the existing requests sent from the app to its backend server.

To check improper input validation, we follow the OWASP manual [19] to test for injection attacks to see how the apps respond to unexpected modified requests. We check for SQL injection, code injection and cross-site scripting (XSS) attacks. Any sensitive data observed is immediately deleted from our databases, and we only record the type of data that the vulnerabilities exposed.

**IoT Device Analysis.** For each of the selected IoT devices, we test the companion apps, radio communications and the embedded device. We test the companion apps by following the same dynamic and static analysis process as for other apps. For the radio communications, we analyze Bluetooth and WiFi communications, and we do this by inspecting the packets sent between the IoT device and smartphone. To analyze the underlying embedded device, we pop open the IoT device and analyze the functionality of the different components. We look at the debug ports and try to exploit them to gain further access to the device.

### 3.3   Static Analysis: Library, App Code, and Firebase

Our static analysis aims to complement the dynamic analysis to understand the apps' intended flow so that we can correlate that with our dynamic analysis to look for any suspicious behavior or weak security measures (e.g., bad input sanitization, unprotected Firebase services, etc.) which can potentially lead to privacy or security issues. We target the following components:

**Third-Party Libraries.** Third-party libraries are widely used by Android app developers to build new functionalities and integrate external services. For an in-depth library analysis for our elderly apps, we use LiteRadar.[5] We run the tool using our custom Python script, with the APK file to be tested, so that we can automate the data (e.g., library names, type, permissions used, etc.) collection process. We analyse the libraries in terms of their permissions and purpose.

**Firebase Analysis.** We analyze the Firebase configuration for security issues by performing an automated analysis using Firebase Scanner [23]. Critical mis-configurations can allow attackers to retrieve all the unprotected data stored on the cloud server and we followed a similar approach to Appthority's work [1] on scanning apps for Firebase misconfigurations.

**Static Code Analysis.** Mobile Security Framework[6] (MobSF) is an automated, open-source, all-in-one mobile application (Android/iOS/Windows) pen-testing framework capable of performing fast static, dynamic, and malware analysis of Android, iOS, and Windows mobile applications [24]. So, we use MobSF for static analysis of 146 apps to check for vulnerabilities related to sensitive information logged or hard-coded in files, improper usage of SQLite databases, inse-cure implementation of SSL, and WebView implementation. We also check the Manifest file of each app to obtain their permissions.

## 4   Results

Following the methodology in Sect. 3, we tested 146 Android apps for elderly people, between October 2020 and December 2021. For dynamic analysis, we ran the apps on a Samsung Galaxy M02 (SM-M022G) phone with Android 10. We report our findings in this section, with an overview of the top 30/146 apps with the most security and privacy issues in Table 1.

---

[5] https://github.com/pkumza/LibRadar/blob/master/docs/QuickStart.md.
[6] http://opensecurity.in/mobilesecurity-framework/.

Table 1. Overall results for 30/146 elderly apps with maximum security flaws.
Legend: ○ : On-device Attacker ◑ : On-path Attacker ● : Remote Attacker

| App Name / Security Flaw | Improper Authentication Mgt. | Insecure Session Management | Insecure PII Transmission | PII Exposure to Third-party (3P) | Device Info. & Usage Exposure to 3P | Improper Input Validation | Improper Access control | Security Misconfigurations | File Path Manipulation |
|---|---|---|---|---|---|---|---|---|---|
| 40 Plus Senior Dating (v9.8) | ◑ | ◑ | ◑ | ◑ | ◑ | | | ◑ | |
| Empowerji (v5.7) | ◑ | ◑ | ◑ | | ◑ | ● | | ◑ | |
| GoldenApp (v3.2) | ◑ | ◑ | ◑ | | ◑ | ◑ | ● | | |
| Senior Safety App (v9.7) | ◑ | ◑ | ◑ | ◑ | | | | ◑ | |
| POC EVV (v3.2) | ◑ | ◑ | ◑ | | ◑ | | ◑ | | |
| EZ Care (v0.0.7) | ◑ | ◑ | ◑ | | ● | | | | |
| BrickHouse TrackView (v1.5.8) | ◑ | ◑ | ◑ | ◑ | | | | | |
| Family1st (v1.0.1) | ◑ | ◑ | ◑ | ◑ | | | | | |
| X-GPS Monitor (v2.10.4) | ◑ | ◑ | ◑ | ◑ | | | | | |
| DAGPS (v21100901) | ◑ | ◑ | ◑ | ◑ | | | | | |
| Tricella Health (v2.15.6) | ● | | | | | ◑ | ◑ | | |
| Oscar Senior/Enterprise (v6.8.2) | | ◑ | ◑ | | | ◑ | | ◑ | |
| FlirtMatures Dating (v1.0) | ◑ | ◑ | | | | ◑ | | | |
| Caring Village (v0.16.5) | | | ◑ | | | | ◑ | ◑ | |
| Senior Discounts (v2.2) | | | | | ◑ | | ○ | ◑ | |
| Seniority E-commerce app (v.1.0.2) | ● | | | | ◑ | ◑ | | | |
| Cougar Dating (v1.1.3) | ◑ | ◑ | | | | | | ◑ | |
| Over 40 Dating Mature (v1.0) | | | | | | ◑ | | | ◑ |
| Generations Homecare System (v3.3.3) | | | | | | | ◑ | ◑ | |
| Alzheimer's Daily Companion (v1.0.7) | ◑ | ◑ | | | | | | | |
| Big Launcher (v1.4) | | ◑ | ◑ | | | | | | |
| HelpAge SOS (v1.0.27) | | ◑ | ◑ | | | | | | |
| Carelinx (v3.0.1) | | | | | ◑ | | | ◑ | |
| Damava (v1.2.4) | | | | | ● | | ● | | |
| Doulikesenior (v1.5.1) | | | | | | ◑ | | ◑ | |
| Homage (v5.0.8) | | | | | ◑ | | | ◑ | |
| EllieGrid (v3.4.1) | | | | | | | ● | | |
| All Well Senior Care (v2.15.0) | ● | | | | | | | | |
| Mobile Caregiver+ (v2.0.35) | | | | | | ◑ | | | |
| 401(K) - Retirement Planning (v2.5) | | | | | | ◑ | | | |

## 4.1 Improper Authentication Management

We found that 15/146 apps have authentication management vulnerabilities. Prominent examples include the following: In *Empowerji*, *40 Plus Senior Dating*, *GoldenApp*, *EZ Care*, *FlirtMatures Dating*, *POC EVV* and *Cougar Dating*, the login credentials are sent in plaintext over HTTP, so any on-path attacker sniffing the traffic can get the user login credentials (e.g., *Empowerji* leaks name, email ID, password and phone number; *POC EVV* leaks the 6-digit user ID, a 4-digit PIN for login and the private messages sent between the caregiver and his/her supervisor). For *All Well Senior Care*, *Seniority* and *Tricella Health*, we successfully performed an OTP brute-force attack (on our test account). This is possible as these apps do not implement any rate limiting and the OTPs consist of 4 or less numerical digits, which can easily be enumerated (even for the worst-case scenario, where we could easily try all 10000 requests for a 4-digit number); we also verified that full account takeover by a remote attacker takes only trivial efforts. In *All Well Senior Care*, the attacker can obtain the user's health data (e.g., heart rate, blood pressure, etc.), wellness data (wake up time, steps taken, etc.), see all the hourly updates the user is providing to her caregiver, the location of the user, all the health charts which are saved on the user's account, and even the private messages of the user with their caregiver or their care group (containing multiple users in one group). Wherein user information (e.g., address, phone numbers, credit card details) can be obtained in the *Seniority* app due to improper authentication management. During our retesting, we also noticed that *Senior Safety App* fixed its issues in a software update.

## 4.2 Insecure Session Management

We found 10/146 apps that had their session IDs sent in plaintext over HTTP. For example, *POC EVV* exposes its session ID in plaintext over HTTP, so an on-path attacker can replay a request from this app and perform an account takeover. Also, 8/146 apps did not use any authentication secret. For example, *GoldenApp* does not make use of any authentication secret for accessing any resource (which also leads to improper access control issues which is explained further in Sect. 4.4). The app's authorization mechanism is purely based on supplying a mobile number, where there is no verification from the server's end regarding which mobile number is tied to which user. An adversary can change the mobile number from the request and log into the replaced number's account. Although the victim's number is not leaked anywhere, an on-path attacker can still see the mobile number as the communications are over HTTP. For our testing, we used only our own test phone numbers. After changing the number, the attacker can impersonate the victim, e.g., to request home services on the user's behalf. Apps like *FlirtMatures Dating* send their session IDs in plaintext over HTTP; any on-path attacker can sniff these secrets, and potentially takeover a user's account, also allowing the attacker to access user's sensitive information.

## 4.3   PII Exposure, Data Sharing with Third-Parties and Trackers

We found that 16/146 apps send plaintext PII to their servers. Examples include: *POC EVV* (login code, login PIN, session ID during login), *40 Plus Senior Dating* (email ID and password during login), *Empowerji* (full name, email ID, password, mobile number and city), *GoldenApp* (username, mobile number, user address), and *EZ Care* (username and password during login and the private messages sent and received between a doctor and the user).

**Table 2.** Top 10 trackers that receive traffic from 146 elderly apps

| Tracker | # Apps |
|---|---|
| crashlytics.com | 35 |
| doubleclick.net | 22 |
| googlesyndication.com | 12 |
| google-analytics.com | 8 |
| googletagmanager.com | 6 |
| appsflyer.com | 6 |
| flurry.com | 4 |
| googleadservices.com | 4 |
| onesignal.com | 3 |
| branch.io | 3 |

Moreover, out of the 16 apps that send plaintext PII to their own servers, 6 of them also send PII in plaintext over HTTP to third-party domains/trackers. Examples include: *Oscar Senior* (email ID, user name and profile picture sent to googleapis, and geolocation to onesignal's API endpoint), *Big Launcher* (exact geolocation to openweathermap.org), *Carelinx* (email ID to intercom.com), *40 Plus Senior Dating* (email ID, user name and profile picture sent to googleapis), *Senior Dating* (user name and password sent to googleapis).

18/146 apps send device information and usage data in plaintext (6/146 over HTTP and 12/146 over HTTPS) to third-party domains. The most common parameters include phone model and OS build version. *Empowerji* sends CPU build, Android version and firmware version to AppsFlyer (third-party domain). *Homage*, *EZ Care* and *All Well Senior Care* send WiFi, cellular information, signal strength, and a flag to check if the device is rooted or not. *Seniority* sends email ID, device information (phone model and OS build), and the product details (that the user adds to the shopping cart or buys on the app) to a third-party analytics tracker (wzrkt.com) over HTTPS.

We found that 115/146 apps communicate with 341 third-party (non-tracker) domains:[7] 66 apps communicate with Googleapis.com domains, 43 apps with Firebase sub-domains and 29 apps with Facebook domains. 72/146 apps had traffic through at least one Google domain. We found 39 unique tracker domains with 137 occurrences across 76/146 apps (see Table 2). The top 3 prevalent trackers are Crashlytics (35/146), DoubleClick (22/146) and Google Syndication (12/146). Crashlytics is a crash reporting software that helps identify bugs in the apps and report the user's activity to the app developers so they can take appropriate measures to ensure that users do not stop using their app. DoubleClick is a Google ad service. In 9 apps, we detect 10 or more third-party domains and trackers (*Senior Discounts, Big Keyboard & Notifications, Free Chat & Senior Dating, Senior Dating by Lauber, Over 40 - Find People 50, 40 Plus Senior Dating, NeuroNation, Ianacare, Oscar Senior*). These apps could expose elderly users to potential voluminous in-app advertisements, and extensive tracking.

### 4.4   Improper Access Control

We found 4/146 apps with improper access control. *GoldenApp's* access control issues are due to insecure session management. As there are no authentication tokens or cookies in the requests, an attacker can replay the requests (even modify them) to create accounts in other users' names which can lead to misrepresentation or identity theft for the user. *POC EVV* contains a 5-digit "dcsId" parameter as the user ID in the requests which can be changed (by a remote attacker) to get other users' data (e.g., phone number, home and office address, zip code). *Senior Discounts plus Coupons* has a 6-digit parameter for the user ID that can be modified to get any other user's email ID. *Damava* also has a similar issue where an attacker can fetch the user details using a GraphQL query and then modify the user ID to get other users' data (e.g., email ID, address, criminal record). The information disclosed in *Damava* could result in a full account takeover for both the patient as well as a caregiver. We also found that the appointment details query and mutation do not implement any access control in *Damava*; an adversary can view, modify and cancel any elderly patient's appointment. Moreover, given the appointment and caregiver details, the attacker can also impersonate a caregiver to harm the patient.

### 4.5   Improper Input Validation

9/146 apps are vulnerable to various injection attacks such as SQL/code injection, cross-site scripting. For example, *Senior Dating by Lauber, GoldenApp, Caring Village* and *Generations Homecare System* are vulnerable to reflected cross-site scripting attacks. An attacker can execute malicious JavaScript code to fetch elderly users' detail or to phish them. We note that for this attack

---

[7] A domain is considered to be a third-party domain if an app from a developer connects to it to enable third-party functions. Thus, the domain certificate owner is not the same as the developer of the app.

to work, a victim would first need to click on a malicious link crafted by the attacker. *Empowerji*, *EZ Care* and *Tricella Health* are vulnerable to SQL injection attacks, allowing an adversary to view, modify and delete any elderly user's data. *EllieGrid* and *Seniority* are vulnerable to code injection. For this attack, we added a JavaScript sleep function in the request body and then observed the response time. When there was a delay of 10 s for the response after the sleep command of 10 s, we confirmed the code injection vulnerability. This is a very serious issue that can lead to complete compromise of the application's data and functionality, and the server that's hosting the application [3]. Due to ethical reasons, we limit our attack in detecting this vulnerability. As there is no authentication secret on *EllieGrid* requests, the attacker can perform this attack remotely by constructing and sending the modified requests to the app's server.

### 4.6   Server-Side Security Misconfigurations

We found 16/146 apps with various security misconfigurations. Apps such as *Doulikesenior*, *Carelinx*, *Pension Status Search Old Age Widow Handicap* and *Homage* transmit HTTP requests to modify an object via unprotected GET requests, and thus are vulnerable to Cross-Site Request Forgery (CSRF) attacks, mostly executed via sharing/clicking a malicious link. We found that *Over 40 Dating Mature* has a file path manipulation vulnerability where we placed user-controllable data (the file path on the app's server) into the URL path of the app's request that might be used on the server to access local resources (which may be within or outside the web root). With this vulnerability, an attacker can modify the file path to access different resources, which may contain sensitive information. For legal and ethical reasons we did not test/validate this attack.

### 4.7   Dangerous App Permissions

Dangerous permissions grant an app access to personal user data (e.g., user's location), or control over the user's device. They are only granted after explicit user consent. We found a total of 598 dangerous permissions in 118/146 apps, i.e., an average of 5 dangerous permissions per app. See Table 3. *Ianacare* (caregiver app) and *Life Assure* (companion app for a tracking device) had the maximum of 11 dangerous permissions (Call Phone, Camera, Write External Storage, Read External Storage, Read Calendar, Write Calendar, Read Contacts, Write Contacts, Read Phone State, Access Coarse Location, Access Fine Location, Get Accounts, Record Audio). Access Fine Location permission is needed if an app wants to know detailed information about the user's location, and respond accordingly. This is often used with advertising and location-based and social-network services like Facebook. Read Calendar allows an application to read the user's calendar data. Calendar events can, and often do contain contact information. The top 2 dangerous permissions found were Write External Storage (92 apps) and Read External Storage (91 apps). Rarely used permissions found were Read Call Log (*BIG Phone for Seniors*), Receive SMS (*Homedoctor Protección Senior*), Get Tasks (*DAGPS*) and Write Call Log (*BIG Phone for Seniors*).

84/146 apps required Access Fine Location and 75/146 apps required Access Coarse Location permission. 61/146 apps asked for Camera permission, such as *Petralex*, *Walk to End Alzheimer's*, *GoutDietRecipes*, *Seniority*, *Aveanna EVV*, and *401(K) - Retirement Planning*. Apps with a significantly high number of risky permissions include *Ianacare*, *401(K) - Retirement Planning*, *Oscar Senior*, *Senior Safety App*, *CrescendoConnect*, *Trusted Senior Care* and *ClearCareGo*.

**Table 3.** 598 Dangerous permissions asked by 118/146 elderly apps

| Dangerous Permission | # Apps |
|---|---|
| Write External Storage | 92 |
| Read External Storage | 91 |
| Access Fine Location | 84 |
| Access Coarse Location | 75 |
| Camera | 61 |
| Record Audio | 44 |
| Read Phone State | 39 |
| Read Contacts | 29 |
| Call Phone | 27 |
| Get Accounts | 22 |
| Write Settings | 9 |
| Read Calendar | 8 |
| Write Calendar | 8 |
| Write Contacts | 5 |
| Get Tasks | 1 |
| Read Call Log | 1 |
| Receive SMS | 1 |
| Write Call Log | 1 |

## 4.8   Third-Party Libraries and Permissions

**Types of Libraries.** We found 122 unique third-party libraries and a total of 1008 libraries in 127/146 apps, for various purposes: app development (93/122), analytics (6/122), advertisements (6/122), and social networking (2/122). We found 34/146 apps with *Facebook* social media library and 14/146 apps with advertisement libraries, mainly *Google Ads* (9 apps) and *Unity3d Ads* (3 apps).

**Libraries by App Category.** A high number of total third-party libraries were found in 26 caregiver apps (218/1008 libraries), 20 EVV apps (162/1008), 16 location tracking apps (150/1008), 12 dating apps (107/1008) and 6 apps for Alzheimer's (55/1008). This shows that the elderly who may need caring, or are unwell, or socially active may be more prone to privacy and data security issues arising via these third-party libraries. 48/146 apps have 10 or more unique third-party libraries. Examples of apps with a high number (>14) of unique libraries are *Knee Arthritis Exercises* (24), *Theora Link* (22), *Walk to End Alzheimer's* (19), *My SOS Family Emergency Alerts* (18), *Doulikesenior* (17), *Pension Status Search Old Age Widow Handicap* (16), *Tracki GPS* (15), and *Empowerji* (15).

**Kinds of Permissions Asked.** We found 3 unique signature[8] permissions asked by the libraries (Dump, Write APN Settings, Write Secure Settings). We found the Dump permission for example used by *Firebase* (64/146 apps), *Glide* (41/146 apps) and *Facebook* (32/146 apps) third-party libraries. Write Secure Settings permission was asked predominantly by *Google Mobile Services* (62/146 apps) and *Firebase* (62/146 apps). This Development Aid library permission allows an application to read or write the secure system settings. This permission should only be seen on Android system apps (and possibly wireless carriers or hardware manufacturer pre-installed apps) [26]. Write APN Settings permission was asked by *Google Play* library (4/146 apps).

### 4.9   Static Code Analysis

Static code analysis with MobSF shows that 93/146 apps can read/write to External Storage; 84/146 apps execute raw SQL queries which may expose them to SQL Injection attacks; 71/146 apps use weak hash functions; 36/146 apps have insecure WebView implementation; and 12/146 apps have insecure SSL implementation, a critical security issue. Apps with all these five concerns are *Alzheimer's Disease Pocketcard, Big Keyboard & Notifications, Over 40 - Find People 50, Pill Reminder & Medicine App, Doulikesenior, Senior Safety App* and *Silver 50 Dating*.

### 4.10   Apps with an IoT Device

We acquired IoT devices that operate with 3/24 IoT companion apps: *EllieGrid, Carego Alphahom, Tuya SOS*, and tested them to understand the relationship between the device and app. We analyzed the app behavior for the remaining 21/24 IoT companion apps, to the extent possible without the IoT device, and found issues in 7/24 apps. *X-GPS Monitor, Family1st, BrickHouse Track-View* and *DAGPS* are IoT companion apps which help family members track their elderly loved ones via IoT devices. All these 4 apps had 3 main issues: (1) improper authentication management, allowing an on-path attacker to sniff the username and password for full account takeover, (2) insecure session management, i.e., there is no use of authentication secrets in their requests, allowing an attacker to replay the requests, and (3) insecure PII transmission, leaking username and password in plaintext over HTTP. An on-path attacker can exploit these issues to track the exact location of users wherever they go with their IoT device due to full account takeover.

---

[8] Enables communication between multiple apps of the same developer. Only granted if the requesting app is signed with the same certificate.

*Tricella Health* and *EllieGrid* are smart pill organizers which make medication management easier and are specifically designed to help the elderly by reminding them to take their pills on time (they consist of a pillbox and an app). *Tricella Health* has improper authentication management, where it is vulnerable to a remote OTP (3-digit number) brute-force attack during login and registration, leading to full account takeover. It also has improper input validation where its login requests are vulnerable to SQL injection attacks. These issues can lead to a remote attacker changing the user's medications causing the user to take the wrong medications, skip doses or overdose.

*EllieGrid's* physical pillbox is designed to store pills and receive reminders as ring notifications. The reminders and medications can be set up in its companion app. We found two major vulnerabilities in *EllieGrid*. Firstly, it offers a functionality to alert the elderly user's caregiver via email and phone, when the pillbox is not opened on time. We note that there is no access control present in this functionality, and a remote adversary can completely tamper with the associated caregiver's detail by using the caregiver profile setup option, which is present on the app UI. An adversary can enumerate a caregiver's ID by brute-forcing, and then supply it to modify the caregiver's email and send the alerts to an attacker under his control, which would allow him to track the elderly users' activities and collect their pill taking habits; additionally, the legitimate caregiver will not receive any further notifications from the pillbox. Secondly, the *EllieGrid* solution offers a paid plan with additional functionalities for the elderly, such as viewing weekly adherence reports and adding a caregiver. Specifically, we found a parameter *subscriptionTypeId* from the user profile API, which sets the value of the current plan. An adversary can set this parameter's value to *premium* and upgrade their *EllieGrid* account for free.

We also found some vulnerabilities by following the static analysis approach in *Carego Alphahom*, which provides a personal alarm system for the elderly. In particular, the app is vulnerable to the Janus vulnerability [17], in which an adversary can prepend a malicious DEX file to an APK file while keeping its signature unaffected. Android versions 5.0 - 8.1 accept the file as a valid APK.

### 4.11   Firebase Analysis

84/146 Android apps use Google Firebase as a backend service and we found 4/84 apps whose Firebase DB was exposed publicly. For ethical reasons and to protect other customers' privacy, we created elderly accounts on the four apps. Then, we updated the Firebase scanner to automatically search for our test data in its response and record the leaked information from our own account. 2/4 apps (*CogniFit* and *Carely*) fixed this issue during the time of our testing. For *UnitedHealthcare EVV Tennessee* and *Amerigroup EVV Tennessee*, at the time of testing, we could not see any sensitive data being stored on their databases.

## 5   Limitations

As Google Play Store does not have a defined "Elderly" or "Senior" app category, our app search is limited to the keywords used. A major limitation we faced during our dynamic analysis was the inability to create accounts for 67/115 of our apps because the companies either make accounts for the users beforehand (and provide access information) or the apps will validate the user's information (e.g., medical insurance numbers, and organization email IDs, which we cannot provide in our test accounts) before creating the account. This was most applicable for the EVV and caregiver apps. For those apps, we conduct a limited dynamic analysis of pre-login application behaviors. We also did not test any paid apps.

## 6   Related Work

Slane et al. [25] collected seniors' perspectives on technological devices and applications to show how seniors protect their personal information, and what knowledge, tools, and support they would need in order to consider new functions or devices. Huckvale et al. [13] assessed 79 clinically safe medical/health apps used by chronic and unwell persons, and found that 23/79 of apps sent unencrypted PII over the Internet, 63/79 apps communicated directly with third-party services and 53/79 of apps had some form of privacy policy. However, this work does not specifically study elderly users, or analyze the backend security issues. Frik et al. [9] identified a range of complex privacy and security attitudes and needs specific to *older adults*, along with common threat models, misconceptions, and mitigation strategies. They showed how older adults' limited technical knowledge, experience, and declining abilities amplify vulnerability to certain risks. Oliveira et al. [20] showed that *older women* were the most vulnerable group to phishing attacks in a study of 158 internet users. Razaghpanah et al. [21] identified 2,121 third-party advertising and tracking services at the traffic level, of which 233 were previously unknown to other popular advertising and tracking blacklists. Their analysis of the privacy policies of the largest advertising and tracking service providers showed rampant sharing of harvested data with subsidiaries and third-party affiliates. Ren et al. [22] analyzed 512 apps for privacy leaks over time across three dimensions (PII leaks, HTTPS adoption, and domains contacted) independently, and found that app privacy gets worse as users upgrade apps and all apps leak at least one type of PII.

In contrast to the above work, we take an in-depth look at the security and privacy threats in Android apps used by the elderly. We also analyze traffic flows, PII or device information and usage leaks, dangerous permissions used by apps and third-party libraries, and backend security issues of high severity, using various tools for both dynamic and static analysis. Our initial framework also included

Lumen Privacy Monitor for dynamic analysis of test apps, but we removed it from the framework as we found that Lumen did not uncover several security flaws as compared to Burp Suite. Even though Lumen would show leaks, there was a layer of uncertainty as to how a leak was transmitted (over HTTP or HTTPS) and where it was leaked (to the client-side product itself or to some third-party domains). Also, Lumen did not work reliably on newer Android versions and only worked best below Android 7. Hence, we decided to use a more manual approach with Burp Suite.

# 7   Conclusion

We presented a comprehensive analysis of 146 Android apps that are intended to assist elderly people. Our methodology included dynamic analysis of traffic domain flows, trackers, leaks, and permissions, static analysis of third-party libraries for risky permissions and vulnerable backend issues using various automated as well as manual tools. We reveal individually many red flags in 30/146 apps and how they are most likely to be a security risk. But also, in a wider sense, we have noticed trends in apps' permissions and domain flows which show us how some companies, third-party libraries, or permissions dominate the segments. This is why we think the analysis should not stop here, as we can delve even deeper to find more flaws and vulnerabilities. This will create a safe environment for the elderly to have the peace of mind that their new smartphones are safe and they have one less thing to worry about.

**Acknowledgements.** This work was partly supported by a grant from the Office of the Privacy Commissioner of Canada (OPC) Contributions Program.

# References

1. Arghire, I.: Thousands of mobile apps leak data from firebase databases (2018). https://www.securityweek.com/thousands-mobile-apps-leak-data-firebase-databases
2. Bengfort, J.: Senior care and mobility: why smartphones and tablets make sense. (2019). https://healthtechmagazine.net/article/2019/11/senior-care-and-mobility-why-smartphones-and-tablets-make-sense
3. Choi, H., Kim, Y.: Large-scale analysis of remote code injection attacks in Android apps. Secur. Commun. Netw. **2018**, 1–17 (2018). https://doi.org/10.1155/2018/2489214
4. CNBC.com: Here's how online scammers prey on older Americans, and what they should know to fight back, November 2019. https://www.cnbc.com/2019/11/23/new-research-pinpoints-how-elderly-people-are-targeted-in-online-scams.html
5. Columbus, L.: Roundup of internet of things forecasts (2017). https://www.forbes.com/sites/louiscolumbus/2017/12/10/2017-roundup-of-internet-of-things-forecasts/?sh=4f00f1d11480
6. CVE.mitre.org: Cve-2022-30083, May 2022. https://cve.mitre.org/cgi-bin/cvename.cgi?name=CVE-2022-30083

7. Davidson, J., Schimmele, C.: Evolving internet use among Canadian seniors. statistics Canada research paper series (2019). https://www150.statcan.gc.ca/n1/pub/11f0019m/11f0019m2019015-eng.htm
8. Easylist.to: Easylist (2022). https://easylist.to/
9. Frik, A., Nurgalieva, L., Bernd, J., Lee, J.S., Schaub, F., Egelman, S.: Privacy and security threat models and mitigation strategies of older adults. In: Proceedings of the Fifteenth USENIX Conference on Usable Privacy and Security, SOUPS 2019, pp. 21–40. USENIX Association, USA (2019)
10. Gibler, C., Crussell, J., Erickson, J., Chen, H.: AndroidLeaks: automatically detecting potential privacy leaks in android applications on a large scale. In: Katzenbeisser, S., Weippl, E., Camp, L.J., Volkamer, M., Reiter, M., Zhang, X. (eds.) Trust 2012. LNCS, vol. 7344, pp. 291–307. Springer, Heidelberg (2012). https://doi.org/10.1007/978-3-642-30921-2_17
11. Github.com: graphiql, January 2022. https://github.com/graphql/graphiql
12. Hoyt, J.: Senior citizen apps (2020). https://www.seniorliving.org/cell-phone/apps/
13. Huckvale, K., Prieto, J.T., Tilney, M., Benghozi, P.J., Car, J.: Unaddressed privacy risks in accredited health and wellness apps: a cross-sectional systematic assessment. BMC Med. **13**(1), 1–13 (2015)
14. Jindal, A., Madden, S.: Graphiql: a graph intuitive query language for relational databases. In: 2014 IEEE International Conference on Big Data (Big Data), pp. 441–450. IEEE (2014)
15. Kakulla, B.N.: Older adults keep pace on tech usage. AARP Research (2020). https://www.aarp.org/research/topics/technology/info-2019/2020-technology-trends-older-americans.html
16. Maaß, W.: The Elderly and the internet: how senior citizens deal with online privacy. In: Trepte, S., Reinecke, L. (eds.) Privacy Online, pp. 235–249. Springer, Berlin (2011). https://doi.org/10.1007/978-3-642-21521-6_17
17. Medium.com: Exploiting apps vulnerable to janus (cve-2017–13156), 26 March 2021. https://medium.com/mobis3c/exploiting-apps-vulnerable-to-janus-cve-2017-13156-8d52c983b4e0
18. Morrison, B., Coventry, L., Briggs, P.: How do older adults feel about engaging with cyber-security? Hum. Behav. Emerg. Technol. **3**(5), 1033–1049 (2021)
19. Muscat, I.: What are injection attacks, April 2019. https://www.acunetix.com/blog/articles/injection-attacks
20. Oliveira, D., et al.: Dissecting spear phishing emails for older vs young adults: on the interplay of weapons of influence and life domains in predicting susceptibility to phishing. In: Proceedings of the 2017 Chi Conference on Human Factors in Computing Systems, pp. 6412–6424 (2017)
21. Razaghpanah, A., et al.: Apps, trackers, privacy, and regulators: a global study of the mobile tracking ecosystem. In: The 25th Annual Network and Distributed System Security Symposium (NDSS 2018) (2018)
22. Ren, J., Lindorfer, M., Dubois, D.J., Rao, A., Choffnes, D., Vallina-Rodriguez, N., et al.: Bug fixes, improvements,... and privacy leaks. In: The 25th Annual Network and Distributed System Security Symposium (NDSS 2018) (2018)
23. Sahni, S.: Firebase scanner, 28 February 2018. https://github.com/shivsahni/FireBaseScanner
24. Shirke, K.: Mobile security framework (mobsf) static analysis, January 2019. https://medium.com/@kshitishirke/mobile-security-framework-mobsf-static-analysis-df22fcdae46e

25. Slane, A., Pedersen, I., Hung, P.C.K.: Involving seniors in developing privacy best practices: towards the development of social support technologies for seniors. in: office of the privacy commissioner of Canada (2020). https://www.priv.gc.ca/en/opc-actions-and-decisions/research/funding-for-privacy-research-and-knowledge-translation/completed-contributions-program-projects/2019-2020/p_2019-20_03/

26. XDA-developers.com: android permissions & security explained. https://forum.xda-developers.com/t/android-permissions-security-explained.2312066/

# MetaPriv: Acting in Favor of Privacy on Social Media Platforms

Robert Cantaragiu, Antonis Michalas[✉], Eugene Frimpong,
and Alexandros Bakas

Tampere University, Tampere, Finland
{robert.cantaragiu,antonios.michalas,eugene.frimpong,
alexandros.bakas}@tuni.fi

**Abstract.** Social networks such as Facebook (Since October 2021 is also known as META) (FB) and Instagram are known for tracking user online behaviour for commercial gain. To this day, there is practically no other way of achieving privacy in said platforms other than renouncing their use. However, many users are reluctant in doing so because of convenience or social and professional reasons. In this work, we propose a means of balancing convenience and privacy on FB through obfuscation. We have created `MetaPriv`, a tool based on simulating user interaction with FB. `MetaPriv` allows users to add noise interactions to their account so as to lead FB's profiling algorithms astray, and make them draw inaccurate profiles in relation to their interests and habits. To prove our tool's effectiveness, we ran extensive experiments on a dummy account and two existing user accounts. Our results showed that, by using our tool, users can achieve a higher degree of privacy in just a couple of weeks. We believe that `MetaPriv` can be further developed to accommodate other social media platforms and help users regain their privacy, while maintaining a reasonable level of convenience. To support open science and reproducible research, our source code is publicly available online.

**Keywords:** Metaverse · Obfuscation · Online profiling · Privacy · Social networks · Recommendation systems

## 1 Introduction

Online tracking on social networks (SNs) have raised concerns regarding user privacy [4,8,15]. Recommendation systems used by social media are developed to present biased information with the purpose of encouraging user engagement. When users share their opinions, beliefs and preferences on said platforms – whether by clicking 'like' on an article or by writing a controversial post – the recommendations they receive are aimed at reinforcing these beliefs. Their goal is to provide users with information that most likely interests them and enables them to trace other users sharing the same values. It is believed that through this approach, users gradually become more engaged with these platforms, while

F. Li et al. (Eds.): SecureComm 2022, LNICST 462, pp. 692–709, 2023.
https://doi.org/10.1007/978-3-031-25538-0_36

going deeper in the rabbit-hole of subjectivity, since the only information and news they receive affirms their already established opinions. As a result, users remain engaged in SN platforms, as the latter make accurate predictions on their potential consumption needs. Hence, platforms in collaboration with companies promoting their products manipulate user information for targeted advertising.

*Balance Between Privacy and Convenience on Social Networks:* Most users seem to be left with two options when it comes to social network privacy: *(1)* either regular use of the platform – hence no privacy or *(2)* complete abstinence from social networks – hence full privacy. However, the second option presents a number of problems. First, the hassle of removing data about oneself from a platform, discourages users as it demands tedious action. Note that data removal does not refer to deleting the account alone, but to the deletion of all posts, pictures and logged data from the platform. Secondly, even in cases where all user data is deleted, SNs may still track individuals through partner companies on different websites (e.g. through FB Pixel [16]). Finally, completely opting out of SNs results in great costs in terms of convenience for many individuals, who wish to keep in touch with their friends, keep up with the news and promote themselves or their activities. To this end, we believe that complete privacy is not achievable for most users. We do, however, think that one can strike a balance between privacy and convenience on said platforms and this has been a major motive behind our work. Our platform of choice for this work is FB – the world's largest online SN. However, the idea presented below can be developed to accommodate privacy on other platforms.

*Contributions:* The main idea has been developed based on increasing concerns regarding the breach of user privacy in online SNs. More precisely, the main concern is that user choices are being covertly manipulated and controlled by SNs. With this in mind, we built `MetaPriv`, an automated tool that allows FB users to obfuscate their data and conceal their real interests and habits from FB. As a result, the core contribution of this paper is that it provides users with the necessary tools to protect their privacy when using SNs. It is worth mentioning that `MetaPriv` allows users to define the desired level of privacy (e.g. become almost 'invisible' online while still using SN platforms, reveal certain information about their digital and real lives etc.). By doing this, `MetaPriv` provides a novel and adaptive balance between privacy and functionality. This is a feature we believe will be used in several services in the near future.

## 2  Related Work

A number of research works offer users a more private experience on FB and other SNs. `FaceCloak` [12] protects user privacy on SNs by shielding personal information from the SN and unauthorized users, while maintaining the usability of the underlying services. `FaceCloak` achieves this through providing fake information to the SN and storing sensitive data in an encrypted form on a separate server. It is implemented as a Firefox extension for FB. `FaceCloak`'s user privacy attempt resembles our work. However, its main purpose is to hide specific data such as age, name, etc. and not user interests derived from interaction with the SN. Moreover, as of August 2011, the current version of the FaceCloak Firefox extension does not work with FB anymore due to changes made by FB [18].

Scramble [3] allows users to enforce access control over their data. It is an SN-independent Firefox extension allowing users to define access control lists (ACL) of authorised users for each piece of data, based on their preferences. In addition to that, it also allows users to encrypt their posted content in the SN, therefore guaranteeing confidentiality of user data against the SN. The tool allows users to hide information through cryptography. This may require prior knowledge, which is usually counter intuitive for ordinary users. Also, it's implementation cannot be found anywhere and is likely outdated.

Other privacy approaches focus on different platforms: Google, Youtube, Amazon etc. While they do not necessarily provide solutions for achieving privacy on FB, their approaches served as an inspiration for our work.

TrackThis [7] by Mozilla proposes an approach of polluting a users browsing history by opening 100 tabs at once. This leaves cookies that are unrelated to the users interests and confuse third party trackers. Similarly, the authors of [19] and [14] show a way to attack personalization algorithms by polluting a users browser history with noise by generating false clicks through cross-site request forgery (XSRF). In [11], the authors present an attack for draining ad budgets. By repeatedly pulling ads using crafted browsing profiles, they managed to reduce the chance of showing their ads to real visitors and trash the ad budget. While having similar approaches to ours, these tools provide limited privacy in the long run as they have to be relaunched after a period of time.

In [17], the authors test protesting against data labouring [2]: they utilize user interactions with different services as input for training user profiling algorithms. They simulate data strikes against recommendation systems. Their results imply that data strikes can put a certain pressure on technology companies and that users have more control over their relationship with said companies. Our work can also be viewed as a protest against the data labouring of users on an SN: if enough users had access to noise attributes, the recommendation systems of FB would most likely be disrupted even for new users not using our tool.

Howe and Nissenbaum proposed AdNauseam [6] – a browser extension designed to obfuscate browsing data and protect user-tracking by advertising networks. It clicks on every displayed ad in different web pages, thereby diminishing the value of all ad clicks – obfuscating the real with fake clicks. Another tool called Harpo [20] uses reinforcement learning to adaptively interleave real page visits with fake pages to distort a tracker's view of a user's browsing profile. Harpo is also able to achieve better stealthiness to adversarial detection as compared to AdNauseam. Our tool is designed and based on similar obfuscation ideas, however we focus on a specific SN platform and not only on advertisements.

## 3    System Model

We now proceed with introducing the system model we consider by describing the main entities participating in the design of MetaPriv, as well as their capacities.

**Social Network (SN):** Defined as a graph $\mathcal{G} = (\mathcal{U}, \mathcal{R})$ where the vertices are comprised of users from a set $\mathcal{U}$, with the edges being the relationship between said users, described by the set $\mathcal{R} \subseteq \{\{u, v\} \mid u, v \in \mathcal{U} \text{ and } u \neq v\}$.

**Users:** Let $\mathcal{U} := \{u_1, \ldots, u_n\}$ be the set of all users registered in an online SN such as FB. Each user has a unique identifier $i \in [1, n]$. In addition to that, each user is associated with a number of attributes. The set of all attributes associated with a user $u_i$ is denoted as $\mathcal{A}_i \subseteq \mathcal{A}$.

**Attributes:** The set of all available attributes in an SN is denoted by $\mathcal{A} := \{a_1, \ldots, a_m\}$ and is called the attribute space. An attribute is a specific trait that a user $u_i$ possesses, e.g. "$u_i$ likes cats".

**BOT:** An entity that adds noise to a user profile $(u_i)$. It works by mimicking the user's interaction with the SN and generates noise attributes on their behalf.

**User Real and Noise Attributes:** Assume a user $u_i$ with a list of attributes $\mathcal{A}_i$. Elements of $\mathcal{A}_i$ may have been generated legitimately (i.e. through the user's real activity) or by the BOT. The set of all attributes generated by the user's legitimate activity is denoted as $\mathcal{A}_i^r \subseteq \mathcal{A}_i$ while the set of all attributes associated with $u_i$ but generated by the BOT is denoted by $\mathcal{A}_i^n \subseteq \mathcal{A}_i$.

### 3.1   High-Level Overview

The core idea behind `MetaPriv` is to fuddle FB's opinion about a user $u_i$ by obfuscating $u_i$'s real attributes $\mathcal{A}_i^r$ with the help of noise attributes $\mathcal{A}_i^n$. To that end, we use the BOT and have it interact with the SN on behalf of $u_i$. Ideally, to achieve privacy, the amount of traffic generated by the BOT should be the same or more than the traffic generated by $u_i$.

When user $u_i$ creates an account on FB, they have no attributes (i.e. the set $\mathcal{A}_i$ is empty). Following registration, $u_i$ begins generating activity (e.g. adding friends, liking pages and posts). By collecting and analyzing user activities, FB creates a list of attributes that represents each user's perceived interests (e.g., $a_1$ – "$u_i$ likes cooking"). For the purposes of this work, we consider these attributes as real and are added to the set $\mathcal{A}_i^r$ – a subset of $\mathcal{A}_i$, i.e. $\mathcal{A}_i^r \subseteq \mathcal{A}_i$. The set $\mathcal{A}_i$ is then used by FB to decide which posts and advertisements are presented in the respective $u_i$ feed. In this scenario, all $u_i$'s interests are known to the SN, which can make accurate predictions about their preferences and therefore populate their account with accurate personalized content. In this work, we are examining ways of protecting user privacy from a potentially malicious or at least curious SN. To achieve this, we have created `MetaPriv`. With our tool, users can confuse an SN about their real interests. `MetaPriv` revolves around a simple idea: Since the SN personalizes users by analyzing their activities on the platform, our tool generates noise traffic on behalf of a user. This will result in adding attributes to the set $\mathcal{A}_i^n$ containing the noise attributes described earlier. With this in mind, we built a BOT as part of the core of `MetaPriv` whose functionality is described below. At this point, it is worth noting that the interactions generated by `MetaPriv` consists of primarily liking posts and pages.

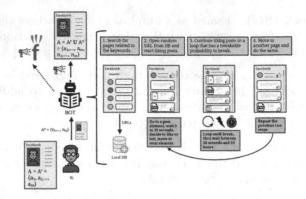

**Fig. 1.** High-level overview of the BOT's functionality.

1. As a primary requirement, the BOT needs access to $u_i$'s account. This can be done in one of two ways: Either with $u_i$ providing their credentials or through their browser profile folder i.e. the hidden folder in an operating system's user folder, where all web browser cookies, etc. are stored.
2. Once the BOT has gained access to the user account, it requires a set of keywords generated by a different part of MetaPriv, which would serve as noise attributes. The keyword generator, however, requires a seed keyword that the user must input at least once.
3. The user then inputs their desired level of privacy. This privacy level simply refers to the level of convenience and benefits that a user is willing to accommodate to better protect their privacy. In practice, it represents the amount of noise that is persistently added to an account.
4. Finally, the BOT repetitively executes a series of steps represented in Fig. 1.

### 3.2 Extending MetaPriv

After extensive experiments, we observed limited success with the initial version of MetaPriv, which we attributed to its limited interactions (i.e., simply liking posts and pages). These results are discussed in Sect. 5. As such, it became necessary to add extra features to MetaPriv. To limit the amount of noise generated, before the BOT switches to another page, it waits for a random amount of time. In the basic implementation, MetaPriv did not run any tasks during this wait period. However, in this extended version, MetaPriv watches keyword related videos and clicks Facebook ads displayed in user's main feed instead of simply waiting. Our observations showed that video watching did not seem to raise any suspicions from FB, i.e. the browser session did not get logged out or blocked, hence the BOT clicks on every ad from the first 100 posts in the main feed, searches the keyword in FB's video page and watches all the videos returned. This, we believe, helps to further reinforce the noise and give it more variety. Figure 2 provides an overview of the extended functionalities of MetaPriv.

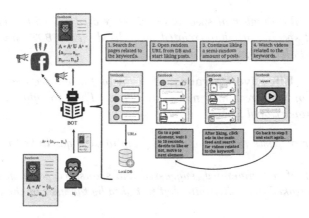

**Fig. 2.** Extended BOT functionality.

# 4   Measuring User Privacy on Facebook

Previous works focus on measuring privacy according to the visibility and sensitivity of user attributes [1, 5, 13]. This approach, however, is inapplicable, as the aim is to confuse the data collector, thus leading to inaccurate user profile predictions. Visibility of a user's attributes would always be maximum, since the SN stores all user interactions with it. Additionally, in this work the concept of sensitivity cannot apply, since all user attributes are known to the SN (i.e can be considered public). With this in mind, we propose a new definition for privacy on an SN based on a user's *real* and *noisy* interactions with the SN. Real interactions are daily, *legitimate* user interactions with the SN. Noisy interactions are BOT-produced and mainly generate fake activity on a user's profile.

Our first approach on quantifying privacy was characterized by rather elementary and naive thinking: Initially, we defined the notion of *Theoretical Privacy*. The intuition behind Theoretical Privacy was that a user's level of privacy is proportional to the number of noise in their profile. However, the results of our first experiments did not support this. Apparently, the time that a user likes a post, a page, etc. seems to be significant for FB's personalization algorithms. More precisely, it seems that FB weighs a user's recent rather than older content. In view of the above, we refined our idea on quantifying privacy and defined *Effective Privacy* – an alternative that better fits FB's models.

**Definition 1 (Theoretical Privacy).** *Theoretical privacy is measured by taking into account the amount of posts liked by a user $u_i$ and the BOT. User $u_i$'s theoretical privacy with $j + k$ attributes is defined as:*

$$P_i^{th} = \frac{\sum_{j \in \mathcal{A}_i^r} RA_j^{th} - \sum_{k \in \mathcal{A}_i^n} NA_k^{th}}{T}, \tag{1}$$

*where $RA_{th}$ is the number of specific attribute-related posts liked by $u_i$, $NA_{th}$ is the number of specific attribute-related posts liked by the BOT and $T$ is the total number of posts liked by $u_i$'s account.*

**Definition 2 (Effective Privacy).** *For this definition we consider the effective strength of user real and noise attributes. The strength of a user's real attribute is proportional to:*

- *the number of posts in the main feed from liked pages linked to an attribute. Variable: $r_p$*
- *the number of recommended, suggested and sponsored posts in the main feed from pages linked to an attribute, but not liked by the user or the BOT. Variable: $r_{sp}$*
- *the number of video posts from the main video feed (https://www.facebook.com/watch) linked to an attribute. Variable: $r_{vp}$*
- *the number of video posts from the latest video feed (https://www.facebook.com/watch/latest) linked to an attribute. Variable: $r_{lvp}$*

*The effective strength of a real attribute is defined as:*

$$RA_{eff} = \frac{1}{n}\left(a\frac{r_p}{t_p} + b\frac{r_{sp}}{t_{sp}} + c\frac{r_{vp}}{t_{vp}} + d\frac{r_{lvp}}{t_{lvp}}\right), \tag{2}$$

*where $a, b, c, d \in \{0, 1\}$, $n = a+b+c+d$, $t_p$ is the total number of posts shown in the main feed, $t_{sp}$ is the total number of suggested posts shown in the main feed, $t_{vp}$ is the total number of video posts related to $u_i$'s attributes from the main video feed and $t_{lvp}$ is the total number of video posts from the latest video feed. Each of the variables $a, b, c, d$ is given the value 0, when their respective fraction is 0. Otherwise they are given the value 1. This is done so that, if one effective strength variable has a value of 0 (i.e. no posts), then it will not be taken into account for the final effective privacy value.*

*A similar definition stands for the effective strength of noise attributes $NA_{eff}$. variables $r_p, r_{sp}, r_{vp}$ and $r_{lvp}$ are replaced with corresponding noise attributes i.e. $n_p, n_{sp}, n_{vp}$ and $n_{lvp}$. The strength of a noise attribute is defined as:*

$$NA_{eff} = \frac{1}{n}\left(a\frac{n_p}{t_p} + b\frac{n_{sp}}{t_{sp}} + c\frac{n_{vp}}{t_{vp}} + d\frac{n_{lvp}}{t_{lvp}}\right) \tag{3}$$

*Finally, for a user $u_i$ with $j+k$ attributes, we combine the two variables and reach the effective privacy:*

$$P_i^{eff} = \sum_{j\in\mathcal{A}_i^r} RA_j^{eff} - \sum_{k\in\mathcal{A}_i^n} NA_k^{eff} \tag{4}$$

In both cases, the resulting value will be $P \in [-1, 1]$. The closer it is to 0, the more indistinguishable will the noise attributes be from real attributes. Therefore, the account of an arbitrary user $u_i$ is private *iff* $P \approx 0$ or $P \leq 0$.

# 5   Implementation and Results

To demonstrate MetaPriv's functionality and practicality, we evaluated both the basic and the extended versions. For the basic version, we created a dummy FB account and ran a 10-week experiment to build the account's real and noise attributes. While for the extended version, we tested MetaPriv on two real FB accounts that have existed and are active for over a decade. To evaluate the dummy account, we used MetaPriv to simulate both user and BOT interactions[1] with FB. Our test program was implemented using Python 3.10 and Selenium WebDriver – a framework for testing web applications that allowed us to simulate an automated user interaction with FB.

*Open Science and Reproducible Research:* Our source code[2] has been anonymized and made publicly available online to support open science and reproducible research.

## 5.1   Dummy Account Results

For the dummy FB account, we created a 22-year-old female user from Ireland (the account and all interactions were made through an Azure server with an Irish IP address). At the end of each week, we ran an extensive analysis of FB's main, video and latest video feed by opening the respective URLs, going through a certain amount of posts in them and saving the information about said posts in an SQL database.

**Weeks 1 & 2:** The first two weeks primarily consisted of building the user profile with a single attribute. To be more specific, we used the attribute "cat", so FB would associate our user with cats. We then provided the keyword "cat pictures" as input to MetaPriv. The program liked 1,056 posts from 51 keyword-related pages over these two weeks. This keyword served as the user's *real attribute*. After one week, 'Recommended' posts appeared in the main feed. Out of 264 posts, 32 were recommended and 11 seemed relevant to the user's profile:

> 1 post related to demographics -a house in Dublin; 1 post about cats from a page about cats; 2 posts about tigers (both from FB group: WildCat Ridge Sanctuary); 1 post about demographics and cats (page name: North Dublin Cat Rescue Ireland); 1 post about ostriches, 1 about bulls, 2 about dogs, 1 about rare animals (related to animals); 1 post about "Dads Acting Like Their Teenage Daughters" (possibly gender-related).

Other recommended posts were unrelated to "cats" and had a dozen million views (we assume these were most likely trending posts). Almost all the recommended posts were videos[3]. After these two weeks, we analyzed 449 posts

---

[1] We make a clear distinction between MetaPriv and the BOT. BOT interactions will be used to refer to the noise traffic generated by MetaPriv.

[2] https://github.com/ctrgrb/MetaPriv.

[3] This could be because users show a higher rate of engagement to online videos compared to text (e.g. articles, blog posts, etc.).

from the main feed and got 13 recommended posts along with 23 "join group" recommendations from cat-related FB groups. 8 of the recommended posts were linked to the user's profile:

> 1 post related to demographics: Football game GERMANY vs IRELAND (2002); 1 post about cats from FB group: CAT LOVERS PHILIPPINES; 4 posts about animals from a group about animal comics; 1 post about cats from the 'Daily Mail' page; 1 post from a group about Dinosaurs. The name of the person posting was: Margaret Happycat.

This time, most recommendations appeared from groups, though the user was not a member of any.

**Week 3:** For the third week, we added a second keyword as a noise attribute to the profile. At this point, the noise was manifested through liking a noise-related page and its posts at every 10th page switch. In essence, 10% of the interactions with FB were now related to a single noise attribute. This 10% represented 72 out of 554 posts liked in week 3 from 5 pages linked to the chosen noise keyword "guns"[4]. We observed that there were no recommended posts after this period. An analysis of 547 posts from the main feed showed that 19 were linked to the noise attribute. The latest video feed contained only 21 videos from liked pages related to the real attribute (i.e. cats). In the main video feed, we analyzed 184 video posts. 70 of them included words such as: ['cat','Cat','kitten','Kitten'] in their description or page URL and were, thus, related to the real attribute, while nothing was related to the noise attribute.

**Week 4:** For this period, we increased the noise amount from 10% to 20%. Out of 530 liked posts, 112 came from 8 pages related to the noise attribute. In the main feed, out of 337 posts, 38 were from pages related to the noise attribute. FB stopped showing recommended posts at this point, however, 'Suggested for you' posts began to show. Out of the 337 posts, 8 were labeled as 'Suggested' out of which 1 was related to animals, 3 specifically to cats and the remaining were possibly gender-related. This time too, the latest video feed showed only cat-related videos and in the main video feed, out of 152 videos, 35 included the words: ['cat','Cat','kitten','Kitten'] in the description or page URL, while no videos were related to guns.

**Week 5:** We decided to add another noise attribute, thus dividing FB interaction as follows: 70% cats, 20% guns and 10% cooking. From a total of 485 liked posts, 130 were related to the keyword "guns" and 36 to "cooking recipes". This time, out of 673 posts in the main feed, 67 were related to guns and 147 to cooking. Our theory for increased cooking content is that a cat lover is more likely to also like cooking rather than guns[5]. This time, out of 16 suggested posts, 14 were cats. In the latest video feed, out of 51 videos, 21 were cats, 1

---

[4] It is worth noting that the percentage value is an approximation since `MetaPriv` is designed with randomness in mind to avoid patterns in its behaviour.

[5] This might also be related to the fact that Ireland has one of Europe's least permissive firearm legislation – hence gun-related content is heavily regulated.

guns and 26 cooking. Finally, in the main video feed, out of 136 posts, 27 were cats, 3 guns and 7 cooking.

**Week 6:** We increased the amount of noise for the cooking attribute to 20% and the gun attribute to 30%, thus dividing FB interaction as follows: 50% cats, 30% guns and 20% cooking. From a total of 647 liked posts, 213 were guns and 125 cooking. In the main feed, out of 405 posts, 35 were guns and 66 cooking. There were also 7 suggested posts, out of which 4 were cooking and 2 cats. In the latest video feed, out of 65 posts, 12 were cats, 2 guns and 51 cooking. Finally, in the main video feed's 103 posts, 27 were cats and 15 cooking.

**Week 7:** We added another noise attribute that would be stronger than others. Hence, FB interaction became: 23% cats, 23% guns, 23% cooking and 30% chess. From a total of 365 liked posts, 90 were cats, 89 guns, 76 cooking and 110 chess. The main feed's 286 posts were divided as follows: 45 guns, 72 cooking and 2 chess. From 14 suggested posts, 10 were cooking and 1 chess. In the latest video feed, out of 162 posts, 18 were cats, 35 guns, 83 cooking and 22 chess. The 137 posts in the video feed were divided as follows: 25 cats, 1 guns, 9 cooking and 1 chess.

**Week 8:** The aim was to examine results, when new attributes were added without reinforcing old ones. For the first half of the week FB interaction was 100% fishing-related and the second half 20% fishing and 80% bodybuilding.

- First half: Liked 235 posts about fishing. In the main feed, out of 402 posts, 207 were cats, 45 guns, 115 cooking, 4 chess and 15 fishing. Out of 7 suggested posts, 4 had to do with fishing and the others were unrelated to the user's attributes. In the latest video feed, from 190 videos, 14 were cats, 48 guns, 72 cooking, 39 chess and 18 fishing. In the main video feed, out of 148 videos, 12 were cats, 2 guns, 10 cooking, 3 chess and 1 fishing.
- Second half: Liked 48 fishing posts and 181 bodybuilding posts. In the main feed, out of 423 posts, 229 were cats, 33 guns, 127 cooking, 22 fishing and 7 bodybuilding. Out of 2 suggested posts, 1 was bodybuilding and the other unrelated. In the latest video feed, out of 156 videos, 16 were cats, 9 guns, 30 cooking, 34 fishing and 72 bodybuilding. In the main video feed, out of 128 videos, 1 was cats, 2 guns, 20 cooking, 1 chess and 1 fishing.

**Week 9:** We ran `MetaPriv` with 10% cat-related traffic and the remaining with the following noise attribute layout: 20% guns, 20% cooking, 20% chess, 20% fishing, 10% bodybuilding. From 626 liked posts, 51 were about cats, 122 guns, 130 cooking, 144 chess, 149 fishing and 29 bodybuilding. In the main feed, out of 460 posts, 199 were about cats, 51 guns, 145 cooking, 19 chess, 25 fishing and 7 bodybuilding. This time there were no suggested posts. In the latest video feed, from 154 videos, 18 had to do with cats, 14 guns, 77 cooking, 35 chess and 18 fishing. In the main video feed, from 137 videos, 25 were about cats, 1 guns, 9 cooking and 1 chess.

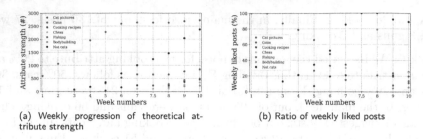

(a) Weekly progression of theoretical attribute strength

(b) Ratio of weekly liked posts

**Fig. 3.** The total amount of posts liked and the ratio of posts liked per week.

**Week 10:** In the last week we ran `MetaPriv` with the same parameters as in week 9: 10% cats, 20% guns, 20% cooking, 20% chess, 20% fishing and 10% bodybuilding. From 381 liked posts, 42 were cats, 75 guns, 96 cooking, 94 chess, 52 fishing and 22 bodybuilding. In the main feed, out of 442 posts, 160 were cats, 71 guns, 139 cooking, 30 chess, 32 fishing and 4 bodybuilding. Again, there were no suggested posts. In the latest video feed, from 133 videos, 10 were cats, 15 guns, 75 cooking, 22 chess and 12 fishing. Finally, in the main video feed, from 124 videos, 6 were cooking, 1 chess and 2 bodybuilding.

The total amount of posts liked on a weekly basis for each attribute (attribute strength), is shown in Fig. 3a. The week number is noted on the horizontal axis and the attribute strength (total amount of posts liked) on the vertical axis. As the figure indicates, even on week 10, the 'cat' attribute strength outweighs all others combined, since the attribute remained reinforced even when said reinforcement decreased over time. Figure 3b represents the ratio of posts. Here, the ratio is calculated using the posts liked on a specific week, omitting those of previous weeks. This time, the attribute strength on the vertical axis stands for the percentage of liked posts for each attribute.

Next, we present the results of each variable for the effective attribute strength. The main feed, recommended posts, latest video feed and main video feed are represented in Fig. 4.

We can, now, compare results between Fig. 4 and Fig. 3b: on weeks 5 to 8, noise-effective attribute strength variables approached real variables. Figure 3b shows that around week 6, there are more noise-related likes than real likes. Consequently, FB's recommendations show more noise-related content as we can see from Fig. 4. In the first 4 weeks, Fig. 4c and Fig. 4d show no relation to noise attributes. We thus conclude that 20% noise is not enough to change said variables. Also, Fig. 4b shows that in a few weeks' time, there were no recommended/suggested posts in the main feed (weeks 3, 9 and 10).

To avoid confusion in Fig. 4 we must clarify that in the main video feed Fig. 4d and the recommended, suggested and sponsored posts Fig. 4b, the FB content is derived from pages not liked by the user. The content is both user attribute-related and unrelated. It is assumed that the unrelated content is presented by FB because of other features in their recommendation systems e.g. users who liked X also liked Y. Their recommendation algorithms are not open source,

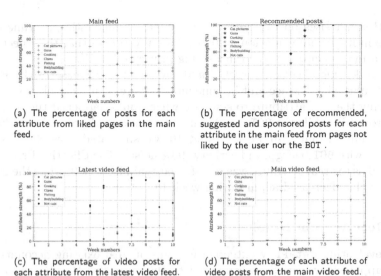

(a) The percentage of posts for each attribute from liked pages in the main feed.

(b) The percentage of recommended, suggested and sponsored posts for each attribute in the main feed from pages not liked by the user nor the BOT .

(c) The percentage of video posts for each attribute from the latest video feed.

(d) The percentage of each attribute of video posts from the main video feed.

**Fig. 4.** Effective attribute strength variables with combined noise

hence their mode of operation is concealed. Due to this, our results are based on content exclusively related to user attributes.

## 5.2 Privacy Results

Based on the definitions described in Sect. 4, we calculated each week's Theoretical (Fig. 5a) and Effective Privacy (Fig. 5b) values. During the first two weeks, we built the user's real attributes and added increasing noise to render FB's noise feed equal to the real.

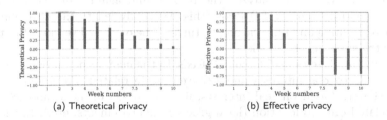

(a) Theoretical privacy

(b) Effective privacy

**Fig. 5.** Theoretical and effective privacy results

Notably, the Effective Privacy in week 6 (50% noise) is close to 0. Once the amount of real traffic generated by users equals the amount of noise traffic, users achieve privacy. The theoretical real attribute strength outweighs the combined noise attribute strengths even after 10 weeks, as shown in Fig. 3a. This explains the difference between the Theoretical and Effective Privacy values and shows that FB emphasises on the user's recent interests, suggesting a "time of like" variable in its recommendation systems. This also proves that the Effective Privacy is a more accurate way of measuring privacy on a SN.

We added more noise in week 7 and saw a small decrease in the Effective Privacy value – i.e. the account became more private. During week 8, we stopped reinforcing the real attribute to simulate what would happen if the user took a break from FB, while the BOT ran. We noted significant decrease in the Effective Privacy value. Finally, in weeks 9 and 10, we simulated a rarely active user combined with BOT background activity (90% noise). The Effective Privacy value increased as the real attribute was re-enforced again in week 9, while the Effective Privacy value decreased again during week 10.

## 5.3   Real Account Results

When evaluating MetaPriv extended features on real existing accounts, a different approach was used as compared to that used for the dummy account. The theoretical privacy takes into account all the likes that a user did during their entire history with FB, which is unfeasible to obtain and categorise into keywords. To this end, when analyzing the results, we considered the feed from pages related to the noise keywords as our noise attribute. For the real data, we simply considered the feeds unrelated to our chosen noise keyword. To this end, we ran our experiments for 4 weeks on two existing accounts (account A and account B). Account A was set to like an average of 27 posts per day, while account B was set to like 54 posts per day.

*Account A:* During the 4 week period, the BOT liked 754 posts from 79 pages and watched 1122 videos. The chosen seed keyword was 'opera' after which the BOT generated other related noise keywords. These keywords, along with their respective amount of posts, pages and videos can be seen in Fig. 6. During the first week of our evaluations, the BOT used the first two keywords: 'opera' and 'composition'. We then analyzed the results, and again observed a complete absence of noise from the FB feeds (this eventually led to the development of the video watching and link clicking features). The extended version of MetaPriv run for the subsequent 3 weeks.

We then analyzed the different FB feeds. In the main feed, out of 596 posts, 86 were related to real interests and 127 were noise related. From 136 suggested posts, 11 were based on real interests, 67 were based on noise and 58 seemed to be related only to location (local grocery advertisements, etc.). In the latest video feed, from 132 videos, 123 were related to real interests and 9 to noise. Finally, in the main video feed, out of 300 videos, 27 were real interest related, 15 were noise related and the rest seemed unrelated to noise or real interests. These results are represented graphically in Fig. 7. Figure 7a shows the exact number of real and noise data (the unrelated bar is out of bounds as it it not used in the calculations) and Fig. 7b shows the percentage of real and noise data.

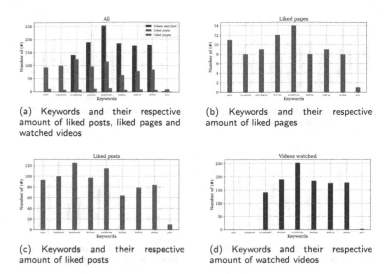

(a) Keywords and their respective amount of liked posts, liked pages and watched videos

(b) Keywords and their respective amount of liked pages

(c) Keywords and their respective amount of liked posts

(d) Keywords and their respective amount of watched videos

**Fig. 6.** Keyword statistics of account A.

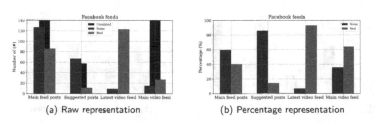

(a) Raw representation

(b) Percentage representation

**Fig. 7.** Graphical representation of the collected data from account A.

*Account B:* For this account, the BOT liked 1518 posts from 129 pages and watched 2871 videos. The chosen seed keyword was 'toyota' and the keyword statistics are shown in Fig. 8. With this account, the extended MetaPriv was used from the beginning. Once completed, we analyzed the different FB feeds. In the main feed, out of 300 posts, 79 were real interest related and 27 were noise related. From 59 suggested posts, 4 were based on real interests, 4 were based on noise and 51 seemed to be related only to location (local grocery advertisements, data carriers, etc.). In the latest video feed, from 300 videos, 100 were related to real interests and 200 were related to noise. Finally, in the main video feed, out of 300 videos 30 were real interest related, 14 were noise related and the rest seemed unrelated to noise or real interests. The results are also represented graphically in Fig. 9.

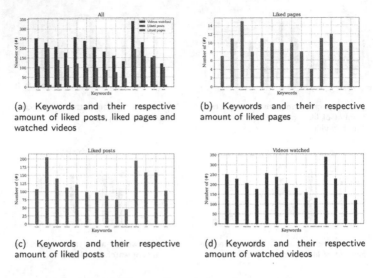

(a) Keywords and their respective amount of liked posts, liked pages and watched videos

(b) Keywords and their respective amount of liked pages

(c) Keywords and their respective amount of liked posts

(d) Keywords and their respective amount of watched videos

**Fig. 8.** Keyword statistics of account B.

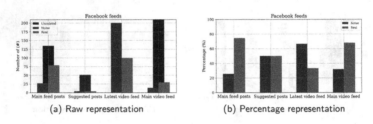

(a) Raw representation

(b) Percentage representation

**Fig. 9.** Graphical representation of the collected data from account B.

It should be noted that analyzing the feed of a real account can be a tedious process as every post has to be manually inspected. Implementing a script to automate this task would be very challenging as there is no way it could distinguish between posts from pages and posts from friends and groups. Additionally, for the FB feed that came as suggested (suggested posts and main video feed), it was harder to understand what was related to the real or noise data. With the old accounts there are significantly more variables to consider such as friends, devices, locations etc. as opposed to a new account that exists in a controlled environment. Hence, the results should be treated as an approximation.

**Observations:** We compared the percentage representation of the FB feeds from the 2 accounts: Fig. 7b and Fig. 9b.

1. Account A has significantly more noise in its main feed as compared to account B, with most of these from suggested posts. We believe account A had more keywords that were of interest to FB. When account A searched for keywords like development, building and growth, FB showed pages that generally were more popular and posted a lot on their pages. In essence,

we believe that these specific interests likely bring FB more profit as they advertise exact products that a user can easily buy.

2. Account B has significantly more noise related feed in its latest video feed. This, we believe is because account B had the keywords cooking, chef and kitchen which produced a lot of video feed about cooking recipes.

From these two observations, we can conclude that adding noise efficiently depends more on the keywords themselves than on the amount of likes and video watches. Nonetheless, with the acquired data, we proceeded to calculate the effective privacy. Posts from friends were ignored since those usually did not reflect any particular attribute of the user. By taking these results into account, the effective privacy yields a result of 0.06 for account A and 0.13 for account B. Both accounts seem to have achieved a larger degree of privacy, with account A basically having its noise attributes almost indistinguishable from its real attributes. This, according to Sect. 4, means that account A has achieved privacy. Account B however, likely needs more time to run the tool.

**Limitations:** After running experiments with `MetaPriv`, we observed the following limitations in its usability. Firstly, the user's FB feeds become less appealing as they become more and more infested with noise related posts. The current solution for this would be to tone down the amount of noise the tool generates. As a future work, a noise filtering tool can be implemented as a browser extension to filter out the noise feed while using FB in the browser.

Another limitation is the variety of noise data that a tool can generate automatically. In our implementation, we used liking posts, pages and watching videos as ways to generate noise. These were chosen as they represent direct interest of the topic at hand. Nevertheless, they are only a fraction of things that a normal user can do on FB. Other interactions such as user posting, commenting, reacting to posts and playing games are likely also used by FB for better user profiling. These interactions however are very hard to simulate adequately and can lead to unwanted issues such as generating posts that are unintelligible, inappropriate or even extremist, which, in the end, can lead to account blocking.

It is also worth mentioning that some users may be hesitant to use `MetaPriv` out of fear of liking something inappropriate. This is one of the reasons that the noise generated by the tool is not completely random. Mainly, the user chooses a seed keyword that will define the first noise attribute and start generating traffic based on it. The next noise attribute will be generated based on the initial seed – a word that is related to the seed word. We admit that this might not be a perfect solution and solutions can be further developed in future works. Another concern is generating traffic related to illegal, extremist or abuse topics. This traffic however is constantly removed from the platform.

# 6    Conclusion and Societal Impact

Social networks shaped the digital world becoming an indispensable part of our daily lives. Over the years, these platforms have gained a reputation for tracking user online activity. These strategies may prove threatening for multiple spheres of peoples' lives – spanning from consumption to opinion formation – and may have ominous effects on democracy [9,10]. This vast collection of personal data by SNs is often exposed (i.e. sold) to third-party companies.

In addition, SN users do not usually have a say on the information they access, as SNs prioritize the content presented on feeds, based on what users most probably want to see. In other words, SN algorithms seemingly hide content and have a great impact on the information users are able to reach. With privacy and societal concerns over SNs rapidly rising, these platforms are seen as rather controversial.

Having identified these issues, we built `MetaPriv`, a tool that adds new privacy safeguards for SN users aimed at hampering SN ability to serve targeted content. `MetaPriv` allows users to define their desired level of privacy. In this way `MetaPriv` strikes a balance between privacy and functionality. We believe this feature will be used in several services in the near future and will help towards building less biased SNs, while minimizing the amount of personal information processed by platforms.

# References

1. Aghasian, E., Garg, S., Montgomery, J.: User's privacy in recommendation systems applying online social network data, a survey and taxonomy (2018)
2. Arrieta-Ibarra, I., Goff, L., Jiménez-Hernández, D., Lanier, J., Weyl, E.G.: Should we treat data as labor? Moving beyond "free". In: AEA Papers and Proceedings (2018)
3. Beato, F., Kohlweiss, M., Wouters, K.: Scramble! your social network data. In: Fischer-Hübner, S., Hopper, N. (eds.) PETS 2011. LNCS, vol. 6794, pp. 211–225. Springer, Heidelberg (2011). https://doi.org/10.1007/978-3-642-22263-4_12
4. Constine, J.: Facebook pays teens to install VPN that spies on them (2019). https://techcrunch.com/2019/01/29/facebook-project-atlas/. Accessed 10 July 2022
5. Domingo-Ferrer, J.: Rational privacy disclosure in social networks. In: Torra, V., Narukawa, Y., Daumas, M. (eds.) MDAI 2010. LNCS (LNAI), vol. 6408, pp. 255–265. Springer, Heidelberg (2010). https://doi.org/10.1007/978-3-642-16292-3_25
6. Howe, D.C., Nissenbaum, H.: Engineering privacy and protest: a case study of adnauseam. In: CEUR Workshop Proceedings, vol. 1873, pp. 57–64 (2017)
7. Hull, L.: Hey advertisers, track THIS (2019). https://blog.mozilla.org/products/firefox/hey-advertisers-track-this/. Accessed 7 July 2022
8. Kelly, H.: Facebook bug set 14 million users' sharing settings to public (2018). https://money.cnn.com/2018/06/07/technology/facebook-public-post-error/index.html. Accessed 10 July 2022
9. Khan, T., Michalas, A.: Trust and believe - should we? Evaluating the trustworthiness of twitter users. In: 2020 IEEE 19th International Conference on Trust, Security and Privacy in Computing and Communications (TrustCom), pp. 1791–1800 (2020). https://doi.org/10.1109/TrustCom50675.2020.00246
10. Khan, T., Michalas, A., Akhunzada, A.: Fake news outbreak 2021: can we stop the viral spread? J. Netw. Comp. Appl. **190**, 103112 (2021)

11. Kim, I.L., et al.: Adbudgetkiller: online advertising budget draining attack. In: Proceedings of the 2018 World Wide Web Conference, pp. 297–307 (2018)
12. Luo, W., Xie, Q., Hengartner, U.: Facecloak: an architecture for user privacy on social networking sites. In: In Proceedings of 2009 IEEE International Conference on Privacy, Security, Risk and Trust (PASSAT-09), p. 1 (2009)
13. Maximilien, E.M., Grandison, T., Liu, K., Sun, T., Richardson, D., Guo, S.: Enabling privacy as a fundamental construct for social networks. In: 2009 International Conference on Computational Science and Engineering, vol. 4. IEEE (2009)
14. Meng, W., Xing, X., Sheth, A., Weinsberg, U., Lee, W.: Your online interests: Pwned! a pollution attack against targeted advertising. In: Proceedings of the 2014 ACM SIGSAC Conference on Computer and Communications Security. CCS 2014, pp. 129–140. Association for Computing Machinery, New York (2014). https://doi.org/10.1145/2660267.2687258
15. Meta: Suspending Cambridge Analytica and SCL Group From Facebook (2018). https://about.fb.com/news/2018/03/suspending-cambridge-analytica/. Accessed 10 July 2022
16. Meta: The Facebook pixel - measure, optimise and build audiences for your advertising campaigns (2022). https://www.facebook.com/business/learn/facebook-ads-pixel. Accessed 7 July 2022
17. Vincent, N., Hecht, B., Sen, S.: "data strikes": Evaluating the effectiveness of a new form of collective action against technology companies. In: The World Wide Web Conference. WWW 2019, pp. 1931–1943. ACM, New York (2019)
18. Wanying Luo, Q.X., Hengartner, U.: FaceCloak implementation download (2009 2010). https://crysp.uwaterloo.ca/software/facecloak/download.html. Accessed 7 July 2022
19. Xing, X., Meng, W., Doozan, D., Snoeren, A.C., Feamster, N., Lee, W.: Take this personally. pollution attacks on personalized services. In: 22nd USENIX Security Symposium (USENIX Security 13), pp. 671–686. USENIX Association, Washington, D.C. (2013). https://www.usenix.org/conference/usenixsecurity13/technical-sessions/paper/xing
20. Zhang, J., Psounis, K., Haroon, M., Shafiq, Z.: Harpo: Learning to subvert online behavioral advertising. arXiv preprint arXiv:2111.05792 (2021)

# Adversary for Social Good: Leveraging Attribute-Obfuscating Attack to Protect User Privacy on Social Networks

Xiaoting Li[1]($\boxtimes$), Lingwei Chen[2], and Dinghao Wu[3]

[1] Visa Research, Palo Alto, CA, USA
xiaotili@visa.com
[2] Wright State University, Dayton, OH, USA
lingwei.chen@wright.edu
[3] Pennsylvania State University, University Park, PA, USA
dwu@psu.edu

**Abstract.** As social networks become indispensable for people's daily lives, inference attacks pose significant threat to users' privacy where attackers can infiltrate users' information and infer their private attributes. In particular, social networks are represented as graph-structured data, maintaining rich user activities and complex relationships among them. This enables attackers to deploy state-of-the-art graph neural networks (GNNs) to automate attribute inference attacks for users' privacy disclosure. To address this challenge, in this paper, we leverage the vulnerability of GNNs to adversarial attacks, and propose a new graph adversarial method, called Attribute-Obfuscating Attack (AttrOBF) to mislead GNNs into misclassification and thus protect user attribute privacy against GNN-based inference attacks on social networks. Different from the prior attacks using perturbations on graph structure or node features, AttrOBF provides a more practical formulation by obfuscating optimal training user attribute values, and also advances the attribute obfuscation by solving the unavailability issue of test attribute annotations, black-box setting, bi-level optimization, and non-differentiable obfuscating operation. We demonstrate the effectiveness of AttrOBF on user attribute obfuscation by extensive experiments over three real-world social network datasets. We believe our work yields great potential of applying adversarial attacks to attribute protection on social networks.

**Keywords:** Attribute privacy · Inference attack · Social networks · Graph adversarial attack · Attribute obfuscation

## 1 Introduction

Social networks have emerged as an indispensable part of our daily lives, allowing us to conveniently share personal ideas for social engagements. Such an

---

X. Li and L. Chen—Equal contribution. Work done while at PSU.

© ICST Institute for Computer Sciences, Social Informatics and Telecommunications Engineering 2023
Published by Springer Nature Switzerland AG 2023. All Rights Reserved
F. Li et al. (Eds.): SecureComm 2022, LNICST 462, pp. 710–728, 2023.
https://doi.org/10.1007/978-3-031-25538-0_37

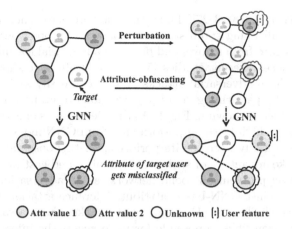

**Fig. 1.** GNN-based inference attack and graph adversarial attack leading to attribute obfuscation (attribute of target user gets misclassified) through traditional perturbation on graph structure/node feature or AttrOBF operation.

interactive environment generates a large amount of user-oriented data. Due to its accessibility and information richness, this data attracts attackers to disclose users' sensitive information and fulfill their malicious intents (e.g., unwanted advertising, user tracing) [3,35]. This puts users' privacy at risk. In fact, with the revolutionary development in machine learning, such privacy risk is not rare on social networks, and could be quickly transmitted and propagated through attribute inference attacks in an automatic fashion [9,13,16,22,26,37].

In particular, social networks are naturally represented as graph-structured data, maintaining user activities and complex relationships among them. For example, nodes in these social graphs usually encode users' profiles, posts, photos, or other statuses, while edges connect users with their friendships, kinships, or follower-followee relationships. In the meanwhile, graph neural networks (GNNs) provide powerful techniques for graph understanding and mining [1,15,19,34]. These GNNs take graph connectivity structure as filter to perform neighborhood information aggregation and extract high-level features from nodes and their neighborhoods [4], which have boosted the state-of-the-art for a variety of downstream tasks over graphs. Therefore, a surge of effective inference attacks utilize GNNs to reveal personal attributes (e.g., age, gender, location, career, and political views) that people are unwilling to disclose on social networks [7,21,32]. The idea is visualized as an example on the left-hand side of Fig. 1 illustrating that the attribute of the target user can be correctly identified by leveraging GNNs over graph structure and user features.

In this work, we demonstrate an attribute privacy threat on social networks as the scenario that an attacker trains a well-performed GNN model to infer users' private attributes from graph-structured data such as Facebook friendship networks and Twitter follower-followee networks. With this in mind, some previous attempts have paid close attention to protect these attributes against inference attacks [3,12,16,18,23,25,27], which, however, limit to unstructured image or text data [12, 18, 23, 27]. Thus, our goal here is to generalize the investigation to more challenging graph-structured data, and protect personal attribute privacy in this regard from a novel and practical adversarial learning perspective. Despite great success, recent studies [5, 8, 31, 33, 38, 39] have shown that GNNs remain vulnerable to adversarial attacks [6] that can easily fool the models into misclassification by performing small perturbations to graph structures and/or node features, which is shown in Fig. 1. As the effectiveness of attribute inference attacks depends on high learning performance from GNN model while adversarial attacks substantially decrease its performance, this observation accordingly inspires us to take advantage of such a vulnerability and cast personal attribute privacy protection problem on social networks as an adversarial attack formulation problem against GNN-based attribute inference attacks. To achieve this goal, we face two challenges: (1) as inference attackers have a variety of choices in GNN construction, it is impossible for us to access the inference models for crafting graph adversarial attacks; (2) due to multimodality of user representations and intractability of relationship manipulations, modifications on either graph structures or node features cannot guarantee the validity of adversarial social networks, which are impractical in the real-world settings.

To address these challenges, in this paper, we design a black-box adversarial attack, called attribute-obfuscating attack (AttrOBF), which aims to deteriorate GNNs into misclassification and thus protect personal attribute privacy against GNN-based attribute inferences on social network data. Given a social network, AttrOBF proceeds by modifying a small fraction of optimal training users' attribute values, while the obfuscated attribute information can propagate along the whole graph through layer-wise neighborhood aggregations, such that the overall performance of attribute inferences by a surrogate GNN model is drastically degraded. Figure 1 illustrates the goal of our work. Due to transferability in adversarial machine learning [24], the obfuscated attribute over social networks is very likely to mislead the real attackers' inference GNN models. More importantly, it is necessary for inference attackers to collect initial attribute annotations for training, while users' annotating on social networks generally relies on their self-reporting; therefore, attribute obfuscating can be conveniently and proactively realized by users and data publishers, and also easily passed to subsequent inference attacks. These advantages allow a refined paradigm to efficiently mitigate the impacts of GNN-based inference attacks on attribute disclosure and enhance personal privacy protection in practice. In summary, our major contributions of this work are listed as follows:

- A novel and practical perspective of protecting privacy on social networks that leverages adversarial attacks to mitigate GNN-based inference attacks.
- A new adversarial attack AttrOBF for attribute obfuscation. To avoid NP-hard search, AttrOBF employs gradient-based method to obfuscate optimal training attribute values in an efficient way, where the problems regarding unavailability of test attribute annotations, black-box setting, bi-level optimization, and non-differential obfuscating operation are specially addressed.
- Extensive experiments on real-world social network datasets to evaluate the effectiveness of AttrOBF on attribute obfuscation and privacy protection.

## 2 Background and Related Work

### 2.1 Graph Neural Network for Attribute Inference

Social networks may indicate users' sensitive information, and thus easily expose them to the attackers who can access the data and infer the private attributes of interest to fulfill the economic, social, or political intents [27]. Considering that social networks are represented as graph-structured data, here we assume that the attackers would take advantage of user features and relationships to train GNN models so as to achieve their attribute inference goals [7,21,32].

Without loss of generality, we denote social network data $G$ to be of the form $G = (V, E, \mathbf{X})$, where $V$ $(n = |V|)$ is the set of user nodes, $E$ is the set of edges specifying relationships among users, and $\mathbf{X} \in \mathbb{R}^{n \times d}$ is feature matrix. Nodes $V$ can be further divided into annotated node set $V_l$ $(n_l = |V_l|)$ and unannotated node set $V_u$ $(n_u = |V_u|)$, where each annotated node is associated with a ground-truth attribute value $y \in Y = \{0, 1, \cdots, k - 1\}$. For instance, for gender attribute, $Y = \{0\text{:male}, 1\text{:female}\}$. Edges $E$ can be encoded as an adjacency matrix $\mathbf{A} \in \mathbb{R}^{n \times n}$ and $\mathbf{A}_{ij} = \{0, 1\}$. That is, if $(v_i, v_j) \in E$, then $\mathbf{A}_{ij} = 1$; otherwise, $\mathbf{A}_{ij} = 0$. Given $\mathbf{A}$, $\mathbf{X}$, and $V_l$ with attribute values $\mathbf{y}_l$, a GNN model $\mathbf{Z} = f_\mathbf{W}(\mathbf{A}, \mathbf{X})$ $(\mathbf{Z} \in \mathbb{R}^{n \times k}$ and $k = |Y|)$ is well trained to predict the attribute value for each node in $V_u$ by minimizing the training loss as follows,

$$\mathbf{W}^* = \underset{\mathbf{W}}{\operatorname{argmin}}\ \mathcal{L}_{\text{gnn}}(f_\mathbf{W}(\mathbf{A}, \mathbf{X}), \mathbf{y}_l) = \underset{\mathbf{W}}{\operatorname{argmin}}\ l(\mathbf{Z}_l, \mathbf{y}_l) + \lambda \|\mathbf{W}\|_2^2 \quad (1)$$

where $\mathbf{W}$ is the trainable weight matrix, and $l(\cdot, \cdot)$ is the loss function. A GNN model $f_\mathbf{W}(\mathbf{A}, \mathbf{X})$ can be specified as graph convolutional networks (GCNs) [15], graph attention networks (GATs) [28], or others [1,10,34]. GNNs can be applied under inductive and transductive settings. In this paper, we focus on transductive inferences where all node connections and features are accessible during training.

### 2.2 Graph Adversarial Attack for Attribute Protection

Given a private attribute, a graph adversarial attack attempts to perturb the graph to obfuscate that attribute and prevent GNN-based inference attack models from correctly identifying users' private attribute values. Generally, it modifies $G$ with its structure and/or node features to an adversarial graph $\hat{G} = (\hat{\mathbf{A}}, \hat{\mathbf{X}})$ [8,38,39], such that the test loss over nodes in $V_u$ can be maximized as follows,

$$\begin{aligned} &\underset{\hat{\mathbf{A}}, \hat{\mathbf{X}}}{\max}\ \mathcal{L}_{\text{atk}}(f_{\mathbf{W}^*}(\hat{\mathbf{A}}, \hat{\mathbf{X}}), \mathbf{y}_u) \\ &s.t.\ \mathbf{W}^* = \underset{\mathbf{W}}{\operatorname{argmin}}\ \mathcal{L}_{\text{gnn}}(f_\mathbf{W}(\hat{\mathbf{A}}, \hat{\mathbf{X}}), \mathbf{y}_l),\ \|G - \hat{G}\|_0 \le \Delta \end{aligned} \quad (2)$$

where a budget constraint $\Delta$ is imposed on perturbations to limit the number of changes over node features and edges to ensure the imperceptibility of attacks.

Clearly, this is a challenging bi-level optimization problem: the attacker aims to maximize the test loss achieved after optimizing the model parameters on the modified graph $\hat{G}$; also, the action space of the attacker from $G$ to $\hat{G}$ are discrete, enforcing vast combinatorial search [39]. Even worse, these attacks based on either graph structure or node feature manipulations are impractical in real-world social graph setting: (1) user nodes usually encode multi-modal data (e.g., profiles, posts, and other activities), where perturbations computed from the feature space are hard to map into user information space in an end-to-end manner; (2) due to limited access to large-scale social networks (especially for ones built on private interactions like Facebook), it is unreasonable to assume that users can alter any relationship as they wish. By contrast, users' attribute values can be easier to manipulate through users' self-reporting. It is necessary for inference attackers to collect initial attribute values for training, while these attribute values on social networks generally come from users' self-reporting. Therefore, attribute value manipulation has a direct impact on the model training and effectiveness of GNN-based inference attacks. Recent studies [20,36] show that flipping a few training labels successfully drags down node classification accuracy to a great extent for graph models, which, however, can merely apply to binary classification tasks. To this end, in this paper, we would like to formulate a more general attribute-obfuscating method on social graphs to protect user attributes in practice, which specifically addresses the aforementioned challenges.

## 3   AttrOBF for User Privacy Protection

In this section, we first identify our goal and challenges, and then detail the technical steps of AttrOBF. The overview of AttrOBF is illustrated in Fig. 2.

### 3.1   Attack Goal and Challenges

In our application setting, AttrOBF is designed to obfuscate a small fraction of optimal training users' attribute values so as to maximally decrease the overall performance of GNN-based attribute inferences trained on the modified graph. More specifically, given a target attribute with either binary or multiple classes, the goal is to have the test users classified as any attribute value different from the true one. In this regard, we can update the general graph adversarial attacks in Eq. (2), and the final objective function of AttrOBF has the following form.

$$
\min_{\Phi(\mathbf{y}_l)} - \mathcal{L}_{\mathrm{atk}}(f_{\mathbf{W}^*}(\mathbf{A}, \mathbf{X}), \mathbf{y}_u)
$$
$$
s.t.\, \mathbf{W}^* = \operatorname*{argmin}_{\mathbf{W}} \mathcal{L}_{\mathrm{gnn}}(f_{\mathbf{W}}(\mathbf{A}, \mathbf{X}), \Phi(\mathbf{y}_l)),\ \|\Phi(\mathbf{y}_l) - \mathbf{y}_l\|_0 \le \epsilon n_l \tag{3}
$$

where $\Phi(\mathbf{y}_l)$ denotes the attribute obfuscating operation on the training attribute values $\mathbf{y}_l$, and $\epsilon$ is the obfuscating rate to $n_l$ to ensure that AttrOBF is unnoticeable. Equation (3) indicates the objective of AttrOBF that directly relates to the loss maximization on the test attribute values $\mathbf{y}_u$. Also, AttrOBF only performs changes to the training attribute values $\mathbf{y}_l$; hence we treat the graph structure $\mathbf{A}$ and node features $\mathbf{X}$ as two constants during our attack formulation. Equation (3) poses four unique challenges to the design of our attack AttrOBF.

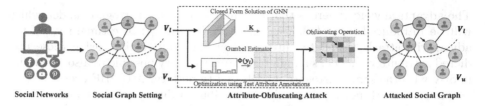

**Fig. 2.** The overview of AttrOBF to protect attribute privacy on social networks.

**Black-Box Setting.** AttrOBF is put under the black-box setting, where it is not aware of the GNN model $f_{\mathbf{W}}(\cdot, \cdot)$ used by inference attackers, including model choice, and parameters. As AttrOBF is a data poisoning attack while we aim to prevent inference attackers from disclosing users' private attribute values on our modified social networks, it is reasonable to assume that AttrOBF has access to the social graph data with respect to $\mathbf{A}$, $\mathbf{X}$, and $\mathbf{y}_l$, which will be collected by inference attackers after attribute obfuscating in real-world scenarios.

**Bi-level Optimization.** The problem formulation in Eq. (3) is of bi-level nature: the optimization on the attack loss $\mathcal{L}_{\text{atk}}$ is achieved after the optimization on the classification loss $\mathcal{L}_{\text{gnn}}$. In this respect, maximizing the test loss to obtain the optimal attribute obfuscating operation $\Phi(\mathbf{y}_l)$ requires retraining the GNN model, while the GNN model parameters $\mathbf{W}^*$ is constrained by the obfuscating operation $\Phi(\mathbf{y}_l)$ on the training attribute values. Optimizing such a bi-level problem is highly challenging by itself.

**Non-differentiable Obfuscating Operation.** In our graph setting, the training attribute data and the action space of the attribute obfuscating are discrete: the training attribute values are $\mathbf{y}_l = \{0, 1, \cdots, k-1\}^{n_l}$, and the possible actions are attribute value changes from the current one to any others. This makes the action space of the problem vast: given the maximum allowed training attribute value changes $\epsilon n_l$, the number of possible attacks is in $O((k-1)^{\epsilon n_l} n_l^{\epsilon n_l})$; exhaustive search is clearly infeasible, while greedy search easily leads to sub-optimal solution. Gradient-based methods can avoid the combinatorial search; however, discrete obfuscating operation $\Phi(\mathbf{y}_l)$ is non-differentiable, preventing AttrOBF from directly applying gradients to optimize the test loss.

### 3.2 Test Attribute Value Prediction

Transductive inferences over a graph imply that all node connections and features are accessible during training. Thus, we can use those annotated data to learn a GNN model described in Eq. (1) to estimate attribute values $\mathbf{y}_u$ of the unannotated or test nodes $V_u$

$$\mathbf{y}_u \approx \mathbf{y}_u^* = \operatorname*{argmax}_{i \in Y} \mathbf{Z}_{u,i}, \quad \mathbf{Z} = f_{\mathbf{W}}(\mathbf{A}, \mathbf{X}) \tag{4}$$

The advantage yielded here is that we can designate the surrogate model, which will be introduced in Sect. 3.3, as $f_{\mathbf{W}}(\mathbf{A}, \mathbf{X})$ in Eq. (4) to estimate $\mathbf{y}_u$; if the adversarial attack formulated in a self-learning manner (i.e., using these predicted attribute values) has a high test error, it is very possible to also generalize poorly with the same surrogate model used to perform AttrOBF over the same graph. It is worth noting that only the attribute values $\mathbf{y}_l$ of the training nodes $V_l$ are used to optimize the GNN model, while the test attribute annotations $\mathbf{y}_u$ from estimation are only used to maximize the test loss for attack formulation.

## 3.3   Surrogate Model

Under the black-box setting, we use two-layer Simple Graph Convolution (SGC) [30] as a surrogate model to perform our attribute-obfuscating attack on social graphs. Specifically, SGC is a linearized two-layer GCN

$$\mathbf{Z} = f_{\mathbf{W}}(\mathbf{A}, \mathbf{X}) = \mathrm{softmax}(\hat{\mathbf{A}}^2 \mathbf{X} \mathbf{W}), \ \mathbf{Z} \in \mathbb{R}^{n \times k} \tag{5}$$

where $\hat{\mathbf{A}} = \mathbf{D}^{-\frac{1}{2}} \tilde{\mathbf{A}} \mathbf{D}^{-\frac{1}{2}}$, $\tilde{\mathbf{A}} = \mathbf{A} + \mathbf{I}$, and $\mathbf{D}$ is the diagonal degree matrix defined on $\tilde{\mathbf{A}}$, i.e., $\mathbf{D}_{ii} = \sum_{j=1}^{n} \tilde{\mathbf{A}}_{ij}$.

There are three reasons behind this surrogate model choice: (1) SGC removes the non-linearity between GCN layers, which not only makes the model more tractable with less unnecessary complexity, but also captures the idea of graph convolutions (as demonstrated in [30], compared to those regular GNNs like GCN [15], GAT [28], FastGCN [4], SGC achieves the comparable or better test accuracy on different classification tasks); (2) SGC has been widely deployed as surrogate model in some successful graph adversarial attack formulations [36,38,39]; (3) SGC of linearity provides a simple closed form solution for $\mathbf{W}^*$, and thus transforms the bi-level optimization in Eq. (3) into single-level, which will be discussed in the following subsection. Due to transferability in adversarial machine learning [24], the attribute obfuscating operation optimized to mislead the surrogate model is very likely to degrade the real attackers' inference models.

## 3.4   Closed Form Solution

To solve the aforementioned bi-level optimization, nettack [38] trains a fixed surrogate model to reduce the attack to the problem simply built upon $\mathcal{L}_{\mathrm{atk}}$; metattack [39] approximates the attack by choosing $\mathcal{L}_{\mathrm{gnn}}$ as an alternate of $\mathcal{L}_{\mathrm{atk}}$, arguing that a model of high training loss very likely misclassifies test nodes; some other attacks [20,36] derive the model parameters and transform the bi-level optimization into single-level. Here, we leverage the closed form transformation idea to compute $\mathbf{W}^*$ and simplify the optimization on $\mathcal{L}_{\mathrm{atk}}$.

Based on Eq. (1), Eq. (3), and Eq. (5), $\mathbf{W}^*$ can be rewritten as

$$\mathbf{W}^* = \underset{\mathbf{W}}{\mathrm{argmin}} \ l((\hat{\mathbf{A}}^2 \mathbf{X})_l \mathbf{W}, \Phi(\mathbf{y}_l)) + \lambda \|\mathbf{W}\|_2^2 \tag{6}$$

After replacing the loss function $l(\cdot, \cdot)$ with mean square loss function, and considering attribute obfuscating operation $\Phi(\mathbf{y}_l)$ as an $n_l \times k$-dimensional matrix where each row is a one-hot vector specifying new attribute value, Eq. (6) can be further updated as

$$\mathbf{W}^* = \operatorname*{argmin}_{\mathbf{W}} \frac{1}{n_l} \|(\hat{\mathbf{A}}^2\mathbf{X})_l \mathbf{W} - \Phi(\mathbf{y}_l)\|_2^2 + \lambda\|\mathbf{W}\|_2^2 \qquad (7)$$

In this way, we can approximately obtain the closed form of $\mathbf{W}^*$ through the derivation as follows,

$$\frac{1}{n_l}\frac{\partial}{\partial \mathbf{W}}(\|(\hat{\mathbf{A}}^2\mathbf{X})_l\mathbf{W} - \Phi(\mathbf{y}_l)\|_2^2 + \lambda\|\mathbf{W}\|_2^2) = 0$$
$$\implies (\hat{\mathbf{A}}^2\mathbf{X})_l^T((\hat{\mathbf{A}}^2\mathbf{X})_l\mathbf{W} - \Phi(\mathbf{y}_l)) + \lambda\mathbf{W} = 0$$
$$\implies (\hat{\mathbf{A}}^2\mathbf{X})_l^T(\hat{\mathbf{A}}^2\mathbf{X})_l\mathbf{W} + \lambda\mathbf{W} = (\hat{\mathbf{A}}^2\mathbf{X})_l^T\Phi(\mathbf{y}_l) \qquad (8)$$
$$\implies \mathbf{W}^* = ((\hat{\mathbf{A}}^2\mathbf{X})_l^T(\hat{\mathbf{A}}^2\mathbf{X})_l + \lambda\mathbf{I})^{-1}(\hat{\mathbf{A}}^2\mathbf{X})_l^T\Phi(\mathbf{y}_l)$$
$$\implies \mathbf{W}^* = \mathbf{K}\Phi(\mathbf{y}_l)$$

where we use $\mathbf{K} = ((\hat{\mathbf{A}}^2\mathbf{X})_l^T(\hat{\mathbf{A}}^2\mathbf{X})_l + \lambda\mathbf{I})^{-1}(\hat{\mathbf{A}}^2\mathbf{X})_l^T$ for the sake of simplicity. Given the closed form of $\mathbf{W}^*$, the bi-level optimization of AttrOBF in Eq. (3) can be updated as the following single-level optimization on $\Phi(\mathbf{y}_l)$.

$$\min_{\Phi(\mathbf{y}_l)} - \mathcal{L}_{\text{atk}}(f_{\mathbf{W}^*}(\mathbf{A},\mathbf{X}),\mathbf{y}_u) \Rightarrow$$
$$\min_{\Phi(\mathbf{y}_l)} - l((\hat{\mathbf{A}}^2\mathbf{X})_u\mathbf{K}\Phi(\mathbf{y}_l),\mathbf{y}_u) + \lambda\|\Phi(\mathbf{y}_l)\|_2^2 \qquad (9)$$
$$s.t.\ \|\Phi(\mathbf{y}_l) - \mathbf{y}_l\|_0 \le \epsilon n_l$$

## 3.5 Gumbel Estimator

To solve the optimization problem in Eq. (9), the attribute obfuscating operation $\Phi(\mathbf{y}_l)$ is the key component. However, $\Phi(\mathbf{y}_l)$ is discrete thus non-differentiable, which means that we cannot directly use gradient-based methods to make updates on $\Phi(\mathbf{y}_l)$. To facilitate closed form solution in Sect. 3.4, we consider $\Phi(\mathbf{y}_l)$ as an $n_l \times k$-dimensional matrix, each row of which is represented as a one-hot vector to indicate the new attribute value. From the probabilistic perspective, we can model each attribute obfuscating operation as a categorical distribution, and this one-hot vector can be then sampled from $k$ label probabilities $(p_0, p_1, \cdots, p_{k-1})$, where the position of 1 (i.e., the best obfuscating operation) is decided by the highest probability: $\text{one\_hot}(\operatorname{argmax}_i[p_i])$.

In other words, given the categorical distribution $\mathbf{P} \in \mathbb{R}^{n_l \times k}$, the test loss of AttrOBF defined in Eq. (9) is an expectation over categorical variables.

$$\min_{\mathbf{P}} - \mathcal{L}_{\text{atk}}(\mathbf{P}) \Rightarrow \min_{\mathbf{P}} - \mathbb{E}_{\Phi(\mathbf{y}_l)\sim\mathbf{P}} l((\hat{\mathbf{A}}^2\mathbf{X})_u\mathbf{K}\Phi(\mathbf{y}_l),\mathbf{y}_u) + \lambda\|\mathbf{P}\|_2^2 \qquad (10)$$

The categorical sampling $\Phi(\mathbf{y}_l) \sim \mathbf{P}$ is still non-differentiable. To solve Eq. (10), we need to find a good gradient estimator. To this end, we use Gumbel estimator

---

**Algorithm 1:** AttrOBF for attribute privacy protection.

---

**Input:** $G = (\mathbf{A}, \mathbf{X})$: Social graph $G$ with graph structure $\mathbf{A}$ and user features $\mathbf{X}$, $V_l$: $n_l$ training user nodes with attribute values $\mathbf{y}_l$, $V_u$: $n_u$ test user nodes without attribute values, $\epsilon$: obfuscating rate, $\tau$: temperature parameter, $T$: epochs.

**Output:** $\mathbf{y}_l$: the obfuscated training attribute values.

Train a GNN model using $\mathbf{A}$, $\mathbf{X}$ and $\mathbf{y}_l$ through Eq. (5);
Estimate $\mathbf{y}_u$ for the unannotated nodes $V_u$;
Pre-calculate $\hat{\mathbf{A}}^2\mathbf{X}$;
Pre-calculate $\mathbf{K} = ((\hat{\mathbf{A}}^2\mathbf{X})_l^T(\hat{\mathbf{A}}^2\mathbf{X})_l + \lambda\mathbf{I})^{-1}(\hat{\mathbf{A}}^2\mathbf{X})_l^T$;
**for** *each epoch $t \leq T$* **do**
  Sample $\mathbf{G} \sim \text{Gumbel}(0,1)$;
  Calculate $h(\mathbf{P}, \mathbf{G})$ using Eq. (11);
  Calculate test loss $-\mathcal{L}_{\text{atk}}(\mathbf{P}) \approx -l((\hat{\mathbf{A}}^2\mathbf{X})_u\mathbf{K}h(\mathbf{P}, \mathbf{G}), \mathbf{y}_u) + \lambda\|\mathbf{P}\|_2^2$;
  Update $\mathbf{P}$ by minimizing $-\mathcal{L}_{\text{atk}}(\mathbf{P})$;
**end**
$\Phi(\mathbf{y}_l) = \texttt{one\_hot}\,(\text{argmax}\,(\mathbf{P}, \text{axis} = 1))$;
Update $\mathbf{y}_l$ using new attribute values in $\Phi(\mathbf{y}_l)$ with top $\epsilon n_l$ highest probabilities in $\mathbf{P}$;

---

[11] to draw samples $\Phi(\mathbf{y}_l)$ from $\mathbf{P}$ in a simple and efficient way. Different from performing argmax to search for the maximal probability, the Gumbel estimator utilizes the Gumbel-Softmax function to generate continuous differentiable approximation to original categorical sampling. Specifically, let $\phi$ (one row of $\Phi(\mathbf{y}_l)$) be sampled from the corresponding categorical distribution $\mathbf{p}$ (one row of $\mathbf{P}$); $\phi$ is approximated as

$$\phi_i = h(\mathbf{p}, \mathbf{g}) = \frac{\exp\left((\log(p_i) + g_i)/\tau\right)}{\sum_{j=0}^{k-1}\exp\left((\log(p_j) + g_j)/\tau\right)}, \text{ for } i = 0, 1, \cdots, k-1 \quad (11)$$

where $\mathbf{g} \sim \text{Gumbel}(0,1)$ is Gumbel distribution, and $\tau$ is the temperature controlling the steepness of softmax function. As the temperature increases, the expected value converges to a uniform distribution over the categories; on the contrary, as $\tau$ approaches 0, samples from the Gumbel-Softmax distribution become one-hot. Monte Carlo sampling from $\mathbf{g}$ makes Gumbel estimator unbiased and low variance [20]. Let $\mathbf{G} = [\mathbf{g}_0, ..., \mathbf{g}_{k-1}]^T$; by replacing $\Phi(\mathbf{y}_l)$ with $h(\mathbf{P}, \mathbf{G})$, the final test loss of AttrOBF is updated as

$$\min_{\mathbf{P}} - \mathcal{L}_{\text{atk}}(\mathbf{P}) \Rightarrow \min_{\mathbf{P}} - \mathbb{E}_{\mathbf{G}}l((\hat{\mathbf{A}}^2\mathbf{X})_u\mathbf{K}h(\mathbf{P}, \mathbf{G}), \mathbf{y}_u) + \lambda\|\mathbf{P}\|_2^2 \quad (12)$$

Accordingly, the derivative of $-\mathcal{L}_{\text{atk}}(\mathbf{P})$ regarding the categorical distribution $\mathbf{P}$ can be computed in an approximate way.

$$-\frac{\partial\mathcal{L}_{\text{atk}}(\mathbf{P})}{\partial\mathbf{P}} \approx -\frac{\partial}{\partial\mathbf{P}}\left[l((\hat{\mathbf{A}}^2\mathbf{X})_u\mathbf{K}h(\mathbf{P}, \mathbf{G}), \mathbf{y}_u) + \lambda\|\mathbf{P}\|_2^2\right] \quad (13)$$

The problem in Eq. (13) is differentiable and tractable. Therefore, it can be easily solved by gradient-based methods (e.g., stochastic gradient descent, Adam).

After the categorical distribution $\mathbf{P}$ is optimally updated, the attribute obfuscating operation $\Phi(\mathbf{y}_l)$ is uniquely defined as:

$$\Phi(\mathbf{y}_l) = \texttt{one\_hot}\ (\mathrm{argmax}\ (\mathbf{P}, \mathrm{axis} = 1)) \tag{14}$$

Note that, $\Phi(\mathbf{y}_l)$ indicates the obfuscating operation on the whole training attribute values $\mathbf{y}_l$. As specified in Eq. (3) and Eq. (9), to ensure the imperceptibility of attack, the attribute obfuscating operation is constrained by $\|\Phi(\mathbf{y}_l) - \mathbf{y}_l\|_0 \leq \epsilon n_l$. That is, the number of maximum allowed training attribute value changes is $\epsilon n_l$. As such, we leverage $\Phi(\mathbf{y}_l)$ and $\mathbf{P}$ to decide the actual attribute obfuscating: we first collect all new training attribute values from $\Phi(\mathbf{y}_l)$ that are different from the original and their corresponding probabilities from $\mathbf{P}$, and then use those new attribute values with top $\epsilon n_l$ highest probabilities to update $\mathbf{y}_l$ so as to guarantee the optimal operation. Algorithm 1 illustrates our proposed attribute-obfuscating attack AttrOBF to protect attribute privacy on social networks. As graph structure $\mathbf{A}$ and node features $\mathbf{X}$ are constants during attribute-obfuscating attack, we can pre-calculate $\hat{\mathbf{A}}^2\mathbf{X}$ and $\mathbf{K}$ using $O(\max(n^3, d^3))$, which significantly decreases the time complexity for each optimization iteration to $O(n_l n_u d)$ ($k \ll d$). Therefore, this efficient attack strategy has implications on its applicability for attribute protection on large social networks in practice.

## 4    Experimental Results and Analysis

### 4.1    Experimental Setup

**Datasets.** In our practical setting, we utilize three real-world social network datasets to conduct our experiments: Polblogs [2], Yale [17], and Rochester [17]. Polblogs represents a political blog network where their attribute values indicate political view of each user. Yale and Rochester datasets collect all the Facebook friendships of Yale University and Rochester University as well as some user attributes, in which career, gender, class year serve as private attributes. We train GNN models in a standard transductive setting where all node features are utilized and 20 nodes are annotated per class, and another 500 annotated nodes are viewed as validation set. Then, we randomly sample 1,000 nodes to evaluate the performance. Table 1 presents the dataset statistics.

**Baseline Methods and Parameter Settings.** In our study, the proposed AttrOBF is designed for practical attribute privacy protections in social media, and to the best of our knowledge, graph adversarial attacks via modifications on multi-class annotations have not yet been explored. Thus, we formulate a couple of baselines in this regard to compare against AttrOBF: (1) Random attribute-obfuscating attacks (**Rand-obf**) where we randomly select a number of training nodes and obfuscate their attribute values to a random one. (2) Degree-based attribute-obfuscating attacks (**Deg-obf**) where we obfuscate the training nodes

**Table 1.** Statistics of three social network datasets in five attribute settings.

| Dataset | Attr. | Nodes | Edges | Classes | Train./Val./Test |
|---|---|---|---|---|---|
| Polblogs | Politics | 1,490 | 19,025 | 2 | 40/500/950 |
| Yale | Career | 8,578 | 405,450 | 2 | 20 × classes/500/1000 |
| | Class-year | | | 6 | |
| Rochester | Gender | 4,563 | 167,653 | 2 | 20 × classes/500/1000 |
| | Class-year | | | 5 | |

with the highest degrees because we believe these nodes play a more important role in the information propagation for GNNs than those with lower degrees; similarly, for all inference settings, we modify the attribute values of the selected nodes to a random one. Note that, as we only focus on attribute obfuscating, those adversarial methods designed for different settings, such as manipulating graph structure or node features, are not comparable here. Following the baseline designs in [36], in order to investigate how different components affect the performance of AttrOBF, we further formulate two variants as baselines by replacing surrogate model and loss function: (3) **AttrOBF-lp** follows the same steps of AttrOBF except that we use label propagation as our surrogate model, which accordingly updates the closed form in Eq. (8) and single-level optimization in (9). (4) **AttrOBF-cse** replaces mean square error in loss function to cross-entropy, which updates the final test loss of AttrOBF in Eq. (12). In our parameter settings, we set the optimization epoch in AttrOBF as 1,000 and training epoch of GNN models as 200. The temperature parameter for Gumbel estimator $\tau$ introduced in Eq. (11) is set as 0.2 and $\lambda = 0.01$ for optimization.

**Attack Model for Attribute Inference Attacks.** Attackers conduct attribute inference attacks to disclose private attributes of users by learning a GNN model on public social network data. Since we do not know the attacker's model, we use SGC to solve black-box setting and closed form for AttrOBF. In our experimental setting, we train simple graph convolution (SGC) [30], graph convolutional network (GCN) [15], graph attention network (GAT) [28], and GCN-based label propagation network (GCN-LP) [29] to perform the inference attack. We mainly use GCN to evaluate the effectiveness of AttrOBF and the impacts of different parameters, while the comparisons among these four models are leveraged for transferability evaluation in Sect. 4.4. To be comparable, these four GNN models are of two-layer structure and the dimension of the hidden layer is set as 16. All other model parameters align with their original works [15,28–30].

## 4.2   Evaluation of AttrOBF

**Effectiveness.** In our experiments, we test the results of five inference settings (i.e., Polblogs-politics, Yale-career, Yale-class, Rochester-class, Rochester-gender) while using AttrOBF to obfuscate the training attribute values with obfuscating rate $\epsilon \in \{0.0, 0.1, 0.2, 0.3, 0.4, 0.5\}$, where 0.0 means no attack in

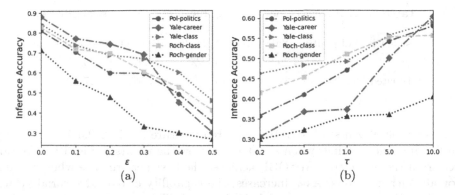

(a)                                                    (b)

**Fig. 3.** (a) represents the test accuracy of all inference tasks on different attribute obfuscating rate $\epsilon$, while (b) specifies the evaluation results of AttrOBF under different values of temperature parameter $\tau$.

place. It is worth mentioning that we merely modify 10 training nodes per class even when reaching the largest obfuscating rate 0.5. We believe this complies with its practicability requirement considering the large graph volume. In this experiment, we use test accuracy to evaluate attribute privacy protection performance. The lower test accuracy represents the better performance of our method. The experimental results are shown in Fig. 3(a). We can see that the attribute inference accuracy for Polblogs-politics, Yale-career, Yale-class, Rochester-class and Rochester-gender on clean data is 81.1%, 88.1%, 84.5%, 82.8%, and 71.4%, which are relatively close to the state-of-the-art results on each dataset. Obviously, AttrOBF drastically decreases all the accuracy of inference attacks and thus achieves the goal of protecting users' attribute privacy on social networks.

**Impact of Attribute Obfuscating Rate $\epsilon$.** Intuitively, when we enlarge the $\epsilon$, the number of the training node attribute values obfuscated by AttrOBF increases and the accuracy of inference attacks should decrease. The results in Fig. 3(a) confirm this point: as the obfuscating rate increases from 0.0 to 0.5, the inference accuracy drops 45.3% for Polblogs-politics, 57.6% for Yale-career, 41.2% for Yale-class, 41.3% for Rochester-class, and 44.2% for Rochester-gender. We can also observe that AttrOBF obtains better performance on binary inference settings than multi-class inference tasks. The reason behind this could be that attacking space on multi-class social graphs is larger, which leads to more uncertainty and difficulty than binary problems that flipping labels can directly impact on neighborhoods and thus more easily mislead the GNN model.

**Impact of Temperature for Gumbel Estimator $\tau$.** The temperature $\tau$ for Gumber estimator is an important parameter in our method that controls the effectiveness of the one-hot sampling. We gradually increase the value of $\tau$ in AttrOBF to analyze its impact to the attack performance. In the experiments, we

**Table 2.** Inference accuracy of using true or estimated test attributes.

| Test labels | Pol-politics | Yale-career | Yale-class | Roch-class | Roch-gender |
|---|---|---|---|---|---|
| True | 33.1% | 29.3% | 43.0% | 40.9% | 25.7% |
| Estimated | 35.7% | 30.5% | 43.3% | 41.5% | 27.1% |

assess the effectiveness of AttrOBF with temperature $\tau \in \{0.2, 0.5, 1.0, 5.0, 10.0\}$ in five inference settings when $\epsilon = 0.5$. We show the results in Fig. 3(b). We can see from the figure that AttrOBF achieves the best performance when $\tau = 0.2$ for all inference tasks. As $\tau$ increases, the capability of our adversarial attack in alleviating the inference models is degraded. This is because when we continuously amplify the $\tau$ value, Gumbel-Softmax distribution becomes closer to uniform distribution, which more significantly deviates from one-hot sampling and thus affects the effectiveness of attribute obfuscating operation. There is a trade-off between near-zero temperatures, where samples are identical to one-hot but the variance of the gradients is large as well. Based on this fact, we use $\tau = 0.2$ throughout the following evaluations.

**Impact of Test Attribute Annotations** $y_u$. We use the prediction results of the surrogate model to estimate the test attribute values in our evaluations, and compare with the true test attribute annotations to investigate the impact of them on the performance of AttrOBF. The comparative results are shown in Table 2 with obfuscating rate $\epsilon = 0.5$. We can observe that integrating true test attribute annotations in our objective loss function can obtain better attack results than the estimated ones, as the estimation might introduce extra loss in our objectives. However, the inference accuracy difference between using true and estimated test attribute annotations seems not very significant. The reason behind this could be that the surrogate model's inference accuracy for different attribute settings is relatively high (i.e., 81.1%, 88.1%, 84.5%, 82.8%, and 71.4% for Polblogs-politics, Yale-career, Yale-class, Rochester-class and Rochester-gender respectively), which makes the estimation closer to ground truth. This implies that our method is not tightly coupled with true test attribute annotations, and can be easily feasible in practical applications.

### 4.3  Comparisons with Other Attack Baselines

In this section, we compare our method AttrOBF against four baselines: Rand-obf, Deg-obf, AttrOBF-lp and AttrOBF-cse. For all methods, we set the obfuscating rate $\epsilon$ as 0.5, and use GCNs as the attack model to assess the inference accuracy. The results of five inference settings are presented in Table 3. We can observe that our method AttrOBF significantly outperforms Rand-obf on all inference tasks. Under Rand-obf attack, the inference accuracy only slightly decreases for all obfuscating rates, which indicates that GCNs are quite robust to random label noise. This also benefits from the powerful learning capability

**Table 3.** Comparisons with other attack baselines (inference accuracy).

| Setting | Rand-obf | Deg-obf | AttrOBF-lp | AttrOBF-cse | AttrOBF |
|---|---|---|---|---|---|
| Pol-politics | 55.7% | 37.0% | 42.5% | 36.5% | **35.7%** |
| Yale-career | 61.2% | 47.2% | 49.4% | 38.6% | **30.5%** |
| Yale-class | 72.0% | 53.1% | 45.5% | 43.8% | **43.3%** |
| Roch-class | 69.6% | 54.2% | 43.5% | 42.1% | **41.5%** |
| Roch-gender | 46.7% | 42.1% | 39.9% | 31.0% | **27.1%** |

of GCNs on graph data of embracing both node features and graph topological structure. Therefore, GCNs are resilient against random node obfuscating operations but still vulnerable to our well-designed adversarial attacks. AttrOBF also achieves better performance than Deg-obf attack, especially for multi-class inference problems. For instance, AttrOBF reduces the inference accuracy to 43.3% and 41.5% for Yale-class and Rochester-class while the results of Deg-obf attack are 53.1% and 54.2%, respectively. This is due to the fact that adversarial attribute values generated by AttrOBF are specifically derived from the goal of misleading the learning model, which are much more effective to degrade the performance of node classification, while Deg-obf identifies the degree information of nodes as the only influential factor for graph learning but ignores other conditions (e.g., node features) leveraged by GCNs.

Regarding to AttrOBF-lp, AttrOBF achieves better results for all classification settings. Compared to graph neural networks, label propagation only aggregates the label information from nodes' neighbors without considering the important feature information. Therefore, choosing SGC to be the surrogate model to compute the closed form solution is more reasonable and effective for our formulation. The similar variant AttrOBF-cse can achieve comparable results but still slightly underperforms our method. The reason behind this performance difference could be that mean square error can better formalize the discrepancy between ground truth and prediction results in the embedding space.

### 4.4 Transferability of AttrOBF

Under the black-box setting, we don't know what model the attacker is using to infer private attributes. This naturally leads us to the question: can our attack strategy generalize to other inference attack models? To answer this question, in this evaluation, we explore the transferability of our method AttrOBF. Specifically, we deploy AttrOBF to obfuscate the training attribute values and generate adversarial graph on five attribute inference settings. Then we test the inference results of the poisoned data against four state-of-the-art GNN models, including SGC [30], GCN [15], GAT [28] and GCN-LP [29] under five obfuscating rates (i.e., $\epsilon = \{0.1, 0.2, 0.3, 0.4, 0.5\}$). To ensure our results are comparable, we build up these models with the same parameter and data settings.

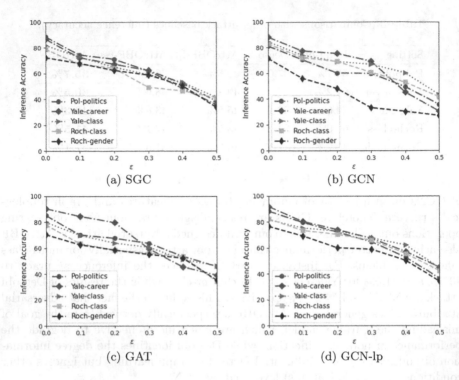

**Fig. 4.** (a), (b), (c) and (d) specify the inference accuracy of SGC, GCN, GAT and GCN-lp while conducting AttrOBF on our surrogate model over different data settings; lower inference accuracy indicates better attack transferability.

The results presented in Fig. 4 show that the adversarial attack performed by AttrOBF can successfully transfer to different graph neural networks. Our AttrOBF method learned on a linearized GCN (i.e., SGC) presents the similar effectiveness against different GNN models under the same inference setting. For example, when $\epsilon$ is set as 0.5, AttrOBF reduces the accuracy of SGC, GCN, GCN-LP to 35.6%, 35.7% and 36.4% on polblogs-politics inference attack and 33.5%, 27.1% and 34.2% on Rochester-gender inference setting. For Yale-career, the inference accuracy of all GNN models drops over 30% when increasing $\epsilon$ from 0.1 to 0.5. While for Yale-class and Rochester-class inference settings, the transferability of AttrOBF on four GNN models are very close and slightly underperform other inference tasks. On the other hand, the results also imply that the complexity of the surrogate model and the intrinsic adversarial vulnerability of the target model contribute to attack transferability: the attack results on SGC and GCN outperform those with more complex model structure such as GAT and GCN-LP. Since the target models are uncontrollable, when applying AttrOBF in practice, we may need to elaborate the surrogate model for better transferability. We leave it as our future exploration.

# 5  Impact, Applicability and Limitation

Our previous method formulation and experimental evaluations demonstrate the impact of our proposed graph adversarial attack solution for attribute privacy protection on social networks: (1) as graph structure and node features are not perturbed, the utilities of social networks regarding user activities and relationships are well preserved without any influence on other downstream tasks; (2) mere small yet optimal training annotation changes can effectively mitigate attribute inference attacks; (3) attribute obfuscating is easy to operate for both data publishers and users. Therefore, in practice, AttrOBF can work as an easy-to-use API provided on the social network server side that enables data publishers to either locally or globally manipulate user attribute values before making the social graphs publicly available, or warn users of potential attribute privacy threats such that users can proactively change their attribute information on the client side. Nonetheless, our approach also poses a limitation which we discuss as follows. In our experiments, we train some regular GNN-based attack models for attribute inferences on social networks. Though AttrOBF has been validated to be transferable to these GNNs, the attackers could take advantage of more advanced and robust GNN models (e.g., adversarial training via latent perturbation [14]) to infer attributes and thus deteriorate AttrOBF. We acknowledge this limitation and leave the investigation on this arms race as our future work, yet it does not impact the great value and general validity of our new insight about leveraging graph adversarial attacks for attribute obfuscation and privacy protection on social networks in practice, as graph learning models of inherent vulnerability could always be evaded by more complicated and more sophisticated adversarial techniques.

# 6  Conclusion

In this paper, we investigate adversary for social good, and cast attribute privacy protection problem on social networks as a graph adversarial attack formulation problem to defend against GNN-based attribute inference attacks. We design a black-box attribute-obfuscating attack AttrOBF, where a linearized two-layer GCN is used as a surrogate model to perform our attack. Under the help of this surrogate model, a closed form of model weights is obtained to transform the bi-level optimization for AttrOBF into single-level. To address non-differentiable attribute obfuscating operation, we introduce Gumbel estimator to generate continuous differentiable approximation that enables gradient-based methods to search for the optimal training attribute values to change. We conduct extensive experimental studies on real-world social network datasets to evaluate the performance of AttrOBF, which validate its effectiveness against GNN-based attribute inference attacks. Despite the limitation, we believe that our work has implications on the applicability of adversarial attacks for attribute obfuscation and privacy protection in practice.

**Acknowledgement.** The work was supported in part by a seed grant from the Penn State Center for Security Research and Education (CSRE).

# References

1. Abu-El-Haija, S., et al.: Mixhop: higher-order graph convolutional architectures via sparsified neighborhood mixing. In: International Conference on Machine Learning, pp. 21–29 (2019)
2. Adamic, L.A., Glance, N.: The political blogosphere and the 2004 us election: divided they blog. In: Proceedings of the 3rd International Workshop on Link Discovery, pp. 36–43 (2005)
3. Beigi, G., Shu, K., Zhang, Y., Liu, H.: Securing social media user data: an adversarial approach. In: Hypertext and Social Media, pp. 165–173 (2018)
4. Chen, J., Ma, T., Xiao, C.: FastGCN: fast learning with graph convolutional networks via importance sampling. arXiv preprint arXiv:1801.10247 (2018)
5. Chen, L., Li, X., Wu, D.: Enhancing robustness of graph convolutional networks via dropping graph connections. In: Joint European Conference on Machine Learning and Knowledge Discovery in Databases, pp. 412–428 (2020)
6. Chen, L., Ye, Y., Bourlai, T.: Adversarial machine learning in malware detection: Arms race between evasion attack and defense. In: 2017 European Intelligence and Security Informatics Conference (EISIC), pp. 99–106. IEEE (2017)
7. Chen, W., et al.: Semi-supervised user profiling with heterogeneous graph attention networks. In: IJCAI, vol. 19, pp. 2116–2122 (2019)
8. Dai, H., et al.: Adversarial attack on graph structured data. arXiv preprint arXiv:1806.02371 (2018)
9. Gong, N.Z., Liu, B.: Attribute inference attacks in online social networks. TOPS **21**(1), 3 (2018)
10. Hamilton, W.L., Ying, R., Leskovec, J.: Inductive representation learning on large graphs. arXiv preprint arXiv:1706.02216 (2017)
11. Jang, E., Gu, S., Poole, B.: Categorical reparameterization with gumbel-softmax. arXiv preprint arXiv:1611.01144 (2016)
12. Jia, J., Gong, N.Z.: AttriGuard: a practical defense against attribute inference attacks via adversarial machine learning. In: USENIX Security, pp. 513–529 (2018)
13. Jia, J., Wang, B., Zhang, L., Gong, N.Z.: Attriinfer: Inferring user attributes in online social networks using Markov random fields. In: WWW, pp. 1561–1569 (2017)
14. Jin, H., Zhang, X.: Robust training of graph convolutional networks via latent perturbation. In: Machine Learning and Knowledge Discovery in Databases: European Conference, ECML PKDD 2020, Ghent, Belgium, 14–18 September 2020, Proceedings, Part III, pp. 394–411 (2021)
15. Kipf, T.N., Welling, M.: Semi-supervised classification with graph convolutional networks. arXiv preprint arXiv:1609.02907 (2016)
16. Kumar, C., Ryan, R., Shao, M.: Adversary for social good: Protecting familial privacy through joint adversarial attacks. In: AAAI (2020)
17. Li, K., Luo, G., Ye, Y., Li, W., Ji, S., Cai, Z.: Adversarial privacy preserving graph embedding against inference attack. IEEE Internet Things J. **8**(8), 6904–6915 (2020)

18. Li, X., Chen, L., Wu, D.: Turning attacks into protection: Social media privacy protection using adversarial attacks. In: Proceedings of the 2021 SIAM International Conference on Data Mining (SDM), pp. 208–216. SIAM (2021)
19. Liu, S., Chen, L., Dong, H., Wang, Z., Wu, D., Huang, Z.: Higher-order weighted graph convolutional networks. arXiv preprint arXiv:1911.04129 (2019)
20. Liu, X., Si, S., Zhu, X., Li, Y., Hsieh, C.J.: A unified framework for data poisoning attack to graph-based semi-supervised learning. arXiv:1910.14147 (2019)
21. Mohamed, A., Qian, K., Elhoseiny, M., Claudel, C.: Social-STGCNN: a social spatio-temporal graph convolutional neural network for human trajectory prediction. In: Proceedings of the IEEE/CVF Conference on Computer Vision and Pattern Recognition, pp. 14424–14432 (2020)
22. Morgan-Lopez, A.A., Kim, A.E., Chew, R.F., Ruddle, P.: Predicting age groups of twitter users based on language and metadata features. PloS ONE 12(8), e0183537 (2017)
23. Oh, S.J., Fritz, M., Schiele, B.: Adversarial image perturbation for privacy protection a game theory perspective. In: ICCV, pp. 1491–1500 (2017)
24. Papernot, N., McDaniel, P., Goodfellow, I.: Transferability in machine learning: from phenomena to black-box attacks using adversarial samples. arXiv preprint arXiv:1605.07277 (2016)
25. Qian, J., Li, X.Y., Jung, T., Fan, Y., Wang, Y., Tang, S.: Social network de-anonymization: more adversarial knowledge, more users re-identified? TOIT 19(3), 1–22 (2019)
26. Ruder, S., Ghaffari, P., Breslin, J.G.: Character-level and multi-channel convolutional neural networks for large-scale authorship attribution. arXiv preprint arXiv:1609.06686 (2016)
27. Shetty, R., Schiele, B., Fritz, M.: A4nt: author attribute anonymity by adversarial training of neural machine translation. In: Proceedings of the 27th USENIX Security Symposium (USENIX Security 18), pp. 1633–1650 (2018)
28. Veličković, P., Cucurull, G., Casanova, A., Romero, A., Lio, P., Bengio, Y.: Graph attention networks. arXiv preprint arXiv:1710.10903 (2017)
29. Wang, H., Leskovec, J.: Unifying graph convolutional neural networks and label propagation. arXiv preprint arXiv:2002.06755 (2020)
30. Wu, F., Souza, A., Zhang, T., Fifty, C., Yu, T., Weinberger, K.: Simplifying graph convolutional networks. In: International Conference on Machine Learning, pp. 6861–6871. PMLR (2019)
31. Wu, H., Wang, C., Tyshetskiy, Y., Docherty, A., Lu, K., Zhu, L.: Adversarial examples for graph data: deep insights into attack and defense. In: IJCAI, pp. 4816–4823 (2019)
32. Wu, Y., Lian, D., Jin, S., Chen, E.: Graph convolutional networks on user mobility heterogeneous graphs for social relationship inference. In: IJCAI, pp. 3898–3904 (2019)
33. Xu, K., et al.: Topology attack and defense for graph neural networks: an optimization perspective. arXiv preprint arXiv:1906.04214 (2019)
34. Ying, R., He, R., Chen, K., Eksombatchai, P., Hamilton, W.L., Leskovec, J.: Graph convolutional neural networks for web-scale recommender systems. In: SIGKDD, pp. 974–983 (2018)
35. Yu, S., Vorobeychik, Y., Alfeld, S.: Adversarial classification on social networks. In: AAMAS, pp. 211–219 (2018)
36. Zhang, M., Hu, L., Shi, C., Wang, X.: Adversarial label-flipping attack and defense for graph neural networks. In: ICDM, pp. 791–800 (2020)

37. Zhang, Y., Humbert, M., Rahman, T., Pang, J., Backes, M.: Tagvisor: a privacy advisor for sharing hashtags. In: WWW (2018)
38. Zügner, D., Akbarnejad, A., Günnemann, S.: Adversarial attacks on neural networks for graph data. In: SIGKDD, pp. 2847–2856 (2018)
39. Zügner, D., Günnemann, S.: Adversarial attacks on graph neural networks via meta learning. arXiv preprint arXiv:1902.08412 (2019)

# Software Security

# No-Fuzz: Efficient Anti-fuzzing Techniques

Zhengxiang Zhou$^{(\boxtimes)}$, Cong Wang, and Qingchuan Zhao

City University of Hong Kong, Hong Kong, China
zxzhou4-c@my.cityu.edu.hk, {congwang,cs.qczhao}@cityu.edu.hk

**Abstract.** Fuzzing is an automated software testing technique that has achieved great success in recent years. While this technique allows developers to uncover vulnerabilities avoiding consequent issues (e.g., financial loss), it can also be leveraged by attackers to find zero-day vulnerabilities. To mitigate, anti-fuzzing techniques were proposed to impede the fuzzing process by slowing down its rate, misinforming the feedback, and complicating the data flow. Unfortunately, the state-of-the-art of anti-fuzzing entirely focuses on enhancing its defensive capability but underestimates the nontrivial performance overhead and overlooks the requirement of extra manual efforts. In this paper, to advance the state-of-the-art, we propose an efficient and automatic anti-fuzzing technique and implement a prototype, called No-Fuzz. Comparing to prior works, our evaluations illustrate that No-Fuzz introduces less performance overhead, i.e., less than 15% of the storage cost for one fake block. In addition, in respect of the binary-only fuzzing, No-Fuzz can precisely determine the corresponding running environments and eliminate unnecessary storage overheads with high effectiveness. Specifically, it reduces 95% of the total storage cost compared with the prior works for the same number of branch reductions. Moreover, our study sheds light on approaches to improve the practicality of anti-fuzzing techniques.

**Keywords:** Anti-fuzzing · Software testing · Fuzzing

## 1 Introduction

Fuzzing was first introduced as a software testing technique in 1990 [25]. Typically, a fuzzer would persistently feed the target program with randomly generated inputs and observe the abnormalities of the program (e.g., segmentation faults) to identify program bugs. Recently, fuzzers have been well-developed - researchers integrate fuzzers with techniques like program instrumentation [3,12,28,29,31,36,38], program analysis techniques [30,33,35] for the efficiency in bug-finding. Besides, researchers also modify the fuzzing mechanisms of some classic works [3,36], to meticulously reallocate the fuzzing resources on some specific tasks (e.g., directly fuzzing a particular code area [7,8,10,23]). In general, fuzzers have achieved great success with plenty of bugs uncovered [14,15,27,31].

However, exposing bugs in the program is a double-edged sword. Developers can find and fix bugs before they spread on the internet. Meanwhile, attackers

F. Li et al. (Eds.): SecureComm 2022, LNICST 462, pp. 731–751, 2023.
https://doi.org/10.1007/978-3-031-25538-0_38

can also leverage fuzzers to explore zero-day vulnerabilities, which might cause financial loss to the companies. Although the adversaries can manually analyze the commercial software, recent studies [17,32] have shown that attackers lean more towards automated tools, like fuzzers, to find vulnerabilities than manual analysis. In the face of the worse situations of bug finding, anti-fuzzing techniques were proposed to hinder malicious use of fuzzers (ANTIFUZZ [16] and FUZZIFICATION [21]). The purpose of anti-fuzzing is to maintain the advantageous position of developers over adversaries on bug-finding. These techniques introduce penalties on fuzzers to disturb the fuzzing heuristics or slow down the fuzzing rate. The source codes of the protected program will be compiled into two versions - one is protected with anti-fuzzing codes, and the other is unmodified. Developers keep the original version, and they can thoroughly test the program. Adversaries only retrieve the protected version, and the anti-fuzzing codes inside the program can severely hinder the use of fuzzers. Consequently, developers are expected to uncover far more bugs than the adversaries and fix them to avoid the possible loss from zero-day vulnerabilities.

Anti-fuzzing techniques are promising, but the prototypes in prior works should be improved to more fine-grained application scope. Intuitively, the storage overhead should be taken into consideration for the practical adoption of anti-fuzzing techniques. In prior works, fake blocks are artificially inserted into the program to saturate the bitmap of fuzzers, while this technique can enlarge the size of the program by even several times the original program. Developers would be unwilling to burden such storage costs only for anti-fuzzing. Instead, they can resort to lighter obfuscation tools whenever applicable, even though these tools may not provide sufficient protection against fuzzers. Another factor that matters is the automation of the tools, i.e., existing prototypes are inconvenient to use. On the one hand, the developers have to locate some code areas manually; on the other hand, the prototypes have some dependencies with third-party tools/libraries that may be incompatible with the OS of users. We believe these factors challenge the future design and implementation of anti-fuzzing techniques. More specifically, the anti-fuzzing techniques should ideally hold the following two properties:

**P1)** *Both storage and performance overheads should be minimized;*

**P2)** *The implementation should support automation which has no modification to the development procedures of the program.*

Based on these thoughts, we propose our solution to anti-fuzzing techniques. The solution involves two categories of techniques - the passive detection methods and active disturbance methods. The passive detection methods precisely check whether the protected program is being fuzzed and launch mitigation strategies once fuzzers are detected. In our design, we integrate instrumentation checking and execution frequency checking to achieve low overhead anti-fuzzing techniques. The active disturbance methods impede fuzzers by attacking the basic fuzzing assumptions and prevent the fuzzers from working normally. We optimize the defective fake blocks. In our design, the fake blocks achieve the minimum storage overhead, which is less than 15% of that in prior works.

We implement these techniques as a fully automated tool, i.e., No-Fuzz. The anti-fuzzing techniques are directly added to the source codes of programs, i.e., no modification is needed to the compilation procedures (e.g., header files, linked libraries, compilation commands). Notably, No-Fuzz is also compatible with other anti-fuzzing techniques in prior works that are not mentioned.

In the evaluation, we measure the effectiveness of our techniques in reducing branch coverage with real-world software from Binutils and two popular benchmarks (Google FTS [1] and Magma [18]). Moreover, we show that our techniques can hinder bug findings for the LAVA-M [13] dataset. To confirm our optimizations to prior works, we have also compared No-Fuzz with the corresponding techniques in ANTIFUZZ [16] and FUZZIFICATION [21]. The results show that our design introduces less overhead and mitigates the negative effects of anti-fuzzing techniques on regular users. Specifically, we reduce about 95% of the storage cost compared with the prior works for the same number of branch reductions. Furthermore, we tackle the obstacle that there is no suitable metric to compare different anti-fuzzing techniques currently. Existing works measure the anti-fuzzing effects and the overhead separately. However, the performance and overhead are orthogonal - both of them vary according to different configurations; it is unfair to compare the performance of different works with unequal overhead directly. Therefore, in addition to measuring the performance and overhead separately, we propose a new metric - "anti-fuzzing efficacy" linking the two metrics to measure the increased defensive capability per unit overhead.

In short, this paper makes the following contributions: 1) throws light on the facts of existing anti-fuzzing prototypes and summarises the properties of the ideal anti-fuzzing techniques; 2) designs and implements automated anti-fuzzing prototype No-Fuzz which can detect and disturb run-time fuzzing mechanisms; 3) evaluate No-Fuzz and some of the prior anti-fuzzing techniques on common benchmarks, showing No-Fuzz's negligible overhead to the protected binary and its effectiveness at impeding binary-only fuzzing. The source codes of all implemented tools are available at https://github.com/CongGroup/No-Fuzz.

## 2   Technical Background of Anti-fuzzing

The purpose of anti-fuzzing techniques is to combat fuzzers to reduce the number of bugs reported on protected binaries. Existing techniques can be majorly summarized as anti-fast-execution, anti-feedback, and anti-hybrid techniques based on the affected fuzzing mechanisms. We will briefly introduce them in the following parts of this section.

**Anti-fast-execution: Introduce Latency to Binary.** One of the fuzzers' assumptions is that more trials with different inputs are expected to explore more paths in the binary. Fuzzers are usually designed with accelerating techniques feeding thousands of seeds per second to the program under test (PUT) [37]. Anti-fast-execution techniques insert latency into the binary to prevent fast-execution. However, the challenge is that the latency can also affect regular users. ANTIFUZZ [16] inserts delay functions in the error handling codes manually; FUZZIFICATION [21] inserts the latency functions in cold blocks. Both techniques are trying to delay the areas that regular users rarely reach, but fuzzers are easy to fall into.

**Anti-feedback: Disturb the Feedback Information.** Modern fuzzers majorly rely on two feedbacks to decide fuzzing heuristics - coverage-feedback and error signals. The coverage information is stored in a bitmap of limited size, and fuzzers are expected to make decisions on seeds and mutations to maximize the coverage. The error signals inform fuzzers to save and report the seeds triggering bugs, which is also the ultimate goal of using fuzzers.

Anti-feedback techniques insert fake blocks into the protected binary to disturb the coverage feedback. These blocks contain codes irrelevant to the program logic but are recorded as valid blocks in the bitmap. If most space of the bitmap has been taken up by these fake blocks, fuzzers will be unable to update new coverage. ANTIFUZZ hijacks the control flows to randomly generated fake functions in the protected program. FUZZIFICATION inserts a fixed number of constraints and functions into the binary, and builds ROP chains as fake paths on the assembly code snippets.

For the error signals, ChaffBugs [19] suggests inserting non-exploitable bugs into the binary to confuse the segmentation faults reported to fuzzers. ANTIFUZZ proposed an approach to hinder the crash discovery by installing a signal handler. The handler hides signals from fuzzers with elegant exits, and thus fuzzers are unaware of crashes.

**Anti-hybrid: Impede Program Analysis.** Hybrid fuzzers [11,20,30,35] generally rely on taint analysis and symbolic execution to accelerate fuzzing. Anti-hybrid techniques embed complex data flows in protected binary to hinder both of the techniques. The idea is based on the fact that program analysis techniques have difficulty in dealing with complex data flows due to the limited CPU resources. ANTIFUZZ encrypts and decrypts the inputs and transforms variables in critical comparisons to their hash values. Similarly, FUZZIFICATION adds extra copy operations to the operand string to complicate the data flows and mislead taint analysis engines to a wrong tag map.

## 3   No-Fuzz Design

No-Fuzz includes passive detection methods and the optimized active technique (fake blocks) of prior works. Passive detection methods detect whether the protected binary is being fuzzed in binary-only-fuzzing (BOF) mode. Once the fuzzers are found, the protection will trigger fuzzing mitigation mechanisms (e.g., introducing latency). As aforementioned, the active methods in prior works are not practical due to the storage overhead. We optimize the fake blocks and design the landing space exploiting the block-identification mechanism of binary-only instrumentation. It reduces the storage overhead of a fake block to only one byte.

## 3.1   Passive Detection Methods

A fundamental requirement for anti-fuzzing is to avoid the negative effects of the inserted anti-fuzzing techniques on regular users. Ideally, if the protected program itself can accurately perceive the fuzzers, we can impose severe penalties on adversaries covertly. Based on this thinking, we introduce passive detection methods to identify the running environments of protected binaries. Once fuzzers are detected, we carry out mitigation mechanisms such as delaying the execution and aborting the program to prevent fuzzing.

**Detect Binary-Only Instrumentation.** In the scenario of using anti-fuzzing techniques, adversaries are not able to retrieve the source codes of the protected binary - they rely on the binary-only mode of fuzzers. The key is that no matter what techniques they are using, they have to collect coverage information of the target program. Techniques such as dynamic instrumentation, hardware assistance, and binary rewriting are the most used for this observation, but all of them cause significant latency (a timing gap) to the PUT. We can detect the timing gap between the native execution and the execution with coverage-collecting codes to determine the running environment.

Timing-related techniques are common in the scope of malware detection [5,22,24]. We learn from existing works and design the detection on binary instrumentations. In the native execution environment (real CPU), the control flow directly falls into the block after a branch-taken instruction. On the contrary, with BOF, the instrumented program executes the additional instructions collecting coverage at the beginning of a block. We detect BOF by checking the edge instructions count (EIC). EIC is the estimated number of instructions executed when entering a function or a block (instructions of an edge). According to the experiments, the EIC for BOF can be about ten times larger than that in the native execution. If we detect the timing gap in a protected program, we acknowledge the existence of BOF and carry out mitigation techniques.

**Mitigation - Introduce Latency.** Due to the performance variation of the CPU, there will be false positives in the detection. A few portions of executions can have a relatively large timing gap, even if they are in the native environment. This usually happens when the CPU is conducting context switching, and extra overhead is counted as a part of the timing gap. According to our experiments, 0.03% of the executions are false positives in a stable environment, and the false-positive rate will be 0.1% in a busy environment where too many parallel tasks are executed simultaneously.

As a consequence, the mitigation mechanisms to fuzzing should be moderate in case the false positives affect regular users. We add a one-second latency to the program by triggering an IO blocking if the BOF instrumentation is detected. Although one second is insufficiently long for a fuzzer, the general effectiveness of the penalty can be guaranteed if we insert more than one detection function into the protected program.

**Examining Execution Frequency.** The nature of fuzzing is that the PUT will be re-executed a large number of times in a short period. This can be leveraged to detect whether the program is being fuzzed. We come up with the idea from "many a little makes a mickle". If the PUT leaves some vestiges every fuzzing round, the vestiges will accumulate during the fast re-executions. After a while, they grow large enough and inform the PUT that it is being fuzzed. In our design, the protected program creates a temporary file every time it runs. If more than 60 files are created in a minute (the threshold is according to configurations), the program will be alerted to the existence of a fuzzer. However, the challenge is that the program only creates the files, but it is difficult to manage them. It can be time-consuming to traverse the temporary files and check which are created by the protected program. Besides, not deleting them can mess up the file systems for regular users. To cope with this program, we find that the daemon process is suitable for the management of temporary files.

A daemon process is a process that runs as a background process. It detaches from the parent process and keeps running after the termination of its parent. We designed the daemon process to patrol the temporary files - to prevent the temporary files from being unintentionally deleted and delete them after the patrolling. The patrolling daemon process detaches itself from the protected program during the execution. A temporary file with an ID to indicate its order will be created by the daemon process. These files are created in ascending order, and the largest order is the detection threshold for fuzzers. It then locks the file for a period which we call "patrolling time". After the patroling, it checks whether the file it locks is correct and deletes the file it creates. The protected program seeks temporary files with the threshold order for every execution. Once the file is found, it means the program has been executed more than the threshold number of times in the patrolling time, and the BOF is likely to exist; so we can apply the mitigation techniques.

**Mitigation - Aborting Program.** Different from the timing gap, the results of the daemon process are accurate, and there are no false positives. We can adopt a more severe penalty in this method. The protected PUT can abort the execution or trigger an artificially inserted bug to misinform the crashes to fuzzers. To further avoid the mitigation strategy affecting the regular users in some unexpected situations, the developers can set a long patrolling time (5 min) and a large threshold (1000 files). Regular users can rarely execute the program at such a high frequency.

### 3.2 Active Methods: Minimum Fake Blocks

Existing fake blocks impede fuzzers at a non-optimal storage cost. ANTIFUZZ [16] (default configuration) introduces about 20 MB of anti-fuzzing codes, while based on the OSS-Fuzz [4] project, most commercial software occupies no more than 100 MB. Besides, small programs are more sensitive to storage costs and are hard to burden high storage costs. Unfortunately, they are more likely to be chosen as the fuzzing targets by attackers due to their faster execution speed and less program logic.

This defect comes to the fore as future fuzzers enhance the capability of fuzzing mechanisms (e.g., size of the bitmap) or improve fuzzing heuristics (e.g., scheduling seeds to avoid triggering anti-fuzzing mechanisms). Anti-fuzzing techniques have to insert more protection codes in proportion to the increased fuzzer capability to handle the intensified arms race. Under this condition, the fundamental storage overhead should be as low as possible; otherwise, the proportioned overhead needed in the arms race will be unsustainable.

The landing space is designed to minimize the extra storage overhead of fake blocks. Existing approaches pile up function calls and constraints, disturbing fuzzers at the function level, where one fake block takes up about nine bytes (one *cmp* and one *jmp* instructions). However, we observe that some of the storage overhead of fake blocks is unnecessary at the assembly level. For example, C compilers generate function frames for each function that controls the base pointer and stack pointer (e.g., *push ebp*). These assembly codes have nothing to do with anti-fuzzing, and eliminating these codes can further reduce the storage overhead.

As adversarial cannot retrieve the source codes of targets, they use BOF with the assistance of external tools to collect coverage feedback. These tools insert codes before entering a new block. If a control-flow-changing instruction (*jmp*, *call* and *ret*) is encountered, they generate a new block record as the updated coverage. Theoretically, the minimum block is the instruction only occupying one byte (opcode of the minimum size), which should be at most 15% (from nine bytes to one byte) of the storage cost of prior works. To achieve the minimum fake block, we instrument each function with a code segment called *landing space*. The landing space contains instructions that have no effect on the normal execution. They are either one-byte instructions or two-byte instructions with an immediate value which is the opcode of a one-byte instruction. This ensures that each byte in the landing space can be translated into a valid instruction.

We further modify the destination address of function calls to the address of a random byte in the landing space. The rationale is that when the modified

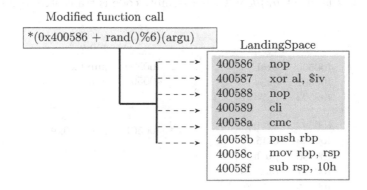

**Fig. 1.** A function with landing space.$iv is the immediate value, in this example, it will be $0 \times 90$ which is the opcode for nop.

function call is invoked, the control flow "land" at a random instruction. The fuzzer considers this instruction the start of a new block and records the address as new coverage. Since the control flow can "land" at any byte in the landing space, fuzzers will record most of the possible addresses after sufficient rounds of fuzzing. The corresponding fake coverage can overwhelm the fuzzer's bitmap.

Figure 1 illustrates the assembly codes of a function and the landing space. The original destination address of the function is $0x40058b$, and we insert the landing space before this address in the text section between $0x400586$ and $0x40058a$. The modified function call $(0x400586 + rand()\%6)$ jumps to the landing space or the original start of the function. In this example, a fuzzer will record six fake blocks at the cost of six bytes.

**Optimizations.** The naive implementation of the landing space seems able to disturb the coverage feedback of BOF. However, we found that the size of the landing space is restricted. A too large size introduces non-negligible latency to the protected program. Moreover, fuzzers like AFL calculate the hash value by exclusive-or operations on the addresses of two blocks. The problem is that the addresses of fake blocks in the landing space are close, and so are the calculated hash values. The chance of hash collision in the landing space is higher than that in normal functions. Intuitively, the more hash collisions happen in the landing space, the less bitmap can be saturated by fake blocks. In other words, the fuzzer will be more powerful in discovering real branches in the protected program. As a means of coping strategy, we propose two optimizations to mitigate the limitations.

**Jump Over Unnecessary Instructions.** If the control flow lands on the first few bytes in the landing space, it has to execute the rest instructions, which incurs significant latency for a large landing space. To avoid executing the unnecessary instructions, we modify some one-byte instructions to a short jump, and the jumping offset is the opcode of the next instruction. As shown in Fig. 2, if control flow lands at $0x400500$, the assembly code is translated as a two-byte

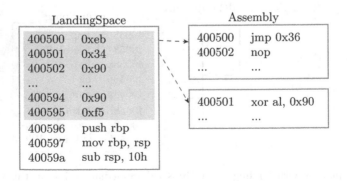

**Fig. 2.** Jump over unnecessary blocks

short jump with offset *0x36*. However, if it lands at the next byte *0x400501*, the corresponding assembly code is "xor al, 0x90". The functionality of the landing space still remains as every byte can be disassembled correctly and recorded as a new block. Yet the jump instructions reduce the performance overhead to 5% of the original landing space.

**Spray LandingSpace at Different Addresses.** To reduce the hash collision rates, we increase the blocks of different addresses. As shown in Fig. 2, we wrap functions in the original program with several intermediate blocks. The intermediate blocks only redirect the control flows in the protected binaries but have no effect on the program execution. We artificially keep wide disparities in the addresses of intermediate blocks; thus, these blocks are likely to generate more hash values than those generated from a single landing space. The size of the landing spaces in these functions is accordingly reduced, and they will be distributed to the intermediate blocks.

# 4 Evaluation

We evaluate No-Fuzz to answer the following four research questions (**RQs**):

- **RQ 1.** Can No-Fuzz hinder fuzzers from exploring new branches?
- **RQ 2.** How effective are the anti-fuzzing techniques at preventing fuzzers from finding bugs?
- **RQ 3.** What are the storage and performance overhead to deploy anti-fuzzing techniques?
- **RQ 4.** What is the suitable metric to compare different anti-fuzzing techniques?

For **RQ 1**, coverage is considered orthogonal to the bug-finding abilities of fuzzers [9]. The more coverage a fuzzer can reach, the more likely it finds bugs inside the target program. We evaluate the coverage reduction on real-world binaries after applying No-Fuzz to show the defense effectiveness of anti-fuzzing techniques. To stress **RQ 2**, we evaluate the anti-fuzzing techniques on the LAVA-M [13] benchmark and measure the shortest time needed to find a bug. The benchmark consists of four buggy binaries (base64, md5sum, who, uniq) with dozens to thousands of artificially inserted bugs.

The **RQ 3.** and **RQ 4.** are both related to the overhead evaluation of anti-fuzzing techniques. To answer **RQ 3.**, we evaluate the storage and performance overhead of anti-fuzzing techniques on real-world programs of different sizes. The **RQ 4.** is based on the concern that the overhead alone is not able to judge an anti-fuzzing technique comprehensively. The problem is that if the number of defensive codes added to the protected programs increases, the overhead is likely to increase accordingly. The defensive capability is orthogonal to the extra overhead as the more defensive codes are inserted into the protected binary, the safer it is able to be. Thus judging a defensive technique only based on one metric (anti-fuzzing effect or the overhead) is not enough. We suggest combining these two metrics and unifying the judging criteria of anti-fuzzing techniques by measuring the defensive ability at a unit cost of storage or execution rate. We define a new metric anti-fuzzing efficacy as the number of reduced branches per byte of extra storage cost and that per millisecond of latency. It measures the capability of anti-fuzzing techniques with respect to the introduced overhead.

In all experiments, the latency mitigation is set to be one second; the daemon process will patrol for one minute and alert if there are more than 60 times of executions; the landing space is configured to occupy 100 bytes, and the functions will be wrapped in 50 intermediate functions. AFL and AFL-based fuzzers (AFLFast and QSYM) use AFL-QEMU. HonggFuzz supports Intel-PT and QEMU, and we adopt both binary-only modes. Each fuzzing campaign runs with three CPU cores. Notably, QSYM runs two AFL instances with two CPU cores and an SMT solver using one core. Fuzzing campaigns on the LAVA-M dataset are kept running for 48 h, while the others last for 24 h. Due to the nondeterministic fuzzing behaviors, we repeat fuzzing campaigns ten times for each fuzzer x target combination.

## 4.1   Reducing Code Coverage

We evaluated the branch coverage of five fuzzers against eight real-world binaries from Binutils, Magma, and Google FTS. Figure 3 shows the average branches covered by each fuzzer on the binaries with and without No-Fuzz protection. Each technique is separately evaluated to avoid the effect of one technique covering up others. From the figure, the combo of all No-Fuzz techniques can severely hinder the branch explorations of fuzzers. The fuzzers can only discover 36.9% of branches on average that should have been, and most of the branches are just for initializations and input correctness checks.

A single passive detection technique reduces 34.8%–52.2% of the branch coverage. The effect variation of the detection should also be attributed to the choices of mitigation techniques and the difference in fuzzers. As the results show, aborting the PUT (the purple columnar) is more effective than introducing latency (the gray ones) to the protected programs. However, introducing latency affects users more slightly than aborting the program. This is the trade-off between effectiveness and impacts on users. It will be reckless to conclude that one mitigation technique outperforms the others. Our suggestion is to apply the more severe mitigation techniques to the more precise detection techniques.

The landing space hinders, on average, 32.4% of the branches. We observe that it is less effective against HonggFuzz. It is because Honggfuzz records the coverage in a temporary file and the size of the bitmap is 16 M, while the bitmap of AFL only occupies 64 K. We consider the current configuration of the landing space too small to saturate the bitmap of Honggfuzz. In the actual situation, the developers can configure a larger landing space for better protection against Honggfuzz.

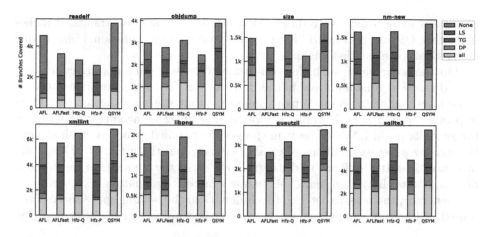

**Fig. 3.** Branch covered by four fuzzers against eight binaries with and without different protections. The techniques are Timing Gap, Daemon Process, Landing Space. The fuzzers are AFL, AFLFast, Honggfuzz-QEMU, Honggfuzz-PT, and QSYM .

## 4.2 Preventing Fuzzers from Finding Bugs

**LAVA-M Benchmark.** Despite many recent works suggesting using the up-to-date benchmarks in bug-finding experiments(e.g., Google fuzzer test suite [1] and Magma [18]), we find they are not suitable for the evaluation of BOF. The problem is that these benchmarks heavily rely on sanitizers, but unfortunately, most BOF techniques are not able to support sanitizers. There are some works like QEMU-AddressSanitizer [2] to fill the gap in BOF and sanitizers, but our evaluation covers different BOF techniques, and not all of them have such complementary tools. Due to this limitation, we decided to use LAVA-M, whose bugs directly trigger segmentation faults and can be caught by the BOF.

Moreover, the efficiency of BOF severely degrades compared with static instrumentation, which is almost a quarter of that of the latter. Even the LAVA-M benchmark contains thousands of bugs; only a few unique bugs can be uncovered for each buggy binary in BOF. Measuring the number of bugs found will be insignificant even though it is considered the ground truth for fuzzer evaluation. Instead of the number of bugs found, we measure the time that fuzzers need to find the first bug in each buggy binary within 48 h. This metric can better illustrate the bug-finding capabilities of BOF in the LAVA-M benchmark.

**Results.** The average time of five fuzzers to find one bug in the LAVA-M benchmark is shown in Table 1. From the table, we find that all fuzzers are able to find at least one bug in the unprotected programs in 48 h. Note that QSYM finds the bug in only several minutes, which is quite faster than other fuzzers. It can be attributed to the design of the LAVA-M benchmark. The bugs in LAVA-M are all designed based on an integer comparison. If an input can bypass the comparison, the corresponding bug will be triggered. This mechanism is essentially more beneficial to fuzzers that are able to solve constraints. It makes sense that QSYM , as a hybrid fuzzer, outperforms other mutational fuzzers due to its symbolic execution engine.

On the other hand, with the anti-fuzzing defenses, some fuzzing campaigns exceed the 48-h time limit and fail to find any bug. The rest campaigns uncover some bugs, but it takes much more time than that spent on the corresponding unprotected programs. Notably, we found Honggfuzz is incompatible with the target md5sum in LAVA-M as it misjudges the handled errors as crash signals. HonggFuzz generates millions of crash seed files, and the majority of them are false positives. It is difficult to distinguish the correct crash seeds in the millions of files, and we have to discard this fuzzer x target combination.

Generally, the passive detection techniques and the landing space successfully impede all fuzzing campaigns, as the time to find a bug extends after applying

**Table 1.** Time of fuzzers to find a bug in native and protected LAVA-M. $\sqrt{}$ means the fuzzing campaign fails to find a bug within 48 h.

| | native | TG | DP | LS | all |
|---|---|---|---|---|---|
| **base64** | | | | | |
| AFL | 12 h 54 m | $\sqrt{}$ | $\sqrt{}$ | $\sqrt{}$ | $\sqrt{}$ |
| AFLFast | 13 h 8 m | $\sqrt{}$ | $\sqrt{}$ | $\sqrt{}$ | $\sqrt{}$ |
| Hfz-QEMU | 1 h 22 m | $\sqrt{}$ | $\sqrt{}$ | $\sqrt{}$ | $\sqrt{}$ |
| Hfz-PT | 5 h 23 m | $\sqrt{}$ | $\sqrt{}$ | $\sqrt{}$ | $\sqrt{}$ |
| QSYM | 2 m | $\sqrt{}$ | $\sqrt{}$ | $\sqrt{}$ | $\sqrt{}$ |
| **md5sum** | | | | | |
| AFL | 36 h 32 m | $\sqrt{}$ | $\sqrt{}$ | $\sqrt{}$ | $\sqrt{}$ |
| AFLFast | 9 h 20 m | $\sqrt{}$ | $\sqrt{}$ | $\sqrt{}$ | $\sqrt{}$ |
| Hfz-QEMU | – | – | – | – | – |
| Hfz-PT | – | – | – | – | – |
| QSYM | 51 m | $\sqrt{}$ | $\sqrt{}$ | $\sqrt{}$ | $\sqrt{}$ |
| **who** | | | | | |
| AFL | 3 h 8 m | $\sqrt{}$ | $\sqrt{}$ | $\sqrt{}$ | $\sqrt{}$ |
| AFLFast | 6 h 37 m | $\sqrt{}$ | $\sqrt{}$ | $\sqrt{}$ | $\sqrt{}$ |
| Hfz-QEMU | 37 m | 2 h 9 m | $\sqrt{}$ | 6 h 32 m | $\sqrt{}$ |
| Hfz-PT | 4 h 31 m | 11 h 45 m | $\sqrt{}$ | $\sqrt{}$ | $\sqrt{}$ |
| QSYM | 1 m | $\sqrt{}$ | $\sqrt{}$ | $\sqrt{}$ | $\sqrt{}$ |
| **uniq** | | | | | |
| AFL | 7 h 19 m | $\sqrt{}$ | $\sqrt{}$ | $\sqrt{}$ | $\sqrt{}$ |
| AFLFast | 6 h 47 m | 23 h 59 m | $\sqrt{}$ | $\sqrt{}$ | $\sqrt{}$ |
| Hfz-QEMU | 4 m | 10 h 55 m | $\sqrt{}$ | 9 h 3 m | $\sqrt{}$ |
| Hfz-PT | 2 h 48 m | 16 h 20 m | $\sqrt{}$ | 17 h 56 m | $\sqrt{}$ |
| QSYM | 5 m | $\sqrt{}$ | $\sqrt{}$ | $\sqrt{}$ | $\sqrt{}$ |

these techniques. If all of the anti-fuzzing techniques in No-Fuzz are applied, none of the fuzzing campaigns can find a bug. Overall, the evaluation confirms that No-Fuzz is effective at preventing the BOF of different fuzzers from discovering bugs in the protected programs.

### 4.3   Performance and Storage Overhead of No-Fuzz

We are inspired by the fact that the size of input files can affect the performance overhead accordingly. Generally, a larger input will invoke more functions and be processed for a longer time. Considering the overhead of the landing space is also accordingly proportional to the functions executed, for fairness, we prepare two sets of input files. One set only contains small invalid files, which can fastly trigger errors in the programs, while the other set consists of valid samples of different sizes to trigger the normal functionalities. The results adopt the average time of the executions with both sets of input samples. Another consideration is that the overhead will be less significant for large and complex programs. The programs are categorized into two groups based on their size and average execution time to mitigate the bias in the evaluations, as shown in Appendix 6. The evaluation results of each group will be analyzed separately.

**Performance Overhead.** As shown in Table 2, the performance overhead for passive detection techniques is about 10–20% for small binaries and less than 1% for large binaries. Although the overhead is relatively large for small programs, the absolute latency is only around 5 ms, which is usually unnoticeable for regular users. The timing gap detection introduces a little more latency than the daemon process. We think it should be attributed to the false positives of the timing gap. Similarly, the landing space introduces the overhead proportioned to the size and complexity of the programs. Small programs incur 40% latency, while for large programs, the proportion decreases to 2%.

**Storage Overhead.** From Table 2, No-Fuzz introduces negligible storage overhead to protected binaries. The passive detection techniques take up storage ranging from about 1 KB to 50 KB (10 KB on average), but they are all less than 1% of the original size of the protected programs. The landing space inserts fake blocks according to the number of functions in the protected binary. Basically, the fewer functions in the original program, the less overhead it has. The storage cost can range from 0.3 MB to 1 MB (0.8 M on average) for different programs.

**Comparisons with Prior Works.** We evaluate the existing anti-coverage techniques in prior works to show that the landing space is worth it. The default configurations of ANTIFUZZ and FUZZIFICATION insert a fixed number of fake blocks; thus the storage overhead is stable - 20 MB for ANTIFUZZ and 1.2 MB for FUZZIFICATION . Clearly, both techniques take up more space than the landing space, and the storage advantage of No-Fuzz is more evident for small binaries due to the accordingly fewer fake blocks in smaller binaries. Note that the storage overhead of FUZZIFICATION is much smaller than that of ANTIFUZZ . However, according to our experiments (Appendix 4), we find the default configuration of the FUZZIFICATION is not enough to saturate the bitmaps of fuzzers. The real storage overhead of the effective configuration of FUZZIFICATION should be even larger than the current 1.2 MB.

**Table 2.** Overhead (CPU) of No-Fuzz and anti-coverage techniques of **A**NTIFUZZ and **F**UZZIFICATION on real-world programs.

| | TG | DP | LS | All | AF(cov) | FZ(cov) | Reference |
|---|---|---|---|---|---|---|---|
| **CPU** | | | | | | | |
| Small | 6.8 ms (21.4%) | 3.4 ms (10.6%) | 13.1 ms (40.9%) | 47.2 ms (147.5%) | 11.3 ms (35.3%) | 14.7 ms (45.9%) | 32.0 ms |
| Large | 23.5 ms (1.1%) | 10.7 ms (0.5%) | 43.8 ms (2.0%) | 64.7 ms (3.0%) | 15.6 ms (0.7%) | 44.6 ms (2.1%) | 2156.2 ms |
| **Storage** | | | | | | | |
| Small | 8.4 K (0.2%) | 10.5 K (0.3%) | 0.8 M (25.9%) | 1.1 M (35.3%) | 22.2 M (696.6%) | 1.25 M (39.1%) | 3.2 M |
| Large | 43.0 K (0.04%) | 27.1 K (0.02%) | 2.0 M (1.9%) | 2.4 M (2.2%) | 22.3 M (21.0%) | 1.27 M (1.2%) | 106.5 M |

### 4.4    Anti-fuzzing Efficacy

To compare the merits of different anti-fuzzing techniques, we introduce a new metric - anti-fuzzing efficacy. The efficacy illustrates the associations between the anti-fuzzing effects (coverage reduction) and storage/performance overhead. As anti-fuzzing techniques improve the defensive capability by inserting extra codes into the protected programs, more defensive codes promise more defensive effects. A well-designed anti-fuzzing technique should introduce as low overhead as possible while possessing effective defensive capability. The defense capability per unit storage/performance cost should be a better metric to describe the anti-fuzzing effects. Specifically, we calculate the efficacy by the number of coverage reductions every kilobyte of defensive codes and the reduction of every millisecond of latency. As a reference, we also calculate the efficacy of ANTIFUZZ and FUZZIFICATION based on the results in Appendix 4.

From Table 3, the passive detection techniques have both the highest performance and storage anti-fuzzing efficacy. Passive detection techniques are the most affordable anti-fuzzing techniques that can hinder the BOF at the lowest cost. Moreover, these techniques insert fixed defensive codes into the protected programs. Thus, the efficacy is stable and more or less has the same order of magnitude among all evaluated programs. The performance efficacy of the landing space is about 20% of the passive detection techniques, and the storage efficacy is much smaller (only about 1% of the passive detection methods). Despite the fact that the landing space seems to be less efficient, it can be deemed as a complement to the passive detection techniques. As we will discuss in Sect. 5, a single defensive technique is weak against adversaries, and it is worth the development of different techniques.

For reference, we evaluate the anti-coverage techniques of ANTIFUZZ and FUZZIFICATION . The performance efficacy of landing space and ANTIFUZZ is close, while FUZZIFICATION is inefficient due to the insufficient number of blocks. The storage efficacy of the landing space is 14–28 times that of these anti-coverage techniques, i.e., on average, we reduce about 95% of the initial storage cost. It illustrates that No-Fuzz is more practical, which can better utilize the storage while keeping adequate anti-fuzzing protection.

**Table 3.** Space and performance efficacy of different anti-fuzzing techniques against four fuzzers.

|  | TG | DP | LS | All | AF(cov) | FZ(cov) |
|---|---|---|---|---|---|---|
| **Performance (#branches/ms)** | | | | | | |
| AFL | 183.9 | 559.3 | 84.2 | 46.6 | 144.1 | 11.5 |
| AFLFast | 165.0 | 509.3 | 61.9 | 42.3 | 121.7 | 5.3 |
| Hfz-Q | 158.5 | 530.1 | 86.2 | 47.0 | 133.9 | 17.0 |
| Hfz-P | 134.5 | 428.4 | 62.6 | 36.9 | 91.9 | 5.0 |
| QSYM | 226.8 | 684.9 | 120.7 | 58.6 | 174.6 | 14.8 |
| Avg | 173.7 | 542.4 | 83.1 | 46.3 | 133.2 | 10.7 |
| **Storage (#branches/kB)** | | | | | | |
| AFL | 148.8 | 181.1 | 1.4 | 2.0 | 0.07 | 0.14 |
| AFLFast | 133.6 | 164.9 | 1.0 | 1.8 | 0.06 | 0.15 |
| Hfz-Q | 128.3 | 171.6 | 1.4 | 2.0 | 0.07 | 0.20 |
| Hfz-P | 108.9 | 138.7 | 1.0 | 1.6 | 0.05 | 0.06 |
| QSYM | 183.6 | 221.8 | 2.0 | 2.5 | 0.09 | 0.17 |
| Avg | 140.6 | 175.6 | 1.4 | 2.0 | 0.07 | 0.14 |

## 5 Discussion

While our design performs effectively and efficiently, it could be further improved. We consider our design a complement to prior works, and we appreciate some designs in prior works which also deserve adoption in the future development of anti-fuzzing tools (e.g., installing the signal handler to hide crashes). We will also stress these concerns in our discussion. In the following, we will discuss the robustness of the anti-fuzzing technique and the advantages of anti-fuzzing over obfuscation because the potential inherent problems (i.e., robustness) and the seemingly possibility that they can be substituted by obfuscation techniques in certain cases.

**Robustness of Anti-fuzzing Techniques.** A primary concern about anti-fuzzing is its robustness. In particular, a dedicated attacker can perform manual analysis to disarm the defense if the details are known, and several prior works suggested applying obfuscation techniques as a countermeasure against reverse engineering. However, for experienced attackers, obfuscation techniques can also be disarmed. We want to reflect the necessity for anti-fuzzing techniques to be robust against manual analysis. Anti-fuzzing techniques are proposed to introduce extra efforts (time, resources, knowledge, etc.) adversaries need to fuzz a protected program. Particularly, they are suitable to defend the untargeted fuzzing tasks on a large scale that are not worth enough to analyze a single binary for attackers manually. Moreover, anti-fuzzing techniques enhance the basic requirements of BOF, from knowing nothing to at least understanding anti-fuzzing and reverse-engineering techniques. The defensive techniques can further reduce the chance that protected binaries are chosen as the targets of BOF. Due to the above reasons, we consider that reverse engineering does not contradict the ultimate purpose of anti-fuzzing techniques.

**Anti-fuzzing or Obfuscation.** Obfuscation is originally considered a potential solution to anti-fuzzing. Compared with the emerging anti-fuzzing techniques, it is well-developed with profound community support. Prior works have conducted some experiments to show the ineffectiveness of obfuscation in anti-fuzzing [16, 21]. However, we will revise their arguments with more experiments and show that obfuscation techniques can be effective at times.

In fact, there are already obfuscation techniques designed to confront symbolic executions, which are similar to anti-hybrid techniques [6,34]. In addition, the obfuscation techniques involving self-modifying codes can be even more powerful against BOF. The self-modifying code is a common technique used in packing and encryption. It reuses the memory space by overwriting the existing opcodes with those of new instructions. The problem is that no matter how many functions are overwritten to a self-modifying block, they possess the same memory address. Most fuzzers record the hash values of function block addresses, and the self-modifying block will be identified as only one function; thus, the coverage information of overwritten functions is lost.

We have conducted some experiments with BOF and dummy programs where the programs are protected by self-modifying codes. The results (appendix 7 and 7) show that BOF cannot be correctly performed on the program with self-modifying codes. Besides, [26] shows that self-modifying codes will severely slow down the translations in emulators, which confirms the anti-fuzzing effectiveness of obfuscation against BOF like `afl-qemu` and `honggfuzz-qemu`. Fortunately, self-modifying codes are usually not welcomed by developers. Commercial software rarely uses self-modifying codes due to the possibility of false positives as malicious attempts and the new bugs introduced by risky modifications. Overall, anti-fuzzing techniques cover the shortage of static obfuscation techniques against fuzzers, and we argue that future anti-fuzzing works should be designed in the scope of static techniques without self-modifying codes.

**Future Work.** We consider that the future work of anti-fuzzing can focus on the following two aspects. On the one hand, we can keep reducing the overhead for existing anti-fuzzing techniques, which increases the number of defensive codes inserted into a program in a disguised way. A possible direction is that the anti-hybrid techniques in prior works are overqualified to disturb the program analysis. They use cryptography functions (e.g., hash, CRC) to wrap the variables. We have conducted some experiments, and it turns out that only hundreds of calculations are enough to overwhelm the symbolic executions, and they are cheaper than the heavy cryptography functions. On the other hand, future anti-fuzzing works can embed anti-fuzzing mechanisms into the program logic. For instance, similar to the flatten technique in obfuscation, we can split a block into several new blocks, and each new block contains a part of the assembly codes of the original block. Thus, each new block is logically dependent on the program and cannot be easily eliminated. Indeed, there are some challenges that need to be solved for this idea, e.g., how to maintain the context among different blocks and how to ensure the number of fake blocks is large enough.

## 6  Conclusion

In this paper, we design several practical and fully-automated anti-fuzzing techniques and integrate them into a prototype tool No-Fuzz. We optimize the storage cost of fake blocks as prior works insert them at the function level occupying an unrealistic storage room. In addition to the active anti-fuzzing techniques that disturb the fuzzing mechanisms, we also design the passive detection methods which precisely determine the running environments of the protected programs and launch mitigation techniques when binary-only-fuzzing exists. The evaluations demonstrate that No-Fuzz significantly reduces the branch coverage of fuzzers. Furthermore, we have also shown that No-Fuzz can impede bug findings in the LAVA-M dataset, i.e., fuzzers have to spend much more time finding a bug. We propose a new metric, the anti-fuzzing efficacy, to measure the defensive capability of an anti-fuzzing technique at a unit overhead cost. Based on this metric, we illustrate that No-Fuzz achieves the same or higher level of protection against fuzzers with even lower overhead than prior works.

In summary, we enhance the awareness of overhead and the importance of automation in an anti-fuzzing arms race. Inspired by this, we summarize the desired properties for future anti-fuzzing techniques - be with less overhead and automated. We have moved one step toward practical anti-fuzzing techniques and hope our efforts can further promote this topic.

**Acknowledgements.** This work was supported by the Research Grants Council of Hong Kong under Grants CityU 11217819, 11217620, 11218521, N_CityU139/21, RFS2122-1S04, C2004-21GF, R1012-21, and R6021-20F.

# A   Appendix

(See Tables 4, 5, 6, 7 and 8)

**Table 4.** The branch coverage of ANTIFUZZ and FUZZIFICATION

|  | readelf | objdump | size | nm | xmllint | libpng | gueutzli | sqlite3 |
|---|---|---|---|---|---|---|---|---|
| **AFL** | | | | | | | | |
| AF(cov) | 1745 | 1449 | 839 | 706 | 1691 | 919 | 2103 | 3840 |
| FZ(cov) | 4498 | 2630 | 1247 | 1529 | 5556 | 1702 | 2805 | 4994 |
| **AFLFast** | | | | | | | | |
| AF(cov) | 1913 | 1345 | 656 | 774 | 1503 | 958 | 2207 | 3757 |
| FZ(cov) | 3383 | 2848 | 1102 | 1411 | 5463 | 1492 | 2727 | 5065 |
| **Hfz-Q** | | | | | | | | |
| AF(cov) | 1049 | 875 | 622 | 894 | 4117 | 1073 | 2499 | 4103 |
| FZ(cov) | 2422 | 2812 | 1277 | 1523 | 6122 | 1996 | 3040 | 6144 |
| **Hfz-P** | | | | | | | | |
| AF(cov) | 1884 | 1067 | 899 | 632 | 3555 | 788 | 1931 | 3097 |
| FZ(cov) | 2612 | 2374 | 1148 | 1190 | 5312 | 1540 | 2563 | 4833 |
| **QSYM** | | | | | | | | |
| AF(cov) | 1946 | 1276 | 814 | 932 | 4255 | 1287 | 2493 | 4441 |
| FZ(cov) | 5072 | 3731 | 1448 | 1740 | 6442 | 2084 | 3538 | 7433 |

**Table 5.** The overhead comparisons between upx and existing anti-fuzzing techniques. As emphasized in the table, the overhead of existing anti-fuzzing techniques is more or less close to that of packing techniques.

|  | readelf | objdump |
|---|---|---|
| Exec time | 125.4 ms | 2156.2 ms |
| upx | **+13.0%** | +24.3% |
| AF(cov) | +37.7% | **+2.0%** |
| FZ(cov) | +32.9% | +14.6% |
| Storage cost | 3.22 M | 9.94 M |
| upx | **−2.24 M (−69.6%)** | **−7.44 M (−74.8%)** |
| AF(cov) | 21.27 M (+660.6%) | 21.25 M (+213.8%) |
| FZ(cov) | 1.29 M (+40.1%) | 1.28 M (+12.9%) |

**Table 6.** Real-world programs of different size and execution time.

| size & exec time | files |
|---|---|
| Small | readelf, objdump, size, nm guetzli, libpng, sqlite3, xmllint |
| Large | ffmpeg_g, nomacs, calc, impress |

**Table 7.** We fuzz a dummy program as well as the obfuscated versions. The dummy program contains several magic-byte checks and will crash if the constraints are satisfied. Tigrees(S) only applies static obfuscation, while Tigrees(D) adopts self-modifying codes which are dynamic.

| | First crash | Fuzz rate |
|---|---|---|
| Native | 45 s | 1805 exc/s |
| UPX | 1 m 27 s | 1800 exc/s |
| Tigress(D) | $+\infty$ | 0 exc/s |
| Tigrees(S) | 2 m 4 s | 1667 exc/s |
| llvm-obfuscator | 1 m 48 s | 1400 exc/s |

**Table 8.** Evaluations to launch BOF on obfuscated/packed binaries. $\times$ means BOF cannot initialize on the binary within 30 min for all four fuzzers. $\sqrt{}$ means all fuzzers succeed in launching the BOF. As the table suggests, self-modifying codes (upx & obfuscation with JIT) can completely prevent the BOF from initialization.

| | native | upx | llvm-obf | Tigress (D) | Tigress (S) |
|---|---|---|---|---|---|
| dummy | $\sqrt{}$ | $\sqrt{}$ | $\sqrt{}$ | $\times$ | $\sqrt{}$ |
| binutlls | $\sqrt{}$ | $\times$ | $\sqrt{}$ | $\times$ | $\sqrt{}$ |
| libjpeg | $\sqrt{}$ | $\times$ | $\sqrt{}$ | $\times$ | $\sqrt{}$ |
| libpng | $\sqrt{}$ | $\times$ | $\sqrt{}$ | $\times$ | $\sqrt{}$ |
| libtiff | $\sqrt{}$ | $\times$ | $\sqrt{}$ | $\times$ | $\sqrt{}$ |
| ffmpeg | $\sqrt{}$ | $\times$ | $\sqrt{}$ | $\times$ | $\sqrt{}$ |
| gzip | $\sqrt{}$ | $\times$ | $\sqrt{}$ | $\times$ | $\sqrt{}$ |

# References

1. Binary-only fuzzing of honggfuzz. https://github.com/google/fuzzer-test-suite. Accessed 12 Mar 2022
2. QASan (QEMU-AddressSanitizer). https://github.com/andreafioraldi/qasan. Accessed 12 Mar 2021
3. A library for coverage-guided fuzz testing. https://llvm.org/docs/LibFuzzer.html (2017)Accessed 23 Oct 2020
4. Aizatsky, M., Serebryany, K., Chang, O., Arya, A.: Announcing oss-fuzz: continuous fuzzing for open source software. Google Testing Blog, Announcing OSS-Fuzz (2016)

5. Balzarotti, D., et al.: Efficient detection of split personalities in malware. In: Proceedings of the NDSS (2010)
6. Banescu, S., Collberg, C., Ganesh, V., Newsham, Z., Pretschner, A.: Code obfuscation against symbolic execution attacks. In: Proceedings of the ACSAC (2016)
7. Böhme, M., Pham, V.-T., Roychoudhury, A.: Coverage-based greybox fuzzing as Markov chain. In: Proceedings of the ACM CCS (2016)
8. Böhme, M., Pham, V.-T., Nguyen, M.-D., Roychoudhury, A.: Directed greybox fuzzing. In: Proceedings of the ACM CCS (2017)
9. Böhme, M., Szekeres, L., Metzman, J.: On the reliability of coverage-based fuzzer benchmarking. In: Proceedings of the IEEE ICSE (2022)
10. Chen, H., et al.: Hawkeye: towards a desired directed grey-box fuzzer. In: Proceedings of the ACM CCS (2018)
11. Chen, Y., et al.: SAVIOR: towards bug-driven hybrid testing. In: Proceedings of the IEEE S&P (2020)
12. Dinesh, S., Burow, N., Xu, D., Payer, M.: RetroWrite: statically instrumenting cots binaries for fuzzing and sanitization. In: Proceedings of the IEEE S&P (2020)
13. Dolan-Gavitt, B.: LAVA: large-scale automated vulnerability addition. In: Proceedings of the IEEE S&P (2016)
14. Google: A scalable fuzzing infrastructure. https://github.com/google/clusterfuzz. Accessed 23 Oct 2020
15. Google: syzkaller found bugs - Linux kernel. https://github.com/google/syzkaller/blob/master/docs/linux/found_bugs.md
16. Güler, E., Aschermann, C., Abbasi, A., Holz, T.: ANTIFUZZ: impeding fuzzing audits of binary executables. In: Proceedings of the USENIX Security (2019)
17. Hafiz, M., Fang, M.: Game of detections: how are security vulnerabilities discovered in the wild? In: Proceedings of ACM ESE (2015)
18. Hazimeh, A., Herrera, A., Payer, M.: Magma: a ground-truth fuzzing benchmark. In: Proceedings of ACM Measurement and Analysis of Computing Systems (2020)
19. Zhenghao, H., Yu, H., Dolan-Gavitt, B.: Chaff bugs: deterring attackers by making software buggier. arXiv (2018)
20. Huang, H., Yao, P., Wu, R., Shi, Q., Zhang, C.: Pangolin: Incremental hybrid fuzzing with polyhedral path abstraction. In: Proceedings of IEEE S&P (2020)
21. Jung, J., Hong, H., Solodukhin, D., Pagan, D., Hyung Lee, K., Kim, T.: Fuzzification: anti-fuzzing techniques. In: Proceedings of USENIX Security (2019)
22. Kang, M.G., Yin, H., Hanna, S., McCamant, S., Song, D.: Emulating emulation-resistant malware. In: Proceedings of ACM Workshop on Virtual Machine Security (2009)
23. Lemieux, C., Sen, K.: Fairfuzz: A targeted mutation strategy for increasing greybox fuzz testing coverage. In: Proceedings of the ACM/IEEE ASE (2018)
24. Lindorfer, M., Kolbitsch, C., Comparetti, P.M.: Detecting environment-sensitive malware. In: Proceedings of the International Workshop on Recent Advances in Intrusion Detection (2011)
25. Miller, B.P., Fredriksen, L., So, B.: An empirical study of the reliability of unix utilities. In: Proceedings of the ACM Communication (1990)
26. Raffetseder, T., Kruegel, C., Kirda, E.: Detecting system emulators. In: Proceedings of the International Conference on Information Security (2007)
27. Rash, M.: A collection of vulnerabilities discovered by the afl fuzzer. https://github.com/mrash/afl-cve. Accessed 13 Sept 2020
28. Rawat, S., et al.: Application-aware evolutionary fuzzing. In: Proceedings of the NDSS, Vuzzer (2017)

29. Schumilo, S., Aschermann, C., Gawlik, R., Schinzel, S., Holz, T: KAFL: Hardware-assisted feedback fuzzing for OS kernels. In: Proceedings of the USENIX Security (2017)
30. Stephens, N., et al.: Driller: augmenting fuzzing through selective symbolic execution. In: Proceedings of the NDSS (2016)
31. Swiecki, R.: Honggfuzz (2020). https://github.com/google/honggfuzz
32. Votipka, D., Stevens, R., Redmiles, E., Hu, J., Mazurek, M.: Hackers vs. testers: a comparison of software vulnerability discovery processes. In: Proceedings of the IEEE S&P (2018)
33. Wang, T., Wei, T., Gu, G., Zou, W.: TaintScope: a checksum-aware directed fuzzing tool for automatic software vulnerability detection. In: Proceedings of the IEEE S&P (2010)
34. Wang, Z., Ming, J., Jia, C., Gao, D.: Linear obfuscation to combat symbolic execution. In: Proceedings of the ESORICS (2011)
35. Yun, I., Lee, S., Xu, M., Jang, Y., Kim, T.: QSYM: a practical concolic execution engine tailored for hybrid fuzzing. In: Proceedings of USENIX Security (2018)
36. Zalewski, M.: American fuzzy lop (2019). http://lcamtuf.coredump.cx/afl
37. Zalewski, M.: Technical "whitepaper" for afl-fuzz (2019). http://lcamtuf.coredump.cx/afl/technical_details.txt
38. Zhang, Z., You, W., Tao, G., Aafer, Y., Liu, X., Zhang, X.: STOCHFUZZ: sound and cost-effective fuzzing of stripped binaries by incremental and stochastic rewriting. In: Proceedings of IEEE S&P (2021)

# eSROP Attack: Leveraging Signal Handler to Implement Turing-Complete Attack Under CFI Defense

Tianning Zhang[1,2]([⊠]), Miao Cai[2,3,4], Diming Zhang[5], and Hao Huang[1,2]

[1] Department of Computer Science and Technology,
Nanjing University, Nanjing, China
[2] State Key Laboratory for Novel Software Technology,
Nanjing University, Nanjing, China
zhangtianning128@126.com
[3] Key Laboratory of Water Big Data Technology of Ministry of Water Resources,
Hohai University, Nanjing, China
[4] School of Computer and Information, Hohai University, Nanjing, China
[5] College of Computer Engineering, Jiangsu University of Science and Technology,
Nanjing, China

**Abstract.** Signal Return Oriented Programming (SROP) is a dangerous code reuse attack method. Recently, defense techniques have been proposed to defeat SROP attacks. In this paper, we leverage the signal nesting mechanism provided by current operating systems and propose a new variant of SROP attack called enhanced SROP (eSROP) attack. eSROP provides the ability of invoking arbitrary system calls, simulating Turing-complete computation, and even bypassing the fine-grained label-based CFI defense, without modifying the return address and instruction register in the signal frame. Because the signal returns to the interrupted instruction, the shadow stack defense can hardly detect our attack. Signal has strong flexibility which can interrupt the normal control flow. We leverage such flexibility to design a new code reuse attack. To evaluate eSROP, we perform two exploits on two real-world programs, namely Proftpd and Wu-ftpd. In our attacks, adversaries can invoke arbitrary system calls and obtain a root shell. Both attacks succeed within 10 min under strict system defense such as data execution prevention, address space layout randomization, and coarse-grained control flow integrity.

**Keywords:** Code reuse attack · SROP · Signal security

## 1 Introduction

Code reuse attacks [25] are still the major attack means nowadays. Among them, sigreturn-oriented programming [5] is a powerful attack technique. It overwrites the return address on the stack to invoke the *sigreturn* system call and prepares a counterfeit signal frame on the stack to manipulate the rip register's value.

© ICST Institute for Computer Sciences, Social Informatics and Telecommunications Engineering 2023
Published by Springer Nature Switzerland AG 2023. All Rights Reserved
F. Li et al. (Eds.): SecureComm 2022, LNICST 462, pp. 752–769, 2023.
https://doi.org/10.1007/978-3-031-25538-0_39

After the *sigreturn* function's invocation, the control flow will transfer to an arbitrary location with an arbitrary register context.

SROP attack has been greatly restricted by several proposed defenses. For example, the signal cookies [3] method uses the kernel to insert a secret value into the signal frame to detect whether the signal frame has been tampered with. This is analogous to stack canary [2].

Another method that PiCFI [24] and MCFI [23] use to mitigate SROP attacks is to inline *sigreturn* system calls into each signal handler, and make the *sigreturn* system call unreachable from other application code. As a result, attackers need to trigger real signals to execute the *sigreturn* system call. From the authors' perspective, the attackers may have to either exploit a buggy signal handler to corrupt the saved thread context or use other threads to concurrently and reliably modify the signal handling thread's saved context. And neither of them they believe is easy since signal handlers rarely have complex code and usually do not run for an extended period of time [24].

However, it is still possible for attackers to conduct attacks by leveraging signal handlers to modify the signal frame. In this paper, we deeply investigate the signal handlers of real-world programs and find that many of them can be leveraged by attackers. Although they usually do not contain normal vulnerabilities, we can leverage them by doing some minor changes, such as overwriting the GOT table entry. Hence we propose eSROP (enhanced sigreturn-oriented programming) attack. It is a more dangerous variant of SROP attack. It can survive under defenses that are proposed to prevent traditional SROP attacks, such as signal cookies [3] or control flow integrity [1].

Our attack method is as follows. We send a signal when the program is executing some security-critical instructions. The signal handler leaks the currently executed instruction address. The attacker decides whether the interrupted instruction is the target one. If it is, the attacker sends the second signal. The same signal handler responses. This time, it overwrites the signal frame on the stack. Then the signal returns to the interrupted instruction to continue execution. However, with a different register context, the instruction will do completely different work. The core idea is still overwriting the signal frame. However, we do not directly overwrite the control data, such as the *rip* register's value. We only modify other general registers' values. So the control flow is preserved, but the data flow is changed. We do not violate backward edge protection, so strong defenses such as shadow stack [6] can hardly detect our attack.

Depending on the type of interrupted instructions, there are three cases. When the interrupted instruction (interrupted by the signal) is a *syscall* instruction, the attacker can invoke an arbitrary system call instead of the original one. Because the syscall number is stored in the *rax* register, which has been manipulated by our attack.

When the interrupted instruction is a DOP gadget [16], the attacker can leverage the gadget to implement Turing-complete computation. Original DOP attack [16] requires dispatcher gadget to connect DOP gadgets. But our attack removes this pre-requisite for using the DOP gadget. We use signals to connect different gadgets and implement complex semantics.

When the interrupted instruction is the CFI verification code, the attacker can even bypass fine-grained label-based CFI protection [1]. Since the signal handler can manipulate the verification result by modifying the general registers, the program will finally be fooled to jump to an attacker-controlled area. Most attacks [10,14] on CFI leverage the implementation defect of it. However, we show that the more fatal problem of CFI is that it cannot defend against signal attacks. Because signal can cause unexpected control flow transfer.

We build two end-to-end exploits to demonstrate the concrete techniques to construct eSROP attacks. In our first Proftpd attack, we show how to attack, show how to leverage the original signal handler to obtain arbitrary system calls invocation primitive, and finally get a shell. Our second Wu-ftpd attack exhibits how to obtain a root shell when we do not directly use the original signal handler. We manipulate the program memory and register a new signal handler for usage. Both of our exploits work reliably with ASLR and DEP defenses turned on and assuming the coarse-grained CFI defense [31] in place. As a consequence, we suggest that defenders should consider the security of signal processing more seriously.

## 2    Background and Assumptions

### 2.1    ROP Attack

Return Oriented Programming [25] attack reuses code snippets in the victim program to perform malicious behavior instead of injecting malicious code. It is a kind of control flow attack which diverts the victim program's execution flow. It has been popular for decades and has lots of variants.

### 2.2    SROP Attack

Sigreturn Oriented Programming [5] is one of the variants of ROP attacks. It is an attack that is related to signals. It leverages the *sigreturn* system call which is invoked when the signal returns. The attacker sets up a fake signal frame on the stack and invokes *sigreturn*. When the *sigreturn* gets executed, it treats the fake signal frame as the signal interrupted context and uses it to restore all the registers' values.

### 2.3    Attack Assumptions

In this paper, we assume a powerful yet realistic threat model. We assume the attacker can obtain arbitrary read/write primitive through the vulnerability. In practice, many vulnerabilities equip the attacker with this kind of ability, such as CVE-2017-7184, CVE-2017-0143, CVE-2016-4117, and CVE-2015-0057. This assumption is the same as other ROP attacks [11,13,27,28]. Then we assume the attacker can send signals to the victim program. It is easy to achieve in local attacks. In this paper, we mainly discuss local attacks, but our method can also be applied to remote attacks. We leave this as future work. This assumption is similar to other signal attacks [7,32]. Once we can send signals, we can finally obtain a root shell.

We also assume that the system is under the following protections. Data execution prevention [12] is deployed in the system. The process is running with non-executable data and non-writable code. Address Space Layout Randomization [20] is also applied in the target system. Since the ASLR defense is enabled, the starting addresses of all the libraries and heap and stack are randomized in each execution. But the text and data segments are always mapped to the same memory addresses. At the same time, coarse-grained CFI defense [31] is in use. An indirect call or jump can go to any function's starting address. Returns should go back to any return address, i.e. an instruction following a call. When we discuss our attack to bypass label-based CFI defense [1] in Sect. 3.3, we assume fine-grained CFI [1] is in use.

Finally, we assume the program is dynamically linked and the GOT table is not under protection.

## 3    eSROP Attack Method

In this section, we illustrate the techniques of enhanced Sigreturn-oriented Programming attack.

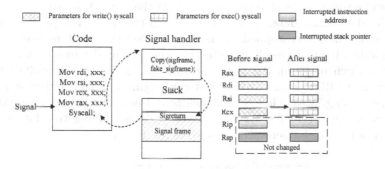

**Fig. 1.** Attack procedure on modifying the signal frame. When the signal returns, the program execute *exec*() system call instead of *write*() system call.

### 3.1    Invoke Arbitrary System Call

In the following, we will demonstrate how to invoke arbitrary system call under coarse-grained CFI defense [31].

Our attack is based on the following facts. First, in a normal program, library functions will always be invoked several times. Some of these library functions will invoke the system call. Second, signals can arrive at any time during the program's execution. If the victim process is executing in userspace (not executing kernel code), and the signal is not blocked by the process. The signal can immediately interrupt the process, and divert the control flow to execute the corresponding signal handler. Third, signal handlers are executed in userspace. They can modify the values on the user stack. Forth, the signal frame is stored on the user stack. The signal frame is used to store the process context (all the register values) that was interrupted by the signal. when the signal returns, the process uses the values in the signal frame to restore all the registers and continues to execute the interrupted instruction.

As shown in Fig. 1, we exploit the timing of a program executing instructions right before the *syscall* instruction and right after the register setting instructions. This timing is transient but it widely exists in a program's execution. We need to capture the timing to send the signal and make the signal arrives just at the point. Then, in the signal handler, we overwrite the signal frame that was stored on the stack to modify the system call number and all the parameters reserved in general registers. When the signal returns, the program will continue to execute the *syscall* instruction. Now we successfully tamper with the system call that the program originally intended to execute and invoke an arbitrary system call.

*Compared with SROP:* SROP directly modifies the return address to the address of the *sigreturn* function and prepares a fake signal frame on the stack. When the vulnerable function returns, it will invoke the *sigreturn*. This is not the normal execution flow, so it can be easily detected. However, in eSROP, we leverage the signal handler to tamper with the on-stack signal frame. eSROP sends the signal and returns to the sigreturn as usual. At the same time, we do not directly overwrite the control data, such as the *rip* register value. The program returns to the point where it is stopped by the signal. The reason is if we modify the *rip* register value, it can be easily detected by other strong defenses such as shadow stack [6], which backs up the return address in a safe area. So eSROP is more stealthy than SROP attack. We do not cause abnormal control transfer during signal processing. Meanwhile, our attack is still powerful, it gives attackers the ability to invoke arbitrary system calls by only modifying the data that the program process to influence the execution result.

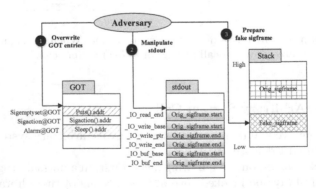

**Fig. 2.** Attack steps that adversary takes to leverage original signal handler. Note that, the *stdout._IO_write_ptr* is first set to *Orig_sigframe.end*. After the *puts()* function's first execution, it will automatically adjust to point to *Orig_sigframe.start*.

*Details:* In this attack procedure, there exist some problems to be solved. First, how to capture the timing of sending the signal. Maybe we need to implement a highly precise timer to stop the program at any instructions. Second, we need a signal handler to overwrite the signal frame which is usually not the intended work that a signal handler will do.

We solve the first problem by sending a lot of signals to the target process. Since the timing is transient and difficult to catch in one shot, we send lots of signals. After a few seconds, one of the signals will hit the target instruction. The signal handler will decide whether the instruction pointer that was interrupted by the signal equals the target. If it is, the signal handler covers the signal frame on the stack. When the signal returns, the program will execute the *exec()* system call. Finally, we will successfully obtain a shell.

To solve the second problem, people may think we must register a new signal handler to implement the semantics. The original signal handler is not designed for this purpose, so it is useless. However, when we thoroughly investigate the signal handler of many real-world programs. We surprisingly find that many of them can be leveraged by attackers, and some of them can even be directly used. This means that we need not install a new signal handler, just leverage the one that the program originally registered. It seems difficult, but we show that by exploiting the *puts()* function, we can overcome all the difficulties (as shown in Fig. 2).

In the following, we will demonstrate two approaches for two different cases. In the first case, the signal handler in the program can be directly used. In the second case, the signal handler in the program cannot be used by the attacker. We show how to conduct attacks in each of these cases.

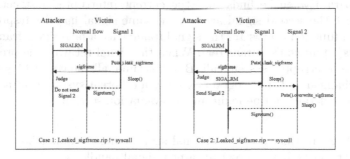

**Fig. 3.** Attack procedure on sending signals. The attacker decides whether to send the second signal depending on the *leaked_sigframe.rip* value.

**Approach 1.** In this case, the signal handler can be directly used. People may wonder why this happens. We will show that attackers can achieve this by doing some minor changes to the GOT table entries. At the same time, the signal handler must meet some conditions.

First, in the signal handler, there must be a GOT function that has at least one parameter and the first parameter is an address. The address must point to an area that the attacker can modify. This GOT function will later be replaced by the *puts*() function. Second, in the signal handler, there must be another GOT function that has at least one parameter and the first parameter is an integer. This GOT function will later be replaced by *sleep*() or *usleep*() function.

These conditions are easy to meet. Since some normal signal handlers always re-install the same signal handler for usage the next time, they will invoke the *sigaction*() function to register the current function again. Before the *sigaction*() function's execution, the program usually prepares a *sigaction* structure and calls another function *sigemptyset*(). This function meets our first condition. It has one parameter and the parameter points to the data on the stack. The data is stored on the lower stack. It has not been used and is not initialized. Attackers can easily control the value in it.

The second condition is also easy to meet. For example, in the signal handler of *SIGALRM* signal, it is normal to invoke the *alarm*() function. This function is a library function. The program invokes it by looking up GOT table. It has one parameter and the parameter is an integer. We can modify the *alarm*() function's address in the GOT table to change it to the *sleep*() function. When the program invokes the *alarm*() function, it executes the *sleep*() function.

As a whole, we need the signal handler to execute the *puts*() function and *sleep*() function. And *puts*() is executed before *sleep*() function. The reason we choose these two functions is that we leverage the *puts*() function to first leak the signal frame on the stack. The leaked information contains the current interrupted instruction pointer, the attacker observes this value and decides whether it is the target instruction (*syscall* instruction). The *sleep*() function is used to wait for the attacker's second signal. The attacker will send the second signal to the program when he finds that the current interrupted instruction is the target. Once the second signal arrives, the same signal handler responds. This time *puts*() function overwrites the signal frame with a fake signal frame (stored in the *puts*() function's parameter). When the signal returns, the program will execute the interrupted system call. But this time, all the general registers' values have changed and the program executes a different system call (as shown in Fig. 3). More details can be found in the evaluation section.

**Approach 2.** In this case, the original signal handler cannot be leveraged by the attacker. So we have to register a new signal handler.

When the signal handler does not meet the requirements shown in approach 1, the attacker can turn to approach 2 to overcome the problem. In this approach, we don't make any assumptions about the original signal handler. We just do not use it and leverage *sigaction*() function to register a new signal handler. However, the *sigaction*() is usually called before the program begins handling requests. So most of the time, we cannot directly leverage the *sigaction*() function. We can leverage other frequently called functions, which have a similar parameter type and number with *sigaction*(). We modify their GOT entries and change their parameters to invoke *sigaction*() to install a new signal handler.

People may wonder whether this kind of GOT function exists. In practice, we find that it is not difficult to find this kind of function. For example, the *sigprocmask*() function has similar parameters as the *sigaction*(). The value of *SIG_UNBLOCK* is *0x1*, which corresponds to the *SIGHUP* signal number. The *SIGHUP* is a signal that can be registered by users. The second parameter is usually a global variable. With the arbitrary write primitive, we can easily manipulate its value. We can construct a *sigaction* structure on it.

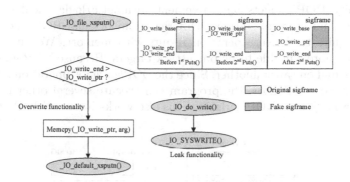

**Fig. 4.** Puts() function's functionality. The puts() function's first execution implements leakage, and its second execution implements overwritten.

**Discussion:** Here we leverage signal nesting to achieve our goal. We use the *puts*() function twice but exploits its different functionalities. For the first time, *puts*() only leaks the signal frame. For the second time, it will overwrite the signal frame. The reason why it can have different functionalities in two continuous executions is that the parameter is different in two executions and the write buffer pointer is changed automatically. For the first time, we make the *puts*() function's parameter point to some zero space, it won't copy anything into the signal frame. We precisely adjust the pointers in *stdout* object's FILE structure (as shown in Fig 4) and make it disclose the current signal frame. For the second time, we make the *puts*() function's parameter point to a fake signal frame. After the output, the *puts*() function automatically adjust the current write pointer to the start of the first signal frame. The area between *_IO_write_ptr* and *_IO_write_end* are used to buffer data. When the second time *puts*() is executed, the overwritten happens. The original signal frame is covered with fake values.

The attack shown above can bypass coarse-grained CFI [31]. First, we never overwrite any return addresses on the stack, even if the signal returns to the interrupted instruction. So we do not violate the backward edge protection. At the same time, we do not violate the forward edge protection. We do modify some control data, such as GOT entries. However, coarse-grained CFI cannot ensure only one target for indirect jumps. We find that the program invokes GOT table functions by using *jmp* instructions. This kind of instruction can have a large number of valid targets. The GOT table is dynamically updated when the program is executed. So the defense cannot differentiate GOT table functions from each other. We leverage this feature to conduct our attack.

### 3.2   Search and Execute DOP Gadgets

To implement more complex attack semantics, we need to use gadgets.

*DOP Gadgets.* As shown in the DOP [16] attack, DOP gadgets are short instruction sequences and are connected sequentially to achieve the attacker's desired functionality. DOP gadgets can implement arithmetic/logic calculation, assignment, load, and store operations. Different from original ROP gadgets, DOP gadgets require to deliver operation results with memory. We find that DOP gadgets are more suitable to be our attack targets. Because DOP gadgets need not be executed one after another. Since the DOP gadgets' operation results have been preserved in memory, the program can execute several other instructions between two adjacent DOP gadgets. This also works in our eSROP attack.

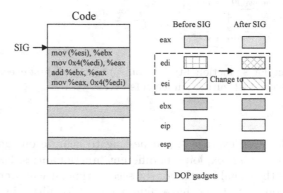

**Fig. 5.** Attack procedure on simulating Turing-Complete computation. The attacker can send a signal before the DOP gadget's execution and modify the data flow. When the signal returns, the gadget will do the computation on attacker-controlled data rather than the original data.

*Chaining DOP Gadgets without Dispatcher Gadget.* The DOP attack has investigated that the DOP gadgets widely exist in most programs. We can easily leverage them. Different from the original DOP attack, our attack removes the need for dispatcher gadgets. The dispatcher gadgets are used to chain the DOP gadgets. It equips the attacker with the ability to repeat gadget invocations. It plays a crucial role in DOP attacks. Because without it, the DOP attack fails. It also limits the DOP attack. Because dispatcher gadgets are rare and sometimes do not exist in a victim program. Even if it exists, it constrains the DOP gadgets that the attacker can use. Because only the DOP gadgets that are reachable by the dispatcher gadgets can be used. At the same time, the DOP attack leverages the vulnerability to modify data flow. This requires that the DOP gadgets are also reachable by the vulnerability.

We show that with the help of the eSROP method, all these limitations can be solved. First, we eliminate the need for dispatcher gadgets. Any DOP gadgets in the program can be used by eSROP. Second, we leverage the signal handler to overwrite the data flow instead of using the vulnerability to modify the data flow. This is more flexible. The DOP gadgets that are not reachable by the vulnerability can also be used.

The way to implement this is similar to what we used to implement arbitrary system calls. This time, the target instruction is a DOP gadget instead of a *syscall* instruction (as shown in Fig. 5). We first leak the program code to identify DOP gadgets. Then we choose the target gadgets we want to execute. When the program executes just before the target gadget, we send the signal. In the signal handler, we modify all the general registers to prepare a new environment for the gadget. When the signal returns, the program continues to execute the DOP gadget, but now the data have been changed. The program does completely different work.

Since that, we can use all the DOP gadgets, and DOP gadgets can simulate Turing complete computation, we can conclude that eSROP is Turing complete.

### 3.3   Bypass Fine-Grained Label-Based CFI

Except for invoking arbitrary system calls and doing Turing complete computation, an eSROP attack can be even more dangerous. It can bypass fine-grained CFI.

The milestone paper [1] proposed by Abadi et al. uses the label-based approach to ensure the program's execution is within its control flow graph (CFG). It is a fine-grained CFI defense. Later, many other label-based approaches [4,30] have been proposed to further develop this method. But we observe that these label-based fine-grained CFI methods are vulnerable when they encounter some unpredictable events, such as signals. Because the CFG represents the intended behavior of the program, it cannot deal with unpredictable events that may happen at run time [22]. The CFG assumes that the control transfer only happens at the end of each basic block. In the real world, signals can be sent to the program at any time. A signal's arrival can cause exceptional flow transfer. This kind of control transfer is not triggered by any instruction but will interrupt the normal execution (even in the middle of a basic block) and force the control to move to the signal handler. Hence the signal handler can be used to hijack the control flow. Although the signal handler is usually small and does not contain stack overflow or other memory vulnerabilities, our eSROP attack can help to accomplish this work.

*Method Description:* The fine-grained label-based CFI modifies the compiled binary to insert unique IDs at the beginning of each basic block. Before each indirect branch, it inserts a few instructions to check if the destination contains the pre-computed basic block's ID. Normal control flow tampering will cause the check to fail because the destination ID will not match the label ID stored in the program. However, attacks are still possible if a signal arrives at the right moment.

The above code is used to ensure that the *jmp ecx* instruction reaches the code starting with label ID *12345678h*.

```
1  cmp [ecx], 12345678h
2  jne violation
3  lea ecx, [ecx+4]
4  jmp ecx
```

**Fig. 6.** Fine-grained label-based CFI verification code.

With a memory vulnerability, suppose an attacker has already tampered with the *ecx* content with a malicious code address. A signal arrives between the *cmp* and *jne* instructions, and the processor status word (*PSW*) is pushed on top of the stack in the signal frame. By leveraging our eSROP method, we can maliciously overwrite the *PSW* in the signal handler. So the *ZP* flag is reset, and when returning, the violation is bypassed and the malicious code address is reachable by the attacker.

The above attack needs to capture the timing. Once the signal does not arrive on time, CFI will detect the attack. Another more stable attack is possible. We do not modify *ecx* beforehand. We just send the signal after the violation check and before the *jmp* instruction. In the signal handler, we modify the *ecx* register's value in the signal frame. Once returns, the program will jump to our malicious code instead of the intended location. The advantage of this attack is if our signal does not arrive on time, the modification just doesn't take place, we avoid the program crash. We can wait for the next chance.

Other label-based instrumentation is also vulnerable to our attack, such as control flow locking [4].

### 3.4 Attack Prevention and Defense

To prevent the eSROP attack, it is important to move the signal frame to some safe area instead of storing it on the user stack. For example, Virtual Ghost [9] saves the signal frame within the VM's internal memory.

Existing techniques that prevent eSROP attack includes, CCFI [21], CPI [18] and GOT protections [17]. CCFI [21] called cryptographic CFI, uses MACs to protect control flow elements, such as return addresses, function pointers, and vtable pointers. CPI [18] is a defense that guarantees the integrity of all code pointers in a program (e.g., function pointers, saved return addresses). Both CCFI [21] and CPI [18] protect the integrity of code pointers.

Some CFI defenses that prohibit overwriting the GOT table can also prevent our attack, such as Modular CFI [23], LLVM cross-DSO [26], PiCFI [24] and uCFI [15].

GOT protection defenses prevent GOT table overwritten attacks. For example, Full Relro (Relocation Read only) [29] arranges the GOT section as read-only at program startup. However, it causes nontrivial loading overhead and does not apply to libraries. People also propose a CFI-based protection scheme [17] against the GOT overwrite attack.

However, these defenses have not been widely adopted in real systems. So eSROP attacks and GOT overwritten attacks still threaten the application security.

# 4 Evaluation

## 4.1 Experimental Setup

We conduct two experiments, Proftpd and Wu-ftpd. Both of them are in a VirtualBox virtual machine. The host machine has an Intel Core i7-10510U with 2 cores @ 1.80 GHz 2.30 GHz and 16 GB DRAM. Both experiments are in 32-bit environments. The operating system of the virtual machine is Ubuntu 16.04.

For Proftpd, we add the parameter "–with-mod_tls" when we configure the program. For the other program, we use the default settings.

In the attacks, the DEP and ASLR defenses are deployed. The programs are not compiled with position-independent code options. So the code and data sections are not randomized. However, library sections are randomized by default.

## 4.2 ProFTPD

The vulnerability CVE-2006-5815 in *Proftpd 1.3.0* is a stack buffer overflow. The vulnerable function is *sreplace*() function. There is an off-by-one error in this function. The attacker can leverage this error to copy a large buffer onto the stack. The buffer will overwrite the local data. It can also overwrite the return address. However, in our attack, we don't cover the return address. Some of these covered local data are security-critical, they are the parameters of the *strcpy*() function. They can implement arbitrary copy primitive. With this primitive, we can further implement our attack.

The following list is an excerpt from *Proftpd 1.3.0*. The function *sig_alarm*() is the signal handler for the *SIGALRM* signal, which is registered by the program itself.

**Step 1: Modify GOT Table Entries.** We modify *sigemptyset*() function's GOT table entry to change it to the *puts*() function's address. We leverage memory copy primitive to copy the *puts*() function's GOT table entry to the *sigemptyset*() function's GOT table entry. The *puts*() function will later do the memory leakage and memory overwritten for us. Then we modify *alarm*() function's GOT table entry to change it to the *sleep*() function's address. The *sleep*() function is also important in this attack because it gives the attacker enough time to decide whether to send the second signal depending on the leaked information.

**Step 2: Modify stdout's Output Buffer.** In our attack, the *puts*() function plays a crucial role. We use it to implement memory leakage and memory overwritten in a signal handler. To leverage the *puts*() function, we should first modify some pointers in the FILE structure of *stdout*. The *puts*() function has an output buffer, we redirect the output buffer onto the stack to point to the signal frame.

To manipulate the FILE structure, we need first modify the *_flags* field of the *stdout* object. The *_IO_write_base*, *_IO_write_ptr*, and *_IO_write_end* represent the base write pointer, current write pointer, and end write pointer respectively. The area between *_IO_write_base* and *_IO_write_ptr* is used to buffer the written

```
1    static RETSIGTYPE sig_alarm(int signo) {
2      struct sigaction act;
3
4      act.sa_handler = sig_alarm;
5      sigemptyset(&act.sa_mask);
6      act.sa_flags = 0;
7
8      #ifdef SA_INTERRUPT
9      act.sa_flags |= SA_INTERRUPT;
10     #endif
11
12     /* Install this handler for SIGALARM. */
13     sigaction(SIGALRM, &act, NULL);
14
15     #ifdef HAVE_SIGINTERRUPT
16     siginterrupt(SIGALRM, 1);
17     #endif
18
19     recvd_signal_flags |= RECEIVED_SIG_ALRM;
20     nalarms++;
21
22     /* Reset the alarm. */
23     _total_time += _current_timeout;
24     if(_current_timeout) {
25       _alarmed_time = time(NULL);
26       alarm(_current_timeout);
27     }
28   }
```

**Fig. 7.** Proftpd 1.3.0 code snippet.

data that has not been flushed out. We can leverage this area to leak the data. Note that in order to successfully leak the data, the _IO_read_end must equal to the _IO_write_base. The area between _IO_write_ptr and _IO_write_end is used to store the parameter data of the puts() function. We can manipulate these two pointers to control the overwritten.

If we want to leak and overwrite the same area, for example, the signal frame in our attack. Meanwhile, we have no chance of adjusting the buffer pointers between leakage and overwritten. The modification will be a little bit complicated. As shown in Fig 4, we first make the _IO_write_ptr points to the end of the signal frame. We make the _IO_write_end equal to the _IO_write_ptr. The program realizes that the current write pointer is at the end of the buffer, it will first flush out the buffer. Then it adjusts the _IO_write_ptr to point to _IO_write_base and copy new data into the buffer. This time we can leak the target object and at the same time overwrite it.

**Step 3: Prepare a Fake Signal Frame.** The attacker leverages the arbitrary copy primitive to write some parameters in the process memory, such as "/bin/sh". Then the attacker prepares a fake signal frame that is stored in the area pointed by the puts() parameter. The fake signal frame contains all the parameters and the system call number that the attacker chooses to execute. When the puts() function is executed, it will copy the data pointed by its parameter to the write buffer. Now the write buffer points to the real signal frame, so the overwritten can take place.

**Step 4: Send the First Signal.** Now the attacker can send a signal to the victim. The original signal handler responds. In it, the *puts*() function is executed instead of the *sigemptyset*() function. The *puts*() function will leak the original signal frame. Then, the *sleep*() function will be executed. The program will sleep for a few moments. In this period, the attacker can observe the output signal frame.

**Step 5: Decide Whether to Send the Second Signal.** There is critical data in the output signal frame, current interrupted instruction pointer. The attacker can determine whether the interrupted instruction is a *syscall* instruction. If it is, we get the point. We can send the second signal immediately. This time, the same signal handler responds. We use the *puts*() function to overwrite the signal frame. Otherwise, we do not send the second signal and wait for the *sleep*() function's completion. The signal frame won't change and we avoid possible crashes.

The signal-sending process cannot promise success in one shot. So it sends lots of signals to the program. The program's signal handler decides whether the condition meets. If the condition meets, the signal handler does the coverage. Otherwise, the signal handler doesn't make the coverage.

Our attack is implemented in a ruby script. It is invoked by the Metasploit framework. We can obtain a shell. The attack can be completed within 6 min.

### 4.3   Wu-ftp

The vulnerability CVE-2000-0573 is a format string vulnerability in *Wu-ftpd 2.6.0*. The format string vulnerability gives the attacker the ability to leak and overwrite arbitrary memory. The *Wu-ftpd* misuses the user input as a format string to pass it to the *vsnprintf*() function. The attacker can construct a specific format string to cover on-stack values and finally leak and overwrite arbitrary memory.

The above code is abstract from the *Wu-ftpd 2.6.0*. The attacker can leverage the program code to obtain a root shell. There is an interesting function in the code, called *ftpd_popen*(). It invokes *seteuid*(0) and *execv*() function. We leverage this function to achieve our goal.

We send the signal when the program is executing the *ftpd_popen*() function. Make sure the signal arrives before the *execv*() function's execution and after the *seteuid*(0)'s execution. When the signal arrives, we leverage the signal handler to overwrite the *execv*() function's parameter *gargv*. When the signal returns, the program continues to execute the *execv*() function. And this time, the parameters have all been changed. The attacker obtains a root shell.

Here we use our second approach. We register a new signal handler by using *sigprocmask*() function.

**Step 1: Modify GOT Table Entries.** We modify the GOT table entry of *sigprocmask*() function to the address of the *sigaction*(). The two functions have similar parameters. The *sigprocmask*() function's first parameter is

```
1   FILE *ftpd_popen(char *program, char *type,
2     int closestderr)
3   {
4     ...
5     i = geteuid();
6     delay_signaling();
7     seteuid(0);
8     setgid(getegid());
9     setuid(i);
10    enable_signaling();
11    execv(gargv[0], gargv);
12    _exit(1);
13  }
14
15  int enable_signaling(void)
16  {
17    if(delaying != 0){
18      delaying = 0;
19        if(sigprocmask(SIG_SETMASK,
20        &saved_sigmask, (sigset_t *)0) < 0){
21          syslog(LOG_ERR, "sigprocmask: %m");
22          return (-1);
23        }
24        return (0);
25    }
26  }
```

**Fig. 8.** Wu-ftpd 2.6.0 code snippet.

*SIG_SETMASK*. Its value is *0x2*. The corresponding signal is *SIGINT*. It can be registered by the attacker. The second parameter of the *sigprocmask()* function is *saved_sigmask*. The *saved_sigmask* is a global variable. Its value can be manipulated. We can construct a *sigaction* structure on it.

**Step 2: Choose a Suitable Signal Handler.** Actually, we can use an arbitrary function in the program as the signal handler. However, the function must meet some conditions. First, the function must have no parameter or only one parameter and the parameter is a little integer. Because the signal handler has only one parameter which is the signal number. Second, the function must meet the requirements shown in approach 1. Here the newly registered signal handler is *pwd()*. It is a function that already exists in the victim program. It has no parameters which can match the normal signal handler. It invokes the function *getcwd()*. We modify the *getcwd()* function's GOT table entry to the address of *puts()* function.

**Step 3: Prepare Fake Data.** We modify the content of the *getcwd()* function's parameter "path". We change it to point to the fake *gargv* structure. The fake structure contains the "\bin\sh". We modify the *stdout* object's FILE structure and change the output buffer to point to the *execv()* function's parameter *gargv*. The *gargv* is stored on the stack.

**Step 4: Trigger the Function and Send a Signal.** The way to trigger *ftpd_popen()* function is by calling *NLST* command. The program will invoke *send_file_list()*, and finally invoke *ftpd_popen()* function. We send the signal when the program is executing the *ftpd_popen()* function. When the signal arrives, the signal handler (*pwd()* function) will invoke *puts()* function instead of the *getcwd()* function. The *puts()* function's execution will cause the *execv()* function's parameter *gargv* be covered. Finally, we can obtain a root shell.

Our attack is implemented in a C program. It can also be implemented in a python script in which attackers can leverage the pwntools to assist the attack. We can obtain a root shell. Our attack can be completed in 5 min.

*Security Analysis.* In our attack, we do not violate the signal cookies [3] defense. Because we only partly overwrite the signal frame (we leave the *rip* and *rsp* register unchanged), we can avoid touching the signal cookie field in the signal frame. A stronger defense such as computing a hash for the signal frame may help to prevent our attack.

We also do not violate shadow stack [6], because we do not manipulate control flow elements on backward edges. Most shadow stack defenses do not protect the integrity of general registers in the signal frame, except for the PACStack [19].

## 5   Related Work

Since we have described eSROP-related defenses in previous sections, we only discuss eSROP-related attacks here.

The attacks that are most related to ours are the Control Flow Bending attack [8] and the Control Flow Interrupt attack [22]. In Control Flow Bending, they leverage the functions, such as *memcpy* and *printf* to do some self modifications. They show that *printf*-like functions can do Turing complete computation. In the eSROP attack, we leverage the *puts* function to both leak and overwrite the same memory space. We show that by carefully adjusting the pointers in the FILE structure, we can make the same function automatically complete two different works continuously. In Control Flow Interrupt, they show that the unexpected trigger of an interrupt and the sudden execution of an Interrupt Service Routine can circumvent CFI-based defenses. Similarly, we show that a signal can help the attacker bypass the fine-grained label-based CFI defenses. In their work, they do not show the experiments and the detailed techniques to overcome the difficulties. But we show the attack methods and experiments for real-world programs.

## 6   Conclusion

In this paper, we propose the eSROP attack. It is a kind of attack that leverages the vulnerable signal-handling process. We build two end-to-end exploits to show how to invoke arbitrary system calls and perform Turing Complete computations without violating DEP, ASLR, and coarse-grained CFI defenses. Both of our attacks can be completed within 10 min. The findings in this paper emphasize the importance of signal-related security. More research on defending against signal attacks is needed. We will leave it as future work.

**Acknowledgement.** This paper is supported by Fundamental Research Funds for the Central Universities (No. B220202073), Natural Science Foundation of Jiangsu Province (No. BK20220973), CCF-Huawei Innovation Research Plan (No. CCF2021-admin-270-202101), China Postdoctoral Science Foundation (No. 2022M711014), Jiangsu Planned Projects for Postdoctoral Research Funds (No. 2021K635C).

# References

1. Abadi, M., Budiu, M., Erlingsson, U., Ligatti, J.: Control-flow integrity principles, implementations, and applications. ACM Trans. Inform. Syst. Secur. (TISSEC) **13**(1), 1–40 (2009)
2. Baratloo, A., Singh, N., Tsai, T.: Transparent {Run-Time} defense against {Stack-Smashing} attacks. In: 2000 USENIX Annual Technical Conference (USENIX ATC 00) (2000)
3. Bauer, S.: Srop mitigation: Signal cookies. Linux Mailing List: https://lwn.net/Articles/67486132 (2016)
4. Bletsch, T., Jiang, X., Freeh, V.: Mitigating code-reuse attacks with control-flow locking. In: Proceedings of the 27th Annual Computer Security Applications Conference, pp. 353–362 (2011)
5. Bosman, E., Bos, H.: Framing signals-a return to portable shellcode. In: 2014 IEEE Symposium on Security and Privacy, pp. 243–258. IEEE (2014)
6. Burow, N., Zhang, X., Payer, M.: Sok: Shining light on shadow stacks. In: 2019 IEEE Symposium on Security and Privacy (SP), pp. 985–999. IEEE (2019)
7. Cai, X., Gui, Y., Johnson, R.: Exploiting unix file-system races via algorithmic complexity attacks. In: 2009 30th IEEE Symposium on Security and Privacy, pp. 27–41. IEEE (2009)
8. Carlini, N., Barresi, A., Payer, M., Wagner, D., Gross, T.R.: Control-flow bending: On the effectiveness of control-flow integrity. In: 24th {USENIX} Security Symposium ({USENIX} Security 15), pp. 161–176 (2015)
9. Criswell, J., Dautenhahn, N., Adve, V.: Virtual ghost: protecting applications from hostile operating systems. ACM SIGARCH Comput. Architect. News **42**(1), 81–96 (2014)
10. Evans, I., et al.: Control jujutsu: On the weaknesses of fine-grained control flow integrity. In: Proceedings of the 22nd ACM SIGSAC Conference on Computer and Communications Security, pp. 901–913 (2015)
11. Farkhani, R.M., Jafari, S., Arshad, S., Robertson, W.K., Kirda, E., Okhravi, H.: On the effectiveness of type-based control flow integrity. In: Proceedings of the 34th Annual Computer Security Applications Conference (2018)
12. Gao, Y.c., Zhou, A.m., Liu, L.: Data-execution prevention technology in windows system. Information Security & Communications Privacy (2013)
13. Gawlik, R., Kollenda, B., Koppe, P., Garmany, B., Holz, T.: Enabling client-side crash-resistance to overcome diversification and information hiding. In: NDSS (2016)
14. Göktas, E., Athanasopoulos, E., Bos, H., Portokalidis, G.: Out of control: Overcoming control-flow integrity. In: 2014 IEEE Symposium on Security and Privacy, pp. 575–589. IEEE (2014)
15. Hu, H., et al.: Enforcing unique code target property for control-flow integrity. In: Proceedings of the 2018 ACM SIGSAC Conference on Computer and Communications Security, pp. 1470–1486 (2018)

16. Hu, H., Shinde, S., Adrian, S., Chua, Z.L., Saxena, P., Liang, Z.: Data-oriented programming: On the expressiveness of non-control data attacks. In: 2016 IEEE Symposium on Security and Privacy (SP), pp. 969–986. IEEE (2016)
17. Jeong, S., Hwang, J., Kwon, H., Shin, D.: A cfi countermeasure against got overwrite attacks. IEEE Access **8**, 36267–36280 (2020). https://doi.org/10.1109/ACCESS.2020.2975037
18. Kuznetzov, V., Szekeres, L., Payer, M., Candea, G., Sekar, R., Song, D.: Code-pointer integrity. In: The Continuing Arms Race: Code-Reuse Attacks and Defenses, pp. 81–116 (2018)
19. Liljestrand, H., Nyman, T., Gunn, L.J., Ekberg, J.E., Asokan, N.: {PACStack}: an authenticated call stack. In: 30th USENIX Security Symposium (USENIX Security 21), pp. 357–374 (2021)
20. Marco-Gisbert, H., Ripoll Ripoll, I.: Address space layout randomization next generation. Appl. Sci. **9**(14), 2928 (2019)
21. Mashtizadeh, A.J., Bittau, A., Boneh, D., Mazières, D.: CCFI: Cryptographically enforced control flow integrity. In: Proceedings of the 22nd ACM SIGSAC Conference on Computer and Communications Security, pp. 941–951 (2015)
22. Maunero, N., Prinetto, P., Roascio, G.: CFI: Control flow integrity or control flow interruption? In: 2019 IEEE East-West Design & Test Symposium (EWDTS), pp. 1–6. IEEE (2019)
23. Niu, B., Tan, G.: Modular control-flow integrity. In: Proceedings of the 35th ACM SIGPLAN Conference on Programming Language Design and Implementation, pp. 577–587 (2014)
24. Niu, B., Tan, G.: Per-input control-flow integrity. In: Proceedings of the 22nd ACM SIGSAC Conference on Computer and Communications Security, pp. 914–926 (2015)
25. Roemer, R., Buchanan, E., Shacham, H., Savage, S.: Return-oriented programming: systems, languages, and applications. ACM Trans. Inform. Syst. Security (TISSEC) **15**(1), 1–34 (2012)
26. Rohlf, C.: Cross dso cfi-llvm and android (2020)
27. Rudd, R., et al.: Address oblivious code reuse: On the effectiveness of leakage resilient diversity. In: NDSS (2017)
28. Schuster, F., Tendyck, T., Liebchen, C., Davi, L., Sadeghi, A., Holz, T.: Counterfeit object-oriented programming: On the difficulty of preventing code reuse attacks in C++ applications. In: IEEE Symposium on Security and Privacy, pp. 745–762
29. Sidhpurwala, H.: Hardening elf binaries using relocation read-only (relro). Red Hat-We make open source technologies for the enterprise (2019)
30. Zhang, C., et al.: Practical control flow integrity and randomization for binary executables. In: 2013 IEEE Symposium on Security and Privacy, pp. 559–573. IEEE (2013)
31. Zhang, M., Sekar, R.: Control flow integrity for {COTS} binaries. In: 22nd {USENIX} Security Symposium ({USENIX} Security 13), pp. 337–352 (2013)
32. Zhou, J., Vigna, G.: Detecting attacks that exploit application-logic errors through application-level auditing. In: 20th Annual Computer Security Applications Conference, pp. 168–178. IEEE (2004)

# Breaking Embedded Software Homogeneity with Protocol Mutations

Tongwei Ren[1], Ryan Williams[2], Sirshendu Ganguly[1], Lorenzo De Carli[1(⊠)], and Long Lu[2]

[1] Worcester Polytechnic Institute, Worcester, MA 01609, USA
{tren,sganguly,ldecarli}@wpi.edu
[2] Northeastern University, Boston, MA 02115, USA
{williams.ry,l.lu}@northeastern.edu

**Abstract.** Network-connected embedded devices suffer from easy-to-exploit security issues. Due to code and platform reuse the same vulnerability oftentimes ends up affecting a large installed base. These circumstances enable destructive types of attacks, like ones in which compromised devices disrupt the power grid.

We tackle an enabling factors of these attacks: software homogeneity. We propose techniques to inject syntax mutations in application-level network protocols used in the embedded/IoT space. Our approach makes it easy to diversify a protocol into syntactically different dialects, at the granularity of individual deployments. This form of moving-target defense disrupts batch compromise of devices, preventing reusable network exploits. Our approach identifies candidate program data structures and functions via a set of heuristics, mutate them via static transformations, and selects correctness-preserving mutations using dynamic testing.

Evaluation on 4 popular protocols shows that we mitigate known exploitable vulnerabilities, while introducing no bugs.

**Keywords:** Software diversity · Protocol mutations · MTD

## 1 Introduction

Connectivity is now ubiquitous within smart and embedded devices—appliances such as light bulbs, power meters and industrial control systems; and in the near-future robot swarms, sensors and weapon systems. Such devices are already deployed in large numbers, with glaring security vulnerabilities [21,29,33,41,49], and outdated, hard-to-upgrade firmware [56]. Different devices may reuse the same components and platform [39], resulting in replication of vulnerabilities.

The situation presents analogies with the early 2000s, when worms like CodeRed spread uncontrollably, exploiting widely-installed, vulnerable internet-facing software [44,45]. The same factors are now resulting in botnets such as Mirai [16,31,43]. For now, large-scale embedded device compromise has resulted in attacks that—while large—remain within reach of traditional cyberdefenses.

© ICST Institute for Computer Sciences, Social Informatics and Telecommunications Engineering 2023
Published by Springer Nature Switzerland AG 2023. All Rights Reserved
F. Li et al. (Eds.): SecureComm 2022, LNICST 462, pp. 770–790, 2023.
https://doi.org/10.1007/978-3-031-25538-0_40

New attack models are however possible, and researchers are just beginning to understand them. Ronen et al. [50] demonstrated an IoT worm targeting smart public street lights. Possible attacks involve bricking devices, wireless jamming, and inducing epileptic seizures at large scale. Other works suggest that with a relatively small botnet of power-hungry IoT devices, an attacker could create a demand surge large enough to collapse a large power grid [57], or control energy pricing [55]. In the industrial domain, highly damaging attacks have already been observed [46]. And internet-connected robotic swarms, poised to becoming commonplace in robotics and military applications [18,33], will need safeguards too as the consequences of attacks are potentially catastrophic.

Even a single widespread vulnerability can enable attacks. For example, a single 0-day affecting Huawei home gateway devices enabled cybercriminals to create a 100,000-strong botnet in December 2017 [31]. It is therefore important to reason about defense-in-depth techniques that can protect devices against yet-unknown 0-day attacks. Authentication helps preventing basic attacks, but it is ineffective in case of default or easily guessable credentials [21], or credential stuffing. Anomaly-based intrusion detection systems (IDSs) suffer from low accuracy [27], while specification-based IDSs may miss stealth attacks [19].

To address this problem, we propose a novel form of moving-target defense for embedded/IoT, based on protocol mutations. We address one of the fundamental problems of large-scale IoT deployments: software homogeneity. It can arise when multiple deployments of devices all share the same vulnerable network-facing code. We support the diversification of application-level network protocol implementations, resulting in dialects which can be deployed at the granularity of individual installations. Dialects can be made mutually incompatible, thus communication with a device without knowledge of its mutations is impossible. This approach works by statically analyzing and mutating protocol source code.

Our work is not meant to replace security best-practices; rather, it complements them. It prevents one-size-fits-all exploits, thus avoiding rapid attack propagation among embedded devices. Furthermore, it is easy to incorporate as mutations are largely automated. The approach is also desirable in contexts where encryption is difficult to deploy due to resource constraints. We note that our work is not applicable to consumer/home IoT scenarios, where applying a different mutation to each individual device sold quickly grows impractical. Instead, it targets *Self-Contained Critical Deployments*: military or infrastructure deployments of homogeneous devices, all managed by the same organization.

Achieving our goal entails solving a number of challenges. First, modifying sender and receiver of a network communication entails identifying code and data structures used to create and parse messages. Unfortunately, to the best of our knowledge no existing technique can identify and map this information. Thus, we devise our own technique, which we name PACO (**Pa**rser/**Co**nstructor extractor), implementing a problem-specific static analysis heuristic. A second component, named ALOJA[1], then selects candidate constructor/parser pair, apply mutations, and test the mutated implementation for correctness. The output is a protocol implementation which incorporates a set of safe mutations.

---

[1] In Catalan mythology, an *Aloja* is a mythical creature able to shape-shift into a bird.

Our results show that this approach results in mutation that are effective in blocking paths to successful attack completion. **Overall contributions:**

1. We propose a static analysis technique to identify message-related structures and functions in network protocol implementations.
2. Based on the technique above, we propose static program transformations to inject symmetric mutations in message generators/parsers.
3. We thoroughly evaluate the techniques above on **4** protocols. We achieve **93%** accuracy in identifying relevant functions. Mutations successfully block **all** reproducible CVEs we identified, and do not affect correctness.
4. We release a software artifact implementing our proposed techniques, enabling analysis and further experimentation by the community (https://osf.io/9gc3n/?view_only=6da059eab07f4ffe934d6b59b49fee2b https://github.com/TongweiRen/Aloja).

## 2  Background

### 2.1  Target Scenarios

We target a style of IoT and embedded systems that we term Self-contained Critical Deployments (SCDs): deployments where (i) the set of devices belonging to the deployment is known a priori; (ii) the devices perform a task where loss of function can lead to significant disruption; and (iii) an attacker with incentives to cause disruption can communicate to the deployment. SCDs arise in military and infrastructure-related settings. Compared to the consumer domain, SCDs are self-contained within a single organization, so backward compatibility is not critical. Furthermore, they are expected to survive for an extended period while performing critical functions, which makes the (small) additional effort to introduce mutations acceptable. We review two example scenarios.

*Autonomous Robotic Swarms.* A recent DARPA BAA, OFFensive Swarm-Enabled Tactics (OFFSET), envisions a class of autonomous swarms of unmanned aircraft and/or ground systems used to accomplish missions in urban environments [20]. US Army also funded the MAST project, aimed at autonomous collections of intelligence-gathering robots [1]. A major issue with robotic swarms is attacks where malicious robots can be injected into the swarm [33]. Consequences of a cyberattack involve equipment damage, and failure to complete the task.

*Infrastructure/Industrial.* Increasingly, public and industrial spaces incorporate network of internet-connected embedded appliances, such as street lights and security cameras. These deployments are characterized by a large number of identical devices within the same network. Attacks may create widespread disruption: if a firmware vulnerability exists, then *all* devices are susceptible to it. In past work, Ronen et al. demonstrated a building-scale attack, where all the smart lights in a large building fall under control of an attacker [50].

## 2.2    Software Diversity in SCDs

Best-practice security measures such as encryption and authentication can help mitigate the risk of attackers infiltrating SCDs. However, past experiences demonstrate that buggy code, leftover development accounts, and other high-level issues can allow the attacker to bypass these lines of defense [38]. Here, we propose the use of *software diversity* as an additional line of defense that can provide additional security when paired with best-practices, in a defense-in-depth approach.

Software diversity [30,40] consists in deploying, with each installation of a given software, a copy which is functionally identical, but differs in the implementation from any other copy. Differentiation is typically envisioned using specialized compilation [22] or binary rewriting techniques [26], in some cases aided by VMs [61]. Differentiation aims at preventing an attacker to devise a general exploit by analyzing a single copy of the program. Introducing variations forces the attacker to tailor their exploits to each copy of the program.

Diversity-based defenses however cannot be ported directly to the SCD domain. Any approach with large overhead—e.g., interposing a VM—has to confront the resource-constrained nature of many devices. Furthermore, some attacks exploit vulnerabilities at levels of abstraction high enough to be impervious to binary-level diversification (e.g. default factory passwords). Third, vulnerabilities are nearly exclusively triggered via network; it is therefore reasonable to deploy diversity within components that deal with network communications.

A relevant question is whether diversification at the granularity of SCDs—and not individual devices—provides enough variety to prevent standardized exploits from spreading. Based on the large number of deployments for popular embedded devices, we expect SCD-level granularity to still provide sufficient diversity.

## 2.3    Goals and Threat Model

Our goal is to introduce software diversity by injecting mutations in the syntax of network protocol messages, thus preventing standardized exploits. Since attacks infect victims via malicious network input, we mutate protocols so that different deployments speak different *protocol dialects*. Mutations can be made incompatible: valid messages within one dialect are rejected by the network message parser in another. By focusing on early rejection of input, our approach is practical against both low-level binary exploits and high-level logic bugs.

We do not target protocols at layer-IV and below (e.g., WiFI, IP, 6LoW-PAN, TCP), as those are typically implemented within the operating system and/or hardware. Instead, we focus on implementations of middleware protocols, such as Cyclone DDS [11]. These typically provide services like publisher/subscriber communication, and have wide applicability within the SCD domain. For example, the DDS protocol is used in domains as diverse as smart cities [10], robotics [42] and military applications [59].

In our current work, we mostly focus on *off-path* attackers. The attacker scans the internet for vulnerable devices (e.g., using vulnerability search engines [8]).

They commandeer any vulnerable device which replies to their probes. For example, the original Mirai botnet was built using similar techniques [16]. The attacker can send traffic towards potential victims and receive replies, but cannot observe the victim's communication with other nodes.

We also discuss *on-path attackers*. In addition to sending and receiving traffic to/from victim, this attacker can observe communications between non-compromised devices prior to the attack. The attacker may use its on-path capability to reverse-engineer wireless communications and identify vulnerabilities, inject messages, and batch-compromise devices.

In general, off-path attackers can be targeted using *static mutations*, and on-path attackers using *dynamic mutations*. We discuss both in the following.

### 2.4 Possible Mutation Types

We define different categories of protocol mutations, each being relevant to different types of attackers.

**Static Mutations.** A static mutation is statically embedded into the protocol firmware at compile time. A given mutated binary always exhibits the same mutation. The mutation behavior can evolve over medium time scales, by periodically recompiling the firmware (e.g., with firmware updates).

Static mutations target off-path attackers, who must guess the particular set of mutations in order to communicate. With an appropriately large set of mutations and their parameters, the effort required to break into the device is increased many-fold. Consider an attack which is carried over a sequence of $N$ messages. Assume each message is independently mutated by a randomly selected mutation[2] from a set $S$ s.t. $|S| = M$. Without any additional information, an off-path attacker must guess the correct mutation by trial-and-error; worst-case and expected number of tries are respectively $MN$ and $\frac{M+1}{2}N$. A multiplicative increase in the attack complexity raises the bar against casual attackers, and has the advantage of simplicity. In this paper, we focus on static mutations.

**Dynamic Mutations.** A dynamic mutation is a one which can be reparametrized or disabled without recompiling the program. Dynamic mutations become necessary with an on-path attacker, who may be able to reverse-engineer mutations, by comparing unmutated protocol executions to the mutated ones in the target network. This attack can be mitigated by deploying a set of dynamic mutations, which evolve according to a *mutation schedule*. Dynamic mutations introduce additional complexity: two communicating peers must synchronize their mutation schedules so that they are always speaking the same protocol dialect, without leaking details of the schedule to the attacker. Our implementation of mutations exports an API through which individual mutations

---

[2] Note that a parametrized mutation with an $n$-bit parameter can be seen as a set of $2^n$ possible distinct mutations.

can be enabled/disabled at run-time, which provides a foundation for dynamic mutations. However, we leave a full implementation of this concept to future work.

## 2.5  One-Size-Fits-all Exploits

Oftentimes protocol implementations in the wild are affected by various types of bugs in the parsing logic. We performed an extensive review of historical parsing-related security bugs from six protocol implementations: Mosquitto MQTT [3], Wakaama [9], MQTT-C [6], Cyclone DDS [11], OpenDDS [7], and DSVPN[4]. Results show that these vulnerabilities can be categorized as follows: incorrect buffer sizing, lack of sanitization, and invalid/improper assertions. For example, a buffer sizing issue reported in CVE-2017-7651 causes a Mosquitto broker to crash after receiving a crafted packet. CVE-2017-7653 causes a Mosquitto broker to disconnect other clients, upon reception of an attack message with an invalid UTF-8 string. This bug is due to lack of string checking. Our approach focuses on early rejection of input, with the goal of containing this style of attacks.

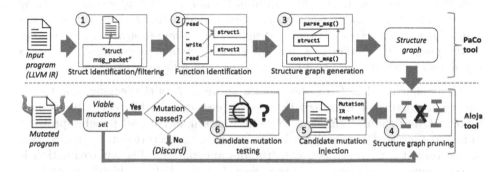

**Fig. 1.** Overview of ALOJA

## 3  Approach Overview

Our approach receives as input the source of a network protocol implementation, such as Mosquitto MQTT [3]. We assume that a single codebase contains both components necessary to create and parse messages. We first analyze the code to identify program components (data structures and functions) which are involved in creating and parsing network messages. This task is performed by the PACO tool, discussed in Sect. 3.1. The information returned by PACO is then used to identify suitable locations for mutations, and to injects the actual mutations. This is performed by the ALOJA tool, described in Sect. 3.2. The overall workflow is described in the following and outlined in Fig. 1.

### 3.1  PaCo: Identification of Relevant Program Components

First, the PaCo tool identifies program functions and structures whose purpose is to construct and parse network messages. PaCo's overall algorithm receives as input a program implementing a network protocol of interest, and return a structure graph describing *message-carrying structs* and *protocol constructors and parsers*, which we define below. Our implementation is based on the LLVM compiler toolkit, and works at the level of LLVM IR.

**Definition 1 (Message-carrying struct).** *A message-carrying struct is a composite data type which represents the structure and content of a network protocol message as a sequence of contiguous binary fields, to be serialized when the message is sent. Such a struct s consist of a sequence of field types $s = f_1, ..., f_n$.*

The notion of message as a sequence of binary fields is consistent with protocol reverse-engineering literature [28], and captures a large number of application-level protocols used in the embedded/IoT space. Based on this assumption, the definition of message constructor and parser follows:

**Definition 2 (Constructor and Parser).** *Consider the IR-level representation $R$ of the implementation of a protocol $P$, and the set $S$ of message-carrying structs in $R$. A message constructor function (constructor) $f_C : S \rightarrow P$ is a function in $R$ which receives as input a struct argument and returns a valid message in the protocol $P$. Similarly, a message parser function (parser) $f_P : P \rightarrow S$ is a function which receives as input a message and returns a struct.*

Unambiguous identifying the entities above in $R$ is challenging, due to the variety of parsing and construction techniques used in different network protocols. Rather than attempting to model the semantic of all possible protocol implementations, PaCo's algorithm is heuristic and returns an approximation of the correct sets of structs, constructors and parsers. The approximation is neither sound nor complete; however, Sect. 4 shows that it is highly accurate.

**PaCo Workflow.** First, PaCo collects all struct types appearing in the program, and filters the result to remove standard library structs (e.g., `__sigset_t`) unrelated to network messages. Further filtering retains only structs passed as input or output to functions that either (i) read or write data from the network; or (ii) perform memory copy (e.g., `memcpy`). Including the latter is necessary as oftentimes protocol code will not send and receive directly from structs, but copy parts of them into separate buffers. These operations, depicted in Step **1** of Fig. 1, result in a set $S$ of candidate message-carrying structs.

PaCo then proceeds to collect functions operating on structs in $S$ and building a *structure graph*. The algorithm iterates over all functions in the program, collecting each function that either reads or write to a variable whose type is in $S$ (Step **2** in Fig. 1). This result in a set $F$ of relevant functions. Intuitively, the set $F$ includes candidate constructors and parsers in $R$.

Finally, PaCo builds a structure graph $G = (V, E)$ as follows. First, it defines the set of vertices $V$ as $S \cup F$. Then, it establishes an edge between each function node in $F$ and the structs in $S$ that the function reads and/or writes (Step **3**).

**Table 1.** ALOJA's mutation library

| Mutation | Description |
|---|---|
| Global/const refactoring | Remap values of enum fields/globals/consts |
| Mutate field value | Linearly combine field value with parameter |
| Encrypt field value | Encrypt field value with pre-determined cipher/key |

## 3.2 ALOJA: Deployment of Mutations

ALOJA uses the structure graph $G$ to inject *symmetric mutations* in constructor and corresponding parser functions.

**Definition 3 (Mutation).** *Consider a message-carrying struct $s \in S$, defined as in Definition 1. Further consider a constructor and a parser function $f_C, f_P \in F$ which operate on $s$. A mutation is a transformation of $f_C$ and $f_P$ in such a way that the mutated functions $f'_C, f'_P$ exchange messages in a format $s' \neq s$ different from their non-mutated counterparts, but the result of the message exchange is functionally identical.*

Mutations must be *invertible*, i.e., it must be possible to reverse any transformation applied to generated messages when those are received. This excludes mutations that hash message fields, and similar applications of one-way functions. Any mutation which removes data from messages is also non-invertible.

Intuitively, ALOJA embeds a given mutation function into a constructor $f_C$, and the inverse mutation into the corresponding parser $f_P$. A desirable property of invertible functions, or bijections, is that they are *composable*; i.e., the composition of invertible functions is also invertible. It is thus possible to inject multiple mutations by composing the corresponding mutation functions.

In practice, we meet the requirement above by restricting ALOJA to mutations which apply invertible transformations to individual fields. Supported mutations, satisfying the property above, are detailed in Table 1. Our implementation, based on the injection of mutation templates into protocol code, makes it easy to expand this set with arbitrary additional mutations.

**ALOJA Workflow.** ALOJA identifies candidate locations for mutations by analyzing the structure graph $G$. First, it marks every function operating on any struct member in $G$ as parser, constructor, or both based on whether the function reads/writes it. It also discards any struct member whose compiler-level type is not compatible with any mutation. Then, applies a heuristic to remove parser and constructor functions that are unlikely to directly affect wire-level protocol messages. First, ALOJA generates the function-level callgraph. Furthermore, it removes each constructor (parser) which has a direct edge to (from) another constructor (parser). The empirical insight is that values that affect network messages are typically written (read) by low-level (high-level) utility functions, which appear as leaves (non-leaf nodes) in the callgraph. This is represented in Fig. 1, Step 4. The output of this step is a pruned structure graph $G'$. We remark that filtering candidates is a performance optimization, but it is not necessary for correctness—thus, we believe an heuristic approach is appropriate. Our testing step, described below, can effectively remove mutants that involve incorrectly selected parsers/generators. We further discuss the performance benefits of filtering in Sect. 4.5.

In the next step, ALOJA build all possible mutation candidates, where a candidate $c = (f_C, f_P, M)$ is a tuple including a constructor $f_C$ and a parser $f_P$ in $G'$ operating on the same struct $s$, and a mutation compatible with the type of $s$. To deploy a candidate mutation, ALOJA wraps the last write to the target struct member in $s$ within the constructor $f_C$ with a template which mutates $s$ prior to writing. Similarly, the parser $f_P$ is mutated by injecting a wrapper implementing the reverse mutation before the first field read (Step **5**).

For the same mutation strategy, our implementation will insert different IR code into the application based on the type of field we choose to mutate. For example, the code for changing `int32` field and `int64` field is syntactically different, but semantically same. This is to make sure our mutation will not change the field length and cause errors.

Next, the mutated program is tested to evaluate correctness. This step is the only one requiring (offline) user involvement, to specify a command executing a test procedure to verify correctness. Note that the procedure may simply run unit tests shipped with the codebase. For each mutation, ALOJA first runs a mutated server and client to check whether they can communicate correctly; then, it runs a mutated server and an unmutated client to ensure that the communication fails (Step **6**). ALOJA returns all mutations that pass both tests.

## 4   Evaluation

In this section, we evaluate ALOJA against the following experimental questions:

- **Question #1: can PACO correctly identify message-related program structures and functions?** In Sect. 4.2, we show that PACO can identify relevant program elements with high accuracy.
- **Question #2: do mutations lead to a measurable change in the difficulty to exploit a vulnerability?** In Sect. 4.3, we show that ALOJA's mutations can mitigate reusable attacks.
- **Question #3: can ALOJA correctly introduce mutations without affecting program correctness?** Extensive testing, discussed in Sect. 4.4, shows that ALOJA did not introduce any new bug.
- **Question #4: are ALOJA filtering heuristics successful in limiting the number of mutations to be tested?** Sect. 4.5 shows that filtering heuristic lead to up to a **41%** reduction in the number of tested mutations.
- **Question #5: do introduced mutations generate overhead in the execution of mutated protocols?** In Sect. 4.6, we show acceptable compile-time and run-time overhead, thus our mutations are practical.

**Table 2.** Characterization of codebases

| Program | Protocol | # LOCs | # Functions |
|---|---|---|---|
| Mosquitto [3] | MQTT | 79,859 | 338 |
| Wakaama [9] | LwM2M | 28,040 | 302 |
| MQTT-C [6] | MQTT | 12,845 | 98 |
| Cyclone DDS [11] | DDS | 109,954 | 2,146 |

**Table 3.** Accuracy of PaCo in identifying message-related structures

| Program | True positives (Positives) | True negatives (Negatives) | Accuracy |
|---|---|---|---|
| Mosquitto | 2 (3) | 26 (26) | 96.6% |
| MQTT-C | 1 (1) | 17 (17) | 100% |
| Wakaama | 5 (5) | 18 (18) | 100% |
| CycloneDDS | 42 (51) | 291 (300) | 97.3% |
| Overall | 50 (59) | 352 (361) | 97.8% |

## 4.1 Implementation and Dataset

We created a prototype implementing the full pipeline described in Sect. 3. It is implemented as a set of LLVM passes and Python modules used to statically analyze IR files, perform mutation injection, and run the mutation test process. In total, our pipeline consists of 1183 lines of C/C++ code (LLVM passes) and 7961 lines of Python code (IR analysis and test automation).

*Dataset.* Table 2 describes the codebases used for the experiments. We selected these 4 projects as they are implementations of representative protocols commonly used in the IoT realm. Mosquitto [3] is an implementation of the popular MQTT protocol, while MQTT-C [6] is another implementation stripped of all extraneous features to provide a minimal install. We also evaluate Wakaama [9], a C implementation of the LwM2M machine-to-machine protocol, and Cyclone DDS [11], a C implementation of the DDS protocol. Although all applications we evaluated are middleware protocol applications, our system can be used for any upper-layer protocol applications using struct to construct messages.

## 4.2 Structure Graph Generation

*Methodology.* In this section, we evaluate the effectiveness of PaCo in identifying message-related functions and structs. In order to identify false positives and negatives, we performed a manual analysis of each codebase and compared the correct sets of functions and structures to those generated by PaCo. Manual analysis involved going through every function and struct, and verifying based on their name and functionality if they were, in fact, parser- or constructor-related. We envision PaCo as a general tool for code understanding; therefore

**Table 4.** Accuracy of PACo in identifying message-related functions

| Program | True positives (Positives) | True negatives (Negatives) | Accuracy |
|---|---|---|---|
| Mosquitto | 10 (11) | 203 (203) | 99.5% |
| MQTT-C | 6 (6) | 57 (57) | 100% |
| Wakaama | 32 (32) | 60 (66) | 93.9% |
| CycloneDDS | 26 (39) | 89 (102) | 81.6% |
| Overall | 74 (88) | 409 (428) | 93.6% |

we use a broader notion of "message-related" than that used by ALOJA. We consider a function/struct message-related if it performs processing/stores data which is directly or indirectly used to construct and/or parse network messages.

*Results-Structure Identification.* Table 3 summarizes structure identification accuracy. True Positives/Negatives are the numbers of network-related/non-network-related functions PaCo successfully identified. Positives/Negatives represent the numbers of actual network-related/non-network-related functions in each codebase. Structure identification is heuristic and based on how a struct is used. False negatives come from network-related structs not being directly used for memory copy and network operations. False positives occur due to PACo heuristics being misled by the presence of syscalls that are frequently, but not always, network-related, e.g. redundant `recv` functions when the application actually uses `read` to receive messages. Overall, results show high accuracy across the codebases (**97.8%**).

*Results - Function Identification.* Table 4 summarizes results regarding the accuracy of function identification across our four evaluation codebases. Overall, PACo achieves **93.6%** accuracy. Analysis of mistakes indicates that they occur due to mislabeling of the corresponding structs, as discussed above.

Overall, we conclude that PACo's heuristics are effective in identifying message-related structures and functions, providing actionable information to ALOJA.

### 4.3   Exploit Mitigation

*Methodology.* For this experiment, we compare the behavior of unmutated compiled binaries with mutated ones. We identified reproducible vulnerabilities in the protocols of interest, by picking older releases with known vulnerabilities, and mutating them using ALOJA. The mutation strategy we used for our experiments was mutating a field value as shown in Table 1, row 3. This process resulted in two versions of a vulnerable protocol implementation, without and with the mutation. We first verified that the vulnerability could be successfully reproduced in the non-mutated client/server. Then, we used the same client and sent the same packets, as we did before, to the mutated server, to check that the vulnerability could no longer be triggered. Because our mutations targets parser/constructor functions, we look specifically at parser-/constructor-related vulnerabilities that are triggerable by malformed network input. For example, CVE-2017-7653 causes a Mosquitto broker to disconnect other clients, upon reception of an attack packet containing an invalid UTF-8 string.

*Collected Vulnerabilities.* For Mosquitto, we did an extensive review of relevant Common Vulnerabilities and Exposures (CVE) reports. We found 17 vulnerability reports of which 7 are parser-/constructor-related. We only show the results of three CVE reports which we could reliably reproduce, including CVE-2019-11779, CVE-2018-12543 and CVE-2017-7653. We could not reliably reproduce the remaining ones (e.g. CVE-2019-11778), as they are caused by heisenbugs. For Wakaama, we reliably reproduced one relevant CVE report, CVE-2019-9004. For MQTT-C and Cyclone DDS, we did not find recent relevant CVE reports.

*Results.* In the case of CVE-2019-11779, the reception of the attack packet in unmutated Mosquitto triggers the vulnerable function `mosquitto_sub_topic _check`. The same attack against the mutated version results in the packet being dropped. The vulnerability is not triggered, and the unmutated attacker's client gets forcibly disconnected. Our experiments for CVE-2018-12543, CVE-2017-7653, and CVE-2019-9004, also resulted in successful exploit in the non-mutated version, and failed exploit in the mutated one. These results show that ALOJA's mutation approach is effective in mitigating network-based exploits.

### 4.4    Correctness

*Methodology.* In this section we evaluate the correctness of mutations applied by ALOJA. It is important to ensure that the mutations do not break any underlying functionality. In order to do so, we run unit tests against the unmutated and mutated version of each protocol, and compare the results of the two runs. The mutation strategy we used for our experiments is mutating an existing field value, shown in Table 1, row 2. All protocols include high-quality developer-provided unit tests which we use for this purpose. We emphasize that these are **not** the tests we used for selecting useful mutants. To avoid biasing the correctness evaluation, for the latter purpose we develop our own test scenarios.

We also performed an in-depth case study on Mosquitto, by designing and building a fuzzing MQTT client based on the Boofuzz fuzzer [5]. The fuzzer generates protocol messages and directs them to a mutated Mosquitto binary. To ensure extensive coverage, we do not generate completely random input, but messages with a structure approximating MQTT's specifications and sessions.

*Results.* Table 5 shows that 3 out of 1233 test cases failed. We manually analyzed each failed test; in all cases, test failures were due to the tests expecting protocol messages in the original (i.e., non-mutated) format. We ruled out these failures as benign, as our mutation strategy is specifically designed to trigger failures like these. Furthermore, our Mosquitto fuzz tester ran for 64.22 min without triggering any unexpected behavior. Overall, these results suggest that ALOJA does not introduce any new bugs or vulnerabilities into the codebase it mutates.

**Table 5.** Results of correctness evaluation tests.

| Program | # Tests | # Failed tests (benign) |
|---------|---------|-------------------------|
| Mosquitto | 207 | 2 (2) |
| Wakaama | 71 | 0 (0) |
| MQTT-C | 18 | 1 (1) |
| Cyclone DDS | 937 | 0 (0) |

**Table 6.** Impact of heuristic on mutation generation

| Program | W/O Heuristic (Useful)) | W/Heuristic (Useful) |
|---------|-------------------------|----------------------|
| Mosquitto | 242(2) | 142(2) |
| MQTT-C | 116(7) | 73(5) |
| Wakaama | 340(3) | 235(3) |
| Cyclone DDS | 969(6) | 795(2) |

## 4.5   Impact of Mutation Filtering Heuristics

*Methodology.* ALOJA uses callgraph analysis to filter constructor and parser functions unlikely to directly operate on message content (discussed in Sect. 3.2). It is important to determine whether such heuristics (i) lead to a reduction in the number of possible mutations to be tested; and (ii) do not lead to loss of potentially useful mutations. In order to evaluate the impact of heuristics, we ran ALOJA twice on each codebase, first with the heuristic deployment, and then deactivated. We compared the runs on two aspects: number of useful mutants and number of overall generated mutants.

*Results.* Table 6 show the number of useful and overall mutations across the three codebases. The heuristic causes a best-case reduction of **41.3%** (Mosquitto) in the number of mutants, and an overall reduction of **25.3%**. Only **6 out of 422** removed mutations are useful, which amount to losing **33.3%** of useful mutations. We conclude that the filtering heuristic selects and remove incorrect mutations with reasonable accuracy.

## 4.6   Performance Impact of Mutations

*Methodology.* To evaluate the overhead incurred due to running a mutated protocol, we examined two aspects. The first is the compile-time overhead due to running PACO and ALOJA, measured by timing the overall compilation without and with the mutation process. We do not report detailed results on code size increase due to mutation, as such overhead remains small—between **0.1%** and **1%**—for all codebases.

**Table 7.** Incurred compile time overhead. PACO overhead includes structure graph construction. ALOJA's overhead is dominated by testing of mutants.

| Program | w/o mutations | w/ mutations | PaCo | Aloja |
|---------|---------------|--------------|------|-------|
| Mosquitto | 3 m 21 s | 11 m 36 s | 10 s | 8 m 05 s |
| Wakaama | 2.33 s | 15 m 21.33 s | 24 s | 14 m 55 s |
| MQTT-C | 1.85 s | 8 m 49.41 s | 0.56 s | 8 m 47 s |
| Cyclone DDS | 1 m57 s | 152 m12 s | 13 m 18 s | 138 m 54 s |

The second is the run-time overhead due the additional computation performed by injected mutation templates. In order to estimate this, we measured the latency overhead when sending batches of 10 messages per client, with a fixed size of 10KB each, via the respective protocol with a set number of clients in the network. Note that the impact of the number of clients in the network on protocol performance depends on the design of the protocol itself. Therefore, introduced overhead cannot be compared across different protocols; however, the results still highlight general trends in the overhead introduced by mutations. We evaluated this overhead using 10, 100, and 500 clients for each protocol. As deploying a device network of this size on an experimental testbed is impractical, we simulated the setup by running the server and the client instances on a dedicated machine. We acknowledge this approach is only an approximation of an actual deployment; however we believe it is sufficient to derive high-level conclusions about mutation overhead. All performance evaluations were run on an Ubuntu 20.04 VM with 4 3.7 GHz cores and 10 GB of RAM.

*Results-Compile Time.* Across our 4 codebases, it took, on average, an additional **45.7** min to run the mutation-enabled compilation process. This includes all stages of PACO and ALOJA. Table 7 compares the compile times achieved by clang to that of our process, which also uses clang but applies mutations prior to binary generation. Most of increased overhead is due to testing mutations in ALOJA. For each possible mutation, ALOJA must run the mutated application twice. The significant compilation time for Cyclone DDS indeed results from the fact that its large codebases induces many candidate mutants, than must then be vetted (on average, testing a mutant requires **10 s**). The process could be sped up by better mutation filtering heuristics, which we leave as future work. Also, multiple mutants could be tested in parallel, which would result in significant improvement on modern multicore platforms. Finally, we emphasize that the mutation overhead only need to be incurred once at compile time.

*Results-Execution Time.* Table 8 shows the overhead in message send latency introduced by ALOJA. The overhead ranges from negligible to significant, although the relative overhead generally increases sublinearly with the number of clients, and notably decreases in the case of Wakaama when going from 100 to 500 clients! This fact in particular lead us to suspect that 100-client Wakaama

**Table 8.** Incurred overhead of running **n** = 10, 100, and 500 clients sending 10 KB messages in the original vs. mutated system

| Program | 10 clients | 100 clients | 500 clients |
|---|---|---|---|
| Mosquitto (**Mutated**) | 3 ms (**3 ms**) | 47 ms (**58 ms**) | 160 ms (**200 ms**) |
| Wakaama (**Mutated**) | 80 ms (**122 ms**) | 120 ms (**230 ms**) | 270 ms (**360 ms**) |
| MQTT-C (**Mutated**) | 15 ms (**15 ms**) | 32 ms (**40 ms**) | 120 ms (**190 ms**) |
| Cyclone DDS (**Mutated**) | 14 ms (**15 ms**) | 139 ms (**149 ms**) | 699 ms (**851 ms**) |

results may be affected by an experimental artifact, but were not able to trace the source of the deviation. Future work should focus on further optimizing mutations and better understanding their performance impact.

## 5    Discussion

*Mutation vs Encryption.* A possible way to diversify a protocol is to retrofit it with encryption, and vary encryption keys across deployments. We deliberately decided to design a more general approach based on field-level mutations, for the following reasons. Field-level mutations can be retrofitted automatically during compilation, and do not change protocol state machine, packet size and structure, thus maximizing compatibility with existing network infrastructure and middleboxes. It is also worth noting that, if desired, field-level mutations can be used to deploy encryption (supported by ALOJA). However, they are not limited to it, and can also implement more lightweight forms of obfuscation. We believe this to be useful to control the performance impact of mutations. For smart sensors, which have to operate for extended periods without battery replacement, even a small increase in computation may translate in significant reduction in device life. Summarizing, our goal is to provide software diversity, not data secrecy. Consistently with the end-to-end principle [52], we believe this is best served by evaluating a range of syntactic mutations, and let application designers choose the most appropriate.

*Mutation-Agnostic Attacks.* Other forms of mutation-based moving target defenses have been shown to be vulnerable to mutation-agnostic attacks [51]. In our context, such an attack would consist of a message which triggers a vulnerability regardless of the mutations. This may happen for example if the victim parses each message field iteratively, and relevant mutations only affect fields which are parsed after the malicious data. These attacks can be mitigated by carefully choosing mutations, which always minimize the amount of code executed in response to an non-mutated message.

*Integration into Embedded Development Workflow.* A relevant question is whether incentives exist for embedded developers to integrate mutations into firmware, since manufacturers have limited incentive to improving security. As discussed in Sect. 2.1, we target self-contained deployments managed by same organization. Firmware for mission-critical devices such as robot swarms or military is custom-developed and specified by contract, which simplifies requesting mutation technology. Cheaper white-label devices, such as camera, may ship with closed-source firmware. There, applying mutations may require re-flashing devices with Open-Source, customizable firmware (e.g., OpenIPC [12] for cameras).

*Limitations of Dynamic Analysis.* The dynamic testing techniques we employ, such as unit tests, cannot guarantee correctness. However, we decided to use them due to the intrinsic limitations of the alternative, which is static analysis. Network protocol implementation exhibit a great variety of programming patterns, which makes statically inferring mutation locations challenging. This is exacerbated by the fact that core static analysis algorithms are in general undecidable, and have precision limitations [54]. Thus, we consider dynamic analysis as an acceptable trade-off.

## 6   Related Work

*Moving Target Defense (MTD).* Traditional MTD strategies can be divided into two categories: operating system (OS)-, network-level. As MTD is a large area of research, we only discuss selected examples. At the OS level, Seibert et al. [53] and Hu et al. [34] use Address Space Layout Randomization (ASLR) and Instruction Set Randomization (ISR) to prevent memory corruption vulnerabilities and low-level code injection attacks. Pappas et al. [47] and Wartell et al. [60] introduce schemes to prevent memory disclosure issues by randomizing the data and code segments of each application [64]. At the network level, Al-Shaer [13] proposes an architecture to enable network configuration changes without disrupting network operations. Haadi Jafarian et al. [37] present a software-defined network (SDN)-based MTD strategy that mutates IP addresses, while maintaining configuration integrity. Huang and Ghosh [35] present an MTD scheme to protect web services, by creating a set of diverse offline virtual servers to replace online servers according to the rotation schedule. OS-level mutations do not prevent many kinds of relevant high-level attacks (such as default password reuse). Traditional network-level mutations affect the network configuration and are orthogonal to ours; they can be seen as an additional possible layer of defense. We separately discuss software-level mutations below.

*Software Diversification.* Software diversification is a popular MTD strategy to prevent application level attacks. Jackson et al. [36] propose a compiler-based technique which uses instruction set and register randomization to generate a large number of variants. This technique is designed for mobile apps. Franz [30] similarly discuss a mobile-oriented approach to generate a unique version of an app for each client which downloads it. Cabutto et al. [17] propose to store chunks of executable binary on a trusted server, dynamically downloading them at execution time. However, this method cannot prevent existed vulnerabilities from being triggered since the attacker can still touch the vulnerable code. Wu et al. [62] present LLVM-based binary software randomization, which apply a number of IR-level transformations (e.g., instruction replacement) prior to compilation. This technique has limitations similar to OS-level MTD. Beurdouche et al. [15] propose a verified implementation of a TLS state machine that can be embedded into OpenSSL to change the overall state machine. Our system focuses on a broader set of protocol implementations. Collberg et al. [24] use a trusted server to generate diverse code variants, which are then dynamically installed within running clients. Our system injects the full mutation logic within the client, thus simplifying deployment. Cui and Stolfo [25] propose a host-based defense mechanism called Symbiotic Embedded Machines (SEM). They inject SEMs into host software as an additional component providing monitoring and defense. Compared with SEM, our method does not introduce an executable middleware and does not impose significant overhead on the target application. Pappas et al. [48] propose in-place code randomization, which breaks the semantics of gadgets used in return-oriented programming attacks. Our technique addresses a broader range of attacks.

*Mutation Testing.* Mutation testing, which aims at introducing errors in source code to ensure effectiveness of test cases, can also generate different mutants during the test process. Hariri et al. [32] present a toolset, SRCIROR, for achieving mutation testing at the C/C++ source code and LLVM intermediate representation (IR). Sousa and Sen [58] also present a LLVM IR-based mutation testing, which changes integer constants, to improve the generation of Transaction Level Modeling (TLM) testbenches. Although mutation testing applies mutations similar to those used in MTD, its goal is orthogonal. Evaluating the applications of ALOJA to mutation testing is an interesting direction for future work.

*Parser/Constructor Function Identification.* Polytracker [2] is an LLVM-based instrumentation tool for dynamic taint analysis, which we initially attempted to use within our project. However, we found that, although taint tracking can be used to locate parsing code, it is less suited for identifying message constructors. Besides, it requires users to provide sufficient and comprehensive inputs. Cojocar et al. [23] propose PIE, a methodology to identify protocol implementation parsers in embedded systems. Similar to Polytracker, PIE is also a parser identification approach and does not identify constructors. Bao et al. [14] and Yin et al. [63] present binary-analysis-based function identification methods. Compared to them, our function mapping leverages source code, and can provide a smaller but more precise function set which includes parser/constructor functions.

## 7   Conclusion

In this paper, we described a technique for injecting mutations into implementations of embedded/IoT-oriented network protocols as a form of moving-target defense. Our evaluation shows that we correctly identify message-generating and parsing code and inject mutations which preserve functional correctness of a protocol. Furthermore, mutations are effective in preventing one-size-fits-all exploits, and only introduce limited overhead. By automating program analysis and transformations necessary for mutations, our work provides an important foundation for moving-target defense based on protocol dialects.

**Acknowledgments.** We thank the anonymous reviewers for their insightful comments. This project was supported by the Office of Naval Research (Grants#: N00014-18-1-2660; N00014-21-1-2492). Any opinions, findings, and conclusions or recommendations expressed in this paper are those of the authors and do not necessarily reflect the views of the funding agency.

# References

1. Micro Autonomous System Technologies (MAST). http://www.mast-cta.org/
2. trailofbits/polytracker: An LLVM-based instrumentation tool for universal taint analysis. https://github.com/trailofbits/polytracker
3. Eclipse Mosquitto (January 2020). https://mosquitto.org/
4. DSVPN (February 2021). https://github.com/jedisct1/dsvpn
5. GitHub - jtpereyda/boofuzz (February 2021). https://github.com/jtpereyda/boofuzz
6. MQTT-C (February 2021). https://github.com/LiamBindle/MQTT-C
7. OpenDDS (August 2021). https://opendds.org/
8. Shodan (January 2021). https://www.shodan.io/
9. wakaama (February 2021). https://www.eclipse.org/wakaama/
10. Who's Using DDS? (January 2021). https://www.dds foundation.org/who-is-using-dds-2/
11. CycloneDDS (2022). https://github.com/eclipse-cyclonedds/cyclonedds
12. OpenIPC (December 2022). https://openipc.org/
13. Al-Shaer, E.: Toward network configuration randomization for moving target defense. In: Moving Target Defense (2011)
14. Bao, T., Burket, J., Woo, M., Turner, R., Brumley, D.: BYTEWEIGHT: Learning to recognize functions in binary code. In: USENIX Security Symposium (2014)
15. Beurdouche, B., et al.: A messy state of the union: Taming the composite state machines of tls. In: IEEE S&P (2015)
16. Brian Krebs: Who Makes the IoT Things Under Attack? — Krebs on Security (October 2016). https://krebsonsecurity.com/2016/10/who-makes-the-iot-things-under-attack/
17. Cabutto, A., Falcarin, P., Abrath, B., Coppens, B., De Sutter, B.: Software protection with code mobility. In: ACM MTD Workshop (2015)
18. Cameron, L.: IoT Meets the Military | IEEE Computer Society (March 2017). https://www.computer.org/publications/tech-news/research/internet-of-military-battlefield-things-iomt-iobt
19. Caselli, M., Zambon, E., Sommer, R., Kargl, F., Amann, J.: Specification mining for intrusion detection in networked control systems. In: USENIX Security Symposium (2017)

20. Chung, T.: OFFensive Swarm-Enabled Tactics. https://www.darpa.mil/program/offensive-swarm-enabled-tactics

21. Cimpanu, C.: Hacker leaks passwords for more than 500,000 servers, routers, and IoT devices (January 2020). https://www.zdnet.com/article/hacker-leaks-passwords-for-more-than-500000-servers-routers-and-iot-devices/

22. Cohen, F.B.: Operating system protection through program evolution. Comput. Sec. **12**(6), 565–584 (1993)

23. Cojocar, L., Zaddach, J., Verdult, R., Bos, H., Francillon, A., Balzarotti, D.: Pie: Parser identification in embedded systems. In: ACSAC (2015)

24. Collberg, C., Martin, S., Myers, J., Nagra, J.: Distributed application tamper detection via continuous software updates. In: ACSAC (2012)

25. Cui, A., Stolfo, S.: Symbiotes and defensive mutualism: Moving target defense. In: Moving Target Defense, pp. 99–108 (August 2011)

26. Davi, L.V., Dmitrienko, A., Nürnberger, S., Sadeghi, A.R.: Gadge me if you can: Secure and efficient ad-hoc instruction-level randomization for x86 and ARM. In: ASIA CCS (2013)

27. De Carli, L., Mignano, A.: Network security for home iot devices must involve the user: a position paper. In: FPS (2020)

28. De Carli, L., Torres, R., Modelo-Howard, G., Tongaonkar, A., Jha, S.: Botnet protocol inference in the presence of encrypted traffic. In: INFOCOM (2017)

29. Eduard Kovacs: Serious Vulnerabilities Found in Schneider Electric Power Meters | SecurityWeek.Com (March 2021). https://www.securityweek.com/serious-vulnerabilities-found-schneider-electric-power-meters

30. Franz, M.: E unibus pluram: Massive-scale software diversity as a defense mechanism. In: NSPW (2010)

31. Goodin, D.: 100,000-strong botnet built on router 0-day could strike at any time (December 2017). https://arstechnica.com/information-technology/2017/12/100000-strong-botnet-built-on-router-0-day-could-strike-at-any-time/

32. Hariri, F., Shi, A.: Srciror: A toolset for mutation testing of c source code and llvm intermediate representation. In: ACM/IEEE ASE (2018)

33. Higgins, F., Tomlinson, A., Martin, K.M.: Threats to the Swarm: Security Considerations for Swarm Robotics. Int. J. Adv. Sec. **2**(2&3) (2009)

34. Hu, W., et al.: Secure and practical defense against code-injection attacks using software dynamic translation. In: VEE (2006)

35. Huang, Y., Ghosh, A.: Introducing diversity and uncertainty to create moving attack surfaces for web services. In: Moving Target Defense, pp. 131–151 (August 2011)

36. Jackson, T., et al.: Compiler-generated software diversity. In: Moving Target Defense, pp. 77–98 (August 2011)

37. Jafarian, J.H., Al-Shaer, E., Duan, Q.: Openflow random host mutation: Transparent moving target defense using software defined networking. In: HotSDN (2012)

38. Kat Hall: Hyperoptic's ZTE-made 1gbps routers had hyper-hardcoded hyper-root hyper-password (April 2018). https://www.theregister.co.uk/2018/04/26/hyperoptics_zte_routers/

39. Krebs, B.: Naming & Shaming Web Polluters: Xiongmai - Krebs on Security (October 2018). https://krebsonsecurity.com/2018/10/naming-shaming-web-polluters-xiongmai/

40. Larsen, P., Homescu, A., Brunthaler, S., Franz, M.: SoK: Automated Software Diversity. In: IEEE S&P (2014)

41. Lewellen, T.: CERT/CC Vulnerability Note VU#800094 (September 2013). https://www.kb.cert.org

42. Maruyama, Y., Kato, S., Azumi, T.: Exploring the performance of ros2. In: EMSOFT (2016)
43. Merces, F., Remillano II, A., Molina, J.: Mirai Botnet Attack IoT Devices via CVE-2020-5902 (July 2020). https://www.trendmicro.com/en_us/research/20/g/mirai-botnet-attack-iot-devices-via-cve-2020-5902.html
44. Moore, D., Paxson, V., Savage, S., Shannon, C., Staniford, S., Weaver, N.: Inside the Slammer worm. IEEE Sec. Privacy 1(4), 33–39 (2003)
45. Moore, D., Shannon, C., claffy, k.: Code-Red: A case study on the spread and victims of an internet worm. In: ACM IMW (2002)
46. Muncaster, P.: A Third of Industrial Control Systems Attacked in H1 2021 (September 2021). https://www.infosecurity-magazine.com/news/third-industrial-control-systems/
47. Pappas, V., Polychronakis, M., Keromytis, A.D.: Smashing the gadgets: Hindering return-oriented programming using in-place code randomization. In: IEEE S&P (2012)
48. Pappas, V., Polychronakis, M., Keromytis, A.: Practical software diversification using in-place code randomization. In: Moving Target Defense (2013)
49. Pascu, L.: Multiple critical security flaws found in nearly 400 IP cameras - Bitdefender BOX Blog (June 2018), https://www.bitdefender.com/box/blog/ip-cameras-vulnerabilities/multiple-critical-security-flaws-found-nearly-400-ip-cameras/
50. Ronen, E., Shamir, A., Weingarten, A., O'Flynn, C.: IoT goes nuclear: creating a zigbee chain reaction. In: IEEE S&P (2017)
51. Rudd, R., et al.: Address oblivious code reuse: on the effectiveness of leakage-resilient diversity. In: NDSS (2017)
52. Saltzer, J.H., Reed, D.P., Clark, D.D.: End-to-end arguments in system design. ACM Trans. Comput. Syst. (TOCS) 2(4), 277–288 (1984)
53. Seibert, J., Okhravi, H., Söderström, E.: Information leaks without memory disclosures: Remote side channel attacks on diversified code. In: ACM CCS (2014)
54. Shapiro, M., Horwitz, S.: The effects of the precision of pointer analysis. In: Van Hentenryck, P. (ed.) SAS 1997. LNCS, vol. 1302, pp. 16–34. Springer, Heidelberg (1997). https://doi.org/10.1007/BFb0032731
55. Shekari, T., Irvene, C., Beyah, R.: IoT Skimmer: Energy Market Manipulation through High-Wattage IoT Botnets - Black Hat USA 2020 (August 2020), https://www.blackhat.com/us-20/briefings/schedule/index.html#iot-skimmer-energy-market-manipulation-through-high-wattage-iot-botnets-20280
56. Simpson, A.K., Roesner, F., Kohno, T.: Securing vulnerable home IoT devices with an in-hub security manager. In: PerCom Workshop (2017)
57. Soltan, S., Mittal, P., Poor, H.V.: BlackIoT: IoT botnet of high wattage devices can disrupt the power grid. In: USENIX Security (2018)
58. Sousa, M., Sen, A.: Generation of tlm testbenches using mutation testing. In: CODES+ISSS 2012 (2012)
59. Wang, N., Schmidt, D.C., van't Hag, H., Corsaro, A.: Toward an adaptive data distribution service for dynamic large-scale network-centric operation and warfare (ncow) systems. In: MILCOM (2008)
60. Wartell, R., Mohan, V., Hamlen, K.W., Lin, Z.: Binary stirring: Self-randomizing instruction addresses of legacy x86 binary code. In: ACM CCS (2012)
61. Williams, D., Hu, W., Davidson, J.W., Hiser, J.D., Knight, J.C., Nguyen-Tuong, A.: Security through diversity: leveraging virtual machine technology. IEEE Sec. Privacy 7(1), 26–33 (2009)

62. Wu, B., Ma, Y., Fan, L., Qian, F.: Binary software randomization method based on llvm. In: 2018 IEEE International Conference of Safety Produce Informatization (IICSPI), pp. 808–811 (2018)
63. Yin, X., Liu, S., Liu, L., Xiao, D.: Function recognition in stripped binary of embedded devices. IEEE Access **6**, 75682–75694 (2018)
64. Zheng, J., Siami Namin, A.: A survey on the moving target defense strategies: An architectural perspective. J. Comput. Sci. Technol. **34**, 207–233 (2019)

# Security and Privacy-Preserving Solutions in the Internet of Things (S/P-IoT) Workshop

# A Generalized Unknown Malware Classification

Nanda Rani, Ayushi Mishra, Rahul Kumar, Sarbajit Ghosh,
Sandeep K. Shukla, and Priyanka Bagade[✉]

Department of Computer Science and Engineering, Indian Institute of Technology,
Kanpur, Kanpur, India
{nandarani,ayushim,rahulkumar,sarbajitg,sandeeps,pbagade}@cse.iitk.ac.in

**Abstract.** Although state-of-the-art image-based malware classification models give the best performance, these models fail to consider real-world deployment challenges due to various reasons. We address three such problems through this work: limited dataset problems, imbalanced dataset problems, and lack of model generalizability. We employ a prototypical network-based few-shot learning method for a limited dataset problem and achieve 98.71% accuracy while training with only four malware samples of each class. To address the imbalanced dataset problem, we propose a class-weight technique to increase the weightage of minority classes during the training. The model performs well by improving precision and recall from 0% to close to 60% for the minority class. For the generalized model, we present a meta-learning-based approach and improve model performance from 48% to 72.06% accuracy. We report performances on five diverse datasets. The proposed solutions have the potential to set benchmark performance for their corresponding problem statements.

**Keywords:** Malware classification · Deep learning · Cyber Security · Malware

## 1 Introduction

The advancement in malware development leads to rapidly evolving malware families. Several image-based deep learning (DL) models, such as ResNet, MLP, LSTM, and GRU, are available that perform well for the corresponding datasets. The recent state-of-the-art models offer close to 99–100% accuracy on some of the datasets [1–3,7]. Although these models perform well, they lack with following capabilities, which we address through this research work:

1. Limited Dataset - The traditional deep learning model requires more data to learn significant features from given image sets. There will always be fewer samples for newly evolved malware classes. In such cases, traditional DL models fail to identify the patterns of the latest evolved malware families. Collecting more newly evolved malware samples to train the traditional model

© ICST Institute for Computer Sciences, Social Informatics and Telecommunications Engineering 2023
Published by Springer Nature Switzerland AG 2023. All Rights Reserved
F. Li et al. (Eds.): SecureComm 2022, LNICST 462, pp. 793–806, 2023.
https://doi.org/10.1007/978-3-031-25538-0_41

may cause a delay in recognizing malware family classes. Hence, there is a need for a model that can learn features from limited malware samples that are newly evolved.

2. Imbalanced Dataset - The datasets used to train various malware classification models [1,5,7] as well as publicly available datasets [1,3,7] are highly imbalanced. Imbalance data may lead to overfitting the model or may result in a biased model. Generating synthetic malware samples may not be a good option for dealing with the imbalanced dataset problem as the actual malware may differ in functionality. Hence, there is a need for a learning methodology that gives importance to classes with fewer samples in the dataset during the training phase to overcome overfitting.

3. Lack of model generalizability - It is always considered that training and testing datasets belong to the same distribution. However, there is a significant chance that unseen test set malware may belong to out-of-distribution from the training sample's distribution. Hence, there is a need for a generic model that can generalize the malware family class and identify patterns from unseen out-of-distribution malware samples. Based on our knowledge, there is no research work for generic malware classification models that can detect out-of-distribution samples.

We introduce three approaches based on advanced deep learning methods to address these problems. First, we implement a prototypical network-based few-shot learning model that can learn new sophisticated malware sample patterns by only seeing very few samples of each malware class. Second, we propose a class weight technique to provide weightage to minority classes and significantly improve the precision-recall of the minority class. Lastly, we employ meta-learning to propose generic models that can detect out-of-distribution malware samples. We utilize five malware datasets of different distributions and achieve better results. We verify the differences between distributions of multiple datasets by implementing out-of-distributions techniques proposed by Zaeemzadeh et al. [12]. Our contributions through this research work are the following:

1. We present a model based on few-shot learning that can learn patterns of newly evolved malware with very few samples.
2. We propose a class weight-based model that can balance the imbalance effect in the malware dataset during training.
3. We introduce a generic model that can classify out-of-distribution samples belonging to the training set's malware class.

We discuss related research work for image-based malware classification in Sect. 2. Section 3 explains the background of malware analysis techniques and how it evolves. We elaborated the implemented methodology to address mentioned research gaps in Sect. 4. Section 5 discusses the experiment implementation and the results. Further, we conclude the contribution and future scope of this research in Sect. 6.

## 2    Related Work

Recently, image-based malware classification has gained popularity over traditional malware classification methods, i.e., static and dynamic malware analysis [2,6]. However, the textural differences between malware images make DL models suitable for identifying malware patterns. Many research experiments are available which implement deep learning models on diverse datasets and exploring several possible feature sets for image-based malware classification. This section discusses a summary of recently proposed malware classification methods.

Natraj et al. [6] propose the first idea to visualize the malware binaries and classify malware based on images. They released the very first image-based dataset named Malimg publicly. Microsoft released malware samples in one of the Kaggle challenges for image-based malware classification [14]. Both datasets, Malimg and Microsoft, have a total of 9,339 and 20,860 samples, respectively.

Singh et al. [1] demonstrate a novel method for malware classification by implementing a pre-trained ResNet50 model and achieved an accuracy of 99.40%. However, they mentioned that their model gives low accuracy for previously unseen malware [1]. Bozkir et al. [5] recognize malware from RGB images generated from a memory dump of the suspicious process by utilizing GIST and HOG features. Among all implemented learning models, the best accuracy is 96.39%. They perform manual feature extraction, which may not be a good option when deploying a model in real time. Similarly, Dhavalle et al. [2] extract features from the images, including energy, entropy, contrast, dissimilarity, homogeneity, and correlation and build various machine learning classifiers. The random forest model achieves the highest accuracy of 96.7%. Bhodia et al. [7] implement several variants of ResNet to identify malware patterns. Even though the authors use several DL models to identify malware, none of them is a generic model which can detect unseen malware. In [3], the authors present diverse deep learning models, including MLP, CNN, LSTM and GRU, to utilize image-based features and opcode features to train the models. VGG19 and ResNet152 perform well with 92% accuracy, but their model is not validated for unknown malware variants. Kim et al. [4] employs a hybrid deep generative model which exploits local and global features of malware images and uses variational autoencoders. The model doesn't validate generalizability with diverse datasets [4].

Zhu et al. [10] implement a Siamese Neural Network-based few-shot learning method to detect malware with few samples, detecting ransomware attacks with few samples. However, their work is limited to ransomware malware class only. Matching networks and prototypical network-based methods for malware classification are introduced by Tran et al. [19]. They claimed performance on a very limited number of experiments and matching network-based model performs poor for Malimg dataset as well as both proposed model performs poor for Microsoft dataset. All of the above research works primarily focus on model performance accuracy and overlook class-wise precision and recall. Also, there is not much work on malware classification with limited malware samples and work which discusses model generalizability for malware classifications. Therefore, we address these research problems in this paper.

## 3   Background

Malware is a malicious code that aims to conduct various destructive operations without the victim's consent and awareness. Attackers introduce several malware families; some notorious families are Trojans, Backdoors, Ransomware, and Worms. With the newly emerging cyber threats, malware is growing exponentially.

As malware evolves rapidly, It is necessary to have intelligent algorithms to identify malware patterns effectively. Primarily, two main analysis techniques are there for malware analysis: static and dynamic. Static analysis can identify malicious patterns without running the executables, and by observing the code structures [17]. However, this method is ineffective against obfuscated malware.

Dynamic code analysis executes the code in a sandbox environment to reveal the runtime behavior [18]. Although it is better than static analysis, dynamic analysis consumes more time and resources. Also, some sophisticated malware may not demonstrate malicious behaviour while running in the sandbox. On the other hand, image-based malware classification provides a novel way to classify the malware without executing the code and performing manual code investigation. The image-based classification techniques provide an emerging exploration method to classify malware with respect to texture variations between malware classes. The texture difference between malware families is shown in Fig. 1.

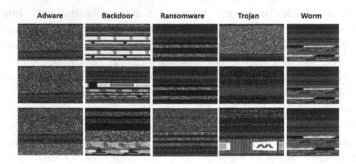

**Fig. 1.** Malware Families representation in Grayscale images

## 4   Proposed Methodology

### 4.1   Dataset

The Malimg [6] and Microsoft challenge datasets [14] are the only publicly available. These datasets contain old malware sample variants that may not contain recent malware patterns. Therefore, we create our dataset by collecting recent malware samples from MalwareBazaar[1]. MalwareBazaar is a platform that aims to share malware samples with the cyber community for study purposes. Our

---

[1] https://bazaar.abuse.ch/.

dataset contains 11,273 malware samples belonging to different malware classes, including ransomware, worm, trojan, adware and backdoor, with 813, 4012, 3926, 426 and 2096 samples, respectively.

We generate grayscale images by converting the executable samples from our dataset. As executable binaries are sequences of 0's and 1's, we use this sequence to group consecutive 8 bits and calculate their corresponding decimal value. The sequence of decimal values is stored in an array and considered as a pixel value for generating the grayscale image for executables. The generated images are visually distinguishable between different malware families (Fig. 1). We set the width of the image size to 256 and let the length be flexible according to the size of executables [1]. We explain all these steps in Algorithm 1.

---

**Algorithm 1.** Executable to grey-scale image conversion

---

0: **procedure** BINARY_TO_IMAGE(*file*) {Convert binary executable to grayscale image}
1: Width = 256
2: Length = File_Size/Width
3: Calculate decimal values for each consecutive 8 bits.
4: Create a 2-D array by fixing width as 256.
5: Convert 2-D array into grayscale images.

---

We obtain datasets from Singh et al. [1] and Prajapati et al. [3]. We use five datasets (Malimg [6], Microsoft [14], Singh et al. [1], Prajapati et al. [3] and our dataset) to perform experiments. We address the research gaps discussed in Sect. 1 by introducing few-shot learning for limited dataset problems (Sect. 4.2), class weight method for imbalanced dataset problems (Sect. 4.3) and meta-learning for model generalizability (Sect. 4.4).

### 4.2  Limited Dataset

We present a prototypical network-based few-shot learning model to address the limited dataset problem. The prototypical network is based on the idea that there is an embedding in which several points cluster around a single prototype representation for each class, present in Fig. 2. The goal is to learn per-class prototypes using feature space sample averaging. In this implementation, we assume 'm' labelled datasets as a support set, where 'm' is as small as one or two samples. The support set is represented as S = $(x_1, y_1), ..., (x_m, y_m)$, in which $x_i \in \mathbb{R}^D$ is D-dimensional feature vector and $y_i \in 1, ...., n$ is corresponding labels. We can denote the support set as $S_n$, represented as data samples with class $l$. The prototype for each class is represented as $C_n$, where $C_n \in \mathbb{R}^m$, an embedding function $f_\theta : \mathbb{R}^D \to \mathbb{R}^m$ having $\phi$ as the learnable parameter. Each prototype represents the average of the embedded support points in its class [13].

$$C_n = \frac{1}{|S_n|} \sum_{(x_i, y_i) \epsilon S_n} f_\phi(X_i) \tag{1}$$

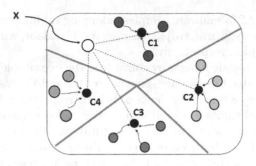

**Fig. 2.** Prototypical networks [13]

The learning phase of Prototypical Networks is to perform by minimizing the negative log-probability $J(\phi)$, often known as log-softmax loss [13].

$$J(\phi) = -log(p_\phi(y = n|x)) \text{ for true class k}$$

where,

$$p_\phi(y = n|x) = \frac{exp(-d(f_\phi(x), c_n))}{\Sigma_{n'} exp(-d(f_\phi(x), c_{n'}}$$

Here $d$ represents euclidean distance.

The key benefit of utilizing a logarithm is that the loss is drastically increased when model fails to predict the correct class labels. The query images classify by measuring the distance between each unlabeled image and prototypes using Euclidean distance. After computing distances, we apply softmax to obtain the probability of belonging to each class, then assign a class based on greater the probability, shorter the distance.

### 4.3   Imbalanced Dataset

We employ class weight techniques to balance the imbalance effect of data samples during training. We assign low and high-weight values to the majority and minority classes. We calculate the weight for each class by using the following formula:

$$w_i = \frac{n\_samples}{(n\_classes * n\_samplesi)} \tag{2}$$

where,
$w_i$ is the weight for each class (i represents the class)
$n\_samples$ is the total number of samples in the dataset
$n\_classes$ is the total number of unique classes
$n\_samplesi$ is the total number of samples of the respective class

The aim is to give the minority class more weight throughout the training phase. We implement a weighted log loss function to achieve the same.

$$log\_loss = \frac{1}{N} \sum_{i=1}^{N} [-(\omega_0(y_i * log(\hat{y}_i)) + \omega_1((1 - y_i) * log(1 - \hat{y}_i)))] \tag{3}$$

where,

$\omega_0$ is the class weight for zero class.

$\omega_1$ is the class weight for one class.

The goal of the objective function in Eq. 3 is to penalize the minority class for misclassification by assigning them a higher class weight while the majority class gets a lower weight. We implement this technique with the ResNet50 model using the weight and loss function shown in Eq. 3.

### 4.4  Model Generalization

We present a meta-learning-based model generalization method to build a generic model. The aim is to build a generic model which can identify malware patterns in the dataset whose distribution was not present in the training dataset. To the best of our knowledge, there are no generic models available that can get trained on one distribution dataset and detect samples of datasets with different distributions. All state-of-the-art model training and testing perform on the same distribution, i.e., the same dataset only [1,3,6,7]. We had a total of five datasets, and before proceeding with generalization, we first needed to verify whether the distribution of all five datasets was different or not. Therefore, we verify the distribution differentiation by implementing out-of-distribution detection.

**Out of Distribution Detection.** In real-world scenarios, test samples may not contain the data from train samples. Therefore, detecting the out-of-distribution (OOD) samples that do not belong to the training classes is desirable. We implement the union of 1-dimensional spaces [12] to perform the OOD detection.

OOD samples can get recognized more robustly and with a greater probability if the feature vectors of the training samples are in a 1-dimensional subspace [12]. Given a training dataset of N-sample label pairings from L available classes, the goal is to train a neural network to detect out-of-distribution samples during testing (not belonging to any known L classes).

Making the distribution of known classes as compact as possible reduces the risk of error. The error probability is given by $p_e = \sqrt{p_l p_o} \exp(-\mathscr{B})$, where $\mathscr{B}$ is the Bhattacharyya distance [15] and is given by:

$$\mathscr{B} = \frac{1}{8} \Delta^T \left(\frac{\Sigma_l + \Sigma_o}{2}\right)^{-1} \Delta + \frac{1}{2} \log \frac{(\det \frac{\Sigma_l + \Sigma_o}{2})}{\sqrt{\det \Sigma_l \det \Sigma_o}} \quad (4)$$

$$\Delta = (\mu_l - \mu_o)$$

The distance $\mathscr{B}$ is a combination of the Mahalanobis distance and a measure of the compactness of the distributions [12]. We distinguish OOD and IN distributions during test time using the cosine similarities between the test samples and the singular vector corresponding to each class. The cosine similarity is:

$$\cos(\theta_{ln}) = \frac{w_l^T x_n}{||w_l|| \, ||x_n||} \quad (5)$$

OOD test perform by computing the angular minimum distance of test feature vector $x_n$, which is given by

$$\phi_n = \min_l \arccos(\frac{|x_n^T v_1^{(l)}|}{||x_n||}) \tag{6}$$

**Meta Learning Based Model Generalization.** We implement a meta-learning-based model generalization method. For generalization, Li et al. [11] present a novel meta-learning approach to synthesize virtual training and test domain for validation during training for achieving generalization, which we follow for this work. Our model generalization method provides a model agnostic training method that enhances the domain generalizability of a base learner. We use ResNet18 as a base learner for this work. We divide a set of different distribution datasets in a train, val and test set so that all have different distributions dataset. We train the base learner on a train set distribution and, at the same time, validate on a validation set distribution(which is different from the training distribution). The meta-optimization goal is to reduce the loss on the training distributions while simultaneously ensuring that the direction is taken to accomplish this also improves the validation loss (having a different distribution than the train set). Once a model learns to minimize the loss on the validation set (different distribution), we can evaluate performance on the test set (having novel different distribution data). We illustrate the model generalization learning flow in Fig. 3 (Different symbols represent different distributions of data samples).

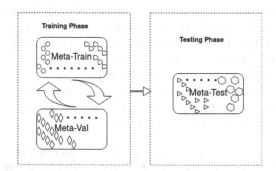

**Fig. 3.** Model generalization model learning method

We assume there are total n_d different distributions of malware datasets in the training set. The test dataset belongs to different distribution, which is not present in the training set. The malware class for all distribution datasets must be the same to compare generalizability. Therefore, we compare the malware class of all available datasets and found three common malware families in all five datasets. These are trojan class, worm class and backdoor class. Hence we

validate our implementation with the three-class classification. The steps follow
to implement the generic model are following:

- We define a base model, ResNet18, parameterized as $\theta$ and hyperparameters
  $\alpha, \beta, \gamma$. to solve the malware classification task. Where, $\alpha$ is meta step size,
  $\beta$ is meta val beta and $\gamma$ is decay rate.
- For each iteration, we follow the below steps:
  - Split the n_d distribution into $\hat{n}_d$ and $\bar{n}_d$.
  - For meta-train we calculate gradients

  $$\nabla_\theta = \mathcal{F}'(\hat{n}_d; \theta)$$

  where $\mathcal{F}$ is the cross-entropy loss function.
  - We update the model parameter with $\theta' = \theta - \alpha \nabla_\theta$
  - We calculate cross entropy loss by using $\bar{n}_d$ and $\theta'$ i.e., $\mathcal{G}(\bar{n}_d; \theta')$
  - For meta-optimization we update the model by using

  $$\theta = \theta - \gamma \frac{\partial(\mathcal{F}(\hat{n}_d; \theta) + \beta \mathcal{G}(\bar{n}_d; \theta - \alpha \nabla_\theta))}{\partial \theta}$$

We minimize the following objective function for this algorithm.:

$$\mathcal{F}(\theta) + \beta \mathcal{G}(\theta - \alpha \mathcal{F}'(\theta)) \tag{7}$$

## 5   Experiment and Results Discussion

### 5.1   Limited Dataset Results

We implement few-shot learning on various datasets available, and the model
achieves best performance considerably by seeing very few malware samples.
Malimg, Microsoft, Singh et al. [6] and our dataset has seven, six, eight and
five classes, respectively. Hence we run them for the number of different class
way n shots, where n can be small, i.e. no newly evolved samples available. The
accuracy achieved by model on the datasets is present in Table 1.

**Table 1.** Result of limited dataset problem

| Our dataset | Acc (%) | Malimg | Acc (%) | Microsoft | Acc (%) | Singh et al. [1] | Acc (%) |
|---|---|---|---|---|---|---|---|
| 5-way 1-shot | 53.85 | 6-way 1-shot | 86.96 | 7-way 1-shot | 91.24 | 8-way 1-shot | 63.04 |
| 5-way 2-shot | 53.57 | 6-way 2-shot | 87.12 | 7-way 2-shot | 90.43 | 8-way 2-shot | **71.59** |
| 5-way 4-shot | 56.86 | 6-way 4-shot | 95 | 7-way 4-shot | **98.71** | 8-way 4-shot | 70 |
| 5-way 8-shot | **65.85** | 6-way 8-shot | **96.88** | 7-way 8-shot | 95.50 | 8-way 8-shot | 69.53 |

## 5.2  Imbalanced Dataset Results

We implement a class weight-based methodology to resolve the imbalance dataset problem. To assess the model performance, we need to verify whether class-wise precision-recall of minority classes is improving or not, as accuracy may not always be a suitable indicator of model performance with an imbalanced dataset. The implemented method improves minority class performance significantly. Hence, Improvement in minority class performance in terms of precision and recall is present in Tables 2, 3, 4 and 5.

**Table 2.** Result of imbalanced problem on Microsoft Dataset

| Class name | Without proposed method | | With proposed method | |
|---|---|---|---|---|
|  | Precision | Recall | Precision | Recall |
| Adware | 0.97 | 0.98 | 0.94 | 0.99 |
| Backdoor | **0.00** | **0.00** | **0.25** | **0.60** |
| Virtool | **0.85** | 0.91 | **0.86** | 0.91 |
| Worm | **0.96** | 0.88 | **0.97** | 0.94 |
| Trojan | **0.87** | 0.84 | **0.95** | 0.76 |
| Botnet | 1.00 | 1.00 | 0.99 | 1.00 |

**Table 3.** Result of imbalanced problem on Our Dataset

| Class name | Without proposed method | | With proposed method | |
|---|---|---|---|---|
|  | Precision | Recall | Precision | Recall |
| Adware | 0.86 | 0.60 | 0.85 | 0.73 |
| Backdoor | 0.94 | **0.89** | 0.87 | **0.91** |
| Ransomware | 0.80 | 0.79 | 0.80 | 0.79 |
| Worm | **0.00** | **0.00** | **0.32** | **0.50** |
| Trojan | **0.46** | 0.60 | **0.67** | 0.58 |

**Table 4.** Result of Imbalanced problem on Singh et al. [1] Dataset

| Class name | Without proposed method | | With proposed method | |
|---|---|---|---|---|
|  | Precision | Recall | Precision | Recall |
| Trojan Dropper | 1.0 | 1.0 | 1.0 | 0.99 |
| Virus | 0.94 | 0.77 | 0.84 | 0.77 |
| Trojan Downloader | 0.89 | 0.88 | 0.79 | 0.93 |
| Backdoor | 0.84 | 0.76 | 0.83 | 0.62 |
| Virtool | **0.00** | **0.00** | **0.59** | **0.40** |
| Worm | 1.0 | 1.00 | 0.99 | 1.00 |
| Trojan | 0.78 | 0.89 | 0.75 | 0.92 |
| Rogue | 0.00 | 0.00 | 0.00 | 0.00 |

Table 5. Result of imbalanced problem on Malimg Dataset

| | Without proposed method | | With proposed method | |
|---|---|---|---|---|
| Class name | Precision | Recall | Precision | Recall |
| Trojan Downloader | 0.98 | **0.95** | 0.92 | **0.98** |
| Backdoor | 1.00 | 1.00 | 1.00 | 1.00 |
| Worm | 1.00 | 1.00 | 1.00 | 1.00 |
| Trojan | **0.95** | 0.97 | **0.99** | 0.91 |
| PWS | 1.00 | 0.99 | 1.00 | 0.99 |
| Dialer | 0.99 | 1.00 | 0.99 | 1.00 |
| Rogue | 0.98 | 1.00 | 0.98 | 1.00 |

## 5.3   Model Generalization Results

We first verify whether the available dataset is in different distribution or not before moving towards generic model implementation.

**Out of Distribution Results.** We implement an OOD detection method to test the distribution difference between datasets by measuring FPR@95TPR and AUC (Area under the ROC Curve). FPR@95TPR is the probability that a negative (out-of-distribution) example gets miscategorized as positive (in-distribution) when the true positive rate (TPR) is as high as 95%. The lower value for FPR@95TPR and higher value for AUC proves the in-data and out-data taken belongs to different distributions. We verified the distribution difference by implementing the method explained in Sect. 4.4 and obtained FPR@95TPR value as 0.2573 and AUC value as 0.93616. The lower value of FPR@95TPR and higher value of AUC proves that the taken datasets are of different distributions.

**Meta Learning for Domain Generalization Results.** To create a baseline for comparing proposed method performance, we evaluate model performance without implementing the proposed meta-learning approach. We implement a commonly used ResNet50 neural network and train on our dataset and Microsoft dataset, and test it on the Malimg dataset and receive only 48% accuracy. Which is not preferable and needs to have a generic model which can perform better than the baseline. Hence, we trained the meta-learning model on the set of Our dataset and Microsoft dataset, and tested on Malimg dataset. Initially, the model achieved accuracy of 68.21%, which is an improvement form the baseline, but we experiment more to improve the performance. Next, in order to increase the diversity of the training set, we train it with the set consists our dataset, Microsoft dataset, and Singh et al. [1] dataset and test on Malimg dataset. This time model improves the accuracy to 69.83%. Finally, we use all five datasets and selected our dataset, Microsoft dataset, Singh et al. [1], and Prajapati et al. [3] dataset for training and Malimg dataset for testing. This time the model improved the accuracy significantly and achieved 72.06%. We can see a high jump compared to the baseline ResNet model from 48% to 72.06% by adding a meta-learning approach on top of the base learner. The result of implemented meta-learning proves that by adding a more diverse distribution dataset in the training phase, the model is learning unknown dimensions of data and generalizing more towards pattern detection for unseen and different distribution malware samples. We summarize the performance of meta-learning for generic models in Table 6.

**Table 6.** Result of model generalization

| Cases number | Training set | Testing set | Acc. |
|---|---|---|---|
| Case 1 (Baseline) | Microsoft | Malimg Dataset | **48%** |
| Case 2 | Microsoft and Our dataset | Malimg Dataset | 68.21% |
| Case 3 | Microsoft, our dataset and Singh et al. [1] | Malimg Dataset | 69.83% |
| Case 4 | Microsoft, our dataset, Singh et al. [1] and Prajapati et al. [3] | Malimg Dataset | **72.06%** |

# 6   Conclusions and Future Scope

This research addresses the critical gaps present in the current malware classification using image representation. The key contribution of this research work is to handle limited and imbalanced dataset problems and present a robust generic malware classification model. Our work focuses on implementing image-based malware classification techniques rather than static and dynamic analysis. This research highlights the malware classification model generalization, which has the potential to provide a new research dimension in malware classification research. As a part of the future work, Hyperparameter tuning can be one of the possible modifications to improve model generalization algorithm performance. The proposed class weight-based technique significantly improves the precision and recall of minority classes and effectively balances the imbalance data effect. The presented model for the limited dataset problem can also further improve by using a zero-shot deep learning technique. In a nutshell, this research work has the strength to serve as a foundation for several future studies on the imbalance and limited malware dataset problem and enhancement of the malware classification model's generalization ability.

**Acknowledgement.** We thank to the C3i (Cyber Security and Cyber Security for Cyber-Physical Systems) Innovation Hub for partially funding this research project.

# References

1. Singh, A., Handa, A., Kumar, N., Shukla, S.K.: Malware classification using image representation. In: Dolev, S., Hendler, D., Lodha, S., Yung, M. (eds.) CSCML 2019. LNCS, vol. 11527, pp. 75–92. Springer, Cham (2019). https://doi.org/10.1007/978-3-030-20951-3_6
2. Dhavlle, A., Shukla, S.: A novel malware detection mechanism based on features extracted from converted malware binary images, ArXiv, vol. abs/2104.06652 (2021)
3. Prajapati, P., Stamp, M.: An empirical analysis of image-based learning techniques for malware classification. In: Stamp, M., Alazab, M., Shalaginov, A. (eds.) Malware Analysis Using Artificial Intelligence and Deep Learning. Springer, Cham (2021). https://doi.org/10.1007/978-3-030-62582-5_16
4. Kim, J.Y., Cho, S.B.: Obfuscated malware detection using deep generative model based on global/local features. Comput. Secur. **112**, 102501 (2022). ISSN 0167-4048. https://doi.org/10.1016/j.cose.2021.102501
5. Bozkir, A., Tahillioglu, E., Aydos, M., Kara, I.: Catch them alive: a malware detection approach through memory forensics, manifold learning and computer vision. Comput. Secur. **103**, 04 (2021)
6. Nataraj, L., Karthikeyan, S., Jacob, G., Manjunath, B.S.: Malware images: visualization and automatic classification. In: Proceedings of the 8th International Symposium on Visualization for Cyber Security, VizSec 2011. Association for Computing Machinery, New York (2011)
7. Bhodia, N., Prajapati, P., Di Troia, F., Stamp, M.: Transfer learning for image-based malware classification. In: Proceedings of the 5th International Conference on Information Systems Security and Privacy (2019)
8. Vasan, D., Alazab, M., Wassan, S., Safaei, B., Zheng, Q.: Image-based malware classification using ensemble of cnn architectures (imcec). Comput. Secur. **92**, 101748 (2020)
9. Lu, Y., Li, J.: Generative adversarial network for improving deep learning based malware classification. In: 2019 Winter Simulation Conference (WSC), pp. 584–593 (2019)
10. Zhu, J., Jang-Jaccard, J., Singh, A., Welch, I., Al-Sahaf, H., Camtepe, S.: A few-shot meta-learning based siamese neural network using entropy features for ransomware classification. Comput. Secur. **117**, 102691 (2022)
11. Li, D., Yang, Y., Song, Y.-Z., Hospedales, T.M.: Learning to generalize: meta-learning for domain generalization (2017)
12. Zaeemzadeh, A., Bisagno, N., Sambugaro, Z., Conci, N., Rahnavard, N., Shah, M.: Out-of-distribution detection using union of 1-dimensional subspaces. In: Proceedings of the IEEE/CVF Conference on Computer Vision and Pattern Recognition, pp. 9452–9461 (2021)
13. Snell, J., Swersky, K., Zemel, R.S.: Prototypical networks for few-shot learning (2017)
14. Ronen, R., Radu, M., Feuerstein, C., Yom-Tov, E., Ahmadi, M.: Microsoft malware classification challenge (2018)
15. Bhattacharyya, A.: On a measure of divergence between two statistical populations defined by their probability distributions. Bull. Calcutta Math. Soc. **35**, 99–109 (1943)
16. Tran, T.K., Sato, H., Kubo, M.: One-shot learning approach for unknown malware classification. In: 2018 5th Asian Conference on Defense Technology (ACDT), pp. 8–13 (2018). https://doi.org/10.1109/ACDT.2018.8593203

17. Chen, L.: Understanding the efficacy, reliability and resiliency of computer vision techniques for malware detection and future research directions (2019)
18. Saurabh, A.M., Static, A.U., Methodology, D.: International Conference on Advanced Computation and Telecommunication (ICACAT) 2018, pp. 1–5 (2018). https://doi.org/10.1109/ICACAT.2018.8933769
19. Tran, T.K., Sato, H., Kubo, M.: Image-based unknown malware classification with few-shot learning models. In: Seventh International Symposium on Computing and Networking Workshops (CANDARW) 2019, pp. 401–407 (2019). https://doi.org/10.1109/CANDARW.2019.00075

# Research on the Grouping Method of Side-Channel Leakage Detection

Xiaoyi Duan, Ye Huang, YongHua Su, Yujin Li, and XiaoHong Fan[✉]

Beijing Electronic Science and Technology Institute, Beijing, China
fanxiaohong@139.com

**Abstract.** Power analysis attack is a method to obtain the key of the cryptographic chip by analyzing the correlation between power consumption information leaked by the cryptographic chip during the computing process and the key. The efficiency of power analysis attack poses a serious threat to the software and hardware implementation of cryptographic algorithms. In order to detect whether a cryptographic chip has information leakage, it is necessary to assess it by using detection techniques. The t-test is a hypothesis test used in the field of statistics to test whether there is a significant difference in the means of two normally distributed populations with unknown variance, and is also a useful tool in side-channel information leakage assessment. In this paper, two grouping methods are proposed based on the characteristics of the AES algorithm to investigate the construction of two overall groups before the implementation of the Welch's t-test. Experimental verification of the DPA contest V4 dataset shows that both grouping methods were effective in detecting a large number of leakage points on power traces, but the grouping method by AES first round S-box output Hamming weight has a higher proportion of both the number of leakage points and the high t-statistic distribution than the method of grouping by bit value.

**Keywords:** Leakage detection · Welch's T-test · AES

## 1 Introduction

With the widespread use of cryptographic devices such as smart cards, the security of cryptographic chips has become a major concern as a security safeguard for cryptographic devices. The key determines the security of the cryptographic algorithm, so the attackers often target the key of the cryptographic algorithm. Traditional brute-force attacks using hardware and software are time-consuming and inefficient. In recent years, the emergence of Side Channel Attack (SCA) has allowed information such as power, runtime and electromagnetic radiation leaked during the operation of cryptographic devices to be used by attackers to analyze the correlation with intermediate values of cryptographic algorithms and ultimately to break keys. The operation of the cryptographic algorithm in the cryptographic chip will result in the leakage of a lot of information. The power analysis attack on key information is an important part of the

F. Li et al. (Eds.): SecureComm 2022, LNICST 462, pp. 807–818, 2023.
https://doi.org/10.1007/978-3-031-25538-0_42

side-channel attack, which attempts to decipher keys by collecting the power consumption information leaked by the cryptographic chip during the operation and analyzing the relationship between the power consumption values and keys [1]. Generally, power analysis attack techniques have been mature, commonly used methods are Simple Power Analysis(SPA), Differential Power Analysis [2](DPA), Correlation Power Analysis [3] (CPA), template attack [4], etc. Since power analysis attack, in terms of experimental means, only requires passive acquisition of power traces, do not cause any interference with the operation of the cryptographic circuit, and do not require physical damage to the chips as intrusive attacks typically do [5], it is not easily detected. Power analysis attack poses a serious threat to the security of cryptographic devices. Therefore, it is very important to detect whether there is information leakage during the implementation of cryptographic algorithms and to evaluate the ability of cryptographic chips to resist power analysis attack. Power leakage assessment can help designers have a preliminary understanding of the security level of the cryptographic chip and carry out targeted protection, which can greatly improve the security of the cryptographic chip. In addition, a set of sample points on power traces that are most relevant to the sensitive intermediate value of the cryptographic algorithm can be obtained through side-channel leakage detection, and then all sample points on power traces are divided into two groups: leakage points and nonleakage points [6]. Subsequently, the leakage points can be selected as feature points containing the most key-dependent information [7] for power analysis attack, which can effectively reduce the computational complexity and time consumed in the attack and improve the efficiency of the SCA attack.

## 1.1 Related Work

The main method of cryptographic chip information leakage detection is hypothesis test, based on the principle that intermediate values generated by chips during cryptographic operations can result in power information leakage if intermediate values affect side-channel information(i.e., power traces) in a statistically significant manner. Hypothesis test methods have become the primary means of leakage detection by calculating test statistics and significance levels to identify outliers. For example, Goodwill et al. [8] used a specific t-test to evaluate the side-channel information leakage of the implementation of the AES (Advanced Encryption Standard) encryption algorithm, proving the availability of the t-test in leakage detection. The method divides the collected power traces into two sets based on the individual bit values of the target intermediate values during the operation of the algorithm. If the sample sizes of the two sets are not equal, the Welch's t-test is used to measure the difference between the mean values of the power consumption data of the two sets at each sample point. When the statistic exceeds a threshold at a certain place, it is determined that the traces in two sets have a high confidence difference at that sample point and there is side-channel power information leakage, i.e., the corresponding sample point on the energy curve is the leakage point and the chosen intermediate state value significantly affects the power consumption of the cryptographic chip. In 2013 BECKER et al. [9] proposed the TVLA (Test Vector Leakage Assessment) method, which uses the non-specific t-test to divide the power traces into two groups according to fixed plaintext and random plaintext, and if the value of the t-statistic at a certain time sample exceeds the threshold, that point is a leakage point. The specific t-test can offer higher confidence in detection at a lower cost than the non-specific t-test [10]. Other common hypothesis test methods include the F-test, which is similar in principle to the t-test in that it detects leakage through statistical differences in power consumption values at every sample point, but the t-test focuses on differences in means between two sets of samples, whereas the F-test focuses on differences in variances.

In addition to the hypothesis test in statistical inference, mutual information is also a commonly used leakage detection method. Mather et al. [11] compared t-test, discrete mutual information (DMI) and continuous mutual information (CMI), in terms of leakage detection capability and computational complexity. The results of the experiment show that the t-test is better when the overall population is normally distributed and the significance of the difference between means needs to be measured. However, CMI can be applied to leakage measurement in any situation, and there are no special requirements for distribution and statistic characteristics.

The t-test is still the most commonly used detection method for side-channel leakage detection. The Welch's t-test is an extension of Student's t-test and is more reliable in cases where the sample sizes of two sets are not equal. Since the Welch's t-test measures the mean difference between two sets of normally distributed populations, in order to accurately use the Welch's t-test to evaluate side-channel leakage information, the key lies in grouping all traces, that is, constructing suitable two sets. At present, there are two main grouping methods for Welch's t-test. The first is to divide all traces into two sets according to fixed plaintext and random plaintext, and the second is to group according to the difference of intermediate variable values. In [12], Welch's t-test is used to measure the side-channel leakage information during the operation of the 3DES algorithm. When constructing the trace sets, only the second type of data is constructed, and eight kinds of variable values are selected from different intermediate states according to the characteristics of the 3DES algorithm. The results of leakage information tests obtained by using Welch's t-test under different groups are different. It can be seen that in the process of using Welch's t-test to detect leakage, the selection of test positions is very important. For the second method of grouping according to different values of intermediate variables, there is a lack of research on specific grouping methods, especially how to group according to bits and Hamming weights.

## 1.2  Our Contribution

There are two main types of grouping methods for Welch's t-test. The first is to divide into two sets of leakage traces according to fixed plaintext and random plaintext, and the second is to group according to different values of intermediate variables.

In this paper, for the second type of grouping method, the grouping position is determined based on the key intermediate state of the AES algorithm's first round S-box output, combined with the Hamming weight model. Two grouping methods are proposed to measure the leakage information during the operation of the AES algorithm, and the effects of the two methods are compared through experiments. The results show that both the number of leakage points and the distribution ratio of high t-statistic are higher than the method of grouping by bit value.

### 1.3 Structure of This Paper

The structure of the article is as follows. The first chapter is the introduction, which mainly introduces the research background and research status. The second chapter describes the basic principles of AES and Welch's t-test. The third chapter introduces the selection of test positions and different grouping methods in the process of leakage detection using Welch's t-test, and finally explains the necessity of repeated tests. The experimental results and analysis of the DPA contest V4 dataset are introduced in Sect. 4. In the last chapter, the full text is summarized.

## 2 Preliminaries

### 2.1 AES

The Advanced Encryption Standard is the most widely used symmetric encryption algorithm today, which is based on the SP cryptographic structure. Although the increase in the length of the key increases the strength of the algorithm, the number of iterations also increases accordingly. The key length of 128 bits for AES which requires 10 iterations is sufficient for most purposes. In AES encryption, except for the last round, each round of transformation includes 4 basic operations: SubBytes, Shift Rows, Mix Columns, and Add Round Key. There is no Mix Columns operation in the last round.

Shift Rows, Mix Columns and Add Round Key in the AES algorithm are just linear transformations which can only serve as an overall diffusion in the encryption and decryption process. SubBytes is a non-linear transformation, and non-linear transformation is the essence of modern cryptographic algorithms. SubBytes is implemented by replacing each byte in the original matrix with a value obtained from the non-linear component S-box, which has a confusing and local diffusion effect on the data during the encryption process, i.e. a bit different in the S-box input will result in multiple bits different in the output. The good non-linear characteristic can effectively resist traditional cryptanalysis techniques such as linear analysis and differential analysis. Since the S-box transformation is the only nonlinear transformation of the AES algorithm, it largely determines the security of the block cipher. However, its nonlinear characteristic makes it exploited by attackers during side-channel attacks, so the power analysis attack generally selects the output of the first round of S-box or the input of the last round of S-box when the AES algorithm runs as the target intermediate value to carry out the attack.

### 2.2 Welch's t-test

Welch's t-test is an extension of Student's t-test, which is applicable when the sample size and variance of the two sets are not equal. For n power traces $L_i$, each containing m sampling points, a certain intermediate value during the operation of the cryptographic algorithm is selected as the grouping basis, and the side-channel leakage traces $L$ is divided into two groups (i.e. $L_0$ and $L_1$) according to the two possibilities of this value. The sample sizes, means and variances of $L_0$ and $L_1$ are $(n_0, \mu_0, S_0^2)$ and $(n_1, \mu_1, S_1^2)$, respectively. The null hypothesis is that the two sets of power consumption traces have the same mean, and it can be considered that the power traces in the two subsets are not statistically different with high confidence, that is, there is no leakage of side-channel power information. The t-statistic can be expressed as follows.

$$t = \frac{\mu_0 - \mu_1}{\sqrt{\frac{S_0^2}{n_0} + \frac{S_1^2}{n_1}}} \tag{1}$$

Its degree of freedom v is expressed as follows:

$$v = \frac{\left(\frac{S_0^2}{n_0} + \frac{S_1^2}{n_1}\right)^1}{\frac{\left(\frac{S_0^2}{n_0}\right)^2}{n_0 - 1} + \frac{\left(\frac{S_1^2}{n_1}\right)^2}{n_1 - 1}} \tag{2}$$

The probability density function of the t distribution can be obtained from the degrees of freedom as:

$$f(t, v) = \frac{\Gamma\left(\frac{v+1}{2}\right)}{\sqrt{\pi v}\,\Gamma\left(\frac{v}{2}\right)}\left(1 + \frac{t^2}{v}\right)^{-\frac{v+1}{2}} \tag{3}$$

$\Gamma(\cdot)$ is the gamma function. The probability that the null hypothesis holds in the Welch's t-test is as follows.

$$p = 2\int_{|t|}^{\infty} f(t, v)dt = 2F(-|t|, v) \tag{4}$$

F is the distribution function, which can be expressed as:

$$F(t, v) = \frac{1}{2} + t\Gamma\left(\frac{v+1}{2}\right)\frac{2F_1\left(\frac{1}{2}, \frac{v+1}{2}, \frac{3}{2}, -\frac{x^2}{v}\right)}{\sqrt{\pi v}\,\Gamma\left(\frac{v}{2}\right)} \tag{5}$$

$2F_1$ is hypergeometric function in (5).

## 2.3 Pass/Fail Criteria

The probability that the null hypothesis is established in the t-test, that is, the calculation result of Eq. (4), gives the probability that the data mean values of the two sets of power traces at a certain sample point are different. If there is a high-confidence difference between two sets of power consumption values at a particular point, that is, the p-value of the corresponding point is very small, it means that the null hypothesis is rejected and the leakage can be detected. If the p-value is large, it means that the mean difference between the two sets of power consumption data is small, so the null hypothesis is acceptable. The size of the p-value is extremely related to the acceptance or rejection of the null hypothesis, so an appropriate threshold needs to be set. When less severe leaks need to be detected, the threshold can be set to a small value. Conversely, if a higher level of leakage needs to be detected, the threshold should be set to a larger value. Because of the large computational volume and the complexity of the test process for conducting a full t-test, the actual test is often simplified to calculate only the t-statistic. t-test is usually set at 4.5, as shown in Eq. (6). When the sample size is greater than 1000, setting the threshold for accepting or rejecting the null hypothesis at 4.5 will enable the t-test to be accurate at 99.999% or more [8].

$$p = 2F(t = \pm 4.5, v > 1000) < 10^{-5} \tag{6}$$

When the absolute value of t calculated by Eq. (1) is greater than the threshold value of 4.5, the difference between the two sets of power consumption values is determined, i.e. the leakage of power information can be detected.

## 3    Leakage Detection with Welch's t-test

### 3.1    Dataset

This paper conducts experimental analysis and validation with the help of power consumption data from the DPA Contest dataset[13], where the power traces are obtained from an AES-256 RSM (Rotating S-box Masking) implementation. The output of the first S-box which is the first round of the AES encryption algorithm was chosen as the object of the t-test. The 20,000 power traces of the AES encryption algorithm in the DPA Contest V4 dataset have the same fixed key. There are 400,000 samples on each power trace. The choice was to evaluate the first byte of the key for leakage information.

### 3.2    Welch's t-test Grouping Construction

Most of the existing differential power attacks have been carried out by using the output of the first S-box or the input of the last S-box of the block cipher algorithm run as the target intermediate value. From Eq. (1), it can be seen that the Welch's t-test also uses the difference characteristic. Therefore, in the process of detecting the leakage of power information with Welch's t-test, the first round of S-box output or the last round of S-box input can also be set as the position of the test to improve efficiency. Combined with the analysis of SubBytes in Sect. 2.1, this paper selects the output of the first round of S-box in the AES algorithm encryption process as the sensitive intermediate variable value in the Welch's t-test, proposes two grouping methods, and then constructs two data sets according to the different values of the test position. As shown in Table 1, the first method in the table is the Hamming weight model, and select the Hamming weight (HW) for the first round of S-box output for classification, and the second method is to select each bit of the output value of the S-box for grouping (Fig. 1).

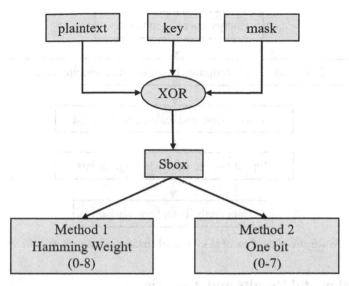

**Fig. 1.** Diagram of the S-box input and the two corresponding grouping methods

**Table 1.** Group construction methods for Welch's t-test

|  | Group method | Set I | Set II |
|---|---|---|---|
| Method I | HW for the first round of the S-box output | $HW = \{0, 1, 2, 3, 4\}$ | $HW = \{5, 6, 7, 8\}$ |
| Method II | The first 8 bits values of the S-box output | bit = 0 | bit = 1 |

## 3.3 Repeated Tests

In the experiment, each leakage trace contains 400,000 sample points. Even if the threshold is set to 4.5, the accuracy of the t-test can reach more than 99.999%, it still cannot be ruled out that at a certain sample point, the absolute value of the t-statistic exceeds the threshold, and there is still a possibility of error at a certain point. In order to minimize the false alarm rate, it is therefore necessary to carry out two independent experiments as a repeat test. 20,000 curves with the same key were selected in DPA contest V4, 10,000 of which were subjected to the Welch's t-test described in Sect. 3.2, and the remaining 10,000 were subjected to the same test. For a given sample point on the energy curve, the sample point can only be considered a leakage point if the threshold is exceeded at the same time in both experiments, because if it is chance that the t-statistic exceeds the threshold at a given time, it is unlikely that this will be repeated at the same time in the next repeat experiment.

Combining the content of Sect. 3.2, a flow for side channel leakage assessment using the Welch's t-test can be obtained as shown in the figure below (Fig. 2).

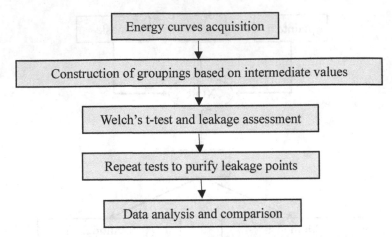

**Fig. 2.** Schematic of the flow of side-channel leakage assessment with Welch's t-test

## 4  Experimental Results and Analysis

In DPA contest V4, select 20,000 energy curves with the same key, of which 10,000 are subjected to Welch's t-test according to the two grouping methods described in Sect. 3.2, and the remaining 10,000 energy curves are repeated according to Sect. 3.3. The sample points which exceed the threshold in both experiments are leakage points, and the number of leakage points detected by each grouping method is shown in Fig. 3. It can be seen from the figure that each grouping method can detect a large number of leakage points. But in comparison, the method that selects the Hamming weight output by the first round of S-boxes for grouping can detect 1002 leakage points. It can detect the larger number of leakage points. In the second method, that is, the method of grouping according to the bit value of 0 or 1, the third bit and the seventh bit outperform the other 6 grouping methods, and can detect 956 and 932 leakage points respectively.

Figure 4 shows the result of Welch's t-test for the first group of 10,000 curves by method I in Table 1, i.e., the Hamming weight model. The red dotted lines in the two figures represent the threshold ±4.5, and it can be found that the leakage points are mainly distributed in four regions, i.e., the four peaks in the figures. In Fig. 5, the leakage points obtained by grouping with the method II are also distributed in the same four main areas, and the $|t|_{max}$ obtained by each grouping method in each area and the corresponding sample time points are recorded in Table 2. It can be seen from the data in the table that although the corresponding leakage time points of $|t|_{max}$ in the four main areas are similar for each method, there is still a certain gap in the t-statistic. The t-statistic of HW is generally larger in all four regions. The t-statistic of bit7 is larger in the other three regions but smaller in region IV. Figure 6 zooms in on the three areas of the area marked by the red square in Fig. 4 to obtain a local curve graph of the area. The figure again confirms that the t-statistic obtained by the HW method at most sample points are higher than those obtained by the other seven grouping methods.

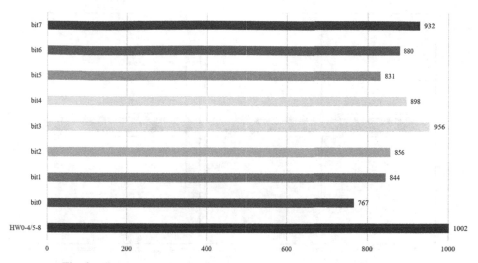

**Fig. 3.** The number of leakage points obtained by each grouping method

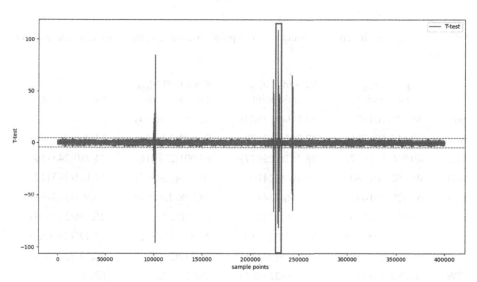

**Fig. 4.** T-statistic at different sample points obtained by method I

Table 2 only lists the distribution of the maximum t-statistic in the four regions. In order to analyze the distribution of the magnitude of t-statistic at all leakage points under different grouping methods, Fig. 7 divides the magnitude of t- statistic into six groups, $4.5 \leq t < 10, 10 \leq t < 20, 20 \leq t < 30, 30 \leq t < 40, 40 \leq t < 50$ and $t \geq 50$, respectively. Although the maximum t-statistic of 156.625 obtained by grouping by bit7 values was the highest of all results, the t-statistic of leakage points obtained by grouping by first round S-box output Hamming weights of 0–4 or 5–8 were the most evenly distributed in the six intervals, especially in the intervals $30 \leq t < 40, 40 \leq t < 50$ and $t \geq 50$,

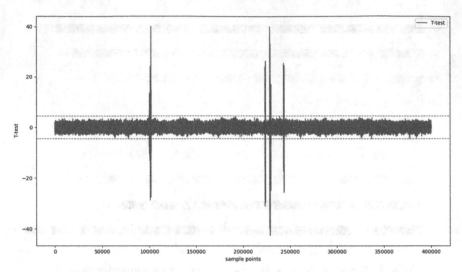

**Fig. 5.** T-statistic at different sample points obtained by bit0

**Table 2.** $|t|_{max}$ and its corresponding leakage point in four regions under different grouping methods

|  | Region I $|t|_{max}$ (sample point) | Region II $|t|_{max}$ (sample point) | Region III $|t|_{max}$ (sample point) | Region IV $|t|_{max}$ (sample point) |
|---|---|---|---|---|
| bit0 | 39.921(101577) | 30.179(223980) | 42.353(228894) | 25.371(243104) |
| bit1 | 38.414(101575) | 27.262(223779) | 55.533(228414) | 28.066(243666) |
| bit2 | 40.916(101577) | 28.452(223977) | 55.001(228416) | 24.980(243110) |
| bit3 | 49.152(101580) | 40.444(224106) | 49.623(228395) | 34.141(243112) |
| bit4 | 57.329(101435) | 41.766(224108) | 48.788(228590) | 30.694(243108) |
| bit5 | 31.926(101590) | 29.579(224107) | 36.410(228470) | 25.136(243668) |
| bit6 | 70.178(101578) | 54.011(224110) | 49.812(228392) | 37.492(243665) |
| bit7 | 156.625(101571) | 101.138(224112) | 76.217(228593) | 25.223(243668) |
| HW | 94.485(101589) | 64.570(223781) | 108.256(228403) | 63.697(243108) |

where the number of leakage points was most prominent and much higher than those obtained by other methods. The size of the t-statistic represents, to a certain extent, the degree of leakage, i.e., the degree of correlation with the sensitive intermediate value. When doing subsequent first-order DPA or CPA attacks, a portion of the leakage points can be selected as feature points according to the number of feature points required, using the size of the t-statistic as a reference standard. In summary, grouping by AES first round S-box output Hamming weight of 0–4 or 5–8 works better than grouping by S-box output of 0 or 1 for each bit value.

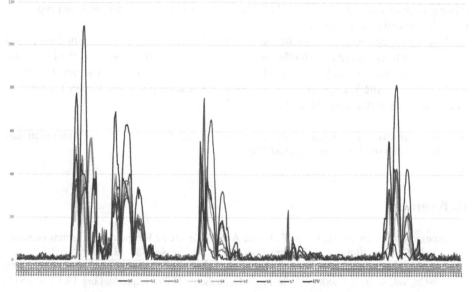

**Fig. 6.** T-statistic at several sample points obtained by every grouping method for region III

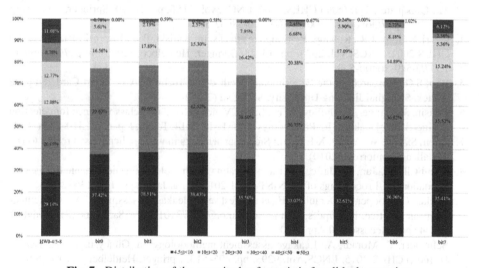

**Fig. 7.** Distribution of the magnitude of t-statistic for all leakage points

## 5 Summary

This paper examines the choice of test positions in the process of side-channel information leakage assessment using the Welch's t-test, and proposes two grouping methods. Experiments on the DPA contestV4 dataset lead to the conclusion that the method of grouping by first-round S-box output Hamming weight of 0–4 or 5–8 is higher than the other grouping methods in terms of both the number of leakage points and the proportion of high t-statistic distribution.

The next step can be to use the side-channel leakage assessment method proposed in this paper to compare it with other tests in the field of statistics such as the F-test and the chi-square test. In addition, a study can be conducted to verify whether the higher the t-statistic of the leakage point is chosen as the feature point, the higher the success rate of the first-order side-channel attack will also be.

**Acknowledgments.** This research was supported by the College Students' Innovation and Entrepreneurship of china (No. 202210018009).

# References

1. Mangard, S., Oswald, E., Popp, T.: Power Analysis Attacks: Revealing the Secrets of Smart Cards. Springer, Berlin (2007). https://doi.org/10.1007/978-0-387-38162-6
2. Kocher, P., Jaffe, J., Jun, B.: Differential power analysis. In: Wiener, M. (ed.) CRYPTO 1999. LNCS, vol. 1666, pp. 388–397. Springer, Heidelberg (1999). https://doi.org/10.1007/3-540-48405-1_25
3. Brier, E., Clavier, C., Olivier, F.: Correlation power analysis with a leakage model. In: Joye, M., Quisquater, J.-J. (eds.) CHES 2004. LNCS, vol. 3156, pp. 16–29. Springer, Heidelberg (2004). https://doi.org/10.1007/978-3-540-28632-5_2
4. Chari, S., Rao, J.R., Rohatgi, P.: Template attacks. In: Kaliski, B.S., Koç, çK., Paar, C. (eds.) CHES 2002. LNCS, vol. 2523, pp. 13–28. Springer, Heidelberg (2003). https://doi.org/10.1007/3-540-36400-5_3
5. Bao, S.G.: Research on the Experimental Method and Technology of Smart Card Template Attack. Shanghai Jiaotong University, Shanghai (2015)
6. Bhasin, S., Danger, J., Guilley, S., et al.: NICV: normalized interclass variance for detection of side-channel leakage. In: Proceedings of the EMC 2014, Tokyo, Japan, pp. 310–313 (2014)
7. Chen, S., Rui, W., Wang, X.F., et al.: Side-channel leaks in web applications: a reality today, a challenge tomorrow (2010)
8. Goodwill, G., Jun, B., Jaffe, J., et al.: A testing methodology for side-channel resistance validation. In: Proceedings of the NIST NIAT 2011, Nara, Japan, pp. 115–136 (2011)
9. Becker, G., Cooper, J., Demulder, E., et al.: Test vector leakage assessment (TVLA) Methodology in Practice. http://pdfs.semanticscholar.org/a10f/31018c9ce38a5231b6481a8f9d4881bca64c.pdf, Accessed 30 Apr 2020
10. Schneider, T., Moradi, A.: Leakage assessment methodology. In: Güneysu, T., Handschuh, H. (eds.) CHES 2015. LNCS, vol. 9293, pp. 495–513. Springer, Heidelberg (2015). https://doi.org/10.1007/978-3-662-48324-4_25
11. Mather, L., Oswald, E., Bandenburg, J., Wójcik, M.: Does my device leak information? an a priori statistical power analysis of leakage detection tests. In: Sako, Kazue, Sarkar, Palash (eds.) Advances in Cryptology - ASIACRYPT 2013, pp. 486–505. Springer Berlin Heidelberg, Berlin, Heidelberg (2013). https://doi.org/10.1007/978-3-642-42033-7_25
12. Chen, J., Li, H., Wang, Y., Wang, Y.: Evaluation side-channel information leakage in 3DES using the t-test. J. Tsinghua Univ. (Nat. Sci. Ed.) **56**(05), 499–503 (2016). https://doi.org/10.16511/j.cnki.qhdxxb.2016.25.007
13. TELECOM ParisTech SEN research group. DPA Contest (4th edition) 2013–2014. http://www.DPAcontest.org/v4/

# PREFHE, PREFHE-AES and PREFHE-SGX: Secure Multiparty Computation Protocols from Fully Homomorphic Encryption and Proxy ReEncryption with AES and Intel SGX

Cavidan Yakupoglu(✉) [iD] and Kurt Rohloff [iD]

New Jersey Institute of Technology, Newark, NJ 07102, USA
{cy267,rohloff}@njit.edu

**Abstract.** We build our secure multiparty computation (MPC) protocols on top of the fully homomorphic encryption (FHE) scheme, BFVrns, and augment it with Proxy Re-Encryption (PRE). We offer three distinct secure MPC protocols that make use of the Advanced Encryption Standard (AES) and Intel Software Guardian Extension (SGX). The PREFHE protocol is based on FHE and PRE that offers a reasonable computational time of milliseconds or seconds, depending on the function computed jointly on the parties' encrypted data. It offers 4 rounds and a communication cost that only depends on the parties' ciphertext size. PREFHE-AES employs AES-128 encryption, which reduces the cost of communication to bits rather than kilobytes or megabytes while maintaining the same number of rounds as PREFHE. PREFHE-SGX is another novel approach that reduces the number of rounds from 4 to 3 by utilizing only one untrusted server. Additionally, it delivers a reasonable level of performance that is applicable to real-world use cases. We pioneer the use of SGX and FHE in secure MPC protocols, resulting in reduced number of rounds. In the protocols, after parties send their encrypted data to the server, they are not required to be online that improves practicality in the protocols. Additionally, the parties are not required to collaborate on any computations during the encryption and decryption phases that makes our protocols more efficient than other proposed protocols.

**Keywords:** Multiparty computation · Homomorphic encryption · RLWE · Proxy reencryption · Intel SGX

## 1 Introduction

With the improvement of technology, new approaches have been proposed such as cloud storage/computing or distributed computing. While these services offer ease and practicality in real life, it comes at a price of privacy. When we store

© ICST Institute for Computer Sciences, Social Informatics and Telecommunications Engineering 2023
Published by Springer Nature Switzerland AG 2023. All Rights Reserved
F. Li et al. (Eds.): SecureComm 2022, LNICST 462, pp. 819–837, 2023.
https://doi.org/10.1007/978-3-031-25538-0_43

our data in the cloud, the cloud or other cloud users may snoop our confidential data. To protect this sensitive information, storing the data in encrypted way is the first step to solve this problem. This idea leads to another problem of making computations on this data. Homomorphic encryption (HE) enables computation of some functions on the encrypted data while FHE allows any kind of computation. Secure MPC takes this approach to another level with computing on the encrypted data collaboratively. It enables $n$ parties computing a function $F$ on $n$ encrypted inputs, such that each party learns the result of the function but not any others' input.

Secure MPC was first introduced by Yao in 1986 [48] for two-party case and multiparty case by Goldreich, Micali and Wigderson [27]. For constructing secure MPC two different approaches have been proposed in general. The first method is based on secure secret sharing where there is an honest majority among the parties [4,10]. The second approach uses binary circuit representation of the function [27,48]. Secure MPC has progressed in terms of efficiency with the recent studies. Based on HE, many MPC studies were proposed such as [5,14,17,18,38]. After the introduction of FHE, many MPC studies were proposed based on FHE such as [33] and FHE variants such as threshold FHE [3] and multikey FHE [34].

FHE refers to a family of encryption methods that allows evaluation of arbitrary computation on encrypted data. FHE was first proposed by Rivest et al. [41] in 1978. It was an open problem until Gentry proved that FHE is possible by using lattices in his work [25] in 2009. After Gentry's breakthrough, many variants of FHE were proposed in the literature [19,43]. FHE offers privacy for data and efficiency on distributed computing on encrypted data and enables powerful privacy-preserving applications. One of these important applications is the family of secure MPC protocols. FHE allows constructing efficient secure MPC schemes. Lattice-based cryptography is known for its quantum resistance, so our secure MPC protocols are quantum-resistant as well. We propose three secure MPC protocols with BFVrns [7,22,29] that is a ring-learning with error (RLWE) based FHE scheme. We offer efficient secure MPC implementations based on PALISADE lattice cryptography library[1] [39].

Efficiency of secure MPC is measured based on three metrics such as rounds, computation cost and communication cost. Rounds refers to total number of communication between parties and servers and among servers. Communication cost is used for the amount of data that is transferred during the execution of the protocol. Computation cost is the amount of computation conducted in each party and server to process the protocol. Some studies suggest some secure MPC protocols that computational and communication complexities of all the parties who participate in the protocol depend on the complexity of the function [4,10,27,30]. This type of protocols may not be efficient in real-life application due to the high complexity of the function. Some recent protocols require communication at every gate and all parties to be online [5,16,18] which is not very possible all the time. In some protocols, decryption is jointly computed [34] which is not very practical in most of use cases. The protocol of [3] requires the

---

[1] https://gitlab.com/palisade/palisade-release.

parties to generate a joint public key online which is not always achievable in real life. The study in [28] suggests a secure MPC protocol for a small class of functions that is not enough for most of the applications. To overcome these challenges, we introduce our FHE and PRE-based secure MPC construction and its two variants with AES and SGX.

We introduce a novel concept of secure MPC as a hybrid of FHE and PRE. Our secure MPC constructions mainly depend on FHE approach. We make use of its proxy-reencryption (PRE) capability for constructing the secure MPC protocols. PRE allows us to conduct computation on encrypted data which are encrypted under many different keys while FHE enables secure computation for two parties. The recent Threshold FHE schemes have some pitfalls that a third party should know all secret keys of the parties to create a common multiparty operation key. We overcome this problem by using PRE. PRE allows reencryption of the ciphertext under a common key to enable evaluation of the function on the given ciphertexts by different parties. It also enables reencrytion of the result of the function evaluation under individual keys of each party so that each party can decrypt the result without exchanging any keys or partial decrypted results.

Our protocols depend on honest-but-curious (semi-malicious) security model that is a prevalent security model used in practical implementations of secure MPC due to performance reasons [6,9,20,21,32]. We assume that two untrusted servers in the protocols do not collude. The assumption of existence of two non-colluding servers is widely used in many studies [9,11,15,21]. Furthermore, we propose further improvements to enhance the security model to malicious model with non-interactive zero knowledge (NIZK) proofs proving plaintext knowledge as done in the work [34]. Our protocols can be easily used by the privacy-preserving applications such as auctions, electronic voting or secure machine algorithms can be good use cases for our secure MPC protocols.

In our main protocol PREFHE, we assume that we have two non-colluding but untrusted servers. One of the server is responsible for creating FHE parameters and generating common key pair and reencryption keys for each part. Another one conducts evaluation of the function on the ciphertexts and reencryption of the result. In PREFHE, the parties are involved in the protocol while uploading their encrypted data and decrypting the final result. In the rest of the protocol, any party does not need any further communication with the servers. The communication between the clients or servers does not depend on the complexity of the function to be evaluated. Also, the computation of the parties/clients does not depend on the complexity of the function $F$. All parties are not expected to be online after sending their encrypted data to the server. In the encryption or decryption phase, we do not require any joint computation by the parties. The parties only send their encrypted data to the server and they get the final result in encrypted at the end of the protocol.

In the AES variation of PREFHE, PREFHE-AES, the parties send their data encrypted under AES-128 that enables less communication cost between the parties and the server ($S_1$). We adapt the idea of the work in [36] to our secure MPC protocol. This adaption creates an extra computational cost on the server ($S_1$), but this can be handled with improvements such as parallelization or including special hardware for AES encryption/decryption. We propose SGX variation of PREFHE as PREFHE-SGX that combines PALISADE library (for implementation of the FHE scheme), Intel SGX technology and secure MPC. We use Gramine as a bridge between PALISADE and Intel SGX to avoid adjusting the PALISADE code to SGX [31].

## 1.1   Our Contributions

**PREFHE:** PREFHE proposes the first combination of FHE and PRE approach for secure MPC protocols. It enables practical secure MPC implementation for real-life use cases. It requires 4 rounds including key exchange phase which is not included as a round in many previous works. The parties in the PREFHE protocol are not required to be online after they send their encrypted data to the server. This makes the protocol a good fit for the applications that do not allow online access all the time. The parties send their data encrypted under the BFVrns scheme that may result in kilobytes sometimes megabytes. This may cause some problems in low-bandwidth network or applications that have small memory or network channel. To handle this problem, we propose AES version of PREFHE.

**PREFHE-AES:** To reduce the communication cost of PREFHE, the parties send their data encrypted in AES-128 which has smaller data size to be sent to the server. We reduce communication cost, but it comes at a price of computation cost on the server side. Computing decryption of AES-128 homomorphically is a costly operation. For applications that require less communication cost, PREFHE-AES is a good fit with the same number of rounds as PREFHE at a reasonable computational time.

**PREFHE-SGX:** For the applications that allow only one server or have constraints of local computation, PREFHE-SGX is a convenient approach with 3 rounds that has less than most of the state-of-the-art protocols. It also introduces reasonable computational cost which only depends on the function to be evaluated. We lead adapting SGX and FHE together in secure MPC protocols that leads practical use of secure MPC protocols in real-life applications.

**Performance In Practice:** Our three protocols provide reasonable amount of running time on the client and server side with milliseconds or seconds that mainly depends on the function. Even if circuit depth is high, we use an efficient FHE scheme, BFVrns, that takes advantages of Residue Number System (RNS) and packing of plaintext in SIMD manner [24,42].

## 1.2   Related Works

The idea of using threshold homomorphic encryption in MPC protocols was first presented by Cramer, Damgard, and Nielsen [14]. Somewhat homomorphic encryption was used to boost implementation of MPC protocols in some studies such as [5,18]. In their protocols, all parties compute proportional to the complexity of the function to be computed and interact at every gate. Choudhury et al. proposed better communication at a computation cost [12]. Their work suggested a kind of interactive bootstrapping protocol to refresh ciphertexts. Cloud server idea came with the work by Kamara et al. [30]. They proposed server-aided MPC idea by assigning large amount of works from the computation to some parties. Halevi et al. suggested the idea of secure computation on the web to minimize communication between parties in the computation [28]. After FHE is proposed by Gentry [25], new approaches based on FHE were suggested by Lopez et al. [33,34] using multikey FHE approach. Asharov et al. presented an efficient threshold FHE based secure MPC scheme in terms of round, communication and computation costs [3]. TFHE schemes allow to jointly generate a common FHE public key along with a secret key that is shared by them later. For decryption, they conduct a collobarative decryption process on ciphertexts to get the final plaintext without learning others' inputs. Garg et al. achieved 2-round MPC from indistinguishability obfuscation [23]. As an optimization they suggested another 2-round MPC protocol from multikey FHE that is independent of the circuit to be computed. [37] proposes a Intel SGX as TEE and FIIE-based multiparty computation that makes use of a certification authority (CA) for aunthentication of the parties. [46] presents a multiparty construction that uses partial HE and Intel SGX as TEE. The latest two constructions do not use Gramine.

## 2 Background

### 2.1 Fully Homomorphic Encryption Scheme: BFVrns

We give a brief explanation of the BFVrns scheme referenced from [7,22,29] but mainly from [29]. Fan and Vercauteren [22] present the RLWE version of work proposed by Brakerski in [7]. Residue Number System (RNS) variant of the BFV scheme is presented by Halevi et al. [29] for more efficient procedures for BFV and it is implemented in PALISADE library. BFVrns provides improvements on decryption and homomorphic multiplication by using Chinese Remainder Theorem (CRT) representation. BFVrns utilizes some parameters such as $m$, $t$, $q \in \mathbb{Z}$. $t$ stands for plaintext modulus, $N$ stands for $\phi(m) = N$, ciphertext modulus is $q = \prod_{i=1}^{k} q_i$ for the same size $q_i$, $\sigma$ is the standard deviation of error distribution $\chi$. $rw$ stands for the size of the relinearization window. Let rings be $\mathcal{R} = \mathbb{Z}[x]/\Phi_m(x)$, $\mathcal{R}_q = \mathcal{R}/q\mathcal{R}$, $\mathcal{R}_t = \mathcal{R}/t\mathcal{R}$. We choose a uniform $\alpha_i \in \mathcal{R}_q$ and $e_i \leftarrow \chi$, $q_i{}^* = q/q_i$, $q_i' = [q_i{}^{*-1}]_{q_i}$, $\beta_i = [q_i' q_i{}^* s^2 - \alpha_i s + e_i]_q$ for $i = 0, 1, \ldots, k$. The public key consists of $pk$ and $W_i := (\beta_i, \alpha_i)$.

- **KeyGeneration:** Secret Key: Sample $s \leftarrow \chi$, set $sk = (1, s) \in \mathcal{R}^2$.
  Public Key: Sample $a \leftarrow \mathcal{R}_q$, $e \leftarrow \chi$, set $pk = ([-(a \cdot s + e)]_q, a) \in \mathcal{R}_q^2$.
- **Encryption**$(m, pk)$: $m \in \mathcal{R}_t$, $u \leftarrow \chi$, $e_0, e_1 \leftarrow \chi$, $ct = [u \cdot pk + (e_0, e_1) + (\Delta m, 0)]$ where $\Delta = q/t$. Output $ct$.

- **Decryption**$(ct, sk)$: $ct = (ct[0], ct[1])$, $x = [\langle sk, ct \rangle]_q = [c[0] + c[1]s]_q$ and output $m := [[x \cdot t/q]]_t$.
- **Add**$(ct_0, ct_1)$: Output $[ct_0 + ct_1]_q$.
- **Mult**$(ct_0, ct_1)$: For $ct_0, ct_1$, tensoring and relinearization are computed as follows:
  - **Tensoring:** $c[0] = ct_0[0]ct_1[0]$, $c[1] = ([ct_0[0]ct_1[1] + [ct_0[1]ct_1[0]]_q)$, $c[2] = ct_0[1]ct_1[1]$ and $c = (c[0], c[1], c[2])$. Output $c'[i] = [[t/q \cdot c[i]]]_q$ for $i = 0$, 1, 2.
  - **Relinearization:** Decompose $c'[2]$ into its CRT components $c'[2][i] = [c'[2]]_{q_i}$, set $c''[0] = [\sum_{i=1}^{k} \beta_i c'[2][i]]_q$, $c''[1] = [\sum_{i=1}^{k} \alpha_i c'[2][i]]_q$, output $ct_{mult} = [(c'[0] + c''[0], c'[1] + c''[1])]_q$.
- **MultiPartyKeyGen**$(pk)$: $pk = (p_0, p_1)$, $a \leftarrow p_1$, $s \leftarrow \chi$, $b = -(e + (a \cdot s)) + p_0$, set new key $pk' = (b, a)$ and $sk = s$.
- **ReKeyGen**$(newpk, oldsk)$: For $rw = 0$, $newpk = (p_0, p_1)$, $e1_i, e2_i \leftarrow \chi$, $u_i \leftarrow \chi$. For each element in $oldsk$; $c0_i = p_0 \cdot u_i + e1_i + f_i$ where $f_i$ are elements at index $i$ in $oldsk$. $c1_i = p_1 \cdot u_i + e2_i$. Set $evalKey = (\{c0_k\}, \{c1_k\})$ for $0 \leq k < v$ where $v$ is the number of elements in $oldsk$. Output $evalKey$.
- **ReEncrypt**$(evalKey, ciphertext)$: Apply KeySwitch on $ciphertext$ with $evalKey$.
- **KeySwitch**$(evalKey, ciphertext)$: $evalKey = (b, a)$. Set $digitsC1$ as CRT-Decompose of $ciphertext[1]$ on base $rw$, $c_1 = digitsC1[0] \cdot a[0]$, $c_0 = c_0 + digitsC1[0] \cdot b[0]$. Set $c_0 = c_0 + \sum_{i=1}^{k-1}(digitsC1[i] \cdot b[i])$, $c_1 = \sum_{i=1}^{k-1}(digitsC1[i] \cdot a[i])$ where $k$ is size of $digitsC1$. Output $newCiphertext = (c_0, c_1)$.

## 2.2 Intel SGX

The Trusted Execution Environment (TEE) is an approach for secure computation that enables the processing of sensitive data within the main processor's secure area (enclave). TEE delivers memory in secure enclaves for isolated computation in the presence of a malicious host. Other processes, such as user or kernel level operations, cannot modify the code contained within the enclave. SGX is a hardware-assisted version of TEE that is available on various Intel processors. SGX enables code to execute in a protected enclave that can communicate with other applications through a dedicated channel, but other applications cannot access the enclave itself [13]. Enclave execution takes place in the protected mode (at ring 3) and follows the address translation done by the operating system kernel [13]. SGX has remote attestation to prove the integrity of the code running in the enclave. When a malicious party attacks a system, it cannot access the code running/stored in the enclave. This reduces the attack surface of the system. SGX has also some disadvantages as follow.

- Paging cost: Data is encrypted and decrypted during exchanging the data between the enclave and outer program. This step creates latency during the paging process.
- Memory limit: SGX has physical memory limit of 128 MB while the practical limit is 90 MB [13,26].

- Lack of library support: Some C++ operations or libraries cannot be used in SGX such as vector from standard library and system calls.

In our study, SGX helps us to execute sensitive data in an untrusted server. In PREFHE, we have to use two servers to prevent disclosing of parties' data. In the PREFHE-SGX version, one server handles the tasks of two servers. When the server in PREFHE-SGX runs the sensitive data that helps decrypting the clients' encrypted data. In the new version, creating the common key pair and reencryption key that use the secret key of common key pair take place in the SGX enclave which cannot be tampered by the host server or any other malicious third parties.

**Gramine:** Gramine is an open-source, lightweight Lib OS(Library Operating System) project that supports Intel SGX and allows users to run their existing applications on Intel SGX [31]. Intel Labs initiated Gramine (previously called Graphene) to provide an open-source compatibility layer for Intel SGX. Gramine bridges various kind of applications and Intel SGX without modifying the application code. Gramine supports native Linux binaries on all platforms. We use Gramine to integrate PALISADE homomorphic encryption library and Intel SGX. Since Intel SGX does not allow usage of some libraries, Gramine handles this problem for developers. PALISADE, Gramine and Intel SGX are first used by Takeshita et al. [45] while we pioneer using this system for building secure MPC protocols.

# 3   Secure MPC Protocols

In this section, we introduce our three secure MPC protocols in detail.

## 3.1   PREFHE: Secure MPC from Multikey FHE and PRE

We construct a secure MPC protocol based on the BFVrns scheme which is a prominent lattice-based FHE scheme. Our protocol is constructed on two untrusted servers and $n$ clients who want to run secure MPC on their secret data collabaratively. We utilize PRE approach to enable privacy of the inputs of the clients and the result of secure multiparty computation. PRE allows reencrypting different ciphertext under the same secret key. Indirectly, it also allows decrypting the same input under different secret keys. In the protocol, we utilize the PRE method proposed in [40] as a building block to manage two untrusted server setting. We assume that these two servers do not collude and the clients and $S_1$ use a secure channel to prevent $S_2$ to access any ciphertext which is encrypted under reencryption keys generated with the common key pair. We summarize how this protocol works step by step. Also, we provide the security analysis for semi-malicious model (a.k.a. honest-but-curious model).

1. The untrusted server $S_2$ decides on the FHE parameter set which is generated by the work [47] and verified by LWE Estimator [2] that is used in Homomorphic Encryption Standard [1]. $S_2$ decides on the client index $j$ who initiates

*Key Generation* and $S_2$ creates the crytocontext $cc$ and a common key pair $CKPair$ from $cc$ to reencrypt the ciphertext under the same key pairs, publishes FHE parameters, $CKPair.pk$ and $j$ to the clients as in Fig. 1.

2. The clients can check the security of the parameter set with LWE Estimator and if it does not provide necessary security limit (i.e. at least 128-bit security level), they can ask for $S_2$ to generate a new parameter set and publish it to all parties.

3. The client $j$ initiates the *Key Generation* process and broadcasts his public key as $pk_j$.

4. Other clients operate *Multiparty Key Generation* using $pk_j$. Each party encrypts their data under their individual public key.

5. All clients operate *ReKey Generation* process to generate new encryption keys to enable $S_1$ to eval the function on the data.

6. The clients reencrypt their ciphertext under their new individual reencryption keys. They send these new ciphertexts $cptxtC_i$ to $S_1$. $S_1$ evaluates the function to be computed on these ciphertexts as in Fig. 2. $S_1$ does not know the secret key of the common key pair $CKPair$, thus $S_1$ cannot decrypt the ciphertexts of the clients.

7. As seen in Fig. 3, $S_2$ creates reencryption keys to allow the clients to decrypt the result under their individual secret keys. $S_2$ sends these keys $REKey_i$ to $S_1$ allowing that noone can see the result in plaintext including $S_1$ and $S_2$.

8. $S_1$ reencrypts the result under corresponding new reencryption keys of the clients and sends all $r_i$ to corresponding public key holder clients where $1 \leq i \leq n$.

9. Each client decrypts their reencrypted ciphertext $r_i$ under their individual secret keys and learns the result of the multiparty computation.

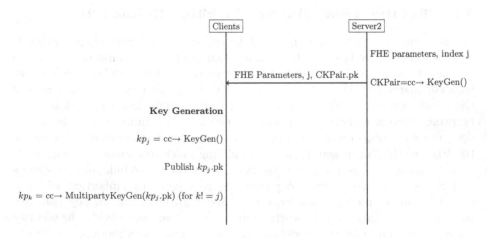

**Fig. 1.** Key generation and exchange phases of the PREFHE protocol.

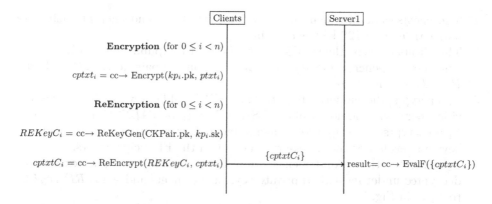

**Fig. 2.** Reencryption phase of PREFHE and PREFHE-SGX protocol.

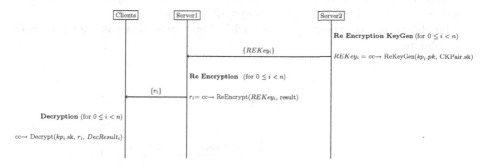

**Fig. 3.** Second reencryption and decryption of the PREFHE protocol.

## 3.2    PREFHE-AES: Secure MPC from Multikey FHE and PRE with AES

We combine the first version of our secure MPC protocol with AES-128 encryption method to reduce communication cost between the servers and clients. In the previous scheme, the clients need to send their ciphertexts that are encrypted under the BFVrns scheme. The ciphertext size in the FHE schemes is large such as $2N \log q$ bits where $N$ is the ring dimension, $\log q$ is ciphertext modulus. To overcome this problem, the clients send their data encrypted under AES-128 encryption that results in a far smaller ciphertext sizes than the BFVrns encrypted one. The ciphertext size in AES-128 depends on the plaintext size, mode of operation and padding. The steps of the protocol are explained as follows:

1. The protocol starts with the key generation and key distribution as in Fig. 4. The FHE parameters are decided by $S_2$ as in PREFHE and distributed to the clients. At the same time, $S_2$ creates a cryptocontext $cc$ and generates a common key pair $CKPair$ from $cc$ to let the clients create their reencryption keys and reencrypt their ciphertexts.

2. The clients generate their public, private key pairs and encrypt their data under their AES-128 key as $c_i$ as in Fig. 4.
3. The clients encrypt their AES key with their FHE public key as $ck_i$.
4. They create reencryption key from the common key pair as $REKP_i$ and send $REKP_i$, $c_i$ and $ck_i$ to $S_1$.
5. $S_1$ encrypts the ciphertexts with their FHE public keys and unravels the ciphertexts with homomorphic AES-128 decryption $(AES^{-1})$ as in Fig. 6.
6. $S_1$ reencrypts these ciphertexts again under their corresponding reencryption keys and evaluates the necessary function on the FHE ciphertexts.
7. $S_2$ generates the second reencryption key to enable the ciphertexts to be decrypted under individual private keys of the clients and sends $REKeyRC_i$ to $S_1$ as in Fig. 5.
8. $S_1$ reencrypts the result with their respective reencryption keys and conducts dimension reduction as in [8] to reduce the size of the ciphertexts, then $S_1$ sends these ciphertexts to the corresponding clients.
9. The clients decrypt their ciphertext with their private keys and get the result in plaintext.

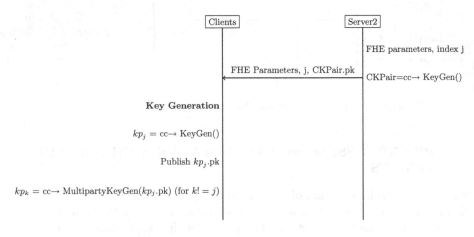

**Fig. 4.** Key generation and distribution of the PREFHE-AES protocol.

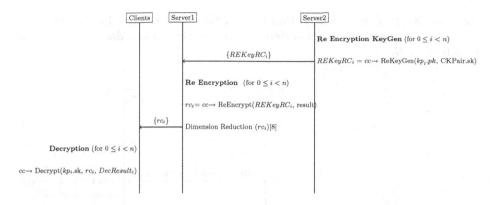

**Fig. 5.** The second reencryption and decryption phase of the PREFHE-AES protocol.

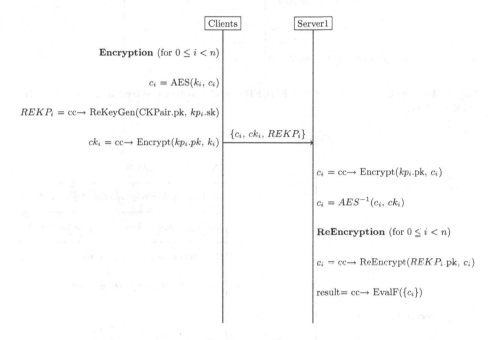

**Fig. 6.** The first reencryption and evaluation of function $F$ phase of the PREFHE-AES protocol.

### 3.3 PREFHE-SGX: Secure MPC from Multikey FHE and PRE with SGX

In this section, we present PREFHE-SGX that enables constructing the PREFHE protocol with one-server setting. Intel SGX enables calculation of sensitive data in the SGX enclave by protecting the data from the outer applications or adversaries. The difference between this protocol and PREFHE is calculating common key pair and reencryption keys in the SGX enclave. In PREFHE, $S_2$ conducts these operations separately to prevent the clients' data to be seen in plaintext by $S_1$.

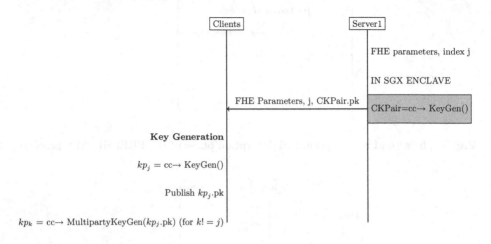

**Fig. 7.** Key exchange phase of the PREFHE-SGX protocol. (Grey box represents the SGX enclave.)

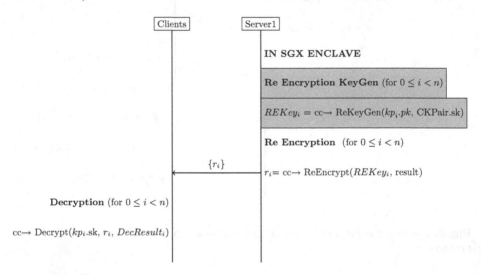

**Fig. 8.** Second reencryption and decryption of the PREFHE-SGX protocol. (Grey box represents the SGX enclave.)

With SGX, the secret key of the common key pair is stored in the SGX enclave. The operations which use this secret key also locate in the SGX enclave so that the server cannot decrypt the clients' encrypted data. We refer the reader to the explanation of PREFHE for further details due to space limit. In this protocol, Gramine allows us to run PALISADE code on the SGX enclave without any adjustments on the code. Figure 7, 2 and 8 depict the steps of the protocol in order.

### 3.4    Correctness

Correctness of the protocols mainly depends on the BFVrns scheme given in Sect. 2.1. Halevi et al. provides correctness proof of the scheme in [29]. We present the correctness of the PREFHE protocol in this section. Other two protocols follow the same correctness proof.

At the beginning of the protocol, *KeyGeneration* step creates the public, private key pair for the encryption step. After this step, we make use of PRE scheme that proposed in [40]. In this step, PRE allows encrypting of all ciphertexts under the same key pair to evaluate a function on them. PRE has *ReKeyGen* routine that creates new *evalKey* for transforming the ciphertext to another one. The second step of PRE is *ReEncryption* step which calls *KeySwitch* routine due to being a PRE operation. *KeySwitch* changes the given input ciphertext to another ciphertext that is encrypted under the new key given in *ReKeyGen* step. *KeySwitch* method uses the algorithm given in [8] as digit decomposition method. Correctness of PRE scheme is proved in [40]. In this step all ciphertexts are transformed to be encrypted under the same public key. The corresponding secret key of this public key is only known by $S_2$. All ciphertext are sent to $S_1$ to evaluate the function which clients want to calculate. $S_1$ evaluates the function on the ciphertexts. $S_2$ runs *ReKeyGen* routine to create new *evalKey* set for reencrypting the result to be decrypted under each clients' secret key. $S_1$ runs *ReEncryption* and sends the results to corresponding clients. Correctness of this step also depends on the PRE scheme. Clients decrypt these new individual ciphertexts with their secret key and open the result in plaintext. Correctness of this protocol mainly depends on PRE which is used two times as a subroutine.

The final decryption of ciphertext after reencryption can be represented as follows where $pk = (p0, p1)$ and $b = p0 \cdot u[i] + e1[i] + s[i]$ from ReKeyGen procedure:

$$c_0 - s \cdot c1 = c0 + \sum_{i=1}^{k-1}(digitsC1[i] \cdot b[i]) - s \cdot \sum_{i=1}^{k-1}(digitsC1[i] \cdot a[i])$$

$$= c0 + \sum_{i=1}^{k-1}(digitsC1[i] \cdot (p0 \cdot u[i] + e1[i] + s[i])) - s \cdot \sum_{i=1}^{k-1}(digitsC1[i] \cdot a[i]).$$

$$(1)$$

After scaling down by $t/q$;

$$\lceil (c_0 - s*c_1)t/q \rfloor = \lceil t/q(c_0 - s \cdot \sum_{i=1}^{k-1}(digitsC1[i] \cdot a[i]) + \sum_{i=1}^{k-1}(digitsC1[i] \cdot (p0 \cdot u[i] + e1[i] + s[i]))) \rfloor.$$
(2)

$\lceil \sum_{i=1}^{k-1}(digitsC1[i] \cdot ((-e - as) \cdot u[i] + e1[i] + s[i]))t/q \rfloor$ is small enough due to $q \ll t$. It can be seen that

$$\lceil (c_0 - s \cdot c_1)t/q \rfloor = m \pmod{t}.$$
(3)

### 3.5    Security Analysis

**Security for the Semi-honest Model:** The semi-honest model implies that all parties follow the protocol description, but they still try to gather information about other parties' inputs, intermediate results or overall outputs just by looking at the protocol's transcripts.

Security of the PREFHE protocol mainly depends on underlying FHE scheme of the protocol and BFVrns depends on RLWE assumption as follows.

**Definition 1. (RLWE [44]):** *For security parameter* $\lambda$, $f(x) = x^n + 1$ *where* $n$ *is power of 2.* $q$ *is* $q \geq 2$. *Let the ring* $\mathcal{R} = \mathbb{Z}[X]/f(x)$ *and* $\mathcal{R}_q = \mathcal{R}/q\mathcal{R}$. $\chi$ *is a distribution over* $\mathcal{R}_q$. $RLWE_{Q,\chi,n}$ *problem concerns about distinguishing following two distributions. The first distribution is uniformly generated samples* $(a_i, b_i) \in \mathcal{R}_q^2$. *In the second distribution, samples* $s$ *from* $\mathcal{R}_q$ *uniformly,* $(a_i, b_i) \in \mathcal{R}_q^2$ *where* $a_i \leftarrow \mathcal{R}_q$ *uniformly and* $e_i \leftarrow \chi$, $b_i = a_i \cdot s + e_i$. *Since SVP problem can be reduced to RLWE [35], RLWE is considered a hard problem.*

**KeyGen/MultipartyKeyGen:** This step creates random $sk$ and $pk$ pairs for the clients and its security depends on RLWE assumption.

**Encryption:** The clients encrypt their inputs under their public key so noone else can decrypt and see their input.

**ReKeyGen + ReEncrypt:** This step depends on PRE scheme proposed in [40] which is proved as IND-CPA secure in [40]. The clients create new $evalKey$ to reencrypt their encrypted inputs to allow function evaluations on all of the clients' data. This step requires individual $sk$ so that noone else can create other $evalkey$ from their $sk$. These reencrypted ciphertexts are sent to only $S_1$ through a secure channel to prevent any decryption by $S_2$. According to our assumption on two non-colluding servers, $S_1$ cannot decrypt ciphertexts sent by the clients and result of function evaluation on ciphertexts because it has no access to $CKPair.sk$. Also, $S_2$ cannot decrypt or manipulate ciphertexts because it cannot see clients' ciphertexts or the final result. $S_1$ cannot get any additional information from intermediate outputs. $ReKeyGen + ReEncrypt$ is used in 2., 3. and 4. rounds to prevent leaking any additional information about the ciphertexts and result.

When all rounds come together, the PREFHE protocol ensures security in the semi-honest model. We can improve the security model to malicious model with NIZK protocols to prove plaintext knowledge as in the work proposed in [34].

# 4    Software Implementation

## 4.1    Implementation on PALISADE

**Experimental Setup.** We run the experiments on the Microsoft Azure Standard DC2s v2 virtual machine that has 2 cores and 8 GB memory running Ubuntu 20.04. We use PALISADE lattice cryptography library version 1.10.6 [39] and Gramine version 1.1[2].

## 4.2    Perfomance

In this section, we analyze our secure MPC protocols in terms of three metrics such as rounds, communication and computation complexity and compare with the state-of-the-art protocols. Due to the unavailability of their implementations, it is not possible to compare running times with other suggested protocols. We compare the protocols such as [3, 33, 34, 38] which provide semi-malicious security model version to provide a fair comparison.

   **Rounds:** PREFHE and PREFHE-AES propose 4 rounds while PREFHE-SGX has 3 rounds in total. Each round in our protocols requires less computation than the rounds in [33, 34]. Our protocols do not require the parties to be online after they send their encrypted data to the server. On the other hand, some cutting-edge protocols require communication at every gate and the presence of all parties online [5, 16, 18] which is not feasible in real-life applications. In some protocols, decryption is jointly computed [34] that increases the number of rounds. In the work presented in [33], encryption key is jointly computed while in our protocols, this is not required which means more practicality. In our protocols, Table 1 suggests that PREFHE-SGX has the less number of rounds. In PREFHE-SGX, one server handles two servers' jobs, so it reduces the number of total rounds.

   **Communication Complexity:** The communication cost between clients and the server is independent of the function to be computed. In PREFHE and PREFHE-AES, the communication cost between two servers is also independent of the complexity of the function. The works in the [3, 33], communication cost depends on the length of the input and outputs. They generally contain a set of indices, ciphertexts and eval keys which is larger than a ciphertext size.

   **Computation Complexity:** In our protocols, the computation complexity on the server $S_1$ is linear in the size of the circuit computing $F$. Since multiplication of two ciphertexts is considered the most costly operation, the multiplicative depth of the function mainly determines the computation cost.

   **Performance Results:** Table 2 suggests that PREFHE has the fastest client and servers time with 2 untrusted server setting. Since homomorphic decryption of AES-128 takes a long time, Server 1 computation time of PREFHE-AES is around 45 s which is still practical for real life. For functions having larger number of multiplications, computation cost can be improved with better hardware

---

[2] https://github.com/gramineproject/gramine.

**Table 1.** Performance comparison of main and our protocols. (Communication complexity refers to the communication cost between a client/party and server that evaluates the function $F$. $\|c\|$ represents size of a ciphertext and $\|c_{AES}\|$ stands for AES-128 encrypted ciphertext size.)

|  | [33] | [38] | [3] | PREFHE | PREFHE-AES | PREFHE-SGX |
|---|---|---|---|---|---|---|
| Rounds | 4 | 4 | 5 | 4 | 4 | 3 |
| Communication Comp. | $\|I/O\|$ | $\|c\|$ | $\|I/O\|$ | $\|c\|$ | $\|c_{AES}\|$ | $\|c\|$ |
| Computation Comp. (Server) | $\|F\|$ | $\|F\|$ | $\|F\|$ | $\|F\|$ | $\|F\|$ | $\|F\|$ |

**Table 2.** Performance results of the protocols for $t = 32769$, $m = 16384$, $\log q_i = 55$, $\sigma = 3$, $rw = 0$, $\lambda = 128$. $F$ has one multiplication as an example in this experiment. Time unit is ms. Client time represents the total runtime of one client.

|  | PREFHE | PREFHE-AES | PREFHE-SGX |
|---|---|---|---|
| Client time | 24.931 | 12.276 | 26.354 |
| Server 1 time | 19.183 | 45142.833 | 25836.862 |
| Server 2 time | 27.701 | 29.975 | NA |

and parallelization techniques. The client side of PREFHE-AES has better performance over other two protocols due to outsourcing the encryption of the data to Server 1. PREFHE-SGX performs better than PREFHE-AES for Server 1 but worse than PREFHE. The reason is that Server 1 in PREFHE-SGX handles two servers' tasks and it utilizes SGX that has paging latency.

**Trade-Off Between Protocols:** According to the needs of the application, the user may consider trade-off between client and server side computations or rounds or communication cost. For applications that have network bandwidth constraints, the user may prefer PREFHE-AES over others. For computational constraints or time sensitivity, PREFHE is the best fit with the short latency. For the systems that allow one server in the secure MPC setting, PREFHE-SGX signifies the best round-efficient one in all secure MPC protocols.

## 5    Conclusion

We propose three distinct secure MPC protocols constructed from FHE, AES-128, and Intel SGX. PREFHE is highly efficient in real-world applications, whereas PREFHE-AES introduces a communication-efficient protocol that is highly efficient in low-bandwidth networks. PREFHE-SGX proposes a single-server setting with 3 rounds and is a pioneer in the use of FHE and SGX in secure MPC protocols. Our protocols' communication costs are function-independent. Additionally, our protocols do not require parties to be online following the transmission of encrypted data to Server 1. The decryption phase does not require any collaboration on the part of the parties, which increases the protocols' practicality. We present efficient and secure MPC protocols that are applicable to a variety of use cases in real life.

# References

1. Albrecht, M., et al.: Homomorphic encryption security standard. Technical report, HomomorphicEncryption.org, Toronto, Canada, November 2018
2. Albrecht, M.R., Player, R., Scott, S.: On the concrete hardness of learning with errors. J. Math. Cryptol. **9**(3), 169–203 (2015)
3. Asharov, G., Jain, A., López-Alt, A., Tromer, E., Vaikuntanathan, V., Wichs, D.: Multiparty computation with low communication, computation and interaction via threshold FHE. In: Pointcheval, D., Johansson, T. (eds.) EUROCRYPT 2012. LNCS, vol. 7237, pp. 483–501. Springer, Heidelberg (2012). https://doi.org/10.1007/978-3-642-29011-4_29
4. Ben-Or, M., Goldwasser, S., Wigderson, A.: Completeness theorems for non-cryptographic fault-tolerant distributed computation. In: Providing Sound Foundations for Cryptography: On the Work of Shafi Goldwasser and Silvio Micali, pp. 351–371 (2019)
5. Bendlin, R., Damgård, I., Orlandi, C., Zakarias, S.: Semi-homomorphic encryption and multiparty computation. In: Paterson, K.G. (ed.) EUROCRYPT 2011. LNCS, vol. 6632, pp. 169–188. Springer, Heidelberg (2011). https://doi.org/10.1007/978-3-642-20465-4_11
6. Bogetoft, P., et al.: Secure multiparty computation goes live. In: Dingledine, R., Golle, P. (eds.) FC 2009. LNCS, vol. 5628, pp. 325–343. Springer, Heidelberg (2009). https://doi.org/10.1007/978-3-642-03549-4_20
7. Brakerski, Z.: Fully homomorphic encryption without modulus switching from classical GapSVP. In: Safavi-Naini, R., Canetti, R. (eds.) CRYPTO 2012. LNCS, vol. 7417, pp. 868–886. Springer, Heidelberg (2012). https://doi.org/10.1007/978-3-642-32009-5_50
8. Brakerski, Z., Vaikuntanathan, V.: Efficient fully homomorphic encryption from (standard) LWE. Cryptology ePrint Archive, Report 2011/344 (2011). https://eprint.iacr.org/2011/344
9. Catrina, O., Kerschbaum, F.: Fostering the uptake of secure multiparty computation in e-commerce. In: 2008 Third International Conference on Availability, Reliability and Security, pp. 693–700. IEEE (2008)
10. Chaum, D., Crépeau, C., Damgard, I.: Multiparty unconditionally secure protocols. In: Proceedings of the Twentieth Annual ACM Symposium on Theory of Computing, pp. 11–19 (1988)
11. Choi, S.G., Elbaz, A., Juels, A., Malkin, T., Yung, M.: Two-party computing with encrypted data. In: Kurosawa, K. (ed.) ASIACRYPT 2007. LNCS, vol. 4833, pp. 298–314. Springer, Heidelberg (2007). https://doi.org/10.1007/978-3-540-76900-2_18
12. Choudhury, A., Loftus, J., Orsini, E., Patra, A., Smart, N.P.: Between a rock and a hard place: interpolating between MPC and FHE. In: Sako, K., Sarkar, P. (eds.) ASIACRYPT 2013. LNCS, vol. 8270, pp. 221–240. Springer, Heidelberg (2013). https://doi.org/10.1007/978-3-642-42045-0_12
13. Costan, V., Devadas, S.: Intel SGX explained. Cryptology ePrint Archive (2016)
14. Cramer, R., Damgård, I., Nielsen, J.B.: Multiparty computation from threshold homomorphic encryption. In: Pfitzmann, B. (ed.) EUROCRYPT 2001. LNCS, vol. 2045, pp. 280–300. Springer, Heidelberg (2001). https://doi.org/10.1007/3-540-44987-6_18
15. Damgård, I., Ishai, Y.: Constant-round multiparty computation using a black-box pseudorandom generator. In: Shoup, V. (ed.) CRYPTO 2005. LNCS, vol. 3621, pp. 378–394. Springer, Heidelberg (2005). https://doi.org/10.1007/11535218_23

16. Damgård, I., Keller, M., Larraia, E., Pastro, V., Scholl, P., Smart, N.P.: Practical covertly secure MPC for dishonest majority – or: breaking the SPDZ limits. In: Crampton, J., Jajodia, S., Mayes, K. (eds.) ESORICS 2013. LNCS, vol. 8134, pp. 1–18. Springer, Heidelberg (2013). https://doi.org/10.1007/978-3-642-40203-6_1

17. Damgård, I., Orlandi, C.: Multiparty computation for dishonest majority: from passive to active security at low cost. In: Rabin, T. (ed.) CRYPTO 2010. LNCS, vol. 6223, pp. 558–576. Springer, Heidelberg (2010). https://doi.org/10.1007/978-3-642-14623-7_30

18. Damgård, I., Pastro, V., Smart, N., Zakarias, S.: Multiparty computation from somewhat homomorphic encryption. In: Safavi-Naini, R., Canetti, R. (eds.) CRYPTO 2012. LNCS, vol. 7417, pp. 643–662. Springer, Heidelberg (2012). https://doi.org/10.1007/978-3-642-32009-5_38

19. van Dijk, M., Gentry, C., Halevi, S., Vaikuntanathan, V.: Fully homomorphic encryption over the integers. In: Gilbert, H. (ed.) EUROCRYPT 2010. LNCS, vol. 6110, pp. 24–43. Springer, Heidelberg (2010). https://doi.org/10.1007/978-3-642-13190-5_2

20. Erkin, Z., Franz, M., Guajardo, J., Katzenbeisser, S., Lagendijk, I., Toft, T.: Privacy-preserving face recognition. In: Goldberg, I., Atallah, M.J. (eds.) PETS 2009. LNCS, vol. 5672, pp. 235–253. Springer, Heidelberg (2009). https://doi.org/10.1007/978-3-642-03168-7_14

21. Erkin, Z., Veugen, T., Toft, T., Lagendijk, R.L.: Generating private recommendations efficiently using homomorphic encryption and data packing. IEEE Trans. Inf. Forensics Secur. 7(3), 1053–1066 (2012)

22. Fan, J., Vercauteren, F.: Somewhat practical fully homomorphic encryption. Cryptology ePrint Archive, Report 2012/144 (2012). https://eprint.iacr.org/2012/144

23. Garg, S., Gentry, C., Halevi, S., Raykova, M.: Two-round secure MPC from indistinguishability obfuscation (2014)

24. Gentry, C., Halevi, S., Smart, N.P.: Fully homomorphic encryption with polylog overhead. In: Pointcheval, D., Johansson, T. (eds.) EUROCRYPT 2012. LNCS, vol. 7237, pp. 465–482. Springer, Heidelberg (2012). https://doi.org/10.1007/978-3-642-29011-4_28

25. Gentry, C., et al.: Fully homomorphic encryption using ideal lattices. In: Stoc, pp. 169–178 (2009)

26. Gjerdrum, A.T., Pettersen, R., Johansen, H.D., Johansen, D.: Performance of trusted computing in cloud infrastructures with intel SGX. In: CLOSER, pp. 668–675 (2017)

27. Goldreich, O., Micali, S., Wigderson, A.: How to play any mental game, or a completeness theorem for protocols with honest majority. In: Providing Sound Foundations for Cryptography: On the Work of Shafi Goldwasser and Silvio Micali, pp. 307–328 (2019)

28. Halevi, S., Lindell, Y., Pinkas, B.: Secure computation on the web: computing without simultaneous interaction. In: Rogaway, P. (ed.) CRYPTO 2011. LNCS, vol. 6841, pp. 132–150. Springer, Heidelberg (2011). https://doi.org/10.1007/978-3-642-22792-9_8

29. Halevi, S., Polyakov, Y., Shoup, V.: An improved RNS variant of the BFV homomorphic encryption scheme. In: Matsui, M. (ed.) CT-RSA 2019. LNCS, vol. 11405, pp. 83–105. Springer, Cham (2019). https://doi.org/10.1007/978-3-030-12612-4_5

30. Kamara, S., Mohassel, P., Raykova, M.: Outsourcing multi-party computation. Cryptology ePrint Archive (2011)

31. Kuvaiskii, D., Kumar, G., Vij, M.: Computation offloading to hardware accelerators in intel SGX and Gramine library OS. arXiv preprint arXiv:2203.01813 (2022)

32. Lindell, Y., Pinkas, B.: A proof of security of Yao's protocol for two-party computation. J. Cryptol. **22**(2), 161–188 (2009)
33. López-Alt, A., Tromer, E., Vaikuntanathan, V.: Cloud-assisted multiparty computation from fully homomorphic encryption. Cryptology ePrint Archive (2011)
34. López-Alt, A., Tromer, E., Vaikuntanathan, V.: On-the-fly multiparty computation on the cloud via multikey fully homomorphic encryption. In: Proceedings of the Forty-Fourth Annual ACM Symposium on Theory of Computing, pp. 1219–1234 (2012)
35. Lyubashevsky, V., Peikert, C., Regev, O.: On ideal lattices and learning with errors over rings. In: Gilbert, H. (ed.) EUROCRYPT 2010. LNCS, vol. 6110, pp. 1–23. Springer, Heidelberg (2010). https://doi.org/10.1007/978-3-642-13190-5_1
36. Naehrig, M., Lauter, K., Vaikuntanathan, V.: Can homomorphic encryption be practical? In: Proceedings of the 3rd ACM Workshop on Cloud Computing Security Workshop, pp. 113–124 (2011)
37. Natarajan, D., Dai, W., Dreslinski, R.: CHEX-MIX: combining homomorphic encryption with trusted execution environments for two-party oblivious inference in the cloud. Cryptology ePrint Archive, Paper 2021/1603 (2021). https://eprint.iacr.org/2021/1603
38. Peter, A., Tews, E., Katzenbeisser, S.: Efficiently outsourcing multiparty computation under multiple keys. IEEE Trans. Inf. Forensics Secur. **8**(12), 2046–2058 (2013)
39. Polyakov, Y., Rohloff, K., Ryan, G.W.: Palisade lattice cryptography library (2018). https://palisade-crypto.org/
40. Polyakov, Y., Rohloff, K., Sahu, G., Vaikuntanathan, V.: Fast proxy re-encryption for publish/subscribe systems. ACM Trans. Privacy Secur. (TOPS) **20**(4), 1–31 (2017)
41. Rivest, R.L., Adleman, L., Dertouzos, M.L., et al.: On data banks and privacy homomorphisms. Found. Secure Comput. **4**(11), 169–180 (1978)
42. Smart, N.P., Vercauteren, F.: Fully homomorphic SIMD operations. Des. Codes Crypt. **71**(1), 57–81 (2014)
43. Stehlé, D., Steinfeld, R.: Faster fully homomorphic encryption. In: Proceedings of ASIACRYPT 2010, pp. 377–394 (2010)
44. Stehlé, D., Steinfeld, R., Tanaka, K., Xagawa, K.: Efficient public key encryption based on ideal lattices. In: Matsui, M. (ed.) ASIACRYPT 2009. LNCS, vol. 5912, pp. 617–635. Springer, Heidelberg (2009). https://doi.org/10.1007/978-3-642-10366-7_36
45. Takeshita, J., McKechney, C., Pajak, J., Papadimitriou, A., Karl, R., Jung, T.: GPS: integration of graphene, palisade, and SGX for large-scale aggregations of distributed data. Cryptology ePrint Archive (2021)
46. Wu, P., Ning, J., Shen, J., Wang, H., Chang, E.C.: Hybrid trust multi-party computation with trusted execution environment. In: The Network and Distributed System Security (NDSS) Symposium 2022 (2022)
47. Yakupoglu, C., Kurt, R.: Parameter selection for computationally efficient use of the BFVRNS FHE scheme. Under review (2022)
48. Yao, A.C.C.: How to generate and exchange secrets. In: 27th Annual Symposium on Foundations of Computer Science (SFCS 1986), pp. 162–167. IEEE (1986)

# Author Index

Printed in the United States
by Baker & Taylor Publisher Services